THAT OTHERS MAY LIVE

THAT OTHERS MAY LIVE

INSIDE THE WORLD'S MOST DARING RESCUE FORCE

SMSGT JACK BREHM
AND PETE NELSON

10 9 8 7 6 5 4 3 2 1

First published in the UK in 2000 by
Ebury Press
Random House, 20 Vauxhall Bridge Road, London SW1V 2SA

Random House Australia Pty Limited
20 Alfred Street, Milsons Point, Sydney, New South Wales 2061, Australia

Random House New Zealand Limited
18 Poland Road, Glenfield, Auckland 10, New Zealand

Random House South Africa (Pty) Limited
Endulini, 5A Jubilee Road, Parktown 2193, South Africa

The Random House Group Limited Reg. No. 954009

A CIP catalogue record for this book is available from the British Library

Design by Leonard Henderson

Hardback edition: ISBN 0 091 87467 X
Australian paperback edition: ISBN 0 091 87468 8
Trade paperback edition: ISBN 0 091 87502 1

Papers used by Ebury Press are natural, recyclable products made from wood grown in sustainable forests

Printed and bound by Mackays, Chatham

DEDICATION

To my wife and best friend, Peggy, whom I love and adore. The greatest gifts God could have given me, my five children: Michele, Elizabeth, Bean (Laura-Jean), Matthew, and Jeffrey. You all supported me in a job I love, regardless of the heartache it could and so often does inflict. "In a box, hon'!"

To the crew of the Jolly 10, for the pain and suffering they and their families endured living up to the motto "That others may live."

To my fellow PJs and "every guy or girl next door" who puts on a set of greens one weekend a month to perform a duty that his or her neighbors could never understand.

And to my mentor, Mike McManus—no words are needed.

CONTENTS

PREFACE

It's intrinsic to the nature of heroism that a hero is the last person who is ever going to call himself a hero, because the chief characteristic of true heroism is selflessness. That is perhaps what distinguishes true heroism from false heroism. False heroism might be the sports star who hits a lot of home runs in a season or scores a lot of points on a basketball court, all wonderful things to behold and cheer for, hugely entertaining, but nobody really puts anything on the line, or risks all that much, playing baseball or basketball. A sports idol is just that, an idol, not a hero. Any local fireman running into a burning house to save so much as a cat or a goldfish is more heroic, in the true sense of the word, than a sports idol. The famous only become role models because we know who they are and what they do. Fame and heroism are two different things.

This is a book about true heroism, deeds committed by a little-known group of men who think of themselves as anything but heroes, men who feel they are only doing their jobs, even when their jobs require them to do extraordinary things. They are called pararescue jumpers, or PJs, men who first came to the public's attention in Sebastian Junger's remarkable best-seller, *The Perfect Storm*. *That Others May Live* is a book about one man, SMSGT Jack Brehm, who serves in the Air Force's 102d Rescue Squadron, part of the 106th Air Rescue Wing, stationed at the Francis S. Gabreski Air National Guard Base in Westhampton Beach, Long Island. It's about Jack's life and times, his family, his adventures, the job he and his peers do, and why they do it. They are not men who, once in a lifetime, rise to the occasion in an emergency and jump into the ocean at great personal peril to save someone from drowning. They are men who train and prepare to do that, and more, on a daily basis.

The book covers a period from 1976 to the present. The reader will notice that in various places in the narrative, the tense shifts from past to present, or from present to past. This is intentional. Certain action scenes seemed best rendered in the present tense, for the purpose of effecting a sense of immediacy, while other scenes and expository information seemed better delivered in the past tense. Places where the tense is intentionally shifted have been marked by a series of eight asterisks.

There are places in the narrative where events have been rendered that took place twenty or more years ago. The reader might wonder about the conversations and events detailed herein, and think, "How could anybody remember what they said twenty years ago?" Indeed, most of us can't remember conversations we had a week ago, or what we had for lunch yesterday. The authors have tried to stay as true as possible to the veracity of events, remaining faithful in spirit, tone, feel, general structure and shape, chronology and import, but we acknowledge that in instances where producing exact verbatim quotations of things spoken long ago was beyond the collective memories of the parties involved we've had to reconstruct scenes and dialogues as best we could, creating conversations that can only approximate what took place in, for example, a loud helicopter among people under tremendous stress in a raging North Atlantic gale or between rescuers suffering from high-altitude hypoxia on an Alaskan mountain peak. Yet it's an ancient truism that a dozen men participating in a single event might, twenty years later, tell a dozen different stories about that event, making any individual narrator's version an approximation, framed by his own particular experience. *That Others May Live* is the story of one PJ's life, referenced by his fallible memories and filtered through his own personal recollections. We did have the benefit of logs, notes, photographs, and journals kept by the author throughout his career to assist us in our renderings, but in the end we must apologize for any instance in which individuals referred to or appearing in the book might feel that the author's version of events varies from their version. This is just one man's story, no more and no less.

It's hard to gauge to what extent one PJ's story might represent the stories of all PJs. Pararescuemen are not only one of the most elite forces in the military, they are one of the more unique groups of people anywhere. They are also as different from one another as any collection of individuals is going to be. Some PJs listen to classical music, some listen to rock, some listen to rap, and some probably listen to voices from outer space. The stereotypical pararescueman gets a testosterone high from being physically fit, and an endorphin high from exercising, and then he gets an adrenaline high after parachuting out of an airplane to a victim in need of medical assistance, and then he gets a spiritual, godlike feeling of omnipotence from saving somebody's life, and then he goes to a bar after the mission and has a few shots of tequila to celebrate, at which point he can become an extremely interesting and relatively unpredictable individual. Every pararescueman will share something with this stereotype, but every pararescueman will deviate from it, too. All share a unique approach to life, a sense of service and commitment to country, and beyond that a true feeling of compassion for their fellow man, which would be rare in any society, at any point in history, but which seems particularly rare in late-twentieth-century America.

ACKNOWLEDGMENTS

I would like to thank my co-author, Pete Nelson, for his ability to turn my crazy life and stories into such an amazing tale. To my agent, Jennifer Gates, thank you for your persistence and overall interest in pararescue. Simply put, without you this story would never have come to life.

To Kristin Kiser, our editor at Crown, thank you for your words of encouragement and all the direction that was needed to make this story flow.

Thank you, Mom and Dad, for giving me a strong foundation on which I was able to build a long and happy life.

To the rest of my large, extended family, and my friends, without your love and support my family and I may not have endured the hard times, but because of you I am blessed with a wonderful life. It is always a pleasure to share my happy times with you all.

I would also like to thank the Rocky Point school district, for their constant support of my children in my many absences over the years.

To my mother- and father-in law, Jane and Warren Stemke, thank you for giving Peggy and me so much support and guidance at our new beginning.

Thank you to all my fellow PJs, who contributed their time, effort and personal stories to paint a better picture of what we do.

—SMSGT Jack Brehm

ACKNOWLEDGMENTS

There are many people I'd like to thank, beginning with the Brehm family, Jack, Peggy, Michele, Elizabeth, Laura-Jean, Matthew, and Jeffrey, who took me into their home and filled me with food, stories, and admiration. Thanks also to Carol Martinsen, Sally Brehm, and Lorraine Fitzpatrick, and to Ken Stanley. From the 106th, I'm grateful for the cooperation and assistance of LTCOL Anthony Cristiano, LTCOL David Hill, CMSGT Alan Manual, MAJ Jim Finkle, Marty Martin, and for the support of all of Jack's friends. From the New York National Guard, I'd like to thank LTCOL Paul Fanning. Thanks to Douglas Thar, USAF Public Communications Division, the Pentagon, and to Bill Vargas, from Pararescueman's Association. From the Coast Guard, I'd like to thank Hugh O'Doherty for the long conversations and for steering me in all the right directions. Thanks to all the PJs who wrote to me with their stories, including John Alexander, Dana Beach, Dave Berrio, Ken Cakebread, Jeff Christopher, Bud Cockerton, Ken Dolan, Monty Fleck, Dan Galde, James Derrick, David Hammer, Greg Hehir, Chris Howk, Craig Kennedy, Jim Lundberg, Dr. Ron Lundrigan, Anthony Negron, Roger Porter, Daniel Routier, Jim Ward, and Dave Young, and apologies to those whose stories I couldn't use, not because they weren't great stories but simply because of the need to limit the scope of what we were trying to cover and say and show.

From Kirtland AFB, I'm grateful for the help given by SGTs Stephens, Copper, McDonald and Lee. From Patrick AFB, thanks to COL Bruce Davis and SMSGT Jeff Curl. At Lackland AFB, I'm extremely grateful for the time given me by men who had a whole lot more on their minds than talking to a journalist, including "cones" Keith Faccilonga, William Moore, Armin Sahdri, Robert Schnell, and Matt White, guys whose commitment and courage thoroughly impressed me. From the Instructors' Cadre, I'm grateful to SMSGTs Tony Alexander, Rod Alne, John Erickson, Blake George, Ross Kilbride, Kevin Kirby, Mike Mahoney, Doug McClure, Craig Showers, Jerry Sowles, and David Swan—thank you all for chatting with me, and for not making me do any pushups. Thanks also to, in Public

Affairs, Irene Witt and to LT Denise Kerr, the best ballroom dancer in the Air Force.

In Alaska, thanks to Bob LaPointe, Carl Brooks, Skip Kula, James Talcott, Mike Wayt, and particularly thanks to Mike McManus, who gave me so much of his time and went out of his way to introduce me to all the people I needed to talk to. He's a truly impressive gentleman and as great a guy as Jack said he would be. Among the PJs, from the class of '78-03, thanks so much to Dave Higgins, Joe Higgins, Randy Mohr, Chuck Matelski, "Slip" O'Farrell, Bill Skolnik, and John Smith, for the stories they shared and, on behalf of all the people they helped who perhaps never thanked them properly, thanks for the careers they had. Any one of these men could have filled a book on his own. Thanks as well to Debbie Judy for telling me about "The Jude."

Farther afield, thanks to Dany Brooks from the U.S. Parachutists Association, and to Dr. Jeffrey T. Mitchell and Don Howell from the International Critical Incidence Stress Debriefing Foundation, for their cooperation and for the vital work they're doing. Thanks to Kim Hong-bin for his bravery and for his efforts conquering the difficulties of trans-oceanic bilingual e-mail, and to Jack Stephens and Matthew Childs for their help with mountaineering questions. Thanks to Jennifer Simpson for her detective work. Thanks in Greece to Tassia Kavvadias, to Park Myoung-Soo, Linda Kim, and to her mother Haeja in Massachusetts for helping with translations, and to Utit Choomuang in Korea for being my main man in Asia. Thanks and a bottomless supply of effusive letters of recommendation to my research assistants Nicky Lewinson and Danielle "She-Should-Have-Her-Own-Sit-Com" Fugazy. Thanks also to my family, whose support has always meant so much to me.

In the publishing world, I'd like to acknowledge Sebastian Junger, whose fine book *The Perfect Storm* first introduced the PJs to the world. At Crown, I'm thankful to the support of the staff, to Rachel Kahan for her read, to editorial director Steve Ross for his enthusiastic support, and especially to Kristin Kiser for having faith in me and for her deft and painless editing. Thanks to supplemental outside readers Alan Gates and Doug Whynott for catching my mistakes, misphrasings, and omissions from draft to draft. At Zachary-Shuster, thanks to Lane Zachary, Todd Shuster, Esmond Harmsworth and thanks, finally, to my reader, agent, and best friend Jennifer Gates, whose vision and inspiration first shaped this project and without whom none of me would have been possible.

—Pete Nelson

PART ONE

1

SHOOTING STARS

As a PJ said to me once, "If you can't get out of it, get into it."

IN A C-130 HERCULES, FLYING AT 26,000 FEET, SMSGT JACK BREHM and five other men are preparing to jump. It's night. Amateurs and recreational jumpers don't jump at night, nor do they jump from 26,000 feet, but Sergeant Brehm is not an amateur. He's a member of the U.S. Air Force's elite pararescue team, a PJ, they're called, short for "pararescue jumper," tasked with rescuing pilots who get shot down behind enemy lines. PJ is the abbreviation used in flight logs when a pararescueman is a member of a flight crew. The pilot is P, the co-pilot is CP, the flight engineer is FE, and so on. It's dangerous to jump at night, and to jump from this altitude, and it's always dangerous to jump behind enemy lines, particularly when the enemy knows they've shot down an American pilot and have dispatched troops to find him. It's considered something of a coup these days to display, in times of war, the picture of a captured pilot on television, but PJs know they're charged with a higher calling than to simply prevent an enemy in Baghdad or Belgrade from gaining the upper hand in a photo-op contest. PJs do what they do "That others may live." This is their motto, their "prime directive." There aren't a lot of people who live by mottoes anymore, but if you're going to live by one, it's hard to think of a better motto. PJs wear maroon berets, and on the metal flash is the image of an angel enfolding the world in its wings.

Before the jump, the men in the C-130 check each other's equipment to make sure everyone has what he needs, and that all is in working order. The only light inside the airplane is red, so that their eyes will be accustomed to the darkness when they jump. They are also equipped with night vision goggles, but they won't use their NVG gear until they're on the ground. The binocular vision of the goggles greatly reduces their peripheral range and impairs depth perception, and they'll need peripheral range and depth perception to make it to the ground safely.

"Two minutes to target," Brehm hears the pilot say over the radio inside his helmet. "Airspeed 125. Scattered cloud deck at 13,000 feet."

"Clouds," one man says. It's unpleasant to jump into a cloud bank, particularly at night.

"Oh well," a second says, "I needed a bath anyway."

"That was you?" a third says. "I thought something died in the oxygen console."

"Gentlemen," the team leader says. Joking soothes the nerves, but it's time to be serious.

The jumpmaster stands by the open door, a large ramp at the rear of the airplane, and holds up two fingers, meaning in two minutes Brehm will step off the end of the ramp and out into the night. The men signal the jumpmaster with a thumbs up to indicate they've heard and understood his message. All eyes are on the jumpmaster. If he doesn't abort the mission in the next two minutes by holding up a closed fist, then it's a go. Brehm, who will be the high man in the stack, is last in line. He is also the oldest man in the line. Someday he'll be too old to do this job. Lately, as he's begun to consider retirement, silly fears or notions have been popping up. Superstitions. "What ifs" that he doesn't particularly care to tell anyone about. The vague notion that he is pushing his luck, a notion that can only come to a man who knows that for the better part of his adult life he has been very lucky. He once predicted he wouldn't live to see thirty, and he was sort of joking when he said it, but not entirely. He is now forty-two years old. There are few men doing this job who are older.

The jumpmaster gives the ready signal by holding his right hand in the air, thumb pointing at the ceiling. Then he gives the jump signal by pointing out the door. On a static line jump, the jumpers would follow each other off the ramp one at a time at one-second intervals, but this is free fall. They jump en masse, stepping off backward to hit the wind square on with their chests.

The adrenaline rush is immediate. As he falls, Brehm feels the same butterflies in his stomach you feel when an elevator starts down, but to a much greater extent. It keeps on coming as he picks up speed, a body-shuddering sensation. At the same time, once he steps out of the airplane, everything becomes suddenly quiet and hushed, which induces a sense of peacefulness.

Then there are the stars in the sky. People who for the first time spend the night sleeping out in the open under clear skies on the Great Plains of the American West, such as the Badlands of South Dakota, for example, feel overwhelmed because they've never seen so many stars before. People who camp high in the Rockies see more stars than people down on the plains see—viewed from ten or twelve thousand feet, the Milky Way becomes a tangible thing, no longer a figure of speech but a great river of light, or some massive migration of fireflies, so distinct and so real that you can't believe the planet Earth is a part of it. *It's* way over there, millions of light years away, and *we're* here, so how could *we* be part of *it?* Brehm is falling from 26,000 feet, almost five miles up—from as high as commercial airliners fly. At 26,000 feet, you see so many stars that you feel like you're one of them, a shooting star, falling to earth. In such thin air, with less atmosphere above you to obscure the view, the stars are brighter and more sharply focused, and there are more of them, and the blackness in between them is blacker and more intense.

"Number one okay," the first man reports to the team leader.

"Two okay."

"Team leader okay."

"Four okay."

"Five okay."

"Six okay," Brehm says.

Jack Brehm reaches terminal velocity, 125 mph, in about ten seconds. He falls a thousand feet in those first ten seconds. He'll fall about a thousand feet every five seconds after that. Terminal velocity describes the point at which the man's wind resistance, the mass of air molecules his body mass displaces as he falls, is equal to the force of gravity that pulls him earthward. Despite the stories of Galileo dropping objects of unequal mass from the Tower of Pisa to prove they fall at the same rate, wind resistance can affect terminal velocity and make objects of unequal mass fall at different speeds. Galileo just couldn't find a high enough tower. An Olympic speed skater in a $500 Speedo bodysuit might fall at a rate of perhaps 135 miles an hour, whereas a lawyer in a three-piece suit would fall more slowly. On a parachute team, you want everybody to fall at the same speed, but short stocky guys will fall faster than tall thin guys, who can tend to float a bit, so often a short stocky guy will have extra fabric sewn into the armpits or the crotch of his jumpsuit to handicap his rate of descent.

At five foot ten and 168 pounds, Brehm is neither stocky nor tall. He'll be in free fall for over two minutes, but he won't really get a sense that he's nearing the earth until around 4,000 feet. Unlike driving down a freeway at 125 mph, there are no telephone poles whizzing past him to indicate his speed or progress. He has a simultaneous sense of motion and motionlessness because he can feel the wind pressing against his body, but he has no point of reference. He knows he's falling, but he can't prove it unless he looks at the altimeter on his left wrist. It takes no strength or concentration to free fall for two minutes. It's nothing like holding your arm out the window of a car moving at 125 mph. It's more like lying on a pillow of air, so restful you could almost fall asleep. At the same time, falling through the sky causes an adrenaline release, the body's natural reaction to impending danger, and any way you look at it, falling five miles to earth is fraught with peril, if only because there's no margin for error. The adrenaline creates a sense of euphoria that can turn some men into adrenaline junkies, installing a craving for risk that can last a lifetime. It doesn't matter how many times you jump—the rush comes every time. You never get used to it. It's also, according to some, the best cure there is for a hangover. Jack Brehm is growing less and less interested in risk, the closer he gets to retirement, but at the same time he certainly likes the rush. He knows he's going to miss it.

"Stay tight but keep your intervals and maintain awareness," the team leader radios, though it's not really necessary, because everyone knows their job.

Each man has a green, six-inch-long Cyalume chemlight attached to the back of his helmet. They need to see each other in the darkness. Each man knows how to fly through the air, turn right, left, slow down, or speed up to avoid getting too close to each other. Still, seeing a team member's chemlight can be difficult if the weather is bad or there are lights on the ground down below. Tonight, because they are falling into heavy cloud cover, no lights are visible below. The lack of ground light adds to the sense of moving but not moving.

To protect his eyes from the wind and cold, Brehm wears a pair of clear plastic eye protectors called boogie goggles. It's very cold at 26,000 feet. The temperature drops about three or four degrees for every thousand feet above ground you go. At night, in a cold winter month, over a place like Kosovo or northern Iraq, the air temperature at 26,000 feet might be as cold as –30°. The wind chill at –30°, moving at terminal velocity, is about –70°. Any exposed skin at that temperature will become frostbitten in seconds. Against the cold, Brehm wears an ECW, or Extreme Cold Weather clothing system, composed of a Gore-Tex jumpsuit, worn over a down-filled jacket and down-filled overalls (sometimes dubbed a "Mr. Puffy" suit), worn over a woodlands green camouflage uniform, and, under that, expedition-weight polypropylene long underwear. He has on insulated Gore-tex boots, polar fleece mittens, and Gore-tex mitten shells. He wears a balaclava inside his helmet and a neoprene face guard. If he were to jump out of an airplane in midsummer over the deserts of Kuwait or Saudi Arabia, he would still wear such cold weather gear.

In addition to being cold, the air is also too thin to breathe. Brehm wears an MBU-12/P pressure-demand oxygen mask, which has a soft, silicone rubber faceplate bonded to a hard plastic shell, which creates a leak-tight seal over his nose and mouth, with a built-in dynamic microphone that allows him to communicate with the other members of his team. The mask is connected to a 106-cubic-inch portable bailout oxygen system, twin bottles of compressed oxygen that Brehm carries in a pouch on his left side. The unit weighs ten and a half pounds and will give him enough air to breathe for thirty minutes. The oxygen will provide him with some minimal protection, if he ever finds himself jumping into a smoke-filled environment, but the main reason to breathe it is to prevent hypoxia. Because the C-130, flying at the same altitude as a commercial airliner, was nevertheless not pressurized (you obviously can't bail out of a pressurized airplane), Brehm has been pre-breathing pure oxygen from a console since an hour before takeoff. C-130 Hercules tankers are built to carry parachutists and cargo, to refuel helicopters in midair, and to fly for long hours in any kind of weather on search missions, but they are not built for comfort.

The team has formed a circle, about thirty feet across. Each jumper faces toward the center of the circle so that they can keep an eye on one another. They'll hold this formation until they reach 6,000 feet, at which point they'll break off, each jumper turning 180 degrees away from the center of the circle. At 5,000 feet, each jumper begins his pull sequence, first looking over his shoulder to make sure the air is clear above him, then waving his arms to warn anybody who might be near him, then looking for his D-ring. In his mind, Brehm rehearses the pull sequence, even though he's jumped over a thousand times. There's a minimum of radio communication between the members of the team during free fall. Brehm hears only the sound of his own breathing and the wind in his helmet.

Still above the cloud deck, Sergeant Brehm looks at his altimeter, attached to his left wrist with a Velcro strap. He's been falling for a full minute, and the top of the cloud bank he's falling into begins at 13,000 feet. This coincidence presents a particularly difficult mental challenge, because the altimeter on his wrist only goes up to 13,000 feet. That is to say, it begins at 13,000, counts down to zero, then starts over again at 13,000, like the orbiting second hand on a clock, but when you jump from 26,000 feet and the cloud deck is at 13,000 feet, both your eyes and your altimeter tell you you're going to hit zero and frap, or go splat on the ground. It can be completely unnerving, and there's a strong urge to pull—many men have done so by mistake—because even though you know you jumped from 26,000 feet, and you trust that your memory of jumping from 26,000 feet is accurate, there is still a voice that questions what you think you know, the same voice we hear when we shut off the stove and leave the house, and two minutes later can't be sure we turned off the stove before we left. You really don't want to space out and get it wrong.

Brehm's altimeter reads 3,000 feet, the needle in the red zone. It means he's at 16,000 feet.

Unless . . . no, I'm at sixteen thousand.

He looks down and sees the cloud deck, illuminated by starlight. He has done this many times before, but it's always eerie. Tonight he sees only an ocean of charcoal gray. Jumping at night, particularly when you're in a cloud, is psychologically demanding because you have no sense of where you came from and no sense of where you're going. Night is, however, the best time to jump if you don't want to be seen, and Brehm does not want to be seen, because this is a military mission.

Compared to other ways of making war, the use of the parachute in military operations is still relatively new. The first successful parachute jump took place in 1783, when Sebastien Lenorman, a French physicist, jumped from a tower. In the early twenties, U.S. General Billy Mitchell staged a display of airborne infantry power at Kelly Field in Texas, dropping six soldiers out of a Martin bomber and proving that they could land safely and deploy within minutes of hitting the ground. The U.S. military leaders watching the demonstration were insufficiently impressed and chose not to develop a paratroops program. The German observers present, however, were quite impressed. The Nazis used paratroops to spearhead their Blitzkrieg assaults during WWII. The Allies didn't really get with it until 1940 and had to play catch-up for most of the war. The U.S. soldiers who dropped behind enemy lines during WWII used round parachutes, which gave them about as much control over where they landed as dandelion seeds in a summer breeze. Men landed in trees, with no way to lower themselves to the ground without breaking a leg, or worse, or they landed in lakes, where they drowned, or they hung up on wires or church steeples, or they landed in the middle of enemy troops, where they were captured or shot. They landed so far apart from each other that collecting themselves into a viable fighting force was often difficult and sometimes impossible.

It's a much more precise state of affairs today. Jack Brehm is, in fact, one of the most precise jumpers in the world, a member of the Air Force STARS demonstration parachute team. Tonight, Brehm is flying a HALO mission, one of the more extreme ways to jump out of an airplane. HALO stands for High Altitude Low Opening. By flying over enemy territory at 26,000 feet, the C-130 Brehm jumped from can avoid being hit by triple A, ground-based antiaircraft armaments, and it can also keep out of range of some SAMs, or surface-to-air missiles, including shoulder-fired Stinger-type missiles, which have a ceiling of about 7,000 feet. More to the point, in a combat zone a plane flying that high might not be taken for a threat, or it might be mistaken for a commercial airliner. An airplane flying in low over a combat zone would be sure to draw a response. If a plane coming in low overflies a river valley behind enemy lines, for example, within hours that river valley could fill with troops looking for any potential threat along the plane's flight path. A HALO jump puts men on the ground in a relatively short period of time while giving the enemy the least warning. The alternative is the HAHO, or High Altitude High Opening jump, where the parachutist does a clear and pull, opening his main chute as soon as he leaves the plane. Pulling from such heights can give the jumper enough drift time that, depending on the prevailing winds, or how strong the jet stream is, he can land as far as fifty miles from where he originally exited the aircraft. A HAHO jump protects the aircraft because it doesn't have to fly over (or anywhere near) the drop zone. The enemy might calculate the aircraft's flight path, but when the potential drop zone is more than fifty miles wide, there's not much they can do. The drawback to a HAHO jump is that the air is so thin at 26,000 feet that when the chute deploys, it can explode open with enough of a jolt to knock the jumper unconscious or rip the chute to shreds. Furthermore, if the jumpmaster or the navigator miscalculates the prevailing winds, or if the winds change, the jumper can miss the drop zone by miles. Each method of jumping has its own kind of beauty, but to someone like Brehm, it's the difference between skiing down a long gentle slope or taking a double diamond run full of moguls at top speed.

A HALO jump is the ultimate thrill.

Jack's altimeter reads a thousand feet.

He braces himself, because although clouds look puffy and soft from below, hitting one from above at 125 mph hurts. It stings, because raindrops may be round on the bottom, but they feel pointy on the top. Clouds may also contain ice crystals. Turbulence inside a cloud can be strong. Clouds often contain significant internal pressure differentials that can make an altimeter reading inaccurate by as much as a thousand feet.

"In the clouds!" the team leader says, even though everybody hits the cloud deck at the same time.

Within a few seconds of entering the cloud, Brehm is damp to the core. His ECW suit is waterproof, but it's like being sprayed with a fire hose. Water under that kind of pressure is going to find a way in—the only thing he could do to stop it would be to wear a scuba diver's dry suit. You don't do any kind of maneuvering inside a cloud, because you might hit someone. You maintain your position and hold your bearing. Jack Brehm experiences a sense of isolation and suspension, a cold nothingness all around him. It's hard to get used to. No matter how many times you've done it, it's still anxiety producing. Brehm stares toward the earth, straining to see something, anything, in the darkness below him, anything to reconnect him to the world.

This could end any time now. Just about now would be fine. How thick is this goddamn cloud anyway? What if this is more than just a cloud? What if it's actually ground fog?

He checks his altimeter again. The dial glows red, but to be safe, he's taped a green chemlight to his wrist to help him read it.

"I'm out," someone says.

Then he's out too. He takes a deep breath. He sees, far off to the south, the lights of a small town. The people in the town are going about their business, watching television, drinking in bars, making love, unaware that unannounced visitors are falling out of the sky just a few miles away. He scans the countryside below, looking for the headlights of any moving vehicles, any sign that they may have somehow been detected.

The circle has lost a bit of its structure in the clouds, but now that everyone's out, they re-form. Falling in formation like this is fairly standard fare at air shows, where professional jump teams put on demonstrations or try to set records for group jumps. It's a bit tougher to do at night, wearing an oxygen mask, carrying a forty-five-pound rucksack, with an M-16 strapped to your side. In a HALO jump, it's not done for show. It's purely practical, in fact essential, to know where your teammates are because everybody needs to deploy their chutes at the right time, and, at the same time. Otherwise you risk having your chute become entangled with someone else's in midair, an event that is usually fatal for both parties.

At 6,000 feet, the team leader gives the command.

"Break off!"

Brehm wheels about and turns away. He checks over his shoulder, waves his arms and, at 5,000 feet, deploys by reaching with his right hand for a steel rectangular ring at his right shoulder. Grasping the ring, he throws his right arm out and forward, as if throwing a right jab at somebody in front of him. This is the moment when he'll find out if he's had a malfunction. If his main chute fails to open, it may be because the pilot chute that pulls the main chute has gotten lodged in the vacuum that forms above a jumper's back as he falls, in which case Brehm needs only to roll his body one way or the other to break the vacuum. If his main continues to fail, he must disengage it by pulling a cutaway handle with his right hand and then his reserve rip cord handle with his left hand, all the while arching his back.

This time, it's not necessary. He's got a good chute.

He's not out of danger. He has to be aware of any malfunctions by other team members because he doesn't want to get hit by somebody else's cutaway chute, nor does he want to fall onto the chute of someone already under canopy. He really doesn't want somebody to fall through his own chute, as happened to a PJ named Scott Gearen, who in 1987 jumped from a CH-46 helicopter from 13,000 feet and opened at 3,500 feet, only to have a man above him crash through his canopy, destroying all but two cells of his parachute. Gearen fell 3,000 feet and hit the ground at an estimated 100 mph. From the neck down, he was okay, taking the brunt of the fall with his head and not his body. If you were going to fall from 3,000 feet and had a choice, you'd probably want it the other way around. According to one account, "An X-ray of his head looked like an exploded view of the human skull. All the bones were there. They just weren't connected." Miraculously, Gearen survived, and he still jumps, but now before he pulls he looks over his shoulder. Twice.

PJs all know Scott Gearen's story.

Brehm looks around for other jumpers. He looks up to check his own canopy. It's dark and hard to see, but everything appears to be okay. His lines are clear. He turns on the flashing strobe light on the back of his helmet, which tells the men in the air with him where he is and what direction he is moving in. He looks down below for the target. He can't see it, but it's the navigator's job to see it, not his. He performs a controllability check to make sure his chute is operating properly, testing his toggles, red nylon loops at the ends of the lines that control and change the shape of his parachute.

"All jumpers report in," the team leader says.

"Nav okay," the navigator says.

"Number two okay."

The team leader is number three.

"Number four okay."

"Number five okay."

"Number six okay. All jumpers have good chutes."

Brehm's ram-air parachute system opens perfectly, as it will about two hundred times, on average, before a malfunction. That is to say, it doesn't matter how old the chute he's using is—if he were to jump two hundred times with a brand-new chute, each time he'd be likely to have a malfunction, anything from impaired steering or breaking to a partial or complete failure to deploy. Some malfunctions can be fixed while falling, but others must be cut away. The old round S-17 static-line, troop-style parachutes are simpler, and have a near zero malfunction rate, but they aren't anywhere near as maneuverable as the MT-1X ram-air chute, a square, double-layered, 375-square-foot chute with an open nose that inflates the chute like an airplane's wing, the curved upper surface providing lift. As the high man, Brehm brakes to allow the others to drop beneath him.

"Nav got a good bearing?" the team leaders asks.

"Turning left ninety degrees to a heading of two-seventy magnetic," the navigator replies.

"Okay, everyone," the team leader says. "Check your position in the stack and let's get some separation. Nav—spiral down and give us some room."

There are essentially two formations that an element can move in while under canopy, either a V-shaped wedge or in a trailing line or stack, with the navigator as low man at the number one position, the team leader somewhere in the middle of the stack, and the high man at the number six position. Each team member needs to keep his eye on the navigator and follow his turns while maintaining his place in the stack. They follow the navigator because ram-air chutes are so highly maneuverable that you can't always tell which way the wind is blowing, the way you might if you were drifting along like a dandelion seed. You want to land into the wind, so that your forward momentum and the ground winds cancel each other out. Unbraked, a ram-air chute flies forward at about thirty mph. You don't want to be flying at 30 mph with a 30-mph ground wind at your back, or you'll hit the ground at 60 mph. It's considerably simpler during a daylight jump, when the navigator can look for smoke or a flag blowing on the ground to see which way the wind is blowing. At night, the jumpmaster, prior to giving the signal to jump, might drop a streamer with chemlights attached to it, or, if he doesn't want the enemy to see chemlights falling out of the clouds, he can attach chemlights that glow in the infrared spectrum, invisible to the naked eye but clearly visible to anyone using night vision goggles.

"Everybody keep your eyes open and look for airplanes," the team leader says. "And bad guys on the ground. Nav—you got any ground references yet?"

"Roger," the navigator replies. "Railroad tracks at twelve o'clock running east west. When we cross them, we got another five klicks to go."

"Number four," number six says. "Where the hell are you going? Bring it back to your left about forty-five degrees."

Brehm watches the ground below him. He sees no muzzle flashes, no tracer bullets, no campfires, no vehicle headlights, nothing to be concerned about, or rather, nothing to be concerned about beyond all the things he always has to be concerned about—trees, telephone wires, rocks, ditches, fences, water, anything he could fly into and hurt himself. The navigator is equipped with an array of electronic gear, including his compass, his radio, and a Global Positioning Satellite locater that's precise to within a few feet, equipment PJs can use to hone in on a downed pilot's locater beacon. Still, all the electronic gear in the world isn't going to help the jumper who misjudges the wind direction and hits a boulder hard enough to crack his helmet open.

"Okay," the navigator calls out. "Nav's got the DZ, two klicks at twelve o'clock. Looking good. Got the target in sight as well. Looks like the ground wind is out of the west. I'm starting to set up on a left base."

"All right," the team leader says. "Set up for landing. Everyone call out any hazards you see. You know how I hate power lines."

They are at 1,500 feet now. Brehm could remove his oxygen, but it's recommended that HALO jumpers breathe pure oxygen until they're on the ground, because breathing pure oxygen helps with night vision. Perhaps the most critical part of the flight is from five hundred feet down, a time at which the men in the element move closer together as they approach the drop zone. This is when an inexperienced jumper can screw up and jeopardize everybody else. An inexperienced jumper might stall his chute, panic, come out of it too fast by letting up on his toggles too abruptly, lurch forward and make contact with the man in front of him, or tangle chutes. Free falling from one hundred feet is just as likely to kill you as falling from 26,000 feet. A jumper might fail to judge where the ground is, flare his chute too soon and collapse it twenty or thirty feet above the ground. If he flares it too late, he could hit the ground too fast. Ideally, the parachutist will approach the ground in a half-braked position, moving with the wind, pass the target at about 1,000 feet, make a flat 90-degree turn into the base leg at eight hundred feet, turn 90 degrees back into the wind at five hundred feet, lower whatever equipment he may be carrying with him at two hundred feet on a twenty-foot strap so that he's not bearing the extra weight when he lands, and hit full brakes about ten feet above the ground, stopping all forward momentum. In a perfect world, your chute will fall gently to the ground, not catch in the wind and drag you along with it. In a perfect world, there are no swirling crosswinds, no obstacles or trees or wires to become entangled in, no turbulence to rock you from side to side, no boulders or rocks to try to land on, and the drop zone is a flat grassy football field. Finally, in a perfect world, there are also no enemy soldiers shooting at you.

"Turning final at eight hundred feet," the navigator reports.

"Number two, watch Nav's canopy on landing," the team leader says. "I'm following you."

SGT Jack Brehm carries a weapon, an M-16A1 rifle. It weighs 7.6 pounds and is worn on a sling over his left shoulder, with the muzzle pointing down. To rig it for jumping, he has duct-tape padding over the muzzle and sights to avoid entanglement with his parachute lines. This also prevents dirt from clogging his weapon if he falls on it while landing. If he had to, Brehm could fire his weapon as he lands, but that's not the idea tonight. That's never the idea. The image of men firing their weapons as they drop to the ground is strictly for the movies. If such a thing were to happen in real life, it would signify a dramatic strategic failure. In fact, if Brehm were ever to fire his weapon in earnest, it would be considered a sign of failure, which is not something you can say about most soldiers. The object of tonight's HALO mission is to get in and get out without being detected or captured. It's a covert SAR or Search and Rescue, as opposed to an overt SAR, which is how the Marines or the Army might attempt to rescue their people, sending in missile- or bomb-bearing jets in advance to clear the area, followed by multiple heavily armed helicopters with mini-guns blazing, followed by a team of men dispersed on the ground to set up a perimeter and blow the bejeezus out of everything that moves, after which the downed pilot can be plucked from the smoldering wreckage. The famous rescue of pilot Scott O'Grady from Bosnia was effected by the Marines something in this manner. PJs train for covert SARs, low-flying clandestine helicopter raids that put one or two guys on the ground to hoist the survivor out of danger under cover of darkness, or HALO or HAHO jumps, methods that risk as few people as possible to get the job done. There's no real rivalry between the services, except that when a rescue comes, everybody wants it. Whether a mission calls for an overt or a covert SAR depends on the situation on the ground.

Brehm, fully trained in tactical operations, is prepared and ready to fire on the enemy if he has to, but the idea is not to be discovered. Sometimes he wishes he had a silencer on his rifle, because then he could use it to shoot rabbits or squirrels for food, if he were ever in survival mode and so far into enemy territory that it would take him days to get out. The problem with a silencer is that if you have one on your weapon, you can be treated as an assassin if you're captured, and assassins are generally not treated well. No one, it goes without saying, wants to be captured or killed, but there is something even less appealing to consider. Every serviceman's worst nightmare is to be captured and then paraded around, either dead or alive, on the streets of someplace like Belgrade or Baghdad. Every soldier remembers the image on Somali television of pilot CAPT Michael Durant being dragged through the streets of Mogadishu, in October of 1993. That image alone helped change the outcome of events because it undermined American public support for what we were trying to do in Somalia. On a personal level, to a soldier, the more elite your unit is, the more you fear being captured and paraded, because it will bring dishonor to your unit, and Jack Brehm is a member of a very elite unit.

"Very elite" is, of course, redundant, but there are a number of military groups that claim, legitimately, to be elite, groups like the Green Berets or the Navy SEALs, and everyone likes to think of themselves as special and unique. The Air Force's pararescue team is unique in many ways. For one thing, it's one of the smallest special operations teams in the military. There are over 600,000 men and women in the U.S. Air Force, and only about three hundred PJs. They're also elite in that they have a single mission and only one basic reason to exist. Since World War I, it has become increasingly true that the key to winning a war has been to control the air above the battlefield, and to do that, you need airplanes with pilots in them, who will occasionally get shot down, despite all the best defense systems and precautions. Experience has shown us that most of the time, dominating the air will not, in and of itself, win a war, but the importance of airpower, particularly in light of recent conflicts like Desert Storm or Operation Allied Force, remains indisputable. For all the technology being developed to guide bombs and cruise missiles and reconnaissance drones, we will probably always need pilots, and pilots and air crews work better when they know someone is going to come get them if they get shot down. The more capable the rescuers, the more confident the pilots.

There are no more capable rescuers than the PJs. No one else knows how to fall five miles from the sky to rescue somebody. No one else trains to make rescues in such a wide variety of circumstances and conditions on a mountaintop, in the middle of the Sahara, or 1,000 miles out from shore in hurricane-tossed seas.

At five hundred feet, Brehm turns into the wind and descends at half-toggle. He watches below him, keeping his eye on his team members' chemlights. The high man's landing is somewhat tricky, with five other team members on the ground before him to avoid, but it's also easier, in that he can watch them land first and learn from their mistakes.

"Nav's in," the navigator calls out.

"Two's in."

"TL in."

"Four's in—shit, that hurts. Goddammit. I flared early again. I'm okay."

It looks fairly clear below, some kind of open field. Brehm tries to read any shifts in the wind, flies right to avoid one of his team members, turns directly into the wind again and lowers his Alice pack at two hundred feet.

"Five's in."

Brehm stalls his chute when he's about five feet off the ground. He lands on both feet, knees bent, but it jars him just a bit because he thought the ground was a few feet closer. He doesn't fall, which is a point of pride with him. He qualified for the Air Force STARS by landing ten consecutive jumps within a three-meter circle and standing up each time, sticking his landings like an Olympic gymnast. He has a number of dreams, but one of them is to land on the pitcher's mound in Yankee Stadium before a World Series game. Right on the rubber.

"Six in," he reports. "Still alive."

He reaches for his cutaway handle to free his chute as soon as he sets down, so that his parachute won't drag him along the ground if it's windy. The temperature is in the seventies. Jack Brehm gathers his chute together and hauls in his gear bag.

"Everybody bring it in and we'll meet on the north side of the target in five," the team leader says. "Good job, boys. Let's clear the DZ."

Brehm sheds his Mr. Puffy suit and unstraps his M-16. He takes off his helmet and his balaclava. He has short red hair, as much mustache as the Air Force allows, and freckles beneath the camouflage paint he wears on his face. There's enough ambient light that he doesn't need his night vision goggles. He collects his gear and rendezvouses with the other members of his team. The team leader is nearly Brehm's age. The rest are all younger, all men in their twenties. It's unusual for someone to remain a PJ for as long as Brehm has, for a variety of reasons. If you ever get knocked unconscious, you're out, because there's always a chance you'll have subsequent blackouts. If your eyes go bad enough, you're out. If you fail to maintain a peak level of fitness and can't pass the annual qualifying physical, you're out. In any rescue, the idea is to land as close as you can to the downed pilot, but sometimes you have to land a considerable distance away and cross miles of often difficult terrain, carrying heavy gear. When you find the pilot, you might have to carry him to where a helicopter can fly in and pick everybody up. In a purely physical sense, pararescue is a young man's game. In an emotional sense, it is, too. Jack Brehm has been doing this for twenty-two years, nearly four times as long as the average PJ's career.

At the rendezvous point, an argument is in progress.

"You're the navigator," number two says. "You're supposed to know these things."

"Don't blame me," the navigator says. "It's not like they gave me a GPS bearing for it."

"Well, I'm not following you then," number five says.

"I'm with him," number four says.

"Doesn't anybody have a cell phone?"

"It's right on the beach."

"No it's not."

"Let's ask the veteran," number two says as Brehm approaches. "Hey, Jack—this guy says Tracers is on 98A after Panama City Beach. I say it's before you get to Panama City Beach."

"Coming from where?"

"From Eglin? Or from Fort Walton Beach?"

"Well, if you take the fork after the bridge, it's before, but then you gotta go another ten miles. The fastest way to get there is to take 98 past Panama City and then circle back on 98A, which becomes Fort Beach Road. Then it's just after the beach. Why?"

"We're debriefing there in an hour," the team leader says. "I suggested the PJ section, but I was outvoted."

"Tonight's amateur night and they get college girls in there trying to make money for spring break," number four explains. Young PJs love strip joints. Old PJs don't mind them, either.

"I'll meet you there," Brehm says. "I need to stop at the motel first and make a phone call."

The training mission is over. They are on the property of Eglin Air Force Base, just outside of Fort Walton Beach, Florida. Dropping men from 26,000 feet is a complicated procedure, requiring all commercial air traffic in the area to be canceled or rerouted, something the Air Force only schedules a couple of times a year. Other teams of men will be falling throughout the evening. Such training missions are exhilarating, but at the same time, preparing for war is a grim business. There is trouble all over the world, in Iraq, in Kosovo, in Bosnia, Croatia, Chechnya, East Timor, the Congo—anywhere that American aircraft fly to police the skies, PJs have to go and stand watch and be ready to launch at a moment's notice.

That others may live.

Brehm's motel is right on the water in Fort Walton Beach. He opens the sliding-glass doors and stands on his balcony watching the ocean. The Gulf of Mexico doesn't smell the same as the ocean in New England. He's tempted to go for a midnight swim, but then he remembers he's done enough for one night. He's not tired. He rarely is after a jump, particularly not after a HALO jump. There's too much adrenaline in his system. The high doesn't go away when the mission ends. In some sense, that's when it begins. It's why guys generally want to go out after a mission and drink beers until the feeling goes away, not that you want the feeling to go away.

It's why his team members are at Tracers, helping college girls raise the funds they need by tucking dollar bills into their garter belts. Anything to further the cause of education. He calls home to Long Island. His wife, Peggy, answers.

"Hey," he says.

"Hi, John," she says, sounding sleepy. "How are you? How'd it go?"

"Did I wake you?"

"I was just resting my eyes."

"What time is it there?" He looks at his watch. "Oh shit. I keep forgetting the Panhandle is in a different time zone here. I'm sorry."

She doesn't mind being woken up. He asks her how his children are. She tells him Bean—Laura-Jean—did pretty good on her progress report. Matthew forgot to feed the puppy again, but Peg reminded him. Molly, the puppy, seems to have learned to pee only on the newspapers, so they're ready for the next step in her training. Jeff is good. The twins are good. Elizabeth, a freshman at Boston University, got A's on two papers she wrote, but that's no surprise because she's always loved writing and is thinking about becoming a writer. Michele and her boyfriend Greg went to the movies—they should be home soon.

Jack tells her there's a debriefing he has to go to at Tracers. She knows Tracers is a strip joint, but it doesn't bother her, because she also knows that there's nothing her husband values any higher than his family and nothing he would ever do to jeopardize that. He tells her he loves her and that he'll be home in three days. He thinks of how many times he's said that before and wonders how many times he'll say it again.

She thinks of how many times he's said that before and wonders how many times he'll say it again.

"Did you see the news?" she asks him.

"No, I didn't," he says. "What's happening?"

She tells him things are going wrong in Iraq. Saddam Hussein is refusing to allow U.N. weapons inspectors to inspect what they want to inspect. There's talk of a renewed bombing campaign. There's also talk of a possible war in Yugoslavia, someplace called Kosovo.

"Well," Brehm says, "with any luck, that'll have nothing to do with me." To be honest, though, part of him wants to go to combat—training to do something your whole life and then never doing it would leave you with a kind of empty feeling. He just jumped out of an airplane from 26,000 feet. There was a reason for that.

She reminds him that he's already scheduled to go to Turkey.

"Peg," he says, "I know. Okay? We can talk about it when I get back."

He hangs up the phone. He's got to start thinking about what he's going to do when he retires. Whenever that's going to be. It would be nice to have one last mission, one major rescue, so that afterward he could say he'd done it all.

It would be nice to go out on a high note.

2

DON'T SIT UNDER THE APPLE TREE

Whenever I go to a foreign country, I try to learn something about the culture before I go. Usually I read about that country's religion. Before I went to Thailand, I read the teachings of Buddha. Before I went to Saudi Arabia, I read up on Islam. All the great religions have the same bottom line. Christians put it this way: "Love thy neighbor as thyself." It makes it hard to understand why there's so much fighting over religion in the world. Pray to Buddha, or Allah, or God, or Jesus—it doesn't matter how you address the envelope. It all goes in the same box.

BILL LOOKS GOOD," PEGGY SAYS. SHE THROWS HER SWEATER ON the bed. "Do you think?"

"He looks real good," Jack says.

"How much weight do you think he lost?"

"Since when?"

"Since you saw him last?"

"I don't know. A lot."

"You said he used to look like Orson Welles."

"He was a big boy."

"I'm glad he looks good."

"He's doing great."

"I'm exhausted. You feel like waiting up for Bean? She told me today she thinks she's old enough to have her curfew extended."

"What'd you tell her?"

"I don't know. She probably is. I told her we could talk about it when you get back."

Peggy doesn't want to say the words "when you get back." Peggy doesn't want to talk about his leaving, but it's like trying to avoid the big blue elephant sitting on your couch. Jack's bags sit at the foot of the bed, unclosed, all but packed. Tomorrow he'll add his toiletries, his shaving cream, toothbrush, razor. Tomorrow night, when she brushes her teeth, Peggy will see the empty hole where his toothbrush ordinarily rests, and it's going to make her want to cry. Tonight is their last night together, and she doesn't want to cry on their last night.

"Did you call Elizabeth?"

"I talked to her yesterday," Jack says. "I'll call her again tomorrow."

"She's not used to being all alone when you go," Peggy says. "Bean was crying. She said it's because her friend didn't call her."

They both know Laura-Jean's weepiness has more to do with the sadness and the strain in the air than anything her friends have said or done to her.

"How's Matty?" Jack asks.

"Hard to read, as usual. Pretending he's cool with everything. He says his lacrosse coach isn't giving him much playing time."

"He will, once he gets to know him."

"He thinks he's too small."

"Tell him size has nothing to do with it."

"Not Matty—the coach thinks he's too small."

"Why? How big is the coach?"

"Not the coach—the coach thinks . . ." Peggy says, before she catches herself and realizes she's being teased. If she weren't so tense, she wouldn't be taken in so easily. She puts her arms around her husband and kisses him. His job is to make her laugh when she gets like this, and he's always been able to. Sometimes she seems like the most serious person in the family. The kids joke all the time, and they like to say to their father, "Why don't you go jump out of an airplane?" Peggy has a sense of humor, but her brow is often furrowed as she tries to think ahead and anticipate any problems, because it's her job, as she sees it, to keep everything in order and moving forward. She has fine eyebrows, beautiful brown eyes, high Slavic cheekbones, a narrow face, soft straight brown hair parted in the middle, cut shorter than she wore it when she was younger, off the neck now. Jack thinks she's beautiful when her brow is knit, and beautiful when she's smiling, but he prefers the latter. She wears the pants in the family, and he wears the parachute, and neither of them would have it any other way, but he knows he makes her worry. He relies on her faith and on her judgment. He could carry a full-grown man on his shoulders for miles, but he knows she's the strong one.

"What did you tell Elizabeth?" Peggy asks.

"I just told her that as far as I know, the mission's still in Turkey. I'm sorry I barked in the restaurant." It's a noise he makes when he's excited. He can't help it.

"I can't take you anywhere."

"Was it really loud?"

"Bill probably didn't think it was, but the couple across the room might have."

"I want to go watch the news for a second."

"Jack . . ."

"Don't worry—the kids are asleep." Peggy isn't afraid that the television will wake the children. She's afraid of what they'll hear, coming from the television, if they should awaken. She's in something of a bind because she knows that the more information she has, the better her decisions are going to be, and that the same thing is true for her kids, but she also knows that for the next three weeks, if not longer, everything on the nightly news regarding the war in Yugoslavia or events in Iraq is going to directly and personally affect every member of her family, each in a different way, none of them positive, and she wants to protect them from that.

"If Bean comes home," Peggy suggests, "switch it to the *Tonight Show.*"

Jack Brehm watches CNN in his living room. It's the third day of the bombing campaign in Yugoslavia—Operation Allied Force, they're calling it. The war seems to have considerable clarity of purpose—to stop, hamper, delay, or deter the Serbian government, led by Slobodan Milosevic, from executing a "cleansing" campaign against the ethnic Albanian/Moslem residents of Kosovo, a southern province of what was once Yugoslavia, between Macedonia and Montenegro in the Balkans. Everybody knows they've done it before, and everybody knows they're doing it again, attested to by footage of endless streams of refugees walking, riding mules, or driving rusted Belarus tractors out of their own country, fleeing Serbian troops who are burning villages, raping women, and executing or taking prisoner men between the ages of fifteen and fifty. The world sat back and watched it happen before, in Croatia and Bosnia, and in Rwanda, and there seems to be a consensus that we can't sit back and let it happen again. Jack agrees. Even Arab countries, with a few notable exceptions, like Iraq, seem to be backing the United States as it leads the NATO alliance in defending the Kosovars. Clarity of purpose, however, does not mean that an operation has structure or definition. Three days in and already the pundits are talking about exit strategies, as if you could know exactly how a war is going to go before you fight it. Brehm's years in the military have taught him to tune out the pundits. He pays attention instead to the physical details. NATO has about 430 aircraft in theater, the CNN announcer says. There are 200 U.S. planes in the air: F-15s, F-16s, F-117 Stealth fighters, British Harriers and Tornadoes, French Mirages, U.S. A-10 Thunderbolts or "Warthogs," AWAC command and control planes, KC-135 and KC-10 tankers, C-130 transports, radar jamming EA-6B Prowlers, B-1 bombers, B-52s and B-2 Stealth bombers, which, with a range of 11,500 miles, have flown all the way from Missouri to Serbia to drop new JDAMs (Joint Direct Attack Munitions) or GPS-guided bombs. There are also Tomahawk cruise missiles and unmanned Predator surveillance drones taking photographs or employing a new JSTARS technology (Joint Surveillance Target Attack Radar System) that sweeps the landscape with radar, looking for movements by tanks or armored personnel carriers. Brehm concerns himself only with the manned aircraft and the weapons the Serbs have to shoot them down, 20mm and 30mm antiaircraft guns, and sixty surface-to-air missile batteries, about two-thirds of those girding Belgrade, mostly Soviet-built Vietnam-era SA-2s and SA-3s, but also several mobile SA-6 batteries and who knows how many SA-7 shoulder-fired missiles.

The experts keep repeating that the Serbs have far more advanced antiaircraft systems than the Iraqis had during Desert Storm, better radar for targeting, and more combat experience. They also have a number of flyable but outdated MiG-21s and perhaps fifteen or twenty state-of-the-art MiG-29s, though on the first day of the war, NATO planes shot down three of the MiG-29s. Last night, they shot down two more MiG-29s attempting to fly into Bosnia. American pilots were reporting little resistance from the ground, wondering why the Serbs weren't launching their SAMs. Then reports of light resistance were proven premature when, only hours before Brehm involuntarily barked in the restaurant, the Serbs managed to shoot down an F-117 Stealth fighter about twenty miles outside of Belgrade. This is the event that holds Brehm's attention, because it's precisely the situation he's trained for over the last twenty years. The experts on CNN are calling the downing a lucky shot by the Serbs, a "golden BB." Jack barked in the restaurant when the TV said the pilot had been rescued.

"Do they know where he is?" Peggy asks Jack, appearing at his side.

"In a hospital in Italy, I guess," Jack says, turning the TV off, because he knows it's going to upset his wife. He puts his arm around her and says, "Let's go to bed."

In the bathroom, though, he's still trying to picture it. He has a fair guess what happened. His guess isn't based on anything the TV reporters have said. The Pentagon has admitted only that PJs were involved and won't say more than that for fear of compromising future operations. Brehm knows how PJs train and how AFSOC (Air Force Special Operations Command) plans such missions. It was either a pair of HH-53s loaded with assorted AFSOC personnel or HH-60s with two PJs, a gunner, and a flight crew—probably the latter, given the short notice and the time that would have been required to plan a joint mission. The HH-60s would have been armed with M-240 machine guns and 7.62mm mini-guns, which are electrically fired six-barreled Gatling guns, capable of putting out 6,000 rounds a minute, and possibly a 50-caliber door gun. Bad guys will sometimes move about, or even fire back, when they hear an M-240 or a 50-caliber machine gun shooting at them, but nobody dares lift his head when a mini-gun lets loose.

The F-117 Nighthawk pilot would have experienced a violent ejection, exiting his aircraft under a force of perhaps four or five Gs. He would have been somewhat disoriented at first. He would have been scared, knowing that whoever shot him down was probably sending troops to look for him. Once on the ground, the pilot would have applied the SERE (Survival, Evasion, Resistance, and Escape) training he was given. He would have found a place to hide. Holed up, he would wonder if the system was working. Are they coming? Tonight? Tomorrow? In civilian rescue work, rescuers can locate victims by honing in on an EPIRB, an Emergency Position Indicating Radio Beacon. There are commercially available emergency signal beacons that transmit GPS (Global Positioning System) data. Businesspeople in restaurants all around the world are already speaking to each other on cell phones with satellite uplinks. Much of the modern communications technology we take for granted was originally developed for military purposes. The system works fairly well for civilian rescues, but in combat, you always have to worry that the wrong people are monitoring your communications.

NATO forces in Operation Allied Force are flying out of Italian bases at Aviano, Cervia, Vincenza, and Brindisi. According to the maps on CNN, the closest friendly country to the site of the crash would have been Hungary, which only recently joined NATO. Wherever they launched from, the helicopters, according to the news, reached the F-117 pilot six hours after he was shot down. The helicopters would have been vulnerable to ground fire. Speed would have been paramount with enemy troops in the area. Once the pilot was located and identified, a PJ would have hoisted down on a cable to pick him up, riding a device called a forest penetrator, a small heavy buoy-shaped steel cylinder with paddles at the bottom that fold down in a Y to form seats. The forest penetrator was designed by the Kaman Helicopter Company in the early sixties to drop through the jungle canopies of Vietnam. To extract a survivor with a penetrator, the PJ places his legs over the injured pilot's as they face each other straddling the cylinder, in effect sitting on the pilot's lap. If the pilot's injuries are too severe, the helicopter will lower a Stokes litter, a caged aluminum basket that can carry someone even if he's unconscious. The helicopters would then have flown out of country, possibly using a different route from the route they flew in on, where ground forces might have been alerted by their ingress. Jack can visualize the whole thing. For all he knows, this is something he might be doing in a matter of weeks or even days.

"Bean told me she wants a piercing for her birthday," Peggy says.

"Oh yeah?" Jack says. He comes back into the moment. Tomorrow night, he'll be five thousand miles away. No sense being a million miles away now, on his last night home. He shuts the faucet off and dries his face. "What'd you say?"

"I told her I'd talk to you about it."

"Offhand, I think I'm against it," Jack says. "Did she say where?"

"I think her tongue."

"Well, that's better than some places, I suppose." He thinks, it's hard to have daughters. Hard to have sons, too, but for different reasons. The twins, Elizabeth and Michele, are drop-dead gorgeous—he remembers taking them to the mall when they were Bean's age and how the boys all looked at them, and how they looked back at all the boys. They were still babies, it seemed, when they first asked to get their ears pierced. At least that was just ears. Then Michele had her tongue pierced. Elizabeth had her belly-button done. What are you going to do?

The next day, Sunday, it's Laura-Jean's birthday, so they all go out to eat breakfast at the Rocky Point Diner. It's the same diner Jack and Peggy went to in high school, before they even knew each other. Say what you want about Long Island, Jack tells people, but it has great diners. When they get home, the answering machine is full of messages from friends, wishing Jack farewell and good luck. Peggy's sister Carol comes over to say good-bye. They don't have to leave for the airport until two or two-thirty, so Jack helps Jeffrey color Easter eggs, and then he plays him in a game of chess. Jack wins, but Jeffrey's game is much improved. Afterward, they wrestle a bit, until Jeffrey starts to cry.

"I'm sorry, buddy," Jack says, holding his son. "Was I being too rough?"

"No," Jeffrey says, sniffing. "I hurt my ribs last night."

"How did you hurt your ribs?"

"I don't know," he says. "I just did."

"I think he just needed an excuse to cry," Peggy tells Jack later, when she gets him aside. "Remember—all reactions today are not real. They're just cover-ups."

Jeff is mad that, again, his father won't be home for his birthday, April first. Bean is mad he has to leave before her birthday dinner tonight. Jack can see that Michele is worried about her mother, in the way Michele puts her arm around Peg or touches her shoulder. Matty is being quiet. Everyone is on edge because of him. As the time to leave arrives, everybody starts to scatter, "The Big Run Away," Peggy calls it, a phenomenon that happens each time he goes away, everybody saying good-bye as quickly as possible and then splitting off, because it's too hard to draw it out. Each kid hugs and kisses Dad and then walks away. It breaks Peggy's heart, each time. Each behavior tacitly acknowledges the fact that Jack's job is inherently risky. Every day he goes to work there's a chance that something might happen, which is something you could say about a fireman or a policeman, but what Jack does is often more extreme than that, and his family knows it. Having him go away on a mission only concentrates the feeling. Sometimes he wonders what they'd think if they really knew the risks he takes, because he knows he's far more aware than they are of what can go wrong when you try to refuel a helicopter in midair or parachute down to a ship adrift in twenty- or thirty-foot seas. His experience and training have taught him to accept those risks, but his family hasn't had the benefit of such experience or training—they've had to learn it the hard way.

He tries to see each of his kids one last time before he goes. Matt is reading. Laura-Jean is going through her closet. Michele and her boyfriend Greg take Jeffrey out into the backyard to distract him. There are ambiguities in life, and then there are those things you know with such an absolute certainty that they anchor you and keep a solid base under your feet, and one of those things, for Jack, is that he loves his children. Sometimes he thinks he loves his children more than other men love their own. That can't be true, but sometimes he feels that way. He hates going away. He's also excited to go away. He also knows that there is no better feeling than saving someone else's life. It's the other thing he does that gives his life purpose. Sometimes the two things conflict. So be it. He throws his things in Peggy's minivan. They pick up Jack's fellow PJ and friend Jimmy Dougherty at his house and begin the hour-long drive to JFK, where Jack and Jimmy will fly commercial to Istanbul.

They arrive at the airport around 4:00. There are televisions everywhere, and it seems like they're all tuned to CNN. Five hundred sorties were flown yesterday, a reporter says, involving two hundred planes attacking ninety targets. There's more footage of the wreckage of the Stealth fighter and Serbian teenagers dancing on the wings, kids Matty's age, sporting signs saying, "We're sorry—we didn't know it was invisible." The pundits say the loss of the $43 million plane is a propaganda coup for the Serbs. Of course, it would have been worse if they could display pictures of the captured pilot. Peggy and Jack both know he's flying to Turkey, where American pilots continue to enforce the northern no-fly zone as part of Operation Northern Watch. Back in December, in response to Saddam Hussein's decision to keep U.N. weapons inspectors from doing the job they were sent to do, allied forces launched an attack on Baghdad that included airplanes and cruise missiles, an escalation in the conflict that might have made bigger headlines if the world weren't so preoccupied with President Clinton's impeachment troubles. With the new war in Yugoslavia, reports of bombing raids in Iraq, which have continued sporadically since December, barely make it into the papers. Both Peggy and Jack know that it's still dangerous to fly over Iraq, and that there's still a chance of U.S. pilots getting shot down in hostile territory. They also know, without having to talk about it, that five hundred sorties over Kosovo in a day are five hundred reasons why Jack might be transferred from Operation Northern Watch to Operation Allied Force.

"Sometimes I think it was easier when the kids were little," Peggy says. She holds Jack's hand. She doesn't want to let go of it.

"How so?" Jack asks.

"I don't know. It was all physical. It was just getting them fed and put to bed at night, and then up and out to catch the school bus in the morning. I thought once they got older, it would be easier, but it's harder. It's all mental now."

"I suppose," Jack says. He wishes there was something else to say. He wants to promise her that he's going to be okay, that he'll be careful. It's nothing he hasn't said a hundred times before. He wishes there was a new way to put it. He wants to repeat what they talked about the night before, how lucky they are, how glad they should be, and how they should appreciate all the great things they have, but he's wary of saying anything that might remotely sound like fated last words. "You've got Michele and Elizabeth to help you—don't be afraid to delegate."

"I know," Peg says. *Why is it worse this time? Or does it always feel like it's worse than before?* She wants to tell him no one has ever loved anyone the way she loves him, that he's her whole life, and that without him she merely functions. It's nothing he doesn't know already. "You'll be in my prayers, you know."

"Yeah, well don't be afraid to delegate in that direction, either," Jack jokes. "We're really lucky, you know."

"It's more than just luck," Peggy says. "Don't you think?"

"What do you mean?"

"I mean, you don't marry somebody you've only known for two months and have it last twenty-one years by accident. God meant for us to be together, you know."

"I couldn't agree more," Jack says. She squeezes his hand and looks at the clock on the wall.

"This really bites."

"I couldn't agree more," Jack says. "I love you big. I'll be very careful, and I'll come home safe. What more can I say?"

"I love you too," she says.

"You want me to walk you back to the car?"

"No," she says. That would make saying good-bye harder. At some point she has to turn and go, and it might as well be now. She hugs him, kisses him, kisses him again, gives him a final hug, turns and walks away. She has to force herself to walk. She resists the urge to look back. Her insides literally ache.

In the car, driving back, she watches the time pass on the digital dashboard clock. Now he's boarding. Now they're taxiing. Now they're in the air. She can't keep the tears back, but why should she? She'll have plenty of time to hold them back in the next three weeks, unless the situation changes, and he's gone for longer than three weeks. . . . She can't bear to follow that line of thought.

"I don't want to do this anymore!" she screams in the car. "I'm too old for this! I don't want to do this anymore! I just don't! I want him home with me."

At Bean's birthday party that night, Peggy tries to be cheerful, and to sing "Happy Birthday" at the top of her voice and make sure that the kids know that everything is going to be okay, that this is just another mission, nothing out of the ordinary. She must be losing her touch, though. Three times during the meal Jeffrey reaches over and pats her arm and says, "Smile, Mom." She thinks about this getting ready for bed that night, that he's just a little boy, a week shy of twelve. That's too young to be worried about your mom, patting her arm and telling her to smile. He shouldn't have so much weight on his shoulders. For as long as she's been a mother, she's tried to protect her children, never by lying to them about the risks their father takes, every time he goes away and each day he goes to work, but by instilling faith in them, and optimism.

She cries again in the shower. It's a safe place to let go. The kids can't hear you, and the tears don't show. After she showers, she puts on one of Jack's shirts, one from the laundry—one that still smells like him—and goes to bed. She sleeps on her side of the bed. Moving over to his side would be bad luck. In her prayers she repeats the phrase that's been running through her head for the last three days, the way a song gets stuck sometimes. She says, *"Please God—watch over him and keep him safe."*

Jack is on an airplane somewhere over the Atlantic. He's thinking the things men think when they are headed into combat zones. He's thinking about his mentor, a guy named Mike McManus, a grizzly old veteran PJ who taught him everything he knows. Mike served in Vietnam but didn't like to talk about it, telling Jack less about combat than he might have preferred, but Jack learned not to press him on the subject. Jack once bought a veteran PJ a beer in a bar and said, well into the conversation, "Didn't you win a Silver Star in Vietnam?" only to see the veteran, a friend for years, bristle and say, "Is that why you bought me this beer?" Jack said no, forget about it, sorry, forget I asked, and he never did get the story. The veterans, he learned, would rather tell drinking stories than war stories. Still, within the pararescue subculture, many of the legendary PJs distinguished themselves in combat, guys like Bill Pitsenbarger, an Airman First Class who received the Air Force Cross posthumously, the first enlisted man to get one, for heroism in Vietnam, or Duane Hackney, one of the most decorated enlisted men in the history of the Air Force, a Vietnam-era PJ who once handed his parachute to one of his rescuees in a burning helicopter, grabbed another parachute and managed to pull the rip cord just as his helicopter exploded, blowing him out the gunner's door. Ted Hawkins. Chuck Morrow. Surfer Johnson. Randy McComb, who went down into the jungle in Vietnam from an HH-53 to pick up a wounded pilot, hoisting him out under heavy ground fire. When the pilot looked up at the vegetation overhead and said, "Shit, I had a hard enough time going through those trees on the way down," McComb loaned him his helmet and visor. They were halfway up the hoist when the helicopter pilot decided he was taking too many bullets and flew out, dragging McComb and the survivor through the trees as they evacuated. McComb hung on to the pilot but lost his eyesight in the escape and had to be hospitalized. He eventually regained his vision. Years later, back home and driving down a country road with his wife, lightning struck a tree, which fell on McComb's car and killed him. His wife escaped without a scratch. *There's a lesson in there somewhere,* Jack thinks.

Jack has heard the names and the stories that go with them. He knows, though he hasn't said this to Peggy, that if he could make one rescue in combat, he could retire a happy man. If he told her that, she'd say, "I thought you were already a happy man," and then he'd say, "I am," and have to explain, even though she already knows a combat rescue is a PJ's raison d'être. It's not that Jack has any particular desire to take part in an armed conflict, and there's no warrior's blood percolating in his veins, but he does have a sincere desire to serve his country, and the action in Kosovo (if that's where he ends up) is something he believes is right. He simply wants to do what he's trained to do for most of his adult life. It's not like poker, but if it were, making a rescue in a combat situation would be playing for higher stakes than he'd ever played for in his life. It's difficult to stop thinking about that. This could be his last chance.

Then he sees the telephone, lodged in the back of the seat in front of him. He wants to call his wife. He wants to be home, lying by her side. He pictures himself as a very old man, lying at her side. He wants that, more than anything, though the future is not in his control. He picks up the phone, then puts it back. There's nothing he can say that she doesn't already know. That's the nice thing about being married to your best friend. There's nothing you can say that she doesn't already know.

3

BOZO WITHOUT A CLUE

When I was a kid, maybe from the time I was ten or eleven, it was rare that a day went by when I didn't go to the beach. Winter spring summer or fall, I didn't care. The house where I grew up was only a block and a half from the Sound. On a clear day, you could stand on the cliffs and look across the Sound about twenty miles or so and see New Haven, Connecticut. In the winter, I'd just walk on the beach with my dog, Irish, who was actually a German shepherd, but we named her Irish anyway. As soon as it got warm enough to swim, in the spring, I'd be in the water, either alone or with my friends, Timmy Lent or Tommy Kitz or maybe the Rayner brothers. It may not have been terribly bright, but we used to dare each other to see how far out we could swim. One time we were probably a couple miles from shore and a guy came along and ordered us to get in his boat. He said, "Do you idiots have any idea how far out you are?" At the time, "far out" was an expression that meant you were hip or groovy, so we laughed, but he said we could get cramps, and that he was going to call the Coast Guard, so we got in his boat. All the way in to shore, he kept scolding us and asking us if our parents had any idea how far out we had been swimming, and as a matter of fact, if they'd known they would have killed us. In retrospect, the guy was probably right. We didn't know anything about the currents, or what was going on out there. I think I was a strong enough swimmer that I would have made it back, but there was no guarantee of that.

I've never been afraid of the ocean. There were times when maybe I should have been, but I think it's because I've always had a healthy respect for it. I know the ocean. I almost feel as at home in the water as I do on land.

Bozo Without a Clue

IN 1976, NORTH AND SOUTH VIETNAM WERE REUNITED, AND SAIGON was renamed Ho Chi Minh City. Nevertheless, the United States was having a good self-esteem year, having extracted itself from Southeast Asia and said good-bye to Richard Nixon. There were the Carter-Ford debates, and there were Mondale-Dole debates too, but for the most part the country was busy recognizing its two hundredth birthday, with bicentennial festivities and tall ships from thirty-one countries sailing off the coasts to assist in the celebration. There were wars in Angola and Lebanon, and ongoing troubles in South Africa and Northern Ireland, but for the first time in a long time U.S. soldiers were completing their tours of duty and coming home safe and sound, to walk on beaches with their girlfriends, or eat at McDonald's, or go to the theaters and watch movies like *All the President's Men*, or *Taxi Driver*, or *Rocky*. Disco ruled the club scene, and the radio played tunes like "I Write the Songs" by Barry Manilow, or "Afternoon Delight" by the Starland Vocal Band, or "The Wreck of the Edmund FitzGerald" by Gordon Lightfoot. *A Chorus Line* ruled Broadway. *Charlie's Angels*, *Rhoda*, and *The Six Million Dollar Man* were on television. The newspapers told us Howard Hughes had died and was purported to have left his money to the Mormon Church, as well as to a Utah gas station attendant named Melvin Dummar. In the sports sections of the daily papers, we read about the Montreal Canadiens winning the Stanley Cup, the Steelers winning the Super Bowl, the Celtics winning the NBA championship, the Cincinnati Reds winning the World Series, and athletes like Franz Klammer and Nadia Comaneci prevailing in the Olympics. Hank Aaron retired with 755 career home runs that year. Gases from aerosol spray cans were causing damage to the earth's ozone layer, according to a National Academy of Science report, and an unknown disease at a Philadelphia American Legion convention killed twenty-nine people and left 151 others stricken. In Uganda, Israeli commandos staged a daring rescue at Entebbe Airport, where seven pro-Palestinian hijackers were holding hostages. Thirty-one people died in the raid, but 103 hostages were saved.

In 1976, on August sixth, John Bernard Brehm, called Jack by his family and friends, turned twenty. He was living at home with his parents, in the town of Shoreham, Long Island, while working a summer job mowing lawns. He'd gone to Suffolk County Community College for two years, and he had an associate's degree in marine biology, but that wasn't taking him anywhere he wanted to go. The house was a comfortable cedar shake–sided four-bedroom ranch on a wooded lot, on a narrow curving road lined with oak trees and pine. He saw *All the President's Men* and *Taxi Driver* and *Rocky* in the theaters that year and liked *Rocky* best. His favorite song on the radio was Paul Simon, singing "Fifty Ways to Leave Your Lover," unless it was Chicago, singing "If You Leave Me Now," even though no one had left him, and considering that he didn't have a girlfriend, no one was likely to leave him soon. He spent time puttering around in his boat, a twelve-foot aluminum Starcraft dinghy with a five-horsepower Evinrude motor on it, fishing for bluefish or stripers in the Sound, sometimes with his dad, or with friends, sometimes alone. Sometimes he'd cut the motor off and just drift.

It was not the only way he was adrift that summer.

In high school, he was mostly interested in girls, though not anyone in particular. He took Barbara Cummings to the prom, where he wore a brown tuxedo with brown velvet trim. He figured he looked pretty swank. He was also interested in cars, one in particular, a gold 1970 Ford Mustang that he bought from his sister Sally for $600. He liked to drive it fast, and knew he could have been more careful, but he wasn't worried about it. His favorite classes in high school were shop and science, and he ran on the track and cross-country teams, but none of this gave him any idea of what he wanted to do or how to make his way in the world. His father, Bernie, had worked as an electrician for thirty years and achieved the rank of Master Chief (E-9) in the Seabees Naval Reserves. Jack's mother, Rosemary, worked as a secretary at Suffolk Community College. Jack's sister Sally, three and a half years his senior, had moved out, but Susan, three and a half years his junior, was still at home, a junior in high school. By 1976, Jack Brehm was beginning to learn what we all learn, once it becomes irrefutably obvious that childhood is over—how uncomfortable you can feel in a comfortable place, like the house you grew up in, when everything starts to inform you you've overstayed your welcome and it's time to go. Mowing lawns was not, he had to admit, a career track.

As a kid, Jack liked riding his bicycle around Suffolk County, sometimes to the Grumman Aerospace facility in nearby Calverton, where he watched the first test flights of their F-14 Tomcat fighters. He liked spending time at the beach, or in the woods, playing war games with his friends, which could become fairly elaborate given that there were so many military veterans in the area with souvenirs their kids could put into play. The girls acted as nurses and carried the wounded off on genuine WWII vintage canvas litters. The boys wore real WWII steel pot helmets. Jack had a toy rifle that was battery-operated and made a *bam-bam-bam-bam-bam* noise when he pulled the trigger. The gun made him the envy of his peers, which included the Gallagher brothers, four of them in all. In war games, the Gallagher brothers often divided up on different sides. Two would be Americans, two would be Germans, and then they would go at each other like cats and dogs, fighting that went beyond play, and usually didn't end until someone was bleeding or crying or both. If Jack learned anything about fighting as a kid, he learned it from the Gallagher brothers.

At twenty, Jack could look out his bedroom window at the woods where they'd played at war and think, "This is crazy—I'm not supposed to be here anymore."

By 1976, Bernie Brehm was as interested in knowing what his son was going to do with himself as his son was. Bernard Brehm was a man of few words, from a time when men weren't expected to talk about their feelings. He'd served in the U.S. Navy in Africa and in the Pacific during World War Two, helping to clear out Japanese tunnels, and knew that the military was a place a young man adrift in the world could turn to for guidance, or at least employment. Despite the fact that his dad was a man of few words, by the autumn of 1976 Jack Brehm was fairly certain that his father was thinking it was time for Jack to get a life. He indicated as much, one morning at breakfast.

"Thought you might be interested in this," Bernie Brehm said, handing Jack an advertisement he'd clipped from Long Island's *Newsday.* It was simply a picture of a man in a helmet and jumpsuit, free falling, the words JUMP TO SAVE LIVES, and a phone number.

"Where is this?" Jack asked.

"I don't know," Bernie said. "Why don't you call the number and find out?"

Jack did. A SGT Jim Langhorn answered the phone. Jack told him he'd seen the ad in the paper. Langhorn invited Jack to drive down to what was then Suffolk County Airport, now Francis S. Gabreski Airport, in Westhampton Beach, just about where the toney part of eastern Long Island begins. Langhorn said he could see him at 1:00. Jack didn't expect anything to happen that quickly, but he checked his calendar and realized that that afternoon, and every afternoon for the rest of his life, was free.

"When you get to the gate," Langhorn said, "ask for the 106th Air Rescue Wing and they'll give you directions."

It was only a twenty-mile drive from Jack's parents' house to the southern shore of Long Island, but Jack had never been there before. Suffolk County Airport serviced the private planes of the wealthy New Yorkers who flew out to the Hamptons for the weekend. The man at the gate directed Jack to a collection of low buildings off to one side of the airfield, including an office building and, across the parking lot, the operations building. Jack parked his Mustang, got out and looked around. He saw ninety flat windswept acres, dry brown grass, and a field of grayish white concrete with lines painted on it, and on the horizon distant water towers and radio towers and low forests of scrub oak with leaves beginning to rust with the approach of autumn. There was a series of eight helicopter pods on the tarmac, odd-looking, ochre-colored barnlike buildings, more like tenement row houses than aviation facilities. He saw two larger hangars, in front of which were parked four Hercules C-130 turboprops, surrounded by service vehicles and movable risers. They were fat, stubby, low-to-the-ground, pugnacious-looking airplanes, painted park-bench green with a matte finish, two large four-bladed propeller engines on either wing and a large dolphinlike hump just above and behind where the pilots sat. They were nothing that made his mouth water, the way the F-14 Tomcat fighter jets he'd watched as a boy made his mouth water, but they were kind of cool-looking airplanes all the same, burly and intimidating.

He asked someone in the parking lot where the administration building was, and then he asked someone in the administration building where Sergeant Langhorn's office was, and only when he saw Sergeant Langhorn's uniform did it dawn on him. He was about to join the Air Force. It made him pause for a moment, but then he looked at the ad again, and the man in free fall, and figured it was something he could do. He told Langhorn, the 106th's recruiter, that he wanted to learn to skydive. Sergeant Langhorn tried to keep a straight face and said, "So you want to be a PJ, do you?"

"I sure do. What's a PJ?" Brehm asked.

"Pararescue," the recruiter said. "That's where you'll learn how to skydive. Scuba dive. Work as a medic. Can you swim?"

"I can swim like a fish. Sir," Brehm added.

"You don't have to call me sir," Langhorn said. "Did they tell you it's possibly the toughest job in the military?"

Jack had to think a moment.

"Well, that's what I want to be," he said. "I saw the ad in the paper." *What the heck? How hard could it be?*

He was clueless.

"Let me see if Sergeant McManus is around," Langhorn said, picking up the phone. "Master Sergeant McManus is in charge of the PJ section here."

Langhorn spoke for a moment, then hung up the phone and told Jack to follow him to the ops building. McManus was in his early thirties, small compared to some of the other guys Jack had seen walking around the base, maybe five-seven, and he bore a vague resemblance to Johnny Weissmuller, the Olympic swimmer and Tarzan portrayer. Brehm didn't know that McManus made Tarzan look like a wuss, but in his green flight suit and polished black boots, he was impressive enough. McManus was less impressed.

The kid looked like a matchstick. Literally, like a match on fire. Jack was a skinny little guy, but the thing that really stood out the most about him, the thing that people noticed first, was his hair. Brehm had a gigantic red afro. McManus had never seen anything like it, except perhaps on Bozo the Clown. He'd seen hippies come in before to enlist, but nobody like this. Yet it was McManus's job to read a man's character, and he liked what he saw in young Jack Brehm. He seemed to have a good attitude and great enthusiasm, right from the start. A fairly small man himself, McManus knew that size wasn't really as important as heart and guts. He never knew when he sent recruits through the Pipeline if they were going to make it, but he thought Jack had as good a chance as anybody. He'd sent guys who looked strong and athletic, and they'd wash out in two weeks. And the hair wouldn't be a problem—military barbers knew what to do with excess hair.

"How much do you weigh?" McManus asked Brehm.

"One-forty," Brehm said. McManus suspected it was more like one-thirty.

"Can you swim?"

"I can swim like fish," Brehm repeated. "I run, too."

"Well," McManus said, looking at Langhorn, "no harm taking the test, I suppose. Good luck, son."

Jack began the preliminary tests on December 20. He had to pass an IQ test as well as meet the physical performance standards, which required him to swim 1,600 yards doing the breast stroke, the side stroke, and the Australian crawl (no problem there), run an eight-and-a-half-minute mile, do six chin-ups, twenty-two push-ups, and twenty sit-ups. By the time he finished, he was exhausted, but happy.

They have to send me to PJ school now. The worst is behind me.

He was clueless.

On February 18, 1977, Jack Brehm joined the Air National Guard and was told he wouldn't be sent to Lackland AFB in San Antonio, Texas, for basic training until March. His friends threw him numerous going-away parties in the interim, where the music blasted, "Keep on a rockin' me baby . . ." and "Take it to the limit . . ." and "Love hurts . . ." and "Show me the way. . . ." At his going-away parties, much alcohol was consumed by all, particularly at a local bar in Rocky Point called the Dry Dock, on Route 25A, a beer joint with live bands on the weekends and disco on the jukebox. Jack wondered if he shouldn't be taking it easy on the beer, maybe focus on getting in shape for what lay ahead, but figured he'd deal with it when the time came, and besides, he wasn't buying—everybody else was. One night at the Dry Dock, a friend from high school named Cathy Cain asked Jack if he knew how to install the speakers she'd just bought for her car. The electrician's son told her no problem, that he'd be happy to help.

The following afternoon, Jack was at Cathy's house, working on her car. Cathy Cain lived with her grandmother, Grandma Jessie Brooks. Her cousin, Margaret Ann Stemke, was visiting. Cathy had invited Margaret Ann—Peggy—to several of Jack's going-away parties, but Peggy hadn't gone to any of them.

"That's him?" Peggy asked. She looked out the window toward the driveway, where she saw a pair of white high-top tennis shoes and a pair of feet sticking out from under the driver's-side door of a white and blue Maverick. "That's the guy who's going away?"

"Yeah," Cathy said. "You wanna meet him?"

There's something mysterious about a man who's had multiple going-away parties thrown for him. Whatever that something was, it wasn't enough to whet Peggy's curiosity.

"I don't think so."

"Oh, come on," Cathy said. "He's a really nice guy."

But Peggy had been seeing a boy named Tim, who had plans, real plans, to become a state trooper, or maybe a park ranger. If things worked out with Tim . . .

"I don't know. . . ."

"Just go out there and say hello," Cathy said. "He's a really nice guy."

In photographs taken at the time, Peggy Stemke looks a little bit like Madonna did before she became *Madonna,* a pre–prima donna Madonna, you could say, with shoulder-length brown hair parted in the middle. She was short, and pretty, not in a big-haired hoop-earringed Long Island sort of way, nineteen years old, working at the power company during the day and drinking in bars at night. She wasn't entirely sure what she was doing with her life, either, but she was pretty sure she'd be doing it in Long Island, unless she could think of something better. She dreamt of seeing the world, and to that end, she was going to travel agent school in New York City, two nights a week.

"So he's a nice guy—so what?"

"Suit yourself. It wouldn't kill you to say hello."

Why not?

She went out the front door and stood by the car, waiting for the head to emerge from beneath the dashboard.

In photographs taken at the time, you can look at Jack Brehm, with his freckles and his easy smile and his gigantic red afro, and think, "This guy has a sweet face." Or you can look at him and think what Peggy thought, the first time she laid eyes on him: *This guy doesn't have a clue. . . .*

She got in her car and drove away without saying a word.

4

SUPERMAN SCHOOL

The first thing I remember was walking in to report to the sergeant in charge, and as I'm standing there, this guy comes in, dripping with sweat, because he's just finished a run, and he's carrying this rock about the size of a football, and he says to the sergeant, "Permission to water my rock, Sergeant?" The sergeant gives him permission, so the guy takes the rock to the water fountain and pours water over it, and then he leaves, without ever taking a sip, and it was like a hundred degrees out that day. I thought, man, what kind of insanity am I letting myself in for?

JACK BREHM, WIDE-EYED AND EAGER, GANGLY AND SPRY, HIS LONG curly red afro intact, arrived at Lackland AFB outside of San Antonio, Texas, in March of 1977. It was the first time, not counting a few trips to Yankee Stadium with his dad and a vacation in Pennsylvania when he was ten, that he'd been off Long Island. He'd never been west of the Mississippi. It was the first time he'd had his head shaved. After six weeks of basic training, he reported to Lackland's Operation Location J, where he would find out whether or not he had what it takes to become a PJ.

There are several names for what Jack was about to go through. One is "Indoc," short for Indoctrination School. In 1977, it was referred to simply as OL-J, short for Operation Location J. Neither term describes it as well as the nickname "Superman School." The idea is to weed out all the candidates who are not supermen, though no one is a superman when he arrives. Some think they are, body builders or star high school athletes who come in, confident that they're big and tough and strong, and that hey can take anything the Air Force can dish out. Most learn they can't. Overconfidence can be self-defeating, because the idea is to identify candidates who can exceed their expectations of themselves. People who come in overconfident often disappoint themselves when the going gets tough, or doubt themselves, and disappointment and doubt can cascade to failure, though nobody flunks out—they simply make it tougher and tougher until you quit. Until you SIE, short for Self-Initiated Elimination. It is, by most measurements, the toughest school in the military, harder than what Navy SEALs or Marines or Army Special Ops candidates go through. At other schools, candidates might say to themselves, "They can beat me, but they can't kill me." At Superman School, the candidates say, "Well, they can kill me, but they can't eat me."

There were about ninety candidates reporting with Brehm, some guys right out of high school, others veterans cross-training from other branches of the service, and all of them volunteers, each with his own reason why he wanted to be a PJ. All of them were motivated by the desire to do good, to serve their country, to challenge themselves, and mainly to save lives. During the Vietnam era, some men who were drafted opted to become PJs because they preferred saving lives to taking lives. The recruiting pitch attracts candidates by promising them they'll jump out of airplanes, but it's far more of an education than a joyride. Becoming a PJ requires a variety of skills, which means candidates have to go to a number of different schools, including scuba school, jump school, free fall school, survival school, paramedic school, helicopter dunker training. They call this succession of schools the Pipeline. Men can apply for admittance to all these schools from other branches of the service, and wait their turn and hope they qualify. Indoc is supposed to prepare candidates physically and mentally for all the other schools. Sending someone through the Pipeline who couldn't handle the physical and mental rigors would waste everybody's time, not to mention the government's money. About 90 percent of all the candidates who make it through Superman School are tough enough to graduate the Pipeline. Ninety percent is also approximately the percentage of the candidates who SIE from Superman School. It's happened that in some classes, only one or two guys finish—there's no quota set by the Air Force. The Navy SEALs program, known for its toughness, graduates about 60 percent, partly because they prescreen their candidates, whereas pararescue takes on all comers. On the other hand, the horror stories and the reputation that precedes Superman School is itself a kind of prescreening mechanism. It's impossible to say how many Navy SEAL candidates would make it through Superman School, but it's a fair bet it wouldn't be 60 percent.

"ALL THE WAY DOWN, AIRMAN BREHM—THAT'S NOT HOW YOU DO A SIT-UP IN THIS PROGRAM! FINGERS INTERLACED BEHIND YOUR HEAD, DIRTBAG! DO YOU WANT TO TRAIN WITH US, OR WOULD YOU RATHER GO HOME?"

"HOO-YAH, SERGEANT . . ."

Brehm met the other candidates, but held off making friends right away, aware that nine out of ten of the guys he met wouldn't be around at the end. Candidates talked about the odds, usually where their instructors couldn't hear them.

"I heard some classes, nobody graduates."

"I heard some guys check into psych hospitals afterward."

"Not me man. I'm making it."

"That's what everybody says."

Most were young, but others were as old as thirty. Most were average size, under six feet. Brehm's roommate was a guy from Long Island named Bill Skolnik, another of Mike McManus's "guard babies." A guard baby is a man sent to Lackland and sponsored by a specific National Guard unit, which then has claims on his services, should he manage to graduate. Skolnik was a Vietnam-era Marine who'd left the service, bummed around, bartended in Tucson for a while, rode his motorcycle for a summer, and realized somewhere along the line that being in the military beat drifting around and sleeping in bushes. When Jack first walked into his room, Skolnik was standing in front of the mirror with his shirt off, exposing a massive upper body, and he was humming the Marine Corps hymn, "From the Halls of Montezuma," while making his pecs dance in the mirror. Jack thought, "This is one built Marine." He felt like 135 pounds of nothing. He wondered how he would ever compete.

"ARE YOU TIRED, BREHM? You look a bit tired, and that's really too bad, because I told you we were doing CHIN-UPS, NOT PULL-UPS—YOU DO KNOW THE DIFFERENCE, DON'T YOU, AIRMAN BREHM? CHIN-UPS IS PALMS FORWARD, PULL-UPS IS PALMS TOWARD YOU—IS THAT TOO COMPLICATED FOR YOU, BREHM?"

"Hoo-yah, Sergeant." Hoo-yah is a PJ expression that means, "Yes, I understand," or, "Yes, I agree," or simply, "Goddamn!"

"WHAT DID YOU SAY?"

"HOO-YAH, SERGEANT!"

Strong as Skolnik was, the instructors at OL-J made him look like a weenie. Most were combat-hardened Vietnam veterans, winding down into peacetime roles. To the young recruits, they seemed liked gods. They reminded Brehm of the characters in the *Sergeant Rock and His Howling Commandos* comic books he'd read as a kid, grossly exaggerated cartoon physiques come to life. They were MSGT Curt Phythian, SSGT Art Morrison, TSGT Steve Wofford, and SSGT Dan Byrd. They were unbelievable, the most awesome physical specimens he'd ever seen, monsters, but the way it worked was, however intimidated or awed Jack felt, he was also inspired, saying to himself, "Hey, maybe I can be like that."

The worst instructor, or the best, depending on your point of view, and whether or not he was in your face, was Sergeant Morrison, a black man dubbed "The Great Dark Shark." The Great Dark Shark was merciless, but not cruel, and had what one candidate recalls were "stone killer eyes." They were the kind of eyes that, when they glared at you from three or four inches away, made you forget to breathe. When the class ran in formation, they sang:

Down at Lackland where the PJs run
There is a sergeant named Morrison.
He stands five-foot-eight with his hair packed down.
His eyes are black and he sure can frown.
If you're a wussy and never bark,
May you know the wrath of the Great Dark Shark.

By the second week, half the candidates had quit. The plan is to start out brutal and then make it harder and harder each week, and the P.A.S.T. is prologue. P.A.S.T. stands for the Physical Abilities and Stamina Test you take to qualify for the privilege of being punished for another nine weeks, an initiation where, all in a three-hour period, you swim twenty-five meters underwater on one breath, swim 1,000 surface meters in twenty-six minutes, run a mile and a half in ten and a half minutes, do eight chin-ups in sixty seconds, and fifty sit-ups, fifty push-ups, and fifty flutter kicks (a flutter kick is a four-count scissors kick), each in under two minutes. The regimen increases in difficulty until by week eight you're doing seventy push-ups, seventy-five sit-ups, thirteen pull-ups, fourteen chin-ups, eighty-five flutter kicks, each in a two-minute period, as well as running six miles in under forty-five minutes, swimming 4,000 meters in eighty minutes, and swimming underwater for fifty meters on one breath. Those are the minimum evaluation requirements. You can earn extra points by exceeding the eval's minimums. Brehm did his best, though there was more to it than just training to make evals. He had to run everywhere he went between exercises. Candidates, broken into eight-man teams, had to run together, carrying a rope wherever they went, to emphasize teamwork. Brehm had to do pull-ups every time he entered the barracks and push-ups every time he exited. He had to do a hundred push-ups every time he screwed up and an instructor caught him, and worse, he had to do a hundred push-ups every time somebody else screwed up. Technically, Brehm wasn't required to perform another man's punishment, but from the start, PJs are taught to work as a team in everything they do. "No one can make it through this program alone," they are told at the beginning. If you don't do another man's punishment with him, you become identified as a non–team player, which makes you a dirtbag, and once the instructors start to think of you as a dirtbag—and they regularly get together to discuss who among the recruits is or isn't a dirtbag—you've basically had it. They'll do whatever they have to do to get you to SIE, and they usually succeed if they don't like you. Jack Brehm's attitude helped him, both his determination and his natural cheerfulness, which made it hard not to like him, such that if he came up a sit-up short or a couple seconds late, the instructors let it pass or gave him a second chance.

"WHO TAUGHT YOU PUSSIES HOW TO RUN? YOU'RE MAKING ME STAND ON THIS TRACK WASTING MY TIME. FIVE MILES! YOU'RE AT THIRTY-FIVE TWENTY, THIRTY-FIVE TWENTY-TWO, THIRTY-FIVE TWENTY-FOUR—YOU LOOK LIKE A BUNCH OF WOMEN RUNNING AROUND OUT THERE ON MY BEAUTIFUL OVAL TARTAN TRACK—PICK IT UP! MAYBE WE SHOULD GET YOU ALL TUTUS TO WEAR NEXT TIME—WHAT DO YOU THINK OF THAT, BREHM? YOU WANNA WEAR A TUTU WHEN YOU RUN?"

"NEGATIVE, SERGEANT."

"THEN PICK IT UP."

"HOO-YAH, SERGEANT."

"WHO'S THAT PUKING ON MY GRASS? DID I GIVE YOU PERMISSION TO PUKE ON MY GRASS, AIRMAN?"

The first major obstacle was "motivation week," otherwise known as Hell Week, the third week of Indoc. Hell Week meant inspections in the middle of the night, sleep deprivation, extra push-ups, extra sit-ups, the first ruck march, hiking with a thirty-five-pound pack, and more calisthenics in a basement room called the Dungeon, a place where Torquemada could have picked up a few pointers on how to torture the human body. The Dungeon was a long, narrow, and dank basement room, lit by a few bare lightbulbs, with a hard concrete floor that recruits scrubbed clean, again and again. There was a mural painted on one of the walls, a cartoon depicting recruits being kicked in the ass by barrel-chested sergeants. Brehm did his exercises on the floor. Sometimes he was allowed to spread a towel beneath him to serve as a cushion, but sometimes not. Sometimes he was allowed to do push-ups outside in a mud puddle, or march in the rain carrying a heavy pack, or run in the Texas sun until he felt like crying, or falling down, or both. Sometimes he was allowed to help carry, along with his team, a 450-pound sixteen-foot length of railroad steel on his daily run—again, to improve his sense of teamwork. Sometimes he ran the obstacle course unencumbered, but sometimes he'd run it carrying another man on his back. Candidates SIE'd in droves during motivation week, guys who lost sight of their long-term goals and focused only on their short-term agonies. Every night at chow, instructors would walk around the tables and lay Self-Initiated Elimination request forms and pens in front of recruits looking particularly weary, saying, "All you gotta do is sign here, and in two hours, you'll be eating steak, or watching some pretty girl wiggle her tits in your face at one of our famous San Antonio strip joints—anybody want to sign?"

Brehm's problem was pull-ups. He was a good swimmer and a good runner, but he lacked upper-body strength. At night, after chow, Brehm would go down into the dungeon and practice his pull-ups, with Skolnik helping him, holding him at the waist and lifting him. Skolnik pushed him, shouting at him, "Come on—you can do this!" as they trained, or simply "Hoo-yah, Brehm" during evals. Candidates helped each other, and took it hard when somebody quit—everybody tried to get everybody else through the ordeal. On the running track, Brehm pushed a guy named John Smith, who was somewhat stockier, bald, older, the only married guy in the bunch, a Vietnam veteran who during the war spent time as a flight mechanic, and later shoveled brass shell casings out the back of an AC-130 "Spector" gunship. Smith in turn helped a guy named Slip O'Farrell, another candidate who was cross-training, a former instructor at the Air Force's survival school in Spokane. The Higgins brothers, D.T. and J.G., pushed each other. The sons of Irish parents, born in Dublin and brought to California as infants, both were of medium build, brown-haired, fair-skinned, and opposite as bookends. J.G. was the serious one, the older brother, always taking responsibility for his younger sibling, trying to keep him out of trouble, which he invariably got into. D.T. had no sense of responsibility whatsoever, perhaps because he didn't need one—his older brother had enough for both of them. D.T. was always late for everything, always screwing up and making everybody do extra push-ups because his shirt wasn't tucked in or his boots weren't shined and under his bed. If you told him to comb his hair, he might comb half of it. During the morning run, D.T. sometimes ran with one eye closed.

"D.T.—what the fuck are you doing running with one eye closed?" Brehm asked.

"I'm conserving energy," he'd reply. "I'm laxin'."

He said "laxin' " because he was too lazy to pronounce the entire word *relaxing*.

Brehm ached at night, but no worse than anybody else. Guys were so sore that they'd walk up and down stairs with their arms folded across their chests so their pectoral muscles wouldn't shake. Jack did calisthenics in his dreams. After practicing pull-ups, some nights his biceps were so taut that he couldn't straighten his arms, but everyone had the same complaints. They talked at night about the Dungeon, and about which instructors were really pricks and which ones were just pretending to be pricks, but they talked mainly about the pool. The pool. Nothing the instructors ever put the recruits through on land compared to what happened in the pool.

"IT'S HOW YOU THINK ABOUT IT THAT MAKES ALL THE DIFFERENCE. MAKE UP YOUR MIND RIGHT NOW THAT IT'S ANOTHER TRAINING DAY AND YOU'RE GOING TO TAKE IT IN THE BUTT. IT'S A MIND-SET, GENTLEMEN. YOUR BODY KNOWS HOW TO DO THIS. YOU GOTTA GO PICK SOMEBODY UP IN A HELICOPTER, PEOPLE ARE SHOOTING AT YOU, YOU GOING TO SIT DOWN AND REST? YOU GOING TO GO OUT ON SICK CALL? IT'S NOT AN OPTION. MAYBE YOU DIE—SO WHAT? AT LEAST YOU DIED DOING SOMETHING WORTHWHILE."

The pool is twenty-five meters long and eight lanes wide, housed under a translucent fiberglass roof which offers some shade, but not enough. On a hot day in August, with a big red Texas sun beating down the walls, the water in the pool can get so warm that it no longer offers relief from the furnace outside. The pool is where the Wizard lives. The "Wonderful Wizard of Wig," some call him. The Wizard is who you see just before you wig out, the eyes you look into just before you pass out underwater and lose consciousness, the guy you think about the night before your weekly water confidence evaluation, when you know you've been screwing it up in training.

Brehm saw guys who were killing it in everything else, strong young men who had no problem with the runs or the calisthenics, but when they got to the pool, they'd lose it. They might appear calm and cool, but then Jack would look down and see that their hands were shaking, or their knees wanted to buckle. The instructors played head games with them, but some guys didn't need it—some guys did it to themselves. Fear of drowning is nearly universal, as natural as breathing, and in fact it's closely related. It's practically a given in the job that, on a watery planet, the majority of a pararescueman's rescues will take place in water, so his mastery over his natural fear of drowning must be absolute. You can push yourself beyond your comfort levels on land to the point of utter exhaustion and still know you have the option of stopping, resting, and recovering. You don't have that option in the middle of the ocean. Particularly not when you're underwater and running out of air.

To get a sense of it, try sitting still and holding your breath for as long as you can. Then try holding it for the same amount of time while walking. Then try it while running. Then try it while running with twin seventy-five-cubic-foot scuba tanks on your back. Now do it after you're already exhausted from exercising all day. Now do it with a 250-pound monster Vietnam vet sergeant on your back, who thinks you're a dirtbag, so he's hammering you, pulling your mask off, pinching your snorkel shut, trying to smoke you—and remember that if you fail to hold your breath, open your mouth, and inhale, you'll fill your lungs with water, not air.

"DON'T EVEN THINK OF SAVING YOURSELF FOR TOMORROW, BREHM. THIS IS THE FIGHT YOU'RE IN NOW. WHAT COMES LATER COMES LATER. YOU'VE ALL GOT A LOT OF WINS UNDER YOUR BELT. START THINKING ABOUT THAT. HOO-YAH—YOU'RE THE BIGGEST BUNCH OF STUDS I'VE EVER SEEN!"

Brehm swam twenty-five meters underwater on one breath in a Speedo with fins. No problem. Then without fins. Easy enough. Then wearing a BC or "buoyancy compensator," an uninflated life preserver. Then wearing a BC and his combat fatigues, each additional item adding weight and resistance, until the twenty-five-meter underwater swim on one breath that took five kicks in a Speedo took eighteen kicks in full gear. He learned to perform tasks underwater while holding his breath, to tie knots, to take his equipment off and put it back on again, always with an exact eye to detail, because there is no margin for error underwater. If he didn't set his mask on top of his fins on the bottom of the pool precisely so, they made him do it again, and again, until he got it right. If he didn't give his instructors the correct "I'm okay" signal each time he surfaced, his left fist clinched in the air above him, they made him do it over. He treaded water wearing a twelve-pound weight belt, while holding his head and both hands out of the pool. At one point, they even tied his hands behind his back and his ankles together and threw him in the pool, "drown-proofing," they called it. To most people, the idea of having your hands and feet tied and then getting thrown into water over your head is the stuff of nightmares. Houdini made a living playing on just such fears. PJs get to where they look forward to it, because they learn that the only real trick is the mental one, where you teach yourself not to panic and eventually come to understand that you can take a deep relaxed breath, sink gently to the bottom, stay there, push to the surface, take another breath, sink to the bottom, surface, breath, sink, and do this almost indefinitely. PJs actually like having their hands and feet tied and getting thrown into the pool, because it gives them a chance to rest, relax, think about girls, sing songs in their heads. They *enjoy* a situation that would panic anybody else.

"JOHNSON—WHY DON'T YOU GET OUT OF THE POOL AND START THINKING ABOUT ANOTHER JOB! CARPENTER—DO YOU REFUSE TO TRAIN? THEN GET IN THE POOL NOW! SUCK IT UP! TODAY, CARPENTER—YOU ARE BECOMING A LIABILITY TO YOUR TEAM, AND THAT IS DISGUSTING!"

The fifty-meter underwater swim is one of the most difficult tasks recruits must accomplish. Brehm had no trouble with it, but others weren't so lucky, and each time they lost their focus or forgot where they were and came up for air, there'd be an instructor screaming in their faces.

"EXPLAIN TO ME WHY EVERYBODY ELSE ON THIS TEAM CAN DO THIS AND YOU CAN'T, CARPENTER? GO BACK AND DO IT AGAIN. DON'T STAND THERE WAITING FOR ME TO SAY IT AGAIN. DO IT NOW!"

Some recruits simply exited the pool, went into the locker room, and faced themselves in the mirror, knowing that by doing so they were out of the program, and that they'd failed and let themselves down. Some went into the locker room and cried. Some threw up. Some, like Jack Brehm, thrived. The PJ record for swimming underwater on one breath is held by a recruit who swam 133 meters and held his breath for two minutes and twenty seconds. An accomplishment like that is as much mental as physical.

"IT'S GOING TO BE WORSE THAN THIS IN SCUBA SCHOOL, GENTLEMEN, SO YOU MIGHT AS WELL GET USED TO IT NOW. COUNT OFF BY TWOS AND PREPARE FOR CROSS-OVERS."

Everyone dreaded cross-overs. Cross-overs tended to force the last few guys to SIE. Cross-overs simply meant that recruits would divide into two teams, facing each other from opposite sides of the pool, and then, at an instructor's signal, each team would swim underwater to the other side, one team swimming low along the bottom of the pool, the other swimming high just beneath the surface. Once across, they would surface, rest for fifteen seconds, then switch positions and cross over again. This would happen perhaps ten times in a set. Recruits would be exhausted by the tenth time. The catch was that as they swam, instructors would pounce on them, push them down and hold them, rip their masks off, kick or punch them, and, in whatever way they chose, try to drown them. Frequently, recruits would "see the Wizard" and either panic and surface or stay down and pass out, at which point instructors would haul the half-drowned recruit out of the pool, resuscitate him and give him oxygen to breathe. Once he was recovered, the instructor would ask him if he wanted to try again.

"Hoo-yah, Sergeant."

"WERE YOU TRYING TO SAY SOMETHING TO ME, DIRTBAG?"

"HOO-YAH, SERGEANT. I'D LIKE TO TRY AGAIN, SERGEANT."

"THEN GET BACK IN THE POOL, AND IF YOU FUCK UP THIS TIME AND PASS OUT, WE'RE GOING TO LEAVE YOU DOWN THERE. . . ."

It was terribly difficult, and sometimes cruel and brutal, but there was never a moment when the difficulty or the brutality or even the cruelty seemed the least bit desultory or pointless—there was always a reason for it. Brehm understood that more and more as the class shrank. No Superman School instructor is ever going to be as cruel or as brutal as the ocean in the middle of a hurricane, or the weather on a mountaintop when it's thirty below and the wind is blowing 100 mph. To rescue someone who's big and strong, you need to be bigger and stronger than he is. To rescue someone who might be panicking in the water, you have to be the last guy to panic in the water. To be part of the solution to a dangerous situation, you can't allow yourself to weaken, or lose hope, or quit, because then you become part of the problem. To save someone who's in such bad shape that he's given up hope, you have to supply him with hope and inspire confidence until he can, if possible, assist in his own rescue. And more than anything else, the point of it all is that you can always do more when you're part of a team than you can on your own.

By the time Jack graduated from Superman School, he'd done twenty-five thousand push-ups, twenty-five thousand sit-ups, eight thousand chin-ups, run over three hundred miles, and swam over seventy-five, much of that underwater. Over eighty candidates who'd started the program washed out. Brehm's class consisted of Bill Skolnik, John "Smitty" Smith (also called "Patches" because of his alopecia, which rendered him virtually bald), Vernon "Slip" O'Farrell, J.G. and D.T. Higgins, Mike Wilkey, Chuck Matelski and Jack's two new best friends, a farm kid from upstate New York named Randy Mohr and a guy from Toledo named Mark Judy. The three of them became known as the Three Musketeers. John Smith, because of his prior service and seniority, became the team leader. O'Farrell, already a sergeant, was second in command.

Brehm owed Skolnik for getting him through, but he wasn't so sure of where Skolnik would end up because he was a bit of a hothead and seemed to enjoy pushing Smith's buttons every opportunity he got. Brehm wrote it off to Skolnik's being an ex-Marine, just an interservice rivalry thing.

As they were packing their bags to head off to jump school at Fort Benning, Georgia, their first stop on the Pipeline, Brehm finally asked Skolnik a question he'd been meaning to ask for some time. Now that the pressure was off, there was no harm.

"Hey, Bill—what was it you did in the Marines, exactly? You never told me."

Skolnik didn't answer at first. Then finally he said, "I worked in the post office."

Brehm laughed.

"You worked in the post office?"

"Yeah—I worked in the fucking post office—you wanna make something out of it, Red?" Skolnik said, stepping toward Brehm. Everyone knew Brehm didn't like to be called "Red."

"No, man—I was just curious. I'd just assumed you'd done something . . ."

"Something what?"

"I don't know. I just didn't think you'd worked in the post office."

"You go where they put you," Skolnik said. "Why do you think I want to be a PJ?"

5

BOZO RETURNS

They call it the Pipeline, meaning you go to a series of schools, and at the end of the series, you graduate and you're a PJ. The class that leaves Indoc doesn't necessarily stay together, because some guys get held back if they become injured or develop medical problems in scuba school or jump school. Other guys from the class ahead of you who were held back might be added to your class. The appeal of pararescue, part of the recruiting pitch they make, is that you get to do all the schools, right in a row. The schools are open to members of other branches of the armed services, but they'll have to go through application processes and seniority situations and waiting lists. They say it can take someone from the Navy about six years, and someone from the Army about eight, to learn what PJs learn in eighteen months in the Pipeline.

From Lackland, you go to Army Airborne School at Fort Benning, Georgia, for three weeks, and then to Combat Divers School in Key West, Florida, where you learn to scuba-dive. That's four weeks. You do one day of underwater egress training—ours was in Norfolk, Virginia, but now it's in Pensacola, where you practice exiting a sunken helicopter in a dunk tank, first with a mask on in daylight, then in the dark, then in the dark upside down, using a HEEDS bottle, a small oxygen tank called a Helicopter Emergency Egress Device. The dunker was invented about five years after we'd left the Pipeline, but it's now part of it.

You do two and a half weeks at Survival School at Fairchild AFB in Spokane, Washington, and five weeks of free fall at the Parachutists School in Fort Bragg, where you do about thirty jumps and you also float in a wind tunnel, where you can practice keeping stable in a free-fall position. Next you do twenty-two weeks at Medic School, also at Fort Bragg, and finally you put it all together in a twenty-week program at Kirtland AFB outside of Albuquerque, New Mexico, where you learn more medical stuff, mostly trauma. Then mountaineering, combat tactics, helicopter insertion and extraction, aerial gunner and ground weapons training. When you're done, they give you the maroon beret that distinguishes PJs from other service groups like, for instance, the Green Berets. When you're done, and you put the maroon beret on for the first time, it's the best feeling in the world.

It's all pretty interesting, but maybe the most interesting part is Survival School. It's probably the toughest program, after Indoc. Psychologically, it's right up there.

BREHM ARRIVED AT FAIRCHILD IN LATE SEPTEMBER OF '77. THE AIR Force developed its Survival School—the only arm of the military to have one—to train pilots and flight crews to survive if they're ever shot down behind enemy lines in part as a response to the situation of the pilots who'd been shot down and held prisoner in North Vietnam. Pilots in Survival School learn how to avoid capture and how, if captured, to avoid becoming a propaganda tool or a casualty in a prisoner-of-war camp. The PJs who go in after downed pilots in combat situations do so with the full intention of getting out again, with the injured pilot, as soon as possible, undetected, and in a perfect world that's how it would work. The fact is that when PJs head into areas of conflict, they are going to the places where the world is the least perfect. They need to learn the same skills the pilots learn, and then some.

Survival School included some academic work, learning in a classroom about how to test a plant to see if it was edible or poisonous, or how to signal an airplane from the ground. The most challenging part came in the last week, when trainees went out in the field and practiced E and E, or escape and evasion techniques. Trainees traveled by bus to the Colville National Forest, about sixty miles north of Spokane in the Selkirk Mountains, at the very northeast corner of Washington State. It has terrain hilly and wooded enough to get lost or to hide in. With Brehm were Mark Judy, Mike Wilkey, and Chuck Matelski, as well as a survival instructor to supervise and observe. The idea was to learn how not to die if a rescue ever went wrong or if they ever got trapped behind enemy lines. Trainees entered the woods equipped with nothing but a flight suit, a parachute, and a pocketknife. One man was allowed to carry matches, but only to be used as a last resort. They were supposed to learn how to start a fire by rubbing sticks together or using a flint. The mission was to spend five days following a map and a compass to a designated location, traveling a distance of perhaps eight or ten miles, without getting caught. Teams of aggressors dressed as Russian soldiers searched for them, both on foot and from the air in HH-1 Huey helicopters, and if they were caught, at whatever stage of the escape and evasion they were in, they'd have to start the program over. Aggressors usually came looking at dusk, with occasional patrols during the day. By midnight or so, Brehm and the others knew the aggressors were pretty much cleared out. Brehm learned things like covering up anything he had on him that might reflect light and give him away—his belt buckle, for instance. He learned how to be quiet. It started out as kind of a game, but it got real very quickly. Particularly the hungrier he got.

The weather was cold for September. They used their parachutes for shelter. The chutes they were given came with white, green, tan, and blaze orange panels for a reason. They could use the white panel to conceal themselves in snow, the green panel in the tropics, the tan panel in the desert, and they could use the orange panel to signal an airplane overhead. Brehm and his team learned how to fashion a parachute harness and a shroud into a rudimentary backpack. The nylon material could be used to catch rainwater or collect morning dew for drinking water. At night, to conceal where they slept, they'd each dig a hole, which they'd cover with the appropriate-color parachute shroud, and cover that with branches or leaves, then crawl in, wrapping themselves in the remaining shrouds for warmth. They also learned how to use their parachute lines to fashion fishing lines and snares to catch animals to eat.

Eating occupied much of their time, or rather, searching for something to eat did. Jack made a mental promise to himself to eat anything there was to eat, and never flinch or falter, because he wanted to keep his strength up at all costs and learn as much as possible. They ate all the edible plants they could find, from roots to wild blueberries. They snared a squirrel, cooked it on a spit and ate it. They turned over a log and found a snake, cooked it and ate it. They found a deposit of turtle eggs and ate them. They found a termite mound. Brehm ate about fifty termites. They didn't taste like chicken—they didn't taste like anything, really. He wasn't too fond of spitting the wings out, because they caught in his teeth and stuck to his uniform. The worst thing he ate was a grasshopper. He never did find out what it tasted like, because he didn't have the courage to bite down. In fact, he thought he could swallow him whole, but it kicked all the way down. Brehm learned that to eat a live grasshopper, first you've got to take the hind legs off. There's not much meat on the legs, anyway—it's not like they're drumsticks on a Thanksgiving turkey.

Such training is intended to make the candidate appreciate the carnivore that he really is and to make him understand what he's capable of when he's really really hungry. He becomes part of the food chain at a primary level, no different from the bird that eats the worm to sustain itself; so if the candidate eats the bird, or if he eats the worm, it's the same thing—one life ends so that another can continue. Going two or three days with nothing substantial in one's belly can make a rational person start to feel capable of rash or desperate acts, as Wilkey found out when he caught a snapping turtle, a big one, maybe the size of a dinner plate. For a while, everyone stood around speculating as to just how much meat the thing might have inside that shell, and just how you were supposed to cook one—in the shell like a lobster or shucked? Finally the question was, how were they going to kill it? It was suggested that somebody pull the head out and somebody else cut it off, until Wilkey decided to do it the old-fashioned way—after all, what would you do if you didn't have a pocketknife? It is, however, a lot harder to bite the head off a snapping turtle than it looks. He bit down as hard as he could, sawing his teeth back and forth, but couldn't sever the spine, and ended up twisting the shell, rotating it clockwise a couple of revolutions while biting down with all his might until the head came loose. Brehm looked on in awe.

"That does it," someone said. "I'm definitely not letting you suck my dick tonight."

Escape and evasion training is also intended to make the pararescueman appreciate what a pilot shot down behind enemy lines might be going through. A PJ undergoing escape and evasion training comes to understand that if the rigors of survival school are hard on him, despite his tremendous physical conditioning, a pilot without that conditioning would have an even more difficult time of it. E and E is serious business, because the alternative to escaping or evading is getting captured and being brought to a prison or POW camp, where a U.S. Air Force pilot is likely to be interrogated and/or tortured. During the conflict in Vietnam in the sixties and seventies, PJs were credited with saving as many as two thousand U.S. servicemen from just such a fate.

By the end of the Pipeline, Jack knew how to parachute out of airplanes, and hoist down from helicopters, and shoot a machine gun, and scuba dive under water, and climb mountains. He'd learned how to diagnose and treat a wide variety of medical problems, how to live in the woods for days without food or water, and how to drink fairly large amounts of distilled spirits in off-base cantinas. He was looking forward to going home to Long Island for a little R&R and a chance to catch up with family and friends before starting the job. He felt strong and young and capable of handling anything life handed him.

The question remained, was he ready for true love?

When Peggy's cousin Cathy got engaged to Tom Bazata, her friends and family decided to throw her an engagement party at the Rocky Point firehouse, one of the few buildings in the area with a hall large enough to hold the clan. It was April 1978, and Peggy was there, along with about seventy other family members and friends. Peggy'd been taking the train into Manhattan two nights a week, a dreary two-hour ride each way, attending travel agent school. She liked looking at maps and brochures from far-off exotic places. Ireland looked good. Greece. Maine, even. Rocky Point was a place she knew by heart. Her father, Warren, was at the party, a switchman at the phone company. Peggy's mother, Jane, was there too. Jane managed Cooper's Stationery in Port Jefferson, just west of Rocky Point. Peggy's older brother Warren Jr. and her sister Lorraine, a year her junior, were talking to Cathy's fiancé Tom by the food table. Peggy's kid sister Carol, fifteen, was being a bit of a pest, asking if Peggy could give her a ride to a friend's house, when Peggy noticed a new face in the crowd, or rather, a vaguely familiar face, one she couldn't place.

She noticed him, first of all, because he was wearing a cowboy hat, and in 1978 you didn't see a lot of cowboy hats in eastern Long Island. You still don't. The Bozo hair was gone. In fact, nearly all the hair was gone. The freckles were still there, but now they were obscured by a deep New Mexico tan. More to the point, something had changed in the eleven months since she'd last seen him. The body was transformed. The 135-pound weakling, formerly built like a matchstick, was now, well . . . ripped.

Cut.

Chiseled.

Buff.

It was instant lust. Jack, Peggy noticed, was wearing blue jeans and a T-shirt and cowboy boots. A tight T-shirt. Probably the same T-shirt he'd worn the last time she'd seen him, but now it was tight across his chest.

His friend, Randy Mohr, was wearing overalls and a derby. She didn't know what to make of the derby. She didn't really care, though—she was far more interested in Jack. Jack and Randy were feeling absolutely bulletproof, young and free and in the best physical condition of their lives. They'd just finished the Pipeline, where they'd jumped and swam and dove and flown and crammed more information into their heads than they would ever have believed possible, plus they had something most guys in their early twenties don't have—a sense of purpose or mission. Randy was on vacation before taking up a posting in Florida. Because Jack had been sent through the Pipeline by the 106th, he owed the Westhampton base a minimum of two years of service, after which he'd be free to apply for positions in other PJ units. But all that would come later. For now they were feeling their oats. They'd never felt such oats.

The next night, Peggy was at the Dry Dock with her cousin Freddie, Cathy's brother, when she spotted Jack over by the jukebox. The room was dimly lit, with dark wooden tables on a dark wooden floor. The only light came from the beer signs in the window, the jukebox, and the light behind the bar. The cowboy hat was gone, but the friend in the derby was there.

"That's him!" she whispered.

"Who?" Freddie said.

"Jack Brehm. You know him, don't you? You went to high school with him. Call him over here."

"Why?"

"Because I'm going to get him to date me," she said.

"What?"

"I'm going to get him to be interested in me," she said. "Call him over here."

Freddie called Jack over. Jack and Peggy chatted for about five minutes, and then Jack went back to his friends.

"Well?" Freddie said teasingly. "Is he interested in you?"

"He's getting there," Peggy said.

A week later, at the Dry Dock again, this time with Cathy, Peggy was standing at the bar when Jack suddenly filled the space next to her.

"Hey," he said.

"Hey," she said, trying to act nonchalant. "What's new with you?"

"Oh, not much," he said. "Just hanging out."

"Who are you here with?"

"My pals, Tom and Tommy."

"You have two friends named Tom?"

"No," Jack said. "One is named Tom and the other is named Tommy."

They chatted animatedly, and Peggy was at her charming best. Making progress. The jukebox played "Boogie Oogie Oogie" and "Three Times a Lady" and "It's a Heartache." Jack listened to Peggy and smiled, but he seemed distracted. He glanced briefly toward the door. When he finally caught the bartender's eye, he ordered two beers. As the bartender brought them, a pretty, dark-haired Italian girl walked past and nodded to Jack to follow her. Nodded in a way that didn't give Jack much of a choice. *Really* nodded. Jack excused himself and said he'd be right back.

"Where's he going?" Cathy said. "Who the hell does she think she is?"

"I don't know," Peggy said.

He said he'd be right back. That means he's interested.

Stephanie was waiting by the jukebox. Jack had been dating Stephanie for a few weeks, but the relationship had gotten extremely heavy, way too fast, and tonight he wanted to go out with the boys. The problem was, it was a Saturday night. You don't want to leave an Italian girl from Long Island sitting home on a Saturday night, and if she catches you, you don't want her to see you talking to some other girl.

"I don't believe you," she said. "You have some nerve. I can't believe you didn't call me."

"I wanted to go out with the guys. . . ."

"The *guys?* That didn't look like the guys you were talking to at the bar. You call that a night out with the guys?"

"She's my friend's cousin. . . ."

"I don't care who she is—I saw the way you were talking to her."

"What way was that?"

"You know which way. Don't be cute with me."

"I don't even know her."

"Does she have a name?"

"Her name's Peggy. Look, Stephanie . . ."

"I thought you said you didn't know her?"

"Well, I know her name. . . ."

"If you want to talk to her, go talk to her. I don't give a shit who you talk to. You wanna talk? Talk! Talk until your lips fall off. I saw the way she was looking at you. If you think . . ."

"Stephanie . . ."

At the bar, the cousins conspired.

"What's he saying to her? Who is she?"

"I don't know. I've never seen her before."

"Did he come with her?"

"I didn't see them come in. They sort of look like they're together. I mean, it looks to me like they're having a fight."

"About what?"

"How the hell should I know?"

"Go over there and find out."

"Find out what?"

"Just find out what's going on."

"Oh, right—I'm supposed to walk over there and say, 'Excuse me, but we were wondering what you two were fighting about. . . .' "

Peggy waited at the bar, while some Bee Gees fanatic—there were many on Long Island in 1978—pumped a week's pay into the jukebox, punching up the numbers for "Stayin' Alive," "Night Fever," "How Deep Is Your Love." The bar was crowded. Loud. Smoky. Cathy was on reconnaissance. Jack was in more of an escape and evade mood.

"All I wanted to do tonight was relax," he told Stephanie, glancing toward Peggy to make sure she hadn't left yet. "It's a little hard to do that with you hanging around in the background."

"The *background*? I'm in the fucking background now?"

"Maybe that was the wrong word . . ."

"Maybe you should just stop talking altogether."

"If you want to stay here, I'll be happy to go somewhere else. . . ."

"Well I'm not happy to stay here, and in fact, I'm leaving—right now!"

Stephanie left the bar. Jack's heart was broken, but then he took a sip of beer, and it was all healed. He noticed Cathy Cain standing nearby. They chatted for a moment, and then she turned and went to the bar.

Where did Cathy go? What was taking her so long?

"He just broke up with his girlfriend," Cathy reported.

"He did?" Peggy said. "That was his girlfriend?"

Gee, that's too bad.

"He says his friends left and he doesn't have a ride home."

"We'll take him home! Tell him we'll take him home."

They drove him home. Getting out of the car, Jack leaned over and gave Cathy a polite kiss on the lips, just a peck, to say thanks for the ride. When it was Peggy's turn for a kiss good night, she made the most of it, because she knew it might be the only chance she'd have. Not that she wanted to appear easy or anything—she wasn't going to *French kiss* a boy the first time their lips ever touched, but she made sure the kiss was longer than he expected, softer than he expected.

Holy shit, Jack thought. His knees were literally weak. All the physical training in the world isn't going to help you when you're kissed like that. *Jesus—was that what I think it was?*

Jack got the message, and called the next day. Jack, Peggy, Cathy, and another friend went to Westhampton Beach that afternoon and parked on Dune Road. They walked the beach. The following weekend, again in a group of people, Jack and Peggy went to the Great Adventure amusement park in New Jersey. That night he slept over in the apartment Peggy was sharing with her sister Lorraine, but that was it—just sleep.

"I tortured him," Peggy recalls. "I wasn't going to get involved with him until I knew he was going to be serious."

They started seeing each other every day. One night, Peggy decided to stop torturing him. Jack took a two-month gig house-sitting for a fellow PJ named George Gonzales, a.k.a. Gonzo. Jack had temporarily moved back home with his parents and was looking for a place of his own, a place where he could have overnight company. Peggy saw him at Gonzo's house and stayed with him there. They had dinner parties, like grown-ups, and invited their friends over, just for drinks, or to watch a new show on television called *Dallas*. It was the end of the sexual revolution, the final days of casual sex, before anybody really knew that unprotected lovemaking could lead to herpes or AIDS or pregnancy. . . .

Well, they knew about the latter. Peggy and Jack knew, but they were young, hot to trot, and sometimes you just feel lucky. And sometimes you're not lucky, or at least you're not lucky in the way you think you want to be lucky.

Peggy came over to Jack's house one night in May. The front door was open, so she walked in and caught him coming out of the shower with just a towel around his waist. Another time, this might have led to something glorious and inspired, but tonight Peggy was crying. Jack asked her what was wrong.

"I don't know if you want to hear this."

"What?"

"I think I might be pregnant," she told him.

"Oh," he said. "Oh shit."

They sat on the edge of the bed, side by side. Jack put his arm around Peggy. She put her head on his shoulder. For two hours they cried, and held each other, and talked about what they were afraid of, both of them acknowledging that this wasn't exactly how they'd ever expected it to happen. Jack knew, without Peggy having to tell him, that one way or the other, she would have the baby, with him or without him. If that was the case, he knew it would be better with him than without him, and he knew that he wanted to do the right thing, and he knew that even though he hadn't known Peggy Stemke all that long, he loved what he knew about her so far. Seeing her deal with this only made him admire her more—her strength, her fairness, and her faith. It wasn't like they were the first couple this had ever happened to—they would figure out how to get through it.

"I'm getting a test tomorrow," Peggy told him. "I guess there's not much we can do until we know for sure."

The next day during her lunch hour Peggy and her friend Maureen drove to the Planned Parenthood Clinic in Patchogue, where her suspicions were confirmed. That afternoon, she and Jack talked about what they were going to do. It was early June, less than two months since they'd first spoken at the Dry Dock. Neither one of them felt they really knew each other all that well, but then, how well did you have to know someone? Lust, it seemed to both of them, wasn't enough to base a partnership on, but hadn't this become something more than that? The way she handled things impressed him. He'd been trained not to panic. Her courage was even more impressive. Jack felt nowhere near ready to become a father and didn't know anyone else his age who was one. That didn't matter. At Superman School he had learned to confront and accept risk. He had learned that he had the power to rise to any occasion that might present itself, but he had learned something more important than any of that. He had learned that there's one thing more important than courage or faith, training, intelligence, intuition, strength, or luck.

Teamwork.

But that had to do with things like hurricanes, earthquakes, typhoons, avalanches, airport raids, terrorist attacks, and all-out combat in a war zone. This was different. This was bigger than that. This was marriage. He needed to talk to somebody, preferably somebody older, with more experience in such matters. Talking to his father was out.

Brehm was wondering if there was anybody at the base he could talk to when he found Mike McManus alone in the locker room. He didn't really know Mike, his NCOIC, very well yet. He was the Non-Commissioned Officer in Charge at the base, responsible for the PJ section. Jack sensed a kind of affinity between them, but then it could be that Mike just liked everybody. Mike outranked Jack, but he never abused his rank. He seemed like a good guy, a fair man. Jack noticed something else slightly odd about McManus—he would hold the door open, not just for women but for everybody, always the last guy to enter a room. Jack decided to confide in him and told him what had happened, expecting some kind of macho advice like, "Screw her—you've got your own life to live—stand up for yourself, PJ!" Instead Mike, who was thirteen years older than Jack, with two kids of his own and a wife, Marie, a schoolteacher, told him he'd do great, that he had the right kind of stuff to be a father.

"I do?" It was exactly what Jack needed to hear.

"Sure."

"Oh."

"Another PJ marriage proposal," McManus said with a smile.

It was a friend at the Dry Dock who finally talked a bit of sense into Brehm, who was having cold feet and thinking of calling the whole thing off.

"Look, man," the friend said, "nobody knows if it's going to work out, down the road, but I know one thing. I know for a fact that you're not going to be able to live in Rocky Point with a kid ten miles down the road in Port Jeff. That's the only definite thing in this equation." Jack nodded. "Look at it this way—if it doesn't work out, it doesn't work out, but at least you gave it a shot. If you don't give it a shot, you'll never know, will you? And you'll never be able to live with that."

Brehm drove to Peggy's parents' house. They were out for the evening. They sat on the front steps.

"So what do you think?" Peggy asked.

"Well," Jack said, "I think we should get married."

"I don't want you to say that just because I'm pregnant."

"I would have said it anyway," Jack told her. "Just not as soon. I love you."

"You know," she said, "you haven't really officially asked me yet."

Brehm got down on one knee.

"Will you marry me?" he said.

"Yes," Peggy said.

It was a warm spring night, late May, no moon but a sky full of stars. They could smell the ocean. There were dishes in the sink containing the remnants of the pasta Peggy had made for dinner. They weren't scared, nor were they without fear. Everything lay ahead of them. Whatever love was, they were going to learn it.

6

THE JOB

Some of the finest men I've ever known served honorably and courageously in Vietnam. That's a given. That's what I know now.

What I knew then was somewhat different. What I knew then was mostly about my cousin Tommy. My sister Sally was closer to him than I was because they were closer in age. His dad walked out when Tommy was little, so my Aunt Gloria had to raise a girl and three boys by herself. My dad ended up being their male role model. I remember watching the draft lottery on television, and I think they'd only drawn something like six numbers before Tommy's birthday came up, and he was given the number four, which meant there was no question he'd be drafted. My Aunt Gloria was hysterical, but my dad, who was a Navy veteran, tried to reassure her that everything would be all right. Nobody could reassure Tommy. We went over there one day, because my mother had bought him a shaving kit, and he was furious, saying, "You guys are just sending me off to war—you don't even care!" I think I was maybe fourteen. My dad and he had some heated debates about the war. Tommy was a really smart kid, with good S.A.T. scores, and I remember he gave my sister a book he'd read called Johnny Got His Gun, *about this soldier who wakes up in a hospital and realizes he doesn't have any arms or legs, and he can't smell or taste or see or hear, and somehow he even realizes he doesn't have a face, and then he remembers that he was in a battle, and now he's in a hospital, but he doesn't know if it's an American hospital or an enemy hospital. After a full year of mental anguish, he finds a nurse who knows Morse code, so he taps out an SOS message in Morse code with his head, and a nurse responds by tapping in Morse code on his forehead, "What do you want?" at which point, his mind just explodes. Something like that. It was a pretty gruesome story, but when I read it, I realized what Tommy was afraid of.*

What we heard from him, once he went to Southeast Asia, was that he hated it from day one, and every letter he wrote said, "I've got to get out of here." He had nightmares. He stood guard and took some fire. There was no welcome-home party for him when he got back, that I can recall, though I remember there were yellow ribbons on my Aunt Gloria's house. When he came back, he was totally different. I had nothing in common with him. Gradually, the family realized he had a drug problem, though all I thought was that he was smoking a lot of pot. One day he and my sister were sitting in the car in the driveway when my Grandma Barbara walked out to the car and got in and announced that she wanted to smoke some marijuana and find out for herself what all the fuss was about. That's the kind of woman she was. So they smoked a joint, and afterward she said, "Well, I still don't see what the fuss is all about."

Tommy died of a heroin overdose. He was in his car. He was twenty-two.

IT WOULD HAVE BEEN A LOT TO HANDLE, JUST LEARNING THE JOB, without a wedding to plan on top of that.

A date was picked. The wedding was to be held on July 28, 1978. The ceremony would take place at Peggy's home church, St. Louis de Montefort, in the town of Sound Beach, with the reception at a restaurant called the Miller Place Inn. Peggy's parents helped make the arrangements. Jack's parents were less enthusiastic, for a couple of reasons. In part, they'd already been burned once when Jack's older sister Sally canceled her own wedding and left her parents with a hefty bill, only to sneak off a month later and marry a man named Vincent whom Bernie and Rosemary Brehm had never met. Now their son was marrying somebody they hadn't met, somebody they didn't know from Eve, a girl he hadn't even invited over for dinner yet to introduce to them in a proper way. Somebody who, as far as they were concerned, was robbing the cradle. She was younger than Jack, but no matter. They were aware of the pregnancy. Jack was as helpful as he could be with the planning and preparations, under the circumstances, given his limited knowledge of weddings and what went on at them. Peggy, coming from such a large family, was more than a little surprised to learn that the first wedding Jack would ever attend would be his own.

Jack felt enormous pressure because of his forthcoming nuptials, and because he also had a new job to learn.

The beginnings of pararescue can be traced back to an emergency that took place on August 2, 1943, when a C-46 developed engine trouble over the jungles of Burma, forcing all twenty-one of its passengers to bail out, including high-ranking Chinese officers, members of the U.S. Office of Strategic Intelligence and a young newsman named Eric Sevareid. A flight surgeon, LTCOL Don Flickenger, and two of his medical assistants, a SGT Harold Passey and a CPL William McKensie, volunteered to parachute into the jungle to rescue the survivors. Jumping was the only way to reach them. Flickenger had jumped from an airplane before. His assistants had not. They landed, treated the survivors, and thirty full days later walked out of the jungle and into civilization. In 1947, the same year that the Air Force became a separate branch of the military, a U.S. B-17 crashed into the jungles of Nicaragua and a doctor named CAPT Pope Holiday jumped in to rescue the pilot, LT Robert Rich. It became apparent to the Air Force that having a team of parachute-trained medical personnel standing ready to give a quick response to emergencies in inaccessible areas was a necessity, particularly when airpower was sure to play a larger and larger role in conflicts worldwide. Pararescuemen made rescues during the Korean War, using helicopters, of the sort seen on the old television program *M*A*S*H*, and SA-16 seaplanes. During the cold war, PJs stood alert to rescue the pilot every time a U-2 spy plane flew, though in the case of the U-2 pilot Francis Gary Powers, shot down over the Soviet Union in 1960, rescue wasn't possible. As the conflict in Southeast Asia grew in the 1960s, so did the need for pararescuemen, which led to the creation of the Pipeline. PJs served nobly in Vietnam and also stood alert, during the 1960s and 1970s, to rescue astronauts for NASA's space program, which continued into the Space Shuttle era.

The purpose of pararescue training is still to rescue pilots who've been shot down behind enemy lines or to come to the aid of service personnel who find themselves in other such dire circumstances, anywhere on the globe. However, to maintain their combat readiness in peacetime, the PJs in addition to their training duties answer calls to rescue civilians, taking on, generally speaking, any task other rescue agencies can't handle, rescues too tough for ordinary measures. Coast Guard ships and aircraft, for example, effect rescues in U.S. territorial waters, within about two hundred miles of the coast, but beyond that, or to get to somebody quickly, you need men who can jump out of airplanes or helicopters that can refuel in midair, such that when the Coast Guard, which is in charge of all off-shore rescues, gets a job they can't respond to they call the Air Force. PJs also assist the Coast Guard when it asks for their help: for example, when John F. Kennedy Jr.'s private plane went down off Martha's Vineyard in July 1999 killing him, his wife, and his sister-in-law. The PJs will launch for famous people or civilians, for U.S. citizens, or for the lowest-ranked seaman on a foreign-registered ship. About 40 percent of pararescuemen are members of the active-duty Air Force, and the rest are members of Air Force Reserve or Air National Guard units. Reserve pararescue units include the 301st RQS (or Rescue Squadron) at Patrick AFB in Florida and the 304th RQS in Portland, Oregon. Guard units include the 129th RQS at Moffett Field in California and the 210th RQS in Anchorage. Jack's unit, the 102d RQS, subsumed by the 106th Air Rescue Wing, was established in 1975 and assigned to cover the northeastern United States and the North Atlantic, operating roughly from Greenland to the north and the Bahamas to the south and about 1,500 miles east to the halfway point between Long Island and Woodbridge AFB in England, where active-duty Air Force PJs were stationed to cover the other half of the Atlantic.

Jack had about 250 co-workers at the base, a number that swelled to over 1,000 on drill weekend, when the 106th's entire complement showed up once a month to train. Other personnel at the base included pilots, mechanics, communications people, recruiters, media relations personnel, motor pool, parachute shop, engine shop, hydraulic shop, electrical shop, security police, central base processing office, medical clinic, mail room, sheet metal shop, auxiliary ground equipment, and life support. Jack worked in the PJ section, on the ground floor of a two-story, World War II–vintage operations building with green shingles and a flat tar roof, hung ceilings, tile floors, fluorescent lights, and little for the eye to rest upon in comfort, save for the old black and white aviation photographs that lined the hallways. There were about eight PJs on the team. Each man had a large closet-sized locker for his personal and professional gear, changes of clothing, extra boots, hats, wet suits, flight suits, combat gear, scuba regulators, packs, camping gear, clean socks, clean underwear, a shaving kit, spare sunglasses, extra car keys, mementos from missions; the inside of every man's locker door was festooned with photographs of *Playboy* playmates, girlfriends, wives, nieces and nephews and children, or the letters their kids had written them while they were away on a TDY, a "temporary duty" tour. In the middle of the locker room were two enormous tables, perhaps six feet across and fifteen feet long, upon which the PJs could assemble their packs and kits and inspect their parachutes before launching on a mission. There was a medical clinic, where the various medications and narcotics they used to treat patients were kept under lock and key, a shower room, an operations dispatch center containing telephones and communication equipment, and a briefing room, something like a small movie theater, with a podium up front, a blackboard, and a retractable movie screen. The rest of the PJ section housed storage bins for all the equipment they might use in the course of a rescue, from parachutes and scuba tanks to climbing ropes and medical kits.

Jack quickly learned that although the ads made the job sound exciting, when nothing exciting is happening the life of a PJ is, relatively speaking, dull as dirt. You do PT, meaning you physically train by running, swimming, or lifting weights because the job requires you to maintain the same level of fitness achieved at Indoc, but beyond that you work in the supply room taking inventory, or you read medical bulletins to stay current as to new procedures or medications, or you read manuals to learn how to operate or repair new equipment or gear, or you read military regulations, or you pack medical kits, inspect alert gear, clean weapons, attend to administrative details, and stare at the telephone.

Altruism explains part of why PJs live for the mission, but the rest is that it breaks the monotony. Jack wanted a mission as soon as possible. Until you make your first save as a PJ, you're still considered a virgin. Until your "cherry mission," the first nontraining mission where you actually rescue or recover somebody, it's all just talk. He waited for something to happen, with the macabre mixed anticipation of the transplant surgeon on New Year's Eve who knows drunk-driving accidents are the best source of transplantable organs, waiting eagerly for the phone to ring, even though he knows it's going to be bad news.

Brehm also wanted a mission because he wanted to have something to say, instead of just sitting there like an idiot, the nights he found himself in the company of veteran PJs with real stories to tell. McManus seemed to have the best stories. From Pennsylvania mining country, he'd worked as a kid as a clown diver, entertaining tourists at fancy Florida hotels. McManus told him how, after Vietnam, he took a group of fourteen front-line PJs fresh out of Southeast Asia and tried to retrain them at Loring AFB, outside of Caribou, Maine, about 150 miles north of Bangor, far from any major population center where they might have done more serious damage. They'd come straight from a war and were all in need of psychological counseling, probably, decompression for sure. They were in jail every week, drinking copious amounts of alcohol and setting things on fire, or stealing fire trucks and Air Force property, getting in brawls at base football and basketball games. "Guys had a lot of energy," Mike said, typical of his tendency to understate. It wasn't until he got everybody into rock climbing that they started to calm down, he explained, adding, "They'd come back from that so tired that they couldn't cause much trouble anymore."

While Peggy worked or looked for apartments (it seemed like the good ones all said, "No kids"), Jack made himself useful at the base during the day and went out at night to an off-base PJ hangout called the Matchbox, a bar about a quarter of a mile from the main gate, so named perhaps because there wasn't a PJ's wife who hadn't thought of burning the place down. If you were a PJ, you stood about as good a chance getting hurt in a brawl at the Matchbox as you did jumping out of an airplane. A PJ, in a brawl, has a special sense of entitlement, in that, as a trained medic, he knows he probably isn't going to do anything to another guy's face that he won't be able to fix later. It wasn't always the most comforting thing to be sitting on a barstool next to Bill Skolnik, probably the best guy you'd want at your side if a fight were to break out, but sometimes it seemed that if he were sitting next to you the odds of a fight breaking out automatically went up. The management welcomed the PJs, despite their bellicose propensities, and often let a group of PJs with four dollars between them drink all night, because they kept the other riffraff in line, the bikers and transients, derelicts, troublemakers, and random skells who drank there because all the other bars in Westhampton Beach were too chic and upscale, catering to the Hamptons crowds, and wouldn't let the Matchbox's clientele in the door. It was easier for management to ask a PJ to throw somebody out the door than call the cops, when calling the cops too many times in a given month could get you closed down as a public nuisance. It was a symbiotic relationship. Sometimes the PJs would apply their escape and evasion training, when one guy would hide under the pool table until the barmaid locked up for the night, and then he'd come out of hiding and let the other guys back in, and they'd drink beer until the sun came up. Once, a member of the 106th arrived at the

Matchbox on his bowling night at 4 A.M., already drunk, only to find the place dark, so he threw his bowling ball through the window and let himself in, unaware that the place had installed silent alarms. He was calmly drinking a beer at the bar when the police arrived, but when management learned it was a guy from the base who'd broken in, they said they wouldn't press charges if he'd agree to fix the window. Another PJ named Dave Lambert was always the first guy to show up for work and the last guy to leave the Matchbox, night after night, and it remained a mystery how he did it, until finally Jack asked him where he lived.

"I'm living in the bushes in front of the Matchbox," Lambert said. It was a warm summer, after all, and a PJ's survival training teaches him how to live in the bushes.

The veterans introduced Jack to a PJ tradition at the Matchbox, the art of "fire-breathing," which involved drinking 151-proof rum—unless Al Snyder was around, and then you had to drink schnapps, because that, and Budweiser, was all he drank. Al was one of the older PJs in the squadron, about thirty-four. Between the demanding physical requirements and the huge amount of time it takes to stay current and qualified in all the various disciplines, the average length of time a PJ stays in the business is about six years. Jack listened to stories of how Mike McManus broke his butt—fractured his sacrum, to be technically correct—jumping out of a C-130 back in May of 1976, though he was jumping again by September, four months after the accident. Jack became aware, both from knowing the man and from hearing what people said about him, that he'd probably never meet anybody as tough as Mike McManus, who was five foot six and 160 pounds of cast iron and willpower. He was also a helluva nice guy, Jack realized, and had seemed to take a liking to his young red-headed recruit.

They stayed up late, shooting pool, taking turns buying rounds or pitchers of beer, telling stories, and Jack absorbed it all and felt enormously lucky to be a part of this group of men. He heard Al Snyder and Bill Hughes talk about one of their finest saves, hauling their friend Don's ass out of the path of a herd of charging bovines during the running of the bulls in the Azores. It wasn't easy to find schnapps in the Azores, but what there was of it, Don had had too much. They talked about a PJ named Bob Harrison, who was boxing in the local Golden Gloves tournament at 155 pounds and doing pretty well for himself. Harrison told of how he and Billy Hughes had gone out in an HH-3 "Jolly Green Giant" and hauled a young couple off a boat that had gotten frozen in the ice of Long Island's

Great South Bay in January of 1977, and how cold it was. Al Snyder had to buy Harrison another schnapps at the thought of it, declining one for himself on the grounds that his wife was about eleven or twelve months pregnant, so he wanted to stay sober in case she needed him to drive her to the hospital. The fact that she was so pregnant hadn't stopped him from coming to the Matchbox, but at least she knew where to find him. Men talked of how long they thought they might be PJs and what they might do when they quit, guys like Mike Durante, Dave Lambert, Carl Frolich, Scott Hursh, Rich Melito, and George Gonzalez. They talked about some of the new guys coming through the Pipeline, guys like John "Mickey" Spillane and Jimmy "Doc" Dougherty, and Dave Ruvola, men McManus had sent to Lackland, knowing he'd get anybody who didn't SIE back to serve with the 106th. They talked about the "Guard bums" on the base. Guardsmen were required to serve one weekend a month and two weeks during the year, thirty-eight days total. Guard bums were the guys constantly scrambling for work, trying to pick up as many man-days as they could, or signing up for as many schools as they could, sometimes, it seemed, to avoid ever having to get real lives.

One night at the Matchbox, they came up with a plan to raise money for the PJ "Fund of Funds" by staging intra-pararescue boxing matches in a ring outside the section after Saturday drill and selling beer at the matches. The idea was to use the money from the Fund of Funds to throw Christmas parties for the base or to buy flowers for anybody whose wife had a baby. The first match was between Scottie "Hurricane" Hursh and Timmy "Mauler" Malloy, and they started a rumor that Timmy had gotten caught doing Scottie's girlfriend, just to spark a little interest. Nobody pulled any punches—both men took a brutal beating, and a lot of beer was sold. Jack was scheduled to fight Dave Lambert the following Saturday until the NCO Club found out the PJs were selling beer without a liquor license and told the base commander, who pulled the plug on the scheme. The next scheme was even better—a "Name That Moon" contest, in which ten PJs formed a human pyramid and then dropped their gym shorts, and then a picture was taken. Pictures were taken of their faces as well. It cost a buck for the chance to match the correct face to the correct moon, and whoever got the most right won half the pot. The Fund of Funds netted over two hundred dollars.

In May, McManus called a briefing in the Ops building and told the squadron there were going to be two missions coming up the second week of June. Neither was anything to get excited about, but one was a bit more interesting than the other. The first mission needed men to fly an HH-3 Jolly up to Burlington, Vermont, in order to get water rescue training for the copilot. The other afforded some "lucky" PJ a chance to be part of history. The Air Force was attempting something that had never been done before, flying helicopters, in this case three HH-53s, across the Atlantic ocean, from Eglin AFB in Ft. Walton Beach, Florida, to Woodbridge, England. The flight would require repeated midair refuelings, and that was always a tricky proposition. Aboard one of the helicopters would be some general, McManus wasn't sure who. They were calling it Operation Volant Vault. The PJs would be "duck-butting" the mission in the C-130 the HH-53s would be taking fuel from, at least until they were halfway across the Atlantic, and then a C-130 from Woodbridge would meet them and escort the general the rest of the way. A duck-butt mission means you serve as an escort, on hand in case anything goes wrong and your services become needed. PJs duck-butt it every time *Air Force One* flies, for example, following behind, ready to go get the president if *Air Force One* were to crash and leave him stranded on a desert island. Because it involved midair refuelings, Volant Vault qualified as an "increased risk mission." It's considered an increased risk any time you have to parachute from a plane, or refuel in midair, or fly in really bad weather, or under combat conditions. Men were assigned to missions for a variety of reasons, from aptitude to availability, but most of the time it was a question of who needed what kind of training.

"I'll go to Vermont, what the hell," Dave Lambert offered. "I hear the maple syrup up there is fresh this time of year."

"Count me in," Scott Hursh said.

"Jack, why don't you and Harrison take the duck-butt?" McManus said. Volant Vault was, of the two, the least preferable mission, an escort service job where nothing was likely to happen, and giving it to Jack was a sign that he was a "newbee" and lacked seniority. Another newbee on the team was Bill Skolnik, who'd had to repeat a course in the Pipeline and finished behind Jack. Jack was glad to see his old friend, both because he was glad to see him and because it meant he wasn't the greenest rookie on the team anymore.

The C-130 tanker took off the afternoon of June 13. It was a Tuesday, a drizzly afternoon, gray and overcast, the same day the Jolly was due to fly back from Burlington, approximately 250 miles due north of Long Island.

McManus and Skolnik had been added to the flight to Vermont, but when Al Snyder asked to go, McManus figured Al needed the opportunity to lead a mission and pulled himself off. That bumped Skolnik as well, because Skolnik needed to qualify on an HH-3, and McManus was the only guy who could have certified him. Skolnik wasn't entirely happy about it, but there was nothing to be done. Peggy drove Jack to the base because she needed his car to run errands. She had a friend who was going into surgery that same night after a horse he had been riding fell and crushed him, and Peggy needed the car in case she had to go to the hospital. She parked next to Scott Hursh's yellow Volkswagen Beetle.

"Hurricane Hursh," Jack said as he got out of the car. He thumped the Beetle on the roof with his fist. "Middleweight champ of the 106th."

"Tell me you're not still thinking of boxing Dave," Peggy said.

"Can't—the commander pulled the plug," Jack said. He was disappointed, because he'd looked forward to having a boxing nickname. Jack "The Ripper" Brehm sounded about right. Oh well. "Why don't you come kiss me good-bye?"

She was happy to oblige. He told her that if everything went off according to schedule, he should be back at the base by 6 P.M. She said she'd meet him there then, or if she couldn't, she'd leave a message with somebody to tell him where she'd be. He thought it was funny, how he was learning new things about her all the time; tonight, for instance, realizing how much he could count on her to be there, to pick him up, or for anything else, really—realizing how reliable she was, and that was a good thing, but it was the kind of thing most people would know before they got engaged to someone, not something they'd discover later. Sometimes when he thought of how little they knew about each other, it scared him, but then he remembered that what little he did know, he liked.

Or loved.

The flight out on the C-130 was uneventful. Brehm and Bob Harrison were joined in the back of the plane by the loadmaster, in charge of the airplane's cargo. There were red nylon benches along the sides to sit on, and whoever wanted to could sit at one of the scanner windows on either side of the aircraft, in front of and below the wings, positions manned whenever a C-130 is used in a SAR, or Search and Rescue mission. There's a console at each window that allows the observer to flick a toggle switch to drop a flare, a smoke signal or a dye package to mark a location, whenever he thinks he might have seen something. The C-130 rendezvoused with the helicopters over the North Atlantic, south of Nova Scotia. There was nothing to see during Volant Vault, just rain and fog out the window, no sky to look at and sometimes no ocean. There wasn't much to do, either, other than check and recheck their gear. They had with them a pair of MA-1 kits, each consisting of a seven-man inflatable raft and its accompanying paraphernalia, as well as medical supplies. They had wet suits, masks, fins, snorkels, and twin fifty-pound scuba tanks. Were they to deploy, they'd be jumping into the ocean with about 160 pounds of gear on. They flew at between 2,000 and 10,000 feet, depending on where the weather was best, but low enough that they didn't need to use supplemental oxygen. The back of a C-130 provides a space about the size of a school bus, plenty of room to be alone with your thoughts. They listened over the intercoms in their helmets as the pilots communicated about weather information or made arrangements to refuel.

The HH-53s would need to refuel perhaps a dozen times between Westhampton and Woodbridge. Crew members on the helicopters were required to don bailout parachutes during air refueling due to the increased chance of a collision. Brehm didn't know it at the time, but his friends Randy Mohr and John Smith, stationed at Eglin, were on one of the helicopters, there to help if anything went wrong. Refueling would be the most dangerous part of the journey. To refuel a helicopter in midair, first the tanker flies out in front of the helicopter, both aircraft slowing their forward speed to about 115 knots. The C-130 unspools a ninety-foot long six-inch-wide reinforced black rubber fuel hose from a pod under either of its wings. At the end of the hose is a device called a drogue, a twenty-five-pound steel coniform "female" receptacle, which the helicopter pilot tries to hit with his probe, a telescoping twenty-foot-long pipe that extends from the lower right side of the chopper. He has to hit the drogue with at least 140 foot-pounds of pressure to connect. It takes 420 foot-pounds of pressure to disconnect. The coupling is self-sealing. The fuel is pumped across from the C-130's own tanks, measured in pounds. The tanker releases the fuel, a high-octane mixture called JP-4 that burns hotter and cleaner than gasoline, at a rate of one thousand pounds a minute. In a perfect air refueling, the chopper's tanks are topped off in one smooth shot, but occasionally contact is broken due to turbulence, so a second attempt must be made. Sometimes if the pilot thinks he's received enough fuel, he'll cut it short and tell the tanker pilot he wants to wait until they reach clearer air, or that he wants to climb or descend to different altitudes, where the flying might be smoother, to try again. The drogue is stabilized by a small basket-shaped parachute, which keeps it from flailing wildly about, but it can still be difficult to hit the drogue, particularly in bad weather with poor visibility. It's a dangerous procedure because the helicopter has to fly so close to the C-130 to make the connection. Once the probe hooks up with the drogue, the pilot can fly off a bit and put some distance between himself and the airplane, but during the actual connecting maneuvers, the rotors of the helicopter miss the C-130's tail stabilizers by as little as twenty feet. Anyone who's flown on commercial airliners knows that aircraft can lurch about in the air due to winds or turbulence, often by a distance greater than twenty feet. A sudden shift in wind direction or a catastrophic wind shear could cause the two aircraft to collide. Pilot error could cause the same thing. The drogue could make contact with a helicopter rotor and knock the chopper out of the sky so fast that nobody would have time to jump to safety.

The HH-53s flew on an east-northeast heading at about 130 knots. Two hours out, they hit "bingo fuel," meaning they were past the point where they could return to shore on their own. They had made three successful midair refuelings without incident when Jack heard the radio in his helmet come to life. He was expecting to hear from the crew flying out to rendezvous with them. His mind was on other things, like where he was going to live, and what kinds of apartments Peggy was finding. He was thinking about whether or not he'd be able to raise a kid on a PJ's salary, or if he'd have to get a second job. Guys raised kids on a PJ's pay, but nobody ever said it was easy. Lots of them took second jobs, as cops, EMTs, prison guards, firemen, bartenders, anything. He was wondering if his parents were going to come around and welcome Peggy into the family. Some of the time, he was not thinking about much at all, staring out the observation window at nothing.

It wasn't a greeting from the tanker from Woodbridge. Instead, it was a communication from the Rescue Control Center at Scott AFB in Illinois, about twenty-five miles east of St. Louis, where all pararescue rescue operations are coordinated. Scott had an urgent message to pass along to the general in the helicopter below. RCC couldn't relay the message directly to the general's helicopter, which lacked the proper high-frequency radio equipment to communicate with RCC directly. The C-130, on a mission, acts as the communication platform for all the other aircraft. Scott didn't know the C-130 accompanying Volant Vault was from the 106th.

"Please inform the general," RCC said, "that an HH-3 from the 106th has crashed outside of Plattsburgh Air Force Base in New York. All seven on board confirmed dead."

"Understood, Scott," the pilot said. He didn't ask for a reason or an explanation. There was a long period of silence. Jack looked at Bob Harrison and pointed to his headset to say, "Are you hearing what I'm hearing?" Harrison nodded. More silence, or rather, the drone of the C-130's four propeller engines and the wind.

"Jolly, this is King," Brehm's pilot said at last. His voice was calm, matter of fact. "Message for the general from RCC at Scott. Please inform that an HH-3 from the 106th Air Rescue Wing has crashed outside of Plattsburgh Air Force Base in New York. Seven confirmed dead."

"Roger, King," the helicopter pilot replied.

Then nothing.

Hearing the news a second time made it sink in. Nobody said anything. There was no message from the general to indicate he understood that the men in the tanker above him had just lost seven of their friends. The decision was made to carry on with Operation Volant Vault. The tanker from Woodbridge met them, and the plane from Westhampton Beach turned around. Jack Brehm had half the Atlantic Ocean to contemplate as they flew back to Long Island. Everyone listened to their radios, awaiting further news, perhaps word that there'd been some kind of mistake, or that a survivor had been found. Everyone lived with his own thoughts, wondering what happened, and whether or not the men in the Jolly had known what was happening to them at the time. *Would it be better to know you were going to crash, and make some kind of preparation with your Maker, if you believed in such a thing, or would it be better to be taken without warning?* Jack Brehm thought only that he'd made some assumptions that he shouldn't have made, and couldn't make again. He'd assumed he was going to see Al Snyder and Scottie Hursh and Dave Lambert again, and now he wasn't. He'd assumed, as young men often do, that he was going to live, if not forever, then for a very long time, and now that wasn't necessarily as sure a thing as he'd thought it was.

He wanted to cry. It would have been quite a natural reaction, he knew, to cry, but he didn't cry, maybe because tough guys aren't supposed to cry, or because nobody else was crying and he didn't want to be the only one, or because it hadn't really sunk in yet. Everything felt suspended, up in the air, literally and figuratively. The closer to Suffolk they got, the more nervous he became, because he knew that once they landed, it would all be confirmed. It sunk in, rather unexpectedly, when he looked out the airplane's right side paratroops door as they landed and saw Scottie Hursh's VW Beetle, and knew that Scottie was not going to get in his car and start the engine and rattle off into the night, the way he had a hundred times before. Somehow, seeing the car made it all concrete and real. Suddenly, everything was irrevocably different. The idea that he could easily have been on the helicopter with the men who died was inseparable from the loss he felt. He'd been lucky, and they hadn't, and it made no sense, and everything was different, and unpredictable, and all he wanted to do was cry. Everyone on the tanker with him was being completely stoical, unemotional, almost blasé about it. What was wrong with them?

When the plane stopped moving and the door opened, he saw McManus standing next to a pickup truck, ready to unload everybody's mission gear and take it back to the Ops building. Jack saw people going about their business, as if nothing had happened, not speaking, and knew only that he had to get away from them, and be alone.

He ran from the plane. It was raining. He ran down the flight line and stopped running when he reached the parking lot, where he sat down on a curb and covered his face with his hands. His sleeve was too wet to dry his eyes with it. Some time later, he wasn't sure how long, he felt someone sit down beside him.

It was Mike. For a moment, McManus didn't say anything. They sat side by side in the rain. McManus had served in Vietnam and knew something about losing friends.

"Hey, man," he said. "You gonna be okay?"

Jack didn't answer. Both men knew that at some level, there was nothing to say. That it would be something they would need to face each in his own way, at his own speed.

"It's part of the job, you know?" Mike said.

"I know," Jack said.

"Take your time," Mike said, "but when you're ready, come on into the section because I'm going to need your help."

In the section, most of the PJs on the team had gathered, the full-timers, McManus, Gonzo, Hughes, Harrison, and the part-timers who arrived after punching out on their full-time jobs—Rich Melito, Jay Jinks, Mike Durante. Somebody was passing beers around. McManus asked who would be available to pull honor guard duty to escort the caskets home.

He also lined up guys to take turns staying with Marlene Snyder and to fend off the press, in case they came around asking questions. His information on the crash itself was sketchy, but as best as he could piece it together, they'd been headed home, following a highway that ran along a valley between mountain ranges, and then they turned back, for whatever reason. Mike didn't know the reason. It was dark, visibility was poor due to fog and rain, and somehow they thought they were farther down the valley than they were. If they'd have been a hundred yards farther south, or a hundred yards farther north, or twenty feet higher in the air, they would have missed everything, but as it was they'd turned and clipped the top of a mountain.

Jack got a ride home from Bob Harrison, forgetting that Peggy was going to come get him. They drove south on Old Riverhead Road and turned right on Montauk Highway. They'd gone about a mile when they passed Peggy, coming the other way in Jack's gold 1970 Ford Mustang. Harrison honked the horn and flashed his lights, but Peggy didn't see them, so he turned around and set off after her, catching her as she turned into the base. Jack ran from the car and threw his arms around Peggy, tears welling up once again in his eyes. She started crying in response, for the wrong reason. She assumed his tears meant that he didn't want to marry her. He assumed that she must have heard about the crash on the news. She hadn't. It took a moment to straighten the matter out. He finally explained to her that three PJs and four crewmen had died in a crash in Vermont.

"This is unbelievable," Peggy said.

"I know."

"No," she elaborated. "I mean, yeah, that's unbelievable too. The reason I was late was that I was on the phone with the hospital." Her friend had died in surgery.

They held each other for a long time.

"Let's get out of here," Jack said.

They went home, dried off, made coffee. They decided they needed to go for a walk. They'd walked about five or six blocks when they saw a church, a small white chapel, set back from the road. They decided they might find some comfort there, a way to get out of the rain in both a literal and a spiritual sense. Peggy was the more religious of the two, but Jack was more than happy to accompany her up the steps. Sometimes you just need to close your eyes and ask the questions, whether or not you get the answers.

The church was locked.

They sat down on the steps and held each other. Everything seemed stacked against them. This was their life, and death was apparently going to be a part of it. It was as if God was sending them a message, and if he was, then the message went something like this: All you've got is each other.

The following week was filled with funerals. On Monday, June 19, Al Snyder was buried in Pine Lawn cemetery, at a ceremony where the surviving PJs surrounded his grave, and then each drank a shot of schnapps, throwing the shot glasses in after his coffin, on top of which was Al's maroon pararescue beret. That same night, his widow gave birth to a boy and named him Alan Craig. Jack and Peggy talked about it that night and tried to imagine what it would be like, to bury a husband and have his child all in the same day. They couldn't imagine. Jack wanted to promise Peggy she'd never have to find out, but if this was the job, how could he promise?

The day after Snyder's funeral, a week after the crash, it was Scottie's turn. Dave Lambert's funeral had already been held in upstate New York, near his parents' home. By now, there'd been enough memorials and funerals and words spoken. The loss was easier to bear, even joke about, and sometimes it seemed like laughter moved the grieving process along faster than tears. The plan was for Brehm and McManus and the others to do a water jump a half-mile off shore and release Scottie Hursh's ashes in the sky over Shinnecock Inlet. On the day of the ceremony, a helicopter was taxied out onto the apron in front of the Ops building. The PJs were suiting up in the locker room, preparing to leave, when the Ops commander, Major Frank, informed the group that the other thousand men of the 106th were standing outside in dress uniforms at full attention.

"Why?" McManus asked.

"They want to salute Scottie's remains as we take him to the plane," Major Frank said.

"Scottie's already on the helo," McManus said.

"I know," Frank said. "What do we do?"

"Well," McManus said, "I suppose we've got to give them something they can salute, don't we?"

Jay Jinks found a rock and put it in a helmet bag, which was carried with great solemnity to the aircraft, and the entire base saluted the rock. Half an hour later, as his family stood on the beach, his fellow PJs gave Scottie "Hurricane" Hursh's ashes back to the sky. All that was left behind was a silver coffee can with the words *Contents: one Scott B. Hursh* typed on a piece of paper Scotch-taped to the side.

7

CHERRY MISSIONS

There was a PJ stationed out in the Pacific Northwest who got handed the worst nickname. It wasn't his fault in any way, but for the first seven or eight missions he went on, either they got there too late or the injuries he treated were too severe and the victims died, so guys started calling him "The Bagger." All he did was put people in body bags. Of course, you learn that you can't save everybody, that you have to accept the fact that your training and your abilities have limitations, and that death is part of the job. Sometimes you develop a dark sense of humor as a coping mechanism, maybe the way doctors or morticians can have dark senses of humor. Still, you really ache to have a good first mission, partly because you've been preparing for it for so long that you blow it out of proportion. You want to get off on the right foot. At any rate, you don't want people calling you "The Bagger." In the rescue business, that's a nickname you hope doesn't stick.

SOMETIMES JACK HEARD ABOUT THE CHERRY MISSIONS OF HIS former classmates on the PJ grapevine. He stayed in touch with Mohr, Judy, and Smith, and they stayed connected to the other guys, more or less. Pararescue constitutes one of the smaller elite forces in the military, never more than about three hundred at any given time. As PJs from one unit join up with PJs from another unit on a training mission or temporary duty tour, eventually they either meet everybody else in pararescue or they've heard of them. There wasn't any sense of competition between Jack and his classmates to see who might "lose his cherry" first, but at the same time, Jack didn't want to be the last.

Slip O'Farrell's first official "save" was barely that. A fishing boat, the *Melba Gal*, had lost its bilge pump and was slowly sinking in the Gulf of Mexico, so O'Farrell's helicopter flew a pump out to them. He'd been posted to Tyndall AFB in Panama City, Florida, an Air Defense Weapons Center where he got assigned to work as a drone jockey, hooking and fishing unmanned Air Force target drones out of the sea, not exactly the kind of rescue work he had in mind, but the Air Force doesn't have that many strong swimmers, so PJs are occasionally used in nonrescue capacities. The helicopter crew would also clear the area before such practice sessions and fly "bikini watch" along the beach to make sure nobody swam out too close to the drone recovery area. The drones were small airplanelike craft with heat generators at the wingtips. Fighter pilots would practice locking on to the drones and firing unarmed heat-seeking missiles at them. The unarmed missiles didn't do enough damage to bring the drones down, so usually the drones would fly back to base when the practice session was over, deploy parachutes, and drop on shore. The exception was when a fighter-jock got lucky and managed to put a missile directly up a drone's tailpipe, which was, naturally, what they all tried to do. When they succeeded, recovery was a bit more difficult. One time a fighter-jock shot down a drone, about five miles out in the Gulf, in a steady rain with twenty-knot winds and seven-foot swells, conditions deemed too difficult for the drone recovery boat on the scene to deploy their swimmer. About six feet of the drone's nose stuck straight up out of the water—the other twenty-four feet were submerged. O'Farrell decided he'd give it a try. He swam to the sinking drone, then dove down about ten feet to find the drone's recovery loop, where O'Farrell attached a cable from the helicopter's cargo sling. He saved the Air Force the cost of the drone, about $250,000, only to be chewed out by the Ops officer when he returned to base for deploying without a second PJ onboard as a safety swimmer.

O'Farrell preferred the term "Sky God" to PJ. His hoo-yah attitude was second to none. He needed all the attitude he could muster for his first real save, which transpired after he'd been reassigned to Kadena AFB in Okinawa. Two crew members on the USS *Thomas Jefferson*, a Polaris-class submarine operating in the South China Sea, had been stricken with an unknown illness. Submarine captains don't like to stop, and they don't like to stay on the surface any longer than they have to, with Soviet spy satellites orbiting overhead, so O'Farrell was forced to hoist down to the conning tower while the ship was under way. The HH-53 pilot had to angle his craft 45 degrees forward into the wind to maintain his position, which blinded him to any hover reference. As a result, O'Farrell could only swing back and forth over the conning tower, while the flight engineer tried to place him gently down. After a few minutes of futility, O'Farrell took off the safety strap and leaned out from the penetrator, intending to drop to the conning tower, something like the way Tarzan used to jump from vines onto the backs of elephants. The difference was that Tarzan didn't have that far to go if he fell off the elephant. O'Farrell would have hit the hull of the ship. If he survived that, he still would have been washed off the deck, sucked through the ship's propeller, and ground into so much Purina shark chow. He made it, climbed into the hatch, and saluted the skipper, reporting in by saying, "Bond—James Bond." O'Farrell told the skipper it would be a lot easier to take his crewmen off the ship if they didn't have to play pendulum. The skipper reversed his engines and stopped the sub long enough to allow O'Farrell to hoist the men off safely.

Chuck Matelski's first assignment took him to Fairchild AFB in Spokane, primarily a base for B-52 long-range bombers, with a few P-38 trainers on hand. PJs at Fairchild flew in HH-1 Huey helicopters, a nonrefuelable two-bladed Vietnam-era airframe, which was considerably smaller than the HH-3 Jolly Green Giants or the HH-60s, but it was capable of carrying two to four litters, depending on how they were arranged. Several of Matelski's early missions involved med-evac'ing premature babies from towns like Boise or Missoula and taking them in portable neonatal units to Spokane, where the only hospital with a neonatal-care facility was located. His first rescue took him deep into the Rocky Mountains of Montana, the Bitterroot Range, where a party of elk hunters had gotten in trouble. It was May 1979. There was still a lot of snow in the higher elevations, but lower down the spring thaw had begun. The hunters had ridden in on horseback, along mountain pack trails far from the nearest road. There were six of them, five hunters in their forties and fifties and an outfitter leading them. They were below the snow line and had come to a clearing when one of them was thrown by his horse. One of the hunters managed to ride out and flag down a highway patrolman, who radioed for rescue, then stayed on the scene to direct the helicopter. Matelski looked down from the helicopter on the Clark Fork and the Kootenai Forest, an endless sea of pine and spruce, hemlock, arborvitae, Douglas fir, and larch. The Huey hovered over trees that were themselves over a hundred feet tall.

He took a long ride down the hoist, through the trees to the site of the accident, next to a riverbed. The victim was a man in his forties, dressed in basic hunting clothes, boots, jeans, and a plaid wool shirt. Matelski determined that the man had fractured his lower back. One of the other hunters was a doctor, who'd managed to stabilize the victim and give him aspirin. Matelski called for a Stokes litter. In the Huey, they hooked up an IV of saline solution, to help administer meds, mostly painkillers, because the hunter was in a huge amount of pain.

Jack practiced following a compass underwater. He shined his boots. He lifted weights in the weight room at the base. He waited for the phone to ring.

Joe "J.G." Higgins's cherry mission was as nerve-wracking as Slip O'Farrell's. Joe was posted to the 67th ARRS at RAF Woodbridge in England. ARRS stood for Aerospace Rescue and Recovery Service, the branch of the Air Force overseeing all PJ operations. Higgins's first mission was a water recovery, in a place called The Wash, a large notch in England's east coast where the Ouse and Welland Rivers empty into the North Sea. British and American pilots use The Wash for bombing practice and strafing runs. An American F-15 fighter had gone down not far from where a British Lightning jet had crashed a month earlier. The plane had simply flown too low, dipped a wing and hit a wave at about 600 miles an hour. There was no hope of survivors, but the Air Force still wanted to bring the bodies up if they could. Finding the plane wasn't going to be easy, not because the waters were deep, but they were extremely murky, with strong currents and heavy tides. A British salvage ship, loaded with sonar and recovery equipment, had been looking for the Lightning jet for weeks. All the PJs had to assist them in their search were wet suits, scuba tanks, and their eyes.

They'd been out about a week diving search patterns from a small boat without much luck, in part because they only had half an hour of slack water between tides. The tide was coming in, so Higgins suggested they drift with the current and tow him along, riding the anchor, a small Danforth anchor with a hinged blade on it. He was clipping along at five or six knots, at a depth of perhaps fifty feet, when he saw something out of the corner of his eye. There was no way to signal the men up top, and the only way he could think of to stop the boat was to jam the anchor in the sand, which jerked the boat to a dead stop and knocked the men on the boat off their feet.

Higgins had to make a quick adjustment as well. To ride the heavy anchor, he'd partially inflated his buoyancy compensator, an adjustable life preserver, something like the opposite of a weight belt. Once he let go of the anchor, his BC immediately started taking him up to the surface. He grabbed the anchor rope and hung on to it, upside down, while he bled the air out of his life preserver. If he'd risen uncontrollably to the surface, he would have gotten the bends, possibly to a fatal extent.

They marked the spot with a buoy and went back the next day to recover the pilots. Pieces of the airplane were scattered across the ocean floor, but a large section of the fuselage was intact, a long dark shape in the cloudy water. The danger lay in the fact that the pilots, who sit in tandem side by side in an F-15, hadn't ejected. The escape pod is something like a space capsule, about the size of a Volkswagen. In an ejection, the pod virtually explodes out of the airplane. A guillotine-like device severs the cables and wiring at the back of the pod, a detonating chord cuts the sheet metal, and then twin rockets, with engines more powerful than those on the jet itself, fire to free the capsule, which is equipped with a parachute and flotation bags. An un-ejected escape pod in a crashed plane underwater is a rather hazardous place to be because there's a chance the pod could blow at any minute. You don't want to be working in the pod and have it fire on you. Worse still, you don't want to be halfway in or halfway out of the pod when it fires.

The window was shattered and the pilot was missing, his body ripped from his seat at impact. The copilot was still in his seat, untouched, as if calmly waiting to be recovered. Higgins had with him cotter pins, which he intended to insert into the escape pod's ejection handles to render them safe. Unfortunately, the ejection handles were too damaged for Higgins to insert the pins. He was scared, but his training in the pool at Lackland had taught him how to recognize fear and what to do about it. He calmed himself down, calculated the risks and assessed the situation. He worked carefully—very carefully—with his partner to extract the copilot. When they got the body out, they bagged it and floated it to the surface. Pieces of the pilot later washed ashore.

Jack bided his time. He watched the Reagan-Carter debates on television, and news of the ongoing hostage crisis in Iran. He practiced low and slowing out of an HH-3 helicopter, jumping into the ocean from ten feet above the surface at ten knots. He also learned that Peggy was having twins. She'd been watching her diet carefully, but felt she was gaining too much weight for it to be a single birth. When Jack put a stethoscope to her belly, he swore he heard two separate heartbeats. Her original obstetrician suggested she was simply overeating, so she found an obstetrician who had a sonogram machine, which told her what they'd suspected, that she'd been eating for three, not two. Jack was impressed with his first real medical diagnosis. He brought two stethoscopes home from work one night and they both listened. They listened the next night too, and the next, and the next. Sometimes he'd fall asleep listening, and wake up with his ears aching from the pressure of the stethoscope.

At work, he listened for the phone to ring. Sometimes when it rang, it was Mark Judy or Smitty telling him they'd heard about someone else from their class.

"You hear about D.T.? Oh man, this one's a beaut. . . ."

Joe Higgins's brother Dave "D.T." Higgins had a mission that was typical D.T. and soon after became the stuff of legend and myth, much of it erroneous, but then, legend and myth have never cared much for the facts. It did indeed involve a tropical island, half-naked island girls and copious amounts of alcohol and island spirits, but it wasn't quite the idyll in paradise PJ folklore has made it out to be.

The call came at 8:30 in the morning. D.T. was stationed at Kadena AFB in Okinawa. There'd been a going-away party the night before for the NCOIC, and the section had boozed it up pretty good. D.T. was in the alert room at the PJ section, reviewing the previous evening's lessons while prioritizing his daily tasks, trying to decide whether to sleep, watch television, or play cards, when the Klaxon sounded, signaling a mission. An airman, part of a six-man weather research team out of Tinker AFB in Oklahoma City, had taken ill, afflicted with a 106° temperature and red spots all over him, while stationed on an island about six hundred miles south of Guam, a place called Woleai Atoll, actually a six-island group in the Carolines, U.S. Trust Territories. It was a jump mission, involving an eight-hour flight on a C-130. PJs love the jump missions the most—some guys go years without getting one. Higgins expected they'd fly there and be waved off and told to go home—that sort of thing seemed to happen all the time. His partner was PJ SSGT Jim Derrick, who was two weeks away from PCS-ing (Permanent Change of Station) back to the States. If they jumped, Higgins and Derrick anticipated a brief mission, twenty-four hours at the most. They arrived around 5 P.M.

From the C-130, the main island looked the size of a postage stamp, perhaps five hundred acres total. Without a good wind line, a jumper could blow right over it. One option was to jump into the water and swim ashore, but the surf looked rough. They noticed a small cultivated field in the middle of the island and decided to try for it, jumping round chutes with a limited steering capability. Higgins missed it.

D.T. hit a coconut palm so hard he broke the faceplate on his helmet. He also broke the tree, which was growing out of a WWII bomb crater, which was full of water, which he splashed into, only to find himself surrounded by twenty "Sumo wrestlers in diapers." The D.T. legend would have it that they were a primitive people, untouched by civilization, though in fact many of them had gone to American universities as part of a program training them to return home to Woleai to run their government, once sovereignty was granted. Derrick landed in a cultivated taro root field which, he soon learned, had been fertilized with human feces, and smelled accordingly. He was immediately surrounded by topless island women, who led him to his partner.

The patient, an Airman First Class named Carmichael, had acute tonsillitis, an inflamed infection that a German nurse who was island-hopping the South Pacific with her husband, their boat moored in the lagoon, had tried to treat by giving Carmichael a shot of penicillin. Unfortunately, he was allergic to penicillin, and in fact to most antibiotics. Higgins and Derrick rehydrated the patient with an IV drip and radioed the Rescue Coordination Center in Guam, where the flight surgeon on call recommended medications that Higgins and Derrick didn't have in their medical kits. Higgins and Derrick applied icepacks to the patient and waited. A Navy P-3 Orion flew out the next day and dropped canisters containing a synthetic penicillin called Keflex and a drug called Solu-Medrol, which Higgins and Derrick added to the drip. The drop was around ten at night. The German nurse's husband had never seen an air drop, and came to the field in the middle of the island to watch. D.T. later learned that the nurse took the opportunity to have an affair on her yacht with one of the weather guys from Tinker. At any rate, the new medications did the trick. Carmichael's temperature was soon down to 102°.

The second trick was getting off the island. The Rescue Coordination Center in Guam arranged for a civilian single-engine Cessna 172 seaplane to fly over from the island of Truk. When he got there, the pilot told Higgins and Derrick it would be such a long flight to Guam that he only had enough fuel to take out two passengers. The patient obviously had to be one of them. Derrick had a wife and family in Okinawa, packing to leave, so Higgins volunteered to stay behind.

He waited to be picked up. He drank beer with the weather guys from

Tinker, whose generator had gone down halfway through their six-month mission, leaving them with nothing to do but get hammered every day and annoy the indigenous population. All the Tinker guys had for food was beer, cases of olives, and do-it-yourself pizza kits, so D.T. made friends with the natives and shared meals with them, mostly rice, dried fish, and fruits. Stories of Higgins lying on the beach sipping piña coladas with beautiful island girls rubbing suntan lotion on him are grossly exaggerated.

The locals, perhaps four hundred natives on the island, were indeed friendly, offering him a fermented coconut milk drink called *tuva,* but it was vile and tasted like rotten eggs. The Woleaian women were friendly as well, even flirtatious, but they came from a part of Micronesia where the definition of beauty is rather different from what it is in the United States, and looked, to Higgins something like big fat ugly Eskimo guys. Higgins claims he wanted nothing to do with them.

Jim Derrick recalls that the women weren't all fat or ugly, and that one, an attractive twenty-five-year-old American Peace Corps volunteer, one of the women who'd greeted him topless when he landed, had joined them (topped) around a bonfire at the weather station, the night before he flew out on the Cessna. She might have been from Boston, or Chicago, or possibly from Seattle—some details simply get lost with the passage of time.

As Higgins tells it, he was stranded. Virtually shipwrecked. A supply ship from Truk was supposed to come get him in three days, but the ship developed problems on route and got pulled into dry dock. After eight days (no point in calling in *right* away), Higgins radioed back to Kadena. The base told him not to worry, they hadn't forgotten about him. He finally hitched a ride on a 140-foot tour boat that was taking Japanese WWII veterans back to the islands they'd occupied to conduct burial ceremonies for the soldiers who'd been left behind. The tour boat took Higgins as far as the island of Yap. Yap had a small commercial airport. Higgins was supposed to catch a flight to Guam, but the Air Force sent his tickets to Truk instead. Eleven days from the time he'd launched from Kadena, D.T. caught a flight to Guam, where he was told he'd have a flight to Okinawa the next day. That flight was canceled. Higgins was told, "Maybe tomorrow." Higgins also didn't have any money on him. For some reason, he did have his checkbook, but he didn't have any ID, no dog tags, nothing, so nobody would take his checks. He also didn't have a change of clothes, which wouldn't have been an issue except that during his stay on Woleai it was hot, so he'd cut the sleeves off his shirt and the legs off his BDU (battle dress uniform) pants, which made him look something like the proverbial guy stranded on a desert island. His beard had grown. His hair was a mess. He was deeply tanned from maintaining a beach watch while he waited to be picked up. Because of how he looked, he couldn't get served in the mess hall. He managed to cash a check for twenty dollars with a colonel who trusted him, money he used to stock up on supplies at the airport snack shop.

Meanwhile D.T.'s teammates at Kadena worried. Information on him was sketchy, particularly after he left Woleai. When he finally landed back at Kadena, a full two weeks after he'd launched on what was supposed to be a twenty-four hour mission, fifty members of the team greeted him at the airfield. Higgins appreciated the welcome-home party, and accounted for his delay, explaining that the natives had seen him falling from the sky, thought that he was a god, and carried him on their shoulders to their village, where they coronated him. His teammates responded by sticking Higgins in a body bag, filling it with ice, and hanging him upside down in a Stokes litter.

Different versions of the story circulated on the PJ grapevine. It figured that if something exotic was going to happen to one of Jack's classmates, it was going to happen to D.T. He heard a rumor that D.T. got busted back to tech sergeant for not getting home sooner, but knew that if it were true, D.T. was the sort of guy who always bounced back. He heard a considerably less amusing story when Randy Mohr called him and told him about his cherry mission.

Randy Mohr, Mark Judy, and John Smith in fact all shared the same cherry mission. Shortly before Thanksgiving 1979, several helicopter and C-130 crews launched from Eglin and headed south across the Gulf of Mexico to Puerto Rico, then flew across the Caribbean to Georgetown, Guyana. The global political situation was a mess. Violence and discord had broken out in Nicaragua, Afghanistan, Yemen, and Iran. Terrorists ruled the headlines. No one knew what to expect in Guyana. Judy manned a C-130 tanker. Smith and Mohr were posted on separate HH-53s. As brand-new PJs, they weren't included or consulted in the planning sessions and didn't know much about their mission other than that an American congressman from California, Rep. Leo J. Ryan, had been killed at a small airport in the jungle, where he'd flown to investigate a religious colony, and that there were apparently "a lot of bodies" at a jungle compound. It was believed that there could still be armed hostiles in the area. On the chance that there were, Smith and Mohr were armed with GAU-5s, a brush gun something like a truncated M-16.

They were housed in an abandoned building at the Georgetown airport. On their first flight to the compound, a three-and-a-half-hour journey, they thought how beautiful Guyana seemed, the jungle canopy below gorgeous to behold, a rolling ocean of foliage. Smith had seen jungles in Southeast Asia, but it was new to Mohr. Smith's helicopter was in a holding pattern at 1,500 feet, about a mile downwind from the compound, when he smelled it. Mohr could smell it from five miles away. Smith thought the smell was something like a compost pile in a garden, only much stronger. Mohr, who grew up in agriculture, compared it to a "really nasty pig farm."

When they landed, they found 917 bodies on the ground, all former members of a religious cult known as the People's Temple, led by a charismatic paranoid psychopath minister named Jim Jones. From their helicopters, looking down, it appeared that a massive quilt had been laid on the jungle floor, bright colors of red, yellow, blue, and green. The rotor wash only kicked up the smell as they landed. Most of the bodies were gathered around a blue-roofed open pavilion. They'd been there for about four days, lying in the equatorial sun, so they were all burned and bloated. In many cases, the soft tissues had swollen so that tongues protruded from mouths, and on many corpses the eyeballs had popped out of their sockets. There weren't as many flies or maggots on the bodies as Smith or Mohr expected. There were Air Force combat controllers on the ground, directing helicopters and setting up landing zones, and there was an army grave registration team at work, identifying and bagging the bodies of the people who'd participated in one of the largest, and perhaps most baffling, mass suicides in history, after Jim Jones decided that the end was near and forced his followers to drink a cyanide-laced punch.

The smell of decaying bodies was overpowering. Some men vomited. Others were issued surgical paper masks, which they could pinch across their noses and treat with liquid peppermint drops to block the smell, but the stench was everywhere, the way a skunk can spray a dog in the backyard and perfume the whole house for days. It came through the masks. It came through the body bags. It was in the mud. Mohr and Smith did without masks, summoning all the hoo-yah they had in them to deal with the sickening conditions. PJs are tasked primarily to rescue survivors, but recovering human remains is also part of their mission, and these were American citizens whose bodies needed to be treated with respect and dignity. It was hard to do that, sometimes, particularly after the second day, when Smith and Mohr discovered the nursery. Smith had kids the same age as some of the children of Jonestown, innocent children who'd had cyanide squirted down their throats from syringes by grown-ups they loved and trusted. What trust more sacred was there to violate? It made him sick, seeing the children.

Mohr had a harder time with it. He'd pick up a small body bag that weighed only fifteen or twenty pounds, and it would make him so angry that he had to kick one of the big bags, knowing he would lay down his life before he'd hurt one of his own kids.

At first they brought the bodies out nine and twelve per flight, but with over nine hundred bodies to recover, that was going to take forever. They were under orders not to stack the bodies on top of each other in the helos, which would have been disrespectful, but they did learn to pack them in sideways, sardine style, until they could bring out up to fifty at a time. At the airport in Georgetown, away from the eyes and television cameras of the media, the helicopters were unloaded and the bodies were placed in metal caskets to be flown back to the States. The PJs were left to consider what it all meant, and they were left with the smell. When it was over, they burned their clothes and buried their gear, and washed and fumigated their helicopters. They showered and scrubbed themselves as best they could, but the stink clung to them. Afterward, they were given three days of R & R on the beaches and in the bars of Puerto Rico, and that helped. Lying on the beach and absorbing the rays of the sun helped them feel clean again. Glasses of vodka and pink grapefruit juice helped them forget about it, but not entirely. Mohr thought of a letter he'd found, written by a woman as she was dying from the cyanide-laced punch. The letter was addressed To Whom It May Concern: *Please understand that we had a good life here. We had everything we needed. We had a hospital, and a bakery, and a pineapple farm, and a hog farm. Please don't think we were all a bunch of lunatics, just because Jim Jones flipped out at the end. The idea he had was a good idea. . . .*

Call him a dumb old farm kid, but Mohr remained unconvinced.

Jack was happy for Randy, and Mark, and Smitty, but he wasn't envious. His own cherry mission had come a month earlier, and afterward he understood something he hadn't understood before.

"Fly where?"

"I can't tell you that," he says, "but then I'll be back. . . ." He can't tell her that things aren't going well, because then she'll worry, and he won't be able to explain exactly how it is that things aren't going well. "I might be back later than expected . . . but then I'll be home. Soon. Okay?"

"Okay."

"I'll try to call again in a week, but I can't promise."

"I know."

"I love you, Peg."

"I love you, John."

The thing is, the not knowing drives her crazy, and the knowing drives her crazy. The news, the war, but mostly the not knowing. Surface mail takes too long and ranges from sporadic to worse, e-mail never gets through, and the phone doesn't do it, even when she connects. *Fifteen minutes? Are they serious?* When it doesn't ring, she wants it to ring, unless it's bad news, and then she doesn't want it to ring. When the light on the answering machine blinks, sometimes she's reluctant to hit playback, but still, not knowing is worse.

That night, she prays again. Same old same old—nothing new about the prayer. *Just keep him safe. That's all I care about. I don't care about me. Just keep him safe. Make him be okay.* It's the same prayer she offered when he flew to Turkey. The same prayer she offered when the Turks denied Jack's team permission to fly, and again when the weather turned them around the first day, and again when the weather turned them back the second day, and again when operations postponed the mission for the weekend. She said it the night the malfunctioning horizontal stabilizer grounded Jack's helicopter, and again when the control tower told Jack's team their diplomatic clearance had expired, and again the next day, when the Turks stopped Jack's team from flying because they needed a hard copy of the orders.

A cynic, or maybe a believer, might say Peggy Brehm's prayers are wasting U.S. taxpayers' dollars, but Peggy wouldn't mind it if it were true.

11

THE BIRD THAT WAS NOT A BIRD

You have to learn mountaineering skills because there's always a chance that a pilot is going to be shot down in a mountainous area where it would be difficult to reach him, even under friendly conditions. We're flying over mountains in Iraq, and in Kosovo, and places where it's easy to hide an antiaircraft battery. Sometimes you're not as worried about the guy getting shot or captured by the enemy as you are that he could succumb to the elements. And if you're racing against time with an enemy patrol trying to reach and capture your guy, whoever has the better mountaineering skills wins.

I climbed Mont Blanc in France back in September of 1982 with a PJ named Rod Alne. We got thrown out of a couple bars one time in the village of Chamonix, a restaurant, because we were told they had menus in English, but when we asked for them, they wouldn't give them to us, which made us think they didn't want our patronage. We also collect souvenirs wherever we go, because our unit had a trophy room, so if you go on a ship, maybe you grab a life ring or a coffee mug with the ship's name on it. In France, my buddy Scott Simpson and I used our mountaineering skills to climb up this hotel's balcony and steal a French flag. A couple days later, the flag had been replaced, so a friend of Rod's, a PJ named Bill Jones, thought he'd climb up and steal that one, except that whoever had put the flag out had figured out how we'd done it the first time, so they greased the railing. When Jones jumped for the railing, he fell two stories to the ground. He was okay, but he was in shock, saying, "I can't believe it—they greased the rail."

Rod got pissed at me when we were climbing an ice face. I was up probably forty or fifty feet, and when I got to the top, I laid my ice ax down instead of sticking it firmly into the ice and double-checking to make sure it was secure. When I bumped it, it went flying down the ice face and landed right at Rod's feet. It didn't hit him, but it could have, and these things weigh maybe four pounds—it could have killed him.

Mountains are dangerous places. You go there because there's no place else you can go where you'll be that tested, and the more you're tested, the more you learn. Sometimes you learn it the hard way, but you learn it.

ON APRIL 1, 1987, APRIL FOOL'S DAY, PEGGY GAVE BIRTH TO HER last child, a boy, Jeffrey. Jeffrey was a sweet, smiling baby. Perhaps because he was still feeling good about his new son, a month later, Jack ran a personal best time of two hours and fifty-one minutes in the Long Island Marathon. Having once predicted he wouldn't live past thirty, every year beyond that milepost seemed like a gift. Almost without noticing the time passing, as if it had sneaked up on him somehow, Jack realized he was now a veteran PJ. He felt comfortable in his job, confident, without anything like the sense of fatigue or burn-out that other PJs retiring early seemed to feel.

One day, a few weeks before Christmas in 1988, McManus asked Jack if he wanted to get a beer at the Matchbox after work, because he had something he wanted to talk to him about, an "opportunity" Mike said. By now Mike was divorced, remarried to a woman named Debra Carnes. Jack had spent many nights at the Matchbox with Mike, talking about women and marriage. He'd seen Mike at his lowest, and was glad to see him so happy again. It was snowing when Jack left the Ops building, three inches already on the ground, but he knew that in eastern Long Island, it was just as likely to rain the day after a snow as stay cold—they would still need luck if they were to have a white Christmas. Mike was already in a booth, nursing a beer, when Jack joined him.

"So what's the opportunity?" Jack asked. "For you or for me?"

"Well," Mike said, "both, if it works out. I've been more or less offered a chance to go up to Alaska and set up a PJ team there. When Debby and I flew up there last month, we really liked the place, so I met with Colonel Taylor, the wing commander there, and we pretty much hit it off. He didn't say so in so many words, but the job is mine if I want it." Jack knew that Mike had never really taken to Long Island, an acquired taste even for people who were born there. He congratulated Mike and told him it sounded like an exciting prospect.

"It depends on what kind of funding I get," McManus said, "but it sounds like we could really do something pretty neat up there." With all the oil money coming in to the Alaskan state coffers, Mike said he had high hopes that he'd be adequately financed, able to order everything he needed to supply his team, instead of taking hand-me-down equipment and used helicopters from the regular Air Force, the way a lot of guard units had to. He had dreams of putting in a professional-quality weight room, maybe even a pool for guys to train in. The governor seemed determined to install a first-class rescue system. Jack was amazed. Mike was nearly forty-five years old, an age when most PJs had retired, and here he was beginning a whole new phase of his career.

"You're going to love it," Jack said. "From what I've heard, Alaska is going to be just your kind of place."

"It could be your kind of place, too," Mike said. "I'm going to need some good experienced PJs up there, so I'd prefer to take the guys I really like with me."

"Who else are you thinking of inviting?" Jack asked.

"Steve Lupenski is one," Mike said. "Some others. I'm not really spreading it around just yet. I figured you'd have to talk it over with Peggy and the kids, but I just wanted to give you the heads up on this as soon as I could. But the other thing would be that once I'm gone, they're going to need a new NCOIC at the base, and you'd be the guy I'd recommend. You'd be pretty much the only guy on my list, as a matter of fact. I know some people are probably going to feel passed over if they hire you for NCOIC, but I'd rather have the best man get the job, not somebody who's simply been here the longest."

"Hmm," Jack said. *Wow* was what he wanted to say.

"I mean," Mike added, "I can't guarantee you anything, and we still have to post the job, so you'd have to go through the application procedures and be interviewed and all that, but there's no rule that says I can't recommend somebody. So think about it and tell me what you want me to do."

As Jack drove home, he had much to think about. He tried to keep the two ideas separate. He was momentarily excited about the idea of going to Alaska, starting fresh in a new place. He pictured the mountains, the forests, the sea, the glaciers, the whole glorious magnificence of the Alaskan experience, but at the same time he couldn't picture relocating. He would talk it over with Peggy that night, but as he drove home he felt as if he already knew what she'd say, and that he was going to agree with her. Her extended family was like nothing he'd ever experienced before, and it was a big factor in why their marriage was as happy as it was. Instant baby-sitters. Instant grown-up company. Instant playmates for the kids. Instant emergency end-of-the-month loans. Car pools to pick the kids up from soccer or cheerleading practice. Readily available emotional support, and plenty of parental eyes, everybody keeping tabs on everybody else's children, much to the chagrin of the children, who felt as though they couldn't get away with anything. It seemed as though if Jack and Peggy moved then her sister Carol would have to move, too, and her sister Lorraine, and her parents, and Jack's sister—as it was, everybody lived within a few blocks of one another. Putting all the kids into new schools seemed harsh. Moving to Alaska might be good for his career, but it would be bad for his family, and his family came first.

On the other hand, becoming NCOIC would also be good for his career, and he wouldn't have to move to do it. He realized that, at first anyway, he'd be learning on the job, and that he was relatively young to be an NCOIC, which meant that there would be guys with more seniority who'd need to be greased or assuaged, but if Mike believed in him (and he knew Peggy believed in him), then he'd be a fool not to believe in himself. He couldn't have asked for a better teacher or role model.

"I think we're going to have to pass on the thing in Alaska," he told Mike the next day, "but I'm definitely interested in the job here."

"Let me talk to Stratameier and Giere," McManus said, referring to the squadron commander and the base commander. "You know you still have to go through the standard selection process," McManus added.

"I understand that," Jack said.

"I'll get back to you."

Jack was excited by his prospects. All the same, Mike's change of station came as a mixed blessing. Jack felt that half the things he knew he'd learned from Mike. Mike had been there when the helicopter had crashed in Plattsburgh. He'd been there when Jack found out Peggy was pregnant. He'd been there when Mark Judy died. He'd been there when Larry Arnott died. And for all the harsh and hard moments, there'd been hundreds of lighter joyous moments, jumps out of airplanes, training runs side by side, Dumb Ass Bare Assed escapades and beers shared in bars all over the globe. Sure they'd see each other again, and stay in touch, but life without seeing Mike on a regular basis was hard to contemplate.

On January 24, 1989, Jack and McManus flew their last mission together. A trawler had overturned in icy cold waters, five miles out from the base on a south-southeast heading. The Coast Guard was on the scene, but they needed medical assistance. Jack joked that given how cold it was, it was sort of a preview for what Mike could expect on his new job. Thermometers at the base registered a mere 24° Fahrenheit. Brehm and McManus low-and-slowed in, entered the water wearing wet suits and swam to a 44-foot Coast Guard ship that had pulled a sailor off a capsized 87-foot fishing boat. The other crewmen had been rescued, but the sailor on the Coast Guard ship was suffering from severe hypothermia and needed to be med-evac'ed to a hospital immediately. Jack and Mike hoisted the victim up, treated him for hypothermia on the helicopter and administered CPR all the way to Stony Brook Hospital, even though the victim had no vital signs and was quite likely dead. The general rule in rescue is, you don't pronounce a cold body dead because cold bodies can sometimes be resuscitated even after being submerged for long periods of time. If the guy warms up and he's still dead, *then* he's dead, which was exactly what the doctors at Stony Brook pronounced him, forty minutes after the HH-3 landed.

There was a farewell party for Mike McManus at the NCO club on the base before he left for Alaska. It was a gloomy winter day, but the wives helped decorate the place to bring in some cheer, Peggy and Barbara Dougherty and John Spillane's fiancée, Laura, stringing up white Christmas lights and *FAREWELL* and *GOOD LUCK*, and *BON VOYAGE* banners. Jack called Major Jeff Frank, who'd been the original squadron commander for the 106th back in 1975, when McManus first came onboard to build the team, and got him to fly up from South Carolina as a surprise. Jack gathered together a number of retired guys who'd been there in '75—Bernie Waters, Dickie Forrestal from the motor pool, Mike's pal despite all the vehicles Mike and his PJs kept wrecking. The PJs wanted to buy Mike a hunting rifle, figuring that's what men going to Alaska need, but they didn't know what kind to buy, so they gave him a cashier's check for $400 and told him to buy a rifle with it, if the idea of hunting appealed to him. There were real gifts, and there were gag gifts. For example, when it was time to clean up after a mission, Mike would always walk from his locker to the showers and back wearing a towel with a slit cut in the middle of it, thrown over his head, something like a terry cloth poncho. He also hated it when he'd leave his shampoo in the showers, so instead, before showering, he'd simply glop a big blue dollop of Head & Shoulders on his pate at his locker and walk around like that, sometimes talking to people or taking phone calls. One gag gift was a new bath towel, with a slit neatly

Twenty-four hours before departing for basic training in February 1977.

No more long hair: Jack's basic training photo.

Jack and Peggy begin their new life together, July 28, 1978.

"Air Force beats Army," July 1977. The class of '78-03 victorious in the Great Chattahoochee Raft Race. *Bottom, from left:* Jack Brehm, John Geerlings, J. G. Higgins. *Top, from left:* Slip O'Farrell, D. T. Higgins, Bob Wagner, John Smith, Mark Judy, Bill Skolnik. (*U.S. Army Photo*)

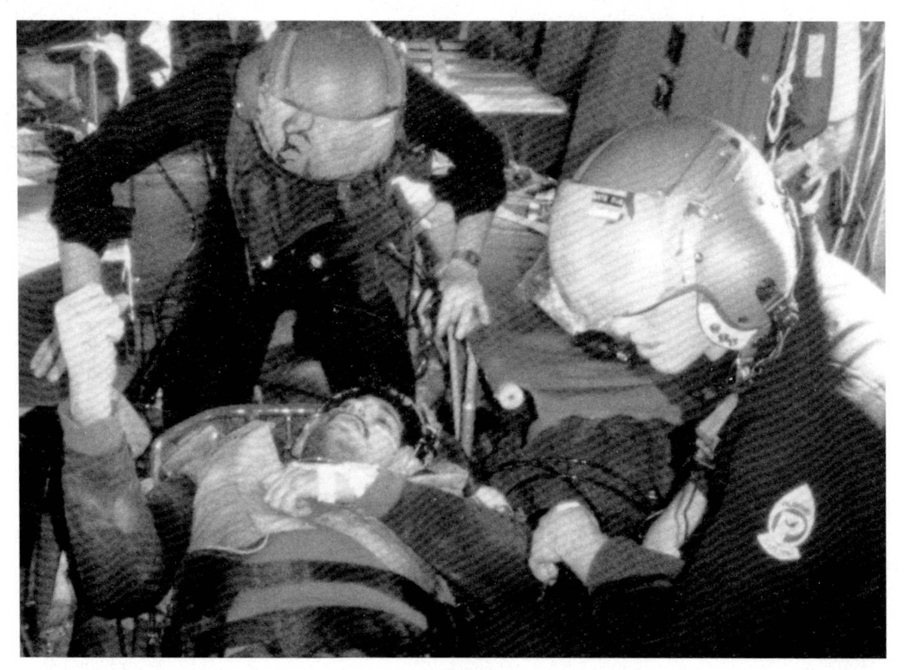

Saving lives is all in a day's work for the PJs. PJ Robert Olson, *left,* and Jack, *right,* monitor Ronald Cunningham's condition, July 14, 1981.

The Jolly 85 that crashed on June 13, 1978, killing all on board, including three PJs from the 106th: Al Snyder, David Lambert, and Scott Hursh. *(106th Combat Visual Information Section)*

Jack gives a tour of an H-60 to Alan Craig Snyder, son of Al Snyder, who died one week before Alan was born. *(106th Combat Visual Information Section)*

COL David Hill, Jr., 106th Wing Commander, and Peggy and Jack at the Senior NCO Academy Graduation in 1994. *(LTC Anthony Cristiano)*

Groundhog Day in Turkey, May 1999. *From left:* Jack, Jonathan Davis, Jimmy Dougherty. (*Rob Marks*)

Peggy's support staff while Jack was in Turkey (celebrating Jack's return). *Top, from left:* Peggy, Jim, Peggy's sister Lorraine, Jack. *Bottom, from left:* Greg, Michele, Peggy's sister Carol, Bean, Jaimie, Elizabeth, Mark.

Above: Jack gets support from mentor Mike McManus as he races his first Ironman-distance triathlon. *(Laura-Jean Brehm)*

Right: Jack's thrill of a lifetime, with daughter Michele at her first jump, 1998. (*Carol Martinson*)

Jack's proudest achievement—the Brehm family. *Top, from left:* Peggy, Matthew. *Middle, from left:* Laura-Jean, Elizabeth, Jeffrey. *Bottom, from left:* Michele, Jack. (*Carol Martinson*)

cut, sewn, and hemmed in the middle, a refinement on the simple tailoring Mike had done on his own towel with his survival knife. When the party moved to the Matchbox after the NCO club closed around two in the morning, Mike showed up wearing nothing but his new towel, buck naked underneath it. A PJ named John Canfield immediately tackled him and wrestled him to the floor, McManus's ass and balls flying all over the place. It was a miracle no one put an eye out.

On the day he left town, beginning the long road trip north to Anchorage, Mike and Debby stopped by Jack and Peggy's house in Rocky Point intending to say a quick good-bye and get on the freeway, but they ended up staying until midnight, drinking beers and talking about old times. Mike brought Jack a parting gift, a pair of brand-new Cochran jump boots, shiny black dress boots for those occasions when a full dress uniform was called for. Jack had always been too cheap or too broke to pony up the forty bucks for dress boots, polishing up his standard Air Force issue jungle boots instead, and Mike had always teased him about it. McManus finally got on the road in the wee hours of the morning, determined not to spend another night on Long Island, only to be harassed on the Long Island Expressway by an insane motorist in what appeared to be a black Monte Carlo. There's nothing particularly uncommon about encountering insane motorists on the Long Island Expressway, but at two in the morning, when it's just you and the lunatic tailgating you at 100 mph and flashing his high beams, when all you're trying to do is leave in peace, it's particularly irritating. McManus wasn't worried for his safety, because he had his weapons in the car with him, and was in fact loading his sidearm, concerned more that the noise from the weapon was going to wake up his wife than about shooting the moron in the Monte Carlo. He finally lost the guy at the Throg's Neck Bridge, and he was happy to see him veer off, but he couldn't help but think it a fitting farewell, and good riddance.

The spring and summer were relatively uneventful. Jack ran the section, thankful that there were no major challenges, just a daily routine of paperwork and training. He knew that Mike had left behind some fairly large shoes to fill, but whenever Jack found himself in doubt about a decision, asking himself "What would Mike do?" usually led him to an answer, and if it didn't, he could always pick up the telephone and go directly to the source. In April, John Spillane married his girlfriend of five years, a woman named Laura Hohman. In May, Jack ran the Long Island Marathon for the eleventh consecutive year. In August, he swam, biked, and ran a half–Iron

Man race, called a Tin Man, in Lake Placid. Search and rescue missions were few, and routine—patients who needed to be med-evac'ed, sailors who were a few days late for dinner and needed to be found. Things stayed quiet until 1990, when Iraqi troops invaded and occupied Kuwait.

A prolonged and complex multinational military buildup followed, preparations for what became Operation Desert Storm, the Gulf War. Active duty Air Force PJs, under the control of AFSOC (Air Force Special Operations Command), were tasked to support tactical combat teams, which meant joining up with combat controllers to establish landing zones, or with the 82d Airborne to seize Kuwaiti or Iraqi airfields. PJs under AFSOC were to parachute in and then perform the functions of old-fashioned field medics, treating anybody who might be hurt in the jump. The Guard and Reserve pararescue units, under the ACC, or Air Combat Command, would ordinarily have been tasked with the traditional assignment of going after downed pilots, but it was decided at the higher levels that the HH-3 and HH-60 Pavehawk helicopters the Guard and Reserve units were flying, aircraft that were rated for low- to medium-risk combat situations, were not going to be safe to fly in the high-risk environment over Iraq. The 106th specifically was deemed non-combat ready, as a unit, because their pilots and mechanics were undergoing conversion training, the squadron recently having switched from HH-3 to HH-60G air frames, and until their training was completed, they weren't going anywhere. There was still a chance, however, that PJs from the 106th might be sent to supplement or replace the active duty PJs in theater.

Guys asked Jack what he thought the chances were that they'd be sent. Prewar propaganda aside, it looked as if it was going to be huge. The newspapers were full of stories about Iraq's state-of-the-art Russian-made air defense systems, their stockpiles of nerve gases and biological weapons of mass destruction, and particularly Saddam Hussein's "crack Republican Guard." Saddam did his part to frighten everybody by speaking of how it was going to be the "Mother of All Battles." The Iraqi army proved, in retrospect, fairly ineffective, managing to stage a partially successful raid on the animals in the Kuwait City Zoo and set a couple hundred oil wells on fire before grabbing the first jeep, bus, bicycle, or skateboard available back to Baghdad, once Desert Storm commenced. Before it started, however, the average American was deeply concerned, if not outright terrified, with what might happen if nerve gases were used, or if Saddam managed to hit Jerusalem with one of his SCUD missiles and do enough damage to draw a nuclear response from Israel. In the early stages of the conflict, PJs from the 106th deployed to Patrick AFB to help fly coverage for an accelerated program of space shuttle launches carrying classified military payloads, meaning, everyone knew, spy satellites to be placed in orbit over the Middle East.

At the Brehm household, it was the first time the kids were old enough to worry about what was going on in the world. The twins were eleven, Laura-Jean was eight, Matt was seven, and Jeffrey had turned three on April first. Elizabeth had developed into the sensitive one, the romantic, easily moved to tears by a story with a sad ending, or better yet by a romantic story with a happy ending. She loved to write—stories, poems, journals, anything as long as she could let the words flow out of her and put them down on the page. She was nonconfrontational, but her emotions were largely evident and accessible, unlike Michele, who played her cards closer to the vest. Michele was confident, willful, more willing to explore and try new things, more self-reliant, more fun-loving, and a better athlete than her twin sister. Elizabeth envied the way Michele didn't care what other people thought, and how she seemed to have a clear sense of reality, of who she was and what she wanted. Both girls were old enough to understand that their father might have to go to the Middle East. Peggy tried to turn the television off whenever she saw the kids watching the news about Desert Storm, but she couldn't keep it off all the time. The White House needed the American public to back the war, and to a certain extent used scare tactics to get the support it needed, emphasizing Saddam Hussein's history of brutality and his prior use of nerve gas on his own people.

If the propaganda campaign worked on grown-ups, it frightened the daylights out of young children. Elizabeth cried. Michele used the tension as an excuse not to do her homework, saying, "I was too upset last night to study." Laura-Jean was the gregarious one, thoughtful of others, sensible and silly at the same time, able to charm her father with little effort, but as the war developed she grew clingy, reluctant to leave her father's side. Even Jeffrey, who was only three, seemed to know that something bad was about to happen somewhere, and that his dad could be involved in it somehow. He was a sensitive child, extremely patient, and a bit of a mama's boy, but neither he nor Peggy seemed to mind. Jeffrey seemed oddly tuned in for someone so young, always staring at the news on CNN whenever he got the chance. Matthew seemed to be handling it well, but Peggy knew that was an act. Matty was the kind of kid who seemed quiet and shy at first, observant and smart but slightly detached or remote, until you got to know him, and then you realized he had the driest sense of humor in the family, a subtle wry wit he used to tease his siblings, usually without seeming mean. He was small for his age group but good at sports like hockey, soccer, or lacrosse, and highly competitive, like his dad, whom he idolized. Admitting Dad was at risk meant admitting Dad was something less than invincible, which wasn't Matthew's position on the matter. Peggy tried to keep her cool but lost it one morning when she was trying to get Matthew out the door and onto the school bus. The phone rang. It was a teacher from the school at Rocky Point.

"How are you doing?" the teacher asked.

"I'm fine. What do you mean?"

"Well, it's just that I heard the 106th was being deployed today."

Peggy's knees weakened. It was all she could do to get Matthew on the bus. As soon as she could, she called Jack at the base, who reassured her that they were not being activated, but rather they had simply been placed on alert.

During the "Mother of All Battles," Jeffrey became obsessed with the pictures on TV, favoring CNN over Barney or cartoons. Pictures of buildings blowing up, or buildings about to blow up, taken from cameras in the nose cones of flying bombs and missiles—what could better capture the imagination of a three-year-old boy? Peggy would say to Jeffrey, "You can't watch this—turn it off," and confiscate the remote control, but sooner or later it would be on again. When Michele won $365 on an Instant Lotto ticket that Peggy cashed for her, she said she wanted to take the whole family to the Great Escape Amusement Park in Lake George. Jack, on alert, couldn't go, but Peggy and the kids went. They went on rides, and played arcade games, ones not involving guns, and stayed in a motel, and ate out in restaurants three meals a day, and forgot about the war that was going to happen, any day.

Desert Storm began in January and lasted until April 6, 1991. The main air campaign was waged in the first month. The 106th waited to be called up, and the PJs were polled for volunteers to deploy in the Gulf on two separate occasions. Jack volunteered both times but was never called. He volunteered without Peggy's knowledge, because he didn't want to worry her prematurely, and because he knew she'd understand if he ever did get called. It wasn't just a sense of duty that made him want to go—it was more a sense of purpose, the thing that gave his life meaning and shape.

Peggy knew that. She also knew Jack was probably volunteering to go without telling her. She was elated when the war ended as quickly as it did.

As the war wound down, Jack got a call from Mike McManus in Alaska, who said that once the squadron was off alert, he had a training mission Jack might be interested in, a team that was going up Mount McKinley in Denali National Park. After all the tension of waiting out Operation Desert Storm, and the disappointment of not going, climbing McKinley seemed, to Jack, like just the ticket.

There was one thing he had to take care of first. Two days before he was due to fly to Kulis Air National Guard Base in Anchorage, Jack's next door neighbor, Carl Waage, called. Carl was a few years older than Jack and lived with his wife, Maryanne, his son Kris, and his daughter Carla. Carl drove delivery trucks for *Newsday.* He and Jack would drink beers in his kitchen and talk about the Mets, and their kids, and the jobs they'd had. Carl had worked as a flagpole painter, not as dangerous as the things Jack did, he said, but scary at times. More dangerous, perhaps, was the job he'd had scraping and repainting the insides of underground storage tanks, which, the doctors thought, was possibly where he'd inhaled the chemicals that had given him a rare degenerative lung disease. Carl was awaiting a double lung transplant, and now that spring had arrived, and the motorcycles or, as doctors call them, "donor-cycles" were coming out of the garages, it looked as if Carl's time on the waiting list was coming to an end. That was, in fact, why he'd called—would Jack mind driving him to the hospital to pick up a fresh pair of lungs?

Jack felt honored, but wondered why Carl hadn't asked his wife. Probably because he didn't want to worry her. Better to call her from the hospital. The lungs were waiting. Jack drove Carl to the hospital. Carl was calm, confident, thrilled that his hospital room had a great view, eager to get it over with, and anxious to hear about Jack's trip to McKinley when he got back.

"Take a lot of pictures," he said. "When you get back, we'll sit on the porch and drink a beer and you can show me your pictures. I'll see you soon."

* * * * * * * *

On the sixteenth of May, three days into his climb of Mount McKinley, his group climbing the West Buttress route, Brehm writes in his diary that he has a slight headache and that he slept only three hours the night before. The entry for Friday, May 17, records the first inkling of trouble: *Arrived*

9,800 feet at 1200 hrs. The whole area from 8,000 feet to 10,000 feet is in a total white-out all day with a light snow falling. Temp. approx. 20 degrees F, winds 10 kts [*knots*]. *The troops are happy we have yet to get stuck in any one place. I'm doing great physically, no blisters, and I feel strong, and you know me, I couldn't be happier. Found out yesterday that a group of Koreans are frozen out at 17,000 feet. One dead, one with frostbite, whole arm, three hypothermic, and one missing.*

But you can't necessarily trust the information you get on a mountain—news items relayed via word of mouth—as climbers pass each other on the way up or down. It's like a big game of telephone, a situation where facts might get distorted, even at sea level—add impaired thinking at altitude to the mix and you can have an obscuring of facts of major proportion. Brehm takes the news of the Koreans with a grain of salt, because it might not be true. His diary entry for May 18 notes, *"There's no place in the world I'd rather be."*

On May 20, they make Windy Corner at 13,500 feet and reach a bowl at 14,000 feet, around 4:30 P.M., a place called Fourteen Camp, which affords them a breathtaking view of Denali National Park and the Alaskan Range. The trip from 11,000 to 14,000 is a bitch, maybe the toughest part of the route. The skies are clear and the sun is intense all day, almost too hot. Brehm's pulse an hour after arriving is sixty beats a minute. On Brehm's rope team are PJ "Skip" Kula and a Navy SEAL named Jack Chapin. PJs Mike Wayt and Steve Lupenski are on team two. PJ Carl Brooks, a British Special Ops guy named Mike Blinkhorn, and a civilian, Brian Abrams, make up team three, while PJs Steve Daigle and Garth Lenz make up team four. Three other guys have gone up the West Rib route, but that's a more technical and thus more dangerous climb, leading through a place called the Valley of Death, where chunks of ice the size of railroad cars can come crashing down, so you have to cross it early in the morning before the sun heats the ice above you. The West Buttress group is for men with less mountaineering experience. Rudolf Kula is a PJ from Cleveland who graduated the Pipeline a few classes behind Jack's, and because he's the PJ with the most experience on McKinley, he's in charge. Lupenski was one of the PJs from the 106th who relocated to Anchorage with McManus to help start up the Alaskan wing. PJ Wayt, a twenty-eight-year-old Japanese-American Air Force brat, is climbing McKinley for the first time, as is Lupenski. It will be Brehm's first climb above 15,000 feet, assuming all goes well. Chapin and Brooks are developing blisters and may not go any farther. The total number of people staying at Fourteen Camp this day is probably about thirty, including three park rangers who've been stationed there for twenty-four days and are due to be replaced and rotated down the mountain. Fourteen Camp, sometimes called Doc Hackett's Camp, after Bill Hackett, one of the first men to climb the West Buttress route back in 1951, is one of two staging areas on McKinley. The other is at 17,000 feet. They are places where you recover and reorganize your thoughts and await news of good or bad weather either above or below you.

All seems well. A diary entry for May 21 records that with an oxygen saturation level of 86 percent, Brehm's pulse, at 8:30 P.M., is sixty-four beats per minute. The entry ends, *"Some Girl Scouts knocked on our tent selling cookies tonight."*

Girl Scouts? The next day Brehm reads the entry and can't remember what he was thinking or why he wrote it down. He might have been dreaming. It's possibly a sign that he needs to rest.

The plan is to spend some time shuttling gear up the mountain and caching it, but mostly the idea is to rest for the next leg of the climb. At 14,000 feet, it takes about three days to acclimate to the altitude. Acclimating to altitude requires a variety of biological adjustments, but the main way the body compensates for the lack of oxygen is by manufacturing additional red blood cells, which carry oxygen from the lungs to the rest of the body. If we could remove the soul from the body and take away the thing that makes us human, we could then think of ourselves as simply an ongoing, enormously complex chemical reaction, a kind of controlled fire, or an assembly of a trillion small fires going on in each individual cell. Without oxygen, fires go out. Chemical reactions slow down. When you're climbing, the thinning air acts like a damper. You can eat three or four times the amount of calories that you might eat at sea level, but without oxygen the fuel inside you only partially burns. The technical term for the general malaise you feel at high elevations is hypobaric hypoxia. It frequently leads to mountain sickness, which generally occurs at 8,000 feet or higher. Affected individuals develop symptoms within four to six hours, reach maximal severity in twenty-four to forty-eight hours. Basic mountain sickness often abates three or four days after exposure. The most common symptom of hypobaric hypoxia is a skull-busting headache, but other symptoms include vomiting, dizziness, labored breathing, and ataxia, or a lack of muscle coordination. Confusion can occur because even the ideas in our heads, including the memories we carry around with us and the dreams we have at night, are themselves chemical reactions that require oxygen. At high altitudes where the oxygen is thin, thoughts and dreams and memories begin to turn fuzzy and lose structure, as if oxygen were the glue holding them together. The psychological symptoms of mountain sickness are things like despondency, irritability, or impaired memory. Thinking becomes work. Sometimes hard work, and it doesn't matter how smart you are to begin with—you get dumber. At 14,000 feet, no matter how fit you are, you get a little bit weaker with each passing day. You sleep at night, but without oxygen sleep does not bring the kind of rest you need and you can wake up feeling more tired than you were when you went to bed. At some point, it requires as much emotional strength to keep going as it does physical strength.

On May 22, the three new park rangers arrive, among them a man named Roger Robinson, who the Alaskan PJs have worked with before. The rangers being replaced head down the mountain to Talkeetna, skiing down part of the way and no doubt feeling better and stronger with each meter they descend. Shortly after their departure, a group coming down the mountain reports bad news. The rumor of fatalities among a team of Korean climbers is false; however, a Korean named Kim Hong Bin is in serious trouble, a second Korean less so. In addition to the Koreans, there are two other parties at 17,000 feet, about twelve people altogether. Kim Hong Bin is an expert skier and one of Korea's leading mountain climbers, a man who made it to 23,600 feet on Mount Everest in 1989 and 23,900 feet on Pakistan's 26,260 foot Mount Nangaparbat in 1990, though no one at Fourteen Camp has any way of knowing this. If they had, they might suspect it could have been a fear of failing to summit three times in a row that got Kim Hong Bin in trouble. From Kim Hong Bin's perspective, how could he turn back, knowing that on his two previous ascents he'd climbed higher than the summit of the mountain he was now climbing?

The staging area at 17,000 feet is a relatively flat narrow plain at the crest of the West Buttress's headwall, an area on the mountain where the angle of ascent increases to 55 or 60 degrees. At the bottom of the headwall is a *bergschrund,* an area of crevasses where the glacier flowing down the mountain breaks off. The vertical slope is mostly ice and bullet-proof snow, sculpted at various locations into *sastrugi* ice, where the ferocious winds create waves and sawtooths and stalactites. From 17,000 feet, it's another 3,320 vertical feet to the summit, a hike of perhaps five horizontal miles. A moderately steep ascending traverse, beginning at 17,200 feet and dubbed the

Autobahn because a German party got in trouble there once, takes you to Denali Pass at about 19,000 feet. You climb a short headwall to a flat area called the Football Field, and then it's a half a mile of plodding up the peak ridge to the summit. Along the way, you may encounter couloirs, knife-edged ridges, frost-fractured schist columns, and snow or ice cornices—no one in their right mind would call it an easy walk, but the degree of incline isn't as steep as the headwall between 14,000 and 17,000 feet. Climbers regularly go from Seventeen Camp to the summit and back in a day. Brehm's party has already cached supplies at 16,030 feet (between 14,000 and 16,030, it's much too steep to cache anything) with the thought of moving the whole show up the following day.

"Is there a problem?" Brehm asks Kula, who explains the situation with the Koreans.

"Koreans?" someone says. "Well, that figures."

"Why?" Jack says. "What's wrong with Koreans?"

It's explained to him that there's nothing wrong with Koreans, except that they seem to come to Alaska with a sense that if they don't make it all the way to the summit, they will then have to return to Korea disgraced and dishonored. Everybody climbs mountains to push themselves and test themselves, but if you push too hard sometimes you flunk the test. A week before, someone at Fourteen Camp says, a group of Koreans at 18,000 feet pulled out when they all got sick.

"The other problem is," a park ranger standing nearby says, "we just got here, and we're not really acclimated, so we don't have anybody who can go get him. We were actually wondering how you guys felt about that."

There is a French helicopter called a Lama, little more than an aluminum frame and a transmission connecting the motor to the rotors, with a place for the pilot to sit, which is light enough to fly to the summit, but the weather has to be perfect, and today it's too windy. Major storm systems crossing the area can be forecast out of Fairbanks, but the mountain generates its own weather as air masses rise up its slopes and cool to form clouds and wind. According to meteorological records, Mount Washington in New Hampshire, only 6,288 feet high, is supposed to have the worst weather in the world, according to measurements taken at the weather station on the summit, with steady 100 mph winds in the wintertime and a world record wind speed of 231 mph measured on April 12, 1934, but that may only be because there are no meteorological records for Mount McKinley, the tallest peak this close to the Arctic Circle. There's no weather station atop McKinley. Brehm and Kula and the others discuss their options. Possibly somebody already camped at 17,000 feet could bring the stricken climber down, but unless that person has training in rescue techniques, the odds are poor that either the rescuers or the victim will make it, particularly if the weather changes.

"Where is he?" Brehm asks the ranger. The ranger points to a place high atop the headwall.

"Right about there, I'm guessing," the ranger says. "At the top of the fixed line."

"What'd they say the symptoms were?"

"They found him unconscious at eighteen and carried him down to seventeen, I think," the ranger says. "That's all I know. I guess they got him in a tent and a sleeping bag."

"Who brought him down?"

"I don't know."

It sounds to Brehm, though he'll reserve his diagnosis until he sees the patient, like high altitude cerebral edema, or HACE, a swelling of the tissue lining the brain at high altitudes that begins as the worst headache you've ever had in your life and ends in unconsciousness and, if left untreated, death. It happens like this. The body responds to hypoxia, or oxygen starvation, by increasing the blood pressure, which accelerates the release of leukotrienes, which increases arteriolar permeability, allowing the passage of fluids into extravascular locations. In other words, your blood pressure rises so high your blood vessels spring leaks. Strenuous exercise only makes it worse, and climbing is strenuous exercise. A guy goes into his tent to rest and doesn't come out, and at first you think maybe he's just sleeping, so you leave him be, but then you can't wake him, and you pry back his eyelids and see two fixed dilated pupils.

Li'l Orphan Annie eyes, PJs call them.

A similar thing can happen to your lungs when the lack of atmospheric pressure induces a pulmonary edema, a swelling of the lung tissues that expresses itself as short or labored breathing, full of crackles and rales, an abnormally fast heartbeat, possibly blue skin, and a general weakness, lethargy, or disorientation. Climbers, to test for the signs of possible pulmonary edema, frequently cough and spit and check their saliva for signs of blood. Pink spit is not good. Body fluids change color at altitude. If your pee turns bright orange, it means you're dehydrated, a condition that can really sneak up on you, because you forget how dry the air around you is.

Mountaintops are like arctic deserts, with near zero percent humidity, air that sucks the moisture out of you, drying out your lungs, particularly breathing as deep and as fast as you do, even when the wind isn't blowing, and when it is . . .

You don't want to think about when the wind blows, and the wind inevitably blows.

There's really only one way to treat altitude sickness. Get the victim lower. It's sort of like the guy who goes into the doctor and says, "My arm hurts when I do this," and the doctor says, "Well then, don't do that."

"We can go," Skip Kula tells the rangers. It makes perfect sense. They are acclimated, prepared, and they have experience in such matters. It isn't why they're on the mountain, but it would make the climb a bit more interesting, Brehm thinks, though it could mean forgetting any summit attempt for the entire party. They've come prepared for a training mission, not a rescue, and don't have all the equipment they need, but rescue equipment is already in place, stored in a chest at 17,000 feet for just such an emergency. The PJs have a single Saber walkie-talkie with them, a National Guard issue sixteen-channel programmable FM radio. The rangers have handheld walkie-talkies and will be able to maintain radio contact with Brehm's group for as long as the batteries last. Batteries don't last very long in extreme cold. Jack Brehm, Wayt, Lupenski, Lenz, Daigle, Kula, Brooks, Abrams, Blinkhorn, and Chapin get in their tents and try to sleep. They awake at 5:30 A.M., the morning of the twenty-third, and leave Fourteen Camp at 7:00 A.M. hoping to reach the Korean by late afternoon. Wayt and Lupenski leave a half an hour before the others, because they've been leading the way and killing it the whole trip, young and in shape and feeling good. Some guys just take to altitude better than others. And then there are the freaks of nature, the guys who in the parlance are simply "genetic," climbers like Reinhold Messner or the late Alex Lowe, guys who could climb to the summit and back in a day. Wayt and Lupenski aren't genetic. They're just young and in shape and feeling good.

Before leaving that morning, Jack Brehm takes his Gore-Tex and pile hat off and applies a heavy coating of sunblock to his already reddened face and neck, SPF 50. With his fair skin, he has reason to worry about sunburn. Inexperienced climbers wear hats and goggles, but they don't realize how fierce the sun can be at that elevation, and don't take into account the fact that it's going to reflect off the surface of the snow and bounce back at you from all angles, and this with considerably less oxygen between you and the sun to block or filter the ultraviolet rays. People get sunburned inside their nostrils, or on their gums if they're walking along with their mouths open, sucking air. Skip Kula once got sunburned on the roof of his mouth. It's particularly important that Brehm, Wayt, Daigle, and Lupenski keep their hats on because before the climb they all shaved their heads at a party at Mike McManus's house, leaving only Jolly Green Giant footprints above the hairline.

They set off toward the headwall. People in Anchorage are still asleep in their warm beds, or eating cornflakes, watching the *Today* show.

Brehm and Kula reach the unconscious body of Kim Hong Bin around 6:30 P.M. after an exhausting eleven-hour climb that took two hours longer than anticipated, with only a few five-minute breaks. Wayt and Lupenski are waiting at the top, eating, rehydrating, and just resting. Lenz, Abrams, Chapin, and Daigle follow at their own pace and will be there soon. Brooks and Blinkhorn took themselves off the rescue and stayed at Fourteen Camp because they were having physical problems. Brehm finds the tent. Kim is tucked inside a sleeping bag. He has one other Korean with him, a man who speaks a very broken form of English. A quick examination of the Korean confirms Brehm's original diagnosis. Hypothermia and cerebral edema. His pupils are dilated and sluggish and he is unresponsive to stimuli. His pulse is extremely slow, as is his breathing, and his core temperature, taken with a rectal thermometer, is down to about 88 degrees. Whoever placed him in his sleeping bag inexplicably left his arms outside the bag. They are now frozen solid. Kula suspects that the Korean's hands, seriously discolored, have somehow been frozen, thawed, and refrozen, which means he's probably going to lose his hands.

"Do you know what happened?" Kula asks the Korean waiting with Kim Hong Bin.

"No," the second Korean replies.

"Who was climbing with him? Was he with you?"

"No."

"He wasn't with you?"

"Alone. Climbing alone."

"Solo."

"Yes. With a partner."

"He was climbing solo with a partner?"

"Yes. But his partner got sick. He went back."

"And you found him?"

"Excuse me?"

"You found him?"

"No. We give him oxygen."

"That's good."

"I'll ask around," Brehm says, hoping he can find someone who knows more about what happened.

No one at Seventeen Camp has come out of their tents to greet the rescuers, so Brehm goes knocking. Tents become insular fortresses on mountaintops, and people rarely visit each other or interact. The tents at 17,000 are even more insular because you have to dig a deep trench to pitch them in, or else they'll blow away. Standing on the Autobahn, looking down, you could have a hard time seeing the camp, even on a clear sunny day, because the tents are so dug in. Brehm has some luck. A Frenchman from one of the other parties says he believes Kim had been placed in his tent by another group two days earlier. He thinks a couple of expedition guides found the guy up by Denali Pass, dazed and vomiting, with a weak pulse and aching lungs, too sick to move. The Frenchman and members of his group took turns checking on Kim, at least until the other Koreans arrived, but there'd been no change. The fact that Kim's arms were outside his bag when the PJs found him indicates to Brehm that no one looked too closely at the injured climber's condition, but it's been Brehm's experience that people often prefer to close their eyes and hope for the best instead of opening them and learning the worst. A second group of Koreans say they couldn't help their countryman because they have a sick climber of their own to attend to, a man suffering from headaches and periodic unconsciousness—the early stages of cerebral edema. The man is barely conscious, but Brehm manages to administer doses of Decadron, a synthetic adrenocortical steroid, to reduce the swelling, and Diamox, a carbonic anhydrase inhibitor that promotes diuresis and controls fluid secretions.

Four hours later, the man is in better shape.

Unfortunately, Decadron and Diamox are tablets and must be given orally every four hours. They work prophylactically as well, but they won't help somebody who's already unconscious. Even if the other climbers at Seventeen Camp had been able to diagnose what was wrong with Kim Hong Bin, there is little they could have done, and perhaps they knew that the only real treatment is to descend. They could have used their body heat to warm up the Korean, but it's an exchange, and what heat he gains you lose. The rule in such situations seems to be this: You have an obligation to help somebody else who's in trouble if you can, but you're not obliged to put yourself in jeopardy, and it's your call as to exactly what that means. Mountaineers have, of course, second-guessed themselves, and each other, for centuries over such things, asking when it's the right thing to do to help and when it's the wrong thing to do, reliving what they could or should have done after a tragedy. Brehm hasn't come to judge anybody. He also hasn't come to second-guess himself.

"This Frenchman over there thinks the guy's been here for a couple days," Brehm says. As he speaks, it begins to occur to him that he's very tired and still has a long night ahead of him.

"That's what the translator tells me," Kula says.

"He said before the guy passed out, he said his lungs ached, so we might have pulmonary edema on top of whatever else."

"This guy's in rough shape. We need to talk about whether or not we can do this."

"Whether?"

"Not whether—how. Let's see what we've got to work with."

The rescue cache is a six- by four- by two-foot wooden container, painted red with a white cross marked on the top of it. A twelve-foot pole with a red flag on the end of it marks the location, in case the box was to be covered over by blowing snow. Brehm and Kula open the box, which is crammed with 600-foot lengths of perlon climbing rope, each with a tensile strength of 1,800 pounds, as well as carabiners, pickets, and snow anchors, called snow flukes. They find a couple of K bottles of oxygen, a spare tent, spare sleeping bags, and a first-aid kit. The rangers had assured them that there would be enough rope to reach Fourteen Camp. A Cascade litter, essentially a seven-foot-long molded plastic bucket, is roped to the back of the box. Brehm unfastens the litter while Skip sorts through the ropes. Garth Lenz and Steve Daigle and the others arrive.

"What's the situation?" Lenz asks.

"The situation sucks," Kula replies. He radios to the park rangers what they've found.

The ground they stand on is bare, windswept pink granite and hard-packed snow, a treeless expanse about the size of a couple of football fields. Looking down, you can see Fourteen Camp, then endless mountain ranges as far as the eye carries. The view from here is legendary. A wounded climber under his own power might be able to descend the same way he'd come up, but an unconscious man has to go down the hard way, lowered on ropes following a couloir or crease in the headwall, which is partly visible from Fourteen Camp. Jack Brehm begins tying lengths of rope together, using a series of double fisherman's knots, but to do so, he's forced to remove his heavy down-filled mittens, leaving only a thin pair of navy blue polypropylene liners between his bare skin and the wind. His fingers are quickly numb, which slows the knot-tying process. His thought processes slow down as well, something he's aware of but can do nothing about, other than to work carefully and double-check each knot he ties to make sure it will hold. Hypoxia robs a man of his ability to reason, like a computer that's not getting enough juice to drive its programs, and that includes spatial reasoning, such that a knot might look fine from one angle and wrong from another. Brehm works carefully, knowing that a flawed brain is, at some level, incapable of accurately measuring or assessing itself. He's tied knots like this a thousand times and has faith that his hands will remember what to do. He hopes muscle memory is more reliable than mental memory—that's what Mike McManus always taught, the reason he wanted his PJs to jump a hundred parachute jumps, just to establish muscle memory—"Fifty jumps is when you're dangerous, because that's when you start to think you know what you're doing. . . ." Jack wonders what Mike's up to, and whether or not anyone has informed him that a rescue is in progress. *Maybe he's watching television right now, or sipping a hot cup of . . .* Then Jack realizes that his focus is drifting, and he tries to concentrate anew on the tasks at hand.

They establish an equalizing triangular anchor system, using snow flukes, an ice ax, and a rock. Each anchor will bear a third of the load, or about two hundred pounds. In theory, any one anchor should be strong enough to hold, were the other two to give way. From above, two men will hold the rope at all times, lowering it hand over hand, braking with a four-carabiner rig. Two men will go down with the litter and guide it over any potential snags, as well as traversing it around obstacles or crevasses, which will be taxing where gravity prefers to pull things down in a straight line. There will be no way for the men going down with the litter to communicate with the men up top, though conceivably the rangers at Fourteen Camp might be able to spot the litter with their binoculars and radio up progress reports. Going down the headwall with the litter is going to be the hard part. Whoever's in the best shape should go. Skip Kula polls his team members. There's no call in this kind of situation for false bravado—claiming to feel better than you actually do is only going to get everybody else in bigger trouble. Jack Brehm and Skip Kula have been working feverishly since their arrival and need to recover. Lupenski and Wayt have been working with them, but they got there first and have had some time to recover. Abrams, the Brit, and Chapin, the Navy SEAL, shake their heads.

"I'm pretty good," Lenz says.

"I could be better," Daigle says.

"I'm fine," Wayt says.

"Same here," Lupenski answers.

"So we can do this?" Kula asks. "Everybody feels good about it?"

Everyone nods.

Steve Lupenski and Mike Wayt will go down with the litter. They are strong as bulls, and as fed, rested, and acclimated as anyone within a thousand miles could be. They've also been displaying sound judgment and are perhaps the most mentally ready members of the group. At this time of year, light will not be a problem, available twenty-two out of twenty-four hours a day. Even at the darkest part of the night, the light will still be greater than a full moon at sea level. Getting him a thousand feet lower might help the Korean, so it's decided to begin lowering Kim Hong Bin immediately. Delay could mean death. Left untreated, high-altitude cerebral edema can often proceed with great rapidity, from stupor to coma to death from massive cerebral hemorrhaging. Hypothermia is an equal danger. Eighty-eight degrees is an extremely low core temperature. Death from hypothermia works like this: First your peripheral blood vessels constrict to prevent the blood from reaching the cooler extremities. Adrenaline is released. Heart rates and respiratory rates increase. Blood pressure goes up. The body generates heat from shivering, which can continue until the core temperature drops to about 86 degrees. The shivering ceases when glucose or glycogen, or the insulin needed for glucose transfer, is no longer available, and there's no fuel left to burn. After the shivering stops, cooling is rapid. Respiration, pulse, and blood pressure decrease, the blood pH decreases, and electrolyte imbalances occur. The heart, which is racing, slows down and becomes highly irregular, sputtering and backfiring like some ancient two-stroke lawn mower engine running on fumes. Electrocardiographic changes occur, with, according to the textbook, "prolonged PR, QRS and QT intervals, obscure or absent P waves, ST-segment and T-wave abnormalities and J or Osborn waves present at the junction of the QRS complex and ST segments." In other words, a last few sparks of the fire that used to be you fly up into the sky, and then the fire goes out. Cardiac and respiratory arrest occurs at around a core temperature of 68 degrees.

If Kim lost consciousness before reaching the shivering stage, it's possibly a good thing because it might mean his body still has some fuel left. However, moving someone that cold can bring on a heart attack. The sleeping bag and blankets they wrap him in before securing him to the Cascade litter insulate him, but sleeping bags only contain and slow the release of your own body heat. They give heat back to you, but they don't generate it. The way you stay warm in an arctic environment is to work up a sweat, get your body temperature up to 101 or 102 degrees, and then trap that heat in the air around you.

"Hang on a second," Wayt says. "Have we got anything to cover the guy's face?"

"Don't block his airway," Kula says. "Just cinch the bag up good."

The temperature is about zero, not terribly cold. Thirty below zero would be about normal for this elevation at this time of year. Jack Brehm and the others are, however, becoming increasingly concerned with the wind, which has been blowing at 15 to 25 knots during the day but which has now increased to 40 to 60 knots, somewhere on the Beaufort scale between a Force 9 gale and Force 11 violent storm. Any winter activities enthusiast knows that the wind layer of your clothing is as important as the insulting layer, perhaps more important. The First Law of Thermodynamics states that energy cannot be created or destroyed. The Second Law of Thermodynamics states that heat will flow from hot to cold objects. Blowing on a cup of hot coffee cools the coffee by increasing the number of cooler air molecules that come in contact with the warmer coffee molecules. The same thing happens when wind blows across the human body. The irony is that up so high, where there's so little oxygen, so much of it can come at you all at once in the form of wind. A 50-knot wind at sea level feels quite different from a 50-knot wind at 17,000 feet—up that high, it feels dangerous, as if your clothes and your skin don't so much stop the wind as filter it as it blows through you and sucks the heat from your core. Even with 99 percent of your body covered, you know a wind like that stands a good chance of killing you. All you can really do is get out of it.

Brehm feels himself weakening as he fights the desire to become lazy and bug out and let somebody else take over, but for his entire career he's never wanted to be the guy who flagged, the guy who dragged the others down by losing enthusiasm. He has a headache. Thinking is becoming difficult. They've done a major climb in eleven hours and haven't had time to stop and rest once they reached their goal. He's anxious. He wishes the wind wasn't picking up. Feeling the wind gusting, Wayt and Lupenski, wearing only wind shells, polar fleece and polypropylene long underwear, decide to don their down insulating layers, just in case. They expect to zip the guy down in an hour or so and probably won't need the extra layer, but you never know. If you have too much insulation on, and you work up a sweat, you can overheat, even in conditions like this. The down makes them bulkier, but that might make them more comfortable and help pad them, if they ever need to sit on or lean against the irregular ice surfaces of the couloir.

"We're set," Wayt says.

"Steve?" Kula asks.

"Let's do it," Lupenski says, looking in the direction of the wind, which seems to be coming down on them from the top of the mountain.

"Don't eat all the cheeseburgers in Talkeetna—save some for us," Brehm says.

"I want to go, too," the Korean translator says, stepping forward. A new development. Kula assesses the change in plans. It's unlikely that Kim Hong Bin is going to wake up and need translating, but the guy, whatever his name is, seems to be in pretty good shape, and it's really up to him.

"You okay?" Kula says. "Are you rested?"

The translator nods.

"When's the last time you ate?"

"Just eat," the translator says. "Much food."

Kula agrees that he can go, as long as he doesn't get in the way or interfere. The translator nods his head to say he understands. Then he tries to pay Mike Wayt a compliment, and probably means to say something like, "You are very brave," or perhaps, "You are very selfless," but what actually comes out of his mouth is, "You are very handsome."

Wayt doesn't know what to say.

They begin lowering the Korean around eight in the evening, letting out a few feet of rope at regular intervals. Mike Wayt works on the Korean's right side, anchored to the lowering rope, just above where it's tied to the litter, with Lupenski on the Korean's left, tethered to the bottom of the litter. The translator follows on his own. Kim Hong Bin weighs about maybe 140 pounds. After the first 150 feet of rope, the three men are out of sight. For the first thirty minutes, Brehm and Daigle at the belaying station can feel the tug of the weight as it descends, but after a certain point the friction of the rope against the rock face and the play in the perlon fibers makes it harder and harder to tell what's going on, the way fishing with a lot of line makes it harder to tell when you've got a bite. You could lose all or part of your load at the other end and not know it unless you start retrieving line. Muscling the litter back up if something were to go wrong down below isn't really an option.

They drop the litter down about five hundred feet, and then the storm hits. It is perhaps nine o'clock. The wind picks up to 60 or 70 knots, with intermittent white-outs. It's ferociously cold. Anyone who hasn't already donned his down insulating layer does so now. Kula tells the others to set up tents as soon as possible. Chapin and Abrams have been digging in, but they are the least familiar with mountaineering, so Kula reminds them to use common sense and to stake everything down so that it doesn't blow away. He tells Daigle that they're going to need to eat. Daigle says he'll see what they've got. Brehm and Lenz pay out line. In wind this fierce, the temptation is overwhelming just to curl up in a ball and protect yourself. Brehm thinks, *If it's this bad for us, it's got to be worse for the guys down below.*

It is. Wayt and Lupenski have by now pretty much given up on zipping the guy down in an hour. It is grunt work, pure and simple, moving the litter, nudging it this way and that, lifting it over obstacles or stopping it from skidding down too fast, looking below them to check where they place their crampons, occasionally stepping on and harpooning their own pant legs, ripping the fabric, down feathers flying. They use the rope as an anchor, but they don't want to let it bear the entire weight of the patient. When the storm hits them, their situation goes from bad to worse. Hard granular snow is pelting down on them from above, to where they can't look up without getting hit in the face hard with a shovelful of pebbles. As long as the line is being payed out from above, they have no choice but to keep moving. Sometimes the white-out conditions cease, and they can see the camp down below, and the lights and shapes of somebody coming up to meet them below the *bergschrund,* but they still have a long way to go. They are tired. They are not comfortable. They have no choice. They keep going.

"The guy's slipping," Lupenski says.

"I've got him," Wayt says. The translator looks on.

"No—he's slipping inside the litter."

Kim Hong Bin has slumped down inside his plastic sled, turned a bit to the side, and his face is clogging with snow. He needs to be repositioned and adjusted, but it's difficult to work with him while the litter itself is moving. On a true rescue mission, they would have a radio with them to tell the team above to stop lowering for a moment, but they don't, so they improvise. Wayt and the volunteer translator take the weight of the litter and hold it in place while Lupenski sees to the patient. He clears his airway, repositions him and tightens the straps holding him in place, then gives Wayt the thumbs up. The procedure takes no more than five minutes. Wayt is having trouble feeling his fingers. It feels as if the temperature is dropping. They move the patient down another fifty feet or so and then the litter stops. They give the line a tug. They realize that somehow they're at the end of their rope, but they still have a long ways to go. There was supposed to be enough rope to reach the bottom. How many sections had there been in the rescue cache? Two? Three? They can't remember. Were they six hundred feet long, or three? They can see a group below them, a long way off. All they can do is wait, totally exposed, while the storm rages all around them.

Above, Brehm rests while Kula and Lenz pay out line. They keep lowering until they're out of rope. Brehm looks over the edge, even though there's nothing to see. The storm is sapping their strength. Skip Kula tells Chapin and the others to start putting up tents, and to be sure to stake everything down in the wind. Then he calls the park ranger at Fourteen Camp on the radio.

"Have you got 'em?" Kula asks.

"Negative," the ranger replies. "We had 'em for a while but then we lost 'em. It's blowing pretty good."

"Say again?"

"Negative," the ranger below says again. "They were maybe a third of the way down the couloir when we lost 'em."

"You're sure about that?"

"Estimated."

"We're out of rope," Kula says.

"You're still short," the ranger says.

"They have to be farther down than that."

"Well, we don't see 'em," the ranger says. "We've got a party going up to meet 'em—maybe they see 'em."

Kula crosses to Brehm.

"We need more rope!" Kula shouts above the wind.

They tie on three sections of their own personal rope, another 450 feet, but they are still short. Brehm goes from tent to tent to scrounge line. The alternative is to wait another twenty-four hours for somebody to bring rope up from below, and they don't have that much time, not with two of their guys and the Korean clinging to the headwall, exposed to the elements. The problem is that loaning your rope to somebody on a mountaintop is not unlike giving your water to somebody in the desert. It may be the most crucial part of your equipment. Nobody will give you all the rope they have, but people usually bring along spares. Brehm manages to borrow one length from the Frenchman, and another from the Koreans.

"Can you see them?" Kula shouts into the walkie-talkie. The wind is howling. His radio is fading.

"Repeat," the ranger asks.

"Can you see them now?"

"Negative."

Brehm is standing at the belaying station when he looks up and sees what he thinks is a large bird flying overhead. A bird or else some kind of low-flying aircraft. There is a kind of Eurasian crow called the chough that nests on Mount Everest at about 27,000 feet. The Everest crows feed on the garbage left behind by climbers, as well as on carrion—on whatever dies up there, which can include the bodies of unlucky climbers. The chough's favorite part of an unlucky climber is the eyes. Neither birds nor airplanes are likely to be found flying above Mount McKinley, so Brehm is puzzled until he realizes, slowly, forcing himself to accept the idea, that it isn't a bird or an airplane, but rather it's the tent they've been attempting to erect for the last hour, blown clean off the mountain. Jack Chapin, the Navy SEAL, used only a single picket to stake down the tent he was working on, and now it's gone. They have two other tents with them, low-profile models made from heavy nylon for just such environments, but it's taken all their best efforts to put up the first one, and now it's gone. Brehm experiences a sinking feeling, a momentary sense of hopelessness, a feeling that even though he knows what further steps to take, it doesn't matter. It's too late. It hurts to breathe. It hurts to swallow. It hurts to blink. He feels nauseated and weak, and senses that he's getting weaker.

Is this how I'm going to die? Brehm briefly thinks. He just as quickly pushes the idea away, but at the very least he feels certain they are about to change over from rescuers to rescuees. To a PJ, there is no worse feeling than that.

Kula calls a meeting. They've sent all their rope down the mountain. They are exhausted after rising at 5:30 in the morning and laboring non-stop since then. They haven't eaten. It's approaching 11 P.M. Somebody has to go down the rope and find out what's wrong, and perhaps establish a second belaying station from a lower elevation. Another poll is taken. Brehm's fingertips are frostbitten from taking his mittens off to tie the knots. Daigle's still not good, and Chapin and Abrams are inexperienced. It's decided that Garth Lenz will go down to see what the problem is.

"We gotta get warm," Skip says. Until Garth Lenz comes back, there's nothing they can do. All six men turn their full attention to getting out of the cold. Perhaps two hours later, they are inside their shelters, heating water over small propane stoves and mixing it with powdered cocoa. The hot fluids raise their core temperatures, and the food they eat refuels them, Ramen noodles, candy bars, rice with Tabasco sauce in it, butter, and dehydrated carbohydrates. Brehm isn't hungry. In today's fitness-conscious culture, most people think of a calorie as something that makes us fat, but a calorie is a unit of heat, not fat, measuring the amount of energy it takes to raise one cc or milliliter of water one degree centigrade at sea level. In extreme cold, you can think of each calorie you eat as perhaps another couple minutes of life. The best source of calories is fat, which is why scientists working at the poles sometimes gnaw on sticks of pure butter as if they're eating a Slim Jim, and why when a polar bear kills a bearded seal he'll eat the fat and leave the muscle tissue. Part of mountain sickness, ironically, includes the loss of appetite, part of the cascade of biological events that makes surviving in extreme cold so difficult. Brehm eats as much as he can force down, and it doesn't taste good, and it doesn't make him feel better, but it's fuel, and he needs fuel.

Before getting into his sleeping bag, Brehm takes his first Diamox tablet. His skull pounds. He tries to think back to the moment when he thought, *Is this how I'm going to die?* Had he felt afraid? Sad? Disappointed? He can't remember anymore. The moment has passed. The wind has blown the memory away, and that's just as well.

Down below, Mike Wayt looks up and sees a tent blowing away in the wind, and his first thought is that somebody must be in it. The wind is blowing hard enough to do that, but the tent drifts out and floats down too slowly for there to be somebody in it. He's not thinking clearly, and he knows it. He also knows they haven't moved in over an hour, and they can't stay where they are. He's exhausted. So is Lupenski. They talk over their situation. The translator looks on. He probably isn't understanding much of what's being said. They decide that Lupenski will climb down to meet the group coming up from below and borrow some rope from them. Wayt and the translator will stay with the litter.

Lupenski moves off to the right, maneuvering around the *bergschrund.* There may well be crevasses covered over with snow that he risks falling into. No one can guess anymore what time it is or how long they've been there. The wind gusts to 80 knots. Wayt watches Lupenski go. He looks up the mountain, where Garth Lenz is descending the rope into a field of *sastrugi* ice. Lenz sees a snag in the line where the rope is coiled up in the rough ice. He has no idea what the situation is down below, but he can see what the problem is here. He frees the line with his ice ax.

Below, the litter goes into sudden rapid free fall. Wayt doesn't know what's happening. The Korean translator is standing below the litter and manages to grab it. Wayt tries to hang on and stop it from falling. He digs his crampons into the ice, but it's no good. They skid down a hundred feet, gaining speed. The translator digs in, and Wayt digs in even harder, because he knows if it goes any faster, they'll never stop it, and if it goes, he goes. Wayt wrestles the litter to a stop and holds it there. The translator trades places with him as Wayt drives his ax into the ice at the bottom of the litter, swinging with all his might. The line above him "esses" down on top of him. What happened? Where is it all coming from?

He calls out for help. He doesn't remember screaming, but perhaps he did. Lupenski returns to the litter and drives his ice ax into the mountain to help secure the package. They pound pickets in and fasten the litter to the pickets with carabiners. Wayt gasps for air, exhausted, still gripping the litter with all his might. Lupenski tells him he can let go.

They reassess their new position. They're off course now, with a large crevasse directly below them. They are getting frostbitten, feeling nauseated, confused, and bone-tired, wobbly legged. They need to rest. The storm hasn't let up. The patient has to be getting worse. Time is running out on him. They pause to regain their strength, but it's waning. Gravity wants to pull the Cascade litter into the crevasse. Wayt and Lupenski use their ice axes as anchors to establish a new belaying station and begin to move the litter sideways, swinging it pendulum-fashion. Lenz reaches them two hours later, about the same time that Roger Robinson, the park ranger, climbs up from below. Then the rest of the group from Fourteen Camp, mostly guides and experienced climbers, reaches them and Mike Wayt and Steve Lupenski finally get a chance to sit. They are utterly exhausted, hands trembling, almost punch drunk and zombified. When

Wayt tries to tell Roger Robinson how tired he is, he overhears one of the others say, in what seems to be disdain, "Yeah, well, we're all tired."

Wayt doesn't have the strength to get up and punch him out, so he can only stare at the guy. He's given everything he has, and this guy wants more?

"We got 'em," Fourteen Camp radios to Skip Kula, about seven the next morning. Nearly twelve hours have passed since the rescue began.

"Say again?" Kula radios back.

"They're good—they made it in," the ranger says, just as Kula's radio goes dead, but that's all Kula needs to know. The weather has cleared. Jack Brehm looks down. He figures the storm must have raged for six or seven hours. At eight, an HH-60 Pavehawk helicopter from the 210th Air National Guard base arrives to ferry Kim Hong Bin to the hospital in Anchorage. From Seventeen Camp, Skip Kula, Jack Chapin, Jack Brehm, Brian Abrams, and Steve Daigle watch in awe as the helicopter lands and takes off below them from 14,000 feet. As far as they know, this is the highest evacuation an HH-60 has ever made. The air is so thin that it seems to take forever for the helicopter to lift off, rotors spinning at top speed for quite some time before the Pavehawk's skids break free from the mountain, giving the appearance that gravity is somehow extra strong today, which is pretty much how everybody at 17,000 feet feels.

Brehm and the others return the borrowed rope, coil up the emergency lines and put them back in the rescue cache, then return to their tents, warming themselves with hot cocoa and noshing down more candy and Ramen noodles and rice with Tabasco sauce on it. Where are Girl Scouts selling cookies when you really need them? They figure they'll see Steve and Mike back in Talkeetna, the closest town to Denali, unless of course they opted to ride the helicopter all the way back to Anchorage. After what they've been through, no one would blame them. May 24 is spent recovering. Brehm fails to even make a diary entry for that day.

Those who'd stayed at 17,000 feet now need to reach the summit. It's called Summit Fever, and it could be the number one cause of death on mountaintops, even though it's not a real disease, not in the medical sense anyway. You've come all this way, probably spent all the money you have and borrowed more to get to the mountain, spent hours upon hours training, pissed off or worried to death half the people who love you, but who you know are nevertheless rooting for you and would share your disappointment if you were to fail. Climbers face up to their physical limitations and fall short all the time, but they also push themselves further than they've ever pushed themselves before because of Summit Fever.

The round trip from 17,000 feet camp to the summit is relatively easy, but you still have to cross snowfields and rugged terrain and a landscape broad enough that you can easily get lost, which is why no one is permitted to summit unless accompanied by someone who's been there before and knows the way. Some parties leave a trail of green bamboo tomato stakes or wands jammed into the snow to mark the way back, but it can still snow hard enough to cover your trail. You travel light and leave behind anything you think you won't need. The sky is clear on May 25, the temperature a balmy zero degrees, winds still blowing between 40 and 60 knots. The remaining rescuers take the Autobahn to Denali Pass, cross the Football Field and make it to the peak at 5:30 P.M., feeling satisfied but not exhilarated. They're glad to summit, but it's a better feeling to know that Steve and Mike and the Korean are down. Besides, once you're on top of a mountain, there's really not much you can do except have your picture taken, catch your breath, drink some water, and start down. It's getting there that's important, not being there. After months of preparation and nervous anticipation, and thirteen days of climbing, they spend a mere ten minutes at the top. Brehm feels the way he sometimes feels at the end of a marathon, an almost religious sense of wonder, apart from any physical weariness or mental exhaustion, at what God has allowed him to accomplish. Briefly, he thinks of Carl Waage, back home in a hospital bed, breaking in a new set of lungs, and offers up a prayer for Carl's speedy recovery. If the theories are correct, prayers offered from 17,000 feet ought to reach their destination quicker than prayers from sea level.

They head down at 5:40 and make it back to their tents at Seventeen Camp by 8 P.M. To their amazement, Mike Wayt and Steve Lupenski are waiting for them.

"What the hell are you doing here?" is all Brehm can say to his old friend Steve.

"What do you think we're doing here?" Steve Lupenski says. "We came here to summit."

Brehm can only admire their determination, not to mention their stamina. Anybody else would have called it a day after hanging on to the side of a mountain for eleven hours.

"What do you mean 'we'?" Chapin says. "My feet look like chopped sirloin."

"We'll go alone then," Wayt says, determined. He doesn't feel one hundred percent, and neither does Steve, but given the shape they were in when they started, they figure 80 percent of a PJ is equal to a hundred percent of anybody else. Skip Kula shakes his head. The rule is, nobody goes to the summit unless accompanied by somebody who's been there before. Brehm knows how disappointed Wayt and Lupenski will be if they don't summit, and he knows that after what they've done, they deserve some kind of reward. It also occurs to him that it would be kind of cool to be able to say he summited Denali twice in two days.

"I'll go with them," Brehm says. "I know the way."

"You sure?"

"I'm sure."

They all spend the night together at 17,000 feet, and at 11:30 the next morning Brehm, Lupenski, and Wayt depart. The weather is clear, and when the sun rises in the sky it gets so warm, perhaps in the mid to high twenties, that Jack and Steve take off their Gore-Tex anoraks and, from the waist up, wear only their underwear. It soon becomes evident that something is wrong with Mike. He isn't saying anything, but he's moving way too slowly, out front, because whoever is moving the slowest goes first. It's even odder because for the whole trip, he's been the one leading the charge. By midafternoon his steps are barely a shuffle, moving him eight inches ahead with each stride, if you could still call them strides. He's resting every five steps, and he appears to be feeling the cold, dressed in full weather gear, though Jack and Steve are overheated. As Mike moves on ahead, Brehm, who is second, stops and waits for Lupenski to catch up to him. It's 2:00 P.M. and they've reached the 19,000-foot mark.

"What do you think?" he says quietly. Lupenski knows what he's referring to.

"What do *you* think?"

"You know him better than I do," Brehm says, "but I don't think he can do it."

"I think maybe you're right," Lupenski says. "He looks like he might be cramping."

"We could hang out for a while and see if he gets better, but we might not make the summit if we do." Brehm calculates that at the rate they're moving, the peak is perhaps another five hours ahead.

"We should turn back."

"You want me to tell him?" Brehm offers. "I'll do it if you want me to."

"I'll tell him," Lupenski says, volunteering for a task nobody relishes. "He's my friend." Brehm watches as Lupenski walks ahead and has a word with Mike. Wayt only listens and nods, and then, without saying a word, he turns around and heads down the mountain, trudging right past Brehm without looking at him. When Lupenski catches up, Jack asks him what he said.

"I told him *I* couldn't make it," Lupenski says.

It's brilliant thinking, particularly when you consider how hard it is to be brilliant at this altitude—better to take the blame himself than make his friend feel as though he was to blame for not making it to the summit. Climbing is something you do as a team, and no one wants to think he let his team down. It's also true that pararescuemen may be among the most competitive sons-of-bitches on the planet, challenging one another on everything from climbing a mountain to eating hamburgers. Mike Wayt doesn't want to go back, but it's the right decision.

As they descend, Mike Wayt doesn't get any better. This is odd. He keeps sitting down in the snow, then getting up, never saying anything about it when he does, and when they ask him how he is, he only grunts. Something seems to be wrong with his stomach, but when they ask him if he's cramping, he shakes his head. They trudge on, and then, at about 4:00 P.M., at about the point where the Autobahn begins, they hit a white-out, a weather system with the upper limit so sharply defined that it seems like they're walking into an opaque lake, or a flowing ocean of milk. Now the cloud cover is at your nose. Two steps forward, you're in over your head and you can't see a thing. Two steps back, the sky is blue again. Roped together, they take their bearings as best they can and head down into the white-out. They locate three tomato stakes somebody left and follow the line, but the fourth stake is missing, and the fifth, and then they don't know where they are. Brehm checks his watch. They wander for two and a half hours, not covering much ground due to Wayt's slowness. The terrain more or less funnels you in the right direction, but if you go too far off line, you can easily fall a thousand feet. Sometimes visibility is perhaps sixty or seventy feet, but most of the time it's less than ten. The whiteness gets to you, too, a disorienting lack of definition to everything, without any frame of reference to tell you not just where you are but who you are. It's also troubling to know that they could walk right past their target, miss it, and keep going. For a while, moving forward and down makes sense, but after a while, moving back, and up, or left, or right, all makes the same amount of sense. What if the tent camp they're looking for is covered with snow? By 6:30, Brehm decides it's futile. He discusses it with the others. They will dig down into the snow, huddle together, and try to wait the weather out. There's a chance the decision could prove fatal, but it seems the best option. They're beginning to dig in when Brehm sees a guy in the distance. Moving closer to him, they hear nylon tents whipping in the wind. The guy, it turns out, is taking a leak. You pee a lot in extreme cold, because your body has better things to do than keep a bladder full of urine warm.

"Hey," the Peeing Man says. "Are you the PJs who rescued the Korean? It figures only maniacs like you would be out in this shit."

Brehm and the others grunt in acknowledgment. The Peeing Man has, in a way, rescued them, but there's really no point telling him that. It turns out they were lost less than a hundred yards from their tent.

Mike Wayt has little to eat at Seventeen Camp. They wait two days for the weather to clear. The wind whips across their tent at 70 or 80 knots. Steve is beat. Mike is hurting and can't eat. Jack Brehm cooks food, and boils water, and spends long periods of time describing, in exquisite detail, all the kinds of food they're going to eat when they get down, thick juicy cheeseburgers with slabs of raw onion and fresh lettuce and tomatoes on a toasted bun, slathered with melted butter and mayonnaise and mustard and ketchup. . . . He stays crisp and motivated, and the others appreciate it, and draw strength from him. At 8:00 P.M. the evening of the second day, the wind slows, so they head down. Brehm's diary notes: *Winds stayed at 30 kts but it is still pretty shaky on the ridge going to the headwall. It took forever to descend the fixed line. Arrived camp 0030, 28 May '91. Made hot chocolate and went to bed. Four nights is too long to spend at 17,000 for anyone.*

They leave Fourteen Camp at 12:30 on the twenty-ninth but hit another white-out at 11,000 feet, stopping at 8,000 feet around 6:30 P.M. An HH-60 flies to the Kahiltna Glacier and picks them up, piloted by Steve Lupenski's brother Al, on the thirtieth at eleven in the morning and flies them to Talkeetna. On the tarmac at the Talkeetna Airport, the group assembles for a team picture. The picture is taken. Mike Wayt tries to smile. He's glad to be down from the mountain, and he hoped this would make him feel better, but it doesn't. He looks around him, at the piles of snow plowed to the edges of the runways, the signs for Hudson Av-Gas, Doug Geeting Aviation, and McKinley Flight Tours, and then it all starts to spin, and he feels as if he's been punched in the gut as he doubles over and falls to the ground. He's flown immediately to Elmendorf Hospital in Anchorage.

The final entry in Jack Brehm's diary is simply the word *BEER*. The exhilaration of coming down off a climb is both psychological and biological: psychological because you can simply feel good for having accomplished a difficult task, biological because your body is no longer under stress and you have residual levels of adrenaline and endorphins in your blood, not to mention the extra red blood cells. You also get to shower and shave for the first time in three or four weeks.

There are several bars on Talkeetna's main drag. They hole up in a place called the Fairview Inn, a historic tavern that's been there since 1923. It has white siding and a tin roof and all anybody really cares about is that the beer is cold. The team needs to do some serious decompressing, but everyone is concerned for Mike Wayt. Somebody calls the hospital and finally learns the diagnosis—he has a bleeding ulcer.

"How could he have a bleeding ulcer?" Daigle asks. They all had complete physicals before going on the climb and would have known if anybody had a bleeding ulcer. "Doesn't that take a long time to develop?"

"Has he been under a lot of stress lately?"

"He's got a new house and a new kid, but I don't think that would do it."

Someone says they heard that sometimes people who experience sheer terror for an extended period of time secrete enough stomach acids to cause bleeding ulcers in a matter of hours.

"How about the Korean?"

"He's okay. He's going to make it."

Lupenski raises his beer bottle in the air.

"To Mikey," he says.

"To Mikey," the rest join in.

At the hospital in Anchorage, Wayt is examined. The doctors find that the pyloric channel that links the small intestine to the stomach has perforated the peritoneal lining of his stomach. The layman's assessment is he busted a gut saving another man's life. When they operate, they remove a foot-long section of his small intestine. The operation is successful, but it will be two years before Wayt's insides feel right again, and five years before he can go for a run without stopping to find a bathroom every five minutes.

That night, lying in bed at the Swiss Alaska Motel, one of Talkeetna's finest, which is not saying a whole lot, Brehm holds the remote control and surfs between channels 2, 11, and 15, picking up bits of a rebroadcast of *M*A*S*H* and the sixth game of the NBA Western Conference finals between the Lakers and the Trailblazers, but the hotel's transponder works only sporadically. Brehm turns the television off and calls Peggy. He relates the whole trip for her, and they talk for over an hour. When he's finished, he says, "Tell Carl that when we're sitting on his porch drinking beers, I'm going to have a good story for him."

"John," Peggy says, "I've got bad news about Carl. He didn't make it."

"When?"

"A week ago. Eight days ago," she corrects herself. "I'm sorry."

As he falls asleep, he thinks that Carl Waage had a great life. He wonders if he appreciated it. Does anybody really appreciate it? He thinks of the view from 17,000 feet, and how the cheeseburger and Coke he ate at the Fairview Inn was the best food he's ever had in his life, and he thinks of Mike Wayt's courage.

12

THE NIGHT THE WIND BLEW

I have no interest in climbing Mount Everest, though I think I could probably do it. But to spend all that time and effort, just to stand at a very high place and hold a flag and have your picture taken? Knowing the risks involved, it sounds pretty stupid to me. Climbing Everest, you know you're rolling the dice on your health, with something like a 60 percent chance of coming back personally injured. In pararescue, you enjoy what you do, diving and jumping and what have you, but you always know you're doing it for a higher purpose than your own personal enjoyment. Sometimes when the daily routine gets to you, because you've had a lot of long boring days in a row doing nothing, sitting around the section waiting for the phone to ring, maybe then you forget what you're doing it for, but not when you're training. You're doing it for other people. Even when you think about dying, I think every PJ eventually asks himself not "Am I going to die in the line of duty?" but "How do I want to die?" And I think every PJ feels like if he's got to die, and he does, he wants to die trying to help somebody.

BY THE END OF OCTOBER 1991, THE FROSTBITE, WHICH HAD darkened Jack Brehm's fingertips after he returned from Mount McKinley, was all but gone. It hurt to dip them in hot or cold water, so doing the dishes or holding a beer could be painful. In regard to the latter, his high tolerance for pain proved useful. It was a gorgeous autumn, the leaves resplendently afire on the hillsides and in the backyards of eastern Long Island. Jack had never missed a Halloween night trick-or-treating with the kids. The morning before Halloween, October 30, Peggy was trying to pin everybody down at breakfast as to what costumes they wanted her to make for them, but so far the only one who knew was Jeffrey, who wanted to be a witch, which meant, Peggy gathered, a black cape of some sort. Matt and Laura-Jean were still undecided. The twins were in sixth grade, and old enough now, they argued, to be allowed to skip canvassing the neighborhood for treats with the rest of the family. Tomorrow night, Elizabeth was going to a sleepover Halloween party at her best friend Emily's house in Sound Beach, one town west of Rocky Point, and was excited about helping Emily plan a scavenger hunt in the neighborhood. Emily wanted to rent a Stephen King movie. Elizabeth didn't like scary movies, didn't like being scared in general, but knew she'd probably be outvoted by the other kids at the party.

Jack got to the base at 7:30 A.M. on the thirtieth. The National Weather Service had issued a coastal flood warning the night before, predicting tides two to three feet above normal, and Nantucket had reported sustained winds of over 45 knots. At 9:05, the Coast Guard's first District Operations Center in Boston had requested assistance from the 106th in searching for a surf caster who'd disappeared off Point Judith, Rhode Island, swept from the rocks after apparently ignoring the coastal flood warnings. A C-130 was launched to look for him. The Coast Guard's Operations Center in Boston also asked, approximately one hour after the call about the fisherman, if the 106th could respond to an EPIRB, or Emergency Position Indicating Radio Beacon, coming from something in the water at 38°32′N and 69°13′W, about 180 miles south of Nantucket. By noon, there was still no word on what the SOS beacon meant. A weather system of some sort appeared to be forming far offshore, but it was moving south and west instead of north and east, the way a hurricane ordinarily moves. Because of it, at 1:00 P.M., an HH-60 crew was put on alert. The PJ section was calm, and outside the skies were blue and the air was warm. Everything seemed to be under control, so around two, Brehm decided to go for a run to the beach and back, a distance of about six miles. It was warm enough that he wore only a T-shirt. The ocean looked rough, with five- to six-foot swells, but nothing outrageous. No one at the 106th knew yet that at 38°32′N and 69°13′W, a 30-foot sailboat, the *Bazaro,* occupied by a lone forty-five-year-old Japanese yachtsman named Mikado Tomizawa, sailing from New York to Bermuda, was foundering in 35-foot seas, taking on water, while the weather around him worsened. No one knew yet that this was the beginning of what would become the "Storm of the Century," written about in Sebastian Junger's *The Perfect Storm.*

As Brehm jogged, a Coast Guard C-130 reached the *Bazaro.* When they did, Tomizawa radioed to them that he was going down. At 2:50 P.M., the 106th was asked to proceed to 37°52′N and 68°44′W, the *Bazaro* having drifted fifty miles since that morning's SARSAT fix, the location determined by the search and rescue satellite that picked up the emergency signal. By 3 P.M., the helicopter pilot for the mission, veteran (and former PJ) CAPT Dave Ruvola, thirty-four, was meeting in the briefing room in the Ops building with his copilot, CAPT Gram Buschor, LTCOL Bob Stack, the C-130 pilot, and the C-130's navigator, all going over aeronautical charts and weather reports. The Coast Guard C-130 on the scene reported a visibility of one and a half miles, winds from the northwest at 22 knots, and 25- to 35-foot seas. Ruvola and Buschor agreed that the HH-60 would need to make four midair refuelings, two going out and two coming back. There were two PJs on the schedule to be on alert that day, Jack's friend John Spillane, thirty-four, and a thirty-two-year-old tech sergeant named Arden "Rick" Smith. Smith was one of the last PJs McManus hired, a truly solid guy and one of Jack's favorites. Jack had flown a mission with him back in October of 1989, when, on the evening of the seventeenth, an earthquake registering 7.0 on the Richter scale rolled the city of San Francisco. PJs from Moffett AFB, outside of Palo Alto, including Jack's old classmate Joe Higgins, were on the scene immediately, searching the collapsed wreckage of buildings and highway bridges for survivors, despite fears of aftershocks. Jack and Rick flew to California the next day in a C-130 to assist in the rescue effort, at the request of RCC at Scott, only to be told ten minutes prior to landing that the request had been canceled. They weren't sure what the confusion was all about, but apparently it had something to do with the State of California wanting to prove it could handle its own emergencies using only state personnel. Whatever the reason, the C-130 from the 106th needed to have some mechanical work done before it could return to base, so Brehm and Rick Smith made the best of it and drove to Lake Tahoe to play blackjack. When they finally flew home, they were met at the base by a local television news crew doing a story on the dramatic return of the heroic earthquake rescue team. Jack saw the news crew's truck parked on the tarmac as they landed. He and Rick talked it over and decided the simplest thing to do would be to refuse all interviews. The local media saw their reticence as an expression of selfless heroism.

Spillane and Smith were in the Life Support section, gathering up the gear they were going to need, when Jack came in from his run. Their gear included cold-water orange Mustang immersion suits, quarter-inch wet suits, LPUs, and survival vests carrying signal mirrors, PRC-90 radios, MK-13 flares, pen gun flares, strobe lights, and survival knives.

"What's up?" Brehm asked.

"Got a mission," Spillane said, filling Jack in and explaining that a Japanese sailor, sailing solo around the world, apparently wanted off his boat. Rick Smith let Spillane do all the talking, Smith being a quiet man who tended to choose his words carefully. Brehm was happy for both of them, because you live for the missions, and even a bit disappointed that he'd been out running and couldn't take the mission himself. It's the NCOIC's job to decide who takes the missions as they come up, according to who's available and who's mission-ready, current with all his qualifications. Spillane and Smith were two of the best he had to send, and it sounded like a gravy mission. It was also going to be their first save using the new HH-60 aircraft, after switching over from the old HH-3s.

"I'll drive you to the AC," Brehm said. It's only about four hundred yards from the Operational Dispatch Center to the helicopter pods, but they needed to make haste, both because the *Bazaro* was foundering and because they wanted to be on site before the sun went down. The blades of the HH-60 Jolly 10 (with the number 110 painted on the side) were already turning when they got there. A C-130 with the number AFR 988 on the tail was taxiing to the runway. The other three C-130s assigned to the wing were down for maintenance. Dave Ruvola was the pilot. Gram Buschor was the copilot. The flight engineer was a Guardsman from New Jersey named Jim Mioli.

"You boys have a good one," Brehm said, shaking hands with his PJs before they left. "I'll see you when you get back."

The two aircraft launched around 3:30, and for the next three hours, the pilot of Air Force Rescue 988 radioed back progress reports, which were noted in the daily log. At 4:25, the tanker passed 700 pounds of fuel to the HH-60, Ruvola making contact with the drogue on the first attempt. Sunset that day came at 4:47 P.M., EST. At 5:00, Jolly 10 took on 900 more pounds to top off its tanks, expecting to be on the scene in another twenty minutes. During the second air refueling, it took Ruvola several tries to hit the drogue, due to increased turbulence. After the refueling, AFR 988 flew on ahead to help relocate the sailboat. The Coast Guard C-130 lost visual contact with it, in seas that had risen to between forty and fifty feet. When the 106th's tanker spotted the sailboat, they dropped MK-6 smoke markers, which Ruvola was able to vector in on, reaching the boat around 6:00. Ruvola and his crew spent the next twenty-five minutes trying to figure out a way to pull Tomizawa off his boat, but the weather was simply too fierce. There was a possibility that they might have to abort. It was a difficult decision, in part because the 106th had yet to abort a mission due to weather, after arriving on site, and in the larger part because the decision posed a potential death sentence for Tomizawa. Hovering directly over the *Bazaro,* Ruvola glanced at his forward airspeed indicator, which told him he was flying in winds gusting from forty to eighty knots, or nearly one hundred miles per hour. The varying wind speeds required him to constantly adjust his power and angle of attack. On two occasions, Spillane, looking out the port-side gunner's window, had to shout to Ruvola to pull up on the collective and put more distance between the helicopter and waves cresting nearly to the Jolly 10's landing gear. Jim Mioli, the flight engineer, looked below and saw waves rising and falling higher and faster than he'd be able to compensate for, even with his hoist operating at high speed, presenting the danger of having slack in the cable with men on the penetrator. Anyone getting a finger or limb caught in a loop in the slack would probably lose the finger or limb. The light was nearly gone. When Mioli told Ruvola he'd be unable to hoist, Ruvola aborted the mission. The *Bazaro* appeared to be riding fairly well in the monstrous seas; Tomizawa was perhaps not in as much danger as he thought, so the C-130 crew dropped him an MA-1 kit, containing a pair of lift rafts and survival supplies, and radioed to Westhampton, at 7:10 P.M., that they'd topped off the Jolly's tanks with their third air refueling and were returning to base. At 7:30, LTC Stack radioed the base for a weather update and was told he could expect an 8,000-foot ceiling with fifteen miles of visibility and low-level wind shear. At virtually the same time, McGuire AFB, just south of Trenton, New Jersey, was receiving weather satellite data indicating that a rain band was forming off the southern shore of Long Island, a finger of the spiraling storm fifty miles wide, eighty miles long, and ten thousand feet thick, rain so dense as to afford zero visibility.

The daily log notes that as they returned to base Spillane and Smith were both granted an extension of CDT, or crew duty time, since it looked as if the mission was going to keep them out longer than a normal crew duty day. The mission status was Ops normal, RTB. With both aircraft returning to base, Brehm's day was done. It was after eight. Before he went home, he drove the PJ truck to Whitney's Deli, about a mile from the gate, across the street from the Matchbox, and bought a six-pack of Budweiser, Rick Smith's beer of choice. Brehm left the truck parked at the helicopter pod, with the six-pack sitting on the seat, and walked back to his car.

When Jack got home, about 9:00, Peggy had just put the twins to bed. Matt, Bean, and Jeffrey had gone down long before. Peggy was making Jeffrey's costume, sewing him a black cape, and told Jack there were leftovers from dinner that he could reheat in the microwave if he was hungry. He was about to do so when the phone rang. It was Mickey's wife, Laura, who was beside herself.

"I just called the base," Laura said, "and they hung up on me. I was asking them when they thought John was coming home and they just hung up on me."

"Who were you talking to?" Jack asked.

"I don't know."

"Laura," Jack said, "just hang on a second and I'll call the base and find out what's going on and then I'll call you back, okay?"

"I mean I know it's probably nothing."

"I'm sure everything's fine. Let me just call them and check it out. I'll call you right back. Sit tight."

Brehm called the base and explained that somebody just hung up on Laura Spillane, and that she was upset about it. When he learned the reason why, his expression changed.

"What?" Peggy said. "What is it?"

"The guy had a Mayday coming in when Laura called," Jack said.

"Why a Mayday?"

"They're ditching the helicopter," Jack said.

* * * * * * * *

In a pararescue unit, a crisis affecting one PJ affects all the other PJs, and their wives and families. When their husbands are gone on a mission, the wives depend on each other in much the same way that their husbands depend on each other. They help each other with car pools and child care. They get together socially and share their worries. They see each other at functions at the base, and at barbecues and pool parties in each other's backyards, and they often wait together at airports, or in hospitals, at awards ceremonies or memorial services. Friendships between wives sometimes outlast their marriages. Being there for each other in times of crisis is something nobody ever has to question—it's a given.

Peggy immediately calls Barbara Dougherty to say they have to get over to Laura Spillane's house. There's trouble on a mission, she says, a helicopter going down, somewhere far out at sea. No, she doesn't know why.

Yes, Mickey is on the helicopter. So is Rick Smith. Somebody should call his wife, Marianne. But somebody from the base should call her first, somebody with more information. Barbara says she needs somebody to baby-sit her kids. Jimmy is three and a half, Diana is two, and Bobby is eleven months. Michele is their regular baby-sitter, so Peggy says she'll wake her daughters up. Both girls are groggy at first.

"Michele, you're going over to Aunt Barbara's to baby-sit. Elizabeth, I need you to stay here and watch the others. I'm going to call and get somebody to come sit with you, but until I do, you're in charge."

The girls think of the other PJs at the base as uncles, and their wives as aunts, particularly the Doughertys and the Spillanes.

"Can you call Carla?" Elizabeth says. Carla Waage is her favorite sitter, their next-door neighbor.

"I'll get either her or Grandma—you want to call Carla? Go ahead and call her."

"How late are you going to be?" Michele asks, putting a raincoat on over her pajamas. Neither she nor Elizabeth have ever seen their mother this frightened before. That scares them, more than anything else. Peggy knows this, and tries to stay level and calm. "Is Dad okay?"

"Your father is fine—he just left for the base. There's been an accident out at sea, and he had to go back. I have to go to Aunt Laura's."

Rain is beating against the windows. Elizabeth looks out at the trees in the front yard, whipping back and forth in the wind like a cheerleader's pom-poms. *Something is happening at sea? What? A plane crash? A sinking ship? Someone is in trouble. Will Dad have to fly out in weather like this? This is bad. This is really bad.*

Jack is in Jimmy Dougherty's truck, the two men racing back to the base. As Jimmy drives, Jack calls Laura Spillane on Jimmy's cell phone. The windshield wipers are beating at full speed, but even then sometimes it's hard to see the road. Before he dials, Brehm tries to think of what to say. This is going to be rough on her. She's five months pregnant, too. They've been friends for years, and she needs to hear the straight truth.

"Laura, it's Jack," he says. "Listen—I'm sorry I couldn't call you before now—I'm in the car with Jimmy and we're headed back to the base. The guy said hanging up on you wasn't intentional and he's sorry, but that's what I'm calling about, because there's been an accident, okay?" He wishes he'd put it differently. He wishes he had more information. "It's not an accident, actually, but something is wrong with the AC and they're going to ditch." He hears Laura gasp. "It's not a crash, Laura—it's a controlled ditch. They're doing it on purpose. It's not like they're out of control."

"Why?" she asks. He wishes he knew the answer to that.

"Probably mechanical failure," he tells her. "We don't know. This is what we practice in the dunk tank down at Virginia Beach."

"Where are they?" she asks.

"I can't answer that. I mean, I would if I could, but I don't know the answer. I don't think they're very far out. They were within one refueling of the base, somewhere south. I'll be able to learn more when I get to the base. I imagine they're getting another bird ready to go as we speak, so Jimmy and I can fly out and pick them up. They've all got survival suits and they've trained for this. Has Peg called?"

"Not yet."

"Well, she will. She's picking up Barbara and then they'll be over. You guys wait by the phone, and I'll call you as soon as I learn anything. And if I have to fly I'll let you know, and then I'll have somebody else call you. So sit tight and hang on. Okay? He's going to be all right."

They both know Jack has to say the words "He's going to be all right," and they both know Jack is not in any position to make any guarantees.

At sea, Dave Ruvola is finding it impossible to hit the drogue with his probe to effect refueling. He's been trying since 8:00. On an ordinary night, in calm air, a circular parachute around the drogue stabilizes it, and a probe light throws a shadow that allows the pilot to center the shadow on the drogue and fly forward into it. Tonight the drogue flails wildly about in the turbulence. Ruvola is afraid the probe could hit one of his rotors. His aircraft is being buffeted around so severely he's afraid he's going to hit the tail of the C-130. Much of the time, he can't even see the drogue in the blinding rain. Much of the time, he can't even see the airplane. Ruvola is wearing NVGs, night vision goggles, a device that electronically amplifies available light. The light enters through a lens and strikes a highly charged photo cathode, which then transfers the charge across a vacuum to a phosphor screen, something like a television screen, where the image is focused, and then the eyepiece magnifies the image. The image is green because the human eye can differentiate more shades of green than other phosphor colors. Night vision goggles are so effective that if you were to put them on in a pitch-black room in your basement, a room so dark you can't see your hand five inches in front of your face, you could not only see your hand, but you could read your palm. On an ordinary night in calm air a helicopter pilot will request that the tanker turn off all its lights during midair refueling, because with night vision goggles on the lights overload the goggles. Tonight, Ruvola asks Stack to turn all his lights on, and he still can't see them, flying less than a hundred feet behind the tanker. There's that much rain. Ruvola and the tanker change altitude several times, looking for better air, but the rain band is almost two miles thick. Ruvola doesn't dare fly any lower than three hundred feet. At 9:10, flying at four thousand feet, and after thirty or forty unsuccessful attempts to refuel, the pilot of Jolly 10 decides he can either make two or three more attempts to hit the drogue, or he can avoid running out of gas and falling out of the sky like a rock by putting his helicopter, as gently as possible, into an ocean that is anything but gentle. There are no parachutes on the helicopter, and bailing out would not be the best option anyway, since it would scatter everyone to the winds. The best option is to let the crew jump out ten feet above the waves. At 9:15, Ruvola tells the tanker to tell the base he's beginning his ditch sequence. His current position is 39°37′W and 71°38′N, about sixty miles southeast of Westhampton, and over twice that from where they left the *Bazaro.* The C-130, itself low on gas, will stay on the scene for as long as it can.

Peggy Brehm and Barbara Dougherty find Laura Spillane in her bathrobe, her distended belly protruding beneath the belt. After hugs, the questions fly. Have you heard anything? Who's called? Who have you called? Who was on the helicopter? Has anyone called Marianne Smith? Carmen Ruvola? Ann Buschor—does anybody know her well? Her husband, the copilot, is new to the unit, so the PJ wives don't know him or his wife as well as they know the others. Somebody who knows her should call. Jim Mioli is single—is there anybody they should contact? Laura is reluctant to tie up the phone, because she doesn't want to miss Jack's call, but she quickly dials Mickey's brothers, and gets her mom on the phone after that. They call the other PJ wives, and everybody exchanges phone numbers. In the kitchen, Peggy makes coffee. They feel better in the kitchen, where the lights are bright. Laura has been preparing the walls to be wallpapered. The smell of plaster dust is in the air. Mickey and Laura have only been in the house for a few months. The living room has a cathedral ceiling, and the floors are bare and there isn't much furniture yet, so when the rain pounds on the roof, it feels as if they're inside a drum. When the wind blows, it feels as if it blows right through the house. The kitchen is a better place to be. A bedroom may be soft and dark, but a kitchen is the most comforting room in any house.

At the base, Brehm is in Ops, the Operational Dispatch Center, and he's on the phone. There are telephones, computers, men operating radios, the SOF's (Supervisor of Flying's) desk, and on the far wall a large magnetic white-board, scored with a grid of black lines where the names of the men assigned to aircraft are posted on magnetic tags. In one group are Ruvola, Buschor, Mioli, Smith, and Spillane, and in another the names of the C-130 crew. The overhead fluorescent lights seem bright but cold. The carpeting in the outer hallway is wet all the way to the front door, as members of the 106th who've heard about the accident report in, shaking their raincoats, everybody trying to gather information and get brought up to speed. Jack is doing the same thing, talking to the Coast Guard's Operations Center in Boston. He's made a list of all the people he has to keep posted. Jim Mioli has a sister in New Jersey, according to his file. Jack dials Laura Spillane's number, but she's too upset to answer her phone. Peggy answers instead.

"Well, the good news is, Gram got off a Mayday call to a Coast Guard cutter, which is apparently only fifteen miles away. Wait a minute." She hears Jack call out to someone else in the room with him, "Fifteen miles or fifteen minutes? Miles." He talks to Peggy again. "Fifteen miles. That's only an estimate, but they think it's about fifteen miles away, and it got the SOS, so they've changed course. That's good."

"What else?" Peggy says. She's not going to say "What's the bad news?" with Laura within earshot.

"It looks like they're going in. Ten minutes ago, they were down to forty pounds, which is like running on fumes. They've already flamed out one engine. You may not need to tell Laura that."

"I know," Peggy says. "What else? What's it like?"

"We don't know. You can probably assume that whatever it's doing here, it's doing the same thing there. Probably worse. Have you talked to the girls?"

"Carla is with Elizabeth. I'm calling my mom as soon as we hang up to go sit with Carla. I'm a little worried about Michele."

"She's tough—she'll be okay."

"There's a Coast Guard cutter, fifteen miles away," Peggy says to Barbara and Laura. "They got the distress call and they're on their way."

Barbara and Laura thank God, and they all wonder how long it will take a Coast Guard cutter to sail fifteen miles. *They can go fifteen miles an hour, can't they? It's not so bad. The boys can last for an hour in the water—they're all incredible swimmers—they can all swim for longer than that.*

Plus they have survival suits and rafts—they'll be okay. Please, God, let them be okay. . . .

Michele is on the couch at the Doughertys' house, in the dark, staring out the window at the wind ripping through the trees. When Peggy calls her, Michele says only that she's okay, and that she's very tired, but she can't sleep. Peggy gives Michele the number at the Spillanes' house. At home, Elizabeth is trying to let the television take her mind off things. She wants to cry. Carla is doing homework at the kitchen table. Elizabeth surfs past a show on A&E called *Living Dangerously*, something about volcanoes, but she isn't in the mood for disasters. TBS is showing a werewolf movie called *The Howling*, but she's not in the mood for that, either. ESPN features the U.S. Women's Body Building Championships, which is only slightly less frightening than werewolves or volcanoes. MTV has Rock 'n' Jock baseball. Larry King is interviewing Brooke Shields. Elizabeth turns the television off. She sits on the couch. She's wrapped herself in a blanket her father brought home from Korea. She feels the storm raging outside and gets angry, thinking her father might have to fly out into it to save somebody. She just wants him to come home. Why is it more important to go save other people than to stay home?

At sea, Dave Ruvola radios his final position at 9:30. He's at 39°51′N and 72°00′W. He tells his crew to bail out. Only Gram Buschor thinks to keep his night vision goggles on for the low and slow, as he looks out, trying to gauge the waves below them. Spillane, Smith, and Mioli go off goggles to perform their pre-ditching duties, throwing the doors open, readying rafts, grabbing canteens and ML-4 kits, called "butt boats." Ruvola's radar altimeter fluctuates between ten and eighty feet. Falling into the crest of a wave, ten feet below, will mean falling the same distance they ordinarily jump from when they low and slow to a rescue site, a reasonably soft landing. Falling into a trough, between waves, dropping eighty feet, will be like hitting a cement parking lot at fifty miles an hour. Fast-roping into the sea isn't an option in an aircraft that might fall at any moment. Mioli shoves a raft out the starboard side door, watches it drop clear out of sight and decides not to jump in after it. Smith and Spillane are at the port-side door, watching the waves below, listening to the helicopter's turbines wind down. Spillane unclips his gunner's belt. Rick Smith is squatting at the door. Spillane puts his arm on his shoulder. Then Smith jumps. Spillane jumps in after him. He's falling. Falling and falling. He's timed it wrong. He's falling way too far.

Peggy gets her mom on the phone and asks her to go over to the house and stay with Elizabeth. Whenever the phone rings, Peggy answers it. Friends who've heard the news call to ask if they can do anything, or bring anything over, food, coffee, anything, but Laura doesn't want anybody else in the house. Peggy worries about Marianne Smith, who has a three-week-old baby to take care of, but Marianne said her brothers and her father are coming to stay with her.

Jack and Jimmy Dougherty rush to ready a second helicopter. They drive the PJ truck to an HH-60 sitting on the tarmac outside its pod and load it full of rescue gear, wet suits, Mustang immersion suits, rafts, medical kits, but the weather is getting worse. The pilots are on the base, somewhere, and should be at the helicopter, preparing for flight, but they're nowhere to be seen. As he drives back to Ops, Jack looks over his shoulder and says to Jimmy Dougherty, "We're not going anywhere—look." The wind is rocking the helicopter back and forth. If the wind gets any stronger, it's going to blow the machine over on its side before it ever leaves the ground. Base commander LTCOL David Hill gives the order that nobody is going to fly until the weather breaks. A ground crew rolls the HH-60 back into its pod. All they can do is wait.

Brehm gets the Coast Guard back on the phone. They tell him that they've launched an HU-25 Falcon jet, which can be on the scene in minutes. The Falcon will look for strobe lights. Each man is wearing a strobe light attached to his survival vest at the shoulder, which he has to activate to make work. Once activated, a white light will blink every one and a half seconds for about twelve hours. Seeing a strobe means someone is alive, or at least that he was alive long enough to activate his strobe. Without self-illumination, a man in the water will be nearly impossible to find. The men in the water also have PRC-90 radios that have a line-of-sight broadcast range as well as receive capability and emit a beacon signal. Brehm knows that AFR 988 stayed on the scene after the ditching but was unable to raise anybody on their radios, before they were forced to RTB with a blown engine of their own. They did pick up a single signal beacon. The Coast Guard launched an HH-65, a short-range recovery helicopter, smaller than an HH-60, from Floyd Bennett Field in Brooklyn, but it was nearly driven into the sea by the winds and had to abort. Jack is told the Coast Guard also launched an HH-3. Unlike the Air Force's HH-3 helicopters, the Coast Guard's HH-3s can't refuel in midair, but they have larger gas tanks than HH-60s and can fly twice as long. Jack calls Peggy and tells her to pass on the good news, that a Falcon and an HH-3 are on the way. He doesn't tell her that nobody's radio is working. He tells her he's going to set the beeper on his watch to go off every thirty minutes to remind him to call.

At Laura's house, Peggy finds some fruit and some cheese and crackers in the refrigerator and sets it out, but nobody is hungry. She's worried about Laura who, five months into her pregnancy, should be taking it easy. They talk about what they know so far.

"The Coast Guard cutter must be getting close. Did Jack say what the name of it was?"

"The *Tamaroa*."

"How big a ship is it?"

"I don't know. It's an ocean-going tug."

"How big are they?"

"You know, Dave Ruvola is a former PJ. I mean if three out of five of them are PJs, they can help each other."

"I can't stand this. I want him to call every five minutes."

"You know what I think?"

"What?"

"I think we're going to be up for a while, and if we are, we might as well get something done."

"You're right. It's better than just sitting around."

"I'd rather do something than nothing."

"Like what? I'm not knitting anything. I hate knitting."

"Why don't we wallpaper?"

"Wallpapering is good."

"We have everything we need. Don't we?"

"I was going to do it tomorrow."

"We wallpaper then."

At Brunswick Naval Air Station in Brunswick, Maine, a Navy P-3 is being made flight-ready. It's equipped with infrared equipment that can detect heat-emitting objects. Ordinarily the equipment would be used to hunt foreign submarines, but a man in a raft presents a pretty good signal. A man alone in the water presents only a head and will be nearly impossible to detect. At sea, the storm worsens. Onshore, television meteorologists wonder if it's premature to predict a "Storm of the Century." Their instruments show a cataclysmic event unfolding in three parts, made up by a high-pressure system over Canada, a hurricane to the south, and an enormous

Great Lakes low sandwiched in between. The Coast Guardsmen are calling it the No-Name Nor'easter.

Jack calls Peggy at 11:00. She tells Jack they're about to start wallpapering the kitchen. She tells him it's hard to wait thirty minutes for news—thirty minutes seems like three hours.

At 11:50, Jack gets the best news so far—the Falcon jet picked up a radio signal on 243.0 megahertz, the international emergency beacon frequency, 14.3 nautical miles downdrift from where the helicopter ditched. The Falcon's dropmaster, wearing NVGs, has also spotted four strobes in the water, three in a group and one a half-mile away, all by itself.

"That's everybody," Peggy says, losing count.

"There's one still missing," Jack says.

"How close is the cutter?"

"I'm not sure, but the Coast Guard HH-3 is only twenty minutes away. To tell you the truth, it's pretty aggravating."

"What is?"

"We want to go and we can't. We don't even have a tanker that's flyable. One's in depot and one's in periodic and the other one's being fixed for something else. The one that just came in blew a gear box."

"Can't you go without a tanker? How far offshore are they?"

"Sixty miles," Jack says. He explains that it may seem close, but without tankers to refuel them, they'd only have fifteen or twenty minutes of loiter time once on scene, and even if they knew exactly where to go, even in good weather there's no guarantee that they'd be able to get a guy up in the helicopter in fifteen or twenty minutes. "Colonel Hill says they're not going to send another HH-60 out in the same conditions we lost the last one in. Actually they're not the same conditions—the weather's getting worse. Apparently."

"I'm sorry," is all Peggy can say. She can hear the anxiety in Jack's voice.

"Everybody's pretty frustrated," Jack says. "We're all just sitting on our hands, waiting for the Coast Guard to call us." Peggy knows Jack's frustration, knows what it's like to feel helpless, waiting for the phone to ring, just as she knows the respect the PJs and the Coast Guard have for each other. The irony of it is that half the time the PJs make a rescue, some local news stations get it wrong and give the credit to the Coast Guard. It's one reason nobody's ever heard of the PJs. "I gotta go, but I'll call again. Call me if you need to, but I'm on the phone almost constantly. I finally got a number for Mioli's sister Cathy in New Jersey—the number we had was wrong."

"I called Lorraine and told her to drive Elizabeth over to Barbara's to stay with Michele. I don't want Michele there all by herself all night."

When Brehm reaches Jim Mioli's sister, she's grateful for the news and says she'll inform the rest of the family. Her concern is for her brother but also for her brother's dog.

"His dog?"

"He takes her everywhere. She's probably in his van. Somebody should walk her. Her name is Maggie."

Jack finds somebody to get the dog. By midnight, the Ops building is crowded with airmen ready to help, pilots and copilots, navigators and mechanics. It feels as if the whole base is present, everybody trying to pull together. Men and women drink coffee, smoke cigarettes, hit the soda machines and the candy machines for sustenance. Everybody wants to pitch in, but Brehm has to send guys home, because the Air Force requires that a flight crew has to rest for twelve hours before a mission, including eight hours of uninterrupted sleep and four hours of uninterrupted non-duty time. Jack recalls that Mark Judy's team was flying two missions in one day. If the whole team spends the whole night in the Ops building, there'll be nobody fit to fly tomorrow, and they may need guys to fly tomorrow, if the weather eases up and lets them.

"Michele," Elizabeth asks her sister. "Do you think Uncle Mickey is in the ocean?"

"Maybe he's at the base."

"Who's in the ocean? Is it PJs?"

"I think so."

"I want to call Dad."

"Don't," Michele says. "They'll call us when they know something."

"I want to call him anyway."

"Elizabeth, no—we can't."

"I want to call Mom."

"She said she'll call. Just wait."

"I don't want to be here. I want to just go home."

"We can't go home."

"I'm scared."

"Don't be."

There are no streetlights. Occasionally a car goes past. Elizabeth can't help but cry, imagining her father's friends in the water, and she can't help but worry that her dad is going to go after them, which makes her cry even more. She hates this, the storm, the darkness, the Doughertys' black dog Patty, which always scared her. Out the window, there's no lightning, no thunder, just a relentless wind-driven rain. Elizabeth finally calls her grandmother, who helps calm her down.

Jack gets good news at ten after midnight and calls Peggy to tell her the Coast Guard's HH-3 is hovering above three men. No, he doesn't know which three men, but he'll call back when he knows.

The Coast Guard doesn't have PJs, but they do have rescue swimmers who can swim with the best of the Navy SEALs or Air Force pararescuemen. The Coast Guard, to state the obvious, trains primarily for water rescues, and its methods differ accordingly. For one, where PJs carry victims up on a penetrator, a Coast Guard helicopter will lower a basket, essentially a five-sided metal cage, into which the victim can swim, either under his own power or assisted by a rescue swimmer. Expectations at the 106th are high, but by 1:00 A.M., Jack Brehm has received the bad news that the HH-3 can't make the rescue. The wind is blowing the basket straight back toward the HH-3's tail. With the pilot working the cyclic and the copilot operating the collective they still can't put the basket in the water. The HH-3 pilot reports that in a hover above the men, his forward speed indicator told him he was flying at 80 knots or 100 mph. What he can do is give the *Tamaroa* accurate locations for the men. The *Tamaroa* is 205 feet long, but waves are cresting above the ship and breaking over its decks. Brehm tries to imagine how high the seas must be. He knows how dangerous it can be, picking people up out of heavy seas. Having a ship on the scene is good, but it's no guarantee of anything. He's worried about hypothermia, which will eventually affect even someone in a survival suit. By now his friends have been in the water for what seems like a very long time. He keeps his worries to himself, and calls Peggy to tell her the Coast Guard cutter is almost there. She's frustrated, and says she thought it was only fifteen miles away. He says it was. She asks what's taking it so long. He says that from the sound of it, they can only make two or three knots, but he's sure they're doing the best they can and adds that you have to also consider that the guys in the water have probably drifted from their original location. Peggy says she's sorry, she knows everybody is doing the best they can.

"I'm worried about Laura—she needs to rest. Someone five months pregnant shouldn't be going through something like this. We finished the kitchen. We're going to bed, but you still have to call us any time you know anything, all right?"

"As soon as I know anything."

"I doubt you'll wake us up. We're bringing the phone next to the bed, so promise me you'll call."

"I will," Jack says.

Peggy, Barbara, and Laura all get into the same queen-size bed. They can't sleep, but they think it might do some good to lie still with their eyes closed. They turn the lights off and hold hands, with Laura in the middle. They listen to the rain and the wind, now hard, now soft, now loud, now quiet. Perhaps it's a natural biological function, a way the body compensates for extreme stress, or acts to relieve it, but somehow, the mood starts to shift from serious to silly. It begins with a heavy sigh, and another, and then a snicker. Eventually hysterical laughter.

"What?"

"Nothing."

"What?"

"Nothing. It's not funny."

"Tell me!"

"I was just thinking what we must look like."

It feels good to laugh. They think about slumber parties they had as adolescents, and how far they've come in their lives since then. Ten minutes later, laughter has dissolved to silent prayer.

Around 1:30, the Coast Guard's HH-3 lands at Westhampton Beach to refuel, and the crew comes into the Ops building to warm up, dry off, use the bathroom, and debrief. They are peppered with questions. They try to describe what it's like out there, how fierce the winds are, how the sea is just a whorl of foam and spray, mountainous waves rolling into each other in infinite combinations. They say it's incredible, unbelievable, that they've never seen anything like it. It was too rough to drop a rescue swimmer. They saw strobe lights, that's all—they can't say who was down below. Eventually, the phone rings at Laura Spillane's house, and Peggy answers. It's another PJ's wife.

"I just wanted to say how sorry I am," she says.

"Why?"

"Well, my father-in-law is at the base," she says, "and he says he was talking to some guys who were saying the conditions are so bad they don't see how anybody could survive."

"Well, it's just really too soon to know," Peggy says. "We don't really know anything yet."

"Well, I know, but my father-in-law says—"

"I'm sorry to cut you off but there's somebody on call waiting—I'll let you know when we know anything."

There isn't another call coming in on call waiting. Peggy just said that. She tells Barbara about the call, but not Laura. When the phone rings again, it's Elizabeth.

"Did I wake you guys up?" Elizabeth says.

"No, hon'," Peggy says. "We're still up. Are you still up? Have you gone back to sleep?"

"We can't."

"Well, you don't have to, if you can't, so don't worry about it, but if you can you should try to sleep."

"When are you coming over?"

"I don't know, hon'—probably in the morning. I'll come and get you as soon as we hear something, but we don't know when that's going to be. You guys are being very brave. How's Michele?"

"She's okay," Elizabeth says. "You haven't heard anything?"

"They flew a helicopter to the scene and now there's a Coast Guard ship that's there, so they should be rescuing people any minute now. Why don't you see if there's something on Nick at Night?"

"Who flew a helicopter?"

"The Coast Guard."

"Is Uncle Mickey in the ocean?"

"Honey, just try not to worry about everything. Your dad and Uncle Jimmy are doing everything they can to get them back—everything is going to be okay. All right?"

"Okay."

"I'm very proud of you. I love you both very much."

"Okay."

At 2:15, the phone rings again. It's Jack.

"They've got one," he says.

"Oh my God," Peggy says, repeating the news for the others, "They've got one! Who? Do they know who?"

"We don't know who . . ."

"John, if you know something, and you're not telling anybody, you have to promise you'll tell me."

"Peggy, honestly, we don't know who it is. I asked the guy at RCC and he said he didn't know. As soon as I hear anything I'll let you know. What I'm telling people now is that they've got the assets at the splash point and they're making recoveries. Right now, that's all we can say."

"But that's good."

"That's very good."

"How many?"

"One."

"No—how many in the water."

"Four. I mean, three, now. There's one still missing, but he's going to be in approximately the same area."

At sea, the *Tamaroa* is risking crewmen every time they put anybody on the deck. The first man they rescue is the copilot, Gram Buschor. They lower a cargo net over the side for him to grab. They haul him aboard and take him inside. His core temperature is 94 degrees, so they immediately begin to warm him by giving him hot fluids and wrapping him in blankets. When Jack learns it's Buschor, his first thought is, if they can get Gram, they can get anybody, primarily because, of the five men on Jolly 10, Buschor is in the worst shape. He doesn't train like a PJ. He's a bit overweight and he smokes. They used to joke that if he ever needed rescue, he wouldn't need flares—they would just look for his cigarette lighter. Everyone else on board was a much better swimmer than Gram Buschor. Brehm's hopes rise. After picking up Buschor, the *Tamaroa* heads for where the HH-3 said the others were. They see strobes in the water. They light flares, aim spotlights, and throw lines overboard with chemlights tied to the ends. They want to come in by drifting down on the men in the water, which means the *Tam'* will have to turn broadside to the waves to make the pickup, a maneuver that in seas that high is terribly dangerous to the ship. On the third try, one of the men in the water manages to grab the net, and they haul him onboard. As soon as he's on deck, they can tell he's in terrible pain. They bring him into a cabin, cut his wet suit off him, give him an IV to rehydrate him and a catheter to measure his urine output. His blood pressure is 140 over 90, and his pulse is 100. Instead of being hypothermic, he's running a slight fever. He's hurting everywhere, and his eyes are glazed. They give him a seasickness patch and Tylenol 3.

The phone rings at Laura Spillane's house.

"John," Peggy says. "I hope this is good news."

"It is," he says. "They've got Mick."

"They've got Mick," Peggy says to the others. She bursts into tears. "Oh my God, they've got Mick, thank God, they've got him. Here—let me put Laura on."

Brehm repeats what he knows. He tells Laura that he's also been told that Mickey is injured. He doesn't really know how badly, but if Mickey was able to swim, and to assist in his own rescue, then maybe he's not hurt so bad. He's receiving medical attention. Jack reminds her that her husband was in great shape before any of this happened, getting ready to run a marathon. He's alive. That's all good news.

By 3:00 A.M., four men have been recovered from the water, and Brehm knows their names. He wants to tell the wives of the men who've been recovered, Carmen Ruvola, Ann Buschor, Laura Spillane, and he wants to tell Jim Mioli's sister, but he dreads telling Marianne Smith that Rick is still out there. Yet he doesn't want her to hear it from someone else, and he knows how the telephone network works. He calls her. The only concrete positive news he has for her is that Mickey remembers seeing Rick leave the helicopter in full survival gear. He says they all have high confidence they'll find Rick. By now, the entire PJ community worldwide seems to know there's been an accident, and that some of their own are in trouble, because units from all over are calling in, offering to send aircraft or men to help in the search. All Brehm can tell them is that the Coast Guard is coordinating the search—anyone with assets to offer should call the First District Operations Center in Boston. The mood at the section is mixed. Knowing they've picked up Dave Ruvola, Jim Mioli, Gram Buschor, and Mickey Spillane has lifted everybody's spirits, but not getting Rick is unacceptable, aggravating at best and infuriating at worst to the PJs who know they have the training and the tools to help but can't use them. Everybody knows that Rick Smith was the strongest swimmer among them, one of the strongest swimmers the PJs have ever produced. It's hard to wait. It should only be a matter of minutes now. The phone should ring, any second. They feel certain.

Four o'clock arrives, and Brehm and the others are nervous again. By 5:00, a collective low-level depression has sunk in, in part simply because people are tired, and spirits can sag when the body gives out and the caffeine doesn't work anymore. Brehm calls Peggy at 5:30, needing support himself before he calls Marianne Smith.

"Everybody thought Rick would be the first guy they got, not the last," Brehm says. "He's the best of all of them."

"What are you going to tell Marianne?"

"Just what we know. It's going to be light soon, and when it is, there's going to be a lot of airplanes going out. We're getting a lot of calls from other units."

Peggy asks the question she's afraid to ask.

"Will you be going?"

"We still can't fly," Jack says. "It's Hill's decision. The math says that Rick's probably blowing away from us, meaning we'd have less loiter time now than we had before. For the moment, it's fixed wings only."

"Have they fixed the tankers?"

"They're working on 'em. How are you doing?"

"Okay," Peggy says. She's relieved, on one level, and saddened on another. "I was going to let your parents sleep a little while longer, but then I wanted to call them before they hear anything on the news and start to wonder. Do they know anything more about Mickey?"

"All we were told is broken bones," Jack says. "Ribs. I'm sure they'll med-evac him as soon as it's feasible. It's still pretty rough out there, I gather. Jim Mioli was hypothermic because he wasn't wearing an immersion suit for some reason."

"It's just unbelievable," Peggy says, looking out the kitchen window to see if the sky has begun to lighten any. "We're all going to go over to Marianne's. My mom is going to get the kids off to school."

"How about the twins?"

"We're still figuring that out. Somebody'll get 'em. Barbara wants to be home when her kids wake up."

Jack calls Marianne Smith after hanging up with Peggy, tells her Rick is not yet recovered and tries to reassure her. Her father has arrived from Delaware, and her brothers are there. He tells her about all the airplanes rushing to the North Atlantic to join the search, C-130s and Talons from Florida, P-3s, Coast Guard Falcons, probably fifteen planes today and more tomorrow if they're needed—every search and rescue asset on the East Coast, basically. He tells her they know that Rick had all his gear when he left the helicopter, a survival vest and a wet suit, and that he could probably survive in a raft for days. Peggy, Barbara Dougherty, and Laura Spillane are on their way over to Marianne's to be with her.

When he calls Marianne back at 7:30 A.M., he wishes he had something to report, but he doesn't. He gives her as much positive information as he can. The Coast Guard is collecting data from marker buoys, including a radio marker buoy the *Tamaroa* dropped into the water where she'd picked the four men out of the Atlantic. The buoy indicates what the Coast Guard calls the datum, a term that describes the central point in a search, calculated from the last point of contact and factoring in how far somebody would drift according to the winds and currents at the site. Finer calculations determine how far from the splash point a man swimming in the water might have drifted in the ten hours since the ditching, against how far a man in a life raft with a higher wind profile might have drifted. He tells Marianne they have a really good idea where to look. The 106th's C-130, AFR 988, has repaired the gear box flux in its faulty engine and is again operational, but their other planes are still grounded with mechanical problems. Jack tells her that in addition to the *Tamaroa,* a high endurance Coast Guard cutter, the 327-foot *Spencer,* is on the scene. The weather at 39°27′N and 72°04′W is still tough, winds gusting to fifty miles an hour, rain and only an 800-foot ceiling to fly in, which will limit the territory any one search plane can cover by narrowing the tracks they have to fly. Jack can hear a television in the background and can only imagine what the morning news is telling Marianne. Overnight, six houses in Westhampton Beach were swept into the sea. Four other homes were heavily damaged. Sailboats off Connecticut, Nantucket, Long Island, and even Daytona Beach, Florida, were lost. Boats were blown ashore in Rhode Island, Connecticut, Virginia, Cape Cod, Martha's Vineyard. Waves are still pounding North Carolina's Outer Banks. Hatteras Island has lost power. The Pilgrim nuclear power plant in Plymouth, Massachusetts, has been shut down as a precaution. Oceanfront homes in Brooklyn, just east of Coney Island, are being battered by the sea, where homeowners are stacking sandbags to protect their property. TV weathermen can't believe the size of this thing, calling the storm an "extra-tropical hurricane," having some of the properties of a hurricane, including a counterclockwise swirling motion, but moving west and south, opposite of the way hurricanes move, and they add that it looks like it's going to stick around a lot longer than a typical hurricane.

Marianne Smith puts Peggy on the phone.

"You must be tired," Peggy says.

"I'm all right," Jack says. "I'm just glad they got Rick."

"What did you say?"

"I said I'm glad they got Rick."

Peggy's heart races.

"John, tell me exactly what it is you're saying," Peggy says.

"Did I say Rick?" Jack says, realizing his Freudian slip. "Oh geez. I meant Mick. Mickey. God. I must be more tired than I thought I was."

"That wasn't good," Peggy says, calming herself, glad she didn't blurt his words out for the others to hear. "Think if it'd been Marianne you were talking to and not me."

"I'm not going to be here much longer," Jack tells his wife. "I'll see you at home."

Neighbors stop by Marianne's to check in on her. They've seen the news on TV. They bring coffee cakes and baked goods. Marianne's oldest girl is seven, and she wants to wear her Halloween costume to school. After getting the kids off and putting the baby down for a nap, Marianne Smith retreats to the kitchen, where she seems extremely somber. Peggy asks her how she's doing.

"He's not coming back," Marianne says, sounding very calm and together. "I just know he's not coming back." Peggy knows what it's like to have that feeling. Twice, when Jack was hurt on the job, both times with broken arms, she'd had premonitions, and knew even before he called home that he'd been injured. Other times, she'd called the base and said, "John—don't fly today—I have a bad feeling." But sometimes he'd flown despite her misgivings and everything had been okay.

"Don't give up," Peggy says to Marianne. "You just can't give up."

* * * * * * * *

Over the next week, the details of the accident were pieced together. After ordering his crew to bail out, Dave Ruvola put the helicopter into the water as softly as possible, kicked out his door, something he'd forgotten to do while the aircraft was still in the air, inflated his life vest, and popped to the surface. He saw Jim Mioli's strobe a short time later and swam to him. Mioli was hurt, so Ruvola tied himself to his flight engineer with a piece of parachute cord and held on to him. The water temperature was in the mid-fifties. In the rush to ditch, Mioli had failed to don his survival suit, and Ruvola knew hypothermia would be a problem in waters that cold. Buschor was relatively unhurt, and had the only working radio among the five of them. Mickey Spillane was in trouble as soon as he hit the water, hard, at perhaps fifty or sixty miles per hour, fracturing his left leg, the radius and ulna of his left arm, the ulna and middle finger of his right arm and hand, cracking four ribs, bruising his pancreas, and rupturing a kidney. He was dazed, semiconscious. At one point, he found the nine-man raft that Jim Mioli pushed out his door, but the water was too rough for Spillane to hold on to it. He eventually grabbed a rubberized sack full of blankets and used that for supplemental flotation. When he saw Ruvola and Mioli's strobes bobbing in the distance, his first thought was that he'd only be a burden if he swam to them, and he felt something like the way he'd felt running marathons, an I'm-in-pain-leave-me-the-hell-alone attitude, until he remembered that his PJ training at Lackland taught him team members should stick together. It took him two hours to swim over to his pilot and flight engineer.

Jack Brehm was back at the base by two the following afternoon, Thursday. During the day, Spillane had been moved from the *Tamaroa* to the *Spencer.* At three o'clock, the 106th asked permission to fly out to the *Spencer* and take Mickey off, but the captain denied them permission, saying the seas were still far too rough to have any helicopters hovering over his decks. Around the same time, a familiar and welcome figure walked into the dispatch center. Mike McManus had flown down from Alaska to take part in a conference in Washington, D.C., and drove up to Long Island as soon as he heard there was trouble. It wasn't the kind of weather you want to be driving in, but that didn't stop McManus. Jack gave his mentor a hug when he saw him. Mike asked what the situation was. Jack filled him in.

"It's rough," Jack concluded. "The pisser is that we still haven't launched the helos. They got the tanker flying again, but Hill says we still have to wait." He added that the primary search area had drifted so far to the south that any helicopter on scene would have to refuel every half hour to avoid going below bingo fuel. As a rule, helicopters only search close to shore. In the mid-Atlantic, you search with fixed-wing aircraft, and once you find what you're looking for, you send helicopters to the exact location of the rescue. Using helicopters to search the mid-Atlantic would be ludicrous.

"I know," Mike said. "It's not just Hill—I heard the generals talking about it in D.C."

"The boys want to fly," Jack said.

"Of course they want to fly," Mike said, "but Hill's got more than just PJs to worry about. You know, you guys could swim in this shit, but the pilots don't train like you. The flight engineers don't train like you. You gonna put those guys in the water?"

"It's nice to have somebody around here who understands," Jack said.

At 5:30 that day, as the light was beginning to fade, a Coast Guard C-130 reported seeing a large patch of green marker dye in the water, with what appeared to be a man in the middle of it, or at least a dark shape that looked like a man. The C-130 dropped another marker buoy, as well as a raft, a flare kit, and radios. The Coast Guard launched an HH-3 to fly to the site. Jack called Marianne to tell her they thought they'd found somebody. An hour later, he had to call her back and apologize, and tell her it was a false alarm. The dye had been dropped by another search pilot to mark something he thought he'd seen. The dark shape was probably just a piece of flotsam. (An article in the New York *Daily News* would erroneously report the next day, November 1, that searchers had spotted a lone individual in choppy seas east of Atlantic City.) There was another false alarm at 9:30 that night, when a Coast Guard helicopter pilot radioed that he'd spotted Smith near the marker buoy the *Tamaroa* had dropped. Jack told Marianne, because she said she wanted to know whenever there was any new information, even if it was a false alarm, but then the Coast Guard pilot corrected himself and said he'd only seen a raft. The weather was still atrocious, bad enough that Elizabeth Brehm and her friend Emily had to cancel the scavenger hunt they'd planned. They bobbed for apples instead, and played games, and ate candy. Some kids wore costumes. Everybody watched the Stephen King movie *It.* Elizabeth thought the movie was okay, but how could it be frightening, after what she'd been through the night before?

Her Uncle Mickey was med-evac'ed from the *Spencer* at eight Friday morning and taken to a hospital in Atlantic City, New Jersey. As soon as they heard, Peggy drove Laura to Atlantic City, leaving at ten in the morning, a five-hour drive. Thirty minutes from the hospital, the two women heard a loud noise when the master brake cylinder blew on Peggy's Plymouth Voyager, so they limped the last thirty miles, driving on the shoulder of the New Jersey Turnpike, listening to the rumble strip beneath the wheels. At the hospital, it was a joyous reunion, tempered by the reality that Mickey was in bad shape, white as a ghost, immobile, with a blank stare on his face. He was, as Peggy Brehm remembers, "in never-never land—he could barely whisper." He was in too much pain to be hugged. Laura held his hand but didn't squeeze it. Peggy drove home that night.

On Saturday, the *Tamaroa* sailed into Shinnecock Inlet for the Coast Guard Station at Hampton Bays. Jim Mioli, Gram Buschor, and Dave Ruvola were met by their loved ones on the docks, then driven to the base for physicals. Mioli and Buschor appeared overjoyed to be home. Ruvola looked distraught, as if, Brehm thought, he might be blaming himself. That afternoon, Brehm, Colonel Hill, and the base chaplain, a guardsman named John Hecht, drove to Marianne's house on the South Shore near the end of the William Floyd Parkway, in the town of Shirley. Her father, stepmother, and two of her brothers were there, as were her children,

Erica, who was seven, Kristin, five, and Caroline, only three weeks old. Marianne looked exhausted, limp. Jack could see the resignation in her face, but he told her they weren't giving up. If anybody could last this long, Rick could, and finally, the weather was getting better. According to the weather patterns, Rick would have blown south, where the water was warmer. The calmer the seas, the easier it was going to be to spot someone. Jack told her to hold on if she could, because nobody was giving up yet. They both knew, however, that realistically, the chances of finding Rick Smith were slim and getting slimmer.

The search lasted a full week, involving hundreds of aircraft and thousands of men, to date one of the largest search and rescue operations in the history of the Coast Guard. There were more false alarms. One plane would see something, drop a raft, just in case it was Rick, and a couple hours later, another plane would call in, saying they'd spotted a raft. The PJs flew out and knifed the empty rafts, so they wouldn't have to investigate them twice. Aircraft from the 106th flew every day, often in a formation of two HH-60s with a tanker between them to serve as a mobile gas station, but the helicopters had to refuel frequently, and every time they did the attention paid to refueling procedures compromised the search. The search area grew larger and larger, as the datum shifted farther and farther away. Areas that had been searched in rough seas were searched again in calm seas. On November 7, the Coast Guard abandoned its search. On the same day, a helicopter from the 106th, Jolly 14, returned from Atlantic City, bringing Mickey Spillane home.

On November 8, nine days after the accident, a Sergeant Mounger from RCC at Scott AFB called to say that the Air Force's search, officially mission 2-2341A, was closed. That evening, Jack Brehm was called into Colonel Hill's office. There'd been a number of debriefings with Dave Ruvola and the other members of the crew of Jolly 10. Speculation as to what happened to Rick Smith was only that—speculation—but the best guess was that he'd probably hit the water as hard or harder than Mickey Spillane had hit it, lost consciousness, and drowned. Another theory suggested he and Spillane may have collided on impact with the sea. A third theory posited that under the stress of preparing to ditch, he may have forgotten to release his gunner's belt and had gone under with the helicopter. Jack wasn't sure what Colonel Hill wanted and was surprised to see a civilian sitting opposite the colonel's desk. The colonel introduced the man and asked him to repeat, for Sergeant Brehm, what he'd just told the wing commander. The man was about thirty, with long scraggly hair, dirty, parted in the middle. He was wearing tennis shoes, jeans, a brown shirt and a jacket over it, and he had a folder in his hands.

"I was telling your colonel," the man said, extending the folder, "that I have psychic abilities, and that I was hoping you'd let me help you. I should tell you that when I do this kind of work, I always anticipate skepticism, but I do have numerous newspaper clippings and documents here, if you'd care to read them, about the times I've worked with various police departments and with the FBI. At any rate, as I was telling Colonel Hill, I think your friend Rick Smith is still alive, because I believe I've seen him."

Brehm took the clippings The Psychic offered and glanced at them without reading them.

"You've seen him?" Brehm said. A skeptic all his life, Brehm didn't believe in psychics. Yet he found himself reserving judgment, reluctant to be the one who says no, this is impossible. He wanted to believe rescue was still possible. Everybody did. This gave him a chance to do that. The Psychic's manner was humble and matter-of-fact, and he sounded reasonable and sincere in his desire to help.

"Yes," The Psychic said. "I've had the vision several times. I see him in the water. There's something shiny on his face, and he's wearing a black suit. And he keeps grabbing for his right leg. I don't know why, but there's something on his right leg. I can give you the coordinates if you'd like."

"Would you mind waiting out in the hall for a second?" Colonel Hill asked The Psychic. When he was gone, Hill asked Brehm what he thought. Hill said he'd called some of the references The Psychic had provided, police departments that said that while the guy hadn't exactly led them directly to what they were looking for, he'd steered them in the right direction, asked good questions, and had indeed proved helpful. Brehm shook his head, more in bewilderment than in doubt.

"I don't know what to think," Brehm said. Brehm knew that there were things in this universe that he couldn't explain. "I guess the shiny thing on his face could be Rick's mask. And he's wearing a black wet suit."

"What about the right leg?" Hill asked. Brehm shrugged.

"I have no idea. I suppose he could be reaching for his knife, or else he's hurt. I don't know what to say. What do you think, Colonel?"

"I don't know, either," Colonel Hill said. "I really don't. Except that I don't see what we have to lose. We've tried everything else. These other people said he'd helped. One voice says 'Why?' and the other says, 'Why not?' The guy says he can give us coordinates."

"Well then . . ."

The next morning at 6:43 A.M., the C-130 AFR 988 took off. AFR 974 and AFR 114 were by now repaired and on standby. The Psychic had explained himself, his purpose, and his vision, to the entire squadron at a preflight briefing. No one expressed any doubts or misgivings about using him. They wanted it to work. No one wanted to cross the line and say, "Forget it, it's over, Rick's gone." The Psychic even requested that he be allowed to fly on the C-130, feeling he'd be able to get a better sense of things if he were actually on the scene. Permission was denied. Instead they let The Psychic speak with the pilot on the radio.

"We're seeing something in the water off to starboard," the pilot radioed back at one point.

"It's going to be a square piece of wood, about two foot by two foot," The Psychic said. Everyone in the Ops room waited.

"It looks like a shipping pallet or something," the pilot radioed in after closer examination. "Just a piece of wood, maybe two foot square."

No one in Ops knew what to say. Some felt chills as The Psychic correctly predicted the sighting. Those who wanted to believe in him saw it as a positive sign. Those who didn't tried to figure out how he could have known. The proof would come when AFR 988 reached the coordinates the psychic had given them. When it did, the anticipation was intense.

"Do you see anything?" The Psychic asked.

"Negative," the pilot said. "Scanners report negative."

"You're certain?"

"As certain as I can be," the pilot said. "Seas maybe ten feet, good visibility. We got nothing."

"Okay," The Psychic said, "that's all right—now, turn east twenty degrees. You should see something white in the water."

Brehm's skepticism returned. If the guy was truly psychic, why wouldn't he just take them straight to Rick? Why send them somewhere, then make them change course? He didn't expect it to make perfect sense, but he did expect it to make *some* sense. For the next ten hours, The Psychic gave the pilot his feelings and impressions, until, at 4:30 in the afternoon, the C-130 was ordered to return to base. Searching the open ocean is an exhausting thing to do. The people manning the scanning windows need a twenty-minute break every hour because focusing and concentrating that hard wears you out. They'd been out for ten hours. By the time they landed, everybody had the feeling they'd been used and misled, if not jerked around outright. Flights had been scheduled for the next two days, but by 8:15 that evening, all flights were canceled, pending reevaluation. The Psychic was politely informed that he'd be called if and when there was any further need for his services.

Marianne called Jack the following afternoon.

"Would you mind coming over?" Marianne asked. "He's here."

"Who is?"

"Well, this guy who says he's a psychic . . ."

Jack was at Marianne Smith's house in a matter of minutes. The Psychic was sitting in her living room, wearing what looked like the same clothes he'd worn the day before. Jack wondered how he'd gotten Marianne's address. He wondered if the guy had slept in his car. He wondered if he lived in his car.

"What's up?" Jack asked, trying to hide his rising ire.

"You're thinking of stopping the search, aren't you?" The Psychic said. *God,* Brehm thought, *you really are a psychic.* "You can't give up hope, Jack." *Don't call me Jack.* "He's still alive. I'm as certain of that as I am of anything. I just can't be of any help unless I can get out there. I'm frustrated, because I'm really having a hard time working from these distances. I just think you'd be crazy to give up now when we're so close."

"Hang on a second," Brehm said. "I want to talk with Marianne."

Jack followed Marianne Smith into the kitchen. Out the kitchen window, he noticed how stark and bare everything was. Before the storm, there'd been leaves on all the trees, but now they'd all blown off, black tree limbs against a cold autumn sky.

"What do you think?" Marianne asked. "He wants to rent a boat and go out there."

"He's going to rent a boat?" Jack asked.

"Well, no," Marianne said. "He wants me to rent the boat."

"Marianne," Jack said, "I hate to put it this way, but I think this is a crock of shit. I think by now we both know Rick is gone, and I think this guy is just some sick jerk who gets a kick out of preying on the hopes of people in tough situations. How else can you explain it? He knows it's going to be hard for you to admit Rick is gone, so he's just . . . I don't know what he's doing. I just think it's a bunch of crap."

"So do I," Marianne said. "I agree. I just needed to hear somebody else say it. Would you mind asking him to leave?"

Brehm confronted The Psychic in the living room.

"Marianne's not interested," he told the man. "I don't know how you found out where she lives, and I don't care—don't bother her again. We don't want your help. Got it? Don't see her, and don't call her. Do we understand each other? So grab your stuff and I'll walk you to your car."

13

KRYPTONITE

The book that came out about the '91 Nor'easter was called The Perfect Storm, *and most of the guys who read it were pretty impressed with how the author got it right. At the time though, we probably wouldn't have agreed that the storm was "perfect" in any way.*

I don't want to defend myself without giving anybody with a different opinion a chance to have a say in the matter. I can live without addressing it. I regret losing Rick, but I don't regret any decisions I made, because I know they were sound. I was thinking as clearly as anybody could. It was time to be practical. Beyond that, there was nothing I could do. If I'd had my druthers, I would have been on the helicopter myself. When they left for the mission, I was jealous. It was going to be a historic mission, the first rescue for the unit using the new HH-60s. The storm caught the whole East Coast unprepared—why should the 106th be any different? After the storm, it was like a mortar round had hit the unit. Guys were devastated, and I understood that, but to be questioned and told your motives were somehow less than clear or righteous, when you know you were trying to do the best by everyone, is horrible. In a way, it was the most traumatic thing that ever happened to me. Everything fell apart.

Humans need answers and reasons for everything. We need to know why horrible traumatic things happen. I think of the U.S. prisoners of war in North Vietnam, guys held for years in hopeless heartbreaking conditions, knowing there was no rational justification for what they were going through. It's your faith, in God or in country or in your family, that gets you through something like that.

In the end, we ask, why was there a storm? We can look at all the meteorological data we want, but in an ontological sense, there's no answer to that question. If we believe in God, we can say, "God sent the storm," but *why* did God send the storm? Why would God choose October 30, 1991, as the night Rick Smith had to die? There's no answer to that, either. But grief invariably poses the question, "Why?" It's human nature to insist that the deaths of the people we love have meaning, because otherwise it would seem that we live in a meaningless universe, where actions and consequences disconnect, and justice goes unserved, and fairness doesn't matter, and things don't make sense anymore. Love seems meaningless, because when all is said and done, love can't really save anybody. Yet because of love, we can't stop asking questions that have no answers, over and over again, until we get angry that we're not getting any answers. We get angry with God, or with Nature, angry with the ocean and the sky. We feel guilty for surviving, angry at ourselves, and enraged at feeling so helpless. We can lash out in defiance, like Captain Ahab with his lightning rods, screaming at God. We can scream at God, or at the ocean, or at the sky, but that usually doesn't satisfy, because unless we get a sign, it's hard to tell when anyone is listening. Then it's human nature to look for someone or something else to blame. Ahab blamed the whale. Some of the PJs at the 106th blamed Jack Brehm.

It makes no sense, but it can, perhaps, be partially deconstructed. It could be argued that the seeds of discord were planted prior to the accident. Even before McManus put Jack's name up to succeed him as NCOIC it was clear in the section that Jack and Mike had a good relationship, one others might envy. Jack admired Mike's courage and toughness, and Mike admired Jack's dedication and spirit. Was McManus ever guilty of favoritism? Probably, if you call it favoritism to give the best assignments to guys he knew could get the job done willingly and cheerfully, guys like Jack, and not to guys Mike had his doubts about, guys prone to acting more out of self-interest than for the good of the team. A handful of PJs who held seniority over Jack questioned Mike's decision to recommend Jack for NCOIC. McManus made the recommendation anyway. Before he left for Alaska, Mike McManus was satisfied that he'd left the unit in the best possible hands.

Yet the feeling in the PJ section among a certain faction was that Jack could have and should have done more to get the PJs in the air the night Jolly 10 ditched. Beginning the very first night, some thought Jack should have gone into Colonel Hill's office and turned his desk upside down if he had to, and pounded his fists and demanded that they be allowed to fly to go rescue their friend. Never mind that the 106th didn't have a flyable refueler, with all four of their C-130 tankers down for repairs. Never mind that that meant any HH-60 arriving on the scene flying without refueling capability would only be able to loiter for fifteen or twenty minutes before it would have to RTB, and even if they knew exactly where to look, in seas that rough there was no guarantee they'd be able to hoist down and pick anybody up in fifteen minutes. Never mind that a Coast Guard HH-3 had already reached the splash point within a few hours of the ditching, but failed to make a pickup due to the weather, and the weather had gotten worse since then. Never mind that when McManus showed up at the base to help out during the search, he backed Jack up one hundred percent, and said that suspension of flying was the right decision, and there was nothing he nor anybody else could have done to reverse it, even if it was the wrong decision. Never mind that it wasn't Jack's call in the first place—it was wing commander Hill's call, and it was the Pentagon's call, too.

Hill had a number of sound reasons to make his decision, but he also had a broader perspective than the PJs had. He was concerned with the entire helicopter crew, not just the PJs, and with the aircrafts. He lived near the base and knew, by listening for them, when his helicopters were late coming home. At 9:00 P.M. the night of the storm he'd been dining in a local restaurant with members of a visiting logistics team when he realized he hadn't heard Jolly 10 flying over and knew it was tardy, at which point he called the base from a pay phone and first learned of the imminent ditching. The logistics team was visiting because the 106th had received a shipment of auxiliary internal fuel tanks for their HH-60s, tanks that would have extended their flying time by about two hours, but the auxiliary tanks couldn't be installed because the shipment was missing the hoses needed to connect the tanks to the HH-60's fuel system. Somewhere along the way, somebody had failed to kit-proof the shipment. It was as if, during the storm, everything that could go wrong did. There was nothing the 106th could do about it but wait for the fuel-line assemblies to arrive.

Hill's perspective was different in another way. He knew that his PJs were upset at not being able to fly the night of the accident, and more so the next day, and he heard them grumble when they learned maintenance wasn't going to be able to install the internal fuel tanks. Hill could see that his PJs, men who could be fairly tightly wound under normal circumstances, were too emotionally invested, to the extent that it might have been a bad idea to fly, even if they'd had tankers available—a Bat 21 mentality was becoming evident. Civilians might recall *Bat 21* as the title of a movie starring Gene Hackman, a fairly inaccurate Hollywood rendition, if you ask most PJs, of an April 1972 rescue in Vietnam of an EB-66 pilot named LTCOL Iceal "Gene" Hambleton who'd been shot down behind enemy lines in the middle of the DMZ, the heart of "bad guy" country, while trying to jam SAM sites during the NVA's Easter Offensive. Bat 21 was the identifying call number of his airplane. By 1972 the North Vietnamese had realized that U.S. forces generally refrained from bombing places where our personnel had been shot down, for fear of hitting our own people. The North Vietnamese used Hambleton's downing as an opportunity to move several armored tank divisions into the area where he was evading, perhaps as many as 10,000 troops in broad daylight. They also knew that somebody was going to come and get him, so rather than capture him they surrounded him and waited, using him as bait to set up a "flak trap." The United States lost several airplanes and a helicopter trying to get Hambleton out, with two HH-53s so shot up they barely made it back to Da Nang, the Air Force thinking all the while, "He's our guy, he's one of us, and he's in trouble, and we gotta go save him." Hambleton was recovered eleven days after being shot down. Lost were two PJs, TECH SGT Allen Avery and SGT William Pearson.

Hill knew being emotionally invested isn't always a good thing. Hoo-yah and gung ho can go too far. There are times when it's foolish to persist, no matter how badly you want to launch—times when courage is counterindicated.

It was a difficult concept for the PJs of the 106th to accept. Some men who might not have stood up to Mike McManus got in Jack Brehm's face. McManus never used Novocain when he went to the dentist. At the end of a night of drinking at the Matchbox, McManus routinely ate his beer glass. Despite his diminutive stature, Mike was somebody you didn't want to take on. "Leadership," Sun Tzu writes in the classical Chinese text *The Art of War*, "is a matter of intelligence, trustworthiness, humaneness, courage, and sternness." Jack had intelligence, trustworthiness, humaneness, and courage, but he didn't have an evil bone in his body. There are occasions when a leader needs to crack a few heads, or eat a few beer glasses, to make a point. Emotions after the accident were out of control. The men suffered from overwhelming feelings of grief and frustration and sadness and an infuriating helplessness. Some tried to self-medicate with alcohol, a poor choice that only made things worse, because alcohol flattens REM (rapid eye movement) sleep, which is the brain's way of processing trauma and healing itself. At the section, cheap shots and low blows abounded. Fingers were pointed. Men whispered behind each other's backs, and meetings were held behind closed doors. One day Jack discovered that somebody had stolen his jacket. Another day, as he prepared to fly to Kuwait on a TDY, he discovered that somebody had hidden a bottle of hooch in his kit bag. Kuwait is an Islamic country where alcohol is strictly forbidden. Smuggling booze into country could have gotten Jack into enormous trouble, had anyone found the bottle. He was lucky to find it and dispose of it, but it became evident that somebody was trying to drive him from the unit.

Jack had men on his side, guys like Jimmy Dougherty and Mickey Spillane, but the argument was dividing the unit. He had Peggy, too, who talked to him and held him and told him he'd done the right thing. She went over the details of the search for Rick with Jack, when he needed to review the decisions made during those difficult hours, but she told him not to second-guess himself, too. She'd never seen him so distraught, a man who'd probably been in about three or four bad moods since the day she met him. Ordinarily, Jack tried, as much as possible, not to bring the office home with him, but now Peggy encouraged him to talk about it, because she could see that what was tearing up the team was tearing him up too.

Colonel Hill knew what was going on, knew someone had stuck a bottle of hooch in Jack's bag, but he couldn't take disciplinary action against anybody without evidence or testimony, and he couldn't get that, because he couldn't crack the "code of silence" that shielded the section, not unlike the way police departments or fire departments sometimes develop a protective code of silence. Hill had also lost a certain amount of face at the awards ceremony that followed the storm. The purpose of the ceremony was to commend people for their efforts and hopefully to initiate a healing process. Air Medals were given to the pilots who flew the search planes, and to the crew members who flew with them. One Air Medal was even given to a parachute packer who'd manned a scanning window on a C-130 for an afternoon. Hill had recommended to Washington that the crew of Jolly 10 receive the Air Force's Airman's Medal for valor in the line of duty. The Airman's Medal is a higher award than the Air Medal. As of the eve of the ceremony, Ruvola, Mioli, Buschor, and Spillane expected the Airman's

Medal. They'd been told that's what they were going to get, and they clearly had a right to feel they deserved it, though they might never have come right out and said so. Hill was informed, the night before the ceremony, that the Pentagon's awards committee had declined the Airman's Medal, ruling that it wasn't an award that could be given out in a noncombat situation. Hill flipped. He picked up the telephone and appealed to the generals above him, arguing that Jolly 10 had ditched in the line of duty—it wasn't as if some irresponsible young fighter jock had trashed an F-15 on a test range out of recklessness or negligence. Several of Hill's superiors agreed with him, but not enough to sway the members of the awards committee. It was too late to call off the awards ceremony, so Hill did the next best thing he could do. Ruvola got an Aerial Achievement Medal. The rest of the crew received Air Force Commendation Medals. Both are lower awards than the Air Medals the scanners were getting.

It did little to assuage the discord in the unit.

Then Dave Ruvola flew to Washington, D.C., in late November to give a special briefing on the accident, and at the hearing he was told he was a hero, and that the Air Force was proud of the way he'd handled himself and saved as many of his crew as he could. Yet when Ruvola mentioned to the man who'd called him a hero, a general, how unfair the meager Aerial Achievement Medal seemed, the general replied coldly, "Well, the bottom line is, you lost the aircraft."

It seemed to Colonel Hill and to Jack Brehm, as well as to many others in the unit, that some sort of mass insanity was afoot, something inexplicable and weird, wrong-headed and bizarre, but nevertheless something that had a life of its own, like an illness that needed to run its course, or a fever that needed to burn itself out. Colonel Hill knew that in the military, once a leader loses the confidence of his men, he loses the ability to lead, and it doesn't matter whether the reasons for that loss of confidence are valid or invalid.

In hindsight, one action that might have been taken, a tool the Air Force had resorted to on other occasions, albeit usually in post-combat situations, would have been to hold a CISD, or Critical Incident Stress Debriefing. CISD was a tool the Air Force, in 1991, was just beginning to be aware of, but one commonly used today. The idea was pioneered by Dr. Jeffrey T. Mitchell, founder of the International Critical Incident Stress Debriefing Foundation, a nonprofit United Nations affiliated organization in Ellicott City, Maryland. Mitchell, currently a clinical associate professor of emergency health services at the University of Maryland, is also a former fireman and paramedic who, in the mid-seventies, began looking at the way emergency workers and rescue teams handle the stress of their jobs. Mitchell looked at the aftermath of a variety of calamities and disasters, from the 1942 fire at the Coconut Grove, a Boston nightclub, to the 1985 Mexico City earthquake and a 1986 midair collision in the skies over Cerritos, California, a gruesome accident involving a private plane and a commercial airliner that left what was thought to be over ten thousand body parts on the ground. He looked at what happens after a crisis to policemen, firemen, medical personnel, anybody who might have come in contact with a traumatic event. Many of them reported one or more symptoms of stress: physical symptoms such as fatigue, dizziness, chest pains, and headaches; cognitive symptoms such as nightmares, uncertainty, hypervigilance, suspiciousness, and the blaming of others; and emotional symptoms such as fear, guilt, panic, denial, irritability, and intense anger to the point of losing emotional control. He found behavioral symptoms such as withdrawal, antisocial acts, inability to rest, and increased alcohol consumption, and he found spiritual symptoms, too, men and women who fought with their God or questioned their basic beliefs, withdrew from their places of worship, and felt empty and lost, without a sense of meaning or purpose. Mitchell observed untreated stress leading to divorce, alcoholism, and suicide attempts. The effect on rescue units was frequently devastating, often marked by an increase in sick days taken, a higher rate of disability claims, and a greater number of qualified people leaving their career fields prematurely and retiring from sheer burnout. In a nutshell, Mitchell found that too often the last thing people who dedicate their lives to saving others remember to do is save themselves. They tell themselves, "It's just part of my job—I'm trained to handle this," when no one can really be trained to handle that much grief and loss and pain, or to pick up the body parts of a fellow human being.

The goal of a Critical Incident Stress Debriefing is to stop the progress of post-traumatic psychological deterioration and stabilize the cognitive and affective processes. First, you reduce the stimulation levels and get everybody to calm down physically by removing them from the source of the crisis—you give them a sense of psychological distance from it. You might break the rescue team up into small groups, those who were directly involved in one group, those more tangentially involved in another, or you might divide them up according to rank, enlisted men in one circle, officers in another. Then you talk about what's going on. You acknowledge that there's a crisis. You don't critique the mission or go over what went wrong and you don't write up reports on anybody—you talk about the emotions you're all feeling, somebody starting simply with "I can't sleep," or "I'm not hungry," or "I'm having flashbacks." You talk about the symptoms, that it's perfectly normal and common to be angry or to look for someone to blame, which is a quick way to release tension and at the same time avoid dealing with it. You talk in general about what stress is, a biological mechanism designed to alert us to imminent danger and protect us from it by preparing us either to fight or flee, but that unlike almost every other species on the planet, humans have a tendency to hang on to the defense mechanism long after the danger has passed.

During the crisis, the men of the 106th spent nine days either waiting in vain for good news, as a storm raged outside, or searching the vast, open ocean, flying long hours, trying to see, trying to concentrate and stay focused. They went without sleep, ate lousy food, drank too much coffee on duty and too much booze off duty, and struggled to contain the things they were feeling, the doubts and the fears, without a clue as to what they were really dealing with. They were dealing with a lot. In fact, after years of field experience, Dr. Mitchell developed a list of things that can stress emergency workers, ranked in order of seriousness, and the worst thing that can happen is to lose a member of your team in the line of duty. It's a clock-cleaner, a proven destroyer of units, time after time, an emotional mortar round, as bad as losing a family member. A rescue team is indeed like a family. PJs spend almost as much time with one another as they do with their families. The bond is made more profound by the fact that frequently their very lives depend on one another. According to Mitchell, the only way losing a team member in the line of duty could be made worse would be if you thought his death was your fault.

And that's exactly how the PJs of the 106th felt.

Someone could have told them, "The worst thing that can happen to a human being just happened to you, and just because you became a pararescueman doesn't mean you gave up being human." The great irony of post-traumatic stress is that, like a Chinese finger puzzle, the harder you fight to escape, the more firmly you're trapped, so you have to do something extremely counterintuitive and quit struggling. PJs would have a harder time doing that than most people. Their strengths would work against them. Self-doubt is, to a PJ, what kryptonite is to Superman, and it's easy to confuse self-examination with self-doubt. The Wizard of Wig at the bottom of the pool at Lackland is real, the embodiment of everything a PJ fears. PJs are taught, from the opening day of Indoc, to deny their emotions. How do you move beyond your comfort level? You deny that you're uncomfortable. How do you keep going when everybody else is exhausted and spent? You deny that you're exhausted and spent. How do you proceed in the face of enormous risk? You deny that you're scared. How do you deal with tremendous physical trauma, patients with gaping head wounds or severed limbs? You pretend it doesn't affect you. How do you deal with the loss of a patient? You tell yourself the guy's number was up, that you don't care. How do you cope with losing a friend? You deny that it happened for no reason, and that there was nothing anybody could have done. You try to figure it out, because we need answers, so badly that we'll supply them even when there are no answers. Denial might work temporarily, but it never works over the long haul. Emotions eventually come out. Sometimes they explode suddenly in ugly painful displays, and sometimes it's more like a slow leak, a debilitating malfunction over a period of years, but either way, inevitably, they come out. The PJs at the 106th got angry at Jack Brehm because they were angry at God, and at the ocean, and the sky, and because they couldn't imagine getting angry at the one person they really were angry at.

Rick Smith.

Anger is a normal part of the grieving process, yet the hardest thing for a bereaved individual to admit is that he's angry at the deceased, pissed off at being left behind and abandoned. We get mad at the people who leave us without asking our permission. Who said they could break off the friendship? We get mad that we can't tell them we're mad. When Tolstoy wrote, "Hell is the inability to love," he didn't mean hell is not knowing what love is, because then we wouldn't know what we're missing. Hell is knowing exactly what love is, and feeling it precisely and fully, with all our hearts, but being unable to express it or give it away. When loved ones die, we can't love them anymore. We can cherish our memories of them, but that's not the same thing. That doesn't do the trick. That doesn't dispose of all the love that keeps building up inside, with nowhere to go until it becomes toxic and dangerous. Rick Smith didn't do anything wrong, he didn't want to die, it wasn't his fault, he was a great guy—how could anybody justify being mad at him? What sense would that make?

But it didn't make sense. It was simply an accident, a random event, in a universe that's sometimes ordered and often random. The universe might not be forgiving, but we can be.

On December 3, 1991, Jack Brehm stepped down as NCOIC. It was for the good of the unit. He'd talked it over with Colonel Hill, who suggested that Jack move aside and let somebody else try to bring stability to the 106th. Jack had the support of a loving family to fall back on, one of the best coping mechanisms there is. Afterward he called Mike, who told him, "Hey man—if you haven't been fired at least three times in this job, you're not trying. All you can do is stay true to yourself."

Jack knew he'd stayed true to himself. There was a sense of peace in that.

After stepping down as NCOIC, Jack moved down the hall in the Ops building and served the unit in Standardization and Evaluation, tasked with making sure everyone in the section was current with his skill levels, training, and qualifications. He worked for a while in the clinic. He enrolled in leadership school for senior NCOs at Gunther AFB in Montgomery, Alabama. At the 106th, an interim non-PJ NCOIC was assigned, CMSGT Ed King, who came from headquarters in Newburgh, New York, to help unruffle feathers and restore a sense of purpose to the team. King helped everybody move on while the application process to find a permanent NCOIC restarted. Eventually, a PJ from outside the unit was brought in, and stability returned. It was exactly the idea of staying true to himself that kept Jack from ever seriously entertaining the idea of quitting. He and Peggy talked about the other things he could do, but when all was said and done, he was trained to save lives. He was good at it. People were alive because of him—how many guys can say that? The idea of throwing away fifteen years of experience was unthinkable. Talking things through with Peggy saved him, as surely as he'd ever saved anybody else. After the bombing of the Murrah Federal Building in Oklahoma City, the divorce rate among the emergency workers involved in the rescue work following the bombing rose by 300 percent; after "the perfect storm" and throughout its aftermath, Jack and Peggy grew closer.

And as disappointed as Jack was at losing the NCOIC position, there was a brighter side. He'd always known that his family was more important than his job, and the transition gave him more time to spend with his family—how could that be a bad thing? He played ball with his kids, and catch, and taught his children how to ride bikes and skateboards. He came to their schools and gave first-aid demonstrations and talked about what it was like to parachute or scuba-dive. He took them to the beach to fly kites or run down the sand dunes. He took them to movies, parades, and fairs. He cheered from the side lines at hockey games and soccer games and basketball games. He took them to dance recitals and baton-twirling competitions, visibly bursting with pride from the front row, tears welling up in his eyes and a huge smile on his face, to where his kids were almost embarrassed that he was there all the time. Attending to his children never seemed to get in the way of giving time to his wife. He and Peggy still held hands everywhere they went, like teenagers, still talked endlessly, and still apologized when they were wrong, knowing the importance of forgiving each other for the mistakes they made.

As keen as he'd been to assume a leadership role, he realized in the end that that wasn't what was important. The team was important. You do what's right for you, and stay true to yourself, as Mike had said, but above that you do what's right for the team. The team needed experienced PJs. Jack still needed the team. In a way, life was simpler under the new NCOIC, CMSGT Alan Manuel, because it allowed Jack to return his primary focus to the mission. All PJs live for the mission, jones for the mission, dream the mission, and Jack was no different. He knew that sooner or later, other leadership opportunities would come along.

* * * * * * * *

Early October. Midafternoon. The Coast Guard's Rescue Control Center in Elizabeth City, North Carolina, notifies the 106th that the captain of a Malaysian freighter, the *Bunga Saga Tiga,* is having heart trouble. It's a jump mission. The ship is sailing from Penang for Calais, France, and is currently 900 miles east of New York in the middle of the Atlantic. Jack Brehm and PJs Sean Brady and Steve Arrigotti fly out in a C-130 and reach the ship around 5:00 P.M. The weather is good for the first 890 miles, but as they circle the ship, a cloud deck at 2,000 feet forces them to jump S-17 round chutes off a static line from 1,000 feet. As he falls, Brehm notes that the sky, the water, the ship, everything is gray, save for the golden sun on the ship's smokestack.

A launch picks them up a couple hundred yards off the *Bunga Saga Tiga's* port beam, in rolling fifteen-foot seas, conditions not terribly harsh or difficult, but the crew on the launch seems edgy, unhappy to be on the open ocean in such a small boat. They're led by the first mate, a thin, short, jittery Malay man in his mid-twenties who speaks broken English, his rank indicated by the epaulets on his shirt, his youth by the wispy mustache on his upper lip. Getting the launch back up to the ship proves a nightmare, a procedure that involves attaching twin chains from a winch on the freighter to hooks at either end of the launch, but the launch's crew manages to hook up to only one of the chains, such that whenever a wave drops out from under the launch, the boat and the men in it dangle at a nearly vertical angle. Brady and Arrigotti opt to climb a rope ladder to the deck of the freighter. Brehm stays with the gear in the launch, and tells them to see to the captain. He'll catch up to them when he can.

When he finally gets onboard, Brehm learns from Brady that the captain is dead.

"For how long?"

"I'm not sure," Brady says. "Not long. I guess RCC called to terminate, but we were already under canopy."

"Swell," Brehm says, noticing a sign on a plaque over the dining hall that reads, *PRAISE BE TO ALLAH.* It's an Islamic ship with an Islamic crew. That means they could be stuck for three or four days on a ship with no beer.

"Guess who called RCC?" Arrigotti says.

"Who?"

"The captain's wife."

"She's onboard?"

"Apparently. We haven't seen her."

Brehm finds the first mate and pulls him aside.

"I'm afraid I've got some bad news," Brehm says. "Your captain has died. I'm sorry for your loss." The first mate doesn't seem particularly grieved. "Do you have a cooler on the ship?"

"A what?"

"A cooler. COOL-ER. Refrigerator. Freezer. Icebox."

"Yes, yes," the mate says, glancing nervously over Brehm's shoulder. "Refrigerator."

"A big one?"

"Big."

"You need to get some men and move the captain's body to the refrigerator," Brehm says. The mate nods. "Have you talked to the captain's wife?"

"No one talk to wife," the mate says.

"What do you mean?"

"No talk. Not allowed. Captain's order."

"Well somebody's got to talk to her," Brehm says, feeling like he's talking to himself. "Please direct me to the captain's quarters."

When he gets there, he sees a woman sitting behind the captain's desk, talking on the phone. She's beautiful, in her mid-thirties, twenty years younger than the captain, with sleek black hair and remarkable dark eyes. Brehm can't tell if she's been crying. Her name is Raji Sekhar. She refers to her deceased husband only as Shaka. After telling her he's sorry for her loss, Brehm asks her a few medical questions, how long her husband suffered, what kinds of pains he reported, what his symptoms were. She answers the questions calmly, but she seems to be in shock.

He wants to say something consoling, but then her telephone rings, and she has to answer it.

At dinner, Brehm asks the cook, using the first mate to translate, whether or not the captain's wife has eaten anything. When he's told she hasn't, Brehm puts together a plate of food, chicken, and teriyaki vegetables, and brings it to her, telling her she should eat. She smiles.

"Please, come in," she says. "Unless you are busy. . . ."

"Busy?" Brehm smiles. "I've got all the time in the world," Brehm says, wondering how and when he'll be able to leave the ship. He can imagine she might need someone to talk to, even if she weren't on a ship where the crew was forbidden to speak with her. There are two black leather couches in the captain's quarters, a Persian rug on the floor (the only rug he's seen on the entire ship), a safe, a bookshelf, a large desk, a pair of nautically themed paintings on the walls (which seems a bit redundant), and a brass lamp. There's a lone picture frame on the desk. A door, sitting ajar, leads to what Brehm presumes is the bedroom, where they found the captain's body. Brehm takes one of the couches. Raji takes the other. Brehm speaks first.

"The first mate said nobody's allowed to talk to you."

"First mate," she says with scorn. She nibbles at a chicken leg. "First buffoon would be more like it."

"You're not too fond of the guy, I guess," Brehm says.

"He's an idiot," she says. "He's the cause of this, you know."

"Of what?"

"Of Shaka's heart attacks," she says.

"How so?"

"Oh," she says, rolling her eyes. "How so indeed. How so is that he was in charge of loading the ship, making sure everything is balanced and what have you, but Shaka was the type of man who attended to everything, you know—he couldn't trust other people, so he had to do it all himself. And especially that man, but this time, he didn't have time to check the First Buffoon's calculations before we sailed. Shaka said he would check the First Buffoon's figures later. When he did, he found out we were overloaded by ten tons. Ten tons! Shaka was furious."

"I don't know much about ships," Jack says. "That's a big problem?"

"Aha! It is indeed a big problem," Raji says, "if you are sailing through the Panama Canal. I've sailed with Shaka since we were first married—do you know what they do in the Panama Canal? They measure your water line, you see, and if you are overweight, you can't go through, because you'll run aground. They won't let you. They make you unload your excess cargo onto a barge, which you have to tow behind you, and then on the other side, you can reload, but they don't just give you the barge—you have to rent one. On top of the delay it causes, it can cost the company half a million dollars. Shaka was beside himself. He was livid. He'd be responsible. He's very respectful to his company—he never makes mistakes like that." She catches herself using the present tense. "We were very lucky—ultimately the weather was too rough to allow the canal authority to mark the water line, so they just waved us through and we didn't run aground, but it didn't make Shaka feel any better. Shaka was a fanatic for details. If it wasn't for the first mate, Shaka wouldn't have had a heart attack. He was too worried about what his First Buffoon was up to. No one respects the mate, you know. The whole crew are idiots. Do you know that the First Buffoon had to pull a knife to get one of the crew members to go out on the launch to pick you up?"

"Really?"

"It's true. It is. I tried to call the Coast Guard after Shaka died to tell them it was too late. I'm sorry you had to come all this way."

"It's not a problem," Brehm says, wishing he could take it back—it was not a problem for him, but the whole situation was clearly hard for her.

"Would you like a glass of wine?" she offers.

"You have wine?" Brehm says. "I didn't think you were allowed to have alcohol on an Islamic ship."

"You're not," Raji says, "But Shaka and I had our secrets. He had a weakness for cigars. I would buy wine whenever we were in port." She crosses to the ship's safe and opens it. "Would you like red wine or white wine?"

Jack tries to remember what he learned in survival school. He had chicken for dinner, and you're not supposed to drink red wine with chicken. He's good to go.

"White."

"Would you like a cigar?" she adds. "I have plenty of them and I am certainly not going to smoke them."

"No thanks," Brehm says. It's no time to be passing around cigars, and particularly not the dead captain's cigars.

She opens the bottle of Chablis and pours him a glass.

"That man is such a fool. I don't know how he got to be first mate. He's too young. He should be home, reading schoolbooks. Where are you from, Sergeant Brehm?" He likes the way she rolls the *R* when she pronounces his name.

"You can call me Jack if you want," Brehm says. "I'm from New York."

"You like New York?"

"Very much."

"Why do you like it?"

"Well, for one thing," he says, "when you're from New York, everywhere you go, people are friendlier." She smiles, but her English isn't good enough to catch the humor.

"I have never been to New York City."

"I'm from eastern Long Island, actually," Brehm says.

"And do you have a family, Jack?"

"I have a wife and five kids," Brehm says.

"Boys or girls?"

"Both. Two boys, three girls. The oldest girls are fifteen."

"My daughter is sixteen," Raji says. "When she was little, I could take her with us, but when she got bigger, I stayed home with her. Now she's fully grown."

"In America, we don't consider sixteen fully grown."

"I was married when I was sixteen," Raji says with a laugh.

"Really?" Brehm says. "Wow. I can't imagine my girls getting married, a year from now. Did you think that was too young?"

"Too young?" she smiles. "I thought that was too old. My friends had all married at fourteen. I thought I'd been passed by. I came home for dinner one night and there was a captain sitting at the table, and I knew right away that he was a captain, and what he was there for. My mother told me, 'Raji, we have a guest for dinner tonight,' and I knew right away."

"How'd you feel about that?"

"I felt very lucky. I didn't know much about the business of ships, but I knew it would be better than marrying a shopkeeper."

She says she loved her husband, despite the fact that the marriage was arranged. She and Jack talk. She asks him about his job. He asks her about her hometown. The way she seems to be handling things reminds him of

Peggy. Eventually, she asks him if he minds if she makes a phone call. She has to call her sister. Brehm sips his wine, drains his glass, and then refreshes it. Raji is speaking in English with her sister, and he tunes it out, until he realizes she is looking at him and answering questions. "Yes," she says, to a question her sister asks. He wonders what it might be. Raji glances at him. Brehm wonders why she keeps giggling. "Yes. Yes, very much." She glances at him again. "Oh, I don't know, maybe thirty or thirty-five—my age. Yes," she says, "he's handsome. He's very handsome. Uh huh. Uh huh. Yes. No, not now . . ."

"My sister is a very bad girl," Raji says, holding her hand over the mouthpiece. "If you were single, I would introduce you."

When Jack Brehm finally leaves, he tells the captain's widow she really needs to eat, even if she doesn't feel like it. He tells her he'll bring her lunch tomorrow.

The next morning, before checking in on Raji he needs to call the base to find out what transportation arrangements have been made to bring him, Brady, and Arrigotti back to the base. He heads for the bridge, hoping to use the ship's satellite telephone. When he gets there, he's greeted by the First Buffoon, who says, "Good morning, Captain." Brehm thinks to correct him, and say, "I'm a sergeant, not a captain," but he lets it go. What's the point?

"Can I use your phone?" Brehm asks.

"Certainly."

"Where should I tell them we're going?"

"Excuse me please?"

"Where are we going?"

"Wherever you want to go, Captain."

Then it dawns on Brehm—the first mate wants the PJ to be captain of the *Bunga Saga Tiga.* From the first mate's point of view, the more responsibility he can pass off, the better. Brehm's first thought is, *You've got to be kidding.* His second thought is, *That might not be a bad way to get home.*

"Let me get back to you on that," Brehm tells the mate. "First I need to use the phone." He wants to add, "And that's an order." He calls the Rescue Command Center in Elizabeth City. He gives his story to the duty officer at RCC, who can't believe it, either.

"They said what?"

"They said they'll take us anywhere we want to go."

"No shit?"

"No shit."

"Do they realize they're probably going to be fined by their company for every day they fall behind schedule?" the duty officer asks.

"Probably not," Brehm says. "The guy's not too sharp."

"Well," the duty officer says, "I don't know what to tell you. If it's okay with them, it's okay with us. I guess your closest port of call is Halifax. When you get there, call the harbormaster and they'll send out a pilot to bring you in."

"Anything else I should know?" Brehm asks.

"Yeah—don't hit anything."

Brehm tells the first officer he wants to go to Halifax. Ten minutes later, he can feel the ship changing course. It's good to be the captain.

The next day RCC calls back and says they've found a ship willing to change course to pick them up in mid-ocean, a smaller freighter that can rendezvous with them at 0200 hours. That way, the *Bunga Saga Tiga* won't have to fall behind schedule. Brehm, Brady, and Arrigotti talk it over. The crew had a hard enough time sending out the launch in broad daylight in relatively calm seas. The weather has worsened, and this time, they'll have to do it at two in the morning. Brehm doesn't want to have to pull a knife on anybody. Maybe if they were transferring to a luxury liner . . . but another freighter? Brady and Arrigotti are against the rendezvous. Captain Brehm makes the executive decision to maintain a heading for Halifax.

He calls the coroner in Halifax to tell him they'll be bringing in a body. The coroner asks him if he's sure the guy is dead. Brehm laughs at the question. "Well, if he wasn't when we put him in the freezer yesterday," Brehm says, "he is now." He makes arrangements with the shipping company to have someone from the company meet the widow at the dock. She'll need a hotel room, airline tickets back to Penang, and somebody has to escort the body home and see to the details to make sure it arrives safely—the widow shouldn't have to do that. Brehm brings Raji dinner that night and explains to her the gist of what he's arranged. He tells her they'll be in Halifax at eight the following evening. The coroner will meet them. There'll be policemen as well, to investigate any possible wrongdoing. She isn't worried. She thanks him. She's more subdued and solemn today, as the reality of it all starts to sink in. There are things you can postpone, at sea, that you can't postpone once you're back on land—it's why so many men go to sea. She thanks him for being so considerate. She breaks out a bottle of Merlot, and they talk for hours, about everything.

"It's really funny, isn't it?" she says at last. "In a way."

"What is?"

"That two total strangers from two entirely different countries and cultures can meet each other in the middle of the ocean and become friends. And then we'll probably never see each other again. Without you, I would have been sitting here in this room, with no one to talk to."

"Surrounded by idiots," Brehm says.

"Yes," she agrees.

The next day in Halifax, the ship is met by the coroner, as well as by two representatives from the Royal Canadian Mounted Police, who are required to investigate the circumstances of the captain's death. Raji has things to attend to, so Brehm says good-bye to her at the dock. A handshake, and then a hug. Brehm recalls the old saying about ships passing in the night. He tells her he and his buddies are joining a couple of Canadian PJs for a night on the town before a flight home in the morning. Raji could probably use a night on the town, but he knows an invitation would probably be inappropriate.

"So take care of yourself, Raji," Brehm says.

"Thank you again for everything," she says. "Wait a minute." She takes a pen and a piece of paper and writes down her address for him. "If you are ever in Penang, you must call me."

"Absolutely," he says, "and if you're ever in Long Island, look me up."

"New York," she says. "Where everybody is friendlier."

"Yeah," Brehm says. "Something like that."

14

DO YOU LIKE VAMPIRE MOVIES?

The ocean has a way of really humbling anybody who thinks he's strong enough to beat it. Sometimes it's something you think is going to be really simple that turns into something you can't control. One time we had what seemed like a fairly straightforward task, a training mission where four of us were supposed to deploy off the PJ boat about four hundred meters from the beach, maybe half a mile down from the Shinnecock Inlet on the southern shore of Long Island, about ten miles east of the base. The idea was to drop to the bottom and follow our compasses to a specific point on the shore. It'd be something like standing in a field or park, picking something across the park four hundred yards away, taking a compass bearing, and then trying to walk to it just looking at the compass and never lifting your head up to see where you're going. The visibility in the water off Long Island can be so poor that when you're on the bottom, you can't see more than three or four feet in any direction. What also happens, though, underwater, is that you can accurately follow a heading, but while you're doing that a current you didn't expect can take you down the shore without you knowing it. Something like walking across that field with a wind pushing you off your line.

It seemed like we were swimming longer than we should have been, and I was running out of air, so I decided to surface. When I did, I found myself right in the middle of the inlet, and the tide was ripping. I couldn't swim out of it. I was wearing twin 72-cubic-foot tanks, which made swimming a bit difficult, and then the waves caught me. I'd played in the surf as a kid a thousand times, so in a way I couldn't believe what was happening to me, because these waves were trying to kill me. The inlet runs between two jetties, made from gigantic granite boulders the size of refrigerators, covered with barnacles and mus-

sels and such—not exactly something you want to get bashed against. The first wave that caught me sent me in backward, so I took the blow on my tanks, but it sort of knocked the wind out of me. I managed to drop my weight belt, but I kept the tanks on for protection because I didn't want to break my back. On the second wave, I hit sideways and tried to break the impact with my arm, and it felt like I broke it, and maybe some ribs as well. I was trying to swim out between waves, but it was impossible, so I figured I'd just try to get myself in a good crash position instead. The third wave threw me up harder than the first two. I tried to grab on to something but I couldn't. That was when I knew that if I didn't figure something out, it was possible I was going to get knocked out and maybe drown. No way could I take a beating like that much longer. I didn't figure anything out, but the fourth wave lifted me up high enough that my tanks wedged between some rocks and I managed to climb out. My dive partner, Mike McManus, had virtually the same thing happen to him. I sat there, feeling equal parts lucky and stupid. I looked down the beach and saw that two of the other guys made the beach. I thought, man, you can't take the ocean for granted. Just when you think you're in control of it, it's going to show you different.

IT'S THE KIND OF MISSION YOU THOUGHT ABOUT, BACK WHEN YOU were going through hell at Lackland and the instructors yelled in your face, "Do you really want to be a PJ? Do you refuse to train? Do you *really* want to be a PJ?" You thought of the reasons why you wanted to be a PJ, and about saving lives, that was the main thing, the really important thing, but sometimes you also fantasized about training missions in Florida, where you'd spend your days scuba diving in the warm Florida waters and your nights drinking beer at open-air beachside bars and nightclubs, all on the Air Force's dime. And those weren't even the off days.

It's Friday, February 23, 1996, another six months to go before Jack Brehm's fortieth birthday, but it's never too soon to start treating yourself right. Particularly when you thought you weren't going to make it to thirty. PJs from the 106th have flown down to cover a space shuttle launch, but Jack needs to get in a few deep dives and a compass swim to knock out his dive requirements for the year. The others take the C-130 back to Westhampton. Jack drives down from Patrick AFB in Cocoa Beach, Florida, just south of Cape Canaveral, to Key Largo to meet up with Mike McManus and some PJs from Alaska. He hasn't seen Mike since Rick Smith's funeral. He also doesn't mind getting away from a winter that has dumped record amounts of snow in the Northeast. It's a year that a lot of northerners have headed for Florida, just to stay sane.

Today Brehm and McManus have three dives planned. They're going south of Pennecamp Coral Reef State Park, diving into a couple of wrecks not far from Mosquito Bank Light #35. The first dive, at 1:30 P.M., takes them down 115 feet to a wreck called the *Bibb.* They spend eighteen minutes at the bottom, exploring the wreck, then ascend, stopping to pause for five minutes at fifteen feet. You have to schedule safety stops into your ascent, and you have to exhale as you rise, because the air in your lungs expands as the water pressure around you decreases. On the surface, your lungs hold about four liters of air, but at sixty-six feet below the surface, those four liters compress to the size of a fist, and you need twelve liters instead of four to keep your lungs inflated. The pressure of the water squeezing your body doubles at thirty-three feet, increasing by a factor of one atmosphere. The scuba tank's regulator is designed to measure the pressure and allow enough air into your lungs to compensate for it. A hundred feet down, at a pressure four times that of the air pressure on the surface, you might have seventeen liters of air in your lungs, but if you rise as little as eight feet without exhaling, the air in your lungs can expand to where a lung might tear or pop a leak. A person in a car accident can suffer from a collapsed lung if he holds his breath when he sees the accident coming, hits the steering wheel or the dashboard, and puts too much pressure on his chest. Think of a lung as a balloon, inflating and deflating inside a jar. The jar represents the chest cavity, an airtight chamber. If the balloon leaks, the air escapes into the chest cavity. The lung then deflates and can't reinflate because there is now air in the chest cavity, and that air has nowhere to go.

The second dive at 2:30 P.M. takes them thirty feet down, to another wreck. They spend thirty minutes on the bottom, then ascend, pausing for four minutes at fifteen feet. The third dive, at 3:30, is identical, diving to thirty feet, with thirty minutes of bottom time and one four-minute safety stop at fifteen feet on the ascent. That night, Jack and Mike hit a few of the local hot spots. Brehm calls Peggy from his motel, the Marina Del Mar, about ten, and they talk about the kids' progress reports, Elizabeth's cheerleading accomplishments (she's the one they throw up in the air, the cheerleading equivalent of a HALO jump), the weather.

"Are you having a good time?" Peggy asks.

"I'm having a great time," Jack tells her. "Tomorrow we're diving into the wreck of an old freighter. They say it's one of the more famous wrecks around here. The water is just beautiful. I think it was eighty-five today. What's it there?"

"I don't want to talk about it," Peggy says. "It's cold."

"Well, it's not cold here."

"I said I don't want to talk about it."

"Is it snowing?"

"I don't want to talk about it."

"After we finished diving today we just lay on the beach. . . ."

"I'm hanging up now," Peggy says. "Be careful tomorrow."

"You know me," he says.

"Yes, I know you," she says. She knows that the thing most likely to get him in trouble is his enthusiasm. "Be careful anyway."

The next day, Saturday, February 24, breaks clear and bright, blue skies and bright sun, perfect diving conditions. Brehm, McManus, and PJ Steve Daigle, who climbed Mount McKinley with Jack, meet at the dive center in the morning. They load their gear onto a wooden 28-foot dive boat, open and flat in the back, allowing divers to step off into the sea. They leave port at around 9:00. They reach the dive site, suit up, and enter the water around 11:00. Brehm is wearing an eighth-inch wet suit (the water is cold a hundred feet down, even in Key Largo) and a single 80-cubic foot scuba tank, which will give him about an hour of air at thirty feet, or twenty or thirty minutes' worth of air one hundred feet down. The wreck they're diving to today, a ship called the *Dwane*, is 120 feet down. They will spend eighteen minutes on the bottom, then ascend, pausing for five minutes at fifteen feet. One hundred twenty feet is fairly deep for a recreational dive, about the limit for a sports scuba certification, but Brehm dove to 115 feet the day before on the *Bibb* and didn't have any problems. His personal deepest dive is 130 feet, done while in scuba school in Key West. One hundred twenty feet is about the height of an eight-story building. As you descend, you can feel the pressure change in a number of ways, as the weight of the water presses on the air-filled cavities of your body. You feel a pain in your ears, until you have to hold your nose and blow your eardrums back out, or sometimes work your jaw until your ears pop and feel normal again. Your mask gets squeezed to your face, so you have to blow air into it through your nose to equalize the pressure. A neoprene wet suit that is a quarter-inch thick on the surface will be crushed at 110 feet to the thickness of a T-shirt, as the light gets murky and the temperature drops.

It takes Brehm and McManus about five minutes to reach the wreck. For Jack, descending is the fun part. When he first enters the water and turns around to look down, a kind of euphoric feeling comes over him because he's weightless and gently falling toward something very beautiful. There's another kind of euphoric feeling, one Brehm is aware of and monitoring himself for. It's called nitrogen narcosis, and it can mean different things to different people. Some people feel light-headed, or lighthearted, buzzed. Some feel intoxicated and giddy, not unlike the way the nitrous oxide the dentist gives makes you feel. The rule of thumb says that every fifty feet you descend is equal to drinking one martini. Some divers feel a sense of tunnel vision, and some people hallucinate. The story goes that Jacques Cousteau, who helped invent scuba diving, felt so happy when he first experienced nitrogen narcosis that he tried to offer his mouthpiece to fish and had to be stopped by his dive partners from doing so, or he might have drowned. Other people feel tense, or even paranoid. Thought processes under the influence of nitrogen narcosis can become as murky as the water; a diver might lose the ability to do long division or other relatively easy math problems, which can lead to diving accidents, especially when conditions below change, forcing the diver to recalculate his dive underwater, say if a swift current or reduced visibility makes the tasks he needs to accomplish take longer or require greater exertion, increasing his air consumption. Sometimes a diver can get a bit loopy, until it seems as if when one thing goes wrong, four things go wrong: he drops his light, and then he drops his compass, retrieving the light, and then he snags his fin on something, and suddenly, he's in trouble. Nitrogen narcosis happens when the nitrogen in the compressed air a diver breathes gets forced or absorbed into the blood and tissues of the body as the pressure increases. What we call "air" is only 21 percent oxygen, 76 percent nitrogen, and 3 percent other gases, and a diver breathes enormous amounts of air when he dives deep.

Nitrogen narcosis is what can happen as a diver descends. The bends can happen when he ascends. A diver gets bent if he comes up without pausing to allow the nitrogen in his blood or tissues to be expelled through his lungs. As the pressure decreases as the diver ascends, the nitrogen in his tissues expands and forms bubbles, something like the way the carbon dioxide in a soda bottle will fizz or foam when you take the cap off the bottle. A diver who ascends without pausing at all, in a panic situation, can get the full-blown systemic bends, which can be fatal, even if he's rushed to a hyperbaric chamber. A hyperbaric chamber treats decompression illnesses by recompressing the victim, which stops the nitrogen from expanding uncontrollably and forces it back into the blood. Once it's in solution in the blood, the lungs can remove it. Even a diver who ascends with caution and planned decompression stops can sometimes take a bends hit in a specific area, where a number of tiny nitrogen bubbles have coalesced to form a larger expanding bubble, sometimes in a joint, in a muscle, or sometimes within the nerve tissue itself, which can be excruciatingly painful. Sometimes there's permanent damage. Researchers today think there are also dive events called micro-bends, which have a subtler effect. Some Navy divers who've dived to extreme depths have been found subsequently to have a neurological condition that seems to permanently rob them of their sense of humor. After a deep dive, some divers find that it can take hours to regain fine motor control over their muscles, and that they can't play the guitar, or write legibly, or they have trouble driving. Perhaps the biggest danger is that you usually don't feel anything happening until you're back on land and you think you're safe. The deepest recorded dive with scuba gear, breathing regular air, is 525 feet. The deepest dive of all time using scuba gear is 925 feet, accomplished in 1996 by two men, Jim Bowden and Sheck Exley, in the Gulf of Mexico, using thirty tanks and fourteen different gas mixtures of oxygen, nitrogen and helium, but even at a depth where the pressure was strong enough to crush a quarter-inch thick cast aluminum battery case, Bowden didn't feel any extraordinary pain. Exley died making the dive.

Today, as he approaches the wreck, Brehm feels good. Confident. Like he's got the best job in the world, but then, he's also felt that sense of satisfaction on dry land. He has a slight case of nitrogen narcosis, but it's nothing he hasn't experienced before. If anything he feels perhaps a bit cocky. Usually he experiences nitrogen narcosis as the equivalent of drinking two beers, nothing dramatic, but definitely pleasant. He tries to caution himself against feeling too cocky. Feeling too good about yourself is as dangerous as feeling scared, both forms of impaired thinking, but it's hard to stop yourself from feeling good about something. He follows McManus as they explore the wreck. The wreck has been picked clean by other divers over the years, no souvenirs to take home to Matt or Jeff, but it is nevertheless interesting. According to reports, there is supposed to be a large grouper living somewhere on the wreck, and Jack wants to find it. At one point, he comes to a wall, about eight feet high, and has to swim up and over it. As he does, he feels a slight ping just above his heart, slightly to the left. It's a small pain. He's felt such pains before, though never in this exact place. Sometimes they go away.

He dives again at noon, a mere forty-foot dive for forty minutes bottom time, into a wreck perhaps three miles away from the first. The second dive goes fine, but when it's over, around two, Brehm realizes he still has the pain over his heart, a very slight ache, but a specifically located ache all the same. He thinks, it's probably nothing.

At nine the next morning, he tries to go for a six-mile run from his motel, heading south on Route 1, but after only a quarter-mile, he feels a sharp stabbing pain in his heart that makes him stop in his tracks, grab his chest and cry out. He bends over. He wonders if he's having a heart attack. He takes his pulse. After a moment, the pain lessens, but he decides to give up on the idea of running. Walking back to the hotel, he is in constant pain, with sharp attacks coming every few seconds. He sees Mike McManus in a coffee shop and joins him.

"What's up, Jack?" McManus says. "You don't look so good."

"I'm not so good," Brehm says, telling McManus his symptoms. He's hesitant to tell McManus just how bad it is. He fears he has a serious problem.

"When did you first notice it?" McManus asks.

"Yesterday, during the first dive."

"It sounds like maybe you took a hit," McManus says. "It's probably not anything serious, but if you are bent, you should go back to the motel and see if you can find a local dive chamber."

Sometimes the symptoms of a dive injury can be so vague that divers don't seek attention for days or weeks. Symptoms can resemble those of a virus: headaches, nausea, fatigue, vomiting, intestinal disturbances, parathesia, muscle or joint pain. On the phone, Brehm hopes to find a local doctor who specializes in diagnosing dive-related injuries, but when he calls the nearest dive chamber in Key Largo, he gets an answering machine, informing him that it's closed because it's Sunday. That sounds a bit odd, for what is ostensibly an emergency medical facility. He leaves his number. No one calls back. He drives with the team back to Patrick at noon. Everyone is laughing and talking about the weekend, so he keeps his complaints to himself. When they stop for gas north of Miami, Mike McManus asks him, out of earshot from the others, how he's feeling. "Like shit," Brehm replies. At 4:30, he calls the emergency room at Patrick, and at 5:30, he sees the flight surgeon, Dr. Ted Foondos, who examines him and asks him a series of questions. Does he feel any joint pains? Any need to cough? Did he feel like he pulled anything, loading or unloading equipment, either onto the C-130 he flew in on or on the boat before or after the dive? Dr. Foondos listens to Jack's chest through a stethoscope. Brehm's heart sounds fine. His breathing sounds normal. Foondos calls Brooks AFB in San Antonio, the Air Force's main medical facility for studying and treating fliers, and consults with a Dr. Mike Ainscough. The conversation lasts about ten minutes.

"We don't think you're bent," Dr. Foondos says at last. "My guy at Brooks agrees. If you were, there ought to be other symptoms. It seems more likely that you pulled a muscle."

"Really?" Brehm says. "You know, Doc, I'm in pretty good shape. . . ."

"I'm going to write you a prescription," Foondos says. "You take these and call me in the morning. Tell me if anything changes."

The prescription is for Motrin.

At 9:00 the next morning, Monday, Jack is back in the doctor's office. The pain has moved. What was once located on his left side, above his heart, seems to have shifted to below his zyphoid process, the bottom of his breastbone, near the diaphragm. How could a muscle pull relocate? Foondos doesn't know, but suggests that if the pain persists, Jack should call his flight surgeon when he gets back to Long Island. Brehm doesn't press the point, but nothing he knows about medicine has ever explained to him how a muscle pull might relocate. By 4:00, Brehm is on a commercial airliner, headed home.

His flight surgeon in Long Island is a Dr. Pasternak, a guardsman and, in civilian life, a cardiologist. When Jack calls him the next day, Tuesday, he's told that the doctor won't be back to the base clinic again until 2:00 Friday. The problem is that now the pain not only persists but it's shifted again, moving from his diaphragm to mid-sternum. Basically it feels as if he's swallowed a large ice cube. This is getting weird, he thinks. At Peggy's suggestion, he locates a dive chamber on Long Island and speaks to a nurse who specializes in dive injuries. He describes the progression of the pain. The nurse is busy, but listens and expresses her opinion when he's done.

"What'd she say?" Peggy asks him when he gets off the phone.

"She says it doesn't seem dive-related," Jack says.

"That's ridiculous," Peggy says. "You're okay, you dive, you're not okay anymore—that's dive-related. Call Dr. Pasternak back."

"I'm seeing him on Friday."

"Well, call him back and get him on the phone. Leave a message and make him return your call. If this is a problem, you're not going to wait until Friday to take care of it."

You sometimes get the sense that if Peggy Brehm had been on the *Titanic,* there would have been plenty of lifeboats to go around, they would have all sailed away fully occupied, and the ship probably wouldn't have struck the iceberg in the first place.

Pasternak returns Jack's call at 7:15 that evening. Jack tells him he originally had a sharp stabbing pain over his heart, which became a dull ache in his diaphragm, which turned into a feeling like he'd swallowed a large ice cube. Pasternak listens and asks some of the same questions Dr. Foondos did. He asks about the dive in question and if anything unusual took place during it. The dive was planned perfectly, and Brehm and McManus and the others dove the plan. No one else on the dive experienced any difficulties, and they followed the same procedures Jack did. Pasternak's over-the-phone assessment matches that of the woman from the dive chamber at St. Agnes. It simply doesn't seem, at least from the way Jack describes it, to be a dive-related injury. They'll know more on Friday when they can meet at the clinic. Until then, he says, Jack should take it easy and skip his daily workouts.

In the interim, the feeling changes yet again. By Friday, it feels as though there's a weight inside his chest, tied to a string around his heart. He thinks he can feel something flapping around loose. Sometimes he almost thinks he can *hear* something flapping around loose, though that's probably unlikely. One night he lets Peggy put her ear to his chest, but she hears nothing but his heart beating. She borrows his stethoscope, but can't tell anything. The last time she put on a stethoscope, they were listening to the separate heartbeats of the twins, Michele and Elizabeth, when they were still in her womb. It reassures her to hear his heart beating. Her concern is for him. His concern is for himself, too, but also for his family, and how he might provide for them in the future, because there are rules regarding what types of injuries might disqualify a man from being a PJ. Getting knocked unconscious, for example, automatically disqualifies you from serving in pararescue, because it's known that one spell of unconsciousness can lead to future blackouts or seizures, and PJs work under circumstances and in situations where they can't afford to black out. Needless to say, between getting sucker-punched in a bar fight or simply going one Kamikaze or Jell-O shot over the line and passing out, PJs do, in some way or other, become unconscious from time to time, so it helps to have a flight surgeon on your side. It also helps to work in hospitals where you can gain access to your own medical records, and it helps to know how to work a bottle of Wite-Out or the delete button on a computer keyboard. Serious injuries, however, can't be hidden, and shouldn't be, and good PJs know that. Lying in bed the night before his examination, Jack hopes it is just a muscle pull, because if it's something else he might have to start looking for a new line of work, and that thought is as uncomfortable as the pain in his chest. The more he thinks about it, the more certain he is that this is a career-ending injury. He tries not to think about it.

Jack meets Dr. Pasternak at the clinic at 4:00 on Friday, March 1. He describes the pain as a loose feeling and says that sometimes he thinks he can even hear it, so Pasternak puts a stethoscope to his chest and listens. Everything sounds normal. He repeats that it doesn't seem to be a dive-related injury, but he knows that Jack is not satisfied with this diagnosis. Brehm knows he probably should be satisfied, because three separate people who ought to know, Dr. Foondos, the dive clinic nurse, and now Dr. Pasternak, have all said the same thing.

"Look," Pasternak says, "why don't you call the physiological center down at Brooks and talk to them? Maybe they can reassure you."

Brehm calls from Pasternak's desk, only to be told that all flight surgeons at Brooks are gone for the weekend. Pasternak recommends that Jack be patient. They can go further with this if the conditions persist, or worsen, but if it's a severe muscle pull it will simply take time to heal. Brehm asks if he should resume his physical training. Pasternak says he can, as long as he keeps it light and stops if he feels any discomfort. Relaxing and not worrying about it sound like good ideas—after all, everybody else is telling him it's minor. Maybe worrying too much about it is the real problem.

Deep down, Jack still thinks he knows better.

On Saturday, Brehm tries to obey doctor's orders and does nothing. The pain and the loose feeling are still there. On Sunday night, he has a hockey game with his team, "The Lost Cause," so he tries to play, but he becomes quickly winded. He thinks it's been so long since he's put in a decent workout that he's gotten rapidly out of shape. On Monday, he manages to run four miles on a treadmill at the small gym in the Ops building at the base, but he can barely maintain a nine-minute mile pace, and he feels very weak.

He feels somewhat better when he wakes up on Tuesday morning. He reports to work. At 7:00 A.M., he tries to go for a six-mile run. He gets a mile and a half before he is fatigued and out of breath. This is not a pulled muscle. He doesn't know what this is, but this is not a pulled muscle. He turns back to the base. A mile from the gate, he decides to go all out and run as fast as he can. He uses the stopwatch function on his watch to time himself.

By the time he reaches the gate, he feels as if he's going to collapse, gasping for air. His time is eight minutes and thirty-three seconds. Now he knows something is wrong. He feels a hundred years old. He's afraid. This is a career-ending injury. The twins are applying to colleges. How will he pay for that? What can he tell them? How will they handle the disappointment?

At the base he showers, dons a flight suit, and finds an empty office with a door he can close behind him. At a quarter to two in the afternoon, he calls Brooks AFB and asks to speak with a flight surgeon from the physiological center. He speaks with a Dr. Butler, who tells him to start at the beginning. It takes Brehm nearly an hour to recite the chronology of the last two weeks. Butler listens patiently and asks a few questions, mainly to make sure he has the dive depths and the times correct. Jack tells him he just tried to run an all-out mile and did it in eight and a half minutes.

"That sounds pretty good to me," Butler says. "I'd love to run an eight-and-a-half-minute mile. How fast would you normally run it?"

"I'm a PJ and a triathlete," Brehm tells him. "I usually run that in less than six."

Jack finishes his synopsis. Finally Dr. Butler reaches an opinion.

"I'm guessing you have medistinal air, probably a pneumothorax," he says. Brehm knows from his paramedic training what that means. He may have a collapsed lung. "I'm going to call Pasternak right now and arrange for you to get some chest X-rays. What's the closest hospital to you?"

Brehm gives Dr. Butler Dr. Pasternak's number, as well as the number to Central Suffolk Hospital. Butler tells him to report to Central Suffolk immediately. Jack clears it with his supervisors and leaves for the hospital.

The X-rays are taken at 4:00. The X-ray technician is a pretty young brunette woman, maybe twenty-five years old. She asks Jack to wait until she develops the film, to make sure the film comes out clear. It does. Ten minutes later, she tells him they're fine.

"They're fine?" Jack says. "What do they show?"

"I'm only the technician," she says. "I can't read the X-rays. I just meant they're fine as in, the pictures came out okay, and I won't need to reshoot them."

"Well when will the doctor be able to read them?"

She shrugs. "The radiologist just left for the day. He'll be back in the morning."

It sounds a bit fishy, since Dr. Butler told him to get to the hospital immediately, but Brehm figures if he could wait nine days, he can wait another twelve hours.

On his way home, he stops off at Barbara Dougherty's house to see how she and the kids are doing. Jimmy is in Turkey on a TDY. She asks Jack if he remembers the Ukrainian sailor her husband recently rescued. Jack says he certainly does. Alexander Taranov. The sailor was from a Ukrainian cargo ship that had rolled over in a storm and was sinking in the mid-Atlantic. Looking down from the airplane, the crew counted thirty-four Ukrainian sailors in the water, holding on to anything that floated, bobbing about in twenty- to thirty-foot seas. The C-130 dropped all the life rafts they had onboard, a total of six, along with survival kits and radios. They managed to make radio contact with the Ukrainians, and told them they'd be back at first light with helicopters and to sit tight. When the HH-60s arrived the next morning at the break of day, they circled the area for thirty minutes, unable to discover a single raft, with no trace of the ship. Finally Dougherty spotted a lone survivor clinging to some flotsam. Dougherty low and slowed in and hoisted Taranov out. The rest of the sailors' shipmates, Dougherty learned, had been killed by sharks during the night or drowned.

"What about him?" Jack asks.

"He's defecting," Barbara Dougherty says. "He's in Manhattan with his lawyer, and he wants to know if I want to come into the city to meet them for drinks. I was wondering if you'd go with me."

Jack says he doesn't feel so good, but he'll go if it will cheer her up. When Laura Spillane calls, checking in, they decide that Laura will go and Jack won't have to, since he's not feeling up to it.

Jack doesn't know that just after he left Central Suffolk Hospital ("Central Suffering," some called it), the twenty-five-year-old X-ray technician had shown Jack's X-rays to a doctor who just happened to be passing by. The doctor said, "I hope this guy is in surgery."

"He's not," she told the doctor. "He just went home."

"When?"

"Two minutes ago"

"Well run out to the parking lot and see if you can catch him," the doctor told her. "This guy should be in surgery. Now."

Jack drives home from Barbara Dougherty's house but passes Peggy coming from the opposite direction. Peggy frantically waves him down and pulls off the road. Jack gets out of the car and sees that his wife has been crying hysterically.

"What's the matter?" he asks.

"You," she says. "A doctor from Texas just called the house and told me he sent you to the hospital with a collapsed lung. Then I called the hospital and they tell me you left—where have you been? Why didn't you call me?"

"They can't read the X-rays until tomorrow," he explains. "There's nothing to tell you until then. I was at Barbara's. I almost went into the city with her. That Ukrainian guy is defecting and he and his lawyer—"

"Nothing to tell me?" Peggy says. "I'm thinking you're in a hospital with a collapsed lung, and you say you have nothing to *tell me*?"

"I didn't know you knew anything," he said. "If I thought you were worried, I would have called."

"How can I know anything if you don't call me?"

"But if you don't know anything, then why would I assume you were worried about—" Jack begins, but quickly abandons this line of reasoning because he knows he's wrong. "I'm sorry. I should have called you."

At home, Peggy asks him again how he feels. She says he doesn't look very well.

"I'm fine . . . I just . . . think maybe I should . . . lie down for . . . a while."

"Listen to you," she says. "You can't even finish a sentence without taking a breath every three words."

The phone rings. It's Dr. Pasternak. He tells Jack his left lung is 80 percent collapsed and that he needs to get to the nearest hospital as soon as possible. Jack tells him that would be Mather Hospital in Port Jefferson, and that he's on his way.

Meanwhile, Peggy has checked the answering machine. There are three messages, one from Jack's NCOIC, Chief Manuel; one from Dr. Butler;

and one from Central Suffolk Hospital. All three messages say the same thing. Get to a hospital, now.

Immediately.

Do not wait.

Peggy drives. Jack doesn't want her to worry, so he tries to tell her that he sees collapsed lungs all the time, and that the procedure to remedy the situation is fairly simple. In the field, lacking anesthesia, he would perform a thoracentesis, inserting a large-bore fourteen-gauge needle, about the diameter of a toothpick, to purge the air in the chest cavity. In a hospital, under anesthesia, a chest tube would be used. The balloon-inside-a-jar analogy isn't quite accurate, because in fact both lungs occupy the same chest cavity, with the heart between them. As one lung collapses, venting air through the tear into the chest cavity, the chest wall around the healthy lung slowly fills with air, restricting the healthy lung's expansion. The pressure in the chest cavity increases with each exhalation, until the damaged lung collapses entirely. Then the pressure begins to push the heart into the healthy lung. If it pushes it too far, it stresses the vena cava, the vein that returns blood to the heart. An artery like the aorta is fairly sturdy, but the vena cava is comparatively flimsy and can easily become twisted or kinked. When this happens, it's called a tension pneumothorax. If the vena cava is constricted completely, no blood can return to the heart, and the patient dies.

Jack tells her only that he sees collapsed lungs all the time.

He reaches the Mather emergency room at ten minutes to seven. He's taken into triage at ten minutes after seven, and at seven-thirty, new X-rays are taken. Peggy is with him, holding his hand, asking him how he feels. He feels fine, really, relieved to be in a hospital and finally getting treatment, but Peggy isn't satisfied that the man she loves is out of danger. It's also true that for all the times in his life that Jack has been in danger, she has never been there with him. She has never been able to do anything about it.

"You're sure you're okay?" she says.

"I'm good," he says. "Really."

She pats his hand. He squeezes hers. She tries to think of what else she can do.

At 8:00, an ER doctor comes by to examine Jack. He asks Peggy to wait on the other side of the curtain. He listens to Jack's chest, and tells him that the new X-rays have revealed that his left lung is 100 percent collapsed and is restricting his right lung by 10 percent. The ER doctor asks the nurse when the thoracic surgeon will arrive. He's told that the thoracic surgeon is due in about twenty minutes.

"This guy doesn't have twenty minutes," the ER doctor says.

Peggy hears this. She throws aside the curtain.

"Look—I don't know what you have to do, but I want you to do it right now," she says.

"Please wait behind the curtain," she's told.

"I'm not waiting behind the curtain," she says. Jack reaches for her hand.

"Peg, it's all right," he says, struggling to breathe. "I don't feel that bad, plus the guy is right here with the needle and he knows what to do with it if he has to. It's not that big a deal."

"Who's going to do this thing?" Peggy asks, turning to the ER doctor. "Are you?"

"We're hoping the thoracic surgeon will arrive shortly," he says.

"What's his name? I want to speak with him."

"It's Dr. Van Bemmelen," the doctor says. "I believe he's on his way to the hospital at the moment."

"He's on his way? You don't know where he is?"

"Peggy," Jack says, "it's going to be all right. Come here."

He puts his arm around her. She kisses his cheek. He whispers to her, "I really think we should just wait until the doctor gets here. I'll be okay until then."

Van Bemmelen arrives at 8:30. He looks at the X-rays, and asks the ER doctor when they were taken. Told that the pictures are half an hour old, Van Bemmelen frowns. He informs Jack that there's no time to wait for an operating room. Unfortunately, that means that there's no time to wait for anesthesia, either. He wants to insert a chest tube immediately.

"Do it," Jack says.

"There's going to be some pain," Van Bemmelen says.

"Do it," Brehm says.

Van Bemmelen picks up a sterilized scalpel from a tray. The idea is to make an incision below Jack's left clavicle and insert the chest tube, a clear plastic tube about the diameter of your index finger. The technical term for it is a thorascotomy.

"Should I be here?" Peggy asks.

"Well," Van Bemmelen asks her, "do you like vampire movies?" She says she doesn't. "Then you might want to step out for a second."

Jack knows she's within earshot, so he doesn't cry out when the surgeon stabs him with the scalpel. He says only, "Oh God . . ." Peggy hears him. It hurts, but it's a good pain, Jack has to admit. When Peggy returns, he's smiling. The chest tube has allowed his left lung to reinflate. Within three breaths, he feels as though it's full again. The tube will stay in for as long as it takes for the tear in his lung to heal.

"Oh my God," she says when she sees the bloody tube sticking out of his chest. "How do you feel?"

"A hundred percent better," he tells her.

"I've got to call the kids," she says.

While she's on the phone, Jack wonders if trying to run a mile in under six minutes was what finally blew the lung open. He probably had a slow leak before that. He feels like a thick-headed idiot. He'd tell Peggy as much, but she already knows.

He doesn't kick himself for showing poor judgment—he's always pushed it, always been a bit reckless, in the belief that luck comes to those who press their luck, and so far he's been right. What nags him is a different idea. Muscle tissue is something you can change through exercise. You can build muscle tissue, and make yourself stronger, but there's nothing you can do to strengthen the tissues in your lungs. The lungs simply grow older, and as the tissue ages, it weakens. You can't help it, and you can't reverse it. The body ages. You lose bone strength, and muscle strength, and brain cells, and who knows what else. You can't help it. You can't reverse it. You can't give in to it, either.

Would his lung have collapsed twenty years ago? Why now? Does it mean anything? Is it a sign, of aging—of mortality? Or of something smaller than mortality—a sign that it's simply time to start thinking about a different line of work?

* * * * * * * *

At home, while he recuperated and waited to return to flight status, Jack signed up for a paramedic class, hedging his bets. If the doctors ruled that he couldn't return to flight status, he might look for work as a medic. He did odd jobs around the house, and he shoveled snow. Lots of snow, snow that filled the backyard and covered the deck. There were eighteen major snowstorms that year. One day, after the snow had piled up at the end of the deck to where it nearly reached the roof, Jack and Jeffrey built an igloo, the kind of snow shelter Jack had learned to build during winter training exercises, complete with a protected entryway and benches inside to sleep on. Jeffrey wanted to spend the night in the igloo, and Jack agreed. Jeffrey went in at 8:00 that night, and Jack joined him long enough to stick a handful of green chemlights in the snow for illumination. He told Jeffrey that he wanted to watch television until ten, and that he'd join him after that. When Peggy learned that Jeffrey was in the igloo all by himself, she decided to keep him company, even though she wasn't really an outdoors enthusiast, and not the kind of person who would ordinarily spend any more time than she had to in a snow shelter. Jack gave her his sleeping bag. She brought a book with her and said she was going to read.

Most people who stay in snow shelters are surprised at how comfortable they are. When Jack went in to get Peggy at ten, she was sound asleep, and so was Jeffrey, so he left them there, safe and warm in their down bags. He turned off the lights. In the backyard, the igloo glowed a dull phosphorescent green in the late winter night.

15

THE HAND OF GOD IN THE HEART OF PITTSBURGH

Mike and I were on a TDY in Thailand in 1988 where we were ordered to teach a Thai captain how to free fall. I believe he's a general or something by now, but at the time, he was still a V.I.P. who wanted to learn how to free fall, and we were chosen to help him. We knew him as Captain Sui Gin. He was in his mid-twenties, maybe five foot six, with a perpetual smile on his face. First of all, in the Pipeline, there's a procedure you have to go through before you can free fall. You go to jump school at Fort Benning and learn how to land and how to jump off a static line. You go to the wind tunnel at Fort Bragg, North Carolina, which is essentially a big hole in the ground with a fan at the bottom with a net over it, and the fan blows air up at 125 miles per hour, and you jump in and learn how to float and how to turn, and how to stabilize yourself, in a safe, controlled environment. You don't just read a few books and then step out the back of an airplane. The guy did wear jump school wings, so we assumed he'd jumped before, but whether he'd ever done free fall remained to be seen. Second, Mike and I didn't have our AFF qualifications, which you need to instruct accelerated free fall, but there was no one else available. Better us than nobody. Third, the guy didn't speak a word of English, which made instructing him slightly more difficult. I pantomimed, and I used hand signals, and I drew the guy pictures—I had no idea how much of it he picked up on. He just sort of smiled and nodded at everything I said. We did this every night for a week. When it came time to jump, to be safe, Mike and I grabbed on to him, one on each arm, and we went out the door with him, but the guy didn't exit square to the wind and immediately he started tumbling, flip-flopping every-

where. Mike wanted no part of it and flew out. It was sort of "Here you go, Jack—let's see how you handle this." I tried to do what I could to get the guy stable, but it was no use, and I was running out of time, so eventually I pulled his main chute and hoped he remembered some of the things I taught him. Away he went, on a square chute he didn't really know how to steer, or brake, riding with the wind. The drop zone was fairly large, a field alongside a country road, but beyond that there were trees and farms and mountains in the distance. If he hit a tree . . . even if he landed in an open field, he could still hit it at thirty miles an hour if he landed with the wind. Mike and I made the DZ without any complications. We had no idea where CAPT Sui Gin went. When we finally caught up with him, he was walking down the road, about four miles away, carrying his parachute under his arm, and he was totally psyched. He wanted to go again. Considering we'd lucked out not killing him the first time, we declined.

But I've always said that Mike and I have led charmed lives. We've both walked away, time and again, from parachute malfunctions and other screw-ups. Sometimes you feel lucky. Other times you feel like there's more than luck involved. Sometimes you feel like maybe somebody's watching over you.

JACK BREHM AND MIKE MCMANUS SHARED A CHARMED EXISTENCE, almost from the start. They'd missed the crash in Plattsburgh, a flight they both could have been on. They survived the pounding on the rocks of Shinnecock Inlet, anecdotally one of the most dangerous inlets in the United States. They were able to bail out of a Thai helicopter after it lost an engine at 10,000 feet. They'd survived hangovers that would have put ordinary men in hospital, and bar fights that would have put ordinary men in jail. McManus had saved Jack's life, simply by teaching him to hang tough. It was McManus who got Jack into running marathons and Iron Man competitions, advising him that the way to get ahead in a race was to imagine that the guy in front of you was a mass-murdering rapist psychopath who wasn't going to stop until he got to your house. There were always going to be other mass-murdering rapist psychopaths to pass, but the point was to focus on the one in front of you, and take them one at a time. Brehm returned the favor by saving McManus's life one night on a visit to Anchorage. The two men were debriefing the day's activities over beers at an Alaskan institution called the Alaskan Bush Company, a strip joint on East International Airport Road just off Old Seward Highway, decorated in Old West Yukon frontier motifs, lacking only swinging doors and someone named Miss Kitty at the door, with a staircase against the back wall that led to the dressing rooms. They were drinking their second beers when Mike described to Jack a weird thing that had been happening to his heart lately, palpitations that came and went and didn't seem to be related to exertion or stress, accompanied by a strange light-headedness. McManus was getting a lap dance at the time, and had a pair of hooters in his face like you read about in books, but Brehm excluded the lap dance from his diagnosis, took a beverage napkin and wrote down the words *Wolff-Parkinson-White Syndrome* with a felt-tipped pen. WPW is essentially a short-circuiting of the heart's electrical system, in which an extra electrical pathway develops between the atria and the ventricles, causing extra contractions that speed the heart rate, easily reparable with surgery but potentially fatal.

"Five bucks says I'm right," Brehm proclaimed. "We just read about it last week in my paramedics class."

An examination by a cardiologist shortly after that was inconclusive, until Mike asked the doctor to look for WPW and proved Brehm's diagnosis correct. McManus carried the beverage napkin in his wallet ever since. McManus was, however, lucky before he ever met Jack, according to a story Brehm frequently tells, when he tries to explain to people why Mike McManus is the toughest guy he knows.

McManus was stationed in Tachikawa AFB in Japan. It was 1968. The section got a call that a fishing boat had had an explosion, five hundred miles off the coast of Japan in the North Pacific. The ship was dead in the water, adrift in a storm. It wasn't known whether there were any survivors on the ship, only that an emergency SOS beacon had been activated. McManus launched in a C-130 at 2100 hours, along with another PJ named Ted Martin. They homed in on the beacon but didn't find the ship until midnight, partly because there were no lights on the boat and partly because the weather was so rough, maybe forty-foot seas and fifty-knot winds. The weather was bad enough that the pilot wanted to abort the rescue, but Mike had flown with him on five other jump missions, and together they had a pretty good track record, and besides, McManus argued, there could be people trapped in the overturned hull of the ship.

The radio operator couldn't raise the ship. Mike concluded that there was nothing left but to go down there and see what happened.

Ordinarily when a jumper leaves an airplane, it suddenly gets very quiet. It was the only time, in Mike's memory, that it ever got louder outside the plane. He heard the ocean literally roaring below him, loud as a freight train, and it scared the crap out of him. He thought, "Oh boy, this is going to be fun."

They deployed from a thousand feet, about two and a half miles upwind from the ship, using round parachutes that couldn't be steered or turned, though McManus did have some control over his rate of descent. Ted Martin immediately had a malfunction, pulled his reserve chute, and sailed off into the night. McManus watched him disappear. He saw the ship below, in a mass of foam, directly on his wind line, and knew he had two choices, either to fly over it and swim back or drop in short and swim to it. He didn't want to hit it, so he decided to drop in short. His landing was rough. He hit the top of a wave with his fins, popped his capewells to release his chute, and immediately did a flip into the sea, smacking the water so hard it ripped the regulator out of his mouth. As a teenager he'd worked as a clown diver, entertaining vacationers in Florida resort pools, so he knew a bit about aquabatics. He'd swam in the open ocean in his early days as a PJ, recovering film cartridges dropped to earth from spy satellites, risking his life for cassettes with signs on the side that said, "If found, please return to . . ." with an address and an offer of a $25 reward for anybody who came across one washed up on a beach, though they were, of course, worth far more than that.

Nothing he'd ever done prepared him for this.

The previous estimate of forty-foot seas proved a tad conservative. The seas were overwhelming, preposterous, ridiculous, hellacious. The Japanese fishing boat drifted away from him in the wind. He swam toward it for a while, but it was no use. It was drifting too fast. He tried to raise the C-130 on his radio, but the radios they gave PJs back then didn't work very well when they got wet, which was most of the time, so he got rid of it because he didn't need the extra weight. He got rid of his scuba tanks for the same reason, dumping them before they beat him to death. He had an inflatable one-man butt boat with him, but the water was too rough to stay in it. The winds were too strong and kept flipping him over. He got back in the water and hung on to the raft. Much of the difficulty came from the fact that there was no pattern or predictability to the waves, the way you can watch waves crashing rhythmically on a beach. Waves lifted him high in the air and dropped him on his face. Waves crashed over his head. He'd take a gulp of air, go under, surface, and wait for the next wave to hit, though they were coming at random, and he never knew when the next one would pound on him. Saltwater blew in his face and down his throat. He threw up frequently. Sometimes he'd ride four or five waves in a row, but then the next one would toss him. He had no sense of time passing, living moment to moment, knowing only that he was growing tired and cold. When he fired a flare the C-130, which was still circling overhead, tried to drop him a twelve-foot in diameter twenty-man raft. Twenty-man rafts weigh about seventy pounds. McManus watched it flip end over end and blow away, skipping like a stone across the surface of the water.

He fired more flares, but there was nothing anybody could do. He knew it would be crazy to send another man in after him. There was no sign of Ted Martin, no other flares in the sky to indicate what might have happened to him. McManus was on his own. For six hours, he fought the ocean. He felt if he could just make it to the morning, he'd be all right. They'd come get him. For six hours, he rode up and down thirty- and forty- and fifty-foot swells, hanging on to his raft while the wind and the waves conspired to rip it from his hands. A wave would crash over him, he'd wait for it to clear, catch a breath, and wait for it to happen again. For six hours.

McManus wasn't a churchgoer and he didn't pray, or at least he wasn't into the "Please help me" approach to deities, but he did talk to the Big Guy from time to time, and felt they had an understanding, that when it was time they'd get it on. McManus believed that God had a sense of humor, and that he was definitely the Big Guy's entertainment that night.

Around 6:00 A.M., as the sky was beginning to lighten, he saw a ship, a Japanese fishing boat, coming toward him, though it was too far away to have seen him yet. The weather was still nasty, twenty-five foot breakers and thirty-knot winds. He had one flare left. He waited, then popped it when the fishing boat was about two hundred yards off. He was in luck. The boat turned toward him.

Ordinarily a boat coming to the rescue of someone in the water will either send out a smaller boat or, more likely, lower a cargo net over the side for him to grab. McManus wasn't sure what they were going to do, and he wasn't sure how much strength he had left to grab any cargo nets.

Enough, he hoped. As the fishing boat approached, he looked for men tending the deck, but in the roller-coaster seas, it was hard to keep a fix on it. He didn't see anybody. When he dropped low, the boat would disappear altogether. Then he'd rise up and see it. Then the entire boat would disappear again behind a wave.

Then suddenly it was upon him, just as a colossal wave lifted him up. The fishing boat plunged into a trough, approaching from his right. The wave crested, then came crashing down on the deck of the ship, carrying Mike with it. He hit hard but managed to hang on to the railing, as the water cleared the decks.

He caught his breath, polling all the parts of his body for broken bones or worse. He was okay.

"Damn," he thought, "I don't know how they did that, but these guys are good."

He gathered himself together for a moment, then took his fins off, threw his butt boat overboard, and walked around to the side of the pilot house, hanging on to the railing lest another wave wash him overboard, in which case they'd have to start over, and he didn't see how they'd be able to catch him twice. The door to the pilot house was closed to the heavy seas, so he pounded on it. There was no answer. He pounded on it again, and then the door opened. There were three Japanese fishermen inside, each of them with eyes wide as saucers.

They hadn't seen him.

They hadn't seen his flare.

They'd only turned in his direction to run with the weather and keep from capsizing. They were in shock, wondering how a small American man in a wet suit had managed to climb onboard their boat in the middle of a typhoon.

The storm raged for three more days. If the fishing boat hadn't picked him up, McManus most likely would have died. Without flares to signal his position, he'd have little hope of rescue. Spotting a lone man floating in the ocean would have been difficult, even in calm seas. A C-130 crew the next day said they couldn't even spot the twenty-man raft they'd dropped him. Ted Martin got picked up by a luxury liner that was riding out the storm and spent the next three days drinking Scotch in the lounge. McManus was transferred to a Japanese Coast Guard cutter, where he helped treat victims of the storm. When they found the boat that had originally emitted the emergency beacon, there were no survivors onboard.

Before he retired, McManus became a member of the Air Force STARS, an expert parachuting team the Air Force uses as a recruiting tool, putting on demonstrations at air shows and football or baseball games. After he left the STARS, McManus got Jack to apply for the vacant position, one which Jack eventually filled by attending a try-out involving jumping and hitting the target ten times in a row, sticking the landing each time. McManus did a jump into a Texas Rangers game at Arlington Stadium in the spring of 1998, executing a perfect hook slide into third base on his landing and getting the thrill of a lifetime. It was a thrill that he wanted his protégé to experience.

Other than as a recruiting tool, stadium jumps have little practical value. If an American pilot were ever to get shot down and eject into the middle of a stadium, there would probably already be somebody there to attend to his medical needs and recover him. At the same time, stadium jumps are among the most difficult PJs or any demonstration jumpers ever attempt. To get a sense of it, put a Cheerio on the floor, maybe ten or twelve feet in front of you, and then imagine trying to fly down into it. The winds involved in a stadium jump are extremely difficult to predict because they change constantly, blowing way across the top of the bowl, swirling in different directions inside the bowl, then shifting again at ground level, where there may be winds blowing in from open loading doors or gaps in the stadium walls. Most stadiums are located in urban areas, surrounded by parking lots, lit barbecue grills from tailgate picnics, lampposts, people, flagpoles, buildings, traffic, and most dangerous of all, those annoying, nearly invisible high-voltage power lines. You train to be as accurate as possible, but nobody in the military trains or draws up plans for jumping into cities or urban areas. Urban insertions are done with helicopters and hoists or fast ropes. In any jump, you have a drop zone (for military training purposes, drop zones must be clear of obstacles for one hundred yards in any direction from the center of the target), but if conditions in the drop zone change or become dangerous, you need to designate an alternate drop zone. If the target zones in stadium jumps are iffy, the alternate drop zones can be even iffier. You don't, however, have a choice—you have to pick somewhere to land. It's one of the more unbreakable laws of parachuting—you must land on the ground the same number of times as you jump out of airplanes.

Brehm's classmate, John Smith, did a stadium jump in Niceville, Florida, near Fort Walton Beach, that went more than a little awry.

Conditions were favorable, a warm autumn night, moderate winds. Smith and a team of PJs from Eglin had executed a practice jump earlier in the day without a hitch. The real jump was scheduled for roughly eight o'clock at night. The plan was to land on the 50-yard line during pregame activities at Niceville High School's homecoming football game. It seemed fairly low risk, flying into a high school stadium, not one of the massive college or professional bowl stadiums full of swirling winds that can give jumpers fits. Smitty was flying a different type of chute from the kind he ordinarily flies, a "sharpshooter" canopy in a vector container, one with a quick-access pilot chute stowed in a pocket on the leg strap of the harness, which he simply needed to grab hold of and throw out into the wind, instead of pulling a rip cord. He exited the plane, saw the aircraft and the stars in the sky, and thought that because it was a night jump it would be wise to locate the hand-deploy early. When he reached for the pilot chute, he couldn't find it. He looked for it, but in the darkness he couldn't tell where it might be. He'd loosened his leg straps during the long wait, crouched in a cramped airplane, and forgot to cinch them down again before he jumped, which may have been a factor. There wasn't time to figure it out. When the emergency beeper went off in his ear, warning him that he'd reached his minimum pull altitude, he immediately went to his reserve canopy. He had a good reserve opening, but by then he was too low to make the target. He started looking for an alternate place to land. The main thing he wanted to avoid were power lines. He saw a brightly lit intersection on a main road that looked pretty good to him and turned toward it, only to see a traffic light change from red to green a few blocks ahead. He saw the oncoming traffic and decided not to challenge any cars or trucks for the right of way. He turned again and headed for a small grove of oak trees. PJs train to land in trees, and in emergencies often prefer to land in trees, which present a fairly consistent set of variables. PJs have special jumpsuits designed for tree landings, akin to the jumpsuits worn by smoke jumpers in Montana and Idaho who fly in to fight forest fires, with low crotches that are reinforced with heavy nylon straps that run beneath the feet and up the inside of the legs. You can kick a man wearing such a suit in the groin and it won't hurt him. Smith wasn't wearing such a suit, which briefly gave him pause, but all things considered, hanging up in a tree was still his safest bet. By now he was too low to maneuver into the wind, so he flew in a deep brakes position, arms straight at his sides, toggles all the way down, to bleed off as much forward speed as possible and enter the tree on a steep vertical descent. At the last moment, however, he saw the last thing he wanted to see—power lines, running through the tree's foliage. He let go of the toggles. The canopy surged dramatically over his head and whipped him up over the power lines, but he hit the tree so hard he broke off a large branch. As Smith fell on the branch, the branch fell on the power lines, causing them to arc, blue sparks flying up into the night. It smelled something like the overheated transformer from an electric train set. The arcing power lines blew out a nearby transformer, which blew out a series of transformers down the line, which blacked out a large part of the city. By the time Smith hit the wires, they were already dead, which was good, because if they weren't, he would have been. He landed on the ground, on his feet, with nothing but a small scratch on his arm.

Brehm got his stadium jump in September of 1998. He had to think hard about it, because he knew the dangers, but Mike had told him what a thrill it was, and Jack couldn't help but fantasize about making a splashy landing in front of sixty thousand people, and many more than that if they showed the game on national television. The whole idea of the Air Force STARS team (Special Tactics And Rescue Specialists) was to get publicity for the Air Force. The plan was to jump onto the field prior to the coin flip and deliver the game ball to the referee at a Pittsburgh Steelers game in Three Rivers Stadium, Pittsburgh. Peggy saw it as an unnecessary risk that Jack didn't have to take, but when she saw the gleam in his eye, she knew there was no stopping him. "The biggest little kid in the world," Randy Mohr had always called him, and he was right. Jack fantasized spiking the ball in the end zone, and he liked the idea of his kids seeing him on television. For a belated eighteenth birthday present, he'd taken his daughter Michele on a jump at a local skydiving club in August, a place where beginning jumpers hooked up in tandem to an instructor. Jack had gone out the jump door of the stripped-down Cessna after her (a plane built in 1956, he noted, the year he was born), and he'd seen the smile on her face when she screamed and gave him a double thumbs-up sign—he was happy for her, because he knew how she felt, but he was also happy for himself, because he knew that for the first time someone in his family finally understood how he felt when he jumped out of airplanes. Fathers hear their teenage children say "You just don't understand me" all the time. Fathers usually have to hold their tongues at such moments, when what they really want to say is, "Well, it would be nice if you understood me, too." Jumping into a stadium, on television, with his children watching, appealed to him. He told Peggy he might even be able to get her tickets to the game.

"I'm a lot less interested in getting tickets to the game than I am in getting you home safe," she said.

"So it's okay for me to go into a war zone but it's not okay to jump into Pittsburgh," he teased.

"It's not okay for you to do, either," she said. "Why don't you get a job in a deli? There's no dishonor in slicing meat, you know."

"This we do, that others may eat salami," he said. "I don't know, Peg—it just doesn't sound the same to me."

* * * * * * * *

A week later, on September 26, Jack Brehm is in the air over Three Rivers Stadium. Six thousand feet below, where the Allegheny, Monongahela, and Ohio rivers meet, Three Rivers Stadium looks smaller than a donut. It's the day before the game, Saturday afternoon, and time for a practice jump. There are four jumpers. Brehm is the third. All will exit the plane at 6,000 feet. The first man will free fall to 4,000 feet and pull, the second to 4,500 feet, Brehm will pull at 5,000 feet, and the last man will pull five hundred feet above him.

It feels wrong from the start. He's used to jumping from much higher altitudes, anywhere from 10,000 to 26,000 feet. He's also used to jumping over water, grass, deserts, even jungles. Below, he sees where I-279 crosses the Allegheny River on the Dusquesne Bridge, and where U.S. 19 crosses the Ohio River on the West End Bridge, and where U.S. 30 crosses the Monongahela River on the Fort Pitt Bridge. The roads are full of cars, which he'd hate to hit. He sees a Navy ship below, the USS *Requin,* now a tourist attraction, docked where the three rivers meet, just south of the stadium. He sees the rooftops of Allegheny Community College on Ridge Road, the Andy Warhol Museum on Sandusky, and the Carnegie Library in Allegheny Square. He sees the tracks of the Conrail railroad running past the stadium, and the skyscrapers of downtown Pittsburgh. He sees the Art Institute, Heinz Hall, Fort Pitt, the Gateway Center, Point State Park, and he sees the pointed steeples of all the nearby churches, St. Mary of Mercy, St. Peter's, Emmanuel Episcopal, and Friendship Baptist. They look like so many pungee sticks, set in the ground to spear him.

He wonders if he's getting too old for this. He and Peggy have talked about his retirement plans and what he might do when he's no longer a pararescueman. He's heard that guys start to psyche themselves out the closer to retirement they get. They start noticing how far out to sea they're going to fly on a mission, and how many air refuelings will be involved, and they start asking what the weather is going to be like when they get there, where before they just went and accepted the dangers, without really worrying about or anticipating them.

Thirty seconds from the drop, he gets the final wind report over his headset. A large scoreboard at the east end of the field marks the twelve o'clock position. A STARS team spotter on the rim of the stadium says winds there are coming from the two o'clock position at eleven knots. A spotter on the ground says winds are five knots from the ten o'clock position.

Brehm exits the plane about a half a mile from the stadium. If something goes wrong, the alternate drop zone will be one of the rivers, whichever river seems closest. He falls to 5,000 feet and pulls, experiencing the familiar and ever-reassuring shock of an opened chute, which yanks him suddenly from a horizontal to a vertical position, feet to earth. His adrenaline begins to pump, then pumps harder when he realizes something is wrong. He looks up and sees that the cells of his chute, a special red-white-and-blue demonstration chute, smaller and faster than the chutes he ordinarily uses, able to turn on a dime and penetrate higher head winds, is only 70 percent inflated. The end cells on the left side of the chute haven't inflated. This isn't an uncommon malfunction, and pumping the brakes usually corrects it.

He pumps the brakes.

It doesn't work.

He's at 4,300 feet.

He realizes he's in a severe left-hand spiral. The city spins beneath him, whirling counterclockwise. It's dizzying. To equalize the curvature of his canopy and fly straight, Brehm has to pull 85 percent right brake and zero left brake. He looks up again, and sees that he has a malfunction called a tension knot, which is not correctable by the jumper, and must be cut away.

He's at 4,000 feet.

You can't deploy a reserve chute until you've rid yourself of a malfunctioning chute—otherwise the reserve will get tangled in the bad chute. The procedure, therefore, is to grab the reserve chute's rip cord with your left hand and grab something called a cutaway handle with your right. The reserve chute rip cord handle is a square aluminum ring, about the size of a cigarette pack. The cutaway handle is shaped differently from a rip cord's

D-ring, so that the two never get confused. The cutaway handle is a small beanbag, about the size of a dill pickle, red fabric filled with sand, attached to the right harness strap with a set of mated Velcro strips. Pulling the cutaway handle flips a series of three interlocking rings, which releases the main. It's attached solely with Velcro, but when Jack tries to pull it with one hand, it won't break loose. It should, but it won't. He goes after it with both hands, which means he has to release the brakes, which again sends him into a severe downward left spiral, but ridding himself of the malfunction is more important. He can't free the cutaway handle from the harness. He absolutely can't pull his reserve until he releases his main.

He grabs the brakes to fly straight again.

He's at 3,700 feet.

He can't land with his malfunctioning chute—he'll die if he tries.

He releases the brakes, spiraling left again. The city rotates beneath him, getting closer and closer. He grabs the cutaway handle with both hands, but just before he does, he offers up a brief sort of prayer, not a formal heavenly address, just the words, "Don't let me die doing something stupid." This time, he pulls as hard as he can on the cutaway handle with both hands. Instantly he feels separation, and transitions back into free fall, face to earth. Now the city rushes at him, antennae and steeples and telephone poles and lampposts, and it all wants to skewer him.

He's at 3,200 feet.

He pulls his reserve and fires it off. He's jerked back to vertical, feet to earth, a small white square chute now open over his head, but he's not out of trouble. He glances to his right, and sees his fancy main chute, so pretty in the colors of the flag, with the words *Aim High Air Force* stitched into it, drifting down toward downtown Pittsburgh. What if it hits somebody? It's not his problem anymore.

He's at 2,700 feet.

He looks for an alternate landing site, but nothing appeals to him, particularly not the cold gray waters of the river below him. When he spots his jump partners, he realizes, to his amazement, that he hasn't lost that much altitude and has maintained his position in the stack. All his maneuverings in the cutaway process must have happened in just a few seconds, though it seemed to take much longer. He decides to try for the stadium.

"We have a cutaway," the voice in his helmet radio says. "Repeat, we have a cutaway and a good reserve deployment."

He thinks, "Thanks for paying attention."

He's at 950 feet.

He follows the number two jumper over the lip of the stadium, crossing the wall at the three o'clock position. He immediately turns left toward the six. It's crazy. He's falling *inside* something. The stadium lights and tiers and seats fly past in a blur. The winds are swirling. It feels as if there are cables everywhere, threatening to cut his suspension lines. He spots the windsock on the 50-yard line, which shows ground winds coming from eleven o'clock at five knots. Turning to land means he has to get close to the far end zone's cable. He hopes he can see it to avoid it. He can't see it—there's too much in the background. He hopes he misses it.

He misses it.

He turns to his final approach at two hundred feet and experiences severe turbulence. It rocks his canopy. He has to release his brakes to stabilize his canopy, but this sends him shooting past the 30-, the 40-, the 50-yard line. As the turbulence subsides, he brakes hard, then makes a final crab to the left to land directly into the wind, at which time he sees a stack of plywood sheets directly in his path at the 20-yard line, just off the field. He manages to land on top of the stack of plywood (instead of hitting the side of it), runs off, jumps, slips on the blue plastic tarpaulin used to cover the field during rains, and slides into the 10-yard line.

Shit damn.

Stadium jumps.

Cheeses.

He's glad to be alive. He feels a tingling in his extremities, the aftereffects of having the crap scared out of him. He is glad Peggy wasn't there to see this. He's glad 100,000 people weren't there to see this. He's glad it wasn't on national television. He is mainly full of disbelief, amazed that he'd come so close to frapping on something so ridiculous, so trivial, a *practice* jump, for a *demonstration*, in *Pittsburgh!* After all the things he's done in his life, to almost die that way . . .

He hears a voice behind him. It's the voice of Wayne Norad, the team chief.

"Sergeant Brehm," Wayne says. "Can you tell me what you did with my five-thousand-dollar United States Air Force STARS parachute?"

"Sorry, Chief," Brehm says. Unbelievable. Does the man not realize what almost happened, or does he know and is simply making light of it? "Not a clue—I had my eyes on the stadium the whole time. I suspect it's somewhere in the heart of Pittsburgh."

Brehm walks to where the other jumpers have gathered. He examines his harness. It's then that he realizes something. He observes the cutaway handle. It looks funny—there are loose threads hanging from it. His first thought is that somebody sewed the knap and hook components of the Velcro together. The knap component is commonly attached to the beanbag, and the hook component is sewn to the harness.

Closer examination reveals that there is no hook component attached to the harness. That is to say, there used to be, but in his panic, or rather, in his desperate effort to pull the cutaway handle, Brehm ripped the stitching from the harness and removed *both* halves of the Velcro. It would take incredible strength to do that.

It would certainly take two hands—or three, he thinks, if you include the hand of God.

That night, Brehm calls McManus to tell him what happened.

"See?" Mike says. "I told you they were fun."

The next day's jump is canceled, due to high winds.

16

ANYONE ELSE BUT ME

Dear Dad,

How are you doing? When are you coming home? Dad do not forget to get me some thing o by the way soon as you left Mom started crying. I love you.

Love,

Jeff

On Sunday, April 11, 1999, the newspapers report that NATO is committing eighty-two more planes to Operation Allied Force, sending over twenty-four F-16s, four A-10 Thunderbolts, six EA-6B Prowlers, thirty-nine KC-130 tankers, two more KC-10 tankers, and seven C-130 transports, bringing the total number of airplanes flying in the Baltics close to seven hundred. A report of explosions at the airport in Montenegro suggests the war might be expanding. The next day, NATO requests an additional three hundred planes. New NATO ally Hungary, where Russian tanks rolled in 1956, stops a convoy of seventy-three Russian trucks headed for Yugoslavia, but the Soviets still seem intent on getting involved. For the first time, Pentagon spokesman Kenneth Bacon suggests that an expanding campaign could require calling up reservists and Guardsmen. By Tuesday, a defense department spokesman is saying reservists could be called up any time, adding that the president has the power to activate up to 200,000 men for as long as 270 days. Logic suggests that if the war expands, and more PJs are needed, that it would be easier for the Air Force to keep in place the men who are already there, rather than fly over troops less prepared.

On Saturday, April 10, Peggy has a luncheon at the base for the Family Support Group. She's been so busy driving her brother-in-law Jim to and from Sloan-Kettering that she's missed the last couple of meetings, and the idea is, after all, that people show up and help each other. She picks up Barbara Dougherty and leaves a note for Matt, telling him what yard work needs to be done. The whole yard needs to be raked out, and particularly the flower beds, where she intends to lay stone instead of mulch this year—it is almost standard that each time Jack goes away, she does something radical to the house, partly to surprise him and give him something to look forward to coming home to, and partly, she supposes, out of some subconscious need to rule the roost by redecorating it. At the support group meeting, they talk about the scholarship fund, but she has a hard time paying attention. On top of everything else, in a week she'll be attending a fund-raiser for Jim that Michele has arranged at the Ramada Inn in Riverhead, a party to help defray his medical costs. Elizabeth will be coming home for it, and says she's bringing her boyfriend Drew—a really nice boy, but isn't the house small enough already? Michele says she and her Aunt Carol will do all the cooking, but there are still a million details to attend to.

When Peggy gets home, around two, she sees that the yard work hasn't been touched.

"Where's Matt?" she asks Michele. "Didn't he see my note?"

"He said he was going to his friend Vinnie's," Michele says, digging into a late lunch she's prepared for herself, white rice and ketchup.

"Vinnie's?" Peggy says. *The nerve of him, to totally ignore my note.* She picks up the phone and dials Vinnie's mother, who says she doesn't know where the boys are.

"Unbelievable," Peggy says.

She gets in her car and goes looking for her oldest son. She drives past Vinnie's house, past the school, past several of Matt's friends' houses. *How dare he? The nerve of that boy! He totally ignored me. He's definitely not afraid of me anymore. How could he? He knows at a time like this we have to pull together. That's what he does—that's exactly what he does—he's just seeing how far he can push, because John isn't here. If John were here, he wouldn't dare. The nerve.* She drives past Vinnie's house again, wondering where they went. To the beach? The park? *Maybe this is just normal? It's normal for a fifteen-year-old boy to rebel—maybe this is nothing to worry about? One thing is clear though—if I don't get control back, the other kids are going to start following Matt's lead. How dare he defy me? I don't need his defiance—this is not the time nor the place for it.*

Then she spots him at the 7-Eleven on Route 25A, where he isn't allowed to go because the traffic is too heavy. She pulls over to the curb. She considers that, at fifteen, it may be time to let him go to the 7-Eleven alone. Vinnie is with him, their bikes leaning against the store window. Then she sees Matt give Vinnie something. Matt looks guilty, suspicious, as if he were making some kind of drug deal. Drugs? She knows him well enough to know that's not it, but it's something. Then Matt spots her, but apparently he thinks she doesn't see him, because he runs away.

Now he's running away from me? He's running *from me? This boy is in big trouble.*

She pulls into the parking lot next to the Rocky Point Diner, down from the convenience store, and waits. She's not in the mood to chase after him, and she has a pretty good idea that if she waits long enough, he's going to come back to get his bike. When he does, she pulls into the 7-Eleven lot and orders him to get in the car.

Now!

He throws his bike in the back.

"Do you have any idea the kind of trouble you're in? Do you have *any* idea? Like it's not bad enough that you ignored my note—what were you up to?"

"When?"

"Now? Just now—at the 7-Eleven."

"Nothing."

"What were you giving Vinnie? I saw you give him something."

"Nothing."

"Don't tell me nothing, I saw you give him something. I want to know what it was?"

"Mom . . ."

"What did you give him?"

"I gave him firecrackers," he finally admits.

"Firecrackers?" she says. "And where did you get firecrackers?" She knows roughly where he got them—everywhere they stopped in North Carolina on the drive home from Myrtle Beach they were selling firecrackers, bottle rockets, Roman candles, and worse.

"I bought 'em at one of the gas stations we stopped at on our way home," Matt says. He'd begged her for fireworks, until she relented and bought him some, a brick of basic Black Cat firecrackers, which she'd wrapped and stored away, telling Matt he wasn't allowed to open them until his father came home.

"You went behind my back, when I was filling up the car with gas, and bought fireworks?" she asks him. He nods. Part of her wants to laugh, because she knows there's probably some sort of genetic attraction to fireworks in the family, some consanguineous appeal, though Matt definitely doesn't get it from her side. She hates fireworks. Back when she was pregnant with Matt, Jack got in trouble at the base when a group of PJs started shooting off their pen guns, which are Vietnam-era flares designed to shoot up seven hundred feet and penetrate the jungle canopy to signal rescue helicopters. They were shooting them in the general direction of the C-130 fleet when the base commander caught them. Another time Jack hurt his eye, playing with fireworks at a Fourth of July beach party. But it wasn't funny then, and it isn't funny now.

"You've made a lot of really bad decisions today, Matthew," Peggy says. "Really bad. And for your information, you now have two hours of yard work and one hour of indoor work ahead of you. Do you understand me?"

"Yes, Mom."

"Do I have to say it again? Have I made myself clear?"

"You've made yourself clear."

The next day, Peggy goes to her sister Carol's house after mass for breakfast and calls home to make sure Matt is doing his yard work. He grumbles, insolent. When she comes home, she finds he's gone back to bed. His cheekiness amazes her. She makes him get up. When she goes to the laundromat to do laundry, her cell phone rings. It's Jeffrey, asking her to settle another argument he's having with his brother. She tries to listen to both of them, but she doesn't even care what it's about, and they're both wrong, and they're both grounded until Jack comes home.

Jeffrey, she can tell, is losing it. He has a two-week limit when Jack is gone, and now his two weeks are up. When school starts again after Easter break, Jeffrey complains that his ribs hurt, enough that he doesn't want to go to school. She makes a deal with him—she'll give him a couple of Tylenol and send him to school, but if he still hurts, he can come home. After he leaves, she calls the school nurse to warn her that he's hit his limit, and that if he comes in, all he'll need is sympathy, maybe an icepack, fifteen minutes of quiet time, and a hug. "If he's really teary," Peggy says, "call me and I'll come get him. He's also not going to be able to concentrate on his schoolwork."

When the nurse calls and says she thinks Jeffrey has a real problem with his ribs, Peggy takes him to the doctor, who says Jeffrey has a strained muscle and bruised cartilage on his rib cage. Peggy doesn't like bringing her children to doctor's visits alone, and again thinks, *I never asked to be the single mother of five.* Jeffrey is actually glad, because his injury means he has two weeks free of yard work, but that night, when Peggy goes to her sister's for Chinese food and some deeply needed "adult time," Jeffrey calls three times, needing to be told what position to sleep in, needing to be told when to take his medicine—needing to know that his mother will come in and kiss him good night when she gets home.

Michele is stressing, too, but seems to be coping. The work she's doing for her Uncle Jim's fund-raiser on Saturday is phenomenal. While working at the Olive Garden, going to school full-time, and finishing up her EMT training, Michele has also been running around to local shops and restaurants getting them to donate prizes and free dinners for two and for four, which she'll be able to raffle off at the fund-raiser. Elizabeth is helping as much as she can from Boston, but she's mainly worried about her mother, worried that she keeps so much to herself. Elizabeth thinks that if her father could only hear the weariness in Peggy's voice and see how worn down and tired she is, maybe this would be his last trip.

Thursday is the worst day of all. Peggy wonders why she's having such a hard time keeping it together, why she can't seem to get a grip. She doesn't want to be alone anymore. It's as simple as that. No other explanation is necessary. Bean left at 4:30 A.M. for a school field trip to Washington, D.C., and that further fragments the family. That afternoon, Jim gets a report on a new CAT scan, which seems to show a four-centimeter tumor on the right plura, the blood vessel near his heart, as well as a blood clot that the doctors are worried about. She knows Jim doesn't need more bad news, two days before his big party. *How much more emotional stress can I handle?* She wants Jack to call, even though the next call isn't scheduled until tomorrow. She feels an overwhelming sadness. She can't allow it to grow, but it seems to get bigger and bigger all the time.

The next day, he doesn't call. Elizabeth is home from school to help with the fund-raiser. Nobody at the dinner table dares to bring up the fact that Jack hasn't called. They try to talk about the good news—further analysis and a second opinion on Jim's CAT scan has revealed that what they thought was a new tumor is nothing more than scar tissue from where the old tumor was removed, and the blood clot is just some surgical Gore-Tex used to patch up the vena cava. They talk about tomorrow's party. They make small talk, and they try to keep talking, because in the silences between the words they can all hear the phone not ringing.

Jack doesn't phone because on Thursday, Groundhog Day finally comes to an end. The team gets a call at 1200 hours to deploy to the Forward Operating Location, somewhere on the border of Turkey and Iraq. They load the aircraft, draw their weapons and taxi out onto the ramp, only to be told that their clearance to fly doesn't come into effect until 1430 hours. Finally, at 1500 hours, they're in the air. After they land and unload the helicopter, there's only time to eat dinner and hit the sack. Brehm can't believe it's taken this long to arrive. There are no telephones at the FOL, which makes him sorry that he won't be able to call home, but there's nothing he can do about it. He's glad to finally get a chance to "play," however, and tries to focus on the task at hand.

The next morning, at 0730, he reports to work. They reload the helicopters, prepare their radios, test their sat-coms, update their intelligence reports, and go over their gear. They don't know how many flights over Iraq they can expect today, but they expect to be told soon. An hour later, the word comes.

"The box will not open today," they're told by headquarters. "Stand down."

"The box will not open today." That's it? That's all? Everyone is pissed off. They're ready. There's nothing they can do to be more ready. They're willing, eager, trained, and if they don't go, they're going to feel as if they've wasted their time.

At noon, they're told to pack up their personal gear because they're going to be replaced. For all the delays in getting them there, it takes the Air Force a mere thirty minutes to land a C-130 to take them back to Incirlik to outprocess.

Brehm can't believe it.

On the flight, he ends up talking to a younger PJ, who asks him if he ever thinks that maybe he's getting too old for this sort of thing.

"What do you mean by that?" Brehm asks the kid.

"I don't mean that you can't do the job—I just mean, you know, that you have, what, five kids?"

"Five," Jack says.

"It just seems like that's a lot to lose."

"Well, of course I don't want to lose it," Brehm says. "I've got a great life—what are you going to do? *Not* have a great life, because there's a chance you're going to lose it?"

"I suppose not," the younger PJ says.

"The way I figure it, I'm forty-two years old, and I've done more stuff than most people do in a hundred years. I mean, that they would do if they lived a hundred years."

"I know what you mean."

"I've been more places."

"Hoo-yah to that."

"What's the point to being alive if you don't believe in something strongly enough to risk your life for it?" The younger PJ doesn't say anything. "I mean, who's to say the day I decide to retire I won't get hit by a car? There's a sign outside the main gate of the base where I work that says, 'YOU ARE ABOUT TO ENTER ONE OF THE MOST DANGEROUS AREAS IN THE WORLD. A PUBLIC HIGHWAY. FASTEN YOUR SEAT BELT AND DRIVE DEFENSIVELY.' I see that sign every day. Who's to say I won't die in a car accident two miles from my house? If that's the case, then I'd rather die rescuing somebody. When and where I die isn't exactly under my control."

He didn't mean to go off on the guy, but standing around for three weeks doing nothing, only to be replaced, has gotten him thinking about what he's doing here. It's weird. He's elated to be going home, and deeply disappointed at the same time. He finds himself thinking of a quote he learned back in high school, his freshman English class, Mr. Snow, the teacher's name was. It was something by Shakespeare, and he can't remember it precisely, but it went something like, "Cowards die many times before their deaths; the valiant never taste of death but once. Of all the wonders that I yet have heard, it seems to me most strange that men should fear; seeing that death, a necessary end, will come when it will come."

He has, in fact, remembered it precisely. If he could remember the context, he'd be aware of the irony. The lines come from Shakespeare's *Julius Caesar,* Act 2, scene 2. The speaker is Caesar, addressing his wife, Calphurnia, on a stormy night full of lightning and thunder, while conspirators are afoot, out to do him harm, and the omens are all bad ("A lioness hath whelped in the street") and she wants him to stay home and play it safe.

"What can be avoided whose end is purpos'd by the mighty Gods?" Caesar wants to know. "Caesar should be a beast without a heart, if he should stay at home today for fear."

Jack arrives at Incirlik and finally manages to call Peg. She happens to be home alone when he calls.

The fund-raiser at the Ramada Inn in Riverhead is a smashing success. They raise over $13,000 to put toward Jim's medical expenses, and everybody is thrilled to see Jim dancing with his wife and to learn that his latest test results are negative. All of Peggy's enormous extended family has shown up, as well as friends from the base, and friends of Jim's from the car dealership where he works. Peggy looks terrific, in a gray-blue dress that flatters her. Michele shines. Elizabeth, in a black velvet skirt slit up the side nearly to the hip, her long curly blond hair cascading down her shoulders, has glammed up and looks like a forties' movie starlet. The food is delicious, large flat pans full of pastas, lasagna, ziti, and salads. They raffle off tickets to Jets games, dinners at local restaurants, free haircuts and manicures and massages, baskets full of Girl Scout cookies and bottles of champagne. The place is decorated with crepe paper and Christmas lights. Matt and Laura-Jean hang out with their friends. Jeffrey has his eye on a pair of walkie-talkies being raffled. Jack and Peggy's next-door neighbor Dennis is a DJ and spins the tunes. The best dancers on the floor are all under six years of age, including one little boy in sunglasses who has disco fever so bad he needs a pediatrician. When friends ask Peggy if she's heard from Jack, she silently shakes her head and bites her lip. When they ask her how she's doing, she says, "Hanging in there, but just barely." Everyone is sensitive that, on an evening when everybody else seems to be coupled up, Peggy is alone.

It's possible that somebody, paying close attention, might notice something slightly different about Peggy, something a bit sly or deceptive in the way she answers questions or glances about the room. Most eyes are on Jim and Lorraine, slow dancing cheek to cheek in the middle of the dance floor.

Elizabeth, her boyfriend Drew, Greg, Bean, and Matty all work in the garden the next day, placing rocks and trying to make things look nice for when Jack comes home. Lorraine and Carol come over for dinner. Carol's kids come, too. After dinner, Michele and Elizabeth and their boyfriends go over to Carol's to watch a movie. They get home around eleven to find Matt watching television.

"Where's Mom?"

"She went to a movie with Aunt Sally," Matt says.

"What movie?"

"I dunno."

"Wow," Elizabeth says. "Good for her."

But it's not like her mother to go to a late movie. When Peggy's not home by 1:00 A.M., Elizabeth starts to worry. It doesn't help to know how upset her mother has been lately, how on edge. She wakes up Michele. They whisper in the hallway.

"Mom's not home."

"What time is it?"

"It's after one."

"Did she say what time she was coming home?"

"To who? Matty was home when she left."

"She's probably at Aunt Sally's."

"Should we call?"

"Not if it's going to wake her up."

"She's probably okay."

"Oh God, of course she is. She probably just zonked out on the couch or something."

"Probably."

But Peggy isn't at her sister-in-law's house, zonked out. She's in a motel room, with her husband. Jack left Turkey at 2:30 in the morning, Saturday, and flew to Italy, from there to Germany, and from there to Baltimore, where he took a tortuous seven-hour bus ride back to the base, where Peggy met him around ten o'clock. She didn't tell anybody at the fund-raiser that Jack was on his way, because she didn't want everybody to get their hopes up when the situation was still subject to change. Mostly, she didn't tell anybody because she wanted him all to herself. She had a right to that. Nobody who really knew what she'd been through could possibly argue with that. When she met him at the airfield, she ran to him and threw her arms around him and felt whole again. It didn't take long for Jack to fill her in on what he'd been up to. It took a lot longer for her to tell him all the things that had been going on at home, but that's the way it usually went when Jack went away—he could spend a month in some foreign country, some exotic distant place, but when he came home, what had been happening in the family in his absence was always more important to him. They talked and talked. Then they didn't want to use words anymore.

Peggy and Jack arrive home Monday morning, April 19, around eleven. Michele and Elizabeth sigh with relief when they see their mom and dad together again. Jack gets Matt and Jeffrey and Bean out of school, and everybody goes to lunch at the diner. Some of the kids are dying to tell Jack everything that happened in his absence. Others are just happy that he's here, home, tangible, and present. Over cheeseburgers and onion rings, everyone's internal emotional guidance system recalibrates. The King is back on his throne, next to the Queen, and there's no longer a power vacuum for everyone to deal with. For the kids, it's as simple as having two sets of eyes watching over them instead of one. They feel safer with two. For Jack, this is the moment he thinks of when he's far away, the image of being surrounded by his family, the thing he carries with him. After a trip it isn't until this moment that he knows he's truly returned to base.

'78-03

I've always had this idea that when we die and meet our maker, God will ask us one question. He'll say, "So—how was it?" If you answer, "Wow, what a ride," he'll welcome you with open arms, but if you complain about all the unfair events that might have caused you an unjust amount of pain, you'll get sent back because you missed the main drift. Life is good. There are bad things in the world. There are situations where you might find yourself out of control or in dire straights, but even then, there is good. It may be hard to find, but it's there.

IN THE MORNING, WHEN JACK BREHM GOES RUNNING, WHETHER HE'S training for a marathon or an Iron Man or just running to stay in shape, he pauses briefly to stretch in the living room of his house. He knows he should pay more attention to stretching, but he just doesn't. Each year, he's a bit sorer and a bit stiffer in the morning, and it's been a while since he ran his personal best marathon time of 2:51, but he can still race with the young guys, and he still enjoys running.

He knocks the sand from his running shoes into the wastebasket. He sees the fireplace he put in, and the ceiling fan, and the grass wallpaper that Peggy put up one weekend in his absence. His entertainment center features a Pioneer turntable, a JVC tuner, a 28-inch Goldstar TV, a Symphonic five-disk CD changer, and a Broksonic VCR, but Brehm doesn't turn any of it on. He hears only the humming of the refrigerator. He glances out the bay window at the weather, and at the vine-strangled oak trees in his front yard. He checks the anniversary clock on the mantel sitting in its bell jar. The clock is surrounded by photographs of his kids, including pictures of Elizabeth and Laura-Jean in their cheerleading uniforms, the blue and white colors of Rocky Point High. Elizabeth's uniform has the word *Eagles* stitched across the chest in gold. It matches her curly blond hair. In a photo album, Jack keeps a picture of Elizabeth flying high in the air, tossed straight up by her fellow cheerleaders. She is smiling as she does the splits, arms straight out from her side as she touches her toes. She never stretched much, either, but when you're that young, you don't have to.

He takes it easy at first, loping down Locust Drive to Eos, where he turns right, then left on King, and right on Odin to Route 25A. He runs east on 25A for a few blocks and turns left on Woodville Road, which brings him back to Long Island Sound. The narrow streets of Rocky Point are lined with old cottages and newly constructed, expansive landscaped homes. He runs past a cottage a PJ purchased years ago. The previous occupants had been Italians, who'd paved their yard with concrete, as was the fashion at the time. The new owner couldn't afford a demolition crew on a National Guardsman's salary, but he could afford a few cases of beer, to give to a bunch of sledgehammer-wielding PJs who tore into the cement only to find that whoever had put it in had reinforced it with any sort of metal junk he could get his hands on, bedsprings and teaspoons, extension cords and chicken wire. It took forever to get it up and out of there. Just as they finished, an old Italian neighbor strolled by to admire their handiwork, and said, "I'm so glad we have young people in the neighborhood again—maybe now we can get some fresh concrete in here."

Brehm likes to run on the beach, on the sand where it's hard-packed above the tide line, marble-sized pebbles the colors of toffee and putty and brick. He runs up and down sand dune cliffs that would make an ordinary runner's thighs burst into flames, but before hitting the beach, he always stops at a cliff above the ocean, where there's a stone bench for people to sit on and gaze out at the sound. It's seventeen miles across to Connecticut. Brehm and Jimmy Dougherty kayaked it once. He puts his feet up on the bench to elevate them and begins his push-ups. He does a hundred push-ups every morning to stay in shape, and then he does one more, for Randy Mohr, and one more, for Mark Judy.

After the space shuttle *Challenger* blew up, a massive effort was made to recover any piece of the spacecraft that might provide a clue as to why the accident happened. The effort included launching an unmanned submarine to search the ocean floor. The submarine found pieces of the *Challenger,* but it also observed a wreckage of a helicopter that could have been the helicopter Mark Judy had gone down in, sitting on the bottom in two thousand feet of water, about fifty miles off Cape Canaveral. A recovery vessel called the *Frank Cable* managed to fasten a line to the fuselage, but the line broke. It was determined that it wouldn't be cost effective to bring the wreckage to the surface, so it was declared a gravesite and left undisturbed.

Jack Brehm runs because he's the last man in his class still serving as a PJ. The others have all moved on to other things.

Randy Mohr thinks about "The Jude" from time to time. After "seeing the light," he moved back to Olean, New York, and took a job at Olean Wholesale, the same place where his dad drove a truck, delivering food to the SureFine chain of supermarkets. Randy had worked there before he enlisted in the Air Force. After leaving pararescue, Mohr spent time on his grandparents' 125-acre horse farm, swimming in the pond and hunting deer on the back acres, and then he married a girl named Diane Gardner, a half Cherokee Indian from nearby Allegheny and someone Randy had played with when they were little kids. She gave birth to a boy, Christian, in July of 1983, and two years later had a girl, Amber-Jude, named after Mark Judy. They bought a huge house in the town of Portville, a "mansion," Mohr says. The town was full of broken homes and dysfunctional families. In junior high school, Christian Mohr got in trouble with some of the other kids at school, including the son of a local cop, who poured ink on Christian's New England Patriots jacket and pressured him into shoplifting a pack of cigarettes, then denied it after Christian got caught. They stole Christian's bicycle, made threats, sprayed graffiti on the garage. To protect his boy, Randy Mohr moved his wife and kids out of their "mansion" to a mobile home on the family horse farm, on a lot behind the big house where his brother lives. Christian hasn't been in trouble since. They have Clydesdales, Arabians, and quarter horses on the farm, even a cow or a bull now and then, all bred for show and sale. They have five-pound bass in the pond and ten-point bucks in the woods. To Randy Mohr, moving his family out of town was a no-brainer, even if it meant going from a mansion to a trailer, because that's what you're supposed to do—live your life "that others may live." He never got an actual save as a PJ, but he still lives the motto—the golden light didn't change that part of it.

He and Jack get together once a year, driving the 370 miles between their houses to drink coffee (Mohr has been on the wagon for eight years) and retell old stories, about the time they were four-wheel driving in the Baja and Jack leapt out of a bush to tackle Mohr, snarling and growling to the point Mohr was convinced he'd been attacked by a bear. They talk about the time Mohr, Jack, the Jude, and Matelski nearly got handed their sombreros in a bar in Juarez, across the border from El Paso, by fifteen or twenty cantinistas after Jack got upset when he paid for a beer with a twenty-dollar bill and the girl wouldn't give him his change. The girl pretended he'd given her a five, then cried *lobo* and screamed bloody murder when Jack said she was cheating him. The bar's patrons rose to defend her, so the PJs went ballistic, breaking pool cues and bottles and throwing bar stools, knowing that the best defense is a good offense. They were allowed to leave after Mohr lifted a stool and threatened to break the mirror behind the bar and destroy half the bar's liquor stock. Jack got his change back, too.

"Jack gets kind of goofy when he drinks," Mohr says. "One time we were in a bar in Long Island, and there was this girl with gigantic ta-tas who was dancing all by herself, really putting on an exhibition, and she was wearing this knit black tube dress, you know, where the only thing holding it up was her boobs, so Jack was drinking his beer and looking at her, and apparently she took offense because she came over and said, 'Why don't you try looking me in the eyes?' Jack was really hammered, so he just kept looking at her boobs and said, 'Oh—you have eyes? And where would those be?' "

Joe Higgins stayed a PJ for eight and a half years. He recalls, with particular fondness, a jump mission six hundred miles west of San Francisco, where a sailor on the research vessel the USS *Dutton* was in need of medical assistance. The call came at three in the morning. They launched at first light. The water was choppy, so heavily whitecapped that they couldn't see the smoke marker they'd dropped to give them wind direction. The *Dutton* dispatched a long boat, which picked them up after they'd been in the water for ten or fifteen minutes. The *Dutton* extended davits over the side to winch the long boat to the deck. It was as they waited to be hoisted out of the water that Higgins noticed a sailor high up on the superstructure of the ship, aiming a high-powered rifle at him and watching him through the rifle's scope.

"What's with the sharpshooter?" Higgins asked the bo'sun.

"Sharks," the bo'sun said.

"Here?"

"Yeah," the bo'sun said. "They're everywhere. This water is full of 'em."

"You might have told us that before we jumped into it," Higgins said.

"We might have," the bo'sun agreed, "but then you might not have come."

While serving with the 129th at Moffett, Joe Higgins got lucky. A lieutenant colonel named Charlie Cross saw something he liked in the young PJ and told him he had a flight slot open. The problem was that to become an officer in the Air Force, you have to have graduated from a four-year college, and Higgins was only two and a half years into his degree. You also have to be twenty-six-and-a-half years old or younger to start the program. Cross said he could waive the college requirement if Higgins promised to finish his degree once he was commissioned, but he couldn't waive the age limit. Higgins started Officer Training School immediately, and from there he went on to flight school. He's currently a lieutenant colonel in the California Air National Guard, where he first flew HH-3E and later HH-60G helicopters, pulling seamen out of the Pacific Ocean and climbers off Northern California's mountainsides. He trained Slovenian pilots in rescue techniques in a program called Partnership for Peace, in which Americans helped retrain military personnel in countries that were once part of, or under the influence of, the former Soviet Union. Higgins recalls a time when Jack Brehm, in Hawaii on a training mission, was waiting in full uniform at a bus stop in downtown Honolulu with a flight engineer who didn't know him very well. A woman at the bus stop asked him what it was he did in the military.

"Well," Brehm said with a mock mysteriousness, "I could tell you, but then I'd have to kill you."

"Don't let him give you that bullshit," the FE said. "His name is Jack Brehm and he's a PJ from Long Island and he's here on a training mission."

"Jack suddenly got this wild look on his face," Higgins recalls, "and then he screamed this blood-curdling scream and said to the woman, 'Now I must kill you!' and leapt at her and proceeded to pretend to strangle her. Jack and the woman had a good laugh out of it, but the flight engineer didn't know what to make of it. He almost had a heart attack. He told me later, 'Your buddy Brehm is kind of wacked,' and I said, 'Yeah, that's about the size of it.' "

Dave Higgins stayed a PJ for twenty years. He stood alert at Edwards AFB in California when the space shuttles landed there, prepared to muscle astronauts out of the cockpit were something to go wrong upon landing. He nearly got washed off the deck of a submarine in the Pacific by a rogue wave while rescuing an overweight seaman with a hernia, "sort of a whiner who I think they just wanted to get off the boat, so on the way back, we practiced our IV sticks on him—you don't get much of a chance to practice that on an actual moving vibrating helicopter—we sort of made a pincushion out of the guy." Another time, D.T. flew to a U.N. observation post on an island in the Yellow Sea off North Korea and treated a father and infant son who'd been burned in a house fire, the HH-60G helicopter accompanied by F-16 fighter planes, given their proximity to the demilitarized zone. Higgins flew with a test team in Hawaii, where PJs from Hickham AFB were charged with recovering whatever hardware had fallen to earth from space and splashed down in the Pacific. He was an instructor at Kirtland for five years. He worked at Hurlburt Field, Florida, in Special Tactics for AFSOC, but didn't care much for the politics of the operations he helped plan there, complicated missions where PJs had to let Command and Control guys help them talk on the radio, while a small company of soldiers rode along to provide security—it seemed as if they were constantly planning for sending twenty guys to do a two-man job. His last administrative job was setting up a pararescue team at Pope AFB in North Carolina. He went to Cuba for the "Great Haitian Vacation," the invasion of Haiti that didn't happen, and pulled a ninety-day rotation in Bosnia in 1995. He retired in July of 1997, but not before seeing his wife, Jill, an Air Force sergeant he'd met when he outranked her, perform so well and win so many awards as a non-commissioned officer that she was recommended for OTS, moving from the ranks of the enlisted to the officers corps, or as Higgins puts it, "She did the impossible." She's a captain now, which means that when she gets transferred somewhere, Higgins has to follow her, but that's all right with him. His sons, Brian and David, are proud of their mother. D.T. is currently trying to finish his undergraduate degree in economics at Campbell University in Buies Creek between Fayetteville and Raleigh, attending classes with kids half his age.

"Going to school at forty sucks," he admits. "I have to read everything at least twice. For every new piece of information you take in, you have to dump something that's already there."

Slip O'Farrell recalls a training exercise in scuba school where he and Brehm were supposed to do high-speed castoffs from the fantail of a patrol boat and then swim 1,000 meters to shore. Brehm lost a fin, hitting the water at about twenty knots. It took the duo forever to reach the beach, where, for losing his fin, an instructor sentenced both Brehm and O'Farrell to two hundred flutter kicks while lying on their twin 72-cubic-foot scuba tanks. "This was the high point of the Pipeline, for me," O'Farrell recalls.

O'Farrell lived in extremes, ever since his instructor at Survival Instructors School showed him how to bite the head off a snake. "I knew then I had found my home." It was living to extremes that finally turned on him. He SIE'd from the PJs in April of 1982, while stationed with the 41st ARRS at McClellan AFB in Sacramento, California. He didn't tell any of the other PJs on his team why he did it. He was reassigned to the base life-support section, two blocks down the street, but for the most part, he avoided his former friends, didn't want to talk about it when he ran into any of them, because he felt guilty for quitting. His gradual fall from grace began when he busted his ass, literally. In Florida, before he was transferred to Okinawa, he and a team of PJs had practiced low-and-slowing from a helicopter, tumbling into the sea at ten knots from a mere ten feet above the water, performing flips and belly flops and cannonballs. It was play, joyful and oblivious. O'Farrell was jumpmastering a low and slow exercise in Okinawa, in a similar playful mood, when he accidentally led two other PJs out of an HH-53 from thirty feet at thirty knots, only to learn he wasn't as tough as he thought he was. He broke his coccyx. Another PJ broke a few ribs.

O'Farrell's fortunes continued to turn. While he waited to heal, he got married "for all the wrong reasons" to a woman he describes as a "beautiful, intelligent, articulate alcoholic" who was being discharged from the Air Force "for all the appropriate reasons." He married her anyway, didn't see a problem. After all, he told himself, he rescued people for a living—why couldn't he save her? He didn't know anything about enabling, or codependency. The marriage was, in a word, tumultuous. In another word, boozy. Extreme. He started turning down temporary duty tours because he was afraid of leaving his wife alone, afraid of what she might do if he wasn't there. For a PJ, the mission was supposed to come first, but it didn't anymore. Worse, he began to fear for his own mortality, in part because of his injury, but to a larger extent because his shattered, shredded marriage made everything seem fragile or doomed. He was spooked. He didn't believe in karma, but he knew his karma was bad. His friends tried to warn him, saying, "Slip, man, you're fucking up," but he only thanked them and walked away. One night, he was supposed to fly aboard a C-130 on a full moonlit night over the California desert, a mission in which the pilots were to use night vision goggles but not terrain-following radar. Without radar, it simply seemed too dangerous. Guys died in training exercises all the time. If an actual rescue were involved, that would have been different, but to die in a training exercise . . .

He quit.

O'Farrell separated from his wife three times before finally divorcing her, fleeing the Air Force, a VA mortgage, a codependent wife—fleeing the whole enchilada. For a while he worked for a private rescue systems company in Colusa, California, where the medical director was Jeffrey MacDonald, known to readers of Joe McGinniss's book *Fatal Vision* as the ex-military doctor who was convicted of killing his wife and family. O'Farrell went from there to delivering oxygen bottles and fixing wheelchairs. "In fourteen months, I went from Sky God to piss-foam," he recalls. After his divorce, he started going to Al-Anon, while attending paramedic school. He worked as a paramedic in Sacramento from 1985 to 1991. He was working in Chico as a paramedic student in 1989 when he met his current wife, Teresa, over an emergency room double overdose, two teenage girls who'd taken barbiturates (they lived). Slip and his family fled the People's Republic of California for the freer expanses of Spokane, Washington, in 1991, where he currently works as an ER nurse, still saving lives and "living by the motto." His daughter is learning to run, swim, jump, dive, climb, and fly. "She can't outshoot me yet," O'Farrell says, "but her ambition is to be a scuba-diving nurse." He tried to sell his parachutes, but they were too old. He uses his scuba gear a few times a year and dreams about pararescue nearly every single night. His deepest regret is that he'll never get to fly his perfect mission, "a last-light low level C-130 jump onto a beeper signal in a blizzard, only to find the survivor hypovolemic and hypothermic, with a grizzly bear sniffing him."

He would probably be the first man ever to bite the head off a grizzly bear.

Mike Wilkey disappeared, last believed to be living in the Salt Lake City area. No one seems to know where he served or where he is now. Chuck Matelski nearly disappeared. After serving for a year and a half at Fairchild, Matelski transferred to Hickham AFB in Hawaii, where he ran the medical supply section. He stayed at Hickham until 1981, then got out. Looking back, he sometimes thinks he should have stayed in, but acknowledges, "Back then, I was stubborn and hard-headed and basically young and stupid. I wanted out to go to school, thinking I was going to be a marine biologist and get a job back in Hawaii. I went to school, but my study habits were poor and my personality wasn't conducive to academics. Part of the problem maybe was that in the Pipeline they build you up to think you're invincible. When I was running with the PJs, we partied up a storm, taking advantage of every bar and girl we could get our hands on. I knew I couldn't do that for twenty years."

After school didn't pan out, Matelski worked as a security guard at a research plant in Santa Barbara, then at a shop that manufactured custom countertops. He took odd jobs in L.A., the Malibu area, doing anything to make money. He stopped drinking in 1992, after waking up from a three-day binge only to hear a voice in his head say, clear as a bell, "That's it." He's currently part owner of a construction company that contracts painting for new construction. He's married to a woman named Anna and has a twenty-one-year-old stepson named Christopher.

Smitty did well for himself. After graduation from the PJ school, John Smith was assigned to the 55th ARRS at Eglin, where he upgraded to jumpmaster and team leader within two years. From Eglin, he was assigned to the 39th at Patrick, where he was part of the Space Shuttle Astronaut Rescue Team. He wrote the rescue procedures for the 099 *(Columbia)* and 101 *(Challenger)* vehicles. From Patrick, Smith transferred to Woodbridge, England, and the 67th ARRS. While there, he participated in the recovery of human remains from an Air India 747 that went down in the Irish Sea. He escorted President Carter to Egypt and President Reagan to Iceland, when Reagan met with Gorbachev. On the same mission, Smitty met Reagan and shook his hand on the tarmac at the airport. Smith led the rescue effort during the U.S. bombing of Libya. He returned to Eglin in 1986, where he stayed a year before moving on to the headquarters of the 23d Air Force at Hurlburt Field, Florida, to work for the Special Tactics Group. There, Smith was in charge of advanced skills training for the entire Air Force Special Operations Command. He participated in Just Cause, Desert Shield, Desert Storm, and Desert Thunder. He was also on the rescue attempt in Bosnia as the primary planner of the mission to extract two French NATO pilots shot down during Operation Deny Flight.

John "Smitty" Smith retired October 30, 1998, after a total of 26 years, 4 months, and 18 days of service. His military decorations include the Bronze star with "V" for valor, the Meritorious Service Medal with four Oak Leaf Clusters, the Air Medal with two Oak Leaf Clusters, the Aerial Achievement Medal with Oak Leaf Cluster, a Joint Service Commendation Medal, an Air Force Commendation Medal with three Oak Leaf Clusters, an Air Force Achievement Medal with Oak Leaf Cluster, and numerous foreign decorations. He was awarded the Sikorsky Winged "S" seventeen times for skill and courage during a life-saving mission using a Sikorsky helicopter. Over the course of his career he was credited with saving the lives of ninety-eight people, twenty-three in combat. One of his favorite missions came on the July 4th weekend of 1983, one of his first assignments out of Woodbridge, a marathon seven-hour flight over the North Atlantic involving three midair refuelings each way in an HH-53 to recover a sailor who'd taken ill aboard an old Boomer-class nuclear submarine. Smith knew the dangers and he knew the story of an unfortunate PJ from the rescue group in Iceland who'd been hoisted down to the deck of a submarine, where the deck tenders had tethered him to the deck for safety because the seas were rough, but the tether they used was too long, such that when a wave washed the PJ off the deck, the forward motion of the sub trapped him underwater. Cutting him loose would have sent him through the screw of the ship. He drowned. Before launching to the Boomer, Smith recalled a sign he'd seen in Jonestown, posted over Jim Jones's throne: "Those who do not remember the past are doomed to repeat it."

The sub's captain refused to surface until the HH-53 was on station. Smith and a fellow PJ named Craig Teeters were hoisted down to the deck without difficulty. They politely but firmly declined when the deck tenders offered them tethers. Down below, the sailor was having cardiac problems, chest pains, skin pallor, fast respiration and rapid pulse, with a blood pressure reading that should have blown the guy's head off. Smith and Teeters were still treating the patient when the captain sent the ship's executive officer to inform them they had fifteen minutes to get the guy off the boat. A Soviet satellite pass was due, and the captain couldn't allow the sub to stay on the surface when that happened. The patient could neither walk to the hatch nor climb up the ladder, so Smith and Teeters fashioned a rope harness for him and lifted him out of the sub. Teeters and the patient went up the hoist first. Smith stayed behind. When the executive officer gave the order to "clear the deck" and asked Smith what his intentions were, he said he'd stay on deck to wait to be hoisted off. The executive officer closed the hatch behind him. Minutes passed. Standing on the deck of the giant ship, he felt quite small and quite alone. It seemed to be taking forever to get the patient off the penetrator. Smith heard the sub's ballast tanks blow just as the HH-53 finally came for him. He felt the submarine sinking into the ocean below him as he grabbed the penetrator. The water came up over the sides of the hull, met in the middle and splashed the bottoms of his feet.

Bill Skolnik began to have problems as soon as he left Lackland. At Jump School in Fort Benning, Georgia, Skolnik, himself an ex-Marine, wanted to show the other Marines training there that PJs were as tough as any Marine. Some branches of the military traditionally consider the Air Force "soft," and others had never heard of the PJs, so to rectify the situation, every time a Marine got dropped for disciplinary pushups, Skolnik dropped with him. To show team unity, every time Skolnik dropped, his fellow PJs dropped too. The Marines didn't want to be shown up, so every time a PJ got dropped, the Marines dropped. Pretty soon the Navy SEALs saw that everybody was doing more pushups than they were, so they started dropping. Then the Green Berets and the Army Rangers got in on it too, even though the PJs were eating the SEALs and the Green Berets for lunch. The interservice competition culminated when the various branches entered a local raft race in which teams paddled about twenty miles down the Chattahoochee river, a race traditionally won every year by the Army Rangers, but this year, the PJs, led by Skolnik, beat them by more than a few boat lengths. The PJs beat the entire field by a distance of two and a half miles. The headlines in the next day's papers read, "AIR FORCE BEATS ARMY," and afterward a Marine captain admitted to Skolnik, "As far as I'm concerned, you PJs are one of the finest groups of military men I've ever had the pleasure to meet."

It would be some time before anybody considered the Air Force "soft" again; nevertheless, Skolnik's enthusiasm and exuberance brought him directly into a personality conflict with John Smith, the team leader, who considered Skolnik's hoo-yahing to be inappropriate and excessive. The personality conflict started small and escalated. Skolnik pushed Smith's buttons, and Smith pushed Skolnik's, and eventually, Smith had enough and recommended to the commander that Skolnik be dropped from the program for disrupting team unity. The commander agreed. Skolnik appealed to McManus, who made some phone calls.

"I always liked Bill's spirit," McManus says. "After all, if it's your son or daughter out there in the middle of the ocean, who do you want going after them—somebody with spirit or somebody without it?"

McManus used his powers of persuasion to get his candidate reinstated, and invited a third party pararescue NCOIC from Scott AFB to interview Skolnik, who agreed that Bill had exactly the kind of attitude pararescue was looking for. Eventually Skolnik was brought back into the Pipeline, but now he was in the class behind Jack. At Scuba School in Key West, Skolnik was with two fellow PJs one night, one of them a young Latino man from Colombia, South America, and they were trying to enter a bar when one of the bouncers told them they didn't admit Cubans. The bouncer probably didn't welcome Skolnik's fist in his face either, but that's what he got. Later, at Kirtland, Skolnik and a PJ named Bill Griffin were involved in an altercation in a twenty-four-hour chow hall on the base where guys coming in from missions at all hours could grab something to eat. Skolnik asked the sergeant behind the counter if he could whip them up some omelets. It was approaching midnight, and the cook was more interested in handing people pre-made sandwiches than relighting the grill.

"You fucking PJs just think you're gods, don't you?" the cook said.

"Yeah, as a matter of fact, we are gods," Skolnik replied.

The cook speculated as to the romantic propensities of Bill Griffin's mother. Skolnik suggested the cook's sister really loved to entertain. In the fight, some witnesses said the cook came over the counter wielding a knife, and most sensible people would agree that it's probably unwise to provoke a cook in his own kitchen, when he knows where all the knives are. Again an investigation ensued, where it was determined that Skolnik hadn't thrown the first punch. His record was, however, beginning to show a troubling pattern of first punches being thrown at him.

Bill Skolnik eventually became a PJ and was assigned to the 106th a few months after Jack Brehm, but he never had a cherry mission. He'd gone on a training mission out of Fort Polk, Louisiana, where he and Bill Hughes practiced escape and evasion techniques in the Louisiana woods, moving twenty-five miles from insertion to pickup point while being searched for by a squad of Special Forces troops. He'd done a good job, and felt good about himself afterward. He asked McManus to put him up for a training mission to climb Mt. McKinley, and was scheduled to go when Mike told him, at a party in the enlisted man's club on the base, that he was going to have to bump him because another PJ with seniority needed the mission more.

Skolnik didn't take the news that he'd been bumped well. He stood by the door, drinking a beer, getting angrier and angrier. Stewing. Then he was bumped again, literally, when a chief master sergeant from maintenance named Dave DeJohn arrived at the party, didn't see Skolnik, and hit him with the door. Skolnik hit DeJohn back, but not with the door. He hit him with a right cross that landed them both on the floor, with everyone there watching him, including the base commander. He knew immediately that it was wrong, a stupid thing to do, but it was too late. He was asked the next day to leave the team.

Today Bill Skolnik is the head wine maker at Leelanau Wineries in Traverse City, Michigan, where he makes pinot noirs, chardonnays, and rieslings. For several years he was the head wine maker at the Osprey's Dominion vineyard, on the north fork of eastern Long Island, and almost every week a C-130 or an HH-60 from the 106th flew over his vineyard, and when they did, his emotions were mixed. In part he felt regret, sorry that one night in an NCO club he'd let Mike McManus down, McManus a man Skolnik loved like a father. For the main part though, whenever the men from the 106th flew overhead, Skolnik simply felt proud to have been one of them, and proud of the work they did, and proud to have been part of it—once a PJ, always a PJ. Hoo-yah.

When Mike McManus retired, Skolnik sent him a case of wine.

Mike McManus, in retirement, is a lion in winter. Mostly he's riding his 1997 Harley-Davidson, a soft-tailed Heritage Springer with a red custom finish and a twin 1400cc engine, with black leather saddlebags and a windshield, crossing the great dry basins of Nevada or slicing up the landscape of Texas's Hill Country. His wife, Debby, might be next to him, riding her Harley Fat Boy. Occasionally he considers his options.

"I don't want to do anything medical," he says. "I suppose I could get a job, but they'd probably want me to come to work on time, and produce something while I'm there, and stay all day. I was never really into fishing. I could take up hunting, but hell, I get moose walking up my driveway. I suppose I could wait for one to walk into my garage and then strangle him."

He lives in a mountainside house above the clouds, at least when the fog rolls in low on the Prince William Sound, south of Anchorage. They have Western art on the walls, Christmas cacti and spider plants in hanging baskets, two fat cats and a German shepherd that barks from the deck at whatever moves below. When the sky is clear he can see the Turnagain Arm, an inlet of Prince William Sound where, when the tide goes out, tourists get stuck in the mud flats on a fairly regular basis. When the tide goes out, the mud dries hard enough to walk on, except in those places where it's not, and then somebody's foot goes through, and then the whole leg goes in, and the person can't get out. Occasionally boats get stranded in the mud, too, but usually it's a hiker who ought to have known better. When the tide roars back in, the sea in the Turnagain Arm rises high above the head of anybody unfortunate enough to be stuck in the mud. It was a PJ from the 210th rescue squadron out of Kulis AFB in Anchorage named

Brent Widenhouse who invented a device to free people from the mud, a three-foot long probe, hooked up to a compressed air tank, which the rescuers insert to pump air into the mud around a victim's foot or leg, making extraction possible by breaking the vacuum.

Mike's last rescue mission came in June of 1997. He and Widenhouse were in a C-130 preparing for a training jump when the pilot reported he'd intercepted a Mayday distress call from a nearby private plane having some kind of engine trouble, hoping to make it to a nearby airfield. There were three people on board, the pilot, another man, and his wife. The C-130 diverted to look for the private plane. They found it, newly crashed in a clearing in a wooded area adjacent to the airfield. McManus and Widenhouse jumped down to the crash site, arriving on scene within minutes of the accident. The airplane was upside down. Widenhouse examined the passenger and reported that he was dead. McManus examined the pilot, who was hanging upside down in a puddle of blood, his head cracked open.

"This guy's bled out," McManus said, looking in the back of the plane. "I thought there were three. Didn't they say three?"

"Shhh—hang on a second," Widenhouse said.

Over the sound of the wind in the trees, they both heard a faint moaning.

"Check that guy again," Widenhouse said.

"Trust me—it's not him."

They widened their search to the area around the plane, until they found a woman in her forties lying in a ditch, thrown about thirty yards from the crash. She was badly hurt, with head and chest injuries, and she was barely breathing. Widenhouse opened her air passage, while Mike radioed for a helicopter. He also asked the C-130 to drop an extra medical kit and a stretcher. The helicopter med-evac'ed her to a hospital in Anchorage. As McManus helped load the stretcher into the helicopter, he winced.

"You okay?" Widenhouse asked him.

"Yeah yeah," he said, declining to add that he'd felt a bit of a twinge then and earlier, especially when his chute opened. The yank a jumper feels when his chute opens to transition him from a free fall to a feet-to-earth position can be severe, but it usually doesn't hurt. Mike felt a twinge, more than a twinge, actually, when his chute opened because he'd broken three ribs in a car accident the day before, information he kept to himself because he had a TDY in Washington, D.C., coming up, a conference on

Search and Rescue that he wanted to attend, and he didn't want to be taken off flight status by some overefficient flight surgeon.

McManus has always had a high threshold for pain, and he's needed it. The most difficult thing he ever had to endure was his divorce. The pain of dealing with his wife's alcoholism was incessant. The intractable futility of it all was hard to accept, because he saw himself as a problem solver. When he moved to Alaska, his kids stayed behind, and that was hard, too, but then life had always been hard. His father hated his job in the steel mill, and came home and drank after work every evening. Among his siblings, Mike's younger brother Ed lives in Florida and doesn't drink at all, but his younger sister Michele died of alcoholism, and his baby brother Marty died of a heroin overdose. Mike's daughter Kelly moved to Anchorage and followed in her father's footsteps by joining the National Guard, where she seems quite happy. He stops by the PJ section at Kulis every once in a while, too, just to check in, or hang around in the day room with the guys. Other times, he rides his Harley. The sound of a 1400cc engine can drown out all kinds of pain.

Jack Brehm runs on the beach. Offshore, Brehm sees a white dinghy, with three men in it, fishing. Back in 1982, PJs from Westhampton on a TDY in Panama went out to rescue a crew of Portuguese fishermen who'd lost their boat in a storm. Their ship had gone down so suddenly that they never managed to send an SOS and weren't looked for until they were overdue in port. Seven men spent five days in a four-man dinghy, without food or water. A team from the 106th jumped when they spotted the dinghy. The men on the boat were delirious, hallucinating, and thought at first that the men falling from the sky were angels descending from heaven to take them away. A month and a half after the rescue, the unit got a letter from the Portuguese captain. His English wasn't the best, but they could make out the gist of what he wanted. They expected he was writing to thank them for saving his crew, but instead, the captain said he wanted money. For a new boat.

"You saved me," he wrote, "now what am I supposed to do?"

Most PJs would reply that once they save somebody's life, their job is pretty much done, and it's really up to the survivor to think of what to do next. Running on the beach, Brehm thinks of the Portuguese captain's letter, because as far as he knows, it's the only time he or anybody else from the 106th has ever heard from somebody they saved. If you ask a hundred PJs, or a thousand, you might not find one who ever received a thank you from a survivor. They don't do it for the glory, and they don't do it for the credit, or the thanks, and they certainly don't do it for the money. They do it, "That others may live," even though they never really know exactly what that means, or how those lives continue.

For Kim Hong Bin, his rescue allowed him to resume his climbing career. In 1992, Kim Hong Bin summited Mount Nangaparbat. In 1997 he summited Mount Elbrus (5,642m) in Europe and Mount Kilimanjaro (5,895m) in Africa. In 1998 he summited Mount Aconcagua (6,962m) in South America and Mount McKinley. He is planing to climb Mount Everest in the spring of 2000 if he can find a sponsor, completing his conquest of mountain peaks on all five continents. Kim's accomplishments are all the more remarkable because after being brought off Mount McKinley in 1991, he lost his hands, and now climbs using prosthetics. When he first came to in the hospital, his hands were bandaged, but he felt as if he had ten full fingers. He had a dream one night that his body was being consumed by cannibals. After a month in hospital, his doctor told him his fingers had turned black and couldn't be saved. He couldn't believe it when he heard it, and he couldn't believe it after the operation. At first he wondered why anybody saved him. Today he is thankful from the bottom of his heart that the PJs saved his life, even though the quality of his life has changed. In 1993, he married his nurse. From 1994 to 1996, he worked at a golf course, but ultimately he was dismissed due to his handicap.

Kim feels that he got in trouble because of poor nutrition. Rather than pack Korean food for the climb, he tried to switch to a Western diet, for example substituting bread for rice, but found the food unappetizing and he missed his spicy Korean condiments. He'd been with a group from the Seoul Chung Hae Mountain Climbing Club, but when they faltered at 13,500 feet, he went on alone. The last thing he remembers before passing out on his way to the summit was being attended to by members of the Sau Mok Po University Climbing Club.

"I think I'm a more careful climber now, and I gather more information and material before I climb. I'm more thorough. I'm thankful the PJs saved me, even though the conditions of my life have clearly changed. It's difficult to find a job in my country with my disability," he says. "Sometimes I wish I'd stayed in Alaska."

As he runs, Jack wonders about a girl in Greece somewhere, unless she's moved to Paris, or maybe New York. He prefers to think she's still in Greece. She's probably twenty-four or twenty-five years old by now. He tries to imagine her life. She has dark hair, unless she's dyed it blond. Maybe she's married by now, with children, maybe a daughter named after her sister, who died when she was two. He wonders if the girl remembers that night, on a boat in the middle of the stormy ocean, when she flew in a helicopter with her mother. He wonders if her mother and father are still around, and if they were there at the wedding. He tries to picture a Greek wedding, but all he knows of Greek weddings are what he's seen in the movies. He pictures a circle of men, holding hands, fingers interlocked above their heads as they step sideways to the music. He can almost see the girl, first in her white wedding dress, laughing with a glass of wine in her hand, then pushing a stroller along some sun-bleached beachfront promenade. He likes to think things worked out for her, though maybe they didn't. Her memories of the night, twenty-one years ago, when she rode in a helicopter are no doubt dim and faded. Maybe all she remembers is that her lungs hurt, and that it was very loud. He's just happy that she has any memories at all. She's probably never heard of the PJs, or of the U.S. Air Force's pararescue program, but that's all right with Jack. As a rule, the people who find themselves flying through the air in the arms of a PJ, being hoisted into a helicopter, usually have more on their minds than making a mental note to remember the names of the guys who are helping them.

There is an exception to the rule. While it's true that civilians almost never say thank you, military survivors do, because they appreciate what's at stake, and know the risks PJs take. As Jack runs, he thinks of one such survivor who recently visited the section. The mission the man flew on remains classified, and will probably remain classified for years—for as long as there's trouble in the Balkans. His F-117 Stealth fighter was shot out of the sky outside of Belgrade on March 27, 1999. He was on a speaking tour, visiting the various pararescue bases around the country, and he stopped by the 106th for a few hours because he had something to say. He spoke of the six hours he spent on the ground, hiding, hearing dogs barking in the distance, wondering if they were military guard dogs looking for him. He spoke of the American flag he'd tucked inside his uniform, and how he knew it stood for the guys who were coming to get him, and for all the people he knew were praying for him, and that gave him the strength he needed to endure. He was a clean-cut kid, a real all-American boy. Jack wondered, upon seeing him, how the Air Force keeps finding pilots like that.

"So I just wanted you guys to know," the pilot concluded, "that sometimes if you're ever sitting around here, frustrated or something because you're not sure what the value of your mission is, I just want you to think about me, and I want you to know that you didn't save just me. You saved my whole flying squadron, all the guys I have on my team, just like you have guys on your team. I was down in the heart of bad-guy territory, and six hours later I was standing in front of my unit. This is the sort of thing that's going to have an impact on them for years to come. And you didn't just save me—you saved my mother. You saved my wife. You may think you saved one guy, but when you do that, you have an effect on a whole lot of people. And all those people are as grateful to you as I am."

Jack runs and realizes that's exactly the point of it all. Every seaman or sailor or mountain climber or heart attack victim he's ever treated or med-evac'ed to a hospital is someone's son or daughter, and possibly somebody else's husband or wife, and if so, likely somebody's father, or uncle, or friend. To save one person is to save the entire web of relationships that depend on that one person, which means that, for Jack, to save one person is to save everything he believes in, the love of a good wife, the adoration of a child, the circle of family and friends that keeps you going and catches you when you fall. To save one person is, by proxy, to save himself. The pilot's speech was more than inspiring, more than motivational. How bad would it be to reenlist, sign on for another six years?

Maybe he'd better talk it over with Peggy first.

Maybe he'd better think about what he's going to say before he talks it over with Peggy.

Jack runs. It's a fine sunny day. He feels glad to be alive. He thinks about the friends he's known and lost, and he's glad to have known them. He thinks about the places he's been and he's glad to have been there. He thinks about the country he serves and is happy to serve it. He thinks about all the love he has in his life and he's thrilled to have it, and hopes only that he can reciprocate. He thinks about his job, and he thinks it's the perfect job, because it allows him to be selfish and selfless at the same time. It lets him do the things he loves, sky dive, scuba dive, but it's not just for him that he does it.

Jack Brehm runs on the beach. He breathes the salt air. He passes a young couple, a boy and a girl, both about twenty, and they remind him of himself and Peggy when they first met. He sees a massive sand cliff rising to his left, a steep slope of heavy wet sand. Someday he will be too old to do this, and then maybe he'll take up golf, but for now, his body still allows him the privilege, so he turns and runs up the cliff, zigzagging, switching back, digging in, sending sand cascading down the slope, and his thighs burn and his lungs aches, but he won't stop. It doesn't feel good to do this, but feels good to have done it. He does it to stay in shape. He does it for the same reason he does everything else.

That others may live.

GLOSSARY

AC Slang abbreviation for "aircraft."
ACC Air Combat Command, headquartered at Langley AFB in Virginia, one of seven commands in the Air Force, along with the Education and Training, Materiel, Reserve, Space, Special Operations, and Mobility Commands.
AFB Air Force Base.
AFF Accelerated Free Fall.
AFSOC Air Force Special Operations Command, headquartered at Hurlburt Field, Florida.
ANGB Air National Guard Base.
AR Air refueling.
ARRS Aerospace Rescue and Recovery Service, the command pararescue fell under in the seventies and eighties. Pararescue now is organized under either ACC or AFSOC.
ARS Air Rescue Service.
BC Buoyancy Compensator, a vest worn by divers that can be inflated with a CO_2 cartridge to increase buoyancy, or deflated to decrease buoyancy.
BDU Battle Dress Uniform.
BENDS An illness that can affect divers if they ascend too quickly, occurring when nitrogen in the bloodstream forms bubbles and expands as the surrounding pressure decreases.
BERGSCHRUND An area of crevasses and cracks where a glacier flowing down a mountain has broken off.
CAPEWELL A clasp that separates a parachute from the harness, used by parachutists to avoid being dragged by ground winds.
CARP Controlled Aerial Release Point, a parachute tactic usually performed at altitudes at or below 800 feet, a way of putting men on the ground in the shortest amount of time.
CDC Career Development Course.
CDT Crew Duty Time.
CEREBRAL EDEMA A hemorrhaging of the tissues surrounding the brain.
CHEMLIGHT A device that supplies illumination via a chemical reaction. Some are shaped like large fountain pens, while others take the form of small disks.
CHOUGH A Eurasian crow, found at high elevations.
CISD Critical Incident Stress Debriefing, a counseling tool usually used to help emergency relief personnel cope with job-related stress.

COLLECTIVE The lever-like control a helicopter pilot uses to change his up/down direction by changing the pitch of the rotor blades.
CORNICE In mountain climbing, an overhang of snow or ice at the top of a ridge or crest.
COULOIR A mountain ravine or gorge.
CP Copilot, as found in a flight log abbreviation.
CRICOTHYROTOMY A surgical procedure where an air passage is cut into a patient's throat.
CYCLIC The stick-like control a helicopter pilot uses to change his forward or backward direction.
DECADRON A synthetic adrenocortical steroid used to reduce swelling in the case of high altitude cerebral edema.
DIAMOX A carbonic anhydrase inhibitor that promotes diuresis and controls fluid secretions.
DNIF The status designation of an airman who is qualified only for Duty Not to Include Flying. The work status an airman is placed in after becoming injured, resulting in his not being able to fly, lasts from one day to two years.
DROGUE The basket on the end of the hose that is extended by a midair refueling tanker, the female receptacle into which the receiving aircraft's probe is inserted to on-load fuel.
DUCK BUTT Slang for a mission in which rescue personnel are assigned to escort another aircraft.
DZ Drop Zone, the designated area where a parachutist attempts to land.
ECW An Extreme Cold Weather clothing system.
ELT Emergency Locating Transmitter, a marker beacon signal given off by a ship or aircraft in trouble.
EPIRB Emergency Position Indicating Radio Beacon, a marker beacon activated by individuals in trouble.
EVAL Evaluations or tests.
FE Flight Engineer, as referred to in a flight log abbreviation.
FLARING The act of stalling one's parachute by entering deep brakes just before touching ground.
FLIR Forward Looking Infrared Radar, a system used to detect enemy movements by picking up heat signatures from ground troops or from the motors of enemy vehicles.
FOL Forward Operating Location.
FRAP Slang for hitting the ground if your parachute fails to open.
GPS Global Positioning System.
HACE High Altitude Cerebral Edema.
HAHO High Altitude High Opening, a parachute tactic where the jumper opens his chute at high altitudes and glides to the target, covering distances of thirty miles or more, depending on the prevailing winds. Supplemental oxygen is required.
HALO High Altitude Low Opening, a kind of parachute tactic where men jump from 25,000–35,000 feet, using supplemental oxygen, and open their chutes at around 3,000 feet, used in covert SARs.

HAS Hardened Aircraft Shelter.
HEED BOTTLES Helicopter Emergency Egress Device, a small oxygen bottle supplying about three to five minutes of oxygen, used by helicopter crew members in case of an accidental submersion.
HOVER REFERENCE A stable reference point which a helicopter pilot needs to fix on, in order to maintain his hover position.
HYPERBARIC High barometric pressure.
HYPERGOLIC Refers to volatile gases that mix in open air and can spontaneously explode.
HYPOBARIC Low barometric pressure.
HYPOTHERMIC Low body temperature.
HYPOVOLEMIC Low blood volume.
HYPOXIA Low oxygen levels.
JDAM Joint Direct Attack Munitions or "smart bombs."
JOLLY Short for "Jolly Green Giant," a nickname for Air Force rescue helicopters.
JSTARS Joint Surveillance Target Attack Radar System.
JUMPMASTER The crewman in charge of telling jumpers when to leave the aircraft.
KINGBIRD A radio designation given to C-130s flying top cover for helicopters.
KLICK Kilometer.
LPU Life Preserver Units, inflatable air pouches worn under the armpits and attached to a vest-like harness.
LZ Landing Zone, the place where a parachutist lands. Also the place designated for a helicopter to land.
MED-EVAC'ED Abbreviation for "medically evacuated," pronounced "med-i-vacked."
MT-IX RAM-AIR CHUTE A square, steerable, double-layered 375-square-foot chute with an open nose that inflates the chute like an airplane's wing to provide lift.
NCO Non-Commissioned Officer.
NCOIC Non-Commissioned Officer In Charge.
NITROGEN NARCOSIS A drunken feeling experienced by divers as they descend, when nitrogen is forced into the bloodstream as the surrounding pressure increases.
NVA North Vietnamese Army.
NVG Night Vision Goggles, a device that electronically amplifies available light.
OD Olive Drab.
OL-J Operation Location J—the site, at Lackland AFB in San Antonio, Texas, where the pararescue indoctrination school is located. Also called Indoc or Superman School.
OTS Officer Training School.
P Pilot, as referred to in a flight log abbreviation.
PCS Permanent Change of Station.
PEN GUN A small flare launcher, about the size of a fountain pen, that can send a signal flare 600 feet up in the air.

PENETRATOR A forest penetrator, designed to penetrate the canopy in the jungles of Vietnam, a milk can–shaped device that can be lowered via a hoist from a helicopter, used to extract survivors.
PHOSPHEGENE An industrial pesticide, similar to the phosgene gases used in WWI.
PJ Pararescue Jumper, a flight log abbreviation.
PNEUMOTHORAX Collapsed lung. A *tension pneumothorax* happens when the pressure inside the chest cavity of a collapsed lung increases to the point that it dislodges the heart and affects the other lung.
PRC Personal Radio Communicator.
PT Physical Training.
PULMONARY EDEMA A hemorrhaging of the lung tissues.
RANK In the Air Force, from bottom to top: Airman Basic, Airman, Airman First Class, Senior Airman, Staff Sergeant, Technical Sergeant, Master Sergeant, Senior Master Sergeant, Chief Master Sergeant, and among the officers, Second Lieutenant, First Lieutenant, Captain, Major, Lieutenant Colonel, Colonel, Brigadier General (one star), Major General (two stars), Lieutenant General (three stars) and General (four stars).
RCC Rescue Control Center. The RCC at Scott AFB, outside of St. Louis, is sometimes referred to as AFRCC, or Air Force Rescue Control Center.
RECON Short for "reconnaissance."
RTB Return To Base, a flight log abbreviation.
RQS Rescue squadron.
SAM Surface to Air Missile.
SAR Search and Rescue. SARs can be covert (men performing HALO or HAHO jumps or flying in low, preferably at night, in helicopters to rescue downed pilots) or they can be overt SARs in which the rescue is made in daylight under protective covering fire.
SARSAT Search and Rescue Satellite, a satellite operated jointly by the United States, Canada, and Russia that picks up EPIRBs and ELTs.
SAR TECH Search And Rescue Technician, the Canadian equivalent of the PJ.
SASTRUGI Ice that the wind has formed into various waves, sawtooths and stalactites.
SAT-COM A radio with a communications satellite uplink.
SCHIST A crystalline rock with a laminar structure that splits easily into layers—for example, slate.
SERE TRAINING A training program used by the Air Force to teach Survival, Evasion, Resistance, and Escape techniques.
SIE Self-Initiated Elimination.
SOF Supervisor Of Flying.
STARS The Air Force's demonstration parachute team, called Special Tactics And Rescue Specialists.
STOKES LITTER A metal basket, used to move an injured or immobilized victim.

TDY Temporary Duty, a tour of duty, often abroad, lasting anywhere from a day to six months.
THORACENTESIS A surgical procedure that purges the air in the chest cavity of a collapsed lung by inserting a large-bore needle into the chest.
THORASCOTOMY A surgical procedure that purges the air in the chest cavity of a collapsed lung by inserting a chest tube into the chest.
TL Team Leader.
TOGGLE The red nylon loop at the end of the lines that a parachutist pulls on to control and change the shape of his chute, thereby steering it.
TRIPLE A Anti-Aircraft Armaments.
VENA CAVA The vein that returns blood to the heart.
WPW Wolff-Parkinson-White syndrome, a short-circuiting of the heart's electrical system, in which an extra electrical pathway develops between the atria and the ventricles, causing extra contractions that speed the heart rate.

ABOUT THE AUTHORS

Jack Brehm has been a pararescue jumper for twenty years. He lives with his wife, Peggy, and their five children in Rocky Point, New York.

Pete Nelson is a prolific author and magazine writer. His articles have appeared in *Harper's*, *Esquire*, *Men's Health*, *Outside*, *Rolling Stone*, *Playboy*, and other publications. He lives in Northampton, Massachusetts. His Web site is: www.pete-nelson.com

Contributors

Deborah J. Anderson
Fearing Research Laboratory
Department of Obstetrics, Gynecology and Reproductive Biology
Harvard Medical School
Boston, Massachusetts 02115

Robert J. Arceci
Division of Paediatrics, Hematology and Oncology
Dana Farber Cancer Institute
44 Binney Street
Boston, Massachusetts 02115

Irene Athanassakis
Department of Immunology
University of Alberta
Edmonton, Alberta, Canada T6G 2H7

Daljeet Banwatt
Molecular Virology and Immunology Program
McMaster University
1200 Main Street West
Hamilton, Ontario, Canada L8N 3Z5

Anna Bartocci
Department of Developmental Biology and Cancer
Albert Einstein College of Medicine
1300 Morris Park Avenue
Bronx, New York 10461

Fuller W. Bazer
Departments of Animal Science and Dairy Science
Institute of Food and Agricultural Sciences
University of Florida
Gainesville, Florida 32611

Kenneth D. Beaman
Department of Microbiology and Immunology
University of Health Sciences
The Chicago Medical School
Chicago, Illinois 60612

Ross S. Berkowitz
Fearing Research Laboratory
Department of Obstetrics, Gynecology and Reproductive Biology
Harvard Medical School
Boston, Massachusetts 02115

Donald R. Branch
Department of Immunology
University of Alberta
Edmonton, Alberta, Canada T6G 2H7

Joyce Brierley
Molecular Virology and Immunology Program
McMaster University
1200 Main Street West
Hamilton, Ontario, Canada L8N 3Z5

Sheila Brown
Division of Comparative Medicine
Clinical Research Centre
Harrow, Middlesex HA1 3UJ England

Philippe Bustany
U 262 INSERM
Clinique Universitaire Baudelocque
123 Boulevard de Port Royal
75674 Paris Cedex 14, France

Gerard Chaouat
U 262 INSERM
Clinique Universitaire Baudelocque
123 Boulevard de Port Royal
75674 Paris Cedex 14, France

Christine Chapeau
Department of Biomedical Sciences
Ontario Veterinary College
University of Guelph
Guelph, Ontario, Canada N1G 2W1

Robert Christopherson
Department of Animal Science
University of Alberta
Edmonton, Alberta, Canada T6G 2H7

David A. Clark
Molecular Virology and Immunology Program
McMaster University
1200 Main Street West
Hamilton, Ontario, Canada L8N 3Z5

Mary Crainie
Department of Immunology
University of Alberta
Edmonton, Alberta, Canada T6G 2H7

B. Anne Croy
Department of Biomedical Sciences
Ontario Veterinary College
University of Guelph
Guelph, Ontario, Canada N1G 2W1

Belinda L. Drake
The Cecil H. and Ida Green Center for Reproductive Biology Sciences
University of Texas
Southwestern Medical Center
5323 Harry Hines Boulevard
Dallas, Texas 75235

Lynn B. Dustin
Renal Division
Brigham and Women's Hospital and the Harvard Center for the Study of Kidney Diseases
75 Francis Street
Harvard Medical School
Boston, Massachusetts 02115

Michel Dy
U 25 INSERM
Hôpital Necker
149 rue de Sevres
75015 Paris, France

Shirley A. Ellis
Institute for Molecular Medicine
John Radcliffe Hospital
Headington, Oxford OX3 9DU England

Christian W. Ertl
Department of Microbiology and Immunology
University of Health Sciences
The Chicago Medical School
Chicago, Illinois 60612

B. L. Ferry

Harris Birthright Centre for Perinatal Medicine
Nuffield Department of Obstetrics and Gynaecology
John Radcliffe Hospital
Headington, Oxford OX3 9DU England

James L. Fishback

Department of Pathology
39th Street and Rainbow Boulevard
University of Kansas Medical Center
Kansas City, Kansas 66103

Gabriel Fulop

Department of Genetics
Hospital for Sick Children
555 University Avenue
Toronto, Ontario, Canada M5G 1X8

Maria Garcia-Lloret

Department of Medicine
University of Alberta
Edmonton, Alberta, Canada T6G 2H7

Thomas J. Gill III

Department of Pathology
University of Pittsburgh School of Medicine
Pittsburgh, Pennsylvania 15261

Anna Grabowska

Division of Cellular and Genetic Pathology
Department of Pathology
University of Cambridge
Tennis Court Road
Cambridge CB2 1QP England

Debbie L. Grissom

Department of Microbiology and Immunology
University of Health Sciences
The Chicago Medical Center
Chicago, Illinois 60612

Larry J. Guilbert

Department of Anatomy and Cell Biology
University of Alberta
Edmonton, Alberta, Canada T6G 2H7

Florina Haimovici

Fearing Research Laboratory
Department of Obstetrics, Gynecology and Reproductive Biology
Harvard Medical School
Boston, Massachusetts 02115

Peter J. Hansen
Departments of Animal Science and Dairy Science
Institute of Food and Agricultural Sciences
University of Florida
Gainesville, Florida 32611

Andrea L. Cortese Hassett
Department of Pathology
University of Pittsburgh
School of Medicine
Pittsburgh, Pennsylvania 15261

Judith R. Head
The Cecil H. and Ida Green Center for Reproductive Biology Sciences
University of Texas
Southwestern Medical Center
5323 Harry Hines Boulevard
Dallas, Texas 75235

Joseph A. Hill
Fearing Research Laboratory
Department of Obstetrics, Gynecology and Reproductive Biology
Harvard Medical School
Boston, Massachusetts 02115

Roger C. Hoversland
Department of Cell Biology and Anatomy
University of Health Sciences
The Chicago Medical School
Chicago, Illinois 60612

Joan S. Hunt
Department of Pathology
University of Kansas Medical Center
39th Street and Rainbow Boulevard
Kansas City, Kansas 66103

M. C. Jackson
Harris Birthright Centre for Perinatal Medicine
Nuffield Department of Obstetrics and Gynaecology
John Radcliffe Hospital
Headington, Oxford OX3 9DU, England

Peter M. Johnson
Pregnancy Immunology Group
Department of Immunology
University of Liverpool
P O Box 147
Liverpool L69 3BX England

Ashley King
Division of Cellular and Genetic Pathology
Department of Pathology
University of Cambridge
Tennis Court Road
Cambridge CB2 1QP England

Radslav Kinsky
U 262 INSERM
Clinique Universitaire Baudelocque
123 Boulevard de Port Royal
75674 Paris Cedex 14, France

Heinz W. Kunz
Department of Pathology
University of Pittsburgh
School of Medicine
Pittsburgh, Pennsylvania 15261

Tina Lavranos
Department of Obstetrics and Gynaecology
The University of Adelaide
Adelaide, South Australia

Joseph D. Locker
Department of Pathology
University of Pittsburgh
School of Medicine
Pittsburgh, Pennsylvania 15261

Y. W. Loke
Division of Cellular and Genetic Pathology
Department of Pathology
University of Cambridge
Tennis Court Road
Cambridge CB2 1QP England

Christopher Y. Lu
Department of Internal Medicine
University of Texas
Southwestern Medical Center
5323 Harry Hines Boulevard
Dallas, Texas 75235

Justin Manuel
Molecular Virology and Immunology Program
McMaster University
1200 Main Street West
Hamilton, Ontario, Canada L8N 3Z5

Dianne B. McKay
Renal Division
Brigham and Women's Hospital and the Harvard Center for the Study of Kidney Diseases
Harvard Medical School
75 Francis Street
Boston, Massachusetts 02115

Andrew J. McMichael
Institute of Molecular Medicine
John Radcliffe Hospital
Headington, Oxford, OX3 9DU England

Andrew L. Mellor
Division of Immunology
National Institute for Medical Research
The Ridgeway
Mill Hill
London NW7 1AA England

Elisabeth Menu
U 262 INSERM
Clinique Universitaire Baudelocque
123 Boulevard de Port Royal
75674 Paris Cedex 14, France

Marianne Minkowski
U 25 INSERM
Hôpital Necker
149 rue de Sevres
75015 Paris, France

Rona J. Mogil
Department of Immunology
University of Alberta
Edmonton, Alberta, Canada T6G 2H7

Don Morrish
Department of Medicine
University of Alberta
Edmonton, Alberta, Canada T6G 2H7

Sandra Peel
Human Morphology
Faculty of Medicine
University of Southhampton
Southampton SO9 3TU England

Karen L. Philpott
Division of Immunology
National Institute for Medical Research
The Ridgeway
Mill Hill
London NW7 1AA England

Jeffrey W. Pollard
Department of Developmental Biology and Cancer
Albert Einstein College of Medicine
1300 Morris Park Avenue
Bronx, New York 10461

Andelka Radojcic
Department of Pathology
University of Pittsburgh
School of Medicine
Pittsburgh, Pennsylvania 15261

Jagdeece Ramsoondar
Department of Animal Science
University of Alberta
Edmonton, Alberta, Canada T6G 2H7

Sohaila Rastan
Division of Comparative Medicine
Clinical Research Centre
Harrow, Middlesex HA1 3UJ England

Charlyne Rebut-Bonneton
U 262 INSERM
Clinique Universitaire Baudelocque
123 Boulevard de Port Royal
75674 Paris Cedex 14, France

Raymond W. Redline
Renal Division
Brigham and Women's Hospital and the Harvard Center for the Study of Kidney Diseases
75 Francis Street
Harvard Medical School
Boston, Massachusetts 02115

C. W. G. Redman
Harris Birthright Centre for Perinatal Medicine
Nuffield Department of Obstetrics and Gynaecology
John Radcliffe Hospital
Headington, Oxford OX3 9DU England

Nancy Reed

Department of Biomedical Sciences
Ontario Veterinary College
University of Guelph
Guelph, Ontario, Canada N1G 2W1

Janet M. Risk

Pregnancy Immunology Group
Department of Immunology
University of Liverpool
P O Box 147
Liverpool L69 3BX England

Sarah A. Robertson

Department of Obstetrics and Gynaecology
The University of Adelaide
Adelaide, South Australia

I. L. Sargent

Harris Birthright Centre for Perinatal Medicine
Nuffield Department of Obstetrics and Gynaecology
John Radcliffe Hospital
Headington, Oxford OX3 9DU England

Robert F. Seamark

Department of Obstetrics and Gynaecology
The University of Adelaide
Adelaide, South Australia

Colleen M. Shea

Renal Division
Brigham and Women's Hospital and the Harvard Center for the Study of Kidney Diseases
Harvard Medical School
75 Francis Street
Boston, Massachusetts 02115

E. Richard Stanley

Department of Developmental Biology and Cancer
Albert Einstein College of Medicine
1300 Morris Park Avenue
Bronx, New York 10461

P. M. Starkey

Harris Birthright Centre for Perinatal Medicine
Nuffield Department of Obstetrics and Gynaecology
John Radcliffe Hospital
Headington, Oxford OX3 9DU England

Ian J. Stewart

Human Morphology
Faculty of Medicine
University of Southampton
Southampton SO9 3TU England

Julia Szekeres-Bartho

Department of Microbiology
Pecs University Medical School
Szigeti Ut Pecs
Pecs 7643 Hungary

Simeon Vassiliadis

Department of Immunology
University of Alberta
Edmonton, Alberta, Canada T6G 2H7

G. M. O. Watt

Harris Birthright Centre for Perinatal Medicine
Nuffield Department of Obstetrics and Gynaecology
John Radcliffe Hospital
Headington, Oxford OX3 9DU England

Thomas G. Wegmann

Department of Immunology
University of Alberta
Edmonton, Alberta, Canada T6G 2H7

Federico A. Zuckermann

The Cecil H. and Ida Green Center for Reproductive Biology Sciences
University of Texas
Southwestern Medical Center
5323 Harry Hines Boulevard
Dallas, Texas 75235

Molecular and Cellular Immunobiology of the Maternal Fetal Interface

1

The Molecular and Cellular Nature of Maternal-Fetal Immune Signaling: An Overview

THOMAS G. WEGMANN and THOMAS J. GILL III

The field of immunology is advancing rapidly due to the use of cellular and molecular cloning technologies to reveal how the various components of the immune system communicate with each other. These advances have resulted in the identification of many gene probes, cell lines, and recombinant molecules that are useful in many specific areas of research. Mammalian reproduction is clearly influenced by cells and products of the immune system, and the most dynamic area of current research in reproductive immunology is concerned with maternal-fetal signaling and how it affects pre- and postimplantation embryos by enhancing or compromising fetal survival. This book reviews the most current work in the field.

The major questions in this area are reflected in headings of the three sections of this book. The first concerns the nature of the fetal major histocompatibility complex antigens expressed at the maternal-fetal interface and that are presumably recognized by maternal immune cells. The second relates to maternal cell-mediated immune effector mechanisms that act at the maternal-fetal interface and have the potential to enhance or to retard placental function and fetal survival. The third focuses on the cytokines and their effects on reproductive tissues. Once again, the effects may have positive or negative characteristics.

This chapter is not intended to provide a comprehensive review of the field, but rather an overview for the reader so that each of the subsequent chapters can be placed within its proper context. For the details of the material discussed in this chapter, as well as for the relevant references, the reader should consult the individual chapters.

The Fetal Major Histocompatibility Complex

It has been known for many years that paternal major histocompatibility complex (MHC) class I antigens are expressed on invasive trophoblast cells at the maternal-fetal interface. The issues of current concern are the exact nature of these molecules and the mechanisms that regulate their expression. An understanding of these points is necessary to comprehend the basis of maternal immune recognition of fetal alloantigens and the ensuing response. In the human, serological studies have shown that extravillous trophoblast expresses class I MHC antigens, whereas villous cytotrophoblast and syncytiotrophoblast do not. Fetal mesenchymal cells express normal class I antigens. The biochemical nature of the antigens expressed on the extravillous trophoblast, which is a fetal tissue in direct contact with maternal tissue, has been a point of controversy. It is clear from serological studies that these antigens do not express conventional class I allele-specific determinants. We are only now gaining an understanding of class I messenger RNA expression in fetal trophoblast tissue. A 45 kDa class I HLA molecule has been identified on both choriocarcinoma and trophoblast cells through cDNA cloning, and although it closely resembles the HLA-C molecule, it is not polymorphic. Levels of expression of messenger RNA for this antigen can be increased in some, but not all tissues by exposure to cytokines, such as gamma-interferon. Also, HLA-G has recently been shown to be present on cytotrophoblast and placental mesenchyme. In addition, a 40 kDa class I molecule has been detected on the surface of both choriocarcinoma and trophoblast cells in humans. A similar class I molecule has been observed on placental cells in baboons and in rats, and there is evidence for expression of an equivalent mRNA in mice. In the latter case, the molecule appears to be encoded by the Q10 locus. However, a relationship between the MHC genes that have been sequenced from cDNA libraries and the cell surface glycoproteins identified by various antibodies remains to be formally established. It has been suggested that there is a higher level of expression of these antigens in the cytoplasm than on the cell surface.

There have been many reports of the potential association of MHC antigen staining with recurrent spontaneous abortion. Most studies have reported an effect of antigen sharing, although some have obtained negative results. By analogy with the recent example of the relationship between HLA-DQ beta chain polymorphism and insulin-dependent diabetes mellitus, restriction fragment length polymorphism analysis might provide further insights into the association between HLA genes and recurrent spontaneous abortion. However, when such an analysis was attempted, using probes for class I, II, and III molecules and for tumor necrosis factor, no association was found. Clearly different molecular approaches are necessary.

We have made substantial progress in understanding the products of the rat MHC that are expressed in the basal trophoblast: an entire cDNA molecule has been cloned and sequenced. It encodes a class I molecule with two glycosylation sites, having a molecular weight (without sugars) of approximately 40 kDa. In addition, cDNA libraries that allow the identification of several deletions related to the growth and reproduction complex (*grc*) have become available in the laboratory. Animals carrying the *grc* exhibit profound effects on reproductive performance, as well as susceptibility to cancer. It will be of great interest to work out the molecular pathway of these effects and the role of the MHC-linked deletions in their pathogenesis.

Progress is also being made in understanding the placental cell expression of mouse MHC antigens, particularly at the messenger RNA level. Previous analyses using monoclonal antibodies to detect cell surface antigens indicated that most paternal antigen expression was concentrated at the insertion of the yolk sac into the lateral aspects of the placenta and in the spongiotrophoblast. An identical pattern of localization was observed when allele-specific H-2 *K* locus probes were used to detect mRNA expression in placental tissue at midgestation. This finding is reassuring because the earlier monoclonal antibody work was subject to the criticism that the antibodies might have cross-reacted with nonclassical class I antigens. Identification of messenger RNA provides strong evidence in this regard, since it is based on the exacting S1 nuclease technique using RNA protection. An interesting result of this work was the finding that both maternal and paternal alleles were expressed at the messenger RNA level. It remains to be determined whether this is also true for class I protein expression at the cell surface. The relationship between this finding and the situation in the rat, in which basal trophoblast cells express only paternal antigens, remains to be established.

These findings show the progress that has been made in the last few years in understanding the nature of the MHC genes expressed in fetal tissues abutting the maternal interface. In the mouse, there seems to be a concordance between surface antigen expression and messenger RNA expression. Although classical class I genes are expressed, unusual class I gene products are also present. This seems also to be true in the rat, and although these data remain to be confirmed in the human, most studies have obtained similar results. Major goals are now to establish a link between this expression and functional aspects of maternal immune recognition and to understand the mechanisms by which this expression is genetically controlled in a tissue-specific manner. Very recent experiments using homozygous beta 2 microglobulin defective mice generated from knockout transgenic mice indicate that mice can successfully reproduce in the virtual absence of MHC class I gene expression on the cell surface. These results put a severe limit on arguments concerning the role of MHC class I antigens in reproduction.

Decidual Effector Cells

In initial studies of effector cells in the maternal-fetal relationship, immunologists confined their attention to the secondary lymphoid organs and blood lymphocytes of the mother. Recently, however, it has been better appreciated that the most important immunological events occur in the local tissues adjacent to the conceptus, including the decidua, draining lymph nodes, as well as more distally in the thymus. Thus, effects detected in the periphery may be only of secondary importance in determining reproductive outcome. There is no doubt that a maternal T cell influx into the decidua occurs at clearly defined times in gestation and that the nature of this cell influx is different in allogeneic and syngeneic pregnancies. In addition, the lymph nodes that drain the uterus are larger in outbred than in inbred pregnancies. The recent development of techniques to isolate relatively pure populations of human and mouse trophoblast cells has helped in assessing the ability of various effector cells to lyse trophoblast. Although attention was initially focused on cytotoxic lymphocytes, there has been a shift in interest toward natural killer cells, simply because cytotoxic T lymphocytes (CTL) are not very effective in killing trophoblast cells. There is little evidence that CTL are present in decidua whereas natural killer cells are present in these areas.

In human decidua, the most abundant lymphoid cell is a large granular lymphocyte that expresses natural killer markers. These lymphocytes do not directly lyse human trophoblast cells in culture, although they can be induced to express cytotoxic activity if exposed to the lymphokine IL-2. These cells also show evidence of natural suppressor activity, although this property is somewhat assay-dependent. Similar observations have been made in the mouse: cytotoxic T lymphocytes (CTL) cannot kill trophoblast target cells, even though the trophoblast expresses the appropriate MHC *K* locus gene product. Indeed, increasing the expression of class I gene products on trophoblast cells by gamma-interferon treatment increases the susceptibility of the cells to destruction by antibody plus heterologous complement, but does not increase their susceptibility to CTL lysis. Nonetheless, the class I antigen can be recognized by T cells because the trophoblast cells can serve as antigen-specific cold target inhibitors. On the other hand, CTL generated in optimal media can kill trophoblast cells, although they are active only on trophoblast cells from 3-day-old cultures and not on fresh tissues. This leads us to question the *in vivo* significance of this observation. Natural killer (NK) cells kill trophoblast targets only if they are exposed to IL-2, but the IL-2-activated NK cells are effective on both fresh and cultured trophoblast cells.

Attention has therefore shifted from cytotoxic lymphocytes to natural killer cells in the decidua, although the physiological significance of either of these cell types remains to be confirmed. There are a number of observations that suggest that a variety of effector molecules can decrease the IL-2 responsiveness of decidual cell populations. Thus, in a healthy pregnancy, these decidual effector cells are unlikely to play a major role, although they may still cause damage in a pathological situation. There is some supporting evidence for this hypothesis from studies in aborting mice, in which increased NK levels have been reported and treatment with anti-NK cell antibody has reduced fetal loss.

The decidua seems to be uniquely susceptible to infection by *Listeria monocytogenes*. If the *Listeria* organisms penetrate the decidua basalis, there appears to be no way that the local macrophages can be triggered for effective bacterial clearance. On the contrary, there is evidence that decidual cell membranes contain a substance that prevents the activation of ordinary macrophages to bactericidal effector cells after direct contact. The exact nature of this substance is unknown, but it does not appear to be a diffusible factor.

Although there is evidence that T cells and large granular lymphocytes, as well as macrophages, reside in the decidua, some of these cells do not appear to be necessary for reproductive function in germ-free animals. Mice that are homozygous for the recessive *scid* and *beige* mutations can reproduce when maintained under barrier isolation. The *scid* mutation prevents the recombinational events that generate T and B cell receptor diversity, whereas the *beige* mutation eliminates virtually all functional natural killer cells. The F_2 hybrid mice that express both mutations have no B or T cells and very few natural killer cells, but reproduce normally under sterile conditions. Both these F_2 hybrids and normal mice raised in a germ-free environment have small placentas, which may reflect an influence of normal microbial flora on placental size. More data, however, are required to examine this interesting issue.

The metrial gland cell represents another cell type that is present between the decidua and the myometrium. It appears to be derived from the hematopoietic cell lineage, although it is not affected by mutations that delete B cells, T cells, NK cells, or colony-forming cells in the spleen. The functions of the metrial gland cell are also unclear, although a role in killing trophoblast cells has been suggested. These cells also appear to release trophoblast growth factor, and this process may be regulated by the immune cell interactions.

The presence of unique effector and regulatory cell populations, including nonspecific suppressor cells, in the decidua has led to studies to define the signals that pass between these cells, and their interactions with the cells of the fetal trophoblast. Recently, a number of effector molecules that influence reproductive function have been identified. The nature and possible role of these cytokines are discussed in the next section.

Cytokines

Although MHC antigens and effector cells that are present at the maternal-fetal interface have been studied for a long time, it is only recently that the importance of cytokines in this setting has been appreciated. Availability of these mediators in recombinant form and the development of specific assays have provided the principal impetus to studies on these molecules. There is now evidence that cytokines, which may be produced by cells of the immune system and by nonimmune tissues, affect both the preimplantation and postimplantation conceptus. It is increasingly apparent that these molecules play a major role in maintaining and/or damaging a pregnancy, and it is becoming difficult to distinguish some of their effects from those of endocrine molecules. Indeed, some of them have complex interactions with well-defined endocrine hormones, which is surprising to both reproductive immunologists and endocrinologists.

The effects of cytokines on preimplantation embryos have been tested in a variety of tissue culture systems. Although not all laboratories have obtained concordant data, some interesting effects have been reported. Under some circumstances, GM-CSF seems to play a role in enhancing the attachment and development of blastocysts, although this role depends on the attachment substrate. On the other hand, most cytokines appear to inhibit the earlier stages of preimplantation development, particularly when used at high concentrations. It may be significant that the uterus and its draining lymph nodes secrete GM-CSF, CSF-1 and suppressor-inducer molecules during the early stages of pregnancy. Monoclonal antibodies against a T suppressor molecule (TSF-1) terminate normal mouse pregnancy specifically and completely, possibly by preventing embryonic implantation. When implantation is experimentally delayed, the normal rise in uterine TSF-1 levels is also delayed. By contrast, treatment of pregnant mice with monoclonal antibodies directed against a suppressor-effector molecule (TSF-3) has no influence on implantation, although it increases fetal weight if administered early in gestation. In larger animals, such as the sheep and the cow, α-interferon and related molecules have been identified in the trophoblast and have been shown to have a direct antiluteolytic effect. They appear to prevent prostaglandin F-mediated destruction of the corpus luteum, which in turn prevents disruption of early gestation. Thus, interferon-like molecules appear to be involved in the maintenance of pregnancy in the sheep and cow, but not in the pig. Their effects appear analogous to those of chorionic gonadotropin in primates. In addition, these molecules also have antiviral and immunosuppressive activity.

The CSF-1 molecule, which has been thought to influence only macrophage growth and function, may also play a major role in reproduction. The uterine content of CSF-1 increases dramatically at the onset of pregnancy or after the induction of pseudopregnancy by steroid treatment. It appears to be synthesized primarily by uterine gland cells, as suggested by *in situ* hybridization studies. Furthermore, messenger RNA coding for the CSF-1 receptor, which represents the *c-fms* proto-oncogene product, is found in the giant cells and the spongiotrophoblast of the mouse placenta. Other evidence indicates that CSF-1, GM-CSF, and IL-3 are growth factors for certain cells within the placenta. For example, GM-CSF seems to stimulate proliferation of day-7.5 pure ectoplacental cone trophoblast and midgestational trophoblast-like cells in the placenta. It does not cause proliferation of cells from the day-16 placenta, however, suggesting that it is active during only a limited time during gestation. The cells that grow out from the placenta in response to cytokine treatment *in vitro* clearly must be characterized further to define their functional relationship to placental cells *in vivo*. These cytokines can also cause the secretion of hormones, such as human placental lactogen, by fetal placental cells. This interface between the immune and endocrine systems clearly warrants further investigation.

Although not all of these effects are due to cytokines released by cells of the immune system, there is evidence that removal of maternal T cells during pregnancy can, in some cases, result in reduced fetal and placental size and spontaneous abortion. In contrast, immunization against paternal alloantigens sometimes leads to increased placental size, increased or decreased fetal size, and an alteration in fetal survival. All of these effects have been observed in mouse models and are strain-dependent. The dramatic increase in the size of the placenta after hyperimmunization is due to changes in the spongiotrophoblast zone. Most intriguingly, the effects of immunization can be reproduced by treatment of mice prone to spontaneous abortion with low doses of recombinant GM-CSF. Whether this is a direct effect or results from a cascade phenomenon remains to be determined.

There has also been progress in understanding the nature of the cytokines that mediate nonspecific immune suppression in the placenta and that correlate with fetal survival. Molecules resembling TGF-β have been identified in the placenta and appear to be produced by the large granular lymphocytes present in the decidua. These molecules have long been identified as nonspecific suppressor cells. The most extensive observations to date have been made in the mouse, but there is also evidence for similar substances in humans. The exact role of these cytokines' *in vivo* remains to be elucidated, but it appears that their levels correlate with survival of individual fetal-placental units within the same uterus. A major effect of the TGF-β-like molecules on immune function appears to be a reduction of IL-2 effects.

This observation may be particularly significant in light of the work described in the previous section, implicating IL-2 as the lymphokine involved in generation of natural killer cells capable of destroying fresh trophoblast. The identification of this unique TGF-β-like molecule suggests the possibility that it or similar substances may be clinically useful immunosuppressive agents.

Conclusions

The progress outlined in this volume indicates the impacts of new cellular and molecular tools on our understanding of the maternal-fetal immune relationship. We are just beginning to understand the molecular nature of the fetal MHC antigens that initiate this interaction, the cellular basis of the maternal effector mechanisms that mediate it, and the cytokines involved in signaling in this interaction.

Many criticial questions remain; three are of particular importance. First, the types of antigens expressed on the surface of the placenta must be studied in more detail. The principal antigens appear to be encoded by the MHC, although a subset do not carry the epitopes of the allele-specific transplantation antigens of the species. There are some differences in opinion as to the maternal or paternal origin of the MHC antigens expressed by the fetal trophoblast. Once this point has been clarified, it will be necessary to define the mechanisms that regulate antigen expression in the placenta and the role of these antigens in cell interactions. These questions are of direct relevance to the field of genetic imprinting, and will have important implications for our understanding of the genetic control of early development. It is generally agreed from work in rats, mice, and humans that class II antigens are not expressed in the placenta, which may explain why the class I antigens that are expressed do not elicit a destructive immune response. The use of transgenic or reconstructed embryos and embryo transfer experiments in conjunction with serological, biochemical, and molecular analysis of MHC antigens in the trophoblast should provide a very fruitful approach to these interesting and perplexing problems.

Second, a detailed characterization of the cells in the decidua and the effector molecules that they produce must be undertaken. This is the first step toward defining the cells that interact in the decidua and the physiological consequences of these interactions. This interplay of stimulation and suppression may be a critical factor in the maintenance of a normal pregnancy, and alterations in this balance may lead to fetal loss. Regulation of the balance between stimulation and suppression is central to much of immunology. However, investigation of these mechanisms in the placenta imposes additional problems of having very limited amounts of material with which to work and of having to perform many critical studies *in situ*. The genealogy of the cells that interact in the decidua must also be defined, but these studies will probably be subject to all of the difficulties encountered in defining blood cell lineages. Nonetheless, systematic descriptive information will be of some practical use. For example, perinatal AIDS is a growing problem, particularly in large urban hospitals. Not all babies born to AIDS-infected mothers are themselves infected, but a substantial proportion are and have a particularly bleak outlook. A great deal more must be known about the basic mechanisms of immune cell traffic and regulation in the decidua in order to develop effective strategies to decrease the fetal infection rate.

Third, cytokines appear to be the language of the hematopoietic/lymphoid system and of the trophoblast/decidua system. This is a surprising and exciting finding, since it indicates that quite distinct physiological systems may use the same effector molecules to mediate their functions. The similarity to the endocrine system is clear, and it may be that there are relatively few such "molecular languages" that are involved in all physiological systems. The interrelationships among these "languages" must also be addressed. Studies of these cytokines are at an early stage, and the chemistry of the molecules and their receptors must be defined in greater detail. In particular, the effects of subtle structural changes on their biological functions must be defined in order to elucidate the differences between stimulator and suppressor effects. This area of research will require an integrated approach, making use of the techniques of protein chemistry, molecular biology, and cell biology, as well as the availability of large amounts of these molecules produced by recombinant DNA techniques. In this way, it should ultimately be possible to assign the proper physiological function to each molecule and its receptor at various stages of differentiation.

The problems of reproductive immunology and genetics mirror some of the major issues in the broader fields of their parent disciplines, and they provide an additional challenge of having to be examined in the content of the trophoblast. Exploring these questions in relation to reproductive biology adds the exciting dimension of their relationship to endocrinology and to developmental biology. As each of these disciplines becomes less parochial, a broader understanding of molecular interactions and the control of physiological functions will evolve. We will also be in a better position to integrate information from different systems, as a wide variety of apparently disparate phenomena are increasingly seen to rely on relatively few effector molecules. The potential applications for the control of reproductive function clearly justify the attention that is now being focused on this area of research.

Part 1

FETAL MAJOR HISTOCOMPATIBILITY COMPLEX

2

Class I Gene Products in the Human Placenta and Extraplacental Membranes

JOAN S. HUNT and JAMES L. FISHBACK

The expression of class I genes by extraembryonic cells is relevant to pregnancy for two reasons. First, the fetus is semiallogeneic to the mother. Full expression of paternally derived major histocompatibility complex (MHC) genes could mediate rejection of the fetus by maternal immune cells. Second, some class I gene products are developmentally regulated (Fahrner et al., 1987) and could be critical to the generation of appropriate cell-cell and/or cell-substrate interactions during placental morphogenesis.

Human placentas and extraplacental membranes are composed of two embryologically distinct cell populations (Faulk, 1983): trophoblast cells arise from the trophectoderm of the implanted blastocyst whereas mesenchymal cells arise from the inner cell mass. Of those two populations, only trophoblast cells are directly exposed to maternal blood and decidua. Trophoblast cells are intercalated between maternal blood and mesenchymal cells in the placenta and between decidua and mesenchymal cells in the extraplacental membranes. Trophoblast and mesenchymal cells demonstrate striking differences in their expression of class I antigens. Trophoblast cells either fail to express class I human leukocyte antigens (HLA) or display unusual class I molecules. In contrast, mesenchymal cells in extraembryonic tissues express a full complement of class I HLA-A, B, C. It has been postulated that trophoblast cells form an immunologically neutral barrier that shields HLA-expressing embryonic cells from alloreactive maternal immune cells (Beer & Sio, 1982).

For the past several years, reproduction immunologists have focused on the mechanisms by which trophoblast cells regulate their expression of class I antigens. In this chapter we will discuss some of the experiments we have performed and supplement our data with findings reported by other investigators. We have used two experimental approaches to explore the question of regulation: *in situ* hybridization to determine intracellular levels of specific mRNA and treatment with interferon-gamma (IFN) to determine if low rates of gene transcription are responsible for low expression. At the end of the chapter we offer some comments and conclusions that seem reasonable at present.

Identification of Class I Antigens

The structure of the 45 kDa class I heavy chains is well described (Juji & Kano, 1984). HLA heavy chains have three extracellular domains (a1, a2, a3) and one intracellular domain. Glycosylation sites and the amino acid sequences coding for allotypic and subclass determinants are located near the junction of the a1/a2 domains. HLA-G, a recently identified nonclassical antigen coded from a gene telomeric to HLA-A (discussed below), is different from other HLA class I heavy chains in that it has a shortened cytoplasmic sequence (Geraghty et al., 1987).

A variety of reagents have been used to identify class I antigens; initially, human HLA antisera from multiparous women were used (Faulk & Temple, 1976). More recently, monoclonal antibodies (mAb) that bind to specific epitopes on HLA class I antigens have been described. W6/32, which binds poorly to isolated heavy chains but strongly to heavy chains associated with beta$_2$-microglobulin (Parham et al., 1979), is a popular reagent for identifying monomorphic determinants of class I antigens. The mAb identifies a 45 kDa class I heavy chains in most types of cells. However, W6/32 precipitates both a novel 40-41 kDa heavy chain and the higher m.w. chain from lysates of trophoblast cells (Ellis et al., 1986; Johnson & Stern, 1986) and the amnion cell-derived AV3 line (Hsi et al., 1988). Although the binding site of a second mAb, 61D2, to monomorphic determinants on class I heavy chain has not been reported, this mAb fails to recognize the lower m.w. chain in AV3 cells (Hsi et al., 1988). A few mAb that recognize specific HLA subclasses have now been reported, including the mAb 4E, which identifies HLA-B and does not require beta$_2$-microglobulin for binding (Yang et al., 1984). Some mAb that distinguish allotypic variants of class I antigens are available, but mAb to the antigens derived from nonclassical class I genes have not been reported.

Class I Genes

In humans, the genes that encode class I heavy chains are found on the short arm of chromosome 6. Class I genes are located either within the MHC (classical HLA-A,B,C) or are telomeric to HLA-A (nonclassical) (Orr & DeMars, 1983). The HLA-A,B,C genes are highly polymorphic and are expressed to a greater or lesser extent by nearly all cells. Their roles in antigen presentation to lymphocytes and graft rejection are well documented.

Recently, intensive efforts have been made to clone the human nonclassical genes and to discover their functions. The murine equivalents (Qa and Tla genes) of the human nonclassical genes have a low degree of polymorphism and, of particular relevance to pregnancy, appear to be developmentally regulated (Lew et al., 1986; Fahrner et al., 1987) and associated with the induction of immunological tolerance (Kress et al., 1983). One gene located between HLA-C and HLA-A has been identified and designated HLA-E (Koller et al., 1988; Mizuno et al., 1988). Two of the nonclassical genes downstream from HLA-A have also been cloned and sequenced, HLA-G (Geraghty et al., 1987) and HLA-F (Geraghty et al., 1990), and the chromosomal organization of the genes in this region has been determined (Koller et al., 1989).

Class I Gene Expression by Inner Cell Mass-Derived Cells in the Placenta and Extraplacental Membranes

If polymorphic class I antigens were not synthesized by the mesenchymal cells in extraembryonic tissues, the expression of those antigens by trophoblast cells would be a less critical question since maternal cell traffic into the placenta is apparently rare. However, mesenchymal cells express both class I and class II antigens (Galbraith et al., 1981). In a recent immunohistological study of mesenchymal cells in the first, second and third trimesters of pregnancy, binding of the mAb 61D2 to class I HLA heavy chains was shown to increase gradually as gestation progressed (Lessin et al., 1988). At the level of gene expression, *in situ* hybridization experiments in our laboratory have demonstrated that mRNA levels for class I heavy chains are related to antigen expression. In comparison with maternal cells, specific mRNA is low in the mesenchymal cells of first trimester tissues (Hunt & Fishback, in press) and high in term tissues (Hunt et al., 1988b). Class II antigens also show gradual increase in expression as pregnancy proceeds to term, although this expression is delayed relative to class I antigens (Lessin et al., 1988).

Class I Gene Products in Placental Villous Trophoblast

It is now well documented that expression of class I MHC antigens by trophoblast cells differs in a number of respects from that of inner cell mass-derived cells. Furthermore, expression differs among trophoblast cell subpopulations, and there appear to be gestation-related differences as well.

Term Placentas

Two trophoblast cell populations can be identified in the placenta. Syncytial trophoblast lines the blood spaces and is bathed continuously in maternal blood. Cytotrophoblast cells, which serve as progenitor cells for the syncytium, lie directly beneath the syncytial layer. In term placentas, cytotrophoblast cells are relatively uncommon.

Syncytial Trophoblast. The first indication that trophoblast cells had unusual patterns of HLA expression came from the studies of Faulk and Temple (1976) and Goodfellow and coworkers (1976). Syncytial trophoblast in term placental villi failed to bind polyclonal reagents to HLA, an observation that has since been confirmed in many laboratories. Regardless of the reagents used, syncytial trophoblast in term tissues does not express class I antigens, and normally fails to bind anti-class II antibodies. An explanation for this highly significant and unusual finding has been provided by the results of *in situ* hybridization experiments performed in our laboratories. When term placentas were fixed in paraformaldehyde, sectioned, and hybridized with pHLA1.1, which is homologous to sequences in the 3′ untranslated end of HLA-B (Koller et al., 1984), syncytial trophoblast was found to contain little if any mRNA for class I heavy chains (Hunt et al., 1988b).

Figure 2-1 shows the results of an *in situ* hybridization experiment using sections of term placenta and an antisense RNA probe for HLA-B (pHLA1.1) under conditions of moderate stringency. Mesenchymal cells contained RNA that hybridized strongly to the HLA probe whereas syncytial trophoblast did not (Fig. 2-1A). One of the controls performed in these studies was pretreatment of tissue sections with RNase, which abolished hybridization (Fig. 2-1B), thus demonstrating that the hybridizing material within the cells was RNA. Low steady-state levels of class I mRNA are clearly responsible for the failure of syncytial trophoblast in term placentas to exhibit class I antigens, although it remains to be determined if these levels are due to low rates of transcription or high rates of degradation.

Cytotrophoblast Cells. In humans, cytotrophoblast cells merge with the syncytium during placental development. Cytotrophoblast cells are therefore uncommon in term placentas and it is difficult to determine with certainty if they express class I antigens using immunohistological techniques. It has also proved difficult, using an *in situ* hybridization approach, to determine if cytotrophoblast cells in term placentas contain class I mRNA. Our impression is, however, that

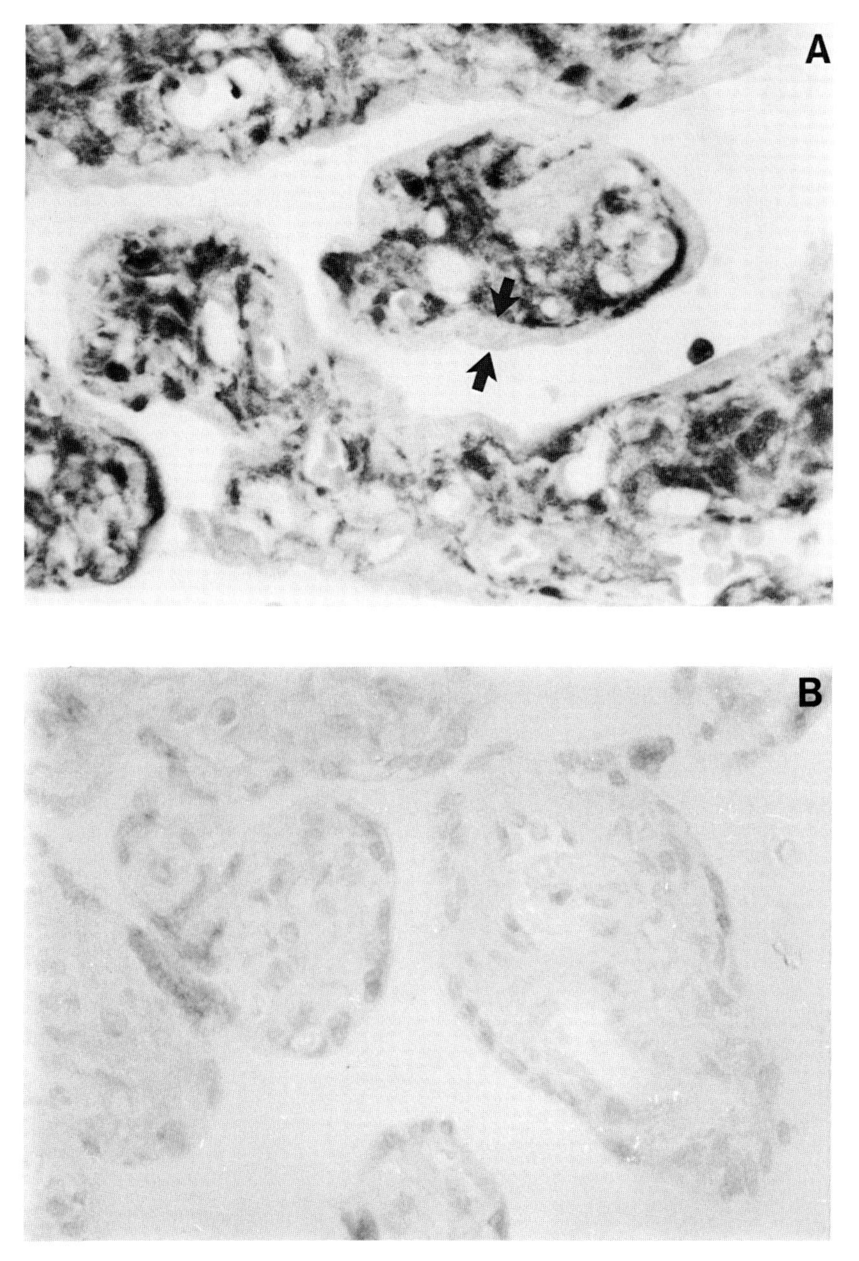

Fig. 2-1. Hybridization of a biotinylated antisense RNA probe, pHLA1.1, to paraformaldehyde-fixed sections of term placenta. (A) Mesenchymal cells in the centers of the placental villi contain class I mRNA. Syncytial trophoblast RNA does not hybridize to the HLA probe (arrows). (B) Pretreatment of tissue sections with RNase abolishes hybridization.

these cells are positive (Hunt & Fishback, in press). Interestingly, IFN treatment of cytotrophoblast cells harvested from term placentas and cultured *in vitro* induces expression of class I antigens and mRNA (Feinman et al., 1987). The mechanism that prevents translation of the mRNA into identifiable class I antigens by cells in intact placental villi remains to be determined.

First Trimester Placentas

The two layers of trophoblast cells are easily distinguished in first trimester placental villi with the cytotrophoblast cells forming a continuous layer beneath the syncytium.

In Situ Hybridization Experiments. In first trimester tissues, syncytial and cytotrophoblast cells contained within the villous are both clearly negative for class I antigens by immunohistology (Sunderland et al., 1981; Hunt et al., 1987). However, we have shown that under moderate conditions of stringency pHLA1.1 hybridizes to RNA in both cell layers (Fig. 2-2A). In first trimester tissues, some mesenchymal cells contained class I mRNA whereas others did not (Fig. 2-2B), a finding that is compatible with immunohistological observations using 61D2 (Lessin et al., 1988) and with the anti-HLA-B mAb 4E (Hunt, et al., 1989). In addition, disrupted villi in the same field with intact villi did not contain hybridizing material.

Recently, we have shown that cytotrophoblast cells both within and external to first trimester placental villi contain class I mRNA (Hunt et al., 1990). Further studies have demonstrated that the messages are transcribed from HLA-G (Yelavarthi et al., submitted). These latter experiments were performed under conditions of high stringency of *in situ* hybridization using two types of probes, a 340 bp biotinylated antisense RNA probe for HLA-G, and an HLA-G-specific oligonucleotide probe. In addition to the cytotrophoblast cells, mesenchymal cells in the centers of placental villi contained HLA-G mRNA, which was not surprising inasmuch as other inner cell mass-derived cells have been shown to transcribe this gene (Shukla et al., 1990).

Experiments in other laboratories performed prior to our most recent *in situ* hybridization studies used the polymerase chain reaction to amplify HLA-G mRNA from chorion membranes (Ellis et al., 1989) and RNase protection assays to identify HLA-G mRNA in the placenta (Wei & Orr, in press). In addition, two dimensional gel analysis has verified the presence of HLA-G proteins in partially purified preparations of trophoblast cells (Kovats et al., 1990). Our *in situ* hybridization results provide unequivocal demonstration of HLA-G transcription by cytotrophoblast cells *in situ*, and also show that the transcripts and proteins identified in these other studies could have been the products of either trophoblast or placental mesenchymal cells.

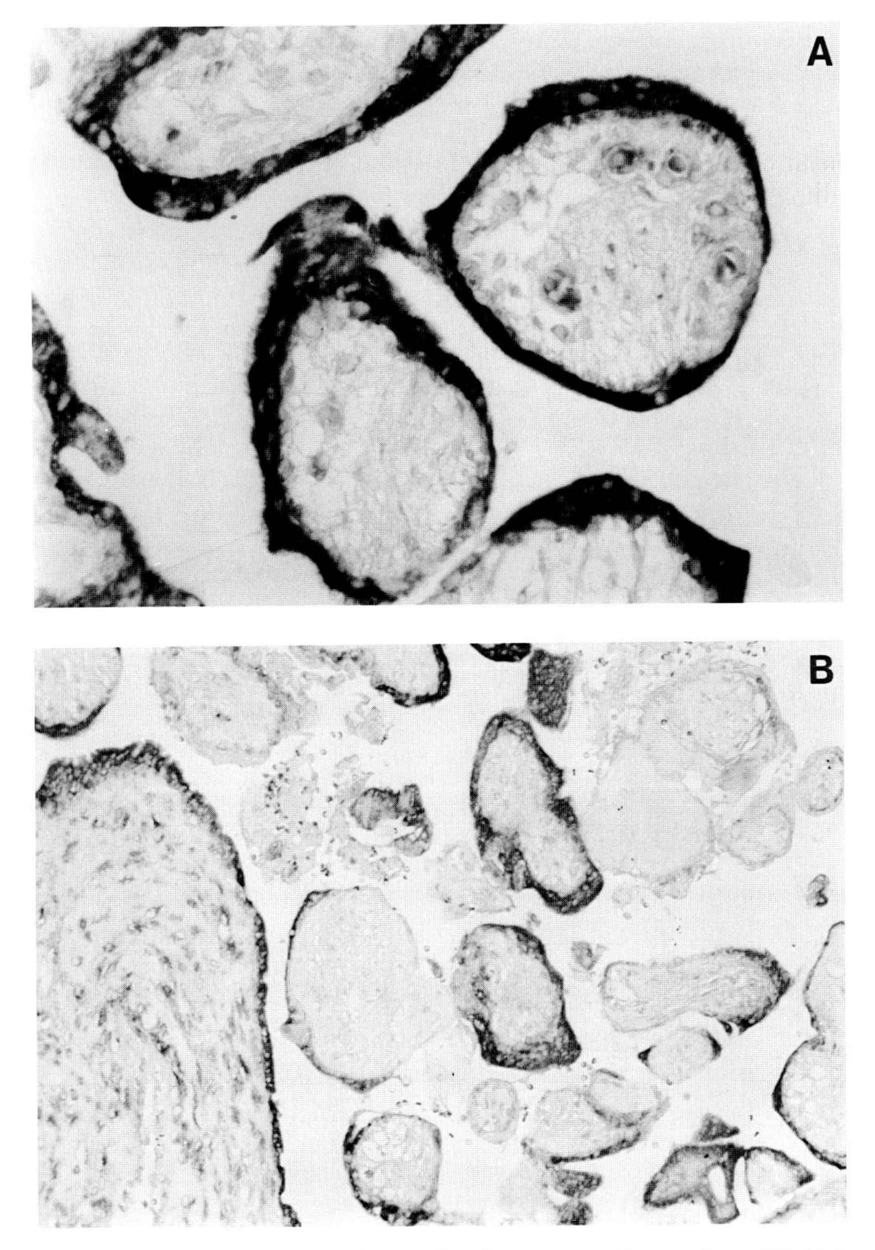

Fig. 2-2. Hybridization of the biotinylated antisense RNA probe, pHLA1.1, to paraformaldehyde-fixed sections of first trimester placenta. (A) Both the syncytial and cytotrophoblast layers of the placental villi contain RNA that hybridizes to the HLA probe. (B) Disrupted villi do not contain RNA that will hybridize to pHLA1.1. Some mesenchymal cells contain class I mRNA whereas others do not.

Interferon Experiments. We attempted to induce class I expression by treating explants of first trimester tissues, which have high viability in culture, for 48 hours with IFN. In most cells, IFN treatment enhances the rate of transcription of the class I genes, with subsequent expression of increased levels of the proteins. Our finding was that neither syncytial nor cytotrophoblast cells were inducible although villous mesenchymal cells were readily up-regulated (Hunt et al., 1987). This unexpected observation has now been explained. HLA-G is apparently the only class I gene transcribed in trophoblast cells *in situ*, and, unlike other class I heavy chains, HLA-G lacks the IFN response element (Geraghty et al., 1990).

Special mechanisms in intact placental villi operate to regulate translation of HLA-G messages into proteins. Although villous cytotrophoblast cells contain class I mRNA, they do not express class I antigens. However, when released from the villus, cytotrophoblast cells appear to gain the capacity to express class I antigens. Few cytotrophoblast cells harvested from first trimester placentas are class I positive whereas cells in continuous *in vitro* culture express the W6/32-binding protein (Loke & Burland, 1988). These observations suggest that constraints imposed by the villus (cell-cell or cell-matrix communications, soluble fetally-derived molecules) may inhibit translation and expression. Similar mechanisms may apply to cytotrophoblast cells in term tissues, as discussed above.

Class I Gene Products in the Extraplacental Membranes

The extraplacental membranes that surround the fetus are made up of layers of chorion membrane cytotrophoblast cells, mesenchymal cells, and amnion epithelial cells. As in the placenta, there is differential expression of class I antigens among these cells.

Chorion Membrane Cytotrophoblast Cells

Extravillous cytotrophoblast cells that migrate from the villous into the placental bed (Sunderland et al., 1981; Wells et al., 1984) and form the chorion membrane (Hsi et al., 1984) express unusual antigens that bind W6/32 and anti-beta$_2$-microglobulin, but not 61D2. Class I antigens on chorionic cytotrophoblast cells also lack binding sites for subclass-specific mAb (HLA-B) (Hunt et al., 1989) and antibodies to allotypic determinants (Redman et al., 1984). Immunoprecipitation studies have shown that the antigens have a lower than expected molecular weight (40 kDa vs. 45 kDa) (Ellis et al., 1986).

Chorion membrane cytotrophoblast cells contained class I mRNA when evaluated by *in situ* hybridization under conditions of moderate stringency (Hunt et al., 1988b) (Fig. 2-3). Recently, by performing *in*

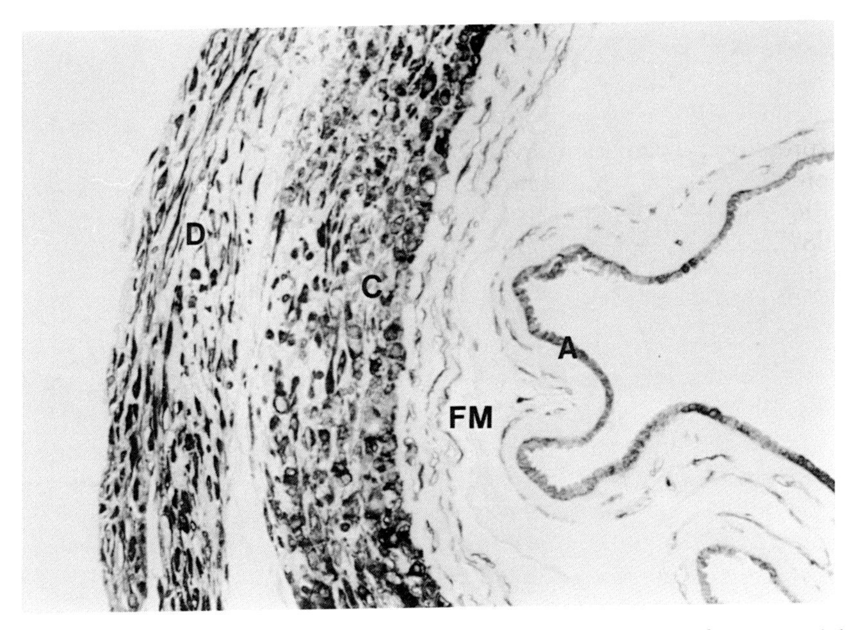

Fig. 2-3. Hybridization of the biotinylated antisense RNA probe, pHLA1.1, to a section of term amniochorion. D, decidua; C, chorion membrane; FM, fetal mesenchyme; A, amnion. All of the cell layers in the amniochorion contain class I mRNA. Levels appeared higher in maternal decidual cells than in extraembryonic cells, as judged by color intensity.

situ hybridizations with an HLA-G specific probe under conditions of high stringency, we have shown that this is HLA-G mRNA (Yelavarthi et al., submitted).

Amnion Epithelial Cells

Although the mesenchymal cells in the fibrous layer between the chorion and amnion membranes are class I HLA positive, there have been conflicting reports regarding class I expression by the amnion cells, which are also derived from the inner cell mass. First reported as class I negative (Hsi et al., 1982), more sensitive immunohistologic technics have shown that amnion cells are often class I positive (Hunt et al., 1988a). Amnion membranes bind W6/32 considerably more frequently than they bind 61D2 (Hunt et al., 1988a) or anti-HLA-B (Hunt et al., 1989).

Amnion cells contain class I mRNA (Fig. 3) (Hunt et al., 1988a), although levels of expression of antigens and mRNA can be regulated by extrinsic factors. IFN enhances class I antigen expression (Hunt & Wood, 1986) and mRNA levels (Hunt et al., 1988a) in amnion cells in tissue explants, whereas epidermal growth factor diminishes mRNA levels (Hunt et al., 1988a). Amnion cells therefore resemble inner cell mass-derived rather than trophoblast-derived cells in their sensitivity to regulation of the rate of transcription of class I genes by IFN. Topographical differences in class I expression have been reported that support the concept that amnion cell class I antigen expression is regulated by extrinsic molecules in normal, untreated tissues (Hsi et al., 1988).

Conclusions

Unusual expression of class I antigens by trophoblast cells has now been extensively documented, although the functional aspects remain to be addressed. Regulation of expression of class I MHC antigens by trophoblast cells may be a major biological adaptation by which the fetus is protected from immune cell recognition and destruction. There is less evidence for this hypothesis in reproduction than in tumor immunology. Diminished class I expression is one of the evasive strategies employed by tumor cells (Hammerling et al., 1987; Nelson & Nelson, 1987). As with syncytial trophoblast, some tumor cells, particularly tumors of epithelial origin (Hammerling et al., 1987), have low to undetectable levels of class I antigens and mRNA (Doyle et al., 1985). Convincing evidence for diminished class I expression as an escape mechanism has been provided by the finding that adenovirus 12 is oncogenic by virtue of its ability to suppress class I production (Vaessen et al., 1986).

Qualitative differences, including the expression of novel class I antigens by tumor cells (Kastern, 1985; Phillips et al., 1985; Lampson & George, 1986) have also been reported, but it is not certain if those antigens are immunogenic. Chorionic cytotrophoblast cells, which express reasonable levels of the 40 kDa class I antigen (Ellis et al., 1986), do not stimulate maternal cells in mixed lymphocyte cultures (Hunt et al., 1984). In addition, amnion cell monolayers can be successfully transplanted across histocompatibility barriers (Akle et al., 1981). Thus, the absence or diminished expression of classical HLA-A,B,C may be critical. The unusual class I antigens expressed by some trophoblast cells may not pose an immunological risk to pregnancy, but may instead play a role in other major events that take place in the placental bed.

Acknowledgments

These studies were studied in part by grants from the Speas Foundation to J.S.H. and J.L.F., and from the National Institutes of Health (BRSG SO7-RR05373, HD26429) to J.S.H. The authors are grateful to H.T. Orr, University of Minnesota, for supplying the class I HLA probes.

References

Akle, C. A., Adinolfi, M., Welsh, K. I., Leibowitz, S., and McColl, I. 1981. Immunogenicity of human amniotic epithelial cells after transplantation into volunteers. *Lancet* 2:1003.

Beer, A. E. and Sio, J. O. 1982. Placenta as an immunological barrier. *Biol. Reprod.* 26:833.

Doyle, A., Martin, W. J., Funa, K., Gazdar, A., Carney, D., Martin, S. E., Linnoila, I., Cuttintta, F., Mulshine, J., Bunn, P., and Minna, J. 1985. Markedly decreased expression of class I histocompatibility antigens, protein, and mRNA in human small-cell lung cancer. *J. Exp. Med.* 161:1135.

Ellis, S. A., Sargent, I. L., Redman, C. W., and McMichael, A. J. 1986. Evidence for a novel HLA antigen found on human extravillous trophoblast and a choriocarcinoma cell line. *Immunology* 59:595.

Ellis, S. A., Palmer, M. S., and McMichael, A. J. 1989. Human trophoblast and the choriocarcinoma cell line BeWo express a truncated HLA class I molecule. *J. Immunol.* 144:731.

Fahrner, K., Hogan, B. L. M., and Flavell, R. A. 1987. Transcription of H-2 and Qa genes in embryonic and adult mice. *EMBO J.* 6:1265.

Faulk, W. P. 1983. Immunobiology of human extraembryonic membranes. In *Immunology of Reproduction.* New York: Oxford University Press, p. 251.

Faulk, W. P. and Temple, A. 1976. Distribution of beta-2-microglobulin and HLA in chorionic villi of human placentae. *Nature* (*London*) 262:799.

Feinman, M. A., Kliman, H. J., and Main, E. K. 1987. HLA antigen expression and induction by gamma-interferon in cultured human trophoblasts. *Am. J. Obstet. Gynecol.* 157:1429.

Galbraith, R. M., Kantor, R. R. S., Ferrara, G. B., Ades, E. W., and Galbraith, G. M. P. 1981. Differential expression of transplantation antigens within the normal placental chorionic villus. *Am. J. Reprod. Immunol.* 1:331.

Geraghty, D. E., Koller, B. H., and Orr, H. T. 1987. A human major histocompatibility complex class I gene that encodes a protein with a shortened cytoplasmic segment. *Proc. Nat. Acad. Sci. USA* 84:9145.

Geraghty, D. E., Wei, X., Orr, H. T., and Koller, B. H. 1990. Human leukocyte antigen F (HLA-F). An expressed HLA gene composed of a class I coding sequence linked to a novel transcribed repetitive element. *J. Exp. Med.* 171:1.

Goodfellow, P. N., Barnstable, C. J., Bodmer, W. F., Snary, D. E., and Crumpton, M. J. 1976. Expression of HLA system antigens on placentae. *Transplantation* 22:555.

Hammerling, G. J., Klar, D., Pulm, W., Momburg, F., and Moldenhauer, G. 1987. The influence of major histocompatibility complex class I antigens on tumor growth and metastasis. *Biochim. Biophys. Acta* 907:245.

Hsi, B.-L., Yeh, C.-J. G., and Fulk, W. P. 1982. Human amniochorion: tissue-specific markers, transferrin receptors and histocompatibility antigens. *Placenta* 3:1.

Hsi, B.-L., Yeh, C.-J. G., and Faulk, W. P. 1984. Class I antigens of the major histocompatibility complex on cytotrophoblast of human chorion laeve. *Immunology* 52:621.

Hsi, B.-L., Samson, M., Grivaux, C., Fenichel, P., Hunt, J. S., and Yeh, C.-J. G. 1988. Topographical expression of class I major histocompatability complex antigens on human amniotic epithelium. *J. Reprod. Immunol.* 13:183.

Hunt, J. S. and Fishback, J. L. 1990. Class I HLA mRNA in extraembryonic cells. In *Trophoblast Research*, vol. 5; *Molecular Biology and Cell Regulation of the Placenta.* New York: Plenum.

Hunt, J. S. and Wood, G. W. 1986. Gamma interferon induces class I HLA and beta-2-microglobulin expression by human amnion cells. *J. Immunol.* 136:364.

Hunt, J. S., King, C. R., and Wood, G. W. 1984. Evaluation of human chorionic trophoblasts and placental macrophages as stimulators of maternal lymphocyte proliferation in vitro. *J. Reprod. Immunol.* 6:377.

Hunt, J. S., Andrews, G. K., and Wood, G. W. 1987. Normal trophoblasts resist induction of class I HLA. *J. Immunol.* 138:2481.

Hunt, J. S., Andrews, G. K., Fishback, J. B., Feess, M., and Wood, G. W. 1988a. Amnion membrane epithelial cells express class I HLA and contain class I HLA mRNA. *J. Immunol.* 140:2790.

Hunt, J. S., Fishback, J. L., Andrews, G. K., and Wood, G. W. 1988b. Expression of class I HLA genes by trophoblast cells: analysis by in situ hybridization. *J. Immunol.* 140:1293.

Hunt, J. S., Lessin, D., and King, C. R. 1989. Ontogeny and distribution of cells expressing HLA-B locus-specific determinants in the placenta and extraplacental membranes. *J. Reprod. Immunol.* 15:21.

Hunt, J. S., Fishback, J. L., Chumbley, G., and Loke, Y. W. 1990. Identification of class I MHC mRNA in human first trimester trophoblast cells by *in situ* hybridization. *J. Immunol.* 144:4420.

Johnson, P. M. and Stern, P. L. 1986. Antigen expression at human maternal-fetal interfaces. In *Progress in Immunology VI.* Orlando: Academic Press, p. 1056.

Juji, T. and K. Kano. 1984. The HLA system. In *Molecular Immunology.* New York: M. Dekker, p. 563.

Kastern, W. 1985. Characterization of two class I major histocompatibility rat cDNA clones, one of which contains a premature termination codon. *Gene* 34:227.

Koller, B. H., Sidwell, B., DeMars, R., and Orr, H. T. 1984. Isolation of HLA locus-specific DNA probes from the 3′-untranslated region. *Proc. Nat. Acad. Sci. USA* 81:5175.

Koller, B. H., Geraghty, D. E., Shimizu, Y., DeMars, R., and Orr, H. T. 1988. HLA-E. A novel HLA class I gene expressed in resting T lymphocytes. *J. Immunol.* 141:897.

Koller, B. H., Geraghty, D. E., DeMars, R., Duvick, L., Rich, S. S., and Orr, H. T. 1989. Chromosomal organization of the human major histocompatibility complex class I gene family. *J. Exp. Med.* 169:469.

Kovats, S., Main, E. K., Librach, C., Stubblebine, M., Fisher, S. J., and DeMars, R. 1990. A class I antigen, HLA-G, expressed in human trophoblasts. *Science* 248:220.

Kress, M., Casman, D., Khoury, G., and Jay, G. 1983. Secretion of a transplantation-related antigen. *Cell* 34:189.

Lampson, L. A. and George, D. L. 1986. Interferon-mediated induction of class I MHC products in human neuronal cell lines: analysis of HLA and b_2-m RNA and HLA-A and HLA-B proteins and polymorphic specificities. *J. Interferon Res.* 6:257.

Lessin, D. L., Hunt, J. S., King, C. R., and Wood, G. W. 1988. Antigen expression by cells near the maternal-fetal interface. *Am. J. Reprod. Immunol. Microbiol.* 16:1.

Lew, A. M., Lillehoj, E. P., Cowan, E. P., Maloy, W. L., van Schravendiji, M. R., and Coligan, J. E. 1986. Class I genes and molecules: an update. *Immunology* 57:3.

Loke, Y. W. and Burland, K. 1988. Human trophoblast cells cultured in modified medium and supported by extracellular matrix. *Placenta* 9:173.

Mizuno, S., Trapani, J. A., Koller, B. H., Dupont, B., and Yang, S. Y. 1988. Isolation and nucleotide sequence of a cDNA clone encoding a novel HLA class I gene. *J. Immunol.* 140:4024.

Nelson, D. S. and Nelson, M. 1987. Evasion of host defences by tumours. *Immunol. Cell Biol.* 65:287.

Orr, H. T. and DeMars, R. 1983. Class I-like HLA genes map telomeric to the HLA-A2 locus in human cells. *Nature* 302:534.

Parham, P., Barnstable, C. J., and Bodmer, W. F. 1979. Use of a monoclonal antibody (W6/32) in structural studies of HLA-A,B,C antigens. *J. Immunol.* 123:342.

Philipps, C., McMillan, M., Flood, P. M., Murphy, D. B., Forman, J., Lancki, D., Womack, J. E., Goodenow, R. S., and Schreiber, H. 1985. Identification of a unique tumor-specific antigen as a novel class I major histocompatibility molecule. *Proc. Nat. Acad. Sci. USA* 82:5140.

Redman, C. W. G., McMichael, A. J., Stirrat, G. M., Sunderland, C. A., and Ting, A. 1984. Class I major histocompatibility complex antigens on human extravillous trophoblast. *Immunology* 52:457.

Shukla, H., Swaroop, A., Srivastava, R., and Weissman, S. M. 1990. The mRNA of a human class I gene HLA G/HLA 6.0 exhibits a restricted pattern of expression. *Nucleic Acids Res.* 18:2189.

Sunderland, C. A., Redman, C. W. G., and Stirrat, G. M. 1981. HLA-A,B,C antigens are expressed on nonvillous trophoblasts of the early human placenta. *J. Immunol.* 127:2614.

Vaessen, R. T. M. J., Houweling, A., and van der Eb, A. J. 1986. Post-transcriptional control of class I MHC mRNA expression in adenovirus 12-transformed cells. *Science* 235:1486.

Wei, X. and Orr, H. T. Differential expression of HLA-E, HLA-F, and HLA-G transcripts in human tissue. *Hum. Immunol.* In Press.

Wells, M., Hsi, B.-L., and Faulk, W. P. 1984. Class I antigens of the major histocompatibility complex on cytotrophoblast of the human placental basal plate. *Am. J. Reprod. Immunol.* 6:167.

Yang, S. Y., Morishima, Y., Collins, N. H., Alton, T., Pollack, M. S., Yunis, E. J., and Dupont, B. 1984. Comparison of one-dimensional IEF patterns for serologically detectable HLA-A and B allotypes. *Immunogenetics* 19:217.

3

Unusual HLA Class I Expression on Human Cytotrophoblast Cells and on a Choriocarcinoma Cell Line

SHIRLEY A. ELLIS and ANDREW J. McMICHAEL

MHC class I molecules are expressed on most mammalian cells and function as restriction elements for cytotoxic T lymphocytes. In the human, the 45 kDa heavy chains, which associate noncovalently with beta$_2$-microglobulin (β-2m) at the cell surface, are encoded by genes located on chromosome 6. Although the products of only three loci (A, B, and C) have been identified serologically, more than 20 class I genes appear to be present in the human genome (Biro et al., 1983). Some of these have proved to be pseudogenes and gene fragments, but it seems likely that some code for functional molecules that may be analogous to the Qa or Tla products in the mouse.

Some Qa gene products exhibit characteristics, such as limited polymorphism, lower molecular weight, glycosylation differences, limited tissue distribution, and phosphatidyl inositol (PI) linkage (Robinson, 1987), that suggest that they may have different functions than classical H-2 antigens. The function of Qa antigens is unknown. Although no true Qa or Tla analogs have been identified in the human, there is evidence for the presence of unusual class-I-related molecules on some activated T cells, although these have not been characterized sufficiently to give a clear indication of their origins or functions (Fauchet et al., 1986). The CD1 antigens, which were thought to be the human equivalent to Tla, have been shown to be coded by a novel gene family related to MHC but located on a different chromosome from the class I genes (Calabi & Milstein, 1986).

The mechanisms by which the mammalian fetus is tolerated during pregnancy, despite expressing paternal MHC antigens, has been the subject of much research and speculation (Bulmer & Johnson, 1983). This situation is unique, and clearly any information concerning the mechanisms involved could enhance our understanding of many aspects of transplantation immunology.

In the human, villous cytotrophoblast and syncytiotrophoblast do not express class I or class II MHC antigens, and it is likely that this is an important part of the mechanism that protects the fetus from maternal immunological attack. However, some populations of extravillous trophoblast in the chorion laeve and placental bed, which lie in close contact with maternal cells, do express a relatively high level of HLA class I antigens (Redman et al., 1984). It is clear from biochemical studies that the HLA class I antigen(s) expressed on these cells is not classical class I. The antigen(s) fails to react with some monoclonal antibodies to monomorphic HLA class I determinants and with all monoclonal antibodies to relevant polymorphic determinants (Ellis et al., 1986). Isoelectric focusing (IEF) data suggest that the molecule may be nonpolymorphic, and it also appears to have a lower molecular weight than classical class I antigens (approximately 40 kDa vs. 45 kDa). Molecules with similar characteristics have been identified on baboon syncytiotrophoblast (Stern et al., 1987).

Various mechanisms have been postulated to play a role in the maintenance of pregnancy, including the induction of tolerance, local suppression of the maternal immune response, and blocking of recognition by T cells of target antigens. The unusual class I molecules expressed on cells within the placenta could play an important role in such mechanisms.

Although extensive work has now been carried out in several laboratories to identify and characterize the functions of these unusual class I antigens, the situation is still unclear. Some of the results of this work and their possible significance are discussed in this chapter.

Evidence for the Presence of Unusual HLA Class I on Trophoblast

Immunohistological Evidence

Binding studies using monoclonal antibodies to various HLA class I epitopes have shown very clearly that some extravillous trophoblast in placental tissues does express HLA class I antigens, in contrast to villous trophoblast (Redman et al., 1984). Positive staining of trophoblast is seen on sections through amniochorion, using monoclonal antibodies against monomorphic determinants of class I, such as W6/32, PA2.6, and BB7.7, and also with monoclonal antibodies against β-2m, such as BBM.1. However, when identical sections are stained with monoclonal antibodies directed against the relevant fetal polymorphic determinants, such as MA2.1 (A2,B17) or ME1 (B7, B27), no staining of trophoblast is seen.

Biochemical Characterization of HLA Class I Antigens

Isolation of Extravillous Trophoblast Cells. Extravillous trophoblast cells can be prepared by enzymatic digestion of chorion membranes after removal of the amniotic epithelium and decidua (Ellis et al., 1986). In this study, serial cryostat sections of the amniochorion of each placenta were made to allow immunoperoxidase staining with a panel of monoclonal antibodies. When antigen expression was studied on isolated extravillous trophoblast cell populations, we found that antibodies to monomorphic class I determinants bound, but that antibodies to appropriate HLA A and B specificities did not.

Analysis of HLA Class I Antigen by SDS Polyacrylamide Gel Electrophoresis (PAGE). Surface proteins on the isolated trophoblast cells were labeled with ^{125}I. Cells were then lysed and immunoprecipitations carried out using monoclonal antibodies against HLA class I antigens. Immunoprecipitated products were analyzed by SDS polyacrylamide gel electrophoresis. Trophoblast preparations consistently showed a β-2m band at 12 kDa together with a heavy chain that had a lower apparent molecular weight than is usually seen on other human cells or cell lines (40 kDa instead of 45 kDa) (Ellis et al., 1986).

Analysis of HLA Class I Antigen by One-Dimensional Isoelectric Focusing (ID IEF). Immunoprecipitates from ^{125}I labeled trophoblast were also analyzed by one-dimensional IEF, a technique that separates HLA A, B, and C heavy chains and β-2m according to their isoelectric points (pI) (Neefjes et al., 1986). Trophoblast material that had been immunoprecipitated with monoclonal antibodies against HLA class I or β-2m consistently showed a single band with a pI of 5.4 (in trophoblast preparations from donors with no shared HLA A, B or C allele) rather than the expected multiple band pattern. β-2m was also seen. A typical result is shown in Figure 3-1 (Ellis et al., 1986).

Conclusions

The evidence suggests that extravillous trophoblast cells express an HLA class I antigen(s) that is nonpolymorphic or has polymorphic determinants that are masked in some way. This molecule also appears to have a lower molecular weight than classical class I antigens. Biochemical evidence is not sufficient to allow more than speculation regarding the nature of this molecule.

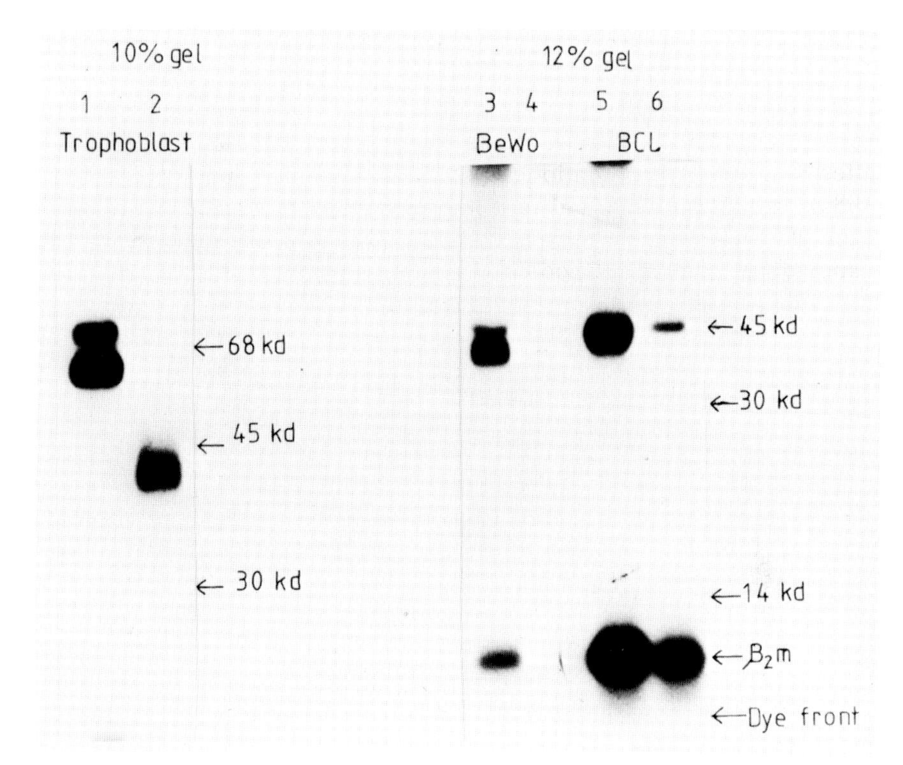

Fig. 3-1. Autoradiographs from two SDS polyacrylamide gels showing immunoprecipitated products from trophoblast (tracks 1 and 2), BeWo (tracks 3 and 4) < and a control B cell line (tracks 5 and 6), with W6/32, anti HLA class I, (tracks 2, 3 and 5), NDOG2, anti placental alkaline phosphatase (track 1) and MHM.5, anti HLA B and C, (tracks 4 and 6). All cells were labeled with ^{125}I.

Evidence for the Presence of Unusual HLA Class I Antigens on a Choriocarcinoma Cell Line

Analysis of Surface Expression of HLA Class I Antigens Using Monoclonal Antibodies

The human choriocarcinoma cell line BeWo was chosen for this study, since preliminary screening showed that it was the only such line tested that expressed any HLA class I antigens. It has not proved possible to obtain a tissue type for this cell line using standard serological techniques. However, it was found that between 70% and 90% of cells bound monoclonal antibodies to HLA class I antigens, as analyzed by flow cytometry (Fig. 3-2). When BeWo cells were treated in culture with recombinant interferon (1000 units/mL for 7 days), surface class I expression increased twofold, although it was

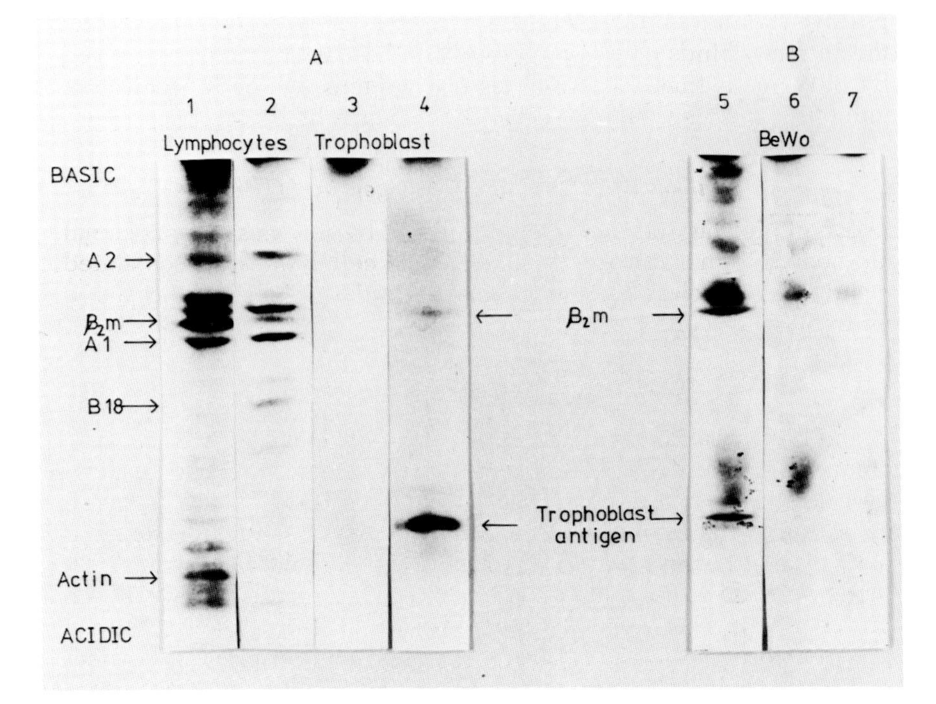

Fig. 3-2. Autoradiographs from two IEF gels. Tracks 3 and 4 show immunoprecipitated products from a trophoblast cell preparation with (track 4) W6/32 and (track 3) an anti CD1 antibody (negative control). Tracks 1 and 2 show products from corresponding maternal and fetal lymphocytes immunoprecipitated with W6/32. Tracks 5, 6 and 7 show products from BeWo cells immunoprecipitated with BBM.1, anti B2m, (track 5), MHM.5 (track 6) and an anti HLA-DR (track 7, negative control).

still not possible to perform serological HLA testing on the cells (Ellis et al., 1986).

Analysis of HLA Class I Antigen by SDS PAGE

SDS PAGE analysis of immunoprecipitated material from ^{125}I labeled BeWo cells demonstrated the presence of a β-2m band and a heavy chain with an apparent molecular weight of 40 kDa when using anti-class I reagents. Similar results were obtained with trophoblast cells (Fig. 3-1). It should be noted, however, that a faint band was also observed at 45 kDa; this could represent a low level of normal class I expression (Ellis et al., 1986, Stern et al., 1988). The monoclonal antibody MHM.5 (Ellis et al., 1985), which recognizes an epitope shared by all HLA B and C antigens, failed to immunoprecipitate the 40 kDa heavy chain from the surface of BeWo cells, despite showing positive staining in flow cytometric analysis. This result suggests that the antibody binds with lower affinity to the class I antigen expressed by BeWo cells than to normal class I antigens, which it readily immunoprecipitates from other class-I-bearing cells.

Analysis of HLA Class I Antigen by 1D IEF

IEF of the material immunoprecipitated by anti-class I monoclonal antibodies from surface-iodinated BeWo cell lysates demonstrated clearly that the class I heavy chain shared the same pI as that found on trophoblast cells (Fig. 3-2).

Conclusions

The BeWo choriocarcinoma cell line clearly expresses a high level of HLA class I antigen(s), as shown by frow cytometric analysis. However, analysis by SDS PAGE and IEF suggests that this class I molecule is unusual in having a low molecular weight and a pI identical to that found consistently in trophoblast immunoprecipitates. Although a faint 45 kDa band is seen on SDS PAGE, suggesting the presence of a low level of normal class I, it seems likely that the predominant class I molecule seen on the BeWo cell surface is unusual and may be similar or identical to the class I seen on extravillous trophoblast cells.

Northern Blot Analysis of BeWo mRNA

RNA was extracted from BeWo cells using a standard method, and poly A+ RNA was then isolated using an oligo-dT column. Samples of mRNA were run on denaturing agarose gels and then transferred to hybridization membranes. Three class I DNA probes were used in this study. p44/2 contains a 5.1 kb insert, including a full-length HLA-A3 gene (Strachan et al., 1984), and should hybridize to any class I sequence. pB550 and pC800 hybridize most efficiently to B and C locus sequences, respectively, but are not locus specific (Strachan et al., 1986). All three class I probes hybridized very weakly to BeWo mRNA, as compared to control B cell line RNA. Of the three probes used, however, the pC800 probe bound most strongly (Fig. 3-3) (Ellis et al., 1989), confirming results obtained previously by Stern et al. (1988).

Detection of HLA Class I Sequences in BeWo cDNA

Construction and Screening of cDNA Libraries

Double-stranded cDNA was synthesized from BeWo mRNA using standard methods (Efstratidis & Villa-Komaroff, 1979; Gubler & Hoffman, 1983). DNA was size-fractionated, and fractions containing the

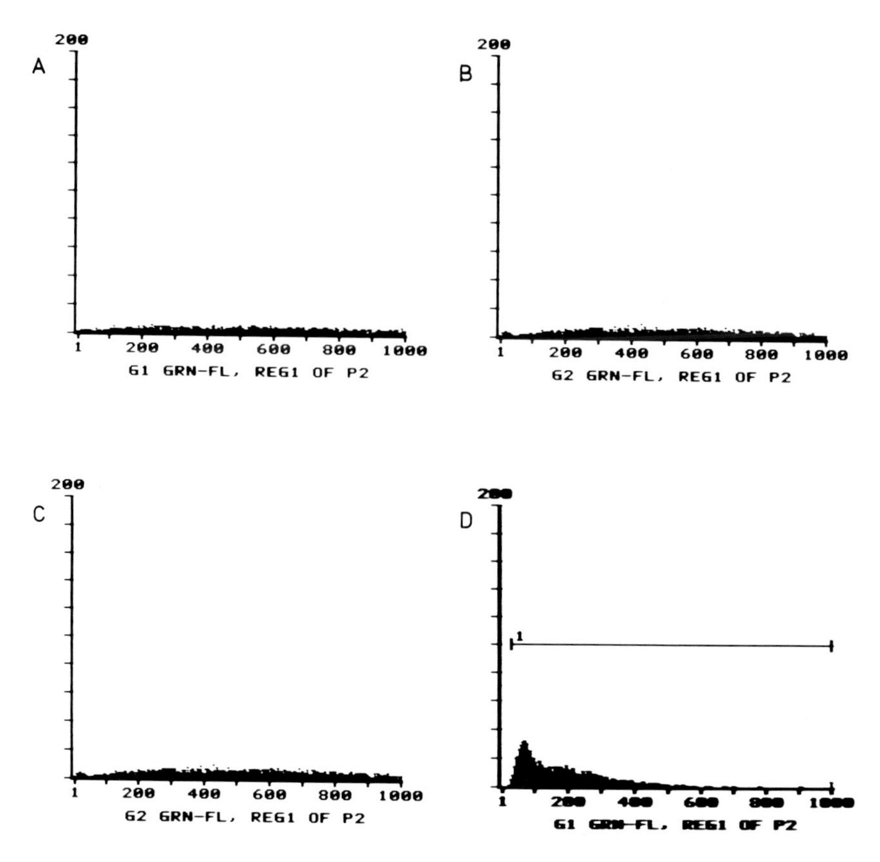

Fig. 3-3. Fluorescence profiles of BeWo cells stained with (A) W6/32; (B) MHM.5; (C) BBM.1; (D) anti CD1 (negative control).

largest fragments were pooled and blunt end ligated into the Sma 1 site of the plasmid vector pAT-X (Twigg & Sherratt, 1980). These constructs were then used to transform competent *E. coli.* Libraries were screened using the class I probe p44/2 (Strachan et al., 1984). When a partial, unique class I sequence was identified, a probe was made (BeWo 200.1), which was used in subsequent screenings.

Identification of a Full-Length C Locus cDNA Clone (Ellis et al., 1989)

Positive inserts were identified and subcloned into the bacteriophage m13. Sequences were determined using the dideoxy chain termination method of Sanger et al. (1977). Specific synthetic oligonucleotide primers were used to obtain complete sequences.

An initial BeWo cDNA library, screened with the p44/2 probe, did not yield any full-length class I sequences. However, three positive clones were sequenced ranging in size from 500 bp to 930 bp, and all showed identical sequences in overlapping regions, indicating that they were derived from the same gene. The probe BeWo 200.1 was made from the 5′ end of the longest clone and was subsequently used to probe for full-length sequences from other BeWo cDNA libraries. Several full-length (1500 bp) positive clones have now been obtained using this approach, and one (BeWo C.1) has been sequenced completely. BeWo C.1 is identical in the overlapping regions (exons 4,5,6,7, and 8) to the shorter clones sequenced previously. We have compared the BeWo C.1 nucleotide sequence with other published HLA A, B, and C sequences (Table 3-1) and conclude that it probably represents a previously unidentified C locus allele, although we cannot exclude that it may be one of eleven serologically distinguishable HLA-C alleles. Figure 3-4 shows the predicted amino acid sequence of BeWo C.1 compared to Cw1, Cw2, Cw3, A2, and B7. There is a particularly high level of homology between the BeWo C.1 sequence and the other C locus sequences, particularly in the "locus-specific" region (amino acids 292–300) within the transmembrane (TM) exon. However, there are several positions throughout the sequence where cBeWo C.1 appears to be unique, particularly in the α1 and α2 domains and the TM region.

Evidence for Other Unusual HLA Class I cDNA Clones

We have used a class I probe to isolate several additional clones from a BeWo cDNA library that are smaller (approximately 1300 bp) than the predicted size of a full-length class I cDNA. Preliminary investigations on one such clone suggest that it constitutes a complete cDNA sequence, as it is intact at both 5′ and 3′ ends and thus is unlikely to be a cloning artifact. Limited sequence analysis indicates that it has similarities to A locus sequences, although it appears to have an aberrant TM region. It is unclear at present whether this sequence codes for an expressed product or is a pseudogene.

Discussion: Significance of BeWo Class I cDNA Clones

Sequence data obtained using clones derived from BeWo cDNA libraries indicate that this cell line expresses a previously unsequenced C locus product. This is likely to be the dominant form of class I made in the cell, because we have isolated several identical clones and our screening protocol is not biased toward C locus sequences. It is conceivable, however, that other class I sequences may be present

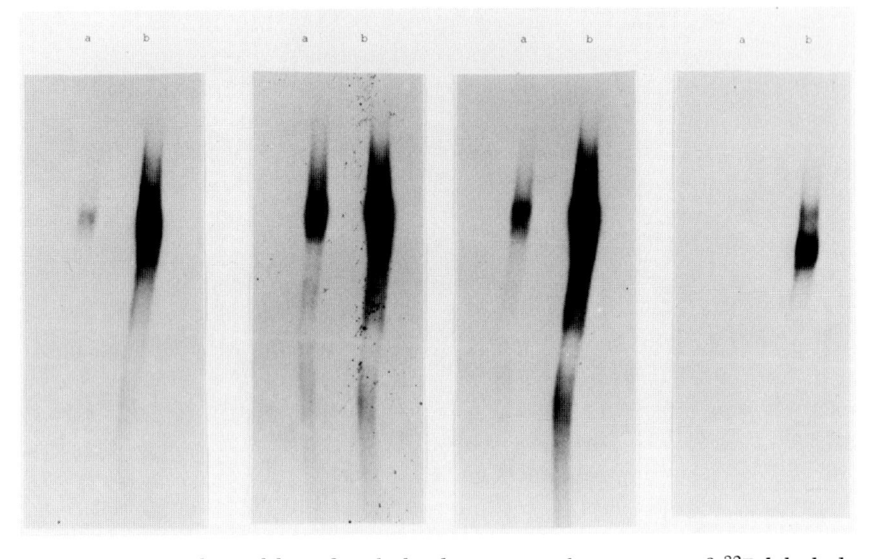

Fig. 3-4. A Northern blot after hybridization with a series of ^{32}P-labeled DNA probes. Lane A shows hybridization to mRNA from the BeWo cell line, lane B to mRNA from a control B cell line. (1) Hybridization of p44/2. (2) Hybridization of pC800. (3) Hybridization of pB550. (4) An HLA class II probe. The membrane was stripped between each hybridization.

at very low levels or may have only limited homology to classical class I. These sequences would therefore be more likely to escape detection. Our preliminary studies of several short positive clones indicate that some of these fall into the latter category.

It is clearly important to determine which of the positive cDNA clones code for surface-expressed HLA class I on these cells. Transfection experiments would go some way to answering this question. It would also be important to rescreen the libraries and to investigate as many positive clones as possible to confirm the apparent lack of expression of classical A and B antigens.

General Discussion

The results described here show clearly that extravillous trophoblast and the BeWo cell line both express easily detectable levels of an unusual HLA class I antigen, which may be the same on both cell types.

Sequences obtained from BeWo cDNA libraries indicate that there are unusually high levels of an unidentified HLA-C locus sequence and no evidence of normal A or B locus sequences. On other cell types, HLA-C antigen expression is generally very low compared to A and

Table 3-1. Amino acid sequences of HLA antigens

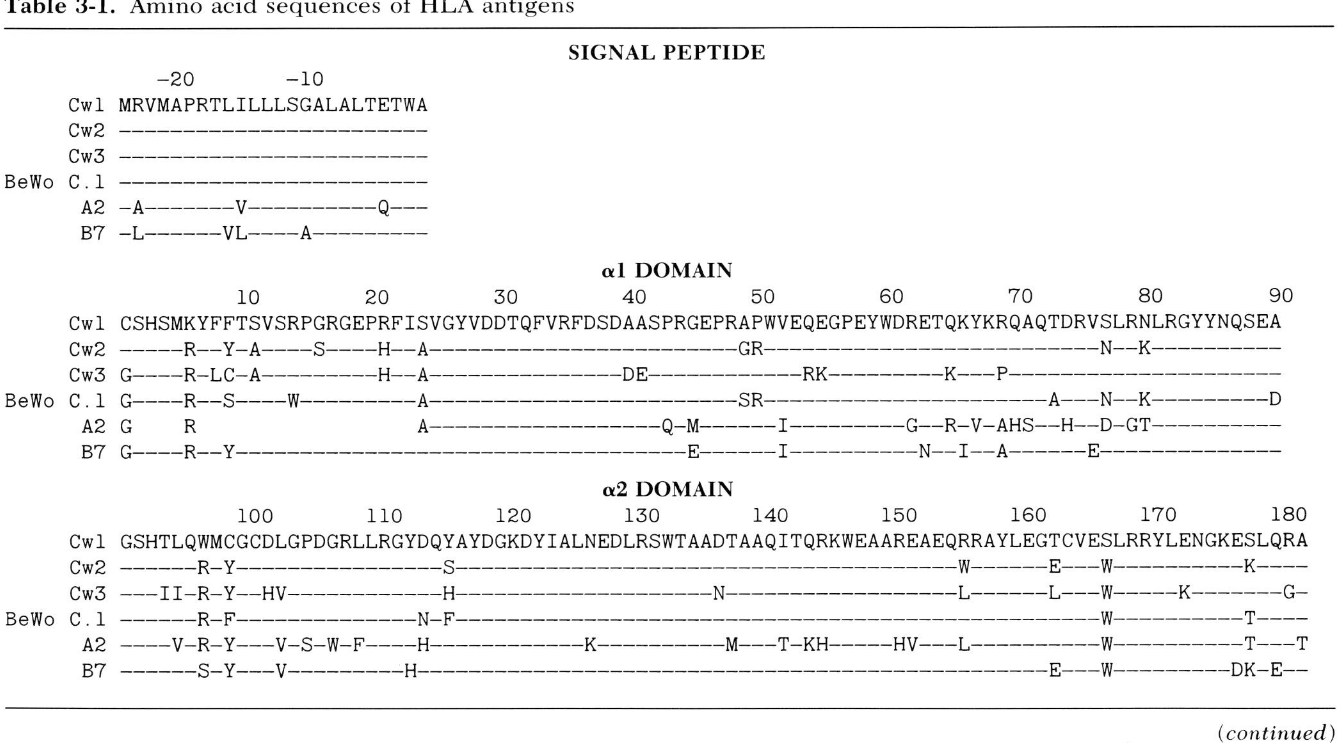

```
                        SIGNAL PEPTIDE

           -20       -10
     Cw1 MRVMAPRTLILLLSGALALTETWA
     Cw2 ------------------------
     Cw3 ------------------------
BeWo C.1 ------------------------
      A2 -A-------V----------Q---
      B7 -L------VL----A---------

                        α1 DOMAIN

                 10        20        30        40        50        60        70        80        90
     Cw1 CSHSMKYFFTSVSRPGRGEPRFISVGYVDDTQFVRFDSDAASPRGEPRAPWVEQEGPEYWDRETQKYKRQAQTDRVSLRNLRGYYNQSEA
     Cw2 -----R--Y-A----S----H--A------------------------GR--------------------------N--K----------
     Cw3 G----R-LC-A---------H--A---------------DE------------RK---------K---P---------------------
BeWo C.1 G----R--S----W---------A------------------------SR----------------------A---N--K---------D
      A2 G    R                 A------------------Q-M------I---------G--R-V-AHS--H--D-GT----------
      B7 G----R--Y-----------------------------------E------I----------N--I--A------E--------------

                        α2 DOMAIN

                100       110       120       130       140       150       160       170       180
     Cw1 GSHTLQWMCGCDLGPDGRLLRGYDQYAYDGKDYIALNEDLRSWTAADTAAQITQRKWEAAREAEQRRAYLEGTCVESLRRYLENGKESLQRA
     Cw2 ------R-Y----------------S---------------------------------------W------E---W----------K----
     Cw3 ---II-R-Y--HV------------H--------------------N------------------L------L---W-----K-------G-
BeWo C.1 ------R-F--------------N-F--------------------------------------------------W----------T----
      A2 ----V-R-Y---V-S-W-F----H------------K----------M---T-KH-----HV---L----------W----------T---T
      B7 ------S-Y---V---------H-------------------------------------------------E---W---------DK-E--
```

(continued)

Table 3-1. Amino acid sequences of HLA antigens (*Continued*)

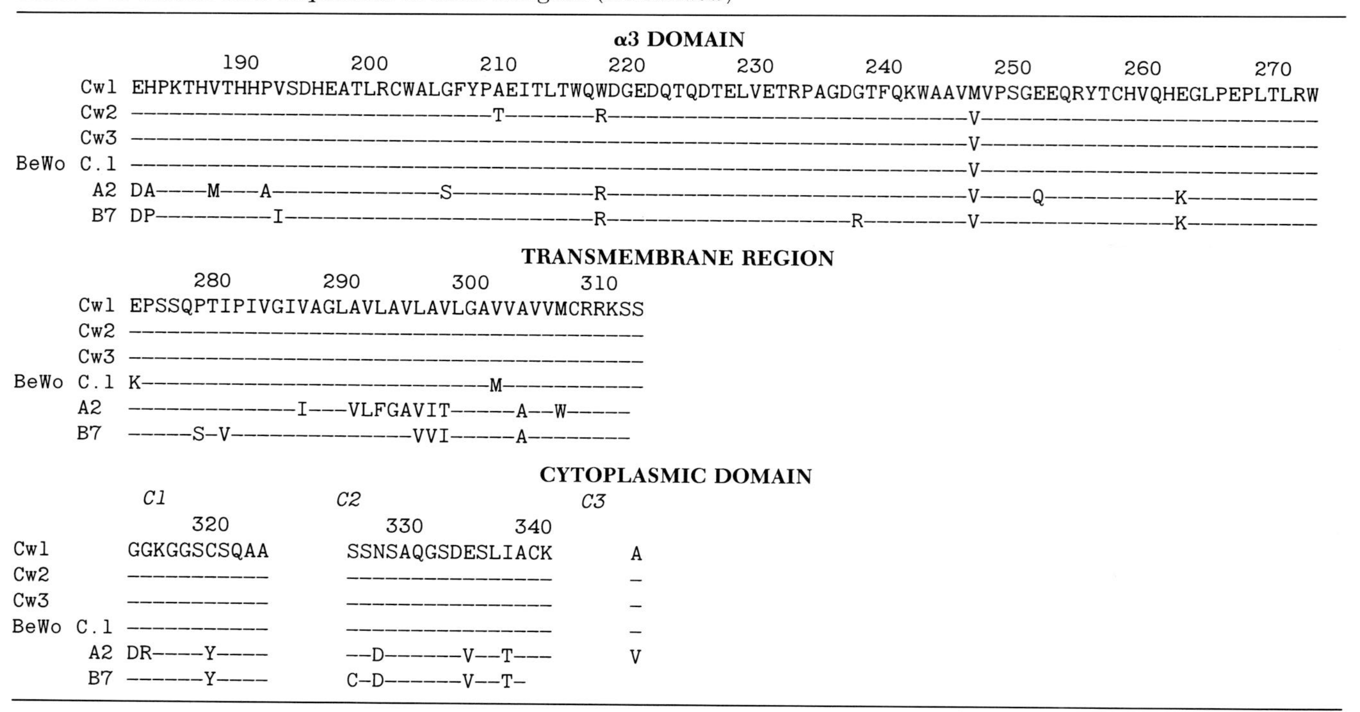

α3 DOMAIN

```
                190       200       210       220       230       240       250       260       270
     Cw1 EHPKTHVTHHPVSDHEATLRCWALGFYPAEITLTWQWDGEDQTQDTELVETRPAGDGTFQKWAAVMVPSGEEQRYTCHVQHEGLPEPLTLRW
     Cw2 ----------------------------T-------R----------------------------V--------------------------
     Cw3 -----------------------------------------------------------------V--------------------------
BeWo C.1 -----------------------------------------------------------------V--------------------------
      A2 DA----M---A-------------S-----------R----------------------------V----Q----------K----------
      B7 DP---------I------------------------R-------------------R--------V---------------K----------
```

TRANSMEMBRANE REGION

```
              280       290       300       310
     Cw1 EPSSQPTIPIVGIVAGLAVLAVLAVLGAVVAVVMCRRKSS
     Cw2 ----------------------------------------
     Cw3 ----------------------------------------
BeWo C.1 K---------------------------M-----------
      A2 -------------I---VLFGAVIT-----A--W-----
      B7 -----S-V--------------VVI-----A--------
```

CYTOPLASMIC DOMAIN

```
          C1             C2                C3
              320        330       340
Cw1      GGKGGSCSQAA    SSNSAQGSDESLIACK    A
Cw2      -----------    ----------------    -
Cw3      -----------    ----------------    -
BeWo C.1 -----------    ----------------    -
      A2 DR----Y----    --D------V--T---    V
      B7 ------Y----    C-D------V--T-
```

B, so this result is clearly unusual. However, the BeWo C.1 nucleotide sequence would encode a protein having the molecular weight of a normal class I heavy chain (approximately 45 kDa), assuming that the mature product is glycosylated normally. This sequence may therefore code for small amounts of a 45 kDa molecule that are expressed on the BeWo cell line, but not on trophoblast. If this is the case, large numbers of cDNA clones that code for the smaller (40 kDa) molecule must be present but escape detection. Alternatively, unusual processing of class I in trophoblast cells could result in expression of a lower MW heavy chain due to posttranslational modification. Finally, alternatively spliced forms of the transcript may be present, although we have so far been unable to detect them. Transfection experiments will help to resolve this problem, as will further screening of trophoblast cDNA libraries with a probe made from the BeWo C.1 sequence.

The importance of HLA-C locus products remains unclear, since they do not generally seem to act as restriction elements and it is assumed that they have distinct functions from A and B molecules or may have no function at all (Gussow et al., 1987). It is interesting to note that a population of murine trophoblast cells, which appears to express normal H-2 antigens, is resistant to lysis by allospecific cytotoxic T cells (Zuckermann & Head, 1987). The current results have not helped to clarify the role of class-I-like molecules on trophoblast. However, they do confirm that such molecules exist, possibly unusual molecular forms, and have provided us with necessary and useful tools to carry out further investigations.

REFERENCES

Biro, P. A., Pan, J., Sood, A. K., Kole, R., Reddy, V. B., and Weissman, S. M. 1983. Sequences of human repetitive DNA, non globulin genes, and MHC locus genes, III. The MHC complex. *Cold Spring Harbor Symp. Quant. Biol.* 47:1079.

Bulmer, J. N. and Johnson, P. M. 1983. Antigen expression by trophoblast populations in the human placenta and their possible immunobiological relevance. *Placenta* 6:127.

Calabi, F. and Milstein, C. 1986. A novel family of human MHC related genes not mapping to chromosome 6. *Nature* 323:540.

Efstratidis, A. and Villa-Komaroff, L. 1979. Cloning of doubly-stranded DNA. In *Genetic Engineering*, vol. 1 (J.K.Stelow and A.Hollander, eds.). New York: Plenum.

Ellis, S. A., Taylor, C., Hildreth, J. E. K., and McMichael, A. J. 1985. An HLA class I monoclonal antibody that fails to bind to all HLA-A antigens. *Hum. Immunol.* 13:13.

Ellis, S. A., Sargent, I. L., Redman, C. W. G., and McMichael, A. J. 1986. Evidence for a novel HLA antigen found on human extravillous trophoblast and a choriocarcinoma cell line. *Immunology* 59:595.

Ellis, S. A., Strachan, T., Palmer, M. S., and McMichael, A. J. 1989. Complete nucleotide sequence of a unique HUA clan I clones product expressed on the human choriocarcinoma cell line. *J. Immunol.* 142:3281–3285.

Fauchet, R., Boscher, M., Bouhallier, O., Merdrignac, G., Genetet, B., Turmel, P., and Charron, D. J. 1986. New class I in man:serological molecular characterization. *Hum. Immunol.* 17:3.

Gubler, V. and Hoffman, B. J. 1983. A simple and very efficient method for generating cDNA libraries. *Gene* 25:263.

Gussow, D., Rein, R. S., Meijer, I., de Hoog, W., Seeman, G. U. A., Hochstenbach, F. M., and Ploegh, H. L. 1987. Isolation, expression and the primary structure of HLA Cw1 and HLA Cw2 genes:evolutionary aspects. *Immunogenetics* 25:313.

Neefjes, J. J., Breur-Vriesendorp, B. A., van Seventer, G. A., Ivanyi, P., and Ploegh, H. L. 1986. An improved biochemical method for the analysis of HLA class I antigens. *Hum. Immunol.* 16:169.

Redman, C. W. G., McMichael, A. J., Stirrat, G. M., Sunderland, C. A., and Ting, A. 1984. Class I MHC antigens on human extra-villous trophoblast. *Immunology* 52:457.

Robinson, P. J. 1987. Structure and expression of polypeptides encoded in the mouse Qa region. *Immunol. Res.* 6:46.

Sanger, F., Nicklen, S., and Coulson, A. R. 1977. DNA sequencing with chain-terminating inhibitors. *P.N.A.S.* 74:5463.

Stern, P. L., Bersford, N., Friedman, C. I., Stevens, V. C., Risk, J. M., and Johnson, P. M. 1987. Class I-like MHC molecules expressed by baboon placental syncytiotrophoblast. *J. Immunol.* 138:1088.

Stern, P. L., Morris, A., McMain, A., Risk, J., Beresford, N., Kenny, T., Hole, N., Strachan, T., Rinke de Wit, T., Wilson, L., Giphart, M., and van Leeuwen, A. 1988. MHC class I expression by developmental tumors: teratocarcinoma stem cells are TCA positive. *Hum. Immunol.* 22:247.

Strachan, T., Sodoyer, R., Damotte, M., and Jordan, B. R. 1984. Complete nucleotide sequence of a functional class I HLA gene, HLA - A3: implication for the evolution of HLA genes. *EMBO J.* 3:887.

Strachan, T., Dodge, A. B., Smillie, D., Dyer, P. A., Sodoyer, R., Jordan, B. R. and Harris, R. 1986. An HLA-C-specific DNA probe. *Immunogenetics* 23:115.

Twigg, A. J. and Sherratt, D. 1980. Trans-complementable copy number mutants of plasmid CoIEI. *Nature* 283:216.

Zuckermann, F. A. and Head, J. 1987. Murine trophoblasts resist cell mediated lysis. *J. Immunol.* 139:2856.

4

Genetic Studies of the MHC Region in Human Recurrent Spontaneous Abortion

JANET M. RISK and PETER M. JOHNSON

The marked polymorphism of molecules encoded by the major histocompatibility complex (MHC) substantially contributes to fetomaternal genetic disparity. MHC-encoded cell surface HLA antigens are the focus of immunological mechanisms of allograft rejection, as well as mechanisms controlling the immune response and T cell restriction. Additional molecules with important immunobiological activities are also encoded within the MHC region, e.g., the closely linked tumor necrosis factor (TNF) α and β genes, the tandem genes for the fourth component of complement (C4A and C4B), as well as other complement factors and the 21-hydroxylase (21-OH) genes (Carroll et al., 1987; Dunham et al., 1987). Factors related to the MHC may therefore be central to immunobiological events allowing survival of the fetal graft in the uterus and successful reproduction of the species. There is evidence from inbred mammalian species suggesting that MHC heterozygotes have superior reproductive capability, which is often interpreted as indicating a reproductive advantage of fetomaternal histoincompatibility and thus a contribution of natural selection to the maintenance of MHC genetic polymorphism. It is discussed in more detail by Beer and Billingham (1977), Gill and Repetti (1979), and Johnson and Ramsden (1988).

Fetal trophoblast cell populations do not constitutively express classical HLA alloantigens (HLA-A,B,C,DP,DQ,DR) at fetomaternal tissue interfaces throughout human pregnancy and may also resist induction of these antigens (Bulmer & Johnson, 1985; Desoye et al., 1988; Hunt et al., 1987; Sunderland et al., 1981). However, extravillous cytotrophoblast strongly expresses a molecule associated with beta$_2$-microglobulin that reacts with most monoclonal antibodies to human class I MHC heavy chain framework determinants but not with monoclonal antibodies to polymorphic determinants of HLA-A or HLA-B

(Bulmer & Johnson, 1985; Redman, et al., 1984). Glycoproteins with a similar antigenic profile have been identified on the BeWo choriocarcinoma cell line, as well as on baboon syncytiotrophoblast, and have been shown to have a slightly lower molecular weight (39-41 kDa) than HLA-A,B,C heavy chains (46 kDa) (Ellis et al., 1986; Johnson & Stern, 1986; Stern et al., 1986). This nonclassical class-I-like MHC molecule may represent the translated product of a novel human class I MHC gene; for example, the HLA-E, −F, or −G genes or structural analogs of a murine Qa region class I gene (Geraghty et al., 1987; Koller et al., 1988, 1989; Mizuno et al., 1988; Paul et al., 1987; Srivastava et al., 1987). Indeed, recent evidence has shown HLA-G expression by BeWo cells and cytotrophoblast (Ellis et al., 1990; Kovats et al., 1990; Risk and Johnson, 1990). Alternatively, unusual products may result from atypical posttranscriptional processing of a class I MHC gene in invasive cytotrophoblast. Recent analysis of some clones selected from a BeWo cDNA library has indicated a close homology with HLA-C (see Chapter 3, this volume). However, maternal anti-HLA-C antibodies do not appear disproportionately often in human pregnancy, although antibodies in placental eluates may identify public HLA-related determinants of limited polymorphism that are distinct from classical HLA alloantigens (Konoeda et al., 1986). In addition, occasional multiparous sera contain antibodies reactive with nonclassical HLA antigens expressed on activated T cells, which are thought to be analogous to murine Qa antigens (Fauchet et al., 1986; Gazit et al., 1984; Mitsuishi et al., 1986; Van Leeuwen et al., 1985).

Studies with inbred mice have shown a high incidence of spontaneous fetal resorption in first pregnancies of CBA/J female × DBA/2 male and B10 female × B10.A male mating combinations. This incidence can be reduced significantly by prior immunization of the females with allogeneic spleen cells. Investigation of this phenomenon using different mating combinations and a variety of congenic or F_1 splenocytes for immunization has shown a critical role for the anti-MHC response that is itself dependent on the allogeneic environment furnished by minor histocompatibility antigens (Chaouat et al., 1988; Kiger et al., 1985; see also further discussion in Johnson & Ramsden, 1988). In humans, a high proportion of conceptuses are not carried to term. Various causes have been suggested for early pregnancy loss, including failure of implantation, karyotypic abnormalities, cervical incompetence, and endocrinological or autoimmune conditions (Johnson & Ramsden, 1988). However, up to 50% of couples who are investigated after three or more consecutive recurrent spontaneous abortions (RSA) have no recognizable reason for these losses. An "immunological" hypothesis proposes that fetal antigens expressed at fetomaternal tissue interfaces normally induce maternal immunoregulatory responses that help to protect the fetus from damaging maternal immune attack. A proportion of women with RSA have been postulated to have abnormalities in their immunological recognition of early pregnancy thereby exposing the fetus to aggressive maternal responses (Beer et al., 1981; Johnson & Ramsden, 1988; Johnson et al., 1986; McIntyre et al., 1986; Rocklin et al., 1976; Scott et al., 1987).

This phenomenon may be related to unusual MHC gene-linked events, and many studies on parental HLA typing in unexplained RSA have now been published (Table 4-1). These data include apparently conflicting results, the statistical significance of which is uncertain. This is not unexpected because of differences between centers in tissue typing methodologies, numbers of antigens tested for identification and numbers of control couples, and the referral and selection of RSA couples. Nevertheless, taken together, these fragmentary data

Table 4-1. MHC Immunogenetics in unexplained recurrent spontaneous abortion (RSA) compared with control couples

Trait	Observation	No. of Couples Studied	References
Individual HLA alleles	No difference	113, 60, 21	1, 2, 3
	Reduced for HLA-B35 & DR3	85	4*
	Increased for HLA-A9	71	5*
	Increased for HLA-A11	26	6*
	Increased for HLA-B35	20	7*
	Increased for HLA-B58	47	8*
	Increased for HLA-A10	29	9
Parental HLA sharing	No difference	113, 60, 85, 115	1, 2, 4, 10
	Increased at HLA-A	71	5
	Increased at HLA-A & B	20, 23, 13, 10	7*, 11, 12, 13
	Increased at HLA-DR/DQ	26, 10, 59, 91,	6*, 13, 14, 15, 16
	Increased at all loci	21, 143	3*, 17*
HLA homozygosity	No difference	60	2
	Increased at HLA-B	85	4
	Increased at HLA-B & C4	113	1*
	Increased at HLA-DR/DQ	59	12
HLA phenotypes	Increased HLA-A2, B12	113	1
	Decreased HLA-A1, B8, DR3	85	4
	Increased HLA-A9(24), DR2	26	6*

* A statistical strength of $p < 0.01$ compared with controls has been reported by the authors. Some effects have only been observed in a subgroup of women (e.g., 1° or 2° RSA patients): see individual references for fuller details.

References: 1. Johnson et al., 1988; 2. Oksenberg et al., 1984; 3. Thomas et al., 1985; 4. Cauchi et al., 1988; 5. Gerencer et al., 1979; 6. Aoki, 1982; 7. Bolis et al., 1984; 8. Vanoli et al., 1985; 9. Jeannet et al., 1985; 10. Smith & Cowchock, 1988; 11. Komlos et al., 1977; 12. Schacter et al., 1979; 13. Beer et al., 1981; 14. Coulam et al., 1987; 15. Reznikoff-Etievant et al., 1984; 16. Lauritsen et al., 1976; 17. McIntyre et al., 1986.

suggest increased parental HLA-B and -DR sharing, as well as HLA-B and C4 locus homozygosity in the female RSA partner. Other studies that have sought to identify a relationship between parental HLA sharing and pregnancy outcome have also yielded conflicting results (Jazwinska et al., 1987; Ober et al., 1987; Unander & Olding, 1983). These associations are weak and inconsistent, and HLA testing is not of clinical usefulness in unexplained RSA. However, these observations could reflect unusual adjacent genetic events within the MHC region (Johnson et al., 1985). Although these couples with RSA are karyotypically normal, there may be more subtle duplications, deletions, mutations, or recombination events within the MHC. Alternatively, a disease-associated gene(s) may be present, which markedly influences biological events critical to viviparity. For example, occasional duplications or deletions of HLA-B or C4 genes can occur in apparently healthy families (Mariotti et al., 1987; Schneider et al., 1986). In our studies, we have therefore used restriction fragment length polymorphism (RFLP) analysis to investigate the MHC region of RSA couples. The degree of polymorphism detected by RFLP can be greater than that defined by serology, and RFLPs can also detect variation in DNA around a given locus. This technique has previously been used to more precisely define HLA associations with some diseases (Cohen et al., 1985).

Patients

Couples with three or more consecutive proven first-trimester spontaneous abortions, each by the same partner, were included in this study. Exclusion of other known causes of RSA was determined by a thorough clinical history and investigation, including karyotypic analyses, hysterosalpingogram, endocervical swab cultures, and thyroid function tests. Women were excluded if they gave a history of an aneuploidic pregnancy loss or had evidence of uterine malformation, persistent infection, detectable serum antinuclear or antiphospholipid autoantibody, other autoimmune disease, or an abnormal complete blood count. HLA-A, -B, -C and -DR tissue typing was determined in all cases, and C4 allotyping was performed for approximately 50% of these couples by electrophoresis and immunofixation as previously described (Johnson et al., 1985, 1988). Primary (1°) RSA couples were defined as having no live birth or pregnancy exceeding 28 weeks gestation, whereas secondary (2°) RSA couples had a single live birth or pregnancy of at least 28 weeks gestation preceding the unbroken series of spontaneous abortions.

Tissue-typed control individuals were drawn from healthy laboratory staff with no previous history of spontaneous abortions.

Table 4-2. DNA probes used in RFLP analysis for RSA couples compared with controls

Probe	Size (kb)	Specificity	Restriction Enzymes Used	Reference
phTNF5	0.85	Human TNFα cDNA	*Eco*RI, *Taq*I	Marmenout et al., 1985
pAT-A	5.3	Human C4A cDNA (cross-reactive with C4B)	*Eco*RI, *Taq*I	Belt et al., 1984
pB_{550}	0.5	3′-untranslated region of HLA-B	*Eco*RI, *Taq*I, *Hind*III	Strachan et al., 1986
p32	7.6	Intact genomic HLA-B7 sequence (cross-reactive with other class I genes)	*Eco*RI, *Hind*III, *Eco*RV	Sodoyer et al., 1985
10-8	2.4	Genomic HLA-DQA1 sequence (cross-reactive with HLA-DQA2 genes)	*Eco*RI, *Taq*I	Trowsdale et al., 1983

RFLP Studies

High molecular weight genomic DNA was isolated from peripheral blood leukocytes (Blin & Stafford, 1976) and digested to completion using 3-10 U/μg of restriction endonuclease (Table 4-2) with overnight incubation at the manufacturer's recommended temperature. The DNA fragments were separated according to size on a horizontal 0.7% agarose gel and transferred onto Hybond-N filters (Amersham) (Southern, 1975). After fixation by exposure to UV light, the filters were probed with DNA probes encoding the gene or part of the gene of interest. Probes were radiolabeled with ^{32}P-dCTP using the random hexanucleotide primer method of Feinberg and Vogelstein (1984). Prehybridization and hybridization were carried out in a mixture containing 50% formamide, 5× standard saline citrate (SSC), 25 mM phosphate buffer, pH 6.5, with 0.5% SDS, 10% dextran sulphate (hybridization only), 5× Denhardt's solution, and 100 μg/ml sonicated denatured salmon sperm DNA. High-stringency washes were used, concluding with 0.1 × SSC, 0.1% SDS at 68°C to remove any non-specifically bound probe. The filter was then autoradiographed (Hoover et al., 1985). Reprobing of filters with different ^{32}P-radiolabeled probes was carried out after washing in 0.1% SDS at 85°C and re-exposure to x-ray film to ensure that all DNA-DNA bonds had been disrupted. Differences in the primary structure of the genetic information in or around the gene being investigated may cause restriction enzyme sites to be lost or gained, thus affecting the DNA fragment banding pattern (polymorphisms). Several probes and restriction enzymes have been used in this study to maximize the amount of information obtained (Table 4-2).

TNF

The TNF α and β genes map within the MHC region on the short arm of chromosome 6 and lie between the class III complement genes and the HLA-B locus (Carroll et al., 1987; Dunham et al., 1987). We initially studied the TNFα gene since (1) the probe recognizes a single gene with only one known polymorphism in humans (Fugger et al., 1989) (2) RFLP has been noted in autoimmune (NZB × NZW) F_1 mice that correlates with reduced TNFα levels (Jacob & McDevitt, 1988), and (3) TNFα may have important stimulatory or cytolytic effects in uteroplacental tissues, particularly on vascular endothelial cells. Recombinant TNF has also been shown to be antiproliferative for human choriocarcinoma cells (Berkowitz et al., 1988), and TNF receptors have been described in the human placenta (Eades et al., 1988).

Typical results using the TNF probe are shown in Figure 4-1 and are summarized in Table 4-3. We have studied 13 control and 68 individuals with RSA. No unusual banding patterns were observed using either the *Eco*RI or *Taq*I restriction endonucleases. These results thus exclude major DNA rearrangements or alterations close to the TNFα gene in RSA couples compared with controls.

C4

The C4A and C4B gene loci lie within the MHC class III gene cluster and were studied because (1) a recessive lethal deletion involving the C4 and 21-OH genes within the murine MHC has been associated with early postnatal death in mice (Shiroishi et al., 1987), (2) low serum C4 levels have been described in women with unexplained RSA (Unander et al., 1987), and (3) an increased prevalence of the C4A3,* B1,* phenotype has been described in unexplained RSA. This could represent homozygosity (C4A3,3 B1,1) or an increased prevalence of null C4Q0 genes in a heterozygous genotype (C4A3,Q0 B1,Q0). It has been difficult to distinguish among these alternatives using serological techniques, especially as there are often only a few immediate family members available for study in couples with RSA (Johnson et al., 1985, 1988). In addition, approximately 60% of the C4 genes serotyped as C4Q0 are deletions rather than nondeleted null alleles (Carroll and Alper, 1987; Schneider et al., 1986).

RFLPs of C4 have been described using the *Taq*I enzyme, and the presence of a 6.4 kb band has been shown to correlate with C4AQ0

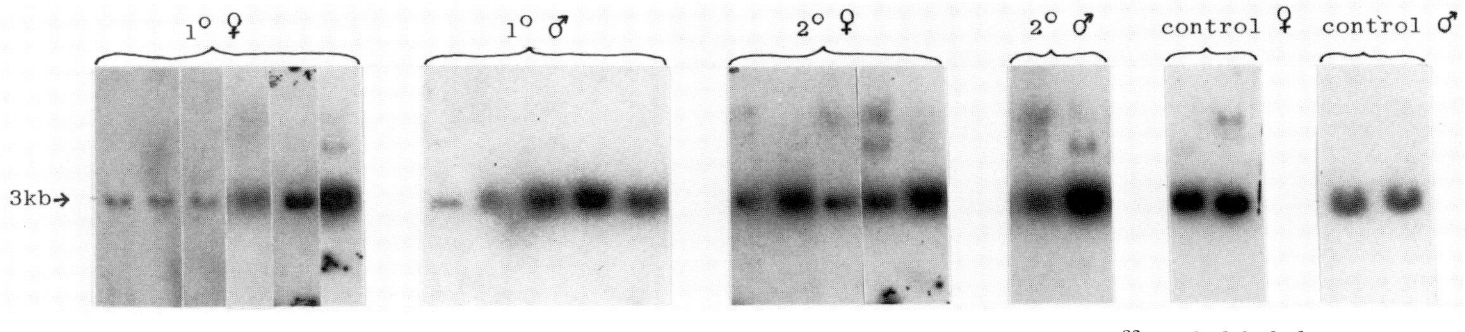

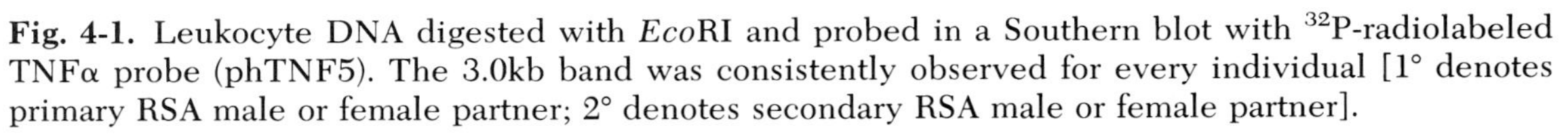

Fig. 4-1. Leukocyte DNA digested with *Eco*RI and probed in a Southern blot with ^{32}P-radiolabeled TNFα probe (phTNF5). The 3.0kb band was consistently observed for every individual [1° denotes primary RSA male or female partner; 2° denotes secondary RSA male or female partner].

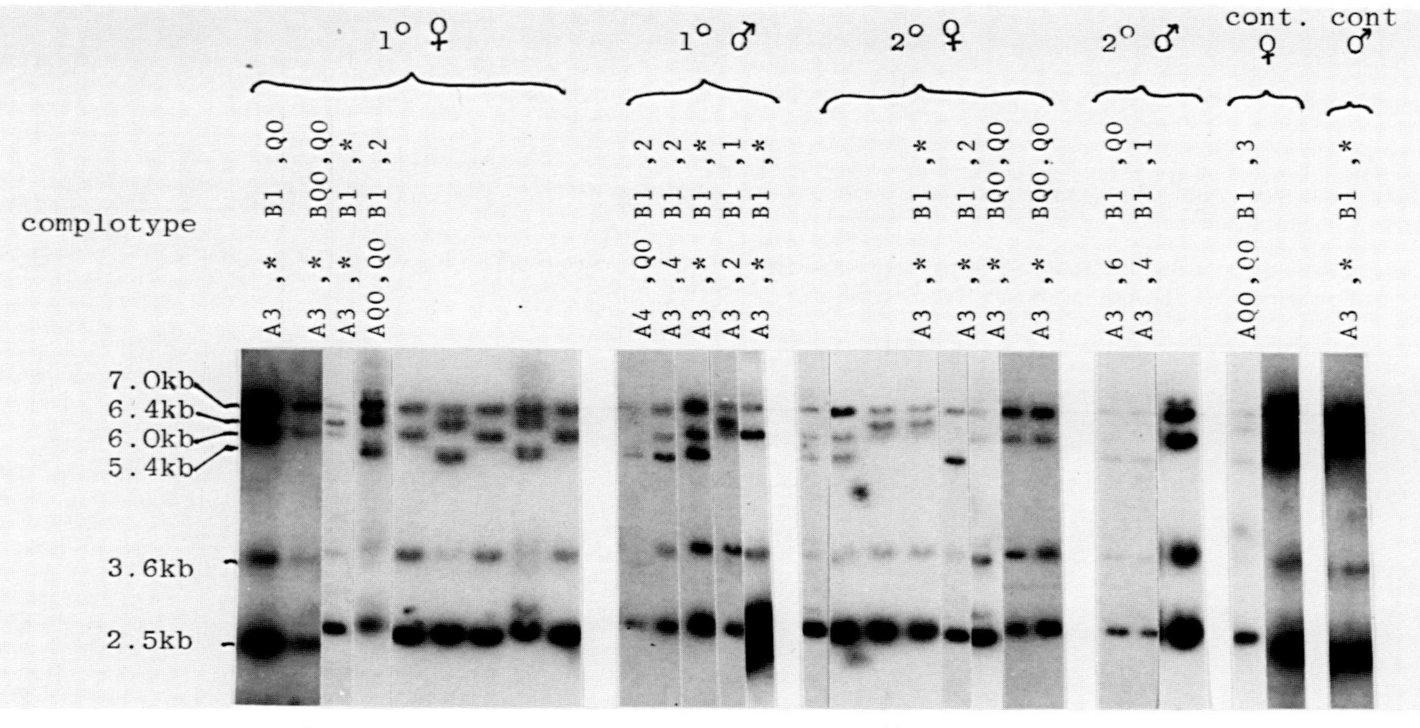

Fig. 4-2. Leukocyte DNA digested with *Taq*I and probed with ^{32}P-radiolabeled C4 probe (pAT-A). Where serologically-defined C4 allotypes were known, these are shown above the corresponding Southern blot track. The 7.0 kb band specifically represents the C4A gene; a 6.4 kb C4B band results when there is a C4A deletion, with loss of the 7.0 kb band if this is homozygous. The 6.0 and/or 5.4 kb bands represent C4B genes depending on the C4B alleles, and the 3.6 and 2.5 kb bands are invariant [1° denotes primary RSA male or female partner; 2° denotes secondary RSA male or female partner; cont. denotes control individual].

Table 4-3. Summary of RFLP results using the TNFα probe (phTNF5)

	Eco*RI		***Taq*I†**	
	♀	♂	♀	♂
1° RSA	26‡	16	10	4
2° RSA	17	9	7	5
Controls	9	4	6	2

* A single major band at 3.0 kb consistently observed for every individual tested (see also Fig. 4-1).

† Three major bands at 1.3, 1.1 & 0.45 kb consistently observed for every individual tested.

‡ Total number of individuals tested.

serotypes caused by a deletion (Schneider et al., 1986). Typical results from our studies are shown in Figure 4-2 and are summarized in Table 4-4. We used the same restriction endonuclease and attempted to correlate the serotypical C4AQ0 phenotype with the presence of the band. There was no unusual occurrence of the 6.4 kb band, denoting a deleted C4A allele, in the study population, which comprised 44 individuals with RSA and 11 controls, as compared with that expected in the general population (Schneider et al., 1986). In all but one case, the 6.4 kb band was observed only when the serotype included C4AQ0 or when it was impossible to exclude the presence of C4AQ0 as in C4A3,*. The only exception was the male partner of a patient with 1° RSA, who had a C4A3,2 serotype. The most likely explanation for the presence of a 6.4 kb *Taq*I band in this individual is a heteroduplication at the C4A locus on one chromosome to produce a C4A(3,2),Q0 genotype; such duplications occur quite commonly (Alper et al., 1986; Carroll and Alper, 1987). Otherwise normal C4 banding patterns were observed for every individual tested (Fig. 4-2 and Table 4-4).

Table 4-4. Summary of RFLP results using the C4 probe (pAT-A)

	Taq*I		***Eco*RI†**	
	♀	♂	♀	♂
1° RSA	17†	9	24	13§
2° RSA	13	5	17	6
Controls	8	8	8	4

* The normal banding pattern consists of a 7:0 kb C4A band with 6.0 and/or 5.4 kb C4B bands. A 6.4 kb C4B band results when there is a C4A deletion. Invariant bands are seen at 3.6 and 2.5 kb. This pattern was consistently observed for every individual tested (see also Fig. 4-2).

† The normal banding pattern consists of 6.4 kb and 5.3 kb bands with or without a polymorphic 3.9 kb band. An 8.4 and/or 7.4 kb band results when there is a C4A deletion. This pattern was consistently observed for every individual other than one 1° RSA male partner (see last footnote).

‡ Total number of individuals tested.

§ One individual gave only an 8.4 kb band (see Fig. 4-3).

Similar results were obtained using the *Eco*RI restriction endonuclease, with no unexpected occurrences of the 8.4 or 7.4 kb bands that appear to denote a deletion of a C4A allele. No other abnormal C4 banding patterns were observed in our 59 RSA and 12 control individuals (Table 4-4). The primary RSA male partner with a C4A3,2 serotype whose *Taq*I banding pattern suggested deletion of a C4A allele, had an *Eco*RI band at 8.4 kb, consistent with heteroduplication giving rise to the C4A(3,2),Q0 genotype. One other 1° RSA male partner (MD) with a C4AQ0, Q0 B1,* serotype showed only a single 8.4 kb band (Table 4-4). However, two other serotypically C4AQ0, Q0 individuals (ML and JR) gave normal 8.4, 6.4, 5.3, and 3.9 kb banding patterns suggesting that MD may have an unusual homozygous deletion around the C4A locus.

Class II MHC

An HLA-DQA1 probe was used for RFLP analyses since transacting regulatory genes for class I MHC antigens are thought to be encoded within the class II MHC region (Salter & Cresswell, 1986) and several of the reported immunogenetic associations with unexplained RSA suggest a role for HLA-DR (Table 4-1). Although polymorphic banding patterns were observed with *Taq*I, all class II MHC banding patterns for 36 RSA and 11 control individuals were compatible with their known HLA-DR types (Table 4-5). Similarly, the normal allelic bands observed with *Eco*RI (Guardiola et al., 1988) were seen in all 56 RSA and 12 control individuals (Table 4-5).

HLA-B

Initial RFLP studies were performed using the full-length HLA-B7 probe (p32). The resulting banding patterns were difficult to interpret even with matched tissue-typed controls because of hybridization to

Table 4-5. Summary of RFLP results using the HLA-DQA1 probe (10-8)

	*Eco*RI*		*Taq*I†	
	♀	♂	♀	♂
1° RSA	23†	12	14	5
2° RSA	15	6	13	4
Controls	8	4	8	3

* The normal banding pattern includes 5.4, 6.7, 11, and 14 kb bands dependent on the HLA-DQ alleles of the individual (Guardiola et al., 1988).

† The normal banding pattern includes 2.6, 4.6, 5.5, 6.1, or 6.8 kb bands dependent on the HLA-DQ (Bidwell, 1988) and HLA-DR (Awad et al., 1988) alleles. For all individuals tested, no unusual banding patterns were observed from those compatible with their known HLA-DR type.

‡ Total number of individuals tested.

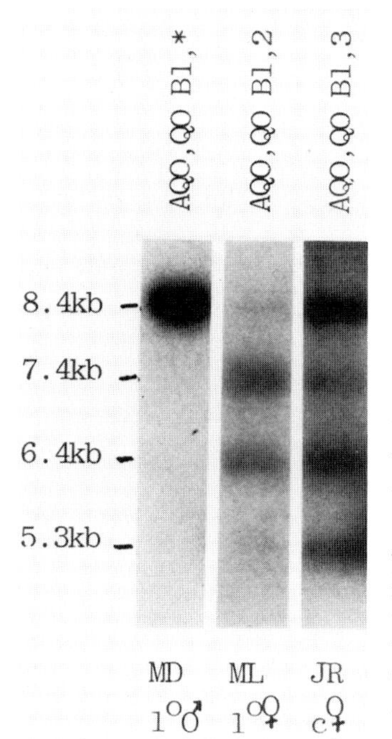

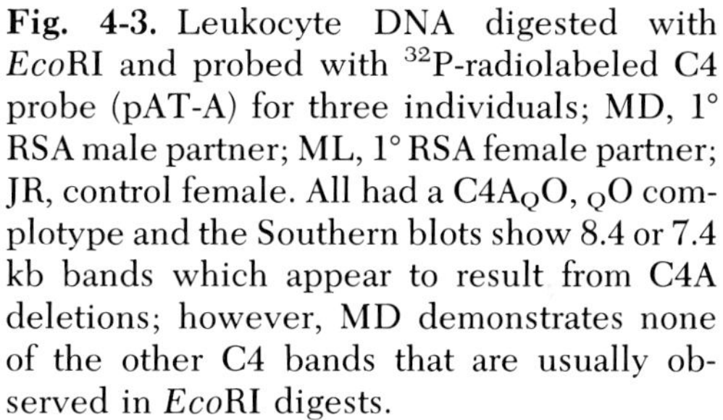

Fig. 4-3. Leukocyte DNA digested with *Eco*RI and probed with ^{32}P-radiolabeled C4 probe (pAT-A) for three individuals; MD, 1° RSA male partner; ML, 1° RSA female partner; JR, control female. All had a C4A_QO, $_QO$ complotype and the Southern blots show 8.4 or 7.4 kb bands which appear to result from C4A deletions; however, MD demonstrates none of the other C4 bands that are usually observed in *Eco*RI digests.

multiple, closely homologous, class I MHC genes (Lucotte et al., 1984). In subsequent studies, we therefore used the short HLA-B locus-specific probe (pB_{550}); this probe corresponds to part of the 3′-untranslated and cytoplasmic region of HLA-B where interlocus homology is minimal and intralocus homology is at its greatest. Many of the reported immunogenetic correlations in unexplained RSA appear to involve HLA-B (Table 4-1). However, only one unusual banding pattern was observed with *Hin*dIII and none with *Taq*I, or *Eco*RI for RSA individuals, compared with the known banding patterns given with each of these restriction endonucleases in normal individuals (Table 4-6).

BeWo Choriocarcinoma Cells

The HLA-B locus-specific probe (pB_{550}) was used in RFLP analysis of BeWo cell DNA compared with peripheral blood leukocyte (PBL) from a DNA tissue-typed (HLA-B8, -B14) individual. Five enzymes (*Eco*RI, *Hin*dIII, *Bam*HI, *Taq*I, and *Pst*I) gave comparable banding patterns with both DNA preparations, whereas RFLPs were detected using *Eco*RV and *Pvu*II. BeWo DNA did not give a 1.0 kb *Pvu*II band, whereas both BeWo and control PBL DNA gave a strong 0.5 kb band (Figure 4-4). Mariotti et al. (1987) have used a similar probe and shown that the 1.0 kb band occurs only in individuals with the HLA-B14 or

Table 4-6. Summary of RFLP results using the HLA-B probe (pB_{550})

	*Taq*I*		*Eco*RI†		*Hind*III††	
	♀	♂	♀	♂	♀	♂
1° RSA	8‡	4	16	7	24	6§
2° RSA	4	2	12	5	8	6
Controls	3	2	6	4	4	5

* Four allelic bands at 9, 4, 3.3, and 2.3 kb consistently observed for every individual tested.
† Invariant band at 6 kb consistently observed for every individual tested.
†† Three allelic bands at 16.5, 15, and 10 kb consistently observed for every individual tested, except one RSA male (see last footnote).
‡ Total number of individuals tested.
§ One individual gave 15 and 13 kb bands.

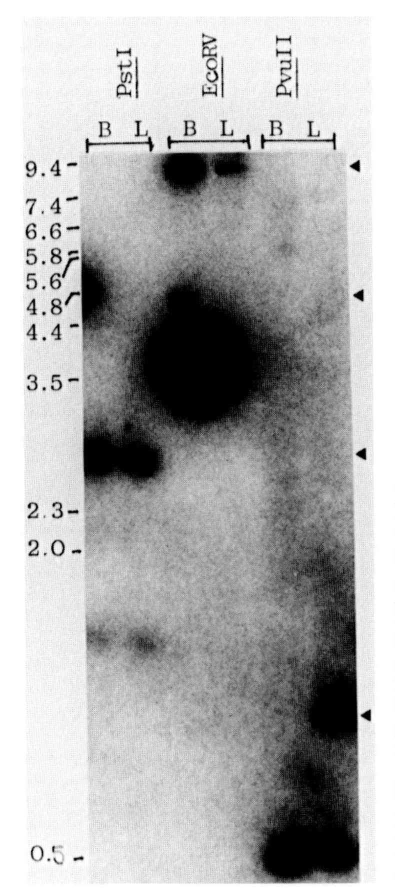

Fig. 4-4. BeWo (B) and control [HLA-B8, B14] peripheral blood leukocyte (L) DNA digested with three separate restriction endonucleases and probed in a Southern blot with ^{32}P-radiolabeled DNA specific for HLA-B [pB_{550}]. The arrows show (i) an 8.6 kb *Eco*RV band correlating with the HLA-B8 alloantigen, (ii) a 4.6kb polymorphic *Eco*RV band observed for BeWo but not the control leukocyte DNA, (iii) a 2.8kb invariant *Pst*I band, and (iv) a 1.0kb polymorphic *Pvu*II band correlating with HLA-B14 or -B40 and observed for the control leukocyte but not BeWo DNA.

-B40 alleles. Thus BeWo cells do not appear to carry either of these HLA-B alleles. Further experiments with additional tissue-typed control PBL DNA preparations have confirmed this observation.

Using *Eco*RV, BeWo DNA gives bands at 8.6 and 4.6 kb, whereas the PBL DNA gave only the 8.6 kb band (Fig. 4-4). Cann et al. (1983) used a full-length class I MHC probe and showed multiple polymorphisms with *Eco*RV. The 8.6 kb *Eco*RV band correlated specifically with the HLA-B8 allele; and our results therefore suggest that both BeWo and control PBL DNA carry the HLA-B8 allele. Experiments with other HLA-B8-positive and HLA-B8-negative PBL DNA preparations have confirmed this observation. The 4.6 kb *Eco*RV band seen with BeWo DNA was also described by Cann et al. (1983), and has been shown to correlate with the HLA-B35 allele (Lederer et al., 1989). This identification of BeWo cells as HLA-B8, -B35-positive is of interest, given their expression of an unusual class I MHC molecule and failure to be lysed by specific alloantisera even after α-interferon treatment (Ellis et al., 1986; Johnson and Stern, 1986). Preliminary RFLP data with BeWo cell DNA using on HLA-C locus-specific probe [pC_{800}] have shown the absence of those polymorphisms characteristic of HLA-Cw5 or -Cw8 (a 7.9 kb *Eco*RI band) HLA-Cw4 (a 2.6 kb *Taq*I band) and HLA-Cw7 (a 1.2 kb *Pvu*II band) (Smeaton et al., 1987; Strachan et al., 1986). Other bands were obtained with the pC_{800} probe and these enzymes, thus indicating the presence of HLA-C gene(s). These results, together with preliminary data using the TNFα and C4 probes do not suggest any unusual alteration of the BeWo cell genome in the MHC region. Previous karyotypic analysis has shown that BeWo cells are trisomic for chromosome 6, with one chromosomal set expressing pronounced rearrangement and extension of the long arm (Sheppard et al., 1985).

Conclusions

We have reviewed evidence for an association between unexplained RSA and MHC immunogenetics that derives from the use of classical serological techniques. In addition, we have carried out RFLP analysis in couples with 1° and 2° RSA and control couples, using DNA probes for the TNFα, C4, HLA-B, and class II MHC genes. No unexpected DNA banding patterns were observed for any of these genes, except in one 1° RSA male partner who may have an unusual deletion around the C4A locus, and in one 1° RSA male who may have an unusual HLA-B 'blank' allele.

The BeWo choriocarcinoma cell line is known to express an unusual class I MHC molecule that may correspond to that normally expressed by extravillous cytotrophoblast cells. Genomic RFLP analysis has shown BeWo cells to carry the HLA-B8 and -B35 alleles and to lack the HLA-B14 and -B40 alleles. These cells also appear to lack the

HLA-Cw4, -Cw5, -Cw7, and -Cw8 alleles, but do possess HLA-C gene(s). However, despite the striking karyotypic abnormalities in these cells, no unexpected MHC gene locus RFLPs were noted.

Acknowledgments

We are grateful to Drs. J. Trowsdale (ICRF, London), R. D. Campbell (MRC Immunochemistry Unit, Oxford), T. Strachan (Dept of Medical Genetics, Manchester), and W. Fiers (Biogen, Gent) for the generous gifts of DNA probes used in this study. This work was supported by research project grants from the Eugenics Society and Birthright, UK.

REFERENCES

Alper, C. A., Awdeh, Z. L. and Yunis, E. J. 1986. Complotypes, extended haplotypes, male segregation distortion, and disease markers. *Hum. Immunol.* 15:366.

Aoki, K. 1982. HLA-DR compatibility in couples with recurrent spontaneous abortions. *Acta Obstet. Gynecol. Jpn.* 34:177.

Awad, J., Navarrete, C., Sachs, J. A., Festenstein, H., Cassell, P. G., Niven, M. J. and Hitman, G. 1988. HLA-DR, DQ and DX alpha RFLPs and their associations with serologically HLA-DR and -DQ antigens. *Immunogenetics* 27:73.

Beer, A. E. and Billingham, R. E. 1977. Histocompatibility gene polymorphisms and materno-fetal interaction. *Transplant. Proc.* 9:1393.

Beer, A. E., Quebbeman, J. F., Ayers, J. W. T. and Haines, R. F. 1981. Major histocompatibility complex antigens, maternal and paternal immune responses, and chronic habitual abortions in humans. *Am. J. Obstet. Gynecol.* 141:987.

Belt, K. T., Carroll, M. C. and Porter, R. R. 1984. The structural basis of the multiple forms of human complement component C4. *Cell* 36:907.

Berkowitz, R. S., Hill, J. A., Kurtz, C. B. and Anderson, D. J. 1988. Effects of products of activated leukocytes (lymphokines and monokines) on the growth of malignant trophoblast cells in vitro. *Am. J. Obstet. Gynec.* 158:199.

Bidwell, J. 1988. DNA-RFLP analysis and genotyping of HLA-DR and -DQ antigens. *Immunol. Today* 9:18.

Blin, N. and Stafford, D. W. 1976. A general method for isolation of high molecular weight DNA from eukaryotes. *Nuc. Acids Res.* 3:2303.

Bolis, P. F., Bianchi, M. M., Soro, V. and Belvedere, M. 1984. HLA typing in couples with repetitive abortion. *Biol. Res. Pregnancy* 5:135.

Bulmer, J. N. and Johnson, P. M. 1985. Antigen expression by trophoblast populations in the human placenta and their possible immunobiological relevance. *Placenta* 6:127.

Cann, H. M., Ascanio, L., Paul, P., Marcadet, A., Dausset, J. and Cohen, D. 1983. Polymorphic restriction endonuclease fragment segregates and correlates with the gene for HLA-B8. *Proc. Natl. Acad. Sci. USA* 80:1665.

Carroll, M. C. and Alper, C. A. 1987. Polymorphism and molecular genetics of human C4. *Br. Med. Bull.* 43:50.

Carroll, M. C., Katzman, P., Alicot, E. M., Koller, B. H., Geraghty, D. E., Orr, H. T., Strominger, J. L. and Spies, T. 1987. Linkage map of the human histocompatibility complex including the tumor necrosis factor genes. *Proc. Natl. Acad. Sci. USA* 84:8535.

Cauchi, M. M., Tait, B., Wilshire, M. I., Koh, S. H., Mraz, G., Kloss, M. and Pepperell, R. 1988. Histocompatibility antigens and habitual abortion. *Am. J. Reprod. Immunol. Microbiol.* 18:28.

Chaouat, G., Clark, D. A. and Wegmann, T. G. 1988. Genetic aspects of the CBA × DBA/2 and B10 × B10.A models of murine pregnancy failure and its prevention by lymphocyte immunization. In *Early Pregnancy Loss: Mechanisms and Treatment* (F. Sharp and R.W. Beard, eds.) London: Royal College of Obstetricians and Gynaecologists, pp. 89-102.

Cohen, D., Paul, P., Le Gall, I., Marcadet, A., Font, M.-P., Cohen-Haguenauer, O., Sayagh, B., Cann, H., Lalouel, J.-M. and Dausset, J. 1985. DNA polymorphism of HLA class I and class II regions. *Immunol. Rev.* 85:87.

Coulam, C. B., Moore, S. B. and O'Fallon, W. M. 1987. Association between major histocompatibility antigen and reproductive performance. *Am. J. Reprod. Immunol. Microbiol.* 14:54.

Desoye, G., Dohr, G. A., Motter, W., Winter, R., Urdl, W., Pusch, H., Uchanska-Zeigler, B., Zeigler, A. 1988. Lack of HLA class I and class II antigens on human preimplantation embryos. *J. Immunol.* 140:4157.

Dunham, I., Sargent, C. A., Trowsdale, J. and Campbell, R. D. 1987. Molecular mapping of the human major histocompatibility complex by pulsed-field gel electrophoresis. *Proc. Natl. Acad. Sci. USA* 84:7237.

Eades, D. K., Cornelius, P. and Pekala, P. H. 1988. Characterization of the tumor necrosis factor in the human placenta. *Placenta* 9:247.

Ellis, S. A., Palmer, M. S. and McMichael, A. J. 1990. Human trophoblast and the choriocarcinoma cell line BeWo express a truncated HLA class I molecule. *J. Immunol.* 144:731.

Ellis, S. A., Sargent, I. L., Redman, C. W. G. and McMichael, A. J. 1986. Evidence for a novel HLA found on human extravillous trophoblast and a human choriocarcinoma cell line. *Immunology* 59:595.

Fauchet, R., Boscher, M., Bouhallier, O., Merdrignac, G., Genetet, B., Turmel, P. and Charron, D. J. 1986. New class I in man: serological and molecular characterization. *Hum. Immunol.* 17:3.

Feinberg, A. P. and Vogelstein, B. 1984. Addendum to a technique for radiolabeling DNA restriction endonuclease fragments to high specific activity. *Anal. Biochem.* 137:206.

Fugger, L., Morting, N., Ryder, L. P., Georgsen, J., Jakobsen, B. K., Svejgaard, A., Andersen, V., Oxholm, P., Karup Pedersen, F., Friis, J. and Halberg, P. 1989. *Nco*I restriction fragment length polymorphism (RFLP) of the tumor necrosis factor (TNFα) region in four autoimmune diseases. *Tissue Antigen* 34:17.

Gazit, E., Gothelf, Y., Gil, R., Orgad, S., Pitman, T. B., Watson, A. L. M., Yang, S. Y. and Yunis, E. J. 1984. Alloantibodies to PHA-activated lymphocytes detect human Qa-like antigens. *J. Immunol.* 132:165.

Geraghty, D. E., Koller, B. H. and Orr, H. T. 1987. A human major histocompatibility complex class I gene that encodes a protein with a shortened cytoplasmic segment. *Proc. Natl. Acad. Sci. USA* 84:9145.

Gerencer, M., Drazancic, A., Kovacic, I., Tomaskovic, Z. and Kastelan, A. 1979. HLA antigen studies in women with recurrent gestational disorders. *Fertil. Steril.* 31:401.

Gill, T. J. III and Repetti, C. F. 1979. Immunologic and genetic factors influencing reproduction. *Am. J. Pathol.* 95:465.

Guardiola, J., Maffei, A., Carrel, S. and Accolla, R. S. 1988. Molecular genotyping of the HLA-DQ gene region. *Immunogenetics* 27:12.

Hoover, M. L., Marks, J., Chipman, J., Palmer, E., Stastny, P. and Capra, J. D. 1985. Restriction fragment length polymorphism of the gene encoding the chain of the human T cell receptor. *J. Exp. Med.* 162:1087.

Hunt, J. S., Andrews, G. K. and Wood, G. W. 1987. Normal trophoblasts resist induction of class I HLA. *J. Immunol.* 138:2481.

Jacob, C. O. and McDevitt, H. O. 1988. Tumour necrosis factor-α in murine autoimmune 'lupus' nephritis. *Nature* 331:356.

Jazwinska, E. C., Kilpatrick, D. C., Smart, G. E. and Liston, W. A. 1987. Fetomaternal HLA compatibility does not have a major influence on human pregnancy except for lymphocytotoxin production. *Clin. Exp. Immunol.* 68:116.

Jeannet, M., Bischof, P., Bourrit, B. and Vuagnat, P. 1985. Sharing of HLA antigens in fertile, subfertile and infertile couples. *Transplant. Proc.* 17:903.

Johnson, P. M., Barnes, R. M. R., Risk, J. M., Molloy, C. M. and Woodrow, J. C. 1985. Immunogenetic studies of recurrent spontaneous abortion in humans. *Exp. Clin. Immunogenet.* 2:77.

Johnson, P. M., Chia, K. V. and Risk, J. M. 1986. Immunological question marks in recurrent spontaneous abortion. In *Reproductive Immunology 1986* (D.A. Clark and B.A. Croy, eds.) Amsterdam: Elsevier Biomedical Press, pp. 239-245.

Johnson, P. M., Chia, K. V., Risk, J. M., Barnes, R. M. R. and Woodrow, J. C. 1988. Immunological and immunogenetic investigation of recurrent spontaneous abortion. *Dis. Markers* 6:163.

Johnson, P. M. and Ramsden, G. H. 1988. Recurrent miscarriage. *Bailliere's Clin. Immunol. Allergy* 2:607.

Johnson, P. M. and Stern, P. L. 1986. Antigen expression at human maternofetal interfaces. *Prog. Immunol.* 6:1056.

Kiger, N., Chaouat, G., Kolb, J.-P., Wegmann, T. G. and Guenet, J. L. 1985. Immunogenetic studies of spontaneous abortion in mice: preimmunization of females with allogeneic male cells. *J. Immunol.* 134:2966.

Koller, B. H., Geraghty, D. E., DeMars, R., Davick, L., Rich, S. S. and Orr, H. T. 1989. Chromosomal organization of the human major histocompatibility complex class I gene family. *J. Exp. Med.* 169:469.

Koller, B. H., Geraghty, D. E., Shimizu, Y., DeMars R., and Orr, H. T. 1988. HLA-E: a novel HLA class I gene expressed in resting T lymphocytes. *J. Immunol.* 141:897.

Komlos, L., Zamir, R., Joshua, H. and Hallbrecht, I. 1977. Common HLA antigens in couples with repeated abortions. *Clin. Immunol. Immunopathol.* 7:330.

Konoeda, Y., Terasaki, P. I., Wakisaka, A., Park, M. S. and Mickey, M. R. 1986. Public determinants of HLA indicated by pregnancy antibodies. *Transplantation* 41:253.

Kovats, S., Main, E. K., Librach, C., Stubblebine, M., Fisher, S. J. and DeMars, R. 1990. A class I antigen, HLA-G, expressed in human trophoblasts. *Science* 248:220.

Lauritsen, J. G., Kristensen, T. and Grunnet, N. 1976. Depressed mixed lymphocyte culture reactivity in mothers with recurrent spontaneous abortion. *Am. J. Obstet. Gynecol.* 125:35.

Lederer, E., Nössner, E., Wank, R. and Schendel, D. J. 1989. Analysis of HLA-B35 variants and B35 haplotypes by isoelectric focusing and Southern blot analysis. *Immunogenetics* 30:63.

Lucotte, G., Coulondre, C., Ngo, K. Y., Salmon, C. and Muller, J. Y. 1984. Polymorphism of HLA class I genes after restriction by endonucleases *Eco*RI, *Eco*RV and *Hin*dIII. *Exp. Clin. Immunogenet.* 1:202.

McIntyre, J. A., Faulk, W. P., Nichols-Johnson, V. R. and Taylor, C. G. 1986. Immunologic testing and immunotherapy in recurrent spontaneous abortion. *Obstet. Gynecol.* 67:169.

Marmenout, A., Fransen, L., Tavernier, J., van der Heyden, J., Tizard, R., Kawashima, E., Shaw, A., Johnson, M.-J., Semon, D., Müller, R., Ruysschaert, M.-R. van Vliet, A. and Fiers, W. 1985. Molecular cloning and expression of human tumor necrosis factor and comparison with mouse tumor necrosis factor. *Eur. J. Biochem.* 152:515.

Mariotti, M., Auffray, C. and Lucotte, G. 1987. DNA polymorphisms associated with HLA-B-like genes and evidence for a duplication of B40 genes detected with an HLA-B-specific DNA probe. *Immunology* 60:475.

Mitsuishi, Y., Falkenrodt, A., Urlacher, A., Tongio, M. M. and Mayer, S. 1986. New human MHC class I antigens segregating with HLA-A antigens detected on some lymphocyte subpopulations. *Hum. Immunol.* 15:175.

Mizuno, S., Trapani, J. A., Koller, B. H., Dupont, B. and Yang, S. Y. 1988. Isolation and nucleotide sequence of a cDNA clone encoding a novel HLA class I gene. *J. Immunol.* 140:4024.

Ober, C. L., Simpson, J. L., Ward M., Radvany, R. M., Andersen, R., Elias, S., Sabbagha, R. and the DIEP Study Group. 1987. Prenatal effects of maternal-fetal HLA incompatibility. *Am. J. Reprod. Immunol. Microbiol.* 15:141.

Oksenberg, J. R., Persitz, E., Amar, A. and Brautbar, C. 1984. Maternal-paternal histocompatibility: lack of association with habitual abortions. *Fertil. Steril.* 42:389.

Paul, P., Fauchet, R., Boscher, M. Y., Sayagh, B., Masset, M., Medrignac, G., Dausset, J. and Cohen, D. 1987. Isolation of a human major histocompatibility complex class I gene encoding a nonubiquitous molecule expressed on activated lymphocytes. *Proc. Natl. Acad. Sci. USA* 84:2872.

Redman, C. W. G., McMichael, A. J., Stirrat, G. M. Sunderland, C. A. and Ting, A. 1984. Class I major histocompatibility complex antigens on human extravillous trophoblast. *Immunology* 52:527.

Reznikoff-Etiévant, M. F., Edelman, P., Mueller, J. Y., Pinon, F. and Sureau, C. 1984. HLA-DR locus and maternal-foetal relation. *Tiss. Antigens* 24:30.

Risk, J. M. and Johnson, P. M. 1990. Northern blot analysis of HLA-G expression by BeWo human choriocarcinoma cells. *J. Reprod. Immunol.* 18:199.

Rocklin, R. E., Kitzmiller, J. L., Carpenter, C. B., Garovoy, M. R. and David, J. R. 1976. Maternal-fetal relation: absence of an immunological blocking factor from the serum of women with chronic abortions. *N. Engl. J. Med.* 295:1209.

Salter, R. D. and Cresswell, P. 1986. Impaired assembly and transport of HLA-A and -B antigens in a mutant TxB cell hybrid. *EMBO J.* 5:943.

Schacter, B., Muir, A., Gyves, M. and Tasin, M. 1979. HLA-A,B compatibility in parents of offspring with neural tube defects of couples experiencing involuntary fetal wastage. *Lancet* 1:796.

Schneider, P. M., Carroll, M. C., Alper, C. A., Tittner, C., Whitehead, A. S., Yunis, E. J. and Colten, H. R. 1986. Polymorphism of human complement C4 and steroid 21-hydroxylase genes: restriction fragment length polymorphisms revealing structural deletions, homoduplications and size variants. *J. Clin. Invest.* 78:650.

Scott, J. R., Rote, N. S. and Branch, D. W. 1987. Immunological aspects of recurrent abortion and fetal death. *Obstet. Gynec.* 70:645.

Sheppard, D. M., Fisher, R. A. and Lawler, S. D. 1985. Karyotypic analysis and chromosome polymorphisms in four choriocarcinoma cell lines. *Cancer Genet. Cytogenet.* 16:251.

Shiroishi, Y. T., Sagai, T., Natsuume-Sakai, S. and Moriwaki, K. 1987. Lethal deletion of the complement component C4 and steroid 21-hydroxylase genes in the mouse H-2 class III region caused by meiotic recombination. *Proc. Natl. Acad. Sci. USA* 84:2918.

Smeaton, I., Summers, C. W., Harris, R. and Strachan, T. 1987. Restriction fragment length polymorphism at the HLA-C locus. *Immunogenetics* 25:179.

Smith, J. B. and Cowchock, F. S. 1988. Immunological studies in recurrent spontaneous abortion: effects of immunization of women with paternal mononuclear cells on lymphocytotoxic and mixed lymphocyte reaction blocking antibodies and correlation with sharing of HLA and pregnancy outcome. *J. Reprod. Immunol.* 14:99.

Sodoyer, R., Nguyen, C., Strachan, T., Santoni, M. J., Damotte, M., Trucy, J. and Jordan, B. R. 1985. Allelism in the HLA class I multigene family. *Ann. Inst. Pasteur* 136C:71.

Southern, E. 1975. Detection of specific sequences among DNA fragments separated by gel electrophoresis. *J. Mol. Biol.* 98:503.

Srivastava, R., Chorney, M. J., Lawrance, S. K., Pan, J., Smith, Z., Smith, C. L. and Weissman, S. M. 1987. Structure, expression, and molecular mapping of a divergent member of the class I HLA gene family. *Proc. Natl. Acad. Sci. USA* 84:4224.

Stern, P. L., Beresford, N., Friedman, C. I., Stevens, V. C., Risk, J. M. and Johnson, P. M. 1986. Class I-like MHC molecules expressed by baboon placental syncytiotrophoblast. *J. Immunol.* 138:1088.

Strachan, T., Dodge, A. B., Smillie, D., Dyer, P. A., Sodoyer, R., Jordan, B. R. and Harris, R. 1986. An HLA-C-specific DNA probe. *Immunogenetics* 23:115.

Sunderland, C. A., Naiem, M., Mason, D. Y., Redman, C. W. G. and Stirrat, G. M. 1981. The expression of major histocompatibility antigens by human chorionic villi. *J. Reprod. Immunol.* 3:323.

Thomas, M. L., Harger, J. H., Wagener, D. K., Rabin, B. S. and Gill, T. J. III.

1985. HLA sharing and spontaneous abortion in humans. *Am. J. Obstet. Gynecol.* 151:1053.

Trowsdale, J., Lee, J., Carey, J., Grosveld, F., Bodmer, J. and Bodmer, W. 1983. Sequences related to HLA-DRα chain on human chromosome 6: restriction enzyme polymorphism detected with DCα chain probes. *Proc. Natl. Acad. Sci. USA* 80:1972.

Unander, A. M. and Olding, L. B. 1983. Habitual abortion: parental sharing of HLA antigens, absence of maternal blocking antibody and suppression of maternal lymphocytes. *Am. J. Reprod. Immunol.* 4:171.

Unander, A. M., Norberg, R., Hahn, L. and Arfors, L. 1987. Anticardolipin antibodies and complement in ninety-nine women with habitual abortion. *Am. J. Obstet. Gynec.* 156:114.

Van Leeuwen, A., Giphart, M. J., De Groot, G., Morolli, B., Festenstein, H., Nijenhuis, L. E. and Van Rood, J. J. 1985. Two different T cell systems in humans, one of which is probably equivalent to Qa or Tla in mice. *Hum. Immunol.* 12:235.

Vanoli, M., Fabio, G., Bonara, P., Eisera, N., Pardi, G., Acaia, B. and Scorza, R. 1985. Histocompatibility in Italian couples with recurrent spontaneous abortions of unknown origin and with normal fertility. *Tiss. Antigens* 26:227.

5

Characterization of the Class I Antigen of the Rat Placenta Encoded by cDNA Clone pARI.5

ANDELKA RADOJCIC, HEINZ W. KUNZ,
JOSEPH D. LOCKER, and THOMAS J. GILL III

The reasons for survival of the fetal allograft, which is intimately exposed to maternal immunocompetent cells, remain unclear. Several mechanisms have been proposed to explain the absence of the classical rejection reaction, and much interest has focused on the maternal-fetal interface of the placenta. One of the main differences between transplanted organs and the placenta is their expression of major histocompatibility complex (MHC) antigens. Class II antigens are not expressed on the placenta of the mouse (Chatterjee-Hasrouni and Lala, 1981; Raghupathy et al., 1981), human (Brami et al., 1981; Sunderland et al., 1981) or rat (Kanbour et al., 1987). There is also differential expression of class I antigens on the trophoblast cell surface (Kanbour et al., 1987): the pregnancy-associated (Pa) antigen with broadly shared determinants is expressed on the cell surface, whereas the classical class I transplantation antigens with private determinants remain inside the cell. The epitopes of the Pa antigen are not recognized by cytotoxic T lymphocytes (CTL), although they elicit alloantibody responses (Ghani et al., 1984, a,b,). The pregnancy-associated (Pa) antigen found in the *a,d,f,b,* and *m* haplotypes of the rat has the characteristics of a class I molecule: the heavy chain of the antigen isolated from lymphocytes has a relative mass of 46 kDa and is associated with β_2-microglobulin. A similar antigen with public determinants has also been found in the human placenta (Ellis et al., 1986; Hunt et al., 1988; McIntyre and Faulk, 1982; McIntyre et al., 1983).

To investigate the nature of the class I antigens in the placenta and the regulation of their expression, we constructed a (WF × DA)F1 hybrid cDNA placental library (Stranick et al., 1986). One of the most abundant clones in the library was chosen for sequence analysis (Radojcic et al., 1989). The deduced amino acid sequence shows the classical class I protein structure, with several features that are specific for the rat antigen. Although it is not yet clear if any of these differences are specific for placental class I antigens, some amino acid substitutions appear to be able to abrogate recognition by maternal immunocompetent cells. The role of these residues in defining the tertiary structure of the antigen and in the presentation of alloreactive epitopes of the placental class I antigen is discussed.

Structure of a Class I Gene and Characteristics of the Class I Transcripts

The class I protein has three extracellular domains, a transmembrane domain by which it is inserted in the cell membrane, and a cytoplasmic domain. The structural organization of the class I gene conforms to the exon-intron organization of the genomic DNA. The typical human and mouse class I gene is 5-6 kb long and is made up of exons (Malissen et al., 1982; Steinmetz et al., 1981). The first exon encodes approximately 20 nucleotides of the 5′-untranslated region and the signal peptide, which is approximately 20 amino acids long. The signal peptide is highly hydrophobic, and it is cleaved after the class I protein has been inserted into the cell membrane. The second and third exons are similar in size (270 nucleotides) and encode the first two extracellular domains (α1 and α2) of the heavy chain. The α3 domain is encoded by the fourth exon, and this domain is the most conserved region of the class I molecule. The homology of the nucleotide sequences of this domain is more than 90% between rat and mouse and more than 80% between rat and rabbit and between rat and human (Radojcic et al., 1989). The α3 domain has also been found to be homologous to β_2-microglobulin and the immunoglobulin constant regions. The fifth exon in the class I gene encodes the highly hydrophobic transmembrane domain that anchors the class I molecules to the cell membrane. mRNA transcripts for soluble class I molecules lack this region and this defect is believed to be generated by alternative splicing of mRNA (Krangel, 1986). Similar posttranscriptional modification has been described for the last three exons of the class I gene (McCluskey et al., 1986), which encode the cytoplasmic domain and the 3′-untranslated region. The class I transcript can also be modified at its 5′-end (Lalanne et al., 1983), which may be another mechanism for generating class I polymorphism at the protein level.

The mature class I mRNA and its corresponding cDNA are 1.6 kb long and contain the sequences of all eight exons (Fig. 5-1). The start codon (AUG) is located after approximately 20 nucleotides of the 5′-untranslated region in the first exon. The eighth exon is over 400 nucleotides in length, although in some cases the translational termination codon (UGA) is present at its 5′ end. Thus, translation may terminate at the end of the seventh exon. The polyadenylation signal

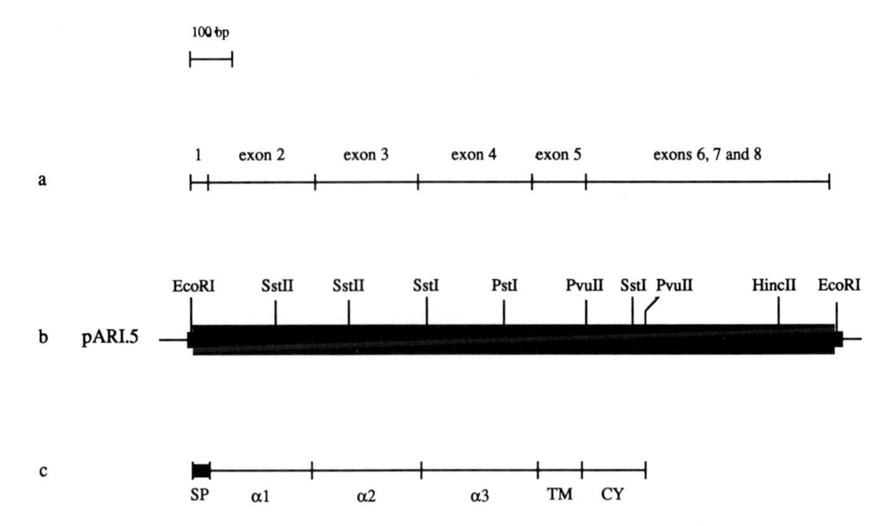

Fig. 5-1. Schematic representation of the exon organization of a class I gene (a); the restriction enzyme map of pARI.5, the rat placental class I clone (b); and their relationship to the domain structure of class I heavy chain (c).

(5′-AAAUAAA-3′) is usually located 400 nucleotides downstream from the stop codon in the mouse (Morita et al., 1985; Taylor et al., 1985).

Characteristics of the Class I Proteins

The class I antigens are glycoproteins found on the surface of nearly all nucleated cells. The heavy chains have relative masses of 42-46 kDa and are encoded by multiple loci within the major histocompatibility complex. Each of the three extracellular domains contains approximately 90 amino acids. The light chain, of relative mass 12 kDa, is β_2-microglobulin, a nonglycosylated molecule encoded on a different chromosome from that encoding the MHC. Class I antigens are the targets of antibodies and cytotoxic T lymphocytes (CTL) during rejection of foreign tissue grafts. They are also involved in MHC-restricted recognition of viral antigens by CTL through formation of antigen-MHC complexes on the target cell surface. In addition to antigen-specific MHC-restricted CTL, CTL can be generated against allogeneic class I molecules. This finding is not unexpected, since class I alloantigens differ from each other in 5-15% of their amino acids.

The third domain of the α chain forms a stable noncovalent interaction with β_2-microglobulin, which is probably very important in class I antigen expression. Although the β_2-microglobulin molecule is highly conserved among species, there appears to be some species specificity. For example, there is a 40-fold enhancement of the surface expression of human class I antigens in mouse mastocytoma cells if the cells are cotransfected with the human β_2-microbulin gene (Perarnau et al., 1988). This effect has been attributed to more efficient association of HLA heavy chains with human β_2-microglobulin molecules, which allows more rapid transport of the HLA molecules from the endoplasmic reticulum to the Golgi apparatus. In addition, class I antigens cannot be expressed in Daudi cells (Sege et al., 1981), which do not produce β_2-microglobulin.

A comparison of MHC class I antigens from different species indicates that they have extensive nucleotide and amino and homologies. Although differences can occur along the whole length of the class I heavy chain, the majority of these differences are localized to the N-terminal 180 residues. Based on sequence analysis, the external domains of the class I molecule can be divided into variable and constant (framework) regions, and most of the variable amino acid residues are found clustered in several positions in the $\alpha1$ and $\alpha2$ domains. The terminal part of the first domain (amino acid positions 60-80) is the most variable region of the class I molecule, and it contains the residues responsible for the allelic differences among class I antigens. The conserved regions of the molecule most likely account for the strong conservation of the tertiary structure of the class I antigens. Highly conserved cysteine residues stabilize the intradomain structure by forming disulfide bridges. These residues lie at positions 101 and 164 in the $\alpha2$ domain and positions 203 and 259 in the $\alpha3$ domain and are conserved in the human (Koller and Orr, 1985), mouse (Morita et al., 1985), and rat (Radojcic et al., 1989). It has also been suggested that the disulfide bridge in the third domain is necessary for receptor-mediated intracellular transport, since disruption of this disulfide bridge interferes with intracellular transport (Miyazaki et al., 1986a).

All class I antigens have N-linked glycans and contain one, two, or three sugar moieties. The specific recognition sequence for glycosylation is Asn-X-Thr/Ser and is found at several conserved positions in the molecule: position 86 in the first domain of the human, mouse, and rat class I antigens (Koller and Orr, 1985; Maloy and Coligan, 1982; Radojcic et al., 1989) and position 156 in the third domain of the mouse and rat class I antigens (Maloy and Coligan, 1982; Radojcic et al., 1989).

The role of glycosylation in class I antigen expression is not yet clear, although it has been suggested that it does not affect antigenicity (Misra et al., 1987a; Parham et al., 1977). Several experiments have shown that tunicamycin treatment, which inhibits glycosylation, does not prevent class I antigen expression (Lindolfi et al., 1985); although a reduction in cell surface expression of the nonglycosylated antigens was observed (Miyazaki et al., 1986b). This suggests that the carbohydrate moieties may play a role in the intracellular transport of the antigen.

Recent crystallographic studies have shown that the human class I molecule HLA-A2 has a twofold rotational axis of symmetry (Bjorkman et al., 1987a, b) and that the α1 domain has the same tertiary folding as the α_2 domain, whereas the α_3 domain has the same tertiary folding as β_2-microglobulin. The α1 and α2 domains form two antiparallel α-helical regions overlying eight β-pleated strands and forming a long groove. Nearly all of the polymorphic amino acid residues in the class I molecule are located around the periphery or in the base of this groove.

Based on the HLA-A2 model, the edges of the groove in the rat placental class I antigen are also the most polymorphic parts of the molecule (Fig. 5-2). Some of these residues are important for antigen and/or T cell receptor (TCR) binding (Tables 5-1 and 5-2), and most

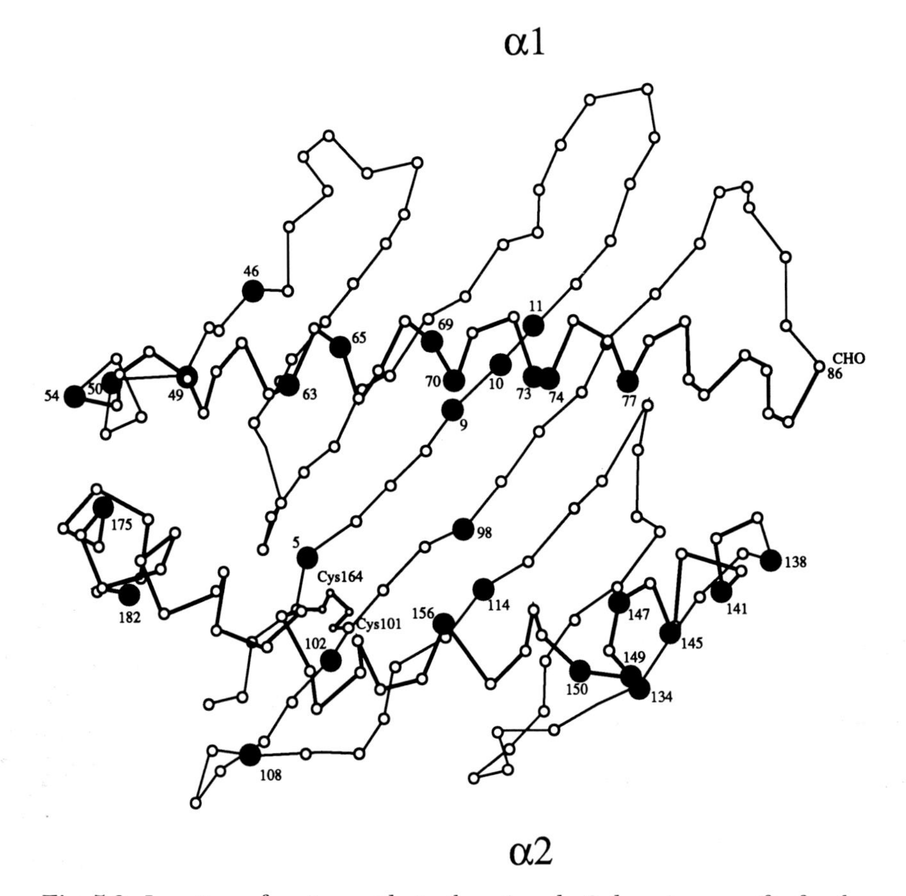

Fig. 5-2. Location of amino acids in the α1 and α2 domains specific for the placental class I antigen encoded by pARI.5 (dark circles). The figure is based on the crystal structure of HLA-A2 defined by Bjorkman et al. (1987a), and it shows the α-carbon backbone structure of the α1 and α2 domains.

Table 5-1. α1 Domain amino acids involved in binding antigenic peptide and/or the T cell receptor*

Class I Antigens	5	7	9	22	24	26	57	58	59	61	62	63	64	65	66	67	68	69	70	71	72	73	74	75	76	77	80	81	82	84
pARI.5	L	Y	D	F	S	G	P	E	Y	E	R	I	T	R	I	A	K	E	S	E	Q	I	Y	R	V	G	T	L	R	Y
H2-K^d	M	.	E	.	.	.	.	.	.	.	E	Q	.	Q	R	.	.	S	D	.	.	W	F	.	.	S	.	A	Q	.
H2-D^b	M	.	E	Y	.	.	.	.	.	.	.	E	.	Q	K	.	.	G	Q	.	.	W	F	.	.	S	N	.	L	.
HLA-B7	M	.	Y	.	.	.	.	.	.	D	.	N	.	Q	.	Y	.	A	Q	A	.	T	D	.	E	S	N	.	.	.
Q10	M	.	E	F	I	.	.	.	.	.	.	E	.	Q	R	.	.	G	N	.	.	S	F	H	.	S	.	.	.	H

* The residues listed have been postulated by Bjorkman et al. (1987b) to contact the TCR and/or antigenic peptides. Amino acid sequence data are pARI.5 (Radojcic et al., 1989), H-2K^d (Lalanne et al., 1983), H2-D^b (Maloy & Coligan, 1982; Reyes et al., 1982), HLA-B7 (Sood et al., 1985), and Q10 (Mellor et al., 1984).

Table 5-2. α2 Domain amino acids involved in binding antigenic peptide and/or the T cell receptor*

Class I Antigens	95	97	99	114	116	143	145	146	147	149	150	151	152	154	155	156	157	158	159	161	162	163	165	166	167	169	171
pARI.5	I	R	S	E	F	T	N	K	L	R	D	G	E	E	R	L	R	A	Y	E	G	E	V	E	W	R	Y.
H2-K^d	F	.	F	L	.	.	R	.	W	Q	A	.	D	.	Y	Y	.	.	.	.	.	.	.	.	.	.	.
H2-D^b	L	Q	.	Q	.	.	R	.	W	Q	S	.	A	.	H	Y	K	.	.	.	.	.	.	.	.	H	.
HLA-B7	L	S	Y	D	Y	.	R	.	W	A	A	R	.	.	Q	R	.	.	.	.	.	.	.	.	.	.	.
Q10	.	W	Y	L	Y	.	R	.	W	Q	A	.	A	.	Y	Y	.	.	.	.	A	.	.	.	.	L	

* See footnote to Table 5-1.

of the variable residues in the rat placental class I antigen are located in the putative peptide binding site and point into the groove (Bjorkmann et al., 1987b). The HLA-A2 variants with differences at positions 66, 152, and 156 bound a synthetic virus antigen, but were not recognized by competent autologous CTL (McMichael et al., 1988). Differences in amino acids at position 9, which lie in the floor of the peptide binding groove, at position 70, and at position 74 are less important for CTL recognition. Although it is not yet clear which amino acid residues are important for TCR binding or may be potential ligands for antigenic peptides, changes in residues that point up or away from the groove could affect interactions with the TCR, whereas amino acid changes in the antigen recognition site could affect antigen binding. Amino acid substitutions outside of the antigen recognition site have no effect on CTL function, e.g., positions 43 and 107 (McMichael et al., 1988).

A number of observations indicate that molecules other than the TCR may facilitate interaction with the class I antigens of target cells. Point mutations in the class I α3 domain can decrease reactivity with CTL (Potter et al., 1987), and residues in this domain are also involved in Lyt-2 recognition. Antibody against these residues inhibits lysis by CTL generated in a primary *in vitro* response (Connolly et al., 1988). Finally, CD8 binds directly to HLA class I molecules (Norment et al., 1988).

The nature of the antigenic determinants recognized by highly specific alloreactive T cells and the mechanism by which this fine specificity is achieved are poorly understood. It is not yet clear whether the same polymorphic segments are equally important as alloantigenic sites for antibodies and for CTL, and some amino acid substitutions probably do not contribute to alloantigenic polymorphisms. It is possible that both the α1/α2 domains and the α3 domain of the class I molecule are involved in specific CTL recognition. Antibodies against an epitope in either the α1/α2 or α3 domains caused slight enhancement of skin graft survival, whereas a combination of antibodies against epitopes in the α1/α2 and α3 domains had a synergistic effect, leading to prolonged graft survival (Connolly et al., 1988).

The amino acids at positions 63 and 73 in the α1-helix and at positions 152, 155, and 156 in the α2-helix play important roles in CTL recognition (Mann et al., 1988). It has also been suggested that alloreactive CTL recognize class I determinants in association with an antigenic peptide that occupies the groove of the class I molecule (Bjorkman et al., 1987b); thus, a class I-antigen complex is recognized by the CTL. The majority of polymorphic residues in class I antigens lie in the peptide-binding site, whereas the most conserved parts are on the surface of the class I molecule and face the solvent.

Finally, some amino acid substitutions in class I molecules may not be recognized by CTL because they are buried within the molecule or fail to bind to the TCR or other critical T lymphocyte surface molecules; nonetheless, these changes could elicit an alloantibody response.

Amino acids in the rat placental class I antigen (Radojcic et al., 1989) can be divided into three groups according to their locations in the molecule: (1) amino acids 5,9,10,11,98,102, and 114, which are located on the floor of the antigen-binding site; (2) amino acids 63,65,69,70, 73,74,77, and 156, which lie on the edge of the antigen-binding groove; and (3) amino acids 46,49,50,54,108,134,138, 141,145,147,149,150,175, and 182, which are located outside the recognition site (Fig. 5-2). Some of these positions have already been identified as important (63,156) or less important (9,70) for antigen binding by the HLA-A2 molecule (McMichael et al., 1988). In the rat class I antigen, amino acids in the first group most likely have no effect on cytotoxicity specificity. Amino acids in the second group are probably responsible for allelic differences and are the most polymorphic positions within and among species. The third group includes the majority of the polymorphic amino acid residues on the side of the α2 domain (134,138,141,145,147,149,150) that face the solvent. The amino acid sequence in this region of the rat placental class I antigen differs significantly from class I molecules of other species and the location of the polymorphic residues is also different. These residues are generally hydrophobic, as are the amino acids in the floor of the antigen-binding side (Fig. 5-3), suggesting that this part of the molecule is also involved in peptide binding with the TCR or with other accessory molecules involved in CTL recognition. It is possible that a single amino acid substitution in the rat placental class I antigen at an immunodominant position could abrogate recognition by CTL.

Conclusions

We have shown that a rat class I clone derived from a placental cDNA library has the same exon organization as other class I genes. The protein deduced from this cDNA clone has all the features of a classical class I molecule: three extracellular domains (each approximately 90 amino acids long); transmembrane and cytoplasmic domains; two glycosylation sites at Asn 86 and Asn 256; and conserved Cys positions at residues 101, 161, 203, and 259. The amino acids of the variable regions are clustered in the same positions as in class I antigens of other species with the exception of positions 134-150 within the α2 domain. These amino acids may be involved in TCR binding.

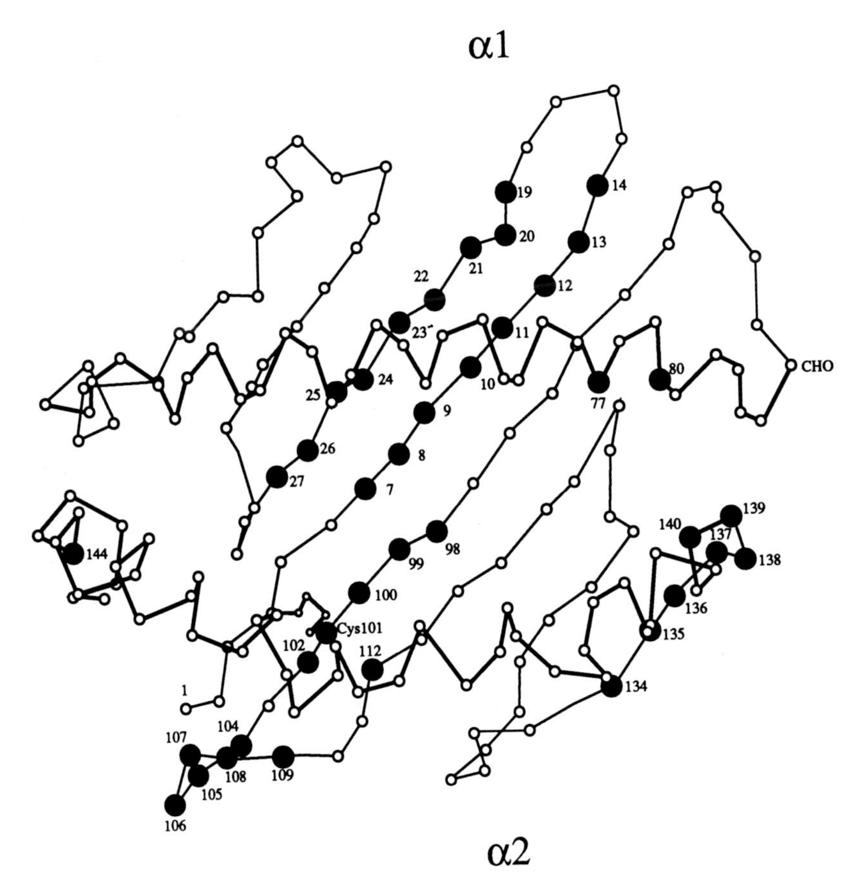

Fig. 5-3. Stereo view of the hydrophobic amino acids in the rat placental class I antigen encoded by pARI.5 (dark circles). The figure is based on the hydropathy plot described by Kyte and Doolittle (1982) and the tertiary structure of the α1 and α2 domains described by Bjorkman et al. (1987a, 1987b).

Acknowledgments

This work was supported by grants from the National Institutes of Health (CA 18659, HD 08662, and HD 0988), the Tim Caracio Memorial Cancer Fund, the Beaver County Cancer Society, and the Pathology Education and Research Foundation.

References

Bjorkman, P. J., Saper, M. A., Samraoui, B., Bennett, W. S., Strominger, J. L. and Wiley, D. C. 1987a. Structure of the human class I histocompatibility antigen, HLA-A2. *Nature* 329:506.

Bjorkman, P. J., Saper, M. A., Samraoui, B., Bennett, W. S., Strominger, J. L. and Wiley, D. C. 1987b. The foreign antigen binding site and T cell recognition regions of class I histocompatibility antigens. *Nature* 329:512.

Brami, C. J., Sanyal, M. K., Dwyer, J. M., Johnson, C. C., Kohorn, E. I. and Naftolin, F. 1983. HLA-DR antigen on human trophoblast. *Am. J. Reprod. Immunol.* 3:165.

Chatterjee-Hasrouni, S. and Lala, P. K. 1981. MHC antigens on mouse trophoblast cells: paucity of Ia antigens despite the presence of H-2K and D. *J. Immunol.* 127:2070.

Connolly, J. M., Potter, T. A., Wormstall, E. M. and Hansen, T. H. 1988. The Lyt-2 molecule recognizes residues in the class I α3 domain in allogeneic cytotoxic T cell responses. *J. Exp. Med.* 168:325.

Ellis, S. A., Sargent, I. L., Redman, C. W. G. and McMichael, A. J. 1986. Evidence for a move 1 HLA antigen found on human extravillous trophoblast and a choriocarcinoma cell line. *Immunology* 59:595.

Ghani, A. M., Gill, T. J. III, Kunz, H. W. and Misra, D. N. 1984a. Elicitation of the maternal antibody response to the fetus by a broadly shared MHC class I antigenic determinant. *Transplantation* (*Baltimore*) 37:187.

Ghani, A. M., Kunz, H. W. and Gill, T. J. III. 1984b. Pregnancy-induced monoclonal antibody to a unique fetal antigen. *Transplantation* (*Baltimore*) 37:187.

Hunt, J. S., Fishback, J. L., Andrews, G. K. and Wood, G. W. 1988. Expression of class I HLA genes by trophoblast cells. Analysis by in situ hybridization. *J. Immunol.* 140:1293.

Kanbour, A., Ho, H.-N., Misra, D. N., MacPherson, T. A., Kunz, H. W. and Gill, T. J. III. 1987. Differential expression of MHC class I antigens on the placenta of the rat. A mechanism for the survival of the fetal allograft. *J. Exp. Med.* 166:1861.

Koller, B. H. and Orr, H. T. 1985. Cloning and complete sequence of an HLA-A2 gene: analysis of two HLA-A alleles at the nucleotide level. *J. Immunol.* 134:2727.

Krangel, M. S. 1986. Secretion of HLA-A and HLA-B antigens via an alternative RNA splicing pathway. *J. Exp. Med.* 163:1173.

Kyte, J. and Doolittle, R. F. 1982. A simple method of displaying the hydropathic character of protein. *J. Mol. Biol.* 157:105.

Lalanne, J. -L., Cochet, M., Kummer, A. -M., Gachelin, G. and Kourilsky, P. 1983. Different exon-intron organization of the 5′ part of a mouse class I gene is used to generate a novel H-2K^{d}-related mRNA. *Proc. Natl. Acad. Sci. USA* 80:7561.

Lindolifi, N. F., Rich, R. R. and Cook, R. 1985. Differential glycosylation requirements for the cell surface expression of class I molecules. *J. Immunol.* 134:423.

Malissen, M., Malissen, B. and Jordan, B. R. 1982. Exon/intron organization and complete nucleotide sequence of an HLA gene. *Proc. Natl. Acad. Sci. USA* 79:893.

Maloy, W. L. and Coligan, J. E. 1982. Primary structure of the H-2D^{b} alloantigen II. Additional amino acid sequence information localization of a third site of glycosylation and evidence for K and D region specific sequence. *Immunogenetics* 16:11.

Mann, D. W., McLaughlin-Taylor, E., Wallace, R. B. and Forman, J. 1988. An immunodominant epitope present in multiple class I MHC molecules and recognized by cytotoxic T lymphocytes. *J. Exp. Med.* 108:307.

McCluskey, J., Boyd, L. F., Maloy, W. L., Coligan, J. E. and Margulies, D. H. 1986. Alternative processing of H-2D^d pre-mRNAs results in membrane expression of differentially phosphorylated protein products. *EMBO J.* 5:2477.

McIntyre, J. A. and Faulk, W. P. 1982. Allotypic trophoblast-lymphocyte reactive (TLX) cell surface antigens. *Hum. Immunol.* 4:27.

McIntyre, J. A., Faulk, W. P., Verhulst, S. J. and Colliver, J. A. 1983. Human trophoblast-lymphocyte cross-reactive (TLX) antigens define a new alloantigenic system. *Science* 222:1135.

McMichael, A. J., Gotch, F. M., Santos-Aguado, J. and Strominger, J. L. 1988. Effect of mutations and variations of HLA-A2 on recognition of a virus peptide epitope by cytotoxic T lymphocytes. *Proc. Natl. Acad. Sci. USA* 85:9194.

Mellor, A. L., Weiss, E. H., Kress, M., Jay, G. and Flavell, R. A. 1984. A nonpolymorphic class I gene in the murine major histocompatibility complex. *Cell* 36:139.

Misra, D. N., Kunz, H. W., Cortese Hassett, A. L. and Gill, T. J. III. 1987a. Comparison of rat MHC class I antigens by peptide mapping. *Immunogenetics* 25:35.

Misra, D. N., Kunz, H. W., Gill, T. J. III. 1987b. Carbohydrate moieties of rat MHC class I antigens. *Immunogenetics* 26:204.

Miyazaki, J. I., Appella, E. and Ozato, K. 1986a. Intracellular transport blockage caused by disruption of the disulfide bridge in the third external domain of the major histocompatibility complex class I antigen. *Proc. Natl. Acad. Sci. USA* 83:757.

Miyazaki, J. I., Appella, E., Zhao, H., Forman, J. and Gzato, K. 1986b. Expression and function of a nonglycosylated major histocompatibility class I antigen. *J. Exp. Med.* 163:856.

Morita, T., Delabre, C., Kress, M., Kourilsky, P. and Jachelin, J. 1985. An H-2K gene of the t^{32} mutant at the T/t complex in a close parent of an H-2K^q gene. *Immunogenetics* 21:367.

Norment, A. M., Salter, R. D., Parham, P., Engelhard, V. H. and Littman, D. R. 1988. Cell-cell adhesion mediated by CD8 and MHC class I molecules. *Nature* 336:79.

Parham, P., Alpert, B. N., Orr, H. T. and Strominger, J. L. 1977. Carbohydrate moiety of HLA antigens: antigenic properties and amino acid sequences around the site of glycosylation. *J. Biol. Chem.* 252:7555.

Perarnau, B. M., Gillet, A. C., Hakem, R., Barad, M. and Lemonnier, F. A. 1988. Human β_2-microglobulin specifically enhances cell-surface expression of HLA class I molecules in transfected murine cells. *J. Immunol.* 141:1383.

Potter, T. A., Bluestone, J. A. and Rajan, T. V. 1987. A simple amino acid substitution in the $\alpha3$ domain of and H-2 class I molecule abrogates reactivity with CTL. *J. Exp. Med.* 166:956.

Radojcic, A., Stranick, K. S., Locker J., Kunz, H. W. and Gill, T. J. III. 1989. Nucleotide sequence of a rat class I cDNA clone. *Immunogenetics* 29:134.

Raghupathy, R., Singh, B., Leigh, J. B. and Wegmann, T. G. 1981. The ontogeny and turnover kinetics of paternal H-2K antigenic determinants on the allogeneic murine placenta. *J. Immunol.* 127:2074.

Reyes, A. A., Schoeld, M. and Wallance, R. B. 1982. The complete amino acid sequence of the murine transplantation antigen H-2D^b as deduced by molecular cloning. *Immunogenetics* 16:1.

Sege, K., Rask, L. and Peterson, P. A. 1981. Role of β_2-microglobulin in the intracellular processing of HLA antigens. *Biochemistry* 20:4523.

Sood, A. K., Pan, J., Biro, P. A., Pereira, D., Stivastava, R., Reddy, V. B., Duceman, B. W. and Weissman, S. M. 1985. Structure and polymorphism of class I MHC antigen mRNA. *Immunogenetics* 22:101.

Steinmetz, M., Moore, K. W., Frelinger, J. G., Taylor, S. B., Shen, F. W., Boyse, E. A. and Hood, L. 1981. A pseudogene homologous to mouse transplantation antigens: transplantation antigens are encoded by eight exons that correlate with protein domains. *Cell* 25:683.

Stranick, K. S., Ho, H. -N., Macpherson, T. A., Locker, J., Kunz, H. W. and Gill, T. J. III. 1986. Regulation of the maternal-fetal response by trophoblast antigen expression. In *Reproductive Immunology* (D.A. Clark and B. A. Croy, eds.) Amsterdam: Elsevier, p. 45.

Sunderland, C. A., Naiem, N., Mason, D. Y., Redman, C. W. G. and Stirrat, G. 1981. The expression of major histocompatibility antigens by human chorionic villi. *J. Reprod. Immunol.* 3:323.

Taylor, S. B., Nairn, R., Coligan, J. E. and Hood, L. E. 1985. DNA sequence of the mouse H-2D^d transplantation antigen gene. *Proc. Natl. Acad. Sci. USA* 82:1175.

6

Analysis of MHC-Linked Genes Affecting Development

ANDREA L. CORTESE HASSETT, JOSEPH D. LOCKER, HEINZ W. KUNZ, and THOMAS J. GILL III

A coordinated interaction among cells is required for species-specific fertilization and normal development of the embryo and fetus. Aberrations in this process can lead to fetal wastage, congenital malformations, retarded development, and malignancy and are presumably mediated by perturbations in normal patterns of gene expression. The immune response to tissue transplants emphasizes the role of genetic control in these processes; many of the genes involved have been conserved throughout evolution and constitute the major histocompatibility complex (MHC). Susceptibility to a variety of diseases in humans (Dausset & Svejgaard, 1977) and in animals (Gotze, 1977) has been associated with certain MHC antigens, although the reasons for this association are not known. Loci controlling a variety of enzymes are closely linked to the MHC in the mouse, rat, and human; in the mouse and rat there are also loci that affect embryological development, the *t*-complex, and growth and reproduction complex (*grc*), respectively. The stable association of these genes indicates that the chromosomal segment carrying them constitutes a multigene family (Snell, 1968), which may be a common property of all mammals (Gill & Kunz, 1979).

The most extensively studied of the genes affecting development is the mouse *t*-complex. The *t*-complex encodes both dominant and recessive genes linked to the MHC, which cause segregation distortion of *t*-haplotypes, sterility in males, embryonic and fetal death, skeletal defects, and suppression of recombination between wild type and *t*-bearing chromosomes (Bennett, 1975, 1981; (Frischauf, 1985; Green, 1981; Klein & Hammerberg, 1977; Lyon, 1981; Silver, 1981). The factor(s) that causes suppression of recombination has been elucidated by the finding that the structure of *t*-chromatin is different than that of wild type over a significant part of the chromosome (Alton et al.,

1980; Artzt et al., 1982b; Silver et al., 1980). The various MHC components have been mapped in the *t*-haplotypes using a combination of classical genetics, serology, and molecular genetics (Shin et al., 1984). These results indicate that the whole MHC region is included in two inversions with the relative positions of its genes intact. In addition, some of the *t*-lethal mutations map very near to, or are interspersed with, components of the MHC. In spite of the extensive genetic and embryological analyses of *t*-chromatin, the genes and gene products responsible for *t*-haplotype-associated effects have yet to be identified (Bennett, 1975; Ginsberg & Hillman, 1975; Silver et al., 1983; Willison et al., 1986).

In this chapter, we summarize our studies on the growth and reproduction complex (*grc*) of the rat in which we begin to explore the molecular basis for its effects.

Growth and Reproduction Complex

Genes affecting growth and development were thought to be peculiar to the mouse until the discovery of the *grc* in the rat (Gill & Kunz, 1979), which has phenotypic properties similar to the partial *t*-semilethal haplotype of the mouse. The *grc* was discovered during studies of B-stock rats (Kunz et al., 1977) in which the $RT1^{l}$ and $RT1^{u}$ haplotypes were segregating: both male and female RT1 homozygotes were small and had fertility defects. The *grc*-bearing animals are propagated by mating heterozygotes or balanced lethals: the grc/grc^{+} was designated the BIL strain; the *grc/grc*, the BIL/1 strain; and grc^{+}/grc^{+}, the BIL/2 strain. To date, no protein product coded by the *grc* region has been detected.

The *grc* in the homozygous state causes sterility in males because of a uniform arrest of primary spermatocytes at the early pachytene stage. It is also associated with decreased body size and testis weight (one-tenth of normal); reduced fertility in females; and partial embryonic mortality. No segregation distortion has been observed (Gill et al., 1983b). The male germ cells in *grc*-bearing rats carry an antigen that is serologically cross-reactive with the t^{s1}-antigen of the mouse, as detected by cytotoxicity testing on rat testicular cells (Artzt et al., 1982b). The *grc* affects the development of both the sperm and the ovum, whereas there is no evidence that *t*-haplotypes affect the development of the ovum. A summary of the immune responsiveness of *grc*-bearing strains is shown in Table 6-1.

The mechanisms by which the *grc* genes act are not known. There are no chromosomal abnormalities detectable by G-banding (Drescher et al., 1980) and no abnormalities of pituitary hormones (FSH, LH, GH), testosterone, testosterone metabolism, or somatomedin C (Gill & Kunz, 1979; Greiner et al., 1980). There is an increase in sulfotransferase activity in the testes of *grc/grc* homozygotes due to decreased

Table 6-1. Immune response of *grc*-bearing strains

Demonstration of humoral immunity
Antibody production using synthetic polypeptides.
Skin graft rejection.
Antibody production in *grc* strains to grc^{+} lymphocytes.
Demonstration of cellular immunity
Skin graft rejection*

* No T cell studies have been done yet.

production of the inhibitor of this enzyme (Lingwood et al., 1985). A similar biochemical defect has been found in the mouse: sperm of *t*-bearing mice express increased galactosyl transferase activity due to decreased levels of its inhibitor (Hashimoto et al., 1983; Shur & Bennett, 1979). The *grc* can interact epistatically with the tail anomaly lethal (*Tal*) gene (Schaid et al., 1982) or with the hood restriction (H^{re}) gene (Gill et al., 1984) to cause embryonic death. This was the first demonstration of lethal epistatic interactions in mammals. Recent studies using *grc*-bearing rats (Melhem et al., 1987; Rao et al., 1984) have shown that these animals can develop preneoplastic hepatocellular nodules after exposure to either of two carcinogens, N-2-acetylaminofluorene (AAF) or diethylnitrosamine (DEN).

RFLP Mapping Studies

The organization of the MHC and *grc* regions of the rat was investigated initially by DNA mapping studies. Molecular analyses were undertaken using mouse cDNA probes to identify restriction fragment length polymorphisms (RFLP) of genomic DNA derived from a selected series of inbred, recombinant, and congenic strains of rats. Because of the probes used and restriction enzymes chosen, a large region of DNA could be examined. Southern blot analysis (Cortese Hassett et al., 1986) was done on liver DNA from the strains listed in Table 6-2. The most informative system used in this study was genomic DNA digested with Eco RI and hybridized with pAG64c (Brickell et al., 1983, 1985; Scott et al., 1983) or pH-2IIa (Steinmetz et al., 1981, a,b). Both probes are mouse MHC class I clones that recognize highly conserved regions of the gene. The polymorphic and nonpolymorphic bands identified by hybridization of pH-2IIa to Eco RI digests are listed in Table 6-3. Between 18 and 25 restriction bands were detected in each strain, and of this number, 9 were nonmappable bands that appeared in every strain. By comparison of the restriction patterns of the recombinants, 17 bands could be assigned to specific MHC regions. These studies used congenic strains to confirm that hybridization differences mapped within the MHC

The assignment of bands to specific regions of the MHC was based

Table 6-2. Genotypes of Rat Strains

Strain	*RT1 Specificities*			
	A	B/D	E	grc
BI	*n*	*a*	*u*	+
BIL	*l/n*	*l/a*	-	*grc/+*
BIL/2	*n*	*a*	*u*	+
R18	*l*	*l*	-	*
R21	*l*	*l*	*u*	+
R22	*l*	*a*	*u*	+
BIL/1	*l*	*l*	-	*grc*
R10	*n*	*l*	-	*grc*
R11	*l*	*l*	*u*	+
YO	*u*	*u*	*u*	+
R16	*a*	*a*	-	*grc*
ACP	*a*	*a*	-	+
DA	*a*	*a*	-	+

Note: RFLP studies have shown the site of recombination to be within the *grc* (Cortese Hassett et al., 1986).

on the comparison of the restriction patterns of inbred strains with those of recombinant and *grc*-bearing strains, and on the comparison of recombinants to their parental strains. Some recombinants contained new bands, and it was assumed that these bands arose directly from the recombinational event and consequently mapped to the region of the site of recombination.

Because of the series of recombinants used in these studies (R10, R18, R21, and R22), RFLP fragments specific for the *RT1.E-grc* region could be identified. Examination of the Eco RI digests of BIL/1 and recombinants R10 and R16, all of which carry the *grc*, showed that 10.8 kb (E15) and 9.8 kb (E16) fragments were always present. In those strains that are grc^+, Eco RI fragments of 6.3 kb (E25) and 4.5 kb (E33) were always present. These findings provide unique RFLP markers to delineate the *grc* region and make it possible to examine this region further. The differences between *grc* (BIL/1) and grc^+ (BIL/2) are illustrated in Figure 6-1.

Additional mapping studies were done using several other restriction endonucleases: Bam HI, Bgl II, Hind III, Kpn I, Pst I, Pvu II, and Xba I (Cortese Hassett, 1987), and representative results with Bgl II and Pvu II digests of DNA are shown in Figures 6-2 and 6-3. Polymorphic restriction fragments could be identified that correlated with the results obtained with Eco RI and Xba I digests. Again, because of the series of recombinants used, specific RFLP fragments could be localized to the *RT1.E-grc* region. The three markers associated with the E^--*grc* region are Bgl II bands of 13.0 kb, 9.4 kb, and 5.6 kb. In addition, unique markers that delineate the *grc* region were

Table 6-3. Hybridization analysis of Eco RI-digested genomic DNA

Band	Kb	BI	BIL	BIL/2	BIL/1	R18	R21	R22	R10	R11	YO	YO.IL.*grc*	YO.IU.*grc*$^+$	YO.IL.*grc* YO.IU.*grc*$^+$	R16	ACP*	Regions Identified
E1†	20.5												+				
E2	20.0	+	+	+	+						+			+	+	+	
E3	19.0	+	+	+	+	+	+	+	+	+	+	+	+	+			
E4	18.2	+	+	+						+	+	+	+	+	+	+	
E5	17.5								+							+	*A*
E6	17.0								+								*E*
E7	16.2	+	+	+	+	+	+	+	+	+	+	+	+	+	+	+	
E8	15.6											+	+			+	
E9	14.4	+	+	+	+	+	+	+	+	+	+	+	+	+	+	+	
E10	14.0									+							*E*
E11	13.2	+	+	+	+	+	+	+	+	+	+	+	+	+	+	+	
E12	12.3	+	+	+	+	+	+	+	+	+	+	+	+	+	+	+	
E13	11.7	+	+	+	+	+	+	+	+	+	+	+	+	+	+	+	
E14	11.5	+	+	+									+				
E15	10.8				+	+			+			+		+	+	+	E^- − *grc*
E16	9.8				+	+			+			+		+	+	+	E^- − *grc*
E17	9.1									+	+		+	+			*E''*
E18	8.6	+	+	+	+	+	+	+	+	+	+	+	+	+	+	+	
E19	8.15								+	+							A—*B/D*
E20	7.8	+	+	+		+	+	+		+	+	+	+	+	+	+	
E21	7.6									+	+		+	+			
E22	7.0		+	+	+	+	+	+		+	+	+	+	+			
E23	6.8	+	+	+	+										+	+	

E24	6.6				+							+					*grc*
E25	6.3	+	+	+		+	+	+		+	+		+	+			$E^u - \text{grc}^+$
E26	6.15														+	+	
E27	6.0				+							+					
E28	5.9								+		+						$A - B/D$ junction
E29	5.6	+	+	+	+	+	+	+	+	+	+	+	+	+	+	+	
E30	5.25														+		*grc*
E31	5.1	+	+	+	+	+	+	+	+	+	+	+	+	+	+	+	
E32	4.8	+	+	+		+	+	+		+	+		+	+			
E33	4.5	+	+	+		+	+	+		+		+		+			$E^u - \text{grc}^+$
E34	4.4	+	+	+	+	+						+		+	+	+	
E35	4.2								+								Recombination site of R10
E36	4.0				+				+			+		+	+	+	*grc*
E37	3.9	+	+	+	+			+		+	+	+	+	+			$A - B/D$ junction
E38	3.75								+							+	
E39	3.68	+	+	+	+	+	+	+		+	+	+	+	+			
E40	3.4									+	+	+	+	+			
E41	3.0									+	+	+	+	+			
E42	2.85									+							E^-
E43	2.7	+	+	+	+	+	+	+		+	+		+	+		+	grc^+
E44	2.25	+	+	+	+	+	+	+	+	+	+		+	+	+	+	
E45	2.0	+	+	+	+	+	+	+	+	+	+	+	+	+	+	+	

* Banding pattern was the same in the DA strain.

† Eco RI-digested bands are sequentially numbered in descending order of size.

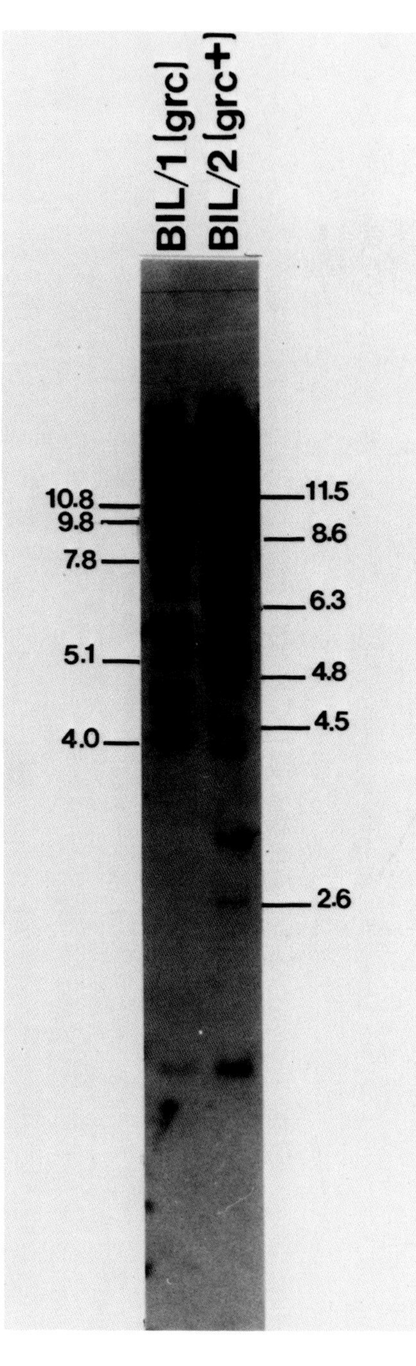

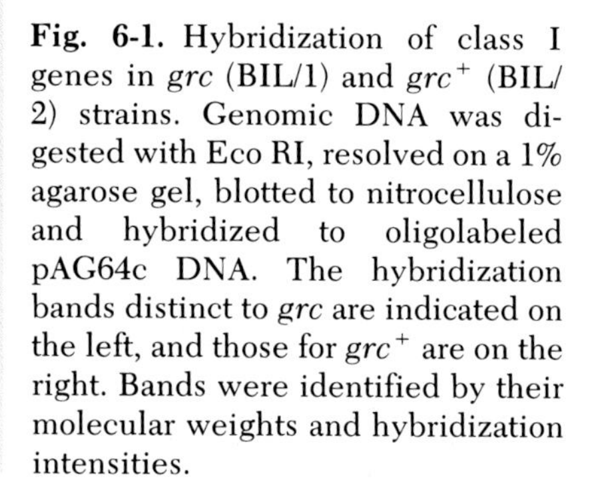

Fig. 6-1. Hybridization of class I genes in *grc* (BIL/1) and *grc*$^+$ (BIL/2) strains. Genomic DNA was digested with Eco RI, resolved on a 1% agarose gel, blotted to nitrocellulose and hybridized to oligolabeled pAG64c DNA. The hybridization bands distinct to *grc* are indicated on the left, and those for *grc*$^+$ are on the right. Bands were identified by their molecular weights and hybridization intensities.

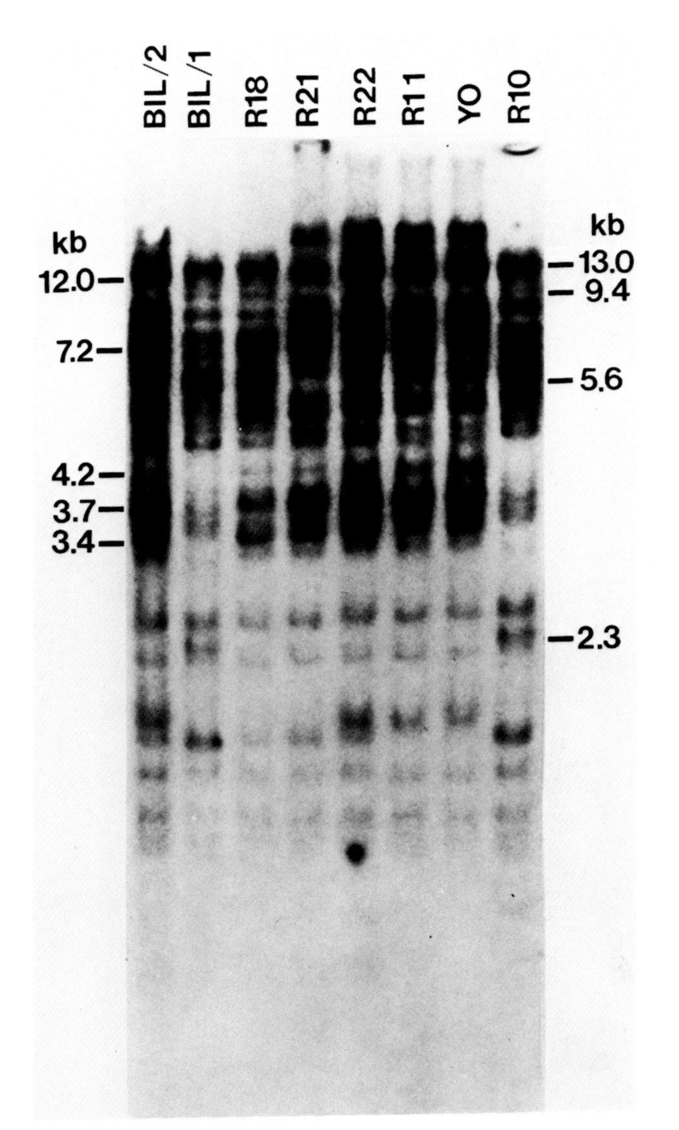

Fig. 6-2. Hybridization of Bgl II-digested genomic DNA. Seven micrograms of DNA were digested with Bgl II, resolved in 0.7% agarose at 40 V for 20 hours, blotted to a nitrocellulose membrane and hybridized to nick-translated pH-2IIa cDNA. The bands were identified by their molecular weights and hybridization intensities. The hybridization bands characteristic of the E^u-*grc*$^+$ region are indicated on the left, and the bands unique to E^--*grc* are indicated on the right.

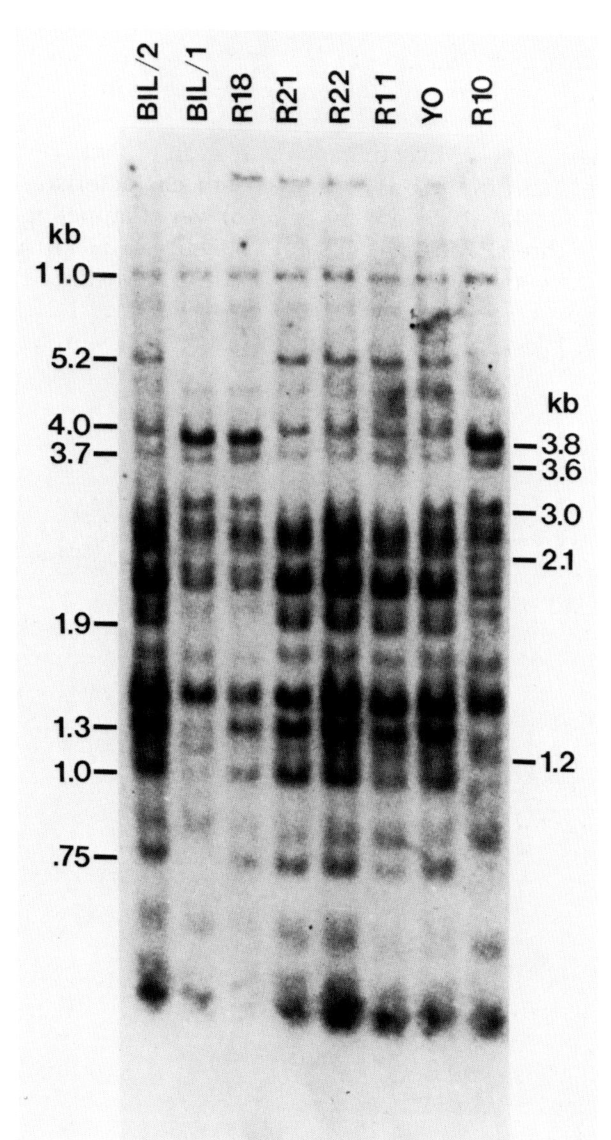

Fig. 6-3. Hybridization of Pvu II-digested genomic DNA. Seven micrograms of DNA were digested with Pvu II, resolved in 0.7% agarose at 40 V for 20 hours, blotted to a nitrocellulose membrane and hybridized to nick-translated pH-2IIa cDNA. The bands were identified by their molecular weights and hybridization intensities. The hybridization bands characteristic of the E^u -grc^+ region are indicated on the left, and the bands unique to E^--grc are indicated on the right.

identified. In those strains that are *grc*$^{+}$, Bgl II fragments of 4.2 kb, 3.7 kb, and 3.4 kb were always present, whereas in *grc*-bearing strains fragments of 7.2 kb and 2.3 kb were seen.

A similar pattern was seen on examination of Pvu II-digested DNA hybridized with the pH-2IIa probe. Four characteristic Pvu II fragments (5.2 kb, 4.0 kb, 3.7 kb, and 1.9 kb) were mapped to the E^{u}-*grc*$^{+}$ region, and three Pvu II bands (3.8 kb, 3.6 kb, and 3.0 kb) were mapped to the E^{-}-*grc* area. In addition, we identified distinct Pvu II bands that were present in *grc*-bearing strains (2.1 kb and 1.2 kb), and three unique markers (1.3 kb, 1.0 kb, and 0.75 kb) that were found in *grc*$^{+}$ strains.

Cloning the *RT1.E-grc* Region

Molecular studies indicate that the class I components of the RT1 system form a large multigene family with a high degree of DNA polymorphism. This contrasts markedly with the low level of serological polymorphism of RT1 (Cramer et al., 1978, 1986; Gill et al., 1983a). In both mouse (Steinmetz et al., 1982) and human (Orr et al., 1982), Southern blot analysis and molecular cloning have been used to show that the number of class I sequences is far greater than the actual number of class I antigens that can be serologically defined. This raises the question of whether the undefined class I genes are pseudogenes (Jeffreys & Harris, 1984; Steinmetz et al., 1981b) or genes differentially expressed during development. In order to approach this question in the rat, we used a similar approach to that taken in other species (Steinmetz et al., 1982; Weiss et al., 1984), generating a cosmid genomic library from the recombinant strain R21 ($A^{1}E^{u}$ *grc*$^{+}$).

We isolated 66 class I clones ranging in size from 26.6 to 55.4 kb with an average insert size of 41.4 kb of genomic DNA (Cortese Hassett et al., 1989). On the basis of Eco RI digestion, 52 of the 66 clones showed partial restriction map overlaps that allowed grouping of the class I clones into clusters, each containing 3 to 18 overlapping clones. A group of ten clones (cluster 1) was localized to the *RT1.E*^{u}-*grc*$^{+}$ region because they contained the Eco RI hybridizing fragments of 6.3 kb and 4.5 kb that are markers for this region (Cortese Hassett et al., 1986). Comparison of the hybridization patterns to class I probes of Eco RI-digested cosmid and R21 genomic DNA confirmed that the clones mapped to the *RT1.E*^{u}-*grc*$^{+}$ region. The class I hybridization patterns of a subset of the clones from cluster 1 is shown in Figure 6-4.

The clones of cluster 1 encompass approximately 41 kb of genomic DNA. Nearly the entire stretch of DNA represented by this cluster is contained in the largest clone 2L1 (41.4 kb), whereas the other nine clones represent subregions of the same genes. The clones in this

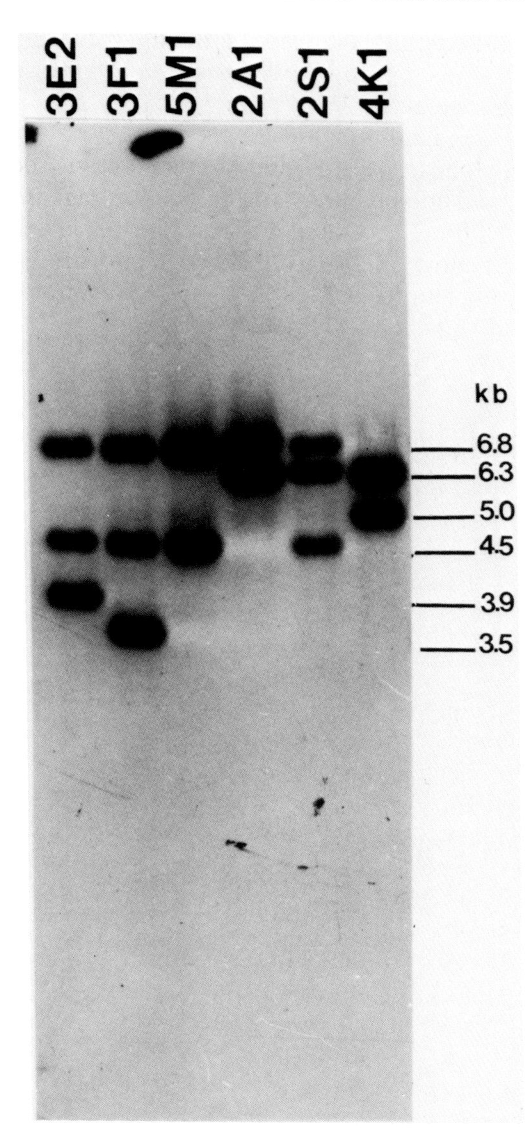

Fig. 6-4. Class I hybridization of a subset of cosmids from cluster 1. One microgram of cosmid DNA was digested with Eco RI, resolved in 1% agarose at 40 V for 16 hours and blotted to a nitrocellulose membrane. The Eco RI fragments were hybridized with 5 ng/ml of pAG64c-insert DNA. The sizes of the class I hybridizing fragments are listed on the far right.

cluster are significantly smaller than most of the other cosmids cloned, and this finding suggests instability in the host vector HB101 or an unusually high density of Mbo I sites in this region of DNA. However, with the exception of two clones that contained a deletion, all of the other clones contained contiguous segments of genomic DNA that appeared to contain four or possibly five class I genes.

The *RT1.E*^{u}-*grc*$^{+}$ region was analyzed further by isolating unique sequence fragments from the cluster 1 cosmids. The first fragments isolated and characterized from this region were of 1.4 kb and 1.7 kb.

These fragments were screened for the presence of repetitive elements by using total rat DNA as a probe, and the specificity of the purified fragments was tested by hybridization to a subset of the cosmid clones. The 1.4 kb fragment hybridized strongly to the 1.4 kb fragment found in all of the clones; some minimal cross-reactivity occurred with other fragments. The specificity of the 1.7 kb fragment was shown to be for the 6.3 kb class I fragment found in four of the ten cosmids in cluster 1. The most likely explanation for this finding is that the 1.7 kb fragment contains flanking sequences or coding regions of the 6.3 kb gene that were not homologous to the mouse cDNA clone pAG64c used in the screening.

To obtain some insight into the organization of the *grc*, these isolated specific sequences were hybridized to genomic DNA derived from five rat strains (BIL/1, R18, R21, R22, and BIL/2). The 1.4 kb and 1.7 kb probes hybridized strongly to specific fragments (1.4 kb and 6.3 kb, respectively) in all strains analyzed except BIL/1, which carries the *grc*. These results indicate that the *grc*-bearing strains have a deletion of at least 3.1 kb (1.4 + 1.7 kb). Since the BIL/1 strain does not express a 6.3 kb band, unlike all of the other strains, the deletion in the *grc* could conceivably be as large as 7-8 kb. The fragments hybridized strongly with the recombinant strain R18 whose site of recombination lies within the *grc* (Cortese Hassett et al., 1986), indicating that these fragments most likely map in the *grc-G/C* region and not in the *E* region.

Discussion

Tightly linked clusters of genes in the mouse have been shown to map predominantly to the *Qa* and *TLa* regions (Steinmetz et al., 1982; Weiss et al., 1984). The number of class I genes differs among haplotypes, particularly in the *Tla* region. Extensive deletions have been reported in the *Qa* region (O'Neil et al., 1986) and in the *TLa* region (Hammerling et al., 1985; LaLanne et al., 1985) without apparent deleterious effects. The identification of four or five tightly clustered genes in cluster 1 of the rat genome suggests that these genes could map to the *Tla* equivalent in the rat, *RT1.G/C*. The *Qa/Tla* genes have been postulated to play a role in the earliest stages of development, and recent studies indicate that the Qa-2 subregion of the MHC encodes the product of the *Ped* (preimplantation embryo development) gene (Warner et al., 1987). The presence of a similar group of genes in the rat suggests that they are biologically important. Thus, the defects seen in the *grc* animals may result from the loss of *G/C* genes that are involved in various stages of development.

Preliminary studies have shown that *grc*-bearing rats have an increased susceptibility to chemically induced carcinogenesis (Melhem et al., 1987). This observation suggests that the deletions may play a role in carcinogenesis, since somatic or germline deletions have been implicated in the inactivation of resistance genes in certain forms of cancer (Hansen & Cavenee, 1988; Weissman et al., 1987). In addition, retrovirus-like sequences have been isolated from the *TL* locus of C57BL/10 mice (Pampeno & Meruelo, 1986), and one sequence has been shown to contain murine leukemia virus-related sequences bounded by long terminal repeats. This finding again suggests a relationship between MHC-linked genes and carcinogenesis.

It has been proposed that a locus in or near the human major histocompatibility complex (HLA) contributes to involuntary fetal loss and neural tube defects (Gill, 1983, 1987; Schacter et al., 1984). The isolation of genes from animal models and the development of specific probes could be used to test this hypothesis. It has been demonstrated in the rat that the MHC-linked *grc* is associated with developmental defects and that strains carrying this complex have an increased susceptibility to cancer. Therefore, the *grc*-bearing rat provides a convenient model with which to explore the relationship between embryogenesis and carcinogenesis.

Acknowledgments

This work was supported by grants from the National Institutes of Health (CA 18659, HD 08662, and HD 0988), the Tim Caracio Memorial Cancer Fund, the Beaver County Cancer Society, and the Pathology Education and Research Foundation.

References

Alton, A. K., Silver, L. M., Artzt, K., and Bennett, D. 1980. Molecular analysis of the genetic relationship of trans-interacting factors at the T/t complex. *Nature* 288:368.

Artzt, K., Lockwood, M., Bennett, D., Kunz, H. W., and Gill, T. J. III. 1982. Serological evidence for a partial t-haplotype in the rat. *J. Immunogenet.* 9:371.

Artzt, K., McCormick, P., and Bennett, D. 1982b. Gene mapping within the T/t complex of the mouse. I. t-Lethal genes are not allelic. *Cell* 28:463.

Bennett, D. 1975. The T-locus of the mouse. *Cell* 6:441.

Bennett, D. 1981. T/t locus, its role in embryogenesis and its relation to classical histocompatibility systems. *Prog. Allergy* 29:35.

Brickell, P. M., Latchman, D. S., Murphy, D., Willison, K., and Rigby, P. W. J. 1983. Activation of a Qa/Tla class I major histocompatibility antigen gene is a general feature of oncogenesis in the mouse. *Nature* 306:756.

Brickell, P. M., Latchman, D. S., Murphy, D., Willison, K., and Rigby, P. W. J. 1985. The class I major histocompatibility antigen gene activated in a line of SV40-transformed mouse cells is H-2D^{d}, not Qa/Tla. *Nature* 316:162.

Cortese Hassett, A. L. 1987. A molecular analysis of the major histocompatibility complex of the rat (RT1) and it's linked regions. Ph.D. dissertation, University of Pittsburgh.

Cortese Hassett, A. L., Stranick, K. S., Locker, J., Kunz, H. W., and Gill, T. J. III. 1986. Molecular analysis of the rat MHC. I. Delineation of the major regions in the MHC and in the *grc*. *J. Immunol.* 137:373.

Cortese Hassett, A. L., Locker, J., Rupp, G., Kunz, H. W., and Gill, T. J. III. 1989. Molecular analysis of the rat MHC. II. Isolation of genes that map to the *RT1.E-grc* region. *J. Immunol.* 142:2089.

Cramer, D. V., Davis, B. K., Shonnard, J. W., Stark, O., and Gill, T. J. III. 1978. Phenotypes of the major histocompatibility complex in wild rats of different geographic origins. *J. Immunol.* 120:179.

Cramer, D. V., Mowery, P. A., Hoffman, S., and Chakravarti, A. 1986. Gene diversity in natural rat populations. *Rat Newsletter* 17:19.

Dausset, J. and Svejgaard, A. 1977. *HLA and Disease*. Baltimore: Williams & Wilkins.

Drescher, C. K., Jargiello, P., Gill, T. J. III., and Kunz, H. W. 1980. Analysis of the giemsa-banding patterns of the chromosomes from rats carrying the genes of the growth and reproduction complex (*grc*). *J. Immunogenet.* 7:427.

Frischauf, A.-M. 1985. The T/t complex of the mouse. *Trends Genet.* 1:100.

Gill, T. J. III. 1983. Immunogenetics of spontaneous abortion in humans. *Transplantation* 35:1.

Gill, T. J. III. 1987. Genetic factors in fetal losses. *Am. J. Reprod. Immunol. Microbiol.* 15:133.

Gill, T. J. III and Kunz, H. W. 1979. Gene complex controlling growth and fertility linked to the major histocompatibility complex in the rat. *Am. J. Pathol.* 6:185.

Gill, T. J. III, Cramer, D. V., Kunz, H. W., and Misra, D. N. 1983a. Structure and function of the major histocompatibility complex of the rat. *J. Immunogenet.* 10:261.

Gill, T. J. III, Siew, S., and Kunz, H. W. 1983b. Major histocompatibility complex (MHC)-linked genes affecting development. *J. Exp. Zool.* 228:325.

Gill, T. J. IV, Gill, T. J. III, Kunz, H. W., Musto, N. A., and Bardin, C. W. 1984. Genetic and morphometric studies of the heterogeneity in the testicular defect of the H^{re} rat. *Biol. Reprod.* 31:595.

Ginsberg, L. and Hillman, N. 1975. ATP metabolism in t^n/t^n mouse embryos. *J. Embryol. Exp. Morphol.* 33:715.

Gotze, D. (ed.) 1977. *The Histocompatibility System in Man and Animals.* New York: Springer-Verlag.

Green, M. C. (ed.) 1981. *Genetic Variants and Strains of the Laboratory Mouse.* Stuttgart: Gustav Fischer Verlag.

Greiner, D. L., Gill, T. J. III, Kunz, H. W., and Gay, V. L. 1980. Reproductive endocrine profile of a strain of rats which exhibits aspermatogenesis and reduced growth. *Biol. Reprod.* 23:564.

Hammerling, U. L., Ronne, H., Widmar, E., Servenius, B., Denaro, M., Rask, L., and Petersen, P. A. 1985. Gene duplications in the TL region of the mouse major histocompatibility complex. *EMBO J.* 4:1431.

Hansen, M. F. and Cavenee, W. K. 1988. Retinoblastoma and the progression of tumor genetics. *Trends Genet.* 4:125.

Hashimoto, U., Suzuki, A., Yamakawa, T., Miyashita, N., and Moriwaki, K. 1983. Expression of GM1 and GD1a in mouse liver is linked to the H-2 complex on chromosome 17. *J. Biochem.* (*Tokyo*) 94:2043.

Jeffreys, A. J. and Harris, S. 1984. Pseudogenes. *BioEssays* 1:253.

Klein, J. and Hammerberg, C. 1977. The control of differentiation by the T complex. *Immunol. Rev.* 33:70.

Kunz, H. W., Gill, T. J. III, Dixon, B., Shonnard, J. W., Davis, B. K., and Hansen, C. T. 1977. Genetic and immunological characterization of naturally occurring recombinant B3 rats. *Immunogenetics* 5:271.

Lalanne, J. L., Transky, C., Guerin, S., Darche, S., Meulien, P., and Kourilsky, P. 1985. Expression of class I genes in the major histocompatibility complex: identification of eight distinct mRNA's in DBA/2 mouse liver. *Cell* 41:469.

Lingwood, C., Kunz, H. W., and Gill, T. J. III. 1985. Deficiency in the regulation of testicular galactolipid sulfotransferase in rats carrying the growth and reproduction complex (*grc*). *Biochem. J.* 231:401.

Lyon, M. F. 1981. The t-complex and the genetical control of development. *Symp. Zool. Soc. Lond.* 47:455.

Melhem, M. F., Rao, K. N., Kunz, H. W., and Gill, T. J. III. 1987. Susceptibility of *grc*-bearing rats to DEN and its relationship to HMP pathway. In *Agents and Processes in Chemical Carcinogenesis.* Sardenia, Italy.

O'Neil, A. E., Reid, K., Garberi, J. C., Karl, M., and Flaherty, L. 1986. Extensive deletions in the Q region of the mouse major histocompatibility complex. *Immunogenetics* 24:368.

Orr, H. T., Bach, F. H., Pleogh, H. L., Strominger, J. L., Kavathos, P., and Demars, R. 1982. Use of HLA loss mutants to analyze the structure of the human major histocompatibility complex. *Nature* 296:454.

Pampeno, C. L. and Meruelo, D. 1986. Isolation of a retrovirus-like sequence from the TL locus of the C57BL/10 murine major histocompatibility complex. *J. Virol.* 58:296.

Rao, K. N., Shinozuka, H., Kunz, H. W., and Gill, T. J. III. 1984. Enhanced susceptibility to a chemical carcinogen in rats carrying MHC-linked genes influencing development (*grc*). *Int. J. Cancer* 34:113.

Schacter, B., Weitkamp, L. R., and Johnson, W. E. 1984. Parental HLA compatibility, fetal wastage and neural tube defects: evidence for a T/t-like locus in humans. *Am. J. Hum. Genet.* 36:1082.

Schaid, D. J., Kunz, H. W., and Gill, T. J. III. 1982. Genic interaction causing embryonic mortality in the rat: epistasis between the Tal and *grc* genes. *Genetics* 100:615.

Scott, M. R. D., Westphal, K. H., and Rigby, P. W. J. 1983. Activation of mouse genes in transformed cells. *Cell* 34:557.

Shin, H.-S., Flaherty, L., Artzt, K., Bennett, D., and Ravetch, J. 1984. Inversion in the H-2 complex of t-haplotypes in mice. *Nature* 306:380.

Shur, B. D. and Bennett, D. 1979. A specific defect in galactosyltransferase regulation on sperm binding to the egg zona pellucida. *Dev. Biol.* 71:243.

Silver, L. M. 1981. Genetic organization of the mouse to complex. *Cell* 27:239.

Silver, L. M., White, M., and Artzt, K. 1980. Evidence for unequal crossing over within the mouse T/t complex. *Proc. Natl. Acad. Sci. USA* 77:6077.

Silver, L. M., Uman, J., Danska, J., and Garrels, J. I. 1983. A diversified set of testicular cell proteins specified by genes within the mouse t complex. *Cell* 35:35.

Snell, G. D. 1968. The H-2 locus of the mouse: observations and speculations concerning its comparative genetics and its polymorphism. *Folia Biol. (Praha)* 14:335.

Steinmetz, M., Frelinger, J. G., Fisher, D., Hunkapillar, T., Pereira, D., Weissman, S. M., Uehara, H., Nathenson, S., and Hood, L. 1981a. Three cDNA clones encoding mouse transplantation antigens: homology to immunoglobulin genes. *Cell* 24:125.

Steinmetz, M., Moore, K. W., Frelinger, J. G., Sher, B. T., Shen, F.-W., Boyse, E. A., and Hood, L. 1981b. A pseudogene homologous to mouse transplantation antigens: transplantation antigens are encoded by eight exons that correlate with protein domains. *Cell* 25:683.

Steinmetz, M., Winoto, A., Minard, K., and Hood, L. 1982. Clusters of genes encoding mouse transplantation antigens. *Cell* 28:489.

Warner, C. M., Gollnick, S. O., Flaherty, L., and Goldbard, S. B. 1987. Analysis of Qa-2 antigen expression by preimplantation mouse embryos: possible relationship to the preimplantation-embryo-development (*Ped*) gene product. *Biol. Reprod.* 326:611.

Weiss, E. H., Golden, L., Fahrner, K., Mellor, A. L., Devlin, J. J., Bullman, H., Tiddens, H., Bud, H., and Flavell, R. A. 1984. Organization and evolution of the class I gene family in the major histocompatibility complex of the C57BL/10 mouse. *Nature* 310:650.

Weissman, B. E., Saxon, P. J., Pasquale, S. R., Jones, G. R., Geiser, A. G., and Stanbridge, E. J. 1987. Introduction of a normal human chromosome 11 into a Wilm's tumor cell line controls its tumorigenic expression. *Science* 236:175.

Willison, K. R., Dudley, K., and Potter, J. 1986. Molecular cloning and sequence analysis of a haploid expressed gene encoding t complex polypeptide 1. *Cell* 44:727.

7

Expression of Major Histocompatibility Complex Class I Genes in Murine Extra-Embryonic Tissues

ANDREW L. MELLOR, KAREN L. PHILPOTT, SOHAILA RASTAN, and SHEILA BROWN

Genes of the class I family of the major histocompatibility complex (MHC) encode cell surface polypeptides that associate with and present peptides to cytotoxic T cells. Hence, they are important genes in the regulation and modulation of immune responses to foreign antigens. As their name suggests, the polypeptides encoded by MHC class I (MHC I) genes provoke strong immune responses when tissues are grafted between genetically disparate individuals of the same species. Graft rejection is mediated by effector T cells, many of which respond directly to the presence of donor MHC I antigens on the surface of cells in the grafted tissues. This allogeneic response to foreign MHC antigens is usually a barrier to successful tissue grafting unless steps are taken to match genes at the MHC.

In mammals, the developing conceptus is in intimate contact with the maternal tissues and blood supply that carry effector T cells. Even though the conceptus inherits MHC genes from the father there is no obvious immunological response by the maternal immune system directed against fetal tissues even though paternal MHC antigens are incompatible with maternal MHC genes; this is generally true as MHC polymorphism is high in many species of mammals. Several models have been put forward in attempts to explain this apparent paradox (Medawar, 1953; Warner et al., 1988). Extra-embryonic tissues, such as placenta and yolk sac, which are derived from embryonic cell lineages, may serve as a protective immunological barrier by expressing paternally inherited MHC antigens that perhaps sequester and prevent access of maternal lymphocytes to the embryo (Hunziker et al., 1984). Alternatively, unresponsiveness to paternally inherited MHC gene products may be maintained by soluble factors secreted by placental tissues (Duc et al., 1985; Voisin et al., 1986) or by suppressor cells (Clark et al., 1983). Finally, the conceptus may escape rejection *in utero* if paternally inherited MHC gene expression is modulated or prevented completely. Yet, previous studies suggest that paternally inherited MHC I antigens are expressed in murine placental and embryonic tissues (Carter, 1978; Chatterjee-Hasrouni & Lala, 1979, 1982; Jenkinson & Owen, 1980) making this last explanation for the lack of fetal rejection unlikely. However, in most of these studies MHC antigens were detected using polyclonal antisera, and positive reactivity may be partially attributable to the presence of nonclassical murine MHC I antigens.

In order to clarify this paradox further and provide more information about the spatial distribution and relative levels of expression of MHC I antigens in murine tissues associated with the developing conceptus, we have studied the transcription of MHC I genes inherited from each parent in these tissues using highly sensitive and allele-specific nucleic acid probes.

Detection of MHC I RNA Transcripts by *In Situ* Hybridization

Preparation of RNA Probes

The spatial distribution and relative levels of MHC I gene transcription in a C57BL/10 (B10) conceptus were ascertained by preparing a ^{35}S-radiolabeled class I RNA probe and hybridizing it to thin sections taken from a developing fetus 13.5 days *postcoitus*. The RNA probe was prepared by subcloning the pH2III cDNA insert (Steinmetz et al., 1981) into the vector pSP64 in both orientations. This allowed synthesis of single-stranded sense (+) or anti-sense (−), mRNA by SP6 RNA polymerase under the control of the transcriptional promoter present in the pSP64 vector adjacent to the pH2III insert (Fig. 7-1). This probe detects all class I genes present in the mouse genome and does not therefore discriminate between MHC I gene transcripts from different MHC genes within this large family.

Localization of MHC I Transcripts Present in Fetal Tissues

The results of hybridizing radiolabeled MHC class I RNA probes to tissue sections from a developing conceptus are shown in Figure 7-2. High densities of silver grains appear in the autoradiographic film over certain regions of the placenta when anti-sense RNA probes are used (Fig. 7-2A & C). Specificity of hybridization of the probe to MHC I transcripts present in the tissues was shown using a probe of the same sense as the mRNA for a negative control (Fig. 7-2B and 7-2D). The greatest density of silver grains is detected over the spongiotrophoblast (s) region of the placenta, although the grain density is also

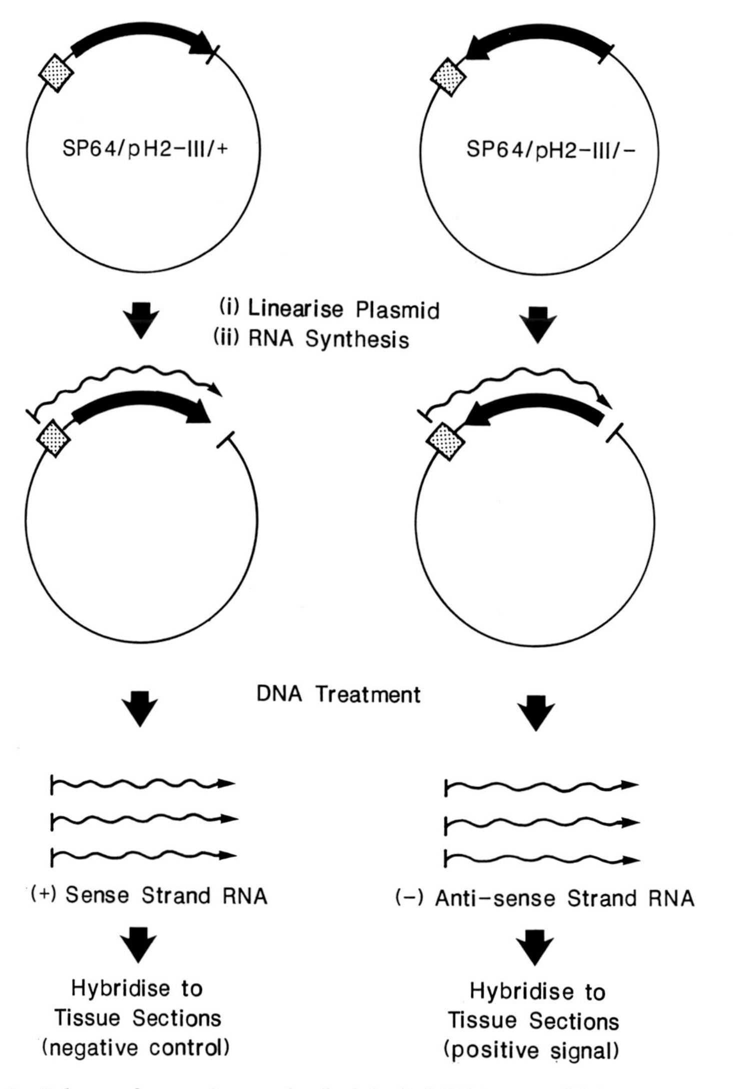

Fig. 7-1. Scheme for synthesis of radiolabeled RNA using SP6 transcriptional promoters (stippled box). Thick arrow indicates position and orientation of pH2III insert in SP6 plasmids.

above background over the decidual (d) and labyrinthine (l) layers. Careful inspection of the yolk sac membranes also reveals clusters of silver grains over the parietal endoderm (p) layer and low, but significant, densities of silver grains over the visceral yolk sac (v) membranes (Fig. 7-2E). Higher densities of silver grains can be seen spread uniformly over the internal face of the uterine wall (u). In contrast, there is no detectable grain density above background over tissues of

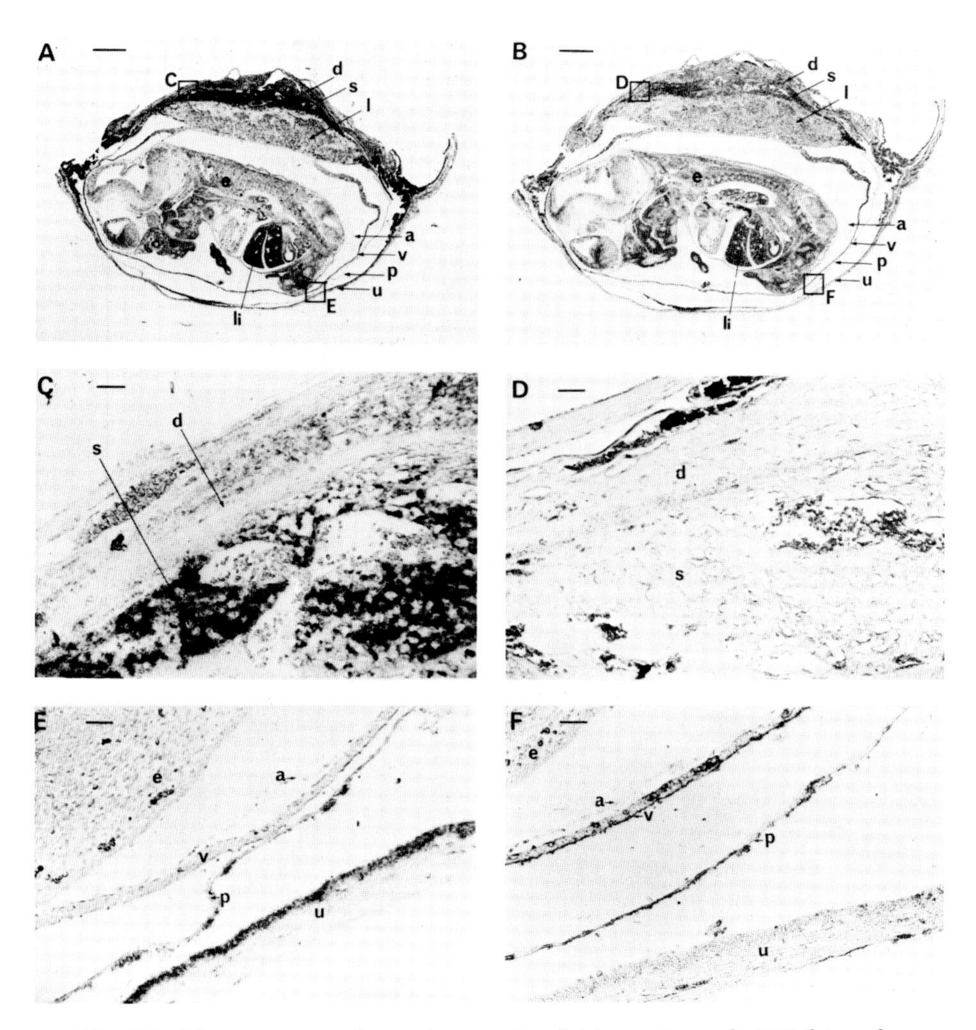

Fig. 7-2. Phase-contrast photomicrographs of thin sections of a B10 fetus after hybridization to MHC Class I anti-sense (A, C & E) or sense (B, D & F) RNA probes. Autoradiographic film was layered over the hybridized sections and exposed for 1 month. Boxes on A and B indicate fields of view on C, E, D and F. Spacebars represent 1 mm on A and B or 50 μm on C, D, E and F. a, amnion; li, liver; for other tissues see text. Histological assignments were confirmed by H & E staining of adjacent tissue sections.

the developing embryo itself, except for the liver (Fig. 7-2A). This shows that there are high steady-state levels of MHC I gene transcripts in certain regions of the placenta, with lower but significant levels in the yolk sac membranes, and very few MHC I gene transcripts in the tissues of the embryo at day 13.5 of gestation.

Table 7-1. Details of mouse strains and MHC haplotypes

Matings	MHC Class I Genes		Genetic Background
(B10 × CBA)F1	K^b D^b	K^k D^k	B10 + CBA
(CBA × B10)F1	K^k D^k	K^b D^b	CBA + B10
(B10 × B10.BR)F1	K^b D^b	K^k D^k	B10
(B10.BR × B10)F1	K^k D^k	K^b D^b	B10
(B10 × B6.bm1)F1	K^b D^b	K^{bm1} D^b	B10(B6)
(B6.bm1 × B10)F1	K^{bm1} D^b	K^b D^b	(B6)B10
B10	K^b D^b	K^b D^b	B10
CBA	K^k D^k	K^k D^k	CBA

Genetic Characterization of MHC I RNA Transcripts

Since the pH2III probe cannot be used to discriminate between different MHC I genes by hybridization, the *in situ* results above did not allow us to determine which genes were being transcribed in extra-embryonic tissues. Genetic characterization of the MHC I transcripts present in extra-embryonic tissues was achieved by (1) extracting RNA from dissected fetal tissues of the conceptus (placenta, yolk sac, and embryo) and subjecting this RNA to S1 nuclease protection analysis using DNA probes specific for particular MHC I genes and (2) setting up matings between mice with different MHC haplotypes and/or non-MHC background genes so that the parental source of MHC I genes could be determined unequivocally (Table 7-1). RNA extracted from tissues was first subjected to Northern blot analysis to determine its integrity and to ensure that RNA concentrations were exactly matched between samples.

Northern Blot Analysis of Conceptal RNA

RNA samples obtained from placenta, yolk sac, and embryo tissues of developing mice at day 13.5 of gestation were separated on a denaturing formaldehyde/agarose gel and transferred to nitrocellulose filters by blotting. Fetal mice from eight different matings were used as sources of RNA for this analysis (Table 7-1). The result of probing these RNA samples with a ^{32}P-radiolabeled MHC class I specific DNA probe is shown in Figure 7-3. High levels of 1.6 kb MHC class I RNA transcripts are present in placental tissues, with lower levels in yolk sac tissues and barely detectable amounts in embryonic tissues. These results are in agreement with the findings of the *in situ* hybridization results presented above.

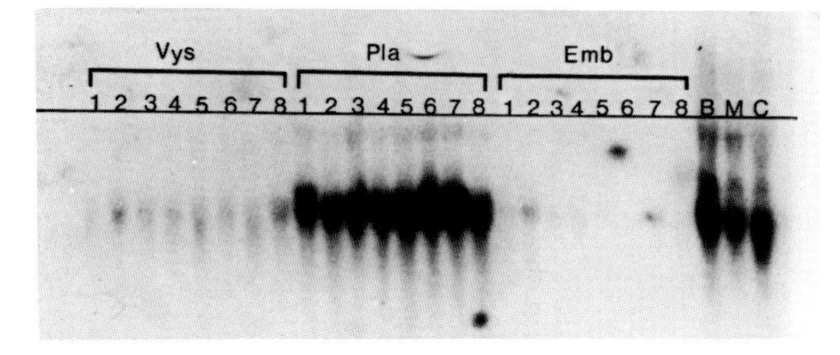

Fig. 7-3. Northern blot analysis of 10 μg samples of RNA extracted from fetal tissue samples. Control RNA samples from B10 (B), B6.bm1 (M) and CBA (C) spleen are also included. Filters were hybridized to a ^{32}P-radiolabeled MHC Class I DNA probe. Vys, yolk-sac; Pla, placenta; Emb, embryo. Numbers refer to the fetal genotypes indicated in Table 7-1.

S1 Analysis of RNA Extracted from Conceptal Tissues

RNA transcripts derived from particular MHC I genes can be distinguished by S1 nuclease protection analysis using end-labeled DNA probes derived from the MHC I gene in question (Philpott et al., 1988). Suitable probes, spanning a highly polymorphic region in exon 3 (Mellor, 1986) and extending beyond the intron/exon boundary (Fig. 7-4B), were prepared from several cloned MHC I genes (H-2K^{b}, H-2D^{b}, H-2K^{bm1}, H-2K^{k}). To carry out S1 nuclease protection analysis, probes were end-labeled and hybridized to RNA extracted from tissues of developing mice with the genotypes indicated in Table 7-1. The results of S1 nuclease protection analysis using a probe derived from the H-2K^{b} gene are shown in Figure 7-4A. Transcripts of the H-2K^{b} gene protect a 207 bp fragment of the end-labeled DNA probe. H-2K^{b} gene transcripts are detected in adult spleen RNA from B10 mice (lane B), but are absent in RNA from CBA mice (lane C), as expected. However, a low level of cross-protection is detected in RNA samples from B6.bm1 mice (lane M).

Protected 207 bp fragments are present in all RNA samples extracted from placental tissues (Pla), except for RNA from CBA mice (lane 8). Since the H-2K^{b} gene is inherited paternally in some cases shown here (lanes, 2, 4, and 6; see Table 7-1), it follows that paternally inherited H-2K^{b} genes are transcriptionally active in placental tissues. Moreover, the level of transcription of this gene is the same irrespective of differences in genetic backgrounds. The quantity of H-K^{b} transcripts detected is slightly, but reproducibly higher for reciprocal matings when the H-2K^{b} gene is inherited only from the mother (lanes 1, 3, and 5). The most likely reason for this is that dissected placental tissue contains some maternal tissue that is closely associated with tissues derived from embryonic cell lineages (Rossant & Croy, 1985).

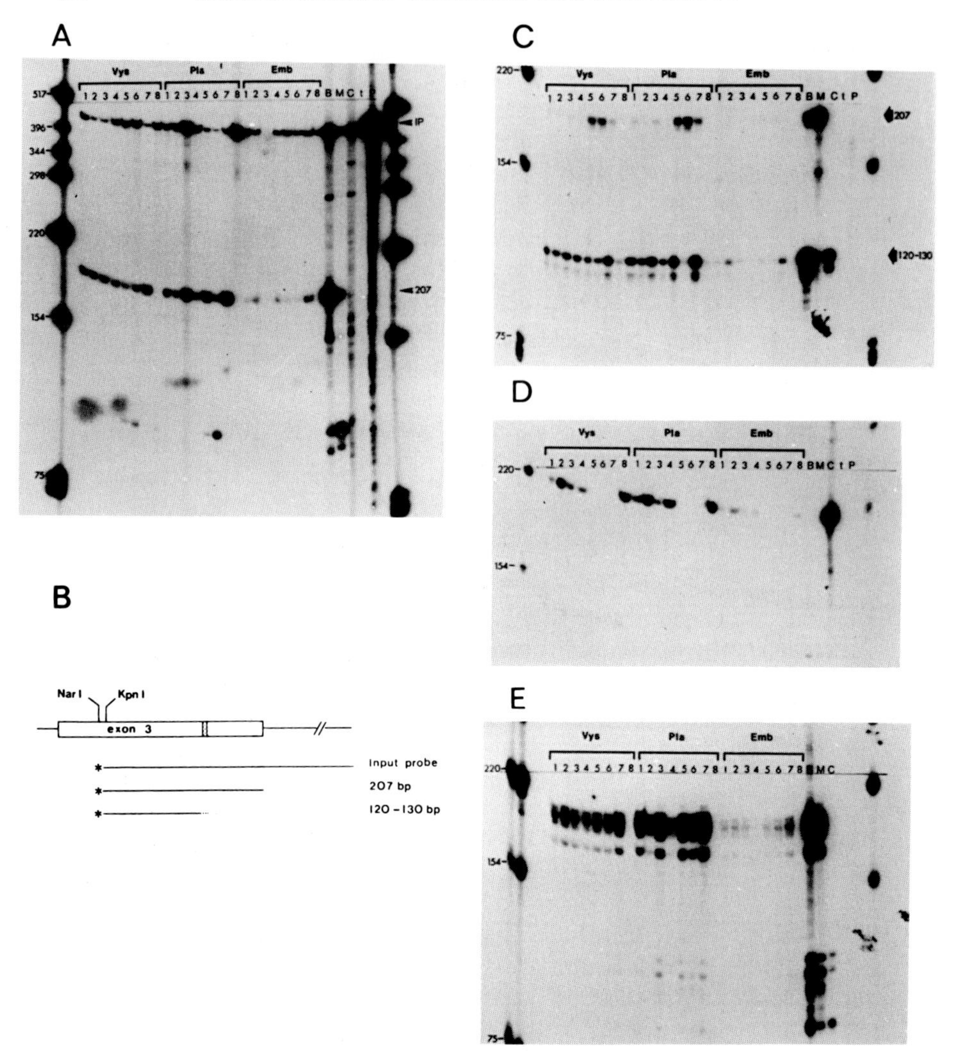

Fig. 7-4. S1 nuclease protection analysis of fetal RNA samples. RNA samples are as indicated in Figure 7-3 except only 2.5 μg of RNA was used for Pla samples. Probes used for S1 analysis were H-2K^{b} (A), H-2K^{bm1} (C), H-2K^{k} (D) or H-2D^{b} (E). Diagram (B) shows how S1 nuclease reduces size of end-labeled (*) input probe to specific size protected by hybridization to RNA transcripts. A polymorphic region in exon 3 (stippled box) prevents protection of non-homologous DNA fragments. For methods see Philpott et al., 1988. Sizes of marker DNA fragments are indicated on the left.

Similarly, H-$2K^b$ gene transcripts are detected in RNA extracted from yolk sac membranes (Fig. 7-4A, Vys). Fewer H-$2K^b$ gene transcripts are present in yolk sac than in placental tissues from the same mice (note that only 2.5 μg of placental RNA was used, whereas 10 μg was used for other tissues). No consistent quantitative difference in amount of H-$2K^b$ transcript is detected among any of the yolk sac RNA samples studied, except for a slightly higher level of H-$2K^b$ transcripts in B10 yolk sac RNA (lane 7). This is explained by the fact that two copies of the H-$2K^b$ gene, one from each parent, are inherited in this case, whereas all other mice inherit a single H-$2K^b$ gene from one parent.

Very few H-$2K^b$ gene transcripts are detected in RNA extracted from embryos (Fig. 7-4A, Emb). This result is consistent with the *in situ* hybridization and Northern blot results presented above.

Similar results were obtained when probes from the H-$2K^{bm1}$, H-$2K^k$, and H-$2D^b$ genes were used to detect homologous transcripts in RNA extracted from placental, yolk sac, and embryonic tissues (Fig. 7-4C–E, respectively). Probes derived from MHC class I genes mapping to the Qa-2 region were also used in S1 nuclease protection analysis of these RNA samples. Transcripts of the Q10 gene (Mellor, 1986) were detected in yolk sac RNA from B10 and CBA concepti (Fig. 7-5, lanes 1 & 2) and at low levels in B10 and CBA embryos (Fig. 7-5, lanes 5 & 6). This last result is probably due to Q10 gene expression in the liver. However, no Q10 gene transcripts could be detected in B10 or CBA placental RNA (Fig. 7-5, lanes 3 & 4). Transcripts of genes encoding Qa-2 antigens (Mellor, 1986) could be detected in placental RNA samples extracted from concepti with a mother of H-2^b (Qa-2^+) haplotype, indicating that maternal Qa-2^+ lymphoid cells are present in the placenta. Low levels of Qa-2^+ transcripts were also detected in the embryonic RNA (data not shown).

Conclusions

We have used the technique of hybridization of a MHC class I RNA probe to thin sections of a developing conceptus 13.5 day *postcoitus*, to study the distribution of H-2 gene transcription in a midgestation conceptus. Our results are rather surprising, since they suggest that the transcriptional activity of these genes is highest in the extra-embryonic tissues constituting the placenta and yolk sac. In contrast, all tissues of the embryo itself, except for liver, have very few H-2 gene transcripts at this period in gestation.

The results of S1 nuclease protection analyses reveal that the H-2 gene transcripts present in extra-embryonic tissues are derived in approximately equal amounts from H-2 genes inherited from each parent. Further, there is no detectable quantitative effect on H-2 gene transcription of different genetic backgrounds. This distribution of H-

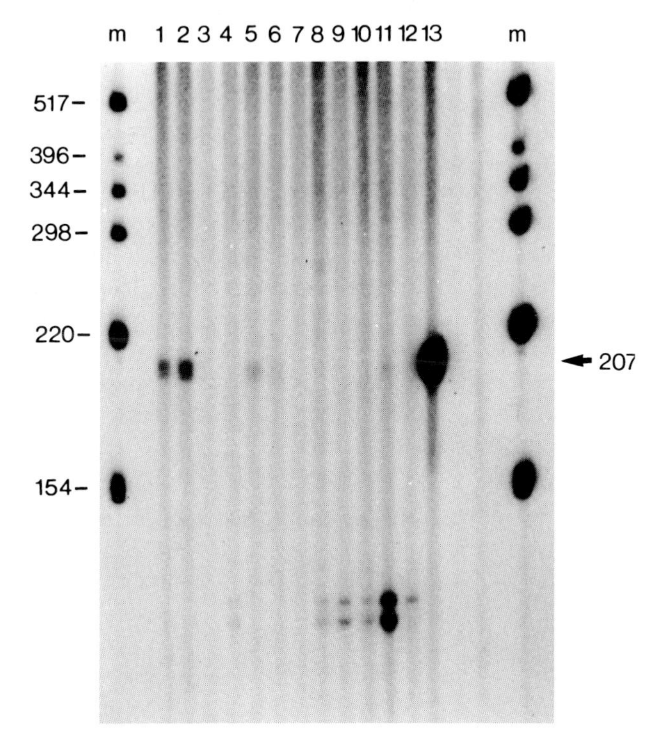

Fig. 7-5. S1 nuclease analysis of fetal RNA samples using a Q10 DNA probe. RNA samples in lanes 1 to 6 are described in the text. Negative control samples are as follows; L cells transfected with B10 Q4 (lane 7), Q6 (lane 8), Q7 (lane 9) genes, untransfected L cells (lane 10), CBA spleen (lane 11), B10 spleen (lane 12). Positive control RNA sample lane 13) is from adult liver.

2 transcripts strongly suggests that there are no unfavorable immunological consequences of expressing paternal MHC class I antigens in the placental tissues, which are intimately associated with the maternal blood supply and thus exposed to the maternal immune system. Indeed, it is very striking that the tissues that contain transcriptionally active H-2 genes are arranged around the developing embryo so as to form a protective layer for the embryo. Paternally inherited MHC I genes are transcribed in relatively high levels, similar to those observed in adult spleen. Since these genes are expressed in cells of embryonic lineages that are intimately associated with maternal blood supply in the placenta, it is unlikely that paternally inherited MHC I antigens would not be accessible to cells of the maternal immune system. Moreover, the distribution of MHC class I transcripts suggest that there is a requirement for expression of paternally inherited MHC I antigens in the immediate vicinity of the maternal blood supply to

the placenta. This may be important in inducing protective immunity for the conceptus against the maternal immune system. It is conceivable that rejection of conceptual tissue, and hence the conceptus itself, does not normally occur because paternally inherited MHC class II antigens are not expressed. Depletion of class-II-bearing cells from grafts has been shown to result in increased graft survival (Billingham, 1971; Silvers et al., 1987). Although there is no evidence for expression of paternally inherited MHC class II antigens in placenta (Chatterjee-Hasrouni & Lala, 1981; Jenkinson & Searle, 1979; Raghupathy et al., 1981), class-II-bearing cells, presumably of maternal origin, are present in the decidual region (Jenkinson & Searle, 1979; Wood, 1980). These cells could potentially function in antigen presentation to maternal helper T cells. Alternatively, the observed lack of response could be due to local suppression in the vicinity of the placenta (Clark et al., 1983; Tawfik et al., 1986) or to the induction of specific tolerance. Some workers have noted that nonclassical MHC I antigens are expressed in extra-embryonic membranes, e.g., the Q10 gene in the yolk sac. It has therefore been suggested that these antigens, which are structurally homologous to H-2 antigens, could interfere with anti-paternal H-2 responses (see Philpott et al., 1988 for a full discussion). In conclusion, it is clear that survival of the conceptus *in utero* is not adversely affected by the presence of high levels of paternally inherited MHC I antigens on extra-embryonic membranes closely associated with the maternal blood supply.

References

Billingham, R. E. 1971. The passenger cell concept in transplantation immunity. *Cell Immunol.* 2:1.

Carter, J. 1978. The expression of surface antigens on three trophoblastic tissues in the mouse. *J. Reprod. Fertil.* 54:433.

Chatterjee-Hasrouni, S. and Lala, P. K. 1979. Localization of H-2 antigens on mouse trophoblast cells. *J. Exp. Med.* 149:1238.

Chatterjee-Hasrouni, S. and Lala, P. K. 1981. MHC antigens on mouse trophoblast cells: paucity of Ia antigens despite the presence of H-2K and D. *Immunology* 127:2070.

Chatterjee-Hasrouni, S. and Lala, P. K. 1982. Localization of paternal H-2K antigens on murine trophoblast cells *in vivo*. *J. Exp. Med.* 155:1679.

Clark, D. A., Slapsys, R. M., Croy, B. A. and Rossant, J. 1983. Suppressor cell activity in uterine decidua correlates with success or failure of murine pregnancies. *J. Immunol.* 131:540.

Duc, H. T., Masse, A., Bobe, P., Kinsky, G. and Voisin G. A. 1985. Derivation of humoral and cellular allo reactions by placental extracts. *J. Reprod. Immunol.* 7:27.

Hunziker, R. D., Gambel, P. and Wegmann, T. G. 1984. Placenta as a selective barrier to cellular traffic. *J. Immunol.* 133:667.

Jenkinson, E. J. and Owen, V. 1980. Ontogeny and distribution of major histocompatibility complex (MHC) antigens on mouse placental trophoblast. *J. Reprod. Immunol.* 2:173.

Jenkinson, E. J. and Searle, F. 1979. Ia antigen expression on the developing mouse embryo and placenta. *J. Reprod. Immunol.* 1:3.

Medawar, P. B. 1953. Some immunological and endocrinological problems raised by the evolution of viviparity in vertebrates. *Symp. Soc. Exp. Biol.* 44:320–338.

Mellon, A. 1986. Molecular genetics of class I genes in the mammalian histocompatability complex. In *Oxford Surveys on Eukaryotic Genes* (N. Maclean, ed.), Oxford: Oxford University Press, pp. 95.

Philpott, K. L., Rastan, S., Brown, S. and Mellox, A. L. 1988. Expression of H-2 class I genes in murine extra-embryonic tissues. *Immunology* 64:479.

Raghupathy, R., Singh, B., Leigh, J. B. and Wegmann, T. G. 1981. The ontogeny and turnover kinetics of paternal MHC antigenic determinants on the allogeneic murine placenta. *J. Immunol.* 127:2074.

Rossant, J. and Croy, B. A. 1985. Genetic identification of tissue of origin of cellular populations within the mouse placenta. *J. Embryol. Exp. Morphol.* 86:177.

Silvers, W. K. and Kimura, H., Desquenne-Clark and Miyamoto, M. 1987. Some new perspectives on transplantation immunity and tolerance. *Immunol. Today.* 8:185.

Steinmetz, M., Frelinger, J. G., Fisher, D., Hunkapiller, T., Periera, D., Weissman, S. M., Uchara, H., Nathenson, S. and Hood, L. 1981. Three cDNA clones encoding mouse transplantation antigens: homology to immunoglobulin genes. *Cell* 24:125.

Tawfik, O. W., Hunt, J. S. and Wood, G. W. 1986. Implication of prostaglandin E2 in soluble factor-mediated immune suppression by murine decidual cells. *Am. J. Reprod. Immunol.* 12:111.

Voisin, J. E., Kinsky, R. G. and Voisin, G. A. 1986. Maternal alloimmune reactions towards the murine conceptus and graft versus host reaction (GVHR). II. Inhibition of priming by placental extracts. *J. Reprod. Immunol.* 9:85.

Warner, C. M., Brownell, M. S. and Ewoldsen, M. A. 1988. Why aren't embryos rejected by their mothers? *Biol. Reprod.* 38:17.

Wood, G. W. 1980. Immunohistological identification of macrophages in murine placental, yolk-sac membranes and pregnant uteri. *Placenta* 1:309.

Part 2

DECIDUAL EFFECTOR CELLS

8

Human Trophoblast-Decidua Interaction *in Vitro*

Y. W. LOKE, ANNA GRABOWSKA, and ASHLEY KING

The relationship between villous trophoblast and maternal systemic immunity has long been a subject of discussion by reproductive immunologists. In recent years, however, the focus of attention has shifted to the interface between extravillous trophoblast and various uterine cells at the placental implantation site. During gestation, the basal decidua is invaded by large numbers of trophoblast cells (Robertson, 1987). However, the functional significance of this migration and the factors that regulate it remain largely unknown. The whole process is undoubtedly finely monitored so that neither rejection nor undue penetration of the uterus by trophoblast ensues. We have recently developed a tissue culture technique that yields extravillous trophoblast (Loke & Burland, 1988), and this has allowed us to study these cells and their interactions with various uterine components *in vitro*. In this chapter, we review data from some ongoing experiments in our laboratory.

Culture of Human Extravillous Trophoblast

A major difficulty with *in vitro* studies of human trophoblast has been the lack of reliable techniques to obtain homogeneous populations of these cells (see review by Loke, 1983). This difficulty is compounded by problems of trophoblast identification because morphological criteria are unreliable for cultured cells, and it is necessary to use other means of characterization (see review by Loke, 1988). We have found immunostaining with a panel of polyclonal and monoclonal antibodies to be highly useful for identification of disaggregated trophoblast cells (Butterworth & Loke, 1985) and trophoblast cells in culture (Loke et al., 1986).

We recently described a tissue culture technique based on the use

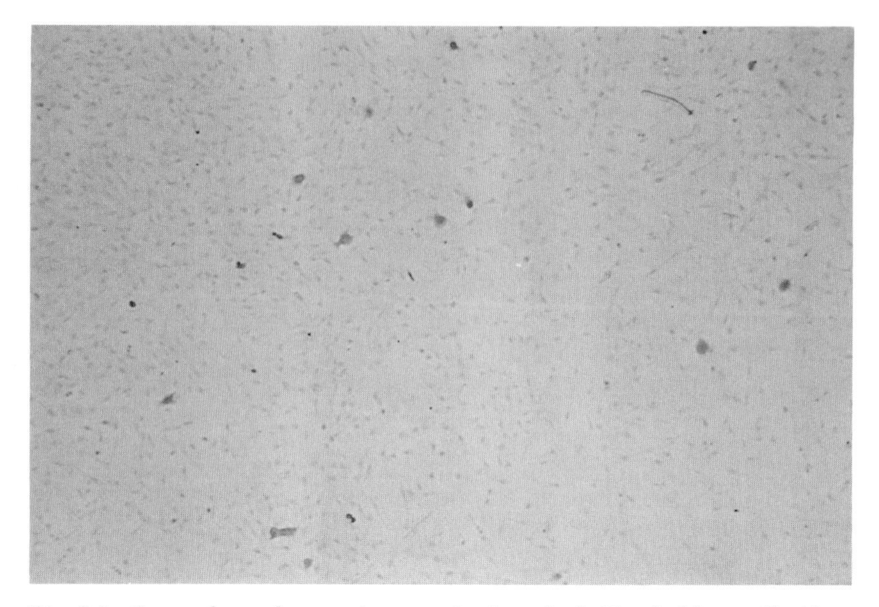

Fig. 8-1. Seven-day culture using standard method. Trophoblast cells identified by Mab PKKl against cytokeratin. (From Loke & Burland, 1988.)

of a modified medium together with a substrate of extracellular matrix, which consistently yields over 80% trophoblast from first-trimester placentas (Loke & Burland, 1988). The improvement in the yield of trophoblast cells as compared to standard culture techniques is very marked (Figs. 8-1 and 8-2). Furthermore, these cells have immunocytochemical characteristics that closely resemble those of extravillous trophoblast (Loke & Butterworth, 1987). They express HLA class I antigens similar to the cytotrophoblast of the cell columns and the interstitial trophoblast that infiltrates decidua. A few synthesize hPL, a property that is associated with the "intermediate" population of extravillous trophoblast as described by Kurman et al. (1984). The multinuclear trophoblast cells formed in culture express HLA class I antigens and cytokeratin microfilaments and stain with both 18B/A5 and 18A/C4 antitrophoblast monoclonal antibodies. They do not produce hCG or hPL. These properties are characteristic of placental bed giant cells, rather than villous syncytiotrophoblast (Table 8-1), suggesting that our system promotes differentiation of trophoblast along the extravillous pathway.

Expression of HLA Class I Antigen by Cultured Human Trophoblast

Although villous trophoblast is devoid of HLA class I and class II antigens, the extravillous population expresses a class I-like molecule that differs from classical class I antigens in many respects (Ellis et

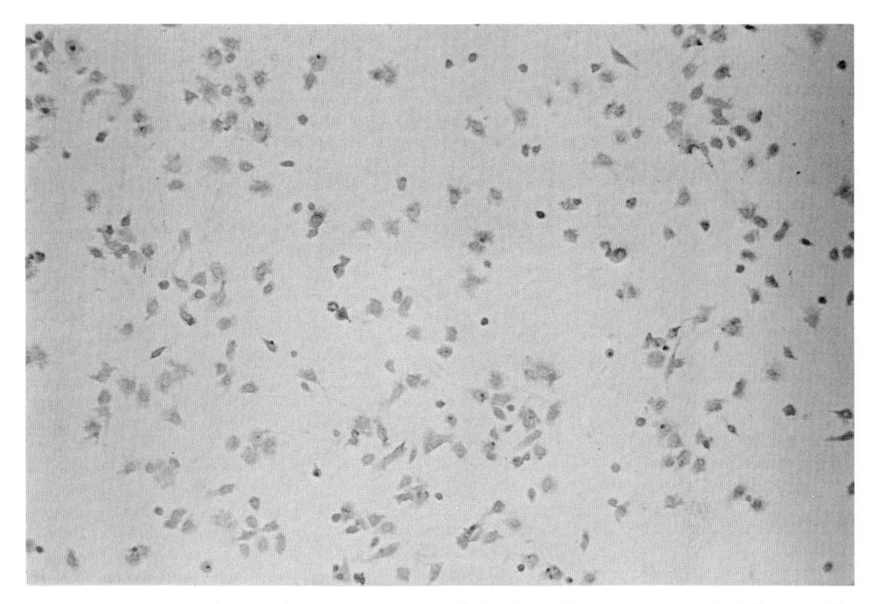

Fig. 8-2. Seven-day culture using modified technique. Trophoblast cells identified by Mab PKKl against cytokeratin. (From Loke & Burland, 1988.)

al. 1986) (see Chapter 3). Since trophoblast cells obtained in our culture system all appear to express this antigen, we have used these cells to characterize this molecule. Our findings are similar to those reported by Ellis and colleagues (1986) using chorionic plate trophoblast: the trophoblast antigen is nonpolymorphic and comprises heavy chains of lower molecular weight than classical class I antigens associated with β_2-microglobulin. In our system, the trophoblast antigen appears to be mainly intracellular with very low levels of expression at the cell surface. It may be argued that this is an *in vitro* artifact due to our culture conditions. We cannot exclude this possibility since we

Table 8-1. Comparison of immunocytochemical staining characteristics among villous syncytiotrophoblast, placental bed giant cells, and cultured multinuclear cells*

	Reaction with Antibodies					
Cell Type	**W6/32**	**PKK1**	**18B/A5**	**18A/C4**	**anti-B-hCG**	**anti-hPL**
Villous syncytiotrophoblast (first trimester)	−	+/−	−	+	+	+
Placental bed giant cells	+	+	+	+	−	−
Multinuclear cells in culture	+	+	+	+	−	−

* From Loke & Burland (1988).

use our trophoblast cells on day 2 or day 3 of culture. If indeed this interpretation is correct, it suggests that we have inadvertently included factors in our cultures that can modify surface class I antigenic expression. This could open up interesting possibilities for further *in vitro* studies of antigenic modulation.

The functional significance of this unusual MHC antigen in relation to the trophoblast-decidua interaction is unclear. We have recently reviewed the literature in this area (Loke et al., 1990). The antigen may simply reflect a stage in the development of extravillous trophoblast and thus be immunologically irrelevant. The molecule lacks polymorphic domains and is not expressed at the cell surface at sufficient levels to trigger maternal alloreactivity. However, it has been proposed by some groups that expression of this antigen by trophoblast is important in determining the success of pregnancy. Wegmann (1987) has advanced the concept of "placental immunotrophism," in which maternal recognition of this class I-like molecule leads to the release of appropriate cytokines by decidual leukocytes, which then directly influence trophoblast growth and function. Decidual leukocytes mainly belong to the NK family, which are normally not MHC restricted. It may therefore not be necessary to have highly polymorphic determinants to activate these leukocytes.

The role of this unusual MHC antigen in nonimmune cellular interactions should also be considered. Contact inhibition of epithelial cell migration appears to be determined by mismatch in certain parts of the MHC (Curtis & Rooney, 1979). This may be relevant to the invasion of extravillous trophoblast by maternal uterine cells. An interaction between class I molecules and cell surface receptors, such as the insulin receptor (Due et al., 1986) and the EGF receptor (Schreiber et al., 1984), has also been reported, and it is possible that the antigen could modify receptor binding activity. Human trophoblast expresses receptors for a variety of peptides. It is possible that the class I-like antigen expressed by extravillous trophoblast could regulate the binding of hormones and other molecules and hence exert a controlling influence on trophoblast growth and differentiation. Thus, the extravillous trophoblast class I antigen could be involved in a range of nonimmunological biological functions.

Interaction Between Trophoblast and Decidual Lymphocytes

There is currently a great deal of interest in the population of bone-marrow-derived cells that infiltrates early decidua. These consist mainly of macrophages and unusual T lineage cells that resemble large granular lymphocytes (LGLs) (Bulmer & Sunderland, 1984). Further characterization of their surface phenotype indicates that they may correspond to the $CD3^-$, $CD16^-$, and Leu $19^{bright+}$ subset of LGLs described by Lanier et al. (1986). Similar cells comprise less than 2% of peripheral blood LGLs, yet form the major population in decidua. Their functions are unknown. LGLs normally possess NK activity and function as effector cells, exhibiting non-MHC restricted killing without prior sensitization. Their main targets are thought to be undifferentiated or transformed cells.

Since extravillous trophoblast cells are relatively immature and express low or aberrant MHC class I antigens, they may be targets for decidual LGLs. We have therefore looked for cytotoxic activity of these decidual effector cells in a ^{51}Cr release assay, using cultured trophoblast cells as targets (King et al., 1989a). Decidual cells isolated by trypsin, collagenase/dispase, or by sieving did not have detectable cytotoxic activity against trophoblast. However, there was demonstrable cytolytic activity against the NK-sensitive cell line K562, suggesting that the lack of trophoblast killing was not due to damage to the effectors during isolation (Fig. 8-3). NK cells isolated from peripheral blood also have no appreciable effect on trophoblast, so it would appear that this refractoriness is an inherent trophoblast characteristic. It may reflect trophoblast membrane rigidity as K562 cells lose their susceptibility to NK lysis if the surface membrane is altered (Roozemond & Bonavida, 1985). Alternatively, trophoblast cells may be able to prevent NK lysis even if recognition occurs. We are now exploring some of these possibilities with cold target competition assays and the single cell conjugate assay.

Given these results, it is perhaps necessary to re-evaluate the functional role of decidual leukocytes in implantation. As stated earlier, proper implantation of the human placenta requires adequate trophoblast invasion. Therefore, although trophoblast cells need to be regulated so that undue myometrial penetration does not occur, they must not be eliminated completely. Decidual cells may exert a cytostatic rather than cytolytic influence. Furthermore, the paradoxical situation whereby decidual leukocytes may actually enhance trophoblast growth by the production of appropriate cytokines has already been mentioned (Wegmann, 1987). As a recent review concluded, "the biology of NK cells should not be viewed through the simple chromium release assay perspective" (Hercend & Schmidt, 1988). We have now initiated trophoblast-decidua co-culture experiments to distinguish between these possibilities.

In the preceding discussion, we have made the assumption that decidual LGLs, because of their abundance, must play some regulatory role in pregnancy. However, we have also observed lymphoid cells with similar phenotypic characteristics in nonpregnant endometrium (King et al., 1989b). The numbers of these cells vary throughout the menstrual cycle with a peak occurring in the late secretory phase (Fig. 8-4). The recruitment of these cells therefore appears to be under hormonal control and is not dependent on the presence of

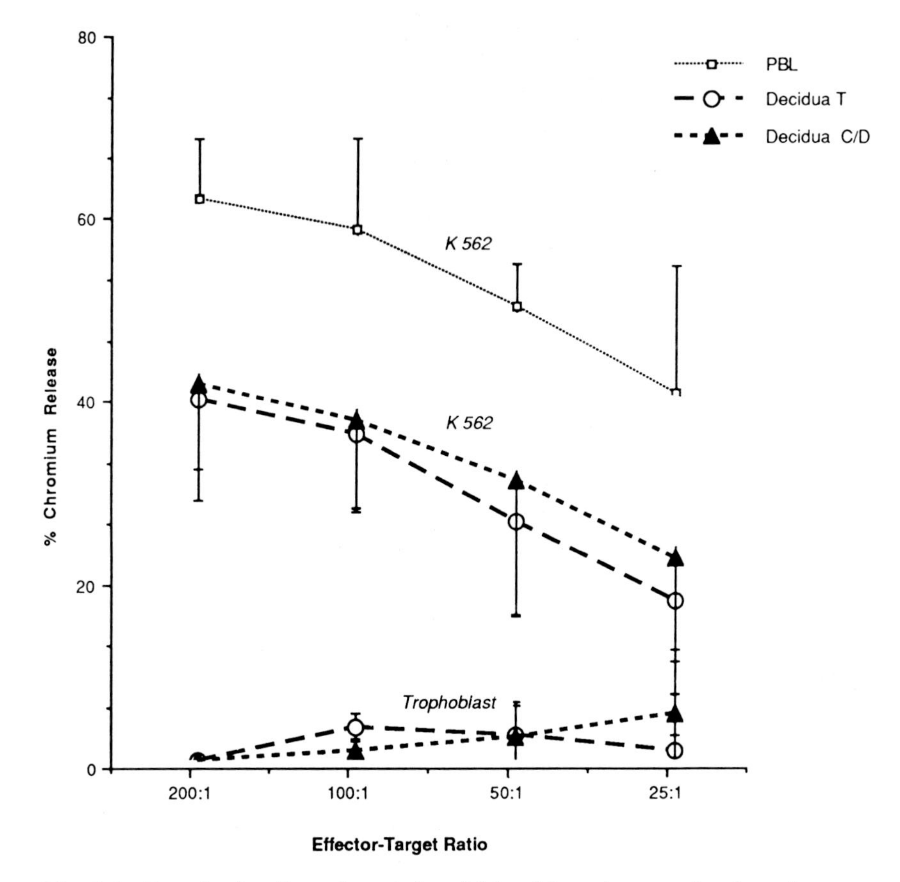

Fig. 8-3. Decidual cells and peripheral blood lymphocytes in chromium release assay against K562 and trophoblast. (From King, Birkby, Loke, 1989a.)

trophoblast. These results considerably weaken the argument that decidual LGLs are present in order to interact with trophoblast. We have noticed that the nuclei of these endometrial leukocytes become progressively karyorrhectic and pyknotic by the late secretory phase of the cycle, signalling imminent cell death. These nuclear changes are not seen in first-trimester decidua, however, indicating that the onset of pregnancy does favor continued survival of these cells.

Laminin in Human Trophoblast-Decidua Interaction

Our observation that trophoblast cells bind to extracellular matrix in culture has prompted us to investigate further the possible role of this protein in trophoblast-decidua interaction (Loke et al., 1989). Laminin constitutes an important component of extracellular matrix

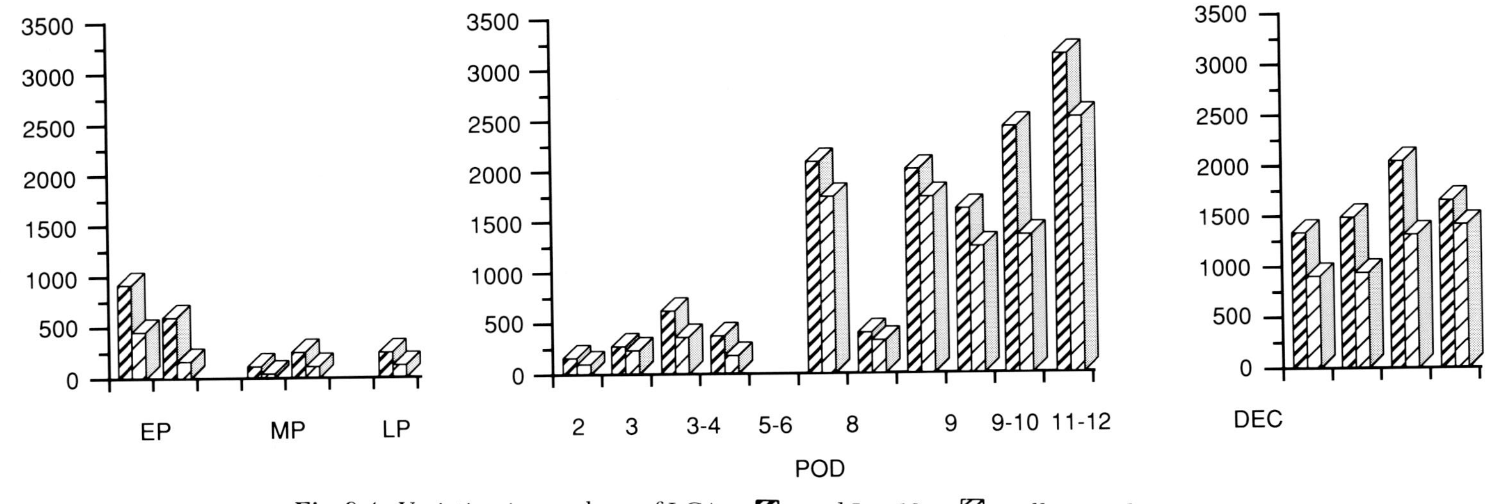

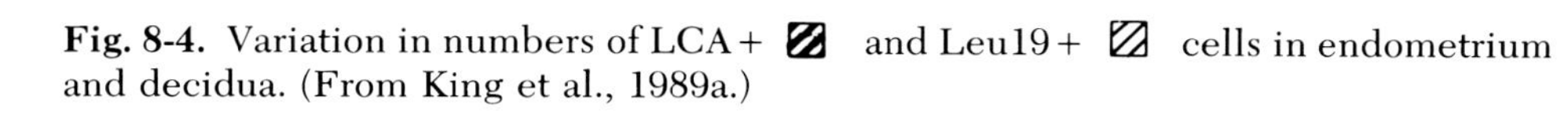

Fig. 8-4. Variation in numbers of LCA+ ▨ and Leu19+ ▨ cells in endometrium and decidua. (From King et al., 1989a.)

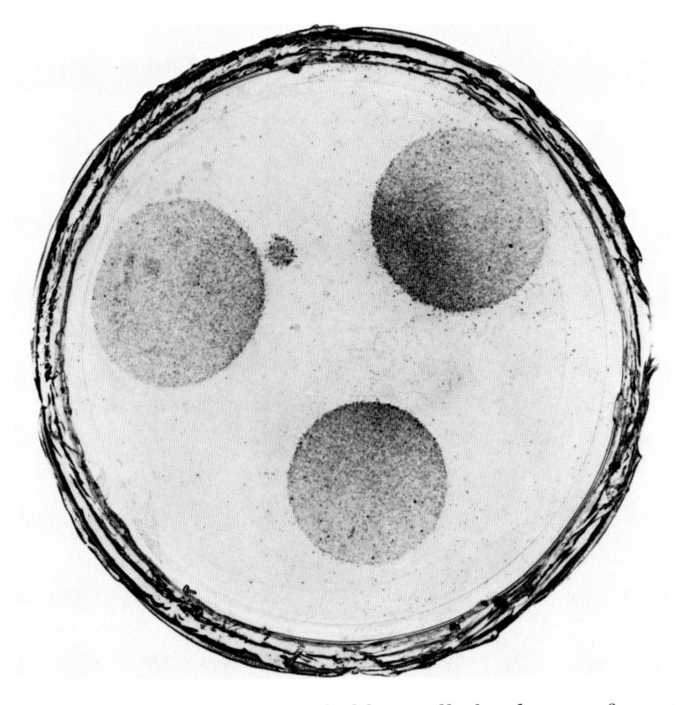

Fig. 8-5. Culture dish showing trophoblast cells binding preferentially to three circular areas coated with laminin (stained with Coomassie blue). (From Loke et al., 1989.)

and is involved in epithelial cell adhesion. We have observed that placental cells attach preferentially to areas of culture dishes that have been coated with laminin (Fig. 8-5), although fetal skin cells show no such preference. The vast majority of placental cells that attach to laminin-coated areas appear to be trophoblast, as judged by immunostaining with a panel of appropriate monoclonal antibodies. Relatively fewer trophoblast cells attach to areas coated with collagen type IV, whereas virtually no cells bind to bovine serum albumin (BSA) coated surfaces. These observations can be quantified over defined grid areas using an eye-piece graticule (Table 8-2). The superior binding efficiency of laminin for trophoblast over collagen type IV and BSA can clearly be seen (Loke et al. 1989).

These observations indicate specificity for the trophoblast-laminin interaction, which may be mediated by laminin receptors expressed on the trophoblast cells. Wewer and colleagues (1987) demonstrated intense immunostaining of invading early extravillous trophoblast by an antibody against the laminin receptor.

We have noted the presence of significant amounts of laminin surrounding individual stromal cells in frozen sections of early decidua (Fig. 8-6), consistent with the findings of Charpin et al. (1985) and

Table 8-2. Number of trophoblast cells adherent to various substrates on day one of culture*

Placental Specimens	Laminin	Collagen Type IV	BSA
1	121	23	7
2	124	41	44
3	79	16	9
4	100	52	19
Total	424	132	79

* From Loke et al. (1989).

Wewer et al. (1985). In the nonpregnant endometrium, very little laminin is present during the proliferative phase, although the protein begins to appear around the second half of the menstrual cycle. This cyclical variation suggests hormonal influence over the production of laminin, as previously suggested by Faber and colleagues (1986).

Invasion of host tissue by cancer cells, has been postulated to occur in a stepwise fashion. In the first stage, tumor cells specifically attach to extracellular matrix components, by specific cell surface receptors such as laminin (Liotta, 1986). Indeed, high-affinity receptors for laminin have been isolated from the membranes of many tumor cells

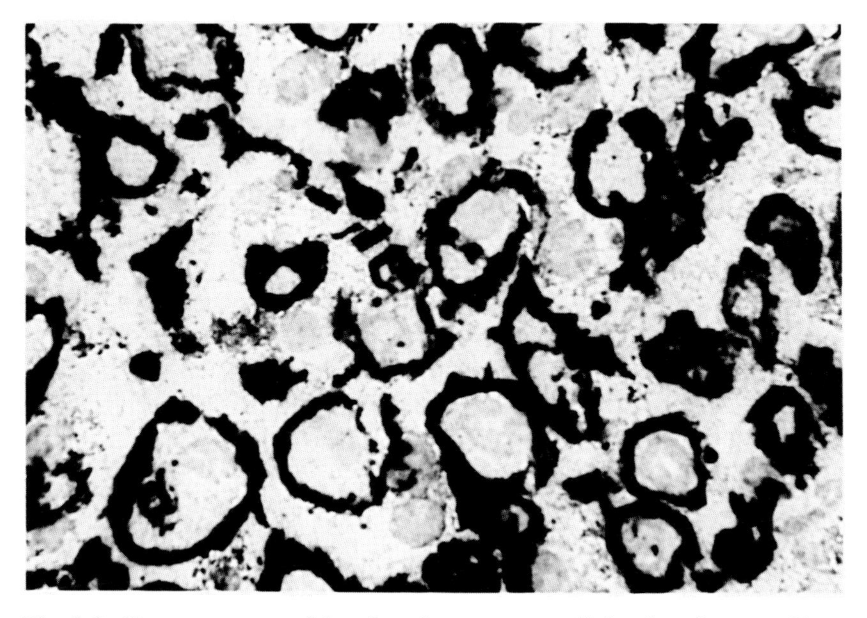

Fig. 8-6. Frozen section of decidua showing pericellular distribution of laminin around stromal cells (stained with rabbit anti-laminin and silver enhanced). (From Loke et al., 1989.)

(Liotta et al., 1984). We have observed preferential attachment of trophoblast to laminin *in vitro*. This, together with the presence of the protein in significant amounts around decidual stromal cells, suggests that laminin may act as an anchoring matrix for invading extravillous trophoblast cells *in vivo*. It is therefore exciting that placental implantation and tumor invasion may utilize similar mechanisms.

References

Bulmer, J. N. and Sunderland, C. A. 1984. Immunohistological characterisation of lymphoid cell populations in the early placental bed. *Immunology* 52:349–357.

Butterworth, B. H. and Loke, Y. W. 1985. Immunocytochemical identification of cytotrophoblast from other mononuclear cell populations isolated from first-trimester human chorionic villi. *J. Cell Sci.* 76:189–197.

Charpin, C., Kopp, F., Pourreau-Schneider, N., Lissitzky, J. C., Lavaut, M. N., Martin, P. M. and Toga, M. 1985. Laminin distribution in human decidua and immature placenta. *Am. J. Obstet. Gynecol.* 151:822–826.

Curtis, A. S. G. and Rooney, P. 1979. H-2 restriction of contact inhibition of epithelial cells. *Nature* 281:222–223.

Due, C., Simonsen, M. and Olsson, L. 1986. The major histocompatibility complex class I heavy chain as a structural subunit of the human cell membrane insulin receptor: implications for the range of biological functions of histocompatibility antigens. *Proc. Nat. Acad. Sci. USA* 83:6007–6011.

Ellis, S. A., Sargent, I. L., Redman, C. W. G. and McMichael, A. J. 1986 Evidence for a novel HLA antigen found on human extravillous trophoblast and a choriocarcinoma cell line. *Immunology* 59:595–601.

Faber, M., Wewer, U. M., Berthelsen, J. G., Liotta, L. A. and Albrechtsen, R. 1986. Laminin production by human endometrial stromal cells relates to the cyclic and pathologic state of the endometrium. *Am. J. Pathol.* 124:384–391.

Hercend, T. and Schmidt, R. E. 1988. Characteristics and uses of natural killer cells. *Immunol. Today* 9:291–293.

King, A., Birkby, C. and Loke, Y. W. 1989a. Early human decidual cells exhibit NK activity against K562 cell line but not against first trimester trophoblast. *Cell. Immunol.* 118:337–344.

King, A., Wellings, V., Gardner, L. and Loke, Y. W. 1989b. Immunocytochemical characterisation of the unusual large granular lymphocytes in human endometrium throughout the menstrual cycle. *Hum. Immunol.* 24:195–205.

Kurman, R. J., Main, C. S., and Chen, H.-C. 1984. Intermediate trophoblast: a distinctive form of trophoblast with specific morphological, biochemical and functional features. *Placenta* 5:349–369.

Lanier, L. L., Le, A. M., Civin, C. I., Loken, M. R. and Phillips, J. H. 1986. The relationship of CD16 (Leu11) and Leu-19 (NKH-1) antigen expression on human peripheral blood NK cells and cytotoxic T lymphocytes. *J. Immunol.* 136:4480–4486.

Liotta, L. A. 1986. Tumor invasion and metastases—role of the extracellular matrix. *Cancer Res.* 46:1–7.

Liotta, L. A., Rao, N. C., Barsky, S. H. and Bryant, G. 1984. The laminin receptor and basement membrane dissolution: role in tumour metastasis. In *Basement Membranes and Cell Movement*, CIBA Foundation Symposium. London: Pitman, pp. 146–162.

Loke, Y. W. 1983. Human trophoblast in culture. In *Biology of Trophoblast* (Y. W. Loke and A. Whyte, eds.). Amsterdam: Elsevier/North Holland, pp. 663–701.

Loke, Y. W. 1988. Immunocytochemical and characterisation of human trophoblast. In *Placental Protein Hormones* (M. Mochizuki and R. Hussa, eds.). Amsterdam: Excerpta Medica, pp. 19–31.

Loke, Y. W. and Burland, K. 1988. Human trophoblast cells cultured in modified medium and supported by extracellular matrix. *Placenta* 9:173–182.

Loke, Y. W. and Butterworth, B. H. 1987. Heterogeneity of human trophoblast populations. In *Immunoregulation and Fetal Survival* (T. J. Gill and T. G. Wegmann, eds.). New York: Oxford University Press, pp. 197–209.

Loke, Y. W., Butterworth, B. H., Margetts, J. J. and Burland, K. 1986. Identification of cytotrophoblast colonies in cultures of human placental cells using monoclonal antibodies. *Placenta* 7:221–231.

Loke, Y. W., Gardner, L., Burland, K. and King, A. 1989. Laminin in human trophoblast-decidua interaction. *Hum. Reprod.* 4:457–463.

Loke, Y. W., King, A. and Grabowska, A. 1990. Antigenic expression by migrating trophoblast and its relevance to implantation. In *Trophoblast Invasion and Endometrial Receptivity: Novel Aspects of the Cell Biology of Embryo Implantation. Trophoblast Research 4* (H. W. Denker and J. D. Aplin, eds.).

Robertson, W. G. 1987. Pathology of the pregnant uterus. In: *Obstetrical & Gynaecological Pathology* (H. Fox, ed.). New York: Churchill Livingstone, pp. 191–207.

Roozemond, R. C. and Bonavida, B. 1985. Effect of altered membrane fluidity on NK cell-mediated cytotoxicity. Selection of inhibition of the recognition or post recognition events in the cytolytic pathway of NK cells. *J. Immunol.* 134:2209–2214.

Schreiber, A. B., Schlessinger, J. and Edidin, M. 1984. Interaction between Major Histocompatibility Complex antigens and epidermal growth factor receptors on human cells. *J. Cell Biol.* 98:725–731.

Wegmann, T. G. 1987. Placental immunotropism: maternal T cells enhance placental growth and function. *Am. J. Reprod. Immunol. Microbiol.* 15:67–70.

Wewer, U. M., Faber, M., Liotta, L. A. and Albrechtsen, R. 1985. Immunochemical and ultrastructural assessment of the nature of the pericellular basement membrane of human decidual cells. *Lab. Invest.* 53:624–633.

Wewer, U. M., Taraboletti, G., Sobel, M. E., Albrechtsen, R. and Liotta, L. A. 1987. Role of laminin receptor in tumor cell migration. *Cancer Res.* 47:5691–5698.

9

Immune Cell Populations in the Human Early Pregnancy Decidua

C. W. G. REDMAN, B. L. FERRY, M. C. JACKSON,
I. L. SARGENT, P. M. STARKEY, and G. M. O. WATT

The term "fetal allograft" is a confusing cliche. Contact with the mother is, in fact, confined to a single highly specialized part of the fetus—the trophoblast. The syncytiotrophoblast lining the chorionic villi is the main fetal tissue in contact with maternal blood. Other forms of trophoblast, including the interstitial, endovascular, and membraneous cytotrophoblast, are embedded directly into maternal tissues. Trophoblast cannot be compared to a conventional allograft because it does not express polymorphic antigens of the major histocompatibility complex (MHC), the main determinants of allograft rejection. Some forms of interstitial trophoblast express an atypical class I MHC antigen (as discussed in Part 1 of this volume). This has now been shown to be the novel HLA antigen, HLA-G (Ellis et al., 1990) of which allotypic variants have not yet been found. No form of human trophoblast has been identified that expresses conventional HLA-A or -B antigens (Redman et al., 1984). Likewise, none expresses class II MHC antigens (Redman, 1983), although membraneous and first-trimester cytotrophoblast cross-react with one antibody that binds to HLA-DP (Starkey, 1987).

Thus, trophoblast does not provide the signals necessary for T cell activation (HLA -D) or the target structures for cytotoxic T cells (HLA-A, -B). In consequence, direct T cell-trophoblast interactions are probably of little or no importance in determining the survival of trophoblast as a graft (Redman et al., 1987).

Immune Cells in the Decidua

Not only do maternal T cells not react directly with trophoblast but they are, during the first trimester, distributed sparsely in the decidua. This does not reflect an overall lack of immune cells, as they are in fact a prominent component of this tissue (Bulmer & Johnson, 1985;

Bulmer & Sunderland, 1984). Of these immune cells, many are macrophages, but most (about 45%) are large granular lymphocytes or LGL (Starkey et al., 1988). In this chapter, we use the term LGL to denote a heterogeneous group of large lymphocytes that are neither T cells nor B cells and do not rearrange either the beta or gamma genes of the T cell receptor (Lanier et al., 1986) or express CD3 (Hercend et al., 1983). They comprise about 10% of peripheral blood mononuclear cells (PBMN) and are found in several organs, including the gut (Ernst et al., 1985) and lungs (Puccetti et al., 1980). Their functions *in vivo* are unknown, but *in vitro* they express natural killer (NK), natural suppressor, and veto activities (Azuma and Kaplan, 1988), as well as antibody-dependent and allogeneic cytotoxicity (Ford et al., 1984). NK cells differ from T cells in that they are not "antigen driven," and they apparently form part of a system for nonspecific immune surveillance that requires no priming.

Phenotype of Human Peripheral Blood LGL

The NKH-1 antigen (CD56) is a marker for all NK cells, but is not expressed on all LGL (Hercend et al., 1985). The antigen corresponds to a 200–220 kDa membrane-associated protein of unknown function. The NKH-1 antibody does not block the cytolytic activity of NK cells (Griffin et al., 1983). The CD16 antigen is associated with the low-affinity Fc receptor (FcRIII), a 50–70 kDa protein expressed by NK cells, peripheral blood neutrophils (Fleit et al., 1982), a very small subset of CD3-positive peripheral blood T cells (Lanier et al., 1985), and some activated macrophages (Fleit et al., 1982). Most but not all NKH-1 positive peripheral blood LGL are also CD16 positive (Perussia and Trinchieri, 1984). There is also a rare CD16-negative subset characterized by a high density of NKH-1 expression (Lanier et al., 1986b). CD16 expression is not a marker for NK activity, although the antigen participates in antibody-dependent cellular cytoxicity, which is blocked by some anti-CD16 antibodies (Perussia et al., 1983a). CD2 (the sheep red cell receptor) is expressed by more than 80% of peripheral blood LGL. It appears to regulate cytolytic activity; anti-CD2 ($F(ab')_2$) enhances NK activity and induces autocytoxicity among NK cells (Schmidt et al., 1988). In addition, anti-CD2 increases IL-2 receptor expression by LGL (Schmidt et al., 1985).

Phenotype of Decidual LGL

We have used antibodies to three markers of peripheral blood LGL (CD56, CD16, and CD2) to characterize the phenotypes of decidual LGL. Maternal decidua (a mixture of decidua basalis and decidual vera) was identified in 15 first-trimester terminations with gestational ages of 7–11 weeks. Using a dissecting microscope, up to 5 g of tissue

Table 9-1. Protocol for dissociation of the decidua

All stages are carried out under sterile conditions, with the Dutch modification of RPMI-1640 containing 1 mM L-glutamine, 50 μg/mL gentamicin, 100 μg/mL streptomycin, and 100 U/mL benzylpenicillin. Enzyme incubations are at 37°C.

1. 15 min in either 0.2 mg/mL type XIV protease (Sigma, Poole, UK) (protocol A) or 1 mg/mL dispase (Boehringer, Lewes UK) (protocol B)
2. 1–2 h digestion in 1.5 mg/mL type IV collagenase and 2 mg/mL type 1-S hyaluronidase (Sigma, Poole, Dorset)
3. Cells filtered through 100-gauge nylon gauze and washed three times by centrifugation with PBS/BSA
4. Overnight incubation at 4°C in 10 mL of DRPMI containing 10% (v/v) fetal calf serum
5. Cells resuspended in 20 mL of 36% Percoll in DRPMI before being layered onto 18 mL of 62.5% Percoll (Pharmacia, Milton Keynes, UK) under 2 mL of PBS
6. Centrifugation at 670 g for 30 min and the cells recovered from the 36%/62.5% interface, washed in a large volume of PBS and resuspended in PBS containing 20 mM glucose and 0.5% BSA

was dissected free of chorionic villous tissue, teased apart, and digested with protease, hyaluronidase, and collagenase as summarized in Table 9-1 (Starkey et al., 1988).

The cells were labeled with a panel of monoclonal antibodies (Table 9-2) and FITC-conjugated rabbit anti-(mouse IgG) (Fab′)2 second antibody. For double labeling the cells were incubated further

Table 9-2. Details of monoclonal antibodies used in this study

Antibody	Specificity	Reference
W6/32	Monomorphic determinant of Class I HLA	Barnstable et al. (1978)
T3*	CD3, associated with T cell receptor	
T11†	CD2, associated with receptor for E-rosettes	
Leu 7	HNK-1 antigen expressed by a subset of NK cells and some CD3-positive lymphocytes	Abo et al. (1983)
NKH1*	200–220 KDa protein on most peripheral blood NK cells	Griffin et al. (1983)
Leu 11c*	CD16, Fc receptor on LGL, granulocytes, and some macrophages	Perussia et al. (1983b)
OKT10	CD38, expressed by B cells, LGL, activated T cells, and macrophages	
CR3/43	Monomorphic determinant of class II HLA	Dick et al. (1984)

* Also used directly conjugated to phycoerythrin.
† Also used directly conjugated to FITC.

with normal mouse serum (10%) to block nonspecific binding to the rabbit anti-(mouse IgG) and then washed and stained with phycoerythyrin(PE)-conjugated monoclonal antibody. FITC-conjugated second antibody alone or PE-conjugated mouse IgG1 were used as controls for single-labeling experiments. For double labeling, controls were stained with FITC-conjugated rabbit anti-(mouse IgG) followed by normal serum and then by PE-conjugated mouse IgG1.

Cells were analyzed on a Coulter EPICS 541 flow cytometer. Forward angle light scatter (FALS), 90° light scatter, and green and red fluorescence were measured. W6/32, an antibody to the nonpolymorphic part of the MHC class I antigen, was used to estimate the total number of cells in the preparations because its epitope is expressed by nearly all maternal cells and most fetal cytotrophoblast. Gates for FALS and 90° light scatter were set using W6/32 labeling to exclude debris and dead cells. The percentage of cells that was antibody positive was calculated by comparison with the appropriate controls using the "Immuno" subtraction program. The results are summarized in Figure 9-1.

The great variability in the results from first-trimester samples could not be explained by differences in gestational age. On average, 45%

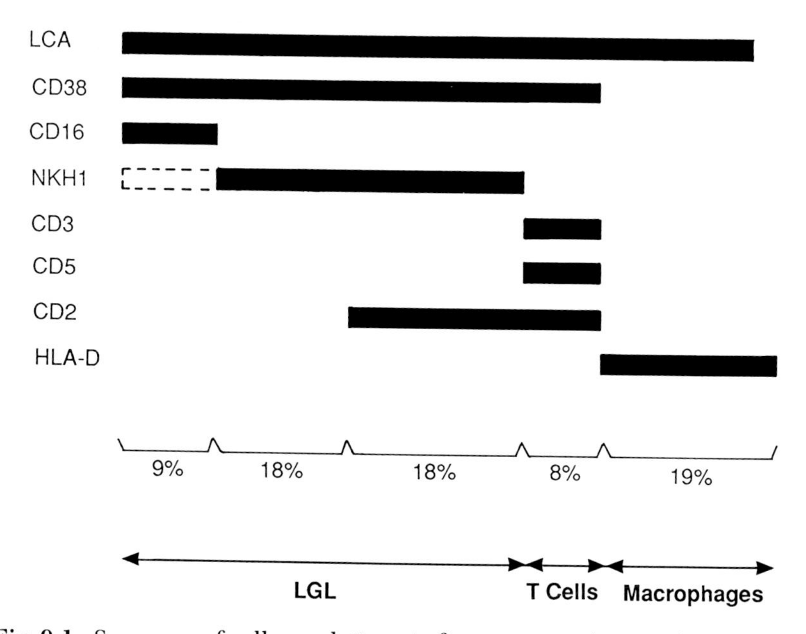

Fig. 9-1. Summary of cell populations in first trimester human decidua. Data from single and double antibody labeling of enzymatic digests of first trimester decidua. The percentage of decidual cells within each subset is indicated at the bottom. LCA—leukocyte common antigen (CD45). (From Starkey et al., 1988 with permission.)

of the cells were LGL, of which most were CD16 negative but positive for NKH1. A minor population of decidual LGL, accounting for an average of 9% of MHC class I-positive decidual cells, was CD16 positive but negative or only dimly positive for NKH1. Leu7, an antibody that binds to cytotoxic T cells and some NK cell subsets (Lanier et al., 1985), did not react with decidual cells. About half of the NKH1-positive cells were also CD2 positive. Macrophages and T cells, comprising an average of 19% and 8%, respectively, of the total, were the other immune cells present in significant numbers.

The majority of peripheral blood LGL are CD16 positive and weakly positive for NKH1 (Lanier et al., 1986b). These have the highest NK activity and seem nearest in phenotype to the decidual CD16-positive cells. The minor subset of peripheral blood LGL that are "NKH1 bright"—largely positive for CD2 but negative for CD16 and CD3—comprise large granular and agranular lymphocytes with only weak NK activity (Lanier et al., 1986b). The NKH1-positive, CD16-negative decidual cells correspond most closely to this minor component of PBL, although only some are CD2 positive.

Thus, the distribution of the subsets of decidual LGL differs significantly from those of peripheral blood LGL, but by analogy, they would still be expected to have NK and ADCC activities.

Isolation of Decidual NKH-1 Positive Large Granular Lymphocytes by Flow Cytometry

Cell populations were labeled for sorting by incubating approximately 40×10^6 decidual cells with 2 mL of PE-conjugated NKH1 monoclonal antibody for 30 min. After washing, the cells were filtered through 40-μm gauze, resuspended at 5×10^6/mL in phosphate-buffered saline (PBS) containing 20 mM glucose and 0.5% bovine serum albumin (PGB), and sorted on an EPICS 541 flow cytometer using a 76-μm tip and the 488 nm line of the argon-ion laser.

A typical two-parameter profile of decidual LGL, labeled with PE-conjugated NKH1, is shown in Figure 9-2. NKH1-positive and NKH1-negative populations were defined by bit-map gating. They were then sorted at 1,500 cells/sec using one droplet sorting.

Details from 23 preparations were summarized in Table 9-3. Before sorting, the decidual cells had a median viability of 81%, the lowest value being 64%. NKH1-positive cells made up a median of 47%, (range: 25–64%) of the unsorted cells, the differences still being unrelated to gestational age. When the sorted populations were reanalyzed on the flow cytometer, the NKH1-positive cells were 98% pure and the remainder contaminated with 6% positive cells. Yields of more than 2×10^6 cells were always obtained, and we generally recovered more than 5×10^6 cells per sample.

It was then possible to use these purified NKH1-positive decidual LGL in functional studies. We analyzed their NK activity and abilities to produce and respond to interleukin 2.

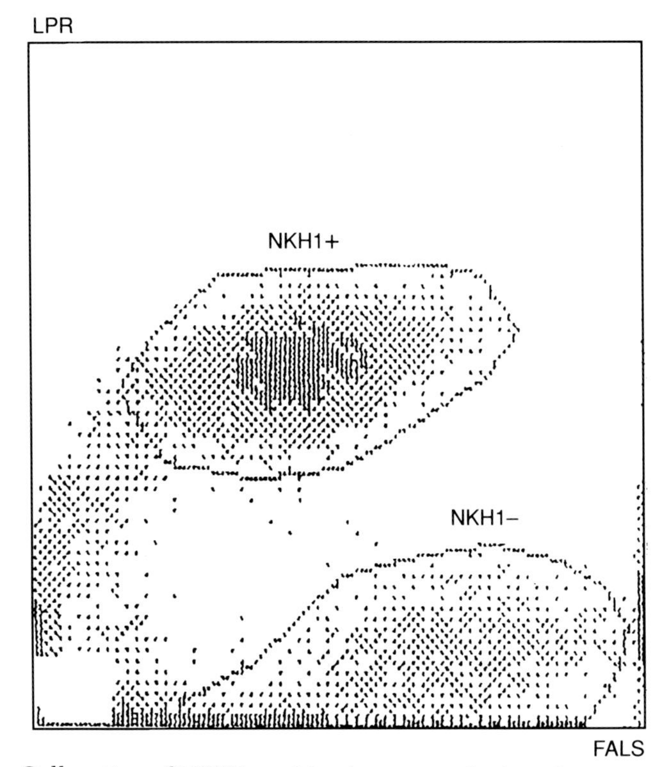

Fig. 9-2. Cell sorting of NKH1-positive large granular lymphocytes. Decidual cells were labeled with PE-conjugated NKH1 antibody and analyzed by flow cytometry using FALS (forward angle light scatter) and LPR (log peak red fluorescence). NKH1-positive and NKH1-negative populations were defined by bit map gating (dotted lines), which excluded dead and aggregated cells and debris, before being sorted using one droplet sorting.

Natural Killer Activity of LGL

LGL can efficiently lyse a wide variety of tumor cells (Kiessling et al., 1975), cells infected with viruses (Santoli et al., 1978), and normal immature cells (Hansson et al., 1979) without prior sensitization and without MHC restriction. Lysis is blocked by anti-LFA-1 antibodies (Hildreth et al., 1983), implying that LFA-1, an adhesion protein, is expressed by LGL (Kohl et al., 1984) and that binding to ICAM-1 (Marlin & Springer, 1987) is important for lytic function. The susceptibility of target cells is increased if they express high mannose or hybrid N-linked oligosaccharides on their surfaces, as is characteristic of rapidly growing and transformed cells (Ahrens & Ankel, 1987). In general the target cells that are most susceptible to NK lysis are those that express no or few MHC antigens (Storkus et al., 1987). NK activity of decidual cells has previously been reported using the leukemia cell line K562 as a target (King et al., 1989), although most murine and human trophoblast are unusually resistant to cell-mediated lysis (see also Chapter 10, this Volume).

Table 9-3 Decidual cells pre- and postsorting with NKH1 antibody

Sample	% NKH1$^+$ve*	% Viability†	Yield‡ (cells × 10^{-6})
Presort‖	47 (25–64)	81 (64–91)	45 (25–109)
Postsort#			
NKH1$^+$ve population	98 (86–99)	83 (55–89)	5 (2–7)
NKH1$^-$ve population	6 (2–13)	80 (50–93)	6 (2–10)

All values are expressed as median values (range) from 23 decidual cell preparations.
* Percentage of NKH1-positive cells determined by flow cytometry.
† Viability assessed by phase-contrast microscopy and trypan blue exclusion.
‡ Cell yield before and after sorting with NKH1 antibody.
‖ Decidual cells before sorting with NKH1 antibody.
Cells obtained after sorting approximately 40 × 10^6 decidual cells with NKH1 antibody. The percentage purity was determined by reanalysis in the flow cytometer.

NK Activity of Decidual Cells

Decidual cells were used as effectors in a routine NK assay, either unsorted or after separation into NKH1-positive and NKH1-negative populations. K562 cells (Lozzio & Lozzio, 1973) were used as NK targets after labeling with 300 μCi of ^{51}Cr (sodium chromate). Target cells (5 × 10^3 in 50 μL DRPMI-NHS) were mixed with different numbers of effector cells in a final volume of 200 μL in microtiter plates. Test combinations, giving effector:target ratios (E:T ratios) ranging from 50:1 to 3:1, were set up in quadruplicate. In addition to spontaneous release, maximum release was determined by incubating target cells with 200 μL of a 5% solution of Triton-X 100 in PBS. After incubation for 6 h, specific ^{51}Cr release was measured and percent cytotoxicity was calculated as follows:

$$\%\ \text{Cytotoxicity} = \frac{\text{test} - \text{spontaneous release}}{\text{maximum} - \text{spontaneous release}} \times 100$$

NK Activity of NKH1-Positive LGL

NK activity was measured using sorted NKH1-positive and NKH1-negative cells, and unsorted decidual cells. The patient's own PBMC were included as a control. Figure 9-3 summarizes the results from 12 experiments. Unsorted decidual cells showed weak NK activity that, as expected, was unaffected by labeling with PE-conjugated NKH1 (data not shown). The NKH1-positive cells showed significantly higher NK activity than unsorted decidual cells ($p < 0.05$) whereas the NKH1-negative population did not kill K562. The NK activity of unsorted PBMC was consistently higher than that of the decidual cell populations.

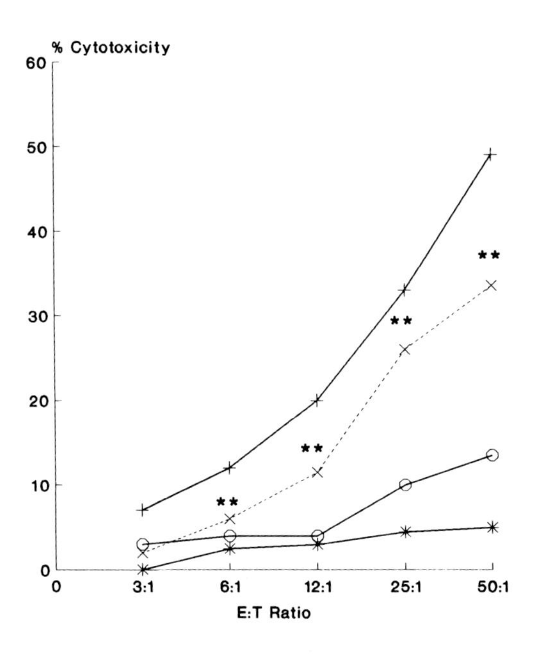

Fig. 9-3. Cytotoxicity of MKH1-positive cells against K562 targets. Unsorted (○—○), and sorted NKH1-positive (×—×) and NKH1-negative (*—*) decidual cells, together with PBMC from the same patients (+—+) were used as effector cells in 6 h ^{51}Cr release assays against K562 target cells. Values are the median % cytotoxicity from 12 experiments. Cytotoxic activity of NKH1-positive cells was significantly greater than both the NKH1-negative and unsorted populations (** $p < 0.01$).

Proliferation of NKH1-Positive LGL in rIL2

The proliferation and activity of LGL are regulated by cytokines including interleukin-2. Peripheral blood NK cells express negligible levels of Tac antigen (Trinchieri et al., 1987; Lanier et al., 1985), but constitutively express a 70 kDa moiety that is unreactive with anti-Tac and appears to be the second subunit of the high-affinity IL2 receptor (Kehrl et al., 1988). The ability of NK cells to respond to IL-2 is biphasic, with short-term enhancement of cytotoxicity followed by a more prolonged proliferative phase. The latter can be blocked by anti-Tac, whereas the former cannot (Kehrl et al., 1988). Immunohistological examination of first-trimester human decidua showed that the infiltrative lymphocytes do not express the Tac antigen (Bulmer & Johnson, 1976). It was therefore of interest to determine the effects of interleukin-2 on decidual cells and their ability to synthesize this cytokine.

Quintuplicate 200 μL cultures (10^5 cells/well in the Dutch modification of RPMI-1640 with 10% normal human serum) of sorted NKH1-positive or NKH1-negative cells or unsorted decidual cells were set up in microtiter plates. Human recombinant interleukin-2 (rIL2; 20 U/mL) was added to each well at the start of the cultures. Control wells contained cells in medium alone. After 2, 4, and 6 days of culture the cells were pulsed with (^3H) thymidine and harvested 18 h later onto glass fiber filters. Isotope incorporation was determined by liquid scintillation counting. Results are expressed as the median counts per minute (cpm) of the quintuplicate cultures.

Figure 9-4A shows that, in the absence of IL-2, NKH1-positive cells did not proliferate for the first 4 days in culture, although their (^{3}H) thymidine incorporation increased fivefold thereafter. Unsorted cells proliferated slowly until the fourth day and less after that time. NKH1-negative cells proliferated more vigorously than either NKH1-positive or unsorted cells, with (^{3}H) thymidine incorporation reaching a peak at day 4 (Fig. 9-4A). When 20 U/mL of rIL2 was added at the beginning of the culture period, the proliferation of all cell types increased. NKH1-positive cells showed the greatest incremental response to IL2, with proliferation peaking on the fourth day and declining slightly thereafter (Fig. 9-4B).

Stimulation indices were calculated as the ratio of (^{3}H) thymidine uptake of cells cultured in rIL2 to that of cells cultured in medium alone. The highest index was seen with NKH1-positive cells, their response peaking on the second day with a 30-fold increase in proliferation and declining thereafter (Fig. 9-4C). The index for unsorted cells was low until the fourth day, but increased slightly by day 6. NKH1-negative cells showed a twofold increase in proliferation, which remained constant throughout the 6-day culture period.

Measurement of IL-2 Production

Quintuplicate 200 μL cultures (10^5 cells/well in DRPMI-NHS) of sorted NKH1-positive or NKH1-negative cells or unsorted decidual cells were incubated in round-bottomed microtiter wells. After 2 and 6 days of culture at 37° in 5% CO_2 in air, 100 μL of the cell-free supernatant was removed and added to round-bottomed microtiter wells containing 100 μL CTLL cells (3×10^5/ml in DRPMI-NHS), a IL-2-dependent mouse cell line (Gillis et al., 1978), which had been grown in the absence of IL-2 for 3 days. After 48 h incubation at 37° in 5% CO_2 in air, each well was pulsed with 0.5 μCi (^{3}H) thymidine, and 18 h later the plates were harvested. The amount of IL-2 released by the decidual cells was calculated from the titration curve of cpm obtained from CTLL cells incubated with 0.001–20 U/mL of rIL2. There was no evidence of IL-2 secretion by any of the three cell populations (Fig. 9-5).

Cytotoxicity and Phenotype of Unsorted Decidual Cells After Culture in rIL2

Unsorted decidual cells were incubated in 24 well plates (Gibco) for 7 days in DRPMI-NHS containing 20 U/mL rIL2 and used as effector cells against K562 target cells in NK assays. In addition their phenotype was examined by flow cytometry, before and after culture in rIL2. Figure 9-6 shows the ability of rIL2 to significantly augment ($p < 0.05$) the NK activity of both PBMC and unsorted decidual cells.

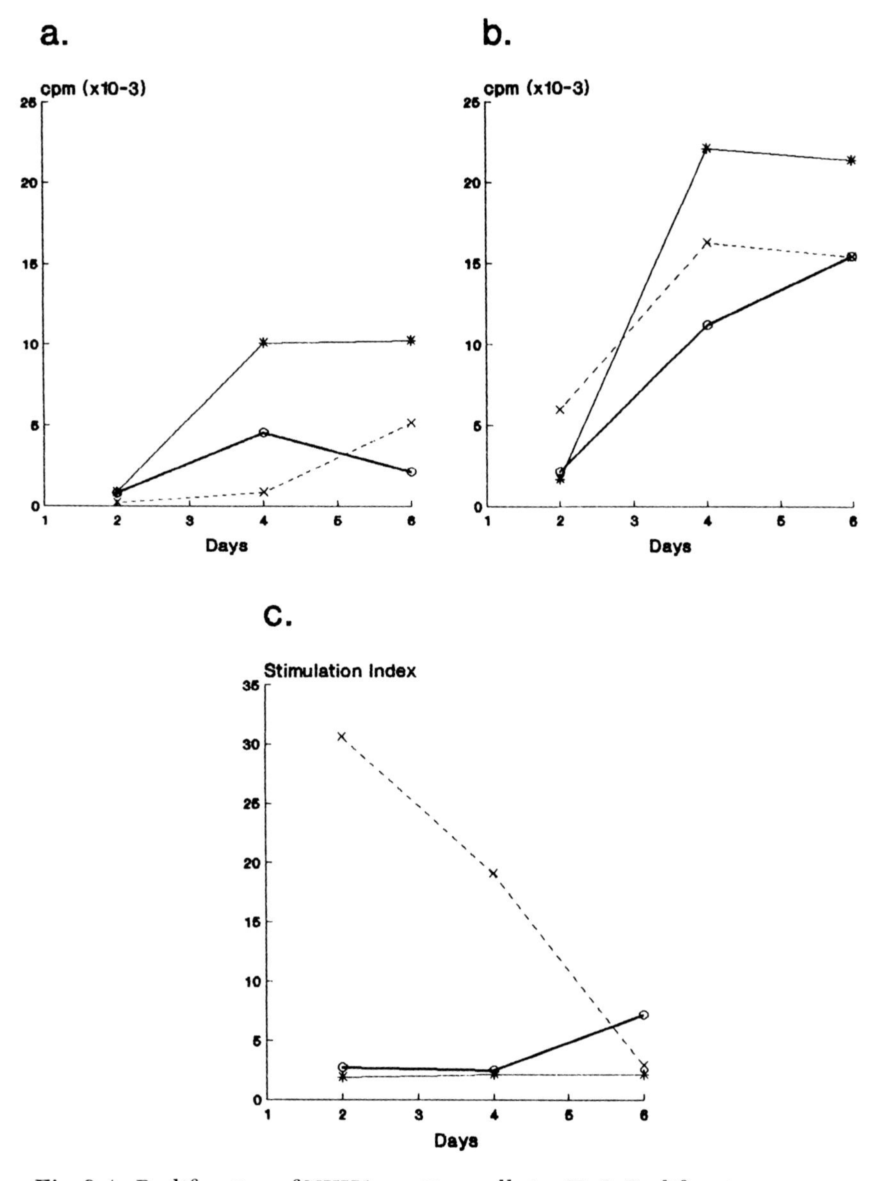

Fig. 9-4. Proliferation of NKH1-positive cells in rIL-2. Proliferation was measured after 2, 4, and 6 days incubation with and without rIL-2. A shows the response of NKH1-positive (×—×), NKH1-negative (*—*) and unsorted (○—○) decidual cells in medium alone, and b shows their responses to 20U/mL rIL-2. The stimulation index shown in c is a ratio of the cpm in the presence of rIL-2 to the cpm in the absence of rIKL-2. The values are median cpm from 6 experiments.

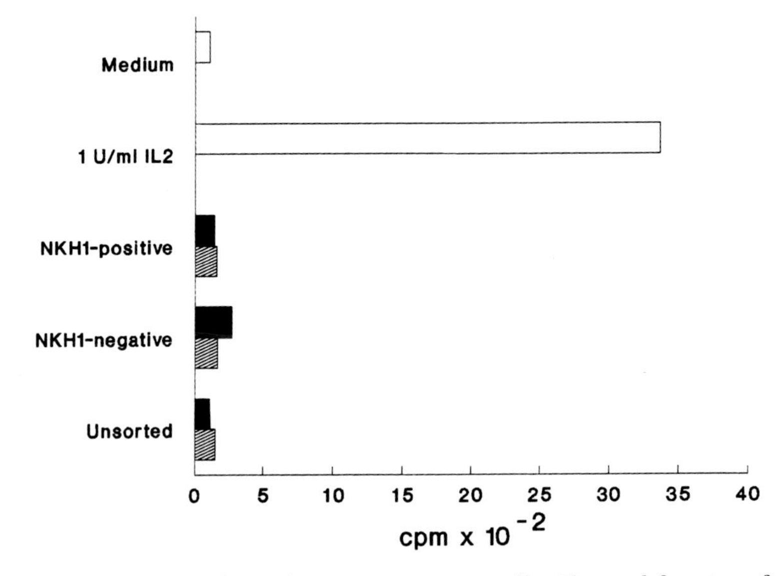

Fig. 9-5. Production of IL-2 by NKH1-positive cells. The proliferation of the IL-2 dependent CTLL cell-line is shown in medium alone, IU/mL rIL-2 and cell-free supernatants from NKH1-positive and NKH1-negative cells and unsorted decidual cells, cultured in medium alone for 2 (black bars) and 6 (hatched bars) days. The values are the median cpm from 6 experiments.

After 7 days in rIL2, the ability of unsorted decidual cells to kill K562 cells at a 25:1 E:T ratio was increased eight times.

PBMC grown in rIL2 also exhibited increased cytotoxic activity against K562 cells, but to a lesser extent, with a 2.6-fold increase in the 3:1 E:T ratio.

Cells were analyzed by flow cytometry before and after 7 days of culture in rIL2. There were significant increases in the proportions of NKH1, CD2, and CD3-positive cells (Table 9-4), although none was statistically significant. In order to determine the contribution of CD3-positive T cells to the enhanced cytotoxicity after culture with rIL2, unsorted decidual cells were cultured in rIL2 (20 U/mL) and then depleted of CD3-positive cells using magnetic beads coated with anti-CD3 antibody. In two experiments, analysis of these samples on the flow cytometer showed that the CD3-positive cells had been depleted from 8% and 10.7%, respectively, to 0%. The cytotoxicity against K562 was only marginally decreased, suggesting that most of this activity is due to LGL (Fig. 9-7).

Discussion

When decidual samples are obtained after termination of pregnancy in the first trimester there is no way of verifying that the pregnancy would have continued successfully to full term; nor can we confirm

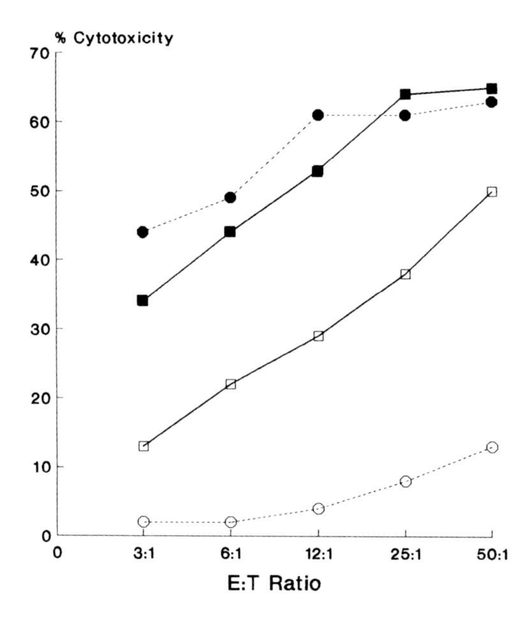

Fig. 9-6. Cytotoxicity of decidual cells after proliferation in rIL-2. The NK activity of unsorted decidual cells before (□—□), and after (■—■) culture for 7 days in rIL-2 (20U/mL rIL-2 on day 0, followed by 5U/mL rIL-2 on day 3 of culture) was measured against K562 target cells in a 6 h ^{51}Cr release assay. Controls were PBMC before (□—□) and after culture in rIL-2 (■—■). The values are the median % cytotoxicity from 7 experiments.

the extent to which the sample is representative of the tissue *in vivo*. These inevitable difficulties may have contributed to the wide variations among individual samples that we observed and that were not related to gestational age. The enzymatic digestion used to prepare the cell suspensions could have caused selective loss of some cell types, as suggested by the observations of Clark et al. (1988) who showed that suppressor activity is lost when proteases are used to disperse murine decidua. However, our results generally confirm those obtained in immunohistological studies of tissue sections (Bulmer & Sunderland, 1984).

The decidua was previously thought to be an endocrine tissue. However, the preponderance of immune cells during the first trimester must change our perceptions of its nature and possible functions. It

Table 9-4. Decidual cell phenotype before and after culture in rIL-2

Time of Assay	Cell No. × 10^{-6} (Viability %)	Antibody-Positive Cells (%)				
		NKH1	CD2	CD3	HLA-D	CD16
Day 0	24 (81)	36 (33–66)	30 (18–54)	0 (0–4)	15 (9–19)	0 (0)
Day 7 (+rIL-2)	15 (67)	50 (30–60)	47 (35–53)	8 (0–11)	12 (6–18)	0 (0)

Note: The percentage of antibody-positive cells was assessed by flow cytometry before (day 0) and after (day 7) culture in rIL-2. Values are the median values (range) from six decidual cell preparations. Viability was assessed by trypan blue exclusion and phase-contrast microscopy.

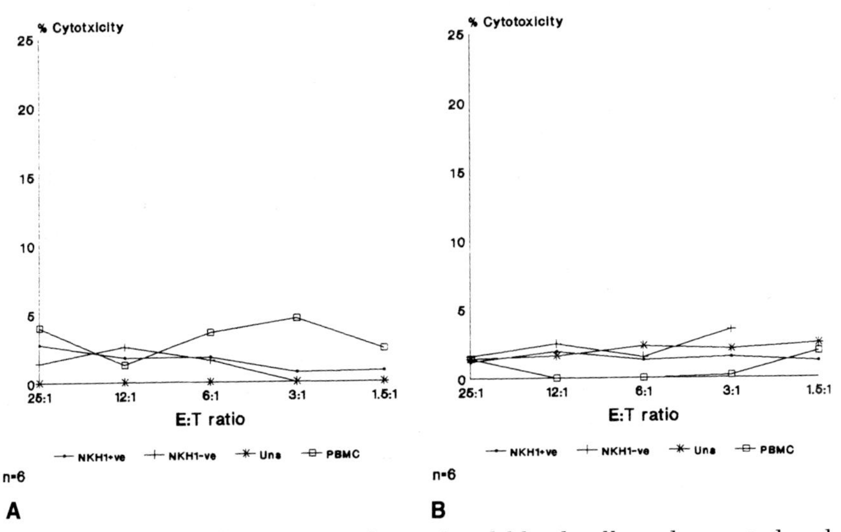

Fig. 9-7. Natural killer activity of peripheral blood cells and unsorted and purified NKH1+ decidual cells. Unsorted (uns) and sorted NKH1+ or NKH1− decidual cells and peripheral blood mononuclear cells (PBMC) were used as effector cells in a 6h ^{51}Cr release assay against trophoblast target cells, comprising either the choriocarcinoma cell line BeWo (A) or trophoblast prepared from term amniochorion (B).

is clear that numerous maternal immune cells are in direct contact with fetal trophoblast and must accommodate to it. Some decidual macrophages and T cells may participate in antigen-driven reactions, but the predominant cell population, comprising NKH1$^+$/CD3$^-$ LGL, is nonadaptive in its responses. Macrophages also have many nonadaptive immune functions. Their relation to trophoblast needs to be determined, both in successful and failed pregnancies.

These cells have lower cytolytic activity than peripheral blood LGL, although it is strongly augmented by interleukin 2. If trophoblast is susceptible to NK lysis, LGL could have an inhibitory effect on implantation and placentation. This inhibition could be physiological, serving to control trophoblast invasiveness, or pathological, causing abortion. However, preliminary experiments using unpurified third-trimester trophoblast and the choriocarcinoma cell line BeWo as NK targets show that, like murine trophoblast, these cells are resistant to NK lysis. This finding is also consistent with the recent report of King et al. (1989). LGL are the major precursors in the peripheral blood of lymphokine-activated killer (LAK) cells (Ortaldo et al., 1986), which can be generated in culture with IL-2, or the combination of IL-2 acting synergistically with TNF (Chouaib et al., 1988). Decidual LGL share at least some of these attributes, and it is possible that IL-2 produced locally within the decidua—for example, in response to infection or to immune stimulation by trophoblast—could lead to generation of cytotoxic activity that might be harmful to trophoblast.

The Fc receptor (CD16) expressed on a minor subset of decidual LGL would be expected to mediate antibody-dependent cellular cytotoxicity (ADCC), as it does in peripheral blood LGL (Lanier et al., 1983; Perussia et al., 1983a). It will be important to determine if human trophoblast is susceptible to ADCC by decidual LGL even if it is resistant to natural killer activity. This question raises the unresolved issue of the extent to which maternal antitrophoblast antibodies cross-reactive with lymphocytes (Macintyre & Faulk, 1986) or otherwise (Davies & Browne, 1985) are produced during human pregnancy.

Alternatively, the LGL may play an immunotrophic role. The cytokines that LGL can secrete are listed in Table 9-5. Undoubtedly this list is still incomplete. In addition, it is not known if one or more subsets of the decidual LGL have special capabilities with respect to cytokine secretion.

In the mouse, the concept of immunotrophism has been developed based on the assumption that the growth factors are T cell derived (Athanassakis et al., 1987). However T cells are a minor component of the human decidua, and the more abundant LGL may therefore prove to be the source of the trophic factors. Of their products, the colony-stimulating factors are perhaps the most relevant. Human trophoblast and choriocarcinoma cell lines express the product of the oncogene c-fms (Muller et al., 1983; Rettenmeier et al., 1986), which is identical with the M-CSF (CSF-1) receptor (Sherr et al., 1985). The effect of M-CSF on growth and differentiation of human trophoblast is not yet known. In the mouse the M-CSF-responsive placental cells are adherent and phagocytic and express nonspecific esterase, although they are negative for the macrophage marker Mac-1 (Athanassakis et al., 1987).

M-CSF is produced by murine uterine glandular epithelial cells (Pollard et al., 1987). Whether the same is true of the human decidua is not known. In addition, macrophages are known to be a source of M-CSF, GM-CSF, and G-CSF (Clark & Kamen, 1987; Nicola, 1987). If LGL or epithelial cells are the sources of the trophic factors, then the stimulus to their production would be either not antigen-driven or

Table 9-5. Cytokines produced by large granular lymphocytes

Interleukin 1	Scala et al. (1984)
Interleukin 2	Kasahara et al. (1983)
Interferon τ	Young and Ortaldo (1987)
TNFα	Peters et al. (1986)
CSF-1	Kasahara et al. (1983)
Leukoregulin	Sayers et al. (1986)

only indirectly so. Otherwise, the stimulus could be entirely non-immune in origin.

It is possible that the LGL inhibit or amplify local antigen-specific maternal immune response to trophoblast. NK cells suppress mixed lymphocyte reactions (Shah et al., 1985), cell-mediated lympholysis (Gilbertson et al., 1986), and plaque-forming cell responses (Shah et al., 1986). On a per cell basis, human NK cells appear to be more inhibitory of B cells than suppressor T cells (Arai et al., 1983). Although trophoblast does not express conventional histocompatibility antigens, maternal immune responses may occur by antigen presentation involving decidual macrophages. The decidual LGL may play an important regulatory role at this level.

Finally it is conceivable that these cells play no role, immunological or otherwise, in the maintenance of pregnancy. Their function may be more prosaic, for example to protect the contents of the uterus from infection. This is unlikely because the numbers of LGL in the decidua regress markedly as pregnancy progresses, so that by full term they are a minor component of this tissue. In other words, they appear to have a function or functions that are specific to the first trimester.

Conclusions

Large granular lymphocytes (LGL) are the most abundant cells in the human decidua during the first trimester. They express the NKH1 antigen that is expressed by all NK cells but not all LGL. We have purified decidual LGL by flow cytometry from cell dispersions labeled with NKH1. Both NKH1-positive cells and unsorted decidual cells have cytotoxic activity against the NK cell target K562, although this activity is weak compared to that of peripheral blood mononuclear cells (PBMC). The NKH1-negative cells have no cytotoxic activity against K562. All three types of decidual cells proliferate in response to recombinant interleukin-2 (rIL2), but none produce significant amounts of IL-2 in culture. When unsorted decidual cells are cultured for 7 days in rIL2, the proportion of NKH1-positive cells increase and NK activity is augmented. Unsorted decidual cells have no cytolytic activity against first- or third-trimester trophoblast targets, or against BeWo, a choriocarcinoma cell line. Decidual LGL have a potential role in regulating the development of the semiallogeneic placenta.

References

Abo, T., Miller, C. A., Gartland, G. and Balch, C. M. 1983. Differentiation stages of human natural killer cells in lymphoid tissues from fetal to adult life. *J. Exp. Med.* 157:273–284.

Ahrens, P. B. and Ankel, H. 1987. The role of asparagine-linked carbohydrate in natural killer cell-mediated cytolysis. *J. Biol. Chem.* 262:7575–7579.

Arai, S., Yamamoto, H., Itoh, K. and Kumagai, K. 1983. Suppressive effect of human natural killer cells on pokeweed mitogen-induced B cell differentiation. *J. Immunol.* 131:651–657.

Athanassakis, I., Bleackley, P. C., Paetkau, V., Guilbert, L., Barr, P. J. and Wegmann, T. G. 1987. The immunostimulatory effect of T cells and T cell lymphokines on murine fetally derived placental cells. *J. Immunol.* 138:37–44.

Azuma, E. and Kaplan, J. 1988. Role of lymphokine-activated killer cells as mediators of veto and natural suppression. *J. Immunol.* 141:2601–2606.

Barnstable, C. J., Bodmer, W. F., Brown, G., Galfre, G., Milstein, C., Williams, A. F. and Ziegler, A. 1978. Production of monoclonal antibodies to group A erythrocytes, HLA and other human cell surface antigens. *Cell* 14:9–20.

Bulmer, J. N. and Johnson, P. M. 1985. Immunological characterisation of decidual leucocytic infiltrate related to endometrial gland epithelium in early human pregnancy. *Immunology* 55:35–44.

Bulmer, J. N. and Sunderland, C. A. 1984. Immunohistological characterisation of lymphoid cell populations in the early human placental bed. *Immunology* 52:349–357.

Chouaib, S., Bertoglio, J., Blay, J.-Y., Marchiol-Fournigault, C. and Fradelizi, D. 1988. Generation of lymphokine-activated killer cells: synergy between tumor necrosis factor and interleukin 2. *Proc. Natl. Acad. Sci. USA* 85:6875–6879.

Clark, D. A., Falbo, M., Rowley, R. B., Banwatt, D. and Stedronska-Clark, J. 1988. Active suppression of host vs graft reaction in pregnant mice. IX. Soluble suppressor activity obtained from allopregnant mouse decidua that blocks the cytolytic effector response to IL-2 is related to transforming growth factor-β. *J. Immunol.* 141:3833–3840.

Clark, S. C. and Kamen, R. 1987. The human hematopoietic colony-stimulating factors. *Science* 236:1229–1237.

Cuturi, M. C., Anegon, I., Sherman, F., Loudon, R., Clark, S. C., Perussia, B. and Trinchieri, G. 1989. Production of hematopoietic colony-stimulating factors by human natural killer cells. *J. Exp. Med.* 169:569–583.

Dalchau, R., Kirkley, J. and Fabra, J. W. 1980. Monoclonal antibody to a human leukocyte-specific membrane glycoprotein probably homologous to the leukocyte-common (LC) antigen of the rat. *Eur. J. Immunol.* 10:737–744.

Davies, M. and Brown, C. M. 1985. Anti-trophoblast antibody responses during normal pregnancy. *J. Reprod. Immunol.* 7:285–297.

Dick, H. M., Steel, C. M. and Dupont, B. 1984. Table of workshop monoclonal antibodies and a synopsis of their principal characteristics. *Dis. Markers* 2:363.

Ellis, S. A., Palmer, M. S. and McMichael A. J. 1990. Human trophoblast and the choriocarcinoma cell line BeWo express a truncated HLA class I molecule. *J. Immunol.* 144:731–735.

Ernst, P. B., Befus, A. D. and Bienenstock, J. 1985. Leukocytes in the intestinal epithelium: an unusual immunological compartment. *Immunol. Today* 6:50–55.

Fleit, H. B., Wright, S. D. and Unkeless, J. C. 1982. Human neutrophil Fcγ receptor distribution and structure. *Proc. Natl. Acad. Sci. USA* 79:3275–3279.

Ford, W. L., Rolstad, B. and Fossum, S. 1984. The elimination of allogeneic lymphocytes: a useful model of natural killer cell activity in vivo? *Immunol. Today* 5:227–228.

Gilbertson, S. M., Shah, P. D. and Rowley, D. A. 1986. NK cells suppress the generation of Lyt-2+ cytolytic T cells by suppressing or eliminating dendritic cells. *J. Immunol.* 136:3567–3571.

Gillis, S., Ferm, N., Ou, W. and Smith, K. A. 1978. T cell growth factor: parameters of production and a quantitative micro-assay for activity. *J. Immunol.* 120:2027–2032.

Griffin, J. D., Hercend, T., Beveridge, R. and Schlossman, S. F. 1983. Characterization of an antigen expressed by human natural killer cells. *J. Immunol.* 130:2947–2951.

Hansson, M., Kiessling, R., Anderson, B., Karre, K. and Roder, J. 1979. NK cell-sensitive T-cell subpopulation in thymus:inverse correlation to host NK activity. *Nature* 278:174–176.

Hercend, T., Reinherz, E. L., Meuer, S., Schlossman, S. F. and Ritz, J. 1983. Phenotypic and functional heterogeneity of human cloned natural killer cell lines. *Nature* 301:158–160.

Hercend, T., Griffin, J. D., Bensussan, A., Schmidt, R. E., Edson, M. A., Brennan, A., Murray, C., Daley, J. F., Schlossman, S. F. and Ritz, J. 1985. Generation of monoclonal antibodies to a human natural killer clone. Characterization of two natural killer-associated antigens NKH1 and NKH2, expressed on subsets of large granular lymphocytes. *J. Clin. Invest.* 75:932–943.

Hildreth, J. E. K., Gotch, F., Hildreth, P. D. K. and McMichael, A. J. 1983. A human lymphocyte-associated antigen involved in cell-mediated lympholysis. *Eur. J. Immunol.* 13:202–208.

Kasahara, T., Djeu, J. Y., Dougherty, S. F. and Oppenheim, J. J. 1983. Capacity of human large granular lymphocytes (LGL) to produce multiple lymphokines: interleukin 2, interferon, and colony-stimulating factor. *J. Immunol.* 131:2379–2386.

Kehrl, J. H., Dukovich, M., Whalen, G., Katz, P., Fauci, A. S. and Greene, W. C. 1988. Novel interleukin 2 (IL-2) receptor appears to mediate IL-2-induced activation of natural killer cells. *J. Clin. Invest.* 81:200–205.

Kiessling, R., Klein, E., Pross, H. and Wigzell, H. 1975. "Natural" killer cells in the mouse. II. Cytotoxic cells with specificity for mouse Moloney leukaemia cells. Characteristics of the killer cell. *Eur. J. Immunol.* 5:117–121.

King, A., Burkby, C. and Loke, Y. W. 1989. Early human decidual cells exhibit NK activity against the K562 cell line but not against first trimester trophoblast. *Cell. Immunol.* 118:337–344.

Kohl, S., Springer, T. A., Schlamstieg, F. C., Loo, L. S. and Anderson, D. C. 1984. Defective natural killer cytotoxicity and polymorphonuclear leukocyte antibody dependent cellular cytotoxicity in patients with LFA-1/OKM-1 deficiency. *J. Immunol.* 133:2972–2978.

Lanier, L. L., Kipps, T. J. and Phillips, J. H. 1985. Functional properties of a unique subset of cytotoxic $CD3^+$ lymphocytes that express Fc receptors for IgG (CD16/Leu-11 antigen). *J. Exp. Med.* 162:2089–2106.

Lanier, L. L., Cwirla, S. and Phillips, J. H. 1986a. Genomic organization of T-cell γ genes in human peripheral blood natural killer cells. *J. Immunol.* 137:3375–3377.

Lanier, L. L., Le, A. M., Civin, C. I., Loken, M. R. and Phillips, J. H. 1986b. The relationship of CD16 [Leu-11] and Leu-19 [NKH-1] antigen expression on human peripheral blood NK cells and cytotoxic T lymphocytes. *J. Immunol.* 136:4480–4486.

Lozzio, C. B. and Lozzio, B. B. 1973. Cytotoxicity of a factor isolated from human spleen. *J. Natl. Cancer Inst.* 50:535–538.

Marlin, S. D. and Springer, T. A. 1987. Purified intercellular adhesion molecule-1 (ICAM-1) is a ligand for lymphocyte function-associated antigen (LFA-1). *Cell* 51:813–819.

Macintyre, J. A. and Faulk, W. P. 1986. Clinical value of research in chronic spontaneous abortion. *Am. J. Reprod. Immunol.* 10:121–126.

Muller, R., Tremblay, J. M., Adamson, E. D. and Verma, I. M. 1983. Tissue and cell type-specific expression of two human *c-onc* genes. *Nature* 304:454–456.

Nicola, N. A. 1987. Why do hemopoietic growth factors interact with each other? *Immunol. Today* 8:134–139.

Ortaldo, J. R., Mason, A. and Overton, R. 1986. Lymphokine-activated killer cells. Analysis of pregenitors and effectors. *J. Exp. Med.* 164:1193–1205.

Perussia, B. and Trinchieri, G. 1984. Antibody 3G8, specific for the human neutrophil Fc receptor, reacts with natural killer cells. *J. Immunol.* 132:1410–1415.

Perussia, B., Acuto, O., Terhorst, C., Faust, J., Lazurus, R., Fanning, V. and Trinchieri, G. 1983a. Human natural killer cells analysed by B73.1, a monoclonal antibody blocking Fc receptor functions. II. Studies of B73.1 antibody-antigen interaction on the lymphocyte membrane. *J. Immunol.* 130:2142–2148.

Perussia, B., Starr, S., Abraham, S., Fanning, V. and Trinchieri, G. 1983b. Human natural killer cells analysed by B73.3, a monoclonal antibody blocking Fc receptor functions. I. Characterization of the lymphocyte subset reactive with B73.1. *J. Immunol.* 130:2133–2141.

Peters, P. M., Ortaldo, J. R., Shalaby, M. R., Svedersky, L. P., Nedwin, G. E., Bringman, T. S., Hass, P. E., Aggarwal, B. R., Hebberman, R. B., Goeddel, D. V. and Palladino, M. A. 1986. Natural killer-sensitive targets stimulate production of TNF-α but not TNF-β (lymphotoxin) by highly purified human peripheral blood large granular lymphocytes. *J. Immunol.* 137:2592–2598.

Pollard, J. W., Bartocci, A., Arceci, R., Orlofsky, A., Ladner, M. B. and Stanley, E. R. 1987. Apparent role of the macrophage growth factor, CSF-1, in placental development. *Nature* 330:484–486.

Puccetti, P., Santoni, A., Riccardi, C. and Herbermann, R. B. 1980. Cytotoxic effector cells with the characteristics of natural killer cells in the lungs of mice. *Int. J. Cancer* 20:153–158.

Redman, C. W. G. 1983. HLA-DR antigen on trophoblast: a review. *Am. J. Reprod. Immunol.* 3:175–177.

Redman, C. W. G., McMichael, A. J., Stirrat, G. M., Sunderland, C. A. and Ting, A. 1984. Class 1 major histocompatibility complex antigens on human extra-villous trophoblast. *Immunology* 52:457–468.

Redman, C. W. G., Arenas, J. and Sargent, I. L. 1987., Maternal anti-fetal immune responses during human pregnancy. In *Reproductive Immunology: Materno-Fetal Relationship* (G. Chaouat, ed.). *Collogue INSERM* 154:25–32.

Rettenmier, C. W., Sacca, R., Furman, W. L., Roussei, M. F., Holt, J. T., Nienhuis, A. W., Stanley, E. R. and Sherr, C. J. 1986. Expression of the human c-fms proto-oncogene product (colony-stimulating factor-1 receptor) on peripheral blood mononuclear cells and choriocarcinoma cell lines. *J. Clin. Invest.* 77:1740–1746.

Santoli, D., Trinchieri, G. and Lief, F. S. 1978. Cell-mediated cytotoxicity against virus-infected target cells in humans. 1. Characterization of the effector lymphocyte. *J. Immunol.* 121:526–531.

Sayers, T. J., Ransom, J. H., Denn, A. C., Herberman, R. B. and Ortaldo, J. R. 1986. Analysis of a cytostatic lymphokine produced by incubation of lymphocytes with tumor cells: relationship to leukoregulin and distinction from recombinant lymphotoxin, recombinant tumor necrosis factor, and natural killer cytotoxic factor. *J. Immunol.* 137:385–390.

Scala, G., Allavena, P., Djeu, J. Y., Kasahara, T., Ortaldo, J. R., Herberman, R. B. and Oppenheim, J. J. 1984. Human large granular lymphocytes are potent producers of interleukin-1. *Nature* 309:56–59.

Schmidt, R. E., Hercend, T., Fox, D. A., Bensussan, A., Bartley, G., Daley, J. F., Schlossman, S. F., Reinherz, E. L. and Ritz, J. 1985. The role of interleukin 2 and T11 E rosette antigen in activation and proliferation of human NK clones. *J. Immunol.* 135:672–678.

Schmidt, R. E., Caulfield, J. P., Michon, J., Hein, A., Kamada, M. M., MacDermott, R. P., Stevens, R. and Ritz, J. 1988. T11/CD2 activation of cloned human natural killer cells results in increased conjugate formation and exocytosis of cytolytic granules. *J. Immunol.* 140:991–1002.

Shah, P. D., Gilbertson, S. M. and Rowley, D. A. 1985. Dendritic cells that have interacted with antigen are targets for natural killer cells. *J. Exp. Med.* 162:625–636.

Shah, P. D., Keij, J., Gilbertson, S. M. and Rowley, D. A. 1986. Thy-1^+ and Thy-1^- natural killer cells. Only Thy-1^- natural killer cells suppress dendritic cells. *J. Exp. Med.* 163:1012–1017.

Sherr, C. J., Rettenmier, C. W., Sacca, R., Roussel, M. F., Look, A. T. and Stanley, E. R. 1985. The c-fms proto-oncogene product is related to the receptor for the mononuclear phagocyte growth factor, CSF-1. *Cell* 41:665–676.

Starkey, P. M., 1987. Reactivity of human trophoblast with an antibody to the HLA class II antigen, HLA-DP. *J. Reprod. Immunol.* 11:63–70.

Starkey, P. M., Sargent, I. L. and Redman, C. W. G. 1988. Cell populations in human early pregnancy decidua: characterisation and isolation of large granular lymphocytes by flow cytometry. *Immunology* 65:129–134.

Storkus, W. J., Howell, D. W., Salter, R. D., Dawson, J. R. and Cresswell, P. 1987. NK susceptibility varies inversely with target cell class I HLA antigen expression. *J. Immunol.* 138:1657–1659.

Trinchieri, G., Matsumoto-Kobayashi, M., Clark, S., Seehra, J., London, L. and Perussia, B. 1984. Response of human peripheral blood natural killer cells to interleukin 2. *J. Exp. Med.* 160:1147–1169.

Young, H. A. and Ortaldo, J. R. 1987. One-signal requirement for interferon-τ production by human large granular lymphocytes. *J. Immunol.* 139:724–727.

10

Immunobiological Features of Murine Trophoblast

JUDITH R. HEAD, BELINDA L. DRAKE, and
FEDERICO A. ZUCKERMANN

The maternal-fetal interface is a composite of tissues of maternal and fetal origin that in most cases exist in apparent harmony throughout gestation. An especially intimate association of cells from these two sources occurs in the hemochorial placenta, which is made up of multiple cell types, including maternal decidua and blood cells and fetal-derived mesenchymal cells, macrophages, endothelial cells, blood, and trophoblast. In attempting to elucidate how fetal-derived cells can invade maternal tissues and survive in the face of maternal defense mechanisms, attention has focused on trophoblast cells, which line the sinuses filled with maternal blood in the exchange area and confront and invade maternal decidual tissue. Early on, it was hypothesized that these cells were antigenically inert, especially with regard to histocompatibility antigens, and thus functioned as an immunological barrier between potentially destructive maternal effectors and vulnerable fetal tissues (Simmons & Russell, 1966; Witebsky & Reich, 1932). However, more recent studies have provided substantial evidence that this simple solution is insufficient. Although some trophoblast cells normally lack histocompatibility antigens, other populations do express these, as well as other antigens (Head et al., 1987). Moreover, effector cells have been discovered that can kill targets (e.g., tumor cells) regardless of MHC antigen expression, such as natural killer (NK) cells, natural cytotoxic (NC) cells, and non-MHC-restricted T cells (Lanier et al., 1986). Finally, there is increasing evidence from both humans and murine models that some pregnancy failure can likely be attributed to destructive maternal effectors (Clark et al., 1987). Thus, the critical questions that arise relative to the maintenance of a quiescent fetal-maternal interface include: (1) the distribution of MHC antigen expression and its regulation in different trophoblast populations and (2) the susceptibility of trophoblast cells to various potential effectors. This chapter deals with these questions in relation to the hemochorial mouse placenta and focuses on work performed with primary *in vitro* cultures of midgestation trophoblast.

Alloantigen Expression on Cultured Trophoblast Cells

The midgestational murine placenta contains several populations of trophoblast: the giant cells scattered along the decidual interface, the cellular spongiotrophoblast through which the major maternal blood sinuses course; and three thin layers (an outer cytotrophoblast layer with two underlying syncytial layers) lining the maternal blood-filled sinuses in the labyrinthine region (exchange area). In order to evaluate trophoblast antigen expression *in vitro*, a method was developed for isolating trophoblast cells from definitive murine placentas (Zuckermann & Head, 1986a). Placentas from 13- or 14-day pregnant animals were carefully dissected away from the decidua and fetal membranes, and the central core of the chorionic plate with its associated fetal mesenchyme was removed. After digestion with neutral protease (dispase), the cells were separated by discontinuous density gradient centrifugation using percoll. Cells collected at the 1.05/1.06 g/mL density interface were placed in culture and the adherent cells characterized. These preparations consistently yield adherent cells with the characteristics listed in Table 10-1. The vast majority of the cells are clearly trophoblast, with very minor contamination by other cells, such as macrophages. There are, not surprisingly, at least two subpopulations of trophoblast. One has alkaline phosphatase activity and is thus likely to be derived from the labyrinth; the other is alkaline phosphatase-negative and is probably spongiotrophoblast. A minority of the cells have transferrin receptors and are likely to be involved in maternal-fetal exchange in the labyrinth.

Table 10-1. Characteristics of percoll-purified murine trophoblast

95% fetal-derived (GPI analysis)
>90% cytokeratin-positive and vimentin-negative
>90% nonspecific esterase-negative
>90% F4/80-negative
>90% Fc receptor-negative
30–45% alkaline phosphatase-positive
20% transferrin receptor-positive

Flow Cytometric Analysis of H-2 Antigen Expression and its Modulation by Interferon (IFN)

Flow cytometry was used to assess MHC antigen expression by these cells after 2 days in culture (Zuckermann & Head, 1986b). A pool of monoclonal antibodies to H-2K^k was used with trophoblast cells obtained from placentas from the H-2^b × H-2^a mating combination (paternal haplotype = K^k, I-A^k, and D^d). Analysis revealed that 30–40% of the cells were positive for H-2K^k, with a wide variation in intensity, but always considerably lower than that of other cells, such as L cells. Trophoblast cells did not express class II MHC antigens. When trophoblast cells were cultured for 48 h with either IFN-α/β or IFN-γ, there was a significant increase—up to 70%—in the number of cells bearing class I antigens, but still no expression of class II antigens. When trophoblast cells were analyzed for both MHC antigens and alkaline phosphatase activity, the alkaline phosphatase-positive population was H-2 negative. The inverse correlation of alkaline phosphatase activity and class I MHC expression suggests that the H-2K expressing population was derived from the spongiotrophoblast, consistent with observations on cells derived from dissected regions of placentas (Jenkinson & Owen, 1980) and a report of alloantibody binding *in vivo* (Singh et al., 1983). Recent *in situ* observations of antigen expression (see Chapter 11) and the presence of mRNA transcripts (Philpott et al., 1988) also support this conclusion. It appears that some trophoblast cells can be induced to express these antigens after IFN treatment, but in a significant population (30% in these cultures), these genes may be repressed irreversibly as apparently are the class II genes in all trophoblast cells.

Effects of Alloantibodies and Complement on Trophoblast

Cultured trophoblast cells were tested for their susceptibility to alloantibodies directed against paternal antigens using an antibody plus complement-mediated ^{51}Cr release cytotoxicity assay (Zuckermann & Head, 1986b). When trophoblast cells of the B10 × B10.A)F_1 phenotype were treated with alloantisera from B6 animals hyperimmunized to A/J antigens, 25–40% were killed in the presence of rabbit complement. Using a monoclonal antibody to the K^k specificity (11.4.1), 20–25% were killed. Cultured trophoblast cells were then treated for 48 h with 1000 U/mL of IFN-α/β and used as targets as before. The lysis with alloantiserum increased to 60% and the monoclonal antibody to over 50%. Similar results were observed with fetal fibroblast cells obtained from the same conceptus. Thus, embryonic cells and placental trophoblast cells are both susceptible to killing by alloantibody directed against paternal alloantigens in the presence of heterologous complement.

Effects of Maternal Antipaternal Immunization *in Vivo*

The ability of a significant proportion of trophoblast cells to bind alloantibody *in vitro* suggested that these cells might be affected *in vivo* by effectors directed against paternal MHC antigens. Because others have reported that alloimmunization of female mice to paternal antigens before or during pregnancy does not affect its outcome substantially (Chaouat & Monnot, 1984; Clarke, 1971), we looked for effects of such immunization not just on delivery of offspring but also on the growth of the placenta and fetus *in utero*. Moreover, to maximize the potential effects of immunization on the fetal-placental unit, some females were intravenously infused during pregnancy with 0.5 mL of rabbit serum as a source of heterologous complement (C′). This serum was exhaustively absorbed with mouse cells to remove natural antibodies and then filter sterilized. The protocols for hyperimmunization of the females and subsequent treatments are given in Table 10-2. Females immunized by this regimen had high serum titers on day 15 of pregnancy (1:512 on average) and significant cytotoxic T cell activity in their spleens.

Two mating combinations were studied—C57BL/6 females mated with A/J males and C3H females mated with DBA/2 males—both gave similar results. Immunization of the females to paternal antigens alone, as expected, had no effect on fetal survival: all had litter sizes (total number of implants) similar to those of unimmunized control animals and very low numbers of late resorptions (0–1.4%). However, those females that received infusions of rabbit serum during preg-

Table 10-2. Immunization protocol

Females alloimmunized	Skin allograft followed 2 weeks later by four weekly intraperitoneal injections of lymphoid cells
Mated	With males allogeneic (immunizing) syngeneic third-party allogeneic
Day 13 of pregnancy	Injected with rabbit serum iv absorbed, high C′ absorbed, inactivated
Day 15 of pregnancy	Sacrified to observe resorptions placental, fetal weights gross, histological changes

nancy had a significantly higher incidence of late resorptions that occurred after the C′ treatment (9.8% and 12.0% for the two groups). The lack of resorptions in unimmunized females receiving C′ and in immunized females injected with inactivated C′ indicated that this was a combined effect of the immunization and C′. Thus, the combination of immunization and C′ could induce pregnancy loss; nevertheless, it is significant that even this tremendous immunological stress was unable to cause failure of the majority of implants.

Despite the inability of the immunizing regimen to cause fetal demise, there was a significant influence on the growth of the allogeneic fetal-placental unit. As seen in Table 10-3, placental weights were increased when the females were immunized to paternal antigens and did not receive C′ or received inactivated C′. Generally, heavier placentas are associated with heavier fetuses (McLaren, 1965); however, in this case, the opposite was found. Fetal weights were lower in the immunized females. When immunized females were infused with C′ during pregnancy, these effects were exacerbated (Table 10-3): placental weights increased even more, and fetal weights were decreased further. No effects on these parameters were seen if the immunized females were mated with either syngeneic or third-party males. To verify that at least some of these changes were the result of maternal alloantibody, some naive C3H females pregnant by DBA/2 males were injected intravenously on day 13 with 6 mg of the IgG fraction of either normal mouse serum or serum from C3H animals hyperimmunized to DBA/2, followed by C′ 1 h later. Two days later, placental weights revealed a significant increase in animals given alloantibodies (182 ± 5.8 mg) compared with normal serum controls (162 ± 5.8 mg). However, fetal weights were unaffected by these treatments. An analysis of DNA content revealed that at least some of the increase in placental weight was due to an increase in cell numbers (0.8 ± .06

Table 10-3. Effects of maternal antipaternal immunization on fetal and placental growth

Female	Male	Immunized to DBA/2	C′ Infusion	Mean Fetal Weight (mg ± SEM)	Mean Placental Weight (mg ± SEM)	Litters
C3H	DBA/2	–	+	222 ± 5	136 ± 6	17
C3H	DBA/2	+	–	208 ± 6	164 ± 4*	18
C3H	DBA/2	+	Inactive	217 ± 9	152 ± 10	6
C3H	DBA/2	+	+	204 ± 5*	176 ± 6†	18

Note: Females were sacrificed on day 15 of pregnancy.
* $p < 0.03$.
† $p < 0.001$ compared with nonimmune control.

mg/placenta in immunized animals vs. 0.5 ± .02 mg/placental in naive animals).

The active immunization of females to paternal antigens often resulted in gross changes in the placenta, with a variety of histopathological effects. These changes were more frequent and dramatic in immunized animals receiving C′. Grossly, the enlarged placentas sometimes showed evidence of extra growth, and most had increased spongiotrophoblast regions along with diminished vascular perfusion in the labyrinthine region, which was usually confined to the outer areas. Histologically, these areas were lacking in maternal but not fetal blood, and the trophoblast cells appeared to be hypertrophied. In some cases, areas of focal necrosis were observed, and there was often neutrophilic margination or thrombosis in some of the larger maternal vessels. Within the placenta itself, however, there was rarely any kind of leukocytic infiltrate. A feature seen in many of the placentas was the accumulation of eosinophilic inclusions within spongiotrophoblast cells, especially near the areas where there was a decrease in maternal blood perfusion. These inclusions are seen in normal placentas to some extent, but were greatly increased in affected placentas, both in the number of cells involved and the inclusions per cell. Their identity is currently unknown.

All of these changes suggest that maternal antipaternal immunization has a detrimental effect on the placenta, which can be exacerbated greatly by the administration of heterologous C′. Nevertheless, the placenta is able to cope with this immunological stress to protect the fetus, except in extreme cases, although often it is small for gestational age. Elucidation of the actual cellular changes occurring in affected placentas will require further investigation.

Susceptibility of Trophoblast Cells to Cell-Mediated Cytotoxicity

The fact that trophoblast cells in culture expressed MHC antigens and could be killed by alloantibody and heterologous complement prompted us to investigate whether these cells might also be susceptible to allospecific cytotoxic T cells (CTL). Moreover, the demonstration that natural killer (NK) cells can be isolated from the pregnant uterus (Croy et al., 1985) suggested that other cellular effectors should also be assessed.

Allospecific CTL

CTL effectors were generated *in vitro* in standard primary mixed lymphocyte reactions, using B10 responders and B10.A stimulators to generate effectors specific for H-2^{a}. In a standard ^{51}Cr release assay, neither heterozygous (B10 × B10.A)F_1 nor homozygous B10.A trophoblast could be killed, even when H-2 antigen expression was increased with IFN treatment (Zuckermann & Head, 1987). Trophoblast cells could, however, compete with specific tumor targets, confirming that the target antigens were not only expressed but were also able to bind to effectors. Similar results were obtained with other strain combinations. To increase effector:trophoblast binding, some assays were done in the presence of the lectin PHA, but trophoblast cells remained remarkably resistant to lysis. This apparent insusceptibility was not altered by treatment of the cells with cyclohexamide to inhibit protein synthesis or neuraminidase. Supernatants from cultured trophoblast cells, even after concentration, did not inhibit normal CTL target killing. Thus, the cultured trophoblast cells seemed to have an innate resistance to CTL-mediated lysis.

Further studies indicated, however, that this resistance could be overcome under certain circumstances (Drake & Head, 1989a). When effectors were generated in GIBCO Opti-MEM medium instead of standard RPMI-1640, they developed a higher lytic capacity toward prototype tumor targets (28.6 lytic units/10^6 cells vs 18.5). These CTL were now able to kill cultured trophoblast cells (43–53% at 100:1 E:T ratio), and the level of killing could be increased by IFN pretreatment, which augments H-2 antigen levels (55–75% at 100:1 E:T ratio). Interestingly, these effectors were not able to kill fresh trophoblast cells.

Natural Killer (NK) Cells

NK cells are non-T, non-B lymphocytes that are capable of lysing a variety of targets, including many tumor cells and virus-infected cells (Lanier et al., 1986). They are characterized phenotypically by the absence of T and B cell markers and the presence of asialoGM1 (Trinchieri, 1986).

Naive and Interferon (IFN)-Activated NK Cells. Spleen cells, a common source of NK cells, were unable to kill cultured trophoblast cells, though they readily killed the prototype NK target, YAC-1 cells, and to a lesser extent, fetal fibroblasts (Zuckermann & Head, 1988). When cyclohexamide was included to prevent the possibility of membrane repair in the trophoblast targets, they remained resistant. Similar results were obtained with spleen cells from animals given poly I:C to activate their NK cells or with spleen cells treated directly with IFN *in vitro* before use as effectors. Such treatments significantly increased YAC-1 target killing, but did not affect trophoblast. Competitive inhibition experiments revealed that trophoblast cells do have the NK target structure and bind to the effectors. Their resistance to NK lysis could not be overcome by neuraminidase pretreatment of the trophoblast, and trophoblast culture supernatants did not contain substances capable of interfering with NK cell killing of YAC targets.

Antibody-Dependent Cell-Mediated Cytotoxicity (ADCC). NK cells bear Fc receptors and are believed to be responsible for ADCC when target cells are pretreated with specific antibody. Therefore, trophoblast cells were exposed to the alloantibodies shown previously to be capable of mediating C′-dependent cytotoxicity (above), followed by naive spleen cells. Although this protocol resulted in efficient killing of tumor target cells, the trophoblast cells remained unaffected (Zuckermann & Head, 1988).

Lymphokine-Activated Killer (LAK) Cells. When naive populations of spleen or peripheral blood lymphocytes are exposed to activated T-cell-derived lymphokine preparations containing interleukin-2, they generate effector cells that are capable of readily lysing a wide variety of tumor targets and some normal cell populations that are normally resistant to NK cell lysis by a non-MHC-restricted mechanism (Rosenstein et al., 1984). These so-called LAK cells are a heterogeneous population containing both cells with NK and T cell markers. LAK cells were generated from murine spleen cells using supernatants from con A-activated rat spleen cells and tested for their ability to kill trophoblast cells (Drake & Head, 1989b). These LAK effectors gave dramatically increased killing of YAC-1 targets and killing of NK-resistant EL4 cells and were able to kill cultured trophoblast cells. Moreover, these cells also killed freshly prepared trophoblast cells. To identify the cell type responsible, LAK cells were depleted selectively of certain cell populations using antibody and C′ before their use as effectors against trophoblast. Anti-CD-8 antibody, which depleted cytotoxic T cells, had no significant effect on trophoblast lysis; however, anti-asialoGM1 antibody pretreatment diminished the lysis of trophoblast cells by 62–74%. Thus, the cells responsible for killing trophoblast in this population were phenotypically NK cells.

Activated NK Cells. To confirm that highly activated NK cells were indeed capable of killing trophoblast cells, effector cells were generated *in vitro* from donor animals with severe combined immunodeficiency (*scid*). *Scid* mice have a developmental defect that renders them incapable of producing mature, antigen-reactive B and T cells, so their spleens are an excellent source of NK cells with little other lymphocyte contamination (Dorschkind et al., 1985). When incubated for several days with IL-2, *scid* spleen cells generate extremely lytic NK effectors. When such cells were tested on YAC-1 cells they killed very efficiently (77–85% at 20:1 E:T ratio) and also lysed NK-resistant tumor targets, such as EL4 and P815. These cells were very effective against both cultured and freshly prepared trophoblast cells (68–76% and 45–50% at 20:1 E:T ratio, respectively).

Comments on Cell-Mediated Lysis of Trophoblast

Other reports of the susceptibility of murine trophoblast to immune effectors have given conflicting results (Chaouat & Kolb, 1985; Smith, 1983) and vary widely in several aspects, including source of effectors, lytic assays used, and, perhaps most importantly, the method of obtaining the trophoblast targets. In some studies, the targets have been rather heterogeneous placental cells that were not fully characterized to determine the proportion of trophoblast cells. There is also some evidence to suggest that susceptibility of targets to CTL lysis may be related to the enzyme used in preparing the cells. When placental cells are exposed to trypsin, killing is observed (Chaouat & Kolb, 1985; Smith, 1983), whereas with collagenase or dispase, there is little or no killing (Chaouat & Kolb, 1985). Thus, some treatments may lead to increased fragility of the cells, resulting in increased vulnerability. All of our studies have been conducted with target cell preparations derived using dispase, a neutral protease that has minimal detrimental effects on the cell, and have been highly characterized to confirm that the vast majority of the target cells belong to the trophoblast lineage. These preparations are also more likely to reflect the properties of trophoblast *in vivo* than are continuous cell lines of placental origin.

Significance of Selective Trophoblast Lytic Resistance to the Maintenance of the Maternal-Fetal Interface

Table 10-4 summarizes the results of testing susceptibility of trophoblast to various effectors. Trophoblast was susceptible to killing by alloantibody in the presence of heterologous complement. However, even though there were significant effects on both fetus and placenta, fetal death only occurred in a small proportion of pregnancies and only if the immunized mothers were given heterologous complement. This suggests that host complement is insufficient to cause destructive effects. Even in this extreme case of immunological insult, the capacity of the placenta to protect the fetus is usually sufficient. With regard to cellular effectors, it appears that the determining factor is the activation state of the effector cells. Murine trophoblast cells

Table 10-4. Murine trophoblast cells *in vitro*

Cannot be killed by	*Can* be killed by
RPMI-generated CTL	OPTI-MEM-generated CTL
Naive or IFN-activated NK	LAK cells
ADCC	IL-2-activated NK cells
LDCC	Alloantibody and C'

are insusceptible to both allospecific and nonspecific killer cells at low or moderate levels of activation, and their resistance would seem to be innate, rather than due to a lack of cell surface target structures, ineffective binding, or secretion of a suppressive factor. This mechanism clearly fails if the effectors have been driven to a highly activated state, most likely due to changes in the lytic mechanism used. There is increasing evidence that cells driven to high levels of lytic activity by IL-2 undergo numerous molecular changes, which include alterations in their lytic mechanisms (Kornbluth & Hoover, 1988; Shanahan et al., 1986). The key role of IL-2 in this change indicates that an extremely important immunoregulatory mechanism at the maternal-fetal interface must be to prevent IL-2-mediated activation of effector cells. Indeed, several such safeguards have been reported in murine decidua, including local production of a soluble factor similar to transforming growth factor-β by suppressor cells, that interferes with activation (Clark et al., 1988). Other decidual cells produce prostaglandin E2, which can accomplish the same end (Tawfik et al., 1986).

These results provide supporting evidence that the most dangerous effector cell for trophoblast *in vivo* is the activated NK cell. It is thus of great interest that the predominant cell type identified at sites of pregnancy failure in rodent abortion models has the functional properties and phenotype of NK cells and that abortion rates can be modulated by influencing NK activity *in vivo* (de Fougerolles and Baines, 1987; Gendron & Baines, 1988). Moreover, decidual suppressor activity appears to be deficient in sites that undergo resorption (Clark et al., 1986). A cause-effect relationship has not been established in these systems, but the current studies suggest that such cells should be evaluated for evidence of activation.

There are several key features of the maternal-fetal interface that appear to be designed to protect the conceptus: (1) poor MHC antigen expression by some trophoblast populations, (2) resistance of trophoblast cells to both nonspecific and specific cellular effectors that they might encounter within the uterus, (3) regulatory processes to prevent IL-2 activation of effectors that trophoblast could not resist, and (4) control of the potential for certain effector cells to enter the decidual area near the interface (Redline & Lu, 1988). All of these taken together suggest that the fetal-placental unit is extremely well protected, and it is unlikely that failure of any one of the above would lead to pregnancy loss. Conversely, it is possible that pregnancy failure results if more than one of these are inoperative. Thus, models of pregnancy failure should be investigated from several aspects to determine which of these apparently important safeguards are intact.

Acknowledgments

The authors acknowledge the technical assistance of Charles Kresge, Deborah Bogue, and Steven Miller and the secretarial assistance of Sandra Finley. This work was supported in part by NIH Grant AI-25227.

References

Chaouat, G. and Monnot, P. 1984. Systemic active suppression is not necessary for successful allopregnancy. *Am. J. Reprod. Immunol.* 6:5.

Chaouat, G. and Kolb, J. P. 1985. Immunoactive products of placenta. IV. Impairment by placental cells and their products of CTL function at effector stage. *J. Immunol.* 135:215.

Clark, D. A., Chaput, A. and Tutton, D. 1986. Active suppression of host-versus-graft reaction in pregnant mice. VII. Spontaneous abortion of allogeneic DBA/2 × CBA/J fetuses in the uterus of CBA/J mice correlates with deficient non-T suppressor cell activity. *J. Immunol.* 136:1668.

Clark, D. A., Croy, B. A., Wegmann, T. and Chaouat, G. 1987. Immunological and para-immunological mechanisms in spontaneous abortion: recent insights and future directions. *J. Reprod. Immunol.* 12:1.

Clark, D. A., Falbo, M., Rowley, R. B., Banwatt, D. and Stredronska-Clark, J. 1988. Active suppression of host-vs-graft reaction in pregnant mice. IX. Soluble suppressor activity obtained from allopregnant mouse decidua that blocks the cytolytic effector response to IL-2 is related to transforming growth factor-β. *J. Immunol.* 141:3833.

Clarke, A. 1971. The effects of maternal pre-immunization on pregnancy in the mouse. *J. Reprod. Fertil.* 24:369.

Croy, B. A., Gambel, P., Rossant, J. and Wegmann, T. 1985. Characterization of murine decidual natural killer (NK) cells and their relevance to the success of pregnancy. *Cell. Immunol.* 93:315.

de Fougerolles, A. R. and Baines, M. 1987. Modulation of the natural killer cell activity in pregnant mice alters the spontaneous abortion rate. *J. Reprod. Immunol.* 11:147.

Dorschkind, K., Pollack, S. B., Bosma, M. J. and Phillips, R. A. 1985. Natural killer (NK) cells are present in mice with severe combined immunodeficiency (*scid*). *J. Immunol.* 134:3798.

Drake, B. L. and Head, J. R. 1989a. Murine trophoblast can be killed by allospecific cytotoxic T lymphocytes generated in GIBCO Opti-MEM medium. *J. Reprod. Immunol.* 15:71.

Drake, B. L. and Head, J. R. 1989b. Murine trophoblast can be killed by lymphokine-activated killer cells. *J. Immunol.* 143:9.

Gendron, R. L. and Baines, M. 1988. Infiltrating decidual natural killer cells are associated with spontaneous abortion in mice. *Cell. Immunol.* 113:261.

Head, J. R., Drake, B. L. and Zuckermann, F. A. 1987. Major histocompatibility antigens on trophoblast and their regulation: implications in the maternal-fetal relationship. *Am. J. Reprod. Immunol.* 15:12.

Jenkinson, E. J. and Owen, V. 1980. Ontogeny and distribution of major histocompatibility complex (MHC) antigens on mouse placental trophoblast. *J. Reprod. Immunol.* 2:173.

Kornbluth, J. and Hoover, R. G. 1988. Changes in gene expression associated with IFN-β and IL-2-induced augmentation of human natural killer cell function. *J. Immunol.* 141:3234.

Lanier, L., Phillips, J. H., Hackett, J., Tutt, M. and Kumar, V. 1986. Natural killer cells: definition of a cell type rather than a function. *J. Immunol.* 137:2735.

McLaren, A. 1965. Genetic and environmental effects on fetal and placental growth in mice. *J. Reprod. Fertil.* 9:79.

Philpott, K. L., Rastan, A., Brown, S. and Mellor, A. L. 1988. Expression of H-2 class I genes in murine extra-embryonic tissues. *Immunology* 64:479.

Redline, R. W. and Lu, C. Y. 1988. Specific defects in the anti-listerial immune response in discrete regions of the murine uterus and placenta account for susceptibility to infection. *J. Immunol.* 140:3947.

Rosenstein, M., Yron, I., Kaufmann, Y. and Rosenberg, S. A. 1984. Lymphokine-activated killer cells: lysis of fresh syngeneic natural killer-resistant murine tumor cells by lymphocytes cultured in interleukin-2. *Cancer Res.* 44:1946.

Shanahan, F., Brogan, M. D., Newman, W. and Targan, S. R. 1986. K562 killing by K, IL-2-responsive NK, and T cells involves different effector cell post-binding trigger mechanisms. *J. Immunol.* 137:723.

Simmons, R. L. and Russell, P. S. 1966. The histocompatibility antigens of fertilized mouse eggs and trophoblast. *Ann. NY Acad. Sci.* 129:35.

Singh, B., Raghupathy, R., Anderson, D. J. and Wegmann, T. 1983. The placenta as an immunological barrier between mother and fetus. In *Immunology of Reproduction* (T. G. Wegmann and T. J. Gill III, eds.). Oxford: Oxford University Press, pp. 229–250.

Smith, G. 1983. In vitro susceptibility of mouse placental trophoblast to cytotoxic effector cells. *J. Reprod. Immunol.* 5:39.

Tawfik, O. W., Hunt, J. S., and Wood, G. W. 1986. Implication of prostaglandin E2 in soluble factor-mediated immune suppression by murine decidual cells. *Am. J. Reprod. Immunol.* 12:111.

Trinchieri, G. 1986. Surface phenotype of natural killer cells and macrophages. *Fed. Proc.* 45:2821.

Witebsky, E. S. and Reich, H. 1932. Zur gruppenspezifischen differenzierung der placentarorgane. *Klin. Wochenschr.* 11:1960.

Zuckermann, F. A. and Head, J. R. 1986a. Isolation and characterization of trophoblast from murine placenta. *Placenta* 7:349.

Zuckermann, F. A. and Head, J. R. 1986b. Expression of MHC antigens on murine trophoblast and their modulation by interferon. *J. Immunol.* 137:846.

Zuckermann, F. A. and Head, J. R. 1987. Murine trophoblast resists cell-mediated lysis. I. Resistance to allospecific cytotoxic T lymphocytes. *J. Immunol.* 139:2856.

Zuckermann, F. A. and Head, J. R. 1988. Murine trophoblast resists cell-mediated lysis. II. Resistance to natural cell-mediated cytotoxicity. *Cell. Immunol.* 116:274.

11

Inhibition of Macrophage and T-Lymphocyte Functions in the Placenta and Decidua During Listeriosis: Implications for Tolerance of the Fetoplacental Allograft

CHRISTOPHER Y. LU, RAYMOND W. REDLINE, LYNN B. DUSTIN, DIANNE B. McKAY, and COLLEEN M. SHEA

Listeria Monocytogenes as a Probe of the Ability of Maternal Lymphocytes and Macrophages to Function at the Maternal-Fetal Interface

In rodent models, special local properties of the placenta and decidua prevent maternal antifetal responses. For example, fetuses residing in the uterus are not affected by ongoing rejection of a genetically identical fetal allograft placed in the maternal thigh (Woodruff, 1958) nor by the presence of maternal antifetal cytotoxic T lymphocytes (CTL) in the spleen (Wegmann et al., 1979). A complete understanding of these and similar observations remains a fundamental unsolved problem in immunology (Chaouat et al., 1983b; Clark et al., 1987; Gill & Wegmann, 1987; Hunziker & Wegmann, 1986).

Many different hypotheses have been proposed to account for these observations (see review, Hunziker & Wegmann, 1986). One postulates that there is active local inhibition of maternal antifetal responses at the maternal-fetal interface (the placenta and decidua). This hypothesis is based on a series of elegant experiments showing that maternal decidual cells and fetal trophoblasts inhibit natural killer, cytotoxic T lymphocyte (CTL), and mixed lymphocyte response activities *in vitro* (see reviews, Clark et al., 1988; Gill & Wegmann, 1987). However, the importance of such active inhibition to events *in vivo* is controversial. Under some conditions, one population of trophoblast cells resists lysis by conventional CTL, or cells with natural killer or ADCC activities (Zuckermann & Head, 1987; Zuckermann & Head, 1988) (see Chapter 10). Survival of this population may therefore not require inhibition of these maternal effector cells. Furthermore, there is controversy about which, if any, trophoblast populations express private *cell-surface* class I MHC antigens that can be recognized by conventional CTL. Although some rodent trophoblast synthesizes private MHC class I molecules (Billington & Bell, 1983; Head et al., 1987; Redline & Lu, 1989), these molecules may remain localized to the cytoplasm where they would not be able to interact with maternal CTL (Kanbour et al., 1987). However, in other systems, private paternal class I MHC antigens are clearly accessible to the maternal immune response (Head et al., 1987; Jenkinson & Owen, 1980; Lala et al., 1983; Raghupathy et al., 1981; Zuckermann & Head, 1986). This issue is further complicated by the nature of class I MHC molecules synthesized by trophoblast. In rats and humans, some cytotrophoblast express a nonconventional monomorphic cell-surface class I MHC antigen that may not be recognized by conventional CTL (Faulk & McIntyre, 1983; Gill et al., 1988; Johnson et al., 1987; Kabawat et al., 1985; Redman et al., 1988). Finally, there are many different types of trophoblast (Loke & Butterworth, 1987; Redline & Lu, 1989). Each may have a different susceptibility to attack by particular components of the maternal immune system. Unfortunately, techniques are currently available to isolate and characterize only a few of the various rodent trophoblast subpopulations.

As an alternative approach we have used *Listeria monocytogenes* as a probe to determine if the maternal immune response is inhibited at the maternal-fetal interface *in vivo*. As discussed below, *Listeria* is ordinarily a powerful stimulus for T lymphocyte and macrophage activation. Our working hypothesis was that the putative local inhibition (see reviews, Chaouat, 1987; Clark et al., 1987; Hunziger & Wegmann, 1986), which ordinarily prevents maternal antifetal responses, would also prevent anti-*listeria* responses at the maternal-fetal interface. Anti-*Listeria* responses and allograft rejection share many common features, including macrophage and T lymphocyte interactions and activation (see reviews, Hahn & Kaufmann, 1981; Strom et al., 1985).

The intracellular pathogen, *Listeria monocytogenes*, is particularly appropriate for analyzing local events in the decidua and placenta. First, it resists killing by antibodies made by maternal plasma cells. To defend the placental-decidual region from *Listeria*, maternal macrophages and T cells must actually infiltrate these tissues and thus would come under the influence of the proposed local immunoregulatory cells (Hahn & Kaufmann, 1981). The T cells must come from the mother rather than the fetus because fetal T cells are not fully competent (Kronenberg et al., 1986). Second, the critical events of listeriosis occur within the first 5 days after infection (Hahn & Kaufmann, 1981). The infection can thus run its entire course during the 19- to 20-day gestation period of the mouse. Third, extensive studies using nonpregnant adult mice and *in vitro* techniques have defined the following events in the host-defense response to *Listeria*. Macrophages that have recently emigrated from the blood vessels ingest

Listeria, but cannot kill them efficiently. However, some bacteria are degraded, and the immunogenic molecules are displayed on macrophage cell surfaces in the context of Ia. T cells recognize the antigen-Ia complexes via their specific receptors, receive accessory signals from mediators, such as interleukin 1 and 6, which are secreted by macrophages (Dinarello, 1989), and then proliferate and secrete lymphokines. Some of these lymphokines, such as gamma-interferon, interleukin-4 (Crawford et al., 1987), and GM-CSF (Grabstein et al., 1986), are known to activate macrophages. These activated macrophages kill *Listeria* efficiently and have increased cell surface expression of Ia antigens (see review, Hahn & Kaufmann, 1981). Our experiments were designed to determine if these T cell and macrophage responses could occur in the placental-decidual region.

The data to be summarized in this review demonstrate the following:

1. *Listeria* are effectively protected from the maternal immune response at the maternal-fetal interface. In contrast, pregnancy does not impair immune functions in the maternal liver and spleen.
2. There are two distinct ineffective anti-*Listeria* responses that account for the increased susceptibility of the maternal-fetal interface to infection. One occurs in the decidua basalis. This region is the most severely influenced by infection, and the ineffective host defense is characterized by the absence of lymphocytes and macrophages. Detailed immunohistological studies indicate that the murine decidua basalis contains a mixture of fetal trophoblast and maternal decidual cells, each synthesizing its own private class I major histocompatibility antigens. The second inefficient response occurs in the chorioallantoic plate where macrophages reach sites of infection, but are not appropriately activated as evidenced by their lack of expression of cell-surface Ia-antigens.
3. Maternal decidual cells by themselves inhibit macrophage functions *in vivo* and *in vitro*. Preliminary results indicate that solid phase molecules embedded in the decidual substratum are responsible for this inhibition.
4. Alpha fetoprotein inhibits macrophage activation, but not chemotaxis in the chorioallantoic plate.

Listeria Find Safe Sanctuary from the Maternal Immune System in the Maternal-Fetal Interface

Figure 11-1 compares the number of bacteria in the maternal lung versus the placental region 6–120 h after a single intravenous injection of organisms. The responses of pregnant mice could be clearly separated into two distinct groups. Placental *Listeria* counts in one group

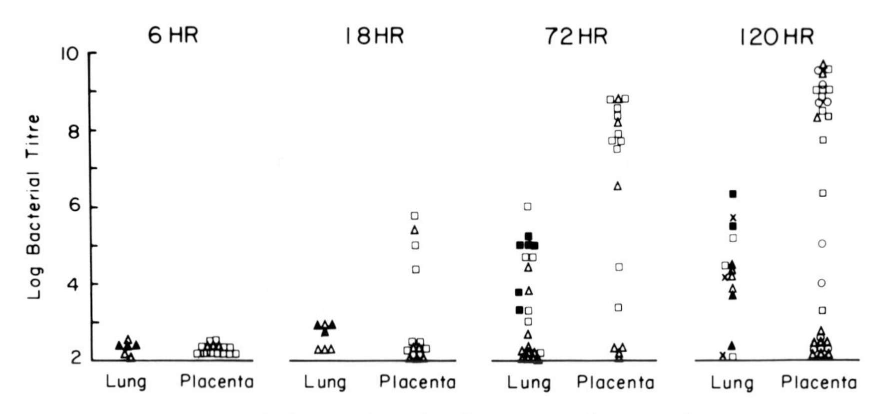

Fig. 11-1. Kinetics of placental and pulmonary infection after intravenous injection of Listeria monocytogenes. The ordinate is the $\log_{10}$ of the total bacteria count for pooled placentas and both lungs from individual animals (number of listeria injected: open triangle, 5×10^4; open circle, 1×10^5; open square, 2×10^5). Lung titers from nonpregnant, age-matched females are also displayed (number of listeria injected: closed triangles, 5×10^4; closed squares, 2×10^5; x's, 2×10^6 [greater than LD_{50}]. The lowest value for bacterial titer on the ordinate, 10^2, represents the threshold of detection of our assay system. (From Redline & Lu, 1987.)

were 1000 to 10,000 times of those in the lung by 120 h after infection. The other group had few or no detectable placental *Listeria*. Table 11-1 shows that the occurrence of placental listeriosis was determined by the number of injected bacteria. If a greater number of organisms was injected, it was more likely that a threshold number of bacteria would reach the placenta. If a threshold number of bacteria did reach the placenta, an overwhelming infection resulted regardless of whether a large or small dose of *Listeria* had been injected.

These data indicated that the placenta was able to contain the

Table 11-1. Relationship of placental *Listeria* infection at 120 h to the initial dose of injected *Listeria**

Inoculum	No. of Pregnant Mice	Placenta Positive†	Log Mean Titer‡ Placenta Positive
5×10^4	10	3	9.1×0.49
1×10^5	10	5	8.2 ± 0.75
2×10^5	10	9	8.4 ± 0.34

Pregnant mice were injected with live *Listeria* on day 14 of pregnancy and killed 120 h later.
* From Redline & Lu, 1987.
† Placenta positive is arbitrarily defined as $>10^4$ in the combined placental tissue from one mother.
‡ Log mean titer ± SEM for placenta-positive subgroup only.

growth of only a small number of *Listeria*. If this threshold was exceeded, overwhelming bacterial proliferation resulted. The anti-*Listeria* responses in maternal liver and spleen were not impaired, suggesting that this inhibition of immunity was localized to the placenta and was not systemic (see Redline and Lu (1987) for details).

Two Different Abnormal Anti-*Listeria* Responses in Different Anatomical Areas of the Maternal-Fetal Interface Are Revealed by Immunohistological Studies and May Account for the Increased Local Susceptibility to Infection

Anatomy

For the purposes of this discussion, the structure of the maternal-fetal interface may be divided into four principal areas (see Fig. 11-2). As discussed below, a different type of anti-*Listeria* response occurred in each area.

1. The *MATERNAL UTERUS* consists of smooth muscle (*myometrium*, or MYO), an epithelial lining (*endometrium*, or EM), and a pregnancy-specific subregion within the myometrium (*metrial gland*, or MG). These tissues consist solely of maternal cells.
2. The *DECIDUA BASALIS*, or DB, is a specialized region of the endometrium that is infiltrated by fetal trophoblastic cells and anchors the placenta to the uterus. This area is perfused by a venous system lined by maternal endothelium (see Fig. 11-2).
3. The *FETAL PLACENTA* comprises maternal blood spaces lined by fetal trophoblastic cells. The *labyrinth*, or L, is perfused by both

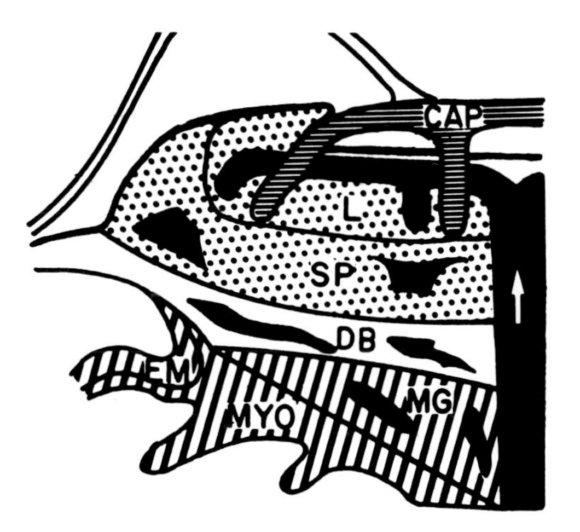

Fig. 11-2. Schematic representation of the normal anatomy of the murine placenta at days 14–19 of gestation. [hatched] Uterus (EM = endometrium, MYO = myometrium, MG = metrial gland); [blank] decidua basalis(DB); [dotted] fetal placenta (L = labyrinth, SP = spongiotrophoblast); [striped] chorioallantoic plate (CAP). (From Redline & Lu, 1988.)

fetal and maternal circulations. The *spongiotrophoblast*, or SP, is perfused only by the maternal circulation.

4. The *CHORIOALLANTOIC PLATE*, or CAP, is nontrophoblastic fetal tissue that is perfused only by the fetal circulation (for details, see Redline & Lu, 1989).

Effective T Cell and Macrophage Anti-Listeria Responses in the Maternal Uterus

As discussed in the first section of this chapter, the most effective anti-*Listeria* response consists of activated macrophages and T lymphocytes. In immunohistological studies, the former can be detected by staining with F4/80, a monoclonal antibody that reacts with all known murine macrophages (Austyn & Gordon, 1981), and 10.2.16, a monoclonal antibody that recognizes the activation marker Ia^k (Oi et al., 1978; Unanue & Allen, 1987). T lymphocytes can be detected by monoclonal antibodies against L3T4, a marker of $CD4^+$ T cells, and Lyt2, a marker of $CD8^+$ T cells. As shown in Table 11-2, activated macrophage and T cells did indeed make up a large proportion of the effective anti-*Listeria* response in the maternal liver and in the endometrium, myometrium, and metrial gland. The latter three tissues are composed only of maternal cells in the mouse (Redline & Lu, 1989). Hence, the maternal immune responses need not be inhibited at these sites to prevent antifetal responses, and the anti-*Listeria* response was also not inhibited.

Inhibition of T Cell and Macrophage Anti-Listeria Responses in the Decidua Basalis

In marked contrast to the maternal uterus, the immediately adjacent decidua basalis had a strikingly abnormal anti-*Listeria* response. Although this was the earliest and most severely infected area of the placental region, there was a striking absence of macrophages and T cells at all stages of infection (see Table 11-2). Granulocytes were the predominant inflammatory cells present. Large numbers of extracellular *Listeria* were seen, indicating an ineffective immune response. Maternal decidual and fetal trophoblastic cells, each synthesizing its own private class I MHC antigens, were intimately intermixed in the decidua basalis (Redline & Lu, 1989; Fig. 11-3A). It was not possible using our immunohistological techniques to determine whether these class I MHC antigens were on the cell surface or within the cytoplasm as suggested by Gill and co-workers (Kanbour et al., 1987). Nevertheless, allogeneic cells were in intimate contact in this tissue, and the inhibition of T cell and macrophage anti-Listerial activities may reflect local immunoregulation that ordinarily serves to prevent maternal antifetal immune responses.

Table 11-2. Cellular composition of inflammatory *Listeria* lesions in different regions of the placenta/decidua*

		Uterus**					
	Liver	EM	MYO	MG	Decidua Basalis	Fetal Placenta	Chorioallantoic Plate
Day3							
Granulocytes†	40‡	5	7	7	42	23	5
F4/80	36	39	17	7	1	1	41
I-A^k	10	28	11	2	2	0	2
L3T4	1	4	<1	0	0	0	0
Lyt-2	0	0	0	1	1	0	0
Day 5							
Granulocytes	19	6	—§	24	33	8	21
F4/80	61	46	—	19	1	0	18
I-A^k	30	38	—	9	2	1	0
L3T4	8	6	—	1	0	0	0
Lyt-2	6	0	—	<1	0	0	0
Day 3 immune‖							
Granulocytes	2	12	20	23	112	22	12
F4/80	63	53	17	9	1	1	28
I-A^k	35	41	27	9	8	0	1
L3T4	7	23	7	5	2	0	1
Lyt-2	4	<1	1	1	<1	0	0
Noninfected#							
Granulocytes	0	0	0	<1	<1	<1	0
F4/80	7	37	9	<1	<1	<1	4
I-A^k	8	19	2	<1	<1	<1	<1
L3T4	0	4	<1	0	<1	0	0
Lyt-2	0	<1	<1	<1	<1	0	0

* From Redline & Lu, 1988.
** EM, endometrium; MYO, myometrium; and MG, metrial gland.
† Granulocytes, MAC-1$^+$ − F4/80$^+$.
‡ Positive nucleated cells/mm^2 × 10^{-2} within lesions.
§ Insufficient myometrium on day 5 placentas for analysis.
‖ Day 3 immune are animals immunized to *Listeria* early in pregnancy, rechallenged with 2 × 10^5 *Listeria* on day 14, and sacrificed 3 days later.
Noninfected baseline tissue density.

*Inhibition of Anti-*Listeria *Macrophage Functions is Unique to Murine Decidua and is a Major Component of the Ineffective Anti-*Listeria *Response.* To our knowledge, the murine decidua is the only site where listeriosis elicits a granulocytic, rather than a macrophage-T-lymphocyte response, at all stages of infection. This may reflect the unique immunological properties of this tissue as a maternal-fetal interface.

Two arguments indicate that inhibition of macrophage functions is a major factor in this deficient anti-*Listeria* response. Inhibition of macrophage functions could account for the absence of both macrophages and T cells. Because macrophages are critical in antigen-induced T lymphocyte proliferation, the deficiency of T cells may reflect the inability of macrophages to reach sites of infection. On the other hand, the deficits in macrophage chemotaxis to *Listeria* located in the decidua basalis cannot be explained by the absence of T cells. A macrophage response against *Listeria* does occur in a variety of T-deficient mice, including the neonate (Lu et al., 1979), neonatally thymectomized and genetically dysthymic nu/nu mice (Lu et al., 1981), and mice with severe combined immunodeficiency (Bancroft et al., 1987). This response is consistent with the known ability of *Listeria* to release bacterial products that are monocyte/macrophage chemoattractants (Galsworthy, 1984), as well as the ability of *Listeria* to activate complement via the alternative pathway and produce C5a, another potent chemoattractant (Van Kessel et al., 1981).

Macrophages and Mature T Lymphocytes are Also Excluded From Noninfected Decidua: Controversies in the Literature. In view of the striking absence of lymphocytes and macrophages in the infected decidua basalis, we examined noninfected tissue and found that macrophages were also absent (Redline & Lu, 1989, Table 11-3). Similar observations have been made by others in rodents using immunohistochemical techniques (personal communication, B. A. Croy and J. R. Head). Furthermore, during implantation in the mouse, macrophages accumulate on the endometrial side of the border between endometrium and decidua, suggesting that they have been attracted to the implantation site but cannot actually enter the decidua (Tachi & Tachi, 1986). At day 10 of gestation, the rat decidua is surrounded by maternal Ia-bearing cells—either dendritic cells or macrophages (Head, 1987)—although they are excluded from this tissue.

In contrast to these findings, Matthews and Searle (1988) reported that antigen-presenting macrophages can be isolated from the normal midgestational murine decidua basalis. One possible explanation for this discrepancy is that our data are based on immunohistochemistry, whereas Searle's data are based on analyzing of dispersed cell preparations. Macrophage survive mechanical and enzymatic dispersion that kills other cell types. Thus, the isolation procedure may preferentially enrich the very small number of macrophages present in decidua. We used staining by monoclonal antibody F4/80 to identify macrophages. As a positive control, we showed the presence of F4/80-positive macrophages in the endometrium and myometrium immediately adjacent to the decidua basalis of the same tissue sections. Although it is theoretically possible that macrophages in the decidua basalis are F4/80-negative, this would be unprecedented (Austyn & Gordon, 1981).

Wood and colleagues (1988) suggest that uterine macrophages play a key role in preventing maternal antifetal responses by secreting prostaglandins and other immunoregulatory substances. The macrophages responsible for this activity were isolated from the uterine wall after

Table 11-3. Regional frequency of leukocyte subsets derived from the mother* and fetus† in day 14–19 pregnant uteri

	Day 14 (N = 2)					Day 17 (N = 3)						Day 19 (N = 2)				
Region	**F4/80**	**MAC-1**	**I-A^k**	**CD4**	**CD8**	**F4/80**	**MAC-1**	**I-A^k**	**CD4**	**CD8**	**B220**	**F4/80**	**MAC-1**	**I-A^k**	**CD4**	**CD8**
Endometrium*	1846	2185	967	132	120	3710	3484	1906	385	158	3	2981	2438	1346	571	139
Myometrium*	707	605	340	18	9	885	567	200	35	24	5	844	680	449	82	34
Metrial gland*	19	80	17	9	6	34	37	10	3	2	1	56	87	31	9	0
Decidua basalis*	8	72	6	5	2	13	28	2	0	1	4	13	17	8	1	0
Spongiotrophoblast*	0	10	1	0	1	1	7	1	0	0	7	2	12	1	0	2
Fetal labyrinth†	146	10	1	3	2	108	17	0	2	2	13	61	54	0	5	5
Allantoic plate†	386	55	0	0	0	444	159	1	0	0	0	377	112	3	0	0
Visceral yolk sac†	415	1	0	0	0	139	20	0	0	0	0	28	8	0	0	0

* From Redline & Lu, 1989.

removal of the placental disc by blunt dissection. We believe, however, that these cells were not located in the decidua basalis. In our hands, immunohistochemical staining showed that the decidua basalis is associated with the placental disc rather than the uterine wall after blunt dissection. In agreement with Wood, we found that the gravid uterine wall, including the endometrium and myometrium, did contain large numbers of macrophages (see Table 11-3).

Reliable *in situ* immunohistochemical studies indicate that the human decidua is unlike that of mice in that it contains large numbers of macrophages (Bulmer, 1987, 1988; Kabawat et al., 1985; Sutton et al., 1983). The basis for this difference is not understood. However, human and murine specimens are not strictly comparable. Our murine specimens were always from midgestation, and the entire placenta and decidua was present, allowing precise anatomical localization. In contrast, the human specimens were either very small biopsies from early in gestation and thus were difficult to orient, or they were from term pregnancies when the biology of the maternal-fetal interface is different from that in midgestation. Furthermore, although humans and mice both have hemochorial placentas, there are numerous structural and functional differences (Mossman, 1987). For example, trophoblast invasion is much deeper in humans and human cytotrophoblast appears to synthesize only a non-polymorphic class I MHC molecule (Johnson et al., 1987; Redman et al., 1988), whereas murine cytotrophoblast synthesizes molecules with private determinants (Billington & Bell, 1983; Head et al., 1987; Redline & Lu, 1989). There are also marked differences in the length of gestation.

Finally, our immunohistological examination indicated that mature $CD4^+$ and $CD8^+$ T lymphocytes were also excluded from the noninfected decidua basalis (Redline & Lu, 1989, see Table 11-3). Recent evidence indicates that various molecules secreted by lymphocytes and macrophages, as well as many other cell types, are trophic for some trophoblast populations (Wegmann, 1987). Our data suggest that there are few conventional T lymphocytes and macrophages present in the decidua basalis at day 14–19 of allogeneic murine pregnancy to mediate such "immunotrophism." However, we have no data on events earlier in gestation.

Restricted Expression of Class I MHC Antigens on Trophoblast During Listeriosis Despite Evidence for Lymphokine Effects in the Decidua Basalis. Despite the absence of macrophages and T cells in the infected decidua basalis, there is evidence that high concentrations of cytokines, such as gamma interferon, do enter this region, perhaps by diffusion from the maternal blood stream or from the neighboring endometrium and myometrium. Maternal endothelial cells express Ia. Private class I MHC antigen expression was elevated on those trophoblast cells that are constitutively class I positive, but was not induced on trophoblast cells that are ordinarily class I negative. No trophoblast became Ia-positive. Thus, despite the evidence for high local concentrations of cytokines, expression of MHC gene products by trophoblast remained tightly regulated, perhaps because inappropriate paternal MHC expression would lead to maternal rejection of these fetal cells.

Deficits in Migration of Monocytes Across Maternal Endothelium Cannot, By Themselves, Account for the Inability of Macrophages to Reach Sites of Infection in the Decidua Basalis. Recent evidence indicates that the binding and translocation of inflammatory cells across endothelium are events subject to various regulatory influences (Springer et al., 1987). Although a defect in the migration of monocytes/macrophages across the local maternal endothelium into the decidua basalis cannot be excluded, this is unlikely to be the entire explanation for the absence of macrophages in infected decidua basalis. Figure 11-3C shows a group of Ia-positive macrophages that have translocated across the endothelium, but are not able to migrate to sites of infection. Numerous granulocytes, on the other hand, have successfully infiltrated the tissue. Furthermore, macrophages did emigrate from myometrial blood vessels but could not cross the boundary between myometrium and decidua (Redline & Lu, 1988; see Figs. 11-3B & D). Finally, the endothelium of the decidua basalis did become appropriately activated during the course of *Listeria* infection, as evidenced by new cell-surface expression of Ia (De Waal et al., 1983; Pober, 1983; Redline & Lu, 1988; Sobel et al., 1984), and the ability to bind intravascular monocytes (Redline & Lu, 1988; Springer et al., 1987).

Deficient Macrophage Activation in the Chorioallantoic Plate (Fig. 11-3 and Table 11-2).

A completely different deficient anti-*Listerial* response was found in the chorioallantoic plate, which consists entirely of nontrophoblastic fetal tissue. Unlike the decidua basalis where few macrophages were present, large numbers of fetal macrophages did reach sites of infection. However, these were not appropriately activated. They did not express Ia, and the presence of extracellular *Listeria* indicated an inability to kill the bacteria efficiently.

Mechanisms Responsible for the Deficient Macrophage Anti-*Listeria* Response in Decidua Basalis

We now discuss mechanisms underlying the abnormal macrophage responses in the decidua basalis and the chorioallantoic plate. There was a different inhibitory mechanism in each tissue (Table 11-4).

Table 11-4. Different anti-*Listeria* responses in three different areas of the maternal-fetal interface

	Maternal Uterus	Decidua Basalis	Chorioallantoic Plate
Tissue	Maternal only	Fetal trophoblast + maternal decidua	Fetal only
Anti-*Listeria* response	Granulocytes Ia^{+}-macrophages T-cells	Granulocytes only No macrophages No T cells	Granulocytes Ia^{-}-macrophages No T cells
Inhibitor	None	Solid phase	alpha fetoprotein

Deciduoma of Pseudopregnancy as a Valid Model of Decidual Cell Function in the Absence of Trophoblast

The decidua basalis is a mixture of maternal decidual cells and fetal trophoblast (Redline & Lu, 1989). To determine if the former can themselves inhibit macrophage functions *in vivo*, we infected deciduoma of pseudopregnancy (dec-pseudo) with *Listeria*. *Dec-pseudo* forms when rodents receive a series of injections that mimic the hormonal environment of pregnancy and are followed by a physical stimulus to the endometrium, such as an intrauterine injection of oil or *Listeria*. The latter is thought to mimic the physical stimulus of implantation. Table 11-5 summarizes the many similarities between the decidua basalis and dec-pseudo. These tissues consist of similar maternal cell types including stromal cells that are believed to have differentiated from endometrial fibroblasts. As discussed below, these decidual stromal cells make solid phase inhibitors of macrophage functions. Both tissues contain non-T, non-B, non-macrophage bone marrow-derived cells. These include the "granulated metrial gland cells" (GMG) with their distinctive large PAS-positive granules (Bell, 1983, 1985). In addition, dec-pseudo and the decidua basalis have a similar basement-membrane type extracellular matrix (ECM) (Wewer et al., 1986) and secrete similar soluble proteins (Nieder & Macory, 1987; Weitlauf & Suda-Hartman, 1988). Finally, endometrial stromal cells in both the decidua basalis and dec-pseudo acquire the ability to form tight junctions (O'Shea et al., 1983).

Of course, there are some differences between these two tissues. Dec-pseudo has no fetal trophoblasts and thus does not have certain functions that depend on trophoblast-decidual cell interactions. Nevertheless, as discussed below, we find that the T-cell-macrophage anti-*Listeria* responses in dec-pseudo and decidua basalis are exactly analogous, and in view of the many similarities in these two tissues (Bell, 1983, 1985; see Table 11-5), we believe that dec-pseudo is a

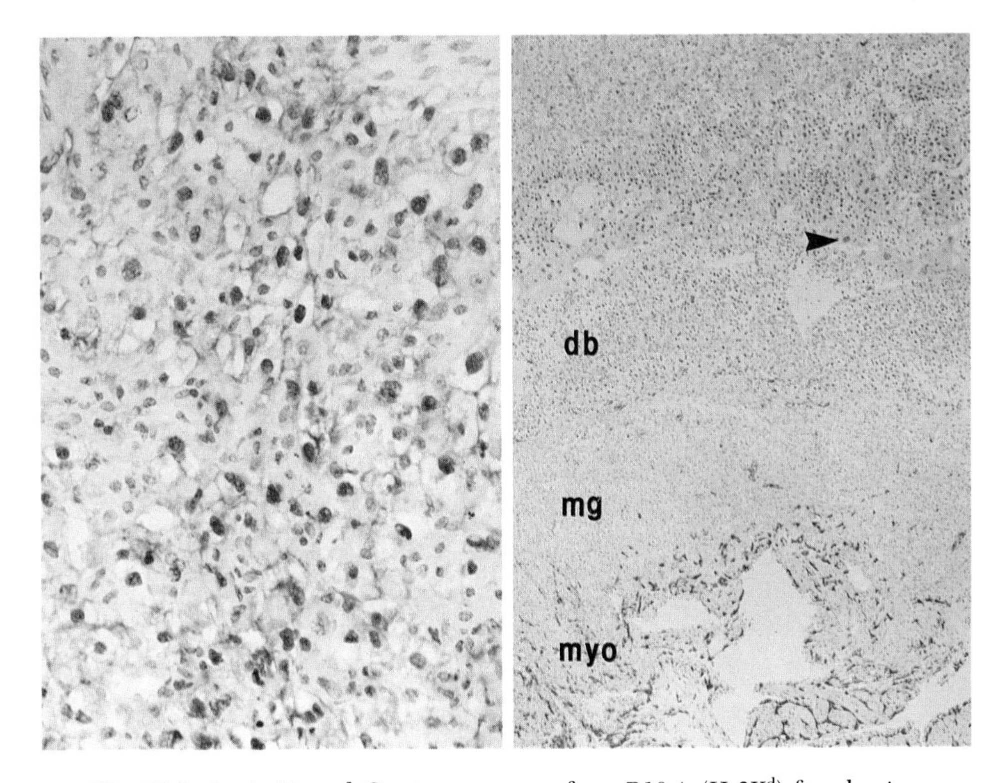

Fig. 11-3. In A, B, and C, uteruses were from B10.A (H-2K^{d}) females impregnated by Balb/c (H-2K^{d}) males and infected intravenously with *Listeria* at day 14 of gestation and sacrificed 3 days later. All frozen sections were developed using the diaminobenzidine chromagen (brown) and counterstained with Gill-2 hematoxylin. See references [Redline & Lu, 1988; Redline & Lu, 1988; Redline & Lu, 1989] for details. (A) *The decidua basalis is a mixture of fetal trophoblast synthesizing paternal Class I MHC antigens (H-2L^{d}), and maternal decidual cells which are H-2K^{d}-negative.* H-2K^{d} on vacuolated fetal trophoblast are stained brown by biotinylated monoclonal antibody 20-8-4S [Ozato and Sachs, 1981], streptavidin-biotinylated peroxidase conjugates, and diaminobenzidine. ×400. (B) *Macrophages are excluded from the murine decidua basalis.* Although *Listeria* were injected intravenously into the mother, none were detectable in this placenta. See reference [Redline & Lu, 1989; Redline & Lu, 1988]. F4/80-positive macrophages (brown color) are frequent in the myometrium (myo), rare in the metrial gland (mg), and essentially absent from the decidua basalis (db). Arrow points to a row of three trophoblastic giant cells which mark the border between the fetal placenta (spongiotrophoblast and labyrinth), above the arrow, and the uterus which lies below the arrow. ×40. See Fig. 11–2 for schematic of anatomy. (*continued*)

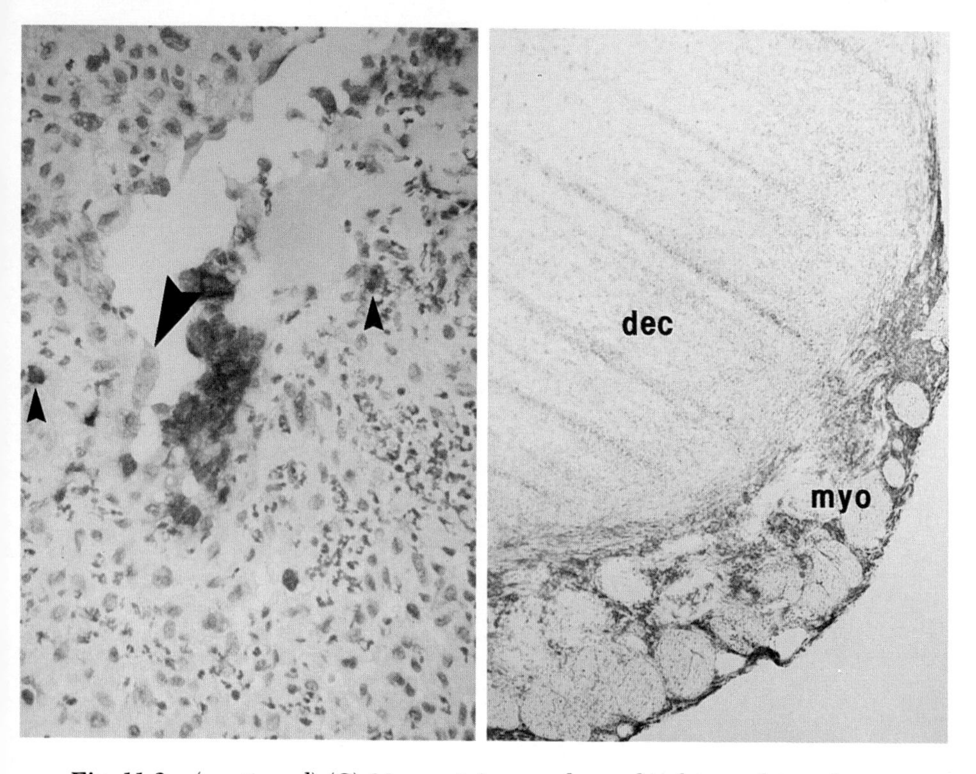

Fig. 11-3. (*continued*) (C) *Monocyte/macrophages bind to and translocate across the activated maternal endothelium of the decidua basalis, but do not penetrate well into the tissue.* Monoclonal antibody 10.2.16 [Oi et al., 1978], anti-I-A^k, stains intravascular monocyte-macrophages (central aggregate of positively staining cells) adhering to the I-A^k-positive endothelium (large arrow). Small arrows show I-A^k-positive macrophages which have translocated through the endothelium but remain in close proximity to the blood vessel. Note granulocytes, on the other hand, have penetrated deep into this heavily infected decidua. See lower and right portions of figure. ×400. (D) *Macrophages excluded from infected deciduoma of pseudopregnancy.* Macrophages detected by monoclonal antibody F4/80 are stained brown and found in the myometrium (myo), but not in the heavily infected decidualized endometrium (dec).

Table 11-5. A comparison of nondecidualized endometrium, true decidua, and deciduoma of pseudopregnancy

	Endometrium	True Decidua	Deciduoma Pseudopregnancy
Hormones	None	Natural	Injected
Trigger	—	Blastocyst	Lm/oil
Cells*		Trophoblast	No trophoblast
	fibroblast	Decidual cells	
	desmin—	stromal cells	
		Desmin +	
		Bone marrow derived	
		LCA +	
		ASGM1 +	
		GMG cells	
ECM†	Fibronectin	Laminin	
	Collagen Type I	Collagen Type IV	
		Entactin/nidogen	
	BM 40—	HS proteoglycans	
		BM 40 +	
Ultrastructure‡	No tight junctions	Tight junctions present	
Anti-*Listeria*§	Macrophages	No macrophages	
	T-cells	No T-cells	

* Bell, 1983; Bell, 1985; Glasser et al., 1987.
† Wewer et al., 1988; Wewer et al., 1986.
‡ O'Shea et al., 1983; Parr et al., 1986; Tung et al., 1986; Welsh & Enders, 1985.
§ Redline & Lu, 1987; Redline et al., 1988.

valid model for studying regulation of macrophages by decidual cells in the absence of trophoblast.

Deficient Macrophage Function During Listeriosis in Deciduoma of Pseudopregnancy is Exactly Analogous to That in the Decidua Basalis

Figure 11-4 indicates that *Listeria* growth in dec-pseudo [E + P group] was 10,000-fold greater than in virgin uteri (no injection group). Immunohistochemical studies indicate that macrophages were excluded from sites of infection as in the decidua basalis (Fig. 11-3B & D). The ineffective anti-*Listeria* response was restricted to the deciduoma and was not a systemic effect of the hormone injections. These mice had normal anti-*Listeria* responses in their spleens and livers after systemic infection.

Deciduoma of pseudopregnancy may be anatomically divided into a "mesometrial" region, located adjacent to the point of entry of the uterine artery into the uterus, and the opposite "anti-mesometrial" region. Decidual stromal cells predominated in the anti-mesometrial

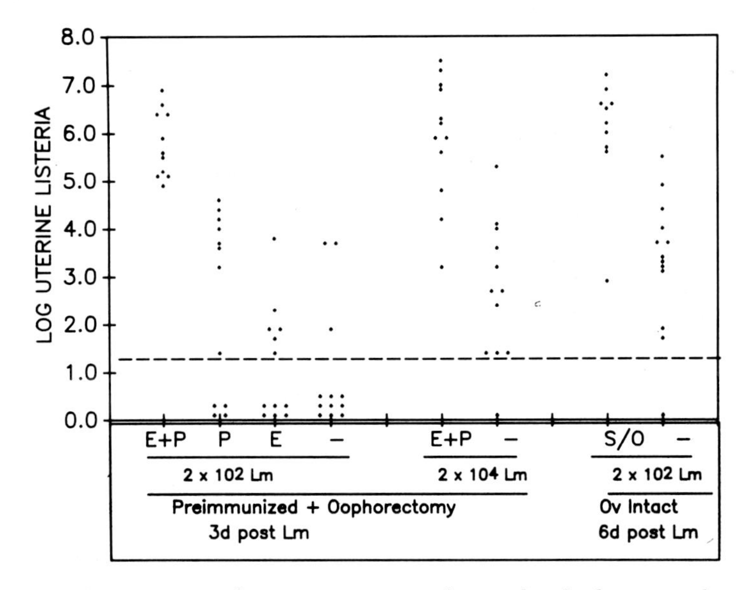

Fig. 11-4. Scattergram of *Listeria* titers within individual uterine horns of mice with and without deciduoma. Dotted line represents threshold of detection (25 listeria) and points below line indicate horns with no listeria detected. A and B—preimmunized and oophorectomized mice treated with complete hormonal regimen of estrogen plus progesterone to induce deciduoma, (E + P), progesterone alone (P), estrogen alone (E), or no hormones (–). Challenged with 2 × 10^2 listeria/ horn (A and C), or 2 × 10^4 listeria/ horn (B). All animals given daily progesterone after challenge with listeria until sacrifice on day 3. Note the predominance of listeria titers in the 10^5–10^7 range in the E + P groups with deciduoma. C—Nonimmune animals with intact ovaries were either superovulated (S/O) or untreated (–), challenged with listeria and sacrificed on day 6. See reference [Redline et al., 1988] for further details.

region. This was the most heavily infected region, where macrophages were excluded from sites of infection. Localization of the abnormal macrophage response to areas where decidual stromal cells predominate is consistent with our data indicating that the substratum formed by decidual stromal cells inhibits macrophage functions *in vitro* (see below). In contrast, the bone-marrow-derived decidual cells were located at the mesometrial region where there were fewer decidual stromal cells, and the anti-*Listeria* response was more normal (Redline et al., 1988).

Overall these data indicate that maternal decidual cells, by themselves, can prevent the anti-*Listeria* macrophage response. These data do not exclude the possibility that some trophoblast populations also inhibit macrophage functions. Indeed, Table 11-2 indicates that the macrophages also did not migrate well to sites of *Listeria* infection in the spongiotrophoblast where there were no decidual cells.

Solid Phase Signals Embedded in the Decidual Substratum Inhibit Macrophage Functions in the Decidua Basalis

Hypothesis. To explain the observed inhibition of the anti-*Listeria* macrophage response in decidua, we have formulated the following hypothesis. Data supporting this hypothesis are discussed in the next section. We postulate that a critical initial signal is ordinarily delivered by the interstitial substratum; this signal informs the monocyte-macrophage that it has left the bloodstream (Brown, 1986). This signal is required to prevent monocyte-macrophage activation in the bloodstream, where the release of superoxides and other toxic inflammatory products would be detrimental. Indeed, after interaction with plastic (Rosen & Gordon, 1987) or fibronectin (Brown & Goodwin, 1988) *in vitro*, macrophages undergo profound changes that may be analogous to those that occur after contact with the interstitial substratum. These changes include large transient intracellular calcium fluxes (Kruskal & Maxfield, 1988), reorganization of the cytoskeleton (Amato et al., 1983; Chaponnier et al., 1987), and activation or inactivation of a number of genes (Collart et al., 1986; Fuhlbrigge et al., 1987; Haskill et al., 1988). Macrophages then acquire new capacities, including the ability to respond to gamma-interferon by expressing cell surface Ia (Beller & Ho, 1982), chemotaxis, increased phagocytic ability (Brown, 1986; Czop, 1986), increased capacity to release superoxides (Kelley et al., 1987), and production of interleukin-1 (Fuhlbrigge et al., 1987) and tumor necrosis factor alpha (Haskill et al., 1988). There is also secretion of enzymes that digest extracellular matrix, allowing macrophage immigration into tissue. The importance of this initial interaction between macrophage and the substratum is illustrated by the inability of macrophages to adhere and spread on Teflon surfaces (Beller & Ho, 1982), which correlates with their inability to be activated by gamma-interferon.

We propose that contact between macrophages and the interstitial substratum of the decidua is inhibitory. Because the decidual substratum contains laminin and fibronectin (Wewer et al., 1986)—extracellular matrix components that ordinarily support macrophage activation (Brown & Goodwin, 1988; Mercurio, 1988; Perri et al., 1985)—inhibitors embedded in the decidual substratum must prevent positive interactions with these matrix proteins. Such *solid phase*, rather than *freely diffusible*, signals are best able to regulate macrophages with the necessary spatial precision. Thus, macrophage functions, including chemotaxis, are inhibited where maternal and fetal cells are intimately intermixed in the decidua basalis. In striking contrast, there is no inhibition in the immediately adjacent endometrium and neighboring myometrium.

Data Consistent with This Hypothesis. After 24–48 h in culture, decidual stromal cells form a confluent substratum of cells and extracellular matrix. We found that this substratum, but not substrata formed by dermal fibroblasts or 3T3 cells, inhibited three macrophage functions *in vitro*: adhesion, spreading, and activation by gamma-interferon. Activation in these experiments was defined by the acquisition of lytic activity against P815 mastocytotoma cells. In murine systems, this well-defined activation function ordinarily requires stimulation by a lymphokine, such as gamma-interferon, and a second signal, such as endotoxin. Decidual stromal cells did not secrete stable soluble inhibitors of these three macrophage functions. Direct contact between macrophages and the putative solid phase inhibitors embedded in the decidual substratum was required (Redline & Lu, 1990).

The putative solid phase inhibitors in the decidua basalis differ from previously described decidual suppressor factors. The latter inhibit T lymphocyte instead of macrophage functions (Hunziker & Wegmann, 1986). They are produced by bone-marrow-derived rather than stromal cells. The suppressor cells inhibit by secreting stable soluble molecules, including PGE2 (Lala et al., 1987; Tawfik et al., 1986) and a TGF-β-like molecule (Clark et al., 1988), rather than by direct contact. Our decidual stromal cells are active after dispersion using dispase, which inactivates some other decidual suppressor cells (Clark et al., 1986). Finally, our decidual stromal cells develop in deciduoma of pseudopregnancy in the absence of trophoblast. Some of the previously described decidual suppressor cells are found only in decidual tissue of true pregnancy (Clark et al., 1986).

The presence of solid phase inhibitors of macrophage activation in decidua is consistent with previous reports that decidua had immunoinhibitory properties. Skin grafts placed on decidua of unsensitized rats and rabbits survive longer than grafts placed in the nondecidualized uterus (Beer & Billingham, 1974; Dodd et al., 1980).

Alpha-fetoprotein Inhibits Macrophage Activation in the Chorioallantoic Plate

Inhibition of Macrophage Activation in the Chorioallantoic Plate

As discussed in the earlier section on different anti-*Listeria* responses, the chorioallantoic plate has an ineffective anti-*Listeria* response that is completely different from the ineffective response in the decidua basalis. In contrast to the decidua basalis, however, large numbers of macrophages do reach sites of infection. However, these macrophages are not appropriately activated as evidenced by their inability to express Ia and kill *Listeria* efficiently.

Several findings indicate that macrophage function in the chorioallantoic plate is actively inhibited. First, during listeriosis, class I

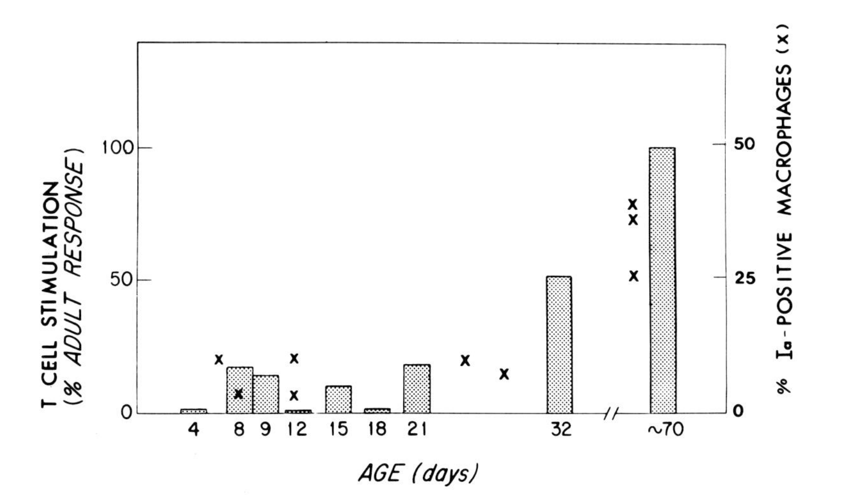

Fig. 11-5. Ontogeny of Ia-positive, antigen-presenting peritoneal macrophages. The abscissa is the age of neonatal mouse donating its resident peritoneal macrophages for study. The left ordinate (stippled bars) gives the ability of macrophages to present heat-killed *Listeria* to adult immune T cells and induce T cell proliferation *in vitro*. The right ordinate ("X") gives the percentage of peritoneal macrophages with cell-surface Ia. See references [Lu, Calamai and Unanue, 1979; Lu, 1984] for details.

MHC antigen expression was increased on fetal stromal cells, and class II antigens were induced on fetal endothelial cells, suggesting the presence of lymphokines, possibly of maternal origin, in the infected chorioallantoic plate (Redline & Lu, 1988). These inhibitors may have prevented the macrophages from expressing Ia in response to these lymphokines. Second, the lack of mature T cell function in the fetus was unlikely to account for deficient macrophage activation in the chorioallantoic plate, because macrophage activation occurs in the absence of T cells in *Listeria*-infected mice with severe combined immunodeficiency (Bancroft et al., 1987).

The chorioallantoic plate consists entirely of fetal tissue and is perfused only by the fetal circulation. We suggest that deficits in macrophage function in this region were caused by the same mechanisms that prevent macrophage activation in the fetus and neonate (Lu & Unanue, 1985). As shown in Figure 11-5, resident peritoneal macrophages in newborn mice are deficient in both Ia expression and antigen-presenting activity. Stimuli such as intraperitoneal gamma-interferon or *Listeria* injections recruit large numbers of Ia-positive macrophages into the peritoneal cavities of normal adult mice, but are ineffective in neonatal mice (Lu & Unanue, 1985). Inhibitory factors in the neonatal environment are responsible for these effects. Thus, when peritoneal macrophages are removed from the presence of these putative inhibitors and cultured *in vitro,* they respond to stimulation by lymphokines in the same way as macrophages from adult mice.

Alpha-fetoprotein in the Fetal and Neonatal Environment Inhibits Macrophage Activation

One inhibitory component of the perinatal environment is alpha-fetoprotein (AFP). This 74 kDa glycoprotein is similar in amino acid composition to albumin and is present at milligram per milliliter concentrations in amniotic fluid and perinatal sera. In the mouse, the serum concentration drops by five orders of magnitude over the first 2 weeks after birth (Bancroft et al., 1987; Crandall, 1981; Kahan & Levine, 1971; Lu & Unanue, 1985; Olson et al., 1977), whereas in humans, AFP levels decrease at the end of the first trimester of gestation.

Data from two laboratories indicate that AFP inhibits macrophage Ia expression at concentrations found in fetal and neonatal sera and mouse amniotic fluid (Fig. 11-6) (Crainie et al., 1989; Lu et al., 1984). These results are consistent with previous observations reporting that mouse amniotic fluid inhibits antigen presentation (Suzuki & Tomasi, 1980), as well as other reports demonstrating immunoregulatory activities of AFP (Murgita & Wigzell, 1983; Tomasi, 1983). However, there is considerable variability in the immunoregulatory activity of various preparations of AFP. This may be attributable to the biochemical heterogeneity of AFP. For example, in the mouse, the five species of apo-AFP differ in the number of covalently bound sialic acid residues (Wong et al., 1988; Zimmerman et al., 1977). In addition, AFP has binding sites for hydrophobic molecules, including polyunsaturated fatty acids.

Of the hydrophobic molecules bound by AFP, all cis-4,7,10,13,16,19-docosahexaenoic acid (DHA) is of particular interest. Fetal rat serum contains a high (150 μM) concentration of DHA that rapidly drops fivefold after birth (Delorme et al., 1984). Since DHA is a major fatty acid constituent of brain and retina, the high fetal serum DHA concentration may be essential to the rapid intrauterine growth of these organs (see review, Salem et al., 1986). The presence of AFP at high levels in fetal, but not maternal, serum and its high affinity for DHA may make it critical in maintaining the high fetal serum concentration of DHA (Crandall, 1981; Hsia et al., 1987).

We find that DHA, at concentrations equivalent to those present in fetal serum, inhibits macrophage activation *in vitro.* Thus, DHA may contribute to perinatal deficits in macrophage function that are, in part, responsible for the increased susceptibility of the chorioallantoic plate and fetus to infection (Dustin et al., 1990).

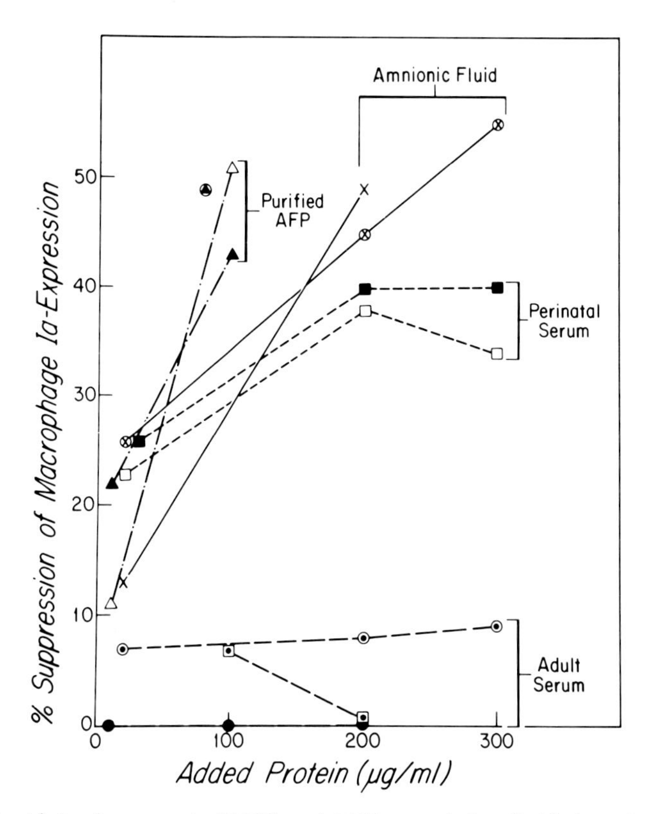

Fig. 11-6. Alpha-fetoprotein (AFP) and AFP-containing fluids (amnionic fluid and perinatal serum) inhibit macrophage Ia expression. Results of three experiments in which macrophages were cultured in the presence of 0.75% lymphokine. Ia expression measured by immunofluorescence. [See Lu, Changelian & Unanue, 1984 for details.]

Summary and Speculations

Infection of the placenta and decidua is a complex event, which involves not only the pathogen, the maternal and fetal immune systems but also immunoregulatory events at the maternal-fetal interface. It can therefore be used as a tool to understand this immunoregulation. *Listeria* is ordinarily a powerful stimulus of T lymphocyte and macrophage activities and was used in our experiments to probe the functional activities of T lymphocytes and macrophages at the maternal-fetal interface. We found two different deficient macrophage anti-*Listeria* responses in different areas of the placental region. One occurred in the decidua basalis, where the fetal placenta is anchored to the maternal uterus. It is one of the few areas in nature where allogeneic cells, each synthesizing its own private class I MHC antigens coexist, without immunological rejection. Macrophages and lymphocytes are excluded from this site. Our data indicate that solid phase inhibitors embedded in the substratum formed by decidual stromal cells prevent macrophage functions. The other abnormal response occurred in the chorioallantoic plate. This consists only of fetal tissue and is not a maternal-fetal interface. In contrast to the decidua basalis, large numbers of macrophages were found at this site. However, these macrophages were not appropriately activated as evidenced by their lack of Ia expression and their inability to efficiently destroy *Listeria*. This area of the placenta is perfused only by the fetal circulation and is therefore exposed to high concentrations of docosahexaenoic acid bound to alpha-fetoprotein. We find that these substances inhibit macrophage activation *in vitro*.

Our data indicate that maternal decidual cells and fetal trophoblast are intimately intermixed in the decidua basalis (Redline & Lu, 1989). Understanding immune responses in this tissue is therefore critical to understanding the maternal-fetal immunological relationship. Our data also indicate that conventional maternal T cells and macrophages are not found in the decidua basalis at midgestation. These cells are excluded even during the powerful stimulus provided by local *Listeria* infection (Redline & Lu, 1988). The most provocative interpretation of this result is that T cells and macrophages cannot immigrate into this tissue, thereby protecting trophoblast in the decidua basalis from the maternal immune response. Furthermore, few trophic interactions between T cells or macrophages and trophoblasts should occur in the decidua basalis.

The maternal-fetal interface has a complex structure. Although our data indicate that T cells and macrophages do not contact trophoblast in the decidua basalis, contact between maternal immunocytes in the blood and trophoblast lining maternal sinusoids does occur in the fetal placenta. Different immunoregulatory mechanisms may be active in different anatomical regions.

Alternative interpretations of our data are possible at the present time. On one extreme, one might argue that the exclusion of T cells and macrophages from the decidua basalis is a spurious result having no importance for the maternal-fetal immunological relationship. Instead, solid phase decidual regulators may be biologically important for morphogenesis of this tissue. Solid phase regulators regulate development of a number of different organs, including the nervous system (Grumet et al., 1985) and kidney (Aufderheide et al., 1987). Such regulators may also mediate communication between the various decidual and trophoblastic cells in the decidua basalis in the course of organogenesis. In line with this argument is the survival of murine ectopic pregnancies where no decidua is present (Nicholas, 1934).

A complete understanding of the maternal-fetal immunologic relationship remains a fundamental challenge to immunologists. We hope that experiments from our laboratory and others will determine if the exclusion of T cells and macrophages from the murine decidua basalis during listeriosis has important implications in addressing this challenge.

Acknowledgments

This work was supported by grants to CYL from the NIH (RO1-HD20188 and RO1-HD24797), the Hood Foundation, and the Hearst Foundation. CYL was a Fellow of the Hartford Foundation and subsequently recipient of a Research Career Development Award (KO4-HD00862). RWR was initially supported by a training grant (7T32AM-07527) and is recipient of a Clinical Investigator Award from the NIH (KO8-HD00864). DBM was supported by a training grant (2T32-DK07527). The authors thank Professor B. M. Brenner for critically reading the manuscript and for his encouragement.

References

Amato, P. A., Unanue, E. R. and Taylor, D. L. 1983. Distribution of actin in spreading macrophages: a comparative study on living and fixed cells. *J. Cell. Biol.* 96:750–761.

Aufderheide, E., Chiquet-Ehrismann, R. and Ekblom, P. 1987. Epithelial-mesenchymal interactions in the developing kidney lead to expression of tenascin in the mesenchyme. *J. Cell. Biol.* 105:599–608.

Austyn, J. M. and Gordon, S. 1981. F4/80 a monoclonal antibody directed specifically against the mouse macrophage. *Eur. J. Immunol.* 11:805.

Bancroft, G. J., Schreiber, R. D., Bosma, G. C., Bosma, M. J. and Unanue, E. R. 1987. A T cell-independent mechanism of macrophage activation by interferon gamma. *J. Immunol.* 139:1104–1107.

Beer, A. E. and Billingham, R. E. 1974. Host responses to intra-uterine tissue, cellular and fetal allografts. *J. Reprod. Fertil.* 21(suppl):59–88.

Bell, S. C. 1983. Decidualization: regional differentiation and associated function. *Oxford Rev. Reprod. Biol.* 5:220–271.

Bell, S. C. 1985. Comparative aspects of decidualization in rodents and human: cell types, secreted products and associated function. In *Implantation of the Human Embryo* (R. G. Edwards, J. M. Purdy, and P. C. Steptoe, eds.). London: Academic Press, Inc., pp. 71–132.

Beller, D. I. and Ho, K. 1982.. Regulation of macrophage populations. V. Evaluation of the control of macrophage Ia expression in vitro. *J. Immunol.* 129:971.

Billington, W. D. and Bell, S. C. 1983. Immunobiology of mouse trophoblast. In *Biology of Trophoblast* (Y. W. Loke and A. Whyte, eds.). New York: Elsevier, pp. 571–596.

Brown, E.. J. 1986. Review: the role of extracellular matrix proteins in the control of phagocytosis. *J. Leuko. Biol.* 39:579–591.

Brown, E. J. and Goodwin, J. L. 1988. Fibronectin receptors of phagocytes. Characterization of the arg-gly-asp binding proteins of human monocytes and polymorphonuclear leukocytes. *J. Exp. Med.* 167:777.

Bulmer, J. N., Johnson, P. M. and Bulmer, D. 1987. Leukocyte populations in human decidua and endometrium. In *Immunoregulation and Fetal*

Survival (T. J. Gill III and T. G. Wegmann, eds.). New York: Oxford University Press, pp. 111–137.

Bulmer, J. N., Smith, J., Morrison, L. and Wells, M. 1988. Maternal and fetal cellular relationships in the human placental basal plate. *Placenta* 9:237–246.

Chaouat, G. 1987. Opinion: placental immunoregulatory factors. *J. Reprod. Immunol.* 10:179–188.

Chaouat, G., Kolb, J. P. and Wegmann, T. G. 1983. The murine placenta as an immunological barrier between the mother and the fetus. *Immunol. Rev.* 75:31–60.

Chaponnier, C., Yin, H. L. and Stossel, T. P. 1987. Reversibility of gelsolin/actin interaction in macrophages. Evidence of calcium-dependent and calcium-independent pathways. *J. Exp. Med.* 165:97–106.

Clark, D. A., Brierley, J., Slapsys, R., et al. 1986. Trophoblast-dependent and trophoblast independent suppressor cells of maternal origin in murine and human decidua. In *Reproductive Immunology: 1986* (D. A. Clark and B. A. Croy, eds.). New York: Elsevier, pp. 219–226.

Clark, D. A., Croy, B. A., Wegmann, T. G. and Chaouat, G. 1987. Opinion: immunological and para-immunological mechanisms in spontaneous abortion: recent insights and future directions. *J. Reprod. Immunol.* 12:1–12.

Clark, D. A., Falbo, M., Rowley, R. B., Banwatt, D. and Stedronska-Clark, J. 1988. Active suppression of host-vs-graft reaction in pregnant mice. IX. Soluble suppressor activity obtained by allopregnant mouse decidua that blocks the cytolytic effector response to IL-2 is related to transforming growth factor-beta. *J. Immunol.* 141:3833–3840.

Collart, M. A., Belin, D., Vassalli, J. D., De Kossodo, S., and Vassali, P. 1986. Gamma interferon enhances macrophage transcription of the tumor necrosis factor/cachectin, interleukin 1, and urokinase genes, which are controlled by short-lived repressors. *J. Exp. Med.* 164:2113–2118.

Crainie, M., Semeluk, A., Lee, K. C. and Wegmann, T. G. 1989. Regulation of constitutive and lymphokine induced Ia expression by murine alphafetoprotein. *Cell. Immunol.* 118:41–52

Crandall, B. F. 1981. Alpha-fetoprotein: a review. *CRC Rev. Clin. Lab. Sci.* 15:127–185.

Crawford, R. M., Finbloom, D. S., Ohara, J., Paul, W. E. and Meltzer, M. S. 1987. B cell stimulatory factor-1 (interleukin 4) activates macrophages for increased tumoricidal activity and expression of Ia antigens. *J. Immunol.* 139:135–141.

Czop, J. K. 1986. Phagocytosis of particulate activators of the alternative complement pathway: effects of fibronectin. *Adv. Immunol.* 38:361–398.

De Waal, R. M. W., Bogmam, M. J. J., Maass, C. N., Cornelissen, L. M. H., Tax, W. J. M. and Koene, R. A. P. 1983. Variable expression of Ia antigens on the vascular endothelium of mouse skin allografts. *Nature* 303:426.

Delorme, J., Benassayag, C., Christeff, N., Vallette, G., Savu, L. and Nunez, E. 1984. Age-dependent responses of the serum non-esterified fatty acids to adrenalectomy and ovariectomy in developing rats. *Biochim. Biophys. Acta* 792:6–10.

Dinarello, C. A. 1989. Interleukin 1 and its biologically related cytokines. *Adv. Immunol.* 44:153–205.

Dodd, M., Andrew, T. A. and Coles, J. S. 1980. Functional behaviour of skin allografts transplanted to rabbit deciduomata. *J. Anat.* 130:381–390.

Dustin, L. B., Shea, C. M., Soberman, R. J. and Lu, C. Y. 1990. Docosahexaenoic acid, a constituent of rodent fetal serum and fish oil diets, inhibits acquisition of macrophage tumoricidal function. *J. Immunol.* 144:4888–4897.

Faulk, W. P. and McIntyre, J. A. 1983. Immunological studies of human trophoblast: markers, subsets and functions. *Immunol. Rev.* 75:139–175.

Fuhlbrigge, R. C., Chaplin, D. D., Kiely, J. M., Valge, V. E. and Unanue, E. R. 1987. Regulation of interleukin 1 gene expression by adherence and lipopolysaccharide. *J. Immunol.* 138:3799.

Galsworthy, S. B. 1984. Immunomodulation by surface components of Listeria Monocytogenes: a review. *Clin. Invest. Med.* 7:223–227.

Gill, R. J., Kunz, H. W., Misra, D. H. and Hassett, A. L. C. 1988. The major histocompatibility complex of the rat. *Transplantation* 43:773–785.

Gill, T. J. III and Wegmann, T. G. 1987. *Immunoregulation and Fetal Survival.* New York: Oxford University Press.

Glasser, S. R., Lampelo, S., Munir, M. I., and Julian J. 1987. Expression of desmin, laminin, and fibronectin during in situ differentiation (decidualization) of rat uterine stromal cells. *Differentiation* 35:132–142.

Grabstein, K. H., Urdal, D. L., Tushinski, R. J., et al. 1986. Induction of macrophage tumoricidal activity by granulocyte-macrophage colony-stimulating factor. *Science* 232:506–508.

Grumet, M., Hoffman, S., Crossin, K. L. and Edelman, G. M. 1985. Cytotactin, an extracellular matrix protein of neural and non-neural tissues that mediates glia-neuron interaction. *PNAS* 82:8075–8079.

Hahn, H. and Kaufmann, S. H. E. 1981. The role of cell-mediated immunity in bacterial infections. *Rev. Infect. Dis.* 3:1221–1250.

Haskill, S., Johnson, C., Eierman, D., Becker, S. and Warren, K. 1988. Adherence induces selective mRNA expression of monocyte mediators and proto-oncogenes. *J. Immunol.* 140:1690–1694.

Head, J. R. 1987. Lymphoid components in the rodent uterus. In *Immunoregulation and Fetal Survival* (T. J. Gill, III and T. G. Wegmann, eds.). New York: Oxford University Press, pp. 46–59.

Head, J. R., Drake, B. L., and Zuckermann, F. A. 1987. Major histocompatibility antigens on trophoblast and their regulation: implications in the maternal-fetal relationship. *Am. J. Reprod. Immunol.* 15:12–18.

Hsia, J. C., Wong, T. T., Trimble, C. E. and Deutsch, H. F. 1987. An in vitro model of placental transfer of polyunsaturated fatty acids—the albumin-AFP exchange system. In *Biological activities of Alpha1-fetoprotein: vol. 1* (G. J. Mizejewski and H. I. Jacobson, eds.). Boca Raton, FL: CRC Press, pp. 205–212.

Hunziker, R. D. and Wegmann, T. G. 1986 Placental immunoregulation. *CRC Crit. Rev. Immunol.* 6:245–285.

Jenkinson, E. J. and Owen, V. 1980. Ontogeny and distribution of major histocompatibility complex (MHC) antigens on mouse placental trophoblast. *J. Reprod. Immunol.* 2:173–181.

Johnson, P. M., Risk, J. M., Bulmer, J. N., Niewola, Z. and Kimber, I. 1987. Antigen expression at human maternofetal interfaces. In *Immunoregulation and Fetal Survival* (T. J. Gill III and T. G. Wegmann, eds.). New York: Oxford University Press, pp. 181–196.

Kabawat, S. E., Mostoufi-Zadeh, M., Driscoll, S. G. and Bhan, A. K. 1985. Implantation site in normal pregnancy: a study with monoclonal antibodies. *Am. J. Pathol.* 118:76–84.

Kahan, B. and Levine, L. 1971. The occurrence of serum fetal alpha-1-protein in developing mice and hepatomas and teratomas. *Cancer Res.* 31:930.

Kanbour, A., Ho, H. N., Misra, D. N., MacPherson, T. A., Kunz, H. W. and Gill, T. J. III 1987. Differential expression of MHC class I antigens on the placenta of the rat. A mechanism for the survival of the fetal allograft. *J. Exp. Med.* 166:1861–1882.

Kelley, J. L., Rozek, M. M., Suenram, C. A. and Schwartz, C. J. 1987. Activation of human blood monocytes by adherence to tissue culture plastic surfaces. *Exp. Mol. Pathol.* 46:266–278.

Kronenberg, M., Siu, G., Hood, L. E. and Shastri, N. 1986. The molecular genetics of the T cell antigen receptor and T cell antigen recognition. *Annu. Rev. Immunol.* 4:529–592.

Kruskal, B. A. and Maxfield, F. R. 1988. Cytosolic free calcium increases before and oscillates during frustrated phagocytosis in macrophages. *J. Cell. Biol.* 105:2685.

Lala, P. K., Chatterjee-Hasrouni, S., Kearns, M., Montgomery, B. and Colavincenzo, V. 1983. Immunobiology of the feto-maternal interface. *Immunol. Rev.* 75:87–116.

Lala, P. K., Kearns, M. and Panhar, R. S. 1987. Immunology of the decidual tissue. In *Immunoregulation and Fetal Survival* (T. J. Gill, III and T. G. Wegmann, eds.). New York: Oxford University Press, pp. 78–95.

Loke, Y. W. and Butterworth, B. H. 1987. Heterogeneity of human trophoblast. In *Immunoregulation and Fetal Survival* (T. J. Gill, III and T. G. Wegmann, eds.)'. New York: Oxford University Press, pp. 197–209.

Lu, C. Y. 1984. The delayed ontogenesis of Ia-positive macrophages: implications for host defense and self-tolerance in the neonate. *Clin. Invest. Med.* 7:263–268.

Lu, C. Y. and Unanue, E. R. 1985. Macrophage ontogeny: implications for host defense, T lymphocyte differentiation, and the acquisition of self-tolerance. *Clin. Immunol. Allergy* 5:253–269.

Lu, C. Y., Calamai, E. G. and Unanue, E. R. 1979. A defect in the antigen-presenting function of macrophages from neonatal mice. *Nature* 282:327–329.

Lu, C. Y., Peters, E. and Unanue, E. R. 1981. Macrophage function in athymic mice: antigen-presentation and regulation. *J. Immunol.* 126:2496–2498.

Lu, C. Y., Changelian, P. S. and Unanue, E. R. 1984. Alpha-fetoprotein inhibits macrophage expression of Ia antigens. *J. Immunol.* 132:1722–1727.

Matthews, C. J. and Searle, R. F. 1988. Antigen presenting capacity of murine decidual tissue in vivo. *J. Reprod. Immunol.* 12:287–295.

Mercurio, A. M. 1988. Expression of extracellular matrixlike glycoproteins by macrophages and other leukocytes. In *Protein Transfer and Organelle Biogenesis*, Orlando, FL: Academic Press, Inc., p. 563–584.

Mossman, H. W. 1987. *Vertebrate Fetal Membranes.* London: Rutgers University Press & Macmillan.

Murgita, R. A. and Wigzell, H. 1983. Regulation of immune functions in the fetus and newborn. *Prog. Allergy* 29:54–133.

Nicholas, J. S. 1934. Experiments on developing rats: I. Limits of fetal regeneration; behavior of embryonic material in abnormal environments. *Anat. Rec.* 58:387–408.

Nieder, G. L. and Macon, G. R. 1987. Uterine and oviducal protein secretion during early pregnancy in the mouse. *J. Reprod. Fertil.* 8187:287–294.

O'Shea, J. D., Kleinfeld, R. G. and Morrow, H. A. 1983. Ultrastructure of decidualization in the pseudopregnant rat. *Am. J. Anat.* 166:271.

Oi, V. T., Jones, P. P., Goding, J. W. and Herzenberg, L. A. 1978. Properties of monoclonal antibodies to mouse Ig allotypes, H-2, and Ia antigens. In *Lymphocyte Hybridomas* (F. Melchers, M. Potter and N. Warner, eds.). New York: Springer-Verlag, p. 115.

Olson, M., Lindahl, G. and Ruoslahti, E. 1977. Genetic control of alpha-fetoprotein synthesis in the mouse. *J. Exp. Med.* 145:819.

Ozato, K. and Sachs, D. H. 1981. Monoclonal antibodies to mouse MHC antigens. III. Hybridoma antibodies reacting to antigens of the H-2b haplotype reveal genetic control of isotype expression. *J. Immunol.* 126:317.

Parr, M. B., Tung, H. N. and Parr, E. L. 1986. The ultrastructure of the rat primary decidual zone. *Am. J. Anat.* 176:423–436.

Perri, R. T., Vercellotti, G., McCarthy, J., Vessella, R. L. and Furcht, L. T. 1985. Laminin selectively enhances monocyte-macrophage-mediated tumoricidal activity. *J. Lab. Clin. Med.* 105:30–35.

Pober, J. S., Collins, T., Gimbrone, M. A. Jr, Cotran, R. S., Gitlin, J. D., Fiers, W., Clayberger, C., Krensky, A. M., Burakoff, S. J. and Reiss, C. S. 1983. Lymphocytes recognize human vascular endothelial and dermal fibroblast Ia antigens induced by recombinant immune interferon. *Nature* 395:726–729.

Raghupathy, R., Singh, B., Barrington Leigh, J. and Wegmann, T. G. 1981. The ontogeny and turnover kinetics of paternal K-2K antigenic determinants on the allogeneic murine placenta. *J. Immunol.* 127:2074.

Redline, R. W. and Lu, C. Y. 1988. Specific defects in the anti-*Listerial* immune response in discrete regions of the murine uterus and placenta account for susceptibility to infection. *J. Immunol.* 140:3947–3955.

Redline, R. W. and Lu, C. Y. 1987. Role of local immunosuppression in murine fetoplacental listeriosis. *J. Clin. Invest.* 79:1234–1241.

Redline, R. W. and Lu, C. Y. 1989. Localization of fetal major histocompatibility complex antigens and maternal leukocytes in the murine placenta. Implications for the maternal-fetal immunological relationship. *Lab. Invest.* 61:27–36.

Redline, R. W., Shea, C. M., Papaioannou, V. E. and Lu, C. Y. 1988. Defective Anti-listerial responses in deciduoma of pseudopregnant mice. *Am. J. Pathol.* 133:485–497.

Redline, R. W., McKay, D. B., Vazquez, M. A., Papaioannoli, V. E., and Lu, C. Y. 1990. Macrophage functions are regulated by the substratum of murine decidual stromal cells. *J. Clin Invest.* 85:1951–1958.

Redman, C. W. G., McMichael, A. J., Stirrat, G. M., Sunderland, C. A. and Ting, A. 1988. Class I major histocompatibility complex antigens on human extra-villous trophoblast. *Immunology* 52:457–468.

Rosen, H. and Gordon, S. 1987. Monoclonal antibody to the urine type 3 complement receptor inhibits adhesion of myelomonocytic cells in vitro and inflammatory cell recruitment in vivo. *J. Exp. Med.* 166:1685–1701.

Salem, N. Jr, Kim, H. Y. and Yergey, J. A. 1986. Docosahexaenoic acid: membrane function and metabolism. In *Health Effects of Polyunsaturated Fatty Acids in Seafoods* (A. P. Simopoulos, R. R. Kifer and R. E. Martin, eds.). Orlando, FL: Academic Press, pp. 263–318.

Sobel, R. A., Blanchette, B. W., Bhan, A. K. and Colvin, R. B. 1984. The immunopathology of experimental allergic encephalomyelitis. II. Endothelial cell Ia increases prior to inflammatory cell infiltration. *J. Immunol.* 132:2402.

Springer, T. A., Dustin, M. L., Kishimoto, T. K. and Marlin, S. D. 1987. The lymphocyte function-associated LFA-1, CD2, and LFA-3 molecules: cell adhesion receptors of the immune system. *Annu. Rev. Immunol.* 5:223–252.

Strom, T. B., Kupiec-Weglinski, J. W. and Tilney, N. L. 1985. On the mechanisms of rejection of vascularized organ allografts: review and an attempt at synthesis. In *Progress in Transplantation, vol. 2* (P. J. Morris and N. L. Tilney, eds.). New York: Churchill Livingstone, pp. 126–146.

Sutton, L., Mason, D. Y. and Redman, C. W. G. 1983. HLA-Dr positive cells in the human placenta. *Immunology* 49:103–110.

Suzuki, K. and Tomasi, T. B. 1980. Mechanism of immune suppression by murine neonatal fluids. *J. Immunol.* 125:2614.

Tachi, C. and Tachi, S. 1986. Macrophages and implantation. *Ann. NY Acad. Sci.* 476:158–182.

Tawfik, O. W., Hunt, J. S. and Wood, G. W. 1986. Implication of prostaglandin E2 in soluble factor-mediated immune suppression by murine decidual cells. *Am. J. Reprod. Immunol.* 12:111–117.

Tomasi, T. B. 1983. Immunosuppressive elements in the fetal and neonatal environments. In *Reproductive Immunology* (T. G. Wegmann and T. J. Gill III, eds.). New York: Oxford University Press, pp. 317–340.

Tung, H. N., Parr, M. B. and Parr, E. L. 1986. The permeability of the primary decidual zone in the rat uterus: an ultrastructural tracer and freeze-fracture study. *Biol. Reprod.* 35:1045–1058.

Unanue, E. R. and Allen, P. M. 1987. The basis for the immunoregulatory role of macrophages and other accessory cells. *Science* 236:551–557.

Van Kessel, K. P. M., Antonissen, A. C. J. M., Van Dijk, H., Rudemaker, R. M. and Willers, J. M. N. 1981. *Infect. Immunity* 34:16.

Wegmann, T. G. 1987. Placental immunotrophism: maternal T cells enhance placental growth and function. *Am. J. Reprod. Immunol.* 15:67–70.

Wegmann, T. G., Waters, C. A., Drell, D. W. and Carlson, G. A. 1979. Pregnant mice are not primed but can be primed to fetal alloantigens. *PNAS* 76:2410–2414.

Weitlauf, H. M. and Suda-Hartman, M. 1988. Changes in secreted uterine proteins associated with embryo implantation in the mouse. *J. Reprod. Fertil.* 84:539–549.

Welsh, A. O. and Enders, A. C. 1985. Light and electron microscopic examination of the mature decidual cells of the rat with emphasis on the antimesometrial decidua and its degeneration. *Am. J. Anat.* 172:1–29.

Wewer, U. M., Damjanov, A., Weiss, J., Liotta, L. A. and Damjanov, I. 1986. Mouse endometrial stromal cells produce basement-membrane components. *Differentiation* 32:49.

Wewer, U. M., Albrechtson, R., Fisher, L. W., Young, M. F. and Termine, J.

D. 1988. Osteonectin/SPARC/BM-40 in human decidua and carcinoma, tissues characterized by de novo formation of basement membrane. *Am. J. Pathol.* 132:345–355.

Wong, L. T., Lu, C. Y., Tinker, D. O. and Hsia, J. C. 1988. Application of high-performance liquid chromatography for the study of the microheterogeneity changes of mouse alpha-fetoprotein in fetal development. *J. Biochem. Biophys. Methods* 15:267–272.

Wood, G. W., Kamel, S. and Smith, K. 1988. Immunoregulation and prostaglandin production by mechanically-derived and enzyme-derived murine decidual cells. *J. Reprod. Immunol.* 13:235–248.

Woodruff, M. F. A. 1958. Transplantation immunity and the immunological problem of pregnancy. *Proc. Roy. Soc. London* 158B:68–75.

Zimmerman, E. G., Voorting-Hawkins, M. and Michael, J. G. 1977. Immunosuppression by mouse sialylated alpha-fetoprotein. *Nature* 265:354.

Zuckermann, F. A. and Head, J. R. 1986. Expression of MHC antigens on murine trophoblast and their modulation by interferon. *J. Immunol.* 137:846–853.

Zuckermann, F. A. and Head, J. R. 1987. Murine trophoblast resists cell-mediated lysis: I. resistance to allospecific cytotoxic T lymphocytes. *J. Immunol.* 139:2856–2864.

Zuckermann, F. A. and Head, J. R. 1988. Murine trophoblast resists cell-mediated lysis. II. Resistance to natural cell-mediated cytotoxicity. *Cell. Immunol.* 116:274–286.

12

Is There an Essential Requirement for Bone-Marrow-Derived Cells at the Fetomaternal Interface During Successful Pregnancy? A Study of Pregnancies in Immunodeficient Mice

B. ANNE CROY, CHRISTINE CHAPEAU, NANCY REED,
IAN J. STEWART, and SANDRA PEEL

The role of bone-marrow-derived cells in the pregnant uterus remains incompletely defined. A variety of lymphoid and lymphoid-like cells have been demonstrated in the uterus during pregnancy (Clark et al., 1984; Croy et al., 1988; Gambel et al., 1985; Lala et al., 1983; Parr & Parr, 1985; Peel et al., 1983; Ritson & Bulmer, 1987). It has been postulated that the functions of these cells range from destruction of the conceptus through suppression of maternal immunity to promotion of trophoblastic activity and fetal survival (Athanassakis et al., 1987; Chaouat et al., 1982; Clark et al., 1984; Croy et al., 1988; Gendron & Baines, 1988). Stocks of mice carrying different, specific, and often well-defined mutations affecting bone-marrow-derived cell lineages are available. Study of immune responses in such animals has contributed significantly to our understanding of lineage relationships of immunocompetent cells and the cellular interactions required for normal function of the immune system (Kindred, 1979; Wu et al., 1968). Similarly, analysis of the distribution and function of bone-marrow-derived cells in implantation sites recovered from immunodeficient mice should provide insights into the relative importance of such cells in the uterus during successful gestation.

The hypothesis that cytokines, released from either T cells (Athanassakis et al., 1987; Wegmann, 1987) or NK cells (Croy et al., 1985, 1988), can increase placental cell function and promote fetal success predicts that immunodeficient animals may have reduced fecundity. Mice provide the best model system in which to address this prediction experimentally because several different immunodeficient mutant stocks are available (Shultz & Sidman, 1987). As well, the short murine gestation period and the easy maintenance of mice as a large population of germ-free animals by use of microisolation caging systems greatly facilitate these studies.

Genetic Mutants

Severe combined immunodeficient (SCID) mice, genotype *scid/scid* (Bosma, et al., 1983), lack mature lymphocytes of both T and B lymphocyte lineages (Dorshkind et al., 1984) and, have moderate depletion in macrophage function (Bancroft et al., 1986; Czitrom et al., 1985; Deschryver-Kecskemeti et al., 1988), but maintain normal levels of nonactivated NK cells (Dorshkind et al., 1985; Lauzon et al., 1986; Tutt et al., 1987). SCID mice appeared to be the most suitable animals for our studies not only because of their severe immunological impairment but also because the mutation is believed to affect *only* pathways of lymphoid maturation (Malynn et al., 1988; Okazaki, Nishikawa, & Sakano, 1988; Schuler et al., 1986). This contrasts with mutations having more pleiotropic effects, such as the *nu* mutation (Cordier & Heremans, 1975; Kindred, 1979; Rebar et al., 1983). To reduce the function of NK cells in SCID mice we crossed SCID males to females of genotype *bg/bg* (Clark et al., 1981; Hioki et al., 1987). The *bg* mutation (Brandt et al., 1981) has been shown to selectively impair splenic NK cell activity (Roder, 1979; Roder & Duwe, 1979) to an extent exceeding that induced by other mutations (Clark et al., 1981; Shultz & Sidman, 1987).

Studies of Fecundity in Immunodeficient Mice

Establishment of scid/scid.bg/bg *Stocks and Study of Their Litter Sizes*

Intercross of C.B-17 *scid/scid* males to C57B1/6J-*bg/bg* females provided animals heterozygous for each mutation. The intercross offspring were randomly paired with each other and their progeny tested for genotype after weaning. Mice negative for murine serum immunoglobulin using Ouchterlony immunodiffusion in gel were identified as *scid/scid*, whereas mice having blood neutrophils containing large (giant) sudanophilic granules were designated *bg/bg* (Bennett et al., 1969). The *bg/bg* genotype was confirmed by coat color dilution in all nonwhite mice. Double mutants were expected at a frequency of 1/16. Typed generation 2 mice were paired randomly to mates of similar genotype. Numbers of offspring produced from these matings and two subsequent random-bred generations are presented in Table 12-1. The data indicate that hybrid vigor resulted from the crossing of the two inbred strains, and in each generation studied to date, no significant influence on litter size could be attributed to the genetically determined immunodeficiency. This study suggests that there is no absolute requirement for either mature B lymphocytes or T lymphocytes during successful murine gestation. Additional impairment in NK cell activity does not interefere with murine pregnancy success.

Table 12-1. Litter sizes of immunodeficient murine breeding pairs

Genotype of Breeding Pair	Number of Litters	Number of Pairs	Offspring Born per Litter
Balb/c (congenic to *scid/scid*)*	266	480	4.6
C57B1/6 (congenic to *bg/bg*)*	181	240	6.7
Intercross of foundation stocks	3	3	8.3
Intercross of generation 1			
+/*scid*.+*bg*	24	10	7.4
Intercross of generation 2			
+/+	12	8	8.5
scid/scid.bg/bg	4	3	8.5
scid/scid.+/*bg*	10	5	7.2
+/*scid.bg/bg*	24	13	8.1
Intercross of generation 3			
scid/scid.bg/bg	25	10	6.0
scid/scid.+/*bg*	14	9	6.4
+/*scid.bg/bg*	13	5	6.4
Intercross of generation 4			
scid/scid.bg/bg	3	3	7.3

* Data from *Handbook on Genetically Standardized Jax Mice*, The Jackson Laboratory, 1980.

Studies of Pregnancy Failure in scid/scid.bg/bg *Mice*

To determine whether embryonic loss was occurring in the immunodeficient mice before parturition, mated animals were sacrificed and numbers of conceptuses and ovarian corpora lutea determined. The data, presented as Table 12-2, further support the conclusion that *scid/scid.bg/bg* mice have no major reproductive impairment.

Trophoblast Morphology in scid/scid.bg/bg *Mice*

To address the question of trophoblast quality in the absence of a mature immune system, conceptuses were recovered from *scid/scid.bg/bg* females and examined morphologically. At day 2.5 of ges-

Table 12-2. Conceptus success compared to ovarian corpora lutea

Genotype of Pregnant Female	Preimplantation*			Postimplantation†		
	Dead	Viable	CL	Dead	Viable	CL
scid/scid.bg/bg	1	8	9	10	130	137‡
scid/scid.+/*bg*		Not tested		0	28	32§
+/*scid.bg/bg*	0	8	9	3	37	35‖

* Day 3.5 of gestation, one pregnancy per genotype.
† Days 8–16 of gestation.
‡ n = 18 litters.
§ n = 3 litters.
‖ n = 4 litters.

tation (day of copulation plug detection was designated day 0.5), morulae were obtained from the oviduct and at day 3.5 of gestation expanded blastocysts were flushed from the uterus. Zonae pellucidae were present at both stages, and no differences in appearance or timing between these preimplantation embryos and those flushed from immunocompetent mice were noted. Nuclei present in blastocyst stage embryos were enumerated and did not differ significantly from the expected number of 64. Histological study of the placenta from days 10 to 15 of gestation indicated successful differentiation of trophoblast giant cells, spongiotrophoblast, and labyrinthine trophoblast, as well as formation of the maternal decidua and metrial gland (Fig. 12-1). No major differences in the sizes of placentas from females of the various genotypes have been noted in preliminary studies, but compared to conventionally raised mice, placentas of the germ-free animals appear small. Quantitative morphometric studies of placentas from larger numbers of animals are required, however, to confirm placental size. These preliminary studies of the reproductive performance of *scid/scid.bg/bg* mice fail to confirm the importance that has been attributed to a functional mature immune system during normal pregnancy. The maternal immune system has been claimed to have effects on the normal functions of the ovaries (Michael, 1983; Michael et al., 1988; Rebar et al., 1983) and the structure and function of the placental trophoblast (Athanassakis et al., 1987; Wegmann, 1987) and uterus (Chaouat et al., 1982).

Bone-Marrow-Derived Cells and the Fetomaternal Interface

The requirement for functional marrow-derived cells to allow successful pregnancy must be re-evaluated in view of our studies of fecundity in *scid/scid.bg/bg* mice. It is possible that bone-marrow-derived cells other than mature B and T lymphocytes and NK cells are necessary for successful implantation and placental growth and function. Alternatively, unique subsets of lymphocytes (Goodman & Lefrancois, 1988) or NK cells may be present in the uterus and retain functional activity. Several populations of bone-marrow-derived cells found at implantation sites need to be considered, including small granulated lymphocytes that have been identified as uterine suppressor cells (Clark et al., 1984, 1986; and Chapter 20, this volume), granulated metrial gland cells (GMG) (Jbara & Stewart, 1982; Stewart & Peel, 1978), and macrophages. In the following sections we review the morphology of implantation sites, including the distribution of GMG cells and macrophages. In addition, we report studies on the differentiation of the metrial gland and GMG cells in immunodeficient mice and on the immune characterization of the metrial gland.

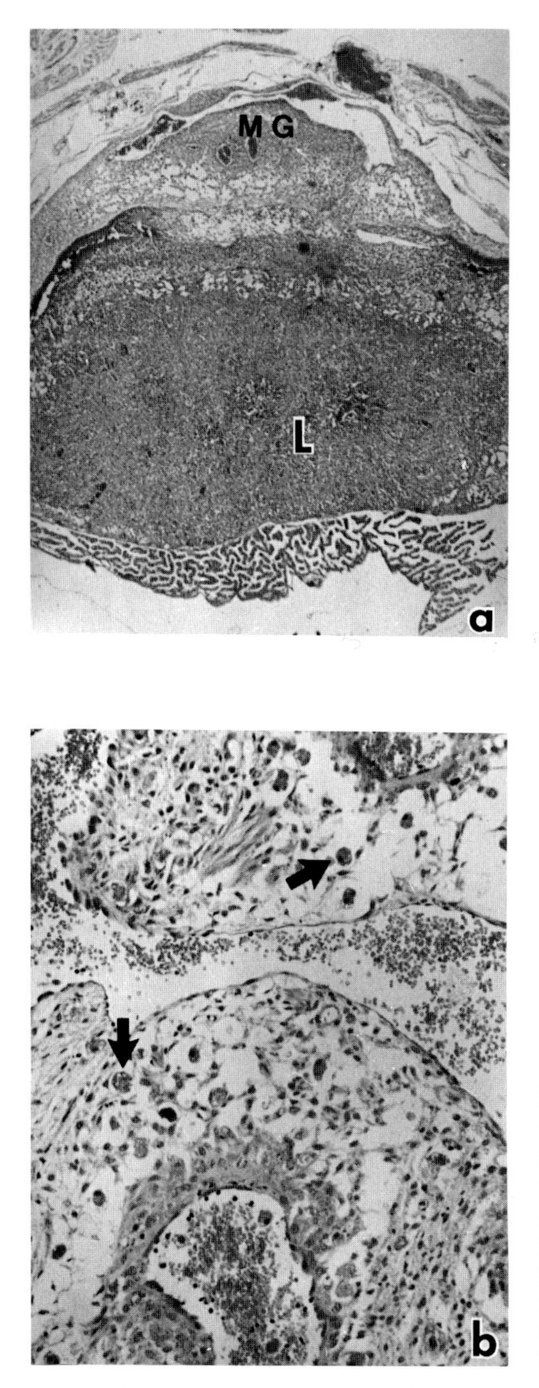

Fig. 12-1. Photomicrographs of (a) the mature placenta and metrial gland (MG) from successful pregnancy in *scid/scid.bg/bg* mouse, day 15 of gestation (×19) and (b) groups of granulated metrial gland cells, indicated by arrows (×125). L = Labyrinthine region.

Review of Morphology of Implantation Sites

In the pregnant mouse the blastocyst hatches from the zona pellucida and becomes oriented within an antimesometrial uterine crypt by day 4 of pregnancy. The blastocyst attaches to the uterine epithelium, initiating local hypertrophy and proliferation of stromal cells. This response is associated with infiltration of bone-marrow-derived cells.

A number of zones of decidua develop in the endometrium, and by day 8 of pregnancy definitive decidual zones have become clear (Fig. 12-2) (Stewart & Peel, 1978). The decidua capsularis lies antimesometrially, forming a cap around the developing embryo, and the decidual basalis lies mesometrially. Between these layers is an intermediate area known as the lateral decidual zone. Decidualization of the endometrium does not extend to the myometrium. A thin layer of stromal cells exists between the decidua and the circular smooth muscle layer of the myometrium and constitutes the basal zone. Proliferation of cells in the basal zone contributes to repair of the endometrium in the postpartum period (O'Shea et al., 1983). By day 7 of pregnancy, proliferation of stromal cells in the mesometrial triangle (at the base of the mesometrium) has initiated formation of the metrial gland (Stewart & Peel, 1982).

Within one day of implantation the uterine epithelium around the implant breaks down, and trophoblast cells lie in contact with maternal blood. Over the next few days there is further development of the trophoblast giant cell zone around the embryo and enlargement of the ectoplacental cone at the mesometrial aspect of the embryo. Beginning at day 10 of pregnancy and continuing for a few days, there is extensive proliferation of trophoblast cells to form the definitive placenta (Jenkinson, 1902; Rossant & Croy, 1985). By day 11 of pregnancy three zones of fetal placenta can be clearly identified; the labyrinthine placenta, the junctional zone (also known as spongiotrophoblast), and the giant cell zone that lies at the periphery of the fetal compartment and is the zone adjacent to the decidua (Fig. 12-2). Development of the labyrinthine placenta, through which maternal blood flows in spaces lined by fetal trophoblast cells, provides an enormous surface area for physiological exchange. It, together with the blood-junctional zone and blood-trophoblast giant cell zone, must be considered as part of the fetomaternal interface rather than just an interface between trophoblast giant cells and decidual cells.

Development of the maternal and fetal compartments of the placenta is not limited to differentiation of decidual stromal and fetal trophoblast cells, but includes the invasion of maternal bone-marrow-derived cells into tissue spaces. In addition, other bone-marrow-derived cells circulate through the placenta in peripheral blood. Many, if not all, of these bone-marrow-derived cells could participate in im-

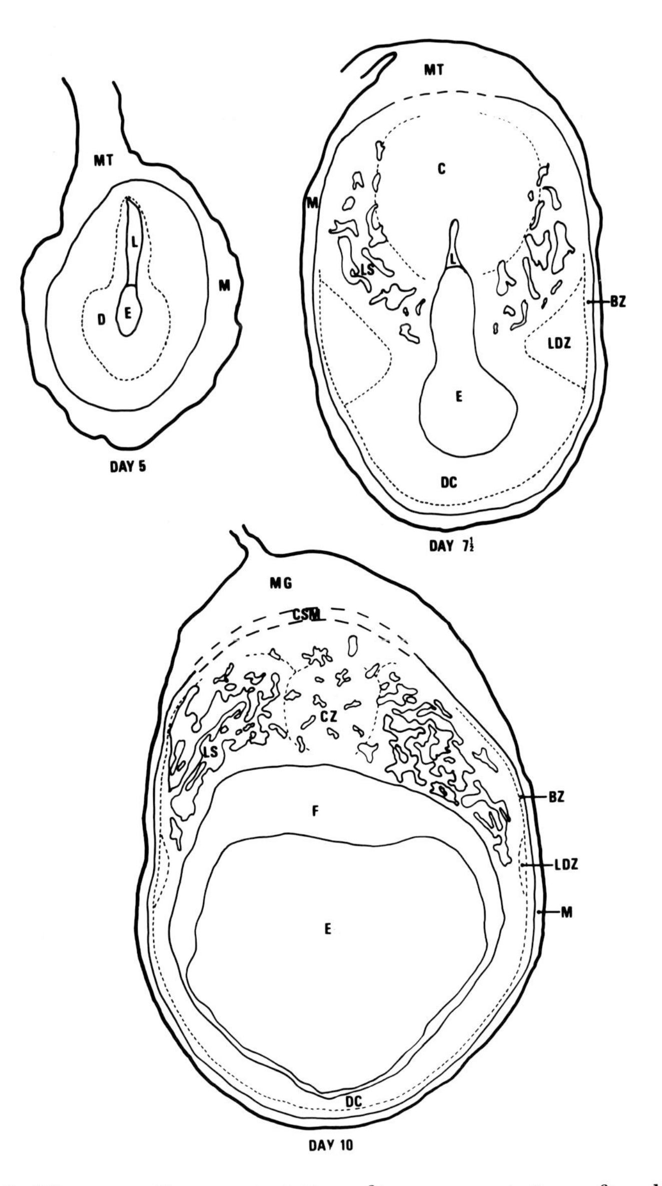

Fig. 12-2. Diagrammatic representation of transverse sections of implantation sites at day 5, day 7½ and day 10 of pregnancy. Basal zone (BZ); circular smooth muscle zone (CSM); compact zone (CZ); differentiating decidual cells (D); decidua capsularis (DC); embryo (E); fetal placenta (F); luminal epithelium (L); lateral decidual zone (LDZ); lateral sinusoids (LS); myometrium (M); metrial gland (MG); mesometrial triangle (MT). (×14). (From Stewart & Peel, 1978.)

munoregulatory mechanisms that might determine the success or failure of an individual conceptus. Most studies of bone-marrow-derived cells involved in pregnancy have been carried out using cells isolated from disaggregated uterine or placental tissues. Although *in vitro* studies have helped to identify immunoregulatory mechanisms in pregnancy, *in vivo* studies are clearly more relevant. The functional contribution of these mechanisms to the success or failure of pregnancy must be determined by whether the bone-marrow-derived cells or their products are present at or can reach appropriate sites within the uterine environment at particular stage(s) of pregnancy to act effectively.

Granulated Metrial Gland (GMG) Cells

For many years it was believed that GMG cells differentiated from fibroblast-like stromal cells in response to the hormonal changes occurring in pregnancy. However, histological studies of the developing decidua and metrial gland of mice (Smith 1966; Stewart & Peel, 1978) and rats (Peel & Bulmer, 1977) suggested that GMG cells may be derived from a precursor cell with lymphocyte-like morphology. Subsequent studies using lethally irradiated, bone-marrow-reconstituted mice provided clear evidence that GMG cells differentiate from marrow-derived precursor cells (Peel & Stewart, 1984; Peel et al., 1983) although their precise stem cell lineage has not been elucidated. At least some GMG precursor cells are present in the endometrium of the nonpregnant mouse (Peel & Stewart, 1984).

In pregnancy, small numbers of GMG cells differentiate throughout the endometrium 1 or 2 days before implantation (Stewart & Peel, 1978, 1981). After implantation, no further differentiation of GMG cells occurs in the interconceptual uterus or antimesometrial decidua. GMG cells present in these regions degenerate within 48 hours (Stewart & Peel, 1981). However, differentiation and proliferation of large numbers of GMG cells continue in the developing decidua basalis. From day 7 or 8 of pregnancy, proliferation of cells in the mesometrial triangle leads to formation of the metrial gland (Stewart & Peel, 1978). Differentiation of GMG cells from agranular precursors and GMG cell proliferation have ceased by day 12 of pregnancy (Stewart & Peel, 1980a).

Although some GMG cells degenerate *in situ* in the decidua basalis and metrial gland, many cross the endothelial lining of blood vessels in these regions and enter the circulation (Stewart & Peel, 1978). Evidence of this migration can be detected beginning at day 8 of pregnancy. Many migratory GMG cells reach the maternal blood spaces of the fetal placenta (Dickson, 1980; Jbara & Stewart, 1982; Stewart & Peel, 1978). Histological studies indicate that an interaction takes place between some GMG cells and layer 1 trophoblast cells lining the maternal blood spaces of the labyrinthine placenta, leading to degeneration of the trophoblast cells involved. Such interactions are evident from early in the development of the labyrinthine placenta, and the frequency of these interactions appears to be highest during the period of development of the labyrinth. Few interactions are apparent by day 17 of pregnancy (Stewart, 1984). *In vitro* studies using time-lapse video recording have confirmed that GMG cells are cytotoxic for some trophoblast cells (Stewart & Mukhtar, 1988).

Macrophages

Studies of macrophage function in murine pregnancy have largely been directed at two issues: immunoregulatory mechanisms in early and midpregnancy and repair of the endometrium in late pregnancy and the postpartum period. Studies of macrophages isolated from disaggregated uterine tissue have suggested that macrophages have immunosuppressive (Hunt et al., 1984) or antigen-presenting functions (Searle et al., 1983). Such roles would likely require involvement of the macrophages at the fetomaternal interface. However, few macrophages are found histologically in the decidua, although they are fairly numerous in the basal zone and in the myometrium (Stewart & Mitchell, 1987).

The contribution of infiltrating macrophages to repair of the uterine wall in late pregnancy and the postpartum period is also controversial. Few macrophages, as defined by expression of the Mac-1 antigen, are present in the decidua basalis and metrial gland during late pregnancy or the postpartum period. However, many cells in these regions appear to have endocytotic activity and probably represent part of the resident stromal cell population (Stewart & Mitchell, 1989).

Differentiation of the Metrial Gland and Granulated Metrial Gland Cells in Mutant and Chimeric Mice

We have used mice that express various mutations affecting hematopoietic and lymphoid lineages to study differentiation of the metrial gland in pregnancy. These studies were intended to assess the lineage relationships of GMG cells and to determine the stringency of the association between the metrial gland, GMG cells, and pregnancy success. Conceptuses in all pregnancies were apparently normal, and we were unable to identify a pregnancy in which the metrial gland failed to differentiate (Table 12-3, Figs. 12-1 and 12-3). Furthermore, GMG cells were always present (Figs. 12-1 and 12-4). Based on studies using *nu/nu* and thymectomized females we can conclude that thymic epithelial stroma is not required for differentiation of the metrial gland or the GMG cell compartment. Similarly, studies of *scid/*

Table 12-3. Differentiation of the metrial gland during pregnancy in immunodeficient and chimeric mice

Maternal Genotype	Defect	Metrial Gland	GMG Cell Appearance
*nu/nu**	Athymic	Present	Normal
Thymectomized +/+*	Athymic	Present	Normal
W/W^v †	Macrocytic anemia Mast cell deficient Defective in spleen-colony-producing stem cells‡	Present	Normal
C57B1/6J *bg/bg*	NK cell deficient	Present	Normal
Random-bred *bg/bg*	NK cell deficient	Present	Normal
C.B-17 *scid/scid*	Improper lymphocyte antigen receptor gene rearrangement	Present	Normal
Random-bred *scid/scid*	Improper lymphocyte antigen receptor gene rearrangement	Present	Normal
Random-bred *scid/scid.bg/bg*	Improper lymphocyte antigen receptor gene rearrangement plus low NK cell activity	Present	Normal
Rat Marrow → Irradiated§ mouse chimera	Mouse hematopoiesis blocked outside of uterus	Present	Normal rat and normal mouse

* Stewart & Peel (1980b).

† Each W/W^v female was grafted with one normal ovary under the kidney capsule, mated to a vasectomized male, and received CD1 × CD1 blastocytes 2.5 days after mating to establish pregnancy (Wordinger et al., 1986).

‡ Wu et al. (1968).

§ Anesthetized, female mice received x-irradiation with 1.5 mm lead shielding of exteriorized uterine horns, followed by 2 × 10^7 male rat bone marrow cells. Pregnancy followed natural matings (for details, see Peel & Stewart, 1984).

scid and *scid/scid.bg/bg* mothers indicate that neither mature B nor T lymphocytes are required for differentiation of the gland or GMG cells and that GMG cells are unlikely to be members of either lineage. GMG cells do not appear to be related to mast cells or neutrophils since their differentiation, morphology, and number are unremarkable during pregnancy in W/W^v and *bg/bg* animals. The presence of apparently normal GMG cells in W/W^v females suggests they are unlikely to be derived from stem cells that give rise to spleen colonies (McCulloch et al., 1964) and subsequently to the major hematopoietic

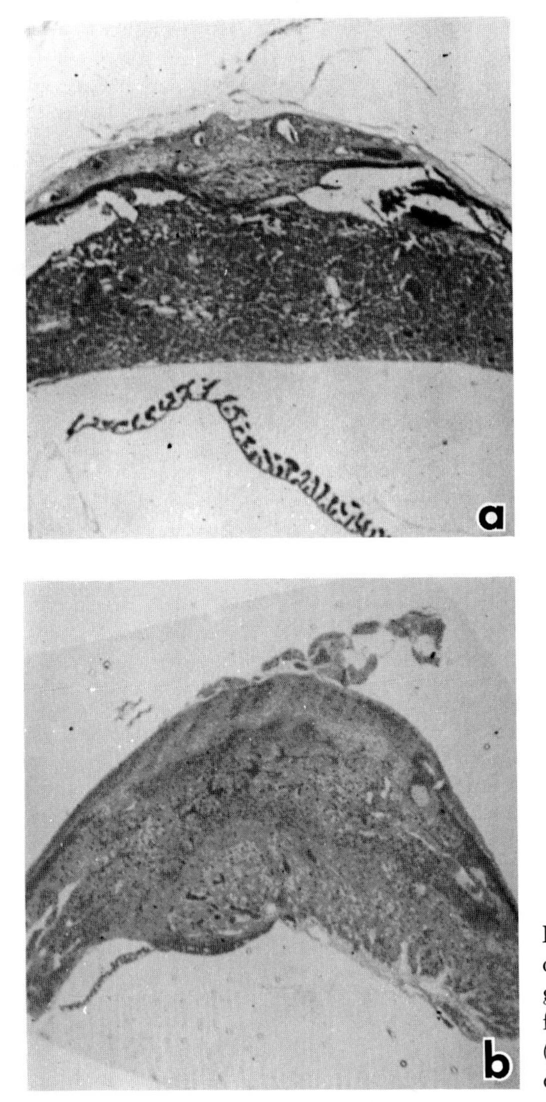

Fig. 12-3. Photomicrographs of the placenta and metrial gland from (a) +/*scid.bg*/*bg* female, day 10 of gestation; (b) C.B-17 *scid*/*scid* female, day 10 of gestation.

and lymphopoietic lineages (Wu et al., 1968). Differentiation of GMG cells in *bg*/*bg* females suggests that they are probably not classical NK cells, despite immunohistochemical evidence that they express asialo-GM1 (Mukhtar et al., 1989; Redline & Lu, 1989) and contain perforin within their granules (Parr et al., 1987). Differentiation of rat GMG cells was observed in chimeric pregnant mice, suggesting that both the metrial gland and GMG cells are essential for murine pregnancy. However, since rat GMG cells did not initiate failure of the murine conceptuses, they may not have direct immunological functions.

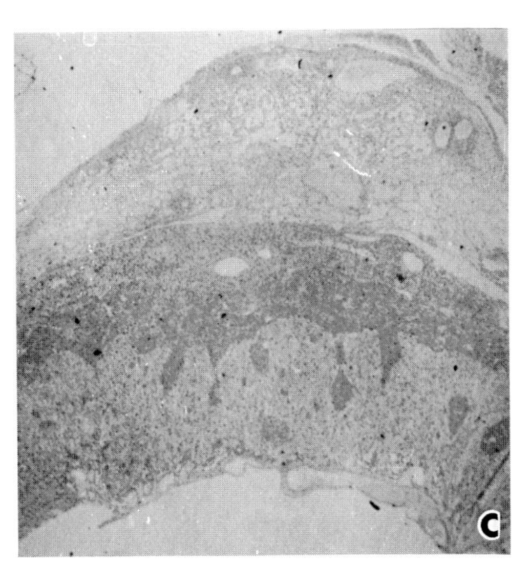

Fig. 12-3. (*Continued*) (c) W/W^v female who received an ovarian transplant under the kidney capsule and, 2.5 days following mating, blastocyst transfers to the uterus, day 14 of gestation. (H&E ×19).

Assessment of Immunological Function of the Metrial Gland

Although the metrial gland has been postulated to be immunocompetent, little functional data has been obtained to support this hypothesis. Indeed, the data presented in Table 12-3 could be interpreted as going against the hypothesis. Therefore, direct assessment of the immunological functions of the metrial gland is essential. Although the metrial gland is readily isolated, it has proven difficult to dissociate it using standard enzymatic or mechanical techniques while preserving the large GMG cells. The development of *in vitro* techniques for culturing gland explants has allowed the collection of almost pure populations of migrating GMG cells (Mukhtar & Stewart, 1988). We have studied supernatants collected from 24-h explant cultures of dissected metrial glands from randombred CD1 mice and evaluated the immunoregulatory activity of this conditioned medium. Metrial gland supernatants suppress mitogen-induced proliferation of splenocytes and block splenic NK cell lysis of target cells, but stimulate proliferation of the NK cell target line YAC (Fig. 12-5). Although no loss of cell viability was observed in these experiments (supernatants made up 5–80% of the final culture volumes), the same supernatants killed 3.5-day blastocysts and 6.5- to 7.5-day ectoplacental cone or embryonic sac outgrowths (Croy & Kassouf, 1989). It must be remembered that metrial gland differentiation has not occurred by the stages of pregnancy at which lytic activity was observed. Decidual cells and later embryonic and placental cells (day 12 of gestation) were not killed by the supernatants. Cytokine activities in metrial-gland-

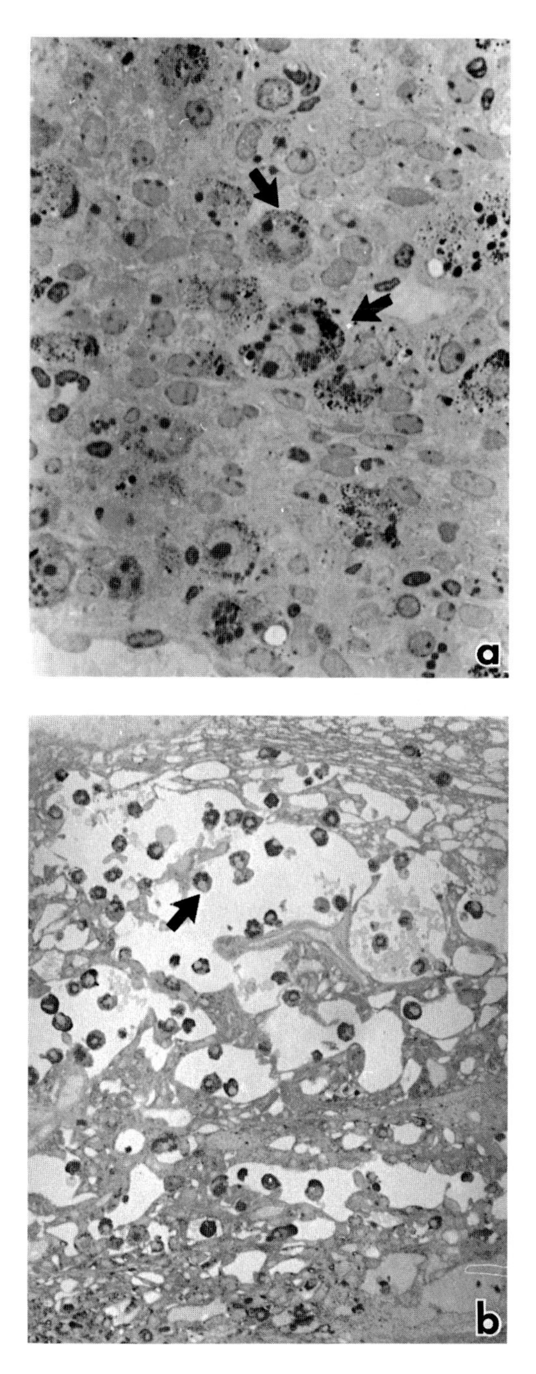

Fig. 12-4. Granulated metrial gland cells (indicated by arrows) from pregnant immunodeficient mice of (a) *nu/nu* genotype (PAS & hematoxylin ×625); (b) WW^v genotype (PAS & hematoxylin ×125).

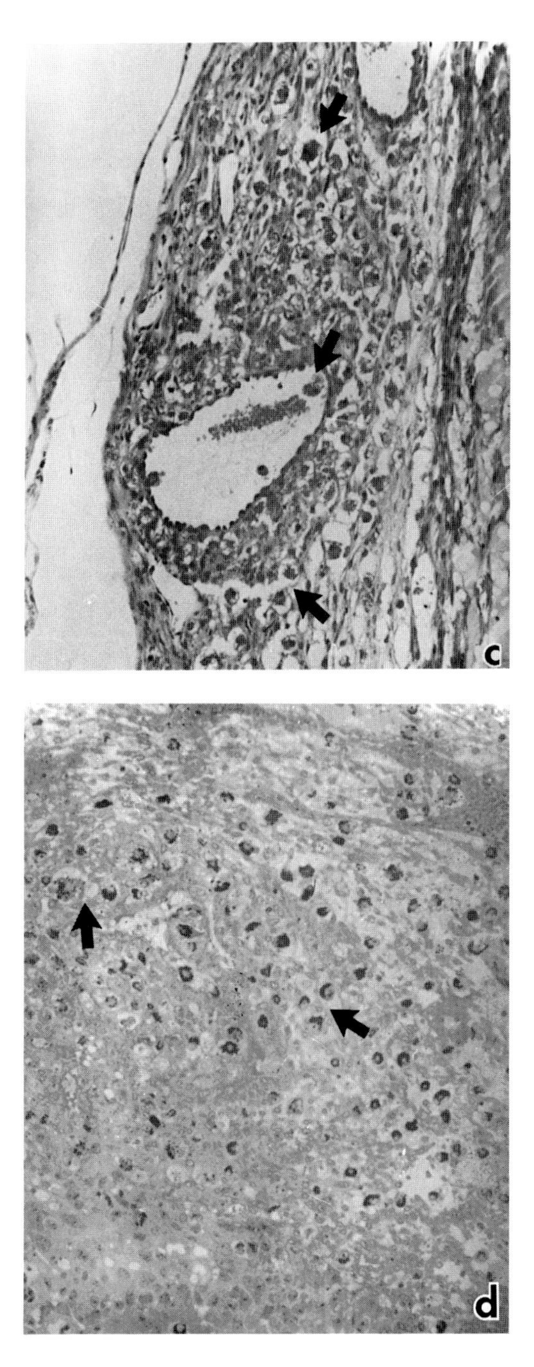

Fig. 12-4. (*Continued*) (c) *bg/bg* genotype (H&E ×125); and (d) C.B-17 *scid/scid* (PAS & hematoxylin ×125).

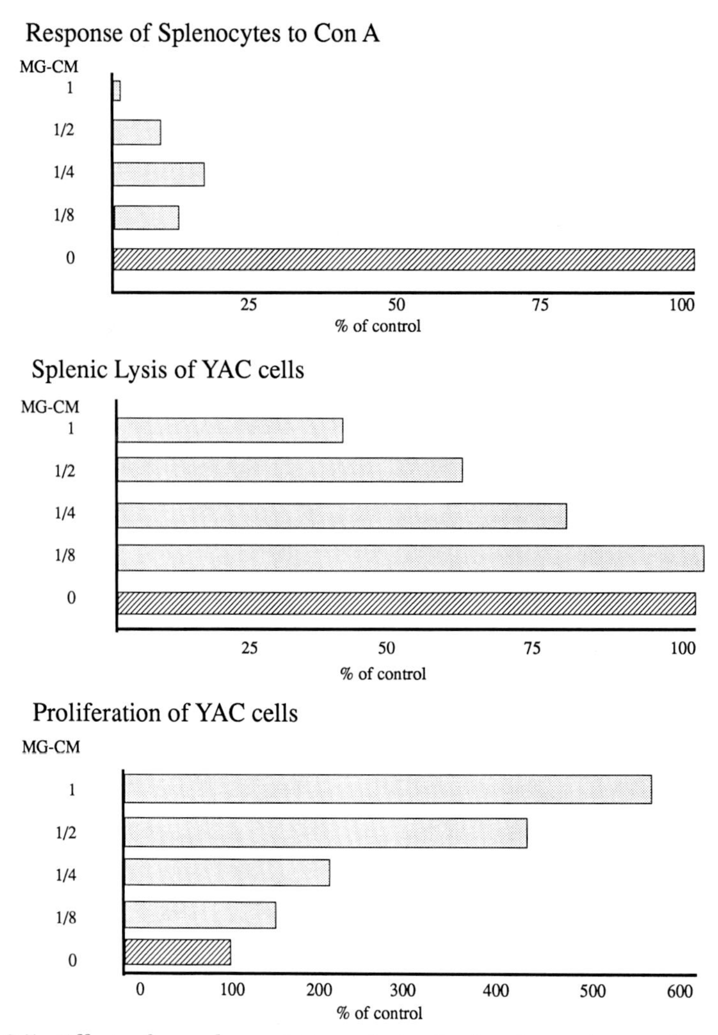

Fig. 12-5. Effect of supplementation of standard cultures by medium/preconditioned by 24 h incubation with explanted metrial glands (MG-CM). All cultures were performed in microtiter plates, containing a total volume of 200 μl/well of RPMI supplemented with 10% fetal bovine serum, antibiotics, buffers and 10^{-5}M 2-mercaptoethanol. Conditioned medium represented 75% of the final volume in each culture. Axis indicates the fraction of 12 day metrial glands from pregnant, randombred CD1 females used for conditioning medium. Abscissa represents the response, relative to control supernatant (24 hour incubated medium containing no tissue) in each assay system. Top panel shows the response of 10^5 CD1 splenocytes to Concanavalin A (3 μg/ml); ^{3}H-TdR present from the 72nd–88th h of culture, 6 replicates/group. Stimulation index in control cultures 39.4. Middle panel shows lysis of ^{51}Cr-labelled YAC target cells during 6 hour incubation at E:T of 50:1 by CD1 splenocytes, 4 replicates/group, mean % specific lysis in control cultures 26.0 ± 2.8; Bottom panel shows proliferation of 1.5 x 10^4 YAC cells, ^{3}H-TdR present from 8th-24th hours of culture, 9 replicates/group. Cell viability in test wells was not different to that in control wells at conclusion of the incubations as assessed by trypan blue exclusion.

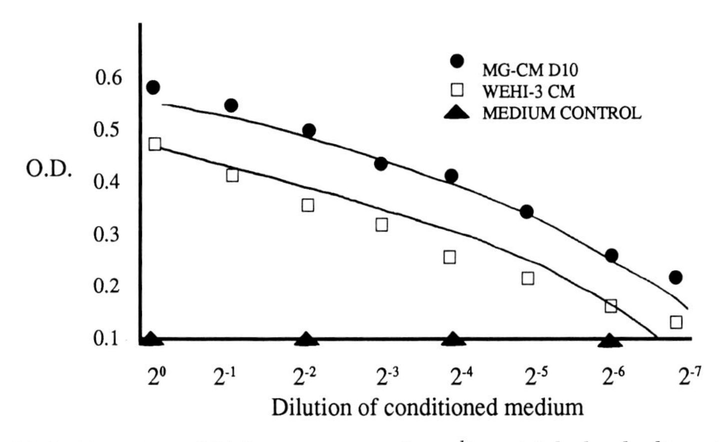

Fig. 12-6. Titration of 24 h supernatant from ¼ metrial glands dissected on day 10 of gestation from CD1 mice using 2 x 10^4 DA.1 cells in a 50 μl culture volume. Control positive lymphokine is from WEHI-3 cells. Axis represents the optical density of a colorimetric reaction using [3-(4,5-dimethythiazole-2-y^1)-2,5-diphenyltetrazolium bromide] and detected at 580 nm (see Branch and Guilbert, 1986); abscissa represents doubling dilutions of supernatants. For WEHI-3 conditioned medium, 2^0 is 5% of total culture volume; for metrial gland conditioned medium (MG-CM) 2^0 is 40% of the total culture volume. Control medium was complete tissue culture medium preincubated without cells. Metrial gland conditioned medium stimulates proliferation of DA-1 cells.

conditioned medium were characterized, based on the ability to support growth of cytokine-dependent cell lines. Supernatants were collected from 24-h cultures of metrial glands collected from randombred CD1 pregnancies on days 8–16 of gestation. All supernatants supported growth of the cell line DA-1 (Fig. 12-6). DA-1 cells are known to grow in the presence of GM-CSF, IL-3, G-CSF, and erythropoietin (Branch & Guilbert, 1986). In preliminary studies, however, incorporation of antibodies against GM-CSF and IL-3 in the assay system did not reduce the stimulatory effect of the metrial-gland-conditioned medium on DA.1 cells. Similarly, we showed that metrial gland conditioned medium did not contain tumor necrosis factors alpha and beta, gamma-interferon or interleukin-2, whereas supernatants were toxic to the CSF-1 dependent macrophage-derived cell line 5.10.14. Further investigations using a radioreceptor assay specific for CSF-1 demonstrated that large amounts of CSF-1 are released from the metrial gland during culture. These data suggest that the metrial gland is an important source of cytokines during normal gestations and is capable of influencing trophoblast function. Studies are in progress to determine which of the cytokines are released by the population of migratory GMG cells (Croy et al., 1990). In preliminary studies, supernatants from cultured metrial glands of *scid/scid.bg/bg* mice were found to have greatly reduced ability to support growth of DA-1 cells. One possible interpretation of this observation is that the immune system enhances the functional activity but not the differentiation of the metrial gland.

Conclusions

We have used immunodeficient animals to study the biological relevance of bone-marrow-derived cells in the pregnant uterus. We made crosses between mice of genotypes *scid/scid* and *bg/bg* to produce animals that lacked Ig and T cell receptor gene rearrangements and had decreased lysosomal enzyme activity. The resulting mice lack serum immunoglobulins and functional T and B cells (MacDougall et al., 1990) and have significantly reduced macrophage and NK cell activity. All males were fertile and the females were able to sustain pregnancy during early adult life (Croy & Chapeau, 1990). The rate of embryonic development in *scid/scid.bg/bg* females appeared normal, and differentiation of a mature placenta, decidua, and metrial gland occurred. These results suggest that normal functioning of B cells, T cells, and NK cells is not essential for successful pregnancy.

Our subsequent investigations of the importance of bone-marrow-derived cells during gestation therefore focused on cells unique to the pregnant uterus, particularly granulated metrial gland cells. Histological study of implantation sites from immunodeficient mice and rat-mouse chimeras revealed that the metrial gland was a constant feature of pregnancy and always contained bone-marrow-derived GMG cells. Supernatants from explant cultures of metrial glands from normal mice on days 8–16 of gestation were found to contain a complex mixture of cytokines that included CSF-1.

Supernatants from metrial glands of *scid/scid.bg/bg* mice, however, were a poor source of activity. These observations suggest that cells of the metrial gland may have important cytokine-related functions that are essential for pregnancy and that these cells may be more important for pregnancy success than lymphocytes of the T, B, or classical NK cell lineages. Definition of the lineage relationships between GMG cells and lymphocytes of T and B and of natural killer/suppressor cell lineages remains an exciting challenge.

Acknowledgments

This work was supported by awards from the Natural Sciences and Engineering Council of Canada, The Ontario Ministry of Agriculture and Food, and by travel support from The Royal Society of London. We thank Drs. S. Yamashiro and L. Guilbert for assistance with the photomicrographs and cytokine assays.

References

Athanassakis, I., Bleackley, R. C., Paetkau, V., Guilbert, L., Barr, P. J., and Wegmann, T. G. 1987. The immunoregulatory effects of T cells and T cell lymophokines on murine fetally-derived placental cells. *J. Immunol.* 138:37.

Bancroft, G. J., Bosma, M. J., Bosma, G. C., and Unanue, E. R. 1986. Regulation of macrophage Ia expression in mice with severe combined immunodeficiency: induction of Ia expression by a T cell-independent mechanism. *J. Immunol.* 137:4.

Bennett, J., Blume, R. S., and Wolff, S. M. 1969. Characterization and significance of abnormal leukocyte granules in the beige mouse: a possible homologue for Chediak-Higashi Aleutian trait. *J. Lab. Clin. Med.* 73:235.

Bosma, G. C., Custer, R. P., and Bosma, M. J. 1983. A severe combined immunodeficiency mutation in the mouse. *Nature* 301:527.

Branch, D. R. and Guilbert, L. J. 1986. Practical in vitro assay systems for the measurement of hematopoietic growth factors. *J. Tiss. Culture Meth.* 10:101.

Brandt, E. J., Swank, R. T., and Novak, E. K. 1981. The murine Chediak-Higashi mutation and other murine pigmentation mutations. In *Immunological Defects in Laboratory Animals* (M. E. Gershwin and B. Merchant, eds.) New York: Plenum Publishing, pp. 99–117.

Chaouat, G., Monnot, P., Hoffmann, M., and Voisin, G. A. 1982. Regulatory T cells in pregnancy. VI. Evidence for T-cell-mediated suppression of CTL generation toward paternal alloantigens. *Cell. Immunol.* 68:322.

Clark, D. A., Brierley, J., Slapsys, R., Daya, S., Damji, N, Chaput, A., and Rosenthal, K. 1986. Trophoblast-dependent and trophoblast-independent suppressor cells of maternal origin in murine and human decidua. In *Reproductive Immunology, 1986* (D. A. Clark and B. A. Croy, eds). Amsterdam: Elsevier Science Publishers, pp. 219–226.

Clark, D. A., Slapsys, R., Croy, B. A., Kreck, J., and Rossant, J. 1984. Local active suppression by suppressor cells in the decidua: a review. *Am. J. Reprod. Immunol.* 5:78.

Clark, E. A., Shultz, L. D., and Pollack, S. A. 1981. Mutations in mice that influence natural killer (NK) cell activity. *Immunogenetics* 12:601.

Cordier, A. C. and Heremans, J. F. 1975. Nude mouse embryo. Ectodermal nature of the primordial thymic defect. *Scand. J. Immunol.* 4:193.

Croy, B. A., Gambel, P., Rossant, J., and Wegmann, T. G. 1985. Characterization of murine decidual NK cells and their relevance to the success of pregnancy. *Cell. Immunol.* 93:315.

Croy, B. A., Waterfield, A., Wood, W., and King, G. J. 1988. Normal murine and porcine embryos recruit NK cells to the uterus. *Cell. Immunol.* 115:471.

Croy, B. A. and Chapeau, C. 1990. Evaluation of the pregnancy immunotrophism hypothesis by assessment of the reproductive performance of young adult mice of genotype *scid/scid.bg/bg*. *J. Reprod. Fertil.* 88:231.

Croy, B. A., Guilbert, L. J., Brown, M. A., Gough, N. M., Stinchcomb, D. T., Reed, N., and Wegmann, T. G. 1990. Characterization of cytokine production by the metrial gland and granulated metrial gland cells. *J. Reprod. Immunol.* 18: In press.

Croy, B. A. and Kassouf, S. 1989. Evaluation of the metrial gland for immunological function. *J. Reprod. Immunol.* 15:51.

Czitrom, A. A., Edwards, S., Phillips, R. A., Bosma, M. J., Marrack, P., and Kappler, J. W. 1985. The function of antigen-presenting cells in mice with severe combined immunodeficiency. *J. Immunol.* 134:2276.

Deschryver-Kecskemeti, K., Bancroft, G. J., Bosma, G. C., Bosma, M. J., and Unanue, E. R. 1988. Pathology of *Listeria* infection in murine severe combined immunodeficiency. *Lab. Invest.* 58:698.

Dickson, A. D. 1980. Migration of metrial gland cells in the mouse. *J. Anat.* 131:255.

Dorshkind, K., Keller, G. M., Phillips, R. A., Miller, R. G., Bosma, G. C., O'Toole, M., and Bosma, M. J. 1984. Functional status of cells from lymphoid and myeloid tissues in mice with severe combined immunodeficiency disease. *J. Immunol.* 132:1804.

Dorshkind, K., Pollack, S. B., Bosma, M. J., and Phillips, R. A. 1985. Natural killer (NK) cells are present in mice with severe combined immunodeficiency (*scid*). *J. Immunol.* 134:3798.

Gambel, P., Croy, B. A., Moore, W. D., Hunziker, R. D., Wegmann, T. G., and Rossant, J. 1985. Characterization of immune effector cells present in early murine decidua. *Cell. Immunol.* 93:303.

Gendron, R. L. and Baines, M. G. 1988. Infiltrating decidual natural killer cells are associated with spontaneous abortion in mice. *Cell. Immunol.* 113:261.

Goodman, T. and Lefrancois, L. 1988. Expression of the γ/δ T cell receptor and intestinal CD8+ intraepithelial lymphocytes. *Nature* 333:855.

Hioki, K., Maruo, K., Suzuki, S., Kato, H., Shimamura, K., Saito, M., and Nomura, T. 1987. Studies on beige-nude mice with low natural killer cell activity. *Lab. Anat.* 21:72.

Hunt, J. S., Manning, L. S., and Wood, G. 1984. Macrophages in murine uterus are immunosuppressive. *Cell Immunol.* 85:499.

Jbara, K. and Stewart, I. 1982. Granulated metrial gland cells in the uterus and labyrinthine placenta of inbred and outbred pregnancies in mice. *J. Anat.* 135:311.

Jenkinson, J. W. 1902. Observations on the histology and physiology of the placenta of the mouse. *Tijid. Nederl. Dierk. Ver.* 2:124.

Kindred, B. 1979. Nude mice in immunology. *Prog. Allergy* 26:137.

Lala, P. K., Chatterjee-Hasrouni, S., Kearns, M., Montgomery, B., and Colavincenzo, V. 1983. Immunobiology of the fetomaternal interface. *Immunol. Rev.* 75:87.

Lauzon, R. J., Siminovitch, K. A., Fulop, G. M., Phillips, R. A., and Roder, J. C. 1986. An expanded population of natural killer cells in mice with severe combined immunodeficiency (SCID) lack rearrangement and expression of T cell receptor genes. *J. Exp. Med.* 164:1797.

MacDougall, J. R., Croy, B. A., Chapeau, C., and Clark, D. A. 1990. Demonstration of a splenic cytotoxic effector cell in mice and genotype *scid/scid.bg/bg*. *Cell Immunol.* 130:106.

Malynn, B. A., Blackwell, T. K., Fulop, G. M., Rathbun, G. A., Furley, A. J. W., Ferrier, P., Heinke, L. B., Phillips, R. A., Yancopoulos, G. D., and Alt, F. W. 1988. The scid defect affects the final step of the immunoglobulin VDJ recombinase mechanisms. *Cell* 54:453.

McCulloch, E. A., Siminovitch, L. and Till, J. E. 1964. Spleen-colony formation in anaemic mice of genotype WW^v. *Science* 144:844.

Michael, S. D. 1983. Interactions of the thymus and the ovary. In *Factors Regulating Ovarian Functions* (G. S. Greenwald and P. F. Terranova, eds.) New York: Raven Press, pp. 445–464.

Michael, S. D., Taguchi, O., and Nishizuka, Y. 1988. Hormonal characterization of female SL/Ni mice: a small thymus gland strain exhibiting ovarian dysgenesis. *J. Reprod. Immunol.* 12:277.

Mukhtar, D. D. Y. and Stewart, I. J. 1988. Migration of granulated metrial gland cells from cultured explants of mouse metrial gland tissue. *Cell Tiss. Res.* 253:413.

Mukhtar, D. D. Y., Stewart, I. J., and Croy, B. A. 1989. Leucocyte membrane antigens on mouse granulated metrial gland cells. *J. Reprod. Immunol.* 15:269.

Okazaki, K., Nishikawa, S-I., and Sakano, H. 1988. Aberrant immunoglobulin gene rearrangement in *scid* mouse bone marrow cells. *J. Immunol.* 141:1348.

O'Shea, J. D., Kleinfeld, R. G., and Morrow, H. A. 1983. Ultrastructure of decidualization in the pseudopregnant rat. *Am. J. Anat.* 166:271.

Parr, E. L. and Parr, M. B. 1985. Localization of immunoglobulins in the mouse uterus, embryo and placenta during the second half of pregnancy. *J. Reprod. Immunol.* 8:153.

Parr, E. L., Parr, M. B., and Young, J. D-E. 1987. Localization of a pore-forming protein (perforin) in granulated metrial gland cells. *Biol. Reprod.* 37:1327.

Peel, S. and Bulmer, D. 1977. The fine structure of the rat metrial gland in relation to the origin of the granulated cells. *J. Anat.* 123:687.

Peel, S. and Stewart, I. 1984. The differentiation of granulated metrial gland cells in chimeric mice and the effect of uterine shielding during irradiation. *J. Anat.* 139:593.

Peel, S., Stewart, I. J., and Bulmer, D. 1983. Experimental evidence for the bone marrow origin of granulated metrial gland cells of the rodent uterus. *Cell. Tiss. Res.* 233:647.

Rebar, R. W., Miyake, A., Erickson, G. F., Low, T. L. K., and Goldstein, A. L. 1983. The influence of the thymus gland on reproductive function: a hypothalamic site of action. In *Factors Regulating Ovarian Function* (G. S. Greenwald and P. F. Terranova, eds.) New York: Raven Press, pp. 465–469.

Redline, R. and Lu, C. 1989. Localization of fetal major histocompatibility complex antigen and maternal leukocytes in murine placenta. *Lab. Invest.* 61:27.

Ritson, A. and Bulmer, J. N. 1987. Endometrial granulocytes in human decidua react with a natural killer (NK) cell marker NKH1. *Immunology* 62:329.

Roder, J. 1979. The beige mutation in the mouse. 1. A stem cell predetermined impairment in natural killer cell function. *J. Immunol.* 123:2168.

Roder, J. and Duwe, A. K. 1979. The beige mutation in the mouse selectively impairs natural killer cell function. *Nature* 278:451.

Rossant, J. and Croy, B. A. 1985. Genetic identification of tissue of origin of cellular populations within the mouse placenta. *J. Embryol. Exp. Morph.* 86:177.

Schuler, W., Weiler, I. J., Schuler, A., Phillips, R. A., Rosenberg, N., Mak, T. W., Keasney, J. F., Perry, R. P. and Bosma, M. J. 1986. Rearrangement of antigen receptor genes is defective in mice with severe combined immune deficiency. *Cell* 46:963.

Schuler, W., Schuler, A., Lennon, G. G., Bosma, G. C., and Bosma, M. J. 1988. Transcription of unrearranged antigen receptor genes in *scid* mice. *EMBO J.* 7:2019.

Shultz, L. D. and Sidman, C. L. 1987. Genetically determined murine models of immunodeficiency. *Ann. Rev. Immunol.* 5:367.

Searle, R. F., Bell, S. C., and Billington, W. D. 1983. Ia antigen-bearing decidual cells and macrophages in cultures of mouse decidual tissue. *Placenta* 4:139.

Smith, L. J. 1966. Metrial gland and other glycogen-containing cells in the mouse uterus following mating and through implantation of the embryo. *Am. J. Anat.* 119:15.

Stewart, I. 1984. A morphological study of granulated metrial gland cells and trophoblast cells in the labyrinthine placenta of the mouse. *J. Anat.* 139:627.

Stewart, I. J. and Mitchell, B. S. 1987. The distribution of macrophages at implantation sites in the mouse uterus in the first half of pregnancy. *J. Anat.* 155:231.

Stewart, I. J. and Mitchell, B. S. 1989. The distribution of macrophages at implantation sites in the uterus of mice in the second half of pregnancy and the early post partum period. *J. Anat.* 164:268.

Stewart, I. J. and Mukhtar, D. D. Y. 1988. The killing of mouse trophoblast cells by granulated metrial gland cells in vitro. *Placenta* 9:417.

Stewart, I. and Peel, S. 1978. The differentiation of the decidua and the distribution of metrial gland cells in the pregnant mouse uterus. *Cell. Tiss. Res.* 187:167.

Stewart, I. and Peel, S. 1980a. Granulated metrial gland cells at implantation sites of the pregnant mouse uterus. *Anat. Embryol.* 160:227.

Stewart, I. J. and Peel, S. 1980b. Granulated metrial gland cells in pregnant athymic mice. *J. Anat.* 131:217.

Stewart, I. and Peel, S. 1981. Granulated metrial gland cells in the virgin and early pregnant mouse uterus. *J. Anat.* 133:535.

Stewart, I. J. and Peel, S. 1982. Changes in the cell population of the pregnant rodent uterus in relation to the differentiation of granulated metrial gland cells. *J. Anat.* 135:111.

Tutt, M. M., Schuler, W., Kuziel, W. A., Tucker, P. W., Bennett, M., Bosma, M. J., and Kumar, V. 1987. T cell receptor genes do not rearrange or express functional transcripts in natural killer cells of *scid* mice. *J. Immunol.* 138:2338.

Wegmann, T. G. 1987. Placental immunotrophism: maternal T cells enhance placental growth. *Am. J. Reprod. Immunol. Microbiol.* 15:67.

Wordinger, R. J., Jackson, F. L., and Morrill, A. 1986. Implantation, deciduoma formation and live births in mast cell-deficient mice (W/W^v). *J. Reprod. Fertil.* 77:471.

Wu, A. M., Till, J. E., Siminovitch, L. and McCulloch, E. A. 1968. Cytological evidence for a relationship between normal hemotopoietic colony-forming cells and cells of the lymphoid system. *J. Exp. Med.* 127:455

Part 3

CYTOKINES

13

In Vitro Models of the Maternal-Fetal Interface

SARAH A. ROBERTSON, TINA LAVRANOS, and
ROBERT F. SEAMARK

To the reproductive biologist interested in improving the efficiency of reproduction in the human or major agricultural species, such as pigs, sheep, or cattle, the loss of early embryos looms large.

It has been estimated that over 50% of human conceptions fail during the preimplantation or early implantation stages (Roberts & Lowe, 1975). Embryonic mortality of 30% is regarded as normal for pigs (Flint et al., 1982), sheep (Kelly, 1984), and cattle (Ayalon, 1978). With the introduction of embryo transfer (ET) procedures, embryonic loss has assumed a new significance. In the human *in vitro* fertilization (IVF) program, the problem is acute as less than one in five of single embryos transferred results in a successful pregnancy (Trounson, 1984).

The complex sequence of morphological and hormonal events that determines the survival and development of the embryo in these early critical stages has only been partly elucidated. There are marked differences among species in both the systemic and local mechanisms involved (see Hodgen & Itskovitz, 1988 for recent references), but it is evident that embryonic survival in all species is critically dependent on the embryo maintaining and further developing the communication formed by the developing egg with the mother (Moor & Seamark, 1986). It is generally assumed that implantation and the subsequent pregnancy will not be successful without the local and systemic changes in the mother that constitute maternal recognition of pregnancy.

Recent developments in microanalytical procedures, particularly the polymerase chain reaction (PCR) (Oste, 1988) and other recombinant DNA microtechniques, allow detailed study of genomic expression in single embryos and the responses of individual somatic cells (see Stewart et al., 1988 for a recent review). These techniques should allow us to achieve a better understanding of the molecular and cellular biology of the embryo-maternal interface. However, owing to the complexity of the situation, *in vivo* application of these techniques would be facilitated if biologically sound *in vivo* models of the implantation process could be established.

The Preimplantation Embryo and its Relationship to the Reproductive Tract Before Implantation

In most eutherian species, the embryo enters the uterus 3 to 4 days after fertilization,where it is at the 8- to 16-cell stage. The intervening period has been spent in the fallopian tube. The functional anatomy of the fallopian tube is complex, and the presence of distinct regions within the tube implies specialization for particular and secretory functions (Beck & Botts, 1974). However, the observation that one-cell preimplantation mouse embryos could continue and complete their development *in vitro* in a simple defined medium (Whitten, 1971; Biggers, 1987), suggests that tubal factors act only in a permissive manner in early embryonic development (Johnson, 1979).

Tubal secretions vary quantitatively and qualitatively throughout the menstrual cycle and contain a wide variety of substances, some of which have been shown to be important in sperm capacitation and fertilization (see Harper, 1988 for recent review). However, evidence of specific embryotrophic factors within these secretions remains tentative. Most data reflect differences in the developmental potential of embryos in the oviductal enviroment *in vivo* and in tubal explants cultured *in vitro*, as compared to development in defined media (Bavister,1988). However, the recent finding that embryos co-cultured with tubal epithelial cells show increased viability and development (Gandolfi & Moor, 1987; Sakkas et al., 1988) provides an important first step in resolving this issue.

By contrast, there is overwhelming evidence that the uterine environment influences embryonic development. The strongest evidence has come from studies of delayed implantation, in which development of the blastocyst can be arrested for periods of days to months and resumes only in response to changes in maternal endocrine status (Weitlauf, 1988).The uterus is best regarded as a potentially hostile environment, and an embryo placed in a uterus that has had inappropriate hormonal preparation will generally fail. On the other hand, embryos can develop in simple medium *in vitro* and at sites other than the uterus *in vivo*. Some embryos appear capable of implanting almost anywhere given the chance, and this has lead to the view that the relatively hostile uterine environment may be a means of controlling implantation.

Due to the anatomical and hormonal complexities of early reproductive events, most studies on the molecular biology of the implantation have been carried out using *in vivo* animal models. Consequently, a variety of mediators have been implicated, including carbon dioxide tension, steroids, histamine, prostaglandins, phospholipids, and a range of embryo and uterus specific peptides and proteins (see Weitlauf, 1988 for a recent comprehensive review). Although *in vivo* studies provide the most physiological system to evaluate the interaction between conceptus and host, significant local factors may easily be obscured by the complex systemic events occurring in preparation for pregnancy. Thus, there is an important role for simpler *in vitro* models.

In Vitro Models of the Maternal Embryo Interface

Murine Models

There are marked differences among species in the events leading to implantation and placentation (see Weitlauf, 1988), reflecting different interactions between the conceptus and maternal tissues. Thus, *in vitro* models of these events will necessarily be species-specific. The best models of the implantation process have been established in the mouse. As early as 1965, Cole and Paul found that mouse blastocysts would develop and implant on various cell monolayers including HeLa and L cells. These embryos exhibited morphological features that differed from those embryos developing in simple medium and more closely resembled events *in vivo*. Similar observations were made by Sherman and his colleagues using a monolayer of mixed uterine cells as a substratum(Saloman & Sherman, 1975; Sherman & Wudl, 1976). Subsequent refinement of the Sherman model using uterine epithelial cells has provided a useful experimental system to gain valuable insights into the cellular biology of implantation (Kubo et al., 1981; Van Blerkom & Chavez, 1981).

Mixed Uterine Cell Monolayer: Effect of Steroids

The initial aim of our present studies was to establish an *in vitro* model to allow further study of the molecular response of the mouse embryo to the maternal environment at implantation. A mixed uterine cell monolayer, similar to that described by Sherman and Wudl (1976), was chosen for use in these studies so as to have representation of the full range of cell types present in the uterus. We found that co-culture of embryos with a mixed cell monolayer established from trypsinized uterine tissue enhanced development as determined by an increased number of embryos progressing beyond the hatching blastocyst stage over 5 days in culture, as compared to embryos cultured in medium alone (Table 13-1). Of particular interest was the finding that inclusion

Table 13-1. Effect of co-culture with uterine cells and steroids on mouse embryonic development *in vitro**

	Steroids†	Blastocyst	Implantation
Control	−	69.5 (308)	43.5 (214)
	+	72.4 (221)	60 (160)
Uterine cells	−	75.9 (613)	73.8 (465)‡
	+	88.9 (910)	97.3 (809)‡

* Results expressed as % of initial number (n) of eight-cell embyros developing to blastocysts and the number of blastocysts developing to implantation state 2 (see Lavranos & Seamark, 1989 for details).
† Progesterone (0.10 μg/mL) plus estrogen (10 μg/mL).
‡ Significant difference from control ($p < 0.001$).

of progesterone and estradiol in the cultures significantly increased the mean percentage of embryos developing to advanced stages (Lavranos & Seamark, 1989), thereby indicating a role for steroid hormones in enhancing the capacity of uterine cells to support preimplantation embryos.

Comparison of Other Cell Types

We next compared the development of eight cell embryos on uterine cells and on monolayers of other cells. The same medium was used in all studies and is designated MEM-FCS. It consisted of MEM supplemented with L-glutamine (1.48 mM), sodium bicarbonate (44 mM), and 10% heat-inactivated fetal calf serum (Lavranos & Seamark, 1989). Our results indicated that human amnion epithelial cells and L cells (ATCC, CC 1) were equally effective as a subtratum, whereas an FL amnion cell line (ATCC, CCL 62) and a monolayer of 3T3 fibroblasts (ATCC, CCL 92) were ineffective (Table 13-2). Human amnion, a tis-

Table 13-2. Effect of co-culture and conditioned medium on mouse embryonic development *in vitro**

Cell Type	Co-Culture	Conditioned Media
Control (MEM-FCS)	54 (411)	—
Uterine	84 (367)†	62 (123)
Amnion	90 (259)†	79 (80)
FL amnion	56 (25)	40 (25)
Fibroblasts		
3T3	48 (30)	12 (31)†
L Cells	90 (259)†	77 (11)†

* Results expressed as % initial number (n) of eight-cell embryos completing developing to posthatching stage.
† Significantly different from control ($p < 0.01$).

Table 13-3. Effect of co-culture and conditioned media on mouse embryonic development *in vitro* as assessed by ^{3}H-thymidine incorporation into hatched blastocysts*

Cell Type	Co-Culture	Conditioned Media
Control (MEM-FCS)	437 ± 15 (15)	—
Uterine cells	526 ± 34 (16)†	395 ± 23 (18)
Amnion	609 ± 22 (20)†	407 ± 16 (20)
FL amnion	515 ± 17 (13)	385 ± 29 (16)
L Cells	482 ± 42 (13)	369 ± 23 (18)†

* For labeling, embryos were transferred into microwells containing 1 μCi ^{3}H-thymidine in 150 μL HEPES buffered medium. Results are presented as mean counts ± SEM (n) incorporated per embryo following 3-h exposure.

† Significantly different from control value ($p < 0.05$).

sue of embryonic origin (see Perry, 1981) has previously been employed in co-culture systems to support neuronal axon development *in vitro* (Davis et al., 1987), and amniotic fluid, which contains hormones and other factors secreted by the amnion, has been used as a culture medium for human embryos *in vitro* (Kirby & Trounson, 1986).

Embryotrophic Factors in Conditioned Media

We did not obtain consistent evidence that soluble embryotrophic factors were produced by uterine cells. These data may not be representative, however, as uterine secretions potentially contain inhibitory as well as stimulatory factors (Toole et al., 1988) (Table 13-3). By contrast, media conditioned by L cells consistently enhanced embryo development. This is of considerable interest as L cells have been identified as a potent source of macrophage colony-stimulating factor (M-CSF) (Stanley et al., 1983). According to the immunotrophism hypothesis (Wegmann, 1988) this lymphokine plays a central role in the development and maintenance of the placenta. A number of molecular species of M-CSF have been described, including a membrane-bound form that may act via cell-cell contact (Rettenmier & Roussel, 1987). One species, which is synthesized by uterine tissues, has been shown to accumulate in fetal tissues and amniotic fluid (Pollard et al., 1987). M-CSF receptors have been found on human choriocarcinoma cell lines and in placenta, possibly indicating a trophic response by the conceptus (Pollard et al., 1987). It thus became of interest to determine whether the effects observed in co-culture could be ascribed to M-CSF or other lymphokines.

Lymphokines as Embryotrophic Factors

Embryo Development in Lymphokine-Conditioned Medium

A comparison of the embryotrophic effects of media conditioned by known lymphokine- or cytokine-producing cells is shown in Table 13-4. In addition to L cells, the other cell lines examined were MLA-144, a gibbon T cell lymphoma that secretes human-like interleukin 2 (hL-2) (Rabin et al., 1981); EL-4, a murine lymphoma that produces interleukin 2 (Il-2) and other CSFs when stimulated with phorbol myristic acetate (PMA); WEHI-3BD$^-$, a murine myelomonocytic cell line that constitutively produces interleukin 3 (IL-3) (Lee et al., 1982); and the murine fibroblast cell line 3T3 (ATCC, CC 1). Murine lung cell conditioned medium (LCCM), a potent souce of granulocyte macrophage colony-stimulating factor (GM-CSF), was also used (Burgess et al., 1977).

To prepare conditioned media, the MLA-144 and WEHI-3B cell lines were grown to an approximate density of $1x10^6$ cells/mL in RPMI-FCS, harvested and resuspended to $1x10^5$ cells/mL in DMEM. Approximately 72 h later the supernatant was collected and clarified by centrifugation and millipore filtration (0.22 μm). A similar procedure was used to prepare EL-4 conditioned medium, although with the addition of PMA (Sigma 10 ng/mL) throughout the period of culture. Murine lung cell conditioned media (LCCM) was prepared according to the method of Burgess et al. (1977).

EL-4 and lung cell conditioned media were dialysed extensively, twice against PBS (pH 7.2) and twice against DMEM to remove PMA and lithium chloride, respectively. All conditioned media were stored at −100°C.

In the experiment summarized in Table 13-4, eight-cell embryos

Table 13-4. Effect of lymphokine-conditioned media (CM) on mouse embryonic development *in vitro**

Lymphokine†	CM	No. of Embryos	1	2
Control (MEM-FCS)	0	87	96.6	67.8
M-CSF	L-Cell	(See Table 13-2)		
GM-CSF	LCCM	83	95.2	65.0
hIl-2	MLA-144	62	98.4	72.6
Il-3	WEHI-3B$^-$	63	100	66.7
Il-2, Il-3 GM-CSF	EL-4	56	98.2	76.8

* Results expressed as % of initial number of eight-cell embryos developing *in vitro* to blastocysts (column 1) and implanting stage (column 2).

† The presence in the conditioned medium of the lymphokines cited was confirmed by use of factor-dependent cell lines (Kelso & Owens, 1988; Rabin et al., 1981) and bone marrow assays (data not shown).

Table 13-5. Effect of lymphokine conditioned media on the rate of attachment of hatching blastocysts *in vitro**

CM	No. of Blastocysts	124 h	140 h	148 h
Control (MEM-FCS)	122	3.1 (98)	94.2 (122)	100 (122)
MLA-144	31	12.5 (24)	90.0 (27)	96.7 (31)
WEHI-3B	29	23 (26)‡	71.8 (28)	100 (29)
EL-4	43	16.7 (30)†	89.7 (39)	90.7 (43)
LCCM	54	33.3 (45)§	96.3 (52)	100 (54)
L cell	37	7.4 (27)	89.2 (33)	100 (37)

* Results expressed as % of hatched blastocysts (n) attaching at specified time post-hCG injection. Embryos were transferred to culture at 72 h post-hCG.
Significant difference from control:
† $p < 0.01$.
‡ $p < 0.001$.
§ $p < 0.001$

(Balb/c x C57 or CBA x C57) were randomly assigned to control or experimental groups. Each group consisted of eight replicates using embryos from four to six mice in each replicate. Ten to twenty embryos were added per well within 15-20 min after recovery from the uterus, and cultures were maintained *in vitro* for a period of 5 days. Wells contained MEM-FCS culture medium alone (1 mL/well) or conditioned media as described above. Observations on embryo development were made once or twice daily, using an inverted microscope. The numbers of embryos achieving morula, blastocyst, or hatching blastocyst stages were recorded (Hsu, 1979).

Interestingly, only L cells conditioned medium showed a clear embryotrophic effect as assessed by the percentage of eight-cell embryos that developed to the blastocyst or implanting stages. However, LCCM had a clear effect on embryo adherence to the plastic culture dishes. In addition, LCCM and to a lesser extent EL-4 conditioned media altered the pattern of trophoblast outgrowth, maintaining a more organized morphology. These observations were confirmed and extended using blastocysts; observations were made on posthatching stages (Table 13-5). These data confirmed that attachment was enhanced in LCCM and in the other conditioned media that contained GM-CSF.

GM-CSF: The Active Embryotrophic Principle in Conditioned Media

To confirm that GM-CSF was the active factor that enhanced attachment, we repeated these experiments using recombinant *E.coli*-derived GM-CSF and yeast-derived M-CSF (Table 13-6). The results clearly indicate that GM-CSF, but not M-CSF, increases the rate of

Table 13-6. Effect of the lymphokines, M-CSF and GM-CSF, on the rate of attachment of hatching blastocysts *in vitro**

Lymphokine U/mL	No. of Blastocysts	124 h	140 h	148 h
Control (MEM-FCS)	162	3.2 (158)	82.9 (162)	100 (162)
M-CSF				
40	87	5.6 (73)	94.3 (87)	100 (87)
200	82	4.7 (64)	89.0 (82)	100 (82)
1000	102	6.9 (72)	94.0 (102)	100 (102)
GM-CSF				
40	69	10.9 (55)†	94.9 (69)	96.3 (69)
200	62	15.9 (44)‡	88.7 (62)	100 (62)
1000	71	10.9 (46)†	93.0 (71)	96.6 (71)

* Results expressed as % of hatched blastocysts (n) attaching at specified time post-hCG injection. Embryos were transferred to culture at 72 h post-hCG.

Significant difference from control:

† $p < 0.01$.

‡ $p < 0.001$.

attachment of hatching embryos and is active at concentrations as low as 40 U/ml.

To measure more accurately the effects of lymphokines on trophoblast outgrowth, implanting embryos were cultured with 1000 U/mL of GM-CSF and/or M-CSF for 48 h (from 120 h post-hCG), and then incubated with 1.0 μCi/mL ^{3}H-thymidine for 6 h. Incorporation of radiolabeling into DNA was assessed by liquid scintillation spectrometry.

In two of three experiments more label was incorporated into embryos cultured in the presence of GM-CSF than control embryos (Table 13-7). The mean incorporation of ^{3}H-thymidine was also in-

Table 13-7. Effect of the lymphokines, M-CSF and GM-CSF, on mouse embryonic development *in vitro* as assessed by ^{3}H-thymidine incorporation into implanted blastocysts*

	Control	M-CSF	GM-CSF	M-CSF + GM-CSF
Experiment				
1	9.7 + 0.56(31)	10.1 + 0.97(27)	10.6 + 0.84(27)†	9.1 + 0.89(27)
2	7.2 + 0.40(51)	9.1 + 0.67(48)‡	8.5 + 0.53(51)‡	7.9 + 0.63(54)
3	4.7 + 0.47(52)	5.2 + 0.53(51)	4.1 + 0.45(26)	4.6 + 0.42(47)

* Embryos (harvested 72 hrs post-hCG) were grown in DMEM in microtiter tray wells to which 1000 U/mL of factor was added at 120 h post-HCG for 48 h. Embryos were pulsed with 1 μCi ^{3}H-thymidine for 6 h and harvested. Results are presented as mean dpm ±SEM (n) ($\times 10^{-3}$).

† Significantly different from control value ($p < 0.05$).

‡ Significantly different from control value ($p < 0.001$).

creased in cultures containing M-CSF although this increase was statistically significant in only one of three experiments ($p < 0.05$).

Effect of GM-CSF and M-CSF on Preblastocyst Stages of Embryo Development. Previous studies of the effects of lymphokines on embryo development have shown that both GM-CSF and M-CSF can arrest embryonic development at preblastocyst stages (Hill et al., 1987). These results are directly at odds with our work. To clarify this point, we cultured one-cell (C57BL x CBA) embryos in HTF medium (Quinn et al., 1985) in the presence of various amounts of recombinant M-CSF and GM-CSF (Table 13-8). There was no evidence of an inhibitory effect of M-CSF or GM-CSF on one- to eight-cell embryos over the range of concentrations tested (40-5000 u/mL) other than at 200 U/mL. This result therefore confirms our previous observations that lymphokine conditioned media have no significant inhibitory effects on embryo development *in vitro.*

Presence of GM-CSF in Uterine Secretions. M-CSF has been identified in the pregnant uterus of the mouse, with a total uterine content of about 500 U on day 5 of pregnancy. This increases approximately 200-fold by term (Pollard et al., 1987). If M-CSF concentrated in the uterine lumen (total volume about 9 microliters at day 5; R. Wales, personal communication) the concentration at the maternal-embryo interface could exceed 5×10^4 U/mL.

To determine if GM-CSF is present in uterine luminal fluid during

Table 13-8. Effect of recombinant-derived GM-CSF and M-CSF on mouse embryonic development *in vitro**

	I		II	
	No. of Embryos	**%**	**No. of Embryos**	**%**
M-CSF				
40 U	66	63.6	42	100.0
200 U	88	43.2†	138	97.4
1000 U	107	63.6	68	100.0
5000 U	101	72.3	73	100.0
GM-CSF				
40 U	47	61.7	29	100.0
200 U	65	40.0†	26	100.0
1000 U	77	73.3	58	100.0
5000 U	86	62.8	54	100.0
Control	117	74.4	87	100.0

* Results expressed as % of embryos completing development from one-cell to eight-cell (column I) and from eight-cell to blastocysts (column II) *in vitro.*

† $p < 0.01$.

day 1 to 5 of pregnancy, female mice were sacrificed and uterine washings obtained by carefully flushing each horn of the uterus with 0.5 mL of serum-free MEM.

GM-CSF activity was assayed using the factor-dependent cell line FD5/12 (Kelso & Owens, 1988). Detectable GM-CSF was present in uterine flushings from two mice on the day following detection of a vaginal plug (day 1) (mean values 7.9 ± 1.0 and 5.6 ± 0.4 U) in one of four mice examined on day 5 of pregnancy (mean value 5.6 ± 0.3 U). The flushings of the other mice examined (day 2, n=1; day 3, n=4; day 4, n=4) contained less than 0.5 U. GM-CSF was undetectable in uterine fluid from three nonpregnant mice (<0.5 U/mL), but was present in three mice after mating to a vasectomized male (day 1 of pseudo-pregnancy) at mean levels of 85.2 ± 2.0, 108.6 ± 3.8, and 94.6 ± 3.3 U/mL respectively.

Uterine levels of M-CSF are known to be under endocrine control, but it remains to be determined whether the uterine GM-CSF activity detected on day 1 in pregnant and pseudo-pregnant mice is of uterine or seminal origin.

Occurrence of GM-CSF in Co-Cultures and Conditioned Media. GM-CSF activity in cultures containing uterine monolayers, prepared as described by Lavranos and Seamark (1989) ranges from 4.7 to >200 U/mL (median value, 59.2 U/mL). Addition of steroids to the cultures did not affect these levels. However, GM-CSF levels in uterine monolayers prepared from mice at days 3, 4, or 5 of pregnancy were significantly elevated over those in cultures from nonpregnant mice. The GM-CSF content of cultures from nonpregnant mice ranged from less than 1 U/mL to 11.6 U/mL. Nonpregnant uterine monolayers did not produce GM-CSF when cultured with steroids. GM-CSF was not detected in conditioned media from amnion epithelial cells and L cells. However, GM-CSF was present in lung cell conditioned medium at a mean level of 2128 U/mL and in EL-4 conditioned medium (mean value 30 U/mL). Trace amounts were also present in WEHI-3B conditioned medium (1.5 U/mL), but none was detected in MLA-144 medium.

T Cells: Source of GM-CSF in Uterine Monolayer Culture? Thy 1.2 positive cells with a T cell morphology were identified in uterine monolayers by indirect immunofluorescence using a monoclonal rat anti-Thy 1.2 antibody (Seralab, UK) and FITC-conjugated sheep anti-rat antibody (Silenus, Australia). Depletion of Thy 1.2^{+} cells from uterine monolayers using the same antibody and rabbit complement resulted in a 2.5-fold reduction in GM-CSF production.

Table 13-9. Effect of including h-LIF (10^3 units/mL) in culture medium on mouse embryonic development *in vitro**

Control	LIF
64 (349)	80 (195)†

* Results expressed as % of initial number of eight-cell embryos (n) completing development to implantation.
† Significant difference from control ($p <$ 0.01).

Myeloid Leukemia Inhibitory Factor (LIF) Is Also Embryotrophic

In addition to M-CSF, L cells secrete differentiation factor (D-factor) a cytokine with physical and biological similarities to myeloid leukemia inhibitory factor (LIF) is a recently discovered hemopoietic regulatory factor that induces differentiation in the M1 myeloid leukemia cell line (Hilton et al., 1988; Gough et al., 1988). We wondered if LIF might have embryotrophic activity due to its similarity to a differentiation restricting factor (DRF) produced by primary embryonic fibroblast cell is or Buffalo rat liver (BRL) cells that are used to maintain embryonic stem cell lines *in vitro* (Moreau et al., 1988). In the absence of DRF, embryonic stem cells (ES) that are isolated as totipotent outgrowths of the inner cell mass differentiate and lose totipotency (Smith et al., 1988). Although it remains to be confirmed that LIF and DRF are identical, specific LIF receptors have been found on both ES and embryonic carcinoma (EC) cell lines. Purified recombinant LIF has also been shown to substitute for DRF in maintaining the totipotency of ES cell lines (Williams et al., 1988).

Addition of human LIF (hLIF), generously provided by Dr. N. Gough at 1000 U/mL, to culture medium (MEM-FCS) significantly increased the number of eight-cell embryos completing development to the posthatching stages (Table 13-9). hLIF had no discernible effect on preblastocyst development (data not shown), and only the posthatching stages appeared to be affected. This affect of hLIF was particularly evident on trophoblast outgrowth, which was measurably greater after 5 days in culture (Table 13-10). Although the morphology of the ICM appeared to be better defined in LIF-treated embryos, no differences in growth were detected.

Concluding Remarks

Our data indicate that many of the embryotrophic effects observed in co-culture studies may be due to lymphokine action on trophectoderm. GM-CSF has been identified in co-culture supernatants and

Table 13-10. Effect of h-LIF on development of mouse embryos in culture*

	Control	+LIF
ICM	9.7 ± 0.26 (24)	10.3 ± 0.23 (12)
Trophoblast	19.12 ± 0.67 (24)	23.1 ± 0.89 (12)†

* Comparison of area of inner cell mass (ICM) and trophoblast of embryos after 5 days in culture (posthatching stage) in the presence or absence of LIF (1000 U/mL). Results expressed as mean area (arbitrary units) ±SEM (n).

† Significant difference from control ($p < 0.001$).

shown to promote implantation of hatched embryos, whereas LIF-like activity in L cell conditioned medium may enhance embryonic survival and development.

Fetal fibroblasts are increasingly used as a substrate for livestock embryos in culture (Gandolfi & Moore, 1987; Weimer et al., 1988; White et al., 1988). In light of our present data, LIF seems likely to be the active embryotrophic factor produced by these cells.

We have shown the presence of Thy 1.2^+ cells in our mixed uterine cell cultures. Our results indicate a relationship between the presence of these cells and levels of GM-CSF. We have also found that GM-CSF is produced by the uterus around the day of implantation and is present in uterine flushings from female mice shortly after mating to vasectomized or intact males. This last result is of particular interest, as mouse semen has been shown to have immunoregulatory effects (Anderson & Tarter, 1982). In addition, several groups have claimed that sensitization of the uterus by seminal factors can reduce early embryonic loss (Stone et al., 1987). The importance and mode of action of GM-CSF, M-CSF, LIF and other lymphokines on the development of pre-embryos clearly warrant further evaluation.

This study therefore supports and extends the immunotrophism hypothesis proposed by Wegmann (1988). According to this hypothesis maternal T cells recognize the alloantigens of the conceptus and are stimulated to produce lymphokines that act on other lymphoid cells and on the trophoblast to promote growth and placentation. *In vivo*, the uterus is heavily infiltrated with lymphocytes prior to implantation. Lymphocyte accumulation may be under hormonal control, and there is preferential retention of T cells within the decidua (Clark et al., 1987; Faulk & McIntyre, 1983). Further infiltration of lymphocytes might be expected at the time of implantation, secondary to changes in vascular permeability at the implantation site (Milligan & Mirembe, 1984).

If validated, the immunotrophism hypothesis has substantiated implications for reproductive medicine. Ectopic pregnancies remain a major health hazard, with an incidence ranging from 1 in 40 to 1 in

300 depending on the location and type of population surveyed. The immunotrophism hypothesis provides immediate insight into possible mechanisms for ectopic pregnancy. There is a significant association of ectopic pregnancy with tubal damage due to infection and endometriosis, which is associated with tubal reflux of uterine fluid.

In IVF programs in which embryo loss remains a major concern, addition of GM-CSF or other lymphokines to culture and transfer media may enhance implantation rates. Alternatively, presensitization of the uterus with semen or other appropriate antigens may prove helpful.

Lymphokines should also be evaluated as adjuvants for culture and transfer media used in livestock embryo transfer programs. Further emphasis should clearly be given to the immunotrophism hypothesis as a basis for designing experimental protocols to investigate ways of overcoming embryo loss.

Acknowledgments

We are grateful to the following people for cell lines: Dr. L. K. Ashman (MLA-144, CTLL, and L cells) and Dr. I. Kotarski (EL4 cells) of the Department of Immunology, University of Adelaide; Professor M. Vadas (WEHI 3 BD and 3T3 fibroblast cells), Institute of Medical and Veterinary Science, Adelaide; and Professor D. Metcalf (FD 5/12), Walter and Eliza Hall Institute, Melbourne. Professor Metcalf also supplied the recombinant yeast-derived murine M-CSF and *E. coli*-derived GM-CSF. LIF was a generous gift from AMRAD Corp. Ltd., Melbourne.

We are grateful to the Swine Compensation Fund of South Australia for financial support for aspects of this study.

References

Anderson, D. J. and Tarter, T. H. 1982. Immunosuppressive effects of mouse seminal components *in vivo* and *in vitro*. *J. Immunol.* 128:535.

Ayalon, N. 1978. A review of embryonic mortality in cattle. *J. Reprod. Fertil.* 54:483–493.

Bavister, B. D. 1988. Role of oviductal secretions in embryonic growth *in vivo* and *in vitro*. *Theriogenology* 29:143.

Beck, L. R. and Boots, L. R. 1974. The comparative anatomy, histology and morphology of the mammalian oviduct. In *The Oviduct and its Functions*. New York: Academic Press, pp. 1–52.

Biggers, J. D. 1987. Pioneering mammalian embryo culture. In *The Mammalian Preimplantation Embryo: Regulation of Growth and Differentiation in vitro*. (A. D. Johnson and C. W. Foley, eds.) New York: Plenum Press, pp. 1–22.

Burgess, A. W., Camakaris, J., and Metcalf, D. 1977. Purification and properties of colony-stimulating factor from mouse lung conditioned medium. *J. Biol. Chem.* 252:1988.

Clark, D. A., Croy, B. A., Wegmann, T. G., and Chaout, G. 1987. Immunological and para-immunological mechanisms in spontaneous abortion: recent insight and future directions. *J. Reprod. Immunol.* 12:1.

Cole, R. J. and Paul, J. 1965. Properties of cultured preimplantation mouse and rabbit embryos and cell strains derived from them. In *Preimplantation Stages of Pregnancy.* Boston: Little Brown and Co., pp. 82–112.

Davis, G. E., Blaker, S. N., Engvall, E., Varon, S., Manthorpe, M., and Gage, F. H. 1987. Human amnion membrane serves as a substratum for growing axons *in vitro* and *in vivo. Science* 236:1106.

Faulk, W. D. and McIntyre, J. A. 1983. Immunological studies of human trophoblast: markers, subsets and functions. *Immunol. Rev.* 75:139.

Flint, A. P. F., Sanders, P. T. K., and Ziecik A. J. 1982. Blastocyst-endometrium interactions and their significance in embryonic mortality. In *Control of Pig Reproduction.* (D. J. A. Cole and G. R. Foxcroft, eds.) London: Butterworth Scientific, pp. 253–275.

Gandolfi, F. and Moor, R. M. 1987. Stimulation of early embryonic development in the sheep by co-culture with oviduct epithelial cells. *J. Reprod. Fertil.* 81:23.

Gough, N. H., Gearing, D. P., King, J. A., Willson T. A., Hilton, D. J., Nicola, N. A., and Metcalf, D. 1988. Molecular cloning and expression of the human homologue of the murine gene encoding myeloid leukemia-inhibitory factor. *Proc. Natl. Acad. Sci. USA* 85:2623.

Harper, M. J. K. 1988. Gametes and zygote transport. In *The Physiology of Reproduction.* New York: Raven Press, pp. 103–134.

Hill, J. A., Haimovici, F., and Anderson, D. J. 1987. Products of activated lymphocytes and macrophages inhibit embryo development *in vitro. J. Immunol.* 139:2250.

Hilton, D. J., Nicola, N. A., Gough, N. M., and Metcalf, D. 1988. Resolution and purification of three distinct factors produced by Krebs ascites cells which have differentiation inducing activity on murine myeloid leukemia cell lines. *J. Biol. Chem.* 263:9238.

Hodgen, G. D. and Itskovitz, J. 1988. Recognition and maintenance of pregnancy. In *Physiology of Reproduction.* (E. Knobil and J. Neill, eds.) New York: Raven Press, pp. 1995–2022.

Hsu, Y-C. 1979. *In vitro* development of individually cultured whole mouse embryos from blastocyst to early somite stage. *Dev. Biol.* 68:453.

Johnson, M. H. 1979. Intrinsic and extrinsic factors in preimplantation development. *J. Reprod. Fertil.* 55:267.

Kelly, R. W. 1984. Fertilization failure and embryonic wastage. In *Reproduction in Sheep.* Canberra: Australian Academy Science, pp. 127–133.

Kelso, A. and Owens, T. 1988. Production of two hemopoetic growth factors is differentially regulated in single T lymphocytes activated with an anti-T cell receptor antibody. *J. Immunol.* 140:1159.

Kirby, C. and Trounson, A. O. 1986. The viability of mouse embryos cultured in human amniotic fluid. Proceedings of the Eighteenth Annual Conference of the Australian Society for Reproductive Biology, Abst 31.

Kubo, H., Spindle, A., and Pedersen, R. A. 1981. Inhibition of mouse blastocyst attachment and outgrowth by protease inhibitors. *J. Exp. Zool.* 216:445.

Lavranos, T. and Seamark, R. F. 1989. Addition of steroids to embryo-uterine monolayer co-culture enhances embryo survival and implantation *in vitro. Reprod. Fertil. Dev.* 1:41–46.

Lee, J. C., Hapel, A. J., and Ihle, J. N. 1982. Constitutive production of a unique lymphokine (IL3) by the WEHI-3 cell line. *J. Immunol.* 128:2393.

Milligan, S. R. and Mirembe, F. M. 1986. The course of the change in uterine vascular permeability associated with the development of decidual cell reaction in ovarectomised steroid treated rats. *J. Reprod. Fertil.* 70:1.

Moor, R. M. and Seamark, R. F. 1986. Cell signalling, permeability and microvascularity changes during antral follicle development in mammals. *J. Dairy Sci.* 69:927.

Moreau, J. F., Donaldson, D. D., Bennett, F., Witek-Giannotti, J., Clark, S. C., and Wong, G. G. 1988. Leukemia inhibitory factor is identical to the myeloid growth factor human interleukin for DA cells. *Nature* 336:690.

Oste, C. 1988. Polymerase chain reaction. *Biotechniques* 6:162.

Perry, J. S. 1981. The mammalian fetal membranes. *J. Reprod. Fertil.* 62:321.

Pollard, J. W., Bartocci, A., Arceci, R., Orlofsky, A., Ladner, M. B., and Stanley, E. R. 1987. Apparent role of the macrophage growth factor, CSF-1 in placental development. *Nature* 330:484.

Quinn, P., Kerin, J. F., and Warnes, G. M. 1985. Improved pregnancy rates in human in vitro fertilization with the use of a medium based on the composition of human tubal fluid. *Fertil. Steril.* 44:493.

Rabin, J., Hopkins, R. F., Ruscetti, F. W., Neubauer, R. H., Brown, R. L., and Kawakami, T. G. 1981. Spontaneous release of a factor with properties of T-cell growth factor from a continuous line of primate tumor T-cells. *J. Immunol.* 127:1852.

Rettenmier, C. W. and Roussel, M. F. 1987. Synthesis of membrane-bound colony stimulating factor 1 (CSF-1) and down modulation of CSF-1 receptors in NIH 3T3 cells transformed by co-transfection of the human CSF-1 and c-fms (CSF-1 receptor) genes. *Mol. Cell. Biol.* 7:2378.

Roberts, C. J. and Lowe, C. R. 1975. Where have all the conceptions gone? *Lancet* 1:498.

Sakkas, D., Batt, P., Cameron, A., and Trounson, A. O. 1988. *In vitro* development of goat preimplantation embryos in co-culture with oviduct epithelial cells. Proceedings Twentieth Annual Conference of the Australian Society for Reproductive Biology, Abst. 48.

Salomon, D. S. and Sherman, M. I. 1975. Implantation and invasiveness of mouse blastocysts on uterine monolayers. *Exp. Cell. Res.* 90:261.

Sherman, M. I. and Wudl, L. R. 1976. The implanting mouse blastocyst. In *The Cell Surface in Animal Embryogenesis and Development.* (G. Poste and G. L. Nicolson, eds.) Amsterdam: Elsevier, pp. 81–125.

Smith, A. B., Heath, J. K., Donaldson, D. D., Wong, G. G., Moreaux, J., Stahl, M., and Rogers, D. 1988. Inhibition of pluripotential embryonic stem cell differentiation by purified polypeptides. *Nature* 336:688.

Stanley, E. R., Guilbert, L. J., Tushinski, R. J., and Bartelmes, S. H. 1983. CSF-1 A mononuclear phagocyte lineage specific hemopoietic growth factor. *J. Cell. Biochem.* 21:151.

Stewart, H. J., Jones, D. S. C., Pascall, J. C., Popkin, R. M., and Flint, A. D. F. 1988. The contribution of recombinant DNA techniques to reproductive biology. *J. Reprod. Fertil.* 83:1.

Stone, B. A., Godfrey, B. M., Seamark, R. F., and Heap, P. A. 1987. Increasing reproductive efficiency in sows by pre-insemination with killed semen. Proceedings of the 43rd Annual Meeting of the American Fertility Society, Abst. 213.

Toole, R. J., Gwazdauskas, F. C., Whittier, W. D., and Vinson, W. E. 1988. Influence of uterine flushings from superovulated cows on *in vitro* bovine morulae development. *Theriogenology* 30:811.

Trounson, A. O. 1984. In vitro fertilization and embryo preservation. In *In Vitro Fertilization and Embryo Transfer.* (A. Trounson and C. Wood, eds.) Edinburgh: Churchill, Livingstone, pp. 111–130.

Van Blerkom, J. and Chavez, D. J. 1981. Morpho-dynamics of outgrowths of mouse trophoblast in the presence and absence of a monolayer of uterine epithelium. *Am. J. Anat.* 162:143.

Wegmann, T. G. 1988. Maternal T cells promote placental growth and prevent spontaneous abortion. *Immunol. Lett.* 17:297.

Weimer, K. E., Casey, P. L., De Vore, D. C., and Godke, R. A. 1988. The culture of equine embryos using new monolayer cultures derived from fetal uterine fibroblast cells. *Theriogenology* 29:327.

Weitlauf, H. M. 1988. Biology of implantation. In *The Physiology of Reproduction.* (E. Knobil and J. Neill, eds.) New York: Raven Press, pp. 231–262.

White, K. I., Rickords, L. F., Southern, L. L., Hehnke, K., Thomson, D. L., and Wood, T. C. 1988. Early embryonic development *in vitro* by coculture with oviductal epithelial cells. Proceedings 44th Annual Meeting of the American Fertility Society, Abst. 421.

Whitten, W. K. 1971. Culture of tubal ova. *Nature* 179:1081.

Williams, R. L., Hilton, D. J., Pease, S., Willson, T. A. Stewart, C. L., Gearing, D. P., Wagner, E. F., Metcalf, D., Nicola, N. A., and Gough, N. M. 1989. Myeloid leukemia inhibitory factor (LIF) maintains developmental potential of embryonic stem cells. *Nature* 336:684.

14

Adverse Effects of Immune Cell Products in Pregnancy

DEBORAH J. ANDERSON, JOSEPH A. HILL, FLORINA HAIMOVICI, and ROSS S. BERKOWITZ

The uterine endometrium is an immunologically dynamic tissue. Large numbers of lymphocytes and macrophages, which mediate cell-mediated immune responses, are present in the human endometrium during the secretory phase of the menstrual cycle and throughout pregnancy (Bulmer & Sunderland, 1984; Kamat & Isaacson, 1987). Mononuclear cells are also present in elevated numbers in cases of endometriosis and uterine infection (Blaustein, 1985; Wheeler, 1982) and in endometrial biopsies of some infertile women (Lint, 1980; Monif, 1982; Xu et al., 1987).

The *immunotrophism* theory holds that products of activated lymphocytes and macrophages serve as growth factors for placental cells and thus may help to initiate and sustain pregnancy (Wegmann, 1984). In this chapter we suggest that activated lymphocytes and macrophages can also release cytokines that adversely affect gestation: we term this concept *immunodystrophism in pregnancy*. We present evidence from our laboratory indicating that certain products of immune cells have toxic or deregulating effects on fetal tissues if present during specific intervals of development. Certain cytokines, such as tumor necrosis factor-α, interleukin-1, and gamma-interferon, which are directly toxic to rapidly proliferating malignant cells *in vitro*, may have similar effects on rapidly proliferating fetal cells. Other cytokines produced by mononuclear cells, including growth factors and differentiation-inducing factors, could disrupt gestation by providing inappropriate growth or differentiation signals. In addition, the maternal immune response to foreign gestational antigens could lead to local immune activation with production of high levels of certain cytokines that have adverse effects in at least some pregnancies. Finally, cytokines produced by immune cells responding to unrelated foreign antigens, such as those expressed on sperm, viruses, or microbes, could result in nonspecific or "innocent bystander" damage to the embryo, fetal membranes, or placenta.

Evidence That Immunological Cytokines Have Adverse Effects in Early Gestation

A number of cytokines produced by activated lymphocytes and macrophages have been identified and characterized (Table 14-1). Recombinant DNA technology has been used to produce many of these mediators in sufficient quantities and purity for use in research. Studies using such recombinant products may help to reveal the role of the immune system in gestation.

We have used *in vitro* models for mouse preimplantation embryonic development and implantation and of mouse and human trophoblast growth to study the effects of immunological cytokines in early gestation. Mixed lymphocyte culture supernatants, which contain a variety of products from activated lymphocytes and macrophages, inhibited mouse embryo development and human choriocarcinoma cell line proliferation *in vitro* (Fig. 14-1A and B), but stimulated subgrowth of trophoblast from mouse blastocysts that had attached to fibrinectin-coated culture dishes (Fig. 14-2A and B). These data suggest that immunological cytokines may have negative or positive effects in early pregnancy, and we speculate that the timing of release of specific cytokines may affect the success or failure of pregnancy.

To assess the influence of individual cytokines on early gestational events, we have studied the effects of several recombinant lymphokines and monokines on various *in vitro* gestational models. These cytokines were obtained from Biogen (Cambridge, MA) and Genzyme (Boston, MA). Most commercially available cytokine preparations have not been fully characterized, and in view of the fragility and susceptibility to antifacts of *in vitro* models of gestational events it is necessary to include extensive controls. These are outlined in Table 14-2.

Mouse Embryo Development in Vitro (Hill et al., 1987)

Two-cell mouse embryos were recovered from female CD-1 mice on day 2 of pregnancy and cultured in BWW medium supplemented with 0.3% BSA and dilutions of various cytokines. Cultures were continued through the blastocyst stage or until day 5 after fertilization (Fig. 14-3). Embryos cultured in the presence of TNF and IL-1 were adversely affected by extremely high levels of cytokines, although no effects were observed with more physiological concentrations of these monokines (1,000 U/mL–1 U/mL). These macrophage factors are therefore probably not cytotoxic to preimplantation embryos *in vivo*.

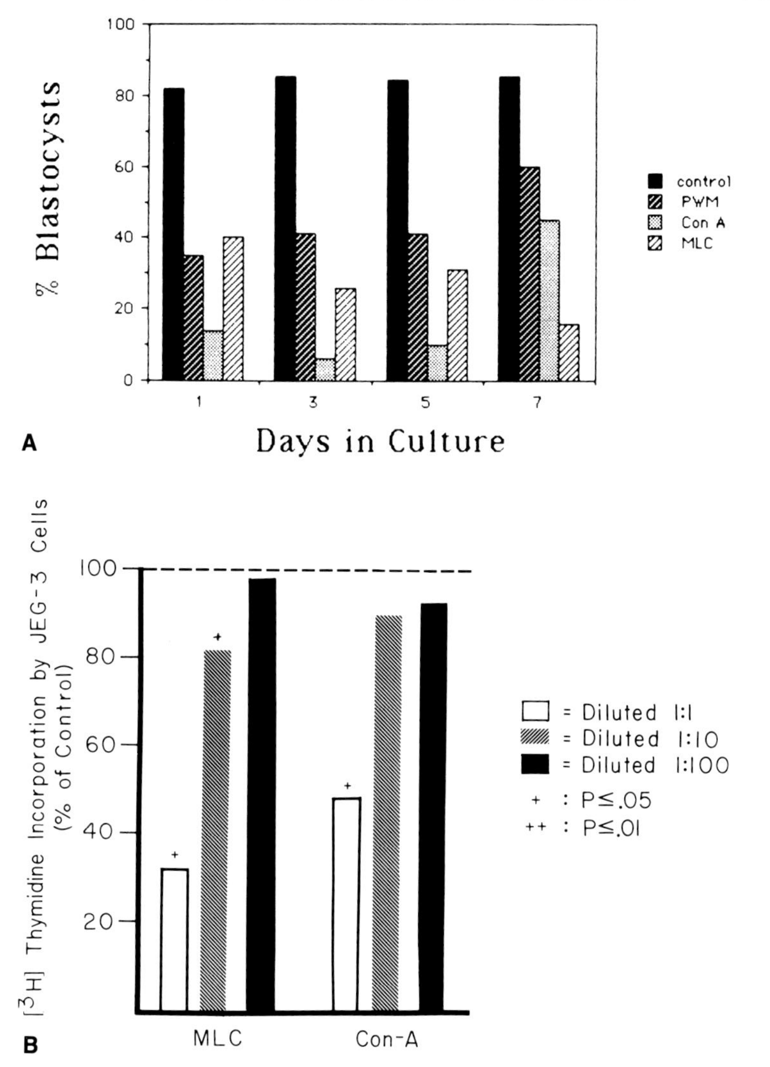

Fig. 14-1. (A) Effects of supernatants of activated lymphocyte cultures on embryo development from the 2-cell to blastocyst stage. Data are presented for supernatants harvested at 1, 3, 5, and 7 days following stimulation with pokeweed mitogen (PWM), Concanavalin A (Con A), or allogeneic lymphocytes (MLC). (B) Effects of supernatants from activated lymphocyte cultures on proliferation of Jeg-3 choriocarcinoma cells. (From Berkowitz et al., 1988.)

The IL-4 preparation available to us was directly toxic to fibroblast cells and may have contained toxic contaminants. We were unable to assess its effects on embryos. Of the other lymphokines tested, recombinant and culture-derived IL-2 had no effects, whereas various preparations of γ-IFN inhibited embryonic development over a wide dose range. These effects were abolished by heat treatment of the γ-

Table 14-1. Properties and activities of principal lymphokines and monokines*

Abbreviation	Name	Principal Cell Type	Principal Activities
IL-1	Interleukin-1	Activated macrophages	Activates resting T cells; stimulates B cell proliferation and secretion of antibody; fibroblast and endothelial cell growth factor activity; stimulates bone resorption; endogenous pyrogen
IL-2	Interleukin-2 T cell growth factor	Activated T lymphocytes	Autocrine T cell growth factor; induces synthesis of other lymphokines; activates macrophages, B cells, natural killer, and other cytotoxic cells
IL-3	Interleukin-3 Mast cell growth factor	Activated T lymphocytes	Supports the growth of pluripotent bone marrow stem cells; growth factor for mast cells
IL-4	Interleukin-4 B cell growth factor; B cell stimulating factor 1	Activated T lymphocytes	Growth factor for B cells; synergizes with IL-3 in promoting mast cell growth; enhances IgE and IgG production; stimulates expression of HLA-DR (Ia) on B cells and macrophages; enhances cytolytic activity of cytotoxic T cells; stimulates resting T cells
IL-5	Interleukin-5 T-cell replacing factor; B-cell growth factor 2 IgA enhancing factor; eosinophil differentiation factor	Activated T lymphocytes	Co-stimulates B cell proliferation; isotype-specific stimulation of IgA synthesis; induces eosinophil differentiation

IL-6	Monocyte-derived BCGF; interferon β_2; B cell stimulating factor	Activated macrophages and T lymphocytes	Induction of B cell differentiation and stimulation of IgG secretion; synergizes with IL-2 to induce CTL differentiation; some antiviral activity
γ-IFN	Gamma-interferon	Activated T lymphocytes	Inhibits viral replication; induces MHC class I (HLA-A, -B, -C) and class II (HLA-DR) antigen expression on a variety of cell types; stimulates NK, basophil, and mast cell activity; cytolytic factor for virally infected neoplastic and reproductive cells *in vitro*
TNF	Tumor necrosis factor-α	Activated macrophages	Direct cytolysis of tumor cells *in vitro* and *in vivo*; toxic to spermatozoa and embryonic and trophoblastic cell lines; stimulates granulocyte ADCC functions; induction of class II MHC antigens on a variety of cell types; stimulates osteoclasts to resorb bone tissue.
LT	Lymphotoxin Tumor necrosis factor-β	Activated T lymphocytes	Same as TNF
CSFs	Colony-stimulating factors		
GM-CSF	Granulocyte, macrophage	Activated T lymphocytes (T_H1 and T_H2)	Stimulates granulocytic and monocytic bone marrow colonies; activates mature granulocytes; affects some reproductive processes *in vitro*
M-CSF	Macrophage CSF-1	Activated macrophages	Stimulates monocytic bone marrow colonies
G-CSF	Granulocyte	Activated monocytes	Stimulates granulocytic bone marrow colonies

* Adapted from Anderson and Hill (1988).

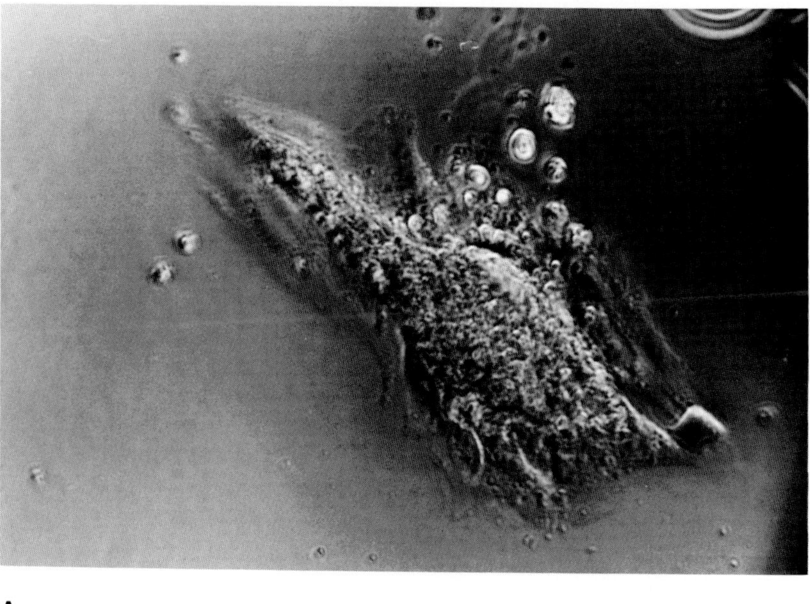

A

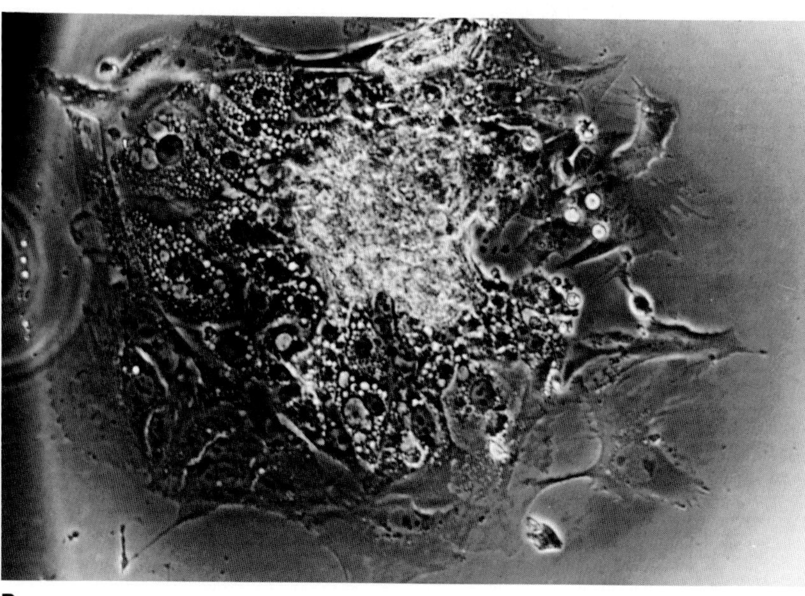

B

Fig. 14-2. Effect of mouse mixed lymphocyte culture supernatant on mouse trophoblast outgrowth *in vitro*. (A) Control outgrowth at 72 h. (B) Outgrowth of blastocyst cultured in mouse MLC supernatant for 72 h.

Table 14-2. Controls that should be performed in cytokine studies*

1. Recombinant and tissue culture products should be dialyzed against the medium used in the test system to remove low molecular weight contaminants and to introduce the optimal physiological medium for the assay.
2. Bioactivity of cytokine formulations should be reconfirmed in classical bioassay systems.
3. Preparations should be assayed for toxic effects in test systems that should not be adversely affected by the recombinant component, i.e., fibroblast proliferative assay.
4. When available, neutralizing antibodies should be used to demonstrate specific inactivation of the biological activity of the preparation. However, polyclonal neutralizing antisera may contain secondary antibodies reactive against other cytokines and toxic contaminants that may have been present in the immunizing mixture.
5. Many of the lymphokines and monokines are heat-labile, whereas most endotoxins are not; heat treatment of such preparations should neutralize the specific activity of susceptible cytokines.
6. Highly purified culture-derived factors, when available, should be assayed in parallel with the recombinant products to demonstrate the same effects with factors of biological and recombinant origin.
7. It is best to use isologous cytokines, i.e., mouse cytokines in mouse model systems, human cytokines in human systems. This is especially critical for IL-4, γ-IFN, TNF, and GM-CSF.

* Modified from Anderson and Hill (1987).

IFN or incubation with specific neutralizing antibody. Recombinant human and murine GM-CSF also inhibited mouse embryo development over a wide range of concentrations. Data from these studies thus provide evidence that products of activated lymphocytes may adversely affect preimplantation events *in vivo*.

To define further the role of cytokines in early events in embryogenesis, we determined the effects of our panel of reagents on proliferation and differentiation of the F-9 mouse teratocarcinoma cell line, which provides an *in vitro* model for mouse embryonic differentiation. Treatment of F-9 cells with retinoic acid and dibutyryl-cAMP induces differentiation from the inner cell mass stage to the parietal yolk sac stage of embryonic development (Strickland et al., 1980). Recombinant tumor necrosis factor at concentrations greater than 100 U/mL and murine-culture-derived γ-IFN at doses greater than 10^4 U/mL inhibited proliferation of undifferentiated F-9 cells *in vitro*, whereas recombinant TNF-X at concentrations $\geq$ 10 U/mL and murine recombinant GM-CSF at concentrations $>$ 10 U/mL inhibited the proliferation of F-9 cells induced to differentiate by retinoic acid and dibutyryl c-AMP. None of these cytokines promoted spontaneous differentiation of F-9 cells or blocked differentiation induced by retinoic acid and dibutyryl-cAMP. Differentiation was judged on the basis of loss of the SSEA-1 antigen and acquisition of laminin expression (Knowles et al., 1980; Solter & Knowles, 1978).

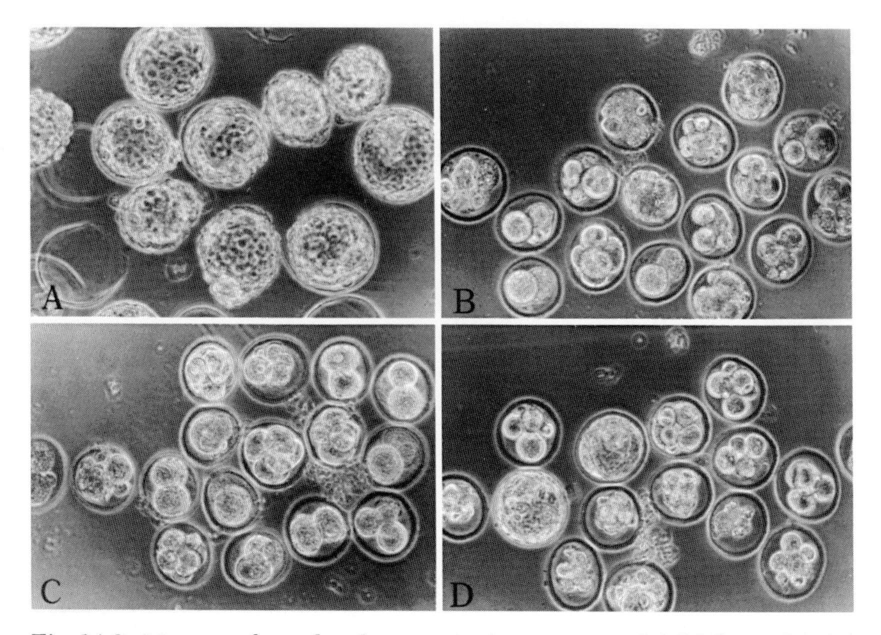

Fig. 14-3. Mouse embryo development in the presence of: (A) Whitten's/0.3% BSA (control); (B) Con-A-stimulated human leukocyte culture supernatant (5 day culture); (C) human culture-derived γ-IFN (1,000 U/mL); and (D) human culture-derived GM-CSF (100 U/mL). (From Hill, Haimovici, & Anderson, 1987.)

Mouse Embryo Attachment and Trophoblast Outgrowth in Vitro (Haimovici et al., 1990)

Various concentrations of cytokines were added to hatched mouse blastocysts, and attachment and trophoblast outgrowth onto fibrinectin-coated culture dishes were assessed after 48 and 72 h in culture. Murine-γ-IFN at concentrations ≥ 100 U/mL significantly inhibited trophoblast outgrowth (surface area control: $4.18 \pm 1.75\ \mu^2 \times 10^{-4}$ vs. $0.92 \pm 1.75\mu^2 \times 10^{-4}$; $p \leq 0.001$). The inhibitory effect of γ-IFN was abrogated by heating or treatment with neutralizing antibody. None of the other monokines or lymphokines had significant effects on trophoblast outgrowth at any concentration tested. However, murine recombinant GM-CSF at concentrations as low as 10 U/mL significantly inhibited blastocyst attachment to fibrinectin-coated dishes *in vitro*.

Choriocarcinoma Proliferation in Vitro (Berkowitz et al., 1988)

We have previously observed that γ-IFN enhances expression of class I MHC antigens and affects the morphology of some choriocarcinoma cell lines (Anderson & Berkowitz, 1986). In a more recent

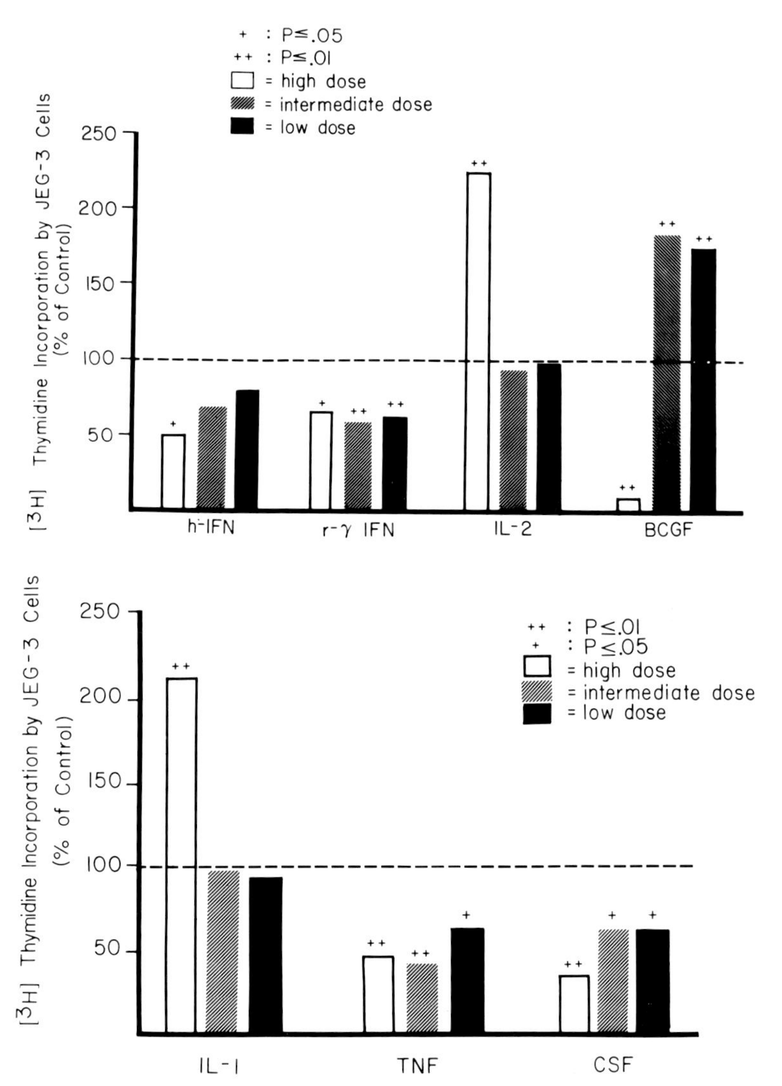

Fig. 14-4. Effects of various cytokines on Jeg-3 choriocarcinoma proliferation *in vitro*. (From Berkowitz et al., 1988.)

study we obtained evidence that γ-IFN at doses ≥ 10^3 U/mL, TNF at doses ≥ 10^2 U/mL, and GM-CSF at doses ≥ 10^2 U/mL significantly inhibited the proliferation of Jeg-3 choriocarcinoma cells *in vitro*, as measured in a 72-h ^{3}H-thymidine incorporation assay. Conversely, some concentrations of IL-1, IL-2, and IL-4 significantly stimulated choriocarcinoma cell line growth *in vitro* (Fig. 14-4A and B). None of these cytokines was overtly toxic to Jeg-3 cells, as assessed by trypan blue exclusion, at the concentrations used in these studies.

Table 14-3. Summary of effects of cytokine panel on reproductive cells *in vitro*

	Two-Cell Embryo	F-9 Undif.	F-9 Dif.	Jeg-3	Trophoblast Outgrowth
Human or mouse γ-interferon	↓	—	—	↓	↓
Human or mouse IL-2	—	—	↑	↑ *	—
Human IL-4	↓ *†	—†	—†	↑	—†
Human or mouse GM-CSF	↓	—	—	↓	—‡
Human or mouse IL-1 β	↓ *	—	—	↑ *	—
Human TNF	↓ *†	↓ †	↓ ↓ †	↓ †	—†

* Effects seen only at high concentrations.
† Tentative result because not all criteria in Table 14-2 were met.
‡ CSF inhibited blastocyst attachment to fibrinectin-coated plastic tissue culture. No effect on trophoblast outgrowth was observed if CSF was added after attachment.

Discussion and Conclusions

We arc only now beginning to study the effects of immunological cytokines on reproductive processes. Preliminary work indicates that these studies are likely to yield large amounts of interesting data, although it will be necessary to develop better *in vitro* models for various aspects of gestation and development. Furthermore, it will ultimately be necessary to confirm all *in vitro* results using *in vivo* systems because *in vitro* cultures lack many factors that may be significant. For example, hormones produced during pregnancy may induce the expression of cytokine receptors or other molecules that interact with cytokines to produce effects that are not apparent *in vitro*. Similarly, observations made with malignant cell lines, such as the F-9 embryonal teratocarcinoma and other available choriocarcinoma cells should be interpreted with caution, as these cells may not accurately reflect the characteristics of their tissues of origin.

Finally, there are undoubtedly many immunological cytokines that remain to be identified and characterized. The unique immunological changes during pregnancy may be accompanied by the production of unique cytokines, possibly by bone-marrow-derived cells in the decidua. Clonal populations of lymphoid cells should be derived from decidua of normal and abnormal pregnancies to allow further characterization of the cytokines produced at the fetal-maternal interface. The possible synergistic effects of combinations of cytokines remain virtually undefined. Immunohistological studies using antibodies specific for individual lymphokines and monokines may also help us to understand better the dynamics of the production of cytokines at the fetal-maternal interface during normal and abnormal pregnancies. This research area may be directly relevant to clinical problems, such as infertility and recurrent miscarriage. In the longer term, a clearer definition of the role of cytokines in mammalian pregnancy may lead to new approaches to promote immunotrophic enhancement of fetal viability and growth and to prevent immunodystrophic effects that may underlie reproductive failure.

Acknowledgments

The authors acknowledge other members of the Fearing Laboratory who have contributed to this work—Heidi Faris, Ling Chen, Janine LaSalle, Tony De Fougerolles, Carol Bacon, Drs. Xu Chong, and Kazue Takahashi—and Ann Collins, who typed this manuscript. This research was supported by NIH grants CA42738, HD23547, HD00815, and HD23775 and by the Fearing Laboratory Endowment.

References

Anderson, D. I. and Berkowitz, R. S. 1985. Gamma-interferon enhances expression of class I MHC antigens in the weakly HLA-positive human choriocarcinoma cell line BeWo but does not induce MHC expression in the HLA negative choriocarcinoma cell-line jar. *J. Immunol.* 135:2498.

Anderson, D. J. and Hill, J. A. 1987. Interleukin-1 and endometriosis. *Fertil. Steril.* 48:894.

Anderson, D. J. and Hill, J. A. 1988. Cell-mediated immunity in infertility. *Am. J. Reprod. Immunol. Microbiol.* 17:22.

Blaustein, A. 1985. *Interpretation of Endometrial Biopsies*, 2nd ed. New York: Raven Press, p. 88.

Berkowitz, R. S., Hill, J. A., Kurtz, C. B., and Anderson, D. J. 1988. Effects of products of activated leukocytes (lymphokines and monokines) on the growth of malignant trophoblast cells in vitro. *Am. J. Obstet. Gynecol.* 158:199.

Bulmer, J. N. and Sunderland, C. A. 1984. Immunohistological characterization of lymphoid cell populations in the early human placental bed. *Immunology* 52:349.

Haimovici, F., Hill, J. A., and Anderson, D. J. 1990. Effects of soluble products of activated lymphocytes and macrophages on mouse blastocyst implantation in vitro. *Biol. Reprod.* In press.

Hill, J. A., Haimovici, F., and Anderson, D. J. 1987. Products of activated lymphocytes and macrophages inhibit mouse embryo development in vitro. *J. Immunol.* 139:2250.

Kamat, B. R. and Isaacson, P. G. 1987. The immunocytochemical distribution of leukocytic subpopulations in human endometrium. *Am. J. Pathol.* 118:76.

Knowles, B. B., Pan, S., Solter, D., Linnenbach, A. Croce, C., and Huebner, K. 1980. Expression of H-2, laminin and SV40T and TASA on differentiation of transformed murine teratocarcinoma cells. *Nature* 288:615.

Lint, T. F. 1980. Complement. In: *Immunological Aspects of Infertility and*

Fertility Regulation (D. S. Dhindsa and G. F. B. Schumacher, eds.). New York: Elsevier-North Holland, p. 13.

Monif, G. R. G. 1982. *Infectious Disease in Obstetrics and Gynecology*. Philadelphia: Harper and Row.

Strickland, S., Smith, K. K., and Marotti, K. R. 1980. Hormonal induction of differentiation in teratocarcinoma stem cells: generation of parietal endoderm by retinoic acid and dibutyryl c-AMP. *Cell* 21:347.

Solter, D. and Knowles, B. B. 1978. Monoclonal antibody defining a stage-specific mouse embryonic antigen (SSEA-1). *Proc. Natl. Acad. Sci. USA* 75:5565.

Wegmann, T. G. 1984. Fetal protection against abortion: is it immunosuppression or immunostimulation? *Ann. Immunol. Instit. Pasteur* 135:309.

Wheeler, J. E. 1982. Pathology of the fallopian tube. In *Pathology of the Female Genital Tract* (A. Blaustein, ed.) New York: Springer-Verlag, pp. 393–415.

Xu, C., Hill, J. A., and Anderson, D. J. 1987. Identification of T-lymphocyte subpopulations in normal and abnormal human endometrial biopsies. Proceedings Society Genecologic Investigation (Abstr.).

15

T-Cell Products in Implantation: Role of Putative Suppressor Factors

KENNETH D. BEAMAN, DEBBIE L. GRISSOM, CHRISTIAN W. ERTL, and ROGER C. HOVERSLAND

Immune Suppression and Pregnancy

The mechanism by which the maternal immune system mediates rejection of a skin graft that expresses paternal histocompatibility antigens, but at the same time sustains a fetal allograft carrying the same antigens remains a central question in reproductive immunology. A number of different mechanisms have been proposed and have been recently reviewed by Beer (1988). They include the hypothesis that the uterus is an immunologically privileged site similar to the hamster cheek pouch or the anterior chamber of the eye. Alternatively, the trophoblast may act as a relatively nonantigenic layer interposed between the fetus and the uterus. We have been primarily interested in regulation of the immune system mediated by suppressor cells. The presence of suppressor cells in decidua was initially reported by Clark and his colleagues some years ago (Clark & MacDermott, 1978; Clark et al., 1984). More recently, suppressor factors have been detected in the fetal-placental unit and the draining lymph nodes (Beaman & Hoversland, 1988; Ribbing et al., 1988). Monoclonal antibodies against suppressor factors were also shown to have pronounced effects on gestation (Beaman & Hoversland, 1988; Ribbing et al., 1988). Effects of immunosuppression on spontaneous abortion of allogeneic or semiallogeneic pregnancies have also been implicated. Several investigators have suggested that the development of blocking antibodies or the generation of suppressor factors may play a critical role in protection of the fetal allograft (Beer, 1988; Voisin, 1980; Chaouat et al., 1985; Clark et al., 1986).

T cell Suppressor Factors

In our initial experiments, we showed that a monoclonal antibody to a T cell suppressor factor (mAB 14-30) terminated pregnancy when the antibody was administered to mice at a dose of 5 mg on each of days 3, 4, and 5 of gestation. This corresponds approximately to the time of implantation (Beaman & Hoversland, 1988; Ribbing et al., 1988). The monoclonal antibody used in these studies was produced against a peptide thought to be responsible for the antigen specificity of suppressor inducer factor (TsF1) (Ferguson & Iverson, 1986). This antibody has been shown to bind to several TsF1-like peptides produced by L3T4-positive cells. Several different TsF1 peptides each with its own antigen specificity have been tested for binding to mAB 14-30. Based on these results, the antibody appears to bind to conserved regions of the TsF1s. The nature of the cells producing the TsF1, the peptides, and antisera have been described by Cone et al. (1988). The characterization of the peptide recognized by mAB 14-30 has been reported by Ferguson and Iverson (1986) and Cone and Beaman (1985). It appears to have a molecular weight of approximately 30 kDa as determined by molecular exclusion chromatography. TsF1 derived from monoclonal cell populations appear homogenous on isoelectric focusing gels, but are heterogeneous when produced by mixed T lymphocyte populations. Their properties thus correspond to those expected of antigen-specific molecules. Like immunoglobulins, they are relatively homogeneous in size and behave as though they contain variable and constant regions.

A second monoclonal antibody, mAb 14-12, recognizes a suppressor affector factor (TsF3) produced by $Ly2^+$ T cells (Ferguson et al., 1988). mAb 14-12 has been shown to increase the resistance of stressed mice to bacterial infections (Kupper et al., 1985).

We initially showed that antibodies to TsF1 reproducibly terminate pregnancy in mice, whereas anti-TsF3 antibody has little or no effect on pregnancy outcome. Antibodies specific for TsF1 detect a protein in the fetal-placental unit (Ribbing et al., 1988), which has many of the properties of TsF1 (Cone et al., 1987; Ptak et al., 1983). Subsequently we showed increased levels of TsF1 in the lymph nodes draining the uterus (DLN) and in the fetal placental unit itself using ELISA and quantitative dot blotting techniques. Although our initial experiments showed no effect of antibodies to TsF3 on pregnancy, we describe here unexpected effects of mAb 14-12 on pregnancy and further characterize the effects of mAb 14-30 on the outcome of pregnancy. We also report some recent experiments in humans using blocking antibodies that specifically suppress the immune response during pregnancy. In these studies we show that the effects of heat-inactivated sera from pregnant women on the MLR (mixed lymphocyte reaction) correlate with the presence of antileukocyte antibodies in the sera (Gilman-Sachs et al., unpublished data).

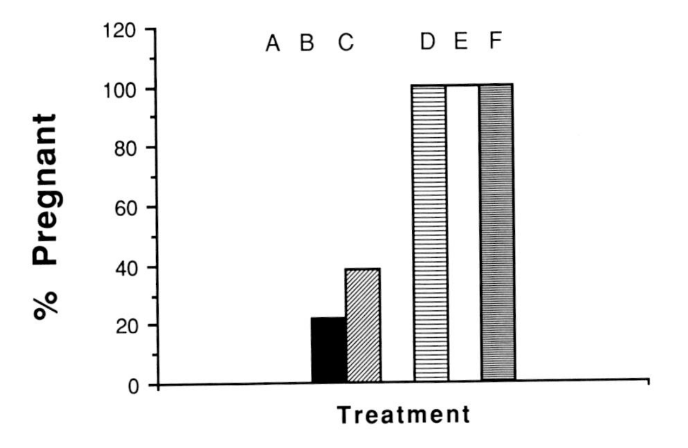

Fig. 15-1. Mated mice were injected on days 3, 4, 5 of pregnancy. Lanes A, B, and C represent groups of animals injected with 10 mg, 1 mg and 0.1 mg of mAb 14-30. Lane D represents uninjected animals; Lanes E and F show animals injected with 150 mg of 15 mg of mAb 14-12, respectively. The number of viable fetuses was measured at day 17 of gestation and is expressed as a percentage. In each case N ranges from 6 to 15 animals.

TsF and Pregnancy

Effects of mAb to TsF1 on Implantation

Antibodies to TsF1 (mAb 14-30) terminate pregnancy in Swiss Webster mice when administered at the time of implantation. However, antibody to TsF3 (mAb 14-12) had no effect on the number of fetuses that were viable on day 17 (Fig. 15-1). Both mAb 14-30 and mAb 14-12 are rat anti-mouse antibodies of IgMκ isotype and were administered at the same concentrations. Likewise, nonimmune rat sera administered at or near the time of implantation had no effects on the outcome of pregnancy. High doses of mAb 14-30 (10 mg per injection) completely abrogated pregnancy, whereas doses of 1 mg and 0.5 mg had intermediate effects, as shown in Figure 15-1. Treatment with mAb had an "all or none" effect on pregnancy in individual animals; pregnant mice each carried 9 to 11 fetuses. In no instance did treatment lead to reduced litter size.

Methods for TsF1 Measurement in Tissues and Sera

Western Blot of TsF1. Immunoreactive protein could be identified in maternal, fetal, and placental tissues. Tissues were harvested at various stages of pregnancy, homogenized, and centrifuged at 12,000 x g. The resulting supernatant was precipitated with ammonium sulfate (50% saturation) and suspended in 100 mM Na acetate buffer, pH 4, and dialyzed against the same buffer at 4°C. The supernatant was then dialyzed into an appropriate sample buffer. Samples underwent electrophoresis and were blotted on nitrocellulose paper as previously described (Beaman & Hoversland, 1988). The protein identified by Western blot in tissues of the fetus, uterus, placenta, and spleen had a molecular weight of approximately 70 bDa when run on SDS-PAGE under reducing conditions. The protein was labile at low pH, further suggesting that it corresponded to TsF1. The protein was extracted as described above and dialyzed into a pH 4 buffer. The resulting supernatant underwent electrophoresis and was blotted as before. After pH 4 treatment, the molecular weight of the putature TsF1 was reduced to 28 to 32 kD as previously reported by Beaman and Cone (1985). These proteins were immunoprecipitated by polyclonal antisera specific for TsF1 or by the monoclonal antibody 14-30. Both the monoclonal antibody and the antisera specific for TsF1 were also able to identify the protein on Western blot analysis.

ELISA of TsF1. The quantities of TsF1 in the conceptus were estimated using an ELISA technique (Cone et al., 1987; Ferguson et al., 1985). In these studies, purified TsF1 was obtained from T cells harvested from ascites fluid as described by Beaman and Cone (1986). The T helper inducer clone, A1.1, provided by Dr. D. R. Green (University of Alberta, Canada) was used in these studies. These cells have been shown to produce TsF1, and one can isolate microgram quantities of TsF1 (Zheng et al., 1988). Our ELISA technique was based on that of Cone et al. (1987). A uniform concentration of 100 nanograms of TsF1/well was used to coat microtiters trays, and two-fold dilutions of TsF or tissue extracts were used as competitors of binding.

Flat-bottomed microtiter trays (Immunlon-Dynatech, McLean, VA) were coated with 12.5 μg of affinity-purified TsF1 in 0.1 M $NaHCO_3$/Na_2CO_3 buffer (pH 9.25) per 96-well tray overnight at room temperature. The plates were then blocked with 100 μL/well of 0.1% bovine serum albumin (BSA) in 0.1 M $NaHCO_3$/Na_2CO_3 buffer (pH 9.25) for 1 h at 37°C. Tissue extracts were prepared as described for Western blots, and the resulting supernatants were diluted serially 1:2 in 0.1 M KH_2PO_4/K_2HPO_4 buffer (pH 7.4) containing 0.1% Triton X-100 and 0.5% gelatin (PBS/Tx/Gel). Alternatively, TsF1 harvested from ascites and purified as described previously was used as a competitive inhibitor. After addition of 100 μL/well of the serially diluted inhibitor, 100μL/well of an appropriate dilution of mAb 14-30 supernatant fluid in PBS/Tx/Gel buffer was added and incubated at 37°C for 1 h. The plates were then washed three times with buffer (0.01 M KH_2PO_4/K_2HPO_4 containing 0.1% Triton X-100), followed by 1-h incubation at 37°C with a 1:1000 dilution of alkaline phosphatase-conjugated anti-rat immunoglobulin antibody (Boehringer Mannheim Biochemicals,

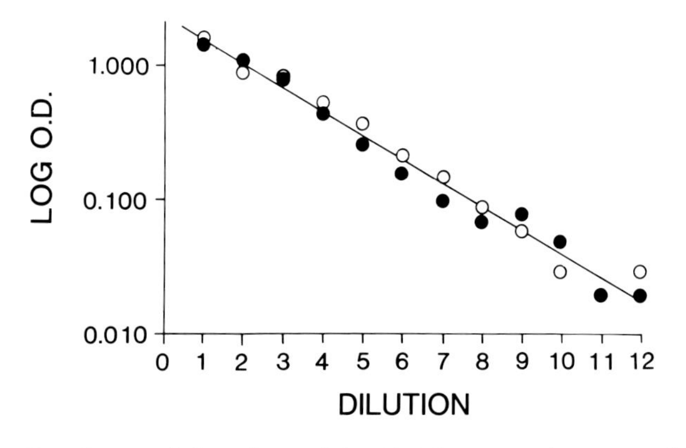

Fig. 15-2. The slopes of the plots of the ELISA were determined by linear regression. The slope y = 2.48 for the determination of TsF binding affinity from T cells and from tissue. The equation for tissue TsF (closed circles) was $y = -2.48 + 2.55x$ with a correlation coefficient of R = 0.972. The equation for T cell TsF (closed circles) was $y = -2.48 + 1.77x$ with a correlation coefficient of R = 0.989.

Indianapolis, IN). This antibody was shown not to react with TsF or mouse tissue extracts. The substrate consisted of 1 mg/mL of p-nitrophenyl phosphate (Sigma) in diethanolamine-HC1 buffer (pH 9.25). The reaction was allowed to develop for 1-3 h at 37°C, and color was determined quantitatively at 0.D. 410 nm on a Minireader II (Dynatech, McLean, VA).

As shown in Figure 15-2, the affinity of the monoclonal antibody for TsF1 extracted from T cell hybridoma A1.1 supernatants or from the day-17 pregnant uterus was identical. A standard concentration of TsF1 isolated from each source was coated on a plate, and twofold dilutions of TsF1 from the T cell hybridoma 51H7D were used as a binding competitor. The slopes of both curves were calculated to be −2.48.

Finally, to increase the range of utility of the assay, data were calculated and plotted as the logit of percent binding versus the log of protein concentration (mg). A standard curve is presented in Figure 15-3. Typically, correlation coefficients ranging from 0.96 to 0.99 were obtained. Concentrations as low as 50 to 100 picomoles per well could be estimated by extrapolation from the standard curve.

We assayed the TsF1 content of various tissues. The values obtained are presented in Table 15-1. Levels ranged from an undetectable amount in muscle to a mean of 34.7 ng/mg protein in lymph node. Interestingly, the amount of TsF1 present in individual lymph nodes varied greatly with the lymph node population studied, whereas the amounts of TsF1 in other tissues showed little variation.

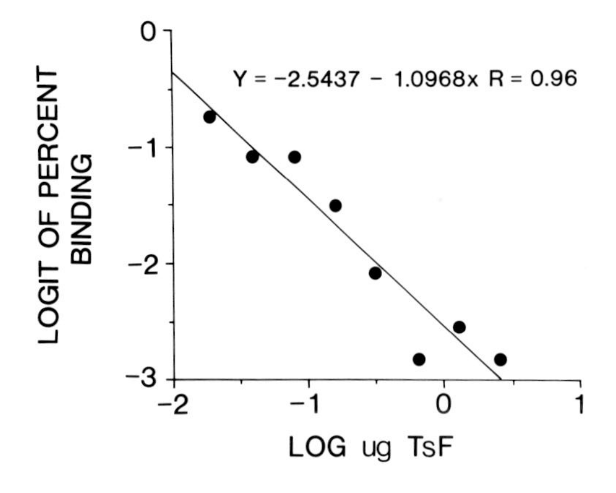

Fig. 15-3. A standard curve generated using the competitive ELISAs. Wells were coated with TsF extracted from uterine tissue. TsF from the same source was used as the competitor for the standard curve. n = 6 in each case, and the correlation coefficient and equation for the line are shown. The data are plotted as the logit of the percent binding.

TsF1 concentrations During Pregnancy

As shown in Figure 15-4, the TsF1 content of the DLN is greatest on days 3 through 6 of pregnancy. Although the amount of TsF1 present later in pregnancy is still substantial, it is much less than that found at or near the time of implantation. The peak level of 820 nanograms of TsF present on day 5 is by far the highest we have encountered under physiological conditions.

Effects of Delayed Implantation on TsF1 Concentrations

Because of the role of steroids in suppression and immunoregulation and the ability of catechol estradiols to induce implantation in oophorectomized mice (Hoversland et al., 1982; Stimpson & Hunter, 1980), we investigated the relationship between TsF1 concentrations and delayed implantation. Previous studies have shown that antipro-

Table 15-1. TsF concentrations in tissues

Tissue	Concentration (ng/tissue)	SE	N
Spleen	20.34	0.32	7
Thymus	9.48	1.77	5
Lymph node	3.58	0.99	8
Uterus	3.58	0.57	5
Uterus* pregnant	152.2	2.52	5
Leishmania-infected lesions	7.21	1.94	3
Normal muscle	ND	ND	5
Normal sera	11.8	2.67	6
Sera pregnant (1)	22.8	4.50	4
Sera pregnant (2)	45.7	5.83	5

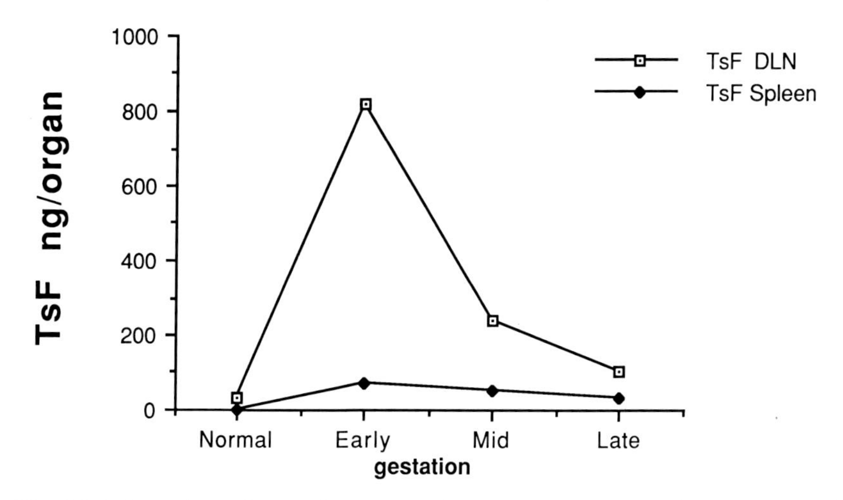

Fig. 15-4. Lymph nodes in the region draining the common iliac artery and lumbar aorta (DLN) were collected from pregnant and nonpregnant animals. The content of TsF1 was determined by ELISA. The amount of TsF is expressed as the mean of at least 5 individual experiments. Early values represent TsF determined on days 4, 5, and 6 of pregnancy. Midvalues include TsF determined on days 8, 9, and 10 of pregnancy. Late values include those determined on days 14, 15, and 16 of pregnancy.

gesterone monoclonal antibodies affected implantation (Rider et al., 1987). Our studies revealed that delaying implantation had definite effects on the concentrations of TsF1 found in uterine tissue (Hoversland; Grissom, & Beaman, unpublished data).

A series of experiments was undertaken to determine the TsF content in various reproductive and lymphoid tissues under conditions of delayed implantation. Two different endocrine states were examined: oophorectomized mice/pregnant mice treated with (1) progesterone alone or (2) progesterone in combination with estrogen. In these studies Swiss Webster mice were mated and then oophorectomized on day 4 of pregnancy, as described by Hoversland, Dey, and Johnson (1982). Animals in the first treatment group were selected at random stages of the estrus cycle and oophorectomized. The day of oophorectomy was designated as day 4, and the animals were injected with 2 mg of progesterone on each of days 7, 8, and 9. The animals were sacrificed after the last injection, and various tissues were examined for their TsF content. A second hormonal treatment group comprised animals treated under the same conditions as above, but also injected with 25 nanograms of estradiol-17B on day 9. The third group was made up of mated animals injected with 2 mg of progesterone on each of days 7, 8, and 9 of pregnancy. The final group included animals mated, oophorectomized on day 4 of pregnancy, and

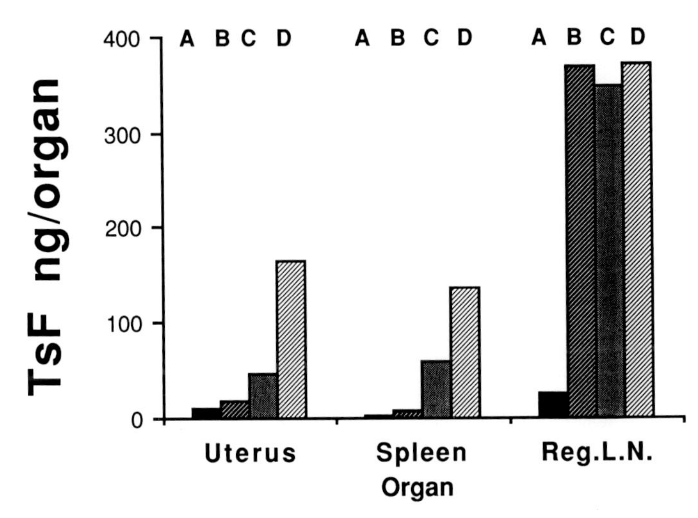

Fig. 15-5. Tissues were taken from female Swiss Webster mice (nonpregnant, Bars A and B; and pregnant, Bars C and D); after treatment with progesterone, Bars A and C, or progesterone plus estradiol, Bars B and D. The concentration of TsF1 was determined 24 hours after the final treatment. The content of immunoreactive TsF was determined by competitive ELISA. The mean of 5 animals was shown.

then injected with progesterone and estradiol as described above. This treatment is hormonally and developmentally equivalent to day 5 of pregnancy. TsF concentrations remained at or below the limit of detection, irrespective of hormonal treatment, when no embryo was present. However, when implantation was induced by estrogen treatment, there was an approximately 30- to 50-fold increase in the amount of uterine TsF1. Estrogen treatment also had similar effects on splenic TsF1 levels. The effect of estrogen administration on the TsF1 content of the regional lymph nodes was somewhat surprising, as there was no correlation with uterine TsF1 concentrations. Administration of estrogen or the presence of an embryo both resulted in a 30-fold increase in the amount of TsF1 detected.

Effects of Anti-TsF3

Intraperitoneal injection of mAb 14-12 into pregnant mice had little effect on the number of viable fetuses. It therefore served as an ideal negative control, because it was of the same isotype as mAb 14-30. However, it was important to determine if high doses of mAb 14-12 had any effect on gestation. When the dose of mAb was increased to 178 μg/injection, we observed a 2.5-fold increase in the day-14 fetal weight (Fig. 15-6). As with mAb 14-30, this effect could be shown only when the antibody was administered early in pregnancy (Fig. 15-7).

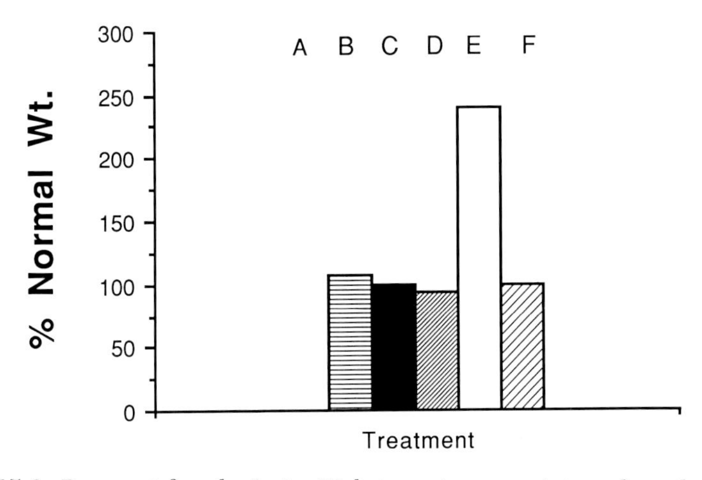

Fig. 15-6. Pregnant female Swiss-Webster mice were injected on days 3, 4 and 5 of pregnancy with 10 mg (Bar A) and 1 mg (Bar B) of mAb 14-30, and the fetal weight of Day 14 of gestation was determined. Control animals, (not injected) are shown in Bar C; or injected with 500 mg of rat immunoglobulin on days 3, 4 and 5 are shown in Bar D. mAb 14-12 was injected on Day 5, 150 mg (Bar E) and 10 mg (Bar F) Day 14 fetal weight was determined for all groups. Values are expressed as percent of normal Day 14 weight (n = 5/group).

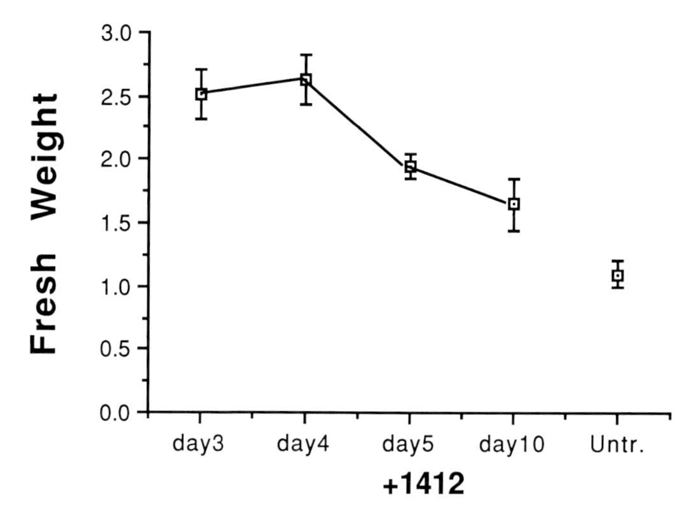

Fig. 15-7. The weight of Day 14 fetuses was determined after injection with 150 mg of mAb 14-12 on the days indicated. The weights of the individual fetuses were determined (n = 5/group).

When mAb 14-12 was administered at later times during pregnancy, its effect on Day 14 fetal weight was decreased.

Treatment with mAb 14-12 also had demonstrable effects in other TsF assays (Ferguson et al., 1985; Kupper et al., 1985; Zheng et al., 1988). The effects of this antibody on pregnancy were directly opposite to those of mAb 14-30. However, they are compatible with the findings of Athanassakis et al. (1987) who showed that stimulation of the maternal immune response had a stimulatory effect on fetally derived placental cells. Possibly a specific response must be turned on in order to turn off a fetus specific immune response. Several groups have described the production of peptides and immunostimulatory lymphokines from cells capable of producing TsF1 (Cone et al., 1988; Green et al., 1987; Ptak et al., 1983). The effects of mAb 14-30 on pregnancy may therefore be mediated through eliciting positive immune response, rather than preventing a response. mAb 14-30 and other similar antisera bind peptides that may themselves combine with other peptides and have other immunoregulatory functions (Cone et al., 1988).

Effects of Antileukocyte Antibodies

We have also studied the effects of antileukocyte antibodies on one-way maternal-paternal MLRs in humans (Gilman-Sachs et al., unpublished data). Our system is based on the observation that women with a history of recurrent abortion may achieve successful pregnancies after immunization with paternal and/or third-party lymphocytes (Beer, 1988; Beer et al., 1987). These studies have shown that successful pregnancies may develop in women who develop MLR-blocking antibodies after leukocyte immunization. Pregnancies could not be sustained in the subset of patients with no response. Blocking antibody therefore represents a third type of suppressive factor, which is able to inhibit a one-way MLR (maternal responder to paternal stimulator) as described above. We have looked for the presence of these suppressor factors in serum, as determined by their effect on MLR responses. The presence of MLC blocking activity correlates closely with the presence of IgG antibodies to paternal lymphocytes (Gilman-Sachs et al., unpublished data). As with other suppressor factors, our results suggest that a positive response must occur before suppression in order for a successful pregnancy to be maintained.

Summary

The administration of a monoclonal antibody to TsF1 terminates pregnancy in mice when given at or before the time of implantation. When this monoclonal antibody was given at other times, no effect on the pregnancy was observed. This antibody affected only the proportion of animals sustaining pregnancy and did not have detectable effects on litter size. High levels of TsF1 were present in uterine tissue or in tissues around the uterus during pregnancy. The highest concentrations of TsF were shown to be in the draining uterine lymph nodes. When implantation of fetus was delayed by hormonal manipulation, a corresponding delay in TsF concentrations was observed. The TsF concentrations in the draining lymph nodes were not affected as dramatically as those in the uterus and spleen when implantation was hormonally induced. This observation may relate to the fact that the draining lymph nodes of that area contain substantial numbers of "normal" lymphocytes which may be stimulated by a variety of external antigens, in addition to "pregnancy-related" subpopulations.

The administration of monoclonal antibody to TsF3 had little or no effect on gestation when the antibody was administered at doses equivalent to those of mAb 14-30. However, when high doses of mAb 14-12 were administered, definite effects on the size of the fetus were apparent. Like mAb 14-30, the effects of mAb 14-12 were greatest when the antibody was administered at or about the time of implantation. The administration of the antibody after day 6 of gestation in the Swiss Webster mouse had less effect.

Studies of T cell suppression of the immune response of females during pregnancy have led to some particularly interesting results. Our findings, together with data indicating that importance of blocking antibodies in suppressing an ongoing immune response in the human immune system, lead to the conclusion that specific suppression of the immune response in pregnancy is important and complex. Although our data emphasize the importance of suppression of the immune response during pregnancy, they point out even more vividly the significance of a fetus specific immune response and the importance of this response in sustaining growth and development of the embryo.

References

Athanassakis, I., Bleackley, R. C., Paetkau, V., Guilbert, L., Barr, P. J., and Wegmann, T. G. 1988. The immunostimulatory effect of T cells and T cell lymphokines on murine fetally derived placental cells. *J. Immunol.* 138:37–44.

Beaman, K. D. and Cone, R. 1986. Production and purification of monoclonal T lymphocyte antigen binding molecules (TABM). *Biochem. Biophys. Res. Comm.* 125:475–483.

Beaman, K. D. and Hoversland, R. C. 1988. Induction of abortion with a monoclonal antibody specific for suppressor T-lymphocyte molecules. *J. Reprod. Fertil.* 82:691–696.

Beer, A. E. 1988. Immunologic aspects of normal pregnancy and recurrent spontaneous abortion. *Semin. Reprod. Endocrinol.* 6:163–180.

Beer, A. E., Quebbeman, J. F., Harrazaki, Y., and Semprimi, A. E. 1987. Immunotherapy of recurrent spontaneous abortion. In *Immunoregulation and Fetal Survival* (T. J. Gill III, T. G. Wegmann, and E. Nisbet-Brown, eds.) New York: Oxford University Press, pp. 286–299.

Chaouat, G. and Voisin, G. A. 1980. Regulatory T cell subpopulations in pregnancy. II. Evidence for suppressive activity of the late phase of MLR. *Immunology* 39:239–248.

Chaouat, G., Kolb, J., Kiger, N., Stansilowski, M., and Wegmann, T. 1985. Immunologic consequences of vaccination against abortion in mice. *J. Immunol.* 134:1594–1598.

Clark, D. A. and MacDermott, M. R. 1978. Impairment of host versus graft reaction in pregnant mice. I. Suppression of cytotoxic cell generation in lymph nodes draining the uterus. *J. Immunol.* 121:1389–1393.

Clark, D., Slapsys, R., Croy, B., Krcek, J., and Rossant, J. 1984. Local active suppression by suppressor cells in the decidua. *Am. J. Reprod. Immunol.* 5:78–83.

Clark, D., Chaput, A., and Tutton, D. 1986. VII. Spontaneous abortion of allogeneic CBA/J X DBA/2 fetuses in the uterus of CBA/J mice correlated with deficient non-T suppressor cell activity. *J. Immunol.* 136:1668–1675.

Cone, R. and Beaman, K. D. 1985. Antigen-binding molecules of T cells: charge heterogeneity and structural ability. *Mol. Immunol.* 22:399–406.

Cone, R., Guardi, D., Danieloff, J., Petty, J., Kobayashi, K., and Cohen, S. 1987. Quantitation of T cell antigen-binding molecules (TABM) in the sera of nonimmunized, immunized and desensitized mice. *J. Immunol.* 138:234–239.

Cone, R. E., Zheng, H., Chue, B., Beaman, K., Ferguson, T., and Green D. 1988. T cell-derived antigen binding molecules (TABM): molecular and functional properties. *Int. Rev. Immunol.* 3:205–228.

Ferguson, T. and Iverson, G. 1986. Isolation and characterization of an antigen specific inducer molecule from the serum of hyperimmune mice using a monoclonal antibody. *J. Immunol.* 136:2896–2903.

Ferguson, T., Beaman, K., and Iverson, G. 1985. Isolation and characterization of a T-suppressor factor by using a monoclonal antibody. *J. Immunol.* 134:3163–3171.

Green, D. R., Chue, B., Zheng, H., Ferguson, T. A., Beaman, K. D., and Flood, P. 1987. A helper T cell clone produces an antigen-specific molecule (T-ABM) which functions in the induction of suppression. *J. Mol. Cell. Immunol.* 3:95.

Hoversland, R. C., Dey, S. K., and Johnson, O. 1982. The ability of catechol estradiols to induce implantation in ovariectomized mice treated with progesterone. *Life Sci.* 30:1801–1804.

Kupper, T., Baker, C., Ferguson, T., and Green, D. 1985. A lesion induced by Ly-2 suppressor T-cells lowers resistance to bacterial infection. *J. Surg. Res.* 38:606–612.

Ptak, W., Gershon, R. K., Rosenstein, R. W., Murray, J. H., and Cone, R. E. 1983. Purification and characterization of TNP-specific immunoregulatory molecules produced by T cells sensitized to Picryl chloride (PCLF). *J. Immunol.* 131:2859.

Ribbing, S. L., Hoversland, R. C., and Beaman, K. D. 1988. T-cell suppressor factors play an integral role in preventing fetal rejection. *J. Reprod. Immunol.* 14:83–95.

Rider, V., Heap, R. B., Wang, M.-Y., and Feinstein, A. 1987. Anti-progesterone monoclonal antibody affects early cleavage and implantation in the mouse by mechanisms that are influenced by genotype. *J. Reprod. Fertil.* 79:33–43.

Stimson, W. H. and Hunter, I. C. 1980. Oestrogen-induced immunoregulation mediated through the thymus. *J. Clin. Lab. Immunol.* 4:27–31.

Wright, L. F., Feinstein, A., Heap, R. B., Saunders, J. C., Bennett, R. C., and Wang, M.-Y. 1982. Progesterone monoclonal antibody blocks pregnancy in mice. *Nature, London* 295:415–417.

Zheng, H., Boyer, M., Fotedar, M., Singh, B., and Green, D. R. 1987. An antigen-specific helper T cell hybridomas produces an antigen-specific suppressor-inducer molecule with identical antigenic fine-specificity: implications for the antigen recognition and function of helper and suppressor-inducer T cells. *J. Immunol.* 140:1351–1358.

16

Interferons Secreted by Sheep Conceptuses are Involved in Maternal Recognition of Pregnancy

FULLER W. BAZER and PETER J. HANSEN

During early pregnancy, sheep conceptuses produce proteins and prostaglandin E_2 (PGE) that are involved in protecting the corpus luteum (CL) from the luteolytic effects of prostaglandin $F_{2\alpha}$ (PGF) released from the uterine endometrium. The secretory proteins of the conceptus appear to exert an antiluteolytic effect by acting directly, in a paracrine manner, on the endometrium, whereas PGE may have a luteoprotective action on the CL (Bazer et al., 1986). Conceptus secretory proteins of sheep do not inhibit uterine production of PGF, but suppress the episodic release of PGF necessary for luteolysis in sheep. In this chapter we show that the major conceptus secretory protein that mediates these changes in PGF release is an interferon alpha molecule called ovine trophoblast protein-1 (oTP-1). We review the biological properties of oTP-1 that allow it to serve as an antiluteolytic protein. We also show that oTP-1 has other biological activities characteristic of alpha interferons, including antiviral and immunosuppressive biological activities.

Ovine Trophoblast Protein-1 is the Antiluteolytic Protein Secreted by Sheep Conceptuses

Moor and Rowson (1966a and b) were the first to establish that infusion of homogenates of sheep conceptuses into the uterine lumen, but not into the utero-ovarian venous drainage, would delay regression of the CL and thus increase the interestrous interval. Unlike the conceptuses of humans and other primates, the sheep conceptus does not regulate CL life span by producing a gonadotropin(s). Ellinwood et al. (1979) determined that sheep conceptus homogenates contained neither chorionic gonadotrophin-like or prolactin-like proteins. In light of these results, it was important to determine if sheep conceptuses secreted a protein that acts as an antiluteolytic agent to block the secretion or action of PGF from the uterine endometrium. In preliminary experiments to identify such a conceptus secretory protein, day-16 sheep conceptuses were cultured in the presence of radiolabeled amino acids. This day of pregnancy was chosen because it represents a time at which conceptus homogenates can extend luteal life span (Rowson & Moore, 1966a and b). The major radiolabeled proteins secreted into the culture medium by day-16 sheep conceptuses, as identified by two-dimensional polyacrylamide gel electrophoresis and fluorography, were initially reported to have molecular weights of about 25 kDa and pI values between 5.0 and 5.5 (Wilson et al., 1979). Based on Sephadex G-200 gel filtration analyses, the molecular weight of these major proteins was determined to be about 20 kDa (Wilson & Bazer, unpublished data). This protein was further characterized by Godkin et al. (1982) as protein X and was later identified as ovine trophoblast protein-1 (oTP-1) (Godkin et al. (1984b) because it was the first major protein shown to be secreted by mononuclear cells of ovine trophectoderm.

Characteristics of oTP-1

Sheep conceptuses secrete oTP-1 between days 10 and 21 of pregnancy. This corresponds to the time interval when the PGF luteolytic signal from the endometrium must be blocked to allow maintenance of the CL (Bazer et al., 1986). oTP-1 has a molecular weight of 19 kDa and exists as three to four isoelectric variants with pI values ranging from 5.3 to 5.7, but it contains no carbohydrate moiety. The isoelectric variants arise from separate mRNAs (Anthony et al., 1988). oTP-1 is secreted by trophectoderm and is taken up by endometrial surface epithelium and superficial glandular epithelium (Godkin et al., 1984a) suggesting that the endometrium is its major site of action. Furthermore, oTP-1 inhibits cAMP production, but has no effect on cGMP and inhibits inositol phospholipid turnover in endometrial tissue. It also strongly amplifies endometrial secretion of at least five proteins, the functions of which have not been determined (Vallet et al., 1987). oTP-1 does not appear to act directly on the CL to influence its life span or level of progesterone production (Godkin et al., 1984a), and there is no evidence that oTP-1 is transported from the uterus into the maternal circulation (Vallet & Bazer, unpublished data).

oTP-1 has high amino acid sequence homology with interferons of the alpha-2 class, which may be important to its biological effects (Charpigny et al., 1988; Imakawa et al., 1987; Stewart et al., 1987). Furthermore, oTP-1 has many of the biological properties of interferons, including antiviral activity equivalent to that of recombinant human and bovine alpha-interferons (Pontzer et al., 1988) and immunosuppressive activity (Newton et al., 1989).

oTP-1 has potent antiviral activity when tested in antiviral assays using either Madin Darby bovine kidney (MDBK) cells (2×10^8) or normal sheep fibroblasts (3×10^8). In the same assays, recombinant bovine interferon alpha 1 and NIH recombinant human interferon alpha 1, had activities of 6×10^7 and 2.2×10^8, respectively, using MDBK cells and 1×10^7 and 2.2×10^8 using normal sheep fibroblasts (see Pontzer et al., 1988). A single sheep conceptus secretes an average of 138 μg (range, 10 to 466 μg) of oTP-1 during a 30-h culture period (Vallet & Bazer, 1988), suggesting that trophoblast is among the most active producers of interferon alpha.

A primary role of oTP-1 during pregnancy is as an antiluteolytic paracrine hormone that inhibits pulsatile secretion of PGF by the endometrium and allows maintenance of the CL. Infusion of oTP-1 into the uterine lumen between days 12 and 14 extends the interestrous interval and CL life span (Godkin et al., 1984a; Vallet et al., 1988). The endometrium of cyclic ewes releases PGF in a pulsatile manner between days 15 and 17 of the estrous cycle, and release of about five episodes of PGF within 24 h is required for luteolysis (Zarco et al., 1988a and b). A mechanism to explain the pulsatile release of PGF by the uterus during luteolysis has been proposed by McCracken et al. (1984). According to this model, estradiol from ovarian follicles induces endometrial oxytocin receptors. Pulsatile release of oxytocin from the posterior pituitary and CL stimulates a corresponding pulsatile secretion of PGF by the uterine endometrium (Flint & Sheldrick, 1986; Hooper et al., 1986), resulting in luteolysis. Fincher et al., (1986) found that pregnant ewes have higher basal concentrations of 15-keto-13,14-dihydro-$PGF_{2\alpha}$ (PGFM) than do cyclic ewes on day 15 (193 ± 30 versus 67 ± 8 pg/mL); Lacroix and Kann (1983) demonstrated higher *in vitro* production of PGF from endometrium of pregnant ewes. oTP-1 is therefore assumed to exert its antiluteolytic effect on the endometrium by inhibiting the oxytocin-induced pulsatile secretion of PGF that causes luteolysis in ewes.

oTP-1 is the Antiluteolytic Protein In Sheep

We developed a protocol to test the total array of conceptus secretory proteins (oCSP) and purified oTP-1 for antiluteolytic activity (Fincher et al., 1986). We infused oCSP or serum proteins into the uterine horns of cyclic ewes between days 12 and 14 at 08:00 and 17:00 h. Additionally, 0.5 mg estradiol was injected intravenously at 07:30 h on day 14, and 10 IU oxytocin was administered at 08:05 h on day 15. This allowed us to determine the effects of oCSP on uterine production of PGF after the uterus had been stimulated by estradiol and oxytocin, which are essential for luteolysis. oCSP inhibited uterine production of PGF in response to both hormones. Similarly, pregnant ewes failed to respond to the luteolytic effects associated with estradiol (Fincher et al., 1986; Kittok & Britt, 1977) and oxytocin (Fairclough et al., 1984). Using this same protocol, Vallet et al. (1988) compared the effects of intrauterine infusion of purified oTP-1, oCSP, oCSP depleted of oTP-1, and whole serum proteins on uterine production of PGF. Purified oTP-1 alone had an antiluteolytic effect equivalent to that of oCSP. oCSP depleted of oTP-1 or whole serum proteins did not inhibit uterine production of PGF in response to estradiol and oxytocin and did not extend the interestrous interval. These results indicate that oTP-1 is the only antiluteolytic protein secreted by sheep conceptuses at day 16 of pregnancy.

Mechanism of Action of oTP-1

Hooper et al. (1986) reported that the pattern of release of oxytocin was similar in cyclic and pregnant ewes. However, oxytocin receptors are significantly reduced or absent in pregnant ewes (McCracken et al., 1984). oTP-1 does not compete with oxytocin for its receptor since tritiated oxytocin was not displaced from its endometrial receptors even by a 100-fold excess of oTP-1 (Flint et al., unpublished data). It was of interest to determine whether oTP-1 blocked the effects of oxytocin on phosphatidylinositol turnover, as this is the second messenger system for oxytocin in endometrium (Flint et al., 1986). Overall, oTP-1 inhibited inositol phospholipid turnover, although it did not prevent the long-term (180 min) effects of oxytocin on phosphatidylinositol turnover in endometrium from ewes on day 15 of the estrous cycle after oxytocin receptor formation (Bazer et al., 1988).

Because functional endometrial oxytocin receptors are absent or present in low numbers in pregnant ewes as compared to cyclic ewes (McCracken et al., 1984), oTP-1 may inhibit synthesis of oxytocin receptors. Although this point has not been directly tested as yet, it is known from other systems that interferons can inhibit receptor synthesis, turnover, and movement within membranes (Faltynek et al., 1984; Taylor-Papadimitriou & Rozengurt, 1985). This last possibility is particularly intriguing since stabilization of receptors within membranes may result in loss of receptor binding without decreasing receptor numbers. Furthermore, production of PGF by endometrium of pregnant cattle, in which an oTP-1-like protein called bovine trophoblast protein-1 regulates CL life span, is stimulated by exposure of the endometrium to oxytocin *in vitro* at 42°C, but not at 39°C (Putney et al., 1988). Thermal stress is known to alter membrane fluidity, phospholipase activity, and inositol phospholipid turnover (Calderwood et al., 1987); such findings are therefore consistent with the hypothesis that conceptus interferons immobilize oxytocin receptors.

Endometrial Receptors for oTP-1 and Interferons

High-affinity, low-capacity binding sites for oTP-1 are present in endometrial membranes (Godkin et al., 1984b), and human interferon alpha will displace oTP-1 from those receptors (Stewart et al., 1987). Knickerbocker and Niswender (1989) found that (1) the concentration and affinity of oTP-1 receptors are not different in caruncular and intercaruncular endometrial tissues of sheep; (2) the numbers of unoccupied receptors are similar in cyclic and pregnant ewes on days 8 and 12, but receptor numbers decreased thereafter for pregnant ewes while increasing to day 16 for cyclic ewes; and (3) the affinity of receptors was similar in pregnant and cyclic ewes on days 8 and 12, but then decreased for cyclic ewes while increasing for pregnant ewes. This study did not determine whether the decrease in receptor numbers in pregnant ewes was due to increased occupancy or down-regulation of oTP-1 receptor levels.

Consistent with the above results of oTP-1 binding studies, Salamonsen et al. (1988) demonstrated that sheep endometrial cells respond to both oTP-1 and recombinant human alpha-interferon *in vitro* as measured by decreased production of PGF and enhanced secretion of endometrial proteins. These endometrial proteins are apparently identical to those amplified when oTP-1 is added to endometrial explant cultures (Vallet et al., 1987).

Similarly, intrauterine infusions of recombinant bovine interferon alpha extended the interestrous intervals in sheep to greater than 19.25 days when 2000 μg was infused daily from days 9 through 19; however, daily infusion of 200 μg of interferon had no effect on cycle length (Lamming et al., 1988). Conversely, it was necessary to infuse only 25 μg of oTP-1 per uterine horn twice daily from days 12 to 14 to extend the interestrous interval to over 25 days (Vallet et al., 1988).

Other Species

Pig conceptuses secrete two major classes of proteins with molecular weights of 20 to 25 kDa (pI values of 5.6 to 6.2) and 35 to 50 kDa (pI values of 8.2 to 9.0) between days 10.5 and 18 of gestation (Godkin et al., 1982). Pig conceptus secretory proteins (pCSP) recovered from cultures of day-15 conceptuses include a protein(s) with antiviral activity (Cross & Roberts, 1988; Beers et al., 1990). In one study 4 mg pCSP plus 4 mg serum proteins or 8 mg serum proteins only was introduced into the lumen of each uterine horn twice daily between days 12 and 15 after intramuscular administration of 1 mg estradiol on day 11 (Harney & Bazer, 1988). Blood samples were collected from the inferior vena cava proximal to entry of the utero-ovarian vein every 15 min between 08:00 h and 11:00 h on days 12 to 17, and plasma was assayed for PGFM, PGE, and progesterone. pCSP had no effect on interestrous intervals or on the concentrations of progesterone in plasma. Peak values for PGFM occurred earlier (day 13) and coincided with initiation of pCSP treatment. Also, pCSP-treated gilts had higher concentrations of PGE (272 ± 35 vs. 154 ± 35 pg/mL) than did serum protein treated gilts. These results do not indicate an antiluteolytic role for pCSP (Harney & Bazer, 1988). Estrogens of blastocyst origin appear to be essential for maternal recognition of pregnancy in pigs (Bazer et al., 1982), and pCSP may therefore play other roles in early pregnancy in this species.

In contrast to the pig, conceptus interferons play an important role in regulation of the CL in cows. The day-17 cow conceptus produces a protein called bovine trophoblast protein-1 (bTP-1) that is immunologically cross-reactive with oTP-1 (Helmer et al., 1987) and has extensive amino acid sequence homology with both oTP-1 and alpha-interferons (Imakawa et al., 1989). Intrauterine infusion of bTP-1 extends CL life span and reduces secretion of PGF from the uterus (Helmer et al., 1989), possibly by inducing an intracellular inhibitor of prostaglandin synthesis (Helmer et al., 1988). Similarly, intrauterine and intramuscular administration of recombinant bovine interferon alpha to cows extends the interestrous interval (Plante et al., 1988, 1989), although the mechanisms involved have not been determined.

Immunosuppressive Properties of oTP-1

A general property of interferons is their ability to inhibit lymphocyte proliferation (Bielefeldt-Ohmann et al., 1987). As noted earlier, oTP-1 has immunosuppressive properties and can inhibit mitogen-induced lymphocyte proliferation (Newton et al., 1989), effects similar to those of recombinant bovine (Bielefeldt-Ohmann & Babiuk, 1986) and human (Bielefeldt-Ohmann et al., 1987) interferon alpha. Exogenous interleukin-2 (IL-2) can reverse the inhibitory effects of bovine, but not human recombinant alpha-interferons. The effects of oTP-1 are most like those of human alpha-interferon, since addition of exogenous IL-2 to PHA-stimulated lymphocytes does not overcome the inhibitory effects of oTP-1 (Newton et al., 1989). Furthermore, oTP-1 blocks IL-2-induced proliferation of lymphocytes primed to express IL-2 receptors by PHA treatment. These immunosuppressive effects of oTP-1 were evident even when oTP-1 was added 24 h after the PHA. This result indicates that oTP-1 affects both early (IL-2 secretion and induction of IL-2 receptors) and late (prolongation of G1 and S + G2 phases of the cell cycle) events in lymphocyte activation (Newton et al., 1989). Balkwill and Taylor-Papadimitriou (1978) have suggested that the antiproliferative effects of interferons may be due to effects on length of the cell cycle. The immunosuppressive and antiproliferative effects of oTP-1 in the pregnant uterus may be biologically important to prevent rejection of the allogeneic conceptus by the mother. This effect may complement the inhibitory effects of a high molecular weight glycoprotein and a low molecular weight protein (10 to 14 kDa) secreted by ovine conceptuses that also inhibit mitogen-induced lymphocyte proliferation and mixed lymphocyte culture responses (Newton et al., 1989). Because oTP-1 is an interferon, it is also assumed to have antiproliferative biological activity.

Conclusions

Sheep conceptuses secrete a protein, oTP-1, between days 10 and 21 of gestation, which is a primary secretory factor responsible for establishment of pregnancy. oTP-1 prevents regression of the CL of pregnancy by inhibiting uterine production of luteolytic amounts of PGF despite the presence of estradiol and oxytocin. oTP-1 does not compete with oxytocin for binding to its receptor or interfere with oxytocin stimulation of the inositol phospholipid second messenger system after oxytocin receptors are formed. oTP-1 is a member of a class of interferon-like proteins produced by conceptuses of sheep, cattle, and pigs that have the structural and biological properties of interferons. In sheep, oTP-1 has antiluteolytic, immunosuppressive, antiviral, and possibly other antiproliferative properties. It remains to be determined whether these properties of oTP-1 and related proteins play a part in the antiluteolytic role of these proteins that contributes to survival of the conceptus.

Acknowledgments

Research supported in this chapter has been supported by NIH Grants HD 10436 and HD20671 and U.S. Department of Agriculture Grants 86-CRCR-1-2106 and 85-CRCR-1871. It has been published as University of Florida Agriculture Experiment Station Journal Series No. R00983.

References

Anthony, R. W., Helmer, S. D., Sharif, S. F., Roberts, R. M., Hansen, P. J., Thatcher, W. W., and Bazer, F. W. 1988. Synthesis and processing of ovine trophoblast protein-1 and bovine trophoblast protein-1, conceptus secretory proteins involved in the maternal recognition of pregnancy. *Endocrinology* 123:1274.

Balkwill, F. and Taylor-Papadimitriou, J. 1978. Interferon affects both G1 and S + G2 in cells stimulated from quiescence to growth. *Nature (London)* 274:798.

Bazer, F. W., Geisert, R. D., Thatcher, W. W., and Roberts, R. M. 1982. Endocrine vs exocrine secretion of $PGF_{2\alpha}$ in the control of pregnancy in swine. In *Prostaglandins in Animal Reproduction II* (L. E. Edqvist and

H. Kindahl, eds.). Amsterdam: Elsevier Science Publishers, pp. 115–132.

Bazer, F. W., Vallet, J. L., Roberts, R. M., Sharp, D. C., and Thatcher, W. W. 1986. Role of conceptus secretory products in establishment of pregnancy. *J. Reprod. Fertil.* 76:841.

Bazer, F. W., Vallet, J. L., and Fliss, M. F. V. 1988. Effects of oxytocin, pregnancy and ovine trophoblast protein-one on prostaglandin F2-alpha secretion and phosphatidylinositol turnover by endometrium in vitro. *Biol. Reprod.* 38 (suppl 1):135 (Abst).

Beers, S., Mirando, M. A., Pontzer, C. H., Harney, J. P., Torres, B. A., Johnson, H. M., and Bazer, F. W. 1990. Influence of the endometrium, protease inhibitors and freezing on antiviral activity of proteins secreted by pig conceptuses. *J. Reprod. Fert.* 88:205.

Bielefeldt-Ohmann, H. and Babiuk, L. A. 1986. Alteration of some leukocyte functions following in vivo and in vitro exposure to recombinant bovine interferon alpha I and gamma. *J. Interferon Res.* 6:123.

Bielefeldt-Ohmann, H., Lawman, M. J. P., and Babiuk, L. A. 1987. Bovine interferon: its biology and application in veterinary medicine. *Antiviral Res.* 7:187.

Calderwood, S. K., Stevenson, M. A., and Hahn, G. M. 1987. Heat stress stimulates inositiol triphosphate release and phosphorylation of phosphoinositides in CHO and Balb C 3T3 cells. *J. Cell. Physiol.* 130:3679.

Charpigny, G., Reinaud, P., Huet, J. C., Guillomot, M., Charlier, M., Pernallet, J. C., and Martal, J. 1988. High homology between trophoblastic protein (trophoblastin) isolated from ovine embryo and alpha-interferons. *FEBS Lett.* 228:12.

Cross, J. C. and Roberts, R. M. 1989. Porcine conceptuses secrete an interferon during the preattachment period of early pregnancy. *Biol. Reprod.* 40:1109.

Ellinwood, W. E., Nett, T. M., and Niswender, G. D. 1979. Maintenance of the corpus luteum of early pregnancy in the ewe. I. luteotropic properties of embryonic homogenates. *Biol. Reprod.* 21:281.

Fairclough, R. J., Moore, L. G., Peterson, A. J., and Watkins, W. B. 1984. Effect of oxytocin on plasma concentrations of 13, 14-dihydro-15-keto prostaglandin F and the oxytocin associated neurophysin during the estrous cycle and early pregnancy in the ewe. *Biol. Reprod.* 31:36.

Faltynek, C. R., McCandless, S., and Baglioni, C. 1984. Treatment of lymphoblastoid cells with interferon decreases insulin binding. *J. Cell Physiol.* 121:437.

Fincher, K. B., Bazer, F. W., Hansen, P. J., Thatcher, W. W., and Roberts, R. M. 1986. Proteins secreted by the sheep conceptus suppress induction of uterine prostaglandin $F_{2\alpha}$ release by oestradiol and oxytocin. *J. Reprod. Fertil.* 76:425.

Flint, A. P. F. and Sheldrick, E. L. 1986. Ovarian oxytocin and maternal recognition of pregnancy. *J. Reprod. Fertil.* 76:831.

Flint, A. P. F., Leat, W. M. R., Sheldrick, E. L., and Stewart, H. J. 1986. Stimulation of phosphoinositide hydrolysis by oxytocin and the mechanism by which oxytocin controls prostaglandin synthesis in the ovine endometrium. *Biochem. J.* 237:797.

Godkin, J. D., Bazer, F. W., Moffatt, R. J., Sessions, F., and Roberts, R. M.

1982. Purification and properties of a major, low molecular weight protein released by the trophoblast of sheep blastocysts at Day 13–21. *J. Reprod. Fertil.* 65:141.

Godkin, J. D., Bazer, F. W., Thatcher, W. W., and Roberts, R. M. 1984a. Proteins released by cultured day 15–16 conceptuses prolong luteal maintenance when introduced into the uterine lumen of cyclic ewes. *J. Reprod. Fertil.* 71:57.

Godkin, J. D., Bazer, F. W., and Roberts, R. M. 1984b. Ovine trophoblast protein-1, an early secreted blastocyst protein, binds specifically to uterine endometrium and affects protein synthesis. *Endocrinology* 114:120.

Godkin, J. D., Bazer, F. W., Lewis, G. S., Geisert, R. D., and Roberts, R. M. 1982. Synthesis and release of polypeptides by pig conceptuses during the period of blastocyst elongation and attachment. *Biol. Reprod.* 27:977.

Harney, J. P. and Bazer, F. W. 1989. Effect of porcine conceptus secretory proteins on interestrous interval and uterine secretion of prostaglandins. *Biol. Reprod.* 41:277.

Helmer, S. D., Hanson, P. J., Anthony, R. V., Thatcher, W. W., Bazer, F. W., and Roberts, R. M. 1987. Identification of bovine trophoblast protein-1, a secretory protein immunologically related to ovine trophoblast protein-1. *J. Reprod. Fertil.* 79:83.

Helmer, S. D., Gross, T. S., Hansen, P. J., and Thatcher, W. W. 1988. Bovine conceptus secretory proteins (bCSP) and bovine trophoblast protein-1 (bTP-1), a component of bCSP, alter endometrial prostaglandin (PG) secretion and induce an intracellular inhibitor of PG synthesis in vitro. *Biol. Reprod.* 38 (suppl 1):153 (Abst).

Helmer, S. D., Hansen, P. J., Thatcher, W. W., Johnson, J. W., and Bazer, F. W. 1989. Intrauterine infusion of purified bovine trophoblast protein-1 (bTP-1) extends corpus luteum lifespan in cyclic cattle. *J. Reprod. Fertil.* 87:89.

Hooper, S. B., Watkins, W. B., and Thorburn, G. D. 1986. Oxytocin, oxytocin-associated neurophysin, and prostaglandin $F_{2\alpha}$ concentrations in the utero-ovarian vein of pregnant and nonpregnant sheep. *Endocrinology* 119:2590.

Imakawa, K., Anthony, R. V., Kazemi, M., Maroti, K. R., Polites, H. G., and Roberts, R. M. 1987. Interferon-like sequence of ovine trophoblast protein secreted by embryonic trophectoderm. *Nature* (*London*) 330:377.

Imakawa, K., Hansen, T. R., Malathy, P. V., Anthony, R. V., Polites, H. G., Maroti, K. R., and Roberts, R. M. 1989. Molecular cloning and characteristics of cDNA's corresponding to bovine trophoblast protein-1. A comparison with ovine trophoblast protein 1 and bovine interferon alpha II. *Mol. Endocrinol.* 3:127.

Kittok, R. J. and Britt, J. H. 1977. Corpus luteum function in ewes given estradiol during the estrous cycle or early pregnancy. *J. Anim. Sci.* 45:336.

Knickerbocker, J. J. and Niswender, G. D. 1989. Characterization of endometrial receptors for ovine trophoblast protein-1 during the estrous cycle and early pregnancy in sheep. *Biol. Reprod.* 40:361.

Lacroix, M. C. and Kann, G. 1983. Discriminating analysis of in vitro prostaglandin release by myometrial and luminal sides of the ewe endometrium. *Prostaglandins* 25:853.

Lamming, G. E., Parkinson, T. J., and Flint, A. P. F. 1988. Evidence that bovine alpha-interferon will prolong luteal function in the ewe. *J. Reprod. Fertil.* (Abstract Series 1):22 (Abst).

McCracken, J. A., Schramm, W., and Okulicz, W. C. 1984. Hormone receptor control of pulsatile secretion of $PGF_{2\alpha}$ from the ovine uterus during luteolysis and its abrogation in early pregnancy. In *Prostaglandins in Animal Reproduction II* (L. E. Edqvist and H. Kindahl, eds.). Amsterdam: Elsevier, pp. 31–56.

Moor, R. M. and Rowson, L. E. A. 1966a. The corpus luteum of the sheep: effect of the removal of embryos on luteal function. *J. Endocrinol.* 34:497.

Moor, R. M. and Rowson, L. E. A. 1966b. The corpus luteum of the sheep: functional relationship between the embryo and the corpus luteum. *J. Endocrinol.* 34:233.

Newton, G. R., Vallet, J. L., Hansen, P. J., and Bazer, F. W. 1989. Inhibition of lymphocyte proliferation by ovine trophoblast protein-1 and a high-molecular-weight glycoprotein produced by the peri-implantation sheep conceptus. *Am. J. Reprod. Immunol.* 19:99.

Plante, C., Hansen, P. J., and Thatcher, W. W. 1988. Prolongation of luteal lifespan in cows by intrauterine infusion of recombinant alpha-interferon. *Endocrinology* 122:2342.

Plante, C., Hansen, P. J., Martinod, S., Siegenthaler, B., Thatcher, W. W., Pollard, J. W., and Leslie, M. V. 1989. Intrauterine and intramuscular administration of recombinant bovine interferon-$alpha_I$-I prolongs luteal lifespan in cattle. *J. Dairy Sci* (in press).

Pontzer, C. H., Torres, B. Z., Vallet, J. L., Bazer, F. W., and Johnson, H. M. 1988. Antiviral activity of the pregnancy recognition hormone ovine trophoblast protein-1. *Biochem. Biophys. Res. Comm.* 152:801.

Putney, D. J., Gross, T. S., and Thatcher, W. W. 1988. Prostaglandin secretion by endometrium of pregnant and cyclic cattle at Day 17 after oestrus in response to in-vitro heat stress. *J. Reprod. Fertil.* 84:475.

Salamonsen, L. A., Stuchbery, S. J., O'Grady, C. M., Godkin, J. D., and Findlay, J. K. 1988. Interferon-alpha mimics effects of ovine trophoblast protein-1 on prostaglandin and protein secretion by ovine endometrial cells in vitro. *J. Endocrinol.* 117:R1.

Stewart, H. J., McCann, S. H. E., Barker, P. J., Lee, K. E., Lamming, G. E., and Flint, A. P. F. 1987. Interferon sequence homology and receptor binding activity of ovine trophoblast antiluteolytic protein. *J. Endocrinol.* 115:R13.

Taylor-Papadimitriou, J. and Rozengurt, E. 1985. Interferons as regulators of cell growth and differentiation. In *Interferons: Their Impact In Biology and Medicine* (J. Taylor-Papadimitriou, ed.). Oxford: Oxford University Press, pp. 81–98.

Vallet, J. L., Bazer, F. W., and Roberts, R. M. 1987. The effect of ovine trophoblast protein-one on endometrial protein secretion and cyclic nucleotides. *Biol. Reprod.* 37:1316.

Vallet, J. L., Bazer, F. W., Fliss, M. F. V., and Thatcher, W. W. 1988. Effect of ovine conceptus secretory proteins and purified ovine trophoblast protein-1 on interoestrous interval and plasma concentrations of prostaglandins F-2a and E and of 13, 14-dihydro-15-keto prostaglandin F-2a in cyclic ewes. *J. Reprod. Fertil.* 84:493.

Vallet, J. L. and Bazer, F. W. 1988. The effect of sire on production of ovine trophoblast protein-one *J. Anim. Sci.* 66 (suppl 1):416, (Abst).

Wilson, M. E., Lewis, G. S., and Bazer, F. W. 1979. Proteins of ovine blastocyst origin. *Biol. Reprod.* 20 (suppl 1):101 (Abst).

Zarco, L., Stabenfeldt, G. H., Quirke, J. F., Kindahl, H., and Bradford, G. E. 1988a. Release of prostaglandin F-2 alpha and the timing of events associated with luteolysis in ewes with oestrous cycles of different lengths. *J. Reprod. Fertil.* 83:517.

Zarco, L., Stabenfeldt, G. H., Basu, S., Bradford, G. E., and Kindahl, H. 1988b. Modification of prostaglandin F-2 alpha synthesis and release in the ewe during the initial establishment of pregnancy. *J. Reprod. Fertil.* 83:527.

17

Colony-Stimulating Factor-1: A Growth Factor for Trophoblasts?

JEFFREY W. POLLARD, ROBERT J. ARCECI,
ANNA BARTOCCI, and E. RICHARD STANLEY

Implantation in the mouse begins with invasion of the trophectoderm through the antimesometrial luminal epithelium of the uterus. This process triggers decidualization in the underlying uterine stroma and allows the continuation of embryonic development (Finn & Porter, 1975). Coincidentally with this invasion of the trophectoderm, the uterine epithelium breaks down. As a result of rapid trophoblast proliferation and migration, derivatives of these cells line the uterine cavity and completely surround the conceptus. This lining is surrounded in turn by maternal decidua. Further proliferation of the polar trophoblasts finally results in the formation of the chorioallantoic placenta with cells of the maternal decidua, extra-embryonic ectoderm, and allantois (Kaufman, 1983; Rossant, 1986). Thus, development of the placenta poses important questions concerning the regulation of the growth and function of these diverse cells, as well as how the fetally derived cells expressing foreign antigens are protected from immunological rejection.

Within the developing placenta there is rapid proliferation of trophoblasts, with doubling times as short as 4.5 hours in humans (Snow, 1978). As the rapid proliferation of several other cell types within tissues appears to be under the control of specific growth factors, it is likely that these factors are also involved in trophoblast proliferation. The chorioallantoic placenta and the uterus have been shown to produce PDGF (Goustin et al., 1985), IGF-1, IGF-11 (Fant et al., 1986), hemopoietic growth factors (Bradley et al., 1971, Burgess et al., 1977), TGFα (Han et al., 1987), and EGF (Adamson, 1987). Trophoblasts have also been shown to express receptors for some of these growth factors, raising the possibility of autocrine or paracrine stimulation. However, detailed studies of the timing of growth factor synthesis in relation to placental growth and development have not yet been reported. Recently, we observed that colony-stimulating factor-1 (CSF-1) was produced in large amounts by the mouse uterus during pregnancy (Bartocci et al., 1986; Pollard et al., 1987). Expression of its receptor (CSF-1R), the product of the c-*fms* proto-oncogene (reviewed in Sherr, 1988), had previously been detected at the mRNA level in murine and human placentas (Müller et al., 1983a and b), by *in situ* hybridization in human placental trophoblasts (Hoshina et al., 1985), and at the protein level on choriocarcinoma cells (Rettenmier et al., 1986). Together these data suggest that CSF-1 is a trophoblast growth factor. In this chapter, we report that the timing and site of expression of CSF-1 and CSF-1R during pregnancy are consistent with such a role for CSF-1 in placental growth and function.

CSF-1

Uterine CSF-1

Site and Timing of Uterine CSF-1 Synthesis. CSF-1 (or M-CSF) is a homodimeric glycoprotein, the molecular weight of which varies from 45 kDa to 90 kDa depending on the source and/or method of preparation. Differences in the molecular weight are due to variable glycosylation and C-terminal proteolysis (Cerretti et al., 1988; Das and Stanley, 1982; Wong et al., 1987). CSF-1 was first described as a circulating growth factor that regulates survival, proliferation, and differentiation of mononuclear phagocytes (reviewed in Sherr & Stanley, 1989). The response of these cells to CSF-1 is pleiotropic. It includes rapid, early morphological changes (Morgan et al., 1987; Tushinski et al., 1982), elevation of protein synthesis, and inhibition of protein degradation (Tushinski et al., 1982). In addition, CSF-1 stimulates the production of cytokines, including IL-2 (Moore et al., 1980), G-CSF (Metcalf & Nicola, 1985), interferons (Moore et al., 1984), and tumor necrosis factor (Warren & Ralph, 1986); potentiates the release of bioactive compounds, such as plasminogen activator (Hamilton et al., 1980; Lin & Gordon, 1979); and induces cell proliferation (Tushinski & Stanley, 1985; Tushinski et al., 1982).

An additional role for colony-stimulating factors outside of the hematopoietic system was suggested initially by the observation of elevated colony-stimulating activity in the pregnant uterus of the mouse (Bradley et al., 1971; Rosendaal, 1975). By using a RIA that detects only biologically active CSF-1, Bartocci, Pollard, and Stanley (1986) showed that a substantial proportion of this colony-stimulating activity is CSF-1 and further that there was a cumulative increase in the concentration of uterine CSF-1 throughout pregnancy. At term this increase was approximately 1000-fold, representing a 10,000-fold increase in amount of CSF-1 per organ (Fig. 17-1). Similar increases in

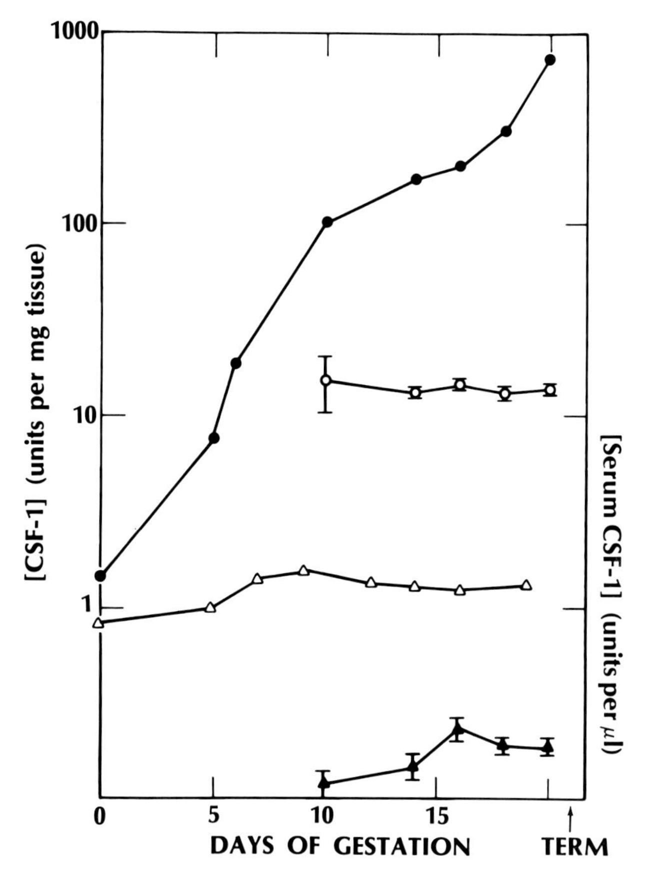

Fig. 17-1. CSF-1 concentrations in the uterus, placenta, fetus and serum during pregnancy. Points represent the means of triplicate determinations of individual C3H/HeJ mice for uterine (●) and maternal serum (△) CSF-1 concentrations. Placental (○) and fetal (▲) CSF-1 concentrations are the means of determinations on three animals performed in triplicate ± SD One unit represents 0.44 fMol of CSF-1. The day that the vaginal plug was detected was designated as day 0 in this figure. (From Bartocci, Pollard & Stanley, 1986, *JEM* 164:956–961, with permission.)

CSF-1 concentrations have been detected in other strains of mice (our unpublished observations).

To determine if CSF-1 was synthesized during pregnancy in these reproductive tissues or had simply accumulated from the serum in which it has a short half-life of 10 min (Bartocci et al., 1987), uterine RNA was isolated and subjected to Northern blot analysis (Pollard et al., 1987) using a cDNA probe to mouse CSF-1 (Ladner et al., 1988). A major 2.3 kb (91%) and a minor 4.6 kb (9%) species were detected in the gravid uterus of endotoxin-unresponsive C3H/HeJ mice, show-

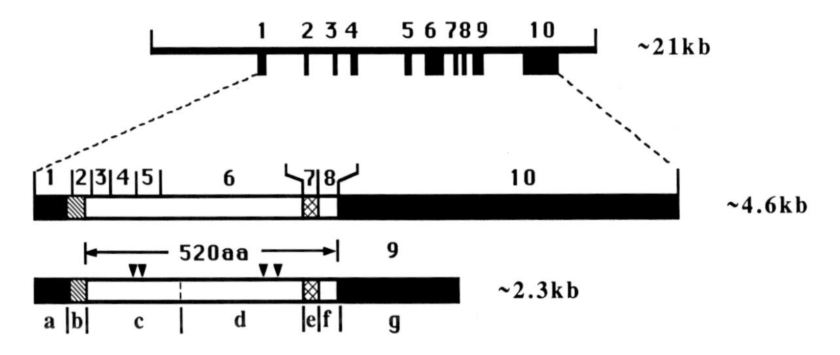

Fig. 17-2. Schematic representation of the two mouse CSF-1 mRNAs. The CSF-1 genomic structure shown is that of the human gene. The numbering of the filled bar indicates the 10 exons of the approximately 21-kb gene. DNA sequencing of two mouse L-cell cDNAs has shown that the 2.3-kb and 4.6-kb mRNA are produced from alternative splicing of exon 8 with either exon 9 or exon 10. Both clones give a 520 amino acid primary translation product. From the DNA sequence analysis and comparison with the partial protein sequence of the mature product the organization of the mRNA has been deduced as follows: a: 5′ untranslated sequence, b: signal peptide, c: mature subunit, d: spacer, e: transmembrane domain; f: intracellular domain, g: 3′ untranslated region. ▼ Potential asn-X-ser/thr N-glycosylation sites. (Data from Ladner et al., 1987 and 1988).

ing that CSF-1 is synthesized in the uterus during pregnancy. Neither of these mRNAs was detected in the nongravid uterus (Pollard et al., 1987). Conversely, in the mouse L-cell line, which is widely used as a source of CSF-1 (Stanley & Heard, 1977), the 4.6 kb species is the predominant form (Pollard et al., 1987). The 2.3 and 4.6 kb mRNAs differ only in their 3′ untranslated region as a result of an alternative use of exons 9 and 10 (Fig. 17-2); (Ladner et al., 1988). The 3 ′ sequence spliced out in the 2.3 kb form contains three repeats, within 58 bp, of the conserved AUUUA sequence shown to confer mRNA instability (Shaw & Kamen, 1986). Although measurements of relative CSF-1 mRNA stabilities have not been made, it is tempting to suggest that in fibroblasts the longer and putatively more unstable form is produced so that levels of CSF-1 can be modulated quickly in response to transient immunological challenges by such agents as endotoxin. By contrast, it might be expected that a constant supply of CSF-1 is required in the uterus over the 19-day period of pregnancy and the more stable 2.3 kb mRNA would be produced. In endotoxin-responsive, randomly bred Schneider mice or inbred C57Bl/6 mice there is relatively more (up to 30%) of the 4.6 kb CSF-1 mRNA species. It is possible that the relative increase in the 4.6 kb species in these endotoxin-responsive mice may be due to endotoxin-induced mRNA expression in uterine fibroblasts.

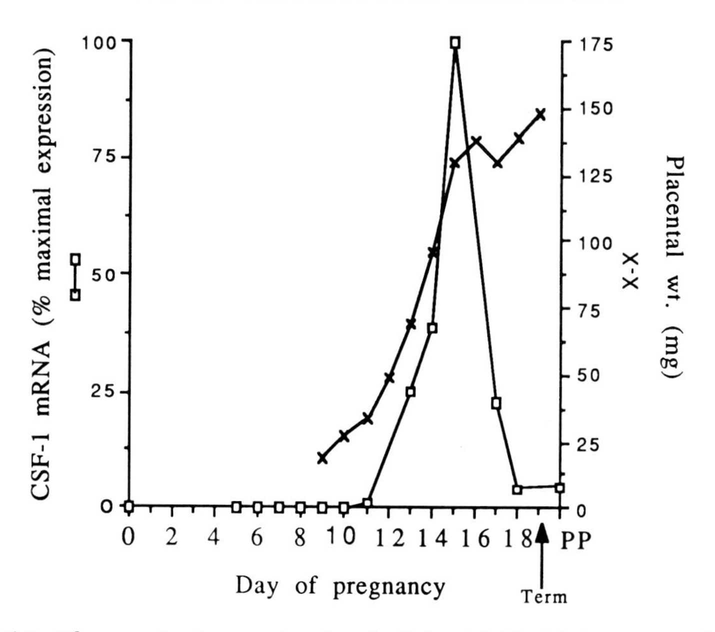

Fig. 17-3. Changes in the uterine level of the 2.3-kb CSF-1 mRNA during gestation. Total Schneider mouse uterine RNA was isolated from individual mice on different days of pregnancy and subjected to Northern blot analysis using a [^{32}P]-dCTP labeled cDNA corresponding to the 2.3-kb CSF-1 mRNA. Following autoradiography CSF-1 mRNA bands were quantitated by densitometry. The blot was reprobed with a radiolabeled ribosomal cDNA and the CSF-1 mRNA levels (□) corrected for differential loading and transfer by the level of 18S rRNA in each individual sample. Placental weights (X) were obtained after dissecting the placenta free of the uterus, embryo and fetal membranes. Values shown are the mean of at least eight placentae. In this figure and all places in the text, day 1 of pregnancy is defined as the day that the vaginal plug was detected. In this strain gestation is 19.1 ± 0.9 days (mean ± SD).

The 2.3 kb species was first observed between days 5 and 7 of pregnancy. Between days 11 and 15, it underwent a further >100-fold amplification to reach a maximum at day 15 (Fig. 17-3). The pattern of the expression of the 4.6 kb mRNA closely followed that of the 2.3kb species. After day 15, both species showed a relative decline, but could still be detected in the postpartum uterus. The period of maximal CSF-1 mRNA amplification coincides with the period of maximal placental growth (Fig. 17-3). *In situ* hybridization using antisense RNA probes derived from the CSF-1 cDNA revealed intense hybridization to the luminal and glandular epithelium (Pollard et al., 1987). The timing of expression was similar to that shown by Northern blotting, with mRNA being first detectable at day 4 and maximal levels observed at days 14 to 15. *In situ* analysis of day 11 uteri also revealed that the CSF-1 mRNA was distributed uniformly throughout the uterus and was not restricted to the regions around the conceptus. Similar conclusions were drawn from Northern blot analysis of RNA isolated from day 7 and 8 implantations and nonimplantation sites (our unpublished data). Therefore, CSF-1 mRNA is expressed in most if not all uterine epithelial cells during pregnancy.

Based on immunological and biochemical data, the CSF-1 synthesized by the uterus appears to be identical to L-cell CSF-1 (Pollard et al., 1987). This is not unexpected because the 2.3 and 4.6 kb mRNAs from mouse L-cells both encode the same protein molecule (Ladner et al., 1988). Analysis of the biosynthesis and release of CSF-1 has been carried out in mouse 3T3 cells transfected with human cDNA clones. It was shown that CSF-1 is synthesized from the human 4 kb clone as a transmembrane glycoprotein that is assembled into disulphide-linked dimers and rapidly cleaved in secretory vesicles to produce the soluble growth factor (Manos, 1988; Rettenmier & Roussel, 1988). These two groups of workers were unable to detect cell surface expression of CSF-1, although Cerretti et al. (1988), using a similar expression vector construct transfected into simian *cos* cells, were able to detect a cell surface form of CSF-1. In humans two molecular clones have been obtained for cDNAs that are smaller than the 2.3 kb species. One, corresponding to a 1.6 kb mRNA, was shown to have lost 298 amino acid residues from the amino-terminal side of the putative transmembrane sequence due to splicing out of the 5′ end of exon 6 and to have an alternatively spliced 3′ untranslated region (Kawasaki et al., 1985; Ladner et al., 1987). The protein product from this clone is processed in a similar manner to that of the 4 kb clone except that the assembled dimers lack the endoplasmic reticulum proteolytic cleavage site. They are therefore expressed on the cell surface from which they are released slowly by extracellular proteolytic cleavage (Rettenmier et al., 1987). A 1.6 kb mRNA species has been detected in mouse liver (Rajavashisth et al., 1987), but not at significant levels in the mouse uterus (Pollard et al., 1987). This species has yet to be molecularly cloned in the mouse. The second human cDNA is approximately 1.9 kb, and its product lacks 116 amino acids as compared to the protein product synthesized from the 4 kb mRNA. The CSF-1 precursor produced in *cos* cells from this 1.9 kb clone is processed in a similar fashion to that of the 4 kb clone, with both soluble and cell surface forms being produced (Cerretti et al., 1988). The presence of the cell surface form of CSF-1 led us to suggest that CSF-1 could act as an adhesion molecule for the attachment of c-*fms*-bearing trophoblasts to the epithelium during implantation and invasion of the maternal stroma (Pollard et al., 1987).

Hormonal Regulation of Uterine CSF-1 Production. Significant elevations of uterine CSF-1 levels are detected by day 5 of pregnancy.

This elevation could also be induced by four daily injections of human chorionic gonadotrophin (HCG) (Bartocci et al., 1986). The HCG effect was abolished by ovariectomy or concomitant administration of the antiprogestin, RU 486 (Bartocci et al., 1986; Pollard et al., 1987), suggesting the involvement of ovarian steroids. To confirm this hypothesis, ovariectomized and estrogen-primed C3H/HeJ mice were treated with estradiol-17β (E_2) and progesterone (P), either individually or in combination, in doses designed to give levels similar to those found during early pregnancy (Finn & Martin, 1982). After 7 days of treatment either E_2 (25 ng/day) or P (1 mg/day) produced a small but significant increase in uterine CSF-1 concentration. There was a synergistic effect of the two hormones when they were administered together, increasing the CSF-1 concentration by 4.2-fold. This increase was further amplified to 14.5 times the control level when the animals were given a decidual stimulus of arachis oil 3 days after the beginning of the hormone treatment. The resulting uterine concentrations were comparable to those found at an equivalent day of pregnancy (Pollard et al., 1987).

Ten ng of E_2 is optimal for the uterine decidual response, but doses of 25 to 50 ng are relatively inhibitory. However, doses of E_2 ranging from 25 to 50 ng gave higher levels of CSF-1 than did a 10 ng dose, suggesting that although the decidual stimulus is required for CSF-1 induction, the maternal decidual response is not itself necessary (Pollard et al., 1987). Removal of E_2 from the $P + E_2$ hormone regime after the fourth day resulted in decreasing in uterine CSF-1 levels to below control levels (Pollard et al., 1987), although P administration alone is reported to be sufficient to maintain the decidual response (Finn & Martin, 1972). Thus, in ovariectomized mice, induction of uterine CSF-1 to levels comparable to day 9 of pregnancy requires the continued synergistic action of P and E_2 and a stimulus to the uterine epithelium capable of eliciting a decidual response.

To confirm that the hormonally induced increase in CSF-1 concentration was due to uterine synthesis, uterine RNA isolated from $P + E_2$-treated mice that had also been given a decidual stimulus was subjected to Northern blot analysis with the mouse cDNA probe. A single 2.3 kb band could be detected at a level comparable to that found at the equivalent day of pregnancy (Pollard et al., 1987; our unpublished data). Thus, treatment with these steroids appears to act principally by inducing an increased level of the alternatively spliced 2.3-kb CSF-1 mRNA.

Placental and Fetal CSF-1

Placental CSF-1 concentrations were 10–100-fold lower than in uterine tissue at an equivalent stage of pregnancy, and did not vary significantly during gestation (Fig. 17–1). Fetal CSF-1 concentrations, although showing some variation throughout pregnancy, were three orders of magnitude less than those in the uterus (Bartocci et al., 1986). These levels were determined in whole fetuses and do not exclude significant tissue-specific expression in the fetus during development. We have also found CSF-1 in amniotic fluid. At day 14, the amniotic fluid CSF-1 concentration was 4070 fmol/mL, and then declined later in pregnancy (our unpublished data). These data confirm results of Azoulay, Webb, and Sachs (1987), who showed high macrophage colony-stimulating activity (presumably CSF-1) in amniotic fluid at days 9–13, which subsequently declined steadily to term.

Although CSF-1 was detected at significant levels in the placenta, only trace amounts of 2.3 kb CSF-1 mRNA were found in Northern blots in two out of six samples tested (Pollard et al., 1987; our unpublished data). No evidence for CSF-1 mRNA expression was found by *in situ* hybridization in the placenta and extra-embryonic membranes (Pollard et al., 1987). Azoulay, Webb, and Sachs (1987), however, found both 2.8 kb and a 4.6 kb mRNA species in the murine placenta at all times of gestation, and Wong et al. (1987) described an $\simeq$ 4 kb species in human term placenta. The reasons for the discrepancy between our data and those of Azoulay, Webb, and Sachs (1987), both obtained in the mouse, are not clear. The variations in transcript size reported by Azoulay et al. (1987) may be due to aberrant mobilities of DNA size markers on formaldehyde gels (Wicks, 1986). However, the mRNA sizes of 2.3 kb and 4.6 kb reported by Pollard et al. (1987) correspond to the sizes of the cDNA clones reported by Ladner et al. (1988). It is possible that the two species were detected by Azoulay, Webb, and Sachs (1987) because of the use of poly A^+ RNA. Alternatively, the placental samples used for mRNA preparation could have been contaminated with small amounts of uterine tissue. Our combined Northern analysis and *in situ* hybridization data show, however, that neither the placenta nor the extra-embryonic membranes are significant sites of CSF-1 synthesis, suggesting that the CSF-1 detected in the placenta and amniotic fluid is largely, if not completely, synthesized in the uterus.

CSF-1 Receptor (c-*fms* Product)

The CSF-1R is a 165 kd transmembrane glycoprotein with tyrosine kinase activity (reviewed in Sherr, 1988; Sherr & Stanley, 1989). It is the cellular homologue of the v-*fms* oncogene that is contained in the Susan McDonough strain of feline sarcoma virus (Sherr et al., 1985). The CSF-1R is selectively expressed at high levels on cells of the mononuclear phagocytic lineage as a single class of high-affinity binding sites (Byrne et al., 1981; Guilbert & Stanley, 1980). In macrophages, CSF-1 binding initially stimulates tyrosine phosphorylation of the receptor. This event is followed by tyrosine phosphorylation of several membrane and cytoplasmic proteins that are presumably involved in mediating the pleiotropic response to CSF-1 (Sengupta et al., 1988).

Before it was known that the CSF-1R was the c-*fms* protooncogene product, v-*fms* was used to determine the pattern of expression of c-*fms* in both fetal and adult tissues. It was found to be expressed in adult spleen and in the inner and outer portions of the placenta (Müller et al., 1983a and b). After the c-*fms* product was identified as the CSF-1R, it was found to be expressed on human choriocarcinoma cell lines (Rettenmier et al., 1986) and trophoblasts (Hoshina et al., 1985). To determine whether the expression of placental cell CSF-1R coincides with the production of uterine CSF-1, we have studied the time course of CSF-1R mRNA expression in the Schneider strain mouse placenta and uterus. Significant expression of a 4.5 kb species was first detected in day 9 placenta. Expression persisted through pregnancy, although with significant tailing off after day 17. The timing of the changes in levels of c-*fms* expression was similar to that observed for CSF-1 mRNA in the uterus.

Before the formation of the placenta, total uterine RNA samples from days 5 to 8 had low but detectable levels of c-*fms* mRNA. Because the uterine samples also contained developing embryos, this c-*fms* expression could be in decidual cells, macrophages, or trophoblasts. To investigate this possibility and to establish which cells of the placenta express the CSF-1R, we performed *in situ* hybridization using a mouse c-*fms* cDNA clone (Rothwell & Rohrschneider, 1987). c-*fms* mRNA was detected on cells of the trophectoderm at day 5 of pregnancy. Thereafter, mRNA levels per cell increased through day 14 to 15 and then declined until term, in a pattern similar to that observed on the Northern blots. In the mature placenta, the highest levels of c-*fms* expression were detected on giant trophoblasts, and this expression continued uniformly on the giant trophoblast layer around the conceptus. Significant expression was also found in the spongiotrophoblast layer and to a much lesser extent in the labyrinth of the placenta (Fig. 17-4; Arceci et al., 1989; Regenstreif & Rossant, 1989). Thus, expression of the CSF-1R in the placenta coincides precisely with expression of uterine CSF-1 mRNA and with periods of rapid placental growth. These data, therefore, strongly support a role for CSF-1 in placental development.

Is There an Immunological Role for Uterine CSF-1?

It has been suggested that T cells can be activated directly by trophoblasts to produce lymphokines, such as GM-CSF and IL-3. These lymphokines, in turn, have been proposed to stimulate trophoblast proliferation and thus may play an important role in placental for-

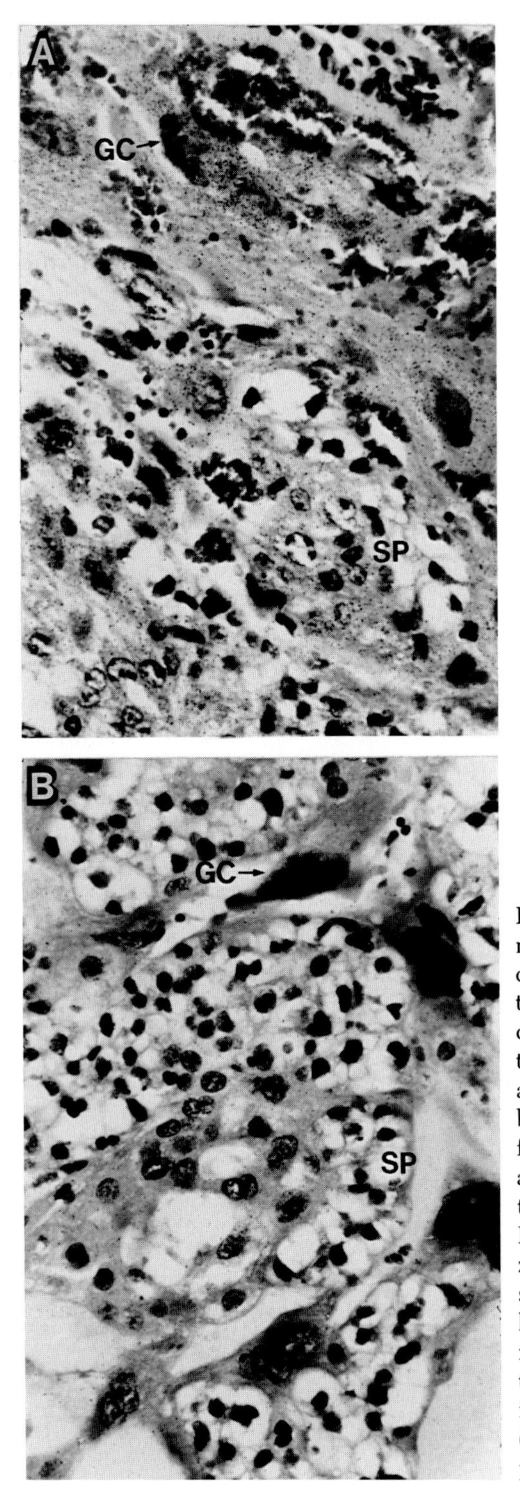

Fig. 17-4. CSF-1 receptor mRNA detected in the placenta by *in situ* hybridization. Day 11 gravid uteri containing placentas and fetuses were fixed, sectioned and subjected to *in situ* hybridization as described before (Arceci et al., 1988) using a [^{32}P]-CTP radiolabeled antisense (A) or sense (B) c-*fms* RNA probe. After hybridization and autoradiography, sections were stained with hematoxylin and eosin. The figure shows transverse sections of the placenta indicating giant trophoblast cells (GC) and the spongiotrophoblast layer (SP).

mation (Wegmann, 1984). This has been termed the immunostimulatory hypothesis (Wegmann, 1984, 1988). CSF-1, although not a lymphokine, has been considered to be part of such a response because of its role in mononuclear phagocyte production and because it can act synergistically with T cell growth factors in hematopoiesis (Athanassakis et al., 1987; Wegmann, 1988). The uniform production of CSF-1 through the uterus suggests, however, that T cell activation does not stimulate local synthesis of CSF-1 at the implantation site. Furthermore, the very early appearance of uterine CSF-1 under control of the female endocrine system suggests that its production serves a physiological rather than an immunological role. Thus, if it were involved in the immunostimulatory response, it would have to be as a syngeristic factor acting with locally produced T cell lymphokines. It has yet to be established whether T cell lymphokines are produced locally *in vivo* and at appropriate times to account for placental growth. Indeed, studies to date have yielded conflicting results (Azoulay et al., 1987; Burgess et al., 1977).

Macrophages also accumulate in the uterus and placenta during pregnancy (Bulmer & Johnson, 1984; Hunt, et al., 1985; Wood, 1980). We assume that the high level of uterine CSF-1 has a role in this accumulation, especially as CSF-1 has recently been shown to be chemotactic for mononuclear phagocytes (Wang et al., 1988). These uterine and placental macrophages may be involved in the regulation of the maternal immune response to the allogeneic fetus (Hunt et al., 1984). Although CSF-1 appears to have little direct effect on the immune functions of macrophages (Nathan et al., 1984) it is not inconceivable that CSF-1 might have an immunological as well as a physiological role in placental biology.

Summary

The trophoblastic expression of the CSF-1R and synthesis of uterine CSF-1 are correlated with the period of maximal placental growth, suggesting that CSF-1 regulates trophoblast growth throughout the entire period of placental development. This hypothesis is supported by the observation that CSF-1 stimulates [^{3}H]-thymidine incorporation into cultured, primary murine placental cells and induces proliferation of cell lines derived from the placenta (Athanassakis et al., 1987; Chapter 18, this volume). In addition, the observed expression of CSF-1R on proliferating trophoblasts, including those of the ectoplacental cone and the spongiotrophoblastic and labyrinthine layers of the definitive placenta, supports such a conclusion. CSF-1 probably has other roles in addition to its effects on proliferation, because it continues to accumulate in the uterus even after the placenta has ceased to grow. Furthermore, the highest expression of the CSF-1 receptor is detected on nonproliferative giant trophoblasts. Although

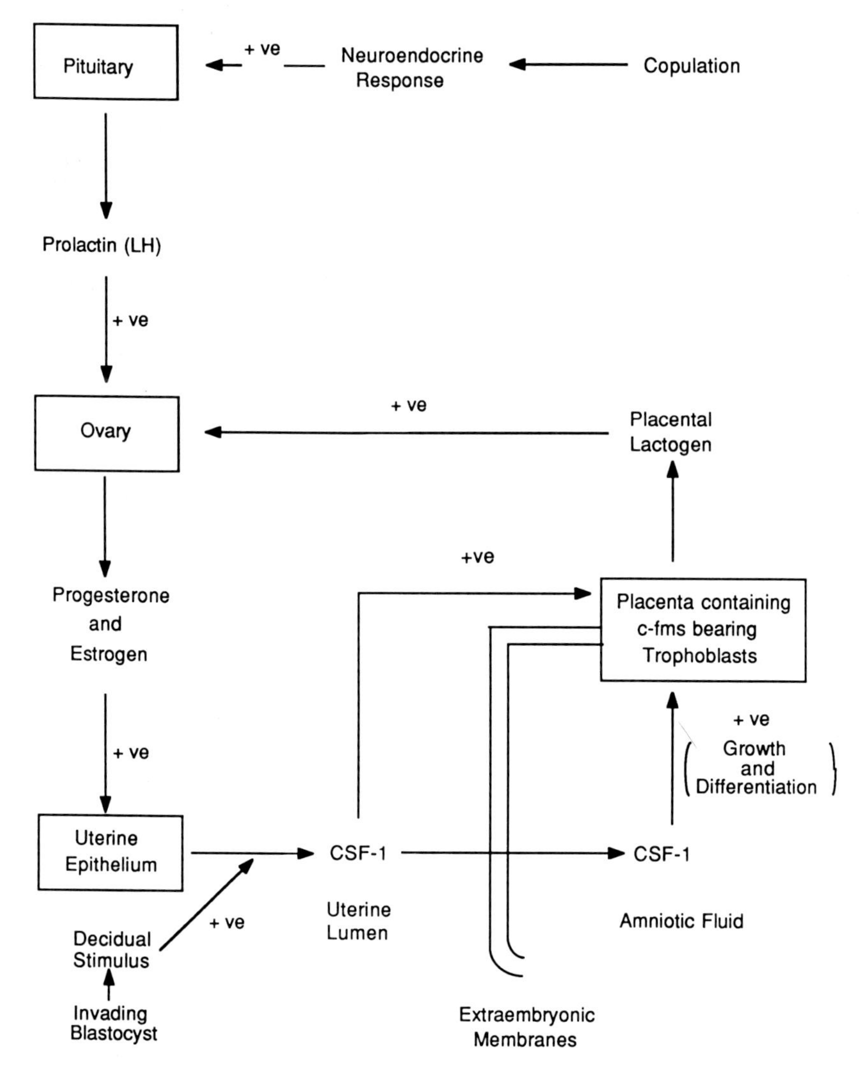

Fig. 17-5. A scheme for the regulation of murine placental development indicating the putative role of CSF-1. The +ve signs indicate a positive induction of hormone or growth factor production.

these giant cells continue to endoreduplicate their DNA (Zybina, 1961) they also have diverse endocrine functions (Soares et al., 1985). Both of these functions may be under the control of CSF-1. In this context, it is of interest to note that CSF-1 has pleiotropic effects on mononuclear phagocytes, promoting their survival, proliferation, and differentiation, as well as regulating them to synthesize other cytokines (Stanley et al., 1983).

Figure 17-5 summarizes our working hypothesis for the regulation of uterine CSF-1 and its involvement in placental development. In the mouse, copulation acts through a neuroendocrine loop to stimulate the pituitary to secrete prolactin (Gunnet & Freeman, 1983). Prolactin probably acts with luteinizing hormone (LH) to allow the maintenance of the corpus luteum and thus the synthesis of progesterone (P). P in turn acts synergistically with E_2 to prepare the uterus for implantation, and at the same time stimulates synthesis of CSF-1 by uterine epithelial cells. Uterine CSF-1 synthesis is enhanced further by the decidual stimulus given by the invading blastocyst. CSF-1 secreted directly into the uterine lumen early in pregnancy stimulates c-*fms*-expressing trophoblasts to grow and invade the uterus. As pregnancy proceeds and the extra-embryonic membranes are formed, CSF-1 is transported by an unknown mechanism across these membranes into the amniotic fluid. Fetal trophoblasts are then stimulated by CSF-1 to grow and differentiate until the mature placenta is formed. During this process, giant cells, perhaps under the influence of CSF-1, produce placental lactogen (PL) 1 and then PL 2 (Soares et al., 1985). PLs act on the corpus luteum to sustain production of both P and E_2, which are required to maintain pregnancy. These two sex steroids further stimulate uterine production of CSF-1. This CSF-1 in turn acts on the trophoblasts, to stimulate their growth and differentiation as appropriate.

In addition to the female sex steroid stimulation of CSF-1 production, the dramatic increase in CSF-1 mRNA observed around day 12 suggests that another stimulus occurs at about that time. Similarly, in the later stages of pregnancy, CSF-1 and c-*fms* mRNA levels per cell begin to decline despite the continuing high P and E_2 levels, suggesting that additional mechanisms may regulate expression of these mRNAs. These diverse roles for CSF-1 in the placenta and the regulation of CSF-1 and its receptor expression through pregnancy remain to be explored.

Acknowledgments

We thank Dr. L. Rohrschneider for the mouse c-*fms* cDNA probe and Frances Shanahan for excellent technical assistance. This work was supported by NIH grants HD25074(JWP), IGM38156(RA), and CA26504(ERS); The Albert Einstein Core Cancer Grant, P30-CA1330(JWP, ERS); and the Lucille P. Markey Charitable Trust (ERS).

References

Adamson, E. D. 1987 Oncogenes in development. *Development* 99:449–471.

Arceci, R. J., Croop, J., Horwitz, S., and Housman, D. 1988. The gene encoding multidrug resistance is induced and expressed at high levels during pregnancy in the secretory epithelium of the uterus. *Proc. Natl. Acad. Sci. USA* 85:4350–4354.

Arceci, R. J., Shanahan, F., Stanley, E. R., and Pollard, J. W. 1989. Temporal expression and location of colony-stimulating factor 1 (CSF-1) and its receptor in the female reproductive tract are consistent with CSF-1 regulated placental development. *Proc. Natl. Acad. Sci. USA* 86:8818–8822.

Athanassakis, I., Bleackley, C. R., Paetkau, V., Guilbert, L., Barr, P. J., and Wegmann, T. G. 1987. The immunostimulatory effect of T cells and T cell lymphokines on murine fetally derived placental cells. *J. Immunol.* 138:37–44.

Azoulay, M., Webb, C. G., and Sachs, L. 1987. Control of hematopoietic cell growth regulators during mouse fetal development. *Mol. Cell. Biol.* 7:3361–3363.

Bartocci, A., Pollard, J. W., and Stanley, E. R. 1986. Regulation of colony stimulating factor-1 during pregnancy. *J. Exp. Med.* 164:956–961.

Bartocci, A., Mastrogiannis, D. S., Migliorati, G., Stockert, R. J., Wolkoff, A. W., and Stanley, E. R. 1987. Macrophages specifically regulate the concentration of their own growth factor in the circulation. *Proc. Natl. Acad. Sci. USA* 84:6179–6183.

Bradley, T. R., Stanley, E. R., and Sumner, M. A. 1971. Factors from mouse tissues stimulating colony growth of mouse bone marrow cells in vitro. *Aust. J. Exp. Biol. Med. Sci.* 49:595–603.

Bulmer, J. M. and Johnson, P. M. 1984. Macrophage populations in the human placenta and amniochorion. *Clin. Exp. Immunol.* 57:393–403.

Burgess, A. W., Wilson, E. M. A., and Metcalf, D. 1977. Stimulation by human placental conditioned medium of hemopoietic colony formation by human marrow cells. *Blood* 49:573–583.

Byrne, P. V., Guilbert, L. J., and Stanley, E. R. 1981. Distribution of cells bearing receptors for a colony stimulating factor (CSF-1) in murine tissues. *J. Cell. Biol.* 91:848–853.

Cerretti, D. P., Wignall, J., Anderson, D., Tushinski, R. J., Gallis, B. M., Stya, M., Gillis, S., Urdal, D. L., and Cosman, D. 1988. Human macrophage-colony stimulating factor: alternative RNA and protein processing from a single gene. *Mol. Immunol.* 25:761–770.

Das, S. K. and Stanley, E. R. 1982. Structure-function studies of a colony stimulating factor (CSF-1). *J. Biol. Chem.* 257:13679–13684.

Fant, M., Munro, H., and Moses, A. C. 1986. An autocrine/paracrine role for insulin-like growth factors in the regulation of human placental growth. *J. Clin. Endocrinol. Metab.* 63:499–505.

Finn, C. A. and Martin, L. 1972. Endocrine control of the timing of endometrial sensitivity to a decidual stimulus. *Biol. Reprod.* 7:82–86.

Finn, C. A. and Porter, D. G. 1975. *Handbooks in Reproductive Biology. Vol. 1: The Uterus.* London: Elek Science.

Goustin, A. S., Betsholtz, C., Pfeifer-Ohlsson, S., Persson, H., Rydnert, J., Bywater, M., Holmgren, G., Heldin, C. H., Westermark, B., and Ohlsson, R. 1985. Coexpression of the *sis* and *myc* oncogenes in developing human placenta suggests autocrine control of trophoblast growth. *Cell* 41:301–312.

Guilbert, L. J. and Stanley, E. R. 1980. Specific interaction of murine colony stimulating factor with mononuclear phagocytic cells. *J. Cell. Biol.* 85:153–159.

Gunnet, J. W. and Freeman, M. E. 1983. The mating-induced release of prolactin: a unique neuroendocrine response. *Endocrinology Rev.* 4:44–61.

Hamilton, J. A., Stanley, E. R., Burgess, A. W., and Shadduck, R. K. 1980. Stimulation of macrophage plasminogen activator activity by colony stimulating factors. *J. Cell. Physiol.* 103:435–445.

Han, V. K. M., Hunter, E. S., Pratt, R. M. Zendegui, J. G., and Lee, D. C. 1987. Expression of rat transforming growth factor α mRNA during development occurs predominantly in maternal decidua. *Mol. Cell. Biol.* 7:2335–2343.

Hoshina, M., Nishio, A., Bo, M., Boime, I., and Mochizuki, M. 1985. The expression of the oncogene *fms* in human chorionic tissue. *Acta Obset. Gynec. Jpn.* 37:2791–2798.

Hunt, J. S., Manning, L. S., and Wood, G. W. 1984. Macrophages in murine uterus are immunosuppressive. *Cell. Immunol* 85:499–510.

Hunt, J. S., Manning, L. S., Mitchell, D., Selanders, J. R., and Wood, G. W. 1985. Localization and characterization of macrophages in murine uterus. *J. Leuk. Biol.* 38:255–265.

Kaufman, M. H. 1983. The origins, properties and fate of trophoblast in the mouse. In *Biology of Trophoblasts* (W. Y. Loke and A. Whyte, eds.). Amsterdam: Elsevier, pp. 23–68.

Kawasaki, E. S., Ladner, M. B., Wang, A. M., Van Arsdell, J., Warren M. K., Coyne, M. Y., Schweickart, V. L., Lee, M. T., Wilson, K. J., Boosman, A., Stanley, E. R., Ralph, P., and Mark, D. F. 1985. Molecular cloning of a complementary DNA encoding human macrophage-specific colony stimulating factor (CSF-1). *Science* 230:291–296.

Ladner, M. B., Martin, G. A., Noble, J. A., Nikoloff, D. M., Tal, R., Kawasaki, E. S., and White, T. J. 1987. Human CSF-1: gene structure and alternative splicing of mRNA precursors. *EMBO J* 6:2693–2698.

Ladner, M. B., Martin, G. A., Noble, J. A., Wittman, V. P., Warren, M. K., McGrogan, M., and Stanley, E. R. 1988. cDNA cloning and expression of murine macrophage colony stimulating factor from L929 cells. *Proc. Natl. Acad. Sci. USA* 85:6706–6710.

Lin, H-S. and Gordon, S. 1979. Secretion of plasminogen activator by bone marrow-derived mononuclear phagocytes and its enhancement by colony-stimulating factor. *J. Exp. Med.* 150:231–245.

Manos, M. M. 1988. Expression and processing of a recombinant human macrophage colony stimulating factor in mouse cells. *Mol. Cell. Biol.* 8:5035–5039.

Metcalf, D. and Nicola, A. 1985. Synthesis by mouse peritoneal cells of G-CSF—the differentiation inducer for myeloid leukemia cells: stimulation by endotoxin, M-CSF and multi-CSF. *Leuk. Res.* 9:35–50.

Moore, R. N., Oppenheim, J. J., Farrar, J. J., Carter, C. S. Jr, Waheed, A., and Shadduck, R. K. 1980. Production of lymphocyte-activating factor (interleukin 1) by macrophages activated with colony stimulating factors. *J. Immunol.* 125:1302–1305.

Moore, R. N., Pitruzzello, F. J., Larsen, H. S., and Rouse, B. T. 1984. Feedback regulation of colony stimulating factor (CSF-1)-induced macrophage proliferation by endogenous E prostaglandins and interferon-α/β. *J. Immunol.* 133:541–543.

Morgan, C. J., Pollard, J. W., and Stanley, E. R. 1987. Isolation and characterization of a cloned growth factor dependent macrophage cell line, BAC1.2F5. *J. Cell. Physiol.* 130:420–427.

Müller, R., Slamon, D. J., Adamson, E. D., Tremblay, J. M., Müller, D., Cline, M. J., and Verma, I. M. 1983a. Transcription of c-*onc* genes c-*ras*^{ki} and c-*fms* during mouse development. *Mol. Cell. Biol.* 3:1062–1069.

Müller, R., Verma, I. M., and Adamson, E. D. 1983b. Expression of c-*onc* genes: c-*fos* transcripts accumulate to high levels during development of mouse placenta, yolk sac and amnion. *EMBO J.* 2:679–684.

Nathan, C. F., Prendergast, T. J., Wiebe, M. E., Stanley, E. R., Platzer, E., Remold, H. G., Welte, K., Rubin, B. Y., and Murray, H. W. 1984. Activation of human macrophages, comparison of other cytokines with interferon-γ. *J. Exp. Med.* 160:600–605.

Pollard, J. W., Bartocci, A., Arceci, R., Orlofsky, A., Ladner, M. B., and Stanley, E. R. 1987. Apparent role of the macrophage growth factor, CSF-1, in placental development. *Nature* 330:484–486.

Rajavashisth, T. B., Eng, R., Shadduck, R. K., Waheed, A., Ben-Avram, C. M., Shively, J. E., and Lusis, A. J. 1987. Cloning and tissue-specific expression of mouse macrophage colony-stimulating factor mRNA. *Proc. Natl. Acad. Sci. USA* 84:1157–1161.

Regenstreif, L. J. and Rossant, J. 1989. Expression of the c-fms proto-oncogene and of the cytokine, CSF-1 during more embryogenesis. *Devl. Biol.* 133:284–294.

Rettenmier, C. W. and Roussel, M. F. 1988. Differential processing of colony stimulating factor-1 precursors encoded by two human cDNAs. *Mol. Cell. Biol.* 8:5026–5034.

Rettenmier, C. W., Sacca, R., Furman, W. L., Roussel, M. F., Holt, J. T., Nienhuis, A. W., Stanley, E. R., and Sherr, C. J. 1986. Expression of the human c-*fms* proto-oncogene product (colony stimulating factor-1 receptor) on peripheral blood mononuclear cells and choriocarcinoma cell lines. *J. Clin. Invest.* 77:1740–1746.

Rettenmier, C. W., Roussel, M. F., Ashmun, R. A., Ralph, P., Price, K., and Sherr, C. J. 1987. Synthesis of membrane-bound colony stimulating factor-1 (CSF-1) and downmodulation of CSF-1 receptors in NIH 3T3 cells transformed by cotransfection of the CSF-1 and c-*fms* (CSF-1 receptor) genes. *Mol. Cell. Biol.* 7:2378–2387.

Rosendaal, M. 1975. Colony-stimulating factor (CSF) in the uterus of the pregnant mouse. *J. Cell. Sci.* 19:411–423.

Rossant, J. 1986. Development of extraembryonic cell lineages in the mouse embryo. In *Experimental Approaches to Mammalian Embryonic Development* (J. Rossant and R. A. Pedersen, eds.). Cambridge: U.K.: Cambridge University Press, pp. 97–120.

Rothwell, V. M. and Rohrschneider, L. R. 1987. Murine c-*fms* cDNA: Cloning, sequence analysis, and retroviral expression. *Oncogene Res.* 1:311–324.

Sengupta, A., Liu, W-K, Yeung, Y. G., Yeung, D. C. Y., Frackelton, A. R., and Stanley, E. R. 1988. Identification and sub-cellular localization of proteins that are rapidly phosphorylated in tyrosine in response to colony stimulating factor 1. *Proc. Natl. Acad. Sci. USA* 85:8062–8066.

Shaw, G. and Kamen, R. 1986. A conserved AU sequence from the 3′ untranslated region of GM-CSF mRNA mediates selective degradation. *Cell* 46:659–667.

Sherr, C. J. 1988. The *fms* oncogene. *Biochim. Biophys. Acta* 948:225–243.
Sherr, C. J. and Stanley, E. R. 1990. Colony stimulating factor-1. Handbook of experimental pharmacology, vol. 95/1. In *Peptide Growth Factors and Their Receptors*, (M. B. Sporn and A. B. Roberts, eds.). Heildelberg/NY: Springer-Verlag, pp. 667–697.
Sherr, C. J., Rettenmier, C. W., Sacca, R., Roussel, M. F., Look, A. T., and Stanley, E. R. 1985. The c-*fms* proto-oncogene product is related to the receptor for the mononuclear phagocyte growth factor, CSF-1 *Cell* 41:665–676.
Snow, M. H. L. 1978. Proliferative centres in embryonic development. In *Development in Mammals, vol. 3* (M. H. Johnson, ed.). Amsterdam: Elsevier, pp. 337–362.
Soares, M. J., Julian, J. A., and Glasser, S. R. 1985. Trophoblast giant cell release of placental lactogens: temporal and regional characteristics. *Dev. Biol.* 107:520–526.
Stanley, E. R. and Heard, P. M. 1977. Factors regulating macrophage production and growth. Purification and some properties of the colony stimulating factor from medium conditioned by mouse L cells. *J. Biol. Chem.* 252:4305–4312.
Stanley, E. R., Guilbert, L. T., Tushinski, R. J., and Bartelmez, S. H. 1983. CSF-1-a mononuclear phagocyte lineage-specific hemopoietic growth factor. *J. Cell. Biochem.* 21:151–159.
Tushinski, R. J. and Stanley, E. R. 1983. The regulation of macrophage protein turnover by a colony stimulating factor (CSF-1). *J. Cell Physiol.* 116:67–75.
Tushinski, R. J. and Stanley, E. R. 1985. The regulation of mononuclear phagocyte entry into S phase by the colony stimulating factor CSF-1. *J. Cell. Physiol.* 122:221–228.
Tushinski, R. J., Oliver, I. T., Guilbert, L. T., Tynan, P. W., Warner, J. R., and Stanley, E. R. 1982. Survival of mononuclear phagocytes depends on a lineage-specific growth factor that the differentiated cells selectively destroy. *Cell* 28:71–81.
Wang, J. M., Griffin, J. D., Rambaldi, A., Chen, Z. G., and Mantovani, A. 1988. Induction of monocyte migration by recombinant macrophage colony-stimulating factor. *J. Immunol.* 141:575–579.
Warren, M. K. and Ralph, P. 1986. Macrophage growth factor CSF-1 stimulates human monocyte production of interferon, tumour necrosis factor and colony stimulating activity. *J. Immunol.* 137:2281–2285.
Wegmann, T. G. 1984. Fetal protection against abortion: is it immunosuppression or immunostimulation? *Ann. Immunol. (Paris)* 135D:301–315.
Wegmann, T. G. 1988. Maternal T cells promote placental growth and prevent spontaneous abortion. *Immunol. Lett.* 17:297–302.
Wicks, R. J. 1986. RNA and molecular weight determination by agarose gel electrophoresis using formaldehyde as denaturant: comparison of DNA and RNA molecular weight markers. *Int. J. Biochem.* 18:277–278.
Wong, G. G., Temple, P. A., Leary, A. C., Witek-Giannotti, J. S., Yang, Y-C., Ciarletta, A. B., Chung, M., Kriz, R., Kaufman, R. J., Ferenz, C. R., Sibley, B. S., Turner, K. J., Hewick, R. M., Clark, S. C., Yanai, N., Yokota, H., Yamada, M., Saito, M., Motoyoshi, K., and Takaku, F. 1987. Human CSF-1: molecular cloning and expression of a 4 kb cDNA encoding the human urinary protein. *Science* 235:1504–1508.

Wood, G. W. 1980. Immunohistochemical identification of macrophages in murine placentae, yolk sac membranes and pregnant uteri. *Placenta* 1:113–123.

Zybina, E. V. 1961. Endomitosis and polyteny of trophoblastic giant cells. *Dokl. Akad. Nauk. SSSR* 140:1428–1431.

18

The Placenta as an Immune-Endocrine Interface: Placental Cells as Targets for Lymphohematopoietic Cytokine Stimulation

LARRY J. GUILBERT, IRENE ATHANASSAKIS, DONALD R. BRANCH, ROBERT CHRISTOPHERSON, MARY CRAINIE, MARIA GARCIA-LLORET, RONA J. MOGIL, DON MORRISH, JAGDEECE RAMSOONDAR, SIMEON VASSILIADIS, and THOMAS G. WEGMANN

Considerable evidence has accumulated over the last 5 years indicating that maternal immune recognition of fetal alloantigens can lead to increased placental and fetal size, as well as improved fetal survival in some strains of mice (Gill & Wegmann, 1987; Wegmann, 1988). Depletion of T cells from animals in midgestation can have the opposite effect, although the magnitude of this effect is somewhat strain-dependent and is not seen in all combinations (Chaouat et al., 1988). Observations of this sort have led us to determine whether maternal T cells or their cytokine products can influence the growth of placental cells in culture. Alternatively, T cells or their products may influence placental cell function. This concept is termed "immunotrophism," and is based on earlier ideas of Clarke and Kirby (1966), although it has been reformulated in light of advances in understanding the molecular basis of immune interactions (Green & Wegmann, 1986; Wegmann, 1984). We now know that a wide range of immune and nonimmune cell-cell interactions can be affected by lymphohematopoietic cytokines. The availability of pure preparations of these mediators makes it possible to test this hypothesis *in vitro* and *in vivo*. The work presented here concentrates on *in vitro* approaches. In an extension of published work (Athanassakis et al., 1987; Mogil & Wegmann, 1988), we report that lymphohematopoietic cytokines stimulate the function, survival, and/or growth of placental cells in the pig and human, as well as in the mouse. In addition, primary cells and cell lines derived from these primary cells appear to show both trophoblast and macrophage characteristics as judged by a variety of criteria. Finally, there is accumulative evidence that cytokine stimulation contributes to continued endocrine activity of these trophoblast-macrophages in culture. This is suggestive of earlier experiments in which exposure of trophoblast cells to human white blood cells in culture led to increased secretion of human chorionic gonadotropin (Dickman & Cauchi, 1978; Kaplan, 1983). In this chapter we critically analyze the apparent interaction between cells of the maternal immune system and the fetal endocrine system that takes place at the maternal-fetal interface. We focus on the characterization of fetal cells that are the targets of the maternal immune system at the interface.

Characterization of Murine Placental Cells That Respond to Lymphohematopoietic Cytokines

Preliminary evidence from our laboratory has demonstrated the existence of a fetal cell type that is derived from the placenta at day 12 of pregnancy, and shares the gross morphological characteristics of both trophoblast and macrophage. This cell is responsive to the colony-stimulative lymphokines GM-CSF and IL-3 and to the macrophage-specific cytokine CSF-1 (Athanassakis et al., 1987). Its responsiveness to colony-stimulating lymphokines and CSF-1, the levels of which increase dramatically during murine pregnancy (Bartocci et al., 1986), suggests that this cell derives from a placental population that is responsive to maternal cytokine signals. Our laboratory has taken two principal approaches to characterize these cells. We have used a panel of monoclonal antibodies that recognize antigens characteristic of epithelial trophoblast (cytokeratin), fibroblasts (vimentin), and macrophages (F4/80, Mac-1, vimentin) (Hume et al., 1984; Lane, 1982; Springer et al., 1979) to determine whether the cells are of ectodermal or mesodermal origin. Our other approach has been to develop cell lines from short-term (1–4 day) cultures to confirm observations made with heterogeneous primary cell populations and to carry out further characterization that is not possible with primary cells because of limited cell numbers.

Characterization of Responsive Cells from Primary Placental Cultures

Because the lymphokine/CSF-1-responsive placental cell has morphological characteristics of both macrophages and trophoblast, we compared its properties after short-term culture with those of bone-marrow-derived macrophages of maternal origin (Table 18-1). Although there is significant overlap between the two populations, there were large differences in expression of the HLA class I and II antigens, cytokeratin, and vimentin, indicating that at least 60% of the placental

Table 18-1. Expression of macrophage, fibroblast, and epithelial markers on murine cells derived from cytokine-stimulated placental and bone marrow cultures

	Percent of Adherent Cells Positive* in Cultures of	
Antigen	**Placenta**	**Bone-Marrow-Derived Macrophages**
Mac-1	79 ± 4	86 ± 8
F4/80	69 ± 2	93 ± 7
Cytokeratin	74 ± 9	12 ± 5
Vimentin	10 ± 2	84 ± 9
Class I D^d	32 ± 7	83 ± 7
Class II Ia^d	19 ± 8	79 ± 2
Mouse IgG†	11 ± 4	4 ± 2
Rat IgG‡	8 ± 1	9 ± 1
None	5 ± 1	8 ± 2

* Fluorescence evaluated visually.

† Mouse IgG was used at the same protein concentration as the mouse anticytokeratin antivimentin, and anti-class I, and II antiodies.

‡ Rat IgG was used at the same protein concentration as the rat anti-Mac-1 and F4/80 antibodies.

cells (those expressing cytokeratin) were not typical hematopoietic macrophages. Double indirect immunofluorescent staining revealed that almost all cytokeratin-positive cells also expressed the macrophage markers, F4/80 and Mac-1 (Table 18-2). Somewhat different data were obtained from experiments to determine how many of these adherent placental cells expressed CSF-1 binding sites, which are expressed specifically on macrophages (Byrne et al., 1981, see chapter 17). To determine whether all cells that responded to CSF-1 by proliferation also expressed the receptor, we carried out concurrent autoradiographic analysis of ^{125}I-CSF-1 binding to the cell surface and ^{3}H-TdR uptake into the nucleus on CSF-1-stimulated placental cells (Table 18-3). This experiment showed that >70% of the adherent placental cells expressed specific CSF-1 binding sites and that essentially the same population proliferated in response to CSF-1 (Table 18-3) or GM-CSF (data not shown).

Although these data suggest the existence of a distinct epithelial cell population with macrophage characteristics, it is also possible that the cytokine-responsive population is an outgrowth of fetal macrophages that are known to be present in the placenta (Wood, 1980). This population may be induced to express cytokeratin under our culture conditions. To exclude this possibility, placental cell preparations were separated by precoll step gradient centrifugation before short-

Table 18-2. Double indirect immunofluorescence staining of fixed cells derived from lymphokine-stimulated placental cultures

	Percent of Cells Staining For		
Antibody Combination	**FITC**	**RITC**	**FITC + RITC**
Mac-1	78 ± 9	—	—
Cytokeratin	—	77 ± 7	—
F4/80	75 ± 4	—	—
PBS	12 ± 6	16 ± 3	—
Mac-1 (F) + Cyt (R)	60 ± 5	68 ± 6	60
Mac-1 (F) + PBS (R)	72 ± 5	6 ± 1	4
F4/80 (F) + Cyt (R)	73 ± 3	65 ± 2	65
F4/80 (F) + PBS (R)	70 ± 4	7 ± 1	5
PBS (F) + Cyt (R)	10 ± 3	71 ± 4	6
PBS (F) + PBS (R)	17 ± 2	14 ± 1	5

Rabbit anti-rat FITC (F) conjugated antibody was used to defect the rat anti-Mac-1 and F4/80 monoclonal antibodies, and goat anti-mouse RITC conjugated antibody was used to detect mouse anticytokeratin antibody. Double-stained cells were first stained with anti-Mac-1 or F4/80 plus FITC and then stained with RITC-conjugated anticytokeratin. Fluorescence was evaluated visually.

term culture. Under these conditions, we identified a small (<10%) subpopulation of F4/80-positive, cytokeratin-negative fetal cells that was distinct from the predominant F4/80- and cytokeratin-positive population (Table 18-4). Thus, classical fetal macrophages coexist in placental cultures as a minor subpopulation. The major population of cytokeratin-positive macrophages displays surface characteristics that suggest that they are derived from a different lineage than the fetal cells.

Table 18-3. Concurrent autoradiographic analysis of ^{125}I-CSF-1 binding and tritiated thymidine (^{3}HTdR) uptake on CSF-1-stimulated adherent placental cells

	Percent Cells with Grains Above		
Labeling Treatment	**Nucleus**	**Outside Nucleus**	**Both**
^{125}I-CSF-1*	—	72 ± 5	—
^{125}I-CSF-1 + CSF-1†	—	9 ± 1	—
^{3}HTdR	67 ± 1	—	—
^{125}I-CSF-1 + ^{3}HTdR	67 ± 10	62 ± 14	62 ± 14

* The nucleus or cytoplasm/plasma membrane of a cell was scored positive when more than ten grains were seen above it. CSF-1-stimulated adherent cells were first incubated with ^{3}HTdR and then processed for ^{125}I-CSF-1 binding at 4°C. Cells having grains over both the nucleus and cytoplasm were considered double positive.

† Blocking of ^{125}I-CSF-1 binding by preincubation with 2 nM unlabeled CSF-1.

Table 18-4. Marker expression on precoll-separated placental cells

Band	Percent in Band	Percent Fetal	Percent Staining For F4/80	Cytokeratin	Vimentin	Control
40%	67 ± 9	95 ± 2	92 ± 1	92 ± 8	33 ± 1	24 ± 4
0%	6 ± 3	73 ± 7	65 ± 4	25 ± 8	15 ± 4	16 ± 4
80%	26 ± 12	0	17 ± 6	14 ± 2	9 ± 1	22 ± 4

Percent fetal cells determined by GPI analysis. Marker expression was tested on adherent cells at day 4 of culture.

Characterization of Lymphokine-Responsive Placental Cell Lines

As an alternative approach to characterization of the lymphokine/CSF-1-responsive placental cell, we established two independent cell lines from long-term cultures of placental cells in the presence of medium condition by the T thymoma cell line EL-4. The EL-4 cell line elaborates a number of T cell lymphokines, including GM-CSF and IL-3 *in vitro*. Detailed characterization of one of the placental lines, FRD, showed it to be almost identical to the major population of lymphokine/CSF-1-responsive placental cells. Thus, it was of fetal origin, (as indicated by its expression of the a × b GPI phenotype). It was also F4/80 positive, Mac-1 positive, cytokeratin positive, and vimentin negative (Table 18-5). Availability of large numbers of homogeneous FRD cells allowed accurate flow cytometric analysis; over 90% of cells were shown to express cytokeratin, Mac-1, and F4/80 (data not shown). FRD cell proliferation was stimulated by CSF-1, GM-CSF, and IL-3 (Fig. 18-1), and FRD also produced estradiol (data not

Table 18-5. Phenotypic characteristics of the placental cell line FRD

Property	Expression
GPI (a × b)	+
Class I MHC	+
Class II MHC	+
Cytokeratin	+
Vimentin	−
Phagocytosis	+
Mac-1	+
F4/80	+
Nonspecific esterase	+
Alkaline phosphatase	−
Acid phosphatase	+
Estradiol production	+

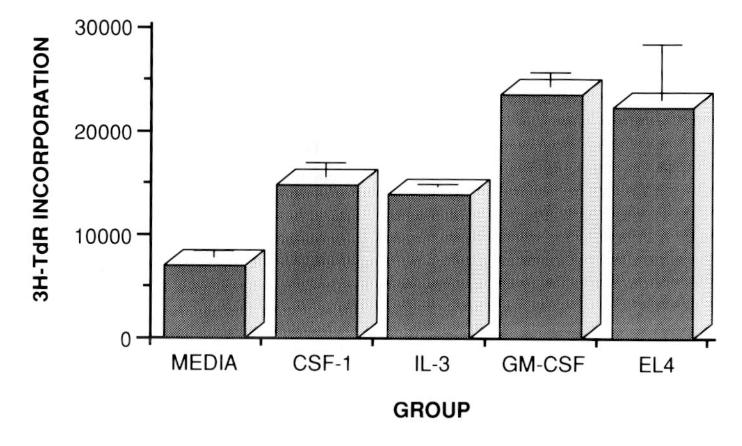

Fig. 18-1. Cytokine stimulation of FRD placental cell proliferation. FRD cells from log-phase cultures were washed 4X with excess L15 medium and added to 0.2 mL cultures at 2.5×10^5 cells/mL in 10% FBS in RPMI 1640 with and without the indicated cytokines or lymphokine preparations (all added at near maximally stimulating levels). Cells were pulsed for the last 18 h of a 3 day incubation period with 1 μCi well ^{3}HTdR.

shown), a property associated with the trophoblast in pregnancy (Bate & King, 1988; Solomon & Sherman, 1975). These data confirm the results obtained with primary cell cultures and strongly suggest that the FRD cell line probably corresponds to an epithelial or trophoblastic macrophage.

It was also possible to analyze mRNA expression in the FRD cell line (Table 18-6). Comparative Northern blot analysis of mRNA from the FRD line and whole placenta showed them to be quite similar. Both strongly expressed c-*fms*, (corresponding to the CSF-1 receptor (Sherr et al., 1985), TNF-α, and IL-1α (Fig. 18-2). Expression at the protein level of the CSF-1 receptor and IL-1 was strongly suggested by the observed proliferative response of FRD to CSF-1 (Fig. 18-1) and the presence of IL-1 activity in FRD culture supernatants (Mogil & Wegmann, 1988). TNF is generally regarded primarily as a cytotoxin, and this view has limited our understanding of its true functions. We have recently shown it to act as part of an autocrine cascade in CSF-1-stimulated macrophages (Branch et al., 1989), and it could therefore serve a trophic role in this context. IL-1 and TNF could therefore both serve as endocrine factors acting on the developing conceptus.

The most interesting property of the FRD line is its ability to stimulate antigen-specific (insulin or poly 18) T lymphocyte hybridomas to secrete IL-2 in an antigen-independent manner (Mogil & Wegmann, 1988) (Fig. 18-3). Antigen-independent activation appears to depend on close cell-cell contact and is not mediated by IL-1 production, since FRD sublines that are unable to support antigen-in-

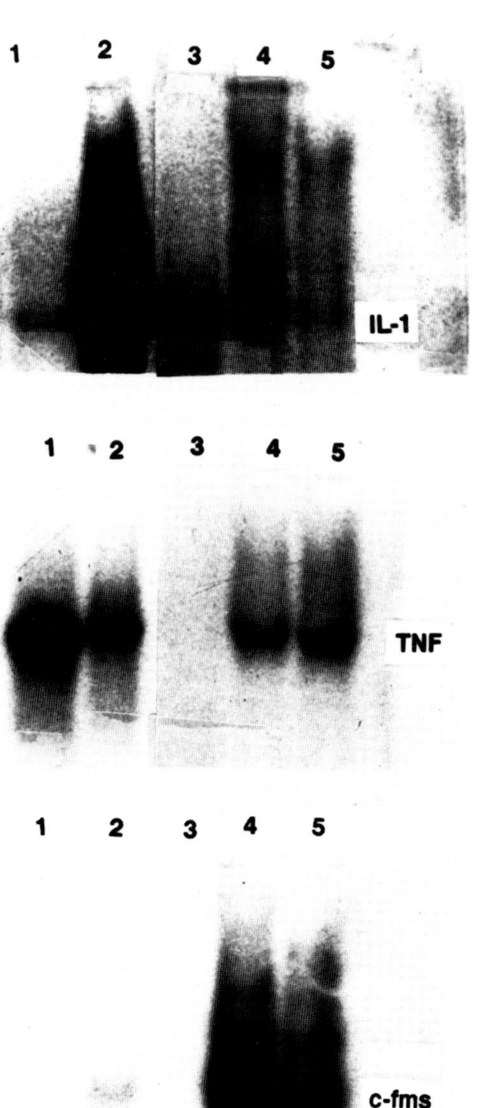

Fig. 18-2. Identification of mRNA encoding IL-1-α, TNF-α and the CSF-1 receptor (c-*fms*) by Northern blot analysis. Methods as described in legend to Table 18-6.

dependent activation still produce significant amounts of IL-1 (data not shown). Thus, the characteristics of the FRD line, which probably corresponds to an epithelial macrophage cell, suggest that cells that possess the ability to directly stimulate adjacent maternal T lymphocytes are present in the placenta.

Taken together, the above observations on murine placental cells indicate the existence of a unique cell of epithelial or possibly tro-

Table 18-6. Northern blot analysis of mRNA from the FRD cell line and whole placenta

Probe	FRD	Placenta (day 14)
IL-1 alpha	+	
IL-2	–	–
IL-3	–	–
IL-5	–	–
GM-CSF	–	–
TNF alpha	+ +	+ +
CSF-1	–	(+)
c-*fms*	+ + +	+ + +
IL-2R (tac)	–	–

Total FRD or C57BL/10J placental RNA was extracted (as described in Chomczynski & Sacchi, 1987 and Chirgwin et al., 1979), and 20 μg was subjected to Northern blot analysis (as described in Shaw et al., 1987). Blots were hybridized to cDNA probes labeled with ^{32}P-dCTP using random oligonucleotides as primers (as described in Feinberg & Vogelstein, 1983) and washed to a final stringency of 0.2 × SSC, 0.1% SDS at 55°C, before autoradiography. Full-length cDNA fragments were obtained from plasmids containing coding regions for IL-1 (Lomedico et al., 1984); TNF-α (Pennica et al., 1985); c-*fms* (Rothwell & Rohrschneider, 1987); IL-2, IL-5, and GM-CSF (Elliot, PhD thesis, University of Alberta, 1987); IL-3 (Yokota et al., 1984); CSF-1 (Ladner et al., 1988); and the IL-2 receptor (Miller, Hooton, & Paetkau, manuscript in preparation).

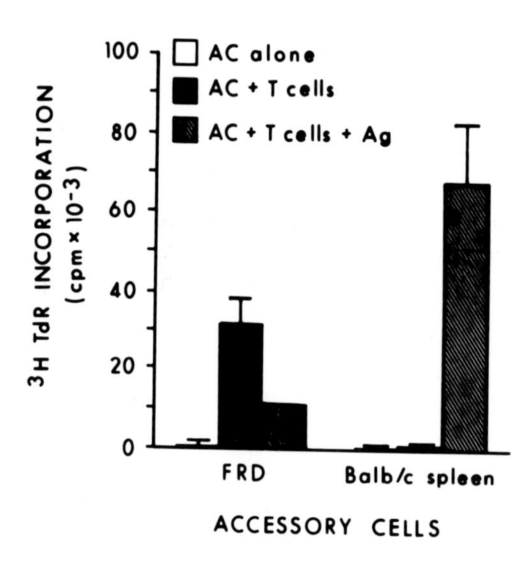

Fig. 18-3. FRD placental cells stimulate A20 T hybridoma cells to secrete IL-2 in the absence of antigen. A20 T cells were cocultured with either irradiated FRD cells or BALB/c spleen accessory cells for 24 hrs in the presence or absence of beef insulin. Supernatants were harvested and assayed for IL-2 on HT-2 indicator cells with the read-out expressed as ^{3}HTdR incorporation (cpm +/− standard error of the mean). Background levels of ^{3}HTdR uptake by HT-2 cells stimulated by A20 T cell supernatant were 2025 +/− 109 cpm.

phoblast origin that is part of the maternal fetal humoral signaling network including hematopoietic macrophages. This cell also expresses many of the physical and functional properties of macrophages. The next section summarizes studies to determine whether similar cells can be found in other species.

Characterization of Placental Cells Able to Respond to Lymphohematopoietic Cytokines in Humans and Pigs

Deliberate immunization of recurrently aborting human females to paternal antigens has been shown to dramatically decrease postimplantation losses (Mowbray et al., 1985). Intrauterine immunization of pigs with killed sperm also reduces the rate of implantation failure (Stone et al., 1987). These observations suggest that specific immunity can be beneficial to pregnancy in at least these two species. We have looked for evidence that placental cells in humans and pigs are responsive to lymphohematopoietic cytokines and may therefore be part of a putative immunotrophic network.

CSF-1 Binding and Stimulation of Term Villous Trophoblast

In humans, studies using primary tissue have provided evidence for the existence of CSF-1-responsive trophoblast cells. Cells isolated by mild proteolysis of the villous trophoblast from term pregnancies were purified by density gradient centrifugation to >95% cytokeratin positivity (<5% were vimentin positive) and then studied for their response to CSF-1, their ability to bind ^{125}I-CSF-1 specifically, and the presence of mRNA encoding the CSF-1 receptor (c-*fms*). Term trophoblast is a nondividing tissue (Pfeiffer-Ohlsson et al., 1984), and it was therefore necessary to measure endocrinological responses. Treatment with recombinant human CSF-1 doubled the production of placental lactogen, a peptide hormone that has been implicated in fetal survival and growth (Talamantes et al., 1980) (Fig. 18-4). The presence of functional CSF-1 receptors on purified trophoblast populations was confirmed by binding studies using ^{125}I-CSF-1. The BeWo choriocarcinoma cell line that has been reported to express large numbers of CSF-1 receptors was used as a positive control in these experiments (Rettenmier et al., 1986) (Fig. 18-5). Autoradiographic analysis showed that 35% of the cells bound CSF-1 (data not shown). As would be predicted from the above data, mRNA extracted from trophoblast cells strongly hybridized to c-*fms* cDNA in Northern blot analysis (data not shown). These data thus show that a significant subpopulation of human primary term trophoblast cells strongly ex-

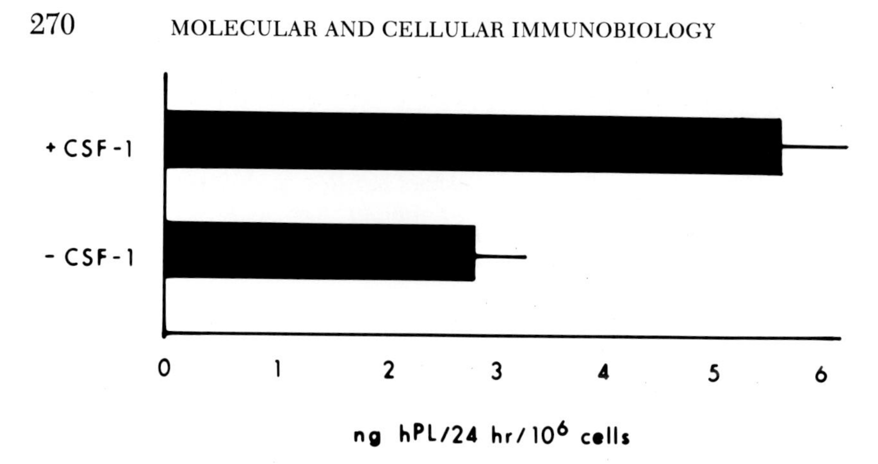

Fig. 18-4. Stimulation of placental lactogen production from term villous trophoblasts by CSF-1. Trophoblasts from term placenta, purified by density gradient centrifugation and selective adherence to yield a 95% cytokeratin positive and 5% vimentin positive population, were cultured in 10% FBS in IMDM for 24 hrs with and without 1000 U/mL pure human recombinant CSF-1. Placental lactogen was measured as described by Morrish et al. (1987), using standards provided by the National Hormone and Pituitary Program.

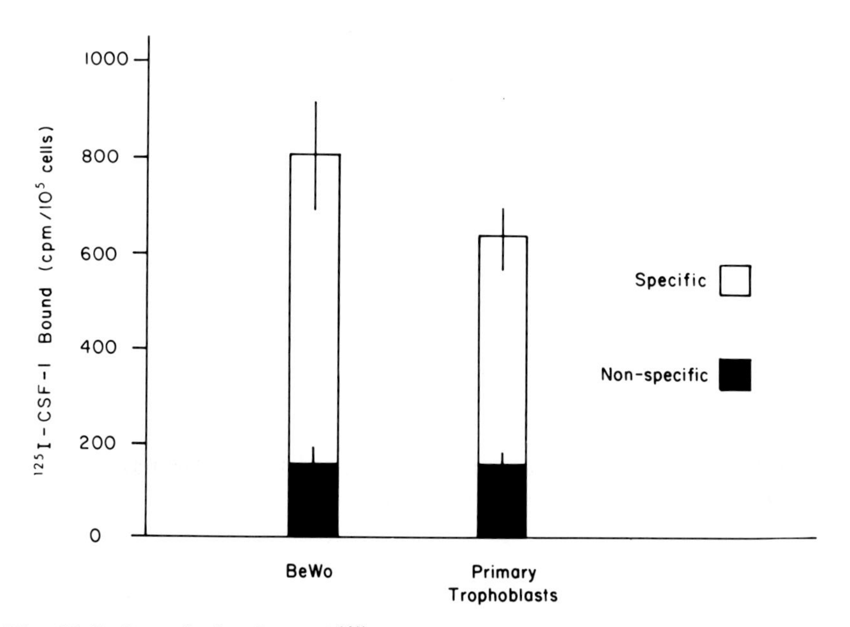

Fig. 18-5. Specific binding of ^{125}I-CSF-1 to human term trophoblasts and to the choriocarcinoma cell line BeWo. Human recombinant CSF-1 was labeled with ^{125}I to approximately 5×10^{18} cpm/mol as described in Stanley and Guilbert (1981). Binding carried out at 2°C for 1 h with 5×10^{6} cpm/mL ^{125}I-CSF-1. Specific binding is that not blocked by preincubation with 1 nM unlabeled CSF-1, (From Stanley & Guilbert, 1981.)

presses the receptor for CSF-1 and can respond to CSF-1 by increased release of an important fetal endocrine factor.

Lymphokine Stimulation of Preimplantation Porcine Trophoblast

In the pig, evidence for a response of trophoblast to lymphokines has come from studies on day 14 preimplantation blastocysts. Porcine trophoblast takes the form of thread-like structures up to a meter in length. By careful cutting of the threads so as to avoid the embryonic disc, single 1-mm sections of almost pure trophoblastic tissue could be obtained. These were placed into individual 1 mL cultures in the presence or absence of crude lymphokine preparations. Lymphokine preparations included medium conditioned by Con A-stimulated pig peripheral blood lymphocytes and supernatant from PMA-stimulated EL-4 cells. Vesicle formation was initiated within 1 day in almost all cultures containing 1% (V/V) of porcine or murine lymphokine preparations (Table 18-7). Early on, compact, free-floating structures were observed in culture, which progressed to highly transparent, multi-lobulated adherent forms before ultimately giving use to adherent monolayers by day 5 of culture. In the absence of lymphokines, the explanted tissue appeared necrotic by day 5 and did not form either vesicles or monolayers. Monolayers grown in the presence of lymphokines produced estradiol-β-17 as measured by RIA (data not shown).

In summary, lymphohematopoietic cytokines (CSF-1 in humans and crude lymphokine preparations in the pig) stimulate trophoblast function in these two species. Taken together, data from mouse, pig, and human models suggest the existence of lymphokine or CSF-1-responsive trophoblastic cells that convert maternal immunotrophic signals into fetal endocrine production.

Table 18-7. Response of preimplantation porcine trophoblast tissue to porcine and murine lymphokine preparation

	Response (Wells out of 24 Maximum)*		
Lymphokine (%)	**Vesicles**	**Monolayer**	**Total**
PBL CM (1%)	12	21	23
PBL CM (0.5%)	10	23	24
EL-4 CM (1%)	5	20	23
EL-4 CM (0.5%)	11	21	22
Medium alone	0	0	0

* Results tabulated at day 3 of culture.

Characterization of Lymphohematopoietic Cytokines Present at the Maternal-Fetal Interface

Although this chapter has been mainly concerned with defining targets for maternal lymphohematopoietic cytokines, we conclude with data showing that lymphokines are present in the decidua abutting the developing conceptus and are therefore potentially available for immunotrophic support of pregnancy. After 3–5 days in culture, mouse decidual cells harvested at day 12 of an allogeneic (C3H × BALB) or syngeneic (C3H × C3H) pregnancy release activities that stimulate growth of the GM-CSF- and IL-3-responsive cell line DA-1 (Branch & Guilbert, 1987) (Fig. 18-6). Most of the DA-1 growth-stimulating activity present in decidual cell supernatants represents GM-CSF, as indicated by the ability of anti-GM-CSF antiserum to block >80% of the DA-1 response. These preliminary experiments confirm the presence of at least one lymphokine at the maternal-fetal interface. More extensive experiments to identify and quantitate lym-

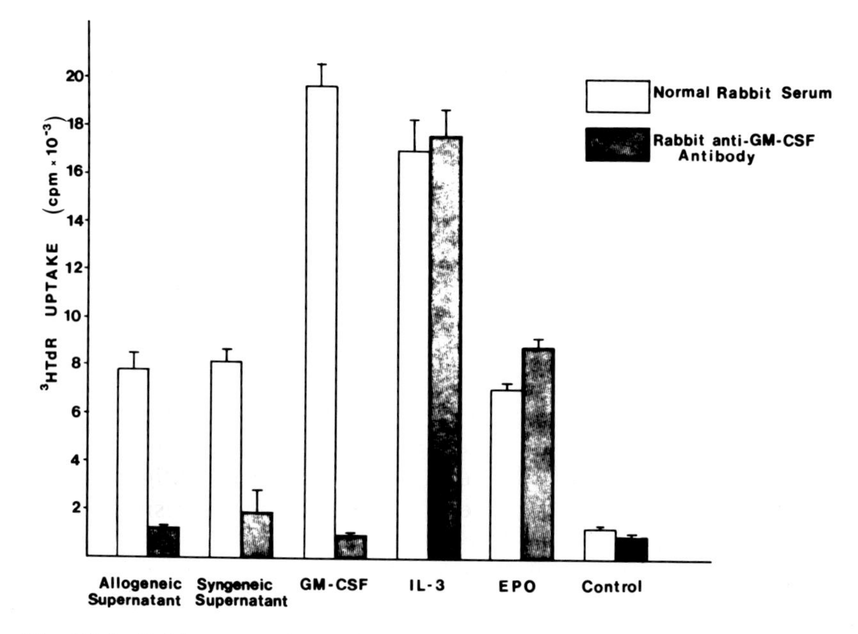

Fig. 18-6. Rabbit anti-mouse GM-CSF antiserum (DeLamarter et al., 1985) blocks growth stimulatory activity of decidual culture supernatants on DA-1 cells. Supernatants were prepared from C3H × BALB (allo) and C3H × C3H (syn) matings at day 13 of pregnancy. GM-CSF (10pg/mL) was used as the positive control for antibody, while erythropoietin (5U/mL) and IL-3(300 U/mL) were used as negative controls.

phokines from decidua of syngeneic and allogeneic pregnancies are currently in progress.

Future Directions

The results described in this chapter have been based primarily on *in vitro* studies using cells derived from the placenta. We have found that growth and function of these cells are influenced by cytokines, which promote the release of steroid and protein hormones involved in fetal survival and growth. It is clear that we have only begun to understand the significance of this immune-endocrine interface. The work needs to be expanded not only to understand the situation in tissue culture more thoroughly but also to determine whether these effects are significant in the living animal. There are suggestions from other systems that these studies will be highly significant. For example, Soares and Telamantes (1983) showed that the level of murine placental lactogen is twice as high in allogeneic as compared to syngeneic placentas. It is tempting to speculate that this is due to the increased immune infiltration in allogeneic placentas, as described by Lala et al. (1986). We have observed that treatment of mice prone to spontaneous abortion with recombinant GM-CSF in midgestation decreases the rate of abortion and leads to an increase in placental size (Chaouat et al., 1988, unpublished data). Does this treatment directly influence endocrine secretion? In humans it is known that human chorionic gonadotropin production decreases immediately before spontaneous abortion (Gill & Wegmann, 1987), and that lymphocytes stimulate human chorionic gonadotropin production from trophoblast tissue *in vitro* (Dickman & Cauchi, 1978; Kaplan, 1983). These observations are directly relevant to the question of whether manipulation of the maternal immune response *in vivo* has effects on fetal endocrine production. If this proves to be the case, it will be essential to assess the influence in hydrids of the maternal immune system on cells of the fetal placenta in relation to pregnancy outcome. It must also be determined whether these effects are obligatory in all pregnancies, or if they represent an ancillary mechanism that may contribute to the success of marginal pregnancies. This latter interpretation would appear plausible, given the experiments reported by Croy et al., (Chapter 12, this volume), showing that *scid-beige* double homozygote mice could breed under germ-free conditions. The immune system may therefore function as an adjunct to the paracrine system of the uterus during pregnancy, using the same or similar cytokines to achieve its effects. Although we do not have answers to these questions as yet, we are confident that they will be addressed in the near future, thereby providing a better understanding of the molecular mechanisms by which the maternal response acts at the maternal-fetal interface.

Acknowledgments

We thank Bonnie Lowen, Anne Smith, Karen Hobbs, and Kevin Atcheson for technical assistance and Debbie Neufeld for preparation of the manuscript. We also thank Cetus Corp. for the plasmid-containing cDNA-encoding mouse CSF-1 and the pure human CSF-1; Genentech Inc. for the TNF-α plasmid; DNAX Corp. for the IL-3 plasmid; John DeLamarter for the anti-GM-CSF antiserum; R. J. Tushinski of Immunex Corp. for recombinant GM-CSF; Dr. V. Paetkau for GM-CSF, IL-2, receptor, and IL-5-containing plasmids; Ann Croy for porcine lymphocyte-conditioned medium; and Dr. L. Honoré for providing human term placenta used in these studies.

References

Athanassakis, I., Bleackley, R. C., Paetkau, V., Guilbert, L. J., Barr, P. J., and Wegmann, T. C. 1987. The immunostimulatory effect of T cells and T cell lymphokines on murine fetally derived placental cells. *J. Immunol.* 138:37.

Bartocci, A., Pollard, J. W., and Stanley, E. R. 1986. Regulation of colony-stimulating factor 1 during pregnancy. *J. Exp. Med.* 164:956.

Bate, L. A. and King, G. J. 1988. Production of oestrone and eostradiol-17 beta by different regions of the filamentous pig blastocyst. *J. Reprod. Fertil.* 84:163.

Branch, D. R. and Guilbert, L. J. 1987. Practical *in vitro* assay systems for the measurement of hematopoietic growth factors. *J. Tiss. Culture Meth.* 10:101.

Branch, D. R., Turner, A. R., and Guilbert, L. J. 1989. Synergistic stimulation of macrophage proliferation by the monokines tumor necrosis factor-alpha and colony-stimulating factor-1. *Blood* 73:307.

Byrne, P. V., Guilbert, L. J., and Stanley, E. R. 1981. Distribution of cells bearing receptors for a colony-stimulating factor (CSF-1) in murine tissues. *J. Cell. Physiol.* 91:848.

Chaouat, G., Menu, E., Athanassakis, I., and Wegmann, T. C. 1988. Maternal T cells regulate placental size and fetal survival. *Reg. Immunol.* 1:143.

Chirgwin, J. M., Przybyla, A. E., MacDonald, R. J., and Rutter, W. J. 1979. Isolation of biologically active ribonucleic acid from sources enriched in ribonuclease. *Biochemistry* 18:5294.

Chomczynski, P. and Sacchi, N. 1987. Single step method of RNA isolation by acid guanidinium thiocyanate-phenol-chloroform extraction. *Anal. Biochem.* 162:156.

Clarke, B. and Kirby, D. R. S. 1966. Maintenance of histocompatibility polymorphisms. *Nature (London)* 211:999.

DeLamarter, J. F., Mermod, J-J., Liang, C. M., Eliason, J. F., Thatcher, D., and Vassalli, P. 1985. Recombinant murine GM-CSF for *E. coli* has biological activity and is neutralized by a specific antiserum. *EMBO J.* 4:2575.

Dickman, W. J. and Cauchi, M. N. 1978. Lymphocyte-induced stimulation of human chorionic gonadotropin production by trophoblastic cells *in vitro*. *Nature* 271:377.

Feinberg, A. P. and Vogelstein, B. 1983. A technique for radiolabelling DNA restriction endonuclease fragments to high specific activity. *Anal. Biochem.* 132:6.

Gill, T. J. III and Wegmann, T. G., eds. 1987. *Immunoregulation and Fetal Survival*. London: Oxford University Press.

Green, D. R. and Wegmann, T. G. 1986. Beyond the immune system: The immunotrophic role of T cells in organ generation and regeneration. *Prog. Immunol.* 6:1100–1112.

Hume, D. A., Halpin, D., Charlton, H., and Gordon, S. 1984. The mononuclear phagocyte system of the mouse defined by immunohistochemical localization of antigen F4/80. Macrophages of endocrine origin. *Proc. Natl. Acad. Sci. USA* 81:4174.

Kaplan, L. 1983. Maternal leukocyte-induced stimulation of hCG release into the media of short-term trophoblastic organ and cell cultures. *ICRS Med. Sci.* 11:893.

Ladner, M. B., Matin, G.A., Noble, J. A., Wittman, V. P., Warren, M. K., McGrogan, M., and Stanley, E. R. 1988. cDNA cloning and expression of murine macrophage colony-stimulating factor from L929 cells. *Proc. Natl. Acad. Sci. USA* 85:6706.

Lala, P. K., Parkar, R. S., Kearns, M., Johnson, S., and Scodras, J. M. 1986. Immunologic aspects of the decidual response. In *Reproductive Immunology*. (D. A. Clark and B. A. Croy, eds.) New York: Elsevier Publishers BV (Biomedical Division), p. 1980.

Lane, E. B. 1982. Monoclonal antibodies provide specific intramolecular markers for the study of epithelial monofilament organization. *J. Cell Biol.* 92:665.

Lomedico, P. T., Gubler, U., Hellmann, C. P., Dukovich, M., Giri, J. G., Pan Y-C. E., Collier, E., Semionow, R., Chua, A. O., and Mizel, S. B. 1984. Cloning and expression murine interleukin-1 cDNA in *Escherichia coli*. *Nature* 312:458.

Mogil, R. J. and Wegmann, T. G. 1988. Immunoregulatory effects of lymphokine-driven placental cells on cloned T cells *in vitro*. *Reg. Immunol.* 1:69.

Morrish, D. W., Bhardwaj, D., Dabbagh, L. K., Marusyk, H., and Siy, O. 1987. Epidermal growth factor induces differentiation and secretion of human chorionic gonadotropin and placental lactogen in normal human placenta. *J Clin. Endocrin. Metab.* 65:1282.

Mowbray, J. F., Liddell, H., Underwood, J. L., Gibbings, C., Reginald, P. W., and Beard, R. W. 1985. Controlled trial of treatment of recurrent spontaneous abortion by immunization with paternal cells. *Lancet* 1:941.

Pennica, D., Hayflick, J. S., Bringman, R. S., Palladino, M. A., and Goeddell, D. V. 1985. Cloning and expression in *Escherichia coli* of the cDNA for murine tumor necrosis factor. *Proc. Natl. Acad. Sci. USA* 82:6060.

Pfeiffer-Ohlsson, S., Goustin, A. S., Rydnert, J., Wahlstrom, T., Bjersing, L., Stehelin, D., and Ohlsson, R. 1984. Spatial and temporal pattern of cellular *myc* oncogene expression in developing human placenta: implications for embryonic cell proliferation. *Cell* 38:585.

Rettenmier, C. W., Sacca, R., Furman, W. L., Roussel, M. F., Holt, J. T., Nienhuis, A. W., Stanley, E. R., and Sherr, C. J. 1986. Expression of the human c-*fms* proto-oncogene production (colony-stimulating factor-1 receptor) on peripheral blood mononuclear cells and choriocarcinoma cell lines. *J. Clin. Invest.* 77:1740.

Rothwell, V. M. and Rohrschneider, L. R. 1987. Murine c-*fms* cDNA—cloning, sequence-analysis and retroviral expression.

Shaw, J., Meerovitch, K., Elliot, J. F., Bleakley, R. C., and Paetkau, V. 1987. Induction suppression and superinduction of lymphokine mRNA in T lymphocytes. *Mol. Immunol.* 24:409.

Sherr, C. J., Rettenmier, C. W., Sacca, R., Roussel, M. F., Look, A. T., and Stanley, E. R. 1985. The c-*fms* proto-oncogene product is related to the receptor for the mononuclear phagocyte growth factor, CSF-1. *Cell* 41:665.

Soares, M. J. and Talamantes, F. 1983. Genetic and letter size effects on serum placental lactogen in the mouse. *Biol Reprod.* 29:165.

Solomon, D. S. and Sherman, M. I. 1975. The biosynthesis of progesterone by cultured mouse midgestation trophoblast cells. *Dev. Biol.* 47:394.

Springer, T., Galfre, G., Secher, D. S., and Milstein, C. 1979. Mac-1: a monoclonal differentiation antigen identified by monoclonal antibody. *Eur. J. Immunol.* 9:301.

Stanley, E. R. and Guilbert, L. J. 1981. Methods for the purification, assay, characterization and target cell binding of a colony-stimulating factor (CSF-1). *J. Immunol. Meth.* 42:253.

Stone, B. A., Godfrey, B. M., and Seamark, R. F. 1987. *Am. Fertil. Soc.* Abstr. 88.

Talamantes, F., Ogren, L., Markoff, E., Woodard, S., and Madrid, J. 1980. Phylogenetic distribution, regulation of secretion, and prolactin-like effects of placental lactogens. *Fed. Proc.* 39:2582.

Wegmann, T. G. 1984. Fetal protection against abortion: is it immunosuppression or immunostimulation? *Ann. Immunol.* (*Inst. Pasteur*) 135D:309.

Wegmann, T. G. 1988. Maternal T cells promote placental growth and prevent spontaneous abortion. *Immunol. Lett.* 17:297.

Wood, G. W. 1980. Immunohistological identification of macrophages in murine placenta, yolk sac membranes and pregnant uteri. *Placenta* 1:309.

Yokota, T., Lee, F., Rennick, D., Hall, C., Arai, N., Mosmann, T., Nabel, G., Cantor, H., and Arai K-I. 1984. Isolation and characterization of a mouse cDNA clone that expresses mast-cell growth-factor activity in monkey cells. *Proc. Natl. Acad. Sci. USA* 81:1070.

19

Immunological and Endocrinological Factors that Contribute to Successful Pregnancy

GERARD CHAOUAT, ELISABETH MENU, JULIA SZEKERES-BARTHO, CHARLYNE REBUT-BONNETON, PHILIPPE BUSTANY, RADSLAV KINSKY, MICHEL DY, MARIANNE MINKOWSKI, DAVID A. CLARK, and THOMAS G. WEGMANN

Survival of the fetal allograft appears to depend on local placental and decidual factors that modulate T cell and natural killer functions (Chaouat et al., 1983). In addition, there is an intrinsic resistance in some placental cells, mostly trophoblast, to conventional cell-mediated lysis (see Chapter 10). The placenta reacts to local immunological stimuli by increased function and by recruiting lymphoid cells into its vicinity. The functions of these cells, which include a high proportion of NK cells, remaining a matter of speculation (see Chapters 9 and 12).

This chapter is concerned with human placental molecules that regulate the development and lytic function of maternal effector cells, which might otherwise pose a threat to the placenta. Some of these molecules are proteins, but steroids are also involved. We present evidence for a progesterone-dependent suppressive pathway that depends on maternal recognition of fetal antigens. In addition, we describe experimental manipulation of pregnancy outcome in the CBA × DBA/2 murine model of pregnancy failure, using activated cells, lymphokines, or specific antisera. This model represents an *in vivo* system with which to test the relevance of some of the above mechanisms. These studies cannot currently be performed in humans for ethical reasons.

Human Placental Factors Regulate CTL and NK Generation

The work described here had its origins in our earlier studies of murine placenta and teratocarcinoma. In this system, we showed that soluble factors were released from murine teratocarcinoma cells and pure ectoplacental cone trophoblast, which blocked mixed lymphocyte culture reactions, the generation of cytotoxic lymphocytes, and certain lytic functions (Chaouat & Kolb, 1984, 1985; Chaouat et al., 1985; Clark & Chaouat, 1986; Kolb & Chaouat, 1985). In an attempt to extend this work to the human system, we have recently begun to use relatively pure human trophoblast populations derived from a variety of sources, including cesarean deliveries and elective pregnancy terminations. Cultured supernatants from these cells inhibit human mixed lymphocyte culture reactions, and this inhibition can be partially reversed if excess interleukin-2 is added at the beginning of culture (data not shown). The same culture supernatants also inhibit the generation of murine cytolytic T lymphocytes in an MLR (Fig. 19-1) (Menu et al., 1989).

In the murine system, teratocarcinoma supernatants proved to be potent suppressors of lymphocyte function (Chaouat et al., 1985). We have therefore tested supernatants from the human choriocarcinoma cell lines—BeWO, JeG, and JAR—for their effects in culture. They appear to be more effective than placental supernatants in suppressing mixed lymphocyte culture reactions and cell-mediated lympholysis,

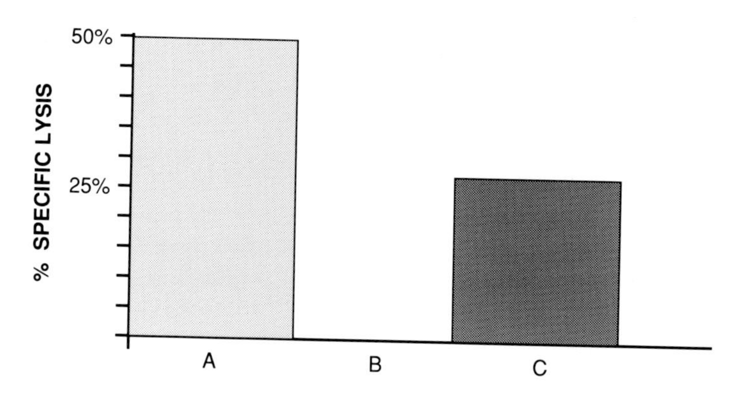

Fig. 19-1. Complete inhibition of human mixed lymphocyte reaction by human placental supernatants. Human lymphocytes were seeded at 5×10^{6}/mL responder versus 5×10^{6}/mL irradiated stimulators in Falcon 3024 culture flasks for 6 days at 37° in a 5% CO2 incubator. Target cells were PHA blasts from the same donor as the stimulator lymphocytes, stimulated with 1 μg/mL PHA (Welcome) for 48 h before the chromium release test (CRT).

After ^{51}Cr labeling, the blasts were used as target cells in a 4-h chromium release assay at a 50:1 effector: target ratio (A) There is a complete inhibition of cell-mediated lympholysis when the culture is performed using a 1:4 dilution of placental supernatant (obtained from 48-h cultures of placental explants from caesarean term delivery) (B) ($p < 0.001$). Note that if the culture is performed with supernatant diluted 1:4 in IL-2 conditioned medium (supernatant from PHA-stimulated human lymphocytes), the inhibition is partially reversed as compared to the MLR/CML performed in S/N diluted 1:4 in normal culture medium (c) ($p < 0.001$).

confirming our results in the mouse. In addition, these supernatants inhibit PHA-induced human T cell proliferation and IL-2-dependent T cell proliferation. They no doubt contain more than one type of suppressor molecule, possibly including suppressor inducer factors. However, we have not found evidence that human trophoblast supernatants are able to induce suppressor T cells, in contrast to our results in the murine system (Chaouat & Chaffaux, 1984). Nevertheless, supernatants from the JeG and BeWO choriocarcinoma cells lines can induce human lymphocytes to become potent suppressors of the mixed lymphocyte culture reaction (Fig. 19-2) (Chaouat et al., 1989). This effect is even seen at a 1:8000 dilution of culture supernatants. Once the educated suppressor cells have been induced, they are effective at ratios as low as 1:250 (suppressor:responder cell). Others have reported negative results in experiments of this type, although this group irradiated its suppressor cell populations with 2500 rads (Saji et al., 1987). We have found that our suppressor cells are inactivated if irradiated at doses higher than 1600 rads (data not shown). We also found that culture supernatants from human trophoblasts, but not the human choriocarcinoma lines, inhibit human natural killer lytic activity in a noncompetitive reversible fashion, as was described for cells derived from the murine placenta (data not shown).

Since the human culture supernatants also inhibited murine lym-

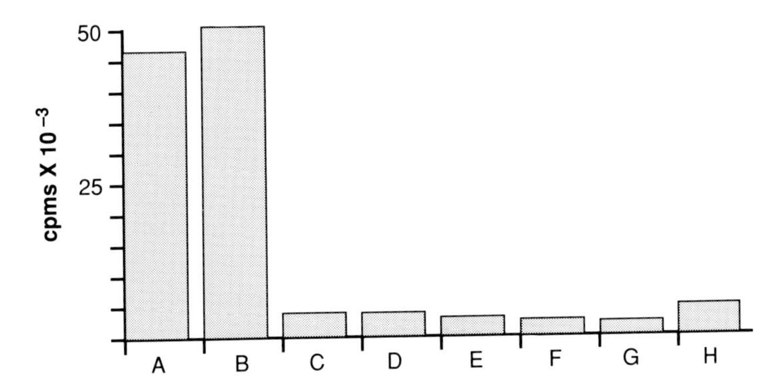

Fig. 19-2. Induction of suppressor cells of the human mixed lymphocyte reaction by culturing lymphocytes for 48 h in the supernatant of the JeG choriocarcinoma cell line. Human MLR performed as in Fig. 19-1, but assessed at day 5 by ^{3}H thymidine incorporation. A: Control MLR B: Response in the presence of cells cultured with human fibroblast S/N (obtained as for JeG S/N) for 48 h. C, D, E, F, G, H same "education" procedure, but using 1:2, 1:500, 1:1000, 1:2000, 1:4000 and 1:8000 dilutions of JeG S/N in culture medium. Cells were then irradiated with 1500 rads and added to the MLR at its initiation so as to achieve a 1:1:1 responder/stimulator/regulator (or control) ratio. Each culture contained 500,000 cells in 100µl in wells of a Falcon 3072 tray. Each data point represents 4 replicates.

phocyte culture reactivity and murine placental supernatant inhibits murine graft-versus-host disease in a popliteal lymph node assay, we tested our human placental supernatants to see if they showed similar activity. Indeed, human placental supernatants caused profound inhibition of popliteal lymph node graft-versus-host reactivity. This was determined by measuring the incorporation of radioisotope into cells removed from draining lymph nodes following footpad injection of allogeneic lymphocytes together with placental cell supernatants. Controls included the same cells injected with control medium or supernatants (Fig. 19-3). We are currently using high-pressure liquid chromatography to identify and purify this material from supernatants.

Our most recent observations indicate that the molecular weight of the material that maximally suppresses IL-2-induced growth of the CTLL cell line is 25 kDa. These data are similar to those obtained in the mouse by Clark (see Chapter 20, this volume) and are compatible with the hypothesis that the activity is due to a TGF-β-like molecule. However, we currently have no direct evidence for this except neutralization assays using anti-TGF-β 2 antisera.

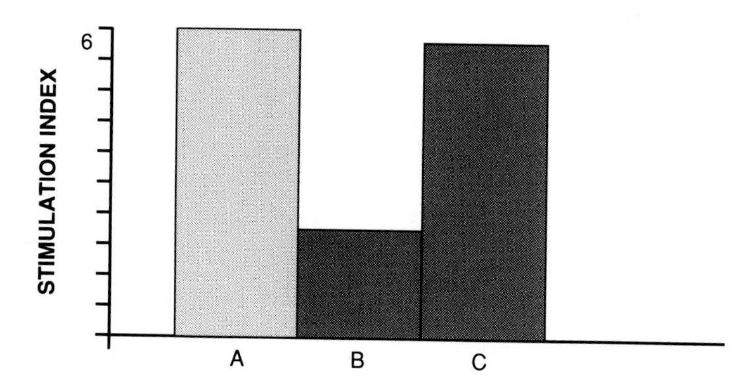

Fig. 19-3. Inhibition by human placental supernatants (obtained from 48 h cultures of placental explants obtained from caesarean deliveries at term) of murine local GVH assessed by the popliteal lymph node assay. To induce a primary GVH, splenocytes from C3H mice were injected in the left footpad of a C3H × Balb/c F_1 mouse. Right and left popliteal lymph nodes were collected on day 5, weighed, and then dissociated mechanically. Proliferation was estimated by seeding cells in 3072 plates in RPMI culture medium in the presence of ^{3}H thymidine. The figure shows the results obtained when GVH was assessed by stimulation index (left PLN weight/right PLN weight). (A) cells injected alone with control medium alone; (B) cells injected with placental S/N; (C) cells injected in conditioned medium from 48 h cultures of human peripheral blood lymphocytes. Similar data were obtained when proliferation was assessed by ^{3}H thymidine incorporation (data not shown).

Steroids as Inhibitors of Lytic Functions

1, 25 Dihydroxycholecalciferol (1,25-$(OH)_2D3$) is a secosteroid hormone that is primarily involved in regulating calcium homeostasis. It is produced by 1-hydroxylation of 25-hydroxycholecalciferol in the kidney. During pregnancy, hydroxylation also occurs in the placenta, contributing to an overall increase of 1,25-$(OH)_2D3$ plasma levels. De Luca and coworkers reported that when rats were placed on a vitamin-D-deficient diet from the time of weaning, a 75% reduction in overall fertility and a 30% reduction in litter size were observed (Halloran & DeLuca, 1979; Halloran et al., 1979). The percentage of pregnant females giving birth to normal litters was reduced by half. Nevertheless, the surviving neonates had apparently normal bone structure.

1,25$(OH)_2D3$ inhibits MLR and decreases cytotoxic T lymphocyte generation from MLR (data not shown). It also inhibits non-MHC restricted (NK) cytotoxicity by peripheral blood lymphocytes (PBLs) (Fig. 19-4) (Rebut-Bonneton et al., 1988).

Progesterone-treated $CD8^+$ T lymphocytes from healthy pregnant women, unlike those from nonpregnant women or patients with idiopathic threatened preterm delivery, release a 34 kDa material that has immunosuppressive activity (Szekeres-Bartho et al., 1985, 1986). A similar material can also be obtained from the splenic lymphocytes of pregnant mice after incubation with progesterone. Most importantly, human or murine embryonic fibroblasts are sensitive to NK-mediated lysis, but this lytic process is blocked by the 34 kDa substance. The 34 kDa material is not produced if the progesterone receptor agonist RU486 is added in culture along with progesterone (Fig. 19-5).

These findings suggested the presence of functional progesterone

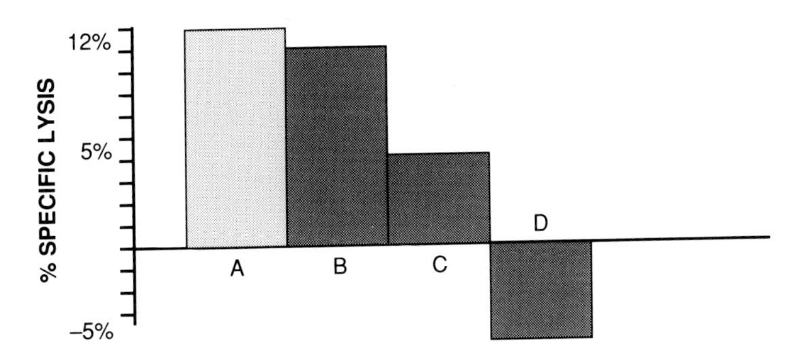

Fig. 19-4. Inhibition by 1,25$(OH)_2D3$ of NK mediated lysis of the K562 taget cell line. Representative experiment at a 50:1 effector:target ratio in a 4 h CRT performed in culture medium (A); or in the presence of 1,25 $(OH)_2D3$ at 10^{-10} (B); 10^{-9} (C); and 10^{-8M} (D) concentrations.

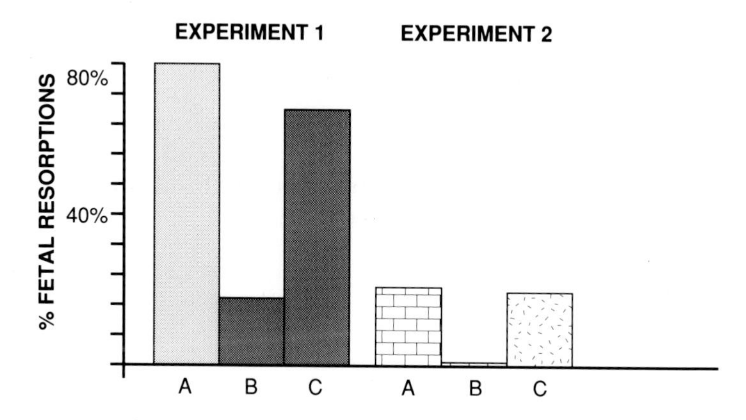

Fig. 19-5. Inhibition of NK mediated lysis of human embryonic fibroblasts by material secreted from cultured lymphocytes of pregnant women after incubation with progesterone. 1×10^7 peripheral blood lymphocytes from pregnant women were cultured for 2 h in culture medium (A), or in culture medium supplemented with 10 μg/mL progesterone (B) or 10μg/mL progesterone + 10μg/mL RU 486 (C). After overnight dialysis, supernatants were added at the beginning of an NK assay against human embryonic fibroblasts. The 100% lysis value is given as a reference point. Note a significant reduction in NK mediated lysis in both experiments with supernatants from progesterone treated lymphocytes (B versus A,$p < 0.001$). Note also that inhibition is reversed if RU 486 is added during the generation of the supernatant.

binding sites on lymphocytes from pregnant women, but not on normal lymphocytes. When lymphocytes were stained with the progesterone receptor-specific antibody mPRI, using an avidin-biotin peroxidase detection system, we found nuclear staining in 14.6 ± 3.7% of lymphocytes from 27 pregnant women compared to 0.47 ± 0.33% lymphocytes from 15 nonpregnant women. CD8 and CD4 cells were then separately depleted by complement-dependent lysis. Elimination of the $CD8^+$ cells was accompanied by a 62 ± 18% decrease in progesterone receptor-bearing cells, whereas depletion of $CD4^+$ cells resulted in a twofold increase in the number of $mPRI^+$ lymphocytes. These studies were carried out in collaboration with Dr. Gy Szekeres, Hotel Dieu, Paris.

These results were confirmed by two-color FACS analysis, staining simultaneously for CD8 (or CD4) and the progesterone receptor. PHA treatment, as well as allogeneic stimulation, resulted in a significant increase in the proportion of progesterone receptor-bearing lymphocytes in nonpregnant individuals (Szekeres-Bartho et al., unpublished data).

These results indicate that $CD8^+$ lymphocytes from pregnant women express progesterone receptors and that these receptors can be induced in normal lymphocyte by mitogenic or alloantigenic stimuli. One must therefore consider the existence of immunosuppressive pathways related to steroid activity when attempting to explain fetal allograft survival.

Positive and Negative Immunomodulation of Murine Pregnancy

The work described above represents an attempt to apply some of the insights derived from our previous work in murine pregnancy to human pregnancy. Many similarities are obvious from this comparison. One very great advantage to murine studies is the ability to perform *in vivo* manipulations to confirm some of the regulatory effects on pregnancy outcome. In the remainder of this chapter, we describe some of our recent findings in this regard, using the CBA × DBA/2 murine spontaneous abortion model. Our original observations indicated that prior immunization of CBA females with BALB/c but not DBA/2 spleen cells resulted in a decrease in spontaneous fetal resorption in this strain combination (Chaouat et al., 1983, 1988). A series of genetic studies led us to conclude that MHC and non-MHC genes were both involved in this phenomenon (Chaouat et al., 1988). We have since gone on to study the effects of a number of immunological manipulations on fetal viability. Some of these treatments have positive effects on outcome, whereas some have negative effects. We consider the positive effects first.

Active spleen cell immunization to prevent abortion results in an increase in placental and fetal size. This led to the development of the immunotrophism hypothesis, which states that products of the maternal immune system, in particular cytokines, can influence placental growth and fetal survival (Wegmann, 1984). Recently we have conducted a series of experiments to test this hypothesis directly. Previous studies indicated that adoptive transfer of either CBA anti-BALB/c antiserum or CBA anti-BALB immune T cells could prevent fetal resorption, as compared to control nonimmune serum or cells. It remained to be shown whether T cells were necessary for this effect *in vivo*. To test this directly, we immunized CBA female mice with BALB/c spleen cells 7 days before mating to DBA/2. Based on our previous experiments, we knew that this immunization leads to active production of antipaternal T cells and antibody. The immunized animals were then treated with anti-L3T4 plus anti-Ly2 monoclonal antibodies in midgestation to deplete their T cells while leaving the antipaternal antibody intact. This abrogated the effect of prior immunization, resulting in a high fetal resorption rate and reduced placental size. This result indicates that maternal T cells are necessary to prevent fetal resorption in this model, even in the presence of actively induced maternal antipaternal antibody (Fig. 19-6, Column D). In addition, we found that autoimmune mice have large placentas,

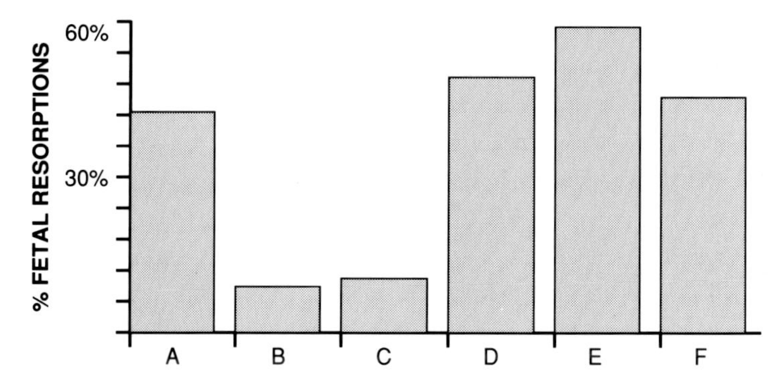

Fig. 19-6. Prevention of fetal resorptions in the CBA × DBA/2 system by adoptive transfer of spleen cells from H-2^k haplotype compatible MRL 1pr/1pr mice but not by spleen cells from control MRL mice. (A) Resorption rates in the CBAx DBA/2 mating. (B) Same mating as A, but mice were immunized against Balb/c splenocytes 7 days before mating. (C) Same mating as A, but mice received 100 × 10^6 splenocytes from MRL 1pr/1pr mice on day 0 (vaginal plug). (D) Same as A, but transfer of spleen cells (100 × 10^6 from non-autoimmune MRL mice. (E) Same as A, but transfer of splenocytes from MRL 1pr/1pr mice on day 0 after depletion of T cells by anti-L3T4 + anti LyT-2 + complement treatment *in vitro*. B and C versus A ($p < 0.01$). D, E and F groups are not significantly different from A ($p > 0.05$).

the size of which is reduced by T cell depletion in midgestation (Chaouat et al., 1988). We therefore asked whether spleen cells from these mice could adoptively transfer the antiabortion effect to CBA/J females who were subsequently mated to DBA/2 males. This was indeed observed, and the effect was shown to be abrogated by prior treatment of the spleen cells with anti-L3T4 plus anti-Ly2 monoclonal antibodies and complement (Fig. 19-6, Column E).

NK cells also seem to be involved in this model of spontaneous fetal resorption (Chaouat, 1986). Baines and his colleagues have also found that resorbing embryos are infiltrated by cells showing an NK-like activity (De Fougerolles & Baines, 1988). Gendron and Baines (1988) have reported that antiasialo GM1 antibody treatment can reduce the rate of spontaneous fetal resorption, and we have also confirmed this result (Fig. 19-7). Further support for a role of NK-like cells has come from the observations of Baines and his colleagues, who showed that poly-IC enhances fetal resorption in the CBA × DBA/2 model, and we have confirmed this result using the less embryotoxic poly I/poly C 12U, provided by Dr. M. N. Thang, Hopital Saint Antoine, Paris (Fig. 19-8). R. Kinsky has also observed a similar enhancement of resorption in CBA × BALB matings, as well as in the BALB × BALB and C57 × BALB strain combinations. In addition, he has obtained

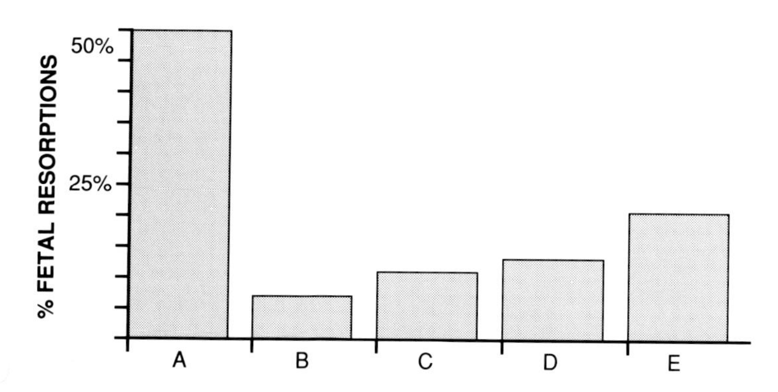

Fig. 19-7. Treatment of CBA × DBA/2 fetal wastage by antiasialo GM1 antiserum. (A) CBA × DBA/2 mating control. (B) CBA × Balb/c (non resorbing strain combination control). (C) CBA immunized 7 days prior to mating against Balb/c splenocytes, and subsequently mated with DBA/2. (D) transfer on day 0 of CBA anti-Balb/c antiserum (0.2 ml i.v.) to CBA/J female pregnant by DBA/2. (D) Same as A, but treated on day 0 with DBA anti-Balb/c antiserum. (E) Same as A, but injected on days 6, 8, and 10 of pregnancy with rabbit anti-asialo GM1 antiserum (0.2 ml). (This serum, plus complement, totally abrogates NK lytic activity of CBA or Balb/c nude splenocytes). p values:B vs A <0.001; C vs A <0.01; D vs A <0.01; E vs A: $0.05 < p < 0.02$

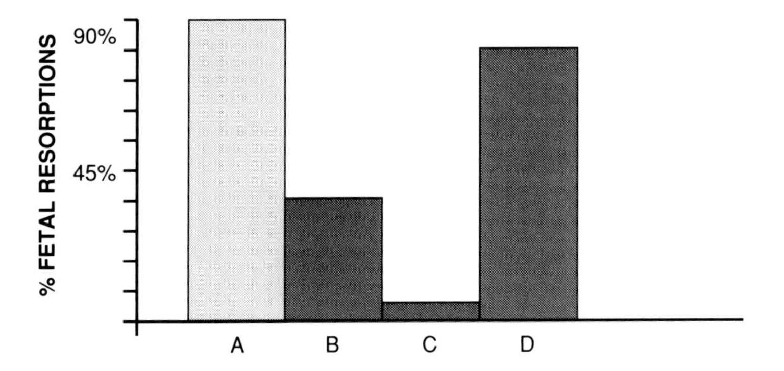

Fig. 19-8. Abortifacient effects of Poly I Poly (C) 12U, an NK cell activator. C3H mice were injected ip with Poly I C12U on day 0 of pregnancy. (A) LPS induced resorption controls (mice received 1 μg of LPS from *Salmonella Enteridis* by ip injection on day 8 of pregnancy (LPS Westphal Difco was a kind gift of Dr Monique Parand and Louis Chedid)). (B) CBA × DBA/2 control mating. (C) Anti Balb/c immunization control ($p < 0.02$ vs B). (D) Poly I C12U injected mice ($p < 0.001$ vs A).

preliminary results indicating that enhanced resorption can be adoptively transferred by spleen cells from isogenic donors activated for 48 hours by poly C 12U, if the cells are transferred 2 days before mating. The effect of the adoptive transfer was abolished if the activated spleen cell population was pretreated with a rabbit antimurine NK antibody (Kinsky et al., unpublished observations, and 1990).

These effects of T cell and NK cell manipulation on fetal survival led us to try to identify the lymphokines involved in enhancing fetal survival. A role for lymphokines and cytokines related to CSF was suggested by experiments in which CSF-1, IL-3, and GM-CSF were shown to enhance trophoblast growth in 12-day placenta and in ectoplacental cone trophoblast (Armstrong & Chaouat, 1989; Athanassakis et al., 1987). We found that GM-CSF was present in decidual cell supernatants (Chaouat, Dy, and Minkowski, unpublished data; Wegmann et al., 1989) and therefore decided to see whether GM-CSF prevented spontaneous fetal resorption when administered during midgestation to CBA females pregnant by DBA/2J males. Even very low doses of GM-CSF were effective in preliminary resorption, with effects seen using 200 or 400 units of purified GM-CSF from the P338 D1 cell line, given ip on days 8, 10, and 12 of gestation. Recombinant GM-CSF (Genzyme) had similar effects when given at a dose of 200 Units ip or iv on the same injection schedule (Fig. 19-9). IL-3 also had comparable effects (data not shown).

All of the above experiments indicate that maternal T cells and their products can influence pregnancy outcome. In addition, cytokines produced by non-T cells, including NK cells, also have significant effects (Chaouat et al., 1988). Just as GM-CSF and IL-3 influence pregnancy outcome positively, there are a number of fairly specific

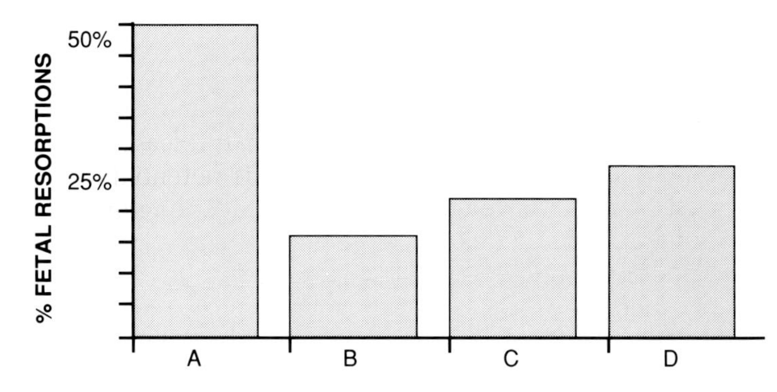

Fig. 19-9. Treatment of resorption by GM-CSF. (A) CBA × DBA/2 mating control (B) CBA × Balb/c mating control ($p < 0.001$). (C) Same as A, but injected ip with GM CSF (from P338 D1) on days 8, 10, and 12 (400 HCSF Units ($p < 0.02$). (D) Same, but Genzyme R-GM CSF (400 GENZYME CSF Units ip on days 8, 10, and 12) $p < 0.05$.

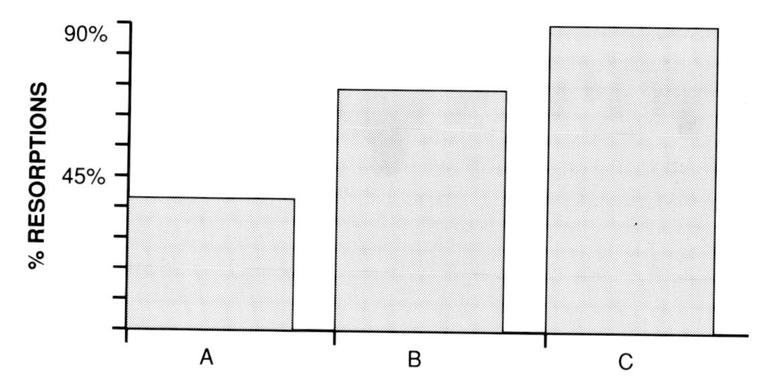

Fig. 19-10. Enhancement of CBA × DBA/2 fetal resorptions by human R-TNF (A) CBA × DBA/2 mating control, (B) human R-TNF (800 Units ip per mouse on day 8). (Human TNF was a kind gift of Dr J Wietzerbin, U 96 Inserm, Institut Curie). (C) LPS control as in Figure 19-9.

agents that adversely influence pregnancy outcome in the CBA × DBA/2 model. One such cytokine is TNF-α. When CBA females pregnant by DBA/2 males are injected with recombinant TNF-α, there is a dramatic increase in the percent of fetal resorptions (Fig. 19-10). There is an even greater effect if the mice are injected with lipopolysaccharide (LPS). LPS was initially described as an abortifacient by Parand and Chedid (1964), and LPS treatment has been shown to increase the production of TNF-α (Parand, 1987). A number of these studies have recently been repeated by Gendron, Baines, and colleagues. Table 19-1 summarizes all known positive and negative influences on the rate of fetal resorbtion in the CBA × DBA/2 model to date.

The work presented here using the CBA × DBA/2 abortion model suggests at least three different mechanisms that may act to prevent abortion after active immunization. The first is a direct trophic effect of lymphocytes and their products on spongiotrophoblast. The second is an indirect effect, mediated through CSF-1 released by macrophages in the decidua. The significance of this potential mechanism may be questioned, however, since Nicklin and Billington (1979) and Redline and Lu (1988), have presented evidence that macrophages are inactivated in the decidua basalis. On the other hand, CSF-1 levels dramatically increase in the uterus during pregnancy, and this factor appears to be synthesized by the uterine gland cells (Bartocci et al., 1986). Perhaps these cells are partially influenced by products or cells of the immune system. A third possibility is that GM-CSF or IL-3 release may lead to a decrease in TNF production or may inhibit LAK cell activation by placental antigens in the decidua or other tissues at the maternal-fetal interface. Interestingly, it has recently been shown that IL-3 strongly inhibits the induction and function of human LAK

Table 19-1. Modifications of CBA × DBA/2 resorption rates

POSITIVE EFFECTS: DECREASES RESORPTIONS			
Clean animal facility		+ + + +	(Hamilton & Hamilton, 1987)
Anti-Balb/c immunization		+ + + +	(Chaouat et al., 1983)
Prior Balb/c mating and pregnancy	1	+ +	(Chaouat et al., 1987; Chavez et al., 1987; Kiger & Bobe, 1987)
	4	+ + + +	(Chaouat et al., 1987, 1988b)
Antiplacental immunization		+ + +	(Chaouat et al., 1987, 1988b)
Good Balb/c × DBA/2 recombinants		+ + to + + + +	(Kiger et al., 1985)
Immune serum (anti-Balb/c) transfer		+ + +	(Chaouat et al., 1985a, 1985b)
Whole immune T cells		+ +	(Chaouat et al., 1985)
Whole immune B cells		+ +	(Chaouat et al., 1985)
Anti-idiotypic treatment		+ +	(Chaouat & Lankar, 1987)
Antiasialo-GM1		+ + +	(Chaouat et al., 1988; De Fougerolles & Baines, 1987)
MRL 1pr/1pr, AKR 1pr/1pr cell transfer		+ + +	(Chaouat et al., 1988, 1989)
IL3		+ +	(Chaouat et al., 1988, 1989)
Natural GM-CSF		+ +	(Chaouat et al., 1988, 1989)
R GM CSF		+ + to + + +	(Chaouat et al., 1988, 1989)
HILDA-LIF-DA		Being tested	(Clark et al., 1989)
NO EFFECTS			
Immunization with BALB non H-2^d congenics			(Kiger et al., 1985)
Immunization with H-2^d cells on non Balb background			(Kiger et al., 1985)
Immunization with some Balb/c DBA/2 recombinants			(Kiger et al., 1985)
NEGATIVE EFFECTS (ENHANCES RESORPTIONS)			
"Dirty" animal facility		+ + to + + +	(Chaouat et al., 1988; Hamilton & Hamilton, 1987)
Aging		+ + to + + + +	(Chaouat et al., 1987; Clark et al., 1987)
Successive DBA/2 pregnancies		+ + to + + + +	(Chaouat et al., 1987, 1988; Clark & Chaouat, 1986)
Some Balb/c × DBA/2 recombinants (Imm, Pregn)		+	(Kiger et al., 1985)
High doses of rIL-2 (CBA and others)		+ + +	(Chaouat et al., Tezabwala & Johnstone, 1986)
High doses of murine gamma-interferon		+ + +	(Chaouat, 1988)

Table 19-1. Modifications of CBA × DBA/2 resorption rates (*Continued*)

NEGATIVE EFFECTS (ENHANCES RESORPTIONS) (*Continued*)		
Poly IC or Poly IC 12 injection	+ + + to + + + +	(Chaouat et al., 1988, 1989; De Fougerolles and Baines, 1987)
Transfer of cells activated by Poly IC	+ + + to + + + +	(Kinsky, 1988, 1989)
Transfer of cells activated by Poly (C (nude or CBA/J) (does not happen if depleted of NKs)	+ + + +	(Chaouat et al., 1988)
LPS-general phenomenon: CBA/J × DBA/2	+ + + +	(Parand, 1964; Chaouat & Parand, 1988)
TNFα	+ + + to + + + +	(Parand, 1987; Chaouat et al., 1987, 1988)

cells (Gallagher et al., 1988). The exact role played by T cells and NK cells in all of these interactions thus remains to be determined.

DISCUSSION

At present it appears that two main factors contribute to fetal survival in the human and mouse models we have been studying. The first is represented by NK-like effector cells or LAK cells, since it is known that trophoblast can be killed by LAK cells or OptiMEM cultured CTLs, which display LAK-like activity (Drake & Head, 1988, 1989). These cells could be activated as a result of local infection or escape from suppression. This is consistent with the abortifacient effects observed after injection of rIL2 (Tezabwala & Johnstone, 1986). Local imbalances in lymphokine regulation could explain the environmental effects on the CBA × DBA/2 model observed by Hamilton and Hamilton (1987). Local active suppression seems to be due in part to TGF-β-like molecules in the placenta and decidua that offset the effects of IL-2 on effector cell activation and function. These effects can be bypassed by addition of excess IL-2. Indeed, it is possible that the suppressor molecules reported here may suppress various types of immune function while serving simultaneously as growth and angiogenic factors for the placenta. In addition, progesterone receptors may be induced on a larger number of cells as a result of maternal antifetal allorecognition. Progesterone itself induces a suppressor factor that reduces NK activity. Reduced maternal anti-paternal allorecognition might result in decreased local active suppression, including that mediated by $Lyt2^{+}$ suppressor T cells, and decreased progesterone-dependent suppression of NK and LAK cell function. Together, their effects could result in the destruction of embryonic fibroblasts by NK and LAK cells and subsequent fetal resorption. Conversely, reduction of local killing activity, decrease in TNF secretion, and optimal CSF production would appear to give a combined effect that ensures optimal placental growth. This in turn would lead to optimal production of immunoregulatory steroids and TGF-β-like molecules and would favor recruitment of decidual suppressor cells by trophoblast. The latter cells could be activated by placental interferons or interferon-like molecules that are known to exist in the placenta (Charlier et al., 1989; Charpigny et al., 1988; Duc Goiran et al., 1987). Interestingly, it is known that GM-CSF and interferons synergize in inducing natural suppressor activity (Cleveland et al., 1988). The success of pregnancy could thus depend on an optimal interaction between all of these pathways. Obviously further evaluation is needed to determine the relative importance of each of these mechanisms.

Additional questions include the nature of the placental antigens that are responsible for recruiting maternal immune cells and the nature of the cells on which these antigens are expressed. Overall, we still have to determine the relative roles of T cells and NK cells in mediating normal placental function, the types of molecules they use to do so, and the nature of the recognition events that lead to this function.

References

Armstrong, D. T. A. and Chaouat, G. 1989. Effects of lymphokines and immune complexes on murine placental cell growth in vitro. *Biol. Reprod.* In press.

Athanassakis, I., Blaeckley, R. C., Paetkau, V., Guilbert, L., Barr, P. J., and Wegmann, T. G. 1987. The immunostimulatory effect of T cells and T cell derived lymphokines on murine fetally derived placental cells. *J. Immunol.* 138:1–37.

Bartocci, A., Pollard, J. W., and Stanley, E. R. 1986. Regulation of colony stimulating factor 1 during pregnancy. *J. Exp. Med.* 164:956.

Chaouat, G. 1986. Placental infiltration of resorbing CBA × DBA/2 embryos. *J. Reprod. Immunol.* suppl 1.

Chaouat, G. and Chaffaux, S. 1984. Placental products induce suppressor cells of graft versus host reaction. *Am. J. Reprod. Immunol.* 6:3–107.

Chaouat, G. and Kolb, J. P. 1984. Immunoactive products of murine placenta. II. Afferent suppression of maternal cell mediated immunity by supernatants from short term enriched cultures of murine trophoblast enriched maternal cell populations. *Ann. Immunol.* (*Inst. Pasteur*) 135C:205.

Chaouat, G. and Kolb, J. P. 1985. Immunoactive products of placenta IV. Impairment by placental cells and their products of CTL function at the effector stage. *J. Immunol.* 135:215.

Chaouat, G., Kiger, N., and Wegmann, T. G. 1983a. Vaccination against spontaneous abortion in mice. *J. Reprod. Immunol.* 5:389–394.

Chaouat, G., Kolb, J. P., and Wegmann, T. G. 1983b. The murine placenta as an immunological barrier between the mother and the fetus. *Immunol. Rev.* 75:31.

Chaouat, G., Kolb, J. P., Riviere, M., and Chaffaux, S. 1985a Local and systemic regulation of maternal antifetal cytotoxicity during murine pregnancy. In *Contributions in Gynecology and Obstetrics, Vol.* 14 (V. Toder and A. E. Beer, eds.). Basel: S. Karger, p. 55.

Chaouat, G., Kolb, J. P., Kiger, N., Stanislawski, M., and Wegmann, T. G. 1985b. Immunological concomitants of vaccination against abortion in mice. *J. Immunol.* 134:1594–1602.

Chaouat, G., Lankar, D., Kolb, J. P., and Clark, D. A. 1987. 2 modeles d'avortements d' origine immunitaire chez la souris de laboratoire: mecanismes abortifs, modalites et mechanismes du traitement par l'immunisation contre un male relie ou non relie suivant les differences antigeniques pere mere. In *Colloque INSERM CNRS Immunologie de la Relation Feto-maternelle,* Vol. 54 (G. Chaouat, ed.). J. LIBBEY. p. 243.

Chaouat, G., Clark, D. A., and Wegmann, T. G. 1988a. Genetics aspects of the CBA/J × DBA/2 J and B10 × B10. A models of murine spontaneous abortions and prevention by leukocyte immunisation. In *Early Pregnancy Loss: Mechanisms and Treatment* (R. W. Beard, and F. Sharp, eds.). Royal College of Obstretrics and Gynecology Press, p. 89.

Chaouat, G., Menu, E., Bustany, P., Rebut-Bonneton, C., and Wegmann T. G. 1988b. Role du placenta dans le maintien de l' allogreffe fetale. *Reprod. Nutr. Dev.* 28:1587–1588.

Chaouat, G., Menu, E., Athanassakis, I., and Wegmann, T. G. 1989. Maternal T Cells regulate placental size and fetal survival. *Reg. Immunol.* 1:

Charlier, M., Hue, D., Martal, J., and Gayle, P. 1989. Cloning and expression of cDNA encoding ovine trophoblastin. Its identity with class II interferons. *Gene.*

Charpigny, G., Reinaud, P., Huet, J. C., Guillomot, M., Charlier, M., Pernollet, J. C., and Martal, J. 1988. High homology between a trophoblastic protein (trophoblastin) isolated from ovine embryos and alpha interferon. *FEBS Lett.* 228:1–12.

Clark, D. A. and Chaouat, G. 1986. Characterisation of the cellular basis for the inhibition of cytotoxic effector cells by the murine placenta. *Cell. Immunol.* 102:43.

Cleveland, M. G., Lane, R. G., and Klimpel, G. R. 1988. Spontaneous interferon beta production. A common feature of natural suppressor systems. *J. Immunol.* 141:2043.

David, V., Bourge, J. F., Guglielmi, P., Mathieu Mahul, D., Degos, L., and Bensussan, A. 1987. Human T cell clones use a CD3 associated surface antigen recognition structure to exhibit both NK-like and allogeneic cytotoxic reactivity. *J. Immunol.* 136:2381.

De Fougerolles, R. and Baines, M. 1988. Modulation of natural killer activity influences resorbtion rates in CBA × DBA/2 matings. *J. Reprod. Immunol.* 11:147.

Drake, B. L. and Head, J. R. 1988. Murine trophoblast cells are susceptible to lymphokine Activated killer (LAK) cell lysis. *Am. J. Reprod. Immunol.* 16:114.

Drake, B. L. and Head, J. R. 1989. Murine trophoblast cells can be killed by allospecific cytototoxic T lymphocytes generated in Gibco OPTI MEM medium. *J. Reprod. Immunol.* 15:1.

Gallagher, G., Wilcox, F., and Al-Azzawi, F. 1988. Interleukin 3 and interleukin 4 each strongly suppress induction and function of human LAK cells. *Clin. Exp. Immunol.* 74:166–171.

Gendron, R. and Baines, M. 1988. Infiltrating decidual natural killer cells are associated with spontaneous abortion in mice. *Cell. Immunol.* 133:261.

Halloran, B. P. and De Luca, H. F. 1979. Vitamin D deficiency and reproduction in the rats. *Science* 204:73.

Hamilton, M. S. and Hamilton, B. L. 1987. Environmental influences on immunologically associated recurrent spontaneous abortion in CBA/J mice. *J. Reprod. Immunol.* 11:237.

Halloran, B. P., Barthel, E. N., and De Luca, H. F. 1979. Vitamin D metabolism during pregnancy and lactation in the rats. *Proc. Nat. Acad. Sci. USA* 76:5549.

Kinsky, R., Delage, G., Rosin, N., Thang, M. N., Hoffmann, M., and Chaouat G. 1990. A murine model of NK mediated fetal resorbtion. *Am. J. Reprod. Immunol.* In press.

Kolb, J. P., Chaouat, G., and Chassoux, D. J. 1984. Immunoactive products of placenta. III. Suppression of natural killing activity. *J. Immunol.* 132:2305.

Menu, E., Kaplan, L., Andreu, G., Denver, L., and Chaouat, G. 1989. Immunoactive products of human placenta. I. An immunoregulatory factor obtained from explants cultures of human placenta inhibit CTL generation and cytotoxic effector cell generation. *Cell. Immunol.* In Press.

Nicklin, S. and Billington, W. D. 1979. Macrophage activity in mouse pregnancy. *J. Reprod. Immunol.* 1:117.

Parand, M. 1987. Role of TNF in non specific stimulation of mouse resistance to infection. Immunobiology. International Conference on Tumor Necrosis Factor and Related Cytokines, Heidelberg.

Parand, M. and Chedid, L. 1964. Protective effects of chlorpromazine against endotoxin induced abortion. *Proc. Roy. Soc. Exp. Biol. Med.* 116:906.

Rebut-Bonneton, C., Menu, E., Denver, L., Andreu, G., and Chaouat, G. 1988. The effects of 1,25,Dihydroxy vitamin D alone or in presence of human placental supernatant on in vitro lymphocyte reactions. *Lymphokine Res.* 7:295.

Redline, R. W. and Lu, C. W. 1988. Specific defects in the anti-listerial immune response in discrete regions of the murine uterus and placenta account for the susceptibility to infection. *J. Immunol.* 140:3497.

Saji, F., Koyama, M., Tameda, T., Negoro, T., Nakamuro, K., and Tanizawa, O. 1987. Effect of a soluble factor secreted from cultured human trophoblast cells on in vitro lymphocyte reactions. *Am. J. Reprod. Immunol.* 13:121.

Szekeres Bartho, J., Kilar, F., Falkay, G., Csernu, V., Torok, A., and Pacsa, A. S. 1985. Progesterone-treated lymphocytes release a substance inhibiting cytotoxicity and prostaglandin synthesis. *Am. J. Reprod. Immunol.* 9:15–24.

Szekeres Bartho, J., Hadnagy, J., and Pacsa, A. S. 1986. The suppressive effect of progesterone during pregnancy: unique sensitivity of pregnancy lymphocytes. *J. Reprod. Immunol.* 7:121.

Tezabwala, B. U. and Johnstone, A. P. 1986. Effects of administration of interleukin 2 in pregnancy. *J. Reprod. Immunol.* suppl 1:47.

Wegmann, T. G. Fetal protection against abortion: is it immunosuppression or immunostimulation? *Ann. Immunol.* (Inst. Pasteur) 135D:309–311.

Wegmann, T. G., Athanassakis, I., Guilbert, L., Branch, D., Dy, M., Menu, E., and Chaouat G. 1989. The role of M-CSF and GM-CSF in fostering placental growth, fetal growth, and fetal survival. *Transplantation Proc.* 21.1.P1,89, 566–569.

20

Role of a Factor Related to Transforming Growth Factor Beta-2 in Successful Pregnancy

DAVID A. CLARK, JUDITH R. HEAD, BELINDA L. DRAKE, GABRIEL FULOP, JOYCE BRIERLEY, JUSTIN MANUEL, DALJEET BANWATT, and GERARD CHAOUAT

The problem of early pregnancy failure and its mechanisms and treatment (Beard et al., 1988) remain unsolved. It is believed that 75% of all human conceptions fail and that approximately 50–60% fail during the preimplantation period or at the time of implantation (Clark, 1988). After implantation, approximately 30% of embroys fail, despite giving rise to at least two elevated beta-hCG tests (Clark, 1988; Wilcox et al., 1988); within the latter group, there are approximately two occult abortions for every clinical miscarriage.

It has been difficult to study the pathophysiology of early pregnancy failure in humans. Hertig, Rock, and Adams (1956) were able to collect a total of 34 early pregnancies (successful and unsuccessful) for histological study from 211 uteri. Functional studies were virtually impossible until recently, owing to difficulties in knowing what to measure and problems in obtaining viable material. For example, it was known that up 50 to 70% of clinical abortus material showed chromosomal anomalies depending upon reproductive history and maternal age (Boue et al., 1975). However, the rate of successful karyotyping was low, and only with the development of techniques for chorionic villous biopsy and oocyte retrieval by follicle aspiration did it become clear that 50–60% of early pregnancy failures may be related to genetic defects (Eiben et al., 1987; Wramsby et al., 1987). In the case of recurrent loss, it is more difficult to implicate random genetic events (Boue et al., 1975), and one must suspect physiological defects. Studies in this area have been facilitated by the development of techniques for biopsy of the early placental bed (Michel et al., 1989). Recently, we have also gained a better understanding of the factors determining success or failure of pregnancy from studies in allopregnant laboratory mice. The developmental kinetics of the mouse are such that the first 4 days postimplantation correspond to the first 16–18 days of human postimplantation embryo growth or 4–5 weeks of gestational age (Rugh, 1968). Therefore, pregnancy failure during the 4-day "peri-implantation" phase of murine pregnancy corresponds roughly to the time period during which occult pregnancy failures occur in humans, whereas failure of mouse pregnancy on or after day 9.5 (5 days post-implantation) corresponds to the timing of most human first-trimester abortions. In the mouse, there are both anatomical and functional differences that distinguish these two phases. In the postimplantation phase, a distinct placenta and fetus are formed, class I MHC-like antigens are expressed on the fetus and on extravillous trophoblast in contact with decidua, and separate maternal-placental and fetal-placental circulations have formed (Clark et al., 1987a, 1988).

Two main types of anatomical defects have been shown to be associated with spontaneous human abortions. Defective fetoplacental angiogenesis occurs in 75–90% of samples (Meegdes et al., 1988). In addition, 60–70% of samples show defective invasion of decidual arteries by extravillous trophoblast (Khong et al., 1987) that does not correlate with the presence of chromosomal abnormalities (Michel et al., in preparation). In all cases, either no embryo was identified by ultrasound examination or the embryo had lost fetal heart activity. This latter situation has a parallel in the murine system. In most abortions, the fetus dies and undergoes necrosis within its trophoblastic sac to produce an anembryonic sac (resorption). In a few instances, however, a formed but deceased "white" embryo is noted. How might such abnormalities come about other than by a genetic defect?

Mechanisms of Pregnancy Failure in the Postimplantation Phase

Defective growth and development can usually be explained by a lack of adequate growth-stimulating factors, by the presence of inhibitors, or by a combination of the two. Recently, there has been considerable interest in the possible role of growth factors in abortion based on the presence of such factors as CSF-1 and GM-CSF in the decidua (Clark & Chaouat, 1989a and b; Pollard et al., 1987) and the presence of CSF receptors in trophoblast subpopulations (Pollard et al., 1987). As well, trophoblast has been shown to respond to growth factors either by production of hormones (see Chapter 18, this volume) or by proliferation (Athanassakis et al., 1987). On the other hand, the concept of inhibition framed conceptually in terms of "rejection of the fetal allograft" must be considered.

Figure 20-1 indicates potential targets for inhibitors that could lead to embryonic death. A direct attack on the fetus by sensitized maternal lymphocytes could potentially lead to rejection, and certainly maternal lymphocytes occasionally colonize the fetus and produce chimeric embryos with either graft-versus-host disease or immunodeficiency

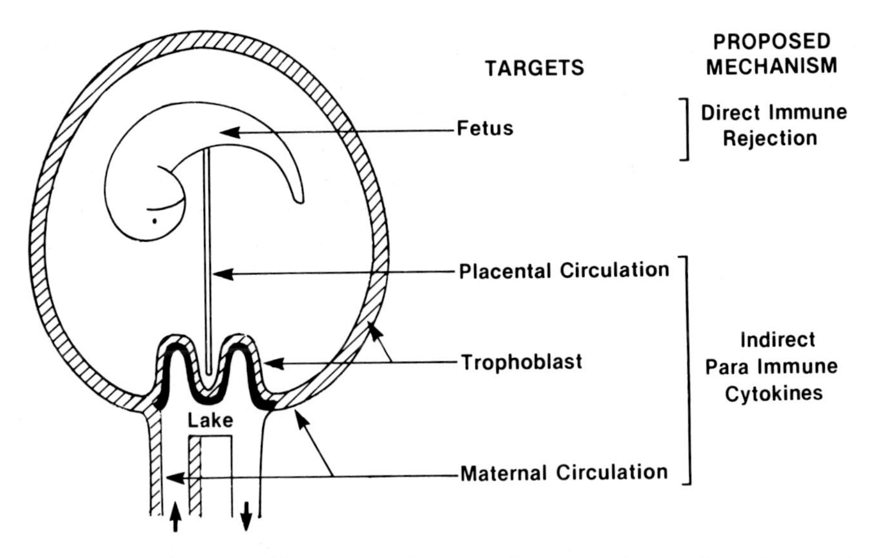

Fig. 20-1. Schematic illustration of potential targets of specific and natural effectors leading to fetal necrosis in postimplantation period (resorption, abortion, rejection). ■ represents MHC-negative syncytiotrophoblast whereas ▨ represents extravillous, largely MHC-positive, trophoblast.

(Ammann, 1986). Maternal antibody can also enter the fetus and produce hemolytic disease (? white embryos). However, for several reasons we do not believe such mechanisms account for the majority of fetal deaths in unexplained pregnancy failure:

1. In the mouse, fetal cells have not been shown to be sensitive to lysis by maternal cytotoxic T lymphocytes (CTL) at the time resorption begins (Croy & Rossant, 1987).
2. Maternal antipaternal MHC alloantibody does not have demonstrated pathogenic effects on the fetus (Bell & Billington, 1983). Similarly, antierythocyte antibody that might produce hemolysis and anemia cannot account for the failure to form a fetoplacental circulation seen in *early* pregnancy failure.
3. The measured frequency with which maternal lymphocytes gain access to the fetus is less than the frequency of resorption (Hunziker et al., 1984).

The second potential target for inhibition/rejection is the trophoblast. Trophoblast is highly resistant to killing by antigen-specific immune effector mechanisms, although a subpopulation may be partially sensitive to alloantibody and CTL *in vitro* (Head et al., 1987; Zuckermann, 1986). Trophoblast may, however, be sensitive to certain types of nonspecific effector cells that are part of the natural defense system involved in surveillance against primitive embryonic-neoplastic cells. Certain types of activated natural effector cells, including lymphokine-activated killer (LAK) cells, can readily lyse trophoblast (Clark et al., 1986b; Drake & Head, 1988). Many natural effector cells produce toxic cytokines, such as tumor necrosis factor-alpha (TNF-α), which causes vascular thrombosis (Shiomura et al., 1988). Trophoblast cells may express receptors for TNF-α (Eades et al., 1988), and a murine placental cell line with trophoblastic features (Slapsys et al., 1988) is susceptible to growth inhibition (but not lysis) by low concentrations. TNF-α (unpublished data).

Other products of the paraimmune defense system may also be relevant effector molecules and these are listed in Table 20-1. Toxic inhibition of trophoblast growth or disruption of either of the circulatory systems shown in Figure 20-1 could result in fetal death and apparent rejection of the fetal allograft. Note that since damage is mediated by inhibitory molecules, minimal cellular infiltration is required. Indeed, the uterine endometrium and decidua contain large numbers of cells, including macrophages that can potentially produce cytotoxic mediators. Conversely, suppression of specific immune effector cells and paraimmune effector activity at the implantation site would protect the conceptus from "rejection" and may therefore be necessary for normal successful pregnancy. In the remainder of this chapter, we summarize the evidence that supports this view.

Table 20-1. Effector molecules

	Mechanism	
Effector Cell	**Direct Contact**	**Indirect**
Classical Immune System: (Antigen Specific)		
Cytotoxic T lymphocyte	+	–
Delayed hypersensitivity T cell	–	TNF-β; Recruit para-immune effectors
Plasma cell	–	Antibody to cell surface; Recruitment
Para-immune System:		
NK cells	+	TNF-α
NK cells + antibody	+	?
Macrophages	+	TNF-α; Enzymes/$O_2^{\cdot -}$
Macrophages + antibody	+	?
NC cells	+	TNF-α
Granulocytes	+	Enzymes; Basic protein
Granulocytes + antibody	+	?

Local Suppression at the Implantation Site

By the fifth day postimplantation in the mouse, potent local suppressor cell activity appears in the decidua (Clark et al., 1986; Canddy, 1987a; Slapsys et al., 1985). These studies show a soluble suppressor activity that inhibits the development of CTLs and LAKs by interfering with the action of interleukin-2 (IL-2) (Clark et al., 1985, 1986c). This mechanism is distinct from the suppression by PGE_2 that has also been postulated to act in decidua (Lala et al., 1988; Parhar et al., 1988). PGE_2-mediated suppression is seen primarily in decidual preparations that have been disaggregated with enzymes (Clark et al., 1986c, 1988; Wood et al., 1988). Since PGE_2 synthesis is normally suppressed by progesterone in decidua (and in the peri-implantation phase in humans), production of high immunosuppressive levels of PGE_2 *in vitro* is likely antifactual, reflecting the trauma of disaggregation and removal of progesterone (Rees et al., 1982; Smith & Kelly, 1988). In contrast, there is good evidence for *in situ* suppression at the implantation site during allopregnancy. In rodents, Sio (1985) has reported histological studies of skin allografts placed either at the choriodecidual junction (implant site) or on decidua in which implantation had been prevented by ligation of the uterine horn before mating. He found that 0/17 skin allografts placed at the choriodecidual junction developed lymphocytic infiltration, whereas skin grafts on non-implant-containing pregnancy decidua were infiltrated by an ongoing immune response ($p = 0.017$). Suppressor cells have been obtained from the uterine venous blood of pregnant mice (Slapsys & Clark, 1982), and several investigators have found that *in vitro* responses of human retroplacental blood lymphocytes are decreased in early pregnancy (Fuchs et al., 1977; Nicholas & Panayi, 1985; Yoshida et al., 1988a and b). Although the local immunosuppressive effect of progesterone could potentially account for some of these observations in humans (Szekeres-Bartho et al., 1985), there is little progesterone production by trophoblast in the mouse (Clark, 1986; Sio, 1985), and the soluble suppressor activity released by placental tissue is only ¼–⅛ of that produced by the associated decidua (unpublished data). Further, the suppressive activity in murine decidual supernatants was unaffected by neutralizing antibodies to PGE_2 and progesterone, but was blocked by antibody to TGF-β (Clark et al., 1988), a molecule that inhibits activation of effector cells by IL-2, IL-3, or IL-1 and prevents the (Ellingsworth et al., 1988; Keller et al., 1988; Sporn et al., 1986; Tsunawaki et al., 1988) respiratory burst of activated macrophages. In addition, TGF-β can block the cytotoxic action of TNF-α on certain target cells (Sugarman et al., 1987). We have found that murine decidual supernatants can also inhibit the response to IL-3 and prevent cytotoxic activation of macrophages by interferon and lipopolysaccharide (LPS) (unpublished data). Suppressive activity can also be obtained from human decidual mononuclear cells, and in both of two experiments this activity was neutralized by anti-TGF-β antibody (Clark et al., 1988; Daya et al., 1985, 1987; Clark et al., 1991). Taken together, these data suggest that a TGF-β like molecule may account for much of the soluble suppressor activity obtained from decidua and may be capable of inhibiting specific immune effectors, as well as nonspecific paraimmune mechanisms.

The distribution of suppressor activity obtained from individual implantation sites for allopregnant (C3H/HeJ × DBA/2) mice (12.5–13.5 days pregnant) showed that resorptions were associated with decreased levels of suppressive activity (Clark et al., 1986a, b, and c, 1990). Overlap of the two distribution curves was noted, however, and although the probability of resorption increased as suppressive activity declines, the resorption rate did not reach 100% when suppression was absent. This may in part reflect the fact that our studies were carried out at days 12.5–13.5 before many resorptions may have occurred. It is more likely, however, that the occurrence of resorption is stochastic and determined by the relative balance between maternal effector activity and local suppression; in the absence of sufficient maternal effector activity, even poorly defended implants might survive (Clark et al., 1986b). Since suppressive activity varied between sites even in the same uterus, the occurrence of partial resorption can also be explained. In an attempt to increase the resorption rate of poorly defended implants, we immunized some of the mice against DBA/2 antigens. Paradoxically, the resorption rate decreased from 26.5% to 11.1% in the immunized mice, and the median level of suppression increased, consistent with the hypothesis that specific immunity may be beneficial and increase local defenses (Clark et al., 1987b, 1990). Additionally, abortion due to a lethal genetic defect was not accompanied by decreased levels of local suppression (Clark, 1988; Clark et al., 1991).

Subnormal levels of local suppression that are reversed by immunization against paternal MHC have also been observed in the CBA/J ♀ × DBA/2 ♂ model for spontaneous abortion (Chaouat et al., 1988; Clark et al., 1986a, 1987c). Although the embryos are infiltrated by cells of CTL and NK phenotypes, resorption begins before the fetal cells become sensitive to CTL lysis. The observation that antibody to asialo-GM1, which is expressed on NK cells and a variety of other natural effector cells including LAKs, prevents resorption suggests that the NK infiltrate may be more functionally relevant (Clark et al., 1991; de Fougerolles & Baines, 1987). Further, TNF-α levels are elevated in resorbing decidua, and injection of recombinant human TNF-α substantially increases the abortion rate (Chaouat et al., 1990; see Chapter 19, this volume). Taken together, these data argue that natural effector cells mediate resorption and that TNF-α provides a "stop" signal. CBA/J mice show spontaneous NK cell activation in response to their bacterial and viral flora, in contrast to some other strains that are low responders (Lanza & Djeu, 1982; Orn et al., 1980), and keeping CBA/J mice under barrier isolation conditions also prevents the high abortion rate (Hamilton & Hamilton, 1987).

Three curious observations made in the CBA/J × DBA/2 system still require explanation:

1. Injection of a monoclonal antibody to the IL-2 receptor (7D4) increases the abortion rate (Clark, 1988; Clark et al., 1991).
2. Injection of low doses of recombinant murine or human GM-CSF reduces the abortion rate (Chaouat et al., 1988; Clark & Chaouat, 1989a and b, in preparation).
3. Injection of anti-T cell antibodies, such as anti-Lyt 2, increases the abortion rate (Chaouat et al., 1988; Clark & Chaouat, 1989a and b; Clark et al., 1989a).

Experiments with Monoclonal Antibodies to the IL-2 Receptor

We initially described the effects of the monoclonal anti-IL-2 receptor antibody 7D4 in the *Mus caroli* to *Mus musculus* blastocysts transfer model. In this system, almost all embryos resorb, and this is associated with infiltration of embryos by maternal cytotoxic T-lineage cells and undetectable levels of local suppression (Clark et al., 1984, 1987b; Croy et al., 1982, 1987). Daily treatment of recipients with antibody 7D4 eliminated most of the cellular infiltration and delayed embryo necrosis, although it did not prevent the development of lesions in placental trophoblast and eventual fetal death. When 7D4 antibody was administered to CBA/J ♀ mated to DBA/2 ♂ (in which partial litter resorption normally occurs) from days 6.5 through 13.5, the final resorption rate increased from 25% to 40.2%. However, this antibody was unable to prevent rejection of a tumor allograft. The lack of an effect may be related to the inability of this antibody to prevent binding of IL-2 to its receptor or to inhibit DTH activity (Kelley et al., 1987). In contrast, the 7/20 anti-IL-2 receptor monoclonal antibody blocks IL-2 binding is a more potent inhibitor of DTH activity *in vivo*, and prevents tumor allograft rejection (Clark et al., 1991; Kelley et al., 1987). Preliminary data suggest that injection of the 7/20 monoclonal into CBA/J mice slightly decreases the abortion rate. This is consistent with the idea that such cytokines as IL-2 may be important in the pathogenesis of resorption in this system. However, one must still account for the increase in resorption seen after treatment with the 7D4 antibody.

In view of the potential importance of nonspecific effector cells, such as LAKs, against trophoblast targets, we have developed an *in vitro* system to generate killer cells directed against the NK-resistant,

CTL-resistant Be6 trophoblast-like cell line (Clark et al., 1986a). Briefly, 1×10^6 splenocytes from nonpregnant female mice were cultured in 96 well plates for 72 h with cytokine-containing supernatants (or pure recombinant cytokines). ^{51}Cr-labeled Be6 target cells were then added to test for cytotoxicity. Decidual supernatants (DS), HPLC-purified decidual suppressor factor (DSF), and TGF-β1 or β2 all inhibited generation of cytotoxic activity. Surprisingly, addition of appropriate dilutions of mAb 7D4 increased the generation of cytotoxic cells. This may be analogous to the boosting of cytotoxic cell generation by culture with anti-T3 antibody (Ting et al., 1988; Tovar et al., 1988). It is possible, therefore, that the increased rate of abortion seen after *in vivo* treatment with 7D4 antibody is due to stimulation of antitrophoblast killer cell activity. Experiments to test this hypothesis are currently in progress.

Effects of Recombinant GM-CSF on the Resorption Rate

Reduction of the resorption rate in CBA/J × DBA/2 matings after treatment with semi-purified GM-CSF was first noted by Chaouat et al. (1988). More recently, these results have been confirmed using low doses of recombinant murine GM-CSF (Chaouat et al., 1990; see Chapter 19, this volume). Although murine GM-CSF stimulates placental cell growth in the system of Athanassakis et al. (1987), purified endotoxin-free human recombinant GM-CSF was unable to stimulate murine placental cell growth *in vitro*. Nonetheless, human GM-CSF treatment reduced the abortion rate *in vivo* (Lea & Clark, 1989; Chaouat et al., 1990; Clark et al., 1991). This observation was particularly puzzling as GM-CSF is not supposed to act across species barriers. However, we have recently noted that low concentrations of murine and human recombinant GM-CSF both inhibit generation of antitrophoblast killer cells *in vitro* (Lea & Clark, 1989; Clark et al., 1991). Further, GM-CSF has been reported to down-regulate IL-2 R expression and to inhibit TNF-α mRNA production in LPS-activated macrophages (Hancock et al., 1988; Vermeulen et al., 1987). GM-CSF may therefore act as a suppressor factor, in addition to its growth-stimulating activities. Abortion in the CBA/J-DBA/2 system depends upon the presence of normal bacterial and viral flora and is associated with TNF-α production; suppression may represent a potential explanation for the antiabortive effect of GM-CSF.

Figure 20-2 summarizes the proposed roles of various cytokines in the regulation of trophoblast and vascular supply essential for pregnancy. The role of the TGF-β-related factor described by us is also shown. In collaboration with Dr. Kathleen Flanders (Chemoprevention Laboratory, NIH-NCI, Bethesda, MD), we have shown that our decidual suppressor molecule is related to TGF-β2 (Clark et al.,

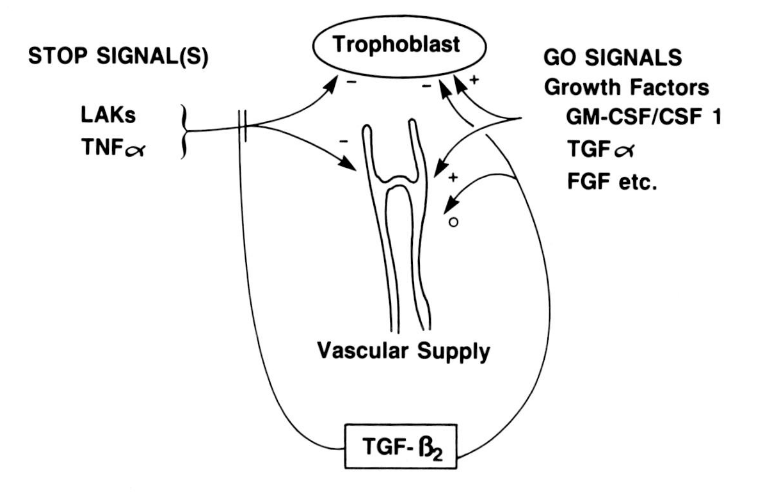

Fig. 20-2. A proposed scheme showing effector cells/mediators, growth factors and TFG-β2-like suppressor factor.

1989b) and is therefore similar to the human glioblastoma suppressor factor that inhibits responses to IL-2 (Siepl et al., 1988). This may be functionally important, since TGF-β2 does not cause the usual TGF-β mediated growth inhibition of vascular endothelial cells (Bensaid et al., 1988; Jennings et al., 1988; Clark et al., 1991) and thus may help the conceptus to develop an adequate vascular supply. Our decidual suppressive factor does appear to inhibit placental cell growth, however, which may be important in limiting trophoblast invasion of the uterine wall. In support of this hypothesis we have observed that most of the suppressor cell activity is located deep within the placental bed and is not primarily in the decidua in contact with trophoblast (Slapsys et al., 1985). In this context, it may be significant that TGF-β2-like suppressor activity is *not* present in supernatants obtained from decidua during the peri-implantation phase of mouse pregnancy when there is rapid trophoblast growth and invasion of decidua.

In vivo Effects of Anti-T Cell Antibodies

In 1987, Athanassakis et al. reported that injections of anti-T cell antibodies reduced the phagocytic activity of placental cells and slightly increased the resorption rate in pregnant mice. A similar reduction in phagocytic activity was noted after injection of anti-Lyt 2 but not anti-L3T4 monoclonal antibodies (Athanassakis & Wegmann, 1986). In the CBA/J × DBA/2 system, treatment with anti-Lyt 2 or a combination of anti-Lyt 2 and anti-L3T4 antibodies on days 7.5, 9.5, and 11.5 of pregnancy dramatically increased the abortion rate (Chaouat et al., 1988; see Chapter 19, this volume). One possible in-

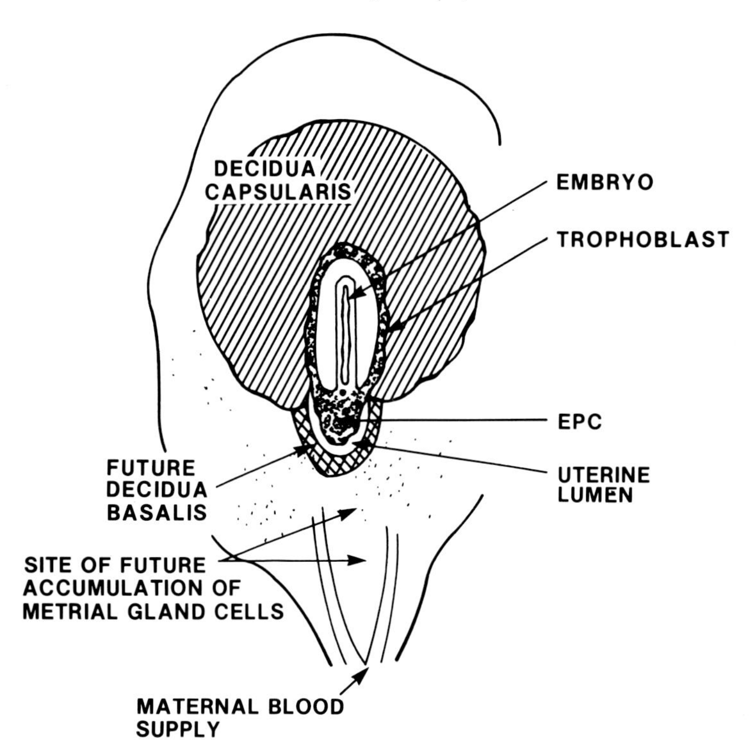

Fig. 20-3. Schematic illustration of peri-implantation murine embryo-uterine relationships. Macrophages and lymphatics are excluded from decidua capsularis. Asialo-GM1-positive cells infiltrate at decidual-trophoblast interface in CBA/J mice pregnant by DBA/2.

terpretation of these data is that the antibody depletes Lyt-2-positive maternal T cells essential for survival of the pregnancy in the post-implantation phase; alternatively, the antibody may stimulate Lyt 2^+ cells with deleterious results. However, we have recently found that a single injection of anti-Lyt 2 antibody on day 6.5 of pregnancy is sufficient to increase the abortion rate (Clark et al., 1989a), suggesting that the antibody may act during the peri-implantation phase (Fig. 20-3). Three observations make this hypothesis attractive:

1. During the preimplantation phase of pregnancy, Lyt-2^+ suppressor cells arise in the endometrium. These cells are large and nonspecific, and unlike classical T cells, are activated by gestational hormones (Brierley & Clark, 1987). Although the level of suppression declines markedly during the peri-implantation period and at the time of implantation, low levels of suppression can still be detected. This activity has recently been shown to be mediated by Lyt 2^+ cells, although it is masked to some extent by a cell pop-

ulation that bears Fc receptors (Clark, 1988). A target population for the anti-Lyt 2 antibody is therefore present in decidua during the peri-implantation period.

2. In the CBA/J × DBA/2 system, asialo-GM1$^+$ cells accumulate in the primary decidua in a proportion of embryos, possibly corresponding to those that will subsequently resorb (de Fougerolles & Baines, 1987; Gendron & Baines, 1988). Although these cells do not inevitably lead to embryo death before day 9.5–10.5, and antiasialo-GM1 antibody may still be protective if given at this time (Clark et al., 1991), there is some evidence that embryo growth and development are retarded during the peri-implantation period (Clark et al., 1986a). We hypothesize that the Lyt-2$^+$ suppressor cells may inhibit the activity of these asialo-GM1$^+$ cells. It is possible that lethal developmental retardation could be produced in some embryos if the levels of Lyt-2$^+$ regulatory cells were disturbed. Whether the Lyt-2$^+$ cells are involved in the production of such suppressive molecules as GM-CSF is under investigation.
3. Ribbing et al. (1988) have shown that injection of a monoclonal antibody to T suppressor inducer factor on days 3.5, 4.5, and 5.5 of pregnancy may cause abortion (see Chapter 15, this volume). Abortion in the peri-implantation period can also be induced by indomethacin (a macrophage activator and inhibitor of decidualization) and IL-2 (Scodras & Lala, 1987; Voth et al., 1987) and poly I:C (de Fougerolles & Baines, 1987; see Chapter 19, this volume). Events in the peri-implantation phase involving suppressor cells may therefore be important in defense of the embryo against elimination by natural effector mechanisms.

Insights from Studies of SCID Mice

SCID Mice have profound deficiencies in T and B cell functions of the classical immune system. They were originally used in reproductive immunology to determine whether *Mus caroli* blastocysts developing in the uterus of *Mus musculus* were aborted by a process of classical immune rejection (Croy et al., 1987). In these studies, the xenoembryos appeared to be aborted at least as quickly as in immunocompetent hosts, and it was therefore clear that nonclassical effector systems were possible mediators of "rejection" (Clark et al., 1987b). Although SCID mice accept many types of grafts, they are known to reject bone marrow allografts (Carlson & Marshall, 1985).

Our studies using mice SCID on the CB17 background have unexpectedly shown that they have a high rate of spontaneous abortion even when raised and mated under barrier isolation conditions (Clark et al., 1989c). In SCID × SCID matings (i.e., CB 17 *scid/scid* × CB17 *scid/scid*), 25% of embryos resorbed, but in CB17 *scid/+* × CB17 *scid/+* (where the females were immunocompetent), the resorption rate

Table 20-2. Natural effector activity of preimplantation murine uterine lining cells from C3H/HeJ mice

		^{51}Cr-Release (mean ± SEM) Using	
Donor	**Cell Yield**	**YAC***	**WEHI-164†**
Control virgin	1×10^5	0	0
Pseudo-pregnant‡	1.5 ± 10^5	3.7 ± 2.0	0
Mated	1.4 ± 10^5	6.4 ± 3.0*	27.3 ± 2.1

* 4-h assay at an effector: target ratio of 100:1.
† 24-h assay at an effector: target ratio of 100:1.
‡ PMSG-hCG was used as described in Brierley & Clark (1987).

was approximately 40%. These results are exactly the opposite of those anticipated if T cells have a positive immunotrophic effect (Wegmann, 1987, 1988). In addition, we observed a deficiency of postimplantation suppressor activity in the decidua of *scid* × *scid* matings and the presence of antitrophoblast killer cells in the spleens of these mice. Indeed, total splenic antitrophoblast killer activity increased dramatically during pregnancy, even in mice co-expressing the bg/bg genotype, which reduces classical NK cell activity (Clark et al., 1989c; see Chapter 12, this volume). These animals in fact produced the highest splenic cytotoxic activity that we have ever measured. Thus, antitrophoblast killer cells are not generated only in *in vitro* systems, these effectors do not appear to be classical NK cells, and their activity is stimulated by pregnancy itself. Indeed, in immunocompetent C3H mice, there is evidence that the presence of the fetus leads to activation of natural cytotoxic cells in preimplantation endometrium (Table 20-2). Gambel et al. (1985) have shown a similar activation of NK-type cells in peri-implantation decidua. Metrial gland cells also appear to kill certain types of trophoblast in the postimplantation phase of pregnancy (Stewart & Mukhtar, 1988). The accumulating evidence therefore suggests that natural effector cells are deliberately activated during pregnancy, and it is tempting to speculate that this represents a mechanism to eliminate those embryos that are least fit, as reflected by low levels of suppressor activity (Table 20-1).

Conclusions

We are rapidly achieving a more precise definition of effector cells and molecules and suppressor cells and molecules involved in the regulation of pregnancy. This, together with techniques for experimentally perturbing suppressor and natural antitrophoblast effector populations *in vivo* in animal systems, should provide the conceptual and technical resources necessary to address the problem of early pregnancy failure in humans.

References

Ammann, A. J. 1986. Fetal and neonatal graft-vs-host and immunodeficiency disease. In *Reproductive Immunology 1986*. Amsterdam: Elsevier, pp. 19–26.

Athanassakis, I. and Wegmann, T. G. 1986. The immunotrophic interaction between maternal T cells and fetal trophoblast/macrophages during gestation. In *Reproductive Immunology 1986*. (D. A. Clark and B. A. Croy, eds.) Amsterdam: Elsevier, pp. 99–105.

Athanassakis, I., Bleackley, R. C., Paetkau, V., Guilbert, L., Barr, P. J., and Wegmann, T. G. 1987. The immunostimulatory effect of T cells and T cell lymphokines on murine fetally-derived placental cells. *J. Immunol.* 18:37.

Beard, R. W. and Sharp, F. eds. 1988. In *Early Pregnancy Loss: Mechanisms and Treatment*. Ashton-under-Lyne: Peacock Press.

Bell, S. C. and Billington, W. D. 1983. Anti-fetal alloantibody in the pregnant female. *Immunol. Rev.* 75:5.

Bensaid, M., Tauber, M. T., Malecaze, F., Prats, H., Bayard, F., and Tauber, J. P. 1988. Effect of basic and acidic FGF and TGF-β in controlling the proliferation of retinal capillary endothelial cells. *Acta Paed. Scand.* 343(suppl):230.

Boue, J., Boue, A., and Lazar, P. 1975. Retrospective and prospective epidemiological studies of 1500 karyotyped spontaneous human abortions. *Teratology* 12:11.

Brierley, J. and Clark, D. A. 1987. Characterization of hormone-dependent suppressor cells in the uterus of pregnant and pseudopregnant mice. *J. Reprod. Immunol.* 10:201.

Carlson, G. A. and Marshall, S. T. 1985. H-2 associated natural resistance against non-syngeneic cells: possible functions of the major histocompatibility complex outside the realm of classical immunology. In *Genetic Control of Host Resistance to Infection and Malignancy* (E. Skamene, ed.). New York: Alan R Liss, pp. 701–711.

Chaouat, G., Clark, D. A., and Wegmann, T. G. 1988. Genetic aspects of the CBA × DBA/2 and B10 × B10.A models of murine pregnancy failure and its prevention by lymphocyte immunisation. In *Early Pregnancy Failure: Mechanisms and Treatment*. Ashton-under-Lyne: Peacock Press, pp. 89–102.

Chaouat, G., Menu, E., Clark, D. A., Minowsky, M., Dy, M., and Wegmann, T. G. 1990. Control of fetal survival in CBA and DBA/2 mice by lymphokine therapy. *J. Reprod. Fertil.* 89:447.

Clark, D. A. 1986. Role of hormonal immunoregulation in reproduction. In *Pituitary Function and Immunity* (I. Berczi, ed.). Orlando, FL: CRC Press, pp. 262–272.

Clark, D. A. 1988. Host immunoregulatory mechanisms and the success of the conceptus fertilized in vivo and in vitro. In *Early Pregnancy Failure: Mechanisms and Treatment* (R. W. Beard and F. Sharp, eds.). Ashton-under-Lyne: Peacock Press, pp. 215–232.

Clark, D. A. and Chaouat, G. 1989a. What do we know about spontaneous abortion mechanisms? *Am. J. Reprod. Immunol. Microbiol.* 19:28.

Clark, D. A. and Chaouat, G. 1989b. Determinants of embryo survival in the peri-and post-implantation period. (K. Yoshinaga, ed.). Boston: Adams Ltd., pp. 171–178.

Clark, D. A., Slapsys, R. M., Croy, B. A., and Rossant, J. 1984. Immunoregulation of host-versus-graft responses in the uterus. *Immunol. Today* 5:111.

Clark, D. A., Chaput, A., Walker, C., and Rosenthal, K. L. 1985. Active suppression of host-versus-graft reaction in pregnant mice. VI. Soluble suppressor activity obtained from decidua of allopregnant mice blocks the response to IL-2. *J. Immunol.* 134:3;1659.

Clark, D. A., Chaput, A., and Tutton, D. 1986a. Active suppression of host-versus-graft reaction in pregnant mice. VII. Spontaneous abortion of allogeneic DBA/2 × CBA/J fetuses in the uterus of CBA/J mice correlates with deficient non-T suppressor cell activity. *J. Immunol.* 136:1668.

Clark, D. A., Croy, B. A., Rossant, J., and Chaouat, G. 1986b. Immune presentization and local intrauterine defenses as determinants of success or failure of murine interspecies pregnancies. *J. Reprod. Fertil.* 77:633.

Clark, D. A., Damji, N., Chaput, A., Rosenthal, K. L., and Brierley, J. 1986c. Decidua-associated suppressor cells and suppressor factors regulating interleukin 2: their role in the survival of the "fetal allograft". In *Progress in Immunology VI* (B. Cinader and R. G. Miller, eds.). New York: Academic Press, pp. 1089–1099.

Clark, D. A., Slapsys, R., Chaput, A., Walker, C., Brierley, C., Daya, S., and Rosenthal, K. 1986d. Immunoregulatory molecules of trophoblast and decidual suppressor cell origin at the materno-fetal interface. *Am. J. Reprod. Immunol. Microbiol.* 10:100.

Clark, D. A., Chaput, A., Slapsys, R. M., Brierley, J., Daya, S., and Allardyce, R. 1987a. Suppressor cells in the uterus. In *Immunoregulation and Fetal Survival* (T. J. Gill III and T. G. Wegmann, eds.). New York: Oxford University Press, pp. 63–77.

Clark, D. A., Croy, B. A., Chaouat, G., and Wegmann, T. G., 1987b. Immunological and para-immunological mechanisms in spontaneous abortion. Recent insights and future directions. *J. Reprod. Immunol.* 12:1.

Clark, D. A., Kiger, N., Guenet, J. L., and Chaouat, G. 1987c. Local active suppression and successful vaccination against spontaneous abortion in CBA/J mice. *J. Reprod. Immunol.* 10:79.

Clark, D. A., Falbo, M., Rowley, R. B., Banwatt, D., and Stedronska-Clark, J. 1988. Active suppression of host-versus-graft reaction in pregnant mice. IX. Soluble suppressor activity obtained from allopregnant mouse decidua that blocks the response to interleukin 2 is related to TGF-beta. *J. Immunol.* 141:3833.

Clark, D. A., Brierly, J., Banwatt, D., and Chaouat, G. 1989a. Hormone-induced pre-implantation Lyt-2+ murine uterine suppressor cells persist after implantation and may reduce the spontaneous abortion rate in CBA/J mice. *Cell. Immunol.* 123:334.

Clark, D. A., Drake, B., Head, J. R., Stedrowska-Clark, J., and Benwatt, D. 1990. Decidua-associated suppressor activity and variability of individual implantation sites of allopregnant C3H mice. *J. Reprod. Immunol.* 17:253.

Clark, D. A., Banwatt, D. K., Manuel, J., Fulop, G., and Croy, B. A. 1989c.

SCID mice in reproductive biology. In The SCID Mouse (M. J. Bosma, R. A. Phillips, and W. Schuler, eds.). Heidelberg: Springer-Verlag, pp. 227–234.

Clark, D. A., Lea, R. G., Podor, T., Daya, S., Banwatt, D., and Harley, C. 1991. Cytokines determining the success or failure of pregnancy. *Ann. NY Acad. Sci.* (in press).

Clark, D. A., Flanders, K. C., Banwatt, D., Millar-Book, W., Manuel, J., Stedronska-Clark, J., and Rowley, B. 1989. Murine pregnancy decidua produces a unique immunosuppressive molecule related to transforming growth factor beta-2. *J. Immunol.* 144.3008.

Croy, B. A. and Rossant, J. 1987. Mouse embryonic cells become susceptible to CTL lysis after midgestation. *Cell. Immunol.* 140:355.

Croy, B. A., Rossant, J., and Clark, D. A. 1982. Histological and immunological studies of post implantation death of *Mus caroli* embryos in the *Mus musculus* uterus. *J. Reprod. Immunol.* 4:277.

Croy, B. A., Crepeau, M., Yamashiro, S., and Clark, D. A. 1987. Further studies on the transfer of *Mus caroli* embryos to immunodeficient *Mus musculus. In Reproductive Immunology: Materno-Fetal relationship* (G. Chaouat, ed.). Paris: INSERM Colloque, pp. 101–112.

Daya, S., Clark, D. A., Delvin, C., Jarrell, J., and Chaput, A. 1985. Preliminary characterization of two types of suppressor cells in the human uterus. *Fertil. Steril.* 44:6:778.

Daya, S., Rosenthal, K. L., and Clark, D. A. 1987. Immunosuppressor factor(s) produced by decidua-associated suppressor cells—a proposed mechanism for fetal allograft survival. *Am. J. Obstet. Gynecol.* 156:344.

de Fougerolles, A. R. and Baines, M. G. 1987. Modulation of the natural killer cell activity in pregnant mice alters the spontaneous abortion rate. *J. Reprod. Immunol.* 11:147.

Drake, B. L. and Head, J. R. 1988. Murine trophoblast cells are susceptible to lymphokine-activated killer (LAK) cell lysis. *Am. J. Reprod. Immunol. Microbiol.* 16:114.

Eades, D. K., Cornelius, P., and Pekala, P. H. 1988. Characterization of the tumor necrosis factor receptor in human placenta. *Placenta* 9:247.

Eiben, B., Borgmann, S., Schubbe, I., and Hansmann, I. 1987. A cytogenetic study directly from chorionic villi of 140 spontaneous abortions. *Hum. Genet.* 77:137.

Ellingsworth, I. R., Nakayama, D., Segarini, P., Dasch, J., Carrillo, P., and Waegel, W. 1988. Transforming growth factor betas are equipotent inhibitors of interleukin-1-induced lymphocyte proliferation. *Cell. Immunol.* 114:41.

Flanders, K. C., Banwatt, D. K., Book, W., Manuel, J., Stedrovska-Clark, J., and Rowley, B. 1987. Murine pregnancy decidua produces a unique immuno-suppressive molecule. *J. Immunol.* 144:3008.

Fuchs, T., Hammarstrom, L., Smith, E., and Brundin J. 1977. In vivo suppression of uterine lymphocytes during early human pregnancy. *Acta Obstet. Scand.* 56:151.

Gambel, P., Croy, B. A., Moore, W. P., Hunziker, T. G., Wegmann, T. G., and Rossant, J. 1985. Characterization of immune effector cells present in early murine decidua. *Cell. Immunol.* 93:303.

Gendron, R. L. and Baines, M. G. 1988. Immunohistochemical analysis of decidual natural killer cells during spontaneous abortion in mice. *Cell. Immunol.* 113:261.

Hamilton, B. L. and Hamilton, M. S. 1987. Effect of maternal-fetal histoincompatibility on the weight of the feto-placental unit in mice; the role of minor histoincompatibility antigens. *Am. J. Reprod. Immunol. Microbiol.* 15:153.

Hancock, W. W., Pleau, M. E., and Kobzik, L. 1988. Recombinant granulocyte-macrophage colony-stimulating factor down-regulates expression of IL-2 receptor on human mononuclear phagocytes by induction of prostaglandin. *J. Immunol.* 140:3021.

Head, J. R., Drake, B. L., and Zuckermann, F. A. 1987. Major histocompatibility antigens to trophoblast and their regulation: implications in the maternal-fetal relationship. *Am. J. Reprod. Immunol. Microbiol.* 15:12.

Hertig, A. T., Rock, J., and Adams, E. C. 1956. A description of 34 human ova within the first 17 days of development. *Am. J. Anat.* 98:435.

Hunziker, R. D., Gambel, P., and Wegmann, T. G. 1984. Placenta as a selective barrier to cellular traffic. *J. Immunol.* 133:667.

Jennings, J. C., Mohan, S., Lınhkhart, T. A., Widstrom, R., and Baylink, D. J. 1988. Comparison of the biologic actions of TGF beta-1 and TGF beta-2: differential activity in endothelial cells. *J. Cell. Physiol.* 137:167.

Keller, J. R., Mantel, C., Sing, G. K., Ellingsworth, L. R., Ruscetti, S. K., and Ruscetti, F. W. 1988. Transforming growth factor beta 1 selectively regulated early murine hemopoietic progenitors and inhibits the growth of IL-3-dependent myeloid leukemia cell lines. *J. Exp. Med.* 168:737.

Kelly, V. E., Gaulton, G. N., and Strom, T. B. 1987. Inhibitory effects of anti-interleukin 2 receptor and anti-L3T4 antibodies on delayed type hypersensitivity: the role of complement and epitope. *J. Immunol.* 138:2771.

Khong, T. Y., Liddell, H. S., and Robertson, W. B. 1987. Defective and haemochorial placentation as a cause of miscarriage; a preliminary study. *Br. J. Obstet. Gynecol.* 94:649.

Lala, P. K., Kennedy, T. G., and Parhar, R. S. 1988. Suppression of lymphocyte alloreactivity by early gestational human decidua. II. Characterization of the suppressor mechanisms. *Cell Immunol.* 116:411.

Lanza, E. and Djeu, J. Y. 1982. Age-independent natural killer activity in murine peripheral blood. In *NK Cells and Other Natural Effectors* (R. B. Heiberman, ed.). New York: Academic Press, pp. 335–340.

Lea, R. G. and Clark, D. A. 1989. The enigma of the fetal allograft: immunosuppression versus immunostimulation. *FASEB J.* 5:A678.

Meedges, B. H. L. M., Ingenhoes, R., Peeters, L. L. H., and Exalto, N. 1988. Early pregnancy wastage: relationship between chorionic vascularization and embryonic development. *Fertil. Steril.* 49:216.

Michel, M. Z., Underwood, J. L., Clark, D. A., Mowbray, J. F., and Beard, R. W. 1989. Histologic and immunologic study of decidual biopsy tissue taken before spontaneous abortion. *Am. J. Obstet. Gynecol.* 61:409.

Nicholas, N. S. and Parayi, G. S. 1985. Inhibition of interleukin-2 production by retroplacental sera: a possible mechanism for human fetal allograft survival. *Am. J. Reprod. Immunol. Microbiol.* 9:6.

Orn, A., Gidlund, M., Ojo, E., Gronvik, K. O., Anderson, J., and Wigzell, H.

1980. Factors controlling augmentation of natural killer cells. In *Natural Cell Mediated Immunity against Tumors* (R. B. Herberman, ed.). New York: Academic Press, pp. 581–592.

Parhar, R. S., Kennedy, T. G., and Lala, P. K. 1988. Suppression of lymphocyte alloreactivity by early gestational human decidua. I. Characterization of suppressor cells and suppressor molecules. *Cell Immunol.* 116:392.

Pollard, J. W., Bartocci, A., Arceci, R., Orlofsky, A., Ladner, M. B., and Stanley, M. B. 1987. Apparent role of macrophage growth factor, CSF-1, in placental development. *Nature* 330:484.

Rees, M. C. P., Parry, D. M., Anderson, A. B. M., and Turnbull, A. C. 1982. Immunohistochemical localization of cyclooxygenase in the human. *Prostaglandins* 23:207.

Ribbing, C. A., Singh, B., and Honore, L. 1988. T-cell suppressor factors play an integral role in preventing fetal rejection. *J. Reprod. Immunol.* 14:83.

Rugh, R. 1968. *The Mouse. Its Reproduction and Development.* Minneapolis: Burgess.

Scodras, J. M. and Lala, P. K. 1987. Reactivation of maternal killer lymphocytes in the decidua with endomethacin, IL 2, or combination therapy is associated with embryonic demise. *Am. J. Reprod. Immunol. Microbiol.* 14:12.

Shiomura, K., Manda, T., Mukumoto, S., Robayashi, K., Nakano, K., and Mori, J. 1988. Recombinant human tumor necrosis factor-a thrombus formation is a cause of antitumor activity. *Int. J. Cancer* 41:243.

Siepl, C., Bodmer, S., Frei, K., MacDonald, H. R., DeMartin, R., Hofer, E., and Fontana, A. 1988. The glioblastoma-derived T cell suppressor factor/transforming growth factor-beta 2 inhibits T cell growth without affecting the interaction of interleukin-2 with its receptor. *Eur. J. Immunol.* 18:593.

Sio, J. 1985. Allograft reactivity and progesterone involvement at the choriodecidual junction. Ph.D. thesis. Dallas: University of Texas.

Slapsys, R. M. and Clark, D. A. 1982. Active suppression of host-vs-graft reaction in pregnant mice. IV. Local suppressor cells in decidua and uterine blood. *J. Reprod. Immunol.* 4:355.

Slapsys, R. M., Richards, C. D., and Clark, D. A. 1985. Active suppression of host-versus-graft reaction in pregnant mice. VIII. The uterine decidua-associated suppressor cell is distinct from decidual NK cells. *Cell. Immunol.* 99:140.

Slapsys, R. M., Younglai, E., and Clark, D. A. 1988. A novel suppressor cell is recruited to decidua by fetal trophoblast-type cells. *Reg. Immunol.* 1:182.

Smith, S. K. and Kelly, R. W. 1988. The release of PGF2-alpha and PGE2 from separated cells of human endometrium and decidua. *Prostaglandins Leukotrienes Essential Fatty Acids* 3:91.

Sporn, M. B., Roberts, A. B., Wakefield, L. M., and Assoian, R. K. 1986. Transforming growth factor-beta: biological function and chemical structure. *Science* 233:532.

Stewart, I. and Mukhtar, D. D. Y. 1988. The killing of mouse trophoblast cells by granulated metrial gland cells in vitro. *Placenta* 9:417.

Sugarman, B. J., Lewis, G. D., Eessalu, T. E., Aggarwal, B. B., and Shepard, H. M. 1987. Effects of growth factors on the antiproliferative activity of tumor necrosis factors. *Cancer Res.* 47:780.

Szekeres-Bartho, J., Hadnagy, J., and Pasca, A. S. 1985. The suppressive effect of progesterone on lymphocyte cytotoxicity: unique progesterone sensitivity of pregnancy lymphocytes. *J. Reprod. Immunol.* 7:121.

Ting, C. C., Hargrove, M. E., and Yun, Y. S. 1988. Augmentation by anti-T3 antibody of lymphokine-activated killer cell-mediated cytotoxicity. *J. Immunol.* 141:741.

Tovar, Z., Dauphinee, M., and Talal, N. 1988. Synergistic interaction between anti-CD3 and IL-2 demonstrated by proliferative response, interferon production, and non-MHC-restricted killing. *Cell Immunol.* 117:12.

Tsunawaki, S., Sporn, M., Ding, A., and Nathan, C. 1988. Deactivation of macrophages by transforming growth factor-data. *Nature* 334:260.

Vermeulen, G., Lehn, M., and Remold, G. 1987. GM-CSF modulates expression of TNF mRNA in human macrophages. *J Leuk. Biol.* 42:546.

Voth, R., Storch, E., Huller, K., and Kirchner, H. 1987. Activation of cytotoxic activity in cultures of bone marrow-derived macrophages by indomethacin. *Eur. J. Immunol.* 17:145.

Wegmann, T. G. 1987. Placental immunotropism: maternal T cells enhance placental growth and function. *Am. J. Reprod. Immunol. Microbiol.* 15:67.

Wegmann, T. G. 1988. Maternal T cells promote placental growth and prevent spontaneous abortion. *Immunol. Lett.* 17:297.

Wilcox, A. J., Weinberg, C. R., O'Connor, J. F., Baird, D. D., Schlatterer, J. P., Canfield, R. E., Armstrong, E. G., and Nisula, B. C. 1988. Incidence of early loss of pregnancy. *N. Engl. J. Med.* 319:189.

Wood, G. W., Kamel, S., and Smith, K. 1988. Immunoregulation and prostaglandin production by mechanically-derived and enzyme-derived murine decidual cells. *J. Reprod. Immunol.* 13:235.

Wramsby, H., Fredga, K., and Liedholm, P. 1987. Chromosome analysis of human oocytes recovered from preovulatory follicles in stimulated cycles. *N. Engl. J. Med.* 316:121.

Yoshida, M., Kanzaki, H., Tokushiga, M., Sato, S., Wang, H. S., Uchida, A., Kasakura, S., and Mori, T. 1988a. Hyporeactivity to mitogens of retroplacental blood lymphocytes in early human pregnancy. *Immunol. Lett.* 17:279.

Yoshida, M., Kanzaki, H., Tokushiga, M., Sato, S., Wang, H. S., Kariya, M., Uchida, A., Kasakura, S., and Mori, T. 1988b. Depression of proliferative response to fetal lymphocytes of retroplacental blood lymphocytes in early human pregnancy. *Immunol. Lett.* 18:155.

Zuckermann, F. 1986. Studies on the role of placental trophoblast in protecting the fetus from immune rejection. Ph.D. Thesis, The Library, University of Texas at Dallas.

Index

‘Then it’s the anniversary of the death of someone you loved in a previous life,’ the older woman had answered.

As though she wasn’t morbid enough on her own account without having to hear nonsense like that.

She didn’t know who her actual mother and father were and remembered little about her life before her faux parents picked her out from the orphanage like an orange, except for how unlike the way she thought a little girl was supposed to be she felt. Today, whatever she could or couldn’t remember, she seemed older to herself than her twenty-five years. What about twenty-five hundred? What about twenty-five thousand? ‘Don’t exaggerate, Ailinn,’ people had always told her. (Twenty-five thousand years?) But it wasn’t she who exaggerated, it was they who reduced. Her head was like an echo chamber. If she concentrated long and hard enough, she sometimes thought, she would hear the great ice splitting and the first woolly mammoths come lolloping down from central Asia. Perhaps everybody – even the abridgers and condensers – could do the same but were embarrassed to talk about it. Unless infancy in the company of real parents had filled their minds with more immediate and, yes, trivial sensations. Our birth is but a sleep and a forgetting – who said that?

Ha! – she had forgotten.

It was a good job that history books were hard to come by, that diaries were hidden or destroyed and that libraries put gentle obstacles in the way of research, otherwise she might have decided to ransack the past and live her life backwards. If only to discover who it was her heart periodically fluttered for.

A sodden old snail appeared from under her bed, dragging a smear of egg white behind it. It was all she could do not to crush it with her bare, ugly foot.

Before chancing his nose outside his cottage in the morning, Kevern ‘Coco’ Cohen turned up the volume on the loop-television, poured tea – taking care to place the cup carelessly on the hall table – and checked twice to be certain that his utility phone was on and flashing. A facility for making and receiving local telephone calls only – all other forms of electronic communication having been shut down after WHAT HAPPENED, IF IT HAPPENED, to the rapid spread of whose violence social media were thought to have contributed – the utility phone flashed a malarial yellow until someone rang, and then it glowed vermilion. But it rarely rang. This, too, he left on the hall table. Then he rumpled the silk Chinese hallway runner – a precious heirloom – with his shoe.

The action was not commemorative in intent, but it often reminded him of a cruelly moonlit night many years before, when after a day strained by something – money worries or illness or news which the young Kevern gathered must have been very bad – his sardonic, creaking father had kicked the runner aside, raised the hem of his brocade dressing gown, and danced an enraged soft-shoe shuffle, his arms and legs going up and down in unison like those of a toy skeleton on a stick. He hadn't known his son was on the stairs, watching.

Kevern pressed himself into the darkness of the stairwell. Became a shadow. He was too frightened to say anything. His father was not a dancing man. He stayed very still, but the cottage thrummed to its occupants' every anxiety – he could sense his parents' troubled sleep through the floorboards under his bed, even though he slept in a room below theirs – and now the disturbance his fear generated gave his presence away.

'Sammy Davis Junior,' his father explained awkwardly when he saw him. His voice was hoarse and dry, a rattle from ruined lungs. Because he spoke with an accent even Kevern found strange, as though he'd never really listened to how people spoke in Port Reuben, he released his words reluctantly. He put two fingers across his mouth, like a tramp sucking on a cigarette butt he'd found in a rubbish bin. This he always did to stifle the letter j before it left his lips.

The boy was none the wiser. 'Sammy Davis Junior?' He too, religiously in his father's presence – and often even when his father wasn't there – sealed his lips against the letter j when it began a word. He didn't know why. It had begun as a game between them when he was small. His father had played it with his own father, he'd told him. Begin a word with a j without remembering to put two fingers across your mouth and it cost you a penny. It had not been much fun then and it was not much fun now. He knew it was expected of him, that was all. But why was his father being Sammy Davis Junior, whoever Sammy Davis Junior was?

'Song and dance man,' his father said. 'Mr Bo Jangles. No, you haven't heard of him.'

Him? Which him? Sammy Davis Junior or Mr Bo Jangles?

Either way, it sounded more like a warning than a statement. *If anybody asks, you haven't heard of him. You understand?* Kevern's childhood had been full of such warnings. Each delivered in a half-foreign tongue. You don't know, you haven't seen, you haven't heard. When his schoolteachers asked questions his was the last hand to go up: he said he didn't know, hadn't seen, hadn't heard. In ignorance was safety. But it worried him that he might have sounded like his father, lisping and slithering in another language. So he spoke in a whisper that drew even more attention to his oddness.

In this instance his father needn't have worried. Kevern hadn't only not heard of Sammy Davis Junior, he hadn't heard of Sammy Davis Senior either.

Ailinn would not have said no to such a father, no matter how strange his behaviour. It helped, she thought, to know where your madness came from.

Once Kevern had closed and double-locked the front door, he knelt and peered through the letter box, as he imagined a burglar or other intruder might. He could hear the television and smell the tea. He could see the phone quietly pulsing yellow, as though receiving dialysis, on the hall table. The silk runner, he noted with satisfaction, might have been trodden on by a household of small children. No sane man could possibly leave his own house without rearranging the runner on the way out.

He had a secondary motive for shuffling the rug. It demonstrated that it was of no value to him. The law – though it was nowhere written down; a willing submission to restraint might be a better way of putting it, a supposition of coercion – permitted only one item over a hundred years old per household, and Kevern had several. Mistreatment of them, he hoped, would quiet suspicion.

At the extreme limit of letter-box vision the toes of worn leather carpet slippers were just visible. Clearly he was at home, the fusspot, probably nodding in front of the television or reading the junk mail which had in all likelihood been delivered only minutes ago, in the excitement of collecting which he had left his tea and utility phone by the door. But at home, faffing, however else you describe what he was doing.

He returned to the cottage three times, at fifteen-second intervals, looking through his letter box to ascertain that nothing had changed. On each occasion he pushed his hand inside to be sure the flap had not stuck in the course of his inspections – a routine that had to be repeated in case the act of making sure had itself caused the flap to jam – then he took the cliff path and strode distractedly in the direction of the sea. The sea that no one but a few local fishermen sailed on, because there was nowhere you could get to on it – a sea that lapped no other shore.

Nothing had changed there either. The cliff still fell away sharply, sliced like cake, turning a deep, smoky purple at its base; the water still massed tirelessly, frothing and fuming, every day the same. Faffing, like Kevern. More angrily, but to no more purpose.

That was the great thing about the sea: you didn't have to worry about it. It wasn't going anywhere and it wasn't yours. It hadn't been owned and hidden by your family for generations. It didn't run in your blood.

He did, however, have his own bench. Not officially. It didn't have his name on it, but it was respected by the villagers of Port Reuben as they might have respected a wall against which the village idiot kicked his heels. *Coco sits here. The silly bleeder.*

They didn't think he was simple-minded. If anything they thought him a little too clever. But there are times in the history of humanity when cleverness might as well be simplicity.

At this hour, and especially at this season, when visitors were infrequent, he usually had the cliffs and the sea that went nowhere to himself. Sometimes Densdell Kroplik, his closest neighbour, would venture out of the reclaimed cowshed he called his bachelor pad and join Kevern briefly on the bench to complain, in the manner of a prophet without honour in his own country, about the madness of the world, the sunken condition of the village, and, by way of proof of both – for he was a self-published chronicler of the times and of this place – his plummeting sales figures. An itinerant barber and professional local, he policed the cliffs and public houses of Port Reuben, barring it to interlopers with his eyes, dressing like a landowner, a fisherman, a farmer, or a fool, depending on what clothes were uppermost on the pile on his floor – sometimes dressing like all of them at once – interposing his tuberous frame between Port Reuben and outside influence. Not so much the gatekeeper, Densdell Kroplik, as the gate. Though history, as another form of over-cherishing the past, was discouraged, he got away with being unofficial custodian of Port Reuben's secrets and teller of its tales, by keeping the narrative short and sweet – certainly shorter and sweeter than his conversation which, especially when he was cutting hair, boiled like the sea. Port Reuben, originally Ludgvennok, had once been an impregnable fortress of the old ways, and now it wasn't. THE END. This was the essence of Densdell Kroplik's *A Brief History of Port Reuben*, with a few maps and line drawings, done in his hand, and a number of comical footnotes, citing himself, thrown in.

No more, strictly speaking, than a pamphlet for visitors he

would rather have stayed away, *A Brief History of Port Reuben* was for sale by the till in every tourist shop. What few tourists there were bought it with their fudge. But for its author it stood between prosperity and ruination, and by that he meant the village's no less than his own. He checked his outlets every day to see how many had been sold, topping up stocks with signed copies from a sinisterly bulging rucksack that also contained combs, scissors, clippers, and shampoos and conditioners made to a secret formula from heather and thistles and wild flowers that grew in his scruffy clifftop garden. This he lugged, with exaggerated effort, as though making a sacrifice of his health to humanity, from shop to shop. Rather than have him engage them in conversation about his sales, which he never considered satisfactory, the shopkeepers kept out of his way, allowing him to load as many of his pamphlets on them as he thought appropriate. A number of them even bought multiple copies for themselves. They did as birthday presents to relations they didn't like. Anything not to have him fulminating against the bastardisation of the times in their shops, blowing out his weather-beaten cheeks, pulling at his knotted polka-dot neckerchief in sarcastic rage, as though that was all that kept his head attached to his body.

On some mornings, in return for the opportunity to rattle on, Densdell would shave Kevern free of charge. Afraid for his throat – because he was sure Densdell saw him as the incarnate proof, if not the prime cause, of Port Reuben's ruin – Kevern made noises of assent to everything he said. But he understood little of it. Once his razor was out, Densdell Kroplik gave up all pretence of speaking a language they shared. He dropped into a dialect that was older and wilder than the cliffs, coughing up sounds as though they were curses, using words Kevern had never heard before in his life and which he believed, half the time, did not actually exist. Rather than make an effort to decipher any of it, he would concentrate on the idea of the wind picking up the invisible hairs

Densdell barbered from him, and spiralling them out to sea in clusters, like dandelion spores.

Little by little the sea claiming him.

This morning, to Kevern's relief, Densdell Kroplik didn't put in an appearance, so he could sit and fret without company. The very seagulls, smelling his anxiety, kept their distance.

He was a tall, skinny, golden-mopped man (though his hair was thinning now), who moved as though apologetic of his height. He was considered, for all his strangeness, to have kind eyes. He unwound himself on to the bench and looked up at the sky. 'Jesus Christ!' he exclaimed, the moment he was comfortable, for no other reason than to pit his voice against those he heard in his head.

Better a voice he could control than a voice he couldn't. He was no visionary, but there were times when he would mistake the sound of a seabird or the distant laughter of fishermen – he didn't doubt it was a mistake – for a cry for help. 'Kevern!' he thought he heard. The two syllables pronounced with equal lack of emphasis. His dead mother's voice. A sick woman's voice, anyway. Quavering and reproachful, having to make itself heard above a jealous, jostling multitude of cries, detached from the person to whom it had belonged. 'Key-vern!'

He hadn't been close to his mother so he guessed this was a trick of longing. He would have liked her to be calling him.

But he recognised a danger in granting this primacy to his imagination: would he know the difference if one day someone really did cry out for his help?

He was not happy, but he was as happy here in his unhappiness, he accepted, as he was ever going to be. The sea confers a grandeur on the smallness of man's dissatisfactions, and Kevern Cohen gratefully accepted the compliment, knowing that his dissatisfactions were no bigger than most men's – loneliness and sense of lost direction (or was it the sense of never having had direction?) – of early-onset middle age. Nothing more. Like his father before him, and he had felt a deeper bond to his father than to his mother, though that wasn't saying much, he turned and carved wood for a living – spindles, newels, candlesticks, bowls, lovespoons for the tourist industry which he sold in local shops – and turning wood was a repetitive and tedious business. He had no family alive, no uncles, nieces, cousins, which was unusual in this part of the world where everyone was as an arm joined to one giant octopus. Kevern was joined to no one. He had no one to love or be loved by. Though this was to a degree occupational – like the moon, a woodturner turns alone – he accepted that it was largely a fault of character. He was lonely because he didn't take or make calls on his utility phone, because he was a neglectful friend, and, worse, an easily dismayed, over-reflective lover, and because he was forty.

Falling in love was something he did from time to time, but he was never able to stay in love or keep a woman in love with him. Nothing dramatic happened. There were no clifftop fallings-out. Compared to the violence with which other couples publicly shredded one another in Port Reuben, his courtships – for they were rarely more than that – came to an end with exemplary courtesy on both sides. They dissolved, that was the best way of putting it, they gradually came apart like a cardboard box that had been left out in the rain. Just occasionally a woman told him he was too serious, hard-going, intense, detached, and maybe a bit prickly. And then shook his hand. He recognised prickly. He was spiny, like a hedgehog, yes. The latest casualty of this spininess was an embryo-affair that had given greater promise than usual of relieving the lonely tedium of his life, and perhaps even bringing him some content. Ailinn Solomons was a wild-haired, quiveringly delicate beauty with a fluttering heart from a northern island village more remote and rugged even than Port Reuben. She had come south with an older companion whom Kevern took to be her aunt, the latter having been left a property in a wet but paradisal valley called, felicitously, Paradise Valley.

No one had lived in the house for several years. The pipes leaked, there were spiders still in the baths, slugs had signed their signatures on all the windows, believing the place belonged to them, the garden was overgrown with weeds that resembled giant cabbages. It was like a children's story cottage, threatening and enchanting at the same time, the garden full of secrets. Kevern had been sitting holding hands with Ailinn on broken deckchairs in the long grass, enjoying an unexpectedly warm spring afternoon, the pair of them absent-mindedly plugged into the utility console that supplied the country with soothing music and calming news, when the sight of her crossed brown legs reminded him of an old song by a long-forgotten black entertainer his father had liked listening to with the cottage blinds down. 'Your feet's too big.'

On account of their innate aggressiveness, songs of that sort were no longer played on the console. Not banned – nothing was banned exactly – simply not played. Encouraged to fall into desuetude, like the word desuetude. Popular taste did what edict and proscription could never have done, and just as, when it came to books, the people chose rags-to-riches memoirs, cookbooks and romances, so, when it came to music, they chose ballads.

Carried away by the day, Kevern began to play at an imaginary piano and in a rudely comic voice serenade Ailinn's big feet.

Ailinn didn't understand.

'It was a popular song by a ja̶zz pianist called Fats Waller,' he told her, automatically putting two fingers to his lips.

He had to explain what ja̶zz was. Ailinn had never heard any. J̶azz, too, without exactly being proscribed, wasn't played. Improvisation had fallen out of fashion. There was room for only one 'if' in life. People wanted to be sure, when a tune began, exactly where it was going to end. Wit, the same. Its unpredictability unsettled people's nerves. And ja̶zz was wit expressed musically. Though he reached the age of ten without having heard of Sammy Davis Junior, Kevern knew of jazz from his father's semi-secret collection of old CDs. But at least he didn't have to tell Ailinn that Fats Waller was black. Given her age, she was unlikely to have remembered a time when popular singers *weren't* black. Again, no laws or duress. A compliant society meant that every section of it consented with gratitude – the gratitude of the providentially spared – to the principle of group aptitude. People of Afro-Caribbean origin were suited by temperament and physique to entertainment and athletics, and so they sang and sprinted. People originally from the Indian subcontinent, electronically gifted as though by nature, undertook to ensure no family was without a functioning utility phone. What was left of the Polish community plumbed; what was left of the Greek smashed plates. Those from the Gulf States and the Levant whose grandparents hadn't quickly left the country while WHAT HAPPENED, IF IT HAPPENED was happening – fearing they'd be accused of having stoked the flames, fearing, indeed, that the flames would consume them next – opened labneh and shisha-pipe restaurants, kept their heads down, and grew depressed with idleness. To each according to his gifts.

Having heard only ballads, Ailinn was hard pressed to understand how the insulting words Kevern had just sung to her could ever have been set to music. Music was the expression of love.

'They're not really insulting,' Kevern said. 'Except maybe to people whose feet are too big. My father never insulted anybody, but he delighted in this song.'

He was saying too much, but the garden's neglect gave the illusion of safety. No word could get beyond the soundproofing of the giant cabbage-like leaves.

Ailinn still didn't comprehend. 'Why would your father have loved something like that?'

He wanted to say it was a joke, but was reluctant, in her company, to put two fingers to his lips again. She already thought he was strange.

'It struck him as funny,' he said instead.

She shook her head in disbelief, blotting out Kevern's vision. Nothing to see in the whole wide world but her haystack of crow-black hair. Nothing else he wanted to see. 'If you say so,' she said, unconvinced. 'But that still doesn't explain why you're singing it to me.' She seemed in genuine distress. 'Are *my* feet too big?'

He looked again. 'Your feet specifically, no. Your ankles, maybe, a bit . . .'

'And you say you hate me because my ankles are too thick?'

'Hate you? Of course I don't hate you. That's just the silly song.' He could have said 'I love you', but it was too soon for that. 'Your thick ankles are the very reason I'm attracted to you,' he tried instead. 'I'm perverse that way.'

It came out wrong. He had meant it to be funny. Meaning to be funny often landed him in a mess because, like his father, he lacked the reassuring charm necessary to temper the cruelty that lurked in jokes. Maybe his father intended to be cruel. Maybe he, Kevern, did. Despite his kind eyes.

Ailinn Solomons flushed and rose from her deckchair, knocking over the console and spilling the wine they'd been drinking.

Elderflower wine, so drink wasn't his excuse.

In her agitation she seemed to tremble, like the fronds of a palm tree in a storm.

'And your thick head's the very reason I'm perversely attracted to you,' she said . . . 'Except that I'm not.'

He felt sorry for her, both on account of the unnecessary unkindness of his words and the fear that showed in her eyes in the moment of her standing up to him. Did she think he'd strike her?

She hadn't spoken to him about life on the chill northern archipelago where she had grown up, but he didn't doubt it was in all essentials similar to here. The same vast and icy ocean crashed in on them both. The same befuddled men, even more thin-skinned and peevish in the aftermath of WHAT HAPPENED than their smuggler and wrecker ancestors had been, roamed angrily from pub to pub, ready to raise a hand to any woman who dared to refuse or twit them. *Thick head*? They'd show her a thick fist if she wasn't careful! Snog her first – the snog having become the most common expression of erotic irritation between men and women: an antidote to the bland ballads of love the console pumped out – snog her first and cuff her later. An unnecessary refinement in Kevern's view, since a snog was itself an act of thuggery.

Ailinn Solomons made a sign with her body for him to leave. He heaved himself out of the deckchair like an old man. She felt leaden herself, but the weight of his grief surprised her. This wasn't the end of the world. They barely knew each other.

She watched him go – as at an upstairs window her companion watched him go – a man made heavy by what he'd brought on himself. Adam leaving the garden, she thought.

She felt a pang for him and for men in general, no matter that some had raised their hands to her. A man turned from her, his back bent, ashamed, defeated, all the fight in him leaked away – why was that a sight she felt she knew so well, when she couldn't recall a single instance, before today, of having seen it?

Alone again, Ailinn Solomons looked at her feet.

ii

A score or so years before the events related above, Esme Nussbaum, an intelligent and enthusiastic thirty-two-year-old researcher employed by Ofnow, the non-statutory monitor of the Public Mood, prepared a short paper on the continuance of low- and medium-level violence in those very areas of the country where its reduction, if not its cessation, was most to have been expected, given the money and energy expended on uprooting it.

'Much has been done, and much continues to be done,' she wrote, 'to soothe the native aggressiveness of a people who have fought a thousand wars and won most of them, especially in those twisted knarls and narrow crevices of the country where, though the spires of churches soar above the hedgerows, the sweeter breath of human kindness has, historically, been rarely felt. But some qualities are proving to be ineradicable. The higher the spire, it would seem, the lower the passions it goes on engendering. The populace weeps to sentimental ballads, gorges on stories of adversity overcome, and professes to believe ardently in the virtues of marriage and family life, but not only does the old brutishness retain a pertinacious hold equally on rural communities as on our urban conurbations, evidence suggests the emergence of a new and vicious quarrelsomeness in the home, in the workplace, on our roads and even on our playing fields.'

'You have an unfortunate tendency to overwrite,' her supervisor said when he had read the whole report. 'May I suggest you read fewer novels.'

Esme Nussbaum lowered her head.

'I must also enquire: are you an atheist?'

'I believe I am not obliged to say,' Esme Nussbaum replied.

'Are you a lesbian?'

Again Esme protested her right to privacy and silence.

'A feminist?'

Silence once more.

'I don't ask,' Luther Rabinowitz said at last, 'because I have an objection to atheism, lesbianism or feminism. This is a prejudice-free workplace. We are the servants of a prejudice-free society. But certain kinds of hypersensitivity, while entirely acceptable and laudable in themselves, may sometimes distort findings such as you have presented to me. You are obviously yourself prejudiced against the church; and those things you call "vicious" and "brutish", others could as soon interpret as expressions of natural vigour and vitality. To still be harping on about WHAT HAPPENED, IF IT

HAPPENED, as though it happened, if it happened, yesterday, is to sap the country of its essential life force.'

Esme Nussbaum looked around her while Rabinowitz spoke. Behind his head a flamingo pink LED scroll repeated the advice Ofnow had been dispensing to the country for the last quarter of a century or more. 'Smile at your neighbour, cherish your spouse, listen to ballads, go to musicals, use your telephone, converse, explain, listen, agree, apologise. Talk is better than silence, the sung word is better than the written, but nothing is better than love.'

'I fully understand the points you are making,' Esme Nussbaum replied in a quiet voice, once she was certain her supervisor had finished speaking, 'and I am saying no more than that we are not healed as effectively as we delude ourselves we are. My concern is that, if we are not forewarned, we will find ourselves repeating the mistakes that led to WHAT HAPPENED, IF IT HAPPENED, in the first place. Only this time it will not be on others that we vent our anger and mistrust.'

Luther Rabinowitz made a pyramid of his fingers. This was to suggest infinite patience. 'You go too far,' he said, 'in describing as "mistakes" actions which our grandparents might or might not have taken. You go too far, as well, in speaking of them venting their "anger" and "mistrust" on "others". It should not be necessary to remind someone in your position that in understanding the past, as in protecting the present, we do not speak of "us" and "them". There was no "we" and there were no "others". It was a time of disorder, that is all we know of it.'

'In which, if we are honest with ourselves,' Esme dared to interject, 'no section of society can claim to have acquitted itself well. I make no accusations. Whether it was done ill, or done well, what was done was done. Then was then. No more needs to be said – on this we agree. And just as there is no blame to be apportioned, so there are no amends to be made, were amends appropriate and were there any way of making them. But what is the past for if not to learn from it—'

'The past exists in order that we forget it.'

'If I may add one word to that—'

Luther Rabinowitz collapsed his pyramid. 'I will consider your report,' he said, dismissing her.

The next day, turning up for work as usual, she was knocked down by a motorcyclist who had mounted the pavement in what passers-by described as a 'vicious rage'.

Coincidences happen.

iii

Ailinn, anyway – whatever the state of things in the rest of the country, and others were now openly saying what Esme Nussbaum had said in her long-suppressed report – had sported a bruise under her right eye when Kevern saw her for the first time, standing behind a long trestle table on which were laid out for sale jams, marmalades, little cakes, pickles, hand-thrown pots and paper flowers.

'Fine-looking girl, that one,' a person Kevern didn't know whispered in his ear.

'Which one?' asked Kevern, not wanting to be rude, but not particularly wanting to be polite either.

'Her. With all the hair and the purple eye.'

Had Kevern been in the mood for conversation he might have answered that there was more than one among the women selling preserves and flowers who had a purple eye. But yes, the black hair – thick and seemingly warm enough to be the nest of some fabulous and he liked to think dangerous creature – struck him forcibly. 'Aha, I see her,' he said, meaning 'Leave me alone.'

Impervious, the stranger continued. 'She'll say she walked into a door. The usual excuse. Needs looking after, in my humble opinion.'

He was dressed like a country auctioneer – of pigs, Kevern thought. He had a pleated, squeeze-box neck, which rippled over the collar of his tweed hacking jacket, and the blotched skin of someone who'd spent too much time in the vicinity of mulch, manure and, yes, money.

'Aha,' Kevern said again, looking away. He hoped his unfriendly demeanour would make it clear he didn't welcome confidentiality, but he mustn't have made it clear enough because the man slipped an arm through his and offered to introduce him.

'No, no, that's not necessary,' Kevern said firmly. He started from all strangers instinctively, but this one's insinuating manner frightened and angered him.

The introduction was effected notwithstanding. Kevern was not sure how.

'Ailinn Solomons, Kevern Cohen. Kevern Cohen . . . but you know each other now.'

They shook hands and the go-between vanished.

'A friend of yours?' Kevern asked the girl.

'Never seen him in my life. I can't imagine how he knows my name.'

'I ask myself the same question.'

They exchanged concerned looks.

'But you're from here, aren't you?' the girl said.

'Yes. But I too have never seen him in my life. You obviously are *not* from here.'

'It shows?'

'It shows in that we have never before met. So you're from where . . . ?'

She flung a thumb over her left shoulder, as though telling him to scoot.

'You want me to go?'

'No, sorry, I was showing you where I'm from. If that's north, I'm from up there. Forgive me, I'm nervous. I've been spooked by what's just taken place. I haven't been here long enough for people to know my name.'

She looked around anxiously – Kevern couldn't tell whether

to get a second look at the man or to be certain he had gone for good. In deference to her anxiety he made light of his own. (He too had been spooked by what had just occurred.) 'You know these village nosey parkers. He's probably an amateur archivist.'

'You have archives here?'

'Well, no, not officially, but we have the occasional crazy who enjoys hoarding rumours and going through people's rubbish bins. I have one as a neighbour, as it happens.'

'And you let him go through yours?'

'Oh, I have no rubbish.'

He enjoyed the sensation of her looking through him. He wanted her to know that any secrets he had, she was welcome to.

'Well I don't think our man was an archivist,' she said. 'He looked too interested in himself. I'd say he was an auctioneer of pigs.'

Kevern smiled at her.

'Which doesn't explain . . .'

'No, it doesn't . . .'

She *was* a fine-looking girl, delicately strung, easy to hurt despite the dangerous thicket of her hair. He thought he detected in himself an instinct to protect her. Absurdly, he imagined rolling her in his rug. Though what good that would have done her, he couldn't have said.

'You don't have an "up there" accent,' he said.

'And you don't have a "down here" one.'

They felt bonded in not sounding as though they were from either place.

Emboldened by this, he pointed to her bruise. 'Who did that to you?'

She ignored the question, going behind the stall to rearrange the flowers. Then she looked him directly in the eyes and shrugged. It was a gesture he understood. Who'd done that to her? It didn't matter: they all had.

Years before, he'd been a choirboy at the church and, because he had a flutey tenor voice ideally suited to Bach's Evangelist, still sang there every Christmas when they performed the expurgated version of the *St Matthew Passion*. He didn't normally attend fetes – he was not a festive man – but several people from the church had urged him to attend. 'Why?' he'd asked. 'Just come along, Kevern,' they'd said, 'it will do you good.' And more flyers publicising the event were popped through his letter box than he could recall receiving for similar events.

On the morning of the fete, the vicar, Golvan Shlagman, even rang to make sure he was coming. Kevern said he was undecided. He had work to do. All work and no play, the Reverend Shlagman quipped. He hoped Kevern would try his best. It wouldn't be the same without his presence. Kevern didn't see why. Why was his presence a matter of significance suddenly? 'We can't do without the Evangelist,' the vicar laughed, though no Mass or Passion was being sung.

Thinking about it later, Kevern thought Shlagman's laughter had been only just the sane side of hysterical.

Had he hysterically laughed Ailinn into coming to the fete, too?

Seeing as they mistrusted strangers equally, didn't speak in the accents of where they resided, and knew a pig auctioneer when they saw one, he asked her out.

She took a minute or two to decide. He, too, was a stranger, she seemed to be reminding him.

He understood. 'A little walk, that's all,' he said. 'Nowhere far.'

On their first date he kissed the bruise under her eye.

He was not a man who raised his arm to women and hadn't been stirred to anger when Ailinn called him thick-headed. He only nodded and smiled lugubriously – it was that dopey-eyed, lugubrious smile that had earned him the nickname Coco, after a once famous clown who sometimes reappeared, accompanied by apologies for the cruelty visited on him, in children's picture books. She was right, when all was said and done. He was a lolloping unfunny clown with a big mouth who didn't deserve her love. And now – she made no attempt to stop him getting up and leaving – he'd lost it.

He reproached himself for being too easily put off. It didn't have anything to do with Ailinn; he lacked the trick of intimacy, that was all. On the other hand, the thickness of her ankles relative to the slenderness of her frame – especially the right one, around which she wore a flowery, child-of-nature anklet – did upset him, and on top of that, like every other village girl, no matter that she came from a village at the other end of the country, she smelt of fish.

But then there *were* other girls in the village, and although they had always treated him with that degree of watchfulness they reserved for people to whom they weren't related, their availability took the edge off his desolation. He was alone, but on any evening he could drop by the Friendly Fisherman and fall into conversation with one or other of them. And at least at the bar the smell of beer took away the smell of fish.

He sat on his bench absent-mindedly, watching the seals flop, enjoying the spray on his face, thinking about everything and nothing, exclaiming 'Jesus Christ!' to himself from time to time, until the sun sank beneath its own watery weight into the sea. It became immediately chilly. Feeling the cold, he rose from the bench and decided to try his luck. Company was company. He called by the cottage first and peered in through the letter box. All was almost well. He was still in, still reading his mail in his carpet slippers, still watching television. And his rug was still rumpled. But his utility phone was flashing vermilion, which meant somebody had rung him. Perhaps Ailinn saying she was sorry, though she had done nothing to say sorry for.

After the falling-out, the saying sorry. That was the way. They had all been taught it at school. Always say sorry.

If it was she who had rung him, should he ring her back? He didn't know.

In agitation, because the knowledge that he'd been rung – no matter by whom – distressed him, he let himself in, discovered the caller had left no message – though he thought he detected the breath of someone as agitated as himself – and locked up again. Fifteen minutes later he was in the Friendly Fisherman, ordering a sweet cider.

iv

The inn was more than usually noisy and querulous. That fractiousness which was being reported as on the increase throughout the country was no less on the increase here. There'd been an incident earlier in the village hall and some of the bad feeling had spilled out into the inn from that. It was Thursday, Weight Watchers day, and one of the village women, Tryfena Heilbron, had refused to accept that she'd put on a pound since the last time she'd been weighed. Words had been exchanged and Tryfena had lifted the scales and dashed them to the ground. 'Next time bring scales that work,' she'd shouted at the weigher who shouted back that it was no surprise to her that Tryfena's husband preferred the company of sweeter-tempered, not to say more sylphlike, women.

By the time news of the altercation reached the Friendly Fisherman the men were involved. Breoc Heilbron the haulier, a dangerous brute of a man even when sober, was drunkenly defending the honour of a wife he didn't scruple at other times to abuse. It struck Kevern Cohen as a sign of the times that men who would once have steered clear of Breoc Heilbron's temper were prepared tonight to needle him, not only man to man, by impugning his capacity to hold his drink, but by referring to his wife's notorious temper and even to her weight. Was he imagining it or did he actually hear someone describe her as a heifer? That heifer, Tryfena Heilbron.

That was how people had begun to talk of one another. That

heifer, Tryfena Heilbron. That lump of lard, Morvoren Steinberg.

Followed by an apology to Morvoren's husband.

And no doubt, that idiot Kevern Cohen.

Kevern tried to remember whether the village had ever in reality been the placid haven pictured in its brochures by New Heritage, that body to which every taxpayer in the country was expected to contribute in return for an annual weekend away from the growing turmoil of the towns. Had it? He didn't think so. Most of the teachers at the village school he had attended had been free with the cane or the slipper before saying sorry. The boys had brawled viciously in the playground. So had the girls. Tourists on their annual weekend breaks were laughed at behind their backs and made to feel unwelcome in the inns, for all that their custom was indispensable to the local economy. But he thought there had been some days when everything was quiet and everyone rubbed along. Whereas now it was never quiet, and no one rubbed along.

He joined in an ill-tempered game of darts with a group of sullenly drunken men, including Densdell Kroplik, failing to hit a single number he was required to hit and having to buy a round of drinks for his team as a consequence.

'Up yerz,' Kroplik said, raising his glass. Kevern laughed, not finding it funny. He wondered again what possessed him ever to let the barber near his throat with a razor.

The other men apologised.

'Not necessary,' Kevern told them.

Densdell Kroplik didn't think it was necessary either. 'Don't yez go apologising for me,' he said, spitting on the floor. 'I do my own, when the time'z right, and thiz izn't.'

Kevern walked away. He wanted to leave, but didn't. His cottage was quiet and he needed noise. A little later, he accepted a challenge to play pool from a handsome, broad-shouldered woman who ran the mug and tea-towel shop in which he sold his love-spoons. Hedra Deitch.

She scattered the balls with an alarming vehemence, called Kevern 'my lover', and made derogatory remarks to him about her husband who was slumped at the bar like a shot animal, coughing out the last of his blood into a pint pot of brown ale.

'That's how he looks when he finishes himself over me,' she said, in a voice loud enough for him to hear.

Kevern wasn't sure what to say.

'Eat shit!' her husband called across to her.

'Eat shit yerself!'

Kevern thought about leaving, but stayed.

'You think he'd be only too glad to give me a divorce,' Hedra Deitch went on. 'But oh, no. We must stay together for the children, he says. That's a laugh. He doesn't give a flyin' fuck for the children and suspects they're not his anyway.'

'And are they?' Kevern asked.

'What do you think, my lover?'

'I can't imagine you passing off another man's children as his,' Kevern said.

She choked on her laughter. 'You can't imagine that, can't you? Then you doesn't have a very vivid imagination.'

Kevern tried imagining, then thought better of it. He went home alone, after submitting briefly to one of Hedra Deitch's muscular snogs. Forcing brutish kisses on people you neither knew well nor cared much for wasn't confined to men. Both sexes broke skin when they could.

A sharp-edged moon lit his way. Once upon a time he'd have been able to hear the sea on a night such as this, the great roar of the ocean sucking at the rocks, breathing in and then breathing out, but the din of voices raised in brawling throughout the village drowned out all other sounds. A quarter of a mile up the road to his cottage he passed the Deitches kissing passionately in a doorway. To Kevern they resembled a single beast, maddened by the need to bite its own mouth. Great fumes of beer and fish rose from its pelt. If Kevern's ears didn't deceive him, Hedra Deitch was alternately telling her weasel husband to eat shit and apologising to him.

The unseasonably warm wind of earlier in the day – smelling of seals and porpoises, Kevern thought – had turned cold and bitter. Something far out to sea was rotting.

He could have done with company, but he knew it was his own fault he had none. 'Company is always trouble,' his father used to say, laughing his demented solitary laugh. But he didn't have to listen to his father. Taking after your father was optional, wasn't it?

He knelt on one knee and peered in through the letter box of his cottage. Shocked by what he saw, he staggered backwards. The cottage had been ransacked. There was blood on the carpet. In the two or three seconds it took him to recover himself, he wondered why he was surprised. This was no more than he'd been expecting. And now the knife between his shoulder blades . . .

He looked again, not afraid of what he'd see. Relieved, he thought.

At last.

But everything was, after all, exactly as he'd left it – the disrespected rug, the teacup, the slippers. There was a blue glow from the television. All was well. He was in. Alone.

It was his utility phone that was flashing the colour of blood.

It sounded like singing. Not a choir, something more random and impatient, a hubbub set to music. He could smell burning but saw no fire, only smoke. Then an enormous rose of flame opened briefly as though, with one supreme effort, it meant to enfold the charred sky in its petals. Against the flame he was able to make out the silhouette of a figure, a slight boy, falling from a high wall. Even before the boy reached the ground the singing grew ecstatic, as though the singers believed their chanting was responsible. 'Down with the enemies of—!' they cried. He couldn't make out the word in the frenzy of its delivery. Life, was it? *Down with the enemies of Life*? Or mice? *Down with the enemies of Mice*? Down with them, anyway. He thought he recognised the keep from whose tower the boy, like a doll with no weight, continued to float and lightly fall to earth. Yes, he knew it. Inside those walls, inside that fire, he had knelt by the body of a mother – he couldn't say, after all this time, if she were his. Her eyes were open but unseeing. Her clothes had been torn from her body. Where her throat was cut a scarlet rose flowered, smaller than the one that had briefly illuminated the sky, but no less remarkable. Its loveliness flowed from it in a stream, running down her breast. He dipped his finger in it, as though it were wine, and put it to his lips. Down with me, he thought.

TWO

Twitternacht

Friday 27th

Ho, HUM . . .

For anyone opening my diary for the first time – and it's for futurity in all its misty uncertainty that I write – ho hum denotes the sound of my mind whirring, not cynicism.

It would appear that he learnt to take these Byzantine precautions from his parents, as they, perhaps, had learnt to take them from theirs, otherwise they denote nothing other than an uncommonly anxious disposition . . .

So concluded the first report on Kevern 'Coco' Cohen I ever wrote. I have a copy in front of me in a black folder. Always wise to keep a copy. I was guessing, I admit that much, but guesswork is an important part of what I have been entrusted to do. Guesswork informed by a knowledge of the ways of men, I mean, a trustworthiness of intuition and a shrewdness of observation, which I flatter myself I possess in as great a measure as any person. Perhaps more. I work – I don't call my observations of Kevern Cohen 'work' – in one of the most trustworthy and ophthalmically demanding professions, as a teacher of the Benign Visual Arts. I am also a painter myself. Landscapes, naturally. Hence their giving me far west Bethesda as my territory. Bethesda with its long history of naive art – spirituality apprehended in the everyday – and of course St Mordechai's Mount which I can see from my studio window and walk to when the tide is out. Modesty should forbid me mentioning my *Seventeen Sketches of St Mordechai's Mount In All Seasons* which enjoy prominence in the Parochial Beauty Rooms at the New National Gallery, but they are my best work to date and I am proud of them. I would have preferred to stay in the Capital, for all its troubles – if only to enjoy the illusion of being at the centre of things and eating a little better – but the position I occupy in the Bethesda Art Academy has its consolations. Head of painting within a department as dedicated to feeling as any in the country is not a job you sniff at. I've heard it argued that Bethesda found it easier than most art colleges to make the journey back from insentience to feeling because for us, feeling never really went away. Conceptualism, or mind-machine art as historians now call it, had always been more of a city than a country fad. It had been practised down here but without any real zest or instinct for it. A few local potters defied the tradition of their craft, forgot or simply refused to remember that a pot's job was to express, in silence and slow time, a flowery tale with sweetness, and set about throwing misshapen objects that had no utility except to offend whoever looked on them by virtue of the obscene acts they depicted. The art, they explained, when they could be bothered to explain anything, lay precisely in the offence. But the joke never took. Obscenities don't shock country people who practise them without thinking twice. And as for the ironies of installation art, you needed department stores all around you to appreciate those, just as you need the colours of a big sky and the changeability of a turbulent sea to understand why painters have to paint. The pursuit of beauty is no mystery when you wake to it each day. And I have always argued that the real sentimentality is not the indulgence of colour but the denial of it. It went missing, anyway. Three generations lived and died without seeing colour except in its lipstick-pink and electric-blue manifestations, flashing tubes and the like, ironic statements about colour and its production, denying the naked sensuousness that makes true lovers of painting believe they are seeing the face of God. But enough of that. You will find my thoughts on the subject – much extended – in many a volume of *Sublime Quarterly*, Bethesda's own art magazine, which can be ordered from any gallery shop in the country and also a good number of the better newsagents. I write under my own name – Edward Everett Phineas Zermansky (Everett to my friends, Phinny to my family) – and am told that I am highly readable.

Well, my wife tells me so, anyway.

Or at least she does when she isn't telling me the opposite. Phinny the Palaverous is how she refers to me to her girlfriends. Who know, of course, she doesn't mean it.

I don't say we fight. But we are not immune to malign influences beyond our kitchen and bedroom. How could we be? Are we not all one family?

That the dry, embittered colourlessness of the conceptual – to return to my theme – helped harden the nation's heart is accepted as a truism by artists of today. Art wasn't the cause or centre of the great desensitisation, for which, of course, all artists apologise, but WHAT HAPPENED, IF IT HAPPENED – or TWITTERNACHT, as I like to call it when I am feeling skittish, by way of reference to . . . well to many things, one of them being the then prevailing mode of social interaction that facilitated, though can by no means be said to have provoked it – WHAT HAPPENED, IF IT HAPPENED, I say, happened, if it did, because as a people we'd anaesthetised the feeling parts of ourselves, first through the ugly liberties with form taken by modernism and second through the liberties taken with emotion by that same modernism in its 'post' form. I say 'we' because there is nothing to be achieved by saying 'they', indeed there is much to be lost, given that 'they' is a policed pronoun today, but when I am certain no one is looking (I mean this figuratively) I poke a finger at the alien intellectualism that brought such destruction first on itself and then, as an inevitable consequence, on all of us. Thus, again, the felicity of my

TWITTERNACHT *jeu d'esprit*, twitter like much else in the same vein that was then the rage, having proceeded from the alien intelligences of the very people who were to lose most by it. Call that irony, a concept of which they, in particular, were overfond, which is an irony in itself. Let's be clear: no one behaved well, but there is such a thing as provocation. The largest beast can be maddened by the smallest parasitic mite. (Especially when it's clever . . . the mite, that is.) I will say no more than that.

Except . . . No, I'll stick to my guns and shut up. 'You talk too much,' Demelza is always saying to me. And I'm a man who listens to his wife.

Perhaps future generations will describe what we do now as a cult of feeling, but better to feel than not to, better to experience love than its opposite. Better, in short, to live now than to have lived then. If the cost of not allowing ourselves to return to that inglorious past, or anything resembling it, is a certain mistrustfulness and vigilance, I happen to think it's a price worth paying. Hence . . . well, hence my doing what I do. My ho humming, as the Divine Demelza calls it. I don't spy on my students or my colleagues. I keep an eye open, that's all. For what? Well, for anything or anyone – how can I best put this? – *left over*. For business dangerously unfinished. For matter out of place, as a famous anthropologist once described dirt. For recidivism. In any of its guises, recidivism is what we fear most. Hence a job of this sort falling to someone teaching at an art college. Because art, for all its adventuresomeness, is also capable of being the most recidivist of human activities, forever falling back in reaction to what was itself a reaction to something else. People can behave like savages when they are allowed to, but only in art do they go so far as to call themselves primitivists. And when the primitivist urge doesn't seize them, the psychoaesthetic urge, the study of human evil – itself another form of primitivism, when you come to think about it – does. So portrait painting is a further recidivism that's frowned on and discouraged – that's in so far as one can discourage anything in a free society. In the main, prize-culture does the job for us. When all the gongs go to landscape, why would any aspiring artist waste his energies on the dull and relentless cruelties of the human face? While not wanting to affect modesty, I suspect I wouldn't be enjoying the favour and seniority I do – I omitted to say that I am Professor Edward Everett Phineas Zermansky, FRSA – had I not from an early age followed nature's laws in the matter of beauty. There are painters who paint more experimentally than I do, without doubt, but of my more troubled colleagues – those who still hanker secretly for the alien and the grotesque, even the degenerate (though they wouldn't dream of pronouncing that term aloud) – I cannot think of one who hasn't had to wait a long time to be given recognition, and even longer to be given tenure.

But to return to the point from which I began, and I don't apologise for my vagrant style – 'Keep up!' I tell my students when I sense they are losing me; 'Keep up!' I even have to tell my wife on those occasions when I catch her glancing at her watch – I don't claim more for what goes into my black folder on Kevern Cohen than it's worth. I say 'I keep an eye open' but I do so only at the lowest level – code name Grey. Think of those I watch as birds, and I am no more than a Sunday twitcher. The work of serious, scientific ornithology is done by others. For which reason, while I am conscientious in my observations, I have never imagined that what I see or what I miss matters a great deal. Until now. Suddenly, I am conscious of having to deliver. It is as though the common house sparrow, on which – to nobody's interest – I've been keeping an eye for some time, has overnight become an endangered species and I am at a stroke indispensable to the species' protection. I won't pretend to knowledge I don't have. All my reports are now more scrupulously monitored than they were before, so I can't say with any certainty that Kevern 'Coco' Cohen – one of the common house sparrows in question – has risen to the top of any pile. I have a feeling about him, that's all. Or rather

I have a feeling that *they* have a feeling. I like the man, I have to say. He has for several years been coming in one day a week to the academy, teaching the art of carving lovespoons out of a single piece of wood. I admire his work, which is exquisite, but there are some who find him a little too good to be true. Not the students; they love his air of grumpy probity as much as I love what he makes, and I am sure that when their opinions are canvassed they will speak of him only in the most glowing terms. But it goes against him with senior members of the college that he doesn't drink with them, spends too much time in the restricted section of the library – not reading a great deal, according to Rozenwyn Feigenblat, our librarian, just staring into space the minute he is a page or two into what he *does* read, as though wondering what he came here for – and is rarely heard to apologise. I don't, of course, mean for reading books, I mean for anything – an act of carelessness or forgetting, a brusqueness, a contradiction. The reason he gives is that as he lives on his own, works in isolation, and so rarely has occasion to lose his temper, he has nothing to apologise for. Not an argument well calculated to win him friends in the common room, because the truth is none of us really think we have anything to apologise for. But the way an institution works is that you go along with the prevailing fiction. And generally – if not individually – the habit of delivering brisk, catch-all apologies is much to be preferred to morbid memory which embalms the past in the Proustian fluids of the maudlin. (Though Proust is no longer read, we still retain the adjective.) My authority for this is the media philosopher Valerian Grossenberger, author of *Seven Reasons To Say Sorry*, whose series of daily lectures for National Radio some years ago can be said to have changed the way we all think. Modern societies had spent too much time, according to Grossenberger, rubbing the twin itches of recollection and penance. In the bad old days, 'never forget' was a guiding maxim – you couldn't move, I've heard tell, for obelisks and mausoleums and other inordinately ugly monuments exhorting memory – but this led first to wholesale neuroticism and impotence and then, as was surely inevitable, to the great falling-out, if there was one. Rather than go on perpetuating the neurasthenic concept of victimisation, Grossenberger argued, the never-forgetters would have done better carving 'I Forgive You' on their stones. In return for which, we might have forgiven them. But that chance came and went. And now who, today, is going to forgive whom for what? Only by having everyone say sorry, without reference to what they are saying sorry for, can the concept of blame be eradicated, and guilt at last be anaesthetised.

Saying sorry, Grossenberger concluded, when he came to address the Bethesda Academy recently – an old man now, but still possessed of his silky powers of reasoning – releases us all from a recriminatory past into an unimpeachable future. We stood and applauded that, not least as it struck us that he was delivering a last eulogy to his own distinguished, emollient career. But if you ask me whether Kevern Cohen stood along with the rest of us, I have to say I don't recall his being present.

I make nothing of it. He might indeed be a man who is so equable of temper that the idea of apology mystifies him. Or he might not yet have got past the 'never forget' stage in his own life. Let us hope that the latter is not the case and agree simply that he's a queer one. 'I find him weird,' my wife said only the other day, after we'd had him over for dinner. 'With those droopy eyes and all that hand washing and tap checking. It's like having What's-he-called over.'

'Lady Macbeth?'

'I said *he*.'

'Pontius Pilate?'

'Yes.'

'As in that fine Dürer—'

'Spare me the lecture, Phinny. Him, yes. But if he's like this in our house, what must he be like in his own?'

'Pontius Pilate?'

'Kevern, you fool.'

'Worse, I don't doubt. Much worse.'

'What I don't understand is how he knows when to stop. While he was helping with the washing-up he kept wandering over to the stove to make sure the gas was off. "I've checked that," I told him, but he said he feared he might have brushed against the taps when he was drying up and it was better to be safe than sorry. But at what point does he decide it's safe?'

'You should have asked him.'

'I did. But his answer was unilluminating. "Never," he said.'

'Never?'

'Never. Isn't that terrible?'

'Yes. But he has to stop sometimes. The man sleeps, for God's sake.'

'I asked him about that, too. Presumably you sleep, I said. So when do you call it a day? At what point are you able to close your eyes? And his answer to that was more unilluminating still. "When I can't stand it any more," he said. And how do you know when that is, I asked. "I just know," he said.'

'Maybe it's when he gets tired. He has the air of a man who tires easily. Men do, you know.'

This irritated her. 'And women don't?'

Which irritated me. 'Of course they do, but we aren't talking about women,' I snapped. 'Or about you.'

We stared angrily into each other's faces.

Why did she, I thought, have to bring her sex into everything?

Why did I, I saw her thinking, have to be so critical of her?

Why were her eyes, I thought, so quick to water up?

Why were mine, I knew she thought, so quickly fierce?

Why did I marry her, I wondered. What had I ever seen in that pallid skin and impertinently, stupidly, retroussé little nose? How could I stop myself, I wondered, from striking her?

Why did she accept me, the witterer I was, I heard her ask

herself. How had she let those ugly crossed teeth of mine ever nibble at her breasts? Why had she ever allowed any part of me to come near any part of her? How much more would it take for her to strike me?

I slunk away.

She followed me into my studio.

I wondered if she was carrying a knife from the kitchen. The carver she'd recently had sharpened. I closed my eyes.

'I'm sorry, Phinny,' I heard her say.

I turned around abruptly. She started. Was she afraid of what I might be carrying? A trimming knife? My razor? A hammer?

'Me too, Demelza,' I said.

We were both sorry, and made love whimpering how sorry we were into each other's ears. I kissed her lovely little nose. She gave me her breast to nibble. Sorry. Sorry. Sorry for what, exactly? Neither of us knew. But without doubt a baseless irascibility had begun to be a fact of our marriage. Had we fallen out of love? I didn't think so. Friends of ours were reporting the same. A querulousness that appeared suddenly from nowhere and vanished just as inexplicably, though each time the period it took for lovingness to return extended itself a little more. We had a formulation for it: things just seemed to be getting on top of us. But why? Why, when we lacked for nothing, when beauty accompanied us wherever we went, when every source of discord had been removed?

It was shortly after this particular exchange of unpleasantries, anyway, that the file code for Kevern Cohen changed from grey to purple. Purple isn't vermilion. We weren't in danger territory. But others, I was now to understand, were reliant on what I knew as a sort of confirmation, let's even say – to be plain about it – as a cognitive intensification, of what they knew or didn't know themselves. Kevern Cohen was becoming a precious commodity.

THREE

The Four Ds

i

It *was* Ailinn who had been ringing him. Against her own instincts. But in line with her companion's, though her companion thought she could go a little further and actually leave a message. 'Even just a hello,' she said.

'When you know me better, Ez,' Ailinn told her, 'you will discover I am not the sort of woman who leaves hellos on men's phones. They pick up or they lose me.'

'And when you know *me* better,' Ez told her, 'you will discover I am not the sort of woman to egg people on to do what they don't want to do. But this is different. You aren't yourself. I've never seen you so down in the mouth.'

'That's because you haven't seen me often. Down in the mouth is not what I do, it's who I am.'

'That isn't true. You were hopeful when you met him. You said you thought you might just have met your soulmate.'

'I did not!'

'Well you said you thought you'd met someone you could possibly get on with.'

'I think that's rather different.'

Brittle-boned and careful with herself, a woman who seemed to Ailinn to quiver with mutuality, Ez leaned in very close. 'Not for you it isn't,' she said, as though the strain for Ailinn of being Ailinn was sometimes more than she could bear for her. 'A man has to be your soulmate before you'll give him the time of day.'

Ailinn raised an eyebrow. She and Ez were not well enough acquainted, she thought, to be having this conversation. She wasn't sure they were well enough acquainted for Ez to be bringing her tea in bed, fluffing up her pillows and patting her hand either, but she put that down to the older woman's loneliness. And consideration, of course. But offering to know so much about the kind of person Ailinn was, her ways with men, what made her happy, when she was and wasn't *herself*, the errands on which she sent her soul, for God's sake – all that seemed to her, however kindly it was meant, to be a presumption too far.

She wasn't angry. Ez didn't strike her as someone who would go through her clothes, or read her letters, or otherwise poke about in her life. She was pretty sure she wouldn't, for example, dream of ringing Kevern to tell him what she'd just told Ailinn. And besides, an older woman could be permitted a few liberties a younger one could not. Wasn't that their unspoken contract – that Ez needed the company of someone who could be almost as a child to her, and Ailinn . . . well she surely didn't need another mother, but all right, someone who could be what she'd never had, an older sister, an aunt, a good friend? Yet even allowing for all that, there was an anxious soulfulness about Ez, a taut emotional avidity that made Ailinn the smallest bit uncomfortable. Why was she sitting on the end of the bed, her body twisted towards Ailinn as though in an act of imploration, her eyes moist with woman-to-woman understanding, the phone in her hand? What in the end did it matter to Ez whether or not she left the village wood-turner a message?

She knew she was lucky to be with someone who cared about her happiness. She wasn't used to it. Her mother by adoption meant well by her but lost interest quickly. She would have had no attitude, or at least expressed no opinion, in the matter of Kevern Cohen. She never spoke of Ailinn's future, a job, possible husbands, children. It was as though she'd given Ailinn a life by rescuing her from the orphanage and that was that. Satisfying her conscience, it felt like, needing to perform a charitable act, and once performed, her responsibility was at an end. What, if anything, followed, was of no consequence or interest to her. So there were levels of concern Ailinn accepted she had still to learn about. Maybe her mother was the way she was with her because Ailinn made her so. Maybe she lacked a talent for being liked. She certainly lacked the talent for being liked by herself. In which case she was grateful to Ez.

And in which case shouldn't she make an effort with the clumsy man who at first had treated her with such gentleness, smiling softly into her face, inclining his head to kiss the bruise under her eye? He was sufficiently unlike the others, anyway, to be worth persisting with.

To hell with it, she thought – though she didn't tell Ez she'd changed her mind; she didn't want her to think it had been her doing – *to hell with it*, and instead of putting down the phone this time when no one answered, she chanced her arm.

Hello. It's Ailinn. You remember? Thick ankles – ring a bell? To be brief about it, because she was sure his time was valuable, she wanted him to know she had inspected herself front on and sideways in the mirror, and OK – she was too thick. And not just around the ankles. He waist was too thick as well. And her neck. She had become, she realised, as overgrown as the garden in which he'd been rude to her and told her it was a joke. She was grateful, by the way, for having the principles of comedy explained. She hoped she would be better able to get a joke the next time he was rude to her.

Anyway, if it was of the slightest interest to him – and why should it be? – she had decided to take herself off to Weight Watchers on whatever day they set up their scales in the village.

That's me. And now you. What do you intend to do about the thickness of your head?

She didn't laugh in order to make it plain that she too had comic ways. She wasn't going to make herself easy for him. If he couldn't read her, he couldn't read her. She didn't want to be with a man who insisted she got his jokes but wouldn't make the effort to get hers. Nor did she want to be with a man who didn't hear how much she was risking. Without risk on both sides, why bother?

Goodbye, she said. Then feared that sounded too final. Or should that be adieu? Unless that came over as desperation. No, goodbye, she said. And wished she'd never bothered.

What good came of love, when all was said and done? You fell in love and immediately thought about dying. Either because the person you had fallen for had a mind to kill you, or because he exceptionally didn't and then you dreaded being parted from him.

That was a joke, wasn't it?

And she got that well enough.

Kevern picked up her message. Relieved and reluctant at the same time – mistrustful of all excitement – he rang her back. He was surprised when she answered.

Oh! he said.

Oh what?

Oh, I never thought you'd be there.

Good, she thought. He imagines I am out and about.

They could hear each other swallowing hard.

Don't go to Weight Watchers, he told her. It's a free-for-all. And besides, you are fine as you are.

Fine? Only *fine*?

More than fine. Perfect. Lovely. She should take no notice of what he had said. There was something wrong with him.

Something wrong in the sense that he said what he thought without thinking through its consequences, or something wrong in the sense that he saw what wasn't there?

He thought about that. Both, he said. And in many more ways besides. Something wrong with him in every possible regard.

So my ankles aren't thick?

No, he said.

And would it matter to you if they were?

This he had to think about too. No, he said. It wouldn't matter to me in the slightest bit. I don't care how thick your ankles are.

So they *are* thick! You have simply decided that to humour me you will turn a blind eye to them at present. Which is generous, but it might mean you will mind them again in the future when you aren't feeling generous or you are in the mood to be funny. And then it will be too late.

Too late for what?

She had said too much.

He waited for her reply.

Too late for us to part as friends.

I promise you, he said.

You promise me what?

That we won't ever part as friends? No good. *That we won't ever part, full stop*? Too good. That I won't mind your ankles in the future, was what he decided to say. Promise.

And now?

Kevern sighed. You win, he said.

I've won, she thought.

She's going to be hard work, this one, he thought.

His other thought was that she was just the girl for him.

ii

The morning after the call he sat on his bench and wondered if he was about to experience happiness and, if so, whether he was up to it. He could have done with someone to talk to – his own age, a little younger, a little older, it didn't matter, just someone to muse with. But enter someone you can muse with and enter, with her, heartbreak. They were as one on this, he and the girl whose ankles he would never again object to, although they didn't yet know it: to think of love was to think of death.

He rarely missed his mother, but he did now. 'What's for the best, Mam? Should I go for it?' But she had always been negative. *What was for the best?* Nothing was for the best – for her the best was not to go for anything, just stay out of trouble and wait to die.

That was the impression she gave Kevern anyway. In fact she lived a secret life, and though that too was wreathed around in death, the very fact that it was secret meant she saw some risk as worth the taking. Was it because she loved Kevern more than she loved herself that she didn't recommend risk to him?

A funny sort of love, Kevern would have thought, had he known about it.

As for his father, any such conversation would have been equally out of the question. 'You always hurt the one you love,' his father had said the first time Kevern was jilted by a girl. Kevern took that to be an allusion to one of the old songs his father listened to on earphones. His father did not normally have that much to say.

'But she's the one who's hurt me,' he answered.

His father shrugged. 'Bee-bop-a-doo,' he said without taking off his earphones. He looked like a pilot who knew his plane was going down.

'I'll go for it, then,' Kevern said to himself, as though after considering all the sage advice no one had given him. But he still wanted to run it all over in his mind.

It infuriated him when Densdell Kroplik appeared up the path, singing to himself, a countryman's trilby pulled down over his eyes, heavier boots on than the weather merited, swinging his rucksack full of unsold pamphlets and nettle conditioner.

'If you want the bench to yourself I'll clear off,' Kevern said. 'I've got work to do.'

'If I'd wanted a bench to myzelf I'd have found un,' Kroplik said.

I see, playing the yokel this morning, Kevern thought. That wasn't his only thought. The other was 'Up yours', though he was not normally a swearer.

His mouth must have moved because Kroplik asked him what he'd said. In for a penny, in for a pound, Kevern decided, taking a leaf out of Ailinn's book. 'I said, "Up yours." I was repeating what you said to me in the pub last night.'

The barber rubbed his face with his hand. 'Yeah, I sayz that sometimes,' he conceded. 'And a lot worse when the mood takes me.'

'I don't doubt it,' Kevern said.

'Like khidg de vey. If you knowz what that means.'

Kevern nodded, saying nothing. It was a way of getting through life: nodding and saying nothing.

'You don't know, though, do you,' Densdell Kroplik went on, enjoying his own shrewdness. 'But I'll give yerz a guess.'

'No doubt it means something like go fuck yourself.'

Kroplik punched the air. 'We'll make a local of yerz yet. Go fuck yerzelf is spot on.'

'I didn't bring up your abusive language to me last night so you could abuse me further,' Kevern said. He heard how pious he sounded but there was no going back now. 'I'd rather not be spoken to like that,' he went on.

'Oh, you'd *rather not*.'

'I'd rather not.'

'Pog mo hoin.'

'Don't tell me . . . Your mother's a fucker of pigs.'

'Close, close. Kiss my arze.'

'You are a mine of indispensable information,' Kevern said, getting up from the bench.

'That's what I'm paid to be. Do you know who the first person was to say pog mo hoin in these parts?'

'You.'

'The *first* person I sayz.'

'No idea. I wouldn't have been around.'

'No, that you wouldn't. So I'll inform yerz. The giant Hellfellen. That's how he kept strangers out. He stood on this very cliff, right where you're standing now, made a trumpet of hiz fist, stuck it in hiz backside and blew the words "kiss my arze" through it, so loud they could hear it three counties away, and you had to have a very good reason to come here after that.'

Kevern was not a folklore man. Mythology, with its uncouth half-men, half-animals, frightened him. And he hated talk of giants. Especially those who used bad language. If there were going to be gods he wanted them to be supreme spiritual beings who didn't fart, who employed chaste speech and otherwise kept themselves invisible.

'We've always known how to extend a warm welcome down here, that's for sure,' he said.

'*We*?' Kroplik made a trumpet of his own fist and belched a little laugh through it. 'Well yes, in point of fact *we* do.'

'So when you tell me to go fuck myself you intend nothing but friendliness by it.'

'Nothing whatsoever, Mister Master Kevern Cohen. Kiss my arze the same. I'm being brotherly, and that's the shape of it. And to prove it I'll give you a free shave.'

On this occasion Mister Master Kevern Cohen declined. 'Pog mo hoin,' he thought about saying, but didn't.

His detestation of swearing amounted almost to an illness. At school, although Latin wasn't taught, one of his classmates told him that the Latin for go fuck yourself was *futue te ipsum* which, for all that it sounded nicer, still didn't sound nice enough. Kiss my arse the same. It wasn't only that he didn't want to kiss anyone or have anyone kiss him there – least of all those to whom it would have been most appropriate to say it – he recoiled from the sound of the word. *Arse*! Even cleansed of Kroplik's brute enunciation it made the body a site of loathing. Swearing was an act of violence to others and an act of ugliness to oneself. It had no place in him.

With one exception he had never heard either his mother or his father swear. The exception – single in type but manifold in application – was his father's deployment of the hissing prefix PISS before words denoting what he most deplored. As, for example, his transliteration of WHAT HAPPENED, IF IT HAPPENED into the raging, ǰestless ǰest-speak of THE GREAT PISSASTER or THE PISSFORTUNE TO END ALL PISSFORTUNES or simply THE PISSASTROPHE. Accompanied always by a small, self-satisfied whinny of triumph, as though putting PISS before a word was a blow struck for freedom, followed just as invariably by a stern warning to Kevern never to put a PISS before a word himself, not in private, and definitely not in public.

Otherwise the worst his father ever let drop in his hearing was 'I think I've forgotten to rumple the bloody hall carpet.'

And even for that his wife reproved him. 'Howel! Not in front of the boy.'

It was something more than distaste for bad language. It was as though they had taken an oath, as though the enterprise that was their life together – their life together as the parents of *him* – depended on their keeping that oath.

They were elderly parents – that explained something. Elderly in years in his father's case, elderly in spirit in his mother's. And this made them especially solicitous to him, watching and remorseful, as though they needed to make it up to him for being the age they were, or the age they felt they were. At the end of his life his father had admitted to a mistake. 'We would have done better by you had we let you be more like the rest of them,' he said. 'We wanted to preserve you but we went about it the wrong way. May God forgive me.'

His mother had died a month earlier. She had been dying almost as long as he'd known her, so her exit was expected, though the means of it was not. In circumstances that could not be explained she had suffered multiple burns while taking a short walk only yards from the cottage. As she didn't smoke she had no use for matches. The day was not hot. There was no naked flame in the vicinity. Either someone had set fire to her – in which event she would surely, since she remained conscious, have pointed a finger of blame – or she had combusted spontaneously – and what counted against that theory was that her torso was not burned, only her extremities. She lay quietly on her bed for three days without complaining and seemingly not in pain. Her final words were 'At last.'

But his father died – aged eighty though looking older – in a slow burn of ineffective rage. On the faces of some old men the flesh sags from lack of expressive exercise, the feeling man behind the skin having no more use for it; but on his father's it grew tighter with approaching death as though the skull beneath could not control its grimaces. On his last night he asked Kevern to dig out an ancient music system he kept hidden under the stairs in a box marked Private Property and got him to play the blind soul singer Ray Charles singing 'You Are My Sunshine' over and over. He shook his fists while it was playing, though Kevern couldn't tell whether at him, at Ray Charles, or at the cruel irony of things. 'What a ȷoke,' his father said. 'What a ȷoke that is.'

He had to unclench his father's fingers when the bitter light finally went out of him.

He let the music go on playing.

Kevern had always known about the box marked Private Property. Its futility saddened him. Would the words Private Property deter burglars? Or were they meant to deter him and his mother? What he hadn't known was how many more boxes marked Private Property – some of them cardboard and easy to get into, others made of metal and fitted with locks, but all of them numbered – his father had secreted under his bed, on the top of the wardrobe, in the attic, in his workshop. Hoarding was proscribed by universal consent – no law, you just knew you shouldn't do it – but he didn't think this could be called hoarding exactly. Hoarding, surely, was random and disorganised, the outward manifestation of a disordered personality. His father's boxes hinted at a careful, systematic, if overly secretive mind. But he'd read that people who kept things, whether they ordered them or they didn't, were afraid above all of loss – the fear of losing their things standing in for their fear of losing something else: love, happiness, their lives. Well he didn't need proof that his father was a frightened man. The only question was what he had all along been so frightened of.

Kevern knew the answer to that while maintaining that he didn't. You can know and not know. Kevern didn't know and knew. There were books in the redacted section of Bethesda Art Academy library with pages torn from them. Kevern sat in what appeared to Rozenwyn Feigenblat, the academy librarian, to be a concentration of profound vacancy, reading the pages that were no longer there.

One of his father's boxes was marked for his attention. Another was marked for his attention only in the event of his considering fatherhood. What he was meant to do with all the others he had no idea. Hoard them, he supposed.

Going through the papers and letters in the box marked for his attention, Kevern discovered a shocking truth about his parents. They were first cousins. That fact wasn't documented or brazenly trumpeted, but it was evident to anyone capable of reading between the lines, and Kevern lived between the lines. He couldn't have failed to gather, from his mother's and father's misery and from remarks they let drop over the years, that they didn't belong down here, that they lived in Port Reuben not out of choice, because they loved the sea or sought a simple way of life, but under duress; but he had never understood the nature of that duress, who or what had brought them and why they stayed. Now he knew. Down here no one would care about their incest (as Kevern considered it to be) even had they got wind of it. Cousins? So bleeding what! We are all one big happy family here. We don't care, my lovelies, if youz is brother and sister.

Kevern didn't miss out on wondering about that too. Was it worse than the letters intimated? Was 'cousins' a euphemism?

Such easy-goingness as Port Reuben and the surrounding villages exercised in the matter of consanguinity was not shared by the rest of the country. Blood needed to be thinned not thickened if there was to be none of that dense, overpopulated insalubriousness that had been the cause of discord. The county was allowed to make an exception of itself only because the authorities didn't take it seriously. A cordon sanitaire could easily be drawn across the neck of the county, cutting it off from the rest of the country; and the existence of an imaginary version of that line – beyond which few aphids (as tourists and even visitors on business were contemptuously known) had ever wanted to stray – already prevented any serious cross-pollution. It was in the overheated towns and cities, where people talked as well as bred too much, that cousins needed to be kept apart. And it hadn't escaped the attention of Ofnow that in acknowledging and encouraging nationality-based group aptitude – popular entertainment and athletics in this corner, plumbing in that – it ran the risk of allowing steam to build up in the enclaves once again. But that didn't apply to Bethesda. The Bethesdans could mate with their own animals as far as the authorities were concerned.

In this, as in so many other matters, Kevern Cohen was not able to be as insouciant as his neighbours. Learning that his parents had been first cousins – if not closer – shook him profoundly. It had nothing to do with legalities: he didn't know whether they'd done wrong in the eyes of the law or not. But their hiding away suggested that they felt they had. And to him it was an animal wrongness: first cousins! – it was too hot, like rutting. They'd run away to breed, and he was the thing they'd bred. Engendered in the steaming straw of their cow-house. Inbred.

He wondered if it explained the oddity of his nature. Was that the reason he had never married and had children of his own? Was he possessed of some genetic knowledge that would ensure his contaminated line would die out?

They'd always been too much of another time for him to feel close to them in the way other sons were close to their parents, so he found it difficult to attribute sins of the flesh to them. What they'd done they'd done. What he couldn't forgive them for was not taking their secret to the grave. Why had they left incriminating documents behind? Shouldn't they have kept him in the dark about what they'd done, as they'd kept him in the dark about almost everything else in their past – where they'd come from, what sort of family theirs was, who they *were*? There were few other papers for him to sort through. Most of the evidential story of their life, other than a number of nondescript notebooks and scrawled-over writing pads he kept for no other reason than that they had kept them, and a locked box which Kevern gave his oath he would open only when it looked likely that he would be a father himself – not before, and certainly not after – had been scrupulously destroyed. So he had to assume that they had deliberately not burned or shredded the handful of letters they had written to each other that proved how closely they were related. But to what end? Did they suppose they were helping him to live a better life? Or were the letters left where he could easily find them in order to give him a reason not to go on living at all? Was it their gift of death to him, like a single silver bullet or a suicide pill?

So much for their delicacy! They had brought him up unable to utter the most commonplace of oaths, a man of refined feeling, a fist of prickles as spiny as a hedgehog, and all along he'd been abnormally sired, a monstrosity, a freak. No wonder he couldn't tell anyone else to kiss his arse or eat shit. He had eaten shit himself.

He made a further unwelcome discovery going through his parents' papers. It wasn't they who had run to this extremity of the country to escape scandal. They had grown up here. Again he was having to read between the lines, but it seemed it was *their* parents, at least on his mother's side, who had bolted. Why that was he couldn't tell. Were they cousins too?

So what, by the infernal laws of genetic mathematics, did that make him? A monstrosity, four or even sixteen times over?

iii

It was Ailinn's adoptive mother's opinion that Ailinn had been abused when she was a little girl. Nothing else quite accounted for her bouts of morose absentness.

Ailinn shook her head. 'I'd remember it, Mother,' she said.

It didn't come naturally to her to call her mother-who-wasn't 'Mother'. And she could see that her mother-who-wasn't didn't care for it either. But she tried. They both did.

'You say you'd remember it, but that depends how old you were when it happened.'

'Believe me, it didn't happen.'

'I believe you that you don't remember, but there's a mechanism in the human heart that helps us to forget.'

'Then mightn't that be because we're meant to forget,' Ailinn replied, 'because it doesn't matter?'

'That's a terrible thing to say.'

Was it? Ailinn didn't think so. What you don't remember might as well not have happened. Remember everything and you have no future. Unless what you remember is mostly pleasant, and it didn't occur to Ailinn to imagine memory as pleasant.

Her own memory went back a long way. She heard the distant reverberations, like echoes trapped in a steel coffin. She just didn't know what it was she was remembering.

'So at the end of your life,' her mother went on, 'when you have little or no memory left . . .'

'That's right, you might as well not have lived it.'

'God help you for saying such a thing. I hope for your sake you won't be feeling that way when you're old.'

Ailinn laughed. 'It could be a blessing,' she said.

But even she knew her cynicism was bravado. Deep within her was a hunger for life to start, to aim herself towards a time when she would not regret having lived. She would outpace memory if she could.

They were at home, drinking tea and dunking biscuits at a scrubbed pine table, looking out over a ploughed field. A crow with a crazed orange eye was hopping with malign purpose from rut to rut. What sort of memory did he have, Ailinn wondered. How many thousands of crows past had it taken to teach him what he knew? And of them, of any of them – what knowledge did he have? Of his own past, even – just yesterday, for example – how much did he know?

Ailinn was nineteen. She had lived in this house how many years now . . . ? Twelve, thirteen? It should no longer, whatever the exact computation, have felt foreign to her. But its dry formality: the teapot with its woolly hat, the floral china tea set, the biscuits carefully arranged on the plate, three ginger, three chocolate digestive, the silver tongs for the sugar cubes, the perfectly ploughed field which, by screwing up one eye, she could move from the horizontal to the vertical plane, as though its parallel furrows were a ladder to the heavens, even her weary-eyed, unsmiling adoptive mother who had never quite become her mother proper – all this was to her the setting for some other nineteen-year-old's life. As for where hers was, that she didn't yet know.

She was artistic. A further reason to think she'd been abused. She drew in pastels: the rising field, the scrubbed table, her would-be mother (not her would-be father who found her skills uncanny and disconcerting), the demoniacal crows – great luminous, visionary canvases which her teachers admired for their ethereal, other-worldly atmosphere, though one of them feared her work was a little too reminiscent of Kokoschka's dreamscapes. 'Where do you go to in your head, Ailinn?' he asked her.

'I don't go anywhere,' she said, 'I just draw what I see.'

She knew she was lying. She did go somewhere. She didn't have a name for it, that was all.

And she didn't know why she went there or what it was a memory or a foreboding, or just an idle fantasy, of.

The paper flowers were a sort of peace offering to her adoptive mother. Something nice to show how much she loved her, how grateful she was, how protected and at home she felt. But even the paper flowers looked as though they'd been picked from some other planet.

iv

Kevern had wondered, when he'd first discovered his depraved inheritance, whether it would put him off sex. That it *should* put him off sex, he didn't doubt. But would it?

The answer was no. Or at least not entirely. He knew he had to take precautions. He couldn't bring into the world a being who might show recessive symptoms of a kind which he – so far, at least – had not. And this meant not only being particular when it came to contraception, but going about coitus gently and considerately. Restoring to the act, maybe, something of the sacred. As it happened, such conscientiousness was not difficult for him: it accorded well with his precise, reluctant nature. He had not been put on earth to fling his seed around.

Ailinn didn't mind that he didn't pile-drive himself into her. It made a change.

'Sleepin' with you is like sleepin' with a woman,' she told him.

Though a clean enunciator out of bed, she made a habit of dropping her gs when verbalising sex. Sleepin', screwin', fuckin', even makin' love. He didn't know why. To rough herself up a bit, perhaps. Or perhaps to rough up him.

'Is that northern speech?' he had asked her.

'Nah. It's *my* speech.' With which she made a triumphant, tarty little fist.

So yes, it was her way of communalising their sex, taking what was special out of it, making it less fragile, putting them both on a more ordinary footing with each other.

Did she find him overscrupulous? Would she have liked him to swear? (Pog mo hoin?)

He unwound himself and sat up. They were in his bed. She had invited him to hers, an altogether more sweetly smelling chamber now that she had got rid of all the spiders and repainted it, with giant paper sunflowers everywhere, but he was uneasy about staying away from his cottage all night. And besides, he lived alone and she didn't.

'So "sleepin'" with me is like "sleepin'" with a woman . . . I'm guessing you mean that as a compliment, though to me, of course, it isn't. Unless you prefer sleeping with women.'

'Never done it,' she said.

'So how do you know it's like sleeping with me?'

'Because sleepin' with you isn't like sleepin' with other men.'

Men! Couldn't she have spared him that?

'How isn't it like sleeping with *other men*?'

'Well you don't seem as though you want to hurt me, for a start.'

'Why would I hurt you? Do you want me to hurt you?'

'No I do not.'

'Then what's the nature of your discontent?'

She slipped out of bed, as though she needed to be upright when he questioned her as hard as this. He tried not to look at her feet.

'I'm not discontented at all,' she said. 'It's hard to describe what I feel. It's as if you don't care, or at least your first care isn't, whether I feel you've entered me.'

'Oh! Would you like me to signal when I have? I could wave a handkerchief.'

He made jokes, she noticed, when he was hurt.

'No, I don't mean that way. I'm really not complaining. It's lovely. I'm not putting this very well but I don't think you care whether you make a difference to me, sexually – *inside* – or not. Most men make a song and dance about it. "Can you feel that? Do you like that?" They want to be sure the conquest of your body is complete. They would like to hear you surrender. It's as though you don't mind whether I notice you're visiting or not.'

'Visiting?'

She took a moment . . . 'Yes, visiting. It's as though you're on a tourist visa. Just popping in to take a look around.'

'That's not how it feels to me. I'm not planning being somewhere else. You need to know that.'

'Good.'

'But it doesn't sound very nice for you.'

'Well it is and it isn't. It's a change not to feel *invaded*. It's nice to be left alone to think my own thoughts.'

'Thoughts! Should you be having *thoughts* at such a time?'

'Feelings, then. You know what I mean – not having to go along with what someone else wants. Not having to be issuing periodic bulletins of praise and satisfaction. But what are yours?'

'What are my thoughts and feelings?'

'Yes. What do you want?'

'Ah, now you're asking.'

'You won't tell me?'

'I don't know.'

'Don't know whether you'll tell me?'

'Don't know what I want.'

But he made her a lovespoon in which the two of them could be recognised, entwined, inseparable, carved from a single piece of wood.

In return for which she made him a pair of exquisitely comical purple pansies, a paper likeness of his face in one, hers in another.

She arranged them in a vase on his dressing table, so that they stared at each other unremittingly.

'When you dust them, do it lightly,' she advised.

'I will sigh the dust away.' He pursed his lips and let out the softest emission of air, as though blowing a kiss to a butterfly.

'I love you,' she told him.

Why not, he thought. Why ever not? 'I love you,' he said.

As he'd told her, he wasn't planning to be somewhere else.

He should not have judged his parents their sin. When the love thing is upon you there's no one who can break you up. And he wasn't even absolutely sure the love thing was upon him – yet.

v

She moved in. Or at least she moved her person in. He cleared space for her to make her flowers in his workshop but she couldn't function in the noise and dust his lathe threw out. So she kept her studio, along with the majority of her possessions, in Paradise Valley. There was an argument on the side of sensible precaution for this anyway, though Ez said she wouldn't take it personally if Ailinn moved out. 'Follow your heart,' she said. But Ailinn thought it was still early for that. She'd been alive long enough to know that hearts were fickle.

Didn't her own jump?

She wanted her mail to go on being delivered to Paradise Valley as well. She had her own letter-box neurosis which she didn't want to clash with Kevern's. She feared letters being lost, postmen being careless about their delivery, just tossing them over the wall into Kevern's little garden, or not pushing them properly through the flap. She wasn't waiting for any communication in particular but believed something, that should have reached her in an envelope, was missing from her life: a greeting, an offer she couldn't have said what of, an advantage or an explanation – even terrible news, but terrible news, too, needed to be faced and not forever dreaded – and the idea that she would not discover it when it came, that Kevern would treat it as junk, or that it would blow away, be blown about the world unknown to her, and leave her waiting, never knowing, was one she found deranging. As a little girl she'd read in comics about a time when people wrote to one another by phone but wrote such horrid things that the practice had to be discouraged. She was glad, at least, that she didn't have to 'angst', as they called it in those comics, about losing phone letters as well. So for the time being, at least, her postal address remained Beck House, Paradise Valley.

If she didn't return to collect what was waiting for her for more than two or three days at a time, however, the weight of expectation and dread oppressed her more than she could bear.

Most mornings, after breakfast, she accompanied Kevern to his workroom, kissed him, breathed in the lovely fresh smell of sawdust – it reminded her of the circus, she said – and either went back to bed with a book or walked down into the valley, singing to herself, alone. But occasionally they would leave the cottage together in order to wander the cliffs or just sit side by side on his bench. She had made the mistake, the first time, of straightening his rug after he'd rumpled it. She saw him wince and then, without saying anything, rumple it again. Thereafter she simply stood by, expressionless, her arms beside her sides, as he locked up, confirmed that he had locked up, knelt to look inside the letter box, stood up, knelt down again to confirm that what he had seen he had seen, put his hand inside the flap, took it out, and then put it back again, looked one more time, then put his keys in his pocket. Sometimes he would send her on ahead so that he could do all this again.

'Don't ask,' he said.

And she tried not to. But she loved him and wanted to relieve him of some of the stress he was obviously under.

'Couldn't I?' she asked once, meaning couldn't she make sure *for* him that everything was OK. Share the burden, whatever it was. Pour the tea, rumple the runner, double-lock and then double-lock again, kneel down and lift the flap of the letter box, peer through (check to see if there was anything for her while she was at it) . . . she knew the routine well enough by now.

'Unthinkable,' he said.

'Just try thinking it.'

He shook his head, not liking her suddenly, not wanting to look at her. She knew. And was glad she was wearing trousers so he could not see her ankles.

But that night, in bed, after exhaustively locking the house from the inside, he tried explaining why she couldn't help him.

'If anything happens it has to be my responsibility. I want at least to know I did all I could. If it happens because of something I have omitted to do, I will never forgive myself. So I make sure.'

'Happens to the house?'

'Happens to the house, happens to me, happens to you . . .'

'But what can happen?'

He stared at her. '*What can happen*. What *can't* happen.' Neither was a question. Both were statements of incontrovertible fact.

They were lying on what she took to be a reproduction Biedermeier bed. He hung his clothes, as now she hung hers, in a fine mahogany wardrobe, two doors on either side of a full-length bevelled mirror, also imitation Biedermeier. It was far too big for the cottage, some of the beam had had to be cut away to make room for it, and she did wonder how anyone had ever succeeded in getting it upstairs. She knew about Biedermeier – it had come back into style. Everyone wanted reproduction Biedermeier. There was a small factory knocking it out in Kildromy, not far from where she grew up. Kildromy-Biedermeier – there was a growing market for it. But she did wonder whether Kevern's furniture wasn't reproduction at all. It looked at once far grander and more worn than anything that came out of Kildromy. Could it be the real thing? Everyone cheated a bit, keeping a few more family treasures than they knew they should.

And this the authorities turned a blind eye to. But if these pieces were genuine, Kevern was cheating on a grand scale. She tried asking him about it. 'This Kildromy-Biedermeier?' He stared at her, lost for words. Then he gathered his wits. 'Yes,' he said. 'Kildromy. Spot on.'

So he was lying. She didn't judge him. If anything, it thrilled her to be a silent party to such delinquency. But it explained why he went to such lengths to protect his privacy. No one was ever going to come to so remote a place, so difficult of access, to steal a wardrobe; but what if it wasn't thieves he feared but, she joked to herself, the Biedermeier police?

Once, although she hadn't mentioned her suspicions, he explained that property wasn't the reason he was careful.

'*Careful*!'

'Why, what word would you use?'

'Obsessive? Compulsive? Disordered?'

He smiled. He was smiling a lot so she shouldn't take fright. He liked her teasing and didn't want it to stop.

'Well, whatever the word, I do what I do because I hate the idea of . . . what was that other word you used once, to describe my lack of sexual attack? – *invasion*.'

'I didn't accuse you of lacking sexual attack.'

'OK.'

'I truly didn't. I love the way it is between us.'

'OK. Invasion, anyway, is a good word to describe what I fear. People thinking they can just burst in here, while I'm out or even while I'm in.'

'I understand that,' she said. 'I am the same.'

'Are you?'

'I always locked my bedroom door when I was a little girl. Every time the wind blew or a tree scratched at my window I thought someone was trying to get in. To get *back* in, actually. To reclaim their space.'

'I don't follow. Why *their* space?'

'I can't explain. That was just how I felt. That I had wrongly taken possession of what wasn't mine.'

There was something temporary about her, Kevern thought. Of no fixed abode. Tomorrow she could be gone.

A great wave of protectiveness – that protectiveness he knew he would feel for her when he first saw her and imagined rolling her in his rug – crashed over him. Unless it was possessiveness. Protectiveness, possessiveness – what difference? He wanted her protected because he wanted her to stay his. 'Well you don't have to feel that here,' he said.

'And I don't,' she said.

He kissed her brow. 'Good. I want you to feel safe here. I want you to feel it's yours.'

'Given the precautions you take,' she laughed, 'I couldn't feel safer. It's a nice sensation – being barred and gated.'

But she didn't tell him there was safe and *safe*. That all the barring and gating couldn't secure her peace of mind. That she kept seeing the pig auctioneer, for example, who had known both their names.

'Good,' he said. 'Then I'll keep battening down the hatches.'

She laughed. 'There's a contradiction,' she said, 'in your saying you want me to think of your home as mine, when you protect it so fiercely.'

'I'm not protecting it *from* you. I'm protecting it *for* you.'

This time she kissed him. 'That's gallant of you.'

'I don't say it to be gallant.'

'You like me being here?'

'I love you being here.'

'But?'

'There is no but. It's not you I'm guarding against. I've invited you in. It's the uninvited I dread. My parents were so terrified of people poking about in their lives that they jumped out of their skins whenever they heard footsteps outside. My father shooed away walkers who came anywhere near the cottage. He'd have cleared them off the cliffs if he could have. I'm the same.'

'Anyone would think you have something to hide,' she said skittishly, rubbing her hands down his chest.

He laughed. 'I do. You.'

'But you're not hiding me. People know.'

'Oh, I'm not hiding you from people.'

'Then what?'

He thought about it. 'Danger.'

'What kind of danger?'

'Oh, the usual. Death. Disease. Disappointment.'

She hugged her knees like a little girl on an awfully big adventure. In an older man's bed. 'The three Ds,' she said with a little shiver, as though the awfully big adventure might just be a little too big for her.

'Four, actually. Disgust.'

'Whose disgust?'

'I don't know, just disgust.'

'You fear I will disgust you?'

'I didn't say that.'

'You fear you will disgust me?'

'I didn't say that either.'

'Then what are you saying? Disgust isn't an entity that might creep in through your letter box. It isn't out there, like some virus, to shut your doors and windows against.'

Wasn't it?

It was anyway, he acknowledged, a strange word to have hit on. It answered to nothing he felt, or feared he might feel, for Ailinn. Or *from* Ailinn, come to that. So why had he used it?

He decided to make fun of himself. 'You know me,' he said. 'I fear everything. Abstract nouns particularly. Disgust, despair, vehemence, vicissitude, ambidexterity. And I'm not just worried that they'll come in through my letter box, but underneath the doors, *and* down the chimney, *and* out of the taps and electricity sockets, *and* in on the bottom of your shoes . . . Where *are* your shoes?'

She shook her head a dozen times, blinding him with her hair, then threw her arms around him. 'You are the strangest man,' she said. 'I love you.'

'*I'm* strange! Who is it round here who thinks trees are tapping at the window to reclaim what's rightfully theirs?'

'Then we make a good pair of crazies,' she laughed, kissing his face before he could tell her he had never felt more whatever the opposite of disgust was for anyone in his life.

vi

Disgust.

His parents had once warned him against expressing it. He remembered the occasion. A girl he hadn't liked had tried to kiss him on the way home from school. It was the style then among the boys to put their fingers down their throats when anything like that happened. Girls, it was important for them to pretend, made them sick, so they put on a dumb show of vomiting whenever one came near. Kevern was still doing it when he encountered his father standing at the door of his workshop, looking for him. He thought his father might be impressed by this expression of his son's burgeoning manliness. Finger down the throat, 'Ugh, ugh . . .' *Ecce homo!*

When he explained why he was doing what he was doing his father slapped him across the face.

'Don't you ever!' he said.

He thought at first that he meant don't you ever kiss a girl. But it was the finger down the throat, the simulating of disgust he was never to repeat.

His mother, too, when she was told of it, repeated the warning. 'Disgust is hateful,' she said. 'Don't go near it. Your grandmother, God rest her soul, said that to me and I'm repeating it to you.'

'I bet she didn't say don't put your fingers down your throat,' Kevern said, still smarting from his father's blow.

'I'll tell you precisely what she said. She said, "Disgust destroys you – avoid it at all costs."'

'I bet you're making that up.'

'I am not making it up. Those were her exact words. "Disgust destroys you."'

'Was this your mother or dad's?' He didn't know why he asked that. Maybe to catch her out in a lie.

'Mine. But it doesn't matter who said it.'

Already she had exceeded her normal allowance of words to him.

Kevern had never met his grandparents on either side nor seen a photograph of them. They were rarely talked about. Now, at least, he had 'disgust' to go on. One of his grandmothers was a woman who had strong feelings about disgust. It wasn't much but it was better than nothing. At the time he wasn't in the mood to be taught a lesson from beyond the grave. But later he felt it filled the family canvas out a little. *Disgust destroys you* – he could start to picture her.

Thinking about it as he lay in Ailinn's arms, trying to understand why the word had popped out of his mouth unbidden, Kevern wondered whether what had disgusted his grandmother – and in all likelihood disgusted every member of the family – was the incestuous union her child had made. He saw her putting her fingers down her throat. Unless – he had no dates, dates had been expunged in his family – that union didn't come about until after she'd died. In which case could it have been the incestuous union she had made herself?

Self-disgust, was it?

Well, she had reason.

But if his own mother's account was accurate, his grandmother had said it was disgust that destroyed, not incest. Why inveigh against the judgement and not the crime? And why the fervency of the warning? What did she know of what disgust wrought?

Could it have been that she wasn't a woman who *felt* disgust in all its destructive potency but a woman who *inspired* it? And who therefore knew its consequences from the standpoint of the victim?

Do not under any circumstances visit on others what you would not under any circumstances have them visit on you – was that the lesson his parents had wanted to inculcate in him? The reason you would not want it visited on you being that it was murderous.

This then, by such a reading, was his grandmother's lesson: Be careful not to be on disgust's receiving end. For whoever feels disgusted by you will destroy you.

Had he wanted to destroy the girl whose attempt to kiss him had been so upsetting that he had to pretend it turned his stomach? Maybe he had.

Kevern 'Coco' Cohen got out of bed and religiously blew the dust off Ailinn's paper flowers.

How many men were there? Six hundred, seven hundred, more? She thought she ought to count. The numbers might matter one day. One at a time the men were led, each with his hands tied behind his back, into the marketplace of Medina, and there, one at a time, each with his hands tied behind his back, they were decapitated in the most matter-of-fact way – *glory be to—!* – their headless bodies tipped into a great trench that had been dug specially to accommodate them. What were the dimensions of the trench? She thought she ought to estimate it as accurately as she could. The dimensions might matter one day. The women, she noted coldly, were to be spared, some for slavery, some for concubinage. She had no preference. 'I will choose tomorrow,' she thought, 'when it is too late.' Grief the same. 'I will sorrow tomorrow,' she thought 'when it is too late.' But then what did she have to grieve for? History unmade itself as she watched. Nothing unjust or untoward had happened. It was all just another fantasy, another lie, another Masada complex. As it would be in Maidenek. As it would be in Magdeburg. She looked on in indifference as the trench overflowed with the blood that was nobody's.

FOUR

R.I.P. Lowenna Morgenstern

i

AILINN KNEW EVEN less about *her* family.

Kevern thought that Ez, the fraught, angular woman with the tight frizzy hair who had brought her down to share the cottage in Paradise Valley, was her aunt, but she wasn't.

'No relative,' Ailinn explained. 'Not even a friend really. No, that's unfair. She *is* a friend. But a very recent one. I only met her a few months before I came away, in a reading group.'

Reading groups were licensed. Because they were allowed access to books not otherwise available (not banned, just not available), readers had to demonstrate exceptionality of need – either specific scholastic need or, if it could be well argued for (and mere curiosity wasn't an argument), general educational need. Kevern was impressed that Ailinn had been able to demonstrate one or the other. But she told him she had simply been able to pull a few strings, her adoptive mother being a teacher.

Books apart, this account of her relations with Ez explained to Kevern why she had made so little ceremony of introducing them. It was as though she had never been introduced to her herself. He was amazed by how anxious she could be one minute, and how devil-may-care the next. 'And you threw in your lot with a woman you'd met in a reading group, just like that?'

'Well, I'd hardly call it throwing in my lot. She offered me a room in a cottage she hadn't ever seen herself, for as long or as short a time as I wanted it, in return for my company, and some help painting and gardening, and I could find no reason to say no. Why not? I liked her. We had a shared interest in reading. And there was nothing up there to keep me. And I reckoned I could sell my flowers just as well down here . . . probably better, as you get more tourists than we do, and . . . and of course there was you . . .'

'You knew about me?'

'My heart knew about you.'

Her arrhythmic heart.

He couldn't tell how deep her teasing went. Did she truly think they were destined for each other? He would once have laughed at such an idea, but not now. Now, he too (so he hoped to God she wasn't playing with his feelings) wanted to think they had all along been on converging trajectories. But no doubt, and with more reason, his parents had thought the same.

She had no memory of her parents – her actual parents – which made Kevern feel more protective of her still.

'No letters? No photographs?'

She shook her head.

'And you didn't ask?'

'Who would I have asked?'

'Whoever was caring for you.'

She looked surprised by the idea that anyone had cared for her. He picked that up – perhaps because he wanted to think that no one had cared for her until he came along. 'Someone must have been looking after you,' he said.

'Well I suppose the staff at the orphanage to begin with, though I have no memory of them either. Just a smell, like a hospital, of disinfectant. I was brought up by a smell. And after that Mairead, the local schoolteacher, and her husband Hendrie.'

'And what did they smell of?'

She thought about it. 'Stale Sunday afternoons.'

'They'd been friends of your parents?'

She shook her head. 'Didn't know my parents. No one seems to have known them. Mairead told me when I was old enough to understand that she and Hendrie were unable to have children of their own and had been in touch with an orphanage outside Mernoc – a small town miles from anywhere except a prison and a convent – about adoption. When they were invited to visit, they saw me. They chose me like a stray puppy.'

She normally liked to say 'like an orange', but there was something about Kevern that made her think of strays.

'I can understand why,' he said, losing his fingers in the tangle of her hair.

She raised her face to him, like one of her own flowers. 'Why?'

'You know why.'

'Tell me.'

'Because to see you is to see no one else.' He meant it.

'Then it's a pity you didn't choose me first.'

'Why – were they unkind to you?'

'No, not at all. Just remote.'

'Are they still alive?'

'No. Or at least Mairead isn't. Hendrie is in a care home. He has no knowledge of the world around him. Not that he ever had a lot.'

'You didn't like him?'

'Not a great deal. He was a largely silent man who fished and played dominoes. I think he hit Mairead.'

'And you?'

'Occasionally. It wasn't personal. Just something men did. Do. Towards the end, before they put him in a home, it got worse. He started to make remarks like "I owe you nothing", and "You don't belong here", and would throw things at me. But his mind was going then.'

'And you never found out where you *did* belong?'

'I belonged in the Mernoc orphanage.'

'I mean who put you there?'

She shrugged, showing him that his questioning had begun to weary her.

'I'm sorry,' he said. Adding, 'But you belong here now.'

ii

As a matter of course, she woke badly. Her eyes puffed, her hair matted, her skin twice its age. Where had she been?

She wished she knew.

At first Kevern thought it was his fault. He'd been tossing and turning, perhaps, or snoring, or crying out in the night, stopping her sleeping. But she told him she had always been like this – not morning grumpiness but a sort of species desolation, as though opening her eyes on a world in which no one of her sort existed.

He pulled a face. 'Thank you,' he said.

'You're not yet the world I wake up to,' she said. 'It takes me a while to realise you're there.'

'So why such desolation?' he wanted to know. 'Where do you return from when you wake?'

'If only I could tell you. If only I knew myself.'

Mernoc, Kevern guessed. He saw an icy orphanage, miles from nowhere. And Ailinn standing at the window, barefooted, staring into nothing, waiting for somebody to find her.

Pure melodrama. But much of life for Kevern was.

And thinking of her waiting to be found, while he was waiting to find, gave a beautiful symmetry to the love he felt for her.

What she'd told him awakened his pity and pity gave him a better reason to be in love than he'd ever had before. There was rapture and then there was responsibility. Each imposed an obligation of seriousness. But together they made the serious sacred.

He couldn't rescue her from her dreams, but he could make waking better for her. The minute he sensed her stir he would get out of bed and open the windows, so that she would wake to light, the smell of the sea, and the cries of the gulls. But sometimes the light was too harsh and the smell of the sea too pungent and the cries of the gulls a mockery. 'They sound the way I feel,' she'd say.

Did that mean that gulls, too, suffered species desolation?

So he had to make a quick decision every morning: whether to open the curtains or keep them closed.

But when the sea was rough they could still hear the blowhole like a giant mouth sucking in and then expelling water. On wild days they would even see the spittle.

'Reminds me of a whale exhaling air,' she said once. 'Do you remember that passage in *Moby-Dick* describing whale-jets "up-playing and sparkling in the noonday air"?'

He didn't.

'But you've read the book?'

He had. Years ago. *Moby-Dick* was one of the classic novels that had not been encouraged to drift out of print – though most editions were in graphic form – the grounds for its remaining available being the interest felt in it by fishing communities, its remoteness otherwise from the nation's calamitous recent history, and the fact that it was from its opening sentence – 'Call me Ishmael' – that the colossal social experiment undertaken to restore stability borrowed its name.

OPERATION ISHMAEL.

'We should read it together,' she suggested when Kevern told her he could remember little of it beyond Ahab and the whale and of course OPERATION ISHMAEL. 'It's my most favourite book in the world,' she told him. 'It's the story of my life.'

'You've been hunting a great white whale? Could that have been me, perhaps?'

She kissed him absent-mindedly, as though he were a child that needed humouring. Her brow was furrowed. 'It wasn't Ahab I identified with, you fool,' she said. 'That's a man thing. I took the side of the whale.'

'Don't worry, men do the same. The whale is more noble than the whaler.'

'But I bet you don't wake to the knowledge that you're the whale.'

'Are you telling me you do? Is that where you've been all night, swimming away from the madness of Ahab? No wonder you look exhausted.'

'I don't know what I've been doing all night, but it's a pretty good description of what I do all day.'

How serious was she?

'All day? Truly?'

She paused. 'Well what am I signing up for if I say "truly"? If you're asking me if I actually hear the oars of the longboats coming after me, then no. But when people describe having the wind at their back it's a sensation of freedom I don't recognise. An unthreatening, invigorating space behind me? – no, I don't ever have the luxury of that. There might be nothing there when I turn around, but it isn't a beneficent nothing. Nothing good propels me. But I call it a good day when I turn around and at least don't see anything bad.'

He couldn't stop himself taking this personally. Wasn't he the wind at her back? Wasn't he a beneficent force? 'I can't bear to think,' he said, 'that you get no relief from this.'

'Oh, I get relief. I get relief with you. But that's the most dangerous time because it means I've forgotten to be on guard. You remember that description of the nursing whales, "serenely revelling in dalliance and delight"?'

He didn't. He wondered whether she was intending to quote the entire novel to him in small gobbets. Something – and this he did remember – that his father had done when he was small. Not *Moby-Dick* – other, darker, more sardonic books. Until his mother had intervened. 'What are you trying to do to the boy?' he had heard her ask. 'Make him you?' Shortly after which his father locked his books away.

'Well, whenever I feel anything of that sort,' she went on, 'whenever I feel calm, at rest, loving and being loved – as I do now – I feel I must be in danger. In my universe I don't know how else to account for being loved. Don't kiss me, I used to say to Mairead when she tucked me up in bed at night. I won't be able to sleep. If you kiss me something terrible will follow. Hendrie wanted to send me to a psychiatrist. Or better still, back to the children's home. Mairead said no. She believed the children's home was to blame. She was convinced that something terrible must have been done to me there.'

'And had it, do you think?'

'Oh God, you and my mother. Something terrible's been done to everybody everywhere. Where's the point of hunting down the specifics? Anyway, I think you can tell when a terror has an origin in a particular event. You might not have a name for it but you can date it. A five-year terror, a ten-year terror . . . This is a thousand-year terror.'

He wondered if she overdid the retrospective panic. If she overdramatised herself. Like him. 'A thousand years is a long time to have been hunted by a one-legged nut, Ailinn.'

'You can make fun of me if you like. I know how crazy it must sound. But it's as though it's not just me, as I am now, or as I was the day before yesterday, who's always running. It's an earlier me. Don't laugh. You're just as barmy in your own way. But it feels like a sort of predestiny – as though I was born in flight. Which I suppose I could have been. It's a pity my real parents aren't around to ask.'

Yes, she overwrote her story. But he loved her. Maybe overloved her. 'We could try to find them,' he said.

'Don't be banal,' she came back sharply, thinking she would have to watch his solicitousness.

He shrank from her asperity. But he had one more question. What he feared when he knelt to check his letter box for the umpteenth time had no features. No person rose up before him. He could weigh the reason for his precautions but he could not picture it. She, though, had Ahab. Was that a way of speaking or did she actually see the man? 'Is he Ahab in the flesh that's coming for you—'

'Wait,' she said. 'Did I say he was "coming for me"? Sounds a bit like waiting for Mairead and Hendrie, doesn't it? Was I waiting for them to "come for me"? You must think my psychology is pathetic, alternating hopes and terrors based on puns—'

'I don't,' he said, afraid that they had begun to judge each other. 'Your psychology is your psychology, therefore I love it. But all I was going to ask was whether Ahab is a generalised idea for you or you actually picture him coming at you with his lampoon.'

'*Lampoon*?'

'Slip of the tongue. You've been making me nervous. *Harpoon*.'

She stared at him. 'You call that a slip?'

'Why, what would you call it?'

'A searchlight into your soul.'

He looked annoyed. 'I let you off your pun,' he said.

She kissed him. 'Yes, you did. But we aren't in a competition, are we, and I'm not making fun of you. It's just that this slip is so you.'

'How so?'

'Well, it's your fear of mockery, isn't it. Your fear of anyone knowing you well enough to poke fun at you.'

She had him here. He had only to deny the justice of the charge to prove it. Touchy? Me?

She had him another way too. Wasn't he her mentor in the matter of a sense of humour? Hadn't he, when she'd been upset with him for teasing her about her thick ankles, lectured her about the nature of a joke? So how much easier-going was he when the joke was on him?

They were in this together, it seemed to her. Skin as fine as parchment, the pair of them. Pride a pin could prick. Hearts that burst when either looked with love at the other.

He could see what she was thinking but decided to be flattered that she offered to penetrate him so deeply. It proved she found him interesting and cared about him.

He excused himself to take a shower. Though he showered frequently, the sounds he made the moment he turned on the water – groans of release (or was it remission?), sighs of deliverance, gaspings deep enough, she feared, to shake his heart out of his chest – suggested it was either the first shower he had ever experienced or the last he would ever enjoy. She had wondered, at the beginning, whether it were some private sexual ritual, demeaning to her, but later she would sometimes shower with him and he made exactly the same noises then. She couldn't explain it to herself. A shower was just a shower. Why the magnitude of his surrender to it? It could have been his death, so thunderous were his exhalations. Or it could have been his birth.

She was relieved when he stepped back out into the bedroom, dripping like a seal. He appeared exhausted.

'There will be more, you know,' she said.

'More what?'

'More showers.'

He expected her to say 'More life'.

'You never know what there will be more of,' he said, 'but that's certainly more than enough about me and who *I* am and what *I'm* in flight from. We began this conversation discussing whales and you – the least whale-like creature I have ever seen.'

'Despite my thick ankles?'

'Whales don't have thick ankles. As didn't Ahab, as I recall.'

'Well he certainly didn't have two.'

If he hadn't loved her before . . .

Best to leave it at that, anyway, they both thought. But he wanted to be sure that she felt safe with him. Still dripping, he pulled her down into the bed and drew the duvet over them.

Gently, protectively.

But were they overdoing this, he wondered.

She'd have answered yes had he asked her.

iii

It was in his lampoon-fearing nature to wonder whether they would be the talk of the village – the slightly odd woodturner who by and large kept himself to himself, and the tangle-haired flower girl from up north who was several years his junior. But the village wasn't exercised by pairings-off, even when the parties weren't as free to do as they pleased as these two were. People who have lived for aeons within sound of crashing seas, and sight of screaming seabirds spearing mackerel, take sex for granted. It's townspeople who find it disarranging.

And besides, the village had something else to yack about: a double murder. Lowenna Morgenstern and Ythel Weinstock found lying side by side in the back of Ythel Weinstock's caravan in pools of each other's blood. By itself, the blood of one would not have found its way, in such quantities, on to the body of the other. So there'd been doubly foul play: not just the murders but this ghoulish intermixing of bodily fluids which was taken by the police to be a commentary on the other sort of fluidal intermingling in which Morgenstern and Weinstock had no doubt been frenetically engaged at the moment their assailant struck.

'Caught in the act' was the phrase going round the village. And no one doubted that it was Lowenna's husband, Ade, who'd caught them. But where was Ade Morgenstern? He hadn't been seen in the village for months, having stormed out of the surgery to which he'd accompanied his wife to have a minor ailment looked at, which ailment, in his view, didn't necessitate the removal of her brassiere. He hadn't seen the brassiere coming off, he had only heard the doctor unhooking it. But his wife had beautiful breasts, as many in the village could testify, and he was a jealous man.

'Breathe in,' he heard the doctor order her. 'And out.' And a moment later, 'Open.'

He was not in the waiting room when his wife emerged fully clothed from her consultation.

Hedra Deitch was less bothered by the question of who was guilty of the crime than its timing. 'If you gotta go, that's as good a moment as any, if you want my view, and that Ythel was a bit of all right,' she told drinkers at the bar of the Friendly Fisherman.

'Rumpy pumpy feels like dying anyway when you've got a husband like mine.'

Pascoe Deitch ignored the insult. 'She always was a screamer,' he put in.

His wife kicked his shin. 'How come you're an expert?'

'When it comes to Lowenna Morgenstern everyone's an expert.'

Hedra kicked his other shin. '*Was* an expert. Who you going to be expert about next?'

Pascoe's expertise, universal or not, caught the attention of the police. Not that he was a suspect. He lacked the energy to be a criminal just as, for all his bravado, his wife believed him to lack the energy to be unfaithful. He masturbated in corners, in front of her, thinking, he told her, about other women – that was the sum of his disloyalty.

'You could feel this one comin',' he told Detective Inspector Gutkind.

'You knew there were family troubles?'

'Everybody knew. But no more than usual. We all have family troubles.'

'So in what sense did you feel this one coming?'

'Something had to give. It was like before a storm. It gave you a headache.'

'Was it something in the marriage that had to give? Did the murdered woman have a lover?'

'Well who else was that lying with her in those pools of blood?'

'You tell me.'

Pascoe shrugged the shrug of popular surmise.

'And did the husband know as much as you know?' Gutkind asked.

'He knew she put it about.'

'Was he a violent man?'

'Ythel?'

'Ade.'

'The place is full of violent men. Violent women, too.'

'Are you saying there are many people who might have done this?'

'When a storm's comin' a storm's comin'.'

'But what motive would anyone else have had?'

'What motive do you need? What motive does the thunder have?'

The policeman scratched his head. 'If this murder was as motiveless as thunder I'm left with a long list of suspects.'

Pascoe nodded. 'That's pretty much the way of it.'

That night he went alone to a barn dance in Port Abraham. His wife was wrong in assuming he was too lazy to be unfaithful to her.

iv

Densdell Kroplik generously offered to sell the police multiple copies of his *Brief History of Port Reuben* at half price on the assumption that it would help with their enquiries. Yes, he told Detective Inspector Gutkind, there were violent undercurrents in their society, but these appeared exceptional only in the context of that unwonted and, quite frankly, inappropriate gentleness that had descended on Port Reuben after WHAT HAPPENED, IF IT HAPPENED – see pp. 35–37 of his *Brief History*. Why Port Reuben had had to pay the price – bowing and scraping and saying sorry – for an event in which it had played no significant role, Densdell Kroplik didn't see. Nothing had happened, if it happened, *here*. WHAT HAPPENED, IF IT HAPPENED, happened in the cities. And yet the villagers and their children and their children's children were expected to share in the universal hand-wringing and name-changing. In his view, if anyone was interested in hearing it, the Lowenna Morgenstern case came as a welcome return to form. In a village with Port Reuben's proud warrior history, people were supposed to kill one another . . . Where there was a compelling argument to do so, he added, in response to Detective Inspector Gutkind's raised eyebrow.

'And what, in your view, constitutes a compelling argument?' the policeman asked.

'Well there you'll have to ask the murderer,' Densdell Kroplik replied.

'And what's this about a proud warrior history?' Gutkind pressed. 'There haven't been warriors in these parts for many a year.'

Densdell Kroplik wasn't going to argue with that. 'The Passing of the Warrior' was the title of his first chapter. But that didn't mean the village didn't have a more recent reputation to live up to. It was its touchy individualism, its fierce wariness, that had gone on lending the place its character and kept it inviolate. Densdell Kroplik's position when it came to outsiders, the hated aphids, was more than a little paradoxical. He needed visitors to buy his pamphlet but on balance he would rather there were no visitors. He wanted to sing to them of the glories of Port Reuben, in its glory days called Ludgvennok, but didn't want them to be so far entranced by his account that they never left. The exhilaration of living in Ludgvennok, which it pained him to call Port Reuben, walled in by cliffs and protected by the sea, enjoying the company of rough-mannered men and wild women, lay, the way he saw it, in its chaste unapproachability. This quality forcibly struck the composer Richard Wagner – if you've heard of him, Detective Inspector – in the course of a short visit he made to Ludgvennok as it was then. In those days husbands and lovers, farmers and fishermen, wreckers and smugglers, settled their grievances, eye to eye, as they had done for time immemorial, without recourse to the law or any other outside interference. Sitting at a window in a hostelry on this very spot, Wagner watched the men of Ludgvennok front up to one another like stags, heard the bacchante women wail, saw the blood flow, and composed until his fingers ached. 'I feel more alive here than I have felt anywhere,' he wrote in a letter to Mathilde Wesendonck. 'I wish you could be with me.'*

Der Strandryuber von Ludgvennok, the opera Wagner subsequently wrote about the village (and dedicated to Mathilde, who had by that time given him his marching orders), was rarely performed; this Densdell Kroplik ascribed not to any fault in the composition but to the lily-livered hypocrisy of the age.

'All very laudable,' Detective Inspector Gutkind conceded. As it happened, he had not only heard of Wagner, a composer beloved of his great-grandfather, but kept a small cache of Wagner memorabilia secreted in his wardrobe in fealty to that passion. He could even hum some of the tunes from his operas and went so far as to hum a few bars of the *Siegfried Idyll* to show Kroplik that he too was a man of culture. Nonetheless, 'All very laudable but I have a particularly savage double murder on my hands, not a few

* Liebling,
The days go by without my hearing from you and I wonder what I have done to deserve your cruelty. Everything I see, I see only that I might relate it to you. Had I only known how wonderful I was going to find Ludgvennok I would not have allowed you to persuade me to come on my own. When I think of all I have written about the regeneration of the human race, and all I have done to further its ennoblement, it cheers me to find a people here who live up to everything I have ever understood by nobility of character. It can sometimes, of course, be as much a matter of what one doesn't find as what one does, that renders a place and a people congenial. Whether by deliberate intention or some lucky chance, Ludgvennok appears to have been released from the influence of those whose rapacity of ambition and disagreeableness of appearance has made life such a trial in the European cities where I have spent my life. Even the ear declares itself to be in a paradise to be free, from the moment one wakes to the moment one lies down – without you, alas, my darling – of that repulsive jumbled blabber, that yodelling cackle, in which elsewhere the ----s make the insistence of their presence felt. Here it is almost as though one has returned to a time of purity, when mankind was able to rejoice in its connection with its natural soil, unspoiled by the jargon of a race that has no passion – no *Leidenschaft*, there is no other word – for the land, for art, for the heroical, or for the rest of humanity.

My darling, I do so wish you could be here with me.

Your R

high-spirited drunks kicking nine bells out of another,' was what he said.

'Your point being?' Densdell Kroplik wanted to know. He was irked that the detective inspector had heard of Wagner, let alone that he could hum him. He wanted Wagner for himself.

He was sitting in his favourite chair by the fire. In all weathers a fire burned in the Friendly Fisherman. And on most evenings Densdell Kroplik, steam rising from his thighs, sat by it in a heavy seaman's sweater warming and rubbing his hands. He cultivated a take it or leave it air. He knew what was what. It was up to you whether you wanted to learn from him or not.

'My point being that it gets me nowhere to be told Port Reuben is back to doing what it has always done best.'

Densdell Kroplik shrugged. 'It might,' he said, 'if you understood more about the passion for justice and honour that has always burned in the hearts of the men of these parts.'

'I doubt that a passion for justice and honour had anything to do with the murder of Lowenna Morgenstern and Ythel Weinstock.'

Densdell Kroplik pointed a red, fire-warmed finger at the policeman. 'Is that something you can be sure of?' he said. 'There was a famous five-way murder here about a hundred years ago. Two local women, their husbands, and a lover. Whose lover was he? No one was quite sure. Am I hinting at pederasty? I might be. All that was certain was that he was an aphid – which makes pederasty the more likely. Buggers, the lot of them. From the north or the east of the country, it doesn't matter which. Somewhere that wasn't here. A pact was what the coroner decided it had been, a love pact born of hopeless entanglement. They'd gone up on to the cliff, taken off their clothes, watched the sun go down and swallowed pills. What do you think of that?'

'What I think is that it doesn't help me with my case,' Gutkind said. 'A pact is suicide, not murder.'

'Unless,' Kroplik went on, 'unless the villagers, motivated by justifiable disapproval and an understandable hatred of outsiders, had taken it upon themselves to do away with all five offenders. In which case it wasn't a mass suicide but a mob attack in the name of justice and honour.'

'And it's your theory that the whole village could have done away with Lowenna Morgenstern and Ythel Weinstock?'

'Did I say that? I'm just a barber with an interest in local history. All I know, from reading what I have read and from using these' – he made a two-pronged fork of his fingers and pointed to his all-seeing eyes – 'is that people have been subdued here for a long time. They have a proud history of torrid engagement with one another which has been denied expression. There's no knowing what people might do – singly or in a group – when their natures rebel against repression.'

'Well you might call it torrid engagement, I call it crime.'

'Then that's the difference between us,' Densdell Kroplik laughed.

After which, to show he was a man who could be trusted, he gave the policeman a free haircut, humming all the while Brünnhilde's final plea to Wotan to let her sleep protected by flame from the attentions of any old mortal aphid.

v

Kevern Cohen stayed aloof from the malicious speculations. He had flirted with Lowenna Morgenstern occasionally, when they had both had too much to drink, and more recently he had kissed her in the village car park on bonfire night. He was no snogger. If he kissed a woman it was because he was aroused by the softness of her lips, not because he wanted to wound them. Breaking skin was not, for Kevern, the way he expressed desire.

Lowenna Morgenstern had a wonderful mouth for kissing, deep and mysterious, the musky taste of wood-fire on her busy tongue.

'Kissing you is like kissing flame,' he had said, bending over her.

'You should have been a poet, you,' she told him, biting his neck until the blood trickled on to his shirt collar.

And now someone had killed her. The man found dead beside her could just as easily have been him.

Ailinn picked up on his sombre mood. 'Did you know these people well?' she asked.

'Depends what you mean by well,' he said. 'I knew her to say hello to. Ythel I'd heard of but never met. He was a pub singer. Not from here. Lowenna was reputed to have a taste for musical talent. Her husband Ade is the church organist. A discontented, jeering man. A hundred years ago he and his brothers would have stood on the cliffs with lamps and lured ships on to the rocks. Then he'd have laughed as they looted the wreckage. If he killed his wife he was just carrying on the family tradition.'

'But then if he did,' Ailinn said, 'he's only wrecked himself.'

'Don't we all,' Kevern said.

She stopped to look at him. They were walking arm in arm in the valley in their wellingtons, splashing in puddles. The trickle of water called the River Jordan had swollen to the dimensions of a stream. The trees dripped. It would have been the height of fancy to think of it as nature weeping, but Kevern thought it anyway.

'What do you mean *don't we all*?'

'Did I say that?'

'You did.'

'Then I don't know. I suppose I was feeling the tragedy of what's occurred.'

'But it's not your tragedy.'

'Well it is in a sense. It's my village.'

'Your village! That's not how you normally talk about it.'

'No, you're right, I don't. Maybe I'm just being ghoulish – wanting to be part of the excitement.'

'I'm surprised it still excites you. Don't you have a lot of this sort of thing down here?'

'Murders, no. Well, a few. But nothing quite as bloody as this.'

'We have them too . . .' She pointed, comically, over her shoulder as she had done the day he met her. As though she were throwing salt. '. . . Up there, if that's north. People are unhappy.'

'I suppose that was all I meant by saying *don't we all*. That we all end up unhappy. You say yourself you walk in fear of unhappiness every hour.'

'Unhappiness? I walk in fear of being hunted to my death.'

'Well then . . .'

'Well then nothing. It's not the same. The whales know who's coming after them, but they still quietly feed their young. You have to risk it. I am still determined to be happy.'

'I was only quoting your own words back to you. *People are unhappy*.'

She put her hands to his face and pulled at his lips, trying to force his melancholy mouth into a smile. 'But we're not, are we? Us? You and me?'

He let her fashion a smile out of him. His eyes burned with love for her. Part protective love, part desire. She could look dark and fierce sometimes, like a bird of prey, a hunter herself, but at others she appeared as helpless as a little girl, the foundling picked out of a children's home in the back of beyond.

'No,' he agreed. 'We're not unhappy. Not you and me. We are different.'

Yes, they were overdoing this.

Later that week he was asked how well he'd known Lowenna Morgenstern.

FIVE

Call Me Ishmael

Friday 3rd

SUDDENLY EVERYONE, AND I mean *everyone*, is taking an interest in my man. Have I said that already? Suddenly everyone's taking *even more* of an interest in my man, in that case. I can't pretend I'm comfortable with this upsurge of curiosity. One guards one's subjects jealously, as one guards one's wife or reputation. If there was more they needed to know, why didn't they just ask me? I have a nasty feeling I'm being superseded, which could mean one of two things: either I'm not up to it, in their estimation, or Kevern Cohen's in trouble too deep for me to fathom. I don't care how this impacts on my good name – I have other fish to fry, when all is said and done – but I'm concerned how Kevern will fare, given all his oddities, without a sympathetic person to keep an eye on him. I like the fellow, as I have said. Whatever is actually going on, it strikes me as cruel that someone so predisposed to paranoia should have all his delusions of persecution and incrimination confirmed. And that's just me I'm talking about . . . Ba boom! as my grandfather would say when he made a bad joke. Back in the days when people liked to make bad jokes. Or any kind of joke, come to that. But to return to me . . . I always liked that silly joke, too, when I was small: 'That's enough of me, so what do *you* think of me?' . . . but to return *seriously* to me, it's hard to tell how I'm regarded 'upstairs'. Certainly no one has – at least in so many words – called my work into question. But 'something a little more definite and up to date wouldn't go amiss' is not exactly the remark of an examiner about to give me an A++ for effort, is it? Tell us something we don't already know, the expressions on their faces said when I first delivered them the news that he had a girlfriend.

I tapped my nose. 'A *regular* girlfriend.'

To whom his intentions, they enquired, after a long, bored silence, are what? It struck me as an odd question. How did I know what his intentions were? Honourable, I guessed, given the man. I was requested, in no uncertain terms, to do better than *guess*. I happen to believe that an intention is a bit like a predisposition to cancer or dementia – essentially genetic. Honourable father, honourable son. Same the world over, even China. Honolable father, honolable son. But families, strictly speaking, are not my territory. To do parents and grandparents you have to have clearance at the very highest level. Mooching about in public records is not generally encouraged. This is a free society, so long as you don't plan to travel – and people are only prevented from leaving the country (or indeed from entering it) for their own good – so access to everything is in principle available to everyone. But the past – especially when it is particularised: the story of you and me and how we got here, the story of Kevern 'Coco' Cohen and whether or not he has inherited the honolable gene – is itself another country. And when it comes to such a country, the powers that be would rather we did not go there. Say sorry and have done is the wisest course, they believe, and I agree with them. Danger lurks in nostalgia. The slogans printed at the foot of the notepaper on which I write my reports – LET SLEEPING DOGS LIE, THE OVEREXAMINED LIFE IS NOT WORTH LIVING, YESTERDAY IS A LESSON WE CAN LEARN ONLY BY LOOKING TO TOMORROW – are reminders rather than threats. So no measures are taken against anyone who does not heed them. Buildings are not barred to you. Doors are not closed in your face. 'Yes, of course' will be the polite rejoinder to any request you make to inspect certificates of birth or death, or voter lists, or even newspapers dating too far back. But the forms you fill in are never read by anyone. Calls are not returned, applications are lost, the person you were talking to in the morning won't be there in the afternoon. If you decide it is easier to forget about it, you will be met with smiles all round. A bottle of champagne tied with a blue ribbon might even be sent to you in the post, together with a note saying 'Sorry we couldn't help. We tried.' But even without these precautions, the consequence of OPERATION ISHMAEL – that great beneficent name change to which the people ultimately gave their wholehearted consent – is that tracing lineage is not only as good as impossible, it is unnecessary. We are all one big happy family now. Zermanskys, Cohens, Rosenthals (that's the head of the academy: Eoghan Rosenthal), Feigenblats (Rozenwyn Feigenblat is the college librarian, and something of a looker I must say) – we acknowledge a kinship which we all tacitly know to be artificial but which works. Apply this simple test: when was the last time anyone was picked on for his name? Precisely. 'We are all Edward Everett Phineas Zermansky!' my students would shout were anyone to persecute me for whatever reason.

We are all Eoghan Rosenthal!

We are all Kevern Cohen!

We are all Lowenna Morgenstern, God save her soul – or at least we were.

If there is anyone alive who is old enough to have an inkling what his parents were called before OPERATION ISHMAEL he will wisely not remember it.

I have heard tell, or at least I have read, that – after an initial period of understandable reluctance, or misapprehension as I would rather think of it – the renaming turned into a month-long street party, young and old dancing with one another in the parks, strangers embracing, people saying goodbye to their old names as they waited for the official documents that would apprise them of their new. A few lucky ones won the right by televised lottery to choose their own from an approved list. But whether they chose or they were given, people entered into the spirit of the change. It was as though they'd been hypnotised. 'You will sleep,' they were told, 'you will fall into a deep carnivalesque sleep wherein you will dance and make merry. At the count of ten you will awake and while you will remember who you were, you will not remember what you were called. One, two . . .' Not literally that, but similar. A moral hypnosis. For our own good. And as with private memories, so with public records: they have been wiped clean. It is sometimes argued, in lowered voices, that if we can't be sure about our neighbours' antecedents, we expose ourselves to . . .

To what? Alien influences?

Well, it was precisely in order to ensure that such a phrase would never be heard again (and I confess I'm as guilty as any other red-blooded patriot when it comes to itching every now and then to use it) that OPERATION ISHMAEL was instituted. It granted a universal amnesty, dispensing once and for all with invidious distinctions between the doers and the done-to. Time must close over the events, and there is no better way to ensure that than to bring everyone together retroactively. Now that we are one family, and cannot remember when we were anything else, there can be no question of a repetition of whatever happened, if it did, because there is no one left to do to again whatever was or wasn't done.

We are all Rozenwyn Feigenblat!

(We are all at least – I confide to you, dear diary – dying for a piece of her . . .)

While no one is listening, allow me to admit that it took a certain ruthlessness to bring us to this point of unanimity. I neither condemn WHAT HAPPENED nor condone it. Let the fact that I was not yet born prove my impartiality. But it needs to be said that we were not alone in our perplexity. What to do with those about whom something needed to be done; how to put a brake on their ambitions; how to express our displeasure with their foreign policy (bizarre that they should have had a foreign policy given that they were foreigners themselves and had what they called a country only by taking someone else's); how to make safe again a world they'd gravely endangered with their migrations, military occupations, and finally weapons of mass destruction – this was something every other civilised country had to make up its mind about, and it is not without some backward-looking pride that I say we made up ours before anybody else. For which credit must go to my fellow professionals – vice chancellors of conscience-stricken universities and professors of the benign arts, painters, writers, actors, journalists, junior untenured academic staff, without whom the campaign to drive them from the face of the earth, to make of them vagabonds and fugitives, a pariah people cursed in every mouth, would not have been conducted in so civilised a manner.

Was there mob violence? I wasn't there, but such a thing does not accord with the view I entertain of this most moderate of countries, home to lyric poets and painters of serene and timeless landscapes. That gross expostulatory rhetoric that has normalised brutality and supremacism in other countries has never disfigured our speech. We do not smudge our canvases in rage. We do not saw at our violins. Whether or not that class of individuals who are the first to throw stones and start fires enjoyed direct acquaintance with the lyric poetry and landscape painting to which they are heirs is immaterial. The effect filtered down to them in language and the habits of contemplation. All of which assures me that, no, there could not have been barbarity. Just the gentle pressure that civilisation itself can exert, the articulated outrage of cultivated people who would not themselves have countenanced, least of all encouraged, inhumanity. Why would they, with so many of the exalted tasks of culture to perform – paintings to finish, lines to learn, lectures to prepare – choose to whip the multitude into acts of ferocity inimical to their own temperaments? Where, apart from any other consideration would they have found the time for it?

'Oh, there's always time,' Rozenwyn Feigenblat bolshily remarked once, when we happened to fall into conversation on this very subject.

I took that to mean that as librarian she knew how much sitting about staring into space we professors and painters are capable of. But then a librarian is not an artist; in her capacity as a filer and notator she will not have grasped the contribution that apparent indolence makes to the creative act.

For an artist, my dear, I wanted to say, to be unoccupied is sacred. What might look like doing nothing is in fact the long wait for beauty to find us. But I could see how that might be misinterpreted. 'If you mean that we sometimes appear bored,' I began instead . . .

She shook her pretty head. 'I'm not talking about boredom,' she said. 'I'm talking about mischief.'

She made it sound like pranks.

'Sexual mischief?' I asked, not wanting to sound too curious.

'Intellectual mischief.'

Not being sure I could trust myself longer in her alluring presence, I let it go at that. Though she left me feeling she had more to say.

What she also left me feeling was that someone should be keeping an eye on her. A position for which, were it vacant, I'd think hard about applying.

But back to Kevern Cohen. What it came down to for me, at least, was that the only reliable way of uncovering Kevern Cohen's intentions vis-à-vis his new sweetheart – short of asking him outright, and I wasn't prepared to do that – was to observe him at close quarters. To which end I invited the lovebirds over for dinner. It would be on his day for visiting the college and I suggested, since he'd mentioned her, that he bring Ailinn down with him, which he was wary of doing to begin with – wariness being his first response to everything – but on discussing it with her he changed his mind. No doubt she wanted to meet his friends, of whom he has few and I can just about be counted one. A half-friend, say. A well-wisher, anyway. An extravagantly beautiful woman, Ailinn, with a tumult of dark hair, like charred straw, and darting, watchful, hawk-like features. She called to mind a seirene, one of those bird women who are painted attacking Odysseus and his crew on vases I have inspected in the National Museum. I am not thinking of the most familiar image, which shows a seirene swooping head first at the ship, her talons at the ready, but rather one of the more serenely musical temptresses, striking her drum or plucking at her harp, surprised, if anything, that Odysseus should want to resist. As Kevern plainly didn't.

'Besotted' was the word my wife and I hit on quite separately, though Demelza did accuse me of stealing it from her.

Ailinn brought us a delicate bouquet of her paper flowers. 'Kitsch, I know,' she said, 'but I make them and could find no fresh flowers in the shops.'

I appreciated the thought and the apology. It must have been difficult for her, taste-wise, visiting the house of a professor of the Benign Visual Arts. I told her they were lovely and pretended to smell them. 'Haven't seen you so skittish in a long while,' Demelza said to me as we were making coffee in the kitchen. 'A pretty face and you go as soppy as Petroc.'

Petroc was our Labrador. Petroc Rothschild . . .

Not really, that was just our little off-colour joke . . .

'I am happy for them in their happiness,' was my reply. She pinched my arm. I let out a little cry. 'What's that for?' 'You know what that's for. Being happy for *them* in *their* happiness. Liar! Why don't you just lick her face?' 'Bitch!' I said. 'Prick!' was her retort.

That night, over an acrimonious nightcap of Benedictine and brandy, we discussed divorce. Discussion had always been something we were good at. You could say it was the glue of our conjugality.

Before they left, Ailinn did say one thing that struck me as surprising. 'Sometimes,' she mused, in answer to my asking how she found it down here, 'this part of the country seems full of eyes.'

'Eyes?'

'Watching eyes.'

'Really?' I said, opening my face to her. 'How do you mean?'

Kevern, too, appeared taken aback by her words. 'I don't know,' she said. 'Something about the way they look at you here. It's not disapproval exactly. It's not even suspicion. It's more as though they're waiting for you to make a mistake or show your real nature.'

'Isn't that just because these communities were cut off from the rest of the country for so long?' I said. 'I feel they look at me like that too. They say you have to have lived here for ten generations before they begin to relax with you.'

'I don't want them to relax with me. I'm not looking for friendship,' she said. 'It's the sense you get that someone's always on your heels. Not following you – just *there*. Waiting for you to give yourself away.'

I noted that for later speculation. *Give yourself away*, eh, young lady. So what are *you* concealing?

Petroc Rothschild must have asked himself the same question because he did not take at all kindly to her, barking when she changed her position too abruptly, and growling most of the time she talked. But then he'd never been overfond of Kevern either.

I enquired whether what she was describing was a recent phenomenon.

'Being here is a recent phenomenon – for me.'

'Of course, of course. I meant did you notice it at once or are you just noticing it now? Has there been a change.'

'I haven't been here long enough to make such fine distinctions,' she reminded me, somewhat sternly, which made me somewhat excited. I like sternness in a woman. Hence Demelza. 'But if you ask me to think about it,' she went on, 'then no, I have not just begun to notice a sense of – I don't know what to call it – *intrusiveness*. Take us' – she put her hand on Kevern's – 'we didn't just meet, we were bundled into each other's arms. Not that I'm complaining about that.'

'I should hope not,' Kevern said, kissing her.

Sweet, but I was more interested, I have to say, in Ailinn's sense of being, as she put it, 'bundled'. Professionally interested.

'So who bundled you?' I asked, but casually, as though I were merely making polite conversation.

'God knows. Some busybody? The village matchmaker? Nobody I'd ever seen before, or since. I don't know if you've seen him again, Kevern.'

He hadn't.

I asked Kevern if he too felt he'd been pushed into meeting Ailinn. He couldn't of course say yes. He had to say he saw her and was smitten. But yes, now we came to mention it, there had been someone hanging around, egging him on. For which, accompanied by another burning look deep into Ailinn's eyes, he was immeasurably grateful.

Petroc growled so loudly that Ailinn started.

'He doesn't mean you any harm,' I assured her.

'I think he does,' she said.

'You don't like dogs?'

'No, not as a rule. We are as one on this.'

'You and the dog?'

'Me and Kevern.'

I told Kevern that I hadn't on his previous visits noticed he was a dog hater, though I kept to myself my conviction that Petroc hated him.

'I'm not. Just not a dog lover. Or at least not inside the house.'

'Are dogs different inside to out?'

'No but I am.'

Concerned that his curtness of manner might offend me – unless she was concerned it might offend Petroc – Ailinn explained him. 'He doesn't like things moving around his legs,' she laughed. 'Not indoors, anyway.'

'That will make it difficult with children,' I observed.

'Impossible,' they said with some vehemence together. 'Quite impossible.'

I am not without subtlety when it comes to reading behind the words people speak. Why the vehemence, I wondered.

'You don't want children?' I asked, casually. I had the feeling they had not talked it over. But I could have been mistaken.

Kevern, anyway, shook his head. 'I am content to be the end of my line,' he said.

'In this, too,' Ailinn added, 'we are as one.'

I didn't, for what it's worth, believe her. Methinks the lady doth protest too much, methought.

Wherever they were on this subject, I considered it worth noting in my report that Kevern 'Coco' Cohen and Ailinn Solomons shared a detestation of dogs.

I would have bet good money against the powers that be knowing *that*.

SIX

An Inspector Calls

i

SOMEBODY HAD SEEN Kevern kissing Lowenna Morgenstern in the car park on bonfire night.

'That shouldn't make me a suspect,' Kevern told Detective Inspector Gutkind. 'If there's a jealous homicidal maniac on the loose that should make me a potential victim.'

'Unless the jealous homicidal maniac on the loose is you.'

'I'm not on the loose.'

'But you have been on the loose, haven't you? No ties, no responsibilities, free to kiss whoever you like.'

Kevern had never before been presented with such a dashing portrait of his life.

'I'm a bachelor, if that's what you mean. Though I am in a serious relationship at the moment.'

'At the moment? How long have you been in this serious relationship?'

'Three months.'

'And that amounts to serious for you?'

'Sacred.'

'Were you in a sacred relationship with Mrs Morgenstern?'

'I don't think a single kiss constitutes a relationship.'

'What would you say it constitutes?'

'A passing thrill.'

'You were aware she was married when you kissed her?'

'I was.'

The policeman waited. '. . . And you had no qualms about that?'

'Not my business. She felt like a kiss, I felt like a kiss.'

'You don't respect marriage?'

'I think it was more that Mrs Morgenstern didn't respect hers. I didn't see it as my job to remember her vows for her.'

'So knowing she wasn't happily married, you took advantage.'

'I don't think, Detective Inspector Grossman—'

'Gutkind.'

'I don't think, Detective Inspector Gutkind, that you can call it taking advantage. You could just as easily say she was taking advantage of my loneliness. But no one was taking advantage of anyone. As I have said – she'd had a few too many tequilas, I'd had a few too many sweet ciders—'

'Sweet cider!' Detective Inspector Gutkind pulled a face.

'And maybe the odd half of lager shandy. I'm sorry if lager shandy disgusts you too.'

'Go on.'

'There's nowhere to go. That's it. She was drunk, I was not entirely sober, she felt like a kiss, I felt like a kiss . . .'

'And whatever you feel like doing, you do?'

Kevern laughed. If only, he thought. 'I think you have a somewhat false picture of me,' he said. 'The clue is in the sweet cider. I am not a man who has a relaxed attitude to pleasure. As a matter of fact, I am not a man who has a relaxed attitude to anything. I have a very unrelaxed attitude, for example, to your being in my house.'

It occurred to him that the picture he was painting was more likely to incriminate him than otherwise. A difficult and lonely neurotic, who laughed where laughter was inappropriate, drank pussy drinks, and was prone to introspection and self-disgust – didn't all murderers fit that bill? And now he was telling the policeman that his presence, here, on the sofa in Kevern's cottage, made him uneasy. Why didn't he just confess to the crime?

'Why do you have an unrelaxed attitude to me being here?' the policeman asked.

'Why do you think? No one likes to be questioned by the police. No one likes to be under suspicion.'

'But you specifically mentioned *your house*. What is it about being questioned specifically in *your house* that upsets you?'

'I'm a very private man.'

'But not so private that you draw the line at kissing other men's wives?'

'I never brought her here.'

'Because?'

'I'm a very private man.'

'And very unrelaxed about a number of things. Did you have an unrelaxed attitude to Mrs Morgenstern's other lovers?'

'I wasn't aware of other lovers.'

'You thought you were special, did you?'

'No. She was known to be free and easy. Nor was I her lover. I didn't think of myself that way.'

'Was that because she repulsed you?'

Kevern laughed. Had he been repulsed? He remembered the bite. It hadn't felt like a repulse.

'It was bonfire night. A few fireworks went off. So did we. It was fun while it lasted.'

'Did you see her go home with Ythel Weinstock that night?'

'I did not.'

'Were you aware that Mrs Morgenstern and Ythel Weinstock were lovers?'

'I was not.'

'Were you aware that he hit her?'

'How could I have been? I didn't know they were intimate.'

'Were you aware that her husband was hitting her?'

'It's something that happens in the village. I wasn't aware of it but I am not surprised. Life in Port Reuben has always been harsh. But now on top of the old cruelties there's frustration. Men are living at the edge of their nerves here. They don't know what they're for. They used to be wreckers, now they run gift shops and say they're sorry. The women goad them. I read that the rest of the country is not much better.'

Worse and worse: now he was painting himself as a moral zealot.

He needn't have worried. Detective Inspector Gutkind also had a dash of moral zealotry in his nature. He believed in conspiracies. It was not permitted to believe in conspiracies (no written law against, of course) but Gutkind couldn't help himself. Conspiracy theorising ran in families and his father had believed in them to the point where he could see nothing else. Gutkind's grandfather had also believed in conspiracies and had lost his job in the newly formed agency Ofnow attempting to root them out. That attempting to root out conspiracies had cost him his job proved there was a conspiracy against him. And behind him was Clarence Worthing, the Wagnerian, Gutkind's great-grandfather who had tasted betrayal to the lees. He fed his resentments and suspicions to his son who fed them to his son who fed them, nicely incubated, to Gutkind. For as far back as the family went, somebody, some group, had been out to get them. Heirlooms in their own way, just as silk Chinese rugs were, romances of family persecution at the hands of conspirators were restricted. It didn't do for any family to be harbouring too many, or indeed any one with too much fervour. Conspiracy theories had fed the suspicion that erupted into that for which society was still having to say sorry. And how could you say sorry when some of the reasoning behind WHAT HAPPENED, IF IT HAPPENED – that conspiracies were sucking the life blood from the nation – remained compelling?

Detective Inspector Gutkind understood why there could be no going backwards in this – and was, anyway, unable to point the finger anywhere but at the odd individual malfeasant, and by its nature individual malfeasance could not amount to conspiracy – but he was a prisoner of his upbringing. He had a careworn build – dapper, the unobservant thought him – lean as though from fretting, with a round face, apoplectic eyes and an unexpectedly wet, cherubic mouth. Had there been a conspiracy to accuse Gutkind of the pederasty that exercised Densdell Kroplik, his mouth would surely have been the basis for it. He looked like someone who pressed his lips where they had no business being pressed.

He smiled at Kevern and wondered if he might be allowed to remove his coat. Kevern could not conceal his awkwardness. It was bad enough that Gutkind was here at all, but a Gutkind without his coat, in his cottage, was more than his nerves could bear. 'Of course,' he said, taking the coat and then not knowing what to do with it, 'that's rude of me.'

He was surprised to see that under his coat Gutkind wore not a jacket but a Fair Isle buttoned cardigan.

Was this to relax the unwary, Kevern wondered. But if that was so, his eyes should have not have looked so combustible as they took in Kevern's person and darted around Kevern's room.

'This Biedermeier?' he asked, running his fingers over the elaborately carved back of the sofa.

Kevern started. 'Imitation,' he said.

'Made down here?'

'Kildromy.'

'That's a long way to go for it.'

'I like the best. I'm a woodworker myself. I appreciate good craftsmanship.'

'It doesn't really go with this cottage, though, does it,' Gutkind went on.

Kevern wanted to say that he didn't think the policeman's cardigan went with his job, but it didn't seem a good idea to antagonise him further. 'It goes with my temperament,' he said.

'And how would you describe that?'

'My temperament? Heavy, ornate and unwelcoming.'

'And out of place?'

'If you like.'

'Would you call yourself a loner?'

'I wouldn't call myself anything. I'm a woodturner, as I think I've told you.'

'Business good?'

'I make candlesticks and lovespoons for the tourist industry. There isn't a fortune in that, but I get by.'

'Why have local people given you the nickname "Coco"?'

'You'd better ask them. But I think it's ironic. "Coco" was the name of a famous circus clown. It must be evident to you that I am not an entertainer.'

'But you entertain women?'

Here we go again, Kevern thought. He sighed and walked to the window. Not knowing what else to do with it, he was still carrying Gutkind's coat over his arm. Though the sea didn't look wild, the blowhole was busy, fine spray from the great white jet of water catching what there was of sunlight. He thought of Ailinn's whale and suddenly felt weary. 'Get the fuck out,' he wanted to tell the policeman. 'Get the fuck out of my house.' If ever there was a time to let go, let rip, let the bad language out of his constricted system, this was it. But he was who he was. Let's get this over with, he thought. 'Is this about the blood?' he asked, not turning his head.

'What blood is that?'

'My blood. Lowenna Morgenstern bit me the night we kissed after the fireworks. She bit me hard. I don't doubt I was seen afterwards with blood on my shirt. I assume that's why you wanted to talk to me.'

'You don't still have that shirt, do you?'

'Well I must have because I haven't thrown any shirt away in a long time. But I'd be hard pressed to remember which shirt I was wearing that night. And whichever it was, it will have been laundered many times since then.'

Gutkind made a perfect cupid's bow of his transgressive lips. He knew why men washed their shirts.

'Oh, come on, Goldberg—'

'Gutkind.'

Goldberg/Gutkind, Kevern wanted to say, *who gives a damn . . .*

'Oh come on,' he said instead, 'you're not telling me that laundering my shirts indicates suspicious behaviour?'

'It could be if it was Mrs Morgenstern's blood and not yours.'

'Aha, and if, having got a taste of spilling her blood once, I couldn't wait to spill it again.'

'Well that's a theory, Mr Cohen, and I will give it consideration. But to be honest with you it's not Mrs Morgenstern's blood that concerns us right now.'

'So whose is it?'

'Mr Morgenstern's.'

'Ah, well I'm glad he's back in the picture. The village gossip mill has had him down as the murderer from day one. He's already been found guilty and sentenced at the bar of the Friendly Fisherman. All you had to do was find him.'

'You misunderstand. It's not Mr Morgenstern's blood at the crime scene I'm talking about. It's Mr Morgenstern's blood all over Mr Morgenstern.'

Kevern shrugged a shrug of only half-surprise. 'That makes it easier for everyone then, doesn't it? Husband kills wife and lover and then kills himself. Case closed. Why are you speaking to me?'

'If only it were as simple as that. It would appear that Mr Morgenstern didn't die by his own hand.'

'What!'

'As you say yourself, Mr Cohen, there's a lot of anger and frustration out there.'

'You're telling me Ade Morgenstern's been murdered now?'

'Well if he didn't do it to himself – which given the manner of his death he couldn't – and if it wasn't natural causes – which it wasn't – and if we rule out the hand of God – which I think we must – that's the only supposition I can make.'

Kevern Cohen shook his head. He couldn't quite muster horror or even profound shock, but he mustered what he could. 'Christ, what's going on in this village?'

Detective Inspector Gutkind showed Kevern a philosophic expression. As though to say, well isn't that precisely what I hoped you might be able to answer.

He didn't write this in his report, but what Detective Inspector Gutkind felt in his heart was this: 'Something smells. Maybe not this, but something.'

ii

Kevern thought he'd better prepare Ailinn for what she might hear. He had, some months before they'd met, he mustered the honour to tell her, kissed the murdered woman. He knew not to say it was nothing. He couldn't have it both ways: if he boasted he was no citizen of Snogland, then he couldn't claim a kiss was nothing. Besides, women didn't like to hear men say that things they did with their bodies and which ought to involve their emotions were nothing. If it was nothing then why do it; and if it was something then don't lie about it. But it wasn't a long kiss and if he hadn't thought about it much the day after – he wasn't going to claim he hadn't thought about it at all – he certainly hadn't thought about it since he'd been with Ailinn who drove all trace of memory of other kisses from his mind.

She was disappointed in him. Not angry. Just disappointed. Which was worse.

'I'm sorry,' he said, 'if I've made you jealous.'

'*Jealous*?'

'I don't mean jealous.'

'What do you mean?'

What did he mean? 'You know,' he said.

'Was there something between you I should be jealous of?'

'No, no.' Here it came – in that case why did he bother to kiss her . . .

'What I feel,' she said, letting him off, 'is that it would have been nice to go on thinking of you as a man who doesn't throw kisses around. Who respects himself or at least his mouth more.'

Kevern tried to think of any man he knew who respected his mouth.

'Well it was no disrespect to you,' he said. 'I hadn't met you. Unless you believe one can demean a person in retrospect.'

She thought about it for longer than he would have liked. 'No, no it doesn't demean me in retrospect,' she said at last. 'It demeans you, which reflects on me, and it takes a little from my fantasy . . . but that was always just girlish nonsense anyway. So no, yes, I'm all right about it, and I thank you for being honest with me.'

Kevern felt he'd been kicked in the stomach. She was no/yes/noing him. Yes, no, she was *all right about it*, which was the language of compromise and disillusionment. And he had shattered her fantasy, which meant her hope to live a life above the common. He had brought her low with his honesty – honesty being the kindest yes/no word she could find for his being a man like every other.

A man like Ahab, even. Demoniacally hell-bent on her unhappiness by simple virtue of his being a man. Except that he wasn't. Yes/no.

He asked her to make love to him, on his bed with the sheets thrown back and the windows open, not to remove all trace of Lowenna Morgenstern's kisses from his lips, but to remove all trace of this conversation. She shook her head. It didn't quite work like that for her. In the open air then. On the cliffs. In Paradise Valley. Let Nature do the job. But she wasn't quite in the mood for that either. She would walk with him, though. A long bracing walk where they could talk about something else. Look beyond them. Not talk about themselves at all. 'We are a bit in each other's heads,' she said.

He knew what she meant but the last thing he wanted to do was walk her out of his.

They walked well together, he thought. Which was a sign of

their compatibility. They were always in step. When one put out a hand the other found it immediately. They stopped to look at the same flowers or to admire the same picturesque cottage. They stooped in unison to stroke a cat or pick up litter. Neither started to speak before the other had quite finished, or at the very moment that the other began a sentence. They talked side by side, like instruments in an orchestra. This wasn't only good manners; it was an instinctive compatibility. Their hearts beat to an identical rhythm.

Had his incestuous parents felt like this at the beginning, he wondered.

He laughed, suddenly, for no reason. Threw back his head and laughed at the sky. She didn't ask him why, she simply threw back her head and did the same. A minute later she seized him by the arm and made him look at her. 'This is very dangerous,' she said.

'You think I don't know that?' was his reply.

He proposed a trip away, a few days' holiday from this degrading village. Gutkind had not asked him to stay put, so he believed he was no more a suspect than all the other men in the county Lowenna Morgenstern had kissed. He was more worried about what the policeman might write in his report about the furniture.

They would pack a couple of bags, drive north, find a city where people didn't know them and weren't murdering one another, stay in a nice hotel that had no view of the sea, go to a couple of restaurants, maybe take in a film, reconnect with each other after the Morgenstern business, no matter that they hadn't come apart over it. Ailinn was surprised to discover he owned a car, which he kept under tarpaulin in the public car park. He had never struck her as a car person. Once she saw him drive she realised she was right. 'You drive so slowly,' she said, 'how do you ever get anywhere?'

'Where is there to get?'

'Wherever it is we're going.'

He hadn't told her. He wanted it to be a surprise. To both of them.

'Let's just drive,' he said, 'and stop when we're tired.'

'I'm tired.'

'Already?'

'I'm tired in anticipation.'

Was this, he wondered, a play on his having been unfaithful to her in retrospect?

He stopped the car and looked at her.

She had a suggestion. 'Let me drive. At least that way we'll arrive somewhere.'

He was worried that she hadn't driven in a while, that she didn't know the roads down here, that she wasn't familiar with the vehicle, that she hadn't studied the manual.

'A car's a car, Kevern!'

Fine by Kevern. He pulled on the hand brake, turned off the engine, and changed seats with her. Not being a car person was one of the ways he had always defined his anomalous masculinity. The men of Port Reuben wanted to kill in their cars; they accelerated when they saw a pedestrian, they revved the engines for the pure aggression of it even when their cars were parked in their garages. Then on Sundays they soaped them as though they were their whores. If they reserved such attention for their cars it was no surprise, Kevern thought, that their wives, the moment they had a drink inside them, were eager to kiss him, a man careless of cars.

Ailinn drove so fast he had to close his eyes.

'Anyone would think Ahab's tailing us,' he said.

'Ahab *is* tailing us,' she told him. 'Ahab's always tailing us. That's what Ahab does.'

It seemed to excite her.

'Couldn't we, on this occasion at least, just let him overtake us?'

She pushed her foot harder on the accelerator and wound down the window, letting the wind make her hair fly. 'Where's your sense of adventure?' she asked.

Questions, questions. . . Why so many feathers among the splintered furniture and ripped clothes, the broken toys, the smashed plates and fragments of glass, the bricks, the window frames, the pages torn from books holy and profane? Feathers from the mattresses hurled from upper windows, of course, but there are sufficient feathers in this single ruined garden to fill a mattress for every rioter in the city to enjoy the sleep of the righteous on. One feather won't lie still. It curls, tickling itself, tries to float away but something sticky holds it to the child's coat to which it has become attached. And where have all the hooks and crowbars appeared from? If the riots broke out spontaneously, how is it that these weapons were so plentifully to hand? Do the citizens of K sleep with crowbars by their beds? They bring them down with gusto, however they came by them, on the head of a man whom others have previously rolled in a ditch of mud and blood and feathers. A ritual bath. They rolled him and then wrung him out like a rag. The sounds of bones cracking and cries for help mingle with the furious triumphant shouts of murderers and the laughter of onlookers. Which prompts another question: when is wringing a man out like a rag funny?

SEVEN

Clarence Worthing

i

ALL WAS NOT well about the heart of Detective Inspector Gofuckyourself. (It wasn't to be supposed he hadn't registered Kevern Cohen's unspoken contempt. He had good ears. He could pick up an unspoken insult from three counties away. So face to face, and knowing nothing of the other's squeamishness in the matter of obscenities, he was hardly likely to have missed what Kevern wished he would do to himself.)

He was overworked – that contributed to his malaise. In his lifetime, at least, the county had never seen so much serious crime. Murders, attempted murders, robberies with violence, infidelity with violence, a seething resentment of somebody or something that issued in behaviour it was difficult to quantify but which he described to himself as a breakdown of respect, in particular a breakdown of respect to him.

He had his theories about the underlying causes but knew to keep them under his hat.

Home for Gutkind was a small end-of-terrace house in St Eber, an inland town built around the county's most important china-clay pit. A white dust had long ago settled on every building in St Eber, giving it, though entirely flat and shapeless, an Alpine aspect that the few visitors to the area had always found attractive. Gutkind's cat Luther, who had been spayed and so had little else to do – 'Like me,' Gutkind sometimes thought – rolled around in this dust from morning to night, going from garden to garden to find more. He would be waiting for the detective inspector when he arrived home, his coat powdered as though with icing sugar, his eyelashes as pale as an albino's, even his tongue white. Gutkind, who had no one else to love, sat him on a newspaper in the kitchen and brushed him down roughly, though he knew that he would be out rolling in someone's garden again as soon as he had eaten. As with the cat, so with the man. Gutkind showered twice a day, more often than that at weekends when he was home, watching the particles almost reconstitute themselves into clay as they vanished in a grubby whirlpool down the plug-hole. It was a form of recycling, Gutkind thought, the clay that had coated his hair and skin returning to its original constituency underground. Otherwise he was not a recycling man. Too many of society's ills were the result of the wrong sort of people with the wrong sort of beliefs finding ways of recycling themselves, no matter how much effort went into their disposal.

Disposal? Detective Inspector Gutkind was not a brute but he believed in calling a spade a spade.

And he was not, in the privacy of his own home, however dusty, a man to say he was sorry.

He had no wife. He had had a wife once, but she had left him soon after they were married. The china clay was one reason she left him, and Gutkind had no desire to move (having to shower so many times a day confirmed his sense of what was wrong with the world), but the other reason she left him was his sense of what was wrong with the world. She discovered for herself what many of her friends had told her – though she hadn't listened at the time – that life with a man who saw conspiracies everywhere was insupportable. 'It's your friends who have put you up to this,' he said as he watched her packing her bags. She shook her head. 'It's your family, then.' 'Why can't it just be *me*, Eugene?' she asked. 'Why can't it be *my* decision?' But he was unable to understand what she was getting at.

Returning home after interviewing Kevern Cohen – yet another person who showed him scant respect – Detective Inspector Gutkind showered, brushed down his cat, showered again, and heated up a tin of beans. He felt more than usually miffed. If I could put my finger on something, he told himself, just *something*, I would feel a damned sight better. But whether he meant put his finger on the motivation of a crime, the name of a criminal, why everything was so twisted from its purpose, why his life was so dusty and lonely, why he hated his cat, he couldn't have said.

He had to have someone to blame. He was not unusual in that. What divided *Homo sapiens* from brute creation was the need to apportion responsibility. If a lion went hungry or a chimpanzee could not find a mate, it was no one's fault. But from the dawn of time man had been blaming the climate, the terrain, fate, the gods, some other tribe or just some other person. To be a man, as distinct from being a chimpanzee, was to be forever at the mercy of a supernatural entity, a force, a being or a collection of beings, whose only function was to make your life on earth unbearable. And wasn't this the secret of man's success: that in chasing dissatisfaction down to its malignant cause he had hit upon the principle, first of religion and then of progress? What was evolution – what was revolution – but the logic of blame in action? What was the pursuit of justice but punishment of the blameworthy?

And who were the most blameworthy of all? Those whom you had loved.

When the sentimental blaming mood was on him – and tonight it roared in his ears the way the sea beside which you had once walked with a lover roared in a treasured seashell – he would climb the stairs to his attic, open an old wardrobe in which he stored clothes he no longer wore but for some reason could not bear to throw away, and pull out a faded periodical or two from the dozen or so which hung there on newspaper sticks, exactly as they had once hung in metropolitan cafés of the sort sophisticated town-bred men and women once patronised in order to drink coffee, eat pastries, and stay up to date with prejudiced opinion. Given that Gutkind kept these periodicals because they contained extended ruminations penned by his great-grandfather, Clarence Worthing, they were, strictly speaking, heirlooms, and exceeded the number of heirlooms – though no one knew exactly what that number was – any one person was permitted to keep. Not being a law exactly, this was not rigorously policed; everyone kept more than they admitted they kept, but, as a detective inspector, Gutkind knew he was taking a bit of a risk and indeed much relished taking it.

He had always dipped intermittently into these publications, enjoying picking up his great-grandfather's thoughts at random, not least because Clarence Worthing had been a cut above the rest of the family, a self-taught thinker and self-bred dandy who had moved in circles of society unimaginable to Eugene Gutkind. He had never met his great-grandfather but had heard tell of him from his grandmother, Clarence Worthing's daughter, something of a lady herself, and a bohemian to boot, who revelled in the fact that she had hardly ever seen her father, so tied up was he in his affairs – in all senses of the word, if Eugene knew what she meant – a whirl of feckless forgetfulness which she put down to his having been rejected as a young man by the only woman he had ever truly loved – a woman who was not her mother. Eugene marvelled that she was not hurt by this. You could not be hurt by such a man, she told him, so stylish was he even when he let you down. Gutkind yearned to have let someone down stylishly. Taking out the newspapers he bathed in the glorious retrospective reflection of his great-grandfather's irresponsibility . . . and pain. By means of Clarence Worthing, Gutkind too became a person to be reckoned with – a man with a tragic past and a liquid way with words and women.

Over and above this he liked reading the Worthing papers for the clarity of their reasoning and on that account read them, again and again, chronologically and therefore, he surmised, systematically. One train of thought in particular engrossed his attention because it seemed to explain something that was crying out for explanation. And tonight Gutkind was of a mood to peruse it again. In the course of it – an extended essay entitled *When Blood Is Thicker Than Water* – his great-grandfather sought to lay the blame for everything he thought wrong with the world, from the moral, political, ethical and even theological points of view, on 'those' who cultivated a double allegiance which was plain for everybody to see but which good manners forced society to turn a blind eye to. In fact, the phrase 'double allegiance' let them off too easily, he argued, for the question had to be asked whether they considered they owed any sort of genuine allegiance to this, or any country in which they'd found themselves, at all.

Or any sort of allegiance to *him*, Gutkind surmised. He didn't mind that his great-grandfather's reasoning reeked of the ad feminam. How else do you measure a great wrong unless you have been on the receiving end of it? If his great-grandfather proceeded from a position of profound personal disappointment – betrayal even – that made his arguments only the more persuasive to Detective Inspector Gutkind.

'Observe their cohabiting customs,' Gutkind's great-grandfather wrote, 'observe them as a scientist might observe the mating habits of white mice, and you will see that however far outside the swarm they wander to satisfy their appetites, for purposes of procreation they invariably regroup. They choose their mistresses and lovers from those for whom they feel neither respect nor compassion and their wives and husbands from their own ranks. As is often reported by innocents who encounter them without knowing by what rules they live, they can be companionable, amusing, even adorable, and in some circumstances, especially where reciprocal favours are looked for, munificent. But this to them is no more than play, the exercise of their undeniable powers and charm for the mere sadistic fun of it. Thereafter their loyalty is solely to each other. Let one of their number suffer and their vengefulness knows no limits; let one of their number perish and they will make the planet quake for it. To some, this is taken to be the proof of the steadfastness of their tribal life, the respect and affection they have been brought up, over many generations, to show to one another. But it is in fact a manifestation of a sense of superiority that values the life of anyone not belonging to their "tribe" at less than nothing. Only witness, in that country which they call their ancestral home (but which few of them except the most desperate appear to be in any hurry to repair to), a recent exchange of prisoners with one of their many enemies in which, for the sake of a single one of their own – just *one* – they willingly handed over in excess of seven hundred! The mathematics make a telling point. Never, in the history of humanity, has one people held all others in such contempt, or been more convinced that the world can, and will, be organised for their benefit alone. It has been said that were the earth to be laid waste, so long as not a single hair of one of theirs was harmed, they would connive in that destruction. That is not a justification for *their* destruction, though others argue persuasively for it. But it does invite us to ask how much longer we can tolerate their uncurbed presence.'

Gutkind so admired the adamantine and yet heartfelt quality of his great-grandfather's prose that he was at a loss to understand why there had been no published collection of his articles or, come to that, why he had not cut a dash in parliamentary politics. Had his notorious social life taken up too much of his time, or were his words too prophetic for the age he lived in? Gutkind knew for himself what it was to be unappreciated and felt for his great-grandfather's sorrows a scalding agony which there was no warrant to suppose Clarence Worthing ever felt himself.

Part of what Gutkind admired about Worthing's work was its conscientious refinement of argument from one article to the next. The refusal of all talk of destruction with which one essay ended, for example, was picked up again in the next with an allusion to 'self-destruction', that being the course on which 'the arrogant, the forward and the vain', as he called them, appeared, paradoxically, to be hell-bent. 'Some worm of divisiveness in their own souls has impelled them – throughout history, as though they knew history itself was against them – to the brink of self-destruction. Imaginatively, the story of their annihilation engrosses them; let them enjoy a period of peace and they conjure war, let them enjoy a period of regard and they conjure hate. They dream of their decimation as hungry men dream of banquets. What their heated brains cannot conceive, their inhuman behaviour invites. "Kill us, kill us! Prove us right!" Time and again they have been saved, not by their own resolution, but by the world taking them at their own low self-valuation and endeavouring to deliver them the consummation they devoutly wish. Only then are they able to come together as a people, mend their divisions, and celebrate their escape as one more proof of the divine protection to which their specialness entitles them. But it is a dangerous game and will backfire on them one day.'

Gutkind heard in this a personal plea by his great-grandfather, to one he had loved without reciprocation, to beware the dragon's teeth she and hers had sowed. He even wondered if it was a coded message. A last-minute warning to her, perhaps, to escape (he had even used that word), to gather up her things and leave, or to go into hiding, before the first shots were fired.

How many messages of this sort, he asked himself, had been sent in this fashion. Not just by Clarence Worthing but by others who had lost their hearts to apparently charming and companionable men and women who proved, when things turned serious, to have been merely trifling with their affections and who, without once looking back, beat a speedy retreat to the bosoms of their own? How much 'saving', for the sake of brief but never to be forgotten embraces, had been going on? Like all theorists of betrayal and conspiracy, Gutkind was a hyperbolist. From the single example of his great-grandfather he extrapolated a whole underground of the hurt, scheming tirelessly, not to say paradoxically, to give another chance to those they knew – knew from their own experience – did not deserve it.

This seemed so plausible to the detective that he began to question whether WHAT HAPPENED had in the end claimed any victims at all. Had it remained an undescribed crime all these years because it was an unsolved crime, and had it been unsolved because it was uncommitted? That made a great deal of sense to him. It explained why the world was not the happier place it should have been, and no doubt would have been, had what was meant to happen happened.

In the early days of Gutkind's courtship his wife-to-be had sent him a graphic letter, imprinted with her lipstick kisses, describing her desires. 'Read and burn', she wrote at the bottom.

Now that he understood these essays of his great-grandfather's as personal missives to a woman he'd loved, he imagined him advising the same precaution. Read and burn.

But this didn't take from the truth of Clarence Worthing's analysis. If anything – since it was designed to win assent even from those it might have hurt, since it was intended to prepare, alert and warn, not rabble-rouse – it made the analysis more compelling. The empathetic Gutkind did figuratively as he was told. He read and burned.

ii

Tonight, he spread out a few more pages of the silver-tongued Clarence Worthing on the kitchen table, blowing on them reverently, a paragraph at a time, to keep them free of dust. How he admired the undeviating strength of his resolution, not compromised by passion but stiffened by it. How wonderful it must have been to know where the wrongness at the heart of life was to be located and what it looked like. Here were no abstractions; here was flesh and blood. His great-grandfather wrote as though the enemy were in the other room, perhaps falsely playing with his children as he wrote, perhaps seducing his wife as he had once been seduced himself. Gutkind felt that he could touch them. Put his arms around them, submit his cheek to their false kisses. He closed his eyes and believed that he could smell them. It was a kind of love. A hatred born of pure fascination. His noble-hearted ancestor had been their friend. He had allowed them into his heart. He had been betrayed by them. Gutkind felt his own heart swell. He almost swooned with this love which was indistinguishable from hate. He closed his eyes and made a perfect pink circle of his lips. Womanly, he felt. Kiss me!

But when he opened his eyes again there was no one there. Only Luther, rolling in the white dust. He felt as though that very dust obscured his vision, fell like a veil over his face, through which he could make out nothing distinct, no person or group of persons, just his own causeless dissatisfaction.

But he needed features and so he conjured them, not from the family journals but from his own immediate experience of what the features of aloof, cold-blooded superiority looked like. Those features belonged to Kevern 'Coco' Cohen.

EIGHT

Little St Alured

i

AILINN DROVE ADVENTUROUSLY but sweetly, ignoring the routine rage of other drivers. They honked her if she didn't pull over to let them pass, and they honked her when she did; she was too fast for some and too slow for others; she lingered too long at traffic lights or she set off too early for those running the lights in opposing directions. A cyclist hammered on the roof of the car, then seeing she was a woman blew her an enraged kiss.

'I'd have turned back by now,' Kevern admitted. 'I'd have killed or been killed.'

'You get used to this as a woman,' Ailinn said.

'You're not turning this into a gender issue?'

'I don't have to. How many women have wound down their windows to scream at me? How many women have shown me the finger?'

'I haven't been counting.'

'You don't need to count. Would that cyclist have blown a kiss at you?'

'All right, I accept what you are saying. But he was young. Any crisis in society manifests itself in the behaviour of young men. So let's go home.'

She wouldn't hear of it. Home was no better, remember. At home men weren't just showing women the finger, they were killing them, and Kevern, or had he forgotten, was suspected of killing a woman himself.

'And a man,' he reminded her. 'Indeed a couple of men. Don't minimise my offence.'

'I don't. But your behaviour doesn't constitute a crisis.'

Kevern tightened his seat belt. 'You'll tell me it's a tautology,' he said, 'but the behaviour of men is the proof we're in crisis.'

'That's a tautology,' she said, finally getting on to the motorway.

She drove at her usual speed, confidently, with a narrowed concentration as though driving through a tunnel. Kevern spoke not one word. After about an hour and a half, as much from a charitable impulse as anything else, she left the motorway again and followed the signs to the small cathedral city of Ashbrittle, at one time home to more ecclesiastical dignitaries than any other town in the country, and for that reason a magnet for Christian tourists. But that was before WHAT HAPPENED, IF IT HAPPENED happened. Subsequently, though the church insisted it had not been specifically instrumental in those events, it had allowed its head to drop. Too much saying sorry, Kevern thought, as he realised where she'd driven them.

'This do?' she asked.

Kevern wound down his window then wound it up again. 'You can smell the disuse,' he said.

'Shall we drive straight out again?'

'No, let's stay. I need to rest my eyes.'

'You haven't been driving.'

'That's what you think.'

They found a motherly bed and breakfast a mile or two outside the town, away from the smell of disuse, and went immediately to bed. Pencil sketches of details of gravestones, lychgates and stoups, arches and columns seen from unexpected angles, hung above their bed. 'Soft clerical porn,' Kevern called it. 'The kitsch to which religion, when no one any longer believes in it, is reduced.'

Ailinn thought he was making too much of it. They were just

pictures. Something had to go on the walls. And how would he have felt had they shown the Saviour bleeding on the cross. He said that would have depended on who'd painted it.

'Let's have a break from judgement,' Ailinn suggested. At least on their first night away. 'We're supposed to be on holiday. Let's just enjoy the relief of not being in Port Reuben. And not being looked at every minute of every day.'

He agreed. 'Or interrogated.'

'Well that's your own fault for kissing married women.'

'You sound like Detective Inspector Gutkind.'

'Did he ask about me?'

'No. Should he?'

'I suppose not. But you'd think I'd be material to his assessment of your character, or at least your circumstances.'

'He was more interested in assessing my furniture.'

She laughed a small laugh then remembered something. 'I was questioned by the police once. Not since I've been with you. Before I left home. I thought they were more interested in my belongings too.'

'What were you questioned about?'

'That was never entirely clear. A burglary, I think. Not for kissing someone in a car park, that I can say. But mainly they wanted the chance to get a look at where I lived. They wondered if I'd held on to any family photographs or letters from before I was adopted. I told them I didn't have any family photographs or letters from before I was adopted for the reason that I had no family. And besides, I knew the law. They said everyone broke the law a bit. I told them I didn't. I told them that if they wanted to know more about me they should try the children's home in Mernoc. And then be so kind as to let me know what they'd found out.'

'And did they?'

'Let me know?'

'Find anything out.'

'No idea.'

She shuddered in his arms, her heart aflutter – 'Someone dear to me has just died,' she said, and then when Kevern sat up in alarm she laughed to reassure him. 'A silly superstition from my part of the world.'

But he was a superstitious man himself. Only a fool, he thought, wasn't. What if her heart had fluttered out of time – an anticipatory flutter – because the someone close to her who had died was him.

A moment later there was a knock on their door. Their hearts leapt together. Who knew they were here?

They needn't have been alarmed: it was only the motherly proprietor wondering if they wanted a hot-water bottle.

They said no.

They had each other.

ii

Ashbrittle was deserted when they went strolling after breakfast. But somehow aflutter too, like Ailinn's heart, as though with affrighted ghosts.

They stared about them. Soul-departed terrace after soul-departed terrace, mocking the moderate, clerical sociability for the expression of which they'd been lovingly designed. Expectant, calling-card residences at which no one called. The stone a melancholy, rusted yellow. The brass doorbells black from never being pushed. A light rain seemed not so much to fall from the sky as rise from the cracked paving stones. A couple of shops selling local-history pamphlets (no one wanted a complete book), pewter goblets, silver spoons featuring the diocesian crest and of course postcards of the cathedral were open, but many more were boarded up. The river had a film of grease on it, like gravy left to go cold. The Bishop's Barn, a one time favourite with tourists, was closed for renovation, but the sign saying so was in need of renovation itself. Graffiti was scrawled on its strong yet quiet Jacobean door. Kevern couldn't read the words or decipher the symbols but to him all graffiti was the language of alienated hate, even when it was urging 'Love'.

They walked in silence under High Street Gate which housed a library, also indefinitely closed for renovation, and found Cathedral Close. 'I have a soft spot for cathedral closes,' Ailinn said, looking around. 'I always feel people must be living such good lives in them.'

'Well maybe they are,' Kevern said. 'That's if anyone is living here at all. It feels as if they've all gone. A plague-bell tolled and they all ran for it. Unless they're on their knees in their cellars, saying sorry.'

Ailinn stopped and told him to be quiet. She could hear music coming from the grandest of the houses. She wanted it to be Bach or Handel but it was only a utility-console ballad wondering where we would be without love.

'In the shit,' Kevern said. To himself. He wasn't going to use language like that to the woman he loved.

She took his arm and moved him on in what, as a devotee of cathedral closes, she knew to be the direction of the main entrance to the cathedral itself. Her early years had been spent in an orphanage that was an adjunct to a monastery. She knew her way around church architecture.

'The gargoyles have been defaced,' Kevern noted, looking up. 'They have no features. No bent noses, no bulging eyes, no pendulous lips.'

'Years of bad weather,' Ailinn guessed.

'Well that's a kind interpretation. But I bet this is deliberate. They've been smoothed over – made to look like nothing and nobody.'

'Botoxed, you reckon?'

He laughed. 'Morally Botoxed. Rendered inoffensive.'

'Still – isn't that better than the way they looked before?'

'Maybe. But they might as well not be here in that case. If they aren't going to remind you of evil, they have no function.'

Ailinn reminded him that their function was to carry water away from the building.

'I meant spiritual function,' Kevern said piously.

Inside, the light struggled to pierce the dust of the stained-glass windows. Far apart from each other, two elderly ladies, dressed in black, prayed, one with her face in her hands.

'There you are,' Ailinn whispered.

'I'm not sure they count,' Kevern whispered back. 'They look as though they've been here for two hundred years.'

'It can take a long time,' Ailinn said, 'for God to answer your prayers.'

'More time than we have.'

'But not more time than they have.'

'And how does he adjudicate between prayers,' Kevern wondered, 'when they are savagely opposed? What if these two are praying for the destruction of each other? How can he satisfy the desires of them both?'

'With difficulty. That's why it takes him so long.'

'I take comfort at least,' Kevern said, 'in there being so few people making their devotions here. It must mean that the rest of them have what they want.'

'God help them,' Ailinn said.

'God help us all,' Kevern agreed.

They let their eyes wander absently over the crucifixes and Bible scenes, neither of them willing to make the effort to determine if any of the art was distinguished. They paused before an elaborately carved stone shrine, virtually a throne, built over a small slab, no bigger than a pillow, which announced itself as containing the blessed remains of *Little St Alured of Ashbrittle, killed by —.*

Kevern took out his glasses to examine the carving. 'Well whatever else, they were wonderful craftsmen,' he said. 'If I could do this with wood . . . such lightness, you think you're looking at flowers. Don't quote me on this, but I almost fancy I can see the poor little bugger's soul ascending to heaven on a tracery of stone petals.'

But Ailinn was more interested in deciphering who the poor little bugger was killed by. 'This hasn't been worn away by time,' she said. 'It's been scratched out.'

'Maybe they decided they had the wrong killer.'

'Then why didn't they replace the name with that of the right one?'

'Could still be investigating. The case might be *sub judice*.'

'After nine hundred years?'

Kevern conceded it was unlikely. 'But then justice, like God, grinds slowly. We should put Gutkind on to it.'

Ailinn knew how Kevern's mind worked. You set it a problem and when it could come up with no answer, it came up with a joke. He had lost interest now in Little St Alured and how he was murdered, and by whom, and why someone or other – an individual with an axe to grind or the depleted might of the church – didn't want anyone to know. She was the curious one. But in the end she too had to admit there were some things that had to remain a mystery.

They took the darkness of the cathedral out with them on to the street.

'This place needs cheering up,' Ailinn said. 'It needs sunshine.'

'It needs something. Pilgrims, I reckon. Believers. Some of the old dogmatism. You can't have a church town without belief and you can't have belief without intolerance.'

'And you think that would liven it up?'

'I do. All this penitential . . .'

'All this penitential what?'

He didn't have the word. 'You know . . . gargoylelessness. If you want God you've got to have the Devil.'

'I'm for neither,' Ailinn said.

'Then this is what you get.'

Glass shatters. They both hear it. She is at one end of the country and he is at another, yet still they hear it. The smashing mania, the shattering of every window in the land. After all the fires, all the beheadings, all the iron hooks and crowbars, the frenzy to kill has not abated. Only now it has become centralised. He is frightened, she less so. She thinks they've done their worst already. He thinks there's always something further they might come up with; he has more admiration for the ingenuity of man; viewing things millennially, he thinks they haven't even started yet. And look, he could be right. This time the mob wears uniforms, and answers to a higher authority even than God. She reads quietly, waiting for the knock. He hides his head. That is how they sit on the train heading east, looking out at the snow, not exchanging a word, she reading, he hiding his head. The train is not a surprise. They were always going to be put aboard this train. There are some among their fellow passengers for whom the train is a relief now that they are finally on it. In the snow everything will be washed away.

NINE

The Black Market in Memory

i

THE FOLLOWING MORNING, chilled by Ashbrittle's faded faith, Kevern – half hoping she would say no – suggested they leave and drive to the Necropolis. The Necropolis was his father's name for the capital.

'Another of his jokes?' Ailinn wondered.

'You could say that, but he might have been in dead earnest.'

'Well I wouldn't know,' Ailinn said, looking straight ahead.

She meant about jokes – since that had been Kevern's first assessment of her: that she didn't get them. But she meant about fathers too.

Neither had visited the Necropolis before. Singly, they wouldn't have dared. It had a bad reputation. Outside the capital people survived the failure of the banks with surprising fortitude; they even took a grim satisfaction in returning to old frugal ways which proved their moral superiority to those who had lived the high life in the capital for so long, washing oysters down with champagne and living in mansions that had their own swimming pools. It was a sweet revenge. In time the Necropolis recovered, to a degree, but its self-esteem, as a great centre of finance and indulgence, had been damaged. WHAT HAPPENED, IF IT HAPPENED – or, as his father called it, THE GREAT PISSASTROPHE – for the most part happened there, and while no one was blaming anyone, a sort of slinking seediness replaced the old strutting glamour. In the Necropolis the divorce rates were higher than anywhere else. So were domestic shootings. Men urinated openly in the streets. Women brawled with one another, used the vilest language, got drunk and thought nothing of throwing up where the men had urinated. You could have your pockets picked in broad daylight. Put up too fierce a struggle and you might have your throat cut. *Might*. It wasn't a daily occurrence, but people in the country were pleased to report that it wasn't unheard of.

Not allowed to remember the glory that had been, the Necropolis put up a cocksure front, belied by the failure of the once great stores and hotels to live up to the past sumptuousness which their premises still evoked. The shops with the grandest windows were not bursting with expensive items. You could get tables at the best restaurants on the day you wanted them. And there was a thriving black-market trade in memorabilia of better times – even, one might say, in memory itself.

Had they not been in love and on an adventure, each emboldening the other, Ailinn and Kevern would not have gone there.

Kevern's father must have warned him against going to the Necropolis a hundred times over the years, but when he tried to recall his actual words Kevern couldn't find any; he could only see the prematurely old man opening and closing his mouth, dressed in his oriental brocade dressing gown, arthritic and embittered, his back to the fire – a fire that was lit in all weathers – angrily smoking a cigarette through a long amber Bakelite cigarette holder, listening with one ear to the footsteps of walkers (snoopers, he called them) passing the cottage to get to the cliffs. Except for when he wore a carpenter's apron in his workshop, he dressed, in Kevern's recollection of him, no other way. Always his brocade dressing gown. Had he just arrived and was waiting for the rest of his clothes to follow, or was everything packed in readiness for departure? Had he for the space of one day in all the years he'd lived in the cottage made peace with the idea that it was his home?

His mother the same, though she didn't dress as though to face down a firing squad. They could have been master and servant, so fatalistically elegant was he, so like an item of her own luggage, a bundle of rags – the bare necessity to keep out the cold – was she.

Whether she had formed an independent view of the Necropolis, or ever been there herself, Kevern didn't know. She didn't talk to him about things like that. The past wasn't only another country, it was another life. But he thought he recalled her seconding her husband, saying, in her weary voice, as though to herself – because who else listened – 'Your father is right, don't go there.'

Kevern suddenly felt guilty realising that he too left his mother out of everything. He put his hand on Ailinn's knee as though in that way, from one woman to another, he could make it up to her – the mother he had trouble remembering.

Ailinn took her hand off the wheel and put it on his. 'Use both hands,' he said, frightened she meant to play pat-a-cake with him while she was driving. 'Please.'

'Well I'm looking forward to this,' she said, hiding her apprehension.

'Me too. I'm looking forward to my first Lebanese.'

'Or an Indian.'

'Or a Chinese.'

'And I can see if I can get my phone fixed,' she said.

'I didn't know anything was wrong with your phone.'

'It rings sometimes and when I answer there's no one there. And occasionally I hear an odd clicking when I'm on the phone to you.'

'How come you've only just mentioned this?'

'I didn't want to worry you.'

'You think someone's listening in?'

'Who would want to do that?'

'Search me . . . Gutkind?'

'Why would he want to listen in to my conversations?'

'Who knows? Maybe he wants to be sure you're not in any danger from me – the lady killer.'

They both laughed.

Kevern didn't mention his crazy thought. That the person bugging her phone might have been his dead father, making sure she was the right woman for his son.

'Is there such a thing as retinal hysteria?' Kevern asked as they approached the city.

Ailinn remembered an old English novel she'd read about a newly and unhappily married Puritan girl visiting Rome for the first time, the stupendous fragmentariness of the pagan/papal city – they were one and the same thing for her – passing in fleshly and yet funereal procession across her vision, throbbing and glowing, as though her retina were afflicted. So yes, Ailinn thought, a person's excited emotional state could affect the way he saw. But why was Kevern's emotional state excited or, more to the point, what did he think he was seeing?

'Zebra stripes,' he said. 'And leopard spots. And peacock feathers. Have we taken a wrong turn and driven into the jungle?'

'You don't think you could be hung-over?'

'You were with me last night. What did I drink?'

'A migraine then?'

'I don't get them. I feel fine. I am just blinded by colour.'

She had been too busy concentrating on the roads, which she feared would be more frightening than any she was used to, to notice what he had begun to notice as they approached the Necropolis. But he was right. The Necropolitans were dressed as though for a children's garden party. The moratorium on the wearing of black clothes, declared in the aftermath of THE GREAT PISSASTROPHE in order to discourage all outward show of national mourning (for who was there to mourn?) was honoured now only in the breach, they thought. Neither Ailinn nor Kevern thought twice about wearing black. But the Necropolis appeared to be obeying it to the letter still, as though seeing in the prohibition an opportunity for making or at least for seeming merry. What neither Kevern nor Ailinn had anticipated was the difference this abjuration of black would make to the look of everything. It was as though the spirit of serious industry itself had been syphoned out of the city.

But it wasn't just the vibrant colours of the clothes people wore that struck them, but the outlandishness of the designs. The further in they drove the more vintage-clothes stalls they passed, until the city began to resemble a medieval funfair or tourney, on either side of the road stalls and pavilions under flapping striped tarpaulins piled high with fancy dress. Kevern rubbed his eyes. 'I don't get it,' he said. 'I've had a policeman snooping around my house in the hope of uncovering a single family keepsake, and here they go about in their great-grandparents' underthings as bold as brass.'

Ailinn laughed at him. 'I doubt the stuff is genuinely old,' she said.

He thought he could smell the mustiness of antiquity on the streets. Mothballs, rotting shawls, old shoes, greasy hats, the forbidding odour of people long forgotten and garments that should have been thrown away. 'What do you mean not *genuinely* old?'

'Like your Kildromy-Biedermeier. I'd say they're fake vintage.'

'What's the point of that?'

'What's the point of your Kildromy-Biedermeier? It's a way of eating your cake and having it. This way they can cock a snook at the authorities without actually doing anything wrong. I think it's fun. Why don't we stop so you can buy me a crinoline and some cowboy boots? And I'll buy you a Prussian officer's outfit.'

'To do what in?'

'Ask me to dance. Take me into the woods. Whatever Prussian officers do.'

'*Did*,' he corrected her. 'There are no more Prussian officers. I hate this playing with everything.'

'Oh, Kevern, where's your sense of fun?'

He smiled at her. It pleased him when she bested him. 'Not everything is amenable to fun.'

'You think we should be solemn about the past?'

'I think we should let it go. What's past is past.'

Had she not been driving she'd have rolled her eyes at him.

But she knew now he did not always say what he believed.

ii

Only as they approached the Necropolis proper did the stalls begin to thin out, though even then they did not vanish altogether. And where stores selling better clothes should have been there were mainly holes in the ground and cranes. Had there been more workmen about, the cranes could have been taken as evidence that massive development was under way, but these too had a vintage air, mementoes of busier days. In accordance with the city's musty festivity, the cranes were festooned with tattered bunting and faded decorations from Christmases or other festivals long past.

At Kevern's instigation – he didn't want to be in the car a moment longer – they checked into a hotel in the part of the city once referred to in the fashion and travel magazines as Luxor, in deference to the opulence of the shopping. Luxor was where most of the grand hotels had been, though there was little of the old glamorous traffic in their lobbies or on the streets outside today. Foreign tourism fell off dramatically after WHAT HAPPENED and had never fully recovered. Who wanted to holiday in the environs of Babi Yar? That this was a reciprocal reluctance it suited the authorities to insist. If visitors didn't want to come and holiday in our backyard, we sure as hell didn't want to holiday in theirs. Where hadn't things been done the stench of which remained abhorrent to the misinformed or oversensitive tourist? Nowhere was safe, when you really thought about it. Nowhere was pleasant. What country wasn't a charnel house of its own history? You were better staying home, if you cared about that sort of thing, with your eyes closed and a cold compress on your forehead. You were better advised to keep to your individual fortress, shuttered and bolted against the movement, in or out, of people, infection and ideas. You contained your own conflagrations, that was the international wisdom, or at least that was the international wisdom as explained by Ofnow. Eventually, we'd all grow less nice in our expectations and things would get back to how they'd been.

In the meantime Luxor retained a little of its old exoticism thanks to the convergence of two accidents of history. Many of the oil rich who had been in the Necropolis, feasting on the decline of the banks (which, by some logic that only the most sophisticated economists understood, made them still richer), and gorging on the best of the new season's fashions, found themselves, when WHAT HAPPENED happened, between the devil of abroad and the deep blue sea of home. They were conscious, even without the advice of their embassies, that WHAT HAPPENED, no matter that they'd welcomed and in some cases been instrumental in it, might easily happen to them next; but equally aware that the revolutionary fervour sweeping their own countries was an even greater danger to them, as a hated elite who could afford to spend half their lives in foreign hotels. What was spring to some was winter to them. Anxious about staying but terrified to leave, they spent what was left of their lives in fretful uncertainty, and now their grandchildren and their grandchildren's children resided where they had been marooned, in a sort of melancholy but pampered limbo, some in the very hotels their grandparents had been staying in when the world convulsed. In the absence of anything else to do, they continued to shop, went on raiding the best stores when the seasons and the windows changed, as it was in their blood to do, but the city had ceased to be a centre of fashion, the clothes were shoddier, the jewellery cheaper, and there was nowhere now for them to return to show off their purchases.

It was a new, rare sight to Kevern and to Ailinn – these idly perambulating gold-ringed men in keffiyehs, paler-skinned, Kevern imagined, than their grandparents must have been, but still with those stern, warrior profiles he had been educated to idealise. The noble generosity of the Arab was as much a given in the citizenship classes Kevern had taken at school, as the free spontaneity of the Afro-Caribbean and the honest industriousness of the Asian. As for the chaste obedience of the women, that was still evident in the modesty of their dress.

'Nice,' Kevern commented, 'to see some black.'

Ailinn said nothing.

As black as ravens, they seemed to her, but nothing like so purposeful, covered from head to foot, only their slow eyes and the gold heels of their shoes visible. She noted with amazement the docility of their bearing as they trailed a step or two behind their men, talking among themselves. Some wheeled perambulators, but in general there were few children. Where was the point in children? And where, anyway, were the nannies? How did it feel, she wondered, to live this privileged life of no design, like a protected species which could forage unimpeded for whatever it liked but with no nest to take its findings back to.

Some of the men smoked hookahs in the lounge of the hotel, morose, looking occasionally at their watches but never at their women who sat staring at their jewelled utility phones, bemused, waiting for them to ring or perform some other once sacred but now forgotten function – totems that had lost their potency. The women allowed their fingers idly to play across the decommissioned keypads. The men too were fidgety, their fingers never far from their prayer beads.

'You should get a set of those, they could calm your nerves,' Ailinn whispered, as they waited for a porter to take their luggage to their rooms. They were travelling light and could have carried their own, but the porters needed employment and where, anyway, was the hurry?

'Are you implying I'm a fretter?'

'You? A fretter!' she laughed, holding on to his arm, then wondering whether, in such a place, it was disrespectful of her to stand so close to a man.

After he'd shown them to their room the porter took Kevern to one side and asked him if there were gramophone records, CDs or videos he was looking for. Bootleg blues bands, rock and roll, comedy – he knew where to lay his hands on anything. Kevern shook his head. What about books that had fallen out of print, bootleg tickets to underground cabarets, souvenir passports of those who hadn't got away before WHAT HAPPENED, IF IT HAPPENED happened, belts and badges worn by the hate gangs of the time, incitement posters, pennants, cartoons, signed confessions . . . ?

Kevern wanted to know who would want such things. The porter shrugged. 'Collectors,' he said.

'No,' Kevern said. 'No, thank you,' remembering the amount of contraband music and words belonging to his father that was hidden away in his loft. It hadn't occurred to him any of it could be worth money.

The bedroom was, or at least had been, ornate. The bed was a four-poster. The carpet vermilion and gold, the drapes similar, sentimental photographs of famous department stores with queues outside adorned the wall. A large bath sat in the middle of the bathroom on gilded griffin's claws, now broken and discoloured. It will topple, Kevern thought, if we get into it together. He didn't like the look of the towels either: though they must once have been sumptuous, each one large enough to wrap an entire bath-oiled family in, they now hung, grey and textureless, over rusted rails.

He went to the window and gazed out towards the park. At school he had read descriptions of the Necropolis written by post-apocalyptic fantasists of a generation before. They were published as an anthology intended as light relief for the pupils, a propaganda joke showing just how wrong people could be when they let their imaginations – and indeed their politics – run away with them. But the anthology was later withdrawn, not because the post-apocalyptics had been proved right, but because the truth was not quite the resplendent rebuttal of their vision it should have been. Kevern remembered the gleaming vistas of technological frenzy dreamed up by one of the writers, citizens of the Metropolis of Zog sitting on brightly coloured tubular benches conversing with their neighbours via bubbles of video speech transmitted faster than the speed of sound by satellite. They had given up talking to one another because talk was too cumbersome. Another envisioned the population living in cages underground, dispersing their seed by means of a carefully regulated system of electronic cartridges which travelled through translucent pipes, along with electricity and water. Otherwise they neither enjoyed nor wanted any other form of human contact. The alternative vision was of devastation – open sewers strewn with the debris of a consumer society that no longer possessed the will or the wherewithal to consume, abandoned motor vehicles with their doors pulled off, electricity pylons which seemed to have marched into the city from the country like an invading army and were now uprooted, bent double like dinosaurs in pain or flat on their backs like . . . Kevern couldn't remember what they were *like*, only that everything was like something else, as though what had destroyed the city was not disease or overpopulation or an asteroid but a fatal outbreak of febrile fantasy-fiction metaphor.

One way or another the destruction wrought by electronics haunted all these writers' imaginations. So much ingenuity and invention bringing so little happiness. In their own way, though, they were optimistic and triumphalist, no matter that they pretended otherwise, each recording the victory of the writers' analogical fancy over nature.

What these writers gloomily and even hysterically prophesied, Kevern thought, was in fact a fulfilment of their private wishes.

Nothing gleamed in the city Kevern looked out on. The

people on the streets had not turned into walking computer screens, riding translucent vehicles that sped along on tracks of spun steel. But neither was it a wasteland that could at least quicken the heart with horror. Yes, the bedecked cranes appeared melancholy, reminding him of drunks fallen asleep in doorways after a party, and after a while the brightly coloured retro clothing of the pedestrians and shoppers began to show as desperate, as though they were waiting for a carnival that was never going to start, but traffic lights worked and, though the cars looked even older than his, they still had their doors, their lights, their windscreen wipers, and – Kevern could clearly hear them from five floors up and through closed windows – their horns. There was no congestion, no sense of drivers fleeing an infected city in one direction, or rushing to join the techno-mayhem from another, so the horn-blowing must have denoted more indurated irascibility than specific impatience. Over in the park, men hooded like Eskimos – saying what things were 'like' went with the apocalyptic territory, Kevern realised – walked ill-tempered dogs, tugging at their leads, wanting them to do what they had come to the park to do and then be off. Every now and then a dog and his master relieved themselves in tandem. Though only the man appeared to relieve himself in anger. An occasional better-off-looking person walking a better-off-looking dog kept his distance, not afraid exactly, but routinely careful. Neither kind appeared to be taking pleasure in the outing. Kevern kept watching, expecting to see an eruption of hostilities, but nothing eventuated. A quiet moroseness prevailed, that was all. An all-pervading torpor that belied the colours, bored the dogs, and made the very light appear exhausted.

Kevern guessed that if you wanted to see blood spilled you had to wait till it got dark.

The pavements on the main roads were unswept, but they weren't the debris-strewn sewers piled with wreckage he'd read about in his school anthology. It wasn't the apocalypse.

There weren't any powerful similes to be made. Nothing was like anything.

So what was it? It was a city seen through a sheet of scratched Perspex. For all the variegations of hue, it had no outlines. People blurred into one another. Kevern wondered if a wife would recognise her husband if she ran into him anywhere but in their home. Would either miss the other if they never *returned* home? And yet they had passed three cinemas and two theatres on the drive in, all advertising romantic musicals. Love – that was the universal subject. Love to play guitars to. Love to dance to. Love to sing about. Old and young, rich and poor, the indigenous and the children of immigrants – love!

Ailinn joined him at the window. 'Well one thing this does do,' she said, 'is make you miss the Friendly Fisherman.'

He couldn't tell if she was exaggerating.

They decided against going out to eat, ordered the Lebanese they'd promised each other – it turned out to be no more than a cold plate of aubergine mushed in a dozen different ways – and went to bed.

The mattress dipped in the middle.

'Christ!' Kevern said ruminatively, looking up at the flaking ceiling.

Ailinn agreed with him. 'Christ!'

iii

They took a late breakfast – mixed mushed aubergines again – in a room that must once have suggested a pasha's pavilion (mosaic tiled floor, mirrors on the ceiling, carpets on the walls), but now looked bored with itself – a street-corner bric-a-brac shop going out of business. Sensing that the permanent residents of the hotel weren't looking for conversation, Kevern and Ailinn kept their eyes lowered. They were served mint tea which Kevern failed to pour from the requisite height. 'It tastes better if you aerate it like this,' the only other person in the breakfast room not in a keffiyeh called across from a nearby table. He was holding his own glass teapot aloft as though he meant to take a shower from it. 'And you get more foam.'

Kevern, feeling like a country boy, thanked him.

'Where are you two from?' the man asked.

Kevern sneaked a look at Ailinn. How did she feel about talking to a stranger? She nodded imperceptibly. 'Port Reuben,' Kevern said.

The man, as broad as a door and dressed like a widely travelled photographer in khaki chinos and a cotton jacket with a thousand pockets, shook his head. 'Never heard of it. Sorry.'

'That's all right,' Kevern said. 'We aren't on the line about it. And you?'

'I'm not on the line about it either.'

If the man was a comedian, Ailinn wondered, how would her thin-skinned lover deal with him.

Kevern worried for her on the same grounds.

He tried a laugh. 'No, I meant where are you from.'

'Me? Oh, everywhere and nowhere. Wherever I'm needed.'

'Then you're needed here,' said Kevern, with a worldly flourish of his arm. 'Should we take sugar with this?'

The man asked if he could join them and joined them without waiting for an answer. The width of him was a comfort to Kevern. You needed a wide man to advise you in a strange place. Ailinn thought the same. He would have made a good father.

It turned out that he was a doctor employed exclusively by this and a number of other nearby hotels to attend to the mental welfare of their long-term guests. 'It keeps me busier than you would imagine,' he said, smiling at Ailinn, as though she, having to deal with the mental welfare of Kevern, would be able to imagine only too easily what kept him busy.

There were questions Kevern wanted to ask but he wasn't sure about the propriety of asking them while there were guests still eating. Reading Kevern's compunction, the doctor, who had introduced himself as Ferdinand Moskowitz, but call him Ferdie, leaned across the table as though to gather his new friends into his wide embrace. 'No one hears or cares what we're talking about,' he said. 'They're miles away. Depression can do that. It can make you indifferent to your surroundings, uninterested in yourself let alone other people.'

'And those who are not depressed?' Kevern asked.

Ferdie Moskowitz showed him a mouthful of white teeth. Kevern imagined him dazzling the Tuareg with them. 'No such animal here. The only distinction to be drawn is between neurotic depression and psychotic depression, and even then those who start out with the milder form very quickly develop the more serious. Dispossession does that.'

'We're all dispossessed in our way,' Ailinn said quickly. She wanted to say it before Kevern did. She could deal with her own pessimism better than she could deal with his. His slighted her. Slighted *them* – the love they felt for each other.

'Yes, and we're all depressed,' the doctor said. 'But in fact few of us are dispossessed as these poor souls are. You must remember that theirs is a culture that had already fallen into melancholy, long before' – he made an imaginary loop with his hand, from which he made as if to hang himself – 'long before you know what.'

'Not what they told us at school,' Kevern said. '*Fierce warrior people*,' he quoted from memory, '*who dispensed largesse and loved the good things in life . . .*'

'Ah, yes – Omar Khayyam via Lawrence of Arabia. *Come fill the cup . . .*'

Kevern closed his eyes, as though savouring something delectable, and tried to remember a line. '*Enjoy wine and women and don't be afraid* – isn't that how it went?'

'We read that at school as well,' Ailinn said, 'only our version was Enjoy but *do* be afraid.'

The doctor made a sound halfway between a cough and a snort.

'As though that was all they ever did,' he said. 'As though, between lying languorously on scented pillows and occasionally riding out to inconsequential battle in a sandstorm, they had nothing to do but wait for us to come and impose our values on them.'

Kevern shrugged. For himself, he wanted to impose his values on no one. He wasn't even sure he knew what his values were.

'Either way,' the doctor continued, 'that's not the real Omar Khayyam. He was a philosopher and a mystic not a hedonist, which of course you can't expect schoolboys – or schoolgirls – to understand. And as for the large-souled warrior of our romantic imagination – he vanished a long time ago, after believing too many lies and too many promises and losing too many wars. Read their later literature and the dominant note is that of elegy.'

'Our dominant note is elegy, too,' Kevern said. 'We've all lost something.'

Ferdinand Moskowitz raised an eyebrow. 'That's an easy thing to say, but you have not lost as the poor souls I treat have lost. At least you can elegise like a good liberal in your own country.'

'I don't think of myself as a good liberal,' Kevern said.

'Well, however you think of yourself, you have the luxury of thinking it in your own home.'

Kevern exchanged glances with Ailinn. Later on they would wonder why they had done that. Other than asking them to call him Ferdie – a name that upset Kevern to an unaccountable degree – what had Moskowitz said to irritate and unite them? Weren't they indeed, as he had described them, people who enjoyed the luxury of home? All right, Ailinn had spent her earliest years in an orphanage and had left the home made for her by her rescuers, but had she not found a new one with Kevern, hugger-mugger on a clifftop at the furthest extreme of the country? 'I cling on for dear life,' Kevern had told her once, making crampons of his fingers, but that was just his exaggerated way of talking. They had found a home in each other. So what nerve had the doctor touched?

'Wherever we live,' Kevern said at last – and his words sounded enigmatic to himself, as though enigma could be catching – 'we await alike the judgement of history.'

Ferdinand Moskowitz rattled his pockets and moved his lips like a man shaping a secret. 'We do indeed,' he said. 'But there are some things we don't have to wait for history to judge.'

'Such as?'

'Such as our using the people you see here – our grandparents using their grandparents – as proxy martyrs. We said we were acting in their interests when all along we were acting in our own. The truth is we didn't give a fig about their misery or dispossession. It was we who felt dispossessed. They were a handy peg to hang our fuming inferiority on, that was all. And once they'd given us our opportunity we left them to rot.'

'This isn't exactly rotting,' Kevern said.

'You haven't seen inside their heads . . .' He paused, then went on, 'Look, I know what you're thinking. These are the lucky ones, the rich and the powdered, born here to parents who were born here. The bombs didn't fall on them, because they financed the bombs. The banks didn't crash on them, because they owned the banks. They were spared the humiliations to which for years their poorer brothers were subjected. But that doesn't mean they don't feel those humiliations. Observe them at your leisure – their lives are sterile and they don't even have the consolation of being able to hate their enemies.'

This was all getting a bit too close to the bone for Kevern. He wasn't sure what to say. People didn't discuss war or WHAT HAPPENED, or the aftermath of either, in Port Reuben. It was not the thing. Not banned, just not done. Like history. WHAT HAPPENED – if WHAT HAPPENED was indeed what they were talking about – was passé. Was this why his father cautioned him against the Necropolis, because in the Necropolis they were still discussing a war that was long over? Was *Ferdie* Moskowitz the disappointment his father wanted to save him from?

'How so?' was the best response Kevern could come up with. This was like arguing through cotton wool. It wasn't that Kevern didn't have a view on the subject, he didn't know what the subject was.

'*How so*? You can't hate in retrospect, that's how so. You can't avenge yourself in retrospect. You can only smoke your pipes and count your beads and dream. And do you know what they fear most? That *our* history will make a mockery of events, extenuate, argue that black was white, make them the villains, ennoble by time and suffering those who made a profession out of their eternal victimhood, stealing and marauding on the back of a fiction that they'd been stolen from themselves.'

The wool descended further over Kevern's eyes. Soon he would not be able to breathe for it.

'*They* being . . . ?' he just managed to ask.

But the doctor had lost patience. No longer a father figure to either of them, he rose, bowed in an exaggerated manner to Ailinn, and left the breakfast room.

A moment later, though, he popped his head around the door and pulled a clownish face. 'The gone but not forgotten,' he said.

The phrase seemed to amuse him greatly for he repeated it. 'The gone but not forgotten.'

'I don't think Ferdie likes me,' Kevern said, after he disappeared a second time.

It was to become a refrain between them whenever Kevern sniffed a predator – 'I don't think Ferdie likes me.'

And Ailinn would laugh.

iv

That afternoon, with a light rain pattering against the scratched Perspex, they decided they would get Ailinn's phone fixed. The best places, the concierge told them, were in the north of the city and he didn't advise driving.

'Is it dangerous?' Kevern asked.

The concierge laughed. 'Not dangerous, just tricky.'

'Tricky to find?'

'Tricky to everything.'

He offered to call them a taxi but Ailinn needed a walk. They wandered aimlessly for an hour or more – Kevern preferred wandering to asking directions, because asking meant listening, and the minute someone said go straight ahead for a hundred metres then take a left and then a hundred metres after that take a right, he was lost. Occasionally a tout, dressed like a busker or a master of ceremonials at some pagan festival, stepped out of a doorway and offered them whatever their hearts desired. 'Do you have anything black?' Kevern asked one of them.

The tout looked offended. He was neither pimp nor racist. 'Black?'

'Like a black tee-shirt or jacket?'

The tout missed Kevern's joke. 'I could get you,' he replied. 'Where are you staying?'

Kevern gave him the wrong hotel. He wasn't taking any chances.

Finding themselves in a part of town where there was actually construction going on, they went into a café to escape the dust. A beefy, furiously orange-faced builder in brightly coloured overalls, covered in plaster, raised his head from his sandwich and looked Ailinn up and down. 'Tasty,' Kevern thought he heard him say. But he could have been clearing his throat or referring to his sandwich. The gesture he made to a second builder who entered the café, however, slowly twirling a probing finger in Ailinn's direction, was unambiguous. The new arrival took a look at Ailinn and fingered her impressionistically in return.

'What's that meant to signify?' Kevern asked them, looking from one to the other.

The builder with the inflamed, enraged face made a creaking motion with his jaw, as though resetting the position of his teeth, and laughed.

'Take no notice,' Ailinn said. 'It's not worth it.'

'You tell him, gorgeous,' the second builder said, opening his mouth and showing her his tongue.

The first builder did the same.

These are the gargoyles I missed in Ashbrittle, Kevern thought.

'Come on. Let's leave them to dream about it,' Ailinn said. She took Kevern by the elbow and led him out.

They were both strangers to the city, but Ailinn felt she could cope better in it than Kevern ever would.

Back on the street the rain was falling more heavily. 'Let's just jump in a taxi, get it sorted and then go home,' she said. 'I think we've been away long enough. I have a migraine coming on.'

It was a vicarious migraine, a migraine for him, a man who didn't have migraines.

Kevern felt guilty. His idea to come away, his idea to mooch about looking into the windows of ill-lit shops and see where they ended up, his idea to go into the coffee shop – his idea, come to that, to ask Ailinn out in the first place, his idea to kiss Lowenna Morgenstern, everything that was making life difficult for Ailinn – his idea.

There were few taxis and those that passed were uninterested in stopping. Kevern wasn't sure if their For Hire lights were on or off, but he thought some drivers slowed down, took a look at them, and then sped off. Could they see from their austere clothes, or their hesitant demeanour, that he and Ailinn weren't from round here and did they therefore fear they couldn't pay or wouldn't tip? Or was it simply something about their faces?

Ailinn had turned white. Seeing a taxi, Kevern made a determined effort to hail it, running into the street and waving his arms. The driver slowed, peered out of his window, drove a little way past them, and then stopped. Kevern took Ailinn's hand. 'Come on,' he said. But someone else had decided the taxi was for him and was racing on ahead of them. 'Hey!' Kevern shouted. 'Hey, that's ours.'

'What makes it yours?' the man shouted back.

He was wearing a striped grey and blue cardigan, Kevern noted with relief, as though that made him someone he felt confident he could reason with. And wore rimless spectacles. A respectable, soberly dressed person in his early thirties. With a woman at his side.

'Come on,' Kevern said, 'be fair. You know I flagged it down before you did. Didn't I, driver?'

The driver shrugged. The man in the cardigan was blazing with fury. 'You don't have to yell and scream,' he said.

'Who's yelling and screaming? I flagged the taxi down before you, and I expect you to accept that, that's all. This lady has a migraine. I need to get her back to our hotel.'

'And I have a wife and tired children to get home.'

'Then you can get the next taxi,' Kevern said, seeing no children.

'If it means so much to you that you have to behave in this insane manner, then take the taxi,' the man said, raising an arm.

Kevern wondered if the arm was raised to call another taxi or aim a blow. He felt a hand on his back. Was it a punch? In his anger, Kevern wouldn't have known if it was a knife going between his shoulder blades. 'Take your hands off me,' he said.

'Calm down, you clown, you've got what you want. Just get yourself into the taxi and pootle off wherever you belong.'

'Get your fucking hands off me,' Kevern said.

'Hey,' the man said. 'Don't swear in front of my children.'

'Then don't you fucking lay your hands on me,' Kevern said, still seeing no children.

What happened next he didn't remember. Not because he was knocked unconscious but because a great sheet of rage had come down before his eyes, and behind it a deep sense of dishonour. Why was he fighting? Why was he swearing? He was not a fighting or a swearing man. And he couldn't bear that Ailinn had seen him in the guise of either.

It was she who had pushed him into the taxi and got them

back to the hotel. 'Your hands are ice cold,' she told him when they were back in their room. Otherwise she said nothing. She looked, Kevern thought, as though made of ice herself.

He didn't know what time it was, but he fell into bed.

'I don't think Ferdie likes me,' he said before he fell asleep.

Ailinn did not laugh.

It was her suggestion, when they woke in the early hours of the morning, that they drive home without even waiting for breakfast. It was clear she didn't want a conversation about what had happened.

'Do you hate me?' he asked.

'I don't hate you. I'm just bewildered. And frightened for you.'

'Frightened?'

'Frightened of what might have happened to you. You didn't know who that man was. He might have been anybody.'

'He was a family man who didn't want his children to hear foul language, that's if there were any children. Though he didn't mind them seeing him pushing a stranger. There was nothing to be frightened of.'

'You don't know that. I was also frightened *about* you. I didn't like to see you like that.'

'Do you want me to explain?'

'No.' She meant no, not now, but it came out more final than that.

'I'm sorry,' he said.

'So am I.'

He couldn't bear leaving right away as she proposed. The thought of driving home in this hostile silence appalled him. You don't leave anywhere like that: it would feel too irresistibly as though they were leaving each other. Better to sit tight, with throbbing temples, and wait for the mood to change. How many marriages might have been saved if only the parties to it had waited – days, weeks, months, it didn't matter – for the mood to change?

'Let's get your phone fixed and then go,' he said.

He wanted to be back where they were before the swearing. And he was anxious to show her that her concerns were foremost in his mind. It was concern for her after all, his desperation to get her back to the hotel so she could sleep off her migraine, that made him fight for the taxi. Unless it was the responsibility he felt for her that had unhinged him. Was he not up to the job of looking after a woman? Did fear of failure unman him?

'I don't care about my phone,' she said.

'But I do. And I'd like an errand to clear my head.'

'To clear *your* head!'

'To clear both our heads.'

'So how do you propose we do this? Go outside and hail a taxi?'

So the punch came, whoever delivered it. But he still refused to capitulate to what it could have meant had he let it.

'I'll get the hotel to call us one,' he said.

He said it firmly. He was not going to allow looking after a woman to emasculate him.

v

It took an hour for a taxi to arrive but when it did the driver swung out of his cab to greet them, bowed low, introduced himself as Ranajay Margolis, looked up at the rain and produced an umbrella as a magician might produce a wand. He insisted on opening the passenger doors for them, one at a time, Ailinn's first.

Struck by his manners, Kevern asked where he was from originally.

Ailinn dug him. He had lived too long in Port Reuben where a black or Asian face was seldom seen. No one had entered the country from anywhere else for a long time. Every person's country of origin – regardless of whether they were a Margolis or a Gutkind – was this one. Wasn't that what made now so much better than then?

Kevern didn't mind the dig. So long as she was digging him they were together.

Ranajay Margolis was amused. He almost danced himself back into his seat. 'I am from here,' he said. 'As for *originally* that depends how far back you want me to go. Where are you from *originally*?'

Kevern held up a hand. He took the point.

Ailinn explained that they wanted to get her phone fixed.

'I'm just the man,' the driver said in his quicksilver manner, turning round frequently and flashing them his snowy teeth, 'but first I'll give you a tour.'

'We don't want a tour, thank you,' she said. 'Just my phone fixed.'

'There are special places for that,' the driver said. 'I know them all. But they aren't easy to find and some of them aren't very trustworthy.'

'We know, that's why we're asking you to take us.'

He bowed as he was driving. 'You sure you don't want a tour?'

'Certain.'

'In that case,' he said, raising a finger like an exclamation mark, as though to punctuate a great idea that had just come to him, 'we will have to go to where the Cohens lived.'

'The Cohens! I'm a Cohen,' Kevern said. He felt a burst of excitement as he said it. Ranajay Margolis had asked him where he was from originally. What if he was from here? Would he encounter people who looked like him on the streets? Uncles, nieces, cousins? Would they be sitting on benches – so many tall, angel-haired 'Cocos' with long faces – minding their language and wondering what their lives amounted to?

Ranajay studied his reflection in the driver's mirror. 'No,' he explained, 'I mean *real* Cohens.'

Kevern offered to show him his ID.

Ranajay shook his head. 'That changes nothing,' he said.

They drove north for about half an hour, along tense, surly streets, past stores selling Turkish vegetables, and then stores selling Indian vegetables, and then stores selling Caribbean vegetables, until they came to a suburb of houses built in a bygone, faraway style, Greek temples, Elizabethan mansions, woodland cottages, Swiss chalets, Malibu country clubs. No film set could have suggested lavish living with so little subtlety. But whatever their original ostentation, the mansions housed more modest domestic ambitions now. Indian children played on the street or stared out at the taxi through upper-storey windows. A handful of men in open-necked shirts played cards under a portico that might once have sheltered foreign dignitaries and maybe even royalty as they drank cocktails. Perhaps because no one could afford their upkeep, some of the grandest dwellings had fallen into disuse. Colonnades crumbled. Corinthian columns that must once have glowed with the phosphorescence of fantasy were dull in the drizzle, in need of replastering and paint. Yet this was no slum. Those houses that were inhabited looked cared for, the neat gardens and net curtains, the atmosphere of quiet industry – even the card-playing was businesslike – mocking the grandeur of those who'd originally occupied them. Many of the garages, large enough to take a fleet of Hollywood limousines – one for him, one for her, and something only marginally smaller for Junior – served as electrical or mechanics workshops and even retail outlets, though it was hard to imagine any passing trade. Signs promised prompt and efficient repairs to utility phones and consoles. Black-eyed adolescent boys sat cross-legged on walls, engrossed in their electronic toys, as though to advertise the competence of their parents' businesses.

The Cohens had lived here, Ranajay had said. What did he mean? Had it been a Cohen colony? Cohentown? He was adamant, anyway, that no Cohens lived here now, and that Kevern's family never had. But who was he to say that? How did he know?

Kevern's parents would never tell him where they had come from. It didn't matter, they'd said. It wasn't important. Don't ask. The question itself depressed and enraged them. Maybe it reminded them of their sin in marrying. But his father had warned him off the Necropolis. 'Don't go there,' he had said, 'it will dismay and disappoint you.' But he hadn't said 'Don't go to *Cohentown*, it will disappoint you.' Just don't go anywhere. Just stay in Port Reuben which – he might have added – will also disappoint you.

He didn't see how he could be disappointed when he had no expectations. But he had been excited when Ranajay had said Cohens had lived here. So there must have been some expectation in him somewhere, some anticipation, at least, that he had known nothing about.

Cohentown – why not?

What do I feel, he asked himself, thinking he should feel more.

What he felt was oppressed, as though there was thunder about.

He asked to be let out of the cab so he could smell the air. 'There's no air to smell,' Ranajay Margolis said. 'Just cooking.'

'Cooking's fine.'

Ranajay was insistent. 'Come. I will take you to the best place to have your phone fixed. I can get you a good deal.'

'Just give me a minute. I want to see if anything comes back to me.'

'You were never here,' Ranajay insisted. 'It's not possible.'

'I think that's for me to decide,' Kevern said.

Ranajay blew out his cheeks, stopped the car, got out with his umbrella, and opened Kevern's door. A group of children looked up, not curiously, not incuriously. He bore no resemblance to them but they weren't amazed by his presence. He had a thought. Were they used to sentimental visitors? Did other members of his family turn up here periodically to find themselves, to smell the air and see what they could remember?

This was silly. There were countless Cohens in the world. There was no reason to suppose that the Cohens whose neighbourhood, according to Ranajay, this had been, were *his* Cohens. But he fancied he would know if he stood here long enough. Birds navigate vast distances to find their way home. They must be able to tell when they are getting close. They must feel a pounding in their hearts. Why shouldn't he, navigating time, feel the same?

Most of the houses had long drives, but one had a front door on the street. He wondered if he dared look through the letter box, see if the silk runner was rumpled, see if the utility phone was winking on the hall table. But there were old newspapers stuffed into the letter box. Looking up, he saw that a number of the windows were broken. The disuse of this house suited him better than the subdued occupancy of the others. In the disuse he might reconnect to a line of used-up Cohens past. He closed his eyes. If you could hear the sea in a washed-up shell why shouldn't he hear the past in this dereliction? You didn't begin and end with yourself. If his family had been here he would surely know it in whatever part of himself such things are known – at his fingertips, on his tongue, in his throat, in the throbbing of his temples. Ghosts? Of course there were ghosts. What was culture but ghosts? What was memory? What was self? But he knew the danger of indulging this. Yes, he could persuade himself that the tang of happy days, alternating with frightful event, came back to him – kisses and losses, embraces and altercations, love, heartbreak, shouting, incest . . . whatever his father and mother had concealed from him, whatever they had warned him would dismay and disappoint him were he to recover any trace of it.

His temples throbbed all right. And since he was not given to migraines they must have throbbed with something else. Recollection? The anticipation of recollection? But it was so much folly. He was no less able to imagine fondness or taste bitter loss while sitting on his bench in Port Reuben. So Cohens had lived here once. And been happy and unhappy as other families had been. So what!

And anyway, *anyway* for Christ's sake! – it came as a shock to him to remember – Cohen was as much a given name as Kevern. He didn't know what his family name had really been when Cohens who were really Cohens roamed Cohentown. Cadwallader, maybe. Or Chygwidden. What was he doing chasing a past associated with a name that wasn't even his?

But then that precisely was the point, wasn't it. No one was meant to know who was, or who had been, who. No one was meant to track himself or his antecedents down. Call me Ishmael. Life had begun again.

Ailinn had come out of the cab and was watching him. 'Are you all right, my love?' she asked.

His relief knew no bounds. She'd called him 'my love'. Which must have meant the wretched taxi incident had been forgiven. He wanted to kiss her in the street. He took her hand instead and squeezed it.

He nodded. 'There's a strange atmosphere of squatting here,' he said, noticing a mother coming out to check on her children, and maybe on him too. He was struck by how softly she padded, as though not to wake the dead. 'They have the air of living lives on someone else's grave.'

'That's a quick judgement to leap to,' Ailinn laughed. 'You've been here all of five minutes!'

'It's not a judgement. I'm just trying to describe what I feel. Don't you think there's a queer apprehensive silence out here?'

'Well if there is, it might be caused by the way you're staring at everyone. I'd be apprehensive if I had you outside my door, trying to describe what you feel. Let's go now.'

'I don't know what it is,' he continued. 'It's as though the place is not possessed by its inhabitants.'

This annoyed Ranajay. 'These people live here quite legally,' he said. 'And have done for long, long times.'

'Don't worry,' Kevern said, 'I'm not claiming anything back.'

'It was never yours,' Ranajay said. 'Not possible.'

Never yours, like yesterday's taxi. Like Ailinn's honour in the café. Did ownership of everything have to be fought for in this city?

Ailinn feared that if Kevern didn't back off, their driver would leave them here. And then let Kevern see how unpossessed by its inhabitants it was. She lightly touched Ranajay's arm. 'I don't think he means to imply it was his,' she said.

Kevern suddenly felt faint. 'Let's get your phone fixed and then go back to the hotel,' he said. 'I've had enough of here.'

He climbed back into the taxi, not waiting for her to get in first.

He had heard his mother's voice. 'Kevern,' she called. Just that. 'Key-vern' – coming from a long way away, not in pain or terror, but as though through a pain of glass. Then he thought he heard the glass shatter. Could she have broken it with her voice?

It made no sense that she should be calling him. She hadn't been a Cohen except by marriage to his father, unless . . . but he wasn't thinking along those lines today, so why should he hear her calling to him in Cohentown?

Calling him in, or warning him to turn away? Away, he thought. He could even feel her hands on his chest. Go! Leave it, your father is right, it will dismay and disappoint you.

Such a strange locution: *dismay and disappoint*. Like everything else they'd ever told him – distant and non-committal. As though they were discussing a life that didn't belong to them to a son who didn't belong to them either.

It had always been that way. Even as they sat on the train going east, looking out at the snow, there was no intimacy. When the train finally pulls into the little station other families will be counted, sent this way and that way, and where necessary ripped from one another's arms. How does a mother say goodbye to her child for the last time? What's the kindest thing – to hang on until you are prised apart by bayonet, or to turn on your heels and go without once looking back? What are the rules of heart-break? What is the etiquette?

Kevern wonders which course his parents will decide on when the time comes and the soldiers subject them to their hellish calculus. Then, as though prodded by a bayonet himself, he suffers an abrupt revulsion, like a revulsion from sex or the recollection of shame, from the ghoulishness of memories that are not his to possess.

Appalled, Kevern hauls himself back from the stale monotony of dreams. Always the same places, the same faces, the same fears. Each leaking into the other as though his brain has slipped a cog. Dementia must be like this, nothing in the right place or plane, but isn't he a bit young for that? So he climbs, so he climbed, so he will go on climbing, back into the taxi taking him away, feeling fraudulent and faint.

Now it was Ranajay's turn to wonder if he'd caused offence. 'I'm only meaning this for your husband's sake,' he said to Ailinn, starting the vehicle up again. 'He could not ever have lived here. There is no one now existing who lived here.'

He looked as though he was going to cry.

'It's all right,' she said, putting an arm around Kevern who seemed to have snapped into a sleep. He hadn't fainted. Just gone from waking to sleeping as if at a hypnotist's command.

Ranajay was beside himself with distress. 'My fault, my fault. I shouldn't have brought you to this part,' he said.

'There is no reason why you shouldn't have brought us here,' Ailinn assured him. She felt she had spent the entire day making life easier for men. 'We asked you to.'

He inclined his head. 'Thank you,' he said. 'I am sure your husband is mistaken. There is no one left from here. They went away a long time ago. Before memory.'

Shut up, she wanted to scream. Shut up now!

But it pleased her that he had called Kevern her husband. *Husband* – she liked the ring of it. *Husband, I come.* Who was it who said that? How she would have felt to hear herself called Kevern's wife she wasn't sure. But OK, she thought, no matter that he had been half-crazed the entire time they'd been away. Yes, on the whole, OK. There were worse men out there.

They never did get her phone fixed. It would take three to five working days for the parts to arrive. And they weren't intending to stay around that long. She'd buy another.

They drove home to Port Reuben later that afternoon in careful, contemplative silence, neither wanting to discomfort the other with so much as a word or a thought. Every subject seemed fraught. They were both greatly on edge, but were still unprepared for what they found on their return. Someone had been inside the cottage.

'I knew it,' Kevern said before he had even turned the key in the door. 'I have known it the whole time we were away.'

'Are you absolutely certain?' Ailinn asked.

It was late and they were tired. The moon was full and a full moon plays tricks with people's senses. He could have been mistaken.

They had to shout over the roaring of the blowhole. No, he wasn't mistaken. He had looked through his letter box and what he had seen he had seen.

His silk runner had been interfered with.

How did he know that?

It was straight.

BOOK TWO

All that most maddens and torments; all that stirs up the lees of things; all truth with malice in it; all that cracks the sinews and cakes the brain; all the subtle demonism of life and thought; all evil, to crazy Ahab were visibly personified and made practically assailable in Moby Dick.

Herman Melville

ONE

A Crazy Person's History of Defilement, for Use in Schools

i

HAD WHOEVER IT was who straightened Kevern 'Coco' Cohen's silk runner been looking for something in particular, something corroborative of Kevern's guilt – no matter, for the time being, what the crime – it was unlikely to have been a little book written by his maternal grandmother, Jenna Hannaford, about which Kevern himself knew nothing. It would not anyway have been found. Jenna's daughter, Kevern's mother, destroyed it when she read it, recognising it to be the work of a crazy person. In that she would have met no resistance from its author. *A Crazy Person's History of Defilement, for Use in Schools* was Jenna Hannaford's own title.

'If you think any school is going to teach that, you're crazy,' her husband told her.

She smiled sweetly at him. She was an elegant woman with a long neck and a mass of yellow hair which she put up carelessly, piling it on top of her head like a bird's nest. He was short, suffered from over-curvature of the thoracic vertebrae and had no hair at all. But it wasn't all beauty and beast. She suffered from depression, had trouble buttoning her clothes because her fingers trembled, and dyed her hair. 'Do you think I don't know that?' she asked.

'Then why are you writing it?'

'Because I'm crazy.'

'Just don't let anyone see it.'

'Of course I won't. Do you think I'm crazy?'

Just don't let anyone was her husband's perpetual refrain. Just don't let anyone see, just don't let anyone hear, just don't let anyone know. He told her not to go out. It was just better that nobody knew she was there, or at least, since everybody did know she was there, just better that nobody saw her. He wasn't afraid she'd run off with someone with a straight back. He was just afraid.

'You worry too much about me, Myron,' she told him.

'I can't worry too much about you.'

'What will be will be,' she said.

She never finished her *Crazy Person's History of Defilement*. Work in progress was how she described it to herself. By that she meant she never expected it to be finished because the subject she was addressing would never be finished. But the other reason she didn't finish it was that she disappeared. Walked out one blowy September afternoon with her head held high, after warning her daughter Sibella not to expect too much happiness and telling her husband to cut down on his smoking, and was never seen again.

Off the cliffs into the sea? An accident? A leap?

Who knew?

Myron Hannaford never forgave himself. He believed in God but only to have someone to castigate himself to. 'I should have worried about her more,' he told Him.

Sibella kept her mother's papers in a little suitcase under her bed, not daring to read through them in case her mother returned and discovered they'd been tampered with. After her father died she was cared for by the boy she'd been brought up with – a relation ten years her senior, she wasn't sure from which side of the family, who longer ago than she could remember had come to live with them by the sea for his health's sake (though he wasn't allowed to go out and breathe the sea air), a gangling, morose, pale-faced fellow with a talent for woodwork (he took over Sibella's father's lathe as automatically as he took over her) and a secret love of syncopated music. When she was old enough, they married. It was never really discussed; it was simply assumed that that was what they would do. Who else was there for either of them?

And in most regards it made no material difference to the life they'd been living before they married.

She had already, in line with ISHMAEL, changed her name from Hannaford to Cronfeld, and as her cousin Howel had changed his to Cohen she didn't feel she had to make too big a change a second time.

On the eve of the wedding Sibella crept out of the cottage with her crazy mother's papers and threw them into the sea.

Because she was a little crazy herself she no sooner threw them into the sea than she knew she shouldn't have. What if a page was washed back up into the village on the tide and found by a fisherman? What if it was swept up into the blowhole and spewed out, paragraph by paragraph, for walkers to find? She scrambled down the rocks to see what she could rescue, then remembered she couldn't swim. There was nothing she could do but hope. As far as she knew, no page ever was recovered from the water in Port Reuben. But from that time forward she lived in a sort of half-absent dread of something turning up, still just about legible, on a roller heading for the West Australian coast or on an ice floe in the South Atlantic, the precise consequences of which for her family could not be foreseen, but without question they would be disastrous.

If you want something to be destroyed for ever, her mother had warned her when she was small, you have to set fire to it and watch it burn away to nothing. It was a frightening time, the little girl knew, though she didn't understand what made it so. Her father had never been more agitated. He wouldn't allow the radio to be played and if anyone knocked on their door they didn't open it. Once, when they heard people coming, he held her to him and put his hand over her mouth. 'If you aren't quiet,' he told her, when the visitors had gone, 'we'll have to put you in a drawer.'

She thought she heard her parents crying in the night.

Her mother's words about the finality of fire stayed in her mind. She asked her if fire burned everything.

'Almost everything.'

'So what doesn't it burn?'

Her mother never took time to deliberate. She had an answer to every question ready, as though she knew it was going to be asked. 'Love and hatred,' she said. 'But I might be wrong about love.'

'How can you burn love?' Sibella wanted to know.

'By burning the people who feel it.'

'So why can't you burn hatred?'

'Because hatred exists outside of people. I liken it to a virus. People catch it. Disgust the same. That's another thing that's flame-proof. It lives for ever. So my advice to you is never to inspire it.'

'Love or disgust?'

'Ha! The cynical answer is "both". But I am not a cynic. Just a pessimist. So my prayer for you is that you will inspire love, but not disgust.'

'How do I do make sure I don't?'

Her mother looked at her and this time thought a while before answering. Then she laughed her crazy woman's laugh. 'You can't!'

It was because she feared her mother was right and that hatred and disgust were indestructible by flame that Sibella threw the book into the sea. It had disgusted her father, it disgusted her mother even as she was writing it, and in so far as she could understand its ravings, it disgusted Sibella. So the bottom of the sea, where it could disgust the fish, was the best place for it.

As for what her mother told her about fire, she tried to live by it thereafter. She sat on the cliffs above the cottage and burned things – papers, letters, photographs, handkerchiefs, wild flowers. Sometimes, after she was married, she thought she would have burned her jewellery had it been flammable.

She had a lot of time, while her husband worked on his lathe and Kevern was at school, in which to worry and remember, though she couldn't remember ever coming to Port Reuben which was not, her mother had once inadvertently let slip, her place of birth.

'So where was my place of birth?' she asked.

'Somewhere else.'

'Where?'

'Somewhere far.'

'Was it nice?'

'Nowhere's nice.'

'Why did we leave?'

Her mother ran her fingers through her distracted hair. 'It seemed a good idea at the time.'

Her father overheard. 'It *was* a good idea at the time,' he said. 'It still is a good idea. We're alive, aren't we? Just don't answer any questions.'

'What questions?'

'And don't *ask* so many questions either.'

And that was all they told her. Her mother kissed her on the head and returned to the kitchen table to go on writing the book that never could and never would be finished. There wasn't much talking in the house. Her father, too, preferred silence to conversation and work to pleasure. Both her parents seemed never to want to finish what they were doing, as though the moment they finished they'd be finished themselves.

She remembered how her mother worked, with a bright light to ease her depression always shining in her face, surrounded by books (which to Sibella's sense only made the depression more intense), twisting loops of her hair around her forefinger, her head propped between two fists when she was thinking, and then her mouth opening and closing as she wrote, occasionally laughing like a hyena, though whether at something she had read or something she had written, something that amused her or something that made her angry – because crazy people laughed when they were angry as well as when they were amused – Sibella was never sure.

'Don't read over my shoulder, Sibella,' her mother would tell her when she tried to find out, 'you're blocking my light,' but in so absent-minded a manner that Sibella felt it was all right to stay where she was and go on reading. She understood little of it at the time, not even the drawings and photographs her mother glued into the book, and wouldn't have sworn that she understood it later when she had all the time in the world to absorb its meanings. But a few elusive phrases lodged in her mind – 'when they saw a moneylender they saw a bloodsucker, for those two defiled substances, money and blood, circulate alike'; 'whoever cleans bodies is hated irrationally for doing what needs to be done'; 'let my child be brought up to the highest level of civilisation, she will still always be thought of as a divine executioner, the child of divine executioners, and must always live in expectation of execution herself' – and they were sufficient to persuade her that it had to be destroyed.

ii

Aged forty-five, and appearing older – while not growing crooked like her father, she had never possessed an iota of her mother's looks – she tried to inspire love, as her mother had hoped she would, and had an almost affair with Madron Shmukler the village butcher. 'You are nothing to write home about yourself,' she told him when he expressed surprise that she attracted him given that she wasn't at all pretty and not remotely his type. He too was forty-five and looked older. They didn't bother to go through the routine of discussing their otherwise-engaged spouses, it was all so predictable. He would deliver meat to the cottage and when the coast was clear they would climb the cliffs separately, as though going in different directions – though there was nowhere for either of them to go – and then meet on Port Reuben Head, which gave them a good view of anyone approaching. Here they would sit on the grass, surprised to be attracted to each other, and half-heartedly – no, quarter-heartedly, she thought – make companionable if perfunctory contact. He would put his hands on her breasts, which were still surprisingly soft under an item of clothing he was unable to name, and she would put her hands inside his trousers. What she found was surprisingly soft too.

Could you call that an affair? Neither of them thought so but they went on doing it, intermittently, until they were too old to climb the cliffs.

She had picked him out at the start of it because he was a butcher and she wanted someone to talk about blood to. Did he feel it polluted him?

'Do I feel it *what*?'

'What I want to know is whether butchers feel unclean. Do they fear they have dirty hands?'

He took his own hands out of her shirt – was it a shirt? – and examined them. 'Look for yourself,' he said. 'You have to wash a lot in my line of work.'

'No, I mean morally unclean. Spiritually . . .'

'Cutting chops?'

'Slaughtering . . .'

'I don't slaughter. I'm more like an undertaker. The animals come to me already dead, but instead of burying them I cut them up and sell them to you.'

Theirs was first and foremost a commercial relationship, he didn't want her to forget. Though later, as a sign of his maturing fondness, he didn't charge her.

He reached for the worn handbag she carried everywhere with her, though she kept almost nothing in it. 'Same with a tanner,' he said. 'Whoever treated the leather for this old thing didn't actually skin the animal.'

She didn't like the way he handled her bag. 'But you're still a link in the chain,' she said.

He stared at her in bafflement. What did she mean? Who was she? What was he doing with her? She was small and round, with flickering blue eyes and discoloured ping-pong-ball cheeks, and wore old-fashioned clothes. She reminded him of Miss Klug, one of his old primary-school teachers, unless what she reminded him of was how Miss Klug had made him feel – embarrassed to be her favourite, but safe. He was nothing to write home about himself, as Sibella had reminded him, but his butcher's brawn and innocent blue eyes had excited a few women over the years, and but for his being married and having four sons, he wouldn't have been embarrassed to be seen with any of them. Sibella, though, was not a woman he wanted anyone to know about. Was she crazy?

'A link in what chain?' he asked.

She laughed, reminding herself suddenly of her mother. 'The defilement chain.'

'I don't know what that means.'

'Do you feel that the part you play in killing animals – I know you don't actually *kill* them – I take your point about undertakers and tanners – but do you feel that there's blood on your hands and that people treat you differently because of it?'

He wondered if that was the longest question he'd ever been asked. He flicked away an ant that was crawling up her leg. 'Why would people treat me differently?'

She remembered the Untouchables of India, photographs of whom her mother found in magazines and pasted into her crazy person's history. Their lowly status, according to her mother, had many explanations but none so telling as their original association with blood. They were their society's ritual murderers, and as such considered unclean. The Burakumin of Japan – information about whom her mother had also collected – the same. Butchers, undertakers, slaughtermen, spillers of blood, killers of gods. And the taboo against touching them could never be broken. They had death on them, and whoever had death on him was outcast. Illogical, because someone had to deal with the dead, the tasks they performed were indispensable and even sacred, but logic had nothing to do with defilement.

'Because they can't forgive the blood,' Sibella said.

Madron shook his head. 'Well that's what you say, but they forgive mine fine enough.'

She shrugged but returned to the subject often. It almost became their love talk. Death, defilement, ritual murderers, sacred executioners.

'Put another record on, girl,' he would say to her.

And she would try. Sometimes, lying with her head against his chest, listening to the hungry screeching of the seagulls, looking up at the undersides of their ugly, torpedo bodies, she would almost succeed.

But she was never free of the sensation that she disgusted him. Which was strange because it was he – a man who dabbled in blood for a living – who was supposed to disgust her.

She loved him, after a fashion, nonetheless. And missed him more intensely than she thought she would when he died, more intensely even than she missed her parents. Was that, she wondered, because in their agitated distance from her they had been half dead already. She could barely remember her mother's disappearance. As for how her father died, she realised with shame that she didn't know. Howel told her it had happened. That she did remember. 'I'll be looking after you now,' he said.

Poor Madron had a heart attack, that was all. One of those quiet ones in the bath. She hoped she hadn't been instrumental in bringing it on. Not by making love, which between them had never been strenuous, but by making him feel dirty. Had she talked his heart into stopping?

She would have liked to kiss his perplexed brow one more time but she understood she couldn't see him. She suffered the terrible fate of all mistresses of married men in that she didn't dare show her face at his funeral.

'Don't show your face.' Where had she heard that before?

It was on the seventh anniversary of his death – almost certainly not coincidentally – that she set fire to her fingers.

TWO

Friends

i

'WE SHOULD NEVER have gone away,' Kevern said to Ailinn when they were inside.

She felt he was blaming her, though the trip had been his idea.

'Can you tell yet if anything's been taken?' she asked.

'It's not what's been taken. I have nothing it would be worth anyone's while to take. It's what's been *seen* that concerns me.'

He stood at the window, not wanting to look around, grinding his fists into his eyes.

'Your feet,' Ailinn said. 'I've only just noticed.'

'What?'

'They're too big.'

He stared at her.

'I'm trying to cheer you up with a joke,' she said.

She stood forlorn in the middle of the little sitting room, not knowing where to put herself, how to help, what to say. When Kevern was at a loss he joked, so she thought she should try the same. But the only effect of her joke was to remind him of something and send him flying up the stairs. She heard him banging about, like a wild animal trapped in someone's loft. After ten minutes he came back down, looking ashen. 'Have they been up there?' she asked.

'*They*?'

'Anyone?'

He fell into an armchair and shrugged. 'Must have been. Everything's too neat.'

'So nothing's gone?'

'Hard to say. My father's records are still there. And I think all his books. That's something. If they wanted to get me on an heirloom charge they'd have taken those. But who knows what they've read, or listened to, or photographed?'

She couldn't help herself. '*They*?'

'I think you should go,' he said.

She went over to him and kissed the top of his head. 'I can't leave you alone in this state,' she said.

'I don't know what you mean by "this state". I am how I always am.'

'Then I can't leave you in that state. Come on – discuss it with me. What do you think's happened?'

He sat forward and dropped his head between his knees. 'Ahab's been,' he said.

One detail he didn't mention: whoever had tidied up his runner had been for a lie-down in his bed.

ii

She didn't want to leave him in any state but she had no choice. 'I need to sleep this one out alone,' he said.

She offered to take the couch but he begged her to go. 'Just for tonight,' he said. 'This is my doing. I was the one who kissed Lowenna Morgenstern.'

'One of the many.'

'You know what I mean.'

'You think this is about her?'

'No. But it's still my fault.'

'You aren't going to do anything silly,' she said.

'Like what? Leave the country?'

She kissed his non-responding lips, noticing for the first time that there were dry serrations in them and that his breath was sour, then she walked back slowly, heavily, through the village to Paradise Valley. I feel a hundred, she thought. A drunken man called out to her. 'I want to bite you,' he said. She laughed. I'm a hundred and he wants to bite me. 'You'll break your teeth,' she dared to call back. But he was too unsteady to take her up on the challenge. A couple snogged violently against a dry-stone wall. Making the beast. A good description of them. A thing of scales and claws. Prehistoric. Kevern and Lowenna, she thought. But she agreed with his assessment that this – supposing he had not imagined it all – was not about Lowenna. As she pushed open the first of the field gates to the Valley a cat ran across her feet. A bad omen according to her adoptive mother. When a cat ran across your feet someone was going on a long journey. And why was that bad? Because you would never see them again.

Her heart fluttered.

Did Kevern's bitter gibe about leaving the country mean anything? Did any of his gibes mean anything? For their own good, people were discouraged from leaving the country – assuming they had any notion of what or where any other country was – but there was always a way if you were desperate, particularly if you lived by the sea and had the money to persuade one of the local fishermen to smuggle you out. You'd never be heard of again. In all likelihood the fisherman would throw you overboard once you were out of sight of the mainland. But at least you'd achieved what you wanted and got away. Why, though, would Kevern want that? He'd told her he loved her. He'd told her he'd never been – and had never in his life expected to be – so happy. So why? And if he wasn't running from the police, who was he running from? Ahab, he'd said. Ahab! Ahab was hers. She felt possessive of him, and angry with Kevern. Before he met her, he had not been troubled by any Ahab. Lampoons, yes. Harpoons, no. What was he doing purloining her terror?

iii

She found Ez up, playing patience and listening to love ballads on the utility console.

'Heavens,' Ez said, 'what brings you home?'

'Trouble.'

'Did the trip go badly?'

'No, the trip went well. Or at least we went well. What we didn't like we didn't like together. It was what we found when we got back.'

Ez put away her cards. 'I'll make tea,' she said, 'unless you'd like something stiffer.'

'Stiffer.'

The older woman poured them a brandy. Rather ceremoniously, Ailinn thought, as though this was a conversation she'd been expecting, was waiting for even, and the brandy had been bought for just such an event. Brandy – when did they ever drink brandy together?

'So . . .?'

'So . . .?'

'So what was it exactly that you found when you got back?'

'Somebody broke into Kevern's cottage while we were away.'

'Was there damage?'

'No. They'd tidied it up.'

'That's an unusual break-in. Was much taken?'

'As far as I could tell – as far as Kevern could tell – nothing.'

'Could you have been mistaken?'

Ailinn was not prepared to tell Ez that Kevern's rug had been straightened, because that would have necessitated her explaining why it was always left rumpled, and that would have been to betray her lover to her friend. She trusted Ez but that was not the point. You don't trust anyone with another person's secrets.

'He's very alert to the slightest change,' she said. 'He knows if anyone's leaned on his gate or sniffed the scent out of one of his roses.'

'Roses? You never said he was a gardener.'

'He isn't. I was being facetious. I'm sorry, I'm upset.'

'Do you know what I think?' Ez said. She was a *do you know what I think* kind of a woman. She assumed people went to her to hear homilies. As, indeed, they often did. 'I think you were both tired after a long drive. And if Kevern is as sensitive to any vibration in the vicinity of his cottage as you say, he was probably anxious the whole time you were away and simply found what he'd feared finding.'

'You are very sure of everything,' Ailinn said. She felt she'd been forced to take a side and the only side she could take was Kevern's.

Ez, she noticed, coloured. For all her intrusiveness, she tried to take a relaxed attitude to Ailinn's worries, half listening, half humouring, in the way of an older person, a concerned relation or a teacher, who knew that things usually worked out tolerably well in the end. The better a friend you were, the more cheerful a front you presented, was Ez's philosophy. A cup of tea, a moral lesson, a hug. She was doctorly, motherly, and even a touch professorial, at the same time. Ailinn had liked the contrarieties of her personality from the moment she met her in the reading group. She dressed modestly, in button-up cardigans and long skirts but liked hobbling about, for short periods, on high heels. Crimson high heels, as though she kept an alternative version of herself under her skirt. She had the quiet, respectful manner of a librarian, and no sense of humour to speak of, but if anything was said which she thought might be designed to amuse her she would choke with laughter, spluttering like a schoolgirl, or throwing back her head and showing how beautiful, before it lost its smoothness, the arc of her throat had once been. She was on her own now but she hadn't always been, Ailinn surmised. There'd been some personal tragedy in her life. A man she'd loved had run away or died. She carried a torch for someone. She burned a little candle in her heart. That was what the crimson shoes were doing – keeping a spark alive. Ailinn even wondered if this was his cottage, whoever he was, or whether they'd had their affair here, in this dripping corner of Paradise Valley where mushrooms would grow out of your shoes if you didn't wear them for a day. Was that why she'd asked Ailinn along – so that she had reason to hold herself together, so that she wouldn't give way to morbidity? In which case Ailinn's falling in love with Kevern and all but moving out of the Valley was inconsiderate. Did that explain the unwonted attentiveness of Ez's manner tonight, the way she appeared to be counting syllables and listening to pauses? Did she *want* to hear that something was amiss between them?

'No, I'm not sure of anything,' she said. 'I was just looking at the situation from all angles.'

'What if it's the police?' Ailinn wondered aloud. 'What if they really do suspect him?'

'But nothing was taken from the cottage, you say.'

'Well that's what Kevern said. But he didn't exactly give himself time to check.'

'You can usually tell.'

'Can you?'

'You can usually tell when something of your own, something that matters to you, has been taken. You just know.'

Ailinn looked at her. What a lot Ez suddenly *just knew*. She took another sip of the brandy. 'What did you do, Ez?' she asked. 'What did you do before you became book-group police?'

Ez laughed – but not, on this occasion, like a young girl. 'That's an amusing concept,' she said. 'I'm sure you didn't think I was policing any of the meetings you came to. I just chose the books.'

'Exactly. You policed what we read. Were you a different kind of policeman before that?'

'I was an administrator.'

'Administering what?'

'Oh, this and that. I kept an eye open.'

'On whom?'

'Good question. Other people who were keeping an eye open.'

Perhaps it was the brandy talking, but Ailinn suddenly propped her elbows on the table, supported her head in her hands and stared hard into her friend's face. 'What's this all about, Ez?' she asked.

'*This*?'

'Why did you bring me here? Why were Kevern and I thrown into one another's arms? Why did you force me to ring him when we'd broken up? Why did someone break into his house while we were away?'

'A: I brought you here because you were – because you are – my friend. B: I am not aware that you and Kevern were thrown into each other's arms. I thought you said it was love at first sight. C: As for Kevern's house – I have no idea why someone would have broken in, just as you have no idea whether anyone actually did.'

'Then why are you annoyed with me?'

'I am not in the slightest bit annoyed with you.' She reached out to stroke Ailinn's cheek. 'I am concerned about you, that's all.'

'Then why are your hands cold?'

'I didn't know they were.'

'And why are you concerned? You are never concerned for me. Not in this way. How many times have you told me I was someone in whom you had absolute faith? And what did that mean, anyway?'

Perhaps it was the brandy talking again, but she began to cry. Not a flood, just a trickle of soft tears that were gone almost as soon as they appeared.

'You're very tired. I think you should go to bed,' Ez said.

'Yes, I think so too. But I won't sleep. I will lie there all night wondering.'

'Wondering who broke in?'

'Wondering whether he was serious when he spoke about leaving the country.'

'Kevern said he was going to leave the country?'

'Not exactly. But he allowed the idea to float before me, like a threat.'

'We need to talk,' Ez said. And this time had Ailinn felt her hands she would have discovered they weren't just cold, they were frozen.

THREE

The Women's Illness

Monday 25th

NOT NORMALLY A diary day, but there are things I have to get down before they escape me.

Bloody Gutkind!

Looking on the bright side, as it is my nature to do, the decline of Gutkind's fortunes, following his most recent act of lumbering zealotry, must herald an improvement in mine. Funny how fate – the divine juggler – balances the fortunes of men with such precision, so that with each rise or fall we vacate space, not just for any old rival, but for someone we have a particular reason for hating. It was to yours truly, anyway, that the powers that be turned to minimise the damage Gutkind was causing. First of all the clown needed to be called off Kevern Cohen, and who better than me, given that I'd taught him briefly (Gutkind, that is) as a mature student, impossible as it is to believe that so unimaginative a man could ever have flirted with the idea of a second career in the Benign Visual Arts, though the Benign Visual Arts, I have to say, did not flirt back – who better, I repeat, than someone with my authority to remind him of the limits of his? Nothing too heavy-handed, just a quiet, *entre nous* suggestion – implicating no one higher up – that he back off. Why break a butterfly on a wheel and all that. Since you're acquainted with him, Professor, you can intimate our disfavour, was the flavour (the flavour of their disfavour is nice, don't you think?) of their communication to me. My knowing

Kevern as well, of course, gave me extra ammunition. 'I've been watching Cohen for some time,' I could get away with saying to Detective Inspector Gutkind, 'and nothing I have seen suggests he would harm a hair of a woman's head, let alone do what was done to poor Lowenna Morgenstern, so please don't bother your own pretty little head about him any further. Kevern Cohen? Mr Lovespoon himself! Are you joking? A policeman of all people should know there are some men who are incapable of committing a murder because they know they'd never get the blood off their hands. Can you imagine our friend Kevern "Coco" Cohen scrubbing underneath his fingernails? He'd be there, crouched over himself, washing until Doomsday. Don't make me laugh, Detective Inspector. The country's crawling with ruffians. Go bag yourself one of those.'

How it was that Gutkind became first an acquaintance and subsequently a student of mine is a story in itself. We met through our wives, is the short of it. They had become friends in the course of attending Credibility Fatigue classes together. And that, too, is a story in itself. It's always the women who go a little wobbly in the matter of WHAT HAPPENED – probably as a consequence of giving or anticipating giving birth, unless it's a more generally diffused hormonal agitation – whereupon some stiffening of their resolve is called for. I can't speak for Mrs Gutkind, who has since left her husband – for which, I have to say, no sane person could blame her – but my wife, Demelza, fell a while back into terribly depressed spirits, questioning the point of saying sorry all the time when by all official accounts (as indeed by mine) there was nothing really to say sorry for, questioning the way we lived our lives, questioning the powers that be, even questioning me, the person who puts food on her table. 'Nothing makes any sense to me,' she'd complain. 'I feel a pall over everything, I feel the children are fed lies at school, I feel I was fed lies at school, I suspect you're feeding lies to your students, we are supposed to have mended what went wrong, except that we are told nothing went wrong, but if it's not safe to go out on to the streets – not safe here, in fucking sleepy Bethesda! – it's as though we're all in a trance, like zombies, pretending, what are we pretending Phinny, what aren't we saying, what aren't you saying, what are these little jobs you say you have to do, other women . . . are you seeing other women? Except I don't feel here' – her hands upon her lovely breasts – 'that you are seeing other women, it feels more as if you've taken to religion or are going out to drink with aliens or someone, is that what you're doing, or are we the aliens, are we from another planet, Phinny, because increasingly I don't feel I'm from this one . . .' And more along such loopy lines.

The doctor, at my instigation, prescribed antidepressants.

Credibility Fatigue classes were my idea too. Between ourselves, dear diary, I'd had a minor professional fling – our both being professors of illusions of sorts – with Megan Abrahamson, the woman who ran the classes in Bethesda, a stern, blue-eyed beauty who'd fallen into a terrible depression herself when she was giving birth to her first child and so knew from the inside exactly what Demelza and others like her were going through. 'What we fear as mothers-to-be,' she explained to me, 'is bringing our child into a dangerous, deceitful world. We see a threat whenever anyone approaches us and we hear a lie in everything that's said. It's the protective instinct gone haywire. So when you learn about WHAT HAPPENED, IF IT HAPPENED you are of a mind to say no ifs or buts about it, it happened, and obviously shouldn't have happened, or we wouldn't all still be so cagey about it, saying sorry while insisting there's nothing to say sorry for. You want, you see, the truth and nothing but the truth for your baby. It isn't you who isn't seeing straight, you think, it's everybody else. In your own eyes you are getting to the bottom of a truth that has been obfuscated, no matter that the person doing the obfuscating is you. It's at this point that I find some straight-talking history, painful as it is, is what's required. "OK, you asked for it," I say. I show them classified documents and photographs: this is what those whom you fear were the innocent victims of what happened were responsible for, I say; this is the damage they wrought, this is the weaponry they unloosed on defenceless peoples, these are the countries they laid waste in their baseless, neurotic, opportunistic fear of being laid waste themselves, these are the bitter fruits of their egoistic policy of "never again", this is how they justified it here, in our parliament and in our newspapers, this is the misery of which they were the authors, these are their faces, these are their words, this is their history, repeated and repeated again wherever they set foot, sorrowful to themselves but a thousand times more sorrowful to those whose necks they trod on and who, when they could finally take no more, trod back, that's if they did, and these are their confessions, the expressions of self-loathing, the acts of self-immolation, the orgy of introverted hate they unleashed on one another as a last expression of an ancient culpability for which they knew, better than anyone else, there could be no redemption. Yes, it breaks the heart, but WHAT HAPPENED, if indeed it happened, was at the last visited by them upon themselves . . .'

I could have kissed her.

In fact I did kiss her.

To what degree these classes put Demelza's concerns to rest I have no idea. She has always been an obstinate, at times even a hysterical, woman. But she certainly turned more placid and glazed-eyed once she'd completed the course. Could have been the antidepressants, I accept, but I like to think that demonstrable truth played its part.

Gutkind and I shared a drink at the bar close to the Credibility Fatigue Centre from time to time while waiting for our wives. He was more angry with his than I was with mine. 'Some bleeding heart has got to her,' he said.

I wondered – *de haut en bas*, professor to police constable, which was all he was in those days – in what way someone had 'got' to her.

He was needled by my asking. 'Women talk to each other,' he said.

His eyes could be too fierce for his complexion. When they blazed, as they were blazing now, they burned out the little natural colour he possessed. In fairness to him I should say that most of the men in the pub we were drinking in looked the same. Coals of fire burning in every face. Just possibly they too were waiting for their wives, though they had the air of frequenting such places as this, as indeed did Gutkind, whereas for me pub-going was an exceptional circumstance. Regulars or not, they knew in their bones I wasn't Bethesda born, they could smell the outsider on me. I came once with Kevern Cohen and I feared there was going to be a lynch party. Two aphids! Why did that make them so angry? If they had to mark their awareness of our difference why didn't they just laugh at us? Or come over to touch our skin? 'Jesus God Almighty, it's skin remarkably similar to ours! Let's be friends.' But no, they snarled and ground their knuckles into the bar, exchanging glances with one another as though each felt it was his neighbour's place to raise an arm against us, and the fact that no one did was a species of betrayal and ultimately shame. Was the impotence they felt another reason for mistrusting us the more? 'Those you don't kill when you should, you end up hating with a fury that is beyond murderousness,' Kevern said as we were urinating in adjoining booths. In fact I was urinating and Kevern was waiting for me to finish. He found it impossible, he confided, to pass water in the presence of another man. 'What about a woman?' I enquired. 'Can any man pass water in the presence of a woman?' he asked, in what was not, I believe, a feigned astonishment. 'Demelza and I do it all the time,' I told him.

I thought he was going to throw up.

It struck me as a good job that no locals were present to witness Kevern's fastidiousness. They would have been still more inclined to lynch him. I have thought about what he said many times. Not on the subject of urinating in company but on the subject of hating those it would have been better that you'd killed. Was he right? And why such murderous hatred in the first place? I could only suppose that the living evidence of someone and somewhere else – the someone and somewhere else those pub regulars could smell on us the minute we entered the room – entirely undermined their confidence in the sufficiency of who and where they were. Are we so precarious in our sense of self that the mere existence of difference throws us into molecular chaos? Is it electrical? And was it even possible that Kevern's inability to pass water in my company had a comparable effect on me? I'm not saying I wanted to kill him on account of his extreme niceness in the matter of a quick piss, but I don't rule out the possibility that I did. Joking. No real danger, of course, because I've read too many poems and seen too much art to be a man of violence – art and poetry being what those troglodytic aphid-haters lacked to turn them from monsters into men.

I didn't convey any of these thoughts to Gutkind, who struck me as a bit of a trog himself, a brooding more than a thinking being anyway. 'She's got it into her head that I see plots everywhere,' he was saying when I returned from my reflections. His wife he was talking about. 'And you've got it into your head that someone's been plotting to get her to think that?' I replied. He eyed me narrowly. I knew what he was thinking. 'Supercilious swine!' But you get that a lot in my profession. The world does not care for professors, even though for a while it was hoped that a number of the worst sort had been thinned out in the purges.

I ordered more drinks and proposed a toast to the course. 'Megan Abrahamson should sort her out proper,' I said, trying to sound like a local. He shook his head, not doubting my confidence but annoyed that a wife of his needed to be sorted out at all. Evidently he took it as a slur on his manhood and position. 'In my line of work,' he said – from which I took him to imply that my line of work wasn't work at all – 'you rarely see an effect without a cause. I don't say every victim has been playing head games with the culprit, but more often than not a crime could have been averted had the victim been more circumspect.' I nodded my approval at his use of 'circumspect'. Fair's fair – if you mark a man down for inconsequence you should also mark him up for vocabulary. 'And if there's a reason why one person's been attacked,' he went on, without showing me any gratitude, 'there sure as hell has to be a reason why a couple of hundred thousand were.'

'If they were.' At any time it seemed necessary to me to throw that in, but with our wives currently receiving corrective instruction from Megan Abrahamson it seemed especially important to be punctilious.

'I grant your if in so far as it relates to eventuation,' Gutkind said, 'but not in so far as it relates to provocation.'

Get him, I thought. But put this sudden turgescence of language down to police school.

I took his point. In the matter of deserts he was an unreconstructed non-iffer. What had happened had had to happen in his little, heretical policeman's book, no ifs about it. Unlike our women, who in their illness feared they were complicit in covering up something terrible, Gutkind believed everyone else was complicit in covering up something grand. No ifs or buts: it had needed to happen and only fell short of a desirable outcome in so far as it could be shown – either on account of faint-heartedness on the one side, or a diabolical cunning on the other – not to have happened at all. That his wife had trouble with the logic of his frustration drove him almost to madness. As I understood it, her comprehension halted at the moment he denied a thing he so patently approved. 'Did it happen or didn't it?' she had screamed at him. Yes, as an idea, he had explained to her, no, as a realisation of that idea. 'So why are we saying sorry?' That was a good question, he agreed. They were saying sorry over the intention. 'Which in that case,' she persisted, 'must have been a bad intention.' No, no, no! It was good intention ineffectively carried out. 'So are we saying sorry for that? Sorry we didn't do it better? That doesn't sound much of an apology to me.' 'Then don't say it for fuck's sake!' Gutkind had exploded. I wouldn't have been surprised to learn he snogged her after that. If only to have something tangible to say sorry for himself.

'All's well that ends well,' I said, as we finished our drinks, more as a way of calming him down than anything else.

'Except it doesn't end, does it?' he said. 'People like our wives won't allow it.'

'I mean it ends well,' I said, 'in that one way or another the thing you desired was achieved.'

I could see he was about to tell me that it hadn't ended to his satisfaction at all. What the hell did he want, this denier with a broken heart – a rerun? I raised my hand to suggest that I was out of steam. Once a man starts comparing your wife to his wife it's wise to bring the conversation to an end. But he must have liked something about me, or been impressed by the advantage an education in the Benign Visual Arts clearly gave me in our conversation, because about six months later he enrolled as a mature student.

Six months after that I failed him. It wasn't that he wrote badly, just that his conspiracy-theorist's view of art made every artist the victim of some other artist's malevolence, Masaccio dying before he was thirty thanks to the machinations of Fra Angelico, Lautrec having been thrown off his horse by Pierre Puvis de Chavannes, Constable . . . but there was no end of it. 'Art isn't war,' I told him when discussing his papers. 'Isn't it!' he said, storming out of my office.

So no matter how much time had passed it wasn't going to be easy, I thought, taking one thing with another, to persuade him to leave Kevern 'Coco' Cohen to me. But when I got to him he was already apprised of the official view of his breaking into Kevern's cottage. 'I know, I know,' he said. 'I've been a naughty boy.'

'Who told you?'

'You're probably more Everett's man than I realise,' Rozenwyn said, noting Kevern's reserve. 'But you tell me when there has ever been a reign of terror that wasn't instigated by intellectuals and presided over by someone possessed of the madness of the artist.'

'You have done a lot of thinking,' Kevern said.

'For a woman, do you mean?'

'Of course not.'

'For a librarian then?'

'No, I don't mean that either.'

But he wondered if he did.

'It's a great intellectual privilege to work in a library,' she reminded him. 'The Argentinian writer Borges was a librarian. The English poet Philip Larkin was a librarian.'

Kevern hadn't heard of either of them.

'All human life is here,' she went on. 'The best of it and the worst of it, mainly the worst. Books do that, they bring out the bad in readers if there's bad already in them.'

'And if there isn't?'

She smiled at him and stroked her pigtail. 'Then they bring out the good. As in me, I hope. I've been able to read a lot here.'

'You should write a book about it yourself,' he said.

'What for? So they can tear the pages out? I am content to know what I know.'

'So why are you telling me?'

She regarded him archly. 'To pass the time.'

He consulted his watch. 'I should be going then,' he said.

'Why don't you look at people when you're talking to them?' she asked suddenly, as though reverting to a conversation they'd been having earlier.

'I didn't know I didn't look at people.' He was lying. Ailinn too would comment on his apparent rudeness. 'But if I don't, it's shyness.'

'Your colleagues think of you as unapproachable,' she went on. 'They think you look down on them. They call you arrogant.'

'I'm sorry to hear it. I carve lovespoons. I have nothing to be arrogant about.'

'There you go . . . the simple carpenter. That's the arrogance they mistrust.'

'I can't do anything about it,' he said. 'I'm sorry if they hate me . . .'

'I didn't say "hate". I said they mistrusted you.'

'For being "uniquely malevolent" . . .'

She laughed. 'No, for being uniquely arrogant.'

He smiled at her. 'That's all right then. As long I'm uniquely something.'

'Well you could do worse. You could be like them. You could read books with pages torn out of them and think you've stumbled upon truth. You could subscribe to a belief system . . .'

'Beliefs kill,' he said.

'Yes, like beauty.'

Their eyes met. She tossed her pigtail from her shoulder – as she must do when she mounts her horse, he thought, or when she climbs into bed. She put a hand out as though to touch his shirt. He thought she meant to move in to kiss him.

'This is the wrong thing to do,' he said.

'I know,' she said in a soft, mocking voice. 'That's why I'm doing it.'

But she was only seeing what sort of an ethicist he was.

'He's more naive than he ought to be,' she wrote the following morning in her report, 'and more fragile. We ought to get a move on.'

They arrived to music, laboured to music, trooped to the crematoria to music. '*Brüder! zur Sonne, zur Freiheit*,' they were made to sing. 'Brothers! to the sun, to freedom.' '*Brüder! zum Lichte empor*' – 'Brothers! to the light.' Followed, maybe, by the Blue Danube in all its loveliness, or a song from *Die Meistersinger von Nürnberg*, not that any of them cared where he was from. Music that ennobles the spirit revealing its ultimate sardonic nature, its knowledge of its own untruth, because ultimately there is no ennobled nature. What was the logic? To pacify or to jeer? Why ice-cream vans, the arrival of which, playing the 'Marseillaise' or '*Für Elise*' or 'Whistle While You Work', excited the eager anticipation of the children? To pacify or to jeer? Or both? Between themselves, the parents cannot agree on the function or the message. The vans, for now, are better than the trains, some say. Shame there isn't actually any ice cream for the children, but be grateful and sing along. Others believe the vans are just the start of it. We have heard the chimes at midnight, they believe.

FIVE

Lost Letters

i

July 8, 201-
Darling Mummy and Daddy,

It was so lovely to be with you last weekend. I am only sorry that you didn't feel the same way about seeing me. I didn't, and don't ever, mean to cause you vexation. What I said came from my heart. And you have always encouraged me to follow my heart. You will say that the opinions of others, especially Fridleif, have made that heart no longer mine, but believe me – that is not true. My decision to take up a secretarial appointment at the Congregational Federation of the Islands is mine alone. It is a purely administrative post and therefore purely secular. I have not left you. Of course I have been influenced by people I have met up here. Isn't that bound to be the effect of an education? Isn't that precisely what an education is for? You, Mummy, said you should never have let me leave home – 'wandering to the furthest ends of the earth like some gypsy', as you chose to put it, though I haven't left the country and am no more than four hours away, even at the speed you drive – but what's happened isn't your fault just as it wouldn't have been your fault had I gone to New Guinea and become a headhunter. I just wish you could consider what I'm doing as a tribute to the open-minded spirit in which you brought me up. My thinking is a continuation of yours, that's all. And I am still your daughter wherever I live and whoever I work with.

Your ever loving

Rebecca

This was the first of a small bundle of letters Ailinn's companion gave her to peruse. 'Don't for the moment ask me how I came by them,' she said, 'just read them.'

'Now?'

'Now.'

The second letter was dated four months later.

November 12, 201–

Dearest Mummy and Daddy,

Up until the final minute I hoped you would turn up. Fridleif had tried to warn me against disappointment – not in a hostile way, I assure you, but quite the opposite. (You would love him if you would only give yourself the chance.) 'You must understand how hard it must be for them,' he said. But I hoped against hope nonetheless. Even as we exchanged our vows I still expected to see you materialise at the church door and come walking down the aisle.

There, it's said. The church *door.*

How did that ever get to be such a terrible word in our family? What did the church ever do to us? Yes, yes, I know, but that was like a thousand years ago. Is there nothing we can't forgive? Is there nothing we can't forget?

Try saying it to each other when you go to bed at night. Church, church, church . . . You'll be surprised how easy it gets. Do you remember the finger rhyme we used to play together? 'Here's the church, and here's the steeple, open the door and see all the people!' The word seemed innocent enough then. No one sent a thunderbolt out of the sky to punish us for saying it.

But if it can't be innocent to you now I'm a big girl couldn't you at least learn to hate it a little less for my sake?

Open the door and see all the people!

Let's get it all over and done with, anyway. I married the man I love in a church. In the presence of God, Father, Son and Holy Spirit we exchanged vows. And I am now Mrs Macshuibhne, the wife of the Reverend Fridleif Macshuibhne. A bit of a mouthful, I agree, but you'd get used to it if you only tried.

Please be happy for me, at least.

Rebecca

'How did you come by this?' Ailinn wanted to know.

'We agreed you wouldn't ask.'

'No, *you* agreed I wouldn't ask.'

'Just go on reading.'

March 24, 201-

Dear Mummy and Daddy,

Still no word from you. Must I accept that you have abandoned me?

What have I done that is so terrible? What shame have I brought on you?

I accept that there was a time when we needed to show solidarity with one another. We were depleted and demoralised. I knew that. Every defection was interpreted as a sign of weakness and exploited – how could I not know that given the number of times I heard it. If they don't even love one another, people said – or we feared people would say, which isn't quite the same thing – why should we love them. But that was a long time ago. No one is trying to exploit us any more. No one even notices us. We are accepted now. We have never been more safe. I know what you will say. You will say what you always said. 'Don't be lulled into a false sense of security. Remember the Allegory of the Frog.' Daddy, if I remembered the Allegory of the Frog I would never stay anywhere* *for five minutes at a time. If I remembered the Allegory of the Frog I would never know a moment's peace. And the water isn't hot here any more. It isn't even lukewarm. Yes, I know you've heard that before. I know it was what our grandparents said the last time. 'Here? Don't make us laugh. Anywhere but here.' Until the eleventh hour, until eleven seconds before the eleventh minute before the clocks stopped for us, as you've told me a thousand times, they ignored the warning signs, laughed at those who told them it was now or never, refused what stared them in the face. Here? Not here! 'And you know their fate, Becky.' Yes, Daddy, I know their fate, and I owe it to the memory of all those who suffered that fate – whom you speak of as though they were family though none of our family perished, I remind you – never to forget it. But that was then and now is now. And that was there and here is here. You used to laugh at me when I came home from university – 'Here she is, our daughter, life president of the It Couldn't Happen Here Society.' And I called you, Daddy, 'honorary chair of the Never Again League'. Well, I don't disrespect you for believing what you believe. It is right to worry. But you cannot compare like with unlike. If you could only see how I am treated up here. The kindness! The consideration!*

The things you fear are all inside your own heads. And I sometimes think such fears make life not worth living. Is it a life to be in terror every day? To start whenever anyone knocks at the door? To recoil in shock from every thoughtless insult? If those are the conditions on which we hold our freedom to be ourselves, marry, bring up our children, worship, then it is no freedom at all. You cannot live a life forever waiting for it to end.

And it is such a waste when we could be so happy. Heaven knows we were happy as a family for so long. If I was with you now we would be happy again. But I can't be with you again without you accepting Fridleif. And what possible reason do you have not to accept him? He is not the Devil. He is not the end of us. Can't we stop all this sectarianism and just live in peace?

All you are doing by rejecting me is making what you dread come true.

Your ever loving daughter,
Becky

PS You are also about to be grandparents.

'This is not going to end well,' Ailinn said.

'Just read.'

September 17, 201-
Dearest Mummy and Daddy,

I will not upset you by sending you a photograph of your grandchild. I accept now, with great sorrow, that there will be no peace between us. But I do owe it to you – and to myself – to explain why I have done what I have done one last time.

Your generation is not my generation. I say that with the deepest respect. I never was and am not now a rebellious child. I understand why you think as you do. But the ship has sailed. My generation refuses to jump at every murmur of imagined hostility. We love our lives. We love this country. We relish being here. And to go on relishing being here we don't have to be as we were before. That's why I have decided to convert. Not as a rejection of the way you brought me up but as a step forward from it. We were always a preparatory people, Fridleif says. And we have done what we were put on earth to do. We have completed our mission and shown the way. We stood out against every manner of oppression, and having conquered it there is no need for all the morbid remembering and re-remembering. I don't say we should forget, I say we have been given the chance to progress and we should take it. It's time to live for the future, not the past. It's time to be a people that looks forward not back.

So why have I decided to embrace my husband's faith? For the beauty of it, Mummy. For the music of it, Daddy. As an expression of the loveliness of life that our grandparents suffered for us to enjoy.

Trust me, I have never been more what you brought me up to be than when I submit to what our people, in their understandably and even necessary touchy sense of separateness, have abjured for centuries – the incense, the iconography, the fragmented light of stained-glass windows, the rapture. We have been accepted and we are ready to join everybody else now. I am, anyway.

Be happy for me.

Your ever loving daughter in Christ,

Rebecca

'I know,' Ailinn said, when Ez told her that Rebecca was her grandmother.

'How did you know?'

'I've been expecting the letter.'

'Is that meant to be funny?'

'No, not at all.'

'So what do you mean?'

Ailinn made a 'leave it' gesture with her hand, wafting whatever she meant away. Wafting it out of the room, wafting it out into Paradise Valley.

'I can tell she was my grandmother, that's all. I can read myself in her. Was there a reconciliation?'

'I'd like you to read the final letter,' Ez said.

Ailinn was reluctant. She couldn't have said why. Maybe it was the word 'final'. But she read it.

May 202-

My Darling Parents,

I am very alarmed by what I have heard is happening where you are. Please write and tell me you are all right. That's all I ask.

Yours in fear,

R

'Now the envelope,' Ez said.

It was stamped, in large purple letters,

RECIPIENT UNKNOWN AT THIS ADDRESS
RETURN TO SENDER

★The Allegory of the Frog

A frog was thrown into a pan of boiling water.

'What do you take me for?' the frog said, jumping smartly out. 'Some kind of a shlemiel?'

The following day the frog was lowered gently, even lovingly, into a pan of lukewarm water. As the temperature was increased, a degree at a time, the frog luxuriated, floating lethargically on his back with his eyes closed, imagining himself at an exclusive spa.

'This is the life,' the frog said.

Relaxed in every joint, blissfully unaware, the frog allowed himself to be boiled to death.

SIX

Gutkind and Kroplik

i

'How do you take it?'

The policeman Eugene Gutkind pouring morning tea for the historian Densdell Kroplik.

'Like a man.'

'And that would be how?'

'Five sugars and no milk. Is this a cat or an albino dog?'

Densdell Kroplik stroking the ball of bad-breathed icing sugar rubbing up against his leg.

'Don't touch it. You'll never get the stuff off your fingers.'

'Like guilt,' Kroplik laughed, sitting forward on the couch, his legs apart, something heavy between them.

A bolt of disgust went through Gutkind's body. Did he really want *that* sitting on his furniture?

He had invited Kroplik round to his end-of-terrace house in St Eber to show him his great-grandfather's collection of Wagner memorabilia. The rarely played composer had brought the two men together, the decline in the popularity of his music confirming their shared conviction that they were living in unpropitious times. Each believed in conspiracies, though not necessarily the same conspiracies.

'Isn't this against the law?' Kroplik asked, leafing through the photographs and playbills and scraps of unauthenticated manuscript that Gutkind had brought out of filing boxes wrapped in old newsprint.

Gutkind wondered how many more jokes on the theme of legality his co-conspiracy theorist intended to make. 'The law is not so small-minded,' he said. 'It winks at a reasonable number of personal items. It's only when they turn out to be an archive that there's trouble.'

Since Kroplik must have had an archive of some size in order to compile even his *Brief History*, this was meant as a friendly shot across his bows.

'So how are you getting on finding the killer of the Whore of Ludgvennok?' Kroplik asked, that being the context in which the name of Richard Wagner had first come up between them. Just a question. He could have been asking whether the policeman had seen any good films lately.

Gutkind put his fingers together like a preacher and lowered his head.

'I presume you're talking about Lowenna Morgenstern?'

Kroplik snorted. 'How many whores do you know?'

'How many whores are there?'

'In these parts there's nobbut whores, Detective Inspector.'

'Then what makes this one different?'

'She's dead.'

Gutkind parted his fingers. There was no denying that Lowenna Morgenstern was dead. But was she a whore? 'Are you telling me,' he asked, insinuating a note of fine scruple, 'that Lowenna Morgenstern sold her kisses?'

'I'm telling you nothing. I'm asking. You found anyone yet? Got a suspect?'

'The process proceeds,' Gutkind said, rejoining his fingers.

'Maybe I'll have more sugar,' Kroplik proceeded in another direction, helping himself to a sixth cube. 'Would your albino dog like one or does he just lick himself when he's in need of something sweet?'

He was disappointed that the detective inspector had stopped asking him who he thought might have murdered Lowenna

Morgenstern, Lowenna Morgenstern's lover and latterly Lowenna Morgenstern's husband. He felt it undermined both his authority and his judgement.

Gutkind passed him a programme for a performance of *Götterdämmerung* at Bayreuth. It had some elegant faded handwriting on the back, a set of initials together with a phone number. Gutkind had some time ago concluded that they were the initials of the woman his great-grandfather had loved to hopeless distraction, and that the phone number was hers. They must have met in the Festspielhaus, perhaps at the bar, or maybe they had even found themselves sitting next to each other, perhaps so transported by the divine music that they rubbed knees though they were each in the company of other lovers. That the woman should have gone to Bayreuth in the first place puzzled Gutkind, all things considered, but the enigma of it made her all the more fascinating, as Clarence Worthing himself must have felt. I too would have fallen for her, Gutkind thought, conjuring the woman's exotic appearance from the archive of his fancy. I too would have been entrapped.

The programme itself was illustrated with several artists' interpretations of the world ablaze. These could have doubled for the state of his great-grandfather's heart. 'I like thinking about the end of the world,' he said. 'You?'

Densdell Kroplik scratched his face. 'We've lived through the end of the world,' he answered. 'This is the aftermath. This is the post-apocalypse.'

Gutkind looked out of his leaded window at the pyramids of grey clay. The land spewing up its innards. The inside of his unloved, unlived-in terrace house no better. Apart from the dusting of clay, there was something green and sticky over everything, as though a bag of spinach had exploded in the microwave, blowing off the door and paintballing every surface – the table, the walls, the ceiling, even the photograph of Gutkind and his wife on their wedding day, she (her doing, not his) with her head scissored off,

Gutkind and his headless bride. Then again, it could just have been mould. Gutkind looked between his fingers. Yes, mould. 'You could be right,' he said.

'I am right. It's the twilight of the gods.'

'Wagner's gods? Here? In St Eber?'

'The gods of Ludgvennok.'

'I don't much care about anybody's gods,' Gutkind said. 'I care more about me.'

'Well it's the twilight of you too, ain't it? Look at your fucking dog, man. What are you doing here, in this whited-out shit-heap, if you'll pardon my Latin, trying – unsuccessfully by your own account – to solve murders that never will be solved? What am I doing over at Ludgvennok, excuse me' – here he spat, trying to avoid the cat – '*Port Reuben*, as I have to call it, what am I doing cutting aphids' hair in Port Cunting Reuben for a living? We were gods once. Now look at us. The last two men on the planet to have listened to *Tristan und Isolde*.'

Eugene Gutkind fell into a melancholy trance, as though imagining the time when he trod the earth like a god, a monocle in his eye such as Clarence Worthing must have worn, in his hand a silver-topped cane, on his arm, highly perfumed . . .

In reality there was spinach on his shoes. 'So who or what reduced us to this?' he asked, not expecting an answer.

'Saying sorry,' Kroplik said. 'Saying sorry is what did it. You never heard the gods apologise. They let loose their thunderbolts and whoever they hit, they hit. Their own stupid fault for being in the way.'

'I'm a fair-minded man . . .' Gutkind said.

'For a policeman . . .'

'I'm a fair-minded man for anyone. I don't mind saying sorry if I've done something to say sorry for. But you can't say sorry if you've done nothing. You can't find a man guilty if there's been no crime.'

'Well look at it this way, Detective Inspector – there are plenty of unsolved crimes kicking about. And plenty of uncaught criminals. Missy Morgenstern's murderer for one. Does it matter if you end up punishing the wrong man? Not a bit of it. The wrongfully guilty balance the wrongfully innocent. What goes around comes around. Pick yourself up an aphid. They're all murderers by association. Hang the lot.'

Detective Inspector Gutkind felt himself growing irritated by Densdell Kroplik's misplaced ire. It struck him as messy and unserious. His own life might have been dismal but it was ordered. It had feeling in it. He offered his guest a whisky. Maybe a whisky would concentrate his mind.

'Let's agree about something,' he said.

'We do. The genius of Richard Wagner. And the end of the world.'

'No. Let's agree about saying sorry. We shouldn't be saying it – we agree about that, don't we?'

Kroplik raised his dusty whisky glass and finished off its contents. 'We do. We agree about most things. And about that most of all. Fuck saying sorry!'

'Fuck saying sorry!'

The air was thick with rebellion.

'Bloody Gutkind!' Kroplik suddenly expostulated.

Gutkind looked alarmed.

'Bloody Kroplik!' Kroplik continued. 'What kind of a name is Kroplik, for Christ's sake? What kind of a name is Gutkind? We sound like a comedy team – Kroplik and Gutkind.'

'Or Gutkind and Kroplik.'

The policeman Eugene Gutkind sharing the rarity of a joke with the historian Densdell Kroplik.

'I am glad,' said Kroplik sarcastically, shifting his weight from one thigh to another, disarranging the cushions on the detective's sofa, 'that you are able to find humour in this.'

'On the contrary, I agree with you. They turn us into a pair of comedians, though our lives are essentially tragic, and for that we are the ones who have to say we're sorry. I find no humour in it whatsoever.'

'Good. Then enough's enough. We are gods not clowns, and gods apologise to no one for their crimes, because what a god does can't be called a crime. *Nicht wahr*?'

'What?'

'*Nicht wahr*? Wagnerian for don't you agree. I thought you'd know that. I bet even your dog knows that.'

The cat pricked the ear nearest to Kroplik. '*Nicht wahr*?' Kroplik shouted into it.

'These days we don't get to hear much German in St Eber,' Gutkind said, as much in defence of the cat as himself.

'Pity. But Gutkind's got a bit of a German ring to it, don't you think? *Gut* and *kinder*?

'I suppose it has. Like *Krop* and *lik*.'

'You see what the aphid swines have done to us? Now we're fighting on behalf of names that don't even belong to us. What's your actual name? What did the whores call you in the good old days? Mr . . . ? Mr What? Or did you let them call you Eugene? Take me, Eugene. Use me, Eugene.'

If Kroplik isn't mistaken, Gutkind blushes.

'Whatever my name was then, I was too young to give it to whores.'

'Your father then . . . your grandfather . . . how did the whores address them?'

These were infractions too far for Detective Inspector Gutkind, Wagner or no Wagner. He was not a man who had ever visited a whore. And nor, he knew in his soul, had any of the men in his family before him. It had always been ideal love they'd longed for. A beautiful woman, smelling of Prague or Vienna, light on their arm, transported into an ecstasy of extinction – the two of them breathing their last together . . . *ertrinken* . . . *versinken* . . . *unbewußt* . . . *höchste Lust!* . . .

Kroplik couldn't go on waiting for him to expire. 'Well mine was Scannláin. Son of the Scannláins of Ludgvennok. And had been for two thousand bloody years. And then for a crime we didn't commit, and not for any of the thousands we did . . . that's the galling part—'

'For a crime *no one* committed,' Gutkind interjected.

Densdell Kroplik was past caring whether a crime had been committed or not. He held out his glass for another whisky. The high life – downing whisky in St Eber at 11.30 in the morning. The gods drinking to their exemption from the petty cares of mortals. Atop Valhalla, dust or no dust.

Gutkind sploshed whisky into Kroplik's glass. He wanted him drunk and silent. He wanted him a thing of ears. Other than his cat, Eugene Gutkind had no one to talk to. His wife had left him. He had few friends in the force and no friends in St Eber. Who in St Eber did have friends? A few brawling mates and a headless wife to curse comprised happiness in St Eber, and he no longer even had the wife. So he rarely got the opportunity to pour out his heart. A detective inspector, anyway, had to measure his words. But he didn't have to measure anything with Densdell Kroplik, least of all whisky. He wasn't a kindred spirit. Wagner didn't make him a kindred spirit. To Gutkind's eye Kroplik lacked discrimination. Not knowing where to pin the blame he pinned it on everyone. A bad hater, if ever he saw one. A man lacking specificity. But he was still the nearest thing to a kindred spirit there was. 'Drink,' he said. 'Drink to what we believe and know to be true.'

And when Densdell Kroplik was drunk enough not to hear what was being said to him, true or not true, and not to care either way, when he was half asleep on the couch with the icing-sugar cat sitting on his face, Detective Inspector Eugene Gutkind began his exposition . . .

There had been no crime. No *Götterdämmerung* anyway. No last encounter with the forces of evil, no burning, and no renewal of the world. Those who should have perished had been forewarned by men of tender conscience like Clarence Worthing who, though he longed to wipe the slate clean, could not betray the memory of his fragrant encounter with Ottilie or Naomi or Lieselotte, in the Bayreuth Festspielhaus. For what you have done to me, I wish you in hell, they said. But for what you have done to me I also wish you to be spared. Such are the contradictions that enter the hearts of men who know what it is to love and not be loved in return. The irony of it was not lost on Detective Inspector Gutkind. They owed their lives to a conspiracy of the inconsolable and the snubbed, these Ottilies and Lieselottes who had imbibed conspiracy with their mothers' milk. They'd escaped betrayal, they who betrayed as soon as snap a finger.

So WHAT HAPPENED, in his view, was that NOT MUCH HAD. They had got out. Crept away like rats in the dark. That was not just supposition based on his cracking Clarence Worthing's code. It was demonstrable fact. If there'd been a massacre where were the bodies? Where were the pits, where the evidence of funeral pyres and gallows trees, where the photographs or other recorded proof of burned-out houses, streets, entire suburbs? Believe the figures that had once been irresponsibly bandied about and the air should still be stinking with the destruction. They say you can smell extinction for centuries afterwards. Go to the Somme. You can see it in the soil. You can taste it in the potatoes.

He had done the maths, worked it out algebraically, done the measurements geometrically, consulted log tables – so many people killed in so many weeks in so many square metres . . . by whom? It would have taken half the population up in arms, and mightily skilled in the use of them, to have wreaked such destruction in so brief a period of time. No, there had been no *Götterdämmerung*.

He takes a swig from the bottle and looks at Kroplik with his head thrown back, his mouth open and his legs spread. What the hell is that inside his trousers? He regrets inviting him over. He is ashamed of his own loneliness. But there is so much to say, and no one to say it to.

He feels subtler than any man he knows. No *Götterdämmerung* does not mean, you fool, that there was no anything. First law of criminal investigation: everyone exaggerates. Second law of criminal investigation: just because everyone exaggerates doesn't mean there's nothing to investigate. In my profession, Mr Kroplik, we don't say there is no smoke without fire. Rumour is also a crime. False accusation – you can go down for that. But that said, there *is* always a fire. Somewhere, something is forever burning. That's why no accusation is ever entirely wasted. Eventually we will find a culprit for any crime. So yes, WHAT HAPPENED happened in that there was minor disturbance and insignificant destruction. To win another of their propaganda wars they did what they had done for centuries and put on another of their pantomimes of persecution. Allowed the spilling of a little blood to justify their disappearing, while no one was looking, with their accumulated loot. A sacrificial people, my great-grandfather called them, and as one of their sacrifices himself, he knew. But they also sacrifice their own. There's a name for it but I've forgotten it. You'll probably know it, Kroplik, you unedifying piss-ant. Like a caste system. You probably didn't know they had a caste system, but my word they did. This one can't light a candle, that one can't go near a body. Some can't even touch a woman unless they're wearing surgical gloves. And some know it's their job to die when the time comes. It's not as unselfish as it sounds. Their children get looked after and they go straight to heaven. Not to lie with virgins, that's someone else. This lot go straight to heaven and read books. For the honour of which they put themselves in the way of trouble, announce themselves in the street by what they wear, hang identifying objects in the windows of their houses where they wait patiently to be burned alive. Here! Over here!

The shouting doesn't wake Kroplik who sleeps like the dead.

I, my rat-arsed friend, Gutkind continues, am a policeman. I know the difference between right and wrong. Wrong is burning someone alive in his own house, I don't care if he invited you in and handed you the box of matches. You can always say no. Sure, you were provoked. Criminals are always provoked. An open door, a short dress, a handbag left unzipped. Don't get me wrong – I sympathise. I'm not beyond a provocation or two myself. Right this minute I'm provoked into violent thoughts by the sight of you snoring on my sofa. But I restrain myself from cutting off your balls. That's what makes me not a villain.

But keep wrongdoing in proportion is another of my mottos. Not everything is the greatest crime in history.

He rubs his face and drinks.

No sir!

And drinks some more.

You'll have your own favourite greatest crime in history, Mr Historian of the Gods of Ludgvennok, but I can tell you this wasn't it. And why wasn't it?

Because of this! He smites his heart.

Would he have done what Clarence Worthing did had he been in his position? Would he have assisted in their escape? Tears flood his eyes. The sublime music swells in his ears . . . *ertrinken* . . . *versinken* . . . *unbewußt* . . . *höchste Lust*! . . . Yes, he and Clarence Worthing are one, made weak and strong by love.

Finishing off what is left in the bottle, he rejoins Densdell Kroplik on the couch where, exhausted by the intensity of his own emotion, he falls immediately asleep on Kroplik's shoulder, the convulsing cat, heaving up fur balls coated in clay dust, between them.

It's only a shame no family photographer is in attendance.

ii

It's Kroplik who wakes first, still drunk. It takes him a moment or two to work out where he is. Though it's only early afternoon it's dark already in St Eber, the shabby pyramids of clay, as though each is lit from within by a small candle, the sole illumination.

Is this Egypt?

Then he notices that the cat has coughed up a puddle of china-clay slime on the lapel of his one smart suit. Or is it Gutkind's doing? It smells as though it's been in Gutkind's stomach. Kroplik clutches his own. He lives on a daily diet of indignity but this is one insult he doesn't have to bear. He has brought his razor along to give the detective inspector a close shave as a token of his friendship and regard. But he is too angry to be a friend. Slime! From Gutkind's poisoned gut! On his one good suit!

He is aware that Gutkind has been ranting at him while he slept. The usual subject – villainy. Was he telling him he knew – teasing him, taunting him with his knowledge. I know the difference between right and wrong Kroplik is sure he heard him say through his stupor. Provocation is no defence. This time . . .

Is this why he was invited over?

It amazes him that Gutkind should have the brains to solve a crime. Yes, he'd as good as laid it out for him a hundred times, but Gutkind had struck him as too dumb to see what was in front of his face.

I've underestimated him, Kroplik decides. I've fatally underestimated the cunt. And laughs appreciatively at his own choice of words. Make a good final chapter heading for the next volume of his history – no, not 'The Cunt', but 'A Fatal Underestimation'.

He thinks about taking out his razor, putting it to Gutkind's throat, and confessing. What would the policeman do then? Throw up some more? Then he has a better idea. He staggers to his feet and closes the curtains. I'll just cut his throat and have done, he has decided.

But it's the cat that gets it first.

SEVEN

Nussbaum Unbound

i

ESME NUSSBAUM LAY in what the doctors called a coma for two months after the motorcyclist rode the pavement and knocked her down. To her it was a long and much-needed sleep. A chance to think things over without interruption. Regain perspective. And maybe lose a little weight.

She wasn't joking about the weight. She was done with looking comfortable and unthreatening. It was time to show more bone. Splintered bone, she laughed to herself, causing the screen to bleep, though she didn't doubt the bone would mend eventually. It wasn't that she'd been incapable of causing discomfort when discomfort needed to be caused. She was known to be a woman who sometimes asked troublesome questions. But there'd been no real spike inside her. She could annoy without quite inspiring fear. Now she fancied being someone else. No, now she *was* someone else. Someone with sharper edges, all spikes. Broken, she was more frightening.

Already her thoughts were unlike any she'd had before. They flew at her. In her previous, comfortable life she would reason her way to a conclusion, which meant that she could be reasoned out of it in time as well. The motorcycle hadn't really been necessary. There were other ways of making her conformable . . .

Comfortable and Conformable – her middle names. Esme C. C. Nussbaum. Always a word-monger, an anagramatiser, a palindromaniac, she now saw words three-dimensionally in her sleep. Comfortable and Conformable cavorted lewdly on the ceiling of her unconsciousness, pressing their podgy bellies together like middle-aged lovers, blowing into each other's ears, two becoming one. She smiled inside herself. It really was a pleasure lying here, waiting for what words would get up to next, what thoughts would come whooshing at her. She liked being the subject of their discussions. It was like listening in to gossip about herself. No, she wasn't as Comfortable or Conformable as she blamed herself for being, was the latest revelation. If she'd been that easy to get on with, what was she doing here, lying in a coma, half dead? She must have put the wind up someone. That was one of the most persistent of her winged thoughts: people frighten easily. Another was: people – ordinary people, people you think you know and like – want to kill you.

She was not herself frightened when such thoughts flew at her. She had once watched an old horror film with her parents about a blonde woman being attacked by birds. They had been terrified as a family. They put their hands over their faces as the birds dive-bombed everyone in the blonde's vicinity. 'Avenging some great but never to be disclosed wrong,' her father said. But lying flat with thoughts flying at her was not like that. She didn't feel assailed. There was no more they could do to her – that partly explained her calm acceptance of their presence, even when they swooped so low she might justifiably have worried for her eyes. But it was more than being beyond terror. She welcomed their violence. It was Conformable with how she felt. They were *thoughts*, after all, which meant they originated in her. If this was herself massing above her, screeching, well then . . . she extended all the hospitality she had to offer. It was about time. A good time, yes, in that she had bags of it to give; but *about* time in the sense that she had wasted too much of it thinking thoughts that were less . . . less what? How nice it was having all the time in the world to find the right word. Less . . . less . . . Esme Nussbaum knew more words than was good for her. She had been the school Scrabble champion; she could finish a crossword while others were still on the first clue; she knew words even her teachers thought did not exist. Now she raided her store for a word that had bird in it, that sounded avian, an av word. Avirulent had a ring, but it meant the opposite of what she needed it to mean. She didn't want to lose the virulence, she wanted to store it. Avile was good – to avile, as she'd had to explain to a sceptical Scrabble opponent in the quarter-finals, meaning to make vile, to debase. But there was no adjective to go with it that she knew of. No avilious. And no noun, no aviliousness. Had there been, then aviliousness was exactly the quality her previous, unwinged thoughts had lacked. They had been too moderate. Too sparing. Yes, she had presented a report, for which they'd killed her – in intention, if not in fact – that spoke of the persistent rage she'd found in the course of monitoring the nation's mood. She had not tried to sugar that pill. We cannot, she had argued, glide over the past with an IF. We must confront WHAT HAPPENED, not to apportion blame – it was too late for that, anyway – but to know what it was and why time hadn't healed it. Yes, she had stood her ground, said what had to be said, done her best to persuade the IFFERS with whom she worked, but that best wasn't good enough. She hadn't followed the logic of her own findings. She had been insufficiently avilious. She hadn't made vile, that's to say she hadn't grasped, hadn't penetrated and presented, even to herself, the vileness of what had been done. Not WHAT HAD HAPPENED but WHAT HAD BEEN DONE.

Ah, but had she gone that far they would have had her run over a second and, if need be, a third time.

Were they that ruthless? Ruthless was not the word Esme Nussbaum would have picked. They were acting out of the best motives. They wanted a harmonious society. Their mistake was not to see that she wanted a harmonious society too. The difference was that they saw harmony as something you attained by leaving things out – contrariety and contradiction, argument, variety – and she saw it as something you achieved by keeping everything in.

Though she had limited access to information that others didn't, she had done no original research into the terrible events which those who did not see as she saw wanted to disown. Research, she thought, had not been necessary. She knew the events to have been terrible simply by their effects. Had they been of less consequence then the aftermath would have been of less consequence too. But the aftermath, of which she too, lying here smashed into tiny pieces, was the bloody proof, brooked no controversy. They could mow her down as often as they liked – and she bore them no malice for it; on the contrary she owed this long reflective holiday to them – but the truth remained the truth. Anger and unhappiness seeped out from under every doorway of every house in every town and every village in the country. Housewives threw open their windows each morning to let out the fumes of unmotivated domestic fury that had built up overnight. Men spat bile into their beer glasses, abused strangers, beat their own children, committed acts of medieval violence on their wives, or on women who weren't their wives, that no amount of sexual frustration or jealousy could explain.

Now that she had the leisure to think, Esme Nussbaum was no longer looking for explanations. You only need an explanation where there's a mystery, and there was no mystery. How could it have worked out otherwise? You can't have a poisoned stomach and a sweet breath. You can't lop off a limb and expect you will be whole. You can't rob and not make someone the poorer, and when it's yourself that you rob then it's yourself you impoverish.

Of the thoughts that flew at her, as the weeks passed, this last was the most persistent, skimming her cheek with its quilled wing, as though it wanted to scratch her into waking – *we are the poorer by what we took away.*

But she was in no rush to come out of her coma where it was

warm and silent – she only saw words, she didn't hear them – and declare what she knew. She had no more reports to write just yet. It was good to look at the world slowly and evenly. You don't need to have your eyes open to see things.

ii

Her father blamed her.

'She couldn't have been looking where she was going,' he said.

'Esme always looks where she's going,' his wife replied.

'Then if it wasn't an accident . . .'

'It *wasn't* an accident.'

'OK, if you say so, it wasn't an accident. In that case someone must have had it in for her.'

'You don't say.'

'The question is—'

'I don't want to hear that question.'

'The question is what had she done wrong.'

'Your own daughter! How dare you?'

He gave a foolish, thwarted laugh, that was more like a belch. He was a near-sighted, jeering man with a hiatus hernia. 'It feels as though something's balled-up in my chest all the time,' he complained to his doctor who recommended Mylanta or Lanzaprozole or Maldroxal Plus or Basaljel or Ranitidine. He took them all but felt no better.

'It's your opinions,' his wife told him, watching in distaste as he banged at his thorax in the vain hope of dislodging whatever was stuck inside him. 'It's your hateful nature paying you back. To speak like that, about your own daughter!'

'People don't have it in for you for no reason,' he persisted.

'Not another word,' his wife said. 'Not another word or I swear I'll cut your chest open with a breadknife.'

The Nussbaums had been having this argument all their married lives. Their mangled daughter was just another opportunity for them to rehearse it all again, their understanding of the universe, what they did or did not believe. What Compton Nussbaum believed was that what happened happened for the best of reasons, there was no effect that didn't have a cause, what people suffered they had brought upon themselves. What Rhoda Nussbaum believed was that she was married to a pig.

'Have you never been sorry for anyone?' she asked him.

'What good would my sorrow do them?'

'That's not an answer to my question. Do you never feel another person's pain?'

'I feel satisfied when I see justice done.'

'What about injustice? What about cruelty?'

He banged his chest. 'Sentimentality.'

'So if I go out and get raped . . . ?'

'It will be your own fault.'

'How so? For being a woman?'

'Well I won't be going out and getting raped, will I?'

More's the pity, she thought.

You don't see your daughter lying as good as dead and blame her for it, Rhoda Nussbaum believed. If I were to kill my husband for what he has just said I would be cleared by any court in the country. The only argument she could see for not killing her husband was that she'd be proving him right – yes, people do get what they deserve.

He'd been a civil servant. '*Servant* gets it,' Rhoda Nussbaum would say when he refused to hear a word against those who employed him. He was proud when his daughter gained early promotion at Ofnow, but turned against her when she turned against it.

'I'm only asking questions,' she would cry in her own defence.

'Then don't,' was his fatherly reply.

She should have found a man and left home for him. But the men she met were like her father. 'Then don't,' they'd say. And the one thing they didn't say no about, she did.

Her mother encouraged her. 'They're all no good,' she said. 'Stay here with me.'

That suited her. She liked her mother and could see that she was lonely. It helped, too, that she was not sentimental about men.

Her father thought she was a lesbian. Many men thought the same. There was something uncanny about her, the seriousness with which she took her work, her obduracy, her pedantry, the size of her vocabulary, the lack of bounce in her hair, the flat shoes she wore, her failure often to get a joke, her unwillingness to play along, her way of overdoing sympathy as though understanding beat snogging. But only her father hated her in his heart. Her being a lesbian was a denial of him. And also, by his own remorseless logic, meant that he was being punished. He didn't know what for, but you don't get a lesbian for a daughter unless you've done something very wrong indeed.

He'd have preferred it had she not come out of the coma.

'You will not tell her she only got what she deserved,' his wife said on the eve of their daughter's removal from the hospital. 'If you want to live an hour longer you will not say it's your own stupid fault.'

He stood at the front door, waiting for the ambulance to arrive. A ball of something even more indigestible than usual was lodged inside his chest.

'Welcome home,' he belched when she was stretchered in. She raised her hand slightly and gave him a faint wave.

I'm doing well, he thought. I'm handling this OK.

Esme thought the same. Not about him, about her. I'm being good. But she knew she'd never be able to keep it up. She'd have to tell him soon enough how wrong he had always been about everything.

Her mother nursed her like a grievance.

'My little girl,' she crooned over her.

Esme told her to stop. She was getting better. In some respects she felt better than she'd ever felt before. Her mother worried that that meant she was preparing to embrace the life of a permanent invalid. But then there was a secret corner of herself that was willing to embrace the life of a permanent nurse. Feed her daughter soup, kill her husband, put up the shutters, smell him rot and hope not to see daylight again.

Esme had never moved out of her parents' house so she was back in her old room. Yet it felt as though she'd been away all her adult life and was revisiting the sanctum of her childhood for the first time in decades. It was the lying down that did that. Lying down and seeing words jerk about above her head. Can one ever return to bed for a long period and not be reminded of being a child? Even the books on her shelves and the magazines on the chest of drawers, bought just before she was run over, even her newest clothes, seemed to belong to a much younger her. Where had she been in the intervening years?

Her mother caught her weeping once. 'Oh, my little girl,' she cried.

'Cut that out!' Esme said. 'I'm not in pain and I'm not sad. I'm just missing something.'

'What?'

'The last fifteen years of my life.'

'You haven't been here that long, darling.'

'I know that. I just can't think what I did with them before.'

In a few weeks she was able to lever herself up by her arms. It would be longer before she could walk, but there was no hurry. Physiotherapists visited her and were disappointed by her slow progress. 'She's regaining strength,' they told her mother, 'but she doesn't seem to have the will to be up and about.'

She wasn't worried about it herself. She still had a lot of thinking to do. Once she was out of the coma her thoughts did not fly at her. She missed that, as people from the country miss birdsong when they move to town. She had to call words to her now. She had to start at the beginning of an idea and puzzle it out. It was like following one end of a ball of thread, uncertain where it would lead her.

Her mother fretted. 'Why are you so quiet?'

'Thinking.'

'You've had a lot of time to think.'

'You can't have too much.'

Can't you? Her mother wasn't sure.

But her father liked her like this. He took it for remorse. Any minute now he expected her to announce that the accident had killed off her lesbian tendencies.

'What's happening in the world?' she asked one morning.

She had got herself over to the breakfast table to join her parents.

'The usual,' her mother said. 'Births, marriages, funerals.'

'What would you have instead?' her husband asked her.

'Something less horrible.'

'We make our beds, we lie in them,' Compton said.

Esme looked from her father to her mother, and back. How long had marriage been a horror to them both? From the first moment of their marrying, forty years before? Had they recoiled from each other even as they exchanged vows? She had never heard them speak lovingly of a time when they didn't dislike each other intensely. So why had they married, and why hadn't they parted? What was it that kept them together? The very magnetism of horror, was that it? The harmony that there is in hatred?

She suddenly saw them as a pair of evil planets, barren of life, spinning through space, in constant relation to each other but never colliding. Did a marriage obey the same unvarying law of physics as the solar system? And society too? Was this equipoise of antagonism essential?

But when the planets in disorder wander . . . Who said that? Esme knew a crossword clue when she saw one. *Disorder wander – prince among men, 6 letters.*

Then she remembered the rest from sixth-form literature. *But when the planets in evil mixture to disorder wander, what plagues and what portents . . . what commotion in the winds . . .*

By these lights her parents had a successful marriage. They hadn't wandered in disorder. They might not have known a moment's happiness together, but at least the winds had stayed quiet.

Now apply this, she reasons, to that commotion whose abiding after-effects had been her study. A raging wind had been loosed, bearing plagues and portents, proof that the planets had wandered badly off their course. Some equipoise of hatred had been lost. You don't kill the thing you love, but you don't kill the thing you hate, either. You dance with the thing you hate to the music of the spheres. And all remains well – relatively speaking; of course relatively speaking, relative to massacre and annihilation – so long as the dance continues. The madness is to think you can dance alone, without a partner in mistrust. Had her mother left her father as she had so often threatened to, what would have become of either of them? She couldn't imagine her mother without her father, so intrinsic to her character was her contempt for him. She existed to denounce him. But he, oh she could imagine him on the streets wielding a machete. WHAT HAPPENED happened, no ifs or buts about it, not because ten thousand men like her father had been abandoned by their wives – though that must have added to the savour of it for some – IT HAPPENED because they forgot, or more likely never fully understood, that those they were killing performed the same function as their wives. It was a catastrophe of literal-mindedness. You don't kill the thing you hate just because you hate it.

As for *why* the hatred, Esme Nussbaum is not concerned to put her mind to that. Not now. Perhaps later when she has more strength. Should she slip back into a coma, she thinks, she'll have the mental space for it.

She is just strong enough, however, to see this one thought through to the end: an essential ingredient of the harmony of disharmony was lost when men like her father went on the rampage. And now, still, all these decades later, they wander in uncomplemented disorder.

She is no longer employed by Ofnow. When Ofnow kills its employees it assumes them to be off the payroll. Her mother has been trying to get her a pension – an endeavour in which she has not been able to count on the support of her husband who understands Ofnow's reasoning – but without success. She knows what their response will be if she pushes them too hard. They will prove her daughter is no longer on the payroll by killing her again.

Sometimes Esme forgets that she is no longer employed by Ofnow and finds herself preparing a new report to take into the office on Monday morning. It will argue that if the country is to enjoy any sort of harmony again, there must be restitution. Not a crude financial recompense to the descendants of those who vanished in the course of WHAT HAPPENED (there can be no talk of victims) – their whereabouts anyway, supposing some exist, are unknown. What she has in mind is making restitution to the descendants, or rather the *idea* of the descendants, of those who remained (there can of course be no talk of culprits either). *Us*, in other words, the living descendants of the living. Restitution in this sense: *Giving us all back what we have lost.*

There will be considerable relief in the office that she is not proposing financial recompense no matter that it cannot possibly be implemented. Blood money presupposes an offence and, since there hasn't been one, blood money isn't on the table. But they won't know what in God's name she means by giving us back what we have lost. *What have we lost*? Explain yourself, Miss Nussbaum. And she will. Gladly.

'What we have lost,' she will tell them, 'is the experience of a deep antagonism. Not a casual, take-it-or-leave-it, family or neighbourly antagonism – but something altogether less accidental and arbitrary than that. A shapely, long-ingested, cultural antagonism, in which everything, from who we worship to what we eat, is accounted for and made clear. *We are who we are because we are not them.*'

They stare at her.

'Remove them from the picture and who are we?'

They are still staring at her.

'We must give the people back their necessary opposite,' she will tell them, heated by her own fierceness, the splintered bones in her body a thousand weapons to slay with.

'And how do you propose doing that, young lady?' someone dares to ask.

Ah, she will say. Now you're asking.

iii

At the very moment Esme Nussbaum was knocked down outside her place of work, her mother fell off a chair on which she'd been standing to dust the bookshelves. Mothers and daughters, especially when no man beloved of either is around to break the current, can be attuned like this.

In the time her daughter was in hospital Rhoda Nussbaum never gave up hope of her coming out of her coma because she could hear her thinking live thoughts. And now that Esme was home, back in the room that had been her nursery, back in her care, her mother heard even more of what was going on inside her head. Planets, marriages, collisions, commotion – she heard all that. Some of her daughter's thoughts and phrases she even recognised as her own. How could it be otherwise? If she was attuned to Esme, then Esme was attuned to her. Even in the womb the baby hears its mother's music. And as an essentially companionless woman, with a rich store of anger in her, Rhoda had confided in her daughter, sometimes in words, sometimes silently, earlier and more frequently than was common or even desirable. Necessary Opposites, for example, was the name of a two-girl, two-boy rock band Rhoda had danced to when she was a teenager. She was pretty certain the band vanished at about the time most hard-rock bands were consensually driven underground, and that would have been a few years before Esme was born. How extraordinary that a phrase that had been lying there in pieces in Rhoda Nussbaum's mind, unused and unreferred to, should suddenly reassemble itself in Esme's. But then again, maybe not. Rhoda had tried to dance her brains out to Necessary Opposites because she didn't like what her brains contained. Was it coincidence? The evil thing she wanted to dance out was all trace of a man in pain – or pretending to be in pain – declaring over and over *I am who I am because I am not them* as though it were an incantation, and begging her to kiss him, forgive him, enfold him, make him better. As though he had a better self she could release.

Hearing the words returned to her in Esme's thoughts did not bring back a long-forgotten event because she had never forgotten it – where she was when she heard them, how they made her feel, the feebleness of her response . . .

EIGHT

Götterdämmerung

i

A BLOOMING, STRONG-JAWED girl of just sixteen, still to meet the husband she can't bear, Rhoda Nussbaum (to be) had a brief affair with a man more than three times her age. Though she called it an affair, there was not much sex in it. Nor much love. It was an affair of curiosity. She was inexperienced, but with a fierce sense of the ridiculous that made her courageous, and he was her schoolteacher. An unattractive man physically, but you don't say no to your teacher. Especially when he wants you to know he's emotionally damaged and you might just be the one to heal him.

'I'm in bits,' he told her when she put her face up to be kissed.

The hands with which he held her shook. At first she thought it was she who was shaking, but she saw the light dancing in his wedding ring like sun on choppy water. 'Make me whole again,' he said, his scraggy beard moving independently of his lips, as though it too was bouncing on a wild, wild sea.

'That's a lot to ask of a pupil you've only ever given B+ to,' she said.

He had no sense of the ridiculous and didn't laugh. He was a folk singer in his spare time and, though they were a long way from any wild, wild sea, sang about fishermen bringing in herrings. The fact that he sometimes brought his guitar to school was another reason Rhoda allowed him to try it on with her. The other girls would be jealous if they found out and Rhoda had every intention of their finding out.

'I just want you to be yourself,' he said.

She swivelled her jaw at him. 'What if I don't know which of my selves to be?'

'You don't have to worry. You're being the self I care best about now.'

Care best about! But what she said was, 'And which self is that?'

'The good and innocent one.'

'Ha!' she snorted. Lacking experience she might have been, but they were in a hotel room drinking cider on the edge of the bed, on the outside of the locked door a frolicsome sign saying LEAVE US ALONE: WE'RE PLAYING, and she knew that while there were many words for what she was being not a one of them was 'innocent'.

'Oh yes you are,' he said, unbuttoning her school shirt. 'Where there's no blood, there's no guilt.'

'There might be blood,' she warned him.

He overcame his surprise to smile his saddest folkie's smile at her. 'That's different. Blood shed in the name of love is not like blood shed in the name of hate.'

She wasn't having any love talk, but she could hardly not ask, 'How do you know? Have you shed blood in the name of hate?'

He let his long horse face droop lower even than usual. 'All in good time,' he said.

He was teasing her, she thought. This was his sexual come-on. *I have done such things* . . . Boys did that but she didn't expect it of a grown man. She liked him less for it and she hadn't liked him much to start with. He shouldn't have supposed she needed him to have terrible secrets. This was terrible secret enough. He was married, her teacher, older than her parents, undressing her, describing the shape of her breasts with his fingers, his touch so intrusively naked he might have been describing them in four-letter words. They were offending against every decency she had been taught.

He thought he guessed what she was thinking. He thought the mention of hate had startled her. But he had guessed wrong. She wanted him to finish a conversation he had started, that was all.

He told her in the end, some three or four visits to the hotel bedroom later. Very suddenly and brutally.

'You'd have been about ten,' he said. They were still dressed, looking out of the window on to a bank of air conditioners. Two pigeons were fighting over a crumb of bread that must have been thrown out of a window above theirs. The room had a worn, padded reproduction of the Rokeby Venus for a bedhead. In the days when the economy boomed and nothing yet had HAPPENED this had been an expensively raffish hotel, softly carpeted for high-heeled assignations. It still spoke knowingly of indulgence and love, but with only half a heart. So great a change in only six or seven years! Now a schoolteacher could afford to bring his pupil here.

A scented candle burned. His guitar case stood unopened in a corner. Was he going to sing to her, she wondered. The sign announcing that they were playing so leave them alone was swinging on the door.

She knew what he was referring to. WHAT HAPPENED, IF IT HAPPENED was the thing that happened when she was about ten. She hadn't known much about it, living too far from any of the centres of conflagration to see anything with her own eyes or hear anything with her own ears. One or two school acquaintances must have been caught up in it because they never showed their faces again, but they hadn't been close friends so their absence didn't impinge on her. Otherwise, apart from her form teacher once bursting into tears, and the headmaster banning all mobile phones and personal computers from the school premises, nothing occurred at school to suggest anything was wrong, and at home her parents remained tight-lipped. There was a blackout imposed by her father, no papers allowed into the house and no serious radio or television, but that had hardly bothered Rhoda aged ten.

OPERATION ISHMAEL, however, in which she went, in a single bound, from Hinchcliffe to Behrens, could not be accounted for without reference to the turbulence it was devised to quiet, and so, one way or another, Rhoda learnt what she had never been taught. Namely that something unspeakably terrible had happened, if it had.

For me to think about when I'm older, she'd decided.

And now older was what she was.

'Yes,' she said. 'And . . .'

He gathered her into his arms. She didn't feel as safe there as she imagined she would when it all started. There was something ghostly about him – he was eerily elongated in body as well as face, as though he had grown too much as a consequence of a childhood illness equivalent to those that stopped people growing at all, bony, with a big wet vertical mouth that hung open despite the attempted camouflage of the beard, showing tombstone teeth. It wasn't difficult to imagine him with the skin stripped from his bones.

Why am I doing this, she asked herself. Why am I here? I don't even like him.

'She would have been about the age you are now, had she lived,' he said.

'She?'

'The girl . . .'

She waited.

'The girl I killed.'

'You killed a girl?'

'Come to bed,' he said.

She shook her head. She wasn't afraid. She just thought he was trying to impress her again. And maybe frighten or arouse her into doing something she didn't want to do.

'How do you mean you killed a girl?'

'How did I do it?'

That wasn't really her question, but all right, how did he do it?

'Not with my bare hands if that's what you think. I left it to others. I stood by and let it happen.'

She released herself. 'What others?'

'Does that matter?'

She pulled the face she and all her girlfriends pulled to denote they were talking to a moron. 'Hello!' she said. *'Does that matter?'*

He reached for her cheek. 'What matters is that I loved and killed for the same reason.' He paused, waiting for a reaction. Was he expecting her to tell him it was all right. *There, there – I forgive you*. 'What attracted me,' he went on, as though he was working out his motives for the first time, 'repelled me.'

'You killed because you were repelled?'

'No, I killed because I was attracted.'

She wanted to go home now.

'Stay,' he said. 'Please stay.'

Rhoda stared into his ugly wet mouth and remembered a skull that had gone round the class during an anatomy lesson. Its mouth, too, though it had once been wired, fell open when the skull was passed from girl to girl.

'You mustn't think I'm going to be violent with you,' he said.

'*She* probably didn't think you were going to be violent with her.'

'I had no choice with her.'

She might only have been a schoolgirl but she knew everyone had a choice. 'That's your excuse,' she said, knotting her tie.

'No, I'm not making an excuse. It just is what it is. Sometimes you have to do something – you can't help yourself – you are drawn into it. You will understand when you're older. You have to destroy to survive. While they live, you can't. Most times it doesn't come to that, but when the opportunity presents itself . . .'

'The opportunity?'

'That's what it was.'

'And she was how old?'

'The girl? I've told you. She'd be about your age now, so then she would have been nine or ten.'

'You went with a girl of nine?'

He had the shakes again, she noticed. 'No, I didn't "go" with her. She was the daughter.'

'Whose daughter?'

'The daughter of the woman I *was* "going" with. It was the mother who attracted me.'

This was getting worse by the second, Rhoda thought. At sixteen, if the words you like to use don't express contempt, they express disgust. Rhoda allowed her teacher to see her rehearsing all of them in her head.

'Wait a minute. Just listen. Let me tell you how it was before you judge me. The mother went for me, not the other way round. I met her at a print shop where I'd gone to get an invitation printed. She was doing the same, only she was arguing over the invitations they'd done for her. They were for the private view of a painter at a gallery I assumed was hers. She wanted me to agree that they'd botched the job. "Look at the colours!" she said. "Did you ever see a woman's breasts that colour?" They looked all right to me, but I agreed because I thought she was genuinely upset—'

'And because you hoped you'd get a look at the colour of hers.'

'No, yes, maybe. That's cheeky of you, but I deserve it. But that's not the point. I was being supportive, that's all. I didn't know then that dissatisfaction was her hallmark, that arguing with tradespeople was just something she did. Like throwing parties. There was a gallery opening or an engagement party or a ruby wedding every week in her world and she paid for most of them. All lavish affairs. Champagne and lobster canapés. She had money to burn. She had everything to burn. She would have burned me had I let her. So it was poetic justice in the end. If you think I lost my mind you'd be right. I lost my mind from the moment I saw her shouting about her invitations. I'd never been with anybody like her. She was older and knew more of the world than I did. A woman with her own art gallery. She was my opposite in every way – unreserved, voluptuous, selfish, faithless, as wild as a cat. She laughed more than anybody I'd ever met, too, but when she wasn't laughing her face would become a mask of tragedy. She had these great, dark, over-painted, sorrowful eyes, as though they told the whole mournful history of her people. That was her explanation, anyway. "We have experienced too much," she would tell me, holding me to her breast, and ten minutes later she was doing a seating plan. "Does nothing mean anything to you for long?" I'd ask her, and she'd say, "Yes, you," or "Yes, my daughter," and once she even said, "Yes, God." She told me she prayed but when I asked her what she prayed for it was always something material – good weather for the opening, the continued absence of her husband ("So that I can have my way with you all weekend" – as though God would help with that), a lightning bolt to destroy the boycotters who milled outside her gallery, chanting against the country whose best painters she represented – though in their presence she merely guffawed her contempt and called them sanctimonious ghouls. "They'll go when they find some other no-hope cause," she told me in front of their faces. There was no guilt or conscience in her. No beauty or inspiration. Don't get me wrong, she was beautiful to look at herself. Dark and soft. Bewitching. Sometimes when I held her I thought she had no bones, her body was so yielding. Though she was obstinate in all our conversations and fought me over everything, in bed she would be anything I wanted her to be. But there was no spiritual beauty. She gave money to charity but the impulse never seemed charitable to me. It was too easy, too automatic. Before my parents ever gave money they would sit around and discuss it for weeks. Should we make a donation here or would it be better spent there? She just wrote a cheque and never thought about it again. She would go to concerts and openings of shows at other art galleries but I never saw her moved. My music she hated. "Caterwauling about fishermen and bumpkins," she called it. I doubt she'd ever eaten a fish. I doubt she'd ever seen the sea, come to that. Or been out into the country. She looked down on people, imitated the accents of the poor, jeered at me even, sometimes, for not having her advantages. And that included a dinner jacket. "You can't come to one of my family events looking like that," she said the first time she saw me in my corduroy suit.

'I wished I didn't have to go to her "family events" or meet her "people" – I never felt at home with them. Was that because they looked down on me? I didn't know. But I always felt they tolerated me, that was all. And if I dared to say a word against them she'd fly at me in a rage. Once she broke two of my teeth. Yet for all the specialness of her "people", for all the superiority of their suffering over anyone else's, she would still affect the airs and graces of a woman who had just taken tea with royalty. These attempts to hide who she was and where she'd come from – her family had sold hats on a street market! – shocked me. And she did it so badly. People laughed at her behind their hands and she didn't notice. No doubt they were laughing at me too. I know what you must be thinking – why did I stay? I was obsessed by her, that's why. The more I hated her the more fascinated I became. I can't explain that. Was she my cruel mistress or my lapdog? I tell you, though you are too young to understand obsession, I was obsessed by the oily sallowness of her skin, her heavy breasts, her swampy lips, the little panting cries she made when I entered her – forgive me – the extravagant way she moved her hands, making up stories, telling lies, transparent fantasies, trying to impress whoever she needed to impress – a room of thirty people or just me, it didn't matter – but it sickened me too.'

He paused as though remembering his manners. Was there perhaps something she wanted to say at this point?

There wasn't. Rhoda thought he was probably right – she didn't have quite the years yet for this.

He took that to be permission to go on.

'There was something ancient about her. I don't mean in

appearance. I mean in what she represented. She went too far back. History should have finished with the likes of her by now. Sometimes when I was making love to her – forgive me, please forgive me, but I have to explain – I felt I was in a sarcophagus making love to a mummy. I thought she would come apart in my hands, under my kisses and caresses, like parchment. Can you be oily *and* dry? Can you be soft *and* brittle? Well she could. That was her power over me. And then she would stir, sit up like someone risen from the dead – Cleopatra herself – and shake her jewellery in my face. That jewellery! She would put those hands up to my cheeks and look at me with longing – or was it loathing? – and I'd hear the jewellery clinking and I wanted to tear it off her. Christ, how badly I wanted to do that! Rip it from her throat and drag it out of her ears. All that false beauty, the impossible way she spoke, her contempt for her marriage, her raving about her precious daughters, her people's tragic past, her pseudo-religiousness, the art she didn't care about – it's a miracle I never did strangle her.'

Rhoda finally found some words. 'So you got someone else to strangle her for you?'

He took a moment to reply. Measuring the silence. 'I let the gallery be burned.'

'With her in it?'

'With the child in it. There were living quarters there. She liked staying there sometimes. It was a treat for her. She could play at shop. Her mother even let her talk to clients sometimes, about the art. She thought it was a great joke. "Out of the mouths of babes," she'd say.'

Rhoda retreated into silence again. *Let the gallery be burned*, did he say? *Let*? She didn't want to know whether that meant he had invited arsonists in or had actually started the fire himself and then failed to put it out. Whatever else, she didn't want to picture him putting a match to the building, knowing there was a child inside. A child who, had she lived, would have been about the age she was now. She didn't want to show her fear.

'It was strange, you know,' he went on, in a different tone altogether now, almost matter-of-fact, 'it was as though it wasn't me doing it. Or if it was me it was me doing it at some other time. Any time in the last, I don't know, two, three thousand years I could have done the same – seen the flames, shaken my head and walked away.'

Very well, he was mad. That somehow made her feel better and even, strangely, less frightened. She had her sanity to defeat him with.

'What do you mean you could have done it two thousand years ago? Are you telling me you're some sort of a vampire?'

'I'm telling you my actions weren't mine alone. I was just repeating what had been done countless times before, and I don't doubt for the same reasons. Would you understand me if I said I'd been culturally primed to do it?'

She brought her hand to her mouth and laughed bitterly up her sleeve, the way everyone did at school when an elder made a preposterous statement. 'Would you understand me if I said I'd been culturally primed to refuse to do my homework?' she gathered the boldness to ask.

He smiled at her smartness. 'Yes, I'd understand and say I hope that's the worst thing you will ever be culturally primed to do.'

'No you wouldn't. You'd say I was letting myself off.'

'It was a necessity,' he said. 'There are such things. It's you or them. You can't both breathe the same air. Some people are too different. *I am who I am because I am not them*, you tell yourself. That's what you fall in love with at first – this clean break with yourself. Because if you are not them, they are not you. But then you realise it isn't anything about them that you love, it's the prospect of your own annihilation. They say before the executed die they fall in love with their executioner. Maybe had she not told me our affair was over, that she'd found a man more suitable to her needs – a financier, I supposed, or a painter, one of her own, anyway – I'd have accepted death at her hands as my consummation. But her timing was wrong. She missed her chance. The world changed while she wasn't looking. One day the streets were quiet, the next the mob was out, shouting, burning, killing. I see from your expression that you know nothing of any mob. You were too young then and you've been well schooled since. But trust me, the gentlest people were suddenly behaving like animals. Was I part of it? Yes and no. I felt what they felt, they felt what I felt, though I believed then and believe now that I acted alone and for my own motives. But the violence didn't surprise me. You'd think the sight of people behaving so unlike themselves would surprise you but it doesn't. Violence quickly comes to look quite normal. Perhaps what I saw was a reflection of the violence in my heart. Perhaps I saw it as more violent than it was because I wanted it to be so. But I couldn't have made up the things that happened. I didn't join in. I even risked my own skin to get to her, to plead with her. *Give me another chance.* That's what she had reduced me to. *Give me another chance! I'll do whatever you like. I'll change.* As though I could ever change into anything she wanted for more than fifteen minutes. As though I could ever be anything but a convenience to her. I ran to the house but found it closed up. Good, I thought, at least they've got away. But then it occurred to me that they might be at the gallery, which at least had shutters. That was two miles away. I ran the whole distance. The shutters weren't down. The crowds had not got that far yet, though the usual boycotters were outside, noisier and more menacing than ever. With the strength that comes from desperation I pushed my way through them and hammered on the window. Little Jesse appeared. Even at that age she was her mother all over again. Same mournful eyes, same heavy cheeks, same rude flirtatiousness. Same indifference to danger. She was even wearing her mother's high-heeled shoes. "Mum's out," she mouthed. I told her to let me in. I'd wait. She said, "Mum doesn't want to see you any more." "What about you?" I shouted.

"Don't you want to see me any more?" She shrugged. Easy come, easy go. I might as well have been a servant or the gardener. A person of no consequence though I'd petted and played with her and bought her presents she didn't need. She eyed me sardonically. Her mother's child. *Don't be pathetic*, I could see she was thinking. I asked who was in the gallery with her. She said no one. She could have been lying but I chose to see her being left alone as proof of her mother's callousness, and as a sign. Nine years old and left to fend for herself. What does that tell you? So should I have cared for her more than her faithless, so-called doting mother did? Whether I could have done anything I don't know. I could have tried to spirit her away. I could have tried to reason with the crowd – *There's only a child in there*. Only an insolent, superior little girl, but a child nonetheless. Unlikely to have made any difference but I could have tried. But the shouts and smell of smoke had a powerful effect on me. I don't say they excited me, but they gave a sort of universality to what I was feeling. *I am who I am because I am not them* – well, I was not alone in feeling that. We were all who we were because we were not them. So why did that translate into hate? I don't know, but when everyone's feeling the same thing it can appear to be reasonableness. Can you understand that? What everyone's doing becomes a common duty. Besides, it wasn't for me to play God. These people had their own God, I thought – let *Him* look after her. So I did nothing when she turned her back on me. Didn't bang on the window. Didn't call her. Didn't warn her. I stood outside for a short while, staring at the inflammatory words painted on the window – GALILEE GALLERIES – as though in a trance. Could have been thirty seconds, could have been thirty minutes, then I walked away.'

He kept his eyes averted from Rhoda's, showing her his long, brittle hands. The hands he hadn't employed to help a child. What did he want her to do – kiss them or break them off at the wrists?

'And now you think it's my duty to let you replace her with me,' she said. She was on her feet, dressed and ready to leave, feeling sick but strong, with her school bag under arm. 'Well you've got another think coming.'

She was relieved to make it out safely on to the street.

ii

She didn't repeat a word to anyone of what she'd been told. There was no point. For one thing, to have spoken of it would have compromised her – what was she doing talking to her teacher about his murderous, obsessional love life in a hotel room? – and for another she didn't expect to be believed. She wasn't sure how much of it she believed herself. He could have made the whole thing up to impress her, or made the second half up to exact an imaginary revenge. You can murder in your thoughts, she knew that. And even if she'd been believed – what then? Where was the crime? What law do you break by walking away? She didn't know much about what had gone on when she was ten, but she'd heard adults talking and knew the slate had been wiped clean. So long as you joined in the chorus of saying sorry, you were in the clear. The past was the past and brought automatic absolution.

As for him, she hoped fervently that he would quit the school, but he didn't. He didn't ask her to go to a hotel with him again either. He just did what he was good at and looked away.

If her presence made him anxious, he concealed it well. She, however, grew morose and began to do badly at school. No one knew why, but she lost interest in her studies and left before she had achieved what had been expected of her. Whereas he appeared, if anything, to prosper. Good divinity teachers were hard to come by.

Not long afterwards, at a concert given by Necessary Opposites, she met Compton who repelled her. The degree to which he made her flesh creep excited her. He was opposite to everyone she cared about, opposite to everything she admired and loved. It was marry him or kill him. And, in anticipation of her daughter's thinking, she saw that it would have been literal-minded of her to kill him.

She didn't tell Compton about her affair with a murderer or a liar or both. She didn't want his hands on her experience, she didn't want to hear him say that the murdered girl got what was owing to her. She was angry enough. Nor did she tell Esme when she was of an age to understand. In Esme's case it wasn't necessary; she picked up the essentials without words needing to be exchanged. There was certainly some rage in her that Rhoda proudly believed was her doing. She'd instilled an appetite for justice that was like a hunger in her own belly. Esme, she was confident, would fight the good fight for her. Esme would show courage where she hadn't. Esme would make someone pay.

swung her legs out of bed and went to stand by the window. It was quiet out there, no wind, no gulls, even the blowhole subdued. The sky was low, without colour or promise. 'God, it can feel dead down here sometimes,' she said.

He remembered his mother saying the same. 'It's like being in a coffin,' she said once. 'With the lid down.'

Was that before or after the free meat, he wondered.

'Look on the bright side,' his father had answered. 'At least there'll be no surprises when they screw you in.'

His light-touched father.

He liked watching Ailinn naked at the window. He'd often thought of carving her, not just in miniature on a lovespoon, but as a candlestick maybe. Would he be able to render the responsiveness of her flesh, the reserves of life that were in her flanks, the strength of her legs? The springiness of her that made him believe in life?

'While we're laying cards on the table,' he blurted out, 'my grandfather was a hunchback.'

She didn't turn around.

'You never told me that before.'

'I never knew before.'

'So how come you know now?'

'Kroplik told me.'

'How does he know?'

'He knows everything. Like your beloved Ez.'

'Does it bother you?'

'To know I'm from crooked stock? Yes. But Kroplik reckons I should be grateful. It was the hunchback who kept us safe.'

'Safe from what?'

'I don't know. Whatever.'

'And how does Kroplik say he managed that?'

'By scaring people and being lucky. Apparently you don't mess with a hunchback. Or at least you don't in these parts.'

'Do you ever wonder . . .' she started to say, then relented.

'Do I ever wonder what?'

'It doesn't matter.'

'Yes it does. Do I ever wonder what?'

'What you're doing here.'

'On earth?'

'In Port Reuben.'

'All the time.'

'Would you want to find out?'

He got up from the bed and moved towards her. He wanted to feel her nakedness pressed into his, the lovely resilience of her buttocks.

'There's a lot I want to find out,' he said. 'But then again there isn't. Mysteries are always so banal when they're solved. You're better off living in uncertainty.'

'You say that, but you couldn't bear not knowing who broke in here and straightened your rug.'

'No. And now I never will find out.' This was a silent allusion, that Ailinn was quick to pick up, to the murder of Detective Inspector Gutkind, the gory details of which were the talk of Port Reuben and beyond. Neither spoke about it. Kevern was happy to have him out of their lives, but he didn't want to put that relief in so many words to Ailinn. He didn't suppose she'd wonder if he'd done it, but then again there was no reason to plant further anxiety. Who knows what anyone will do in the end? Who would have thought he'd kiss Lowenna Morgenstern? Who would have thought his mother had a secret life? And now Ailinn . . .

'Certainty might be banal, but better that, any time, than the immeasurable stress of uncertainty,' Ailinn said, reading his mind.

'So you're pleased to know now how you came to be in an orphanage? You don't wish that Ez had never told you?'

'Hardly "pleased", but yes, I believe I am better off for knowing, banal though you consider it all to be.'

'I didn't say that what happened to you was banal.'

'Don't apologise. I'm not offended. It *is* banal. But I would rather know it than not.'

'And you'd rather know that Ez was instrumental in our meeting?'

'Rather it had happened some other way, but rather know than not know that it happened the way it did.'

'We should drink to Ez, then.'

Was he being sarcastic, or just slow to take the measure of what she was trying to tell him?

He went downstairs to open a bottle and returned with two full glasses.

'To Ez,' he said.

She still couldn't decide. Sarcastic, or unfeeling, or stupid?

And then he noticed that Ailinn's eyes were red. Not with weeping, more with the strain of looking.

'You look as though you've seen a ghost,' he said.

And that was when she told him.

What will it take? The same as it has always taken. The application of a scriptural calumny (in this instance the convergence of two scriptural calumnies) to economic instability, inflamed nationalism, an unemployed and malleable populace in whom the propensity to hero-worship is pronounced, supine government, *tedium vitae*, a self-righteous and ill-informed élite, the pertinaciousness of old libels – the most consoling of which being that they'd had their chance, these objects of immemorial detestation, chance after chance (to choose love over law, flexibility over intransigence, community over exclusiveness, and to learn compassion from suffering) . . . chance after chance, and – as witness their moving in scarcely more than a generation from objects of immolation to proponents of it – they'd blown them all. Plus zealotry. Never forget zealotry – that torch to the easily inflamed passions of the benighted and the cultured alike. What it won't take, because it won't need – because it never *needs* – is an evil genius to conceive and direct the operation. We have been lulled by the great autocrat-driven genocides of the recent past into thinking that nothing of that enormity of madness can ever happen again – not anywhere, least of all here. And it's true – nothing on such a scale probably ever will. But lower down the order of horrors, and answering a far more modest ambition, carnage can still be connived at – lesser bloodbaths, minor murders, butchery of more modest proportions.

From an unwritten letter by Ailinn's great-grandfather Wolfie Lestchinsky to his daughter Rebecca.

BOOK THREE

Meet . . .
Merowitz, Berowitz, Handelman, Schandelman
Sperber and Gerber and Steiner and Stone
Boskowitz, Lubowitz, Aaronson, Baronson,
Kleinman and Feinman and Freidman and Cohen
Smallowitz, Wallowitz, Tidelbaum, Mandelbaum
Levin, Levinsky, Levine and Levi
Brumburger, Schlumburger, Minkus and Pinkus
And Stein with an 'e-i' and Styne with a 'y'

Allan Sherman, *Shake Hands With Your Uncle Max*

ONE

The Least Little Bit of Umbrage

i

'So I WAS right all along to think it,' Kevern said after a silence that seemed to Ailinn to go on for a period of dark time that could not be calculated in minutes or hours or even days . . .

'Right to think what?' she asked at last before her own life ran out.

'That Ferdie didn't like me. Ferdie has never liked me.'

It was four o'clock in the morning, the time no living thing should be awake. There was not a sound from the sea where Kevern had looked for seals and not found any – drowned were they? drowned in some communal act of self-murder? – and where he imagined that even the fish, after eating well, must be now sleeping. They had tried talking in bed but Kevern needed to be able to pace about, so they had gone downstairs to the little kitchen. Ailinn sat at the table in her dressing gown, absent-mindedly banging her fists together. Kevern made tea, walked up and down, and made more tea. They had toasted all the bread they had and eaten all the biscuits. Ailinn couldn't face sardines or pilchards so Kevern opened tins of baked beans, cherry tomatoes, tuna in olive oil, mushroom soup and sweet-corn. These he mixed in a large bowl to which he added salt, pepper and paprika. No thanks, Ailinn had said. He was not wearing any clothes. In response to Ailinn's concern that he was cold, and then that he would scald himself, he said he wanted to be cold and wanted to scald himself. How you see me is how I feel, he told her.

Vulnerable, she could understand, but she wanted him to know he wasn't – they weren't – in any danger.

'Can Ez be trusted?' he asked.

'To do what?'

'To keep quiet.'

It was a difficult question to answer. 'No one means us any harm,' she repeated.

He laughed. 'Don't forget Ferdie. Never forget Ferdie.'

She was not inclined to follow him into Ferdie territory. She knew that he was preparing to go through the names of everyone he thought had ever harmed him or meant him ill – a list that could take them through many more nights like this – and still at the end of it scratch his head and say he didn't understand what he'd done to offend them. It appeared to give him consolation to go on saying 'I don't think Ferdie likes me,' and she feared he would repeat it and repeat it until she was able to direct him on to another course.

'There is no point even trying to make light of any of this,' she said. 'I know that you only joke when you are at your most anxious.'

'Joking? Who's joking?'

He no sooner said those words than he knew he had to cross his js no longer.

Could this be called a liberation, then? It was too early to say.

He was past the point of marvelling at how much made sense to him now. He had always known . . . that was to be his defence against the horrors of surprise . . . he had always known *really*, at some level, below consciousness, beyond cognition, he had always known *somewhere* . . . not everything, of course not everything, not the half of it, but enough, for the news to be as much confirmation as shock . . . though whether that was confirmation of the worst of what he'd half known, or the best, or just something in the middle, he was yet to find out. But he hadn't been to sleep and was wandering his kitchen naked, drinking tea and eating bean and tuna soup, so it had to be admitted he was not exactly taking it lightly.

By comparison, Ailinn, banging her fists together like cymbals, was relaxation itself.

'Ferdie didn't like you, either,' he reminded her.

'Darling, I don't give a shit what Ferdie thought.'

'You should. The world is full of Ferdies.'

'*Your* world is full of Ferdies.'

'So you're OK about all this, is that what you're telling me?'

She had put herself in a false position. No she didn't feel OK about *all* this, but then Kevern still didn't know the full extent of it. She couldn't hit him with more than she'd hit him with already. This was part one. Part two would come when she thought he was good and ready. Give me time, she'd told Ez. Wouldn't it be best to strike while the iron's hot, Ez had said, but the metaphor was too close to the literal truth. It would have been like branding and braining him. I'll need time, she insisted. As for what she did tell Kevern about – their sudden consanguinity – then yes, the revelation did feel more a blessing than a curse to her. But however their histories had converged, their antecedent narratives were different. To put it brutally, she had none. Ez had simply filled the blanks in for her. And something was better than nothing. Whereas for Kevern, well he had to set about reconfiguring a densely peopled chronicle, reimagining not just himself but every member of his family. And pacing the kitchen with no clothes, trying for jokes that weren't funny even by his family's standards of deranged unfunniness, he didn't appear so far to be making a good job of it.

'I'll be OK,' she said, 'when you're OK.'

He stopped his pacing and leaned against the stove. 'Be careful, for Christ's sake,' she warned him.

'What did they see?' he asked suddenly, as though addressing another matter entirely, as though he had just strolled into the room with an incidental question in his mind. 'I'm not asking what they thought – they thought what they'd been taught to think – but what did they *see* when my hunchbacked grandfather popped his nose out of this cottage to sniff the poisoned air? What did they see when my mother went shopping in her rags? Or when my father crept into the village to sell his candlesticks to the gift shops? Or when you and I, come to that, first went strolling arm in arm through Paradise Valley? What do they see when they see us now?'

'Who's "they"?'

He wouldn't even bother to answer that. She knew who 'they' were. 'They' were whoever weren't them. The Ferdies.

'What do we look like to them, is what I'm asking. Vermin?'

'Oh, Kevern!'

'*Oh, Kevern* what? *Oh, Kevern, don't be so extreme*. Do you think I could ever outdo in extremity those who did what they did? But to understand how they could ever do it requires us to see what they saw, or at least to imagine what they saw.'

'Maybe they didn't see anything. Maybe they still don't. Has it occurred to you that we just aren't there for them?'

'*Just*! That's a mighty big "just", Ailinn. I think I'd rather be vermin than "just" not there. And even if you're right, it still takes some explaining. How do you make a fellow mortal not there? What's the trick of seeing right through someone? An indifference on that scale is nothing short of apocalyptic – or it is when it comes to getting rid of the thing you don't see, going to pains to obliterate what isn't there. But I don't think you're right anyway. I think they must see something, the embodiment of a horrible idea, the fleshing out of an evil principle that's been talked about and written about for too long, mouldy like something that's crawled out of its own grave.'

'You are in danger,' she said, 'of describing the horror you see, not the horror they do.'

'Why should I see horror?'

'Don't be naive.'

'How am I being naive?'

'When Hendrie raised his hand and told me I had been with them too long, that I didn't belong there, that he wished they'd never rescued me from the orphanage, I saw what he saw. An outcast ingrate – with big feet – whom no one could possibly love. That's the way it works.'

'I'm sorry about the feet. I love your feet.'

He dropped to his knees and thrust his head under the table where her feet were, and kissed them. I could stay here, he thought. Never come back up.

But he did come back up. That was the grim rule of life, one always came back up . . . until one didn't.

She was smiling at least. Gravely, but a smile was still a smile.

'Take my point, Kevern,' she said.

'I take your point. And I don't hate myself, if that's what you're getting at.'

'That's not what I'm getting at. I don't hate myself either. But criticism rubs off. How could it be otherwise? Sometimes the glass through which others look at you tilts and you catch a little of what they see. It's understandable that you wish you'd made a better impression.'

'*Impression*! You make it sound like a children's story – *The Little Girl Who Should Have Made a Better Impression*. I'm not that little girl, or boy. I don't crave anybody's respect – except yours. I'm not trying to understand what people see when they see me – when they see *us*, Ailinn – because I think I ought to improve my appearance. I've no desire to wear a better aspect. I want to understand what they see on the principle that one should know one's enemies. I want to know what they see so I can hate them better.'

She fell silent – not bruised by the vehemence of his words but because she wondered whether she was wrong not to feel what he felt. Was it feeble of her to reject resentment, even on behalf of her poor great-grandparents? This queer exhilaration she was experiencing – as though her life could be about to start at last and never mind where she'd been before – was it disloyal? Was Ez sending her on a fool's errand whose futility was the least of it? Was it wrong? Was it treasonable?

But no. Whatever she was doing, right, wrong, feeble, gullible, treasonable, Kevern's way was plain bad. Bad for him. Bad for his mental state. Bad for them. Bad for their future together. *Bad*. 'This is unhealthy,' she said at last.

'It's a bit late for health.'

'You are also not being honest with yourself. You say you need to understand how others see you, but your curiosity isn't dispassionate. It isn't divided equally between those who don't like you and those who do. You're only really intrigued by those who don't.'

'Hardly surprising is it, given what I've just discovered, if it's those who don't like me I'm interested in right now. My friends I can think about later.'

Friends? Did he have friends? His recent conversation with Rozenwyn Feigenblat – not a word of which he'd mentioned to Ailinn – came back to him. She saw him as friendless – worse than that, she saw him as courting friendlessness. And now here was Ailinn saying the same. Why was his nature quite so pervious to women?

'It's not right now I'm talking about,' she persisted. 'You've always paid more attention to your enemies.'

'Ailinn, I didn't know I had enemies until five minutes ago.'

'That's ridiculous. Who do you lock your door against? Who are you frightened of being invaded by? You have lived in a world of enemies all your life.'

'You can talk, you and Ahab.'

She waved Ahab away. 'Now he's found me I'll deal with him,' she said.

'It's as easy as that?'

'No. But it's good to confront him now he's out of the shadows.

It's good to turn and face him. Look him in the eyes. Your point – know your enemy. OK, Ahab – do your worst. And it turns out he isn't even called Ahab.'

'No, he's called Ferdie – who frankly I find more frightening.'

'That's because you want to go on being frightened. You know no other way.'

'Are you calling me a coward?'

'No. I'm sure it takes bravery to live with fear as you do.'

'That's patronising. I don't "bravely" live with fear. It's not something I choose. I have no choice.'

'You do – you have the choice not to wallow . . .'

'You think this is wallowing?'

She did, yes she did, but declined to answer. She dropped her head between her fists, and this time beat the cymbals against her ears.

He wondered if he ought to get dressed. The first squeeze of narrow light was showing out to sea. He wasn't ready for day, but if it had to come he should go and greet it. The cliffs would be a good place to be, on his bench, side by side with Ailinn, looking out to the dead, consoling sea. It wouldn't change anything but weather was preferable to the cottage, and the great sea justified his fears. The world was terrifying.

'Will you walk with me?' he asked, in his gentlest voice. She was right, he knew she was right, morbidity was his nature. So what was new?

'Of course I will,' she said, putting an arm around him. Not everyone was his enemy, she wanted him to know. But the gesture made them both feel isolated. They had each other, but who else did they have?

It was only when they were on the bench that she realised he hadn't double-locked and double-checked that he'd locked the door of his cottage. Had he kicked the Chinese runner? She didn't think he had. She should have been pleased but she wasn't. What was he without his rituals?

There was rain in the air. That squeezed sliver of light had been an illusory promise. Below them, the blowhole was clearing its throat in readiness for a day of tumult. A couple of gulls threw themselves like rags into the wind.

'What now?' he said suddenly.

'Do you want to go back in?'

'No, I meant what are we going to do with the rest of our lives?'

She knew but couldn't tell him. 'We can do whatever you'd like to do,' she lied.

'Well we can't just carry on as though nothing's happened.'

'Why not? How much has changed really?'

'Everything,' he said. 'Absolutely everything.'

'You'll feel differently in a few days. You'll get back into the swing of things.'

'What swing of things? I never was in the swing of things. I was waiting. Just waiting. I didn't know what I was waiting to happen or find out, but I now see that the waiting made for a life of sorts.'

'*Of sorts*! With me? Is that the best you can say of our time together – *a life of sorts*?'

He put his arm around her waist but didn't pull her to him. 'Not you. Of course not you. I don't mean that. We are fine. We are wonderful. But the me that isn't us, that wasn't us, when all is said and done, before I met you – before the pig auctioneer – that solitary me . . . where do I go with it from here? I waited and I waited, scratching away at bits of wood, and now I know what I was waiting for and it's . . .'

'It's what?'

He didn't know. Above him the raggedy gulls screamed desolately. Was it all just thwarted greed or did they hate it here as much as he did? He looked up to the sky and cupped his ears as though the birds might tell him what to do with himself from this moment on.

'Nothing,' he said at last. 'What it is is nothing. In fact it's worse than nothing.'

'You could try feeling pride,' she said.

'What?'

'Pride. You could decide to wear it as a badge of honour.'

'What do you suggest I do? Change my name back?'

'That's a black joke, Kevern,' she said.

He agreed. 'The blackest.'

'Then why did you make it?'

He shrugged. 'Why did you speak of pride and honour? Where's the honour, please tell me? You might as well ask this ant which I am about to tread on to view all the previous years of his ant life with pride.'

'It's not to his shame that you stamp on him.'

'I disagree with you. It is his shame, his fault, for being an ant. We have to take responsibility for our fate. Even an ant. What happens to him is his disgrace.'

She was shocked to hear him speak like this. It felt like a blasphemy to her. Perhaps he needed to blaspheme. Perhaps that was his way of working the shock of it all out of his system. Nonetheless she couldn't let his blasphemies go unchecked. 'You aren't saying what you really mean,' she said. 'You can't honestly think that your mother's and father's life was a disgrace.'

'They were in hiding for the whole of it. Yes, it was a disgrace.'

'And what about those who had nowhere to hide? Their parents and grandparents? Mine?'

'The trodden generations? A disgrace.'

'Then it's up to you to restore respect.'

'Me? I am the greatest disgrace of all.'

ii

Esme Nussbaum sits at the window of her room and watches rain drip from the ferns. Even when it's not raining anywhere else it rains in Paradise Valley and even when it doesn't rain in Paradise Valley the ferns go on dripping.

There is nothing more I can do, she tells herself. It's no longer in my hands. But it's in her brain, and with that she wills them on, the harbingers of her bright new equilibrium of hate.

Senior officials from Ofnow are on the phone to her every day. They want to know how it's proceeding. The population is still tearing itself apart – why, in her very neck of the woods there has been another brutal murder, a double murder, a policeman and his cat, for God's sake: what maniac would kill a cat? – so they need good news. She tells them this thing must run its course. Yes, she has other irons in the fire, but this is the best bet and, trust her, she won't take her eye off it for a moment. But she has to remind them that the complex structure of conflict that was Rome wasn't built in a day and that there'll be no immediate visible effect even if all does go well. They don't agree with her. They think the country will feel a different place the minute it learns that WHAT HAPPENED, IF IT HAPPENED was only, after all, a partial solution. They don't expect a uniformity of response. After years of saying sorry there's no knowing how the public will react but, by Esme's own analysis, the news itself – a few well-judged publicity photographs, the odd teaser interview, not giving too much away, in celebrity and gossip magazines – should begin to restore the necessary balance of societal antagonism. 'Just give us some tidbits we can definitively leak,' they tell her, meaning that the wedding, the conception, and the birth can wait. The child of course is crucial – *For unto us a child is given* – but even the promise of it should suffice for the moment.

I'm on it, Esme tells them.

There is one among the importunates whose excitement at the prospect of a cultural rebirth – musicals with wit, reject-rock, hellishly sardonic comedies, an end to ballads – is so intense he can barely express it in coherent sentences. So frequently does he call her that Esme is beginning to wonder whether he isn't himself one her scouts had missed. I have to tell you, she tells him, that reigniting popular culture is not high among my objectives. He baulks at 'popular'. The serious theatre, too, needs a shot in the arm, he reminds her. Imagine hearing complex, warring sentences on the stage again. Imagine paradox and bitterness and laceration. Art as endless disputation, bravura blasphemy – Oh, the bliss of it, Ms Nussbaum! Alternatively, imagine the *Herzschmerz* of a violin and piano sonata, played as only they can play it, as though for the final time. She warns him against premature recidivism. You know about things you shouldn't know about, she says sternly, and you make unwarrantable assumptions about my politics. I have no desire to restore a status quo from which so many suffered. To regret WHAT HAPPENED is not to throw the baby out with the bathwater. Something needed to happen, even if what did exceeded decency and proportionality. But nor must we force those who have been providentially spared back into demeaning stereotypical patterns. *Herzschmerz* indeed! I repeat, I am indifferent to the entertainment implications of this project. Not dismissive, just not engaged. My concern is not bebop but the physics of societal mistrust. You cannot have a one-sided coin. If what I am seeking comes about, we will once again enjoy the stability of knowing who we're not.

Her importuner laughs, optimistic despite what she has said to him, imagining he has heard irony. But he is wrong. Irony is not something Esme Nussbaum does.

It has occurred to her, of course, to worry for Ailinn should things not come about as she intends or, indeed, should it come about too well. What if the years of saying sorry have bred an antagonism even deeper than before? Could Ailinn find herself the object of violent suspicion long before the desired equilibrium has time to take hold?

But Esme is in the grip of a passion to do good, and all other concerns, including Ailinn's safety, are subjugated to the more immediate task of bringing that good about.

There is still some way to go. The problem is Kevern. Not the facts about the bloodline. The facts are fine. So easy of confirmation, in fact, it is a wonder the Cohens were able to go on living for so long in Port Reuben unmolested. The problem is the flakiness. She isn't any longer sure that he is suitable. She puts this down to poor preparation. Those who have been making him their study have not done their job well. They have not adequately assessed his character. They have been looking through him, or past him, not *at* him. But it's her fault too. When she came down to Paradise Valley it was with a view to scrutinising them both. So what went wrong? Ailinn went wrong. Or rather Ailinn went too right. Esme wonders if her vile father had her number after all. Was she indeed a lesbian? She didn't think so, but without question she'd found the girl engrossing. And while she was engrossed in the one she failed to keep tabs on the other. Perhaps Kevern had been exercising the same magic. Perhaps he too had blinded those charged exclusively with watching him. Is that their inherited gift, Esme catches herself asking. Are they charmers? Do they beguile? She stills her thoughts. If she's not careful she'll be understanding too well why WHAT HAPPENED happened.

Kevern is not her last throw of the dice. Neither, come to that, is Ailinn. Little by little, fragile shoots of hopefulness have shown themselves in remote corners of the country. Nothing showy, naturally, no salt-rose or topaz, but here and there, a violet by a mossy stone, a dark thing between the shadow and the soul, wasting its sweetness on the desert air. And these will certainly be significant when it comes to procreative negotiations further down the line. But they are not her first choice. Ailinn and Kevern remain her first choice.

There is another consideration when it comes to Kevern. Esme has given voice to this more than once, in private while watching the ferns drip and when irked by all the problems associated with his character. Who needs the little prick, she has wondered, surprised by her own violence. Expletives came to her often when she lay in her coma, but they haven't visited her much since.

What she means by this is that while Ailinn must be the real McCoy, and must, short of a miracle, have a father for the child, it might not be absolutely essential to that child's being the real McCoy that the father is the real McCoy as well. She has been hampered by having no one to ask and very few intact books to consult but she has beavered away and believes she can now confirm Ailinn's grandmother's understanding of the law of matrilineality: yes, it is indeed the case, as Rebecca thought when she defied her husband, that the McCoys, as it amuses her to call them while she bites her fingernails, look only to the mother for transmission of authenticity. Thus, though there's no knowing who Ailinn's father was, and though her grandfather Fridleif was unacceptable in every possible regard, the fact that she is in direct, unbroken line of matrilineal descent from her grandmother, who appears to have ticked all the boxes herself, is sufficient to make her what Esme wants her to be. That being the case, who needs that little prick Kevern Cohen?

No, no one *needs* him. That's the point to which Esme's rough scholarship has brought her. But still and all it will be better in every way if he can be roped in. His presence as Ailinn's agitated, unsmiling consort will help Esme to the composite effect she is looking for. Kevern does not, she is confident, photograph well. There are many aspects of character the camera can lie about, but stand-offishness is not one of them. A man so aloof that he accepts no kinship with the human race looks exactly that when he's photographed – an unquiet thing, displaced and determined to stay that way. Furthermore, if she can sell him the whole box of tricks, or at least keep the pairing to the degree that he will buy into engagement, marriage and the rest of it, she will be able to arrange them a traditional wedding – she will officiate herself if she has to – whose antiquated self-absorption will enrage as many as it pleases. Including, she has no doubt, Kevern Cohen. He will not behave well at his own wedding. She has come across the ritual of the bridegroom breaking a glass. Kevern, she is confident, will stamp it to smithereens. He will make a sardonic speech, compromising his love for Ailinn (she doesn't doubt its genuineness) with savage jokes that no one will enjoy. Yes, the more she thinks about his studied prickliness, the more she wants to keep him. Ailinn is a woman of immense charm. What no one wants is for people to fall in love with her to the degree that no equilibrium of hate is re-established. Kevern, on the other hand, even should he somehow succeed in not being wholly detestable, will not inspire devotion. In Kevern the people will have no difficulty recognising their own antithesis.

iii

Black Friday

Demelza has left me. My mistake – though in the course of our final argument she told me I had made more mistakes than she could count – was to leave my diary where she could find it. Unless my mistake was to confide quite so many sexual secrets to its pages.

Wrong again, she said, when I confessed to that. Your mistake was to have *had* so many sexual secrets.

She says there's no other man. Do I believe her? No, I do not. My money's on Kevern 'Coco' Cohen. I can't say I ever did care much for him but now I know him for what he is I suspect he has been scheming to squirm his way between Demelza's legs all along. The metaphor of the reptile, by the way, is not mine. There was man, there was woman and then there was the all-knowing snake. I can't be blamed for the theology of that parable when it was they who told it about themselves. Enter knowledge into the paradisal world of love and innocence – in other words enter them with their obscene obsession for knowing everything – and that's happiness gone for ever. No wonder they shunned the human form and painted abstract robotical horrors.

Well, we thought we'd scorched that particular snake, but here it is again writhing between my wife's legs. And the crazy thing is that I've been instrumental in its rebirth. Had I seen what he was about years ago, before the Wise Ones rewrote the manual, I could have penned a damning report and that would have been that. There were enough clues, God knows. The never saying sorry. The never being out of the library. The furtive tap-turning and hand washing – what was he trying to wash off, I'd ask Demelza. Now it's clear: his own snake slime. Slime that is now inside my wife. No wonder she was evasive when I tried to talk to her about him. And no wonder, come to think of it, she suffered Credibility Fatigue. I know now just what was fatiguing her.

It's a good job I am civilised. I count to a hundred. I pat Petroc, pat a couple of students in the same spirit, take out my sketches of St Mordechai's Mount and remember when my mind was last given over to the contemplation of unsullied loveliness. I have an idea for a new series of watercolours – Eden. The Garden before the introduction of the snake. Just Demelza and I doing as we are told, unaware of our nakedness, alone under the trees, except maybe for Petroc. Speaking of whom, should I not have smelt a rat when he was snarling around Kevern 'Coco' Cohen's feet smelling something worse? 'Petroc!' Demelza used to cry, calling him off. 'Down, Petroc. Naughty boy. Down! I'm so sorry, Mr Cohen.' Mr Cohen! *I'm so sorry, Mr Cohen*. I bet she was. Poor Petroc. Disparaged for expressing his nature and keeping us safe from harm.

I wouldn't put it past him – the snake, not the dog – to have made her offerings of lovespoons. Portraits. Full-length. Top to toe. The pair of them entwined in lime wood. Not exactly likenesses. He doesn't do likenesses. A likeness is not primitive enough for his depraved aesthetic. They prefer a touch of the ape to show through. But likeness enough to be compromisingly recognisable. Probably shown them to our students, too, while lecturing on the intricacy of their carving – *intricate* all right! – hoping they would make out Demelza despite the monkey features and scoff at me. Where did they do it? Here, when I was teaching? Or did she go over there on days when she said she needed to do some shopping? On the floor of his workshop, would it have been? On a bed of sawdust? If only I'd been less trusting. I should have smelt her hair when she returned. Should have gone searching for shavings in her underwear drawer. Or better still should have had my way with that wild-haired piece of his while he was otherwise engaged. It must be assumed – forgive the fancy talk: I'm preparing my defence – I must assume that she too is to be numbered among the degenerates, though the flowers she made were beautiful enough. Veering on the odd, as you'd expect, even the macabre, but still close enough to nature to be lovely. So what would she have been like, that bird-woman of his with the hawk face? Sharp claws she'll have, I bet. A tongue wet with blood and little nibbly teeth. Mandibles – is that the word? *Rotten juice and mandibles* – who said that? *The shitty magma of rotten juice and mandibles* . . . blah, blah, blah . . . ring a bell? . . . *the passion of the termite* . . .

. . . it must, methinks, have been one of those resurrected samizdat pamphlets from before WHAT HAPPENED that did the rounds of the country's common rooms not all that long ago, probably as a medical corrective to our periodic recrudescences of unseemly guilt. All very well saying sorry sorry sorry sorry sorry – I have always been at the forefront of the apologising party myself, so long as we aren't apologising for anything we have actually done – but a little puncturing of the windpipe of our dutifulness is no bad thing, as many of us felt, hence the reappearance of these short samizdatty things, if that's the right expression, inflammatory trifles, anyway, from those on the front line and who knew the problem of termite infestation for themselves, that brightened our lives for a while before we grew dutiful again.

When a thing is heartfelt it stays with you. '*Ich hab' im Traum geweinet*' . . . '*Où sont les neiges d'antan*' . . . You don't forget sentiments like those. They express the quintessence of regret. But quintessence of scorn can melt your bones as well. Like those lines about shitty magma . . . the termites being everywhere, selling everything, keeping everything, destroying everything, weaving their web, was it, yes, *weaving their web in the shadows* . . . then eliminating, dissuading, pursuing whoever might cause them the least little bit of umbrage – that's the phrase – to a final bloody course of reckoning, tee-dum tee-dum . . . *The least little bit of umbrage*. Can there be a more telling description of the disproportionality of Kevern 'Co-co-cocksucking' Cohen and his kind, can there be a better atomisation of their crazed thin-skinned sensitivity, than that? *The least little bit of umbrage.* That imagined sliver of a slight in retaliation for which they'd have shaken the whole planet to its foundations . . . if we'd let them.

It would come as no surprise to learn the snake believes he's been caused the least little bit of umbrage by me, though where and how I can't imagine, and deny all charge and knowledge, but believes it anyway, I bet he does, in return for which he deposits his slime in my sweet, gullible and far too forgiving, not to say slime-receptive, Demelza. He will treat you as he's treated me, I tell her. They are incapable of gratitude . . . But she denies all knowledge of him. You think I'd want to be with another man after you, she says. You think I'm that big a fool? But my mind races with suspicions of them both and that's enough for me. On my hands and knees I pursue the spattered trail of rotten juices to my bed.

That I have no recourse, short of a private feud which, as the older and more easily hurt party, I am sure to lose, has been made plain to me in a communication from up there. They don't exactly confirm my suspicions as to Demelza (though they blaze them forth as to everything else), but the warning is unequivocal: stay away. It's actually even blunter than that. You have made a balls-up, move aside. No mention of Mrs Snake but I take the injunction to include her. Stay well clear of them both. Pretty much what I told Detective Inspector Gutkind. So you could say that in death he must be enjoying his revenge. As for when I will be enjoying mine, God alone knows. I am not, anyway, to have the consolation of confronting either of them. Not a cold word into his ear, not a warm whisper into hers; no bite from those mandala mandibles; no last sniff of her paper flowers.

My hand is forced. I will away to beauty . . .

No, not Rozenwyn Feigenblat. The beauty of natural things – tidal flats, sunsets, unsullied by all the subtle demonism of life and thought . . .

iv

Ailinn Solomons, looking at the moon, and listening to her jumping heart, wondered at what was happening to her. She had returned, briefly – she didn't want to leave Kevern on his own for too long – to Paradise Valley where there were still things to find out, sort out, have out, and was sitting on a cold mossy bench, hugging herself against the chill damp, listening to Ez clattering about rather obviously in the kitchen. 'Do I feel any different?' she asked herself. Ez had been lending her books relevant to that question, or at least fragments of books, dog-eared, singed, defaced, some of them crayoned over as if by a class of three-year-old delinquents. Although they purported to have been written – whenever it was they were written – from the inside, by those in the know, or at least by those who knew others in the know, each work, no matter how little of it there was, contradicted the one before. It was her forebears' austerity of conscience, according to one writer, that had always troubled humanity and explained the hostility they encountered wherever they went. They demanded too much. They set too high a standard. A second writer understood their defining characteristic as a near irresponsible love of the material world, and it was this that had landed them in hot water. Offered the spirit, they chose matter. Offered emotion, they chose reason. This one said they were deeply pious; that one found them profoundly sacrilegious. They were devoted to charity, yet they amassed wealth regardless of how they came by it. When they weren't consumed by self-regard they suffered a bruising sense of worthlessness. They saw the universe as a reflection of the God that loved them above all people, but moved through it like strangers. When she came to the alienation they felt in nature she recognised herself at last. She had never been comfortable on a garden seat in her life. She disliked the damp newsprint smell of vegetation, detested snails and worms, felt threatened by the icy indifference of the moon, and feared the irregular rhythm of her heart which also, surely, was a thing of nature. So while she didn't feel any different after reading all Esme had given her to read, she at least understood why she felt the same.

Esme called out to her from the kitchen. She had, since morning, been making chicken soup to an ancient recipe she'd found in a cookery book that must have been as old as creation and wondered whether Ailinn wanted to eat it inside or out. Ailinn didn't want to eat it at all, so reverentially had Esme prepared it, with so much sacrificial ardour had she dismembered the chicken, so full of spiritual intention was her dicing of the carrots, so soulfully did she look at her through the steam rising from the pan, but decided that as she had to eat it somewhere she would eat it out. Compound the discomfort.

They ate silently for a short while, balancing the soup plates on their knees. Esme sneaked looks at her.

'Are you enjoying it, my love?

My love!

'Am I meant to?'

'Well I've made it for you in the hope you will.'

'No, I mean is it part of my preparation?'

Esme winced.

'Will it count against me,' Ailinn continued, 'if I don't? Will it prove I'm a fake?'

'Well I won't tell,' Esme said.

'Forgive me, I am not able to finish it,' Ailinn said at last, putting the plate on the ground between her ugly feet. 'There is something more pressing than soup.'

Esme started in alarm. It irritated Ailinn how easily she could worry her. She had only to express the slightest disquiet for Esme's entire system of defences to be activated. She's too close to me, she thought. There's more of her inside my skin than there is of me.

'What is it that's more pressing?' Esme asked. She could have been asking how long Ailinn had known she only had an hour to live.

'Matrilineality,' Ailinn said.

'Could you explain that?'

'Matrilineality? After all you've said to me on the subject! My love' – take that, Ailinn thought – 'it's you who are the authority.'

'No, I meant could you explain what bothers you about it.'

So, Ailinn, shivering under the cold moon, did.

If fathers bore so little responsibility for the defining characteristics of their progeny, as Esme said they did, in what sense were they their progeny at all? There seemed to be a carelessness here that belied the otherwise strict code of kinship into which Ailinn had now been drawn. Had it really mattered not at all what sort of seed her father had put into her mother, and her grandfather into her grandmother? Was it merely incidental? She felt the pull of contradictory impulses: pleased to be incontrovertibly what she was, but disappointed she had got there, so to speak, so easily, with so few caveats as to fathers. In an odd way it devalued her new-found affiliation. 'I would want a child of mine to be validated on both sides,' she told Esme.

'I want that for you too,' Esme assured her.

Fearing that Esme intended to embrace her, Ailinn moved her chair away, pretending she was trying to make herself more comfortable.

'But . . . ?'

'But we don't always get what we want.'

'You moved heaven and earth to keep us together, Ez,' she reminded her. 'You wouldn't let me walk away from him. "Ring him, ring him," you urged me. My soulmate, you had the nerve to call him when you knew nothing of my soul. And when I told you he was walking away from me you turned as white as your blouse. What's changed?'

Esme Nussbaum was relieved that Ailinn couldn't see her blush. 'Nothing's changed. I care about your happiness as much as I ever did. More. But you've taken what I've had to tell you remarkably well – far better, truly, than I dared to hope you would. I couldn't imagine you ever dealing with this on your own, yet you have.'

'Not have, *am* . . . I'm a work in progress, Ez.'

'I understand . . .'

'And I'm not on my own.'

'Are you saying that Kevern is with you on this every inch of the way?'

'I never said *I* was with me on this every inch of the way. I haven't chosen this, remember. And I haven't seen through to the end of all it means. You have to face the fact that I probably never will. I can't give you a guarantee for life.'

'I know that and I'm not pressuring you. If you and Kevern can work this out together there's nothing I'd like more.'

'Matrilineality notwithstanding?'

'Matrilineality is not my invention. It just happens to be the way it works.'

'And the way it works makes Kevern redundant?'

'Not at all. The future I envisage requires mothers and fathers.'

'For the look of the thing.'

This time Esme would not be denied. She leaned across and stroked the girl's arm. 'Ailinn, this is all about the "look" of the thing. You are no different today from who you were a year ago, a month ago even. What's changed is how you appear. How you appear to yourself and how you will appear to the world. It's all illusion. Identity is nothing but illusion.'

'I shouldn't worry in that case that I don't like chicken soup?'

'I'd like you not to worry about anything.'

Ailinn wondered why she'd made a joke. Was it Kevern's doing? 'If it's all illusion,' she continued in a different vein, 'why has it caused so much misery?'

'I've had a long time to think about this,' Esme said, pausing . . .

'And?'

Ailinn marvelled at her own impatience. She had lived in ignorance of just about everything for a quarter of a century; now she needed answers to questions she could never have imagined she would ask, and she needed them at once. The pity of it was that the person in the best position to answer those questions seemed to have all the time in the world. In fact Ailinn was wrong about this. Esme, too, was a cauldron of impatience, but did not want to frighten Ailinn off with her intensity. So both women sat with frayed nerves, listening to the clocks furiously ticking in their brains.

'We are dead matter,' Esme continued at last, 'indeed I was very nearly dead matter myself when I realised this – we are dead matter until we distinguish ourselves from what's not dead. I was alive, I told myself as I was lying there. Very nearly dead, but alive. And it made me more alive to realise that. I wasn't the me I'd been, but nor was I the me they wanted me to be, which was no me at all. Only when we have a different state to strive against do we have reason to strive at all. And different people the same. I am me because I am not her, or you. If we were all red earthworms there'd be no point in life. Identity is just the name we give to the act of making ourselves distinct.'

'So you're saying it's irrelevant what our identities really are? As long as we assume one and fight against someone else's.'

'I'd say so, yes. Pretty much.'

'Isn't that a bit arbitrary?'

'Perhaps. But isn't everything? It's just chance that we're born to who we're born to. There's no design.'

'So why fight for who we are?'

'For the sake of the fight itself.'

'Then isn't that a bit violent, as well as arbitrary?'

'Life is violent. I had to fight death to be alive.'

'But if "who we are" is arbitrary, and if we fight for whatever cause we just happen to be to born to, for no other reason than the fight itself, then it didn't have to be me you picked for this . . .'

'I didn't pick you, Ailinn.'

'All right. Describe it how you like. But if there is no identifiable me then it doesn't matter whether I am it or not. I don't have to be the real deal because there is no real deal. You could have hit on anyone.'

Esme bit her lip. 'You'll do it better,' she said.

They fell silent. Something crawled across Ailinn's feet. She wondered if it was Esme's red earthworm, that made life meaningless. She shuddered. Esme offered to go inside and fetch her a shawl. Ailinn shook her head. She could have been shaking Esme off her.

'If you're asking me to do this without Kevern,' she said suddenly, 'I'm afraid I can't. No, it's feeble of me to put it like that. If you're asking me to do this without Kevern, I'm afraid I *won't*.'

Esme felt as though all her splintered bones had been crushed a second time. She remembered what it took to distinguish herself from the dead.

'In that case we will have to make sure you do it with him,' she said.

TWO

Shake Hands With Your Uncle Max

i

IT WAS HEDRA Deitch who was the first to congratulate him.

'On?'

'Don't be like that,' Hedra said, wrinkling up her nose.

Kevern had dropped into her souvenir shop to see if her stock of lovespoons needed replenishing. She didn't sell many. Painted earthenware garden statuary, pressed-flower pictures, and Port Reuben tea towels and coffee mugs accounted for most of her trade. 'Cheap and cheerful, like me,' was how she described her business. But she thought a small selection of Kevern's lovespoons lent her shop a more upmarket feel, and she welcomed the opportunity his visits gave her to be suggestive with him. He wasn't like the other men in the village. You had to work a bit harder with him. She had snogged him once that she could remember, at the end of a wild night in the pub, when they were both drunk. She had done it to enrage Pascoe but she had enjoyed it too, after a fashion. He had a softer mouth than she expected. No biting. And no slapping. On his part, that is. So she was glad enough to return to Pascoe's rough indifferent gnawing later.

But Kevern was one of those men who got under your skin by not adequately taking you in. So he remained a challenge to her.

It was Ailinn's idea that Kevern do something practical such as checking on his outlets, no matter that there was no pressing financial reason to do so. He had not been down into the village, not seen a living soul since she'd told him the first part of what she had to tell him, and that was two weeks ago. He had gone into a decline, rapid even for a man who declined easily. He agreed to Ailinn's suggestion only because he knew it would make her, at least, feel better. He wasn't expecting to feel better himself. He didn't want to feel better. He owed it to what he'd been told to feel worse. That was what living a serious life meant, wasn't it, honouring the gravity of things by not pretending they were light? Rozenwyn Feigenblat had told him he was an ethicist, not an artist. He agreed with her. An artist owed a duty to nothing except his own irresponsibility. It was OK for an artist to frolic in the water, no matter how bloody the waves or how high the tide rose. An ethicist had an obligation to drown.

Just go for the walk, Ailinn had said. Just go for the exercise. See someone who isn't me. 'There isn't someone who isn't you,' he'd said. Whereupon she'd pushed him out of the cottage.

He meant what he'd said. There wasn't anyone who wasn't her, and if there were he didn't want to see them. And even she, since she'd become the bearer of bad news, was not always a welcome sight to him now.

But most of all he hadn't gone out because he hadn't wanted to be seen.

Was that because he believed he suddenly looked different? No. He trusted he looked exactly the same: the man he had always been, in decline as he had always been. The difference today was that he understood what they'd seen when they'd looked at him in the past.

He exchanged stiff greetings with people he barely knew. He had lived here all his life, in a village of fewer than two thousand souls, and yet there were still people who were lifetime residents themselves whose names he didn't know. His parents had taught him well in one regard. Remain a stranger to the place, they had said. Say nothing. Ask for nothing. Explain yourself to no one.

But they had also cautioned him to go unnoticed, and in that he could scarcely have fared worse. Everyone knew who he was – Kevern 'Coco' Cohen, the man with the sour expression who sat on his own bench above the blowhole, saying nothing, asking for nothing, explaining himself to no one.

And now here was Hedra Deitch, coming out from behind her counter to look him up and down, surveying him in that hungry way of hers, wondering if he'd do for whatever her itchy nature needed at that moment, something or other that her shot-beast of a husband couldn't provide. Shame he wasn't an artist. He'd have provided it and painted her later.

But why the congratulations? Was she being sarcastic, welcoming him to a knowledge of himself the whole village had possessed for years? Was she applauding his cottoning on finally – Kevern, the last to know about Kevern?

'Don't be like what?' he said.

She put one hand on her hip, as though to answer his coquettishness. 'Don't be pretending you aren't proud.'

He was not a man who ever asked people what they meant. He would rather puzzle over their words for months, and still not get to the bottom of their meaning, than ask them for a simple explanation. Did he not want to know or could he not bear to appear uncomprehending? This was a time to wonder whether he'd ever in his whole life understood a word that had been said to him. Clearly he hadn't ever understood his parents. Could it be that he had missed the point of what Ailinn had been saying to him too?

If only . . .

But when the news was bad . . . then he understood.

And Hedra? He prepared his face to pretend to get her meaning – a half-smile and a philosophic widening of the eyes that would cover every eventuality: from a declaration of undying to love to news that she had a terminal disease.

'I'm not pretending anything,' he said. 'And I'm certainly not pretending I'm not proud. I have nothing to be proud about.'

She moved a step closer. Was she about to kiss him? *Then be proud of this, my lover . . .*

Funny how often, for a man who didn't consider himself lovable, he thought a woman was about to kiss him. Was it hope? Was it dread? Or did he think of himself as the unsmiling princess, waiting to be kissed back into warm life by a frog?

'I don't reckon your missus would be pleased to hear you got nothing to be proud about,' Hedra said.

He increased his half-smile to a three-quarter smile and opened his eyes a little wider. 'My missus . . . ? What's Ailinn got to do with this?'

It was then she made a cradling motion with her arms, beaming like the Virgin Mary, rocking a little one to sleep.

'Come on!' she taunted him. 'You don't have to be coy with me. I know you're proud. Daddy!'

There, in the middle of the shop, with people watching, he snogged her brutally.

ii

Ailinn barely recognised him when he returned.

'My God, what's happened?' she said.

He felt that his face had grown to twice its length. He couldn't bear the weight of his jaw or control the movement of his tongue. He pointed to it. I have no words, the gesture meant. There are no words . . .

She put her arms around him and he remained enfolded in them. But he was unresponsive. This wasn't the first time she had held him, drained of life, but never before had she felt she couldn't at least thaw him back to something like good humour.

She made him tea which he drank without waiting for it to cool, almost in a single gulp.

'You are carrying our baby,' he finally said.

Now it was she who couldn't speak.

He waited for her to drink her tea. She could take all the time she liked. Time was not their problem. Then, looking beyond her, he repeated his words, without anger, without feeling. 'You are carrying our baby.'

'How do you know?'

'It's the talk of the village.'

She didn't believe that. The village had better things to talk about.

'What do you mean?' she asked. 'What do you *actually* mean?'

'I mean that it's known in the village that you are carrying our baby. I presume it's ours.'

'That's a low blow,' she said quietly.

'Yes. It's a low blow.'

Among the thousand things that hurt her at this moment was the knowledge that he wasn't looking for reassurance and so there was nothing she could reassure him with – not tenderness, not devotion, nothing. Yes, it was his baby, and that only made it worse. There would not now be a moment when suspicion could dissolve in mutual delight. That joy was lost to them.

'It isn't just,' he said, 'that the village knows before I do.'

'I understand. I'm sorry. I have told no one.'

'No one?'

'I have told no one in the village.'

'Which means you have told someone?'

'Yes.'

It wasn't necessary for either of them to speak the person's name.

'And it isn't just that either,' he said. 'Though that is no small thing.'

'I know. I am so very sorry.'

He was listening to the logic of his thoughts, not the progress of her apology.

'We had an understanding.'

'I know we did, darling.'

'We had an understanding that no child would "come along" to surprise either of us. We both, I thought, were taking the necessary precautions.'

She wondered whether she should remind him that accidents happen, that no precaution was ever foolproof, but she couldn't bear even to essay a lie. 'We were,' she said.

'And then you weren't . . .'

She could find no extenuating explanation. '. . . And then I wasn't.'

'Did you think I would *come round eventually*?'

She heard the banality, heard how insulting to him it was to think it, but yes, she had thought precisely that. *He would come round* . . . At the far reaches of sanity she still thought it.

'I hoped.'

'And you didn't discuss it with me *why* . . . ?'

She said nothing.

'Given your *hope* for me eventually,' he persisted, 'why didn't you at least try me initially?'

There was no way back from this. 'I couldn't risk it.'

'Couldn't risk my saying no?'

'Exactly.'

'The risk being?'

In a gesture of desperation, she ran her hand through her hair. He could hear it crackle. He used to love stirring up an electrical storm in her hair. Combing it through with his fingers and watching the sparks fly. Now it was a site of desolation. Her desperation was more than he could bear. He thought his chest would break apart – not for himself, for her. For himself he felt only sullen anger. It was dark, where he was. A black corner of stoppered fury. But it was worse for her. He was that kind of a man: he thought everything was worse for a woman. Especially a woman he loved. Was that a form of contempt? He didn't know. He simply thought the pain for her was greater, perhaps because for her there was still hope mixed up in it. And there wasn't for him. He had flattened out; there was nothing now he could reasonably hope for. Only her to be all right, not to suffer, and she was distraught beyond the point of help.

'The risk,' she said, reading his thoughts, 'was that you would express your refusal so vehemently that there would be no going back from it.'

'And then?'

'And then we would lose the future I wanted for us.'

'The future you wanted for us, or others wanted for us?'

'Both.'

'But the future you wanted for us was once the future I wanted for us, and that didn't include – Ailinn, as I recall it positively excluded – a child.'

She hung her head. 'It did.'

'So what changed?'

'*I* changed.' It wasn't a good enough answer. She heard its inadequacy hang in the air between them, the way a lie can be detected on a phone line, in a crackle of silence.

'This baby,' he said – and in that phrase she heard his final disowning of it – 'it isn't just any baby, is it?'

'I don't know what you mean.'

'You do. It isn't just a future for you and me, is it? It's *the* future.'

'Is that so terrible?'

'Yes, if that means what I think it means.'

'Well it's your choice of words, Kevern.'

'But not my choice of future.'

'And what's your choice of future? To die out?'

'I've died out.'

That was the moment, with a clarity and sadness that all but made her poor arrhythmic heart stop, when she saw her life without him. 'Well I haven't,' she said.

There was, to the dismay of both of them, vigour in it.

Kevern remembered the box his father had made him promise he would open only in the event of his being about to be a father himself. He was sure he knew what it would contain. The word DON'T. But he didn't open it to find out.

iii

They did have one last conversation. He begged for it. A final night wrapped around each other.

'It promised so much,' he said, waiting for the dawn to break. 'We promised each other so much.'

She'd been over it and over it with him. Didn't *this* promise so much?

She could have killed him – would have killed him had she not cared deeply for him – so perverse were the words he chose. What was she offering him if not a future? What was she carrying if not promise?

'What was our promise?' she asked him. Not looking any longer for a fight. Just wanting to hear him say it. One more time. What would it have been?

'The promise of not knowing what it would be,' he said.

'Kevern, that's just a riddle.'

'Ah, then . . .'

They said nothing for another hour, simply held on to each other. But she was not prepared to give up without a fight, no matter that the fight was lost. She had told him all there was to know, all that she knew anyway. But she still wanted him to see he didn't have to commit as she was committed. Couldn't he come along for the ride? Be her consort? Look on from the sidelines . . .

'At the misery you're preparing for our child?'

She wouldn't let him get away with that. 'You can't have it both ways,' she said. 'You can't disown the child *and* call it yours.'

Was she right? He lay, listening to the quivering of her atria. Would she bequeath the child her troubled heart, he wondered. If she did, she did. Better that than what he had to bequeath.

'I'm simply saying you could stay out of whatever you want to stay out of.'

All of it, he thought. But he said, more gently, 'That being?'

'The politics.'

'The politics?'

'The journey . . .'

'Oh come on, Ailinn. I never expected that of you. *Journey*, for Christ's sake.'

'Then what word would you use?'

'I wouldn't. But I'll give you "mission" if you must have a word. A misguided mission to change what can never change. And actually, you know, it's even worse than that. It's a mission to repeat what should never be repeated.'

'And why are you so sure it will be repeated?'

'Because that's the law of it. Your heart, my love, is a live, tumultuous thing. Most human hearts are stone. And the immutable law I speak of is engraved on all of them.'

'You let them win once you decide it's immutable.'

'They have won already. They won a long time ago.'

'We could do so much to change this.'

'I don't want to change this. I want it to go on being. It's the only vengeance we have left – our refusal to stay around. Hand them the victory, I say, and let them see how empty it is.'

'And that's the future you say you promised me?'

'I thought it was the future we promised each other.'

'Don't you see how empty that would be for us too?'

He thought about it. For a long time, stretched out beside her, lying on her shoulder, bringing her on to his, kissing her face, her ears, her eyes, he thought about it. It was morning when he spoke. 'At least it would have been an emptiness of our deciding,' he said.

She was back in Paradise Valley by the time he rose. He breathed gently on the vase of paper flowers she had brought him as her moving-in present, barely daring to touch them, then he walked out on to the cliffs. He looked down into the great mouth of the blowhole. It was sucking so hard he needed to stand back from the edge. He felt it could reach up and gulp him down whole, like Hedra Deitch subjecting him to one of her snogging kisses.

But he didn't have to submit, even to Hedra. A life was owned by the person who lived it, he believed. What happened didn't always happen because you wanted it to, but what you made of it was your responsibility. Help there was little and gods there were none. We are the authors of our own consequences, if not always of our own actions.

The credo of a serious man. You could be too serious, he didn't doubt that. But his birthright was his birthright. No one can make me, he thought, feeling the spray on his cheeks.

Though even that turned out not to be entirely true. Distinct from the sucking of the sea and the screaming of the gulls he heard his mother calling to him. Her old, frayed, faint, reproachful cry.

'Key-vern . . . Key-vern . . .'

He put his ear to the wind. He had always been a good boy. When your mother called . . .

'Key-vern,' she called again.

He smiled to hear her voice.

'What is it, Ma?'

'Jump,' he heard her say.

Not feeling he should make her say it twice, he put his fingers to his lips, as though blowing her a kiss, and jumped.

Ailinn felt her heart crash into her chest. Esme Nussbaum heard it from the other end of the room and turned to look. She scowled.

They both knew.

'This is not a good way to start,' Ailinn said, 'with anger between us.'

'On the contrary,' Esme said, 'this is the best possible way to start.'